HANDBOOK FOR
Clinical
Memory
Assessment
OF OLDER ADULTS

HANDBOOK FOR

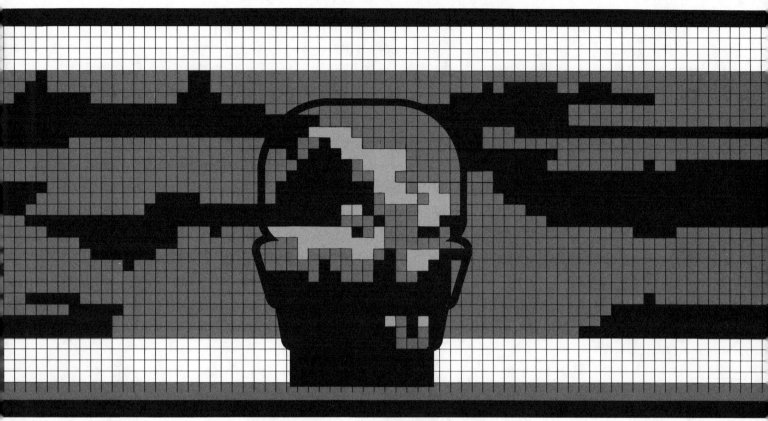

Clinical Memory Assessment

OF OLDER ADULTS

Leonard W. Poon

Editor

Associate Editors

Thomas Crook   Barry J. Gurland

Kenneth L. Davis   Alfred W. Kaszniak

Carl Eisdorfer   Larry W. Thompson

American Psychological Association
Washington, DC 20036

Copies may be ordered from:

American Psychological Association
Order Department
P.O. Box 2710
Hyattsville, MD 20784

Library of Congress Cataloging-in-Publication Data

Handbook for clinical memory assessment of older
    adults.

    Includes bibliographies and indexes.
    1. Memory, Disorders of—Age factors. 2. Memory,
Disorders of—Diagnosis. 3. Neuropsychological tests.
4. Alzheimer's disease—Diagnosis. I. Poon, Leonard
W., 1942-   . II. American Psychological Association.
[DNLM: 1. Alzheimer's Disease—diagnosis. 2. Depres-
sion—diagnosis. 3. Memory Disorders—diagnosis.
WM 173.7 H236]
BF378.A33H36 1986   618.97'6858075   86-26523
ISBN 0-912704-42-X

55,511

Contents

Foreword

This volume on clinical memory assessment was conceived to honor the late George A. Talland. The Massachusetts General Hospital Psychiatry Service is delighted to have George Talland honored in this way. I am especially pleased by this recognition because George was my friend.

George Talland came to Boston during the peak of the Freudian frenzy. Everything was colored with the psychoanalytic brush. There was little experimental psychology. Eclecticism was in hiding. Even amnesia, memory defects, and Korsakoff's syndrome were explained by repression, suppression, and denial. It's extraordinary to look back on that time and to believe that it really existed in that form. I assure you that it did. In 1954 into the department of Erich Lindemann came George Talland with his keen intelligence, his quick epigrammatic sense of humor, and a strong suspicion that the answer to human behavior was not to be found in the annals of psychoanalysis.

George was a good-looking man: blue eyes, pale complexion, shock of brown hair, about six feet tall, trim, and of regal bearing. I always imagined that he was of noble birth. Actually, I know little about the circumstances of his birth aside from the fact that he was born in Budapest, Hungary, in 1917. He received BA and MA degrees in economics from Cambridge University and a PhD in psychology from the University of London. When he spoke—generally so softly that it was necessary to strain to hear him—it was in clipped British tones superimposed on a Budapest base. He was a terrific talker in individual conversation or in small groups. Somehow his presence was diminished in large lecture halls.

When he came to Massachusetts General Hospital (MGH), George was given a suitable room on the third floor of the Bulfinch Building—a room that at one time had been the room of Oliver Wendell Holmes, MGH physician.

George could be brusque and put people off—he was quick to anger and was occasionally condescending. He was an unlikely friend for a young man of Irish extraction born and bred in the Midwest. However, underneath the sometimes forbidding exterior, George was a warm, sensitive, and loyal friend. He and I ate lunch together every day for a number of years.

He had a knack of listening to others that impressed me and served as an example for me. He could draw people out and was genuinely interested in what they had to say—unless it was foolish or uninteresting. He did not suffer fools gladly. Perhaps it is from this fact that his largely undeserved reputation for arrogance grew.

He could on occasion be sarcastic and cutting. Coming as he did from the citadel of British organic psychiatry, the Maudsley, it was tempting for him to unleash the powers of his tongue against the bastion of analytic psychiatry that much of Boston had become.

For the most part he worked quietly in his lab, but, unlike a lot of lab workers, he was also extremely interested in clinical phenomena, so he cultivated the acquaintance and sometimes the friendship of the clinicians practicing around him at MGH. He developed a particularly strong relationship with the neurologists Maurice Victor and Raymond Adams, who were interested in his work with memory. Unfortunately, no one in psychiatry seemed to share this interest.

In order to convince himself that psychodynamic psychiatry was nonsensical (at least I always thought that this was his reason), he took on a couple of patients to treat under the supervision of two analysts, John Nemiah and Peter Sifneos; and to the great surprise of all three, George turned out to be a sensitive, understanding therapist despite the fact that he never believed that Freudian dogma had anything to do with his therapeutic successes.

When I think about what George Talland would have liked to be remembered for, I think of three things. One was his joy in his work. He took a delight in his discoveries and was eager to share them with others. He worked at a time when research on memory disorders was about as popular as the study of the ancient dialects of the Fertile Crescent. Despite the lack of enthusiasm surrounding him, he was able through endless small conversations to muster among his compatriots a good deal of enthusiasm about his work. In 1961, the American Academy of Arts and Sciences awarded its annual monograph prize to him for his best-known book, *Deranged Memory*.

The second thing for which we who knew him remember George is his interest in people. It is unusual, at least in my experience, to find somebody with as inventive and active a mind as George's who is not always wanting to hold center stage, to hog the limelight. George developed a natural talent for listening, despite the fact that he loved to talk.

Finally, he enjoyed the world. He loved books, paintings, music, Hungarian food, and fine wine. He was one of the most gracious hosts I have ever encountered.

In my own fading memory bank there are a number of dinners at George's house that stand firm and unfaded; I can remember the table, the guests, and, above all, the conversations.

George maintained his dignity and graciousness through a long terminal illness. He died in 1968. I have never stopped missing him. I join you in honoring him. He took pleasure in intellectual exchange. There could be no better way of commemorating his memory than with this comprehensive Handbook.

Thomas Hackett
Boston, Massachusetts
June 1986

Preface

The major objective of this Handbook is to provide directions to psychologists, psychiatrists, neurologists, and other health care professionals for making informed decisions about clinical memory assessment. The Handbook is intended to answer basic questions about memory diagnosis: What underlying theoretical and clinical issues are important in the selection of an assessment instrument or battery? What types of tests are available, and how have these tests been validated with available theoretical and clinical evidence?

Although this Handbook concentrates on memory assessment of older adults, many of the issues are also applicable to clinical memory assessment in general. In the care and treatment of the elderly population, abnormal decline in both memory and intellectual functioning is a major diagnostic landmark of Alzheimer's disease and related disorders, diseases that are commanding attention from health care professionals and public policymakers alike. Although standardized memory test batteries are available, there is no consensus among clinicians about the selection of tests to identify the loci of memory dysfunction and to evaluate treatment efficacy. These problems of instrument selection are also common in the diagnosis of other clinical syndromes in which memory and cognitive functioning are compromised.

To meet the stated objectives, the Handbook is divided into five sections. Each section is edited by a clinician or researcher noted for his contribution in the specific area. Section I gives context to the Handbook by providing an integration of experimental and clinical precepts in memory assessment and by outlining a broad public health and public policy perspective on clinical memory testing in the diagnosis and treatment of Alzheimer's disease and related disorders. Section II defines the issues in test selection from theoretical and clinical perspectives. Section III reviews the different types of instruments available for the evaluation of symptoms and complaints. Section IV evaluates instruments for detecting depression and for differentiating depression from observed aging effects in performance. Finally, Section V reviews a variety of validation methods, including longitudinal data, clinical outcome, and anatomical, physiological, neurochemical, and genetic information. Three indexes are included for the benefit and convenience of the reader. First, an alphabetical author index is included. Second, a comprehensive subject index was constructed to guide the reader to specific terms and concepts in memory assessment. Finally, a test index was included so that the reader can cross-reference specific tests mentioned in the chapters with their usages and findings.

The most effective way to achieve an overall perspective of the Handbook is first to examine the introductory chapter in each section. These chapters serve to guide readers through the various substantive issues in the respective sections.

This book is the second of a series of books and conferences dedicated to the memory of George A. Talland, who made a significant contribution to the field of memory and aging prior to his premature death in 1968 at the age of 51. The first book, *New Directions in Memory and Aging,* published in 1980, was devoted to the exploration of theoretical issues related to aging. Dr. Talland was a friend and colleague of many of the contributors in this second volume who gathered to present and discuss their ideas at the Memorial Conference prior to consolidating them into chapters for this Handbook.

The concept of a series of memorial conferences and edited volumes honoring Dr. Talland's contributions was enthusiastically endorsed by Thomas G. Hackett, MD, Chairman of the Psychiatry Department at the Massachusetts General Hospital, in which Dr. Talland spent a large portion of his research career. Dr. Hackett has authored this volume's foreword, describing George Talland, the person and researcher. Dr. Talland began the work of the laboratory that is now known as the Mental Performance and Aging Laboratory. It has been directed subsequently by James L. Fozard, PhD, from 1968 to 1978 and by myself from 1978 to the present. (It moved with me in July 1985 to the Gerontology Center at the University of Georgia.)

I would like to acknowledge the many individuals

and institutions that made possible the conference and this edited Handbook. I wish to acknowledge the continuous encouragement and support from Thomas G. Hackett, MD; Howard Chauncey, PhD, DMD, the Associate Chief of Staff for Research and Development at the Veterans Administration Outpatient Clinic, Boston; and Leonard Jakubczak, PhD, the project officer at the National Institute on Aging. The implementation of the conference and the edited volume was made possible by Conference Grant 1R13 AG 04032 from the National Institute on Aging. During the editing process, I moved from Boston to Athens, Georgia. The support and resources from the Gerontology Center at the University of Georgia made the final publication steps possible.

I also wish to acknowledge the generous support of Michael Pallak, PhD, the former Executive Officer, and Gary VandenBos, PhD, Associate Executive Director for Communications, of the American Psychological Association (APA). I thank them for publishing and marketing this Handbook, which we hope will have far-reaching impact on memory diagnosis for the disciplines of psychology, psychiatry, and neurology, as well as for other health care professions. The leadership of Brenda Bryant, the manager of Special Publications at APA, and the meticulous technical assistance of Alice Markham, Deanna D'Errico, Pam Presar, and Donna Stewart at APA have been invaluable. I am grateful to the contributors, editors/co-organizers, and the conference staff in persevering throughout the three years needed to complete this project from start to finish. The administrative aspects were directed with efficiency and a sense of humor by my wife Billie Poon, MA, MDiv., who fulfilled similar responsibilities for the first conference. Billie performed beyond the call of duty in coordinating the copyediting and rewriting of manuscripts with each contributor. Without her help this publication would not have been possible. Patricia Tun, PhD; David Lowe, BA; and Virginia Ranauro all contributed significantly to the smooth execution of the conference and the management of manuscripts for the Handbook.

Finally, this Handbook is primarily the result of the substantive leadership from the section editors, co-organizers, and friends: Barry Gurland, MD; Carl Eisdorfer, PhD, MD; Thomas Crook, PhD; Larry Thompson, PhD; Alfred Kaszniak, PhD; and Kenneth Davis, MD. Over the three-year period, we drew from our collective clinical and research experiences to select chapter topics and contributors, and in the long editorial process we worked as a team to shape and reshape the contents for the readership. I believe George Talland would be satisfied with this effort.

Leonard W. Poon
Athens, Georgia
June 1986

Contributors

Marilyn S. Albert, PhD Assistant Professor, Departments of Psychiatry and Neurology, Division on Aging, Massachusetts General Hospital, Harvard Medical School

Raymond T. Bartus, PhD Professor, Department of Psychiatry, New York University School of Medicine; Director, Geriatric Research Program, Lederle Labs, Pearl River, New York

Robert M. Bilder, PhD Instructor of Clinical Psychology, Department of Psychiatry, Columbia University College of Physicians and Surgeons; Chief Neurologist and Assistant Research Director, New York State Psychiatric Institute Division at Creedmoor Psychiatric Center, Queens Village, New York

Robert I. Block, PhD Associate Research Scientist, Department of Anesthesia, University of Iowa, Iowa City

Jeffrey Borenstein, MD Resident, Department of Psychiatry, New York University School of Medicine

Jack Botwinick, PhD Professor, Departments of Psychology and Neurology, Washington University

Roland J. Branconnier, MA, PhD candidate Research Consultant, Laboratory of Neuropsychology, Tufts Medical School; Executive Director, Institute for Psychopharmacologic Research, Brookline, Massachusetts

Paul R. Braun, BS Study Coordinator, Department of Neurology, Veterans Administration Medical Center, Allen Park, Michigan

Samuel D. Brinkman, PhD Clinical Neurologist, Neuropsychology Clinic, Abilene, Texas

Nelson Butters, PhD Professor, Department of Psychiatry, University of California School of Medicine, San Diego; Chief, Psychology Service, Veterans Administration Medical Center, San Diego, California

Catherine Buttinger, MD Resident, Department of Psychiatry, Albert Einstein College of Medicine

Donna Cohen, PhD Professor of Gerontology, School of Public Health, and Associate Director, Gerontology Center, University of Illinois at Chicago

Suzanne Corkin, PhD Associate Professor, Department of Brain and Cognitive Sciences, Massachusetts Institute of Technology

Thomas Crook, PhD President, Memory Assessment Clinics, Inc., Bethesda, Maryland

Peter S. Cross, MPhil Research Scientist, Center for Geriatrics and Gerontology, New York State Office of Mental Health, New York, New York

Walter R. Cunningham, PhD Professor, Department of Psychology, University of Florida

Laura Cushman, PhD Assistant Professor, Division of Rehabilitation Medicine, University of Rochester

Warren L. Danziger, PhD Research Assistant, Department of Neurology, Washington University

Kenneth L. Davis, MD Chief, Psychiatry Service, Veterans Administration Medical Center, Bronx, New York; Professor, Department of Psychiatry, Mount Sinai School of Medicine

Mony J. de Leon, EdD Assistant Professor, Department of Psychiatry, New York University Medical Center; Director, Neuroimaging Research, Geriatric Study and Treatment Program, New York University Medical Center

Frank H. Duffy, MD Associate Professor, Department of Neurology, Children's Hospital Medical Center, Harvard Medical School

Daniel D. Dunn, PhD Psychologist, Psychiatry Service, Veterans Administration Medical Center, Bronx, New York

Carl Eisdorfer, PhD, MD Professor and Chairperson, Department of Psychiatry, and Professor of Psychology, University of Miami; Director, University Center on Aging, University of Miami

Richard C. Erickson, PhD Professor, Department of Medical Psychology, Oregon Health Sciences University; Staff Psychologist, Psychology Service, Veterans Administration Medical Center, Portland, Oregon

Steven H. Ferris, PhD Associate Professor, Department of Psychiatry, New York University School of Medicine; Executive Director, Aging and Dementia Research Program, New York University Medical Center

Charles Flicker, PhD Research Assistant Professor, Department of Psychiatry, New York University School of Medicine

Paula Altman Fuld, PhD Associate Professor, Department of Neurology (Psychology), Albert Einstein College of Medicine; Director, Division of Neuropsychology, Department of Neurology, Montefiore Hospital Medical Center, Bronx, New York

Dolores Gallagher, PhD Clinical Assistant Professor, Department of Psychiatry, Stanford University School of Medicine; Associate Director for Education and Evaluation, Geriatric Research, Education, and Clinical Center, Veterans Administration Medical Center, Palo Alto, California

Ajax E. George, MD Professor, Department of Radiology, New York University Medical Center; Director, Computed Tomography, New York University Medical Center

Michael J. Gilewski, PhD Adjunct Assistant Professor, Department of Gerontology, University of Southern California; Staff Clinical Psychologist, Psychology Service, Veterans Administration Outpatient Clinic, Los Angeles, California

Elkhonon Goldberg, PhD Associate Professor of Psychiatry (Psychology), Albert Einstein College of Medicine; Director, Division of Neuropsychology, Department of Psychiatry, Montefiore Medical Center, Bronx, New York

Eric Granholm, BA Graduate Student, Department of Psychology, University of California at Los Angeles

John H. Growdon, MD Associate Professor of Neurology, Harvard Medical School; Neurologist, Department of Neurology, Massachusetts General Hospital, Boston, Massachusetts

Barry J. Gurland, FRCP (London), FRC Psychiatry John E. Borne Professor of Clinical Psychiatry and Director, Center for Geriatrics and Gerontology, Columbia University Faculty of Medicine and The New York State Office of Mental Health

M. Janice Gutfreund, MA Doctoral Candidate, Department of Psychology, Michigan State University

Thomas P. Hackett, MD Draper Professor, Department of Psychiatry, Harvard Medical School; Chief, Psychiatry Service, Massachusetts General Hospital, Boston, Massachusetts

Judith O. Harker, PhD Research Psychologist, Human Memory Research, Veterans Administration Medical Center, Sepulveda, California

Thomas B. Horvath, MD, FRACP Vice-Chair/Department of Psychiatry, Mount Sinai School of Medicine; Clinical Director, Department of Psychiatry, Veterans Administration Medical Center, Bronx, New York

Diane Howieson, PhD Assistant Professor, Department of Medical Psychology, Oregon Health Sciences University; Head, Neuropsychology Section, Psychology Service, Veterans Administration Medical Center, Portland, Oregon

F. Jacob Huff, MD, Assistant Professor of Psychiatry and Neurology, University of Pittsburgh; Neurologist, Falk Clinic, University of Pittsburgh

Earl Hunt, PhD Professor, Department of Psychology, University of Washington

Terry L. Jernigan, PhD Assistant Professor, Departments of Psychiatry and Radiology, School of Medicine, University of California at San Diego; Staff Psychologist, Psychology Service, Veterans Administration Medical Center, San Diego, California

Celeste A. Johns, MD Department of Psychiatric Research, Long Island-Hillside Medical Center, Glen Oaks, New York

Alfred W. Kaszniak, PhD Associate Professor, Department of Psychology, University of Arizona

Colleen M. Kelley, PhD Assistant Professor, Department of Psychology, Williams College

Youngjai Kim, PhD Psychologist, Long Island Jewish-Hillside Medical Center, Glen Oaks, New York

John W. Largen, Jr., PhD Adjunct Clinical Assistant Professor, Department of Psychology, University of Houston; Clinical Neuropsychologist, Department of Psychiatry, Kelsey-Seybold Clinic, Houston, Texas

M. Powell Lawton, PhD Director of Research, Philadelphia Geriatric Center, Philadelphia, Pennsylvania

Maryann Martone, BA Graduate Student, Department of Neurosciences, University of California at San Diego

Gloria McAnulty, PhD Research Associate, Department of Neurology, Children's Hospital Medical Center, Harvard Medical School

Richard Scott McDonald, PhD Associate Director of Medical Research, Sandoz Research Institute, East Hanover, New Jersey

E. Jeffrey Metter, MD Staff Neurologist, Neurology Service, Veterans Administration Medical Center, Sepulveda, California; Associate Professor in Residence, Department of Neurology, School of Medicine, University of California, Los Angeles

Richard C. Mohs, PhD Associate Professor, Department of Psychiatry, Mount Sinai School of Medicine; Psychologist, Psychiatry Service, Veterans Administration Medical Center, Bronx, New York

Margaret A. Naeser, PhD Assistant Professor, Department of Neurology, Boston University School of Medicine and Boston Veterans Administration Medical Center

George Niederehe, PhD Assistant Professor, Gerontology Center, University of Texas Mental Sciences Institute and Department of Psychiatry and Behavioral Sciences, University of Texas Medical School, Houston

Mary Jo Nissen, PhD Assistant Professor, Department of Psychology, University of Minnesota

Leonard W. Poon, PhD Professor of Psychology, Director, Gerontology Center, and Chair, Faculty of Gerontology, University of Georgia; Clinical Associate, Psychiatry Service, Massachusetts General Hospital, Boston, Massachusetts

Allen Raskin, PhD Director, Psychology Division, Lafayette Clinic, Detroit, Michigan

Barry Reisberg, MD Associate Professor, Department of Psychiatry, and Clinical Director, Aging and Dementia Research Program, New York University Medical Center

Walter H. Riege, PhD Chief, Human Memory Research, Veterans Administration Medical Center, Sepulveda, California; Research Psychologist (Professor), Department of Psychiatry and Biobehavioral Sciences, School of Medicine, University of California, Los Angeles

Wilma G. Rosen, PhD Associate Clinical Professor of Medical Psychology, Department of Psychiatry, Columbia University; Director, Neuropsychology Unit, Division of Psychology, Department of Psychiatry, Neurological Institute, Columbia-Presbyterian Medical Center, New York, New York

Carl Salzman, MD Associate Professor, Department of Psychiatry, Harvard Medical School; Director of Psychopharmacology, Massachusetts Mental Health Center, Boston, Massachusetts

Mohammad Sarwar, MD Associate Professor, Section of Neuroradiology, Yale University School of Medicine

Nancy A. Sherman, PhD Assistant Psychologist, Department of Psychiatry, Veterans Administration Medical Center, Bronx, New York

Eliahu Sinaiko, PhD   Research Statistician, Aging and Dementia Research Program, New York University Medical Center

Martha Storandt, PhD   Professor, Departments of Psychology and Neurology, Washington University

Edith V. Sullivan, PhD   Research Scientist, Ashton Graybiel Spatial Orientation Laboratory, Brandeis University

Larry W. Thompson, PhD   Faculty, Division of Gerontology, Stanford University; Director, Gerontology Research Programs, Menlo Park Division, Veterans Administration Medical Center, Palo Alto, California

Herbert Weingartner, PhD   Chair/Department of Psychology, George Washington University; Director, Cognitive Studies Program, National Institute of Mental Health, Bethesda, Maryland

Betsy E. White, MPH   Graduate Student, Department of Psychology, University of Southern California

Robert S. Wilson, PhD   Associate Professor, Department of Psychology and Social Sciences, Rush-Presbyterian-St. Lukes Medical Center, Chicago, Illinois

Jessica Wolfe, PhD   Assistant Professor of Psychiatry, Department of Psychiatry, Tufts University School of Medicine; Research Clinical Pyschologist, Psychology Service, Veterans Administration Medical Center, Boston, Massachusetts

Jerome A. Yesavage, MD   Associate Professor, Department of Psychiatry and Behavioral Science, Stanford University; Associate Chief of Staff for Rehabilitation, Veterans Administration Medical Center, Palo Alto, California

Elizabeth M. Zelinski, PhD   Assistant Professor, Departments of Gerontology and Psychology, University of Southern California

Global Perspectives on Clinical Memory Testing

Barry J. Gurland, *Section Editor*

Leonard W. Poon, Barry J. Gurland, Carl Eisdorfer, Thomas Crook, Larry W. Thompson, Alfred W. Kaszniak, and Kenneth L. Davis

CHAPTER

1

Integration of Experimental and Clinical Precepts in Memory Assessment: A Tribute to George Talland

My principal method of research is the laboratory experiment; my primary object of observation is achievement in performance; from there I infer mechanisms and processes. At the same time, working in a hospital and with patients, I have enough respect for clinical tools to employ them where they can point to problems as well as answer questions. (p. vi)

Those are the words George Talland used to describe his approach to research in *Deranged Memory: A Psychonomic Study of the Amnesic Syndrome* (1965), a volume summarizing 5 years of clinical observation and experimental study on a group of patients in the chronic state of Korsakoff's disease. Talland was a pragmatist in the use of experimental and clinical tools. He was also an integrator and a consolidator of not only his own work but also the work of his peers in academic and clinical research and practice. At the time of his premature death in 1968, Talland was at the peak of his productivity. His work is a legacy to all who are currently studying memory disorders and developing memory assessment tools.

Talland's effort as an integrator of knowledge in the last two years of his life is noteworthy. In October 1967 he finished editing *Human Aging and Behavior* (1968b), a volume that consolidated and highlighted theories and research of prominent investigators such as Canestrari, Craik, Davies, Eisdorfer, Rabbitt, Riegel, Schaie, Surwillo, Szafran, and Talland himself.

At that time Talland knew he was dying of cancer, and yet he pushed on to finish two projects. The first project was an international conference on the pathology of memory that was held in October 1967. The purpose of the conference was twofold: (a) to enable the academic scientist to become better acquainted with the variety of memory disorders commonly encountered by the clinician and (b) to acquaint the clinician with the academic scientist's current thoughts on how memory operates and on how its processes are measured. Some of the distinguished participants in the conference were Barbizet, Broadbent, Bruner, Cofer, Cronholm, Geschwind, Hecaen, Kral, Miller, Posner, Postman, Pribram, and Zangwill. Talland was too sick to edit the proceedings, and he died before the book, *The Pathology of Memory,* was published in 1969 (Talland & Waugh, 1969). The book was edited by Dr. Nancy Waugh at his request.

Talland's final project was the writing of a Penguin Science Series book, *Disorders of Memory and Learning* (1968a). The editor of the book, Graham A. Foulds, wrote in the editorial foreword: "After I had received the completed manuscript and suggested that he might expand certain parts, particularly his own work on the Korsakoff psychosis, he wrote to say that I had caught him at a bad time and he regretted that my suggestion could not be followed" (p. 10). Within two months George Talland was dead.

Talland had strong opinions about principles and methods in the study of memory, memory disorders, and memory assessment. Some of his opinions were not in accordance with the zeitgeist, but that did not stop him from expressing them. In retrospect it is obvious that the man was ahead of his time, and many of his principles and concepts are reflected in the contents of this Handbook. If there is a lesson to be learned from Talland's research approach, it is from his dedication to integrating clinical observations with laboratory performance. He insisted that both are needed to present a clear picture of the clinical syndrome and to test causal hypotheses; one or the other alone often skims the surface of a memory dysfunction and is apt to be misleading.

In this spirit of bridging clinical and experimental knowledge, we, the editors and authors in this Handbook, present and review issues that we believe are pertinent to researchers and clinicians who are involved in the study of memory disorders and who need to assess the integrity of memory functions in older adults.

Why Is Memory So Difficult To Assess?

Although there are numerous standardized memory assessment batteries, there is no general agreement among clinicians about which battery provides the appropriate sensitivity and specificity in diagnosing memory dysfunctions in older adults (Erickson, Poon, & Walsh-Sweeney, 1980). For example, the Wechsler Memory Scale was found to have limited power for detecting specific deficits; it has been criticized for lacking a measure for long-term retention, for not differentiating modality-specific memory functions, and for not being validated for the elderly population (Erickson & Scott, 1977; Erickson et al., 1980). The Guild Memory Test (Gilbert, Levee, & Catalano, 1968) was found by some clinicians to be too complex for people with more than a mild deficit, and the Randt Memory Test (Randt, Brown, & Osborne, 1980) was found lacking in the measurement of nonverbal memory. The clinician's dilemma in test selection is further delineated in chapters 8 (Erickson & Howieson) and 33 (Riege, Harker, & Metter) of this Handbook. The problem of test sensitivity and specificity is illustrated by the common complaints among clinicians that the results of some memory tests bear no resemblance to the everyday memory functioning of the patient.

Why is memory so difficult to assess? We believe there are three primary reasons: (a) the multidimensional nature of memory (cf. in this volume, Hunt, chapter 6; Corkin, Growdon, Sullivan, Nissen, & Huff, chapter 16; Kaszniak, Poon, & Riege, chapter 17), (b) the large number of variables that can affect memory functioning (cf. Kaszniak & Davis, chapter 27), and (c) the variable range of responses that can be considered normal (cf. Gurland & Cross, chapter 2; Cunningham, chapter 4; Erickson & Howieson, chapter 8). The many factors that can influence memory make it clear why the level of functional memory is fluid and subject to intra- and interpersonal variability. George Talland wrote:

> Occasional failures in recall or a temporary difficulty in learning need not be taken as symptomatic of a disorder in a function. All our functions are exercised within limits and, with such heterogeneous and often complex functions as remembering and learning, the limits are wide. Every so often one's performance can exceed as well as fall short of those mean values that correspond to the

bulk of one's efforts and achievements. We infer a disorder from a permanent or extensive disability in comparison with previous performance or in comparison with a suitably defined control group. (1968a, p. 24)

When there is a memory dysfunction, and especially in its early stages, the fluid nature of memory makes it a challenge to estimate the probability of dysfunction and to isolate the locus of its disorder. Memory is involved in practically all aspects of our daily lives, and yet people tend not to think consciously or intentionally about how they acquire and remember information until they perceive that there is a problem—for example, naming problems or excessive blocking during retrieval (Bowles, Obler, & Poon, in press). Consequently, studies have shown that patients do not articulate memory complaints accurately (Poon, Fozard, Treat, & Popkin, 1978; Zelinski, Gilewski, & Thompson, 1980; Gilewski & Zelinski, chapter 11, this volume).

On the other hand, clinician-scientists are not immune to misclassifying the degree of cognitive and memory dysfunction in diagnosing cases of possible Alzheimer's disease and related disorders (ADRD) in older adults. The percentage of misdiagnosis has been estimated to be between 10% and 50% (Garcia, Reding, & Blass, 1981; Gurland & Toner, 1983; Ron, Toone, Garralda, & Lishman, 1979). Although memory and cognitive dysfunction is only one of several presenting factors in ADRD, this level of misdiagnosis indicates that there is a genuine need to improve current understanding of memory and cognitive assessment, diagnostic criteria, and selection of diagnostic instruments. The need to upgrade clinicians' understanding of memory assessment should be taken as a serious challenge, given the public health implications of misdiagnosing individuals in cases of ADRD that Gurland and Cross discuss in chapter 2 of this Handbook.

Basic Ingredients of Memory Assessment

A perusal of the chapters in this Handbook should provide a picture of the diversity of approaches in the study of memory functioning in older adults. These approaches can be divided roughly into three classes: (a) neuropathological approaches with concomitant psychological models (e.g., Goldberg & Bilder, chapter 7), (b) descriptive approaches of psychological functions without reference to neuropathology (e.g., Hunt, chapter 6), and (c) observational approaches that fit data within available neuropathological and psychological frameworks (e.g., Talland, 1968a). These approaches have accounted for an exponential increase of information on memory functioning and memory disorder in old age in the last two decades (Poon & Welford, 1980). The bulk of the literature is concerned with experimental studies of normative aging processes; studies of clinical memory dysfunction constitute the next largest category. At present the literature contains little translation of research findings into effective diagnostic tools.

Memory assessment fulfills at least three clinical purposes. The primary purpose is to contribute to the medical diagnosis of a syndrome in which memory and other cognitive processes are in question (e.g., Korsakoff's syndrome and ADRD). Second, it contributes to the localization of possible brain lesion. Finally, it contributes to the treatment and management of individuals with memory problems. Chapters in this Handbook, particularly those in Section II, are designed to crystallize the pertinent diagnostic issues from the perspectives of the different approaches in the study of memory functioning as well as from the clinician's perspective in evaluating change and treatment efficacy.

Some basic concepts about memory should be kept in mind in selecting test instruments and in interpreting results. First and foremost, it is important to realize that memory is a consolidation process, and tests of this consolidation process must reflect the real-life demands on the individual. This would mean that ability to perform rote learning and immediate retrieval of new information may not be representative of an individual's entire repertoire of abilities. Furthermore, other sources of information besides memory tests can provide data on memory capabilities. That is, information about environmental influences, personality type, general and specific health and biomedical status, nutrition, premorbid intelligence, and other intrinsic and extrinsic factors all can contribute to a picture of an individual's memory functioning.

What basic ingredients should a clinician be cognizant of in the design of a memory assessment battery? We would like to identify the basic ingredients by borrowing and adapting a diagram used by Jenkins (1979) and adapted by Smith (1980) that spells out the pertinent factors in cognitive research (see Figure 1-1). These factors are equally pertinent in memory assessment.

The first factor describes the characteristics of the individual: a person's age, health and biomedical status, education, intelligence, depression, environmental

influences, skills, knowledge, self-rating of memory, and so on. It is imperative to have this sort of basic information for interpreting test results and for comparing an individual's score against normative data. The impact of some of these individual-difference variables is outlined in this Handbook. For example, chapters in section V contain hypotheses and data on the influences of anatomical, physiological, neurochemical, and genetic factors on memory functions. Knowledge about what an individual thinks about his or her memory is important in memory assessment. Researchers frequently observe the so-called "self-fulfilling prophecy"—complaining individuals frequently perform poorly to justify their complaints (Poon et al., 1978). The severity of memory complaints could also provide some indication of an individual's level of depression (see Section IV). Instruments to assess memory complaints are summarized in chapter 11 (Gilewski & Zelinski). Finally, it has been demonstrated that an individual's education, general intelligence, occupation, and skills could influence the level of performance (see Poon, 1985, for a review). In cognitive aging research, age differences could be under- or overestimated if these variables are not properly controlled (Poon, Krauss, & Bowles, 1984), and similar under- and overestimation of deficits might occur in individual assessment if these variables are not considered.

The second critical factor in memory assessment is the criterion task, the actual test and its dependent measure(s) used to measure performance. For a particular task, it is important to note that different dependent measures evaluate different aspects of a process and may contain different levels of sensitivity. When performances of young and elderly adults are compared, for example, recognition recall is less sensitive to age differences than is free recall (Schonfield & Robertson, 1966). When drawing conclusions about differences in memory performance, one must keep the specific dependent measure in mind.

Another crucial aspect of the task factor to consider in interpreting results is the relative complexity of the task. It has been empirically demonstrated that 60-year-olds, in comparison with 20-year-olds, perform disproportionately worse when the complexity of the task is increased (Cerella, Poon, & Williams, 1980). This phenomenon can also be demonstrated when depressed subjects are compared with nondepressed control subjects (see Weingartner, chapter 22, this volume). The lesson to be learned is that the magnitude of the difference in deficits between a patient and a control subject could vary from negligible to significant, depending on the relative complexity of a task or test. To complicate the diagnostic picture further, task complexity could interact with the severity of dysfunction, an individual difference characteristic. These sorts of possible interactions must be kept in mind when interpreting an individual's scores with some established norms.

The third factor in memory testing—the nature of the test stimuli, verbal or nonverbal—dictates the type

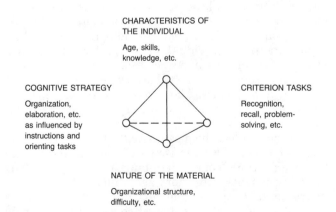

CHARACTERISTICS OF
THE INDIVIDUAL

Age, skills,
knowledge, etc.

COGNITIVE STRATEGY

Organization,
elaboration, etc.
as influenced by
instructions and
orienting tasks

CRITERION TASKS

Recognition,
recall, problem-
solving, etc.

NATURE OF THE MATERIAL

Organizational structure,
difficulty, etc.

Figure 1-1. Basic ingredients in memory assessment. Adapted from Jenkins (1979) by permission.

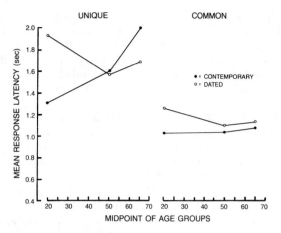

Figure 1-2. Mean response latencies for the unique and common versions of contemporary and dated exemplars for the 20-, 50-, and 65-year old groups. Adapted from Poon and Fozard (1978) by permission.

of processing to be measured. One dimension of the stimuli, the familiarity, is especially critical in the evaluation of memory functions in older adults. Figure 1-2 effectively demonstrates that the familiarity of the test stimuli can influence the magnitude and direction of age differences (Poon & Fozard, 1978). The time each subject took to name the pictures of objects was measured, and the objects presented to a young and an older cohort were varied in datedness and uniqueness. The figure shows that there is no age difference in the response latencies of naming familiar objects. A classic aging function was observed when young, middle-aged, and older adults were asked to name objects that were representative of the 1970s (e.g., a computer card and a digital clock). However, the direction of this aging function was reversed when the stimuli that were more familiar to the elderly sample than to the young sample were employed. It is interesting to note that because the middle-aged group was equally familiar with both sets of stimuli, there was no difference in the naming latencies. Cohort-specific effects have also been demonstrated with memory for words and for prose (see Poon, 1985, for a review). One lesson to learn is that the use of some neutral or unfamiliar stimuli may exaggerate the degree of memory difficulty for older people and that therefore the observed deficit could be the result of the stimuli employed rather than an indication of a flawed memory process.

The final factor in memory assessment is the measurement of cognitive strategies used to perform the task, and this, of course, is dependent on the nature of the stimuli and the criterion task employed to measure the cognitive process. Poor performance could be a result of inefficient strategy, especially in the performance of novel and unfamiliar tasks. Strategies and processes could be inferred from the qualitative profile of a set of psychometric tasks. However, laboratory-based information-processing tasks may be more efficient in separating and identifying underlying factors contributing to a response (Kaszniak et al., chapter 17). For example, poor or slow retrieval could be due to

slow motor initiation, slow retrieval, or both. Poor retrieval could be due to poor discrimination of stimuli or to a conservative criterion in response selection. Poor recall could be a function of inefficient encoding strategies or of difficulty in separating the gist from the details. Poor spatial memory performance could be due to an inefficiently derived solution as a result of an individual's preference for a verbal solution. Because effective treatment of dysfunction presupposes an understanding of the underlying processes in both the neuropathological and the psychological domains (Corkin et al., chapter 16), it is imperative that the assessment procedure identify the mechanisms underlying the flawed processes as well as the remaining intact functions.

Informed Decision Making in Test Selection

Given the basic ingredients for memory assessment, are there specific criteria for test selection? Are some tests better than others? How many tests are sufficient to evaluate all of the basic ingredients involved in memory functioning?

As mentioned earlier, the authors of the 40 chapters in this volume could possibly offer 40 different answers to the questions just raised. Furthermore, if one were to poll the seven editors of this volume, it would be clear that they differ in orientation and therefore would offer different answers to these questions. We, the editors, want to emphasize that there is no one correct answer to these questions. Because memory tests are used to confirm clinical hypotheses, a number of tests may be appropriate if they are suitable for the milieu of the individual and provide a qualitative profile of underlying mechanisms that are the basis of the clinical hypothesis. The selection of a test or a set of tests should therefore be guided by the prototypical behavioral symptoms of the disease, the hypotheses of the clinician, and the previously demonstrated sensitivity and specificity of a test, as well as by psychometric properties of the test. This process necessitates informed decision making on the part of the clinician. A standardized memory test may be completely appropriate for one individual but provide incomplete data about another individual. This philosophy argues against the relative appropriateness or usefulness of one standardized memory battery (or task) against another, and it places the responsibility for selecting effective assessment instruments squarely on the clinician.

In order to select the most cost-effective instruments, a clinician needs a wide range of information on the following: (a) memory functioning, including the four basic ingredients of memory assessment; (b) available instruments or paradigms for different assessment purposes; and (c) demonstrated sensitivity of specific tests in evaluating change, in relating to other biologic or behavioral markers, and in clinical diagnosis. Chapters in Sections II to V of this Handbook were designed to provide these perspectives for informed decision making.

As an exercise, we would like to demonstrate how the information contained in Sections II to V may be used to select instruments for performing three essential functions in clinical memory assessment: (a) systematic intake of signs and symptoms, (b) classification of severity of symptoms, and (c) examination of hypotheses about possible deficits and their underlying mechanisms.

Intake of Signs and Symptoms

Three clusters of instruments that have been reviewed in this Handbook are available to assist clinicians to systematically outline the nature of memory problems. These instruments were developed from three different perspectives. From the study of metamemory (the effects of the feeling-of-knowing) in cognitive psychology, investigators from the laboratory have developed a series of metamemory questionnaires that had been adapted for use as memory complaint questionnaires in clinical situations. An exhaustive outline of these questionnaires is presented in Table 1 of chapter 11 (Gilewski & Zelinski). Furthermore, information on scales that have been used with the elderly population, scaling and psychometric properties, and their commonalities in 10 different dimensions of metamemory are reviewed in that chapter.

From clinical studies of geriatric drug trials, rating scales have been identified (McDonald, chapter 13) that have been used to examine treatment-related changes in memory and cognitive functions in older adults. Mini-status examinations that are reviewed in chapters 12 (Reisberg et al.) and 14 (Ferris, Crook, Flicker, Reisberg, & Bartus) are also applicable. Scales are identified that focus on a single facet of cognitive and noncognitive factors (e.g., attention–concentration, anxiety, or sleepiness) as well as on the multiple facets of psychopathology (e.g., withdrawn depression, cognitive dysfunction, psychotic distortion, agitation, and hostile suspiciousness).

Because memory complaints and depression are highly correlated (Thompson, chapter 19), assessment of depression during the intake interview may clarify the etiology of the observed signs and symptoms, thereby providing leads toward hypotheses of dysfunction. A summary of popularly employed observer- and self-rated depression scales is presented in Table 1 of chapter 21 (Yesavage). Detailed reviews of six specific interviewer-administered scales (Gallagher, chapter 20) and four self-rating scales (Yesavage, chapter 21) are included. In the cognitive assessment of older adults, the impact of depression is important and controversial. Chapters in Section IV provide detailed rationales, theoretical perspectives, approaches for separating depression from aging effects, and sometimes conflicting data to illustrate the pitfalls and problems of the concomitant effects of depression on cognition. All clinicians who are involved in cognitive assessment should read this section.

We believe that the preceding information should provide clinicians with a solid basis for making informed decisions for selecting or designing initial intake protocols. Concrete recommendations are made in the various chapters for selecting instruments in different assessment situations.

Classification of Severity of Symptoms

A practical question for the clinician is, "How benign or malignant is a pattern of observable symptoms and behaviors, given what is now known about ADRD?" The question itself is simple enough; however, the answers may not be so simple in light of what is known of (a) the variability of behaviors across individuals, (b) the overlap of symptomatologies and the absence of well-defined knowledge of different types of mental disorders associated with old age, and (c) the absence of definitive criteria in the description of syndromes. Given the above caveat, several chapters in the Handbook describe data of functional decline in ADRD and provide rationale for scale construction in the classification of the severity of decline.

Chapters 28 (Storandt, Botwinick, & Danziger), 29 (Wilson & Kaszniak), and 30 (Rosen, Mohs, & Davis) provide longitudinal data on the rates of progressive decline on ADRD over the course of 2.5, 3, and 1.5 years respectively. These data are quite difficult to obtain, owing to problems of patient dropout during the study, and they provide a rare glimpse of the rates of change in different types of functioning.

Two chapters also provide some insight in the construction of scales that attempt to classify the severity of the observed symptoms. Reisberg and his colleagues (chapter 12) have proposed to define stages of cognitive impairment in the Global Deterioration Scale (GDS). The idea is that major symptoms or phases of ADRD are identifiable and that these phases are differentiable by psychometric instruments and by physiological and biochemical measures. Three major phases have been identified: forgetfulness, confusion, and dementia. These phases are further refined into seven substages—no cognitive decline (GDS = 1) to late dementia or very severe cognitive decline (GDS = 7). In another effort, Rosen and her colleagues (chapter 30) discuss the Alzheimer's Disease Assessment Scale (ADAS) that they constructed, which also evaluates cognitive and affective disturbances in addition to behavioral disturbances. Both developments deserve close scrutiny when a severity classification scale is needed for preliminary screening.

Hypothesis Testing

When it is suspected that the observed memory dysfunction is due to problems in the acquisition of new information (secondary memory), for example, what test(s) should one employ to confirm this hypothesis? This step is most important, because when tests are appropriately selected and efficiently employed, they will provide a fine-grained analysis of the problem. This step is also controversial because there are differences in opinion about test selection.

At least five historical factors have contributed to the diversity of hypothesis-testing approaches in the study of memory functioning. First, intellectual and cognitive functioning have been studied by two different traditions: the psychometric and the information-processing traditions (e.g., see chapters 14 and 17). Each of these traditions tends to follow somewhat different assumptions and theoretical and methodological approaches. Second, as mentioned earlier, approaches to the study of memory changes and developmental differences can be divided roughly into those that are based on neuropathological changes and those that are not. Approaches to assessment could therefore be based on either a psychological or a neuropsychological model. Third, the diagnostic link between brain and behavior is not well established (see Riege et al., chapter 33), and different hypothesis-testing approaches could account for different models of the brain–behavior relationship. Fourth, theories on memory and on memory and aging have changed and fluctuated with new information and knowledge over the decades (see Poon, 1985, for a review). These changes have also affected the thinking regarding the emphasis of relevant factors in memory assessment. Finally, there are psychiatric models (e.g., motivated forgetting and repression, Talland, 1968a) that could account for post-traumatic psychogenic amnesia and other forms of amnesia.

Because of the diversity of hypothesis-testing approaches, a patient may be tested with different sets of diagnostic instruments when he or she is evaluated by different clinicians. The different methods of diagnosis may come to similar conclusions, and again they may not, given the rate of misdiagnosis and of differences in opinions of different clinician-scientists (see Gurland & Cross, chapter 2). Although clinicians tend to stay with one orientation for hypothesis testing (e.g., psychometric or information-processing), most will employ methods that have been demonstrated to show sensitivity for a particular process.

Chapters 14 to 18 provide in-depth reviews of psychometric, neuropsychologic, and information-processing approaches to the analysis of possible underlying memory dysfunctions. These chapters should provide a sound initial basis to make informed judgments for hypothesis testing. From the perspective of the brain–behavior relationship, chapter 16 (Corkin et al.) and chapter 7 (Goldberg & Bilder) provide a concise rationale for the neuropsychological approach. For those clinician-scientists who are interested in the evaluation of treatment effects, chapter 16 provides a review of brain regions affected by ADRD, known neurotransmitters affected by ADRD, and corresponding behavior affected by the respective brain regions and neurotransmitters. A set of tests is recommended to examine hypotheses regarding changes in the brain–behavior relationship. A complementary review of the diagnostic link between brain and behavior dysfunctions as well as a recommendation of a multivariate test approach is provided in chapter 33 (Riege et al.).

Chapter 17 (Kaszniak et al.) provides the theoretical and practical bases for the use of information-processing procedures for fine-grained analyses of behavior. This chapter begins by listing the pertinent reviews of literature on memory and aging in the last decade; it also examines the use of information-processing paradigms for studying underlying memory mechanisms in normal aging, in ADRD, and in focal brain lesions. It should be emphasized that information processing is not a set of concrete tests or procedures; rather, it is an approach to the study of cognition based on cognitive psychological models. The test procedure can be innovative and flexible and must be guided by theoretical or clinical hypotheses.

Finally, chapter 14 (Ferris et al.) examines common psychometric memory tests for subject assessment and selection as well as for evaluation of treatment effects. Examples of psychometric tests that closely simulate everyday behavior are presented, and criteria for choosing tests for subject selection and for treatment evaluation are discussed. Chapter 15 (Mohs, Kim, Johns, Dunn, & Davis) presents data from paradigms that have been shown to be sensitive to specific memory processes in ADRD. Chapter 18 (Branconnier) demonstrates how computer-based information-processing paradigms can be effectively packaged for clinical use. These chapters provide a comprehensive background for making informed decisions in selecting tests from initial evaluation of symptoms and for testing of hypotheses regarding possible locus of dysfunction.

Integration of Experimental and Clinical Precepts

Talland placed two quotes on the front page of his prize-winning book, *Deranged Memory: A Psychonomic Study of the Amnesic Syndrome* (1965). We believe that these quotes are most appropriate in introducing our effort to delineate the state of the art of clinical memory testing in older adults. The first quote comes from T. S. Eliot in *The Family Reunion*:

We do not like to look out of the same window,
 and see quite a different landscape.
We do not like to climb a stair,
 and find that it takes us down.
We do not like to walk out of a door,
 and find ourselves back in the same room.
We do not like the maze in the garden,
 because it too closely resembles the maze
 in the brain. (cited in Talland, 1965, p. ii)

The authors in this book show our readers different views from the same window, as well as the same view from different windows. We constructively criticize existing approaches and methods, and we also show from our own work that we, too, have walked up and down, inside and outside, and sometimes have found that we have not gone very far. Most of all, the search for cost-effective clinical memory assessment tools does indeed closely resemble a journey through a maze. We would like to emphasize that there is no one correct way of solving the maze of clinical memory assessment and that integrating cumulative information from different perspectives can stand us all in good stead.

We reiterate and wholeheartedly applaud Talland's recommendation that clinical observations in collaboration with laboratory performance are necessary to present a clear picture of the clinical syndrome. Systematic observation and clinical interview can provide clues that cannot be discovered by any other means. Laboratory performance tests, without some clue or hypothesis, cannot begin to cover in a cost-effective manner representative samples of behavior that are relevant to everyday remembering.

Studies presented throughout this Handbook, especially those in Section V, show that the study of memory dysfunction and the validation of memory assessment instruments are difficult and tedious tasks. In applying research findings to clinical assessment, we carefully delineate possible methodological and theoretical pitfalls that can contribute to variability in neuroanatomical measures (Jernigan, chapter 35; Brinkman, Largen, Cushman, & Sarwar, chapter 36), in behavioral measures (Hunt, chapter 6; Ferris et al., chapter 14; Thompson, chapter 19), and in the relationship between neurologic and behavioral measures (Kaszniak & Davis, chapter 27; Riege et al., chapter 33). With few exceptions, most of the studies employed relatively small numbers of subjects, reflecting the difficulty in recruiting patients within a set of usually stringent inclusive criteria, and in many instances reflecting the problem of attrition in longitudinal follow-up that is often beyond the control of the investigators. Issues of subject sampling, study replication, and result generalization are noted in the discussion of the sensitivity of specific paradigms in clinical diagnosis.

By and large, one may take comfort in knowing that when diagnostic instruments are judiciously selected, it is possible to obtain some measure of sophistication in identifying and differentiating patterns of performances between control groups and patient groups over time (e.g., chapters 28 to 30), with different clinical presentations across patient groups (e.g., chapters 31 to 34), and with some reliable degree of association to other anatomical, physiological, and biochemical measures (e.g., chapters 35 to 40). This level of sophistication can be obtained only with close collaboration among biomedical and behavioral scientists and among researchers and clinicians. Of course, we have just begun to understand the reciprocal impact of the brain and behavior. From both biological and behavioral perspectives, scientists are starting to learn more about aging processes, individual differences, and an individual's utilization of biological and psychological resources to deal with the environment. All of this information is beginning to be related to our knowledge about memory and memory disorders with older adults

and to increase the sensitivity of our diagnostic instruments for hypothesis testing.

We begin this Handbook on clinical memory assessment with the second quotation selected by George Talland, with which he probably intended to give aid and comfort to those following his footsteps, attempting to unravel the secrets of the brain and its concomitant behavior. The quotation is by Karl R. Popper in *The Logic of Scientific Discovery:*

Science never pursues the illusory aim of making its answer final, or even probable. Its advance is, rather, towards the infinite yet unattainable aim of ever discovering new, deeper, and more general problems, and of subjecting its ever tentative answers to ever renewed and ever more rigorous tests. (Cited in Talland, 1965, p. ii)

References

Bowles, N. L., Obler, L., & Poon, L. W. (in press). Aging and word retrieval: Naturalistic, clinical, and laboratory data. In L. W. Poon, D. Rubin, & B. Wilson (Eds.), *Everyday cognition in adulthood and old age.* New York: Cambridge University Press.

Cerella, J., Poon, L. W., & Williams, D. (1980). Age and the complexity hypothesis. In L. W. Poon (Ed.), *Aging in the 1980s: Psychological issues* (pp. 332–340). Washington, DC: American Psychological Association.

Erickson, R. C., Poon, L. W., & Walsh-Sweeney, L. (1980). Clinical memory testing of the elderly. In L. W. Poon, J. L. Fozard, L. S. Cermak, D. Arenberg, & L. W. Thompson, (Eds.), *New directions in memory and aging: Proceedings of the George A. Talland Memorial Conference* (pp. 379–402). Hillsdale, NJ: Erlbaum.

Erickson, R. C., & Scott, M. (1977). Clinical memory testing: A review. *Psychological Bulletin, 84,* 1130–1149.

Garcia, D., Reding, M., & Blass, J. (1981). Overdiagnosis of dementia. *Journal of the American Geriatrics Society, 29,* 407–410.

Gilbert, J. G., Levee, R. F., & Catalano, F. L. (1968). A preliminary report on a new memory scale. *Perceptual and Motor Skills, 27,* 277–278.

Gurland, B., & Toner, J. (1983). Differentiating dementia from nondementing conditions. In R. Mayeux & W. G. Rosen, (Eds.), *The dementias* (pp. 1–17). New York: Raven Press.

Jenkins, J. J. (1979). Four points to remember. A tetrahedral model of memory experiments. In L. S. Cermak & F. I. M. Craik (Eds.), *Levels of processing in human memory.* Hillsdale, NJ: Erlbaum.

Poon, L. W. (1985). Differences in human memory with aging: Nature, causes, and clinical implications. In J. E. Birren & K. W. Schaie (Eds.), *Handbook of the psychology of aging* (pp. 427–462). New York: Van Nostrand Reinhold.

Poon, L. W., & Fozard, J. L. (1978). Speed of retrieval from long-term memory in relation to age, familiarity, and datedness of information. *Journal of Gerontology, 33,* 711–717.

Poon, L. W., Fozard, J. L., Treat, N. J., & Popkin, S. J. (1978) From clinical and research findings on research to intervention programs. *Experimental Aging Research, 4,* 235–254.

Poon, L. W., Krauss, I., & Bowles, N. L. (1984). On subject selection in cognitive aging research. *Experimental Aging Research, 10,* 43–49.

Poon, L. W., & Welford, A. T. (1980). A historical perspective. In L. W. Poon, (Ed.), *Aging in the 1980s: Psychological issues* (pp. xiii–xvii). Washington, DC: American Psychological Association.

Randt, C. T., Brown, E. R., & Osborne, D. P., Jr. (1980). A memory test for longitudinal measurement of mild to moderate deficits. *Clinical Neuropsychology, 2,* 184–194.

Ron, M. A., Toone, B. K., Garralda, M. E., & Lishman, W. A. (1979). Diagnostic accuracy in presenile dementia. *British Journal of Psychiatry, 134,* 161–168.

Schonfield, D., & Robertson, B. A. (1966). Memory storage and aging. *Canadian Journal of Psychology, 20,* 228–236.

Smith, A. D. (1980). Cognitive issues: Advances in cognitive psychology of aging. In L. W. Poon, (Ed.), *Aging in the 1980s: Psychological issues* (pp. 223–227). Washington, DC: American Psychological Association.

Talland, G. A. (1965). *Deranged memory: A psychonomic study of the amnesic syndrome.* New York: Academic Press.

Talland, G. A. (1968a). *Disorders of memory and learning.* Harmondsworth, Middlesex, England: Penguin.

Talland, G. A. (1968b). *Human aging and behavior.* New York: Academic Press.

Talland, G. A., & Waugh, N. C. (1969). *The pathology of memory.* New York: Academic Press.

Zelinski, E. M., Gilewski, M. J., & Thompson, L. W. (1980). Do laboratory tests relate to self-assessment of memory ability in the young and old? In L. W. Poon, J. L. Fozard, L. S. Cermak, D. Arenberg, & L. W. Thompson (Eds.), *New directions in memory and aging: Proceedings of the George A. Talland Memorial Conference* (pp. 519–544). Hillsdale, NJ: Erlbaum.

Barry J. Gurland and Peter S. Cross

CHAPTER

2

Public Health Perspectives on Clinical Memory Testing of Alzheimer's Disease and Related Disorders

Public health aspects of Alzheimer's disease and related disorders (ADRD) are reviewed and their implications for clinical memory testing discussed. We draw attention to its high and increasing prevalence; the substantial extent to which it accounts for morbidity and mortality rates among the elderly; the high costs of caring for victims with respect to both public and private expenditures, in terms not only of material but also of human resources. The public health aspects of ADRD have specific relevance to the field of clinical testing of memory. Particular issues discussed include the need for more precise epidemiological and other research data, for descriptors of the disease and its consequences that adequately reflect its attendant disability and service needs, for avoiding costly and distressing misdiagnosis or unnecessary admission to institutions, and for systematic assessment that will enable the service system to work in a more coordinated and efficient manner.

Introduction

This chapter addresses the public policy and public health questions raised by Alzheimer's disease and related disorders (ADRD) and the role of clinical memory testing in the diagnosis and management of the disease. Since compromised memory and cognitive function is one of several important benchmarks of ADRD, the field of clinical memory testing has specific public health relevance. Clinicians need to employ tests to make diagnostic and treatment plans for an individual patient, while public health planners need tests to make decisions for the protection and improvement of the health and well-being of the community. This chapter addresses the public health perspective. The bulk of the chapters in this volume will address clinical evaluation issues.

The symptoms of Alzheimer's disease and related disorders have been described for over two thousand years, more precisely classified during the past century and a half, but widely acknowledged only over the recent decade. In the Greco-Roman era, statesmen and philosophers addressed the legal implications of impaired judgment due to advanced age, and physicians described the symptoms of intellectual deterioration (Lipowski, 1981). The separation of dementia from other mental disorders and its subclassification began in the 19th century. Around the turn of the century, Alzheimer identified the typical neuropathology of the disease that now bears his name. The clinical features and pathology of the related conditions that produce dementia, particularly the arteriosclerotic or multi-infarct variety, have been delineated mainly during the present century. Despite this long history of clinicopathological discovery, public awareness of this disorder is a recent phenomenon.

A current definition of dementia emphasizes a general decline in intellectual competence after maturity, with symptoms specifically affecting memory, orientation, abstract thinking, judgment, personality, emotional control, and functional capacity. Alzheimer's dementia (AD), also known as "primary degenerative dementia" (American Psychiatric Association, 1980), has the added characteristics of an unknown etiology, an age-related incidence, a distinctive neuropathology

Preparation of this chapter was supported in part by Administration on Aging Grant OHD AOA 90-AT2155/03. Requests for reprints should be sent to Barry Gurland, Center for Geriatrics, Gerontology and Long Term Care, 100 Haven Avenue, New York, New York 10032.

(diffuse degeneration and atrophy of brain tissue with excessive numbers of neurofibrillary tangles and senile plaques concentrated in the cerebral cortex and hippocampal regions of the brain), a strong tendency toward an insidious onset, a chronic course, irreversible progression, and premature death.

Each of the disorders related to Alzheimer's can be distinguished by characteristics of the clinical picture, etiology, neuropathology, or response to treatment. The most common related varieties of dementia are multi-infarct, normotensive hydrocephalus, Pick's disease, Creutzfeldt-Jakob disease, Guam-complex, alcoholic, pugilistica, and those associated with Parkinsonism, Huntington's chorea, and Down's syndrome.

Although age-related, AD is not restricted to those who are elderly; it can occur in the presenile period (prior to age 65) as well; in fact, when first described, this disorder was viewed as occurring only in the presenile period. AD probably accounts for the great majority (about 75%) of dementias occurring in the general population. Apart from the effect of age, little is known about the etiology of AD, although many possibilities are being explored, including changes in immunity, aluminum toxicity, and a transmissible slow virus. Some series of familial cases clearly have a genetic pattern (Heston, 1981). A close relationship between brain changes and the behavioral impairments has been demonstrated (Tomlinson, Blessed, & Roth, 1970), and the pathophysiology of the condition is rapidly being elucidated with reference to cholinergic and other neurotransmitter pathways: characteristically distributed alterations occur in the activity of choline acetyltranferase and acetylcholinesterase. Experimental pharmacological treatments have been based on these pathophysiological findings.

The Perspective of Public Health

The tragic consequences of AD or a related dementia are readily evident to those who observe the course of the condition, whether as a close relative or friend, a health care professional, or a research worker. Yet consideration of individual cases gives only one perspective on the problems imposed by this cluster of diseases. A different perspective, that of public health, focuses on the broader problems faced by society.

Public health issues are more than the sum of the effects of individual cases. When the magnitude of the problem exceeds a critical threshold, the commonweal is undermined, the functioning of society is threatened with disruption, and pressures mount for a response by societal systems, including the health and social care system. This position has been reached by the problems of ADRD partly as a result of a recent increase in the prevalence of the condition and partly because of a heightened social awareness of consequent problems and a recognition of the inadequacy of the current responses to the problem. The public health aspects of ADRD have burst into prominence.

If the public health view is that of societal concerns about ADRD, then its corresponding research arms are primarily epidemiology, health services research, and the sociomedical sciences. These efforts, together with clinical experience and the results of biomedical research, shape the public health perspective. This perspective is intended to influence reforms in delivery and quality of health and related social care, to guide the allocation of resources, and to suggest further lines of productive research.

From this preamble it can be anticipated that this chapter will draw attention to the high and increasing prevalence of ADRD; the substantial extent to which it accounts for morbidity and mortality rates among the elderly; the high public and private costs of caring for victims, in terms not only of material but also of human resources; the many ways in which the formal health and social care system is inappropriately structured, staffed, and financed for the care and management of this chronic, multifaceted disorder with medical, psychiatric, and social ramifications; the vital role of the informal support network and alternatives to institutional placement in controlling costs of services or improving the quality of life and care for patients; and the need for research that will lead to early and effective prevention and treatment of ADRD.

The specific issues surrounding clinical memory testing for compromised memory and cognitive function that reflect the public health perspective include the need for more precise epidemiological and other research data; for descriptors of the disease and its consequences that adequately reflect its attendant disability and its service needs; for avoiding costly and distressing misdiagnosis and unnecessary admission to institutions; and for systematic assessment that will enable the service system to work in a more coordinated and efficient manner.

Human and Financial Costs

The prominence of ADRD as a public health concern derives both from the great number of people who are victims of ADRD with its attendant suffering, disability, and death, and from the still greater number who are indirectly affected. The direct victims are at an overall prevalence for definite dementia of about 7% of those aged 65 or older. Prevalence rises steeply during old age from well under 1% at age 65 to more than 20% for those over age 85. Yearly incidence rates rise from less than 0.5% at ages 60 to 64 to over 3% for those over age 80 (Gruenberg, 1978; Hagnell, 1966; Sluss, Gruenberg, & Kramer, 1981). ADRD is now the 4th leading cause of death (after cancer, heart disease, and stroke) (Tower, 1978); it cuts life expectancy by between one half to two thirds and leads to over 60,000 deaths annually (Katzman, 1976). Probably the brunt of the mortality falls on those who are physically ill, possibly by direct effect of central neurological impairment on the homeostasis of vital organ systems, or through inappropriate treatment of a physical condition because of indifference, poor communication, unnoticed drug interactions, or concomitant overadministration of psychotropic drugs (Tower, 1978).

Among those indirectly affected are foremost the family members who bear the burden and expense of caring for dependent and sometimes behaviorally troublesome patients. At least two thirds of all patients with ADRD reside at home. Numbers of cases of ADRD alone do not suggest the dimensions of the burgeoning problem of caring for these patients; one must also take into account the ratio of size of the group with ADRD to the size of the group who must care for and support them (a type of dependency ratio). ADRD progressively impairs the capacity of the victim to be independent. As their condition deteriorates, ADRD victims become unable to carry out such tasks of caring for themselves as managing accounts, shopping, cooking, doing household chores, dressing, grooming, going to the toilet, maintaining continence, walking, feeding themselves, and communicating. Victims also become insufficiently alert to simple dangers and unmindful of the necessity of following health-care regimes such as taking medications.

Someone, usually a spouse or child, must provide personal assistance, supervision, encouragement, and reminders to compensate for these deficits. Apart from the physical labor and emotional demands involved, the helper may have to forego a job or social activities. Moreover, accessory symptoms of ADRD may add to the strain on the caregiver; for example, the victim may be aggressive and destructive, wander at large, be up all night, scream, or be incontinent. At this very concrete level, the dependency ratio is an indicator, albeit rough, of severe personal difficulties inflicted by ADRD on individuals not themselves direct victims of the condition.

There is a further manner in which the dependency ratio is a measure of societal burden due to ADRD. Private or public funds must be expended to pay for care when an informal support network is unavailable or is overwhelmed. When the funds derive from the public purse through general revenues or special levies, or when health insurance premiums are generally affected, the societal burden is spread. The size of the population engaged in productive employment relative to the financial costs of supporting patients with ADRD through the formal health and social services will again be reflected by the dependency ratio.

Basing an estimate of the number of ADRD cases on a prevalence rate of 1% for those 65 to 74, 10% for those 75 to 84, and 20% for those 85 and over, and assuming that the informal caregivers are drawn from those 45 to 65 years old, the ratio of potential informal caregivers to potential dependents has changed from 47 in 1960 to the current ratio of 35. The projection for the year 2000 is that this ratio will fall to 32.

The staff of long-term care facilities and home health agencies also have to cope with the frustrations of treating an often inexorably progressive condition. In nursing homes a large fraction—perhaps a majority—of all residents suffer from a dementia. They tend to be more impaired in basic self-care than other residents, to have longer stays, to present more behavioral difficulties, to be prescribed more psychotropic medication (National Center for Health Statistics, 1979). Most of the hands-on care is provided by minimum-wage labor. Staff turnover is rapid. Nearly three quarters of all nursing home beds are controlled by profit-making firms. Extensive attempts at government regulation and inspection of those facilities have likely been effective in raising the quality of care over the past decade, but the quality of care remains a focus of concern (Vladeck, 1980).

The taxpayer subscribes to the necessary public cost of service and research. One main expenditure is on nursing home care. In 1980, over 1.3 million persons were in nursing homes (National Center for Health Statistics, 1984). Total expenditures were 21.6 billion dollars (10.3 billion in private funds; 11.3 billion in public funds) (Freeland, Calat, & Schendler, 1980). If it is assumed that half of all residents are demented, then over 5.6 billion dollars in public expenditures can be attributable to ADRD. Nursing home costs were projected to rise to 42 billion dollars in 1985 and over 75 billion in 1990 (Freeland et al., 1980). Private expenditures for nursing home care are a major source of catastrophic health expenses to families (Congressional Budget Office, 1977).

The magnitude even of current costs of nursing home care is such that pressure to contain them has become a dominant feature of public discussion. Hopes that cheaper alternatives to institutional care might be devised that would at the same time improve care and cut costs were already waning as the results of the first formal comparisons of these alternatives to institutional care were published (Weissert, 1978; Weissert, Wan, Livieratos, & Katz, 1980).

Studies of the community-resident elderly have repeatedly found that the demented use a large proportion of health and personal social services. A study of a probability sample of elderly New Yorkers living at home (Gurland, Dean, Gurland, & Cook, 1978) found that of the one tenth of the sample most dependent on others, nearly half had a dementia that was a primary reason for their dependency. In the Newcastle upon Tyne study (Kay, Bergmann, Foster, McKechnie, & Roth, 1970), the 6% of the sample of the community-resident elderly diagnosed as demented, upon several years' follow-up, had accounted for over one half of all time spent by the sample in residential homes and nearly one third of all hospital admissions. (This despite their considerably greater mortality during the follow-up period.)

Less directly affected are those who, although not victims or in contact with one, are nevertheless aware of being at increased risk for developing the disease. There is a 30% risk of developing severe ADRD, given survival to age 80 (Sluss et al., 1981). The risk for first-degree relatives of the earlier onset cases is increased over fourfold. Given the high level of risk for ADRD, many of those surviving (or hoping to survive) to old age fear that they may become demented.

The importance of ADRD as a public health problem will grow with the increasing proportion and number of elderly people in the population. The number of those over 65 increased by over 20% in the 1970-to-1980 decade and is projected to increase 18% in this

(1980-to-1990) decade (U.S. Census, 1976). Studies appear to be in substantial agreement regarding the rate of increase of prevalence rate of ADRD with increasing age (Sluss et al., 1981).

It is this steep increase of prevalence with increasing age, together with the past and projected increases in the numbers of the old, and especially the very old, that has given rise to recent talk of an "epidemic of dementia" seen variously as an "approaching epidemic" (Plum, 1979), a "quiet epidemic" ("Dementia, the Quiet Epidemic," 1978) or, most ominously, a "deluge" (Wells, 1981).

There is evidence that the prevalence of ADRD has been rising also as the victims of ADRD are assisted to live for longer periods of time. According to Gruenberg (1978), the average duration of the course of ADRD rose from 3 to 5 years in Lundby between the period 1947 to 1957 and 1957 to 1967.

The Social Support Network

For every patient with ADRD who is more or less permanently institutionalized (usually in a nursing home), there are at least two living in the community who are being cared for by kin (almost always a spouse or child). The patients in institutions are as a group sicker than those in the community with respect to the stage of illness and the extent of disturbing behavioral accompaniments of the disease (Bergmann, Proctor, & Prudham, 1979). A further key difference between the two groups is in the extent of the social supports available to them.

The widowed are several times more likely than those with spouses to be in an institution, and the never-married more likely still. Those without children are at higher risk of being institutionalized than are those with a child, and having several children lowers the risk of institutional admission still further (Brody, Poulshock, & Masciocchi, 1978; Greenberg & Ginn, 1979).

The cohorts who will become aged over the next 50 years differ only slightly from the cohorts who are now already old, with respect to their propensity to marry. However, they will have markedly fewer children. Couples now already old had on average about five children, those about to become old had three, and those who will become old in the next century will have had but two (U.S. Census, 1974). So there will be markedly fewer children available to support the elderly.

And even these fewer children may be less well situated to care for their aged parents. Middle-aged married women now go to work—in the past 30 years their participation in the labor force has risen from 11% to over 45% (U.S. Census, 1973). It may be difficult for women to leave the labor force when necessary to care for kin, as is shown by the fact that over 30% of the mothers of preschool children now work, leaving the care of their children to others.

Spouses, who are the primary support of the dependent elderly living in the community, are also disproportionately female. The great difference in life span between men and women, together with the fact that women typically marry men older than themselves, results in a highly unbalanced sex ratio in old age. As recently as 1930, there was roughly one man for every woman in the elderly population; today the ratio is only 0.7, and it will become slightly more skewed over the foreseeable future (Treas, 1977, 1981). For a man this means a greater chance of having a living spouse to care for him in the event of need. However for a woman—and especially for the quite elderly woman most at risk for dementia—the chances of having a spouse to rely upon will grow smaller.

It seems only reasonable to expect a further weakening of normative and legal constraints against placing a parent or spouse in an institution. Persons now in long-stay institutions for the aged grew up in an era that was still quite alive with the stigma of the county poor house and the fear of the dole—they had not generally placed their own parents in institutions in old age. (Filial responsibility was then still commonly a legal obligation). Few people, even today, enter a nursing home without lingering regrets, on the part of both the new resident and the family, that perhaps care could have been provided in the community. Having placed their own parents in old-age institutions in greater numbers than ever before (the proportion of elderly people in nursing homes has more than doubled in the past 20 years), the generations who are about to become candidates for such placements will be still less reluctant. The burden of care for the demented, now still borne largely by the families of the demented, may shift further onto the shoulders of non-family-members and become increasingly a public rather than a private burden.

This shift has direct implications for the manpower needs of those professions and organizations now playing major roles in the care of the demented. Nursing home personnel—including physicians, administrators, nurses, nurses' aides, and physical, speech, and occupational therapy workers—will all be in increasing demand. A similar array of personnel work in the home health care sector, which will continue to expand (Fountain, 1976).

For some of these groups, notably physicians, the manpower supply over the next several decades is likely to be adequate, but the needs of the elderly imply a redirection of training within the profession to emphasize geriatric care and research (Institute of Medicine, 1978). For others, especially nurses' aides, growth may need to be especially rapid (U.S. Bureau of Labor Statistics, 1982).

Accuracy of Diagnosis

Inaccurate diagnosis of ADRD can lead by several paths to untoward public health consequences. When the clinician prejudiciously regards the impairments of the elderly as due to aging itself, the symptoms of ADRD may be attributed to "senility" rather than to a specific disease; thus the prevalence of the condition will be underestimated, the victim may not attract the

health care resources and management suitable for a patient and the caring family, and those subtypes of ADRD (such as multi-infarct or alcoholic dementia, or normotensive hydrocephalus) that are sometimes controllable or remediable may be missed. When the diagnosis of ADRD is incorrectly made, the identification of remediable conditions that resemble the syndrome picture of ADRD may not be intensively investigated, and the opportunity for effective intervention then may be overlooked; this is especially true with regard to states of depression or acute confusional states, which, if left untreated, can lead to unnecessary morbidity, mortality, and excessive utilization of acute and long-term care.

Statistics on dementia are still too crude to satisfy fully the public health approach to etiology, needs assessment, intervention, and prevention. Uncertainties arise as a result of inconsistencies in criteria for assessment and diagnosis, differing degrees of rigor in exclusion of confounding disorders (such as pseudodementia), lack of clarity in the distinctions between morbid and normal age-related changes in memory, and biases of performance on tests (see Eisdorfer, chapter 3, and Thompson, chapter 19, this volume). Redressing these inadequacies requires an upgrading of the role of memory testing.

Tests of memory and other cognitive functions are a conventional part of a contemporary diagnostic investigation of a possible case of ADRD. When seen from the vantage point of public health, with respect to the probabilities of inaccurate diagnosis in large populations, the use of simple tests and diagnostic criteria (see Reisberg et al., chapter 12, this volume) in the consulting room appears to reduce the rate of misdiagnosis, especially if combined with specific inquiries about the symptoms of depression and the routine use of selected laboratory investigations for metabolic and blood abnormalities. Brain-imaging techniques, particularly computer-assisted tomography, improve diagnostic accuracy by detection of space-occupying lesions and, to a lesser extent, by suggesting the possible presence of brain atrophy.

At present, neuropsychological testing has not been demonstrated to reduce diagnostic errors with respect to ADRD. Concepts and measures of memory dysfunction are being refined to an impressive degree, as reviewed in Kaszniak & Davis, chapter 27, and Crook, chapter 10 in this volume. However, the sensitivity and specificity of memory tests in relation to the diagnosis of dementia needs to be clarified.

One difficulty in achieving adequate *sensitivity* (the proportion of true cases so identified by the test) is that memory testing—even when that term is used in a broad sense to include assessment of orientation, learning, and information processing—is only one of several important aspects of diagnosis (see Eisdorfer, chapter 3, this volume). Language deficits are said to occur early in the dementing process (Rosen & Mohs, 1982; see also Rosen, Mohs, & Davis, chapter 30, this volume), and other changes of diagnostic relevance take place in personality and motivation, judgment, emotional control, visuospatial ability, motoric activity, and competence in everyday activities as well as in laboratory tasks. Without including much of this information in assessment, many cases, especially early ones, might be missed.

Specificity (the proportion of noncases so identified by the test) is even more of a challenge to memory assessment. It is well to remember that, even were the reliability of the memory test quite high, if the test were applied in a population in which dementia is relatively rare (e.g., less than 10%), the number of false positives would greatly outweigh false negatives (Shrout & Fleiss, 1981). Indeed the false positives may exceed true positives in many instances. Only by inclusion of other aspects of diagnosis (e.g., history, onset, associated impairment) can the group of tested positives be winnowed to a group in whom the diagnosis of a dementing condition is confidently established (see Eisdorfer, chapter 3, this volume).

There is ample evidence that misdiagnosis of ADRD does occur in medical practice to an important extent. Reviews of misdiagnosis (Garcia, Reding, & Blass, 1981; Gurland & Toner, 1983) show a frequency of misdiagnoses ranging from under 10% to over 50%. These misdiagnoses are not restricted to nonspecialist settings but occur also at the hands of neurologists, psychiatrists, and internists.

Short of the presence of pathological material, an irreducible uncertainty is probably inherent in diagnosis. However, given that biopsy is not widely regarded as an ethically acceptable risk, and autopsy comes, of course, too late for clinical purposes, there must be a continued search for better diagnostic aids. Some of these may be found in better imaging techniques such as positon emission tomography or nuclear magnetic resonance, or in neurophysiological approaches such as neurometrics, or perhaps in neurotransmitter analysis. A key issue is whether clinical testing of memory can enable diagnosis to reach a satisfactory level of accuracy without undue reliance on expensive technology.

Comprehensive Evaluation

Even accurate diagnosis is usually inadequate for the purpose of deciding on a suitable plan for case management. Comprehensive evaluation (see Erickson & Howieson, chapter 8, this volume) is a better guide to management decisions and includes, beyond diagnosis, information on the course of the condition, previous response to treatment, concomitant and complicating conditions, functional abilities and disabilities, the strength of social and financial supports, and environmental factors, as well as on the range of services and sites available and affordable. In a strict sense, clinical tests of memory occupy one niche within the structure of comprehensive evaluation; in a broader sense, tests of the conditions that affect memory should be directed not only at memory and related cognitive functions but also at the causes and effects of memory disturbance (see Riege, Harker, & Metter, chapter 33, and Butters, Martone, White, Granholm, & Wolfe, chapter 34, this volume). By these tokens, clinical memory testing involves, for example, an assessment of depression to rule out pseudodementia (Gurland, Golden, & Challop, 1982) and an assessment of performance levels in the activities of daily living (see Crook, chapter 10, and Gilewski & Zelinski, chapter 11, this volume) to arrange appropriate disposition and personal assistance and to follow progress of the condition.

With ADRD now more in the public consciousness, with increasing concern over costs, and with rapidly expanding research, one can expect efforts to standardize and routinize the assessment/diagnostic process (see Cunningham, chapter 4, this volume). In research settings these pressures will arise from the felt need to ensure comparability across studies. Standardized memory tests may also play a direct role in determining eligibility for services or to prevent ADRD patients from being discriminated against in gaining nursing home admission.

The cost of an initial evaluation of a possible case of ADRD is now in the region of a thousand dollars, allowing for a clinical history; a phenomenological, neurological, and physical examination; routine laboratory testing; a computed tomography scan; and a session of neuropsychological testing. If through this process a single case of misdiagnosis is avoided and a remediable condition detected and successfully treated, it is likely that a prolonged institutional stay will be obviated and a saving of perhaps tens of thousands of dollars of public money will be effected. Cost–benefit or cost–effectiveness analyses along these lines (see Cohen, chapter 9, this volume) should be pursued with respect to clinical testing of memory in the present and potential state of the art.

Overlap Between Normal and Morbid

A specific test for morbid, as opposed to normal, aging changes in memory (see Kaszniak, Poon, & Riege, chapter 17, this volume) would allow further investigation of the public health concern about the possible rapid rise in ADRD with increasing age. There is apparently about a fivefold increase in incidence in the old-old (i.e., older than 80) as compared with the young-old (ages 65 to 79); this possibility is serious, given that already one in four people in the United States reaches 85 years of age. An alternative hypothesis (Mortimer, Schuman, & French, 1981), suggested on the basis of hospital admissions data (an uncertain basis) and pathology in unselected populations (Matsuyama & Nakamura, 1978; Tomlinson & Kitchener, 1972), is that the rise in incidence levels off sometime after age 75. Further examination of this hypothesis will require tests that are specific to morbid memory changes and are unbiased by other characteristics, such as education, that differ between age cohorts. An illustration of the kind of specific test needed is found in a study (Osborne, Brown, & Randt, 1982) in which 24-hour delayed recall was found to be affected by both morbid changes in memory and by aging, while 3-minute recall was specific to ADRD.

Longitudinal Studies of Memory Performance

The course of ADRD, typified by slow and unrelieved progression (see Rosen et al., chapter 30, this volume), is a major factor in its public health impact, as well as being a key element in diagnosis. For these reasons, the usefulness of tests of memory and other performance characteristics of ADRD can be enhanced by more emphasis on longitudinal patterns. Time and sequence patterns of performance deficits delineate differences among acute, chronic, and invariant conditions. Acute conditions suggest the presence of a confusional state due to a cause which is usually remediable and outside of the brain tissues (e.g., electrolyte disturbance, hidden sepsis, drug side effect, endocrinological imbalance, anemia, other metabolic deviation, space-occupying mass in the cranium). Invariant traits may reflect a lifelong impairment such as mental retardation. It is the chronic condition that is most consistent with the course of ADRD.

The diagnosis of ADRD implies also a decline from previous functioning (Schoenberg, 1981; see also Storandt, Botwinick, & Danziger, chapter 28, and Wilson & Kaszniak, chapter 29, this volume). Rarely, however, are the results of premorbid psychometric testing available. Sometimes these are inferred from a comparison of tests that are change sensitive to those that are relatively impervious to change. However, the reliability and validity of retrospective accounts of memory change have not been sufficiently explored. Even contemporaneous self-ratings of memory or informant reports may correlate poorly with laboratory measures (Kahn, Zarit, Hilbert, & Niederehe, 1975; see also Gilewski & Zelinski, chapter 11, this volume). Some promising correlations have been reported in which changes *relative* to past performance are determined (Rabbitt, 1982) and in which informant reports in this respect are taken (Baddeley, Sunderland, & Harris, 1982).

Prospective longitudinal assessments must contend with practice effects (see Kaszniak, Poon, & Riege, chapter 17, this volume), which are generally marked for memory testing. In one recent study (Luhr & Gurland, 1984) in which three tests of memory and cognition were given to elderly subjects at bimonthly interviews for over a year, practice effects were found in all tests. Nevertheless, against the background of performance improvement due to practice, persistent longitudinal patterns of memory impairment were noted, and these were distinguished from episodic impairments due to depression and acute confusional states.

Longitudinal approaches (see Storandt et al., chapter 28, and Wilson & Kaszniak, chapter 29, this volume) can also aid in documenting, and, by extrapolation, in predicting, the course of illness. Longitudinal patterns should also assist in the elucidation of possible subtypes of dementia. ADRD with an onset after age 75, for example, seems to have less effect on shortening life than ADRD of early onset (Mortimer et al., 1981), with as yet undetermined importance for subtyping. Such information on the duration of survival in a state of dependency is of particular use for planning appropriate health and social services and types of care settings for the population or for the individual.

Subtypes

The etiological and clinical subtypes within ADRD have differing public health implications. High rates of alcoholic dementia suggest different preventive efforts than high rates of multi-infarct dementia. Rates of AD point to the need for intensifying research on this condition of unknown origin. Subtypes attributable to familial and genetic factors, to a transmissible agent, to a surgically relievable obstruction of cerebrospinal flow, or to another identifiable disorder such as Parkinson's disease or Huntington's chorea, each focus public health attention and policy on specific modes of prevention, intervention, manpower development, resource allocation, public education, future projections of need for services, and so on. Therefore, the contribution of psychometric classification (see Cunningham, chapter 4, this volume) to public health analysis is advanced by greater specificity in terms of subtypes of ADRD (see Cohen, chapter 9, this volume).

About one half of cases of dementia are primarily of the Alzheimer's type, and appreciable proportions (20% to 25%) are multi-infarct and alcoholic (Tomlinson, Blessed, & Roth, 1970; Wells, 1979). Various secondary dementias, some of them remediable, account for a substantial minority (about 20%) of cases. However, these proportions vary in certain settings (Hutton, 1981) and subgroups.

Not yet clear is the extent to which psychometric tests (for the purposes of subclassification) supplement, confirm, or substitute for other clinical information on changes in intellectual level and personality; associated possible causes; the rate, pattern, and duration of the course of the disorder; the response to specific treatments; and special and laboratory investigations. Ideally, the precision and reliability of psychometric testing (see Cunningham, chapter 4, this volume) should replace less rigorous types of information or allow screening of patients for more expensive procedures.

Biases in Test Results

Performance on memory and cognitive tests is not free of the influences of education and socioeconomic status. This hampers public health policy formulation because it is not yet known whether prevalence differences between certain sociocultural groups reflect differing vulnerabilities to ADRD or are only an artifact of the assessment process. Differences have been found between sociocultural and educational groups in rates of poor performance on memory tests as well as between geographically distinct groups. Particularly low rates of poor performance, for example, have been found in disadvantaged and in rural groups (Akesson,

1969; Primrose, 1962; Wilder & Gurland, 1982), and lower rates have been found in London than in New York (Gurland et al., 1983). These results, if taken at face value, would provide useful leads to etiology and prevention; but it is unlikely that these avenues will be vigorously explored until the indicators of ADRD are shown to be culture fair or free of cultural bias.

One analysis of age, education, and scores on a mental status questionnaire of a representative elderly community sample showed that educational level falls with age and partly accounts for the rise with age of errors on a scale of disorientation and memory (Gurland, 1981).

Early Dementia

Accurate identification of *early* cases of dementia would be of signal importance to public health efforts in prevention as well as to the individual's and the family's desire to anticipate and plan appropriate responses to the disease. However, the extreme variation in prevalence estimates of mild or early cases in different surveys of the general elderly population attests to the difficulty of correctly identifying ADRD early in its course. Whereas prevalence of severe or established cases is reported fairly consistently in the range of 3% to 8%, estimates of the early or mild cases range from less than 5% to over 20% (Gurland, Dean, Cross, & Golden, 1980). The Newcastle study of the elderly (Kay, Beamish, & Roth, 1964) found on follow-up that the diagnosis of early dementia was often in error. Thus, at present, public policymakers cannot rely confidently on the frequently quoted statistics of between 5% and 10% incidence for early dementias; much less can clinicians base the management plan for an elderly person on the uncertain basis of a diagnosis of early dementia.

Part of the problem is definitional. The term *early* may refer to mild but definite cases, to definite cognitive decline but with insufficient confirming signs of dementia, or to poor performance on cognitive tests with a decline only inferred because there is no firm evidence that the subject had a prior better performance level. Nielson (1962) defined mild dementia as "patients who are able to take care of themselves, and who are characterized by a definite decline in the level of performance, but who have their basic personality and judgement well preserved, and a relatively good insight into the nature of these changes" (p. 312). Thus, factors in addition to memory changes characterize his definition. Reisberg, Ferris, and de Leon (1982) defined early dementia in their Global Deterioration Scale (GDS) and distinguished it from mild cognitive decline, which they termed "early confusional" [state]. A key criterion is that the patient can no longer survive without some assistance; in this there is either a contradiction or a subtle refinement of Nielson's definition. In either event, there are in Reisberg's definition several references to performance levels of specific memory and other cognitive tasks that lead one to ask to what extent memory tests can solely define this condition of early dementia. For the present, a conservative view is that the diagnosis of dementia, whether early or mild or any other variety, can safely be made only when clear-cut, real-life performance deficits are evident.

Dysfunction, Disability, and Handicap

The most important public health aspect of dementia is probably not impairment of memory or other cognitive function, nor death, but prolonged disability. The consequences of such disability are evident in both the personal and the public spheres. For the individual victim there is loss of independence, inability to pursue work or interests, and constriction of leisure and interpersonal activities, with sometimes a tormenting anguish and fear at the loss of coping capacity and erosion of customary gratifications. Public relevance is seen in the loss of productive work by the victims, perhaps preceding the onset of manifest dementia by some years (although this is not yet well documented); in impairment of competence of public officials (many high offices—for example, legislative and judicial offices—are occupied by those of an advanced age); in decisions on surrogate management; in medicolegal issues of competence to stand trial or bear witness; in the need for consent for participation in research or receipt of treatment; and in formal and informal manpower and service considerations.

Clarification is needed of the usefulness and limitations of memory testing in addressing these issues of impairment of function and of the possible controls over intervening and interactive factors that would enhance the contribution of memory testing. It would be helpful to have specification of which memory and cognitive tests illuminate which aspects of disability in dementia (see Eisdorfer, chapter 3, and Kaszniak & Davis, chapter 27, this volume). Useful in this direction would be studies relating disability to batteries of tests (including tests of semantic and episodic or procedural and declarative memory, constructional tasks, orientation, information processing, and the like). As an illustration of the kind of work that is relevant to this issue, correlations have been shown between, on the one hand, specific tests of memory, motivation, and visuopractic skills and, on the other, specific difficulties in dressing (Weintraub, Baratz, & Mesulam, 1982).

Another good example of a broad attempt to relate cognitive performance and disability is found in a study of the difficulty experienced by older people in group conversations as opposed to dialogue (Rabbitt, 1982). The elderly subjects were matched with younger subjects on dialogue efficiency; both were asked to recall each sentence of a group conversation and who had said it. It appeared that difficulty in group conversation was due partly to failures in immediate memory, partly to failures in attentional selection, and partly to slight hearing loss not resulting in deafness but making the work of listening harder.

As of now, correlations between memory tests and disability are probably not high enough and the intervening variables not sufficiently specified to allow the disability to be calculated from results of memory testing alone. The disability must be measured independently and directly. Nor can estimates be made of *excess* disability among populations with observed levels of cognitive performance and disability, given that the expected relations are not yet precisely specified.

The uncertain relationship between memory testing and disability also leaves open whether improvements in disability can or must be effected through the medium of treating the memory difficulty (Weintraub et al., 1982). For example, behavioral speed may be just as severely affected by ADRD (and aging) as is memory or learning (Perret & Birri, 1982); thus, it may be that changing the demand of the environment with respect to speed can lead to adaptation by the afflicted patient without improving memory as such.

Clinical and Public Health Conflicts

It is advisable to keep in mind the distinction between the interests of the public health and the clinical arenas so that research may take both into consideration. Clinicians need tests that help them to plan treatment and management of the individual patient; the tests should be acceptable to the patient, readily available, and reimbursable or inexpensive. Public health planners need tests that can be used on large groups, are readily administered on a large scale, are straightforward to analyze, and, again, are not too expensive.

The clinician expects testing to facilitate or increase the accuracy of diagnosis and evaluation for prognosis, treatment, and case management. The public health professional expects a test to provide persuasive evidence for designing and funding programs in service delivery, manpower training, and research. Because new public health programs must often justify their additional costs and overcome the inertias and vested interests of the health and social system, the data provided for public health policy should be at least as good as that developed for clinical decision making.

The clinician may gain a good deal of rapport with patient, family, and staff through the employment of treatments for memory disorders that are experimental in nature; public health interventions, however, with their highly visible costs and effect on raising expectations of benefit, can be counterproductive if they are ineffective. Thus, the evaluation of interventions for ADRD should be methodologically at least as precise in the public health as in the clinical setting.

These clinical and public health distinctions can also be seen in the interpretation of results of trials of drug treatments for memory disorder. Any sign of improvement will be welcome clinically. From the public health viewpoint, however, it is changes that reduce requirements for personal assistance, management, and institutionalization that are pertinent; improvements that result in a longer survival for dementia patients without changing the above requirements may be seen as not very helpful from the public health viewpoint.

It is of great moment to the public health sector that the clinical assessment of memory and other cognitive functions contribute as fully as possible to public policy and to changes in the current health care system that will improve the quality of care for the victims of ADRD and their families.

References

Akesson, H. (1969). A population study of senile and arteriosclerotic psychoses. *Human Heredity, 19,* 545–566.

American Psychiatric Association. (1980). *Diagnostic and statistical manual of mental disorders* (3rd ed.). Washington, DC: Author.

Baddeley, A., Sunderland, A., & Harris, J. (1982). How well do laboratory-based psychological tests predict patients' performance outside the laboratory? In S. Corkin, K. L. Davis, J. H. Growdon, E. Usdin, & R. J. Wurtman (Eds.), *Alzheimer's disease: A report of progress in research* (pp. 141–148). New York: Raven Press.

Bergmann, K., Proctor, S., & Prudham, D. (1979). Symptom profiles in hospital and community resident elderly persons with dementia. In F. Hoffmeister & C. Muller (Eds.), *Brain function in old age*. Berlin: Springer-Verlag.

Brody, S. J., Poulshock, S. W., & Masciocchi, C. F. (1978). The family caring unit: A major consideration in the long-term support system. *Gerontologist, 18,* 556–561.

Congressional Budget Office. (1977). *Catastrophic health insurance*. Washington, DC: U.S. Government Printing Office.

Dementia, the quiet epidemic. (1978). *British Medical Journal, 1,* 1.

Fountain, M. C. (Ed.). (1976). Working with older people [Special issue]. *Occupational Outlook Quarterly, 20*(3).

Freeland, M., Calat, G., & Schendler, C. E. (1980). Projections of national health expenditures: 1980, 1985, 1990. *Health Care Financing Review, 1*(3), 1–29.

Garcia, D., Reding, M., & Blass, J. (1981). Overdiagnosis of dementia. *Journal of the American Geriatrics Society, 29,* 407–410.

Greenberg, J., & Ginn, A. (1979). A multivariate analysis of predictors of long-term care placement. *Home Health Care Services Quarterly, 1,* 75–99.

Gruenberg, E. M. (1978). Epidemiology of senile dementia. In B. S. Schoenberg (Ed.), *Neurological epidemiology: Principles and clinical applications* (pp. 437–455). New York: Raven Press.

Gurland, B. J. (1981). The borderlands of dementia: The influence of sociocultural characteristics on rates of dementia occurring in the senium. In N. E. Miller & G. D. Cohen (Eds.), *Clinical aspects of Alzheimer's disease and senile dementia* (pp. 61–80). New York: Raven Press.

Gurland, B., Copeland, J., Kelleher, M., Kuriansky, J., Sharpe, L., & Dean, L. (1983). *The mind and mood of aging: The mental health problems of the community elderly in New York and London*. New York: Haworth.

Gurland, B., Dean, L., Cross, P., & Golden, R. (1980). The epidemiology of depression and dementia: The use of multiple indicators of these conditions. In J. O. Cole & J. E. Barrett (Eds.), *Psychopathology in the aged* (pp. 37–60). New York: Raven Press.

Gurland, B., Dean, L., Gurland, R., & Cook, D. (1978). Personal time dependency in the elderly of New York City: Findings from the U.S.–U.K. Cross-National Geriatric Community Study. In *Dependency in the elderly of New York City* (pp. 9–45). New York: Community Council of Greater New York.

Gurland, B. J., Golden, R., & Challop, J. (1982). Unidimensional and multidimensional approaches to the differentiation of depression and dementia in the elderly. In S. Corkin, K. L. Davis, J. H. Growdon, E. Usdin, & R. J. Wurtman (Eds.), *Alzheimer's disease: A report of progress in research* (pp. 119–125). New York: Raven Press.

Gurland, B., & Toner, J. (1983). Differentiating dementia from nondementing conditions. In R. Mayeux & W. G. Rosen (Eds.), *The dementias* (pp. 1–17). New York: Raven Press.

Hagnell, O. (1966). *A prospective study of the incidence of mental disorders*. Stockholm: Scandinavian University.

Heston, L. L. (1981). Genetic studies of dementia: With emphasis on Parkinson's disease and Alzheimer's neuropathology. In J. A. Mortimer & L. M. Schuman (Eds.), *The epidemiology of dementia* (pp. 101–114). New York: Oxford University Press.

Hutton, J. T. (1981). Results of clinical assessment for the dementia syndrome: Implications for epidemiologic studies. In J. A. Mortimer & L. M. Schuman (Eds.), *The epidemiology of dementia* (pp. 62–69). New York: Oxford University Press.

Institute of Medicine. (1978). *Aging and medical education*. Washington, DC: National Academy of Sciences.

Kahn, R. L., Zarit, S., Hilbert, N. M., & Niederehe, G. (1975). Memory complaint and impairment in the aged. *Archives of General Psychiatry, 32,* 1569–1573.

Katzman, R. (1976). The prevalence and malignancy of Alzheimer's disease: A major killer. *Archives of Neurology, 33,* 217–218.

Kay, D., Beamish, P., & Roth, M. (1964). Old age mental disorders in Newcastle upon Tyne. Part 1: A study of prevalence. *British Journal of Psychiatry, 110,* 146–158.

Kay, D., Bergmann, K., Foster, E., McKechnie, A., & Roth, M. (1970). Mental illness and hospital usage in the elderly: A random sample followed up. *Comprehensive Psychiatry, 11,* 26–35.

Lipowski, Z. J. (1981). Organic mental disorders: Their history and classification with special reference to DSM-III. In N. E. Miller & G. D. Cohen (Eds.), *Clinical aspects of Alzheimer's disease and senile dementia* (pp. 37–45). New York: Raven Press.

Luhr, J. C., & Gurland, B. J. (1984). *Practice effects in behavioral testing of elderly hypertensive patients*. Unpublished manuscript. Center for Geriatrics and Gerontology, New York.

Matsuyama, H., & Nakamura, S. (1978). Senile changes in the brain in the Japanese: Incidence of Alzheimer's disease neurofibrillary change and senile plaques. In R. Katzman, R. D. Terry, & K. L. Bick (Eds.), *Alzheimer's disease: Senile dementia and related disorders* (pp. 287–297). New York: Raven Press.

Mortimer, J. A., Schuman, L. M., & French, L. R. (1981). Epidemiology of dementing illness. In J. A. Mortimer & L. M. Schuman (Eds.), *The epidemiology of dementia* (pp. 3–23). New York: Oxford University Press.

National Center for Health Statistics. (1979). *The national nursing home survey: 1977 summary for the United States* (DHEW Publication No. PHS 79-1794). Washington, DC: U.S. Government Printing Office.

National Center for Health Statistics. (1984). *Trends in nurs-*

ing and related care homes and hospitals: United States, selected years 1969–1980 (Vital and Health Statistics Series 14, No. 30). Washington, DC: U.S. Government Printing Office.

Nielson, J. (1962). Geronto-psychiatric period-prevalence investigation in a geographically delimited population. *Acta Psychiatrica Scandinavica, 38,* 307–330.

Osborne, D. P., Jr., Brown, E. R., & Randt, C. T. (1982). Qualitative changes in memory function: Aging and dementia. In S. Corkin, K. L. Davis, J. H. Growdon, E. Usdin, & R. J. Wurtman (Eds.), *Alzheimer's disease: A report of progress in research* (pp. 165–169). New York: Raven Press.

Perret, E., & Birri, R. (1982). Aging, performance decrements, and differential cerebral involvement. In S. Corkin, K. Davis, J. H. Growdon, E. Usdin, & R. J. Wurtman (Eds.), *Alzheimer's disease: A report of progress in research* (pp. 133–139). New York: Raven Press.

Plum, F. (1979). Dementia: An approaching epidemic. *Nature, 279,* 372–373.

Primrose, E. (1962). *Psychological illness: A community study.* London: Tavistock.

Rabbitt, P. (1982). Development of methods to measure changes in activities of daily living in the elderly. In S. Corkin, K. L. Davis, J. H. Growdon, E. Usdin, & R. J. Wurtman (Eds.), *Alzheimer's disease: A report of progress in research* (pp. 127–131). New York: Raven Press.

Reisberg, B., Ferris, S. H., & de Leon, M. J. (1982). The global deterioration scale for assessment of primary degenerative dementia. *American Journal of Psychiatry, 139,* 1136–1139.

Rosen, W. G., & Mohs, R. C. (1982). Evolution of cognitive decline in dementia. In S. Corkin, K. L. Davis, J. H. Growdon, E. Usdin, & R. J. Wurtman (Eds.), *Alzheimer's disease: A report of progress in research* (pp. 183–188). New York: Raven Press.

Schoenberg, B. S. (1981). Methodological approaches to the epidemiologic study of dementia. In J. A. Mortimer & L. M. Schuman (Eds.), *The epidemiology of dementia* (pp. 117–131). New York: Oxford University Press.

Shrout, P. E., & Fleiss, J. L. (1981). Reliability and case detection. In J. K. Wing, P. Bebbington, & L. N. Robins (Eds.), *What is a case? The problem of definition in psychiatric community surveys* (pp. 117–128). London: Grant McIntyre.

Sluss, T. K., Gruenberg, E. M., & Kramer, M. (1981). The use of longitudinal studies in the investigation of risk factors for senile dementia–Alzheimer type. In J. A. Mortimer & L. M. Schuman (Eds.), *The epidemiology of dementia* (pp. 132–154). New York: Oxford University Press.

Tomlinson, B. E., Blessed, G., & Roth, M. (1970). Observa-tions on the brains of demented old people. *Journal of Neurological Sciences, 11,* 205–242.

Tomlinson, B. E., & Kitchener, D. (1972). Granulovacuolar degeneration of hippocampal pyramidal cells. *Journal of Pathology, 106,* 165–185.

Tower, D. B. (1978). Alzheimer's disease-senile dementia and related disorders: Neurobiological status. In R. Katzman, R. D. Terry, & K. L. Bick (Eds.), *Alzheimer's disease: Senile dementia and related disorders* (pp. 1–4). New York: Raven Press.

Treas, J. (1977). Family support systems for the aged: Some social and demographic considerations. *Gerontologist, 17,* 486–491.

Treas, J. (1981). The great American fertility debate: Generational balance and support of the aged. *Gerontologist, 21,* 98–103.

U.S. Bureau of Labor Statistics. (1982). *Economic projections to 1990* (Bulletin 2121). Washington, DC: U.S. Government Printing Office.

U.S. Census. (1973). *Census of population: 1970 subject reports, final report PC(2)-6A.* Employment status and work experience. Washington, DC: U.S. Government Printing Office.

U.S. Census. (1974). *Population of the United States: Trends and prospects: 1950–1990.* Washington, DC: U.S. Government Printing Office.

U.S. Census. (1976). *Demographic aspects of aging and the older population in the United States* (Current Population Reports, Series P-23, No. 59). Washington, DC: U.S. Government Printing Office.

Vladeck, B. C. (1980). *Unloving care: The nursing home tragedy.* New York: Basic Books.

Weintraub, S., Baratz, R., & Mesulam, M. M. (1982). Daily living activities in the assessment of dementia. In S. Corkin, K. L. Davis, J. H. Growdon, E. Usdin, & R. J. Wurtman (Eds.), *Alzheimer's disease: A report of progress in research* (pp. 189–192). New York: Raven Press.

Weissert, W. G. (1978). Cost of adult day care: A comparison to nursing homes. *Inquiry, 15,* 10–19.

Weissert, W. G., Wan, T., Livieratos, B., & Katz, S. (1980). Effects and cost of day care services for the chronically ill: A randomized experiment. *Medical Care, 18,* 567–584.

Wells, C. E. (1979). Pseudodementia. *American Journal of Psychiatry, 136,* 895–900.

Wells, C. E. (1981). A deluge of dementia. *Psychosomatics, 22,* 837–840.

Wilder, D., & Gurland, B. (1982). *Some comparisons of the Los Angeles Hispanic elderly with other populations interviewed using the CARE.* Unpublished manuscript, Center for Geriatrics and Gerontology, New York.

Issues in Clinical Memory Assessment

Carl Eisdorfer, *Section Editor*

CHAPTER

3

Conceptual Approaches to the Clinical Testing of Memory in the Aged: An Introduction to the Issues

In this chapter on clinical significance of memory assessment, I address the conceptual approaches to clinical assessment through memory testing. According to my Funk and Wagnall's dictionary (1943), the word *conceptual* refers to concept, "an abstract general notion or idea, also any notion combining elements into the idea of one's subject." Simply put, then, I present a number of notions related to clinical memory assessment.

Three approaches are synthesized in memory testing: First, experimental cognitive psychology as it merges into studies of clinical syndromes. Second, the scientific and professional traditions of measurement psychology, with its technical background of test construction, validity, reliability, and factor-analytic studies. This area has expanded to include the neuropsychological approach to brain–behavior measurement. Third, a background of medicine, with its centuries-old tradition of clinical care and differential diagnosis and treatment, more recently based on empirical studies of psychopathology and behavior using standard examination procedures.

One need not be at the bedside to make significant clinical contributions. The history of medicine includes numerous examples of major advances made by basic scientists that were relevant to patient care and were rapidly incorporated into widespread practice. A particular model, that of the clinician–scientist (whether biomedical or psychosocial) is often proposed for medical school faculties, although it may be waning in clinical psychology training. The importance of good science in support of patient care cannot be emphasized enough.

The relatively limited role played in traditional medicine by the psychological (and social) scientist reflects a problem in the use of clinical memory assessment that must be addressed. The relevance of the behavioral sciences for the medical clinician is still only marginally appreciated, perhaps because of the paucity of a so-called third faculty group in the behavioral sciences, as exists in other branches of clinical teaching. If the basic researcher is the first faculty and the clinician the second, the third faculty are those who are active in basic research and who also serve as clinicians and educators themselves, thus bridging the gap between the laboratory and the bedside. What is called for, of course, is a body of clinical research that connects basic concepts and data to a level of practice that has demonstrated value in the care of those in distress.

Conceptualization and careful laboratory study of memory are therefore of potentially great clinical significance, although some scientists in the cognitive laboratory may have little interest in the problems of clinical care, and some clinicians may have little interest in the elegance of cognitive research paradigms. The tradition of tests and measurements with its concerns for valid and reliable measures, of standardization, of relevant subpopulations, and the like should be of great concern to the clinical psychologist using the output of these measures. Because not all clinicians can assess the validity and reliability of the tests, they use clinical professional standards that are established and maintained for clinical tests. To complicate this process, the relative decline in the status of assessment in clinical psychology practice and the tendency of clinical investigators to develop and use their own idiosyncratic laboratory techniques have compromised the generalizability of clinical research output in cognitive evaluation.

Modern (medical) diagnosis involves the collection and use of a range of information to understand and clarify the problems besetting a sick person. The information includes symptoms, that is, the patient's reported (subjective) experiences; signs, that is, those factors emerging as normal or atypical in the physical examination of a patient; and associated findings from the clinical laboratory. In synthesizing these data, the clinician must exercise decision-making skills that are crucial to the differential diagnosis of the disease. But as Feinstein (1967) pointed out, there are really three general categories that the thoughtful clinician must consider. First is an understanding of the *disease* as an impersonal entity, second is an understanding of the *host* as a unique complex, and third is an understanding of the *illness*—the specific pattern of signs and symptoms presented by the individual host.

The clinician must ask a series of questions:

1. What do I know? That is, what information do I have from previous contact with the patient as well as from current report and examination?

2. What could it be? That is, what are the various disorders that could cause this problem in the patient and are consistent with laboratory data?

3. What more do I need to know? That is, what laboratory or other data are needed to clarify issues and narrow the spectrum of diagnoses?

4. Given the new data, what are the most likely diagnoses?

5. What is causing or is likely to have caused the disease or dysfunction?

6. What can I do? Will the disease affect others? Is it contagious? Does it have implications for the family? Is it occupationally related?

7. What will be the effect of what I do on the problem as presented, on the disease or disorder diagnosed, on the patient, and on those around the patient, both proximally and distally?

8. What is the role of memory testing in addressing these questions?

It is in the treatment and management of the patient and affected others that the clinician exercises his or her socially designated role, and it makes the clinician the penultimate pragmatist. Clinicians are fundamentally committed to finding the appropriate treatment, cure, or management of patients, to relieve them of the problems they presented with and of any problems that emerged during evaluation (or secondary to the treatment itself). Diagnosis, with its implication regarding cause, is the easiest way of ensuring that a particular therapeutic strategy is appropriate. It provides a strategy to ensure that the clinician has not overlooked some alternate approach or wasted time and resources on hit-or-miss therapeutic ventures that have the potential for side effects and lack the value of therapeutic gains. This presupposes, of course, a clear understanding and differentiation of the diagnosis, and it also pre-

supposes that clinical memory testing has practical value; for indeed if it is otherwise, then however heuristic or interesting the findings may be to the investigator, it is unlikely that the clinician will reexpose a patient to the experience.

As scientist-clinicians, we must be concerned about the provisional nature of any clinically established diagnosis. A diagnosis can only reflect what is known at the state of the art, but researchers have the responsibility to enlarge that scope through increasing the data base—by treating each patient as a clinical experiment that may improve the pool of information that is relevant to the host disease or illness in question. Let us pursue this further.

Arriving at a diagnosis is akin to conducting an experimental procedure. It involves defining the problem by using an initial data set and then using those data to specify a hypothesis in the form of a general diagnostic impression—for example, pneumonia, a metabolic lesion, or a dementia. Initially, the general nature of the problem and of its somatic or systemic locus is identified. The process usually proceeds rapidly to the collection of data for the differentiation of the disorder to identify which among the competing hypotheses (diagnostic alternatives) can best account for the available data. In the diagnosis of pneumonia, its pathogen can be identified—that is, whether it is bacterial, viral, mycotic, and so on—and if bacterial, whether it is pneumococcal (statistically the most probable cause) or is caused by some other bacterial organism. In the case of dementia, clinicians will wish to know if the dementia is reversible and whether it is caused by physical agents or disease or by some psychiatric disturbance such as depression. Also included in the diagnosis might be whether permanent alteration of the central nervous system (CNS) is likely, whether the memory disturbance will be persistent, and perhaps which among the competing etiologies is at the root of the problem.

Further specification in the case of a patient with pneumonia may include the culturing of the pathogen and sensitivity testing to a range of available antibiotics. This testing may be used in fact to shortcut the diagnostic process and move rapidly to treatment by getting to the point of specification early. The notion here is that optimally, clinical testing should help not only with the differentiation of the disorder but also with the therapeutic strategy itself. This notion, of course, is consistent with my earlier comment that the clinician is of necessity a pragmatist. In the instance of memory testing, clinicians should raise the question of diagnosis, differentiation, and specification, not only for treatment but also to clarify etiology and possible outcome.

The issue of intervention is a corollary of diagnosis. In order for the effect of intervention or the natural history of a disorder to be assessed and monitored, the entities to be measured must be carefully isolated and calibrated. According to Feinstein (1967), this process is a crucial basis for clinical judgment. Once the variables have been identified and isolated, clinicians must agree on a scale of measurement and make intervention decisions accordingly. I have called such an approach, as applied to the behavioral sciences, the microanalysis of behavior. It is very much in the tradition of George Talland, who worked to specify patterns of the amnestic processes and their relationship to specific syndromes of known etiology. It is his leadership in memory testing, apart from his extraordinary qualities as a man, that is honored in this book.

In the description of factors involved in clinical judgment, I alluded to the potential for an intervention to have widespread consequences. This implies another notion, namely that clinicians should be in a position to extract the functional value of test data. What is the "real-world" significance of a given test profile? Does it help us determine the functions that can be performed at work or at home? Can we use it to develop intervention strategies for cognitive support or identify deficits in day-to-day functions so that we can alert the family of the patient? What is the value of testing for crucial functional questions such as the ability to drive a car, consent to or reject surgery, maintain financial control of one's assets, change a will, and so on? Maximization or circumscription of a patient's participation in his or her own affairs requires skills, and others who are involved in the patient's affairs should understand the issues involved.

In a review of psychological assessment, Schaie and Stone (1982) suggested that four answers may be given to the question "Why assess?" One is to diagnose behavioral disorders; two, to evaluate a patient's ability to function independently, which is relevant to legal questions of competence; three, to evaluate a patient's ability to work and perform; and four, to provide baselines from which to follow an intervention.

Another question is whether clinical memory testing can become based on a stronger relationship with experimental cognitive psychology so that clinicians may disaggregate the components of memory deficit in order to identify functional and physical lesions with greater precision. As an initial undertaking, it would be desirable to develop a battery of tests such that identifiable patterns of performance will characterize particular subgroups of patients. As an example, diabetes is characterized by frequent urination. A readily identifiable property of the urine produces sweetness in diabetes melitus or blandness in diabetes insipidus, and this distinction leads easily to the differentiation of two very different diabetic disorders. Indeed, their etiologies, pathogenesis, and management are remarkably dissimilar. The differentiation of the urinary quality helped clinicians eventually to understand the metabolism of the organ system affected.

In the case of the most frequent irreversible dementing syndrome, Alzheimer's disease (AD), can careful memory testing disaggregate that disorder? Is the work of Cohen and her associates correct (Cohen, Eisdorfer, & Walford, 1981)? That is, is there a subtype of AD with attentional deficit as the dominant feature whereas another form of the disease is characterized by associational deficits? Can more definitive memory testing differentiate what electron microscopy now does not, that is, the difference between possible sub-

types of disease, between early- and late-onset disease, or among genetically labeled patient groups? Is a more experimental psychological orientation to the disorders of memory needed that is based less on current data than on newly conceptualized approaches to the structure of memory and learning?

In his classic monograph, *Diseases of Memory*, Ribot (1882) stated,

> Facts collected at random are very unequal in value; the most extraordinary are not the most constructive, the most curious are not the best sources of light. Physicians, to whom we owe them for the most part, have described and studied only from a professional standpoint. A disorder of memory is to them only a symptom, and is so recorded; it serves to establish a given diagnosis and prognosis. It is the same with classification; the observer is content with associating each case of amnesia with the morbid state of which it is the effect; thus we have amnesia from softening of the brain, hemorrhage, cerebral disturbance, or intoxication.
>
> From our point of view, however, diseases of memory must be studied by themselves, as morbid psychical states, through which we better understand the same elements in a healthy condition. As to classification, we are forced to arrange them according to external resemblances. Our knowledge of the subject is not sufficiently advanced to permit us to undertake a natural classification— that is by cause. (pp. 7–8)

Of more recent vintage is the approach of the cognitive clinical psychologist whom we honor here. In describing the psychopathology of memory, George Talland (1965) indicated that its theoretical analysis could be conceptualized at three levels: at the neuropathological level, with brain lesions as the point of departure; at the psychological level, which proceeds without reference to neuropathology; and in the "observations of behavior both clinical and experimental and some attempt more or less systematic, to order them within a conceptual frame of reference" (p. 261). It is this third line of attack that characterized Talland's work in *Deranged Memory* and that indeed was the orientation of most of his work.

This then leads me to some final comments. It seems to me that what is needed is to develop a system of clinical memory testing that at once contributes to, interfaces with, and expands existing knowledge of the psychopathologic causes of memory deficit. The prospect of doing so, however, raises some very important questions.

• Can the diseases and the structure of memory be understood well enough for a proper evaluation to be organized that can identify possible differences in the patterns of memory loss among the diseases affecting memory?

• Can the clinical examination of memory help clinicians to discriminate among diagnostic entities across the range of individual differences, accounting for variables such as age, motivation, circumstance of testing, education, standardization sample, and so on?

• Can reliable and valid tests of cognition and memory be created so that scientist-clinicians reach a consensus on a standardized procedure for investigating and evaluating clinical memory?

• Can a protocol be developed that is functionally relevant?

• If developed, will such a schema be used by clinicians in psychiatry, psychology, neurology, and related fields?

The next six chapters in this Handbook provide six different perspectives to assist the reader in finding answers to the preceding questions. Chapter 4 (Cunningham) addresses the important psychometric perspectives necessary to construct or choose sensitive and meaningful memory tests. Chapter 5 (Lawton) provides a contextual perspective in describing the influences of psychosocial influences on cognitive testing. Chapter 6 (Hunt) outlines one experimental perspective of cognition on which tests of memory ability could be based. Chapter 7 (Goldberg & Bilder) provides clinical examples of neuropsychological perspectives in committing errors of omission and commission in evaluating amnestic syndrome. Chapter 8 (Erickson & Howieson) outlines the clinician's perspective in measuring change and treatment effectiveness. Finally, chapter 9 (Cohen) addresses the psychopathological perspectives in differential diagnosis of AD.

In a paper entitled "The Assessment of Organic Impairment in the Aged: In Search of a New Mental Status Examination" (Eisdorfer & Cohen, 1982), I wrote:

> Strategies of intervention and attempts to evaluate older persons have not been incorporated into government policy or health care practice. A part of the difficulty is the failure to understand the nature of the cognitive impairment, the lack of any available yardstick against which to judge improvement, and the concomitant general reluctance to deal with complex problems of a chronic, slowly deteriorating population. (p. 346)

It is probably the case, too, that there are as many demented persons outside of institutions as there are inside, that the outside community contains even more individuals who are mildly impaired.

With the projected increase in the number and proportion of the aged population (Myers, 1975), the impact of cognitive disability as a significant component of health and social problems is becoming a major national problem. The development of a technology with a more precise instrumentation for measuring the changing abilities of the older population at risk is an important social as well as scientific priority, and, it should be added, such technology is an absolutely essential but missing clinical tool.

References

Cohen, D., Eisdorfer, C., & Walford, R. L. (1981). Histocompatibility antigens (HLA) and patterns of cognitive loss in dementia of the Alzheimer type. *Neurobiology of Aging, 2*(4), 277–280.

Eisdorfer, C., & Cohen, D. (1982). The assessment of organic impairment in the aged: In search of a new mental status examination. In E. I. Burdock, A. Sudilovsky, & S. Gershon (Eds.), *The behavior of psychiatric patients: Quantitative techniques for evaluation* (pp. 329–351). New York: Marcel Dekker, Inc.

Feinstein, A. R. (1967). *Clinical judgment*. Baltimore, MD: Williams & Wilkins.

Funk & Wagnall's College Standard Dictionary of the English Language. (1943). Chicago: Wilcox & Follett.

Myers, R. (1975). *Social security*. Homewood, IL: Richard D. Irwin, Inc.

Ribot, R. (1882). *Diseases of memory*. New York: Appleton.

Schaie, K. W., & Stone, V. (1982). Psychological assessment. In C. Eisdorfer (Ed.), *Annual review of gerontology and geriatrics* (Vol. 3). New York: Springer.

Talland, G. A. (1965). *Deranged memory: A psychonomic study of the amnesic syndrome*. New York: Academic Press.

Walter R. Cunningham

Psychometric Perspectives: Validity and Reliability

Issues of validity and reliability in clinical memory assessment of the elderly are considered. Five barriers to progress in developing validity criteria are identified: These are: the indeterminate dimensionality of memory; the diversity of aging phenomena; problems in specifying diagnostic criteria for different memory functions; process versus individual differences in research orientations; and the need for effective teams of experimental psychologists, psychometricians, and clinicians. Construct, predictive, content, and face validity are discussed in this context. It is argued that construct validity is the most important kind of validity. Issues related to reliability are considered briefly.

Over the past three decades, there has been an increasing awareness of the needs of elderly people in American society. In the area of memory assessment, professional psychological practice with the elderly lags well behind what is scientifically and technically possible. The purpose of this chapter is to discuss issues concerning the validity and reliability of measures in the context of clinical memory assessment.

Ideally, the criteria for validity of a measurement instrument should be based on a clear concept of the phenomenon to be measured. A major problem for practicing clinical psychologists who must evaluate memory functioning in the elderly on a day-to-day basis is that the dominant instrument was based on a rather vague and unsystematic concept 40 years ago. The time is more than ripe to move beyond this early effort and to bring the full weight of modern cognitive science, recent developments in psychometrics, and increased awareness of these advances in clinical psychology to bear on the problem of improving clinical memory assessment of the elderly.

Clearly, this task will not be easy. A number of problems are involved. This chapter identifies five barriers to progress in developing criteria for validity and reliability in this area. But for these problems someone might have developed a more adequate instrument,

perhaps 20 or 30 years ago, and then there would be less need for this book.

Barriers to Progress

There seem to be five major barriers to specifying rigorously validity criteria for clinical instruments of memory functioning. (Although there may be other barriers, these five are doubtless sufficient to account for the sluggish progress in this field.) These barriers are (a) the indeterminate dimensionality of memory, (b) the diversity of aging phenomena, (c) the lack of full specificity of diagnostic categories for various memory functions; (d) the fact that the overwhelming majority of memory research is process oriented rather than oriented toward individual differences; and (e) the rareness of effective cooperation between experimental psychologists, psychometricians, and practicing clinicians.

Memory is a multidimensional phenomenon, but the extent of its dimensionality is not well understood. This issue is complicated by the numerous competing (and sometimes redundant) models and theories of memory. Estimates of the number of such models range from 15 to 40. Terminology is often redundant or inconsistent. Sometimes the same term refers to different phenomena in different models, and sometimes different terms refer to the same phenomenon. For example, Kinsbourne (1980) questioned the distinction between attention and input, and even suggested that awareness may be tantamount to encoding. Along the same lines, some models indicate that both intermediate and long-term functions should be assessed, yet other models indicate that any information remembered for 5 minutes will be remembered for 5 years. Although other examples are possible, clearly redundancies exist across various conceptualizations and theories of memory. Thus, the same phenomena may be masquerading under different names in different theoretical accounts. Research is badly needed to develop individual-difference measures of various memory operationalizations to be used in correlational studies of the structure of memory, in an effort to identify redundancy. It appears that more research in factor analysis is needed to identify an approximate structure of memory. Such work would provide a basis for further research, as is discussed later.

The second major obstacle to progress concerns the nature of aging. Although behavioral researchers almost always use chronological age at an operational level, they only rarely provide an explicit definition of what they mean by "aging" (Birren & Cunningham, 1985). Some researchers focus on primary, or normal, aging, but others want to investigate a combination of primary and secondary (disease-related) aging. It might be a mistake to force a premature consensus regarding a definition of aging, but a genuine consensus would help scientific efforts. It is important to realize that there is not a strong consensus regarding the basic nature of aging even among biologists (Finch & Hayflick, 1985). (For a more extended discussion of one approach to defining aging, see Cunningham, 1981.)

Researchers' operational procedures, such as screening experimental subjects for perceptual limitations, are not always consistent with the concept of aging employed and are often inadequate. For example, a common phrase in the research literature is "The subjects were active, community-residing volunteers assumed to be in good health." Because brief and easily administered ratings of health status have recently been shown to have a considerable degree of validity (see, e.g., LaRue, Bank, Jarvik, & Hetland, 1979; Mossey & Shapiro, 1982), such measures should be routinely used in research with the elderly.

A closely related problem concerns the fact that most psychological research draws on positively biased volunteer samples. In contrast, elderly patients at clinics typically have multiple health or behavioral problems in addition to the primary presenting problem. At some scientific meetings it seems that various professionals are talking about different groups. An academic researcher, who usually sees only very healthy and capable elderly people who have volunteered for complicated and lengthy research activity, is likely to view the elderly as having fewer problems than does a clinical psychologist working in nursing homes. Therefore, professionals working in different settings occasionally can greet one anothers' perceptions of the elderly only with considerable consternation.

A third aspect of this general problem of validation is that there are multiple outcomes of aging, some of which are normal and others of which result from disease or other causes not universal to the elderly population. Because our concept of aging lacks specificity, and also because the dimensionality of memory is not determinate, deducing specific predictions about the effects on memory of normal aging or a variety of other conditions is truly problematic. Remedying this problem will require a crisper, or at least a consistent, definition of what is meant by aging, an assessment of the dimensionality of memory functioning, and a coherent, specific theory linking the phenomena of aging to memory factors. Further, there is a need for explicit theories explaining why a particular disease state or behavioral abnormality (such as extreme depression) should be linked to some aspect of memory. Some psychologists tend to think of relationships between memory problems and disease states as empirical concerns. However, the analytical question of why a particular relationship exists is important also, although often this issue will take an investigator beyond the confines of his or her traditional discipline. Until such conceptualizations are developed, there will continue to be a "by gosh and by golly" quality to applied efforts in this area.

A fourth major obstacle to progress in validation concerns the gap between process-oriented research and clinically oriented research. Clinically oriented research investigates individual differences and tends to focus on the relationships (usually correlations) between performance on a given task and some external variable, such as the presence or absence of a given disease. Process-oriented research usually is aimed at achieving a deeper and more analytical understanding of the nature of the task by conducting experiments in which some aspect (process) of the task is manipulated (see Kausler, 1982, Chapter 5, for a more extended discussion).

There is a wealth of experimental evidence concerning various aspects of memory. There are also some extant ideas about the structure or dimensionality of memory. Given the need for better clinical tests of memory to be used with the elderly, it is only logical that an important piece of progress in this area would involve the translation of process-oriented variables into psychometrically adequate tests of individual differences. This is absolutely essential because clinical evaluation involves the use of individual difference measures, in part, to arrive at a diagnostic conclusion. It seems reasonable to assume that many psychometrically adequate tests of individual differences in memory can be based on the available process-oriented research, but concepts must be translated and tests developed. In some cases, this work may be fairly easy. In fact Guilford (Guilford, 1967; Guilford & Hoepfner, 1971) has already developed many such measures. It is likely, however, that some translations may be very difficult and slow in coming, either because individual differences in some processes are small or because measuring some memory processes reliably may require too many trials to be practical.

If these problems are to be overcome, there must be an active and continuing cooperation between experimental psychologists, clinicians, and psychometricians. This is particularly true with regard to the translation of process-oriented research into individual differences measures. The tendency for these specialists to remain isolated groups is the fifth major obstacle to a full validation of memory measures for the elderly. The experimental memory literature is a vast and foggy jungle; it is unlikely that any nonspecialist can effectively forge a path through this jungle. But it is the clinician who most clearly perceives assessment needs, practical constraints, and realities of the testing situation. And the psychometrician is needed to bridge the gap between experimental and clinical work, not only by developing professionally competent tests but also by developing a structural basis from which possible measures can be systematically selected.

Kinds of Validity

Construct Validity

Construct validation may be thought of as a continuing exploration of the meaning of a scientific construct. This process has three major components, according to Nunnally (1978):

> (1) Specifying the domain of observables related to the construct; (2) from empirical research and statistical analyses, determining the extent to which the observables tend to measure the same thing, several different things or many different things (usually by applications of factor analysis); and (3) subsequently performing studies of individual differences and/or controlled experiments to determine the extent to which supposed measures of the construct produce results which are predictable from highly accepted theoretical hypotheses concerning the construct. (p. 98)

Will Rogers used to say that he was not a member of an organized political party—he was a Democrat. When assessing construct validity, psychologists are usually a little like Rogers's Democrats: One psychologist may make up a test, a second may include the test in a factor-analytic battery, and a third may carry out a series of controlled experiments with a version of the test as a dependent variable. This process usually goes on haphazardly for many years. Concerted, programmatic efforts by well-qualified teams of researchers are the exception rather than the rule. This tendency is unfortunate. Construct validity is by far the most important kind of validity. It is the most strategic (far-reaching) kind of validity because it makes measures much easier to use. Empirical results from measures with construct validity are usually easier to interpret, and such measures can be applied in practical situations more effectively. Also, only after the structure of the memory domain has been specified will certain kinds of questions be efficiently researched. For example, which aspect of memory is most sensitive to the early stages of alcoholism? Unless the approximate number of dimensions of memory is known, it is not possible to carry out a comprehensive and efficient research program to answer this question.

There are two major approaches to researching construct validity: structural research and manipulated experiments. There has been much manipulative research investigating memory, but less structural research. (In contrast, in the area of intelligence, there is a wealth of correlational studies of structure, but comparatively little controlled research.) In the area of memory, the enormous experimental literature has provided a great deal of insight into how memory works, and this is certainly important. The dearth of structural research is unfortunate because a prerequisite for developing systematic memory testing is at least an approximate knowledge of the dimensionality and structure of memory.

Structural research on memory measures began several decades ago. For example, Thurstone and Thurstone (1941) reported a rote memory factor, which is today the best replicated factor of memory. Guilford's (1967) Structure of Intellect (SOI) model included memory as one aspect of intellectual operations. The other operations in the SOI model were evaluation, convergent production, divergent production, and cognition. Because there were six products (units, classes, relations, systems, transformations, and implications) and four content areas (figural, symbolic, semantic, and behavioral) in the SOI model, it predicted 24 memory factors. However, relatively little research has been carried out in the social-behavioral content area, and Guilford recently acknowledged that the products in his model have less empirical support than the operations and content areas. If distinctions between products and the insufficiently researched area of social-behavioral memory content are eliminated, only three memory factors are left. Undoubtedly, more are needed.

Although research on memory factors has been sporadic, the existing literature provides a basis for further work. For example, factor analysis is very effective for identifying redundant operationalizations. Although specialists sometimes disagree about the optimum number of factors from a given analysis, the picture can usually be clarified by a series of linked studies in which, by design, new factors are allowed to emerge through the use of new variables. Unfortunately, this programmatic approach to factor analysis is not often followed. Another important point is that an explicit goal should be set: to identify broad common factors and to avoid narrow factors born of similar forms of the same test.

The battery of factor-referenced tests developed by the Educational Testing Service (ETS) is an example of what can be accomplished. Many years ago, ETS organized a conference to consider which factors of intellectual abilities were well established, using the accepted scientific criterion that a factor is well established if it has been replicated in two or more laboratories by two or more investigators. Specialists in psychometrics and intelligence testing were able to arrive at a substantial consensus regarding which ability factors were well established. ETS has continued to support this project, and the Kit of Factor Referenced Tests (Ekstrom, French, & Harman, 1976) is an invaluable aid to researchers in the area of intelligence. Although this project has focused on intellectual abilities, recent work has already identified four memory factors (Visual, Span, Associative, and Meaningful Memory). A concerted effort would probably identify more memory factors.

Conclusions from manipulated experiments can augment and substantiate the meaning of a given variable in relationship to other variables, in addition to elucidating the underlying processes involved in a given type of memory. Unfortunately, the wealth of information from experimental studies is not coherently organized. Organization does not come easily, because the field is theoretically diverse. An attempt to review the literature systematically would be a desirable step toward creating a more coherent viewpoint on the construct validity and the dimensionality of memory measures.

Predictive Validity

Predictive validity indicates the degree to which a test can estimate some behavior (the criterion) external to the measuring instrument (Nunnally, 1978). Predictive validity is more concrete than construct validity, which is not only abstract but sometimes downright ethereal.

Researchers who study predictive validity assume that the criterion is the basis of evaluation but often do not focus sufficiently on it. Is the criterion reliable? Is it sound to assume that it is the best practical yardstick against which to evaluate the test? Often, criterion development is by far the most difficult aspect of studying predictive validity.

For example, a common problem in industrial and educational research is that supervisors' or teachers' rating procedures may not be sufficiently reliable to provide a suitable evaluation of tests. Medical ratings and categorizations may well have similar problems. Often, careful attention to developing an effective rating system is needed prior to a study of predictive validity.

Another problem is defining and specifying the diagnostic categories a test predicts. Clearly, it is important to have as homogeneous a research group as possible. However, when working with a condition such as Alzheimer's disease, which remains primarily a diagnosis of exclusion, the researcher inevitably will include at least some borderline cases, which will detract from the precision of the study. Yet another problem has to do with multiple conditions. A sample of subjects with one type of cardiovascular disease, for example, may have other conditions as well, thus potentially biasing validity estimates. The usual solution to this problem is to screen groups elaborately to ensure that subjects in a given diagnostic group approximate having only one serious medical problem.

A more subtle, though potentially important, aspect of the predictive validity of memory tests is the ability to predict everyday behaviors or subjective perceptions of memory (metamemory). There is increasing interest in measuring individuals' perceptions of their own memory functioning. A closely related area of interest is how significant others (e.g., spouses or institutional caregivers) perceive memory functioning. Which aspects of memory are most related to an individual's own complaints about memory? Which aspects are most apparent to others? This kind of information could be of value to clinicians, but little research with the elderly has investigated such questions. Part of the problem is that these questions would be much easier to research if there were an existing taxonomic structure from which measures could be drawn systematically. Research on everyday behaviors and the subjective evaluation of memory has the potential of being a very important application of experimental psychology to everyday life.

Content Validity

Content validity is evaluated by a rational appeal to the manner in which a test was constructed (Nunnally, 1978). Perhaps the clearest example of a test with content validity is a spelling test constructed by taking a random or systematic sampling of words studied in a children's spelling workbook. Because the items were systematically sampled from a specified domain, the test is thought to have content validity. This kind of validity appears to be relatively unimportant for research on memory (because it is hardly ever applicable), although a rather weak appeal to content validity was one of the rationales for the Wechsler Memory Scale (WMS) (Wechsler, 1945).

Face Validity

Although not a major kind of validity in a technical sense, face validity deserves a few comments. Face validity means the tests appear valid. Face validity, which is sometimes dismissed as "phony validity," is relevant to memory testing for two reasons. First, the clinician's approach must be plausible to the client and so must the clinical procedures. If the situation is not plausible, the client may not cooperate or give his or her best efforts, which may bias the test results and the evaluation. Second, old people generally are not so docile as sophomore psychology majors, who are often veterans of many exotic and unusual procedures conducted in the name of academia. It is well documented that some elderly people will not perform tasks that they view as trivial or ridiculous. Some of these people probably have a need to escape from a situation they view as threatening, but others are simply asserting common sense. Thus, measures of clinical memory do need some reasonable degree of face validity.

Reliability

Reliability is probably best thought of as consistency either across occasions or within occasions. For example, does a test yield consistent results at different times? Most researchers think the more reliable a test is, the better, but reliability is more of a trade-off than is validity. Higher levels of reliability can almost always be achieved by increasing the number of items on the instrument, but the test then requires more time of the patient, the experimental subject, and the psychologist. Therefore, the appropriate degree of reliability depends on the situation and the time requirements. For example, in a controlled experiment in which only one dependent measure is used, the subject's time is not overburdened, and if the sample for the study is small, then a reliability of 0.9 is undoubtedly needed. In contrast, in a factor-analytic study involving many variables and batteries lasting 2 to 3 hours, shorter instruments and reliability coefficients of 0.6 are not unusual or inappropriate. For clinical evaluation in which several tests are combined for an overall composite, individual test reliabilities of 0.8 seem reasonable. However, if a given test is to stand by itself in making a contribution to the evaluation, a reliability of 0.9 should be the standard. Clearly, this situation obtains when a pattern or scatter of scores from a battery is used for diagnosis, but this standard is not used so commonly as it should be in such cases.

An important topic in this context is the reliability of measures in specific groups such as diagnostic categories. The reliability of a psychological test is best assessed using a sample that is as heterogeneous as possible, given the test's intended application. Also, unless it can be assumed that the behavior itself is relatively consistent, an unambiguous adjudication of the test's reliability is not possible. Occasionally, reports are critical of a given instrument because it fails to yield reliable results for a particular sample of psychotics, but the correct inference is that the test is not reliable in this sample. Thus, if the behavior is inconsistent, the test, no matter how well constructed, cannot be reliable. It would be incorrect to conclude that the test is unreliable in general. It is important to recognize that reliability of psychological tests is not an absolute quantity but varies across samples and situations. When assessing the memory of the elderly, clinicians need to know the reliability of a test for both community-dwelling elderly and impaired groups.

In several studies with large samples, I have had a chance to compare a number of reliability coefficients for different cognitive abilities. The reliability of test performance of the community-resident elderly seems to be very slightly less consistent than that of young adults. However, because the range of scores for most elderly groups is slightly greater than for young adults (and reliability estimates are usually quite sensitive to the range of scores), the observed reliability coefficients are roughly the same. Thus, it appears that for most tasks, reliability is adequate.

Conclusions and Recommendations

To have adequate construct validity, a test must be anchored in a structural theory of memory functioning that is reasonably comprehensive in identifying broad, common factors. Probably the most crucial problem with the WMS and its revisions is that they are not based on such a taxonomic structure. There is probably not a single development that would be more useful to the rational development of memory test batteries for the elderly than the creation of such a structure.

For each variable assessed by the test battery, there should be substantial evidence from controlled studies that the given measures perform as predicted from processing models of memory. In order to be included in the battery, each selected test should have at least one (and hopefully many) predictive relationships to real-world criteria, including but not limited to other measures of individual differences, such as age, diagnostic categories, types of brain damage, treatment effects, and various subjective reports of memory functioning. The tests selected should also have reasonable face validity and should not make elderly subjects uncomfortable or disinclined to cooperate. Undoubtedly, some factors of memory that will be identified will have little or nothing to do with real-world criteria. There would not be much point in including tests for such factors in clinical batteries.

A sustained program of factor-analytic research on memory would probably identify 10 to 15 broad memory factors, which would probably be too many for a standard clinical battery. A modular approach is possible: Three or four of the best-validated tests could be used as a standard, time-efficient battery, and a dozen or so other tests with appropriate standardization and norms could be held in reserve to be used when an extensive clinical evaluation is required.

References

Birren, J. E., & Cunningham, W. R. (1985). Research on the psychology of aging: Principles, concepts and theory. In J. E. Birren & K. W. Schaie (Ed.), *Handbook of the psychology of aging*. New York: Van Nostrand Reinhold.

Cunningham, W. R. (1981, August). *The Cascade Model of intellectual abilities in late adulthood*. Paper presented at the meeting of the American Psychological Association, Los Angeles.

Ekstrom, R. B., French, J. W., & Harman, H. H. (1976). *Manual for Kit of Factor Referenced Tests*. Princeton, NJ: Educational Testing Service.

Finch, C. E., & Hayflick, L. (1985). *Handbook of the biology of aging*. New York: Van Nostrand Reinhold.

Guilford, J. P. (1967). *The nature of human intelligence*. New York: McGraw-Hill.

Guilford, J. P., & Hoepfner, R. (1971). *The analysis of intelligence*. New York: McGraw-Hill.

Kausler, D. H. (1982). *Experimental psychology and human aging*. New York: Wiley.

Kinsbourne, M. (1980). Attentional dysfunctions in the elderly: Theoretical models and research perspectives. In L. W. Poon, J. L. Fozard, L. S. Cermak, L. W. Thompson, & D. Arenberg (Eds.), *New directions in memory and aging*. Hillsdale, NJ: Erlbaum.

LaRue, A., Bank, L., Jarvik, L., & Hetland, M. (1979). Health in old age: How do physicians' ratings and self-ratings compare? *Journal of Gerontology, 34*, 687–691.

Mossey, J. M., & Shapiro, E. (1982). Self-rated health: A predictor of mortality among the elderly. *American Journal of Public Health, 72*, 800–808.

Nunnally, J. C. (1978). *Psychometric theory*. New York: McGraw-Hill.

Thurstone, L. L., & Thurstone, T. G. (1941). Factorial studies of intelligence (*Psychometric Monograph* No. 2).

Wechsler, D. A. (1945). A standardized memory scale for clinical use. *Journal of Psychology, 19*, 87–95.

M. Powell Lawton

Contextual Perspectives: Psychosocial Influences

This chapter discusses cognition as it is related to other facets of general well-being, referred to as "the good life." A review of research indicates that on a bivariate level, the cognitive functioning of older people is related to health, functional health, interaction with friends, meaningful time use, and psychological well-being, but not with amount of family interaction and only in scattered fashion with perceived quality of life. Multivariate analyses of five studies indicate that direct independent relationships remain between cognition and functional health and between cognition and interaction with friends. The relationships between cognition and time use and psychological well-being were indirect. It is concluded that cognition is an essential component of the general well-being of the elderly and that the clinician should explore the extent to which other facets of well-being vary with cognitive state.

Most of the chapters in this book are devoted to sharpening the constructs and the instruments for measuring one specific form of cognition—memory. This focus tends to narrow the range of inquiry in a much-needed way. By contrast, this chapter looks beyond memory and beyond cognition in order to search for the place of cognition in the totality of what I have called "the good life" (Lawton, 1983f). Cognition and memory are portrayed as only two members of a total transactional context of person and environment. The context is transactional because causality is mutual rather than unidirectional. This chapter emphasizes the centrality of cognition in suggesting that cognition directly and indirectly affects other domains of functioning. It must be understood, at the same time, that the reciprocal effects whereby domains such as social interaction, activities, or psychological well-being affect cognitive performance, are equally probable.

In order to understand how elemental cognition is, we have to see the framework within which the system of the person in the environment functions and develop a rationale for examining cognition and its associations with all the other facets of the good life. It is also necessary to understand how existing empirical research has addressed cognition and its function in the

context of the good life. Research done at the Philadelphia Geriatric Center showing the place of cognition in a general model of well-being will be presented.

In attempting to describe the major aspects of life, I have suggested that the entirety of life may be viewed in evaluative terms as "the good life," divided into four sectors: behavioral competence, perceived quality of life, psychological well-being, and objective environment (Lawton, 1983f). While these four sectors can be differentiated conceptually and empirically, they have substantial areas of overlap. (See Figure 5-1) Examples of the separate domains for each of the four sectors are shown in Table 5-1.

One can see that cognition is one of five domains of behavioral competence (discussed at greater length in Lawton, 1972, 1982a). Cognition, in turn, has the many facets familiar to all, such as learning, problem solving, and memory (each of which may also need to be differentiated into subdomains, as Cunningham suggests in this volume for memory, Chapter 4). I think that research dealing with many of the sectors and domains of the good life has become so specialized that we are overlooking opportunities to determine the interrelationships among domains and sectors. We therefore risk losing opportunities both to understand the whole person and to understand cognition as a process.

Cognition and Functional Assessment

Clinicians have long recognized that a brief set of questions about orientation and general information affords an efficient means for screening gross degrees of

Some of the research reported in this chapter was supported by Grant AG00895 from the National Institute of Aging, Grants MH30665 and MH35312 from the National Institute of Mental Health, and Grants 93P57436 and 90-AR-006 (Leonard E. Gotteman, principal investigator) from the Administration on Aging.

Table 5-1. Examples of Domains in the Four Sectors of the Good Life

Behavioral competence	Perceived quality of life	Psychological well-being	Objective environment
Self-rated health	Satisfaction with:	Depression	Income
Health conditions	• income	Anxiety	Number of family
Health behavior	• family	Happiness	Number of friends
Functional health (ADL)	• friends	Positive affect	Housing quality
Cognition	• housing	Negative affect	Neighborhood quality
Time use	• neighborhood	Congruence	
Social interaction	• time use	Life satisfaction	
		Morale	
		Self-esteem	

cognitive impairment. Impaired people need to be identified in many situations where there is no specialist available to perform an in-depth assessment. The popularity of the Kahn-Goldfarb Mental Status Questionnaire (MSQ) (Kahn, Pollack, & Goldfarb, 1961) and many similar instruments attests to this need. Essentially the same rationale lies behind the need for functional assessment in general. "Functional assessment is an evaluation of the most important aspects of the behavior and the objective and subjective worlds of the person through standardized methods that can be applied by people who have a wide variety of backgrounds and training" (Lawton & Storandt, 1984, p. 258). Thus, in addition to providing a large increase in information at relatively small cost, functional assessment attempts to be comprehensive in its coverage of the major facets of well-being.

Psychologists have hardly begun to learn all that can be learned from the patterning of levels of well-being as measured by full-range assessment packages. For example, the Duke Older Americans Resources and Services (OARS) functional assessment questionnaire (Center for the Study of Aging and Human Development, 1978) has the capability of yielding a profile of scores: measures of social, economic, mental, and physical well-being; and proficiency in the activities of

daily living (ADL). The relationship between cognition and other domains of well-being might be expected to vary as a function of the state of health or of the presence of a particular disorder. "Crossover" relationships, that is, a concurrence of two symptoms that are not usually thought of as indicators of the same syndrome, are very frequent. For example, Golden, Teresi, and Gurland (1982–1983) found that a report of being "sad or depressed," while a good indicator of depression, occurred in 39% of the dementia cases as well, while 19% of their depressed people did not know how long they had lived in their area. In clinical use, it is thus clearly beneficial to be able to see whether a measured cognitive impairment is matched by impairments in other areas, whether this disability stands alone in an otherwise competent person, or whether some other pattern exists.

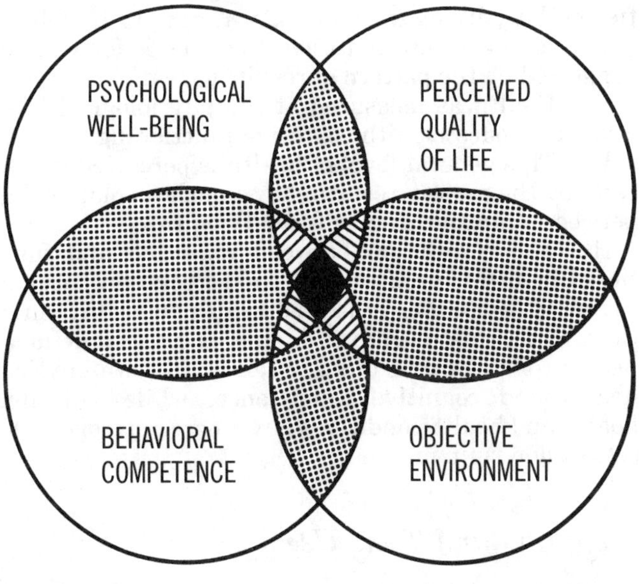

Theoretically, the productive questions concerning how cognitive performance fits in with the other facets of the person are even more numerous. Each person's lifelong range of cognitive competence is likely to be minimally reflected in some areas of functioning, for example, psychological well-being, because an individual builds life goals, expectations, and coping styles around the self-perception, and ideally, acceptance of this relatively stable range of cognitive competence. Changes in cognitive functioning are a very different matter. A decline in cognitive efficiency, especially if perceived by the person, will disturb the self-perceptions and self-acceptance of his or her accustomed functional levels in many domains of living. To understand the functioning person, we must be able to observe when such rearrangements among the facets of the good life do and do not take place. A landmark research finding illustrating this point came in the National Institute of Mental Health's (NIMH) original Human Aging Study (Birren, Butler, Greenhouse, Sokoloff, & Yarrow, 1963), which demonstrated relative autonomy among several levels of functioning among the healthiest of the subjects, but measurably greater interdependence of levels among the less healthy subjects.

Empirical Studies of the Domains of Well-Being

The major problem of either a literature review or a more formal meta-analysis is that one must often use research designed for purposes other than the one

Figure 5-1. The four sectors of the good life. Reprinted from Lawton (1983f) by permission.

being currently addressed (see Okun & Stock, 1984). However, using existing literature as a foundation to shed new light on the relationship has several limitations. First, memory as such has rarely been explicitly assessed in research that also assessed other aspects of the good life. Therefore, this review will focus on cognition rather than memory. Second, since cognitive functioning was often not the focus of the research to be reviewed, the cognitive measures are frequently either brief (for example, the ubiquitous MSQ) or factorially impure (such as the Wechsler Adult Intelligence Scale [WAIS], Wechsler, 1958). Third, imprecision born of the typical functional assessment battery's need to obtain the maximum amount of information in the least amount of time characterizes many measures in other domains. Fourth, what can be gleaned from existing studies is typically bivariate relationships (correlations, chi-squares, or mean differences) where the influences of additional factors can not be determined. Finally, the studies reviewed do not represent the universe of all reports that present correlations between cognition and well-being, but, rather, those collected by the author in his recent readings. Despite these problems, one of the strengths of a critical review is that where robust relationships do, in fact, exist, they will show through across the many variations in measures, samples, and research designs. The strategy for this section will be to present a compact review of findings from the recent literature regarding the relationships between the cognitive measures and each of the other domains of well-being. The text will comment about the limitations of the findings and the possible meaning of the findings.

Table 5-2 shows the bivariate relationships between various measures of cognition and other indicators of behavioral competence or psychological well-being (column labeled "other measures") as reported in a number of studies by diverse investigators. For complete descriptions of the many measures used, the original sources must be consulted.

Where multiple indicators of a single construct were used on the same group of subjects, a median of those correlations is presented, so that the same subjects are shown in Table 5-2 only once for the correlation between any pair of constructs.

Cognition and Health

It has been accepted as axiomatic that physical health and cognitive functioning are highly related, and there are few data that contradict this basic notion. Less clear are conclusions regarding the size of the relationship, the variations in the size of the relationship as a function of the range of variation in measures, the type of cognitive measure, and the type of health measure. The issue of the range of variation deserves a comment that applies to all types of the relationships discussed in this chapter. Where both the cognitive measure and the other measure of well-being are age-related, the bivariate relationship calculated on subjects across a wide age span will, of course, be substantial. If knowledge regarding the relationship between cognition and

another domain independent of age is required, multivariate treatment or analysis within age group is required. The same reasoning applies when both cognition and the second variable are health related. Once more, the necessity of multivariate analysis is clear.

The type of cognitive measure used is an obvious source of variation in the size of the relationship between cognition and health. For example, scores on the MSQ would have so little variance in a normal sample that their relationship to contextual factors would be minimal. Analyses of the contribution of the type of cognitive measure to the health–cognition relationship will not be attempted here but will be left to others with greater expertise in this area (see, e.g., the methodological critique by Siegler, Nowlin, & Blumenthal, 1980).

Type of health measure is a major focus of study in its own right (see Lawton, 1984, for an extended discussion). The Philadelphia Geriatric Center's Multilevel Assessment Instrument (MAI; Lawton, Moss, Fulcomer, & Kleban, 1982) distinguishes and provides indexes for measuring self-rated health, health conditions, health behavior, and functional health (activities of daily living, ADL). Self-rated health is known to share much conceptual space with psychological well-being; a meta-analysis of 231 such correlations showed a median correlation of .32 (Okun & Stock, 1984). By contrast, the median correlation between self-rated health and cognition in the studies displayed in Table 5-2 is .15 (all were statistically significant). Health conditions are much more difficult to scale than self-rated health. Laboratory measures are objective but apt to reflect a narrow band of physical health. Nonetheless, diverse measures of physiological functioning have displayed significant relationships with both fluid and crystallized cognitive measures (Birren et al., 1963; Heron & Chown, 1967). Table 5-2 shows consistent but low correlations between checklist measures of self-reported health conditions and MSQ-type measures (median .12, range .05 to .22). Notably higher correlations were found between MSQ scores and activities of daily living (median .325, range .15 to .49).

The following are tentative hypotheses for testing, suggested by the pattern of results shown in the table:

H1. Health as measured at the physiological level covaries modestly with cognitive functioning.

H2. This general level of health is perceived veridically by the person, resulting in a modest relationship between cognition and self-rated health.

H3. The correlation between cognition and functional health is greater than the correlation between cognition and either self-rated health or health conditions. This relationship is higher because functional health competence is directly caused by both physical health and cognitive competence, while self-rated health and health conditions have more heterogeneous sets of determinants.

Cognition and Time Use

Time use, that is, the way people spend their discretionary time exclusive of informal social contact, was

Table 5-2. Relationships Between Cognition and Domains of the Good Life

Domains of the Good Life	Source	r_o	Cognitive Measure	Other Measures
Health				
• self-rated health	Lawton (1983a)	.19	Interviewer rating	MAI self-rated health
	Lawton (1983b)	.15	WAIS Comprehension, DS	MAI index
	Lawton (1983c)	.14	MSQ	MAI index
	Lawton (1983d)	.13	WAIS Comprehension	MAI index
	Palmore & Luikart (1972)	.20	WAIS total score	Single rating
• health conditions	Golden et al. (1984)	.22	CARE dementia index	CARE somatic index
	Lawton (1983a)	.11	Interviewer rating	MAI health conditions
	Lawton (1983b)	.05	WAIS Comprehension, DS	MAI index
	Lawton (1983c)	.13	MSQ	MAI index
	Lawton (1983d)	.12	WAIS Comprehension	MAI index
	Lawton (1983e)	.12	WAIS Comprehension	MAI index
• functional health	Lawton (1983a)	.17	Interviewer rating	MAI ADL index
	Lawton (1983b)	.27	WAIS Comprehension, DS	MAI ADL index
	Lawton (1983c)	.42	MSQ	MAI ADL index
	Lawton (1983d)	.32	WAIS Comprehension	MAI ADL index
	Lawton (1983e)	.18	WAIS Comprehension	MAI ADL index
	Lawton & Brody (1969)	.38	MSQ	PSMS ADL index
		.48	MSQ	IADL index
	Linn (1983)	.49	Mini-Mental State	PAMIE ADL
		.31	WAIS	Disability scale
	Quinn (1982) Group 1	.16	MSQ	PSMS
	Group 2	.44	MSQ	PSMS
	Group 1	.33	MSQ	IADL
	Group 2	.15	MSQ	IADL
	Golden et al. (1984)	.34	CARE dementia index	CARE ADL index
• other health indicators	Baer & Gaitz (1971)	.16	Spitzer MSS-Memory	Physician rating
	Birren et al. (1963)	.39	Verbal Factor I	Vital capacity
		−.29	Verbal Factor I	Systolic blood pressure
	Lawton & Brody (1969)	.35	MSQ	Physician rating
Time use	Golden et al. (1984)	.28	CARE Dementia index	CARE activity index
	Lawton (1983a)	.18	WAIS Comprehension, DS	MAI activity index
	Lawton (1983b)	.18	Interviewer rating	MAI activity index
	Lawton (1983c)	.30	MSQ	MAI activity index
	Lawton (1983d)	.52	WAIS Comprehension	MAI activity index
	Lawton (1983e)	.34	WAIS Comprehension	MAI activity index
	Palmore (1981) Duke I males	.30	WAIS total score	Activity index
	females	.51	WAIS total score	Activity index
	Duke II males	.25	WAIS total score	Organizations frequency
	females	.22	WAIS total score	Organizations frequency
	Reichard et al. (1962)	.40	Test factor	Organizations frequency
		.22	Test factor	Activity index
Interaction with family	Lawton (1983a)	.00	Interviewer rating	Aggregate interaction
	Lawton (1983b)	−.02	WAIS Comprehension, DS	Aggregate interaction
	Lawton (1983c)	.14	MSQ	Aggregate interaction
	Lawton (1983d)	.02	WAIS Comprehension	Aggregate interaction
	Lawton (1983e)	.03	WAIS	Aggregate interaction

Continued

Note. Acronyms for test names are MAI—Multilevel Assessment Instrument; WAIS—Wechsler Adult Intelligence Scale; MSQ—Mental Status Questionnaire; CARE—Comprehensive Assessment and Referral Evaluation; ADL—Activities of Daily Living; DS—Digit Symbol; PSMS—Physical Self-Maintenance Scale; IADL—Instrumental Activities of Daily Living; PAMIE—Physical and Mental Impairment Evaluation; MSS—Mental Status Schedule; PGC—Philadelphia Geriatric Center; LSI—Life Satisfaction Index.

Table 5-2; continued

Domains of the Good Life	Source	r_o	Cognitive Measure	Other Measures
Interaction with friends	Golden et al. (1984)	.27	CARE dementia index	CARE isolation index
	Lawton (1983a)	.15	Interviewer rating	Aggregate interaction
	Lawton (1983b)	.22	WAIS Comprehension, DS	Aggregate interaction
	Lawton (1983c)	.29	MSQ	Aggregate interaction
	Lawton (1983d)	.39	WAIS Comprehension	Aggregate interaction
	Lawton (1983e)	.25	WAIS	Aggregate interaction
	Linn (1983)	.20	Mini-Mental State	PAMIE withdrawal score
		.18	WAIS total score	Social participation index
	Palmore (1981) Duke I males	.24	WAIS total score	Family and friends interaction
	females	ns	WAIS total score	
	Duke II males	ns	WAIS total score	Family and friends interaction
	females	.17	WAIS total score	
Psychological well-being	Birren et al. (1963)	.00	WAIS	Depression rating
		.00	WAIS	Morale rating
	Golden et al. (1984)	.16	CARE dementia index	CARE depression index
	Lawton (1983a)	.18	Interviewer rating	PGC Morale Scale
	Lawton (1983b)	.30	WAIS Comprehension, DS	Positive affect
		.30	WAIS Comprehension, DS	Negative affect
		.19	WAIS Comprehension, DS	PGC Morale Scale
	Lawton (1983c)	.18	MSQ	PGC Morale Scale
	Lawton (1983d)	.37	WAIS Comprehension, DS	Positive affect
		.22	WAIS	Negative affect
		.13	WAIS	Rosenberg Self-Esteem Scale
	Lawton (1983e)	.11	WAIS Comprehension, DS	Positive affect
		.14	WAIS	PGC Morale Scale
	Linn (1983)	.08	Mini-Mental State	PAMIE anxiety scale
		.01	Mini-Mental State	LSI
		.08	WAIS	Hopkins checklist, anxiety
		.11	WAIS	Hopkins checklist, depression
		.09	WAIS	LSI
	Palmore (1981) Duke I males	ns	WAIS Verbal	LSI
		ns	WAIS Performance	LSI
	Duke I females	ns	WAIS Verbal	LSI
		.24	WAIS Performance	LSI
	Duke II males	ns	WAIS Verbal	Affect Balance
		ns	WAIS Performance	Affect Balance
	Duke II females	.27	WAIS Verbal	Affect Balance
		.22	WAIS Performance	Affect Balance
	Palmore & Luikart (1972)	.05	WAIS	Cantril ladder
	Tobin & Lieberman (1976)	.26	6-test composite	Life satisfaction
		.20	6-test composite	Anxiety index
		.16	6-test composite	Depression index

Note. Acronyms for test names are MAI—Multilevel Assessment Instrument; WAIS—Wechsler Adult Intelligence Scale; MSQ—Mental Status Questionnaire; CARE—Comprehensive Assessment and Referral Evaluation; ADL—Activities of Daily Living; DS—Digit Symbol; PSMS—Physical Self-Maintenance Scale; IADL—Instrumental Activities of Daily Living; PAMIE—Physical and Mental Impairment Evaluation; MSS—Mental Status Schedule; PGC—Philadelphia Geriatric Center; LSI—Life Satisfaction Index.

hypothesized to be more complex than health and cognition, because it is more dependent on extrapersonal factors (Lawton, 1972). Primary among these extrapersonal factors are socioeconomic status (SES) and environmental opportunity, both of which are also related to cognitive functioning. Thus SES, like chronological age, is another essential covariate that must be taken into account in order to comprehend the basic relationship between cognition and time use.

The measurement of time use is much less developed than is measurement in other domains of behavioral competence (Lawton, 1985). The literature reports that such measures as counts of discretionary activities, time budgets, and organizational participation have been used as indicators of time use. Because the components of this domain are as yet poorly articulated, it is premature to examine the differential effects of different time-use measures on the size of the cognition–time use relationship.

Because of the great heterogeneity both in the measurement of time use and in the types of samples used, it is not surprising to find a wide range of correlations between cognition and time use in the several studies summarized in Table 5-2 (.18 to .52), but the median is respectably high (.29).

The following hypotheses may be profitably tested:

H4. A substantial portion of the variance shared between cognition and time use in older people is statistically explainable by lifelong SES. The causal sequence is complex. First, people make lifelong choices of uses of time that are consistent with their basic cognitive competence. Second, basic cognitive competence no doubt influences attained SES. Finally, SES affects the choice of ways to spend one's time because status itself constrains or facilitates particular choices.

H5. Another portion of the variance shared between cognition and time use in older people is explainable by *changes* in cognitive competence associated with pathology or other factors arising in later life. Impaired cognition is likely to lead to a change in activities. This source of variance might be approached by studying how the time use–cognition relationship varies with the types of cognitive measures (e.g., crystallized vs. fluid intelligence). In such investigations, it would be important to make the distinction between lifelong and present cognitive functioning and between earlier and present SES in terms of how each might condition the relationship between present cognitive functioning and present time use.

H6. Variance in health contributes to the relationship between cognition and time use. That is, an interaction between health and cognitive status may occur such that when health is poor, time use is more strongly affected by cognition than when health is good, a hypothesis receiving some support in the NIMH Human Aging Study (Birren et al., 1963).

Cognition and Social Behavior

Because social behavior intermeshes the personal systems of multiple individuals, this domain may be the most complex level of behavioral competence (Lawton, 1972). Measurement is relatively unstandardized in this domain, but typically consists of measures of frequency of interaction with family and friends (Lawton, 1986). Although most published research has mixed these two quite different classes of informal relationships, there is ample reason to recommend keeping them separate, because their influences on psychological well-being have been shown to differ. In the research reviewed for this study, the relationship between level of family interaction and cognition was essentially zero. The relationship between contact with friends (in some studies this category included family) and cognition ranged from .15 to .39, with a median of .21.

The first three hypotheses regarding social behavior parallel those for time use:

H7. Lifelong SES and cognitive competence are potent determinants of amount of contact with friends in later life.

H8. Change in cognitive competence in later life affects amount of contact with friends.

H9. Variance in health contributes to the relationship between cognition and social behavior. Again, poor health is suggested as potentiating the relationship between cognition and social behavior; that is, in poor health, high cognition will be more positively related to social behavior and low cognition more negatively with social behavior, as compared to the situation when people are in good health.

H10. Family contact, being determined powerfully by affective bonding and social obligation, does not covary with cognitive functioning.

Cognition and Psychological Well-Being

Psychological well-being has been studied at length, resulting in the identification of many varieties of psychological well-being, (e.g., life satisfaction, morale, or happiness), although certainly there are more labels than there are conceptually and empirically differentiable domains (Lawton, 1982b). The many different measures used as indicators of both cognition and psychological well-being, the diversity of samples, and perhaps the lesser robustness of the relationships between cognition and psychological well-being are all factors that play some part in the inability to summarize easily the findings of a substantial number of studies. Small but significant associations between cognition and psychological well-being were found in several studies at the Philadelphia Geriatric Center (discussed in a following section), by Tobin and Lieberman (1976), and among female subjects in the first Duke Longitudinal Study (Palmore, 1981); few significant relationships were found by Birren et al. (1963) in the Human Aging Study, by Linn (1983), among male subjects in the first Duke Longitudinal Study (Palmore, 1981), or in subjects of either sex in the second Duke study (Palmore, 1981). Across all those listed in Table 5-2, the median r is .135, range .00 to .37.

H11. The bivariate relationship between the generalized construct psychological well-being and cognition is dependent on more "third-variable" influences than are other such bivariate relationships. The influence of such factors as SES, health, and age needs to be considered jointly when the relationship between cognition and psychological well being is tested.

H12. The independent multivariate relationship between psychological well-being and cognition is smaller than relationships between other domains of well-being and cognition.

Cognition and Perceived Quality of Life

The literature search yielded the least amount of research data on this type of bivariate relationship.

What little there is suggested a low positive relationship between cognition and most domains of perceived quality of life, although more instances of zero relationships were found in the case of environmental satisfaction than in other domains of perceived quality of life.

The following hypotheses might be pursued:

H13. Persons with greater lifelong and contemporary cognitive competence are more satisfied with most domains of their everyday lives.

H14. The domains of perceived quality of life in which satisfaction is most related to cognition are analogous to the domains in which behavioral competence is most highly related to cognition: Time use and interaction with friends. Less related to cognition is family satisfaction.

H15. Environmental satisfaction shows no net relationship to cognition, because of offsetting forces. Objective environmental quality tends to be higher among the cognitively more competent, thus leading to greater satisfaction. Competent persons are, however, more critical, and less competent persons are more accepting of situations that have a low probability of change (Campbell, Converse, & Rodgers, 1976; Carp, 1975).

Multivariate Relationships Between Cognition and Well-Being

Some multivariate studies in gerontology have examined some of the foregoing relationships (see Palmore, 1981; Palmore & Luikart, 1972). Because there are so few such studies, and not all of those that exist are relevant for the present purpose, the multivariate results presented here derive solely from the several studies performed at the Philadelphia Geriatric Center, and thus have limited generalizability. The five data sets (also cited in Table 5-2) were derived from interview studies of noninstitutionalized elderly populations. Although the specific instruments used varied somewhat across the studies, a common set of constructs was measured in each project. Most of the data derived for Figure 5-2 has not been published. Reports have been published giving further methodological details for some of the studies, however.

In study A, a local-area random sample of 1269 Social Security recipients were interviewed (Gottesman, 1974; Lawton, 1983a). Study B consisted of random samples of tenants ($N = 494$) from five publicly assisted housing projects for the elderly (Lawton, 1983b). The standardization population for the MAI came from Study C (Lawton, 1983c; Lawton, Moss, Fulcomer, & Kleban, 1982); the four subsamples represented community residents, public housing tenants, in-home service recipients, and people on an institutional waiting list ($N = 590$). Study D involved 284 subjects in subsamples of community residents, life-care community residents, congregate residents, and clinically depressed patients (Lawton, 1983d; Lawton, Kleban, & diCarlo, 1984). For Study E, 232 community residents

stratified by sex and living arrangement (lived alone vs. with spouse) were interviewed (Lawton, 1983e).

The Analytic Strategy

The multivariate causal model (Figure 5-2) is a preferable way to approach some of the hypotheses framed earlier. The analysis of covariance structures as made available in the LISREL computer program (Jöreskog & Sörbom, 1978) is the ultimate preferable approach, a task that is under way with these data sets. However, path models of the conventional variety are presented here; these analyses illustrate the points to be made here, without offering definitive tests of the entire models.

Background factors. While gender and race have not figured strongly as important factors in the relationships between cognition and other forms of well-being, they were seen as desirable to control, in the form of covariates, before examining the other relationships. Education, despite its ambiguous meaning for the current cohort of elderly (whose opportunities for education were often very limited), is probably the best single proxy one can find for long-term SES. (Occupational status of the main wage earner in the household proved to account for less variance in dependent variables than did education of the subject.) Current income (adjusted for household size) reflects lifelong SES strongly but also reflects contemporary economic status and presumably environmental opportunities. In order to begin to test any hypotheses about the differential effects of lifelong versus present SES, better variables to represent the construct at two stages of life will be required. For the present purpose, education and income are used simply as covariates in order to highlight better the independent influence of present cognitive functioning on the other variables. Age is highly problematic as a covariate, because it is known to be intrinsically associated with health, some forms of cognition, and perhaps other variables in the model. In fact, a whole set of analyses is warranted without the control for age. However, age is used as a statistical control in these analyses in order to determine the variance contributions of nonchronological age factors to variations in behavioral competence within the older age range.

Exogenous variables. The main exogenous variables (residualized with respect to the five background variables) are health (measured in these studies as health conditions) and cognition; the association between health and cognition is assumed to be accounted for by factors outside the model. Another exogenous variable is family interaction. This variable is assumed to be causally unrelated to health and cognition. Finally, in the absence of any variable in the data sets representing objective environment, perceived environment, the last exogenous variable, is not only a domain of perceived quality of life but also is used here as a proxy for objective environment.

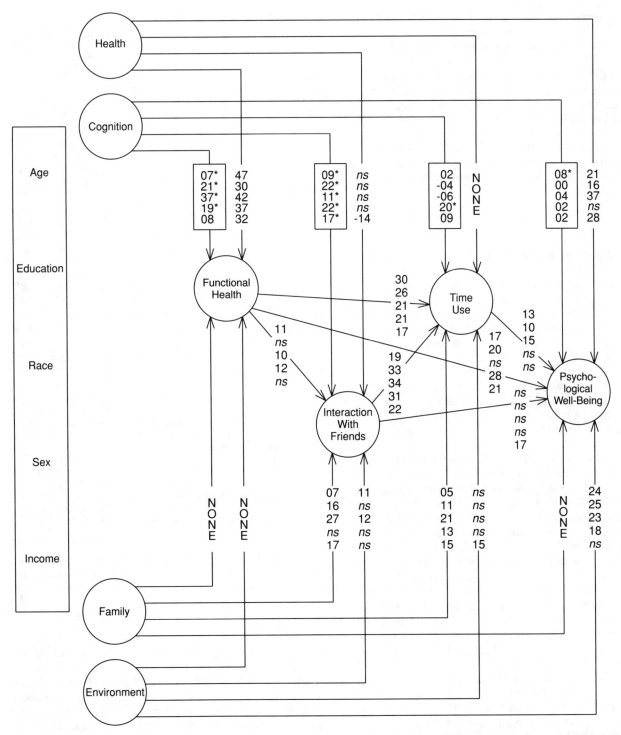

Figure 5-2. Causal model of well-being. Figures are path coefficients. Coefficients showing the direct effects of cognition are boxed. All such coefficients are shown (asterisks indicate those where $p < .05$), but only significant coefficients ($p < .05$) are shown for the paths between other variables. Rectangular paths connect exogenous and endogenous variables. Diagonal paths connect endogenous variables to one another. The path analyses used the five demographic variables in box at left as control variables, but for clarity their coefficients are omitted. (Data come from Lawton, 1983a, 1983b, 1983c, 1983d, 1983e).

Endogenous variables. Functional health (activities of daily living, or ADL) is hypothesized to be affected by both health and cognition, but not by family interaction or perceived environment. Cognition is hypothesized to affect interaction with friends both directly because of the cognitive demands of the social relation-ship and through functional health. Time use, even with background factors controlled, is hypothesized to be directly affected by family interaction, cognition, functional health, and perceived environment. The effect of health on time use, however, is indirect, through functional health, since it is dependency in ADL tasks that is primarily responsible for the restriction of discretionary activities. Interaction with friends leads to social activities and thus is hypothesized to affect time use directly. Finally, the ultimate dependent variable, psychological well-being, is hypothesized to be directly affected by health, functional health, interaction with friends, and time use. The observed small bivariate relationship between cognition and psychological well-being is hypothesized to be accounted for by the relationship between cognition and functional health, interaction with friends, and time use, so there should be no direct effect and the sizes of the indirect effects should be small.

Results

Figure 5-2 shows the results of the 5 complete path models; the figures are path coefficients. Only the significant coefficients are shown, except for those referring to cognition. The direct effects of cognition on each of the other model elements are denoted by the boxed path coefficients. The rectangularly drawn paths represent paths from exogenous to endogenous variables. Diagonally drawn paths represent paths between endogenous variables.

The full models are presented in the figure in order to illustrate the multivariate complexity of the relationships, but only the results dealing with cognition are discussed here. These results are shown in Table 5-3.

The first section of Table 5-3 shows the zero-order relationships between cognition and all other variables. There are no surprises in the pattern of relationships with background variables: The correlations of cognition with age, income, and education are substantial, those with sex and race trivial. A low but consistent relationship between cognition and a health-conditions checklist was found, but no consistent relationship was found between cognition and either interaction with family or perceived environmental quality. By contrast, every correlation between cognition and the endogenous variables is significant, and most are relatively high by survey-research standards.

The second section shows the partial correlations between cognition and the exogenous variables, with the effects of the five background variables removed. Because both cognition and the exogenous variables have substantial correlations with either or both age and SES, it is not surprising that every correlation shrinks after the background variables are controlled.

The last section shows standardized regression (path) coefficients between cognition and the endogenous variables (derived from a set of reduced-form regression equations). Each endogenous variable was used as a dependent variable; the background variables, the exogenous variables, and the endogenous variable(s) with causal priority (there were none in the case of ADL) were used in stepwise fashion as independent variables. With this maximum control over mutually causal influences, cognition still is significantly associated with ADL (4 studies) and with amount of contact with friends (5 studies). By contrast,

Table 5-3. Relationships Between Cognition and Background, Exogenous, and Endogenous Variables[a]

Variables	Study[b]				
	A	B	C	D	E
Background					
Age	−13*	−24*	−28*	−38*	−21*
Sex	−05	04	−07	01	−15
Education	19*	30*	39*	48*	47*
Current income	14*	39*	20*	33*	41*
Race	09*	02	03	—[c]	04
Exogenous					
Physical health	11*	05	13*	12	12
Interaction with family	00	−02	14*	02	03
Perceived environment	12*	−05	−02	08	18*
Endogenous					
Activities of daily living	17*	27*	42*	32*	18*
	(11)*	(19)*	(—)[d]	(20)*	(06)
Interaction with friends	15*	22*	29*	39*	25*
	(11)*	(21)*	(—)	(23)*	(15)
Time use	18*	18*	30*	52*	34*
	(11)*	(10)*	(—)	(33)*	(13)
Psychological well-being	18*	12*	18*	23*[e]	14[f]
	(15)*	(06)	(—)	(10)	(01)

[a]Values are zero-order correlation coefficients except for those in parentheses, which are partial correlations after 5 background variables were controlled. Decimals omitted.
[b]Letters refer to Lawton 1983a, 1983b, 1983c, 1983d, 1983e references.
[c]Too few nonwhites for reliable estimate.
[d]Partial correlations not available for Study C.
[e]A measure of positive affect showed a correlation of .37*.
[f]A measure of positive affect showed a correlation of .11.
*$p < .01$.

the relationships between cognition and time use and between cognition and psychological well-being are clearly weaker.

Conclusion

Two conclusions may be drawn, subject to testing in other samples. First, older people who are functioning well in the cognitive sphere are likely to be characterized as living the good life in many other ways, as seen in the zero-order relationships. This conclusion has implications for clinical practice and service. To some extent, a brief measure of cognitive functioning may constitute one window to the larger state of well-being of the older client. Cognition is not an area of functioning set apart from others. The set of simple bivariate associations in fact constitutes the best possible summary data to characterize the way people function in everyday life. People speaking to us in clinical settings do not control for SES and do not communicate the nature of indirect effects very well. Those who are privileged in one domain of well-being are likely to be similarly privileged in other domains; the reverse is also implied.

When research rather than clinical assessment is

the focus, the zero-order relationships are a poor vehicle for understanding the intricacies of causal influences. The first set of controls shown in Table 5-3 tells us that not everything is explained by lifelong ascribed statuses or socioeconomic position. People who are cognitively intact are still more likely to perform everyday activities well, have more interactions with friends, engage in more nonobligatory activities, and perhaps have greater psychological well-being. The full path analysis shows further findings that are consistent with some of the causal hypotheses. Both health conditions and cognition independently affect the quality of performance of everyday activities. While social activity with friends is associated with several background factors and with health, further variance in the amount of interaction with friends is contributed by current cognitive performance level. The tendency for the cognitively impaired to engage in fewer activities is strongly affected both by SES and by health, especially impairment in ADL. Thus there is slight evidence in favor of an independent causal link between cognition and activity, except indirectly. Similar reasoning may be applied to the association between cognition and psychological well-being.

Clinical practice would be improved if clinicians had a clearer idea of where current cognitive performance fits into the total picture. The levels of interdependence among the domains of the good life, while substantial, are still relatively low in variance-percentage terms. The occurrence of an indicator of impaired memory in clinical testing should constitute a signal that further information is necessary regarding how far this one disability has invaded the other domains of the good life. For example, impaired memory within a context of preserved social relationships and high life satisfaction may well justify a laissez-faire approach to other psychosocial interventions. But if a person with the same degree of memory disturbance is socially isolated and depressed, an "excess" psychosocial disability exists, which is treatable by behavioral intervention. Intervention possibilities will be enlarged by knowing better the scope of well-being that could potentially be affected by explicit cognitive training or by counseling that focuses on a person's perception of her own cognitive skills. Because the time when practitioners can improve memory in dementia patients directly still seems distant, it is very likely that criteria for reflecting intervention will be more appropriately chosen from this larger class of indicators of the good life.

Two thoughts relevant to further research needs will conclude this chapter. First, the strong suggestion is made to researchers in cognition and aging to embed a set of efficient functional-assessment measures (e.g., the Duke OARS, the Comprehensive Assessment and Referral Evaluation, CARE [Golden, Teresi, & Gurland, 1984], or the MAI) in their research. Substantial differences are likely in the covariation patterns linking cognition with other indicators of well-being, depending on the type of cognitive function being tested. We need to be able to perform meta-analyses and secondary data analyses on data sets that have used a variety of different measures representing the cognitive domain. The MSQ and the WAIS are inadequate to test these differential patterns of covariation.

Second, researchers with a strong interest in the psychosocial area need in turn to include cognitive measures in their batteries, measures whose choice is guided by the differential covariation analyses that are planned. It is difficult to imagine any situation in which the relationship between a psychosocial variable and cognitive functioning would not be relevant.

References

Baer, P., & Gaitz, C. M. (1971). Survival of elderly psychiatric patients. In E. Palmore & F. Jeffers (Eds.), *Prediction of life span* (pp. 153–166). Lexington, MA: Lexington Books.

Birren, J. E., Butler, R. N., Greenhouse, S. W., Sokoloff, L., & Yarrow, M. (1963). *Human aging* (Public Health Service Publication No. 986). Washington, DC: National Institute of Mental Health.

Campbell, A., Converse, P. G., & Rodgers, W. (1976). *Quality of American life*. New York: Russell Sage Foundation.

Carp, F. M. (1975). Ego defense or cognitive consistency effects of environmental evaluation? *Journal of Gerontology, 30,* 707–716.

Center for the Study of Aging and Human Development, Duke University. (1978). *Multidimensional functional assessment: The OARS methodology* (2nd ed.). Durham, NC: Duke University Press.

Golden, R. R., Teresi, J. A., & Gurland, B. J. (1982–1983). Detection of dementia and depression cases with the Comprehensive Assessment and Referral Evaluation interview schedule. *Journal of Aging and Human Development, 16,* 241–254.

Golden, R. R., Teresi, J. A., & Gurland, B. J. (1984). Development of indicator scales for the Comprehensive Assessment and Referral Evaluation (CARE) interview schedule. *Journal of Gerontology, 39,* 138–146.

Gottesman, L. E. (1974). Needs, costs, and effects of home services among the aged. Washington, DC: Administration on Aging.

Heron, A., & Chown, S. (1967). *Age and function*. Boston: Little, Brown.

Jöreskog, K. G., & Sörbom, D. (1978). *LISREL: Analysis of linear structural relationships by the method of maximum likelihood*. Chicago: International Educational Resources.

Kahn, R. L., Pollack, M., & Goldfarb, A. I. (1961). Factors related to individual differences in mental status of institutionalized aged. In P. H. Hoch & J. Zubin (Eds.), *Psychopathology of aging*. New York: Grune & Stratton.

Lawton, M. P. (1972). Assessing the competence of older people. In D. Kent, R. Kastenbaum, & S. Sherwood (Eds.), *Research, planning and action for the elderly*. New York: Behavioral Publications.

Lawton, M. P. (1982a). Competence, environmental press, and the adaptation of older people. In M. P. Lawton, P. G. Windley, & T. O. Byerts (Eds.), *Aging and the environment: Theoretical approaches* (pp. 33–59). New York: Springer.

Lawton, M. P. (1982b). The well-being and mental health of the aged. In T. Field, A. Stein, H. Quay, L. Troll, & G. E. Finley (Eds.), *Review of human development* (pp. 614–628). New York: Wiley-Interscience.

Lawton, M. P. (1983a). *Need, costs and effects of home services among the aged*. Unpublished data from Grant 93P57436 from the Administration on Aging, Philadelphia Geriatric Center.

Lawton, M. P. (1983b). *The changing service needs of older tenants*. Unpublished data from Grant 90-AR-006 from the Administration on Aging, Philadelphia Geriatric Center.

Lawton, M. P. (1983c). *Assessment and the mental health of the elderly*. Unpublished data from Grant AG00895 from the National Institute of Aging, Philadelphia Geriatric Center.

Lawton, M. P. (1983d). *Perceived psychological well-being in the aged*. Unpublished data from Grant MH30665 from the National Institute of Mental Health, Philadelphia Geriatric Center.

Lawton, M. P. (1983e). *Old and alone*. Unpublished data from Grant MH35312 from the National Institute of Mental Health, Philadelphia Geriatric Center.

Lawton, M. P. (1983f). Environment and other determinants of the well-being of older people. *The Gerontologist, 23*, 349–357.

Lawton, M. P. (1984). Investigating health and subjective well-being: Substantive challenges. *International Journal of Aging and Human Development, 19*, 157–165.

Lawton, M. P. (1985). Activities and leisure. In M. P. Lawton & G. Maddox (Eds.), *Annual Review of Gerontology and Geriatrics*: Vol. 5 (pp. 127–164). New York: Springer.

Lawton, M. P. (1986). Functional assessment. In P. M. Lewinsohn & L. Teri (Eds.), *Clinical assessment and treatment of the older adult*. New York: Springer.

Lawton, M. P., & Brody, E. (1969). Assessment of older people: Self-maintaining and instrumental activities of daily living. *The Gerontologist, 9*, 179–185.

Lawton, M. P., Kleban, M. H., & diCarlo, E. (1984). Psychological well-being in the aged: Factorial and conceptual dimensions. *Research on Aging, 6*, 67–97.

Lawton, M. P., Moss, M., Fulcomer, M., & Kleban, M. H. (1982). A research and service-oriented Multilevel Assessment Instrument. *Journal of Gerontology, 37*, 91–99.

Lawton, M. P., & Storandt, M. (1984). Assessment of older people. In P. McReynolds & G. J. Chelune (Eds.), *Advances in psychological assessment* (Vol. 6, pp. 236–276). San Francisco: Jossey-Bass.

Linn, M. W. (1983). *Cooperative study of nursing home care and psychiatric hospitalization*. Unpublished data, Veterans Administration Hospital, Miami, FL.

Okun, M. A., & Stock, W. A. (1984). Research synthesis of the health–subjective well-being relationship: Introductory comments. *International Journal of Aging and Human Development, 19*, 8–83.

Palmore, E. (1981). *Social patterns in normal aging: Findings from the Duke Longitudinal Study*. Durham, NC: Duke University Press.

Palmore, E., & Luikart, C. (1972). Health and social factors related to life satisfaction. *Journal of Health and Social Behavior, 13*, 68–80.

Quinn, J. L. (1982). *Triage II: Coordinated delivery of services to the elderly* (Vol. 1). Wethersfield, CT: Triage.

Reichard, S., Livson, R., & Peterson, P. G. (1962). *Aging and personality*. New York: Wiley.

Siegler, I. C., Nowlin, J. B., & Blumenthal, J. A. (1980). Health and behavior: Methodological considerations for adult development and aging. In L. W. Poon (Ed.), *Aging in the 1980s: Psychological Issues* (pp. 599–612). Washington, DC: American Psychological Association.

Tobin, S. S., & Lieberman, M. A. (1976). *Last home for the aged*. San Francisco: Jossey-Bass.

Wechsler, D. (1958). *The measurement and appraisal of adult intelligence*. Baltimore, MD: Williams & Wilkins.

Earl Hunt

6

Experimental Perspectives: Theoretical Memory Models

Tests of memory ability should be based on a theory of cognition in which memory is only one of several aspects of thinking. The dominant theory in cognitive psychology today is the production activation model. It is based upon the idea that cognition is a type of computation, and that computation can be modeled by the action of productions, actions that are to be taken when patterns are recognized. The production activation model identifies specific functions that operate on information in working or long-term memory. Paradigms for testing these functions in isolation can be developed. Testing memory functions in isolation, however, may not provide an accurate assessment of a person's ability to use memory in familiar, extralaboratory situations. The reason is that a person's memory capability is determined jointly by the ability to handle information in the abstract and the amount that a person knows about the content of the information being processed. Experimental studies are described that emphasize the distinction between these two kinds of memory capability. Testing to evaluate information-handling capabilities in the abstract is appropriate when the purpose of testing is to evaluate alterations of brain processes, or when testing is done to diagnose memory failures in a person whose general ability is already known to be poor. Tests that assess a person's ability to function in familiar situations are more appropriate if the goal is to determine general mental competence.

Failures in episodic memory are so closely associated with old age that we tell jokes about age and memory. The jokes have more than a grain of truth in them. On the other hand, there are substantial individual differences in the extent of memory loss with age. When dealing with an individual it is not enough to know that, on the average, certain types of memory deteriorate as one grows old. Measures of individual performance are needed. An evaluation of memory may be required to estimate how a person will function in society. Certain patterns of memory performance provide cues for the differential diagnosis of various pathologies. Also, the evaluation of memory at different stages of life tells us something about the aging process.

There is clearly a market for tests of memory. How should they be constructed?

An analogy to medical evaluation is useful. Most medical tests are based on theories of the systems being evaluated. Theoretical analyses define the variables to be measured and the properties of an ideal measurement. Actual measurements are compromises between the ideal and pragmatic constraints, such as cost or invasiveness. Cardiovascular measures provide good examples. They are based upon a model of the cardiovascular system as a closed hydraulic system, consisting of a pump and pipes of varying diameters. Measures such as the familiar blood pressure cuff make sense within the hydraulic model, and make sense more generally because the model is correct.

In this chapter the measurement of memory is treated from a theoretical point of view. An idealized model of memory is presented and used to define the parameters of memory performance. The goal of this exercise is not to deduce what procedures must be used to evaluate memory, but rather to deduce theoretical limits that establish the characteristics of an allowable measure of some aspect of memory. The applied psychologist's problem is to find measures that are both theoretically allowable and pragmatically realizable. The problem is harder than the problem of designing cardiovascular measures, because our models of memory are much more complex than the hydraulic model that describes the cardiovascular system. The complexity is probably inevitable, for no one has yet proposed a verifiable, simple theory of mental processes. It is not at all clear that such a theory is possible.

The Production Activation Model of Memory

The model of memory presented here is a generalization of a model that has been developed, in slightly different forms, to explain a variety of aspects of human cognition, ranging from complex problem solving (Newell & Simon, 1972) to the control of attention (Hunt & Lansman, 1984). The present description is most similar to Anderson's ACT* model (Anderson, 1983a, 1983b) and to the Production Activation model developed by my associates and myself (Hunt, 1981; Hunt & Lansman, 1984; Hunt & Pixton, 1982). The intent of this paper is to focus on themes that are common to all production selection models, rather than to focus on the differences between particular models within the class. To avoid circumlocution, the term *production activation model* will be used to refer to the entire class of models.

Elements of a Production Activation Model

Production activation models are based on the truism that thinking is the manipulation of an internal representation of an external environment (Newell, 1973). The models distinguish between a *working memory* storage area that holds information about the current situation and a *long-term memory* storage area that contains records of the past. *Memory processes* transfer information from one area to another. These processes can be thought of as rules for taking actions in particular situations, for example, for recalling semantic information about small, furry animals when seeing the visual stimulus CAT. The fact that rules are being executed implies the existence of some sort of brain "machinery" that does the necessary operations. The operations themselves fall into two broad classes: pattern recognition and information transfer. The complementarity of the two types of operations can be seen by examining further the memory processes required for thought.

Figure 6-1 shows the information flow assumed in a production activation model. Information from the external environment is presented directly to long-term memory, where it is recognized as an example of a class of previously learned items. For instance, the visual stimulus provided by a small, furry animal might be recognized as an example of a *cat*. As a result of the recognition process, information from long-term memory that has been associated with the instantiated concept is made available to working memory. Continuing with the example, recognizing an animal as a "conceptual" cat will make active knowledge about cats in general. As a result, the information in working memory consists of much more than a representation of the distal stimulus in the environment.

The contents of working memory are continually examined, recognized, and evaluated by further long-term memory processes, producing further augmentation of the information in working memory. External actions occur when the configuration of information in working memory instantiates a pattern that is associated with an external response. This means that the system is capable of selecting a response that is appropriate in context. The sight of a cat on one's lap might

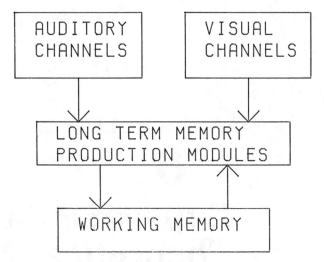

Figure 6-1. The flow of information between the external world, long-term memory, and working memory.

initiate stroking motions, while the sight of the same cat near one's canary could trigger grabbing motions.

The recognition and evaluation processes that reside in long-term memory are represented by a set of rules, called *productions*. A production consists of a pattern and an associated action. A production can be written as

$$\text{Pattern x} \rightarrow \text{Action y,} \qquad (1)$$

where the pattern is a rule for classifying stimulus complexes (including the contents of working memory) and the action is some well-defined action that the system can take. Two classes of actions are of interest: actions that result in overt responses, and actions that rearrange the contents of working memory.

A *production system* is a set of instructions for executing a task. Table 6-1 contains an example, a production system for dealing with a traffic light. Readers not already familiar with the production notation are urged to examine the table carefully. Note in particular the productions concerning yellow lights. These illustrate an important capability of production system models: *goal = directed problem solving*. Working memory may contain symbols indicating goals. The goal will have been created by previously executed actions. Goals become part of the stimulus complex and may exert an influence on problem solving.

The production system notation was imported into psychology from computer science, where productions are used as a device to describe computations.

Most psychological models that use the production notation differ from the computer science models in the way that the pattern recognition step is defined. In psychological models the pattern recognition process is represented by a continuous valued function that computes the extent to which a particular stimulus situation satisfies the pattern, rather than as a boolean function that states whether or not the situation is an example of the pattern. For instance a robin and a chicken are both birds, but a robin, being closer to the

Table 6-1. A Set of Productions for Driving Near Traffic Lights

Preconditions	Action
Light is green	→Drive through
Light is yellow and close to intersection	→Drive through, rapidly
Light is yellow and distant from intersection and no goal to hurry	→Decelerate
Light is yellow and distant from intersection and goal to hurry	→Accelerate, check other cars
Light is red and no goal to hurry	→Stop
Light is red Cars crossing intersection	→Stop
Light is red and goal to hurry	→Check for other cars
Light is red and goal to hurry and no cars crossing intersection.	→Drive through light

psychological prototype of a bird, has a higher value on a "birdness" dimension than does a chicken. Thus it seems more psychologically realistic to allow a stimulus to activate several patterns partially, than to say that each stimulus exactly instantiates one and only one pattern.

Formal notation helps clarify these ideas. Consider a production rule, such as rule (1) stated earlier, whose preconditions form pattern x. Let s be a stimulus situation, defined by the state of external stimulation, working memory, or both. Stimulus s is said to activate pattern x by some amount $f(x,s)$, where $0 \le f(x,s) \le 1$, depending upon the resemblance of s to x. A given stimulus may simultaneously activate several patterns. Continuing the example, the stimulus "chicken" would activate the patterns "bird," "pet," and "barnyard animal" to varying degrees.

The degree to which a production is activated at any time, t, will be determined by three variables: its activation level immediately prior to t (at time $t - 1$ in a discrete time approximation), the extent to which the production's pattern is activated by the stimulus situation s that is present at time t, and the extent to which related productions are activated at time $t - 1$. Making the activation of a production dependent upon the concurrent activation of related productions is a concept that can literally be traced back to Aristotle's theory of association of thoughts (Anderson & Bower, 1973). Computationally, let $x(t)$ be the activation level of pattern x at time t, and let $A(t) = \{x(t)\}$ be the set of activation levels of all productions in long-term memory. The value of $x(t)$ is determined by

$$x(t) = f(x(t),s) + g(A(t - 1)) \quad (2)$$

where $g(A(t - 1)$ is a function that depends on the joint levels of activation of all productions at time $t - 1$, just prior to stimulus presentation.

Finally, what determines whether the action associated with a particular production will be taken? Production activation models must include a *conflict resolution rule* that selects certain productions on the basis of their activation levels. Let $X(t)$ be the set of selected productions. Then

$$X(t) = h(A(t)), \quad (3)$$

where h is some rule for selecting members of A. For instance, a simple rule would be to select the production with the highest activation level. If a production is included in $X(t)$, its action is taken at that time. The cycle then continues.

The various production activation models that have been proposed all satisfy the description just given. They differ in their definitions of the f, g, and h functions. Given the level of generality of the present discussion, however, these differences need not concern us.

Codes

In the terminology of computer science, the ideas of working memory, long-term memory, and production activation are *architectural concepts*. They refer to the manipulation of information without describing the information structures being manipulated. Architectural concepts alone are not sufficient for a theory of memory. The way that information is coded in memory must also be specified.

Psychological production system models generally assume that at least three different codes may be used to hold information in memory. Two are closely tied to the form of input. Anderson (1983b) refers to codes for spatial and temporal location, while Hunt (1981) refers to auditory and visual codes. In addition, both models contain an abstract semantic code that is not tied directly to the modality in which information is received. Information is translated into this code by productions that recognize and interpret statements in the codes tied to sensory modalities. Similarly, other productions translate from the internal semantic code to the external codes.

The Processes of Memory: An Illustration

Although the discussion to this point has stressed the structural aspects of memory, production activation models envisage memory as a highly dynamic process. A formal presentation of the details would be inordinately lengthy. Instead, an informal scenario will be offered to illustrate the basic idea.

Suppose that are you eating a Sunday brunch in a restaurant. Your companion calls your attention to a large man who is entering. A second man comes from the kitchen to greet him. Your companion says:

That is Joe DeMonster, the famous professional football player. At college, he majored in consumatory nutrition and became a famous gourmet. The other man is Monsieur Pierre, the chef. Every Sunday he prepares him a triple order of eggs benedict, right before the game. Last Sunday he had his usual meal, and then made five sacks of the opposing quarterback. It didn't seem to bother him at all.

Readers only mildly familiar with American football (and brunches) will have little trouble in understanding this vignette. Suppose further, though, that the scenario is to be comprehended by a robot whose "brain" is programmed as a production system. What would this production system have to be capable of doing? How would information have to be manipulated so that the robot would know what was going on?

The robot would have to have access to a considerable amount of linguistic knowledge. Words are initially sensed as sound or letter patterns. They must be recognized and replaced by their semantic equivalents. The structure of strings of linguistic terms must be recognized in order to extract the meaning of each sentence from its surface structure. To do this the robot must have available sophisticated word processing productions in long-term memory, and must use them to construct a meaningful representation of what is going on. Let us examine some of the requirements the production system must meet.

The need to retrieve word meaning from long-term memory is obvious. Word meaning, alone, is insufficient, because some words serve as place holders for terms previously defined in context. This sort of word definition is called *anaphoric reference*. Anaphors are understood only by retrieving meaning from working rather than from long-term memory. Consider the pronoun "he" in the sentence "At college he . . . ." This anaphor can be resolved by a simple search of working memory, since at the time the anaphoric reference is encountered there will be only one possible referent in memory. The more complicated resolution of "he" and "him" in the sentence beginning "Every Sunday . . . " requires the use of knowledge about what chefs do and what eating habits are. This means that the robot must have a production system that can blend semantic knowledge about words with pragmatic knowledge about what makes sense in the episode at hand. Finally, consider the very first word of the speech, the pronoun "That . . . ." It is an *exophoric* reference, that is, a reference within a linguistic message to some nonlinguistic entity that is presumed to be present in working memory. The robot must have the productions required to coordinate between its internal representations of the linguistic and visual stimuli. The amodal semantic used in most production system models of human thought provides the common core by which communication is accomplished.

Of all the processes just mentioned, the process of retrieving word meanings seems the simplest. But even it has hidden complexities. The retrieval of word meanings seems "automatic" in the sense that we are not aware of it, but the process is not simple. Consider the information processing needed to understand the next to final sentence in the story, "Last Sunday he made five sacks . . . ." In American English "sacks" can mean either "bags," as in "paper sacks," or, as it does here, it can mean "tackles of a football quarterback behind the line of scrimmage." The meaning is immediately apparent in context. If the robot is built like a human, both semantic referents of "sacks" will be aroused, and the production system will select the one appropriate for the context.

The word "it" in the final sentence in the passage (". . . it did not bother him . . . ") once again illustrates the importance of context. From a strictly linguistic point of view, "it" should refer to the last named event, and "him" to the last named male person. If so, though, the sentence would mean "Having been tackled behind the line of scrimmage did not seem to bother the quarterback at all." Although this sentence is linguistically acceptable, it makes no sense in the context of a football game. Furthermore, the listener "knows" (i.e., can immediately retrieve from memory) the pragmatic conversational rule that unusual or palpably false statements are not made unless they are marked by some special signal, such as a wink or a laugh. In terms of the production activation model, long-term memory must contain productions that demand that an interpretation of a statement make sense in context. A robot that could deal with conversation would have to have a very sophisticated memory system indeed.

Let us review briefly what all this means. A robot that could comprehend the example would have to be capable of retrieving information from both working memory and long-term memory. These capabilities are abstract, in the sense that they can be defined without reference to the content of the information being retrieved. In order to make the correct retrievals, however, the robot would have to know a great deal about the meaning of the information being manipulated. Put more abstractly, a distinction must be made between context-free and context-sensitive capabilities for handling information.

Memory involves storage as well as retrieval of information. Some storage is synonymous with the development of working memory structures. To comprehend a message, one must build information structures in working memory that incorporate both the linguistic interpretation of the message and the nonlinguistic information that is related to it. Without such an incorporation the sentences become gibberish. Information structures must also be built in long-term memory, in order to maintain some continuity between the present and the past. These structures appear to be a highly selective record of the information that has been perceived. To continue with the DeMonster example, suppose that on the following day you (or the robot) were asked, "Did anything interesting happen during your brunch?" You might reply by recounting the gist of the episode, selectively emphasizing those features that appeared important to you. You would probably correctly state that the player ate a very large meal and then played well. You would be somewhat less likely to remember the precise meal the player ate, or the details of the incident that indicated that he played well. Peripheral details, such as the chef's name, would be even less likely to be recalled. One of the major unsolved puzzles in memory research is whether selective recall is due to failures to perceive information (in the model, to incorporate it into a working memory structure), failures in transferring information from working memory to long-term memory, or failures in retrieving information that has been stored in long-term memory and that can be recalled in some circumstances but not in others.

A scenario is a pedagogical device, not scientific evidence. There is ample evidence for all of the memory retrieval and storage phenomena illustrated by the DeMonster scenario (Klatzky, 1975). In more formal terms, any device that executes human-like cognitive acts, using a production activation system as its reasoning mechanism, must be capable of executing the following processes:

1. Recognizing patterns in order to match its productions to the current contents of working memory.

2. Constructing working memory representations from linguistic and nonlinguistic input. This process must be executed rapidly enough to keep up with the presentation of information to the system.

3. Scanning working memory, to resolve anaphoric and exophoric references.

4. Summarizing information in working memory, to keep the storage requirements in bounds.

5. Storing information in long-term memory. This process consists of two subprocesses: constructing new productions and inserting these productions into a network of associations with existing productions. The latter subprocess must be able to alter the associations between productions that already exist in long-term memory.

Implications of Production Activation Models for Memory Testing

The production activation model implies a functionalist approach to memory testing. It assumes two processes of memory (storage and retrieval), two locations (working memory and long-term memory), and three types of code (auditory, visual, and semantic). Specific memory functions are identified by combinations of process, location, and code, for example, retrieval of visual information from working memory.

This analysis immediately suggests a taxonomic approach to memory testing. In such an approach, a memory test developer attempts to construct behavioral procedures that isolate each of the possible memory functions. For example, one might try to develop a pure test of the ability to retrieve visual information from working memory. Such an approach to memory testing bears more than a passing resemblance to Guilford's (1967) *Structure of Intellect* approach to the more general problem of intelligence testing. The functionalist approach has its merits and demerits, and both are worth considering.

The functionalist approach works best when the memory system is thought of as a mechanical system for storing and retrieving information, without regard to the content of the information being handled. Such a view is appropriate if one wants to focus on memory as a phenomenon of the brain. For instance, tests of narrowly defined memory functions are particularly useful when the goal of testing is to characterize the effects of a precise insult to the brain, such as a localized lesion. The functional approach is less useful when one is concerned with the effects of memory loss upon global powers of the mind, that is, the total mental competency provided by combining how a person handles information with the content of the information that the person has. To drive the point home, an elderly football fan would probably remember more about the DeMonster scenario than would a 23-year-old Russian ballerina.

A narrow functionalist approach is inappropriate for evaluating global mental capacity, because there are trade-offs between different parts of the memory system. Limited working memory capacity may be more than compensated for by efficient encoding of information in the productions stored in long-term memory. When assessing a person's total memory capacity, the appropriate question may not be "How well do all this person's memory functions work in isolation?" but rather "How well is this person's memory system functioning as a whole?" The second question is far harder to answer than the first.

The next section expands on these themes. First some comments are made about tests of specific functions. The remarks are meant to illustrate areas of concern, rather than to describe how each function should be evaluated. A theoretical analysis of the integration between different memorial functions is then offered, and the implications of that analysis for testing are explored.

Testing Different Aspects of Memory

Working Memory Functions

If the production activation model of thought is at all accurate, working memory functions must be major determinants of mental action. This is so because the information structures in working memory constitute the thinker's internal representation of what is going on. This includes both a record of the stimuli that have been presented in the immediate past and a record of how these stimuli have been interpreted. Measures of limits on working memory structures should thus provide information about our capacity to comprehend the world as it is presented to us. Some possible tests of working memory will be illustrated. Linguistic examples will be used to make various points. The principles being illustrated apply to nonlinguistic applications of memory as well.

The size of working memory has traditionally been measured by memory span tests, in which people are asked to recall strings of letters, words, or other verbal stimuli. Span tests are included in many of the widely used assessment batteries, including the Wechsler Memory Scale (Matarazzo, 1972). Furthermore, the apparently limited length of the average person's memory span is one of the classic constants of psychology, the famous "Magic Number Seven, plus or minus two." (Miller, 1956).

Despite the ubiquity of memory span tests, memory span is probably not a good measure of the ability to retain useful information in working memory. The reason for this statement, which flies somewhat in the face of a long tradition of measurement, is that a person's memory span can be altered drastically without altering general mental performance. Shallice and Warrington (1970) reported a case of a brain-injured individual who had an effective memory span of zero, but who could carry on a conversation. At the other end of the scale, some people have dramatically increased their apparent memory spans, but only in specialized contexts. The current "record holder" demonstrated a memory span in excess of 80 digits (Chase & Ericsson, 1981)! The person who achieved this amazing performance did so by developing a strategy that worked only for memorizing digits. His memory span for other material was quite normal.

The fact that exceptional memory span is specialized suggests that the memory span test itself is a rather specialized problem-solving situation, and that performance on a memory span test may not be a measure of a vital intellectual capacity that is required in a wide range of tasks. The same point can be made, with somewhat more precision, by experimental studies. Independent studies by Klapp, Marshburn, and Lester (1983) and by Lansman (1978) used essentially the same design. Normal young adults were shown strings of letters. They then attempted to solve a simple problem that required the use of working memory. Finally they recalled the letter strings. In both series of experiments it was found that the presence of the letter recall task slowed problem solving, but that increasing the number of items to be recalled did not produce a further increase in the interference between memory load and problem solving. Klapp et al. went further. They manipulated the time between the presentation of the letter strings and the presentation of the problem to be solved. A delay of a few seconds in problem presentation eliminated the effects of the memory task on the problem-solving task. They concluded that problem-solving ability was reduced while information about the letter strings was being consolidated in working memory but that retaining information after it had been consolidated did not conflict with concurrent problem solving.

People are seldom called upon to retain information in working memory in isolation; they retain information in order to use it. A person's effective memory in a particular situation will depend upon the extent to which the other things the people are doing at the time interfere with the act of memorization. A study by Kerr, Condon, and McDonald (1983) illustrated this dramatically. Kerr et al. had people perform gross motor balancing acts, such as standing in an unusual posture, while doing a conventional verbal short-term memory task or while constructing a visual image. Performance on the verbal memory task and the concurrent balance task were independent, whereas there was mutual interference between the imagery and the balance task. Two conclusions can be drawn from Kerr's study. One is that the control of motor actions is itself a problem-solving ability that interferes with visual working memory. Making this point was the purpose of Kerr et al.'s study. The second point is that the extent to which a concurrent activity interferes with working memory depends upon how the information in working memory is coded. Evidently different processing resources are involved in the maintenance of visual and verbal representations in working memory.

These results do not support the idea that there can be a behavioral procedure that will test the size of working memory. The effective capacity of working memory will depend upon the way in which information is presented and the role of the memorized information in whatever concurrent task a person is doing. Furthermore, there may be large individual differences in the skill with which people cope with memory demands in particular situations. The production activation model of cognition emphasizes the joint importance of a structural capacity for holding any information and a learned, subject-matter-specific capacity for coding information in an efficient way, in order to reduce the load on memory structures.

An obvious conclusion from these arguments is that working memory capacity should be tested in contexts that are important in a person's life. Linguistic situations are particularly important because, as was shown above, language comprehension relies heavily on working memory. In part, this is memory for coded information, the propositional structure of a message rather than a message itself. On the other hand, verbatim information must be held briefly, while the propositional structure is being extracted. For instance, it appears that normal readers retain in working memory a substantially verbatim record for roughly two sentences (Glanzer, Fischer, & Dorfman, 1984). This suggests that a test of the ability to retain information in working memory while reading would be a useful measure of one's ability to comprehend some aspects of speech. Daneman (1983) has developed a testing procedure that does just this. The examinee is shown a series of sentences and then asked to recall the last word of each sentence. Here is a simple example.

Sentences presented:

The dog followed the man through the door.

My mother prepared a steak and kidney pudding.

Recall:

The correct answer is "door, pudding."

The measure is the maximum number of sentences that can be presented while recall remains perfect. Daneman regarded this as a measure of a person's ability to hold information in working memory while processing linguistic input, an example of the point that one's effective memory should be evaluated in a specific setting. As such, the measure works. Daneman and her colleagues have reported correlations in the .8 range between performance on this test and on tests of the ability to resolve anaphoric references.

The logic of Daneman's procedure could be extended to other tasks. For instance, one could construct a test of spatial working memory, by asking a person to observe items placed in different locations, then execute a spatial or motor task, and finally to recall the item locations. To my knowledge, no such test has been constructed.

In Daneman's procedure the linguistic material to be processed during the memory task is essentially independent of that task. Memory could also be tested by observing how a person copes with realistic situations that vary the demand on working memory in a systematic way. This can be illustrated with a linguistic example. Imagine that an examinee hears the following sentences and then must answer the question indicated.

Sentences presented:

John entered the restaurant.

He was a tall and haughty man who appreciated good food.

Question:

Who was a tall and haughty man?

The memory requirements of the task can be extended, as in the next example.

Sentences presented:

John entered the restaurant.

The hostess eyed him with curiosity.

He was a tall and haughty man who appreciated good food.

Question:

Who was a tall and haughty man?

The second task differs from the first in the length of the retention interval between the introduction of a subject and an anaphoric reference to it. Even more complications could be introduced. Furthermore, the logic of the example is not restricted to verbal information. The same approach to memory testing could be applied to the evaluation of memory requirements in spatial and motor tasks, such as driving. What problems would be encountered in developing and using such tests?

One objection is that there are no adequate norms for such procedures, whereas there are norms for traditional memory span measures. This objection is spurious. If a test cannot be justified on a theoretical basis, the existence of normative data is irrelevant. If a test can be justified on a theoretical basis, normative data should be obtained.

A more serious objection has to do with the theoretical interpretations of such measurements. A test of "realistic working memory" places the examinee in a "dual task" situation: Information must be retained while the person is doing some nonmemory task. People will differ in their ability to execute the nonmemory task. If so, their memory scores may reflect differences in the ability to do the nonmemory task, rather than differences in "pure" memory ability. Consider again the last two sentences of the restaurant scenario, in which an anaphoric reference crossed over a sentence about "getting quarterback sacks." The anaphor might be resolved incorrectly because a person had a poor memory, or because the person did not have the knowledge required to understand the reference to "quarterback sacks."

The example is extreme, for certainly no one would propose that a jargon-filled question be used in testing. The general point is quite serious. In order to measure performance in dual-task situations the examiner must have a specific model of how the two component tasks interact (Ackerman, Schneider, & Wickens, 1984). In some cases measurement requires fairly elaborate testing using a variety of single- and dual-task conditions (Hunt & Lansman, 1982). Such procedures will seldom fit into the constraints of clinical testing situations.

Assessing Encoding and Storage in Working Memory

Encoding is the process by which information is changed from an original representation into an augmented one. A good example is the replacement of a visual or phonetic code for a word by a code that includes information about word meaning. Encoding depends upon two things: having the appropriate codes (i.e., productions) in long-term memory and having efficient brain mechanisms for comparing representations in working memory to the patterns stored in long-term memory. The latter process appears to be a stable individual characteristic (Hunt, 1983).

Encoding processes have to be executed rapidly in order to be effective. A listener must recognize speech sounds at the speed with which they are presented in normal conversation, and a viewer must recognize physical situations, such as red lights and barking dogs, as they occur in that person's world. In fact, the conventional memory span task may well be a measure of encoding rather than a measure of the size of a working memory structure. Dempster (1981) concluded that individual differences in digit span are determined primarily by individual differences in the speed of encoding the symbols to be retained rather than by individual differences in the ability to retain symbols once they are encoded.

Two principles must be kept in mind when constructing tests of encoding ability. The first is that the encoding processes associated with each type of memory code are almost certainly distinct. This conclusion can be argued on neuropsychological grounds alone. Insults to the brain may produce selective loss of the ability to code speech symbols or visual patterns (Walsh, 1978). The second principle is that any test of an encoding process is valid only if the person being tested knows very well the meaning of the symbols being encoded. In terms of the production activation model, recognition should be achieved by the activation of a single production, rather than by the piecing together of the results of several activations. Again illustrating by example, most readers of English recognize the meaning of the word *cat* by a simple encoding, whereas many people will infer the meaning of *subcritical* by combining the encoded meanings of *sub* and *critical*. In more empirical terms, pattern recognition should meet the criteria for automated responding; it should be as rapid as possible and take place without conscious control.

Experimental psychologists have devised a number of procedures to evaluate the speed of automated pattern recognition. A factor analytic study of several such procedures showed that they all tap a single "reference to memory" factor (Hunt, Davidson, & Lansman, 1981). The clearest marker for the factor is the *lexical decision* task, in which a person is shown a string of letters and asked whether or not the string forms a word. Hertzog, Raskind, and Cannon (in press) have extended this work by showing that tests of speed of access to memorized information show a selective impairment in the elderly, beyond that observed in motor reaction time tasks. This suggests that the evaluation of encoding ability may be important in research on aging.

For the purposes of clinical testing, though, virtually all of the experimental psychologists' measures share a common fault. They measure the time between stimulus presentation and the completion of a simple motor response, either throwing a lever or pressing a button. Therefore test scores are contaminated by two effects. Practice has a substantial influence on the speed of virtually all motor responses. Experimental psychologists typically give their subjects a good deal of training on the use of the apparatus before beginning the testing procedure. This may not be feasible in a clinical setting. A more subtle effect is the *speed–accuracy trade-off*. In encoding, information about the stimulus is accumulated from memory over a measurable time period, usually about half a second. A person who is willing to identify a stimulus on the basis of relatively little information will respond faster than one who is more cautious, but the first person will make more errors. It can be quite difficult to disentangle individual differences in performance that are due to differences in efficiency of encoding from individual differences in the way in which people trade off speed and accuracy (Pachella, 1974).

An alternative to using tasks that require speeded responding is to use tasks that the subjects find familiar, but to modify them in some way to emphasize the encoding process. An interesting possibility is to measure encoding in reading by using the Rapid Single Visual Presentation (RSVP) technique. In RSVP, passages are presented, one word or phrase at a time, on a computer-controlled screen. The dependent measure is the participant's comprehension level at various presentation rates. An analagous procedure can be used for verbal comprehension, by speeded presentation of tape-recorded speech. Technological advances in the development of computer-generated speech may make this method of presentation much easier to use than it has been in the past. Apparently very little research has been done using either RSVP or compressed speech comprehension as measures of a person's ability to encode information.

Storage is the process of placing a representation of presented information into long-term memory. In a sense, successful storage is the criterion against which other measures of memory must be compared, since the purpose of observation must be to acquire a memorial record. Encoding and storage are intimately related, because what we remember of an event will depend very largely on how it was interpreted at the time it was observed. In part, the automatic encoding processes just described will determine the interpretation. However, automatic memory references and encoding processes are not all that determine event interpretation. Furthermore, they may not be the most important determiners of individual differences in interpretation and storage. Sternberg and Powell (1983) referred to the study of encoding processes in comprehension as placing an emphasis on "bottom up" processing, since encoding studies stress the dependence of comprehension upon simple, stimulus-driving recognition processes. They pointed out, correctly, that in studies of normal adults, individual differences in encoding processes account for a relatively small proportion of the variance between individuals. Correlations between measures of encoding and reading comprehension range from .3 to .4 in young adults.

The term *schema* is used to refer to a preexisting memory structure that is used to organize incoming information (Bartlett, 1958; Schank & Abelson, 1977). An example would be a schema for, say, a detective story or a news broadcast. People are much better able to store facts if they have a schema that can be used to organize them. In a widely cited study, Chase and Simon (1973) showed that expert chess players could retain more information from a glance at pieces on a chess board than could novices. However, the experts had an advantage only if the pieces were in plausible, legal chess positions. This observation, and further details of the study, convinced Chase and Simon that the experts fitted the information on the board into preestablished schemas for familiar chess situations. Chiesi, Spilich, and Voss (1979) reached a similar conclusion about the organization of memory in a study that was, on the surface, far different from Chase and Simon's work. College students listened to a simulated broadcast of a few innings from a baseball game. Subjects who were baseball fans were able to comprehend and recall much more information than subjects who were not baseball fans. The fans' advantage was restricted to recalling information that was relevant to the game.

These two studies are the tip of an iceberg of relatively recent work, all of which points to the same conclusion. Working memory holds more than a jumble of isolated codes. A memorial representation is a data structure consisting of coded terms and relations between them. Incoming stimuli are assigned meaning in such a way that they fit into slots in a developing structure, be it the representation of a chess match or a baseball game. A person's ability to form a reasonable configuration of information in working memory depends very much upon the availability of suitable schemas for the material to be memorized.

People have schemas for the things they are familiar with. This prosaic fact poses a difficult problem for the clinical assessment of memory. Many clinical tests are based on procedures developed either by experimental psychologists or by psychometricians. For good reasons, the psychologists and psychometricians have avoided test situations where performance depends upon a person's idiosyncratic experiences. As a result, most test procedures place the examinee in a relatively unfamiliar situation. Such tests are useful in determining memory functioning in context-free situations. The information that the tests provide can be used to indicate damages to the brain structures involved in memory, because such structures presumably exert context-free influences on memory. What context-free tests do not provide is an assessment of whether or not a person's memory is adequate for daily life.

How should a person's functional memory be assessed? In order to predict whether or not a person can cope with the memory demands of daily activity, the clinician must determine how well each patient can use the schemas that the environment requires. A psychological assessment procedure must be tailored to the individual being assessed. The medical model for testing is not appropriate. Blood pressure is blood pressure for everyone, but the meaning of a memory test may vary from person to person. In extreme cases, of course, customization of tests may not be necessary. Gross, easily illustrated memory defects do appear in Alzheimer's disease, hippocampal damage, and Korsakoff's syndrome. Evaluating the subtler defects associated with normal aging, exhaustion, or drug use is a qualitatively different problem.

Long-Term Memory Functions

The interpretations of the world that are built in working memory depend heavily on expectations about the world that are retrieved from long-term memory. Is there any way to evaluate the retrieval process directly? Learning is also an essential part of human activity. Can the learning process itself be evaluated?

The production activation model distinguishes between two kinds of retrieval from long-term memory. *Direct retrieval* occurs when a single production is activated and, as part of its action, places some information into working memory. Direct retrieval is part of pattern recognition. *Indirect retrieval* occurs when the system is given the goal of finding a particular piece of information, and the first response to the cue is not the answer. Indirect retrieval can be thought of as a problem-solving activity, in which the goal is to locate information in long-term memory that satisfies some criterion for relevance. The initial cues produce further cues, via direct retrieval, that in turn produce other cues, until the necessary information is found. What guides this problem-solving activity?

When information is presented, it will be coded in a particular way, not in all possible ways. The cues present at the time of retrieval must reactivate the cues noticed and stored at the time of memorization. Tulving and Thompson (1973) referred to this phenomenon as *encoding specificity*. They illustrated it by citing studies of the memorization of arbitrary material. Encoding specificity may be much more important when meaningful material is to be memorized than when we are dealing with arbitrary lists or paired associates. People seem to take a very narrow view of what they are to learn, when they learn something.

Research on problem isomorphs illustrates this point. Two problems are isomorphic if they have the same underlying structure, although they have different surface characteristics. For instance, the procedures involved in balancing a personal checkbook are identical whether the account is in U.S. dollars or British pounds. In studies of problem isomorphs, participants solve a series of somewhat more subtle isomorphic problems. Each problem has a different surface structure. For example, there are problems with the same underlying logical structure that can be presented as problems in algebra or as problems in fitting together pieces of a jigsaw puzzle (Hunt, 1978). Investigator after investigator has found remarkably little transfer from one problem isomorph to another (Gick & Holyoak, 1983; Hayes & Simon, 1974; Hunt, 1978; Reed, Ernst, & Banerji, 1974). Why? The surface structure of a problem provides perceptually dominating cues, so, in the absence of specific instruction to do otherwise, almost all people code solutions as procedures to be triggered by surface cues. Those few that do abstract general problem-solving rules are able to transfer learning appropriately. Unfortunately, though, transfer is hard to achieve. With discouragingly few exceptions, people learn procedures in fairly narrow contexts. They recall problem-solving procedures only when the original context is reinstated. Failure to recall a problem-solving procedure that a person once knew can be taken as evidence for a failure of a retrieval mechanism only if the examiner is convinced that the examination situation contained sufficient cues to reinstate the context of the original learning, as it was perceived by the subject.

Learning can be thought of as the ability to create new data structures in memory. Extreme cases of failures of learning occur in pathological cases (e. g., hippocampal damage) and are easy to recognize. Smaller changes in the ability to learn are much harder to evaluate, because, once again, the efficiency of a memory process depends upon the context in which memory is to operate.

From a theoretical perspective, learning something new is equivalent to creating new productions in long-term memory. Anderson (1982) has developed a detailed model of production construction. His argument is too long to be presented here, but his major conclusion is relevant. The construction of new procedures (i.e., new productions) is itself a complex problem-solving action. The learner must examine the productions currently in long-term memory to see if they can be merged, specialized, or otherwise modified to deal with a new experience. Learning, in this sense, is a metacognitive act. The system executes a problem-solving program (a production system) that takes as its objects some of the contents of its own long-term memory. By implication, learning will be disrupted either if the system somehow loses access to its metacognitive program or if it becomes incapable of executing that program due to some "biological" disruption, such as a loss of the ability to ignore interrupting stimuli while a problem is being solved.

These observations pose yet another difficult problem for the clinical assessment of memory. Useful memory is intimately tied to the ability to learn meaningful material. But meaningful learning is as hard to study as problem solving because meaningful learning *is* problem solving. Although there is a theoretical literature on learning as problem solving, any proposal for clinical testing based on that literature would, at present be sheer speculation. This is unfortunate, because what a clinician really has to know is a person's ability for meaningful learning, not that person's ability to learn nonsense syllable lists. Although there is some indication that the two abilities may be correlated in clinical populations, (Sunderland, Harris, & Baddeley, 1983), a great deal of research remains to be done.

A second kind of learning involves rearrangement of the associations between productions in long-term memory, without changing the productions themselves. For example, if one repeats a sequence of actions over and over again, the cue for the first action in the sequence will eventually become a sufficient cue to trigger subsequent actions without requiring the production of cues provided by the earlier responses in the sequence. This kind of "learning" can often be illustrated by situations in which it leads to minor slips in performance, such as a typist's typing the word *ration* instead of *ratio*. More generally, when a single cue is sufficient to initiate a response very quickly, and apparently without effort, the responses are said to be *automated* (Schneider & Shiffrin, 1977).

The conditions under which automated learning takes place are not at all clear. Some authors maintain that at least some automation can occur without conscious awareness (Hasher & Zacks, 1979), whereas others have asserted that a controlled, problem-solving

stage in learning is a necessary phase in automation (Fisk & Schneider, 1984). It is not necessary to resolve the controversy here. What is important is to consider the clinical implications. If there are two kinds of learning, they may depend upon two different processes and respond to different variables. In terms of the production activation model, it is necessary to distinguish between information that is to be stored as a modification to the set of productions that are already available, and information that is to be stored as a modification of the associations between existing productions.

The construction of new productions is equivalent to meaningful learning, as described above. The difficulty of evaluating such learning has already been described. Evaluating the ability to automate learning is much easier, at least theoretically. Operant conditioning could be looked on as a sort of procedure for the development of automation. Scanning paradigms, which were originally used to define automation, have been heavily studied. These are situations in which people spend hours, over several days or weeks, learning to detect targets in stimulus arrays. Eventually detection will become automated. Performance in scanning situations can thus be looked on as the criterion for the ability to achieve automatic learning. The logic of using scanning paradigms to evaluate automation is impeccable, and in theory these paradigms could be used to study individual differences in memory acquisition. The problem is a practical one. On the one hand, the patient time required to study the development of automation is seldom available. On the other hand, if a process takes days to develop, it just cannot be studied without extensive observation.

Conclusion

What conclusion should a person interested in memory assessment draw from this extended discussion of memory theory? By far the most important conclusion is that there is never going to be a single measure that will tell us how well a patient's memory works. The sort of picture that one needs depends upon the purpose of testing. What are the major considerations?

In cases where the purpose of testing is to establish the mechanisms of action of a particular variable that influences memory, then the reasonable thing to do is to test those functions, in isolation, that the variable is thought to influence. For instance, it is obvious that physical variables have physical consequences. Hippocampal lesions do not change the content of the information in a person's memory, but they may well influence the content-free mechanisms that operate on that information. By the same token, education will not change the content-free mechanisms that the brain has for information handling, but education can change information content. A test for possible hippocampal damage would not be the same as a test of the ability to recall history facts after instruction in economics!

A good case can be made for the testing of isolated functions if the purpose of assessment is to determine, in great detail, the sort of memory impairment that may be found in a specific case. This would be useful if one were planning a course of rehabilitation therapy, for it would be important to know what functions were impaired in a patient whose memory was already known to be deficient in a global way. Quite a different assessment procedure would be in order if the purpose of testing was to estimate how well a person might function in a particular life context. In this case the examiner would have to be concerned with the effectiveness of functioning of the integrated memory system, not the effectiveness of its parts in isolation. If the clinician looks to the theoretician for guidance here, the clinician will find the theoretician at a somewhat hazy "cutting edge" of memory research. Models of the functioning of integrated memory systems are being developed, and it may be that they will lead to the development of realistic, theoretically defensible assessment procedures. Creating these procedures is an endeavor that will require close cooperation between theoretically oriented experimental psychologists and all those specialists who deal with clinical populations. Reconciling theoretical purity with pragmatic constraints will not be easy. The alternative, to use tests that we know make little sense, hardly seems attractive.

References

Ackerman, P. L., Schneider, W., & Wickens, C. D. (1984). Deciding the existence of a time-sharing ability: A combined methodological and theoretical approach. *Human Factors, 26*(1), 71–82.

Anderson, J. R. (1982). Acquisition of cognitive skill. *Psychological Review, 89*, 369–406.

Anderson, J. R. (1983a). A spreading activation theory of memory. *Journal of Verbal Learning and Verbal Behavior, 22*, 261–295.

Anderson, J. R. (1983b). *The architecture of cognition.* Cambridge, MA: Harvard University Press.

Anderson, J. R., & Bower, G. H. (1973). *Human associative memory.* Washington, DC: Winston.

Bartlett, F. (1958). *Thinking.* New York: Basic Books.

Chase, W. G., & Ericsson, K. A. (1981). Skilled memory. In J. R. Anderson (Ed.), *Cognitive skills and their acquistion* (pp. 141–189). Hillsdale, NJ: Erlbaum.

Chase, W. G., & Simon, H. A. (1973). The mind's eye in chess. In W. G. Chase (Ed.), *Visual information* (pp. 215–282). New York: Academic Press.

Chiesi, H. L., Spilich, G. J., & Voss, J. F. (1979). Acquisition of domain-related information in relation to high and low domain knowledge. *Journal of Verbal Learning and Verbal Behavior, 18*, 257–274.

Daneman, M. (1983). The measurement of reading comprehension: How not to trade construct validity for predictive power. *Intelligence, 6*, 331–345.

Dempster, F. N. (1981). Memory span: Sources of individual and developmental differences. *Psychological Bulletin, 89* 63–100.

Fisk, A. D., & Schneider, W. (1984). Memory as a function of attention, level of processing and automatization. *Journal of Experimental Psychology: Learning, Memory and Cognition, 10*, 181–197.

Gick, M., & Holyoak, K. (1983). Schema induction and analogical transfer. *Cognitive Psychology, 15*, 1–38.

Glanzer, M., Fischer, B., & Dorfman, D. (1984). Short term storage in reading. *Journal of Verbal Learning and Verbal Behavior, 23*(4), 467–486.

Guilford, J. P. (1967). *The nature of human intelligence.* New York: McGraw-Hill.

Hasher, L., & Zacks, R. (1979). Automatic and effortful processes in memory. *Journal of Experimental Psychology: General, 108*, 356–388.

Hayes, J. R., & Simon, H. A. (1974). Understanding written problem instructions. In L. Gregg (Ed.), *Knowledge and cognition* (pp. 167–200). Hillsdale, NJ: Erlbaum.

Hertzog, C., Raskind, C. L., & Cannon, C. J. (in press). Age related slowing in semantic information processing speed: An individual differences analysis. *Journal of Gerontology.*

Hunt, E. (1978). Qualitative sources of individual differences in complex problem solving. In J. M. Scandura & C. J. Brainerd (Eds.), *Structural process models of complex human behavior. Proceedings of the NATO Advanced Study Institute on Structure/Process Theories of Complex Human Behavior* (pp. 573–602). Rockville, MD: Sitjhoff & Noordhoff.

Hunt, E. (1981). The design of a robot mind: A theoretical approach to issues in intelligence. In M. Friedman, J. P. Das, & M. O'Connor (Eds.), *Intelligence and learning* (pp. 459–478). New York: Plenum Press.

Hunt, E. (1983) On the nature of intelligence. *Science, 219*, 141–146.

Hunt, E., Davidson, J., & Lansman, M. (1981). Individual differences in long term memory access. *Memory and Cognition, 9*(6), 599–608.

Hunt, E., & Lansman, M. (1982). Individual differences in attention. In R. Sternberg (Ed.), *Advances in the psychology of human intelligence* (Vol. 1). Hillsdale, NJ: Erlbaum.

Hunt, E., & Lansman, M. (1984). *A unified model of attention and problem solving* (Technical Report). Seattle: University of Washington, Department of Psychology.

Hunt, E., & Pixton, P. (1982). A general model for simulating information processing experiments. *Proceedings of the 4th Annual Conference of the Cognitive Science Society* (pp. 160–163). Ann Arbor, MI.

Kerr, F. B., Condon, S. M., & McDonald, L. A. (1983). Cognitive spatial processing and the regulation of posture. *Journal of Experimental Psychology: Human Perception and Performance, 11*, 617–622.

Klapp, S. T., Marshburn, E. A., & Lester, P. T. (1983). Short term memory does not involve the "working memory" of information processing: The decline of a common assumption. *Journal of Experimental Psychology: General, 112*, 240–264.

Klatzky, R. (1975). *Human memory.* San Francisco: Freeman.

Lansman, M. (1978). *An attentional approach to individual differences in immediate memory.* Unpublished doctoral dissertation, University of Washington, Seattle.

Matarazzo, J. D. (1972). *Wechsler's measurement and appraisal of adult intelligence* (5th ed.). Baltimore, MD: Williams & Wilkins.

Miller, G. A. (1956). The magical number seven, plus or minus two: Some limits on our capacity for processing information. *Psychological Review, 63*, 81–97.

Newell, A. (1973). Production systems: Models of control structures. In W. G. Chase (Ed.), *Visual information processing* (pp. 463–526). New York: Academic Press.

Newell, A., & Simon, H. (1972). *Human problem solving.* Englewood Cliffs, NJ: Prentice-Hall.

Pachella, R. G. (1974). The interpretation of reaction time in information processing research. In B. H. Kantowitz (Ed.), *Human information processing: Tutorials in performance and cognition* (pp. 41–82). Hillsdale, NJ: Erlbaum.

Reed, S. K., Ernst, G. W., & Banerji, R. (1974). The role of analogy in transfer between similar problem states. *Cognitive Psychology, 6*, 436–450.

Schank, R., & Abelson, R. (1977). *Scripts, plans, goals and understanding*. Hillsdale, NJ: Erlbaum.

Schneider, W., & Shiffrin, R. M. (1977). Controlled and automatic human information processing: I. Detection, search, and attention. *Psychological Review, 84*(1), 1–67.

Shallice, T., & Warrington, E. K. (1970). Independent functioning of verbal memory stores: A neuropsychological study. *Quarterly Journal of Experimental Psychology, 22*, 261–273.

Sternberg, R. J., & Powell, J. S. (1983). Comprehending verbal comprehension. *American Psychologist, 8*, 878–893.

Sunderland, A., Harris, J. E., & Baddeley, A. D. (1983). Do laboratory tests predict everyday memory? A neuropsychological study. *Journal of Verbal Learning and Verbal Behavior, 22*, 341–357.

Tulving, E., & Thompson, D. M. (1973). Encoding specificity and retrieval processes in episodic memory. *Psychological Review, 80*, 352–373.

Walsh, K. W. (1978). *Neuropsychology: A clinical approach*. Edinburgh, Scotland: Churchill Livingstone.

Elkhonon Goldberg and Robert M. Bilder

CHAPTER

7

Neuropsychological Perspectives: Retrograde Amnesia and Executive Deficits

Two types of dangers have to be dealt with in the assessment of memory: (a) potential errors of omission—failure to detect an amnestic syndrome, and (b) potential errors of commission— automatically assuming that poor performance on a memory task necessarily signifies presence of a primary amnestic syndrome.

The first type of error is illustrated in Part I in the example of retrograde amnesia. *Retrograde amnesia is underemphasized both in clinical assessments and in brain–behavior theory, and its incidence in clinical populations is probably underestimated. The assumption that remote memory deficits are invariably secondary to recent memory deficits is not universally valid. An amnestic syndrome exists in which retrograde amnesia is central. Examination of this syndrome suggests that access to several types of remote memories can be impaired. New techniques for systematically assessing retrograde amnesia must be designed and introduced into routine diagnostic batteries.*

The second type of error is illustrated in Part II in the example of the executive syndrome. *In this syndrome, performance on what are presumably memory tasks can be severely disrupted, without necessarily involving poor storage or retrieval. The executive syndrome is characterized by different phenomenology of recall failures than are primary amnesias; and deficits of recall or recognition, while present, are not central to this syndrome. Poor performance on memory tasks in this syndrome is secondary to a more fundamental deficit of selectivity of cognitive control.*

Memory disorders are among the most common cognitive consequences of central nervous system (CNS) disease, regardless of etiology. They are conspicuous in patients with tumors (e.g., pituitary adenomas), vascular conditions (e.g., aneurysms of the anterior communicating artery), infectious diseases (e.g., herpes simplex encephalitis), degenerative diseases due to substance abuse (e.g., Korsakoff's syndrome), anoxia, and head trauma. Memory deficits are central also to the geriatric dementias.

Psychometric properties (internal consistency, reliability, standardization) have been given much consideration in the development of techniques for memory assessment. Considerably less attention has been paid to the ethological and construct validity of assessment methods. The most widely used assessment methods fail to address the complaints of patients and at the same time fail to elicit responses that would more adequately reflect the diversity of cognitive mechanisms that may be responsible for memory dysfunction. A patient, for instance, may be unable to learn a list of unrelated words, but this finding may fail to explain why the patient forgets the names of acquaintances or misplaces money.

The constricted nature and limited ethological salience of the assessment technique (i.e., list-learning task) results in a limited range of possible types of memory dysfunctions that can be elicited. Given that memory is not a unitary construct, such isolated measures, no matter how reliable and standardized, will fail to provide insight into the nature of the patient's deficits and will fail to detect the significance of certain dimensions of memory pathology.

Another issue often underemphasized in the studies of deranged memory is the issue of the cognitive composition of the deficit. It is often assumed that deficient performance on a memory task necessarily implies impaired storage and/or retrieval. In fact, it is entirely possible that deficient encoding strategies (Buschke, in press) or executive control (Goldberg & Costa, 1986; Luria, 1976) contribute to poor performance as much as or more than faulty storage and/or retrieval. The common failure to recognize such contributions to poor performance on a task designed to measure memory may lead to an erroneous formulation of the nature of the deficit. An error of commission of sorts occurs because of the incorrect conclusion that a primary amnesia is present, whereas, in fact, encoding and/or executive deficits are at the core of the problem.

The difficulties of cognitive assessment of the dementias are compounded by the fact that multiple cognitive deficits are usually present; each of them is easily confounded and obscured by others. This problem is to be expected given the diffuse or multifocal distribution of lesions in most dementias. Assessment is further confounded by the fact that, although multidimensional, the cognitive deficits in dementias are often not very pronounced in magnitude along any single cognitive dimension. This complex, multidimensional nature of the dysfunction makes it difficult to establish a nomenclature of the salient cognitive phenomena that need to be elicited in the neuropsychological examination in order to arrive at an appropriate diagnosis.

To this end, it may be profitable to utilize knowledge of *potentially salient phenomenology* of cognitive disorders derived from studies of more focal, neurological, or neurosurgical populations. The cognitive deficits that characterize these populations are generally more discrete, less multidimensional, and at the same time more pronounced, in terms of there being (fewer) cognitive dimensions. This reflects the relatively more discrete and focal nature of the lesions involved.

The value of utilizing knowledge of "focal" cognitive pathology for understanding dementias is not in drawing etiological or even syndromal similarities, but rather in identifying types of cognitive impairment that surely exist in the dementias as components of more complex syndromes but because of syndromal complexity are likely to be overlooked or underemphasized. Identifying potentially salient cognitive impairments also provides a framework for developing assessment techniques that may tease apart the relevant dimensions of cognitive compromise in the context of multidimensional dysfunction.

The purpose of this chapter is to draw the reader's attention to some of those cognitive deficits that affect performance on memory tasks and that are likely to be ignored or misinterpreted. Although cognitive deficits due to head trauma serve as the material for illustrations, we believe that the phenomena presented are relevant to dementias.

Two separate, distinctly different types of poor performance on mnestic tasks will be discussed. One of them is often ignored, thus leading to an error of omission. The other one, on the contrary, is likely to lead to an erroneous conclusion of the presence of a primary amnesia, thus leading to an error of commission.

I. Assessing Retrograde Amnesia: A Possible Error of Omission

Although memory deficits have long been the focus of neuropsychological studies, investigators have traditionally concentrated on anterograde amnesia (the inability to learn and retrieve new information, that is, information encountered after the onset of the pathological condition). Retrograde amnesia (the deficient retrieval of old information, presumably learned long before the onset of the pathological condition) has drawn considerably less attention, and relatively little is known about it. Consequently, the incidence and severity of retrograde amnesia in brain-damaged populations is probably considerably underestimated (Butters, 1983, in press). Explanations that have been offered to account for this underemphasis include methodological difficulties in constructing valid assessment instruments to measure retrograde amnesia (Erickson, 1978; Poon, 1985) and lack of a theoretical framework to account for such major phenomena as the temporal gradient of the deficit that often characterizes retrograde amnesia (Butters, 1983).

An additional, perhaps more critical reason for this relative lack of interest in retrograde amnesia is the longstanding assumption that the severity of the deficit of remote memory (retrograde amnesia) can never exceed the severity of the deficit of recent memory (anterograde amnesia). In other words, it has been assumed that (a) in progressive brain disease (e.g., dementia), retrograde amnesia develops more slowly than, or in parallel with, anterograde amnesia, and that in recovery from an acute condition (e.g., head trauma), the recovery from retrograde amnesia is more rapid and complete than, or occurs in parallel with, the recovery from anterograde amnesia (Barbizet, 1970; Benson & Geschwind, 1967; Milner, 1966; Sanders & Warrington, 1971; Squire & Slater, 1978; Teuber, Milner, & Vaughan, 1968). In cases of posttraumatic amnesia, clinicians generally expect a relatively rapid and complete disappearance of retrograde amnesia and a relatively slow and often incomplete recovery from anterograde amnesia.

These assumptions inevitably led to the formulation of the principle that anterograde amnesia is the center of the amnestic syndrome, and retrograde amnesia is a dependent, peripheral component. A few cases challenging the validity of this general neurological and neuropsychological principle have been reported, but documentation of the deficits has been sparse, and the evidence has usually been dismissed as anecdotal.

Recently, however, several well-documented cases have demonstrated that the "paradoxical" pattern is indeed possible, that is, dense and severe retrograde amnesia may exist without severe anterograde amnesia (Butters, 1979; Goldberg, Antin, et al., 1981; Roman-Campos, Poser, & Wood, 1980). The existence of an amnestic syndrome in which retrograde rather than anterograde amnesia plays the central role should lead to a reexamination of memory assessment methodologies and point out several inadequacies in clinical approaches to deficits of remote memory.

We now present a detailed report of a case in which retrograde rather than anterograde amnesia dominated the clinical picture, and discuss its implications.

A Case Study

A 36-year-old, right-handed, college-educated male had an open skull fracture in the right parieto-occipital and temporal areas, with herniation of the right hemisphere and compression of the left mesencephalon at the tentorial notch. In surgery, a small portion of the macerated brain was removed, the dural laceration was sewn over, and the bone-plate replaced.

For two days the patient was comatose and had dilated pupils. Subsequently, there was right hemiparesis with spasticity of the distal upper right extremity and a right Babinski's sign, and a left superior quadrantanopsia.

Six weeks later, a computerized tomography (CT) scan revealed considerable ventricular enlargement, and a ventriculoatrial shunt was performed, connecting the right temporal area with the foramen of Monroe. Repeated CT examinations during the period of recovery revealed symmetrical mild to moderate ventricular enlargement, a region of rarefaction in the right mid- and posterior-temporal areas adjacent to the craniotomy site, a small region of rarefaction along the left mid-temporal convexity, and a narrow band of hypodensity approximately 2 centimeters long in the median and left paramedian zones, extending from the ventral tegmental portion of the upper mesencephalon (where the midline was reached and crossed) caudally to the ventral portion of the ponto-mesencephalic junction. There was prominence of the Sylvian fissure bilaterally. The sulci were of normal size, and no midline shift was noted anywhere in the brain. The ventriculo-atrial shunt tip remained in place. The CT findings were consistent with multiple parenchymal changes, both posttraumatic and surgical; these were consistently observed throughout several CT examinations during a 2½-year posttraumatic follow-up.

Five months after the accident, systematic observations of the patient's behavior began. Several features were prominent in the clinical picture at this early stage of recovery:

1. The patient was disoriented to time, place, and person.

2. The patient exhibited a severe mixed aphasia. His speech was anomic, grammatically primitive, and limited to several overlearned automatisms. The patient's comprehension was relatively intact, and he was able to answer simple questions (in short, lexically and syntactically impoverished sentences) and respond to simple instructions. There was no deficit of articulation: he was able to repeat words on command and "read," albeit with little or no comprehension.

3. The patient had profound anterograde amnesia. He was unable to retain the names of persons over 2-to-3-minute periods, or even recognize them. His visuospatial memory appeared to be more intact, in that he was able to find the dining room, entrance, and other points of reference on the ward.

4. The patient had profound retrograde amnesia. He recognized his parents, both in person and in photographs, but he did not recognize his wife, his children, or his business associates. When questioned about his age and occupation, he would report that he was 16 or 17 years old and that he was a high school student. He would give the correct name of the high school he had attended and his parents' address as his residence. He responded negatively when asked about his subsequent college and business career.

The Pattern of Recovery

During the course of recovery, the patient became fully oriented to time, person, and place. A virtually complete restitution of language functions took place, so that only a very mild dysnomia for nouns was occasionally observed. The right hemiparesis completely resolved but the left superior quadrantanopsia persisted.

The amnestic syndrome observed in our patient at this early stage of recovery was quite severe but qualitatively not unusual in that both profound anterograde and profound retrograde amnesias were present. We expected a typical course of recovery: a "shrinkage" of the temporal extent of retrograde amnesia with ultimate complete recovery (with the exception of the memory for the short segment of time immediately surrounding the accident), and a much slower recovery from anterograde amnesia, probably incomplete so that the patient would be permanently impaired with respect to his ability to learn and/or retrieve new information.

In fact, the opposite happened. The patient's ability to learn new information improved steadily, so that he became able to maintain continuity of events around him. He knew the names of people around him, could keep track of his daily and weekly activities, began to watch television and read newspapers, and was able to monitor and temporally interrelate events in the world at large. By the end of the observation period, the degree of his anterograde amnesia was clinically and practically inconsequential.

The patient's retrograde amnesia, in contrast, failed to show any recovery with respect to either its temporal extent or its density. The patient remained profoundly impaired with respect to personal information: He maintained that he was about 17 years of age, attended high school, and had never held a job or had a family of his own. The patient's fund of general knowledge was also impaired and failed to reveal even moderate recovery: He was unable to answer trivial questions such as "What is the capital of France?" or "Who wrote *King Lear*?"

As the extent of his anterograde amnesia diminished, the patient was increasingly able to relearn much of the information lost to him. He was reacquainted with his wife and children. His life history covering the 20-year period of amnesia was reconstructed for him, and he was able to retain it. This knowledge, however, lacked any sense of authenticity for the patient, and he would invariably draw the distinction between what he "knew" and what he "had been told" about himself.

We had to conclude, on the basis of clinical observations, that a most unusual pattern of recovery from posttraumatic amnesia was taking place: There was considerable and near complete recovery from anterograde amnesia and no recovery from retrograde amnesia.

The clinical picture of retrograde amnesia was puzzling also with respect to the type of information to which access had been lost. It is usually assumed that retrograde amnesia, when present, affects predominantly or even exclusively only information that is embedded in a temporal context. In other words, only memory for *events*, both personal and public, is assumed to be defective. Such knowledge for events was clearly impaired in our patient, but in addition to that, loss of access to nontemporally encoded information (that which can be termed *facts*) was also present. The distinction between temporally coded and nontemporally coded information roughly (but not precisely) corresponds to the distinction between *episodic* and *semantic* information. It is usually assumed that in retrograde amnesia, access to episodic information is impaired, whereas access to semantic information remains intact.

In our patient, however, while access to episodic information was clearly lost (extending over a period of about 20 years), there was also loss of access to certain domains of semantic information. To the extent that one can make a distinction within the body of semantic information between singular and generic knowledge, our patient apparently had impaired access to singular semantic information but intact access to generic semantic information. Indeed, his knowledge of the lexicon, numeric concepts, and generic geometric concepts was not impaired.

Information regarding facts (e.g., "London is the capital of England"), unlike information regarding events (e.g., "Johnson succeeded Kennedy as president of the United States"), lacks inherent temporal quality, and in this sense the requirement of temporal encodedness is not implicit in such information. Nevertheless, even knowledge for facts can be characterized in terms of the time and circumstances of its acquisition by the subject. In this sense, amnesia for events and amnesia for facts can be compared in terms of their temporal extents. When such comparison was made for our patient, it appeared that the temporal extent of his retrograde amnesia for facts exceeded that of his retrograde amnesia for events. Indeed, his amnesia for personal and public events extended back to about the age of 17, whereas he was unable to retrieve trivial facts such as "Paris is the capital of France" and "Shakespeare was the author of *King Lear*," which must have been learned at a much earlier age by an urban upper-middle-class person who attended excellent schools.

Once we concluded that the patient presented an unusual case of retrograde amnesia without anterograde amnesia of comparable severity, we were further puzzled by his ability to relearn and retain newly learned information over very long periods of time. Indeed, assuming that the patient had a relatively intact capacity to learn and retain new information and a severely impaired capacity to retrieve old information, one would expect that as successfully learned new information became old, the patient would lose access to it. One would assume further that the only mechanism for maintaining effective access to such information would be continuous rehearsal; and the amount of information that can be simultaneously rehearsed is limited. In other words, only the limited amount of information that can be maintained in the secondary memory via rehearsal would be available for retrieval over long periods of time. Once information enters the unlimited capacity of tertiary memory, the access to it should be lost. This is not what happened with our patient. He was able to learn large amounts of information and retain it over very long periods of time. It was clear that the amount of information learned or relearned after the accident (which could be retrieved by the patient at will) far exceeded the limited capacity of secondary memory.

Long-Term Neuropsychological Follow-Up

In order to document these clinical observations, a systematic longitudinal study of the patient using standard neuropsychological procedures was designed. We discuss those components of the study that are immediately relevant to the issues of memory.

Recent memory was assessed using several word list learning tasks (Buschke Selective Reminding Technique [Buschke, 1973]) and the Wechsler Memory Scale (Wechsler, 1945).

Remote memory was assessed using three instruments:

1. *Boston Retrograde Amnesia Questionnaire.* (Albert, Butters, & Levin, 1979) This questionnaire is chronologically organized and measures the subject's memory for important public events and personalities that were significant in specific decades. The battery consists of three parts: verbal active recall, verbal recognition, and nonverbal recognition ("famous faces"). Only those segments of the battery (decades) that correspond to the subject's conscious life are used. Normal control subjects answered at least 80% of the questions on this battery correctly.

2. *Personal Events Questionnaire.* With the help of the patient's family, we compiled a chronology of important events in the patient's life. The chronology included specific events and information from the time the patient attended elementary school up to the period immediately preceding the trauma. Schools attended, places of employment, names of friends, teachers and business associates, and vacation destinations were included. For each time segment, questions were constructed in pairs equated as far as possible for significance and type of information.

3. *General Knowledge Battery.* This battery was designed by E. Goldberg, R. Bilder, and L. Gerstman (unpublished test, 1980) to complement the first two batteries. Unlike those chronologically organized batteries, it was designed to assess the knowledge of trivial facts that lack inherent temporal quality. In order to further describe the nature of the memory deficit in our patient, we consider the organization of this battery in some detail.

The battery consists of two parts: verbal and nonverbal. The nonverbal part (60 questions) assesses, in a forced multiple-choice format, the ability to make associations between pictures based on old, overlearned general knowledge. It covers three thematic domains:

culture, geography, and symbols. Problems in the cultural domain involve presentation of a well-known architectural or artistic "standard" stimulus (e.g., a picture of Winchester Cathedral); the subject's task is to choose one of four alternative stimuli that is "most related" to the standard (e.g., a picture of "Big Ben" versus the Statue of Liberty, a Hindu temple, or an Aztec ruin). Geography problems require matching the unlabeled silhouettes of countries that are in closest proximity (e.g., Spain is matched to France, not Japan). For the domain of symbols, a standard stimulus symbol is presented (e.g., a treble clef); the subject's task is to select one of four pictorial stimuli that is "most related" to the standard (e.g., a violin versus various woodworking tools).

The verbal part (240 questions) covers the same three thematic domains and consists of an active recall section and a multiple-choice section. The verbal multiple-choice section is composed of three subsections, each of which is characterized by a different level of confusability among the multiple-choice items. For instance, if the question is "Which city is the capital of country X?" the highest level of confusability would be represented by a multiple-choice answer array consisting of the names of the correct capital and of three incorrect capitals of countries on the same continent. The intermediate level of confusability would be represented by a multiple-choice array consisting of the name of the correct capital and three names of geographical entities, none of which is the name of a city (e.g., names of rivers or mountains). The lowest level of confusability would be represented by the name of the correct capital city and three proper names that are not geographical entities (e.g., names of famous historical personalities).

In addition, the General Knowledge Battery (both active recall and multiple-choice sections) is organized into two halves equated both for thematic composition and difficulty of the questions. The availability of two equivalent administrations can be valuable for various assessment and experimental purposes.

The battery was administered to 20 normal control subjects matched to the patient with respect to age, educational and socioeconomic status, and region of residence. All control subjects answered at least 95% of the questions correctly.

Table 7-1 summarizes the patient's performance on memory tests at about 10 months and about 2½ years posttrauma. All tests of recent memory (anterograde amnesia) demonstrated considerable impairment at the initial testing and revealed significant improvement when the results of the first and the second testing were compared and at the second testing reached (Wechsler Memory Scale) (Wechsler, 1945) or approached (Buschke Selective Reminding Technique) (Buschke, 1973) the normal range. The Wechsler Memory Quotient was consistent with and changed in parallel with the Wechsler Adult Intelligence Scale (WAIS) IQ, a finding usually construed as indicating that anterograde amnesia does not constitute an outstanding feature of cognitive impairment.

The tests of remote memory (retrograde amnesia), on the other hand, revealed profound impairment at both

Table 7-1. Performance of Patient With Retrograde Amnesia 10 Months (T_1) and 2½ Years (T_2) After Injury

Task	T_1	T_2	z
Wechsler Memory			
Total score	53.2	69.4	2.18*
Buschke Selective Reminding			
Total recall	53.1	91.5	4.67**
Long-term storage	36.1	80.0	5.55**
Long-term retrieval	20.0	74.6	7.51**
Consistent retrieval	0	56.2	9.25
Boston Retrograde Amnesia			
Recognition	36.7	43.3	0.75
Recall	11.7	30.0	2.47*
Famous faces	27.4	39.7	1.58
General Knowledge Battery			
Verbal recall	58.3	66.7	0.84
Verbal recognition	64.8	59.3	−0.69
Visual recognition	30.8	28.5	−0.18

$*p < .02.$ $**p < .0001.$

Note. Scores are expressed as percentages of maximum possible scores. One-tailed tests of difference between two proportions with correction for chance in the case of multiple-choice tasks were used. Reprinted from Goldberg, Antin, et al., (1981) by permission. Copyright 1981 by the American Association for the Advancement of Science.

the first and the last testing sessions. No appreciable improvement was observed, except on the recall part of the Boston Retrograde Amnesia Questionnaire, on which the absolute levels of performance were the lowest and, therefore, on which a "floor effect" was likely to have been observed.

In the multiple-choice sections of the General Knowledge Battery, the quality of performance was inversely related to the degree of confusability. Such an effect is usually construed as evidence that retrieval (access to engrams) rather than storage (presence of engrams) is impaired. It also indicates that our patient's deficit of retrieval was not complete: Obviously some clues were intact, enabling the patient to discriminate less plausible from more plausible choices.

Psychometric examination of the patient's memory impairment thus agreed with the clinical picture. Initially, both profound anterograde and profound retrograde amnesia were present. Subsequently, there was significant recovery from anterograde amnesia but not from retrograde amnesia. After 2½ years, no or very little anterograde amnesia remained, while severe retrograde amnesia was still present. In all likelihood, this severe retrograde amnesia was due to deficient retrieval rather than to the destruction of engrams. The retrograde amnesia was pronounced for both personal and public events and for facts.

We also attempted to document the patient's puzzling ability to retain large amounts of new information over very long periods of time. We pretested the patient on the General Knowledge Battery. Once the degree of impairment was established, we trained the patient on one of the two equivalent halves of the battery—in other words, we taught him the correct answers to the questions until he reached a criterion. The other equivalent half of the battery remained "untrained"; it was used only periodically to allow longitudinal comparisons with the "trained" half; and when it was used, we did not offer the patient any feedback to his responses.

We then retested the patient periodically on both halves of the battery for about a year after he learned the trained half to criterion. Figure 7-1 presents results of this study for two sections of the battery. The effect of training remained significant over the whole period of retesting; the level of performance on the trained half was significantly higher on retests than on the initial pretest level. Performance on the untrained part of the battery, on the other hand, remained at the same level during the periodic retests as during the initial pre-test.

Thus, the effect of learning remained strong over a very long period (about a year). The results of this formal study thus support the clinical observations of the patient's considerable ability to relearn.

Discussion

This case study raises more questions than it answers. It does, however, teach certain lessons.

First, this case underscores the value of phenomenology for understanding brain pathology and its relationship to cognitive deficits. Some of the most important advances in neuropsychology and cognitive neuroscience can be credited to case studies of one or of a few patients with striking, unanticipated phenomenology that could not be accounted for by existing theories and for whose assessment no standard, routinized psychometric procedures were available. The studies by Sperry and Bogen of split-brain patients, by Penfield and Milner of patients with temporal pole resections, and by Goldstein and later Luria of patients with prefrontal lesions are examples of such insights. Studies of this sort invariably raise more questions than they answer, but in the process they open new domains of inquiry into brain–behavioral relationships and provide points of departure and direction for whole sets of more systematic, "large-N" studies. Each of the aforementioned studies had been such a point of departure for inquiry into the roles of hemispheric interaction and mechanisms of recent memory and anterograde amnesia and into the role of the frontal lobes in executive control and its disintegration, respectively.

More specific lessons derived from the presented case follow:

1. Retrograde amnesia can be an outstanding or central component of the amnestic syndrome, not always just being concomitant to anterograde amnesia. Therefore, it should be studied and assessed in patients carefully and in its own right.

2. The implicit assumption that retrograde amnesias are homogeneous is probably incorrect, and the possible scope of retrograde amnesias is greater than is usually assumed. Indeed, various types of anterograde amnesia have been specified and various aspects of anterograde amnesia are routinely assessed. With respect to retrograde amnesia, on the other hand, only access to chronological, temporally encoded information is usually tested, and adequate assessment techniques have been developed for this aspect only (Albert, Butters, & Levin, 1979; Marslen-Wilson & Teuber, 1975; Sanders & Warrington, 1971; Seltzer & Benson, 1974; Squire & Slater, 1975).

Access to other types of overlearned information is presumed to be intact in patients with amnesias and as a rule is not assessed systematically. In our patient, however, both the memory for events and the memory for facts were impaired, the latter possibly being even more impaired than the former in terms of the temporal extent of the amnesia, with respect to the time of acquisition of information. We are currently developing a set of procedures to assess retrograde amnesia systematically with respect to various types of overlearned information, and we are testing these procedures on patients with amnestic syndromes of various etiologies and loci of brain damage.

3. There may be more than one system that can subserve access to remote storage. Paradoxically, this conclusion is made plausible by strengths rather than deficits in our patient. Although he never regained access to the old information learned prior to the head injury, he could maintain access to new information even when it became old, provided that it was learned after the head injury. We can only speculate about the compensatory or alternative mechanisms that came into play, but the observation clearly lends support to recently formulated hypotheses of the multiplicity of memory systems (Goldberg, 1984; Mishkin, 1982; Mishkin, Spiegler, Saunders, & Malamut, 1982). The potential relevance of such theorizing to the issues of remediation of impaired memory functions is unclear at this time but should be ascertained further.

Aside from these general considerations regarding the relevance of the just-described observations to the study and assessment of memory, some specific considerations may be of particular relevance to the study of amnestic syndromes in geriatric dementias. Older patients rarely report the kind of clear-cut dissociation between lucid access to old, overlearned information and deficient ability to learn new information that is often seen in classic amnesias. Instead, they report, among other things, difficulties in recalling overlearned telephone numbers and names of people and in following overlearned directions (Poon, 1980). These complaints may be indicative of retrograde amnesia, yet they cannot be validated directly by the psychometric paradigms commonly employed in standardized assessment of memory functions (e.g., word list learning, paired-associate learning), because these paradigms study recent rather than remote memory.

In our patient, the extensive retrograde amnesia was attributed to a lesion in the ventral tegmental area of mesencephalon that destroyed nuclei from which reticular pathways ascend into the mammillary bodies and

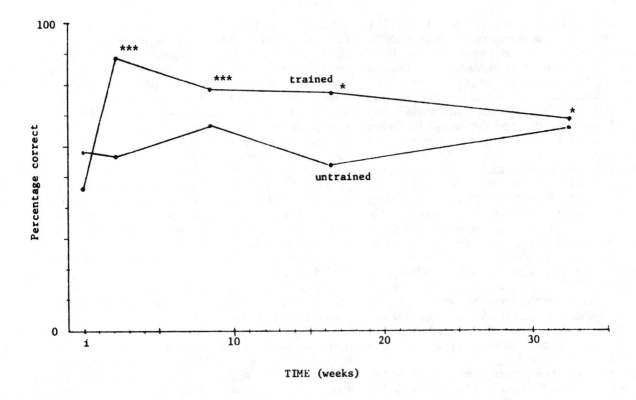

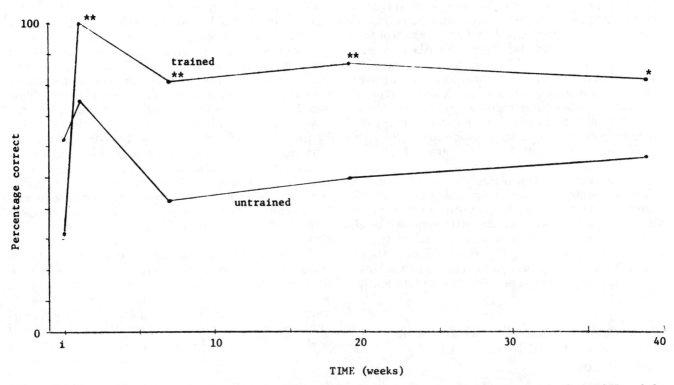

Figure 7-1. Comparison between performances on the trained vs. untrained parts of two sections of the General Knowledge Battery: verbal active recall section (top); visual section (bottom). Initial levels of performance (before the beginning of training) are indicated on the abscissa by i. Different from initial performance at (*=.05, **=.01, ***=.001) level of significance.

hippocampi. A more detailed discussion of focal findings in the patient, of the rationale for the neuroanatomical formulation, and of the hypothesized neural mechanisms responsible for the cognitive deficit has been presented elsewhere (Goldberg et al., 1981; Goldberg, Hughes, Mattis, & Antin, 1982; Goldberg, Mattis, Hughes, & Antin, 1982). The importance of these areas in memory function was subsequently demonstrated in animal models (Oades, 1981). The structures involved are proximal to the bottom of the third ventricle and to the fourth ventricle. The third ventricle is usually found most dilated on radiological examination of Alzheimer's patients (de Leon et al., 1980). Given this pattern of ventricular dilation and hence possible tissue atrophy around the walls of the ventricle, it is probable that the mesencephalic areas affected in our patient are also at risk in patients with Alzheimer's disease (AD).

Given the high density of nuclei and pathways in the ventral mesencephalon and the fact that these are reticular nuclei and pathways, the critical size of a lesion capable of producing profound cognitive deficit is probably quite small (Goldberg, Hughes, et al., 1982). In other words, an amount of tissue loss that would not be sufficient to produce an appreciable cognitive deficit in most parts of the brain probably would be sufficient to lead to a deficit if the lesion were located in the ventral mesencephalon. It is therefore possible that a strategically located vascular event in the vertebro-basilar circulation (which provides most of the blood supply to the pons and ventral mesencephalon) may also produce severe retrograde amnesia.

Ischemic attacks in the vertebro-basilar circulation are not uncommon, and they constitute the postulated mechanism of transient global amnesia (Fogelholm, Kivalo, & Bergstrom, 1975; Mathew & Meyer, 1974; Poser & Ziegler, 1960). Persistent retrograde (but not anterograde) amnesia secondary to an episode of transient global amnesia has been described recently (Roman-Campos et al., 1980). It has been suggested that a small infarction in the mesencephalon occurred concurrently with the ischemic attack and was responsible for the residual retrograde amnesia (Goldberg, Hughes, et al., 1982). All of these considerations lead one to suspect that an amnestic syndrome to which retrograde amnesia is central can develop also in the context of multiple-infarct dementia.

In conclusion, it is hoped that the mechanisms and deficits of remote memory, long underemphasized in neuropsychology, cognitive psychology, and neurophysiology, will be accorded due attention both by clinicians and by basic cognitive and neuroscientists, and that as a result, new insights will be gained both into normal brain–behavioral relations and into diseases of the central nervous system, including the dementias.

II. Assessing Executive Deficits in Memory: A Possible Error of Commission

Performance on tasks involving recall can be conspicuously deficient following prefrontal damage in humans (Luria, 1976). Removal of the frontal lobes in animals leads to considerable deficit of delayed responses, whereas the ability for immediate responses remains intact (Jacobsen, 1935). This pattern led to early formulations implicating the frontal lobes as the "seat of memory."

Konorski (1973), Konorski and Lawicka (1964), Pribram (1961), Weiskrantz, Mihailovic, and Gross (1960), and others demonstrated, however, that experimental animals with frontal lobes removed also manifested behavioral disinhibition and were highly distractible by irrelevant ongoing stimuli. If the flow of ongoing irrelevant stimulations was reduced, or the excitability of the nervous system was diminished pharmacologically, then the performance on memory tasks improved dramatically. Luria (1976) and Tsvetkova (1966) have demonstrated that in patients with prefrontal lesions, the very structure of mnestic activity suffers, rather than the more elementary aspects of storage and retrieval per se. The mnestic processes lose their purpose-oriented, hierarchically organized nature. These findings led to the revision of the earlier assumption of the frontal lobes being the "seat of memory." Instead, it has been proposed that the learning deficit observed following prefrontal lesions is secondary to a more general impairment of executive control.

In this section, we describe various types of deficits in recall that were seen following damage to the prefrontal areas. It is not our purpose to ascertain the degree of impairment of storage and retrieval per se in prefrontal pathology. Instead, we attempt to demonstrate that regardless of the condition of these two memory processes, an entirely different type of deficit contributes to the grossly distorted performance of patients with frontal damage on tasks of recall. Both new learning and utilization of old, overlearned information may suffer as a result of the deficit. This deficit is executive in nature and can be described best as an inability to selectively subordinate the process of retrieval to the task at hand. This lack of selectivity of recall can take the form of a field-dependent associative behavior that is not subjected to "editing" either by the context of the task or by the nature of the specific material to be recalled; or it can take the form of perseveration, resulting in impaired transition from the previously appropriate engram or class of engrams to the currently appropriate one in the recall sequence. More often than not, both manifestations of deficient selectivity are present in the performance of the same patient.

We now present samples of recall by a patient with severe deficit of executive control with features of both field-dependent behavior and perseveration, and we discuss the implications for understanding possible sources of recall deficits. The following observations have been discussed in greater detail by Goldberg and Costa (1986) and by Goldberg and Tucker (1979).

A Case Study

A 24-year-old, right-handed male patient, a graduate student of engineering, sustained an open head trauma that resulted in fracture of the frontal bone. In subsequent surgery, the fractured bone was removed and the resection of both frontal poles took place. The patient was studied 2 weeks to 6 months after the accident by E. Goldberg at the Burdenko Institute of Neurosurgery in Moscow. The "field-dependent" quality of the patient's recall can be illustrated best by his immediate recall of orally presented stories. (The samples have been translated from Russian.) The story, "A Hen and Golden Eggs," was read to the patient as follows:

A man owned a hen that was laying golden eggs. The man was greedy and wanted to get more gold at once. He killed the hen and cut it open hoping to find a lot of gold inside, but there was none.

After hearing the story, the patient's recall was as follows:

A man was living with a hen . . . or rather the man was the hen's owner. She was producing gold . . . The man . . . the owner . . . wanted more gold at once . . . so he cut the hen into pieces but there was no gold . . . no gold at all . . . he cuts the hen more . . . no gold . . . the hen remains empty . . . so he searches again and again . . . no gold . . . he searches all around . . . in all places. The search is going on with a tape-recorder . . . they are looking here and there, nothing new around. They leave the tape-recorder turned on, something is twisting there . . . what the hell are they recording there . . . some digits . . . 0,2,3,0 . . . so, they are recording all these digits . . . not very many of them . . . that's why all the other digits were recorded . . . it turned out to be not very many of them either . . . so, everything was recorded . . . and I'll tell you what . . . there were only 5–6 digits there . . . (E.G.: Have you finished?) Not yet, I'll finish soon . . . so, there were only 5–6 digits there . . . When they took bus #5 and went down Lefortoff Drive . . . so, you get there and transfer to bus #5 . . . (E.G.: You better finish!) Not yet! Wait a moment! So you take bus #5 and get to the Bauman Square . . . from the Bauman Square you go further on . . . further on. Here you take off . . . and again you take bus #5 . . . I'll make it precise . . . so you take off . . . and take bus #5 . . . and you get to cafeteria . . . number 5 point 6 . . . (The monologue continued for another 40 minutes.)

Another story, "A Lion and a Mouse," was read to the patient as follows:

A lion was asleep and a mouse was running around making noises. The lion woke up, got very angry, caught the mouse and was about to eat him up, but then he decided to be kind and let the mouse go. A few days later, hunters caught the lion and tied him to a tree with ropes. The mouse learned about it, ran down, gnawed the ropes and set the lion free.

The patient's subsequent recall was as follows:

So the lion made friends with the mouse. The mouse was caught by the lion. He wanted to strangle him but then let him go. The mouse started dancing around him, singing songs and was released. After that the mouse was accepted in his house by . . . lions, various animals. After that he was released, so to say he hadn't been captured, it was like if he were captured but he was still free. But after that he was completely released and was walking free. So, he was released by the lion completely, after the lion listened to him, and he was released to all the four directions. He didn't run away and remained to live in his cave, then the lion caught him once again, in some time . . . I don't remember it quite exactly. So, he caught him, and released again. Now the mouse got out of there to his moor (a slang expression for a secure place), to his railroad station. The mouse goes further and further and tells about his railroad station . . . and there is another mouse and the third one at the station . . . so the mouse opens the door to this . . . What's his name? Hullo! Hullo! How are doing? Okay, more or less . . . all set. Glad to find you . . . I have an apartment . . . and a house . . . and a room. The bigger mouse asks the small one: How are you doing? How is it going? So it was all right, I had a lot of friends. They often meet . . . but the friendship broke apart, so you tell him that I'm sorry for those short rendezvous . . . Or you don't tell anything." (The story ends with the two friends drinking beer in a railway station bar.)

The patient's storage and retrieval of the first story were both, by and large, adequate; the initial segment of the patient's monologue contains most of its content virtually undistorted. The initial segment of the patient's second monologue was, at least in part, adequate as well. However, in each case, having conveyed the original story, or its fragment, the patient began to deviate from it until there was no resemblance between the original story and the content of the monologue. The patient rambled for 40 to 60 minutes for each monologue. An inability to terminate an activity once it has begun is commonly observed in various behaviors (writing, drawing, etc.) of patients with frontal damage. Often such "inertia of termination" co-occurs with "inertia of initiation." It was very difficult to coax the patient to start recall. When instructed to recall the story, he responded, "I have told it already," or "There was nothing in this story." However, once he started, he could not terminate the process. The frequent co-occurrence of both forms of inertia in the same behavioral sample may indicate that they are two manifestations of the same cognitive deficit.

The patient's verbal output obviously was not controlled by the text engram in his memory, because both the engram and its availability for retrieval were reasonably intact; yet the discrepancy between the patient's monologue and the original story is quite profound.

The question then arises regarding the mechanism underlying the patient's ability to manufacture a lengthy monologue in response to a short story. Perseverations constitute an obvious factor, and the patient's monologue was plagued with them. Perseverations, however, can at best account for the least productive aspects of the patient's monologue: repetition of a few verbal or thematic clichés. But the patient's monologues were not entirely repetitive. They obviously had some development: Long chains of events were invented by the patient in the most bizarre combinations. Thus, perseverations alone can hardly account for such creative components of the monologues.

The phenomenon of field-dependent behavior is commonly observed in frontal patients. As a rule, this term is used to describe the frontal patient's tendency to react to incidental stimuli that occur in their external sensory field instead of accomplishing the behavioral task. The structure of the monologues under discussion is somewhat reminiscent of this behavior, and we will use the term *verbal field-dependent behavior* to refer to the mechanism proposed to explain this structure. By verbal field-dependent behavior we mean any behavior in which the subject, instead of following the task of communication at hand (recalling a story, describing a picture, etc.) in a selective way, is distracted by stimuli that happen to appear in the physical environment, or by out-of-context associations prompted by the subject's internal network of semantic or episodic representation. These distractors become incorporated into the subject's monologue, distracting it from its original direction.

Analysis of prefrontal monologues reveals several types of such distractors:

1. *External stimuli* (objects in the sensory field, actions of surrounding persons, etc.). The inclusion of the tape recorder in the first of the two described monologues is an example. (One of the authors was taping the patient.) Another example of such external intrusion is the patient's recall of the story, "A Dove and the Pigeons." The story was read to the patient as follows:

A dove learned that pigeons were fed very well. So the dove dyed herself white and flew to the pigeons. The pigeons accepted her and the dove began to live among them. But one day the dove cried out the way doves do, and the pigeons realized that she was an imposter and chased her away. The dove tried to join other doves but was not accepted by them either, because she was white.

The patient then recalled: "Pigeons are well-fed, and the dove envied them. So she flew to the dove-cote. But the net was too thick so she couldn't even pull her head through it" (points to the net that guards his bed).

2. *The patient's own condition.* Thus, in recalling the story "A Dove and the Pigeons," the patient projected his own verbal exhaustion.:

A dove, or rather a pigeon, or rather a dove learned the dove language, flew to her pigeons and told her that she learned to speak the dove language. She went on talking, some time passed, and a pigeon asks the dove: "Where did you learn to speak this way, how could you make it? How long can you talk this way?" And the dove answers that she can talk a year, two, maybe three—and that's it . . . I'm telling you all precisely . . . they ask the dove, "How could you learn to talk this way?" . . . So, they ask the dove, "How long can you talk?" And the dove answers that she can talk a year, two, well, three at most and that's it. A year

passes, two, three, the dove gets exhausted, she doesn't know what else to say. A year passes, two, three . . . the dove's lexicon gets exhausted. (A long perseveration follows.)

3. *Out-of-context episodic associations.* The patient's introduction of "route 5" in the first monologue illustrates this type of intrusion. All of the subsequent details correctly described the bus route 5 in the city of the patient's residence.

4. *Lexical out-of-context associations.* The patient's recall of the story "A Dove and the Pigeons" illustrates lexical out-of-context associations:

So the dove flew back to the doves, but they did not accept her either. Then she flew to her . . . little fledglings . . . brought them food . . . looked at them . . . then looked into the mirror . . . at the girl Dove . . . and she started dancing around the mirror . . . because she was pretty . . . it was the girl's silk that was pretty . . . so she looked at her . . . wedding dress. (The monologue continues.)

The dove became "a girl Dove." The Russian word for dove is also a common female first name.

5. *Semantic out-of-context associations.* The patient's recall of the story "A Lion and a Mouse" illustrates semantic out-of-context associations:

A hunter caught the lion . . . and tied him to the tree . . . a mouse came and untied him . . . so, the lion is free . . . Now, the hunter caught the lion again . . . So, they are in trouble . . . they got together once . . . and another time . . . there is nothing good . . . they got together once again . . . everyone got together . . . and they discuss how to save the hostage lion . . . and the mouse tells them: "Don't you run away" . . . (A person with a white coat enters the room) . . . The doctor will come . . . and prescribe what to do.

Although the doctor included in the monologue was an external stimulus in the subject's visual field, the subsequent statement ("prescribe what to do") was apparently an introduction of a common cliché associated with a doctor.

Thus, at least five types of intrusions can influence the recall of patients with frontal damage. Only the first kind (1) is localized in the external physical field; the other four, in one way or another, belong to the patient's internal representations. These can be semantic (4,5), episodic (3), or dynamic (2). In this case, the patient's essentially executive deficit, verbal field-dependent behavior, interfered with his performance on a memory task involving new learning, thus simulating anterograde amnesia.

Perseveration

We will now illustrate how another executive deficit, perseveration, may interfere with utilization of overlearned generic knowledge, thus simulating retrograde amnesia. The disruptive effect of perseveration on the patient's utilization of old storage can best be illustrated by his performance on the task of drawing common geometric figures (e.g., circle, cross, triangle, square) following verbal instructions. It is safe to assume that engrams of such generic images had been established in the patient's long-term memory well before the accident at age 24. Indeed, when asked to name such figures, identify them in a multiple-choice display, or draw them following verbal instructions, the patient could accomplish the task with respect to all of the figures employed.

The patient's performance changed drastically, however, when he was asked to draw geometric figures following a rapid succession of verbal commands, that is, when the name of a new figure was presented verbally as soon as the patient completed the previous one. The patient's performance under these conditions revealed "perseverations of elements," illustrated on parts a and b of Figure 7-2. The patient could draw the initial figure accurately, but this figure, or a component of it, was merged with every subsequent figure in the sequence.

This phenomenon resembles the well-known phenomenon of "homogeneous interference" common in primary amnesias of various etiologies (Luria, 1976). Homogeneous interference, however, is typically observed in tasks of new learning that involve episodic information. It does not affect the domain of lexical knowledge of otherwise generic representations. Here, on the other hand, we observe perseverations of elements in the context of utilization of overlearned, categorical storage that clearly deals with generic representations bordering on lexical knowledge and embraces the kind of information to which access is usually intact in typical primary amnesias.

A related phenomenon, which has been termed "perseveration of activities" (Goldberg & Tucker, 1979), is illustrated in parts c and d of Figure 7-2. The patient was instructed to draw a circle, a square, and a triangle and then to write a sentence (which did not include names of geometric figures). Both tasks were performed flawlessly. However, when the patient was subsequently instructed to draw the same geometric figures, the correct forms were accompanied by the terminal letters of the Russian names of the corresponding shapes:

КРУГ, КВАДРАТ and ТРЕУГОАЬНИК

respectively (part c of Figure 7-2).

Perseverations between different categories of stimuli can be identified in part d of Figure 7-2. The patient first drew geometric figures and then performed simple arithmetical computations. Both tasks were performed flawlessly. However, when subsequently instructed to draw the same geometric figures as before, the patient replaced them with mathematical symbols. As in the previously described situation, the distortions were not random. A multiplication sign "x" appeared instead of a "cross," with the perceptual similarity being apparent. The two subsequent replacements can naturally be interpreted semantically: Choices of specific items made by the patient in a wrong category were facili-

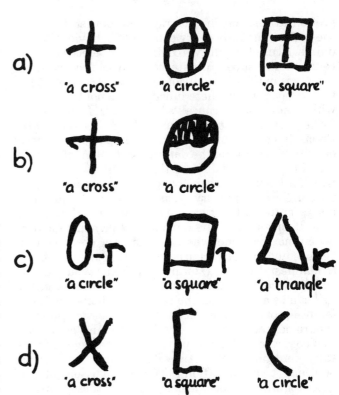

Figure 7-2. Examples of perseveration on tasks of drawing graphical sequences. a,b—perseveration of elements; c,d—perseveration of activities. Reprinted from Goldberg and Tucker (1979) by permission.

tated by the similarity of verbal labels. The Russian term for the bracket drawn is *square bracket,* and the term for the parenthesis is *circle bracket.*

Unlike the previously described type of perseveration, this one can hardly be explained in terms of interference between graphical elements of specific figures. Rather, these manifestations seem to reflect confusion between whole semantic categories (part d of Figure 7-2) or types of activities (part c of Figure 7-2). Such interference at superordinate levels between overlearned domains of engrams or types of processes is totally atypical for classic amnesias.

The perseverations described have all the hallmarks of an executive rather than a primarily amnestic deficit. They can be potentially interpreted as manifestations of amnesia, because these phenomena bear some resemblance to the phenomenon of interference that plagues the retrieval processes in classic amnesias. Yet, they are set apart from the latter by the type of information that they may affect, which includes semantic, generic, overlearned information bordering on lexical knowledge, thus leading to a considerably greater depth of deficit than in classic amnesias.

Discussion

Unlike retrograde amnesia, described in the first part of this chapter, the executive deficits described in this part are in no danger of being overlooked in the clinical assessment of a patient. These deficits, which are commonly but not exclusively seen following damage to prefrontal cortices, are flagrant and devastating, and they affect virtually every domain of behavior that requires focused cognitive control and selectivity. Because of the superordinate position of the executive functions in the hierarchy of cognitive processes, it has been proposed that these functions are not comparable with traditionally conceived cognitive faculties but rather cut across them (Luria, 1976; Teuber, 1964). Precisely because of the pervasive impact of executive deficits on cognition, the danger exists of misinterpreting them as the deficit of that cognitive dimension, which a particular cognitive task at hand purports to measure, be it memory, visuospatial processing, language, or motor functions. In the context of this discussion, it means that the diagnosis of primary memory deficit may be made, whereas in fact the observed poor performance on a task purported to measure memory is a manifestation of a totally different syndrome, to which executive rather than memory deficit is central.

It can be argued that the retrieval deficits and interference-proneness characteristic of classic amnestic syndromes, and the lack of selectivity and perseveration observed in the executive syndrome, belong to the same continuum of "retrieval failures" (L.D. Costa, personal communication). The comparison of the neurocognitive mechanisms behind these various kinds of deficit is beyond the scope of this chapter. On a syndromal level of analysis, however, the two types of deficits are distinctly different. The executive deficits of recall usually appear together with a cluster of impairments that can be observed outside the domain of memory. These include motor perseverations, echopraxia, echolalia, field-dependent behavior, and motor and ideational inertia, which can take two forms (usually co-occurring): inertia of initiation and inertia of termination of activity. Judgment, intra- and interpersonal insight, conceptual thought, and problem-solving abilities are usually grossly impaired. Emotional control is deficient: Either flat affect, indifference, and aspontaneity are observed; or behavioral disinhibition and oscillation of affect within an inordinately broad range, from euphoria to sham rage are seen (Damasio, 1979; Luria, 1980; Teuber, 1964). These behavioral symptoms constitute, in combination, a severe executive syndrome.

Poor performance on memory tasks can be a part of the executive syndrome, although it is hardly a central part, and is usually considered as a secondary or derivative rather than a primary component (Luria, 1980). Patients afflicted with the executive syndrome are at least as impaired on tasks that do not involve recall or recognition as they are on those that do. This constitutes a major difference between the executive syndrome and primary amnesias: In the latter, by definition, deficits of recall and recognition are the central manifestations, although usually not the only ones. It is important to correctly identify an executive deficit and to be aware of its potential to masquerade as a primary amnesia.

Numerous investigators (Damasio, 1979; Luria, 1980; Teuber, 1964) have pointed out a paradox associated with the executive syndrome: It has a devastating impact on real-life functioning, yet it is difficult to diagnose with standard psychometric techniques. Although some neuropsychological tests (e.g., Wisconsin Card Sorting, Trail Making, Word Fluency) are considered quite sensitive to this deficit (Lezak, 1983), they are not necessarily specific and thus leave ample room for diagnostic confusion. Clinical practitioners are probably best advised to familiarize themselves with excellent clinical descriptions of this syndrome (Blumer & Benson, 1975; Damasio, 1979; Luria, 1980; Teuber, 1964), and to develop sensitivity to the qualitative cognitive, personality, and affective features that characterize it. Algorithmic, quantitative diagnostic procedures are certainly desirable, but there are situations when they cannot yet replace expert judgment.

Two main variants of the executive syndrome have been described. They are characterized by two different but overlapping constellations of symptoms: one by predominant inactivity and affective flatness, the other by predominant behavioral and affective disinhibition. These two behavioral patterns have been classically associated with, respectively, dorsolateral prefrontal or orbitofrontal damage. Mixed cases also exist (Blumer & Benson, 1975; Hecaen & Albert, 1978; Luria, 1980). Milder cases are frequently observed that do not necessarily include all of the symptoms at a significant level of severity.

It is important to distinguish between the cognitive–behavioral and the neuroanatomical characteristics of the executive syndrome. Although historically it has been postulated that only focal lesions in the prefrontal cortex can produce the cognitive–behavioral entity described, recent findings obtained both on animal models and on neurological and psychiatric populations have indicated that other conditions are also capable of producing the syndrome. These include lesions in the ventral mesencephalon (Goldberg, Mattis, et al., 1982; Oades, 1982), a subpopulation of chronic schizophrenia (Flor-Henry, 1976; Kolb & Whishaw, 1983), and biochemical disorders affecting the mesolimbic-mesocortical dopamine systems (Brozoski, Brown, Rosvold, & Goldman, 1979; Simon, Scatten, & LeMoal, 1980).

It has been proposed that dementias of old age, including Alzheimer's disease, are characterized by heterogeneity and multiplicity of cognitive profiles and courses (Cohen, Eisdorfer, & Walford, 1981). It is quite possible that executive deficits are central to some of the dementias. Increased numbers of tangles and plaques have been found in the dorsolateral prefrontal cortex of patients with AD, but it was not among the most severely affected regions (Brun & Gustafson, 1976). However, to the best of our knowledge, no pathological studies of the orbitofrontal cortex (another site critical for the integrity of executive control) have been conducted with AD patients. Future studies of correlations between various executive cognitive and affective deficits and the number of tangles and plaques in well-defined areas of anterior cortex, both dorsolateral prefrontal and orbitofrontal, may shed further light on cognitive–pathological subtyping of dementias of old age.

The very construct of memory probably has to be revised in view of recent findings and postulations to the effect that deficient performance that has been traditionally ascribed to poor retrieval or storage capacity may in fact be attributable to other impairments. Buschke (in press) proposed that deficient encoding capacity or deficient utilization of encoding strategies may be a major contributing factor—and so, evidently, may deficient executive control be a factor.

References

Albert, M. S., Butters, N., & Levin, J. (1979). Temporal gradients in the retrograde amnesia of patients with alcoholic Korsakoff's disease. *Archives of Neurology, 36,* 211–216.

Barbizet, J. (1970). *Human memory and its pathology.* San Francisco: Freeman.

Benson, D. F., & Geschwind, N. (1967). Shrinking retrograde amnesia. *Journal of Neurology, Neurosurgery and Psychiatry, 30,* 539–544.

Blumer, D., & Benson, D. F. (1975). Personality changes with frontal and temporal lobe lesions. In D. F. Benson & D. Blumer (Eds.), *Psychiatric aspects of neurologic disease* (pp. 121–136). New York: Grune & Stratton.

Brozoski, T. J., Brown, R. M., Rosvold, H. E., & Goldman, P. S. (1979). Cognitive deficit caused by regional depletion of dopamine in prefrontal cortex of rhesus monkey. *Science, 205,* 929–932.

Brun, A., & Gustafson, L. (1976). Distribution of cerebral degeneration in Alzheimer's disease: A clinico-pathological study. *Archiv für Psychiatrie und Nervenkrankheiten, 223,* 15–33.

Buschke, H. (1973). Selective reminding for analyses of memory and learning. *Journal of Verbal Learning and Verbal Behavior, 12*(5), 543–549.

Buschke, H. (in press). Control of cognitive processing. In N. Butters & L. Squire (Eds.), *The neuropsychology of memory.* New York: Guilford Press.

Butters, N. (1979). Amnesic disorders. In K. M. Heilman & E. Valenstein (Eds.), *Clinical neuropsychology* (pp. 439–474). New York: Oxford University Press.

Butters, N. (1983). *Retrograde amnesia in amnestic and dementing syndromes.* Paper presented at the Fourth Annual Meeting of the New York Neuropsychology Society, New York.

Butters, N. (in press). Alcoholic Korsakoff's syndrome: An update. *Seminars in Neurology.*

Cohen, D., Eisdorfer, C., & Walford, R. L. (1981). Histocompatibility antigens (HLA) and patterns of cognitive loss in dementia of the Alzheimer type. *Neurobiology of Aging, 2,* 277–280.

Damasio, A. (1979). The frontal lobes. In K. M. Heilman & E. Valenstein (Eds.), *Clinical neuropsychology.* New York: Oxford University Press.

de Leon, M., Ferris, S., George, A. E., Reisberg, B., Kricheff, I. I., & Gershon, S. (1980). Computed tomography evaluations of brain–behavior relationships in senile dementia of the Alzheimer's type. *Neurobiology of Aging, 1,* 69–79.

Erickson, R. C. (1978). Problems in the clinical assessment of memory. *Experimental Aging Research, 4,* 255–272.

Flor-Henry, P. (1976). Lateral temporal-lymbic dysfunction and psychopathology. *Annals of the New York Academy of Science, 280,* 777–795.

Fogelholm, R., Kivalo, E., & Bergstrom, L. (1975). The transient global amnesia syndrome: An analysis of 35 cases. *European Neurology, 13,* 72–84.

Goldberg, E. (1984). Papez circuit revisited: Two systems instead of one? In N. Butters & L. Squire (Eds.), *The neuropsychology of memory* (pp. 183–193). New York: Guilford Press.

Goldberg, E., Antin, S. P., Bilder, R. M., Gerstman, L. J., Hughes, J. E. O., & Mattis, S. (1981). Retrograde amnesia: Possible role of mesencephalic reticular activation in long-term memory. *Science, 213,* 1392–1394.

Goldberg, E., Bilder, R., & Gerstman, L. (1980). *General Knowledge Battery.* Unpublished test.

Goldberg, E., & Costa, L. D. (1986). Qualitative indices in neuropsychological assessment: An extension of Luria's approach to executive deficit following prefrontal lesions. In I. Grant & K. M. Adams (Eds.), *Neuropsychological assessment of neuropsychiatric disorders.* New York: Oxford University Press.

Goldberg, E., Hughes, J. E. O., Mattis, S., & Antin, S. P. (1982). Isolated retrograde amnesia: Different etiologies, same mechanisms? *Cortex, 18,* 459–462.

Goldberg, E., Mattis, S., Hughes, J. E. O., & Antin, S. (1982). *Frontal syndrome without a frontal lesion: A case study.* Paper presented at the Fifth European Meeting of the International Neuropsychological Society, Deauville, France.

Goldberg, E., & Tucker, D. (1979). Motor perseverations and long-term memory for visual forms. *Journal of Clinical Neuropsychology, 1,* 273–288.

Hecaen, H., & Albert, M. L. (Eds.). (1978). *Human neuropsychology.* New York: Wiley.

Jacobsen, C. F. (1935). Function of frontal association areas in primates. *Archives of Neurology and Psychiatry, 35*(3), 558–569.

Kolb, B., & Whishaw, I. (1983). Performance of schizophrenic patients on tests sensitive to left or right frontal, temporal or parietal functions in neurological patients. *Journal of Nervous and Mental Disease, 171,* 435–443.

Konorski, J. (1973). The role of prefrontal control in the programming of motor behavior. In J. D. Maser (Ed.), *Efferent organization and the integration of behavior* (pp. 175–201). New York: Academic Press.

Konorski, J., & Lawicka, W. (1964). Analysis of errors by prefrontal animals in the delayed response test. In J. M. Warren & K. Akert (Eds.), *The frontal granular cortex and behavior.* New York: McGraw-Hill.

Lezak, M. (1983). *Neuropsychological assessment* (2nd ed.). New York: Oxford University Press.

Luria, A. R. (1976). *The neuropsychology of memory.* Washington, DC: Winston Press.

Luria, A. R. (1980). *Higher cortical functions in man* (2nd ed.). New York: Basic Books.

Marslen-Wilson, W. D., & Teuber, H.-L. (1975). Memory for remote events in anterograde amnesia: Recognition of public figures from newsphotographs. *Neuropsychologia, 13,* 347–352.

Mathew, N. T., & Meyer, J. S. (1974). Pathogenesis and natural history of transient global amnesia. *Stroke, 4,* 303–311.

Milner, B. (1966). Amnesia following operation on the temporal lobes. In C. W. M. Whitty & O. L. Zangwill (Eds.), *Amnesia* (pp. 137–160). London: Butterworths.

Mishkin, M. (1982). A memory system in the monkey. *Philosophical Transactions of the Royal Society of London, B298,* 85–95.

Mishkin, M., Spiegler, B. J., Saunders, R. C., & Malamut, B. L. (1982). An animal model of global amnesia. In S. Corkin, K. L. Davis, J. H. Growdon, E. Usdin, & R. J. Wurtman (Eds.), *Alzheimer's disease: A report of progress in research.* New York: Raven Press.

Oades, R. D. (1981). Types of memory or attention? Impairments after lesions of the hippocampus and limbic ventral tegmentum. *Brain Research Bulletin, 8,* 221–226.

Oades, R. D. (1982). Search strategies on a holeboard are impaired in rats with ventral tegmental damage: Animal model for test of thought disorder. *Biological Psychiatry, 2,* 243–258.

Poon, L. W. (1980). A systems approach for the assessment and treatment of memory problems. In J. Ferguson & C. B. Taylor (Eds.), *Comprehensive handbook of behavioral medicine* (Vol. I, pp. 191–212). New York: Spectrum Publications.

Poon, L. W. (1985). Differences in human memory with aging: Nature, causes, and clinical implications. In J. E. Birren & K. W. Schaie (Eds.), *Handbook of the psychology of aging* (pp. 427–462). New York: Van Nostrand Reinhold.

Poser, C. M., & Ziegler, D. K. (1960). Temporary amnesia as a manifestation of cerebrovascular insufficiency. *Transactions of the American Neurological Association, 85,* 221–223.

Pribram, K. H. (1961). A further analysis of the behavior deficit that follows injury to the primate frontal cortex. *Experimental Neurology, 3,* 432–466.

Roman-Campos, G., Poser, C. M., & Wood, F. (1980). Persistent retrograde amnesia deficit after transient global amnesia. *Cortex, 16,* 509–518.

Sanders, H. I., & Warrington, E. K. (1971). Memory for remote events in amnestic patients. *Brain, 94,* 661–668.

Seltzer, B., & Benson, D. F. (1974). The temporal pattern of retrograde amnesia in Korsakoff's disease. *Neurology, 24,* 527–530.

Simon, H., Scatten, B., & LeMoal, M. (1980). Dopaminergic A10 neurones are involved in cognitive functions. *Nature, 286,* 150–151.

Squire, L. R., & Slater, P. C. (1975). Forgetting in very long-term memory as assessed by an improved questionnaire technique. *Journal of Experimental Psychology: Human Learning and Memory, 104,* 50–54.

Squire, L. R., & Slater, P. C. (1978) Anterograde and retrograde memory impairment in chronic amnesia. *Neuropsychologia, 16,* 313–322.

Squire, L. R., Slater, P. C., & Chace, P. M. (1975). Retrograde amnesia: Temporal gradient in very long-term memory following electroconvulsive therapy. *Science, 187,* 77–79.

Teuber, H.-L. (1964). The riddle of the frontal lobe function in man. In J. M. Warren & K. Akert (Eds.), *The frontal granular cortex and behavior.* New York: McGraw-Hill.

Teuber, H.-L., Milner, B., & Vaughan, H. G. (1968). Persistent anterograde amnesia after stab wound of the basal brain. *Neuropsychologia, 6,* 267–282.

Tsvetkova, L. D. (1966). Disturbance of text analysis in patients with frontal lobe lesions. In A. R. Luria & E. D. Homskaya (Eds.), *The frontal lobes and regulation of psychological processes.* Moscow: Moscow University Press.

Wechsler, D. (1945). A standardized memory scale for clinical use. *Journal of Psychology, 19,* 87–95.

Weiskrantz, L., Mihailovic, L., & Gross, C. (1960). Stimulation of frontal cortex and delayed alternation performance in the monkey. *Science, 131,* 1443–1444.

Richard C. Erickson and Diane Howieson

CHAPTER

8

The Clinician's Perspective: Measuring Change and Treatment Effectiveness

Clinicians serve particular social functions that bear on their decision making. The selection and use of formal tests of learning and memory takes place in this context. In addition, a number of complex problems must be considered when the clinician-researcher attempts to measure treatment effectiveness, not all of which have been resolved in the literature.

Establishing a procedure for measuring change in memory functioning resulting from treatment efforts is a difficult task, particularly for the clinician who must operate with constraints imposed by clinical demands and limited resources. In addition, the number of published reports that explicitly relate to this topic is extremely limited. Consequently we intend to make a preliminary exploration of relevant issues in this chapter (cf. Erickson, 1978) but will not attempt to identify a specific strategy for measuring change and treatment effectiveness (cf. Erickson, Poon, & Walsh-Sweeney, 1980). There are three reasons for this. First, the issue of treatment effectiveness only adds to a discussion of memory assessment that is already overburdened with unresolved issues. Second, important issues related to the documentation of change and treatment effectiveness in the broader arenas of psychotherapy and behavioral interventions are themselves unresolved (Harvey & Parks, 1982). Third, the demonstration of the clinical effectiveness of treatment procedures involves more than the successful completion of a rigorously designed outcome study.

In the first section of this chapter, we briefly discuss the social function of the clinician and how it bears on clinical decision making. Then we review some problems of selecting formal tests of learning and memory and discuss factors that clinicians must consider in assessing treatment outcome. We conclude with a plea for greater efforts to organize and synthesize the literature.

The Social Role of Clinicians

Clinicians enjoy prestige and serve important social functions in the world today. Social expectations help shape how clinicians understand and do their work. To the extent that clinicians are oblivious to the impact of these expectations, they will be blind to the limitations of their theories and procedures (cf. Parsons, 1964, chapter 10; Sarason, 1981).

Features of Clinicians' Assigned Role

Faced with a patient who has a complaint (in this case, a memory complaint), the clinician's assigned task is threefold: to diagnose the problem, to render a prognosis, and to prescribe treatment. In diagnosing the problem, the clinician assigns a technical label that "explains" the patient's behavior. In developing a prognosis, the clinician indicates what the patient might expect in the future. In prescribing treatment, the clinician proposes a course of action that should correct the disorder or at least prevent the patient and others involved with the patient from engaging in actions that will make matters worse.

In the course of rendering their expert opinions, clinicians help reduce the ambiguity and anxiety associated with unidentified disturbing phenomena and further one course of action over another. Indirectly, they serve as judges, assigning "blame" for disorders to patients, the mistaken actions of others, pathological biological processes, or some combination of the three. On

We would like to thank Muriel D. Lezak for her thoughtful recommendations for revising portions of this chapter.

the basis of clinicians' pronouncements, patients may be relieved of certain social responsibilities, exonerated or censured, or restored to full social and vocational functioning.

Four features of the clinicians' assigned role bear highlighting. First, clinicians are charged with the task of rendering decisions that have immediate and long-term consequences for specific patients and for other persons close to them. Second, clinicians function as experts whose pronouncements carry more weight than statements made by persons not regarded as expert, whether their recommendations are accepted and acted on or not. Third, clinicians must make their decisions in the face of severe time and money constraints. Complaints about skyrocketing medical costs notwithstanding, the resources for answering important questions are limited. Fourth, clinicians are held accountable for their decisions in immediate and concrete ways. Errors in clinical judgment can result in personal embarrassment, professional censure, or unfavorable malpractice judgments.

Given these considerations and given the fact that the scientific bases for much of what clinicians are called on to do are limited, clinicians must bridge the gap between the known and the unknown with a mix of common sense, theoretical deductions, plausible analogies, and clinical experience, while remaining aware that they may need to defend their decisions at any time. When they must defend themselves, they face "juries" composed not of the scientific community in any immediate sense but of professional peers, patients and their families, the community, and "lawyers and accountants."

Clinical Decision Making

Clinicians are using clinical judgment when they say that a patient's memory is impaired or has improved. The judgment rests on a process of clinical reasoning, an elaborate but not necessarily esoteric process of hypothesis generation, evidence gathering, and decision making. There are several more or less adequate paradigms that describe how clinicians proceed: problem solving (or information processing), judgment, and decision making (Elstein & Bordage, 1979)—and a literature suggesting that clinical judgments are not value free (Abramowitz & Dokecki, 1977). We will not detain ourselves, however, except to make note of the fact that the clinician's way of proceeding is complex, not well articulated, geared to the demands of the specific clinical situation as it unfolds, and subject to certain systematic biases—most notable, a premature restriction of the range of alternatives (Elstein & Bordage, 1979; Hunt & MacLeod, 1979).

Clinicians use judgment to select and weigh the evidence, and will use formal test procedures to the extent that they are reliable and valid and appear plausible and cost-effective. For example, a clinician may not undertake formal testing if the problem is obvious enough, if the prescribed treatment provides results that are satisfactory to all parties, or if the clinician perceives that he or she is not likely to be called on to defend his or her decision. Thus, clinical judgment is not based on test scores alone; it is also based on other data such as chart notes, history, behavioral observations, and reports from significant others.

Selecting the Right Tests

Selecting tests to be used with the aged to assess the change in memory functioning that results from treatment is difficult (Erickson et al., 1980). There is no generally accepted procedure for assessing memory disorders. This disagreement exists in part because there is no comprehensive, well-accepted model of how memory works (see, e.g., Baddeley, 1976) and because no single test detects impairment resulting from memory disorders of all etiologies. Successful memory performance is dependent on many cognitive operations, and a breakdown in any of these may result in impaired performance. An understanding of the differences and similarities in the memory disorders associated with various neurological diseases is a necessary starting point for developing assessment procedures.

Another problem is that, in practice, there are no appropriately comprehensive and standardized clinical tests; some memory tests have certain advantages while others have different advantages. For example, the memory test most commonly used in the United States, the Wechsler Memory Scale (Wechsler, 1945), has the advantage of volumes of normative data from years of use, yet the battery does not meet contemporary standards for providing complete measures of memory functioning, which will be discussed more fully later.

Memory tasks developed for research purposes have helped indicate how memory functioning may break down (see chapter 6); however, most of these tasks are unknown to clinicians, research test materials are not generally available, and normative data are too limited to be clinically useful. For example, memory research in the 1970s focused on the encoding capacities of persons with memory difficulties. Yet most widely used clinical procedures provide no data about the encoding capacities of the person being examined. More recently, research efforts have shifted to study of episodic as well as semantic memory, but clinicians have too few guidelines for assessing episodic memory.

In general, clinicians are interested in memory tests that identify memory deficits, provide information useful for counseling or rehabilitation, and are sensitive to changes in functioning (see chapter 9). Tests should document both strengths and weaknesses in memory functioning so that clinicians can suggest compensatory strategies for memory-impaired persons. Clinical memory tests also should be minimally stressful, nonredundant, and cost-effective. A number of more specific criteria are discussed here.

Test Requirements: Clinical and Theoretical Usefulness

There are at least eight considerations for determining whether a memory test is clinically and theoretically useful.

1. The most important requirement is that a test assess both immediate and delayed recall of newly learned material. Clinicians often make this assessment by asking patients to repeat three words and recall them after 5 minutes. This brief screening task is too simple to detect memory problems in some cases, however, and it employs a very short delay. An ideal procedure would use material that requires at least three repetitions to acquire and would assess retention of that material for several hours. Some memory disorders produce impaired acquisition, whereas others do not. Delayed recall of newly acquired information is impaired in persons with almost all memory disorders; and, generally speaking, the longer the delay, the more impaired the performance. Unfortunately, most clinical tests do not assess delayed recall after an interval of more than an hour, possibly because of the difficulty in scheduling a patient's return for testing after an extended delay. Memory problems for some patients will be missed without this extended assessment. The newly developed New York University (NYU) Memory Test (Randt, Brown, & Osborne, 1980), however, uses delays of up to 24 hours.

2. Using a range of stimulus materials is important because patients with unilateral lesions may have material-specific memory disorders that depend on the side of the brain that has been injured. Material-specific memory disorders in patients with surgical trauma of the temporal lobes have been described (e.g., Milner, 1968): Left-hemisphere lesions produce verbal memory deficits, and right-hemisphere lesions produce nonverbal memory deficits. This pattern also has been reported following unilateral electroconvulsive treatment (Berent, Cohen, & Silverman, 1975; Halliday, Davison, Browne, & Kreeger, 1968). Most studies of stroke patients have not compared recall for verbal and nonverbal material, but one study of short-term memory (Kim, Royer, Bonstelle, & Boller, 1980) found that left-hemisphere stroke patients performed worse on verbal memory span tasks, whereas right-hemisphere stroke patients performed worse on nonverbal memory span tasks.

Alternatively, it has been suggested that unilateral brain damage produces modality-specific memory disorders. For example, Butters, Barton, and Brody (1970) found that patients with right-parietal lesions had deficient retention of both verbal and nonverbal material presented visually while they retained auditory material relatively well. Conversely, patients with either right or left temporal lobe excisions showed deficits in auditory short-term memory for verbal material, while performance was intact on visual, verbal, and nonverbal short-term memory tasks (Samuels, Butters, & Fedio, 1972). Unfortunately, few studies have adequately examined the issue of material versus modality specificity.

Most patients with bilateral or diffuse brain dysfunction have general memory deficits that are not specific to the nature of the stimulus material. In these cases, it is necessary to use only a limited variety of stimulus materials during memory testing.

3. To delineate the nature of a memory defect in terms of underlying cognitive operations, clinicians could examine encoding, storage, imagery, retrieval, rehearsal, organization strategies, and other cognitive operations that alter the memory process and influence recall (see chapter 6). Time constraints and other practical considerations, such as fatigue, will prevent examination of all of these functions in all patients, but a clinician who knows the nature of a memory disorder can make an informative selected examination.

For example, Craik and his colleagues (Craik, 1977) have demonstrated that poor memory performance of older persons on verbal tasks is associated with failure to organize and encode the semantic properties of the stimulus material and failure to use mediators. Also, older persons use inferior rehearsal strategies (Sanders, Murphy, Schmitt, & Walsh, 1980). Older persons perform better on recognition than on free-recall tasks (Craik, 1977; Perlmutter, 1979; Schonfield & Robertson, 1966; Smith, 1975), suggesting that deficient retrieval ability is at least a component of the memory impairment. Demented patients have memory deficits far beyond age-related declines; their recognition performance, although better than their free recall, is worse than expected for their age. Consequently, measures of recognition are useful for identifying memory disorders associated with dementia (Branconnier, Cole, Spera, & DeVitt, 1982). Since recognition performance of demented patients improves under conditions of partial cuing (Miller, 1975; Morris, Wheatley, & Britton, 1983), retrieval deficits appear to contribute to their recognition as well as free-recall difficulties.

During the past decade, efforts have been made to identify characteristic features of other types of memory disorders. Butters and Cermak (1980), for example, have extensively studied the memory disorder associated with Korsakoff's syndrome. The memory defects include impaired encoding and, perhaps secondarily, retrieval. Patients with Korsakoff's syndrome use inferior rehearsal strategies (Sanders et al., 1980); many more strategy variables have yet to be examined. Also, these patients have a striking lack of insight regarding their memory disorder. In contrast, patients with herpes encephalitis (Mattis, Kovner, & Goldmeier, 1978) and Huntington's disease (Butters & Cermak, 1980) appear to have a memory storage deficit and generally are aware of their memory difficulties.

By examining the various steps in the memory process, clinicians can better characterize deficits and suggest ways that patients can improve functioning by employing appropriate compensation strategies.

4. Memory tests that provide qualitative as well as quantitative information are desirable because qualitative features may characterize certain disorders. For

example, in a recent study, Fuld, Katzman, Davies, and Terry (1982) proposed that the occurrence of intrusion errors in a word list task is a distinguishing feature of the performance of Alzheimer's patients. Further data from larger samples are necessary to establish the diagnostic value of this measure (Branconnier, 1982). Many memory tests score only the number of correct items recalled and disregard erroneous recall. Assessment of qualitative features of data also may provide information about a patient's biases and strategies for performing a task.

5. The assessment procedure should include memory tests that have demands similar to those for everyday behavior. A prose recall task is similar to the daily task of trying to recall conversation. On the other hand, some memory tests, such as learning a list of consonant trigrams, bear little similarity to everyday behaviors. The recall of meaningless material would not be expected to relate to everyday behaviors as much as the recall of familiar material.

6. An assessment should include measures of an individual's memory performance during daily functioning as well as the person's performance on standardized memory tests. Both self-evaluation of memory functioning and evaluation from another reliable observer who has frequent contact with the individual are valuable components of an assessment procedure. The metamemory questionnaire developed by Zelinski, Gilewski, and Thompson (1980) was developed to compare patients' self-assessments of memory functioning with their performance on standardized memory tests (see Gilewski, chapter 11). This questionnaire could be completed by an observer who is familiar with the patient.

7. An examination of remote memory is not necessary in all cases. Remote memories usually are relatively well retained in a wide variety of brain diseases that produce memory impairments, such as early Alzheimer's disease, stroke, and hypoxia. Some brain diseases, such as closed-head injury and Korsakoff's syndrome, produce limited retrograde amnesia from the onset of the illness or injury. Huntington's disease produces a remote memory impairment that extends over many decades with approximately equivalent losses for each decade interval (Albert, Butters, & Brandt, 1981).

8. Usually it is not necessary to examine short-term memory unless the clinician is looking for an attentional disorder or dementia. Good short-term memory under conditions of continuous attention is characteristic of persons with a variety of memory deficits. For example, patients with the classic amnestic disorder, Korsakoff's syndrome, have forward digit spans well within the normal range (Talland, 1965). However, if their attention during memory tasks is distracted for 15 or more seconds or if they are required to retain information for more than 30 or 40 seconds without distraction, their performance level drops substantially (Butters & Cermak, 1980). In rare cases (e.g., Warrington & Shallice, 1969), patients may have selective impairment of verbal short-term memory.

Test Requirements: Standardization and Availability of Normative Data

Three criteria for selecting tests concern standardization and the availability of normative data.

1. Clinicians should use tests with established reliability and validity and with appropriate norms (see chapter 4). Adults' performance on many memory tests declines with age, so age-graded norms are necessary. Also, memory performance on many tests correlates with intellectual ability, and sex is a significant variable on some memory tests. Some memory tests have norms for particular patient populations, such as patients with Alzheimer's disease.

2. Because the usefulness of any diagnostic screening test depends on its discriminative validity (Branconnier et al., 1982), clinicians need tests that have well-established false-positive and false-negative rates. Such information enables clinicians to judge whether failure on a test indicates a pathological state or whether adequate performance indicates intact memory (Erickson, 1978).

3. Clinicians should select tests that have procedures adjusted for the aged (or appropriate for the diagnostic group in question). Many memory tests present material at the same rate for all subjects despite many studies showing that older persons are slower to process information. The NYU Memory Test was designed with the elderly in mind. It measures orientation and memory for old learned information, words, digits, paired associates, a short story, pictures of familiar objects, and incidental memory for the titles of the subtests. The relatively small amount of information to be learned (e.g., only 6 paired associates and recognition of 7 pictures) is appropriately adjusted for the memory-impaired older adult. The procedures of the Fuld Object-Memory Evaluation's Bag Test (Fuld, 1980) has been dramatically adjusted to assure processing by the elderly. In this test, the person pulls common objects from a bag one at a time and names them; this procedure is used to guarantee that the person has attended to and recognizes each item. Then the person is asked to recall as many objects as possible.

Test Requirements: Treatment Evaluation

Two additional selection requirements seem important for studying the course of memory disorders and treatment effectiveness.

1. Because memory performance of older people may vary greatly from one person to another, clinicians should use within-subjects paradigms. They therefore should select tests that have multiple forms for test-retest purposes. In fact, clinicians often must assess treatment at least three times for each person. Unfortunately, few memory tests provide multiple forms: Benton's (1974) Revised Visual Retention Test and Rey's Auditory Verbal Learning Test (translated in Lezak, 1983) have three forms, and the NYU Memory

Test has five forms. The Wechsler Memory Scale has two forms, but they do not appear to be of equal difficulty (Bloom, 1959) and would not be interchangeable (Lezak, 1983).

2. Obviously, testing instruments should be sensitive to changes in memory functioning, faithfully reflecting improvement (whether spontaneous or due to medical or behavioral treatments), decline, or fluctuations in the clinical course of various illnesses. Clinicians need to be alert to potential floor and ceiling effects.

Problems Involved in Selecting Memory Tests

There are so many criteria to consider when selecting tests of memory functioning that clinicians can easily provide incomplete or faulty evaluations. One common pitfall is to select and generalize from too narrow a range of tests. For example, short-term recall and delayed recall are not equally sensitive measures of memory disturbance, and the kinds of materials used may determine the degree of impairment measured.

Although clinicians want to avoid too narrow a range of memory tests, examinations should be as brief as possible. It is impossible to assess any one person's memory performance using the full spectrum of known variables. A clinician can select the subset of possible tests most sensitive to the particular disorder under investigation. For example, a clinician who is studying a memory disorder associated with Alzheimer's disease might concentrate on tests that measure immediate and delayed (from a few minutes to several hours) recognition and free recall. It would be useful to examine encoding and rehearsal strategies and to note the types of errors obtained. In contrast, the clinician would not need to vary the modality or type of material presented or to provide more than a cursory examination of remote memory.

A related problem is the choice between a fixed battery of memory tests and a composite of various independent tests (see Erickson & Scott, 1977, Erickson et al., 1980, and Lezak, 1983, for reviews of currently available memory batteries). Memory batteries have the advantage that data for all of the subtests have been obtained from the same normative sample. When independent tests with different normative samples are compared, it is impossible to know whether fluctuations in performance from test to test reflect differences in the individual's performance level or the use of different normative samples.

However, fixed batteries have numerous disadvantages. A preset battery of tests is not constructed to answer questions of particular importance in a given case. There are no provisions for extending assessment in some areas or shortening assessment in others, so examiners may obtain too limited data and waste time. Similarly, fixed batteries often have procedural constraints: Instructions, pacing, and other procedural factors usually cannot be varied to meet individual needs.

In attempts to meet criticisms and improve testing procedures, some clinical researchers have introduced procedural revisions or provided needed norms for the popular Wechsler Memory Scale (Hulicka, 1966; Klonoff & Kennedy, 1966; Power, Logue, McCarty, Rosenstiel, & Ziesat, 1979; Russell, 1975). Other researchers have responded to the failings of the old batteries by creating new batteries, such as the Guild Memory Test (Crook, Gilbert, & Ferris, 1980; Gilbert & Levee, 1971; Gilbert, Levee, & Catalano, 1968) and the NYU Memory Test. Unfortunately, these newer batteries are not above criticism, whatever their virtues. For example, the NYU Memory Test was designed with alternative forms for longitudinal studies, including studies of treatment effectiveness. It has definite advantages over the Wechsler Memory Scale: It provides measures for both learning and retention on a variety of tasks, it obtains recall for several delay intervals, and it includes measures of incidental learning. However, this test battery has the same disadvantage as the Wechsler Memory Scale in that it is highly verbal (Lezak, 1983). It was designed for assessment of the elderly and might be expected to produce a ceiling effect, at least on some subtests, when used in other applications with younger patients suspected of having memory problems. Also, the story recall subtest appears to be more similar to a word-list task than a prose task, and the scoring for "gist" gives credit for near-verbatim recall without regard to distortions in meaning or structural organization of the recall. Finally, the reliability and validity of the battery have not yet been established.

The rigidity of well-standardized testing procedures also introduces problems. In order to eliminate confounding variables such as distractibility, poor motivation, or confusion, and thereby maximize a subject's performance, skilled clinicians may want to adjust test procedures. But modification of assessment procedures from person to person may introduce variability that undermines standardized test norms. Clinicians must weigh the pros and cons of sacrificing standardized procedures in order to meet an individual patient's need.

Assessing Change and Treatment Effectiveness

How do the issues discussed to this point bear on the process of evaluating whether a change has taken place in an aging patient's memory functioning or whether treatment for memory impairment has been effective? To shed some light on the problems facing clinicians, in this section we characterize in four steps how clinicians proceed: (a) diagnosing the problem; (b) determining functional goals; (c) selecting appropriate, feasible, and cost-effective interventions; and (d) measuring the outcome. The section ends with a brief review of outcome studies.

Diagnosis

In diagnosing a problem, a clinician attempts to identify, collect, and synthesize relevant information about the patient's experiences, capabilities, and social and physical environments. The clinician uses this information to help "explain" the disorder and suggest a corrective course of action. The risk of jumping to conclusions on the basis of inadequate data is great for several reasons.

First, a memory complaint already represents a "diagnosis" that the patient or persons close to the patient have rendered in response to the patient's problems of daily life. The complaint may represent little more than a formulation designed to elicit attention and help from the clinician as an identified social agent, a formulation made plausible by cultural beliefs about aging and by the social acceptability of memory complaints as an explanation for failures in family and social functioning.

Second, a memory complaint is often vague, representing the belief of the patient or significant others that the patient is not processing or retrieving information as well as usual. As the results from memory complaint questionnaires illustrate, people's beliefs about their own performance are stable but not entirely accurate (Herrmann, 1982). A memory complaint may be made in addition to or in the absence of other physical complaints or mood disturbances. The relationships among depression, memory complaints, and memory functioning outlined by Gallagher, Thompson, and Levy (1980) illustrate some of the possibilities.

Third, a memory complaint sets in motion a complex of clinical assessment procedures that will be more or less systematic and comprehensive, depending on the knowledge and skills of the clinician in question. As Engel (1977) noted, the medical model can make practitioners oblivious to important information, and, as Haynes (1983) observed, every assessment system is based on underlying assumptions that influence the types of instruments employed, the populations and phenomena to which these instruments are applied, the types of data acquired, the inferences derived from these data, and the intervention programs based on such inferences. Given the possible assessment systems (medical, psychophysiological, intellectual, neuropsychological, personality, behavioral, etc.) and the intricacies involved in executing adequate protocols as well as the limitations of the most organized diagnostic systems (Strupp, 1978), the diagnostic task seems overwhelming.

In addition, clinicians are only beginning to conceptualize problems in living as resulting from interactions between the organism and the environment, rather than as determined by the organism (or some isolable organismic variable) or by the environment. Failure to appreciate the influence of family dynamics or to assess potential social–environmental supports and stressors can result in imprecise or erroneous formulation of a problem. Understandably, clinicians may fail to do a "total person assessment" (Erickson et al., 1980), with the result that patients will receive wrong treatment or a needlessly gloomy prognosis. The problem is that clinicians must approach their work intuitively rather than systematically because of the inadequacy of available models.

For the clinician, the diagnosis should always be a "working diagnosis," a conceptualization that helps him or her relate most effectively to the problem presented. Diagnosis is a continuing process that itself contributes to the effectiveness of treatment.

Functional Goals

A second step, one not necessarily carried out in the course of achieving the first step, is the articulation of the functional goals sought by the patient or involved others. In this step clinicians ask, "If the problem is remedied, to what extent will the patient's quality of life and ability to cope with the challenges of the environment be improved, and what will be the cost to the family and the community?" Most of our favored laboratory tasks and psychometric tools do not address the relationship between test results and functional levels of daily living (Erickson et al., 1980; Gallagher et al., 1980; Schaie & Schaie, 1977), although there are reasons to suppose that such relationships exist (Heaton & Pendleton, 1981). Functional assessments such as those developed by Lawton (Lawton, Moss, Fulcomer, & Kleban, 1982) and Pfeiffer (Duke University Center for the Study of Aging, 1978) represent more or less independent undertakings and further illustrate the conceptual complexity of the clinical task.

Selecting appropriate functional goals lands clinicians in the middle of a value-laden debate that is not readily resolved (cf. Erickson, 1972; Strupp, 1978). Clinicians may wish to see themselves as negotiating value-free contracts with their patients, but this is likely to be the case only when a patient's problem is private and the patient is going to pay the total bill. To the extent that social and financial costs are incurred by other parties, their values and interests will impinge. In a case involving an institutional setting, as many as six conflicting interests may be represented: The patient, who may or may not be inconvenienced or troubled by the memory impairment; the family; neighbors; third-party payers, for whom the cost of treatment or institutionalization may be a concern; the staff of the hospital or nursing home, who may be troubled by the disruption of normal ward procedures; and clinicians, who, in addition to being brokers in the system, may have their own agendas. The success of a settlement may hinge not on improving memory functioning as measured by memory tests so much as on satisfying the complaints of all of the involved parties.

Successful outcomes are commonly thought to involve a return to normal and independent functioning. As clinicians address chronic debilitating disorders, success may instead be marked by the slowing of a patient's functional decline. In such cases, the challenge may be to prevent or minimize surplus disabilities (Levy, Derogatis, Gallagher, & Gatz, 1980) and to help patients and their families better manage difficult situations, not to fix things "as good as new."

Interventions

Once the problem has been identified and functional goals have been established, the clinician is faced with the task of selecting or creating effective interventions to achieve the goals. Effective solutions to many clinical problems, particularly psychosocial problems, may derive from common sense and pragmatics rather than from logico-empirical processes. Even so, the selection of an avenue of intervention will be constrained by the working diagnosis, the breadth of the assessment, and beliefs about the possibility for constructive change. Fortunately, whatever their biases about particular patients, clinicians who make whole person assessments can offer helpful prescriptions whether or not gain will be recorded in terms of memory functioning as measured by traditional memory tests. The issue is not whether change can take place, but where clinicians can intervene in the total system (see Butler & Lewis, 1982; Zarit, 1980):

• A 70-year-old woman and her children fear that she is becoming senile because she has mislaid some important items and forgotten to pay some bills. Careful history-taking reveals that she has had this trouble all her life and the family's concerns rest on cultural folklore about aging. Reassurance may assuage their concerns, but the benefits of such an approach are not reflected on tests of learning and memory.

• A brain-injured patient is taught to use an appointment book, a daily schedule and checklist, and a special pillbox, all of which improves her functioning and sense of well-being (Fowler, Hart, & Sheehan, 1972). Formal testing, however, does not reflect the improvement.

• A reality orientation program instituted in a nursing home reduces hassles for patients and staff alike, but does not change formal test scores (Campos, 1984; Letcher, Peterson, & Scarbrough, 1974; Zepelin, Wolfe, & Kleinplatz, 1981).

• The muddled wanderings of a lonely old man are corrected by registering him in a day-care program. Despite the fact that the quality of his life is improved and the concerns of his neighbors are met, no changes show up on memory tests.

• A patient with chronic deteriorating disease marked by progressive memory loss is taught mnemonic strategies (cf. Poon, 1980). Follow-up testing shows no change, but the patient might have changed for the worse if his condition had been untreated.

• A successfully treated depressed patient no longer has complaints about her memory, much to her relief and the relief of her family, but her memory test scores show no change.

• An Alzheimer's patient is given a drug to enhance memory functioning. Test scores show slight, statistically significant improvements, but no meaningful improvement is observed in his everyday life.

Formal memory test scores do have a place in evaluating change and treatment effectiveness, and there is a need for better instruments. In the final analysis, however, such test scores must relate to the felt needs of the patient and involved others or they will be of little use to the clinician. As the foregoing examples illustrate, improved psychosocial functioning and consumer satisfaction may count for more than improved scores on learning and memory tests.

Outcome

The practice of psychotherapy was well established before systematic questions about its efficacy were raised. Eysenck's (1952) famous challenge precipitated discussion that shows no signs of abating; an excellent review of the history of this discussion may be found in Bergin and Lambert (1978). Thus far, two conclusions have been established, both of which are relevant to the issues discussed in this chapter: Psychological interventions are effective, and, with few exceptions, there is little reason to favor one intervention over another (Luborsky, Singer, & Luborsky, 1975; Smith, 1982; Smith & Glass, 1977).

Space does not permit even a listing of the problems faced in evaluating treatment effectiveness, problems that are as conceptually complex as they are logistically challenging. Problems encountered in designing research protocols to measure change over time have been discussed by Campbell and Stanley (1963), Isaac and Michaels (1971), Kratochwill and Mace (1983), and Schaie (1977). Relationships among outcome measures are only moderate (Erickson, 1975; Strupp, 1978), so investigators must consider the variety of available measures as well as their interrelationships (Raskin & Jarvik, 1979; Waskow & Parloff, 1975). As Eysenck's ostensibly straightforward question, "Is psychotherapy effective?" has been unpacked, complex literatures have emerged on nonspecific factors in treatment outcome and on therapist and patient variables, as well as evaluations of various treatment approaches and analyses of given approaches to see which components account for the effects. Succinct reviews of the literature may be found in the *Handbook of Psychotherapy and Behavior Change* (Bergin & Garfield, 1971; Garfield & Bergin, 1978), the 1981 APA *Master Lectures* (Harvey & Parks, 1982), and the recently published *Clinical Psychology Handbook* (Hersen, Kazdin, & Bellack, 1983).

Researchers have scarcely begun to articulate useful ways of addressing complex questions about outcome, while clinicians are continuing to create plausible and ostensibly useful interventions: For example, a few years ago Herink (1980) catalogued some 250 different psychotherapies. Discussion is divided between studies attempting to identify factors common to all psychotherapeutic interventions and studies attempting to evaluate the efficacy of particular treatment strategies (Kazdin, 1983).

The relevant literature also considers issues related to program evaluation, addressing the problems of effectively executing therapeutic procedures in clinical settings (Hargreaves & Attkisson, 1977; Sechrest &

Cohen, 1979; Suchman, 1967; Weiss, 1972). Recently, Hayes (1983) articulated ways in which clinicians can use individual cases as information sources so that they can produce as well as consume clinical knowledge.

Here we restrict our comments to two important issues: specificity and clinical effectiveness.

Specificity. A memory complaint expresses a concern regarding failed functioning that is designed to elicit help from health care givers. Precisely what is involved remains to be assessed and the cause or causes postulated. That we researchers are focusing our attention on the problem of memory impairment here should not distract us from the fact that we have not yet specified the outcome question. The problem has perennially been one of specifying all relevant elements in the outcome question (Erickson, 1972, 1975; Strupp & Bergin, 1969). Precisely what is the disorder to be treated? What are relevant therapist and patient variables? Which intervention(s) will be applied? What outcomes are intended? How will they be measured? How often and for how long? Complete specification of all relevant issues may well render the outcome questions too complex to be answerable (Smith, 1982).

Clinical effectiveness. The relationship between outcome research and program evaluation has been poorly articulated. Generally speaking, a contrast has been made between the scientist–academician who does pure research and the artisan–practitioner who does applied research (cf. Kiesler, 1971)—with the latter considered second class.

The reality of the relationship is more complex, however. Research conditions may not be generalizable to clinical operating conditions. This problem has been discussed at length by Hayes (1983), Kazdin (1982, 1983), and Kratochwill and Mace (1983) and in several special methodological sections in the *Journal of Consulting and Clinical Psychology* (1978, 1981). These discussions will be very helpful to clinical investigators. Most important, Kazdin noted that an adequate plan for outcome research involves not only basic research but also controlled trials under clinical conditions and clinical replications extending treatment to practice.

Kazdin's discussion prompts two additional observations concerning bridging the gap between outcome research and program evaluation. First, researchers are caught in a bind from which there appears no evident escape. The more carefully they conceptualize, implement, and monitor outcome research (i.e., the more internally valid the research is), the less generalizable it may be to clinical practice (i.e., the less externally valid it may be); but the more research procedures allow for clinical exigencies, the less explicable and replicable the results may be. Kazdin's excellent discussion of three landmark studies (Paul & Lentz, 1977; Rush, Beck, Kovacs, & Hollon, 1977; Sloan, Staples, Cristol, Yorkston, & Whipple, 1975) illustrates this problem, as do the points he makes about analogue research.

As he notes, analogue research constitutes one pole on the continuum of clinical research and is favored by

Kazdin because it circumvents many of the methodological, practical, and ethical issues associated with research in clinical settings. However, the advantages analogue research offers are offset by some disadvantages in terms of generalizability: It uses subjects that bear little resemblance to target populations, and their problems, motivations, and expectancies are not typical. In addition, the therapists, settings, and manner in which the treatment is delivered are not representative of clinical practice. Elegantly designed and painstakingly executed outcome studies may bear faint resemblance to the clinical practices they purport to justify.

Our second observation about bridging the gap between outcome research and program evaluation is that outcome research must address not only whether the intervention works and whether its effects can persist but also the extent to which patients and their significant others will continue to maintain the treatment regimen. Only recently has serious attention been given to the fact that an alarming proportion of patients do not follow good health care practices (Haynes, Taylor, & Sackett, 1979; Stone, Cohen, Adler, et al., 1979). Because what clinicians ask memory-impaired patients and their families to do may require significant behavioral changes, clinicians cannot ignore problems of treatment compliance. There is really little point in investing great efforts in demonstrating what *can* be done under ideal conditions (outcome research) if this proves to be a far cry from what *will* be done under clinical conditions (program evaluation).

A Sampling of Outcome Studies

Creating and evaluating the effectiveness of clinical interventions designed to ameliorate memory dysfunction among aging and brain-injured persons are only part of the larger problem of evaluating psychotherapy and technologies for behavior change. Researchers who are unaware of the many complex problems involved in the larger enterprise are likely to underestimate the magnitude of the task facing them. But there have been some preliminary efforts to evaluate the effectiveness of behavioral and pharmacological interventions.

Existing discussions regarding behavioral interventions for memory disorders (see Carroll & Gray, 1981; Cermak, 1980; Poon, 1980; Schaffer & Poon, 1982; Winograd & Simon, 1980; Zarit, Zarit, & Reever, 1982) do not provide the definitive answers clinicians need. It remains to be seen whether and with whom current interventions will produce enduring and generalizable effects and whether these interventions will prove feasible in clinical practice (Lewinsohn et al., 1977; Poon, 1980; Poon, Walsh-Sweeney, & Fozard, 1980; Zarit et al., 1982).

In recent years an attempt has been made to determine whether the memory defect associated with Alzheimer's disease could be ameliorated by the administration of drugs, most commonly drugs that boost cholinergic activity of the central nervous system. The treatment has been assessed by measuring performance on one or more memory tests before and during drug administration (Brinkman et al., 1982; Davis & Mohs, 1982; Etienne, Dastoor, Gauthier, Ludwick, & Collier, 1981; Mohs & Davis, 1982; Pomara et al., 1983; Thal, Fuld, Masur, & Sharpless, 1983; Wettstein, 1983). These studies have employed a double-blind, placebo-controlled crossover design. Two studies (Etienne et al., 1981; Kaye et al., 1982) collected at least two baseline measures in an attempt to allow the patients to adapt maximally to the test situation. However, most studies have not indicated whether the drug affected behavior nondiscriminately in general or whether any changes in memory performance during the examination correlated with meaningful changes in memory functioning in the patient's usual environment, as measured by systematic data from a reliable observer in daily contact with the patient.

Conclusion

Numerous obstacles prevent the development of a clinical protocol or an orderly set of clinical protocols, that practicing clinicians can understand and use to measure change in memory functioning resulting from treatment. The available information is too uncoordinated to be useful. Synthesizing and organizing this information will be an enormous task. Moreover, experimentalists and clinicians are heading in opposite directions (Erickson, 1977). Most experimentalists are busily pursuing endless analyses, multiplying the number of potential "culprits" for various clinical memory disorders. Thus, although some experimentalists have attempted to organize what is known by developing theories or writing review articles, the analytic impulse has outstripped the synthesizing impulse. As assessment procedures multiply, clinicians' use of these procedures will become increasingly haphazard. Efforts at systematizing the concepts comparable to our efforts at analysis are overdue.

As experimentalists and clinicians interested in the problem of how people process and organize information, we are singularly equipped not only to describe empirically how clinicians develop and organize information but also articulate and prescribe how they might do it more efficiently and effectively. Much remains to be done, although Hunt and MacLeod (1979) provided a rare example of such an effort. It will take hard work to order and synthesize the material now available, but the rewards will be great: Patients will be better served, and clinical approaches will be less haphazard. To echo the comments of Parloff and Dies (1977; cf. Schaie & Schaie, 1977), the present challenge is far more clinical–conceptual than research–technical.

References

Abramowitz, C. V., & Dokecki, P. R. (1977). The politics of clinical judgment: Early empirical returns. *Psychological Bulletin, 84,* 460–476.

Albert, M. S., Butters, N., & Brandt, J. (1981). Development of remote memory loss in patients with Huntington's disease. *Journal of Clinical Neuropsychology, 3,* 1–12.

Baddeley, A. (1976). *The psychology of memory.* New York: Basic Books.

Benton, A. L. (1974). The Revised Visual Retention Test (4th ed.). New York: Psychological Corporation.

Berent, S., Cohen, B. D., & Silverman, A. J. (1975). Changes in nonverbal learning following a single left or right unilateral electroconvulsive treatment. *Biological Psychiatry, 10,* 95–100.

Bergin, A. E., & Garfield, S. L. (Eds.). (1971). *Handbook of psychotherapy and behavior change: An empirical analysis* (2nd ed.). New York: Wiley.

Bergin, A. E., & Lambert, M. J. (1978). The evaluation of therapeutic outcomes. In S. L. Garfield & A. E. Bergin (Eds.), *Handbook of psychotherapy and behavior change: An empirical analysis* (2nd ed.). New York: Wiley.

Bloom, B. L. (1959). Comparison of the alternate Wechsler Memory Scale forms. *Journal of Clinical Psychology, 15,* 72–74.

Branconnier, R. J. (1982). Diagnostic considerations in Alzheimer's disease: Predictive value of intrusion errors as a differential diagnostic sign of Alzheimer's disease. *Annals of Neurology, 12,* 317.

Branconnier, R. J., Cole, J. O., Spera, K. F., & DeVitt, D. R. (1982). Recall and recognition as diagnostic indices of malignant memory loss in senile dementia: A Bayesian analysis. *Experimental Aging Research, 8*(3–4), 189–193.

Brinkman, S. D., Smith, R. C., Meyer, J. S., Uroulis, G., Shaw, T., Gordan, J. R., & Allen, R. H. (1982). Lecithin and memory training in suspected Alzheimer's disease. *Journal of Gerontology, 37,* 4–9.

Butler, R. N., & Lewis, M. I. (1982). *Aging and mental health* (3rd ed.). St. Louis: C. V. Mosby.

Butters, N., Barton, M., & Brody, B. A. (1970). Role of the right parietal lobe in the mediation of cross-modal associations and reversible operations in space. *Cortex, 6,* 174–190.

Butters, N., & Cermak, L. S. (1980). *Alcoholic Korsakoff's syndrome.* New York: Academic Press.

Campbell, D. T., & Stanley, J. C. (1963). *Experimental and quasi-experimental designs for research.* Chicago: Rand McNally.

Campos, R. G. (1984). Does reality orientation work? *Journal of Gerontological Nursing, 10*(2), 52–64.

Carroll, K., & Gray, K. (1981). Memory development: An approach to the mentally impaired elderly in the long-term care setting. *International Journal of Aging and Human Development, 13,* 15–35.

Cermak, L. S. (1980). Comments on imagery as a therapeutic mnemonic. In L. W. Poon, J. L. Fozard, L. S. Cermak, D. Arenberg, & L. W. Thompson (Eds.), *New directions in memory and aging: Proceedings of the George A. Talland Memorial Conference* (pp. 507–510). Hillsdale, NJ: Erlbaum.

Craik, F. I. M. (1977). Age differences in human memory. In J. E. Birren & K. W. Schaie (Eds.), *Handbook of the psychology of aging* (pp. 384–420). New York: Van Nostrand Reinhold.

Crook, T., Gilbert, J. G., & Ferris, S. (1980). Operationalizing memory impairment in elderly persons: The Guild Memory Test. *Psychological Reports, 47,* 1315–1318.

Davis, K. L., & Mohs, R. C. (1982). Enhancement of memory processes in Alzheimer's disease with multiple-dose intravenous physostigmine. *American Journal of Psychiatry, 139,* 1421–1424.

Duke University Center for the Study of Aging. (1978). *Mul-*

tidimensional functional assessment: The OARS methodology (2nd ed.). Durham, NC: Duke University Press.

Elstein, A. S., & Bordage, G. (1979). Psychology of clinical reasoning. In G. C. Stone, F. Cohen, N. E. Adler, et al. (Eds.), *Health psychology: A handbook* (pp. 333–367). San Francisco: Jossey-Bass.

Engel, G. L. (1977). The need for a new medical model: A challenge for biomedicine. *Science, 196*, 129–136.

Erickson, R. C. (1972). Outcome research in mental hospitals: A search for criteria. *Journal of Consulting and Clinical Psychology, 39*, 75–77.

Erickson, R. C. (1975). Outcome studies in mental hospitals: A review. *Psychological Bulletin, 82*, 519–540.

Erickson, R. C. (1977). Problems in clinical memory testing. In *Toward comprehensive intervention programs for memory problems among the aged* (Technical Rep. No. 77–01). Boston: Veteran's Administrative Outpatient Clinic, Geriatric Research, Educational and Clinical Center.

Erickson, R. C. (1978). Problems in clinical assessment of memory. *Experimental Aging Research, 4*, 255–272.

Erickson, R. C., Poon, L. W., & Walsh-Sweeney, L. (1980). Clinical memory testing of the elderly. In L. W. Poon, J. L. Fozard, L. S. Cermak, D. Arenberg, & L. W. Thompson (Eds.), *New directions in memory and aging: Proceedings of the George A. Talland Memorial Conference* (pp. 379–402). Hillsdale, NJ: Erlbaum.

Erickson, R. C., & Scott, M. L. (1977). Clinical memory testing: A review. *Psychological Bulletin, 84*, 1130–1149.

Etienne, P., Dastoor, D., Gauthier, S., Ludwick, R., & Collier, B. (1981). Alzheimer's disease: Lack of effect of lecithin treatment for 3 months. *Neurology, 31*, 1552–1554.

Eysenck, H. J. (1952). The effects of psychotherapy: An evaluation. *Journal of Consulting Psychology, 16*, 319–324.

Fowler, R. S., Jr., Hart, J., & Sheehan, M. (1972). A prosthetic memory: An application of the prosthetic environment concept. *Rehabilitation Counseling Bulletin, 16*(2), 80–85.

Fuld, P. A. (1980). Guaranteed stimulus-processing in the evaluation of memory and learning. *Cortex, 16*, 255–271.

Fuld, P. A., Katzman, R., Davies, P., & Terry, R. D. (1982). Intrusions as a sign of Alzheimer's dementia: Chemical and pathological verification. *Annals of Neurology, 11*, 155–159.

Gallagher, D., Thompson, L. W., & Levy, S. M. (1980). Clinical psychological assessment of older adults. In L. W. Poon (Ed.), *Aging in the 1980s: Psychological issues* (pp. 19–40). Washington, DC: American Psychological Association.

Garfield, S. L., & Bergin, A. E. (Eds.). (1978). *The handbook of psychotherapy and behavior change* (2nd ed.). New York: Wiley.

Gilbert, J. G., & Levee, R. F. (1971). Patterns of declining memory. *Journal of Gerontology, 26*, 70–75.

Gilbert, J. G., Levee, R. F., & Catalano, F. L. (1968). A preliminary report on a new memory scale. *Perceptual and Motor Skills, 27*, 277–278.

Halliday, A. M., Davison, K., & Browne, M. W., & Kreeger, L. C. (1968). A comparison of the effects on depression and memory of bilateral E.C.T. and unilateral E.C.T. to the dominant and non-dominant hemispheres. *British Journal of Psychiatry, 114*(513), 997–1012.

Hargreaves, W. A., & Attkisson, C. C. (Eds.). (1977). *Resource materials for community mental health program evaluation* (2nd ed.). Rockville, MD: National Institute of Mental Health.

Harvey, J. H., & Parks, M. M. (Eds.). (1982). *Psychotherapy research and behavior change*. Washington, DC: American Psychological Association.

Hayes, S. C. (1983). The role of the individual case in the production and consumption of clinical knowledge. In M. Hersen, A. E. Kazdin, & A. S. Bellack (Eds.), *The clinical psychology handbook* (pp. 181–195). New York: Pergamon Press.

Haynes, R. B., Taylor, D. W., & Sackett, D. L. (Eds.). (1979). *Compliance in health care*. Baltimore, MD: Johns Hopkins University Press.

Haynes, S. N. (1983). Behavioral assessment. In M. Hersen, A. E. Kazdin, & A. S. Bellack (Eds.), *The clinical psychology handbook* (pp. 397–426). New York: Pergamon Press.

Heaton, R. K., & Pendleton, M. G. (1981). Use of neuropsychological tests to predict adult patients' everyday functioning. *Journal of Consulting and Clinical Psychology, 49*, 807–821.

Herink, R. (Ed.). (1980). *The psychotherapy handbook*. New York: New American Library.

Herrmann, D. J. (1982). Know thy memory: The use of questionnaires to assess and study memory. *Psychological Bulletin, 92*, 434–452.

Hersen, M., Kazdin, A. E., & Bellack, A. S. (Eds.). (1983). *The clinical psychology handbook*. New York: Pergamon Press.

Hulicka, I. M. (1966). Age differences in Wechsler Memory Scale scores. *Journal of Genetic Psychology, 109*, 135–145.

Hunt, E. B., & MacLeod, C. M. (1979). Cognition and information processing in patient and physician. In G. C. Stone, F. Cohen, N. E. Adler, et al., (Eds.), *Health psychology: A handbook* (pp. 302–332). San Francisco: Jossey-Bass.

Isaac, S., & Michaels, W. B. (1971). *Handbook in research and evaluation*. San Diego: Robert R. Knapp.

Journal of Consulting and Clinical Psychology, 1978, *46*(4).

Journal of Consulting and Clinical Psychology, 1981, *49*(2).

Kaye, W. H., Sitaram, N., Weingartner, H., Ebert, M. H., Smallberg, S., & Gillin, J. C. (1982). Modest facilitation of memory in dementia with combined lecithin and anticholinesterase treatment. *Biological Psychiatry, 17*, 275–279.

Kazdin, A. E. (1982). Methodology of psychotherapy outcome research: Recent developments and remaining limitations. In J. H. Harvey & M. M. Parks (Eds.), *Psychotherapy research and behavior change* (pp. 151–193). Washington, DC: American Psychological Association.

Kazdin, A. E. (1983). Treatment research: The investigation and evaluation of psychotherapy. In M. Hersen, A. E. Kazdin, & A. S. Bellack (Eds.), *The clinical psychology handbook* (pp. 265–284). New York: Pergamon Press.

Kiesler, D. J. (1971). Experimental designs in psychotherapy research. In A. E. Bergin & S. L. Garfield (Eds.), *Handbook of psychotherapy and behavior change* (pp. 36–74). New York: Wiley.

Kim, Y., Royer, F., Bonstelle, C., & Boller, F. (1980). Temporal sequencing of verbal and nonverbal materials: The effect of laterality of lesion. *Cortex, 16*, 135–143.

Klonoff, H., & Kennedy, M. (1966). A comparative study of cognitive functioning in old age. *Journal of Gerontology, 21*, 239–243.

Kratochwill, T. R., & Mace, F. C. (1983). Experimental research in clinical psychology. In M. Hersen, A. E. Kazdin, & A. S. Bellack (Eds.), *The clinical psychology handbook* (pp. 197–221). New York: Pergamon Press.

Lawton, M. P., Moss, M., Fulcomer, M., & Kleban, M. H. (1982). A research and service-oriented Multilevel Assessment Instrument. *Journal of Gerontology, 37*, 91–99.

Letcher, P. B., Peterson, L. P., & Scarbrough, D. (1974). Reality orientation: A historical study of patient progress. *Hospital and Community Psychiatry, 25*, 801–803.

Levy, S. M., Derogatis, L. R., Gallagher, D., & Gatz, M. (1980). Intervention with older adults and the evaluation of outcome. In L. W. Poon (Ed.), *Aging in the 1980s: Psychological issues* (pp. 41–60). Washington, DC: American

Psychological Association.

Lewinsohn, P. M., Glasgow, R. E., Berrera, M., Danaher, B. G., Alperson, J., McCarty, D. L., Sullivan, J. M., Zeiss, R. A., Nyland, J., & Rodrigues, M. R. P. (1977). Assessment and treatment of patients with memory deficits: Initial studies. *JSAS Catalog of Selected Documents in Psychology* (Ms. No. 1538), 7, 79–80.

Lezak, M. D. (1983). *Neuropsychological assessment* (2nd ed.). New York: Oxford University Press.

Luborsky, L., Singer, B., & Luborsky, L. (1975). Comparative studies of psychotherapies. *Archives of General Psychiatry, 32,* 995–1008.

Mattis, S., Kovner, R., & Goldmeier, E. (1978). Different patterns of mnemonic deficits in two organic amnestic syndromes. *Brain and Language, 6,* 178–191.

Miller, E. (1975). Impaired recall and the memory disturbance in presenile dementia. *British Journal of Social and Clinical Psychology, 14*(1), 73–79.

Milner, B. (1968). Disorders of memory after brain lesions in man: Material-specific and generalized memory loss. *Neuropsychologia, 6,* 175–179.

Mohs, R. C., & Davis, K. L. (1982). A signal detectability analysis of the effect of physostigmine on memory in patients with Alzheimer's disease. *Neurobiological Aging, 3,* 105–110.

Morris, R., Wheatley, J., & Britton, P. (1983). Retrieval from long-term memory in senile dementia: Cued recall revisited. *British Journal of Clinical Psychology, 22,* 141–142.

Parloff, M. B., & Dies, R. R. (1977). Group therapy outcome research, 1966–1975. *International Journal of Group Psychotherapy, 27,* 281–319.

Parsons, T. (1964). *Social structure and personality.* New York: Free Press.

Paul, G. L., & Lentz, R. J. (1977). *Psychosocial treatment of chronic mental patients.* Cambridge, MA: Harvard University Press.

Perlmutter, M. (1979). Age differences in adults' free recall, cued recall, and recognition. *Journal of Gerontology, 34,* 533–539.

Pomara, N., Domino, E. F., Yoon, H., Brinkman, S., Tamminga, C. A. & Gershon, S. (1983). Failure of single-dose lecithin to alter aspects of central cholinergic activity in Alzheimer's disease. *Journal of Clinical Psychiatry, 44*(8), 293–295.

Poon, L. W. (1980). A systems approach for the assessment and treatment of memory problems. In J. Ferguson & C. B. Taylor (Eds.), *Comprehensive handbook of behavioral medicine* (Vol. 1, pp. 191–212). New York: Spectrum Publications.

Poon, L. W., Walsh-Sweeney, L., & Fozard, J. L. (1980). Memory skill training for the elderly: Salient issues on the use of imagery mnemonics. In L. W. Poon, J. L. Fozard, L. S. Cermak, D. Arenberg, & L. W. Thompson (Eds.), *New directions in memory and aging: Proceedings of the George A. Talland Memorial Conference* (pp. 461–484). Hillsdale, NJ: Erlbaum.

Power, D. G., Logue, P. E., McCarty, S. M., Rosenstiel, A. K., & Ziesat, H. A. (1979). Inter-rater reliability of the Russell revision of the Wechsler Memory Scale: An attempt to clarify some ambiguities in scoring. *Journal of Clinical Neuropsychology, 1,* 343–346.

Randt, C. T., Brown, E. R., & Osborne, D. P. (1980). A memory test for longitudinal measurement of mild to moderate deficits. *Clinical Neuropsychology, 2,* 184–194.

Raskin, A., & Jarvik, L. F. (Eds.). (1979). *Psychiatric symptoms and cognitive loss in the elderly.* New York: Hemisphere.

Rush, A. J., Beck, A. T., Kovacs, M., & Hollon, S. (1977). Comparative efficacy of cognitive therapy and pharmacotherapy in the treatment of depressed outpatients. *Cognitive Therapy and Research, 1,* 17–37.

Russell, E. W. (1975). A multiple scoring method for the assessment of complex memory functions. *Journal of Consulting and Clinical Psychology, 43,* 800–809.

Samuels, I., Butters, N., & Fedio, P. (1972). Short-term memory disorders following temporal lobe removals in humans. *Cortex, 8,* 283–298.

Sanders, R. E., Murphy, M. D., Schmitt, R. A., & Walsh, K. (1980). Age differences in free recall rehearsal strategies. *Journal of Gerontology, 35,* 550–558.

Sarason, S. B. (1981). *Psychology misdirected.* New York: Free Press.

Schaffer, G., & Poon, L. W. (1982). Individual variability in memory training with the elderly. *Educational Gerontology, 8,* 217–229.

Schaie, K. W. (1977). Quasi-experimental research designs in the psychology of aging. In J. E. Birren & K. W. Schaie (Eds.), *Handbook of the psychology of aging* (pp. 39–58). New York: Van Nostrand Reinhold.

Schaie, K. W., & Schaie, J. P. (1977). Clinical assessment and aging. In J. E. Birren & K. W. Schaie (Eds.), *Handbook of the psychology of aging* (pp. 692–723). New York: Van Nostrand Reinhold.

Schonfield, D., & Robertson, B. (1966). Memory storage and aging. *Canadian Journal of Psychology, 20,* 228–236.

Sechrest, L., & Cohen, R. Y. (1979). Evaluating outcomes in health care. In G. C. Stone, F. Cohen, N. E. Adler, et al. (Eds.), *Health psychology: A handbook* (pp. 369–394). San Francisco: Jossey-Bass.

Sloan, R. B., Staples, F. R., Cristol, A. H., Yorkston, N. J., & Whipple, K. (1975). *Psychotherapy versus behavior therapy.* Cambridge, MA: Harvard University Press.

Smith, A. D. (1975). Partial learning and recognition memory in the aged. *International Journal of Aging and Human Development, 6,* 359–365.

Smith, M. L. (1982). What research says about the effectiveness of psychotherapy. *Hospital and Community Psychiatry, 33,* 457–461.

Smith, M. L., & Glass, G. V. (1977). Meta-analysis of psychotherapy outcome studies. *American Psychologist, 32,* 352–360.

Stone, G. C., Cohen, F., Adler, N. E., et al. (Eds.). (1979). *Health psychology: A handbook.* San Francisco: Jossey-Bass.

Strupp, H. H. (1978). Psychotherapy research and practice: An overview. In S. L. Garfield & A. E. Bergin (Eds.), *Handbook of psychotherapy and behavior change* (2nd ed.) (pp. 3–22). New York: Wiley.

Strupp, H. H. & Bergin, A. E. (1969). Some empirical and conceptual bases for coordinated research in psychotherapy: A critical review of issues, trends and evidence. *International Journal of Psychiatry, 7,* 18–90.

Suchman, E. A. (1967). *Evaluative research.* New York: Russell Sage Foundation.

Talland, G. A. (1965). *Deranged memory.* New York: Academic Press.

Thal, L. J., Fuld, P. A., Masur, D. M., & Sharpless, N. S. (1983). Oral physostigmine and lecithin improve memory in Alzheimer's disease. *Annals of Neurology, 13,* 491–496.

Warrington, E. K., & Shallice, T. (1969). The selective impairment of auditory verbal short-term memory. *Brain, 92,* 885–896.

Waskow, I. E., & Parloff, M. B. (Eds.). (1975). *Psychotherapy change measures.* Rockville, MD: National Institute of Mental Health.

Wechsler, D. (1945). A standardized memory scale for clinical use. *Journal of Psychology, 19,* 87–95.

Weiss, C. H. (1972). *Evaluation research.* Englewood Cliffs, NJ: Prentice-Hall.

Wettstein, A. (1983). No effect from double-blind trial of physostigmine and lecithin in Alzheimer's disease. *Annals of Neurology, 13,* 210–212.

Winograd, E., & Simon, E. W. (1980). Visual memory and imagery in the aged. In L. W. Poon, (Eds.), *New directions in memory and aging* (pp. 485–506). Hillsdale, NJ: Erlbaum.

Zarit, S. H. (1980). *Aging and mental disorders.* New York: Free Press.

Zarit, S. H., Zarit, J. M., & Reever, J. E. (1982). Memory training for severe memory loss: Effects on senile dementia patients and their families. *The Gerontologist, 22,* 373–377.

Zelinski, E. M., Gilewski, M. J. & Thompson, L. W. (1980). Do laboratory tests relate to self-assessment of memory ability in the young and old? In L. W. Poon, J. L. Fozard, L. S. Cermak, D. Arenberg, & L. W. Thompson (Eds.), *New directions in memory and aging: Proceedings of the George A. Talland Memorial Conference* (pp. 519–549). Hillsdale, NJ: Erlbaum.

Zepelin, H., Wolfe, C. S., & Kleinplatz, F. (1981). Evaluation of a year-long reality orientation program. *Journal of Gerontology, 36,* 70–77.

Donna Cohen

Psychopathological Perspectives: Differential Diagnosis of Alzheimer's Disease and Related Disorders

Differential diagnosis and treatment of the dementias of later life is an interdisciplinary challenge. Cognitive assessment is one of several essential evaluations to distinguish diseases of the Alzheimer type, vascular dementias, and related disorders, and psychological testing also provides the empirical basis to devise a treatment plan for patients with different forms of dementia. Unfortunately, cognitive and behavioral information is underutilized in patient care. Specific research priorities are discussed, including information needed to develop an adequate classification to overcome the limitations of DSM-III, to test the hypothesis of the heterogeneity of dementia, and to improve our ability to care for people—to maximize their functional effectiveness and quality of life throughout the course of illness.

In his memoirs Luis Bunuel wrote, "You have to begin to lose your memory, if only in bits and pieces, to realize that memory is what makes our lives. Life without memory is no life at all . . . . Our memory is our coherence, our reason, our feeling, even our action. Without it we are nothing . . ." (Sacks, 1984, p. 14). Individuals afflicted with Alzheimer's dementia and related disorders undergo progressive and substantive losses in memory and other areas of cognition accompanied by changes in affect and behavior. The cognitive and behavioral losses are devastating, and the costs in the loss of human resources and the agony of patients and their families are incalculable.

Alzheimer's disease and other forms of nonreversible dementia afflict several million older persons in the United States alone, and perhaps 10% of the world population over age 65. Although research efforts have intensified in many areas—epidemiology, etiology and pathogenesis, diagnosis and clinical course, treatment, family issues, and systems of care, little is known about the dementias of later life, including the exact nature and course of the cognitive losses. As a consequence, early and accurate diagnosis is often a challenge.

However, early and accurate diagnosis of the cause of memory and cognitive impairments is essential. First, not everyone with cognitive impairment has Alzheimer's disease. As many as 20% to 30% of individuals referred for memory problems have a reversible and treatable dementia, which can be determined only by a comprehensive diagnostic workup. Second, although Alzheimer's disease is the most common dementia of later life, there are other forms of irreversible dementia; accurate differential diagnosis is necessary to develop an effective care plan.

Because progressive cognitive impairment from a previously higher level of functioning is the hallmark of Alzheimer's disease, a cognitive examination is one of the necessary components of a complete workup to establish the differential diagnosis. In this chapter I will review the contribution of cognitive evaluation to the differential diagnosis of Alzheimer's disease and related disorders. The clinical differentiation of the dementias of middle and later life is often difficult (Nott & Fleminger, 1975; Todorov, Go, Constantinidis, & Elston, 1975), and the differential diagnosis of primary neuronal degeneration of the Alzheimer type is currently made by a process of exclusion, the elimination of all other testable causes of dementia (Eisdorfer & Cohen, 1980).

The Interdisciplinary Challenge of Differential Diagnosis

A middle-aged or older person with complaints of memory problems or objective evidence of dementia often presents a complex dilemma to the clinician (Blazer, 1982; Cohen & Eisdorfer, 1985; Jefferson & Marshall, 1981). The complexities multiply with increasing frailty and with the number of medications and chronic illnesses. During the process of differential diagnosis, a series of important questions must be answered in order to ascertain the presence, severity, and cause of cognitive impairment.

If the individual complains about memory problems, are the complaints supported by objective evidence? Do the complaints signal a depressive disorder or is there another problem? If serious impairments are obvious, what is the cause or causes? Have metabolic disorders, cardiovascular disorders, hypoxia, normal-pressure hydrocephalus, nutritional deficiencies, toxins, drugs, infections, trauma, demyelinating disease, depression, inflammatory disease, and other disorders that are known to cause dementia been thoroughly evaluated? If any one or more of these are suspected to cause dementia, will appropriate treatment and therapy reverse the cognitive deficits, either partially or completely? If more than one chronic problem, for example, uremia and heart disease, has existed in the same person for a long time and cognitive losses are occurring gradually, are the neuropsychiatric symptoms due to the long-standing illness, or could Alzheimer's disease also be present?

Does the individual show any noticeable symptoms that identify any of the diffuse parenchymatous diseases—for example, Pick's disease, Creutzfeldt-Jakob disease, Parkinson dementia complex, Huntington's chorea, spinocerebeller degeneration, progressive myoclonic epilepsy, Hallervorden-Spatz syndrome, progressive supranuclear palsy, or any of several others? Is there any reason to suspect Wernicke-Korsakoff encephalopathy? Is there evidence for global transient amnesia or transient ischemic attacks (TIAs)? If so, are they basilar or carotid TIAs? Is there a clinical history of cerebral infarcts or current evidence of focal motor, sensory, and visual signs? Does the individual show signs of multi-infarct dementia or lacunar dementia?

Eisdorfer and Cohen (1980) developed a clinical checklist and research diagnostic criteria (RDC) for Alzheimer's disease to classify patients after a comprehensive evaluation, including a careful medical history and drug inventory, a physical examination, psychiatric and neurological evaluations, and psychological testing for cognitive performance and emotional status, as well as appropriate laboratory tests. A research clinical diagnosis requires that several conditions be satisfied. There must be evidence of a gradual onset and progression of cognitive deterioration over a minimum 6-month period. Mental status testing must show significant cognitive impairment in at least three of the following areas: learning, attention, memory, orientation, calculation, comprehension, abstraction, and judgment. Individuals must also be impaired in at least one of the following areas: the ability to work, to relate to family, to relate to peers, or to function socially. Finally, they must satisfy the medical exclusion criteria for all testable physical and psychiatric causes of cognitive impairment and have an Ischemic score (Hachinski, Lassen, & Marshall, 1974) of 4 or less to exclude the probable diagnosis of vascular dementia.

Contributions of Cognitive Assessment to Differential Diagnosis

Differential diagnosis is an interdisciplinary challenge, and the assessment of cognitive functioning is theoretically one of several essential evaluations to distinguish Alzheimer's disease, vascular dementias, and related disorders. Clinical psychological testing complements the physical, psychiatric, and neurological examinations as well as the many laboratory tests. Theoretically, cognitive test results could provide characteristic psychological profiles for diagnostic subcategories. In reality, we do not yet have the empirical data base necessary to characterize the cognitive deficits of specific dementia subtypes. However, the results of careful psychological testing in conjunction with other biomedical examinations provide valuable information to arrive at a presumptive consensus diagnosis.

Currently, there are no psychological test batteries or rating scales specific for Alzheimer's disease. Several brief mental status examinations are used to document the presence of impairment—the Mini-Mental-Status examination (Folstein, Folstein, & McHugh, 1975), the 10-question Mental Status Questionnaire (Kahn, Goldfarb, Pollack, & Peck, 1960), or the Blessed (Blessed, Tomlinson, & Roth, 1970). None of these instruments, however, was constructed to be more than a quick screening instrument to detect gross deficits. Each one evaluates only limited dimensions of cognition, including the individual's awareness of personal biographical information (birthdate, birthplace), general information (place of testing, president), ability to follow simple instructions, and short-term memory for sentences, objects, or words. These mental status instruments are therefore limited in the range of intellectual behaviors they examine, and they ignore the variability of impairments observed in dementia.

Likewise, until recently, standardized psychometric testing had had limited utility in making diagnostic decisions (Alexander, 1973; Bayles & Boone, 1982). Fuld and her colleagues (Fuld, Katzman, Davies, & Terry, 1982) have reported evidence that verbal intrusions are a behavioral characteristic of Alzheimer's disease, and Branconnier (1982) has reported that the occurrence of intrusions in a patient with dementia greatly increases the probability of a correct diagnosis of Alzheimer's disease. More recently, Fuld (1984) has proposed that almost half of patients meeting research diagnostic criteria for Alzheimer's disease show a characteristic profile of scores on subtests from the Wechsler Adult Intelligence Scale (WAIS). Her profile was derived originally from an analysis of test data from young adults treated experimentally to temporarily induce a deficiency in the cholinergic system of the brain (Drachman & Leavitt, 1974). Brinkman and Braun (1984) confirmed the occurrence of this WAIS profile in approximately half of the Alzheimer cases tested. This is an exciting finding for further research, but it is also important to remember that half of the patients did not exhibit this profile.

There are no cognitive scales specific for multi-infarct dementia. Multi-infarct dementias are easily recognized in most patients because of a clinical history of cerebral infarcts as well as the presence of focal neurological signs and symptoms. A symptom checklist, the ischemic score, developed by Hachinski (Hachinski et al., 1975) and modified by Rosen, Terry, Fuld, Katzman, and Peck (1980), is used to assign patients to a category of probable multi-infarct dementia. The ischemic score does not identify patients with Alzheimer's disease.

The cognitive deficits in cerebrovascular dementias usually reflect the areas of the brain that are destroyed. Deficits often occur abruptly and may either stabilize or improve after a stroke has occurred. In general no consistent pattern of cognitive deficits is observed in multi-infarct dementias (Fuld, 1978; Perez et al., 1975). Feigenson (1978) reported that 37% of more than one thousand patients referred to a stroke rehabilitation unit displayed aphasia and perceptual difficulties. Although discrete language and perceptual deficits do not define a generalized dementia syndrome per se, these symptoms significantly affect the quality of life (Boller, 1981).

The clinical assessment of cognition is necessary for the differential diagnosis of dementias today. However, clinical cognitive research is urgently needed to develop assessment batteries that when used in conjunction with the medical technology will improve our standards of differential diagnosis for Alzheimer's dementia and the different forms of cerebrovascular dementias. There may even be more than one type of Alzheimer's dementia. The results of clinical, neuropathological, biochemical, and genetic studies suggest that Alzheimer's is a heterogeneous disease (Whitehouse et al., 1982; Cohen, Eisdorfer, & Walford, 1981). Many major physical and psychiatric disorders have multiple forms—infectious diseases, leukemias, diabetes, pneumonia, and mental retardation, to mention only a few. The empirical analysis of subgroups of dementia is essential if we are to achieve success in identifying the biological, psychological, and environmental realities of successful treatment. Therefore, advancements in our understanding of heterogeneity is the empirical basis of improved differential diagnosis.

Clinical cognitive assessment in the diagnostic evaluation contributes a valuable but often underutilized data base to develop a set of treatment goals to optimize the functional effectiveness and quality of life for the individual and the family. Regardless of the type of dementia, cognitive remediation techniques in the early and middle stages may enhance the individual's ability to compensate for losses (Wilson & Moffat,

1984). The differential between Alzheimer's and vascular dementias may have important implications for several dimensions of management, rehabilitation, and treatment. As stated earlier, whereas Alzheimer's dementia is characterized by progressive losses, certain cognitive skills affected by a stroke may actually improve with time.

Our understanding of Alzheimer's dementia and related disorders is in its infancy. We need to develop theoretical models of behavioral change as a guide for future empirical studies of the nature and course of cognitive impairment. Over the past decade Alzheimer's dementia has gone from a little-known disease to a widely publicized one. With the anticipated biological revolution, we should see breakthroughs in our understanding of etiology and pathogenesis as well as technical advancements in diagnosis and treatment (Blass, 1984). But will we see a behavioral revolution in our understanding of the hallmark of dementia—the devastating cognitive dysfunction?

It would be exciting to see an acceleration of cognitive and behavioral research that might yield a paradigm for the microanalysis of behavior concurrent with the technology that measures the biological substrate of memory, attention, and learning. Knowledge about the precise nature of cognitive impairments throughout the course of dementia will not only contribute to clinicians' understanding of cognitive mechanisms, but will also enhance their ability to provide care. Even after the anticipated biological revolution, strategies will still be needed to care for these patients. The general treatment goals will remain the same—to maximize functional effectiveness and quality of life throughout the course of the illness.

Some clinicians have questioned the necessity for theoretical models of cognitive impairment, intensive cognitive assessment, and clinical research in the psychology of dementia. The realities of trying to care for people living through the human disasters of Alzheimer's disease and related disorders make many clinicians suspicious of the practical contributions of academic theorizing. Alzheimer's disease and related disorders leave flesh and bone intact (at least in the beginning) but crush judgment and emotions. They rob individuals of their sense of self, the process whereby new experiences are turned into knowledge (Cohen & Eisdorfer, 1986). The loss of self gradually destroys the richness of life experience; impairs recall, fantasy, imagination, and foresight; and destroys the fabric of human communication and interactions. It is often painfully difficult to care for and work with patients as they lose their ability to function. Real tension exists between the practice community and the academic community. Researchers frequently do not treat patients, especially over long periods of time, and clinicians often do not understand the implications and limitations of research studies. Both have an important role. Clinicians must deliver state-of-the-art health care using practical and reliable diagnostic criteria as well as treatment strategies to optimize the quality of life. Researchers must find a better way to provide health care.

Problems With DSM-III and the Classification of Dementia

Although differential diagnosis is the initial step to help patients, clinicians' concepts of dementia in later life and the current knowledge base limit our capacity to confidently complete this process of clinical decision making. DSM-III further confuses decision making. The diagnostic categories for cognitive disorders in DSM-III not only reflect the current paucity of knowledge, but the classification also does not even reveal what is known.

The problems raised by our methods of differential diagnosis and by the clinical assessment of cognition are both practical and theoretical. The quantitative training of psychologists in statistics and research design as well as psychometrics has led to the creation of a variety of tests that are meant to help in clinical assessment and diagnosis. However, very few tests have been developed for the evaluation of dementia. Several mental status examinations have come to be useful to document the general level of cognitive impairment, but they are of little value for differential diagnosis of the nonreversible dementias, because many symptoms of cognitive impairment are similar across different dementias.

If our long-term objective as independent scientists is to clarify the diagnosis of late-life dementias, should we not work out a system of patient classification based upon psychological theory and empirical evidence rather than rely on a medical diagnostic system based on a form of consensus as in DSM-III? Dementia is defined in DSM-III (American Psychiatric Association, 1980) as an overall decline in intellectual functioning characterized by impairments in memory, judgment, and abstraction, accompanied by aphasia, agnosia, or apraxia, any or all of which are sufficient to interfere with work and social functioning. In DSM-III, Organic Mental Disorders replaces the DSM-II category title Organic Brain Syndrome (OBS). OBS was seen essentially as a syndrome with a number of manifestations, and it was defined either as psychotic or nonpsychotic, acute or chronic. These distinctions are dropped in DSM-III, which includes nine different organic mental disorders: Intoxication, Withdrawal, Delirium, Dementia, Amnestic Syndrome, Delusional Syndrome, Hallucinosis, Affective Syndrome, and Personality Syndrome.

These categories are inadequate for the differential diagnosis of middle-aged and older persons with cognitive impairments. They have little meaning in the context of what little is known about the etiologies and pathogenesis of the reversible and nonreversible dementias. Although these nine categories certainly can be used to classify patients, they lack a rational theoretical organization for the classification of a significant cognitive impairment in the aged. For example, the most common form of dementia is primary neuronal degeneration of the Alzheimer type, accounting for more than 50% of the dementias. DSM-III defines dementia according to the signs and clinical course of Alzheimer's dementia, but it does not clarify the role of multi-infarct dementias or mixed dementias. Multi-infarct dementia, originally associated with multiple infarctions but now used to refer to all vascular causes of dementia (Caplan, 1979), appears to affect 20% of the cognitively impaired aged. Another 12% to 15% have a mixed dementia, with pathological signs of Alzheimer's and cerebrovascular disease.

DSM-III was intended to be an atheoretical consensus nomenclature for clinicians, particularly psychiatrists. The more than 200 disorders and conditions have been grouped into 18 distinguishable groups. These groups of disorders are categorized along each of five axes. Briefly, each of the five axes represents a different dimension of information. Axis I is the clinical syndrome that is the focus of attention. Axis II specifies the personality disorders that may occur in adults, adolescents, or children (where relevant). Axis III is reserved for physical disorders relevant to Axis I or Axis II. The diagnostic complexities inherent with the aged who manifest cognitive dysfunction and several chronic illnesses with neuropsychiatric features make the simplicity of this axis questionable. Axis IV allows a coding, on a 7-point scale, of the severity of the stressors that are judged to be contributing to or precipitating the disorders on Axis I or II. This axis requires more specificity if it is to be useful for the dementias. Axis V represents the highest level of premorbid functioning of the individual within a year of the presenting problems or conditions. This estimate of adaptive functioning, also on a 7-point scale, is used primarily for prognosis. It has little utility for nonreversible dementias. If redefined, however, it could provide a much needed estimate of a patient's competency.

Many criticisms of DSM-III have focused on the categorical approach and the weight attached to the traditional medical model. The results of psychological assessments are virtually excluded from being incorporated into the diagnostic dimensions. Several authors (Eysenck, Wakefield, & Friedman, 1983; Schacht & Nathan, 1977) have argued that the coding of medical disorders enlarges the domain of psychiatry and restricts the input of nonmedical professionals. Spitzer (1981) has defended the medical focus of DSM-III as necessary to make it consistent with the revisions in the International Classification of Diseases (ICD). He also has urged psychologists to construct their own classification to supplement or compete with DSM-III!

Given that DSM-III is a reality, psychologists, including those studying and caring for the aged, cannot ignore it. However, it is time to recast the clinical diagnostic criteria for Alzheimer's disease, vascular dementias, and related disorders. Present standards for Alzheimer's disease and related disorders (Eisdorfer & Cohen, 1980) need to be modified to be applicable to the manifestation of these disorders throughout the latest years. More precise criteria can also be developed to quantify the characteristics of these diseases and their subgroups. Although the validity and utility of DSM-III for the classification of the entire range of psychopathology in the aged is controversial (Blazer, 1982; Cohen & Eisdorfer, 1984; Eisdorfer &

Cohen, 1983), this discussion will be restricted to the dementias.

DSM-III is primarily a professional manual and secondarily a scientific one. The pressures that influenced DSM-III will also influence DSM-IV and succeeding manuals. The obvious pressures are the practical concerns of professionals to communicate with each other and to define the legitimate boundaries of the profession. Health insurance carriers also need to find the manual acceptable for reimbursement of appropriate health care costs. In general, these various concerns are probably best dealt with through consensus.

However, what about the influence of research on the revision of DSM-III? History clearly shows that it takes time for scientific findings to find professional application (Eysenck & Eysenck, 1980). What information is needed? What are the research priorities for clarifying the diagnostic criteria for Alzheimer's disease and related disorders that are listed in DSM-III?

First, categorical assessments must be replaced with dimensional assessments to obtain a profile of cognitive changes. The degree of cognitive and behavioral deficiencies should be measured along a scale or scales with known reliabilities and validities. However, the battle to include a global assessment scale of dementia will probably be a long one, even though there are some embryonic scales that are ripe for modification and refinement (Cohen, Eisdorfer, & Holm, 1984; Cole & Dastoor, 1980; Reisberg, Schneck, Ferris, Schwartz, & de Leon, 1983; Rosen, Mohs, & Davis, 1984). Intelligence, which is probably the best established behavioral dimension, is not even systematized in DSM-III. DSM-III continues to provide several heterogeneous and arbitrarily defined categories, even though scores of intelligence or dementia would provide much clearer information. Combining scores for adaptive behavior with scores for the level of dementia would provide more information than categories such as "mildly retarded" or "mildly demented."

Second, psychological assessments must be considered in conjunction with treatment options. Although pharmacologic agents are not yet available to cure, reverse, or halt the progression of Alzheimer's dementia, there are treatment options (Cohen, Kennedy, & Eisdorfer, 1984; Eisdorfer & Cohen, 1981; Yesavage & Karasu, 1982). Unfortunately, most cognitive research is characterized by two parallel empirical approaches—one that attempts to describe cognitive performance and the other that tries to improve cognitive skills. More research is needed to understand how to mobilize cognitive skills and functional effectiveness.

Third, cognitive assessments must be based on observable behavior rather than on subjective impressions of clinicians. A microanalytic analysis of cognition is lacking that is not only based on knowledge of the course of cognitive changes in dementia but is also clinically useful (Cohen & Eisdorfer, 1979). Assembling all of the pieces of the puzzle in the differential diagnosis of an older patient requires time, patience, and the synthesis of behavioral and biological data into a consensus diagnosis. At the present, the profile of cognitive deficits is one piece of the puzzle.

Someday, cognitive strengths and deficits may be incorporated into the differential diagnosis with more precision. For the moment, clinicians must use DSM-III, but they should at least recognize its limitations. Intensive research is the key to improving standards for diagnostic decision making and empirically derived health care. The careful analysis of attention and memory as well as behavioral dysfunction, in the finest tradition of George Talland, may uncover the early warning signs of dementia. In the case of multi-infarct dementia, early detection of vascular illness may even prevent the onset of dementia.

Diagnosis of Vascular Dementia

Although vascular disease is not the major etiology of dementia, it causes cognitive impairment in a significant group of individuals (Feigenson, McCarthy, Greenberg, & Feigenson, 1977; Fisher, 1965b). Early diagnosis is crucial, because appropriate interventions may arrest or even prevent the development of dementia. The exact prevalence of vascular dementia is not known. However, the incidence of clinical stroke increases between ages 45 and 85, and the rate of increase seems to double every 10 years (Baum & Robins, 1981).

There were 1.7 million stroke survivors in the United States in 1978; 75% were between the ages of 55 and 84. The population at risk for vascular dementia based upon the survivors of clinical stroke alone is substantial. The results of neuropathological analysis show that cerebral infarcts are even more prevalent than the clinical studies suggest (Fisher, 1965a; Jorgensen & Torvak, 1966). A substantial number of patients show postmortem evidence of ischemic disease although no history of clinical stroke or focal findings is evident. Thus, subclinical cerebrovascular disease in the aged brain may lead to multi-infarct dementia even in the absence of clinical stroke.

Identification of risk factors associated with cerebrovascular disease would be helpful to understand multi-infarct dementia (Cohen & Eisdorfer, 1984). It is possible that the risk factors for multiple infarcts are similar to stroke, but they need not be. The best information on risk factors in stroke is derived from the Framingham Study, in which subjects have been followed for more than 30 years. Risk factors for cerebrovascular disease are hypertension and the presence of impaired cardiac functioning (e.g., coronary heart disease, arrhythmias, or congestive heart failure), and diabetes (Kannel, 1971, 1982; Wolf, Dawber, & Kannel, 1978; Wolf, Kannel, & Dawber, 1978). The risk for stroke also increases with the number of abnormalities present in an individual.

Individuals with hypertension have seven times as much cerebrovascular disease as normotensives. Borderline elevation of blood pressure doubles the incidence (Wolf, Dawber, & Kannel, 1978). The risk of stroke increases threefold in all age groups when coronary heart disease is present (Wolf, Kannel, & Dawber,

1978). Patients with chronic atrial fibrillations are at an 8.5-fold increased risk!

Risk factor management in the United States has led to a decline of 45% in the incidence of stroke over the last 25 years (Garraway, Whisnant, Furlan, et al., 1979; Garraway, Whisnant, Kurland, & O'Fallon, 1979). However, stroke prevalence is the figure with the greatest influence on multi-infarct dementia. Prevalence has not changed very much, as a result of the increasing numbers of older persons and decreased mortality for strokes. Mortality resulting from cerebrovascular disease and myocardial infarction has also declined (Kannel, 1982), and close to half of this decline has occurred since 1972 when therapy for borderline hypertension became aggressive. If risk factor management continues, the result may be a decrease in the subset of older persons at risk for multi-infarct dementia.

Is clinical cognitive assessment an appropriate focus for the differential diagnosis of vascular dementia? In light of a 20% reduction in the aged over the last 10 years due largely to a decrease in stroke and heart disease, the answer is yes, more than ever. Clearly, the manipulation of risk factors is an important approach in the struggle to eliminate multi-infarct dementias, but this crusade will take time. Until we have achieved this goal, the quest for earlier recognition of cerebrovascular disease and subtle behavioral impairments must continue. There is no reason to believe that improved differential diagnosis will depend more on vascular parameters than on cognitive and emotional indicators. Our technology for the latter is simply less sophisticated than the former, and there are those who believe that machines and basic science are more "scientific" than behavioral and clinical science.

Cognitive Evaluation: A Complex Challenge for Caring

The older individual with dementia brings an impaired mind to the diagnostic and therapeutic relationship, which alters our usual ways of communication. Clinicians must learn the language of the cognitively impaired aged, and just as important, we must allow them to teach us. Trust, patience, honesty, and hope must be exchanged between the patient and the clinician. With the aged, these transactions must occur or care will be impossible. The diagnosis may be accomplished, but the patient's needs and true capabilities may never be realized.

Whether we are scientists or clinicians, or whether we wear both hats, there is no substitute for the empirical research that must be done to learn the earliest signs of significant cognitive impairment, to determine whether characteristic cognitive profiles exist for dementia subgroups, and to identify the limits of cognitive remediation and enrichment. In order to accomplish this, we need to establish a special relationship with the patient. Although so many of the deficits are painfully obvious, individuals even in moderate and severe stages surprise us with their capacity to perform. Robert Cancro's (1983) observations from 26 years of caring for schizophrenics could easily be applied to our experience with dementia patients:

We must let the patient play Virgil to our Dante, even though we understand no Latin. It is only with this attitude of openness and trusting uncertainty, initially on our part, that we may bridge the gap in communication and find our way through the inferno together. (p. 280)

Loss of intellectual prowess manifests itself in behaviors such as language difficulties and apraxia, impaired memory and attentional mechanisms, and deficient executive processing, all of which are progressively but inevitably affected. Within the limits of their remaining cognitive skills, however, patients have the right to help make decisions, participate in their care, and choose how they will live their remaining years. The outcome of the clinical process of differential diagnosis should be more than a classification of the dementia subtype. The clinical cognitive measures should also allow us to derive an index of "sliding competency." The clinician has a responsibility to monitor the changing competency and needs of the patient to help both the patient and the family to redefine goals and live with dignity.

References

Alexander, D. A. (1973). Some tests of intelligence and learning for elderly psychiatric patients: A validation study. *British Journal of Social and Clinical Psychology, 12,* 188–193.

American Psychiatric Association. (1980). *Diagnostic and statistical manual of mental disorders* (3rd ed.). Washington, DC: Author.

Baum, H. M., & Robins, M. (1981). National survey of stroke: Survival and prevalence. *Stroke, 12,* 159–168.

Bayles K. A., & Boone, D. R. (1982). Potential of language tasks for identifying senile dementia. *Journal of Speech and Hearing Disorders, 47,* 210–217.

Blass, J. (1984). Staging of Alzheimer's disease. *Journal of the American Geriatric Society, 32,* 4.

Blazer, D. (1982). *Depression in late life.* St. Louis, MO: Mosby.

Blessed, G., Tomlinson, B. E., & Roth, M. (1968). The association between quantitative measures of dementia and of senile changes in the cerebral grey matter of elderly subjects. *British Journal of Psychiatry, 114,* 797–811.

Boller, F. (1981). Strokes and behavior: Disorders of higher cortical function following cerebral disease, disorders of language and related functions. *Stroke, 12,* 532–534.

Branconnier, R. J. (1982). Predictive value of intrusion errors as a differential diagnostic sign of Alzheimer's disease. *Annals of Neurology, 12,* 318.

Brinkman, S. D., & Braun, P. (1984). Classification of dementia patients by a WAIS profile related to central cholinergic deficiencies. *Journal of Clinical Neuropsychology, 6*(4), 393–400.

Cancro, R. (1983). Toward a unified view of schizophrenic disorders. (pp. 265–280). In M. R. Zales, (Ed.), *Affective* and schizophrenic disorders (pp. 265–280). New York: Brunner/Mazel.

Caplan, L. R. (1979). Chronic vascular dementia. Primary Care, 6, 843–848.

Cohen, D., & Eisdorfer, C. (1979). Cognitive theory and assessment of change in the elderly. In A. Raskin & L. F. Jarvik (Eds.), Psychiatric symptoms and cognitive loss in the elderly. New York: Halstead Press.

Cohen, D., & Eisdorfer, C. (1984). Risk factors in late life dementia. In M. Marois (Ed.), Senile dementias in the 21st century (pp. 221–237). New York: Plenum Press.

Cohen, D., & Eisdorfer, C. (1985). Major psychiatric and behavioral disorders in the aged. In R. Andres, E. Bierman, & W. Hazzard (Eds.), Principles of geriatric medicine (pp. 867–908). New York: Oxford University Press.

Cohen, D., & Eisdorfer, C. (1986). The loss of self—a family resource for Alzheimer's disease and related disorders. New York: Norton.

Cohen, D., Eisdorfer, C., & Holm, L. (1984). Mental status examinations: Utility for the diagnosis and management of the older adult with significant cognitive dysfunction. In M. Albert (Ed.), Clinical neurology of aging. New York: Oxford University Press.

Cohen, D., Eisdorfer, C., & Walford, R. L. (1981). Histocompatibility antigens (HLA) and patterns of cognitive loss in dementia of the Alzheimer type. Neurobiology of Aging, 2, 277–280.

Cohen, D., Kennedy, G., & Eisdorfer, C. (1984). Phases of change in the patient with Alzheimer's dementia: A conceptual dimension for defining health care management. Journal of the American Geriatric Society, 32, 11–15.

Cole, M. G., & Dastoor, D. (1980). Development of a dementia rating scale: Preliminary communication. Journal of Clinical Experimental Gerontology, 2, 46–63.

Drachman, D. A., & Leavitt, J. (1974). Human memory and the cholinergic system: A relationship to aging? Archives of Neurology, 30, 113–121.

Eisdorfer, C., & Cohen, D. (1980). Diagnostic criteria for primary neuronal degeneration of the Alzheimer type. Journal of Family Practice, 11, 553–557.

Eisdorfer, C., & Cohen, D. (1981). Management of the patient and family coping with dementing illness. Journal of Family Practice, 12, 831–837.

Eisdorfer, C., & Cohen, D. (1983). Late-onset schizophrenia and paranoia in the elderly. In L. Grinspoon (Ed.), Psychiatry update (Vol. 2). Washington, DC: American Psychiatric Association.

Eysenck, M. W., & Eysenck, H. J. (1980). Mischel and the concept of personality. British Journal of Psychology, 71, 191–204.

Eysenck, H. J., Wakefield, J. A., & Friedman, A. F. (1983). Diagnosis and clinical assessment: The DSM-III. Annual Review of Psychology, 34, 167–193.

Feigenson, J. S. (1978). Definition of dementia. Stroke, 9, 523.

Feigenson, J. S., McCarthy, M. L., Greenberg, S. D., & Feigenson, W. D. (1977). Factors influencing outcome and length of stay in a stroke rehabilitation unit: Part 2. Comparison of 318 screened and 248 unscreened patients. Stroke, 8, 657–662.

Fisher, C. M., (1965a). Lacunae: Small deep cerebral infarcts. Neurology, 15, 774–784.

Fisher, C. M. (1965b). Pure sensory stroke involving face, arm and leg. Neurology, 15, 76–80.

Folstein, M. F., Folstein, S. E., & McHugh, P. R. (1975). Mini-Mental State: A practical method for grading the cognitive state of patients for the clinician. Journal of Psychiatric Research, 12, 189–198.

Fuld, P. A. (1978). Psychological testing in the differential diagnosis of the dementias. In R. Katzman, R. D. Terry, K. L. Bick (Eds.), Alzheimer's disease: Senile dementia and related disorders (pp. 185–193). New York: Raven Press.

Fuld, P. (1984). Test profile of cholinergic dysfunction and of Alzheimer-type dementia. Journal of Clinical Neuropsychology, 6(4), 380–392.

Fuld, P., Katzman, R., Davies, P., & Terry, R. D. (1982). Intrusions as a sign of Alzheimer's dementia: Chemical and pathological verification. Annals of Neurology, 11, 155–159.

Garraway, W. M., Whisnant, J. P., Furlan, A. J., Phillips, L. H., Kurland, L. T., & O'Fallon, W. M. (1979). The declining incidence of stroke. New England Journal of Medicine, 300, 449–452.

Garraway, W. M., Whisnant, J. P., Kurland, L. T., & O'Fallon, W. M. (1979). Changing pattern of cerebral infarction: 1945–1974. Stroke, 10, 657–663.

Hachinski, V. C., Iliff, L. D., Zilhka, E., DuBoulay, G. H., McAllister, V. L., Marshall, J., Ross-Russell, R. W., & Symon, L. (1975). Cerebral blood flow in dementia. Archives of Neurology, 34, 632–637.

Hachinski, V. C., Lassen, N. A., & Marshall, J. (1974). Multi-infarct dementia: A cause of mental deterioration in the elderly. Lancet, 2, 207–210.

Jefferson, J. W., & Marshall, J. R. (1981). Neuropsychiatric features of medical disorders. New York: Plenum Press.

Jorgensen, L., & Torvak, A. (1966). Ischemic heart disease in an autopsy series: Part I. Prevalence, location, and predisposing factors in verified thrombo-embolic occlusions and their significance in the pathogenesis of cerebral infarction. Journal of Neurological Science, 3, 490–509.

Kahn, R. L., Goldfarb, A. I., Pollack, M., & Peck, A. (1960). Brief objective measures for the determination of mental status in the aged. American Journal of Psychiatry, 117, 326–328.

Kannel, W. B. (1971). Current status of the epidemiology of brain infarction associated with occlusive arterial disease. Stroke, 2, 295–318.

Kannel, W. B. (1982). The meaning of the downward trend in cardiovascular mortality. Journal of the American Medical Association, 247, 877–880.

Nott, P. N., & Fleminger, J. J. (1975). Presenile dementia: The difficulties of early diagnosis. Acta Psychiatrica Scandinavica, 51, 210–217.

Perez, F. I., Rivera, V. M., Meyer, J. S., Gay, A., Taylor, R. L., & Mathew, W. T. (1975). Analysis of intellectual and cognitive performance in patients with multi-infarct dementia, vertebrobasilar insufficiency with dementia, and Alzheimer's disease. Journal of Neurology, Neurosurgery, and Psychiatry, 38, 533–540.

Reisberg, B., Schneck, M. K., Ferris, S. H., Schwartz, G. E., & de Leon, M. J. (1983). The Brief Cognitive Rating Scale (BCRS): Findings in primary degenerative dementia (PDD). Psychopharmacology Bulletin, 19(1), 47–50.

Rosen, W. G., Mohs, R. C., & Davis, K. L. (1984). A new rating scale for Alzheimer's disease. American Journal of Psychiatry, 14(11), 1356–1364.

Rosen, W. G., Terry, R. D., Fuld, P. A., Katzman, R., & Peck, A. (1980). Pathologic verification of the ischemic score in the differentiation of dementias. Annals of Neurology, 7, 486–488.

Sacks, O. (1984, February 16). The lost mariner. New York Review of Books.

Schacht, T., & Nathan, P. E. (1977). But is it good for the psychologists? Appraisal and status of DSM-III. American Psychologist, 32, 1017–1025.

Spitzer, R. L. (1981). Nonmedical myths and the DSM-III.

APA Monitor, 12, 33.

Todorov, A. B., Go, R. C. P., Constantinidis, J., & Elston, R. C. (1975). Specificity of the clinical diagnosis of dementia. *Journal of Neurological Science, 26,* 81–98.

Whitehouse, P. J., Price, D. L., Struble, R. G., Clark, A. W., Coyle, J. T., & DeLong, M. R. (1982). Alzheimer's disease and senile dementia: A loss of neurons in the basal forebrain. *Science, 215,* 1237–1239.

Wilson, B. A., & Moffat, N. (Eds.). (1984). *Clinical management of memory problems.* Rockville, MD: Aspen.

Wolf, P. A., Dawber, T. R., & Kannel, W. B. (1978). Heart disease as a precursor to stroke. In B. S. Schoenberg (Ed.), *Advances in neurology* (Vol. 19). New York: Raven Press.

Wolf, P. A., Kannel, W. B., & Dawber, T. R. (1978). Prospective investigation: The Framingham Study and the risk of stroke. In B. S. Schoenberg (Ed.), *Advances in neurology* (Vol. 19). New York: Raven Press.

Yesavage, J., & Karasu, T. B. (1982). Psychotherapy with elderly patients. *American Journal of Psychotherapy, 36,* 41–55.

Instruments for the Evaluation of Symptoms and Complaints of Memory Dysfunction

Thomas Crook, *Section Editor*

Thomas Crook

10

Overview of Memory Assessment Instruments

Remarkable progress has been made in memory research during recent years, but this progress is not reflected in many of the tests employed by clinicians and clinical investigators. The most widely used standardized memory test today is probably the Wechsler Memory Scale, which was published in 1945 and includes items from much earlier tests such as the Army Performance Test of World War I and even earlier scales developed by Binet. Clearly, more sophisticated measures are available for both clinical and research applications.

The need for state-of-the-art assessment instruments is particularly apparent for the large and rapidly expanding elderly population. Memory complaints are extremely prevalent among even healthy aged individuals, and serious memory impairment may result from a wide range of medical and psychiatric disorders.

Of particular concern is the devastating memory loss resulting from dementing disorders such as Alzheimer's disease (AD). Psychometric instruments are extremely useful in these disorders for both diagnostic assessment and assessment of clinical change. The latter application is particularly important in the search for an effective treatment for AD and related disorders. For example, the effects of pharmacologic treatments now under investigation are quite subtle and may be missed entirely without sophisticated assessment instruments. Such a mistake could lead to the incorrect rejection of a hypothesis that might lead to the eventual development of clearly effective compounds. Alternatively, misinterpretation of activating or other nonspecific drug effects as effects on memory may lead to costly and unproductive efforts to develop more potent analogues of the compound under study. Similar issues regarding sensitivity and specificity of psychometric instruments are also applicable to the evaluation of other treatment alternatives to improve cognitive functioning of older persons.

The following chapters were developed to identify state-of-the-art assessment instruments for different clinical and research applications. Chapter authors were asked to recommend specific instruments, to consider the strengths and limitations of the measures selected, and to outline promising directions for future instrument development. In some cases, such as the selection of behavior rating scales, the task is relatively straightforward. In other cases, however, particularly in the selection of psychological performance tests, the task can be approached from various perspectives. For example, the neuropsychologist's perspective on memory testing is likely to differ from that of the psychologist whose background is in standardized educational and clinical testing, and both of these perspectives are likely to differ from that of the experimental psychologist with a background in information processing. Clearly, there is no "correct" perspective and no single test or test battery that is appropriate in all situations. Thus, the reader is presented with somewhat different views in different chapters on psychological testing and is asked to consider the relative merits of different approaches against the particular demands of the assessment task at hand.

A brief review of the section may point the reader to chapters of particular interest. Chapter 11, by Gilewski and Zelinski, deals with the task of assessing memory complaints among elderly persons living in the community. Gilewski and Zelinski discuss the importance of obtaining self-report data on memory function in this population and review 10 scales that have been employed in studies with elderly subjects. The authors recommend specific scales for different clinical and research applications and identify two general-purpose scales that will be of interest to clinical investigators.

Following the Gilewski and Zelinski chapter, Reisberg and his colleagues (chapter 12) discuss the utility of specific psychometric instruments in the initial evaluation of elderly patients. The authors discuss the clinical symptomatology seen in AD—the major dementing disorder of late life—and identify instruments that may be of diagnostic utility, as well as others that may be useful in identifying the stage to which the disorder has progressed. Instruments discussed in chapter 12 will be of interest to both clinicians and clinical investigators.

In chapter 13, McDonald turns to the use of observer rating scales in treatment assessment. He discusses characteristics of behavior rating scales and reviews eight scales for assessing drug effects on a range of psychiatric symptoms seen in late-life dementing disorders. McDonald argues that the scales reviewed can provide valuable data in assessing treatment effects but that no single scale is an adequate source of data on treatment efficacy.

Chapters 14 through 18 consider psychological performance tests for use in assessing treatment effects. Although there are substantial areas of agreement among investigators on this issue, different perspectives clearly exist. In chapter 14, Ferris and colleagues advance the argument that tests used as treatment outcome measures should be as closely related as possible to the actual behavioral impairments in daily life that necessitated treatment. They outline a "face-valid" treatment assessment battery and identify other tests that are useful in selecting patients for study. The authors also describe a visuospatial recall test that maintains face validity but that is homologous to preclinical measures that are used to identify compounds with potential for treating cognitive disorders. A somewhat different approach to test selection is reflected in chapter 15 by Mohs and colleagues. In this case the strategy of the authors is to establish the sensitivity of performance tests to clinical change in AD by administering measures to patients at 6-month intervals as the disease progresses. They recommend several recall and recognition measures that are sensitive to clinical deterioration in AD and thus are presumably sensitive to clinical improvement resulting from drug treatment.

In chapter 16, Corkin and her colleagues describe a neuropsychological approach to assessing treatment effects in late-life dementing disorders. This perspective holds that measures should be selected on the basis of sensitivity to lesions in the specific neuroanatomical regions affected by the disorder under study or of sensitivity to neurochemical deficits known to occur in the disorder. The authors recommend an extensive treatment assessment battery composed of 27 separate tests. Readers may find the entire battery or various specific tests included in the battery to be of interest. Tests recommended include measures of attention, perception, memory, language, and praxis. Although the chapter focuses specifically on treatment assessment, it will also be of substantial interest to clinicians.

A perspective on test selection quite different from that provided by Corkin and her colleagues is presented in chapter 17 by Kaszniak and his colleagues. In this chapter the issue of test selection in treatment assessment is approached from the information-processing tradition within cognitive psychology. This approach holds that the effectiveness of cognitive processing can be measured by carefully controlling and manipulating information presented to the subject and by partitioning his or her response into different components that reflect different processes. This approach deserves careful consideration in treatment studies, because the paradigms described allow the investigator to examine very subtle effects of drugs on specific parameters of memory and other cognitive functions.

The final chapter, addressed to test selection in treatment assessment studies, is by Branconnier (chapter 18). Rather than representing a particular academic perspective on test selection, Branconnier discusses the advantages of a computerized test battery. Many of the tests described in previous chapters employ computerized administration and scoring procedures, but the battery described by Branconnier is an explorable, comprehensive battery that may be of interest to clinicians and clinical investigators.

In general, then, the following eight chapters provide the reader with specific recommendations concerning the selection of state-of-the-art psychometric instruments for use in assessing memory and other cognitive impairments in elderly individuals. Few tasks are more important in psychology and psychiatry today than understanding and developing effective treatments for the dementing disorders of late life. The continued development and refinement of clinical assessment instruments will greatly facilitate this task and hasten the day when the dementing disorders of late life will no longer be frightening realities, but simply memories.

Michael J. Gilewski and Elizabeth M. Zelinski

CHAPTER

11

Questionnaire Assessment of Memory Complaints

In this chapter, we critically review the questionnaires that have been used to assess memory complaints in older adults and recommend which are the most appropriate for both clinical and research applications. To document the external validity of memory complaint questionnaires, we review studies that have investigated the relationship between questionnaire scores and both performance on laboratory memory tests and memory complaints as assessed by other methods. We conclude with suggestions for the future development of questionnaires, focusing on the content and wording of items, the type of judgment required of the subject, scaling, and the number of dependent measures.

Memory complaints are thought to reflect the memory problems that people experience in everyday life. This chapter focuses on questionnaires designed to measure a person's assessment of his or her own memory functioning in everyday situations. Self-assessment of memory complaints is important for a number of reasons.

First, there is evidence for a reliable correlation between memory complaints and performance on laboratory memory tests among the community-dwelling elderly (Riege, 1982; Zelinski, Gilewski, & Thompson, 1980). Older people who report more memory problems often perform worse on memory tests than do people who report fewer problems. Second, memory complaints provide valuable information for detecting dementia. Reisberg et al. (chapter 12, this volume) found an interaction between impairment and complaints. At all levels of impairment as measured by the Global Deterioration Scale, relatives' judgments correlated well with patients' scores on the scale. For patients with mild or no impairment, there was a strong relationship between patients' self-reports and spouses' reports of memory problems, but at more severe impairment levels, patients tended to overestimate their memory abilities. Thus, the discrepancy between patients' self-assessments and actual performance as judged by more objective observers may be a factor in differentiating a pathological process from normal aging. In addition, patients' complaints may be early warning signs of developing problems. As Erickson and Howieson (chapter 8) indicate, memory changes may be incipient without being measurable by memory tests. Longitudinal follow-up to complaints can thus serve as a useful index in detecting cognitive deterioration.

Third, self-reports of memory can be useful in differentiating depression and dementia. Depressed people tend to complain about their memories even though they have no performance deficits, whereas patients with dementia overestimate their memory ability on self-report instruments. Thus, comparing memory complaints and memory performance can be important in differentiating depression and dementia in old age.

Fourth, memory complaints are important phenomena in their own right. Complaints provide useful information about how people view their general cognitive functioning as they age. Their perception of their memory capabilities may influence their performance on memory tasks (Poon, Fozard, & Treat, 1978). Therefore, it is useful to have self-assessment data to control for this influence. Finally, for many older people, memory questionnaires appear to be less threatening than laboratory tests, and the greater face validity of questionnaires compared with memory tests may increase cooperation during assessment.

Choosing the appropriate questionnaire with which to assess elderly adults becomes a critical decision because there are so many reasons for obtaining self-reports of memory functioning. In this chapter, we review 10 memory complaint questionnaires, discuss the external validity of them, and make suggestions for

This research was supported in part by National Institute on Aging research grant 1 R01 AG4114 awarded to Elizabeth Zelinski.

selecting the most appropriate instrument for a community-dwelling population. We conclude with recommendations for future development of questionnaires.

Review of Questionnaires

Since the late 1970s, a number of questionnaires to assess memory complaints have been developed, and most of them have been reviewed by Herrmann (1982). We focus here on 10 questionnaires that have been employed in studies with elderly subjects. Table 11-1 outlines the features of these questionnaires. They have been divided into two categories: (a) questionnaires for which no psychometric properties (i.e., factor structure, reliability, and validity) have been examined and (b) questionnaires for which at least some psychometric properties have been examined. Cunningham (chapter 4) elaborates on the necessity of establishing adequate validity and reliability for all

assessment instruments. Our treatment of questionnaires with no examined psychometric properties reflect the importance of investigating such properties. We describe such questionnaires but do not recommend them for widespread use in assessing memory complaints in the elderly.

Additional criteria we consider important for evaluating a questionnaire for clinical or research use include the number and types of items, the availability of a published version of the questionnaire, the suitability of dependent measures for a clinical or research situation, the availability and adequacy of norms for older adults, and the utility of the instrument for assessing an older adult population. Although we judge certain characteristics as strengths or weaknesses, the person using a particular instrument must make the final determination of its usefulness. For instance, although we may determine that a certain instrument has too few items to assess memory complaints adequately, in some situations, such as when a screening

Table 11-1. Descriptive Features of Ten Memory Assessment Questionnaires

Author(s)	Questionnaire	Number of Items	Items Published?	Scaling	Dependent measure(s)
Psychometric properties not examined					
Perlmutter (1978)	Memory Questionnaire	60	Yes	4 & 10 pts.	5 composite scores
Zarit et al. (1981)	Memory Complaints Questionnaire	12	No	3–11 pts.	Total score
Niederehe et al. (1981)	Metamemory Questionnaire	134	No	varies	—
Hulicka (1982)	Self-Assessment of Memory Questionnaire	45+	No	—	Total score
Psychometric properties examined					
Herrmann & Neisser (1978) and	Inventory of Memory Experiences (IME)	72	Yes	7 pt.	Part F: 8 factor scores & total score Part R: 3 section scores
Herrmann (1979)	Short Inventory of Memory Experiences (SIME)	32	No	7 pt.	Part F: 8 factor scores Part R: 2 section scores
Zelinski et al. (1980) and	Metamemory Questionnaire	92	Yes	7 pt.	9 scale scores
Gilewski et al. (1983)	Memory Functioning Questionnaire (MFQ)	64	No	7 pt.	7 scale scores
Goldberg et al. (1981)	Wadsworth Memory Questionnaire (WMQ)	35	No	5 pt.	—
Riege (1982)	Memory Self Report	30	Yes	4 pt.	4 category scores
Sunderland et al. (1983)	Everyday Memory Questionnaire	35	Yes	5 pt.	Total score
Dixon & Hultsch (1983b)	Metamemory in Adulthood	120	No	5 pt.	8 factor scores

instrument must be administered to hundreds of patients, brevity may be the most important consideration. Therefore, in addition to our recommendations, needs in a particular research or clinical setting must be taken into account.

Questionnaires for Which Psychometric Properties Have Not Been Examined

Perlmutter's Memory Questionnaire. Perlmutter (1978) was the first to publish a self-report questionnaire on memory for use with the elderly. Her Memory Questionnaire consists of 60 items, summarized by five composite scores, one for each of the following categories: memory problems, memory demands, expectation of memory change with age, use of memory strategies, and memory knowledge. Table 11-2 lists several sample items. Perlmutter has published only the one study on the Memory Questionnaire, although she has included some of the instrument's questions in two other studies (Perlmutter, 1979; Perlmutter, Metzger, Nezworski, & Miller, 1981).

As the first questionnaire designed specifically for the elderly, Perlmutter's instrument has served as a prototype for subsequently developed questionnaires. For example, Niederehe, Nielsen-Collins, Volpendesta, and Woods (1981) drew from Perlmutter's items in developing their own instrument. Nevertheless, Perlmutter's Memory Questionnaire has some serious drawbacks: There is no published information on scoring procedures; the composite scores are based on varying numbers of items, ranging from one item (memory demands) to 40 items (memory problems) (M. Perlmutter, personal communication, September 13, 1983); and no one has examined the instrument's psychometric properties. Finally, Perlmutter does not expect any further development or use of the questionnaire.

Table 11-2. Sample Items From Perlmutter's Memory Questionnaire

Category	Sample item
Memory problems	11. How often do you forget names?
Memory demands	3. How often in your daily activities do you need to rely on your memory?
Expectation of memory change with age	43. Do you think your memory will get worse when you get older?
Use of memory strategies	16. How often do you write reminder notes?
Memory knowledge	49. Do you find it easier to remember organized things than unorganized things?

Note. Reprinted from Perlmutter (1978) by permission.

Zarit et al.'s Memory Complaints Questionnaire. Zarit and his colleagues (Zarit, 1982; Zarit, Cole, & Guider, 1981; Zarit, Gallagher, & Kramer, 1981) developed a clinically oriented questionnaire for assessing memory complaints. Their Memory Complaints Questionnaire is based on Kahn, Zarit, Hilbert, and Niederehe's (1975) clinical interview. The questionnaire's 12 items are presented in Table 11-3. Three kinds of scales are used: 3-point scales ranging from 0 to 2, 4-point scales ranging from -1 to $+2$, and 11-point scales ranging from 0% to 100%. To calculate the total score, item 11 is reduced from an 11- to a 3-point scale, and then the first 11 items are summed. Higher scores reflect more complaints.

This instrument is the briefest formal questionnaire designed for use with the elderly and is probably most useful when a brief index of memory complaints is needed. Another benefit is that in several studies with community-dwelling elderly subjects, Zarit and his colleagues (Orr, 1983; Zarit, 1982; Zarit, Cole, & Guider, 1981; Zarit, Gallagher, & Kramer, 1981) have exam-

Table 11-3. Zarit et al.'s Memory Complaints Questionnaire

1. Do you have any trouble with your memory?

2. Has your memory changed since you were younger?

3. Do you have trouble remembering things that happened a few minutes ago?

4. Do you have trouble remembering things that happened a few days ago?

5. Do you have trouble remembering things that happened many years ago?

6. Which would you say you remember better, things that happened in the past or things that happened recently?

7. How do you find out that you have forgotten something?

8. Do you have any trouble remembering any of the following? (six situations, such as trying to recall someone's name).

9. Compared to other people your age, how would you rate your memory?

10. How do you react when you forget something?

11. If 100% indicated a perfect memory and 0% a terrible memory, what percent would you score *your memory?*

12. What score would you have given your memory when you were younger, say in the 20s or 30s?

Note. Reprinted from an unpublished questionnaire (Zarit et al., 1981) by permission.

ined the relationships between memory complaints as measured by this questionnaire and depression, memory performance, and the effects of memory training.

However, there are weaknesses in the instrument. First, there is no information on its reliability. Second, there is no rationale for the inclusion of the particular items in the questionnaire. Although the items appear to sample different aspects of everyday memory functioning, with only 12 items it is likely that specific memory problems will be missed. Third, each item is so general as to be ambiguous and open to different interpretations. If this is the case, a total score will not be representative of the items, and the use of a total score may lead to misleading results. It is also unclear whether all items measure the same construct, because the internal structure of the questionnaire has not been investigated. Finally, the 3-point scales used with most of the items in the questionnaire restrict the variance of responses, which may also lead to misleading results.

Because of the instrument's brevity and its utility for an older population, the Memory Complaints Questionnaire could be an important contribution to the field, pending further psychometric development (e.g., obtaining test–retest reliability, examining internal consistency and testing for unidimensionality, and correlating the questionnaire with a more comprehensive self-report instrument). A brief, reliable index of memory complaints would satisfy a critical need for many clinical and research situations.

Niederehe et al.'s Metamemory Questionnaire. Niederehe et al. (1981) developed the Metamemory Questionnaire, sample items of which are given in Table 11-4. The questionnaire consists of 134 items tapping the following areas: (a) general problems and concerns; (b) circumstances surrounding memory difficulties, such as when and where the difficulties occur; (c) metamemory knowledge; (d) use of strategies; (e) beliefs about age-related changes in memory; and (f) the personal significance attached to memory. The questionnaire is designed as an interview, but it can be self-administered.

This instrument is probably one of the most comprehensive developed to assess everyday memory functioning and metamemory. The open-ended questions throughout the questionnaire elicit considerable qualitative information, which may be desirable in certain clinical settings. But the instrument's strengths—its length and the inclusion of open-ended items—can also be considered weaknesses. A long questionnaire may be impractical in some research endeavors, especially if memory complaints are only one aspect of a study. Also, the questionnaire does not lend itself to quantification. Although Likert-scale ratings are required on some items, relying on these items alone would result in incomplete information. Therefore, the only way to evaluate group differences is to analyze data item by item. This problem alone makes the Metamemory Questionnaire inappropriate for most research purposes. In sum, although this questionnaire is unsuitable for research in its present state of development, it holds promise for effective use in certain clinical situations.

Table 11-4. Sample Items From Niederehe et al.'s Metamemory Questionnaire

Category	Sample item
General problems	1. Do you have problems (troubles, difficulties) with your memory? (Yes/No) What kind of troubles do you have? (open-ended response)
Circumstances of difficulties	12. How often do you have difficulty remembering any of the following things? (17 possibilities, such as people's names, with rating on a 5-point scale)
Metamemory knowledge	19. In your experience, which item in the following pairs is *easier* to remember? (10 pairs such as "organized things or unorganized things")
Strategy use	21. In order to help yourself remember something later on, how often do you use any of the following *methods?* (11 methods, such as "writing yourself reminder notes," with rating on a 4-point scale)
Beliefs about memory and age	36. Do you think people's memory generally changes as they get older? (Yes/No) How? (open-ended response)
Personal significance of memory	54. What would it (or does it) *mean* for you if your memory were to become weak? (open-ended response)

Note. Reprinted from an unpublished interview/questionnaire (Niederehe et al., 1981) by permission.

Hulicka's Self-Assessment of Memory Questionnaire. Hulicka (1982) reported pilot work using a questionnaire including more than 45 items. Sample items are not available. The questionnaire focuses on (a) present memory for 17 categories of memory items, such as appointments and names; (b) whether a person had difficulty remembering, at least twice in the past year, any of 16 events, such as appointments or what someone said; (c) overall memory efficiency; (d) overall current memory efficiency compared with that of the same person 5 to 10 years ago, that of the average person, that of the average young adult, and that of the average same-aged person; and (e) signs of memory problems, such as having trouble keeping the memory of two or more events distinct or taking longer to remember. A total score is obtained. No technical data have been reported, so there is insufficient information to evaluate this instrument, and we do not recommend its use.

Questionnaires for Which Psychometric Properties Have Been Examined

In this section we focus on questionnaires for which psychometric properties have been evaluated. Table 11-5 summarizes the psychometric investigations of these questionnaires.

Herrmann and Neisser's Inventory of Memory Experiences. Herrmann and Neisser (1978) standardized their Inventory of Memory Experiences (IME) on 205 undergraduate students. The questionnaire is divided into two sections: Part F, which includes 48 items concerning frequency of forgetting, and Part R, comprising 24 items tapping various aspects of remembering. Table 11-6 presents sample items from both parts. Part F items measure how often forgetting occurs, using a 7-point scale ranging from *always* to *never*. The authors originally assumed that Part F measures eight abilities. However, in a principal components analysis of data from the undergraduates, they identified eight factors that were different from the a priori categories and did not correspond well to the hypothesized structure.

In some instances, items from different a priori factors loaded on the same principal component. For instance, the Absentmindedness component consisted of two items from the a priori category of absentmindedness, four items from forgetting of intentions, and one from conversations. Also, several items from the a priori category of absentmindedness loaded either on another factor (one item on People), on more than one factor (one item on both Absentmindedness and Places), or not on any factor (two items). The eight principal components obtained were Rote Memory, Absentmindedness, Names, People, Conversations, Errands, Retrieval, and Places. Scores are calculated for each a posteriori factor and for the total Part F. In a short-term longitudinal follow-up 4 to 5 months later, 41 of the undergraduates were retested with the IME. Test–retest reliabilities of the items ranged between .15 and .74, with a median of .49. The reliability for the total Part F score was .68.

Part R of the IME is divided into three categories of eight questions each: recall of childhood experiences; memory for specific past events, such as the last time one went to the doctor; and use of memory in conversa-

Table 11-5. Psychometric Properties of Six Memory Assessment Questionnaires

Questionnaire	n (Age range)	Factor analysis	Reliability	Reported use with older adults
Inventory of Memory Experiences (Herrmann & Neisser, 1978) and Short Inventory of Memory Experiences (Herrmann, 1979)	205 (undergraduates)	Part F: 8 principal components	.15–.74 test–retest (items)	Cordoni (1981) Goldberg et al. (1981) Tenny (1982) Chaffin & Herrmann (1983)
Metamemory Questionnaire (Zelinski et al., 1980) and Memory Functioning Questionnaire (Gilewski et al., 1983)	903 (16–89)	3 common factors	.82–.93 internal consistency (scales) .22–.64 test–retest (scales)	Zelinski et al. (1980) Popkin et al. (1982) Gilewski (1983) Gilewski et al. (1983) Lott & Scogin (1983)
Wadsworth Memory Questionnaire (Goldberg et al., 1981)	123 (51+)	6 common factors	—	Goldberg et al. (1981)
Memory Self-Report (Riege, 1982)	60 (21–84)	4 clusters	.80 (interrater)	Riege (1982)
Everyday Memory Questionnaire (Sunderland et al., 1983)	102 (16–65)	Unidimensional construct	—	Harris & Sunderland (1981) Rabbitt (1982)
Metamemory in Adulthood (Dixon & Hultsch, 1983b)	378 (18–81)	9 correlated factors	Internal consistency .61–.91 (7 scales) .28–.76 (activity scale)	Dixon & Hultsch (1983a, 1983b)

Table 11-6. Sample Items From Herrmann and Neisser's Inventory of Memory Experiences

Factor	Sample item	Factor	Sample item
	Part F		Part F
1. Rote Memory	45. Think of times when you have called somebody on the phone, using a phone number that you have called several times before. How often do you find that you must *look the number up again* because you don't remember it?	7. Retrieval	48. How often when someone mentions a name that sounds familiar to you (it "rings a bell"), do you find that you cannot identify it; that is, you can't say who the name belongs to, or why it seems familiar?
2. Absentmindedness	18. How often are you unable to find something that you put down only a few minutes before?	8. Places	8. Suppose you were going back to some place (such as a friend's house) where you have been only once before. Would you have to ask for directions?
3. Names	7. How often do you find that just when you want to introduce someone you know to someone else, you can't think of their name?		
			Part R
4. People	39. When you are in a restaurant and want to speak to your waiter or waitress, how often do you forget what he or she looked like (so you don't know which waiter or waitress to call)?	R-1. Childhood memory	1. Do you remember any *toys* that you had as a young child? (Don't count any toys you have kept until now.) Think of whatever toy you remember best. How well do you remember what it was like?
5. Conversations	28. When you are telling someone a joke or a story, how often do you forget the punch line or ending before you get to it?	R-2. Memory for personal events	9. Do you remember the last time you went to see a doctor? About how long ago was it? How well do you remember that time?
6. Errands	3. If you go to the supermarket to buy four or five things (without a written shopping list), how often do you forget at least one of them?	R-3. Memory in conversations	18. When you or your friends have seen the same movie or TV shows, do you ever talk about it afterwards? If you do, how well do you remember the show?

Note. These sample items are also items from the shortened SIME, except R-3, which has been dropped from the SIME. Reprinted from Herrmann and Neisser (1978) by permission. Copyright Academic Press Inc. (London) Ltd.

tions. Each item is rated on a 7-point scale ranging from *not at all* to *perfectly*. Herrmann and Neisser (1978) reported a reliability of .46 for Section R-1 (Childhood Memory) and a reliability of .47 for Section R-3 (Memory in Conversations). They did not report a reliability estimate for Section R-2 (Memory for Personal Events), nor did they report the factor analysis of Part R, because the "results were not particularly illuminating" (p. 40). Herrmann (1979) developed a shortened version of the questionnaire, the Shortened Inventory of Memory Experiences (SIME), with three questions for each factor from Part F and four items each from Sections R-1 and R-3.

Four studies have reported use of the IME or SIME with older adults, and three of these have examined differences between younger and older age groups. Cordoni (1981) administered a modified IME to young, middle-aged, and old adults and failed to obtain age differences on any of the questionnaire's dependent measures. Cordoni also factor-analyzed Part F for both young and old adults. Although the same number of factors was extracted in each of the two groups, the factor structure was different in the two groups. Also, the factor structure in Cordoni's young group did not match the factor structure for Herrmann and Neisser's (1978) young subjects.

Chaffin and Herrmann (1983) investigated age differences with the SIME, and Tenny (1982) investigated age differences using only the 10-item absentmindedness scale. In both studies, young subjects reported having somewhat better memories than did the old subjects on some items, and old subjects reported having somewhat better memories than did the young subjects on others. Overall, there were no age differences in memory complaints, which is contrary to findings in other studies, as we discuss later.

One benefit of using the IME and SIME is the number of studies, most involving younger people, with which results can be compared (Chaffin & Herrmann, 1983; Crovitz, 1982; Herrmann, 1979; Herrmann & Neisser, 1978; Shlechter & Herrmann, 1981; Shlechter, Herrmann, Rubenfeld, Stronach, & Zenker, 1982). Despite wide use of the instrument, it has two major drawbacks. First, the factor structure is unstable across samples and across age groups. Second, the IME and SIME were not developed specifically for an older adult population, and the items tend to tap the kinds of memory failures that are universal to all age groups, such as calling someone by the wrong name. Despite the apparent universality of the items, results indicate that neither version addresses the particular kinds of memory problems older people report as increasing with age.

Zelinski et al.'s Metamemory Questionnaire. Zelinski et al. (1980) published a 92-item questionnaire, with nine a priori scale scores: general rating, reliance on memory, retrospective functioning, frequency of forgetting, frequency of forgetting when reading, remembering past events, seriousness, mnemonics usage, and effort made to remember. Sample items from this questionnaire can be seen in Table 11-7. All items are rated on 7-point Likert scales, with higher scores indicating a more positive self-evaluation of memory. A study of the questionnaire's internal consistency reported Cronbach's alphas for the scales ranging from .82 to .93 for 639 adults ranging in age from 16 to 89 (Gilewski, Zelinski, Schaie, & Thompson, 1983). A similar range for alpha was obtained with a sample of 196 people (Gilewski, 1983). Thus, sample size was not responsible for the robust alphas. Test–retest reliabilities of the scales over a 3-year period ranged from .22 to .64.

A factor analysis of the items (Gilewski et al., 1983) yielded three correlated common factors: frequency of forgetting, seriousness, and mnemonics/retrospective functioning. The factor analysis permitted a reduction of the questionnaire from 92 to 64 items, and the abbreviated version was renamed the Memory Functioning Questionnaire, or MFQ. The factor structure of the seven a priori MFQ scale scores was replicated in a young group (ages 29–39) and an old-old group (ages 71+). In a young-old group (ages 55–70), three different factors emerged: frequency of forgetting, general rating, and mnemonics usage. The retrospective and seriousness scales did not load on any of the three factors.

The Metamemory Questionnaire has several advantages over other questionnaires. Investigation of its

Table 11-7. Sample Items From Zelinski et al.'s Metamemory Questionnaire

Scale	Sample item
1. General rating	1. How would you rate your memory in terms of the kinds of problems you have?
2. Reliance on memory	2. How often do you need to rely on your memory without the use of remembering techniques, such as making lists, when you are engaged in . . . (a) social activities?
3. Retrospective functioning	3. How is your memory compared to the way it was . . . (b) one year ago?
4. Frequency of forgetting	4. How often do these present a memory problem for you . . . (a) names?
5. Frequency of forgetting when reading	5. As you are reading a novel, how often do you have trouble remembering what you have read . . . (a) in the opening chapters once you have finished the book?
6. Remembering past events	6. How well do you remember things which occurred . . . (a) last month?
7. Seriousness	7. When you actually forget in these situations, how serious of a problem do you consider the memory failure to be . . . (a) names.
8. Mnemonics	9. How often do you use these techniques to remind yourself about things . . . (a) keep an appointment book.
9. Effort made to remember	10. How much effort do you usually have to make to remember in these situations . . . (a) names.

Note. These sample items are also on the shortened Memory Functioning Questionnaire (MFQ); the reliance and effort items, however, have been dropped from the MFQ. Reprinted from Zelinski et al. (1980) by permission of Lawrence Erlbaum Associates.

psychometric qualities has been as thorough as for any other memory self-report instrument. Furthermore, this questionnaire has been administered to more elderly adults than any other instrument, and normative data are based on extensive sampling. Studies in which this instrument has been used with the elderly have looked for correlations between self-reported memory functioning and depression, memory performance, and intelligence (Gilewski, 1983; Lott & Scogin, 1983; Popkin, Gallagher, Thompson, & Moore, 1982). Significant relationships have been found among depression, memory performance, and memory complaints.

Despite these advantages, the instrument has problems. First, because all analyses of internal structure have indicated multiple dimensions (Gilewski, Zelinski, & Thompson, 1978; Gilewski et al., 1983), we have always analyzed scale scores. The absence of a total score may be undesirable in some research projects. Another drawback may be the questionnaire's length. Even the shortened version may be too long for some assessment situations. A third weakness is that the factor structure of the MFQ is not the same for all age groups. This may pose problems for some research projects. In general, though, there are many advantages to using this instrument because of its extensive analysis of structure and reliability and its widespread use in an older adult population.

Goldberg et al.'s Wadsworth Memory Questionnaire. Goldberg et al. (1981) developed the 35-item Wadsworth Memory Questionnaire (WMQ) for adults over age 50. Factor analysis identified six common factors: (a) General Forgetting, (b) Distress, (c) Spatial Memory Problems, (d) Concentration and Problem Solving, (e) Social Situations, and (f) Disorientation. Each factor accounted for approximately equal variance (about 16%). Table 11-8 shows the item with the highest load-ing on each factor. All items are responses to the question "How often is this a problem for you?" Judgments are made on a 5-point scale ranging from *not at all* to *very much.*

The major benefits of this questionnaire are that it is brief and that all of the items relate directly to every-day experience. At present neither the questionnaire nor the results of the factor analysis have been published. Also, reliability of the instrument has not been reported, and there is no reported use of the instrument with younger adults. Even though the authors identified the factor structure, they never incorporated factor scores or other summary measures in their analyses. Rather, they reported results item by item. Although this questionnaire has benefits, because it is unpublished, its widespread use is unlikely, and public scientific evaluation of it is difficult.

Riege's Memory Self-Report Questionnaire. Riege (1982) devised the 30-item Memory Self-Report. Sample items are provided in Table 11-9. Items are rated on a 4-point scale ranging from *almost never* to *almost always.* Twenty of the items are scored and summarized into four category scores describing short-term, interference–delay, perceptual–spatial, and imaginal memory processes. The four categories each contain five questions. Interrater reliability was at least .80 for assigning the questions into the four categories. A cluster analysis also yielded the same four categories (W. H. Riege, personal ommunication, July 12, 1983).

The shortness of this questionnaire may be an asset, but the major benefit of the Memory Self-Report is that the categories identified may relate to specific types of laboratory tasks. Nevertheless, Riege (1982) did not test people completing the questionnaire on the laboratory memory tasks that matched the conceptual organization of the questions. Although the organization of the questionnaire seems promising, the utility of the conceptual organization is unknown. Another draw-

Table 11-8. Items With the Highest Factor Loadings From Goldberg et al.'s Wadsworth Memory Questionnaire

Factor	Item with highest loading
1. General forgetting	Are you finding it harder to remember where you put things?
2. Distress	Would you say that your memory problems cause you a great deal of distress?
3. Spatial memory problems	Do you become confused or lose direction when shopping, trying to find a bus stop, or looking for a street address?
4. Concentration/ problem solving	Does it seem to take more time lately to grasp the meaning of new ideas?
5. Social	Do you find it difficult paying attention to what someone is saying to you?
6. Disorientation	Have you often found yourself not knowing what time of day it is?

Note. Reprinted from unpublished questionnaire (Goldberg et al., 1981) by permission.

Table 11-9. Sample Items From Riege's Memory Self-Report

Memory category	Sample item
Short-term	10. If the telephone directory assistance gives you a number, can you dial it without writing it down?
Interference–delay	11. Can you shop for groceries without a list and not forget any item?
Perceptual–spatial	4. In a large department store do you usually remember which entrance you used?
Imaginal	9. In the dark can you distinguish between your car key and your house key?

Note. Reprinted from Riege (1982) by permission.

back is that little technical information, such as the results of the cluster analysis, has been published. There is also no information on test–retest reliability. Riege's instrument thus has several unique assets but is hampered by incomplete psychometric development.

Sunderland et al.'s Everyday Memory Questionnaire. Sunderland and his colleagues (Baddeley, Sunderland, & Harris, 1982; Sunderland, Harris, & Baddeley, 1983) developed the Everyday Memory Questionnaire, which consists of 35 items divided into 5 sections: (a) speech, (b) reading and writing, (c) faces and places, (d) actions, and (e) learning new things. Sample items are listed in Table 11-10. Each item is rated on a 5-point scale for the frequency of the situation's occurrence. The questionnaire was developed for use with a brain-injured population, but it has been used in two studies with older adults (Harris & Sunderland, 1981; Rabbitt, 1982).

A unique feature of this questionnaire is that it includes a series of parallel forms and can be administered as a checklist or as a questionnaire. On the checklist version, a person checks the frequency of each forgetting incident on a daily basis or as prescribed by the clinician or researcher. The questionnaire includes questionnaire and checklist forms for a relative to corroborate responses of the target person. This additional information is ideal when using the instrument with people whose self-reports might have questionable accuracy, such as older adults with dementia.

Sunderland et al. (1983) have examined some of the instrument's psychometric properties. They submitted the items from the different forms to multidimensional scaling and cluster analysis but could not identify any subgroups of items. Although they did not report esti-mates of internal consistency, they indicated that 77% of all the items had correlations greater than .30 with a total score. Given the apparent internal consistency and the absence of multiple dimensions, they concluded that the instrument measures a unidimensional construct.

Despite the advantages of the instrument, namely, alternate forms, brevity, and unidimensionality, it has questionable utility for an older adult population. Young subjects (ages 20–36) reported more memory failures than did two samples of older adults (ages 69–80 and 50–60) (Harris & Sunderland, 1981). These results are contrary to those obtained with instruments developed specifically for older adults. The source of this discrepancy needs to be identified before the Everyday Memory Questionnaire can be recommended for widespread use in an elderly population.

Dixon and Hultsch's Metamemory in Adulthood Questionnaire. Dixon and Hultsch (1983b) developed the 120-item Metamemory in Adulthood Questionnaire. Sample items from this instrument appear in Table 11-11. Each item is rated on a 5-point scale. The authors identified eight a priori scales: strategy use, knowledge of memory tasks, knowledge of memory

Table 11-10. Sample Items From Sunderland et al.'s Everyday Memory Questionnaire

Section	Sample item
A. Speech	1. Forgetting the names of friends or relatives or calling them by the wrong names.
B. Reading and writing	14. Forgetting the meanings of unusual words.
C. Faces and places	18. Forgetting where you have put something. Losing things around the house.
D. Actions	24. Forgetting to do some routine thing which you would normally do once or twice a day.
E. Learning new things	30. Unable to remember the name of someone you met for the first time recently.

Note. Reprinted from Sunderland et al. (1983) by permission.

Table 11-11. Sample Items From Dixon and Hultsch's Metamemory in Adulthood Questionnaire

Dimension	Sample item
1. Strategy	107. Do you write appointments on a calendar to help you remember them?
2. Task knowledge	1. For most people, facts that are interesting are easier to remember than facts that are not.
3. Knowledge of memory capacity	2. I am good at remembering names.
4. Perception of age change	17. The older I get the harder it is to remember things clearly.
5. Activities supportive of memory	72. How often do you read newspapers?
6. Anxiety and memory	9. I find it harder to remember things when I am upset.
7. Achievement motivation and memory	69. It's important that I am very accurate when remembering names of people.
8. Locus of control and memory	79. Even if I work on it my memory ability will go downhill.

Note. Reprinted from Dixon and Hultsch (1984) by permission.

capacity, perception of change in memory, activities supportive of memory, memory and anxiety, memory and achievement motivation, and locus of control in memory abilities. The internal consistency (Cronbach's alpha) of seven of the scales ranged between .61 and .91 across three samples (*n* = 378). For the activities scale, the alpha was smaller, ranging from .28 to .76 across the three samples. Dixon and Hultsch factor-analyzed their questionnaire and obtained nine correlated factors. Seven of the factors matched the a priori scales. The strategy scale, however, broke down into two factors: Retrieval and Physical Reminder.

The Metamemory in Adulthood Questionnaire has some positive features. It is probably as comprehensive as Niederehe et al.'s Metamemory Questionnaire, and, like the latter instrument, it taps metamemory. However, Dixon and Hultsch's instrument is unique in its attempt to measure personality factors as they relate to self-reported memory. The questionnaire was developed through a sequence of psychometric analyses. The authors began with 206 items and proceeded to examine content validity, internal consistency, and factor structure. Finally, they obtained estimates of internal consistency from three independent samples. Nevertheless, the thoroughness of the instrument may also be a weakness. In most research or clinical situations in which batteries of questionnaires or tests are administered, time constraints may not allow for the use of a lengthy instrument. In addition, test–retest reliability estimates need to be obtained, and an examination of factor structure in different age groups would determine more fully the utility of the questionnaire. In general, because of its comprehensiveness and extensive psychometric evaluation, Dixon and Hultsch's instrument is an asset to the field.

Summary

We have reviewed 10 questionnaires that have been used to assess memory complaints in the elderly. The psychometric properties of 6 have been investigated. Each questionnaire has advantages and disadvantages, and it is likely that the specific clinical or research setting will be the determining factor in deciding which instrument is the most appropriate to use. However, we can offer some guidelines for making that decision.

We generally do not recommend those instruments whose psychometric properties have not been examined. An exception is the Niederehe et al. Metamemory Questionnaire (1981), which could be employed as an in-depth interview when the benefits of obtaining extensive qualitative information far outweigh the disadvantage of unknown psychometric properties. Because it is brief, the Memory Complaints Questionnaire (Zarit, 1982; Zarit, Cole, & Guider, 1981; Zarit, Gallagher, & Kramer, 1981) is the most useful of the remaining questionnaires whose psychometric properties have not been investigated, but further development of the instrument is necessary.

The two questionnaires developed for younger adult populations are of questionable validity for an aged population. Researchers using the IME (Herrmann & Neisser, 1978) and SIME (Herrmann, 1979) and the Everyday Memory Questionnaire (Sunderland et al., 1983) with young and old age groups have found no age differences and no more complaints about memory among the young than among the old. This finding is contrary to results obtained with other questionnaires: Older adults generally report more memory complaints than do younger people. Chaffin and Herrmann (1983) and Harris and Sunderland (1981) hypothesized that complaints might be related to activity level: More active people might have more complaints than less active people, because their increased activity would result in more situations encountered in daily life and increased stress, both of which could negatively affect everyday remembering. Young people were compared with young-old and middle-aged adults, who were thought to be more active than old-old adults, but the same results were obtained—the young adults had more memory complaints than the older ones.

One possible source of this discrepancy is the way questions are phrased. For instance, Question 1 of Sunderland et al.'s Everyday Memory Questionnaire involves the frequency of "forgetting the names of friends or relatives or calling them by the wrong names." A comparable question on the IME is, "How often do you find that just when you want to introduce someone you know to someone else, you can't think of their name?" In fact, there are several questions about names on each of these two instruments. The other questionnaires generally have only one question each on names, and as can be seen in Table 11-12, the wording for name items is almost always more general on these other questionnaires than on the two questionnaires normed on younger adults. There is evidence that younger people think in more specific terms than do older people (see, e.g., Birren, 1969), and perhaps this observation can account for the discrepant results. Young adults would be expected to report more complaints than old adults when questions request specific information, and older adults would be expected to complain more when questions are general. However, this hypothesis has not been directly tested by having young and old adults respond to specific and general types of memory questions.

Another possibility is that the IME, SIME, and Everyday Memory questionnaires tap into memory failures that occur in people of all ages or failures that are more likely to be noticed by young adults, while ignoring the kinds of failures that are more likely to be reported in an older population. Regardless of the reason, results from these questionnaires do not generalize to an elderly population in the same way that results from other questionnaires in the field do. Until this discrepancy is resolved, we cannot recommend these two instruments for use with older adults.

Two questionnaires hold some promise, despite inadequate psychometric evaluation. Both the WMQ (Goldberg et al., 1981) and the Memory Self-Report (Riege,

Table 11-12. Items Assessing Forgetting of Names

Questionnaire	Item
Younger target population	
Everyday Memory Questionnaire	1. Forgetting the names of friends or relatives or calling them by the wrong names.
Inventory of Memory Experiences	7. How often do you find that just when you want to introduce someone you know to someone else, you can't think of their name?
Older target population	
Metamemory in Adulthood	2. I am good at remembering names.
Wadsworth Memory Questionnaire	Do you forget names of new people you meet, even after being introduced several times?
Metamemory Questionnaire (Niederehe et al.)	12. How often do you have difficulty remembering any of the following things . . . (a) names?
Memory Questionnaire	11. How often do you forget names?
Memory Complaints Questionnaire	8. Do you have trouble remembering any of the following . . . someone's name?
Metamemory Questionnaire (Zelinski et al.)	4. How often do these present a memory problem to you . . . (a) names?
Self-Assessment of Memory Questionnaire	No sample item available, but her item appears to be similar to those by Niederehe et al., Zarit et al., and Zelinski et al.
Memory Self-Report	No question on names

1982) are brief and have been developed specifically for use with older people. The conceptual organization of Riege's questionnaire is also promising as a means of built-in external validation, especially vis-à-vis laboratory memory tasks. Unfortunately, little technical information has been published on these instruments, and their reliability has not been established. Therefore, the disadvantages of these instruments may outweigh their advantages.

The two remaining questionnaires are probably the most applicable for general clinical and experimental use. The MFQ (Gilewski et al., 1983) and the Metamemory Questionnaire (Zelinski et al., 1980) have the following advantages: extensive investigation of internal structure and reliability, adequate norms,

and use with both clinical and nonclinical elderly populations. We recommend the shorter version, the MFQ, because its content was empirically derived from the parent Metamemory Questionnaire. One minor caveat is that the factor structure of the questionnaire in a young-old age group differed from the structure in younger and older age groups. However, this problem affects only the general rating, seriousness, and retrospective functioning scales. Another drawback in certain situations is that total scores have not been developed for the Metamemory Questionnaire and MFQ.

Dixon and Hultsch's (1983b) questionnaire has an advantage over the MFQ because it taps into aspects of metamemory beyond everyday memory complaints. Some research situations may require information on memory knowledge and knowledge of memory capacity. Also, in some clinical and research situations, the instrument's coverage of the relationship of memory functioning to personality variables may be desirable for a researcher who may be interested in the relationship between anxiety and memory complaints. Only Dixon and Hultsch's Metamemory in Adulthood Questionnaire contains items on this relationship. Drawbacks include the instrument's length and the lack of investigation of test–retest reliability and of factor structure across age groups. Also, this questionnaire has been employed in only one study other than the validation study (Dixon & Hultsch, 1983a).

External Validity of Memory Complaint Questionnaires

Given that there are questionnaires one can employ in a specific assessment situation, it is helpful to know what memory complaints relate to for purposes of external validation and identification of moderator variables. Several criteria have been used to validate self-reported memory functioning. The most frequently employed criterion is performance on memory tasks. The strongest reported relationships between complaints and performance are canonical correlations of .67 between a set of complaint variables and a set of performance measures (Riege, 1982; Zelinski et al., 1980). Hulicka (1982) also reported significant negative correlations between memory complaints and logical memory (as measured by the Wechsler Memory Scale), digit span recall, and free recall, but not between complaints and performance on a paired-associates task. Finally, Dixon and Hultsch (1983a) described significant relationships between self-reported memory and text recall.

Several studies investigating complaint–performance relationships have reported inconclusive or negative results. Kahn et al. (1975) found only 6 of 36 complaint–performance correlations to be significant. Perlmutter (1978) found only 2 of 10 correlations to be statistically reliable. In two studies, Zarit and his colleagues (Zarit, Cole, & Guider, 1981; Zarit, Gallagher, & Kramer, 1981) found only one significant correlation out of 23. When one of the authors of this chapter related self-reported memory functioning to memory performance, intelligence, and depression factors, only the relationship between self-report and depression was reliable (Gilewski, 1983). The source of discrepant findings may be in the tasks employed as measures of memory performance. Memory for texts (both stories and essays), nonverbal tasks, delayed tasks, and historical facts seems to have a reliable relationship with memory complaints. Recall of word lists and similar tasks involving immediate episodic memory are less likely to be related to memory complaints.

Other assessment techniques, such as diaries, can be external criteria for memory complaint questionnaires. Unfortunately, no studies of this kind have been conducted with elderly adults. Shlechter and Herrmann (1981) observed, in a college sample, a relationship between both open-ended and close-ended diary responses and the total score for the SIME. In open-ended diaries, people listed memory failures in a blank notebook, and in close-ended diaries, they responded to specific questions, such as how often they forgot names of people. There were no relationships between diary responses and the SIME factor scores, except when the questionnaire was administered after the diary was completed. In an adult, brain-injured population, Sunderland et al. (1983) found significant correlations among all four assessment methods: patient questionnaire, patient checklist, relative questionnaire, and relative checklist. All of these methods assessed the identified patient's everyday memory functioning. Thus, there may be a reliable relationship between different methods of assessing everyday memory in younger adults, but such a relationship has not been established in an older adult population.

Although they are not obvious external criteria for validation of memory complaints, two moderator variables demonstrate a reliable relationship with memory complaints. These variables are the relationship between memory complaints and depression and the differences in complaints at various stages of old age. Every study that has examined the relationship between depression and memory complaints in the elderly has found a significant one (e.g., Gilewski, 1983). More memory complaints are associated with higher levels of depression. Also, every study investigating memory complaints in young-old (ages 55–70) and old-old (ages 71+) adults has found age-group differences (see, e.g., Gilewski, 1983), although the nature of the differences varies across studies. In some instances, young-old adults report more complaints than do old-old ones, whereas in other instances, the old-old adults complain more. The complaint–depression relationship is discussed in the next section. The source of the age-group differences is not known, but similar age group differences are also found with other variables, such as memory performance (see Gilewski, 1983).

Recommendations for Future Development of Questionnaires

As a step toward establishing a second generation of questionnaires, researchers should examine several important issues arising from investigation of the current instruments. The first issue concerns the content, or dimensions, of the items in the questionnaires. Everyday memory is vast and complex. We researchers obviously cannot tap into every aspect of memory functioning, but we can focus either on one (e.g., frequency of forgetting) or on several dimensions. Both types of questionnaires are probably useful. Of all dimensions covered by the questionnaire items reviewed in this chapter, the most prevalent is frequency of forgetting. Table 11-13 lists the other dimensions and their relative frequencies among the questionnaires used with older adults. After frequency of forgetting, perceived change across time, or perception of differences in memory ability compared with other age groups, is clearly the second most frequent dimension among the questionnaires. This category also includes beliefs about memory and aging. The other dimensions are strategies and mnemonic usage, the only dimension that shows few or no age differences; seriousness, or personal significance, of memory failures; overall judgment of memory functioning; memory, or metamemory, knowledge; demands on memory in daily life; memory for past events; effort made when forgetting occurs; and the relationship of memory to personality traits. One future task, therefore, is to decide which and how many of these dimensions are most important to include in a questionnaire on everyday memory functioning.

Another issue involves the wording of items. Examination of how items are worded on the questionnaires reviewed here reveals that most are worded negatively (e.g., "How often do you forget such and such?" "How serious is it when you forget in this or that situation?"). Even when questions are worded more positively (e.g., "How good is your memory for people's names?"), it is clear that the response scale has a positive and a negative end point. And often the low and high ends of the scale remain positive or negative throughout an entire questionnaire.

As mentioned in the previous section, every study that has examined the relationship between depression and memory complaints in the elderly has found a significant, positive relationship. This relationship has been observed both when depressed and normal people are compared and within subjects, as depressed people improve over the course of treatment (see, e.g., Popkin et al., 1982). Significant relationships between the two factors have also been observed in community samples in which depression levels are subclinical.

It is widely known that depression and negative thinking are correlated (see, e.g., Beck, Rush, Shaw, & Emery, 1979). There are three situations that could account for the correlation between depression and memory complaints: (a) Depression is the result of interpreting events in negative ways, (b) negative thinking is secondary to depressed moods, or (c) both depression and negative cognitions are locked in a vicious cycle. Memory complaints or complaints in general would be secondary to negative thoughts and beliefs. Thus, it is important to realize when looking for complaints on our questionnaires that those who complain most, among whom are the depressed, will report the most complaints. Lott and Scogin (1983) recruited sub-

Table 11-13. Dimensions Tapped by Memory Questionnaires

Dimension	Questionnaire
Frequency of forgetting	(10) All
Change in memory over time/perceived differences between age groups	(8) Inventory of Memory Experiences, Memory Complaints Questionnaire, Memory Questionnaire, Metamemory in Adulthood, Metamemory Questionnaire (Niederehe et al.), Metamemory Questionnaire (Zelinski et al.), Self-Assessment of Memory Questionnaire, Wadsworth Memory Questionnaire
Seriousness of memory failures	(5) Inventory of Memory Experiences,[1] Memory Complaints Questionnaire, Metamemory Questionnaire (Niederehe et al.), Metamemory Questionnaire (Zelinski et al.), Wadsworth Memory Questionnaire
Strategies and mnemonics usage	(4) Memory Questionnaire, Metamemory in Adulthood, Metamemory Questionnaire (Niederehe et al.), Metamemory Questionnaire (Zelinski et al.)
Overall judgment of memory functioning	(4) Memory Complaints Questionnaire, Metamemory Questionnaire (Niederehe et al.), Metamemory Questionnaire (Zelinski et al.), Self-Assessment of Memory Questionnaire
Memory knowledge	(3) Memory Questionnaire, Metamemory in Adulthood, Metamemory Questionnaire (Niederehe et al.)
Demands on memory in daily life	(3) Memory Questionnaire, Metamemory Questionnaire (Niederehe et al.), Metamemory Questionnaire (Zelinski et al.)
Memory for past events	(2) Memory Complaints Questionnaire, Metamemory Questionnaire (Zelinski et al.)
Effort when forgetting occurs	(2) Inventory of Memory Experiences,[1] Metamemory Questionnaire (Zelinski et al.)
Relationship of memory to personality traits	(1) Metamemory in Adulthood

[1]Cordoni's (1981) adaptation of the Inventory of Memory Experiences.

jects in two ways: advertising for older people with memory complaints and advertising for older people who would participate in miscellaneous research projects. Although the groups did not differ in levels of self-reported depression or memory performance, the group who responded to the ad for people with complaints reported more complaints on the Metamemory Questionnaire (Zelinski et al., 1980).

If, on the other hand, we researchers want realistic estimates of people's everyday memory functioning, we need to alter how the questions are asked. We must control for social desirability in items, avoid response sets, and word questions so as to maximize accurate judgments. For instance, rather than simply asking an individual to rate on a scale from *always* to *never* how often he or she forgets car keys, we could ask the person how often he or she has forgotten them over the past month—namely, never, once, twice, three times, or four or more times.

The wording of questions also points back to the issue encountered when discussing the Herrmann and Neisser (1978) and the Sunderland et al. (1983) ques-

tionnaires. Employing very specific items may fail to yield age differences, but using more general ones often does yield age differences. At this time, it is unclear which type of questionnaire is the more appropriate assessment tool. However, sensitivity to age differences may be an important matter when considering some of the basic reasons for assessment of memory complaints in old age—differentiation of depression, dementia, and normal aging, and early detection of cognitive deterioration. To this end, ubiquitous complaints, like forgetting names at parties, are not as important as forgetting names in important social situations that lead to embarrassment and social withdrawal. There is a major difference between forgetting a name of a former classmate at a high school reunion and forgetting the name of one's own son or daughter who has come to visit.

Wording of questions leads to a third issue, namely, the type of judgments desired. Our sense is that we researchers have been trying to get at fairly accurate estimates of everyday memory functioning. We appear to be seeking an index of strengths and weaknesses on memory in daily life. Other types of judgments, however, may be just as important. One may consider it important to examine attitudes or beliefs about one's memory independent of actual memory problems. Attitudinal information could be covaried with judgments of frequency of forgetting to obtain more accurate self-reports. A third type of judgment is that provided by relatives and other judges who can view an individual's functioning from an external perspective. These judgments can be used to corroborate those of the client. Knowledge that other information will be available to compare with an individual's self-report may make those self-reports more reliable.

The fourth recommendation for future research involves scaling. To date, almost every questionnaire used with the aged has employed Likert scales ranging from 3 to 10 points, with 5- and 7-point scales the most frequent. There is no hard and fast rule about an ideal length, but 5 or 7 points generally provide sufficient variance for comparison with other variables.

Although Likert scales are adequate, they can be improved, especially if we desire accurate judgments. One way to improve them is to use behaviorally anchored rating scales that would make the scale judgment the same for everyone. Harris (1979), for example, has offered the ordinal frequency scale shown in Table 11-14. Another alternative is to employ the technique Lewinsohn and his colleagues (MacPhillamy & Lewinsohn, 1982; Teri & Lewinsohn, 1982) use with the Pleasant and Unpleasant Events Schedules. On their 3-point scales, each point is associated with a particular frequency. A zero means that the event has not been experienced in the past 30 days; a 1 refers to a few times, namely, 1 to 6 times in the past month; and finally, a 2 refers to often or seven or more times in the past month.

Finally, how many dependent measures should a questionnaire provide? One overall memory index? A subscore for each factor or dimension? Obviously, one score would be the most economical for relating self-reported memory functioning to other variables. Such a score might serve the same function as an IQ score. However, like intelligence, everyday memory functioning is multidimensional. No less than a profile of subscores could portray a person's memory functioning to any degree of accuracy. Nevertheless, a problem arises in relating subscores as a set to other variables. Only canonical correlation or regression of sets of variables can be used. Such analyses often demand more subjects than some research projects warrant. The number of scores is thus an issue that is not easily resolved, but it must be considered.

Conclusion

Because science is a social enterprise, researchers and clinicians need to help us collaborate to develop and evaluate assessment tools that will help us understand self-reported memory functioning in the elderly. Although we can employ some of the existing instruments in our research and clinical work, a second generation of questionnaires to assess memory self-reports is clearly a necessity.

Table 11-14. Harris Ordinal Frequency Scale

A. Never
B. About once in my life
C. More than once in my life but less than once a year
D. About once a year
E. More than once a year but less than once a month
F. About once a month
G. More than once a month but less than once a week
H. About once a week
I. More than once a week but less than once a day
J. About once a day
K. More than once a day

Note. Reprinted from Harris (1979) by permission.

References

Baddeley, A., Sunderland, A., & Harris, J. (1982). How well do laboratory-based psychological tests predict patients' performance outside the laboratory? In S. Corkin, K. L. Davis, J. H. Growdon, E. Usdin, & R. J. Wurtman (Eds.), *Alzheimer's disease: A report of progress in research* (pp. 141–148). New York: Raven Press.

Beck, A. T., Rush, A. J., Shaw, B. F., & Emery, G. (1979). *Cognitive therapy of depression.* New York: Guilford Press.

Birren, J. E. (1969). Age and decision strategies. In A. T. Welford & J. E. Birren (Eds.), *Interdisciplinary topics in gerontology: Vol. 4. Decision making and age* (pp. 23–36). New York: S. Karger.

Chaffin, R., & Herrmann, D. J. (1983). Self reports of memory performance by old and young adults. *Human Learning, 2,* 17–28.

Cordoni, C. N. (1981). Subjective perceptions of everyday memory failures. *Dissertation Abstracts International, 42,* 2047B. (University Microfilms No. 8121287)

Crovitz, H. F. (1982, November). *Towards measuring real-world forgetting in real time.* Paper presented at the meeting of the Psychonomic Society, Minneapolis, MN.

Dixon, R. A., & Hultsch, D. F. (1983a). Metamemory and memory for text relationships in adulthood: A cross-validation study. *Journal of Gerontology, 38,* 689–694.

Dixon, R. A., & Hultsch, D. F. (1983b). Structure and development of metamemory in adulthood. *Journal of Gerontology, 38,* 682–688.

Dixon, R. A., & Hultsch, D. F. (1984). The Metamemory in Adulthood (MIA) instrument. *Psychological Documents, 14,* 3.

Gilewski, M. J. (1983). Self-reported memory functioning in young-old and old-old age: Structural models of predictive factors (Doctoral dissertation, University of Southern California, 1983). *Dissertation Abstracts International, 43,* 4170B.

Gilewski, M. J., Zelinski, E. M., Schaie, K. W., & Thompson, L. W. (1983, August). *Abbreviating the Metamemory Questionnaire: Factor structure and norms for adults.* Paper presented at the meeting of the American Psychological Association, Anaheim, CA.

Gilewski, M. J., Zelinski, E. M., & Thompson, L. W. (1978, September). *Remembering forgetting: Age differences in metamemorial processes.* Paper presented at the meeting of the American Psychological Association, Toronto.

Goldberg, Z., Syndulko, K., Lemon, J., Montan, B., Ulmer, R., & Tourtellotte, W. W. (1981, August). *Everyday memory problems in older adults.* Paper presented at the meeting of the American Psychological Association, Los Angeles.

Harris, J. E. (1979, December). Everyday cognitive functioning: The need for assessment and some basic methodological issues. In J. E. Harris (Chair), *Assessment of cognitive functioning in everyday life.* Symposium conducted at the meeting of the British Psychological Society, London.

Harris, J. E., & Sunderland, A. (1981, September). *Effects of age and instruction on an everyday memory questionnaire.* Paper presented at a conference of the British Psychological Society, Cognitive Section on Memory, Plymouth, England.

Herrmann, D. J. (1979, December). *The validity of memory questionnaires as related to a theory of memory introspection.* Paper presented at the meeting of the British Psychological Society, London.

Herrmann, D. J. (1982). Know thy memory: The use of questionnaires to assess and study memory. *Psychological Bulletin, 92,* 434–452.

Herrmann, D. J., & Neisser, U. (1978). An inventory of everyday memory experiences. In M. M. Gruneberg, P. E. Morris, & R. N. Sykes (Eds.), *Practical aspects of memory* (pp. 35–51). New York: Academic Press.

Hulicka, I. M. (1982). Memory functioning in late adulthood. In F. I. M. Craik & S. Trehub (Eds.), *Advances in the study of communication and affect: Vol. 8. Aging and cognitive processes* (pp. 331–351). New York: Plenum Press.

Kahn, R. L., Zarit, S. H., Hilbert, N. M., & Niederehe, G. (1975). Memory complaint and impairment in the aged: The effect of depression and altered brain function. *Archives of General Psychiatry, 32,* 1569–1573.

Lott, C. L., & Scogin, F. (1983, November). *Relationship of memory complaint and memory performance.* Paper presented at the meeting of the Gerontological Society of America, San Francisco.

MacPhillamy, D. J., & Lewinsohn, P. M. (1982). The Pleasant Events Scale: Studies on reliability, validity, and scale intercorrelations. *Journal of Consulting and Clinical Psychology, 50,* 363–380.

Niederehe, G., Nielsen-Collins, K. E., Volpendesta, D., & Woods, A. M. (1981, November). *Metamemory processes and perceptions: Depression and age effects.* Paper presented at the meeting of the Gerontological Society of America, Toronto.

Orr, N. (1983). *Longitudinal change in memory performance and self-reports of memory problems in older adults.* Unpublished master's thesis, University of Southern California, Los Angeles.

Perlmutter, M. (1978). What is memory aging the aging of? *Developmental Psychology, 14,* 330–345.

Perlmutter, M. (1979). Age differences in adults' free recall, cued recall, and recognition. *Journal of Gerontology, 34,* 533–539.

Perlmutter, M., Metzger, R., Nezworski, T., & Miller, K. (1981). Spatial and temporal memory in 20 and 60 year olds. *Journal of Gerontology, 36,* 59–65.

Poon, L. W., Fozard, J. L., & Treat, N. J. (1978). From clinical and research findings on memory to intervention programs. *Experimental Aging Research, 4,* 235–253.

Popkin, S. J., Gallagher, D., Thompson, L. W., & Moore, M. (1982). Memory complaint and performance in normal and depressed older adults. *Experimental Aging Research, 8,* 141–145.

Rabbitt, P. M. A. (1982, January). *How good do you think you are?* Paper presented at the meeting of the Experimental Psychology Society, London.

Riege, W. H. (1982). Self-report and tests of memory aging. *Clinical Gerontologist, 1*(2), 23–36.

Shlechter, T. M., & Herrmann, D. J. (1981, April). *Multimethod approach to investigating everyday memory.* Paper presented at the meeting of the Eastern Psychological Association, New York.

Shlechter, T., Herrmann, D., Rubenfeld, L., Stronach, P., & Zenker, S. (1982, April). *An investigation of people's knowledge of their everyday memory abilities.* Paper presented at the meeting of the Eastern Psychological Association, Baltimore, MD.

Sunderland, A., Harris, J. E., & Baddeley, A. D. (1983). Do laboratory tests predict everyday memory? A neuropsychological study. *Journal of Verbal Learning and Verbal Behavior, 22,* 341–357.

Tenny, Y. V. (1982, August). Misplacing objects in the aged and the young. In T. M. Shlechter, D. J. Herrmann, & M. P. Toglia (Chairs), *A symposium on current trends in everyday memory research.* Symposium conducted at the meeting of the American Psychological Association, Washington, DC.

Teri, L., & Lewinsohn, P. (1982). Modification of the Pleasant and Unpleasant Events Schedules for use with the elderly. *Journal of Consulting and Clinical Psychology, 50,* 444–445.

Zarit, S. H. (1982). Affective correlates of self-reports about memory of older people. *International Journal of Behavioral Geriatrics, 1*(2), 25–34.

Zarit, S. H., Cole, K. D., & Guider, R. L. (1981). Memory training strategies and subjective complaints of memory in the aged. *Gerontologist, 21,* 158–164.

Zarit, S. H., Gallagher, D., & Kramer, N. (1981). Memory training in the community aged: Effects on depression, memory complaint, and memory performance. *Educational Gerontology, 6,* 11–27.

Zelinski, E. M., Gilewski, M. J., & Thompson, L. W. (1980). Do laboratory tests relate to self-assessment of memory ability in the young and old? In L. W. Poon, J. L. Fozard, L. S. Cermak, D. Arenberg, & L. W. Thompson (Eds.), *New directions in memory and aging: Proceedings of the George A. Talland Memorial Conference* (pp. 519–544). Hillsdale, NJ: Erlbaum.

Barry Reisberg, Steven H. Ferris, Jeffrey Borenstein, Elia Sinaiko, Mony J. de Leon, and Catherine Buttinger

CHAPTER

12

Assessment of Presenting Symptoms

The major mental disorders in the aged are associated with a few notable pathologic syndromes. Excellent, brief, standardized instruments have been available for several years for the assessment of all the major pathologic syndromes with the exception of cognitive impairment. In recent years, clinical instruments for the assessment of cognitive decline in Alzheimer's disease, and in other geriatric pathologies with cognitive concomitants, have been developed.

The rationale, validation, and utilitarian aspects of these clinical assessments, and their relationship to mental status and psychometric measures of cognitive dysfunction, are discussed. The relationship between these clinical assessments of cognitive pathology and the phenomenology of the disease processes that they are designed to measure are explored with particular reference to our recently acquired and rapidly expanding knowledge of Alzheimer's disease and other dementing or pseudodementing disorders of the senium.

Introduction

The major mental disorders of the aged are (a) Alzheimer's disease (AD) (referred to in the psychiatric nomenclature as primary degenerative dementia, American Psychiatric Association, 1980); (b) dementia associated with cerebrovascular accidents and multi-infarct dementia; (c) geriatric affective disorder and, in particular, involutional depression; (d) involutional psychoses; (e) idiopathic Parkinson's disease; (f) chronic schizophrenia; and (g) chronic toxic brain disease, especially associated with alcohol-induced brain disease. These disorders are associated with a few notable pathological behavioral syndromes. Specifically, these pathologic syndromes are cognitive dysfunction, depression and anxiety, psychosis, and the extrapyramidal syndrome.

The assessment of presenting symptomatology in each of these syndromes in the aged has been complicated by a variety of factors. These have included

(a) overlap among the various geriatric mental disorders with respect to symptomatology; (b) the absence of clinical description for some of the most important disorders presenting in the senium and, in some instances, a paucity of clinical knowledge with respect to the specific presentation mode in the elderly of the otherwise well-described disorders; and (c) the absence of any criteria for the description of some of the most severe and hence, paradoxically blatant, yet unquantifiable, symptom syndromes with which these patients are likely to present.

Each of the above issues has been most urgently represented in recent years with respect to the assessment of presenting symptomatology in the patient with AD. Nevertheless, despite the formidable epidemiologic dimensions of this important disorder of the senium, ignorance has traditionally been most apparent in this area. Hence, a constructive approach with respect to the resolution of some of the conundrums outlined above might begin with this traditionally very-difficult-to-assess entity and proceed outward to a discussion of the more general phenomena. Consequently, we shall begin with an overview of general assessment instrumentology for presenting symptoms in the elderly, and the traditional strengths and weaknesses of these instruments.

One major omission in these instruments was, as we shall discuss, in the area of cognition, an area of particular relevance, of course, with respect to efforts to develop useful assessments of AD symptomatology. Ideally, if such instruments were to be developed, they would need to be developed in such a way as to reflect the symptomatology in the disease entities they were

This work was supported in part by grants AG 03051 and AG 01344 from the National Institute on Aging and by grants MH 38275 and MH 29590 from the National Institute of Mental Health.

to be designed to measure. Hence, for example, the range of cognitive symptomatology assessed ideally should relate in some congruent way to the range of cognitive deterioration in the dementing disorders of the senium. Before such disorder-specific or disorder-relevant instruments could be developed, the global nature of pathology in the disorder, such as in AD, would need to be described. Once the global disease entity had been described, then more specific, and stage-specific, descriptions could be developed. Having accomplished these disorder-specific tasks, the relevance of traditional and more general, less disorder-specific instruments for assessment of the newly described disease entity could be reexamined. Conversely, the relevance of disorder-specific instruments for other geriatric mental disorders could be studied. It is this process, which has now been applied to AD and which has general relevance with respect to the presentation of geriatric mental syndromes, that will be described in some detail in this chapter.

Excellent, brief, standardized, and widely accepted clinical rating instruments for the assessment of the syndromes of depression and anxiety, psychosis, and the extrapyramidal syndrome have been in wide usage for many years. These include the Hamilton (1960) scale for depression and anxiety, the Brief Psychiatric Rating Scale (BPRS; Overall & Gorham, 1962) for psychosis, and the Simpson-Angus scale for extrapyramidal symptomatology (Simpson & Angus, 1970), among others. The assessment instruments just enumerated frequently serve not only in the evaluation of the respective behavioral pathological syndromes, but also as diagnostic tools. Hence, a Hamilton Depression Scale score of 18, or greater, clearly reveals the existence of a significant depression syndrome concomitant, and also serves to support a diagnosis of major affective disorder.

Instruments for the assessment of the syndrome of cognitive dysfunction in the elderly are less universally accepted at the present time. This is, in part, a result of the very recent awakening of scientific and medical knowledge and interest in the area of cognitive dysfunction in the elderly and, in part, a result of the severe limitations of many of the traditionally utilized assessments. Because cognitive dysfunction is perhaps the most frequently encountered behavioral pathologic syndrome in the elderly, it is fitting that the issues surrounding the clinical evaluation of this syndrome be explored in detail in this chapter. Inextricably interwoven issues with respect to the diagnosis and differential diagnosis of AD, the major illness causing cognitive impairment in the elderly, also require systematic discussion. The borderlands between AD and normal age-related cognitive functioning must be carefully described. Finally, the differential diagnosis of these disorders from geriatric depression and the other mental disorders of the senium that have been enumerated also requires systematic discussion.

A clinical diagnosis of AD is arrived at in precisely the same way as a clinical diagnosis of any other mental disorder—specifically, by reference to the unique onset, course, and clinical presentation of this disease entity.

The onset of AD is insidious. As is the case with other clinical illnesses with an insidious onset, family members may trace the origins to a specific event at a particular time that served to alert them to the illness process. Once aware of the illness, family members generally observe a gradually progressive process, although plateau periods are also noted.

The clinical course and presentation of AD have been described in detail only in the past few years. Until very recently the increases in medical understanding with respect to the pathophysiologic nature of AD were not accompanied by improved clinical understanding of the disorder. Indeed, a consensus conference, the proceedings of which were published in 1981 (Miller & Cohen, 1981), demonstrated that medical and scientific understanding of the clinical syndrome, in terms of phenomenology, progression, and prognosis, had not advanced notably since the descriptions of Rush (1793) and Esquirol (1838).

In this decade, however, the clinical manifestations of the illness have begun to be described in greater detail. For example, case histories of AD in its early, middle, and late stages were published in 1981 (Reisberg, 1981). More specifically defined stages of the illness process in terms of their clinical manifestations were described in 1982 (Reisberg, Ferris, de Leon, & Crook, 1982). The implications of these clinical, stage-specific, descriptions of normal aging and progressive Alzheimer's disease (PDD), in terms of the differential diagnosis of the major dementing disorders of the senium, were also described in 1982 (Reisberg & Ferris, 1982). Guidelines for physicians on the management of the illness process as it progresses were also published that year (Reisberg, 1982). Recently, preliminary prognostic concomitants of specific stages in the illness process were also described (Reisberg, Ferris, Shulman, et al., in press). Simultaneously, other laboratories have described in unprecedented detail some of the clinical processes associated with AD. For example, Mace and Rabins (1981) highlighted many of the management issues posed by the evolution of the disease process and, in particular, the impact of the illness upon the family constellation.

Hence, in the past few years, a comparatively large amount has been learned about the clinical syndrome of AD. Formerly, physicians diagnosed the illness strictly in terms of "what it was not" (i.e., in medical terminology, it was a diagnosis of exclusion). Presently, it is possible for physicians to diagnose this illness in the same fashion as all other illnesses (i.e., in terms of the unique onset, course, and presentation of the condition in its various stages, as it evolves). It is this unique process that we shall summarize in the following section. The subsequent sections will examine the impact of the recently acquired knowledge of the clinical concomitants of normal aging and AD on the utility of previously developed mental status and psychometric assessments. The final section will reevaluate the differential diagnosis of cognitive disorders in the elderly, taking into consideration the rapidly accruing new knowledge in the field.

I. Assessing the Stage of Cognitive Decline: Clinical Assessment Instruments

Assessing Global Clinical Symptomatology in Normal Aging and Alzheimer's Disease: The Global Deterioration Scale

The clinical symptomatology of persons with cognitive decline consistent with normal aging or with AD varies depending upon the magnitude or "stage" of cognitive impairment. Within each stage, symptomatology is fairly consistent. The global clinical characteristics of each stage of cognition in normal aged and in those with mild to severe AD can be seen in the Global Deterioration Scale (GDS) for age-associated cognitive decline and AD, which is summarized in Table 12-1.

Previous investigations have revealed strong, significant relationships between progressive decline on these global clinical parameters and independent behavioral, neuroradiologic, neurometabolic, and neuroimmunologic assessments in subjects with normal aging and progressive primary degenerative dementia (PDD) (de Leon et al., 1983; Ferris et al., 1980; Nandy, Reisberg, Ferris, & de Leon, 1981; Reisberg et al., 1982).

Initial prognostic concomitants of these global clinical stages of normal aging and AD in community-residing outpatients have also recently been published (Reisberg, Shulman, et. al., 1983). Longitudinal investigations of aging and dementia subgroups have continued in our laboratory, and more extensive prognos-

Table 12-1. Global Deterioration Scale (GDS) for Age-Associated Cognitive Decline and Alzheimer's Disease

GDS stage	Clinical phase	Clinical characteristics	Diagnosis
1 = No cognitive decline	Normal	No subjective complaints of memory deficit. No memory deficit evident on clinical interview.	Normal
2 = Very mild cognitive decline	Forgetfulness	Subjective complaints of memory deficits. No objective deficits in employment or social situations. Appropriate concern with respect to symptomatology.	Normal aged
3 = Mild cognitive decline	Early confusional	Earliest clear-cut deficits. Decreased performance in demanding employment and social settings. Objective evidence of memory deficit obtained only with an intensive interview. Mild to moderate anxiety accompanies symptoms.	Compatible with incipient Alzheimer's disease
4 = Moderate cognitive decline	Late confusional	Clear-cut deficit on careful clinical interview. Inability to perform complex tasks. Denial is dominant defense mechanism. Flattening of affect and withdrawal from challenging situations occur.	Mild Alzheimer's disease
5 = Moderately severe cognitive decline	Early dementia	Patients can no longer survive without some assistance. Patients are unable during interview to recall a major relevant aspect of their current lives. Persons at this stage retain knowledge of many major facts regarding themselves and others. They invariably know their own names and generally know their spouses and children's names. They require no assistance with toileting or eating, but may have some difficulty choosing the proper clothing to wear.	Moderate Alzheimer's disease
6 = Severe cognitive decline	Middle dementia	May occasionally forget the name of the spouse upon whom they are entirely dependent for survival. Will be largely unaware of all recent events and experiences in their lives. Will require some assistance with activities of daily living. Personality and emotional changes occur.	Moderately severe Alzheimer's disease
7 = Very severe cognitive decline	Late dementia	All verbal abilities are lost. Frequently there is no speech at all—only grunting. Incontinent of urine; requires assistance toileting and feeding. Loses basic psychomotor skills (e.g., ability to walk).	Severe Alzheimer's disease

Note. Reprinted from Reisberg, Ferris, de Leon, and Crook (1982) by permission. Copyright 1982 by the American Psychiatric Association.

Table 12-2. Aging and Dementia: Results of a Longitudinal Study of Community-Residing Subgroups

Clinical status at baseline	n	Age (Years: mean ± SD)	Sex	Follow-up interval (Days: mean ± SD)	Follow-up status[1]	Percentage with negative outcome
Forgetfulness phase (GDS = 2)	40	68.80 ± 5.29	21 M 19 F	1252 ± 151	40 Community residing 2 Clinically worsened[2] 38 Clinically unchanged	5.0
Early confusional phase (GDS = 3)	32	71.09 ± 6.79	16 M 16 F	1310 ± 181	30 Community residing 3 Clinically improved[2] 3 Clinically worsened[2] 24 Clinically unchanged 1 Institutionalized[3] 1 Deceased	15.6
Late confusional phase (GDS = 4)	22	72.32 ± 5.75	4 M 18 F	1342 ± 212	10 Community residing 4 Clinically worsened[2] 6 Clinically unchanged 6 Institutionalized[3] 6 Deceased	72.7
Early dementia phase (GDS = 5)	6	72.33 ± 7.37	3 M 3 F	1505 ± 242	3 Community residing 1 Clinically worsened[2] 2 Clinically unchanged 2 Institutionalized[3] 1 Deceased	66.7
Middle dementia phase (GDS = 6)	6	72.50 ± 3.83	5 M 1 F	1523 ± 201	0 Community residing 4 Institutionalized[3] 2 Deceased	100.0

Note. Adapted from Reisberg, Ferris, Anand, Buttinger, et al. (1984) by permission. Copyright 1984, American Psychiatric Association. Also adapted from Reisberg, Ferris, Shulman, et al. (in press) by permission.
[1]Negative outcome is defined as clinical worsening (i.e., an increase in GDS score of 2 or more), institutionalization, or death.
[2]Clinical change is defined as a change of 2 or more from GDS scores at baseline.
[3]In nursing homes.

tic data are presently available (see Table 12-2) (Reisberg, Ferris, Shulman, et. al., in press). Summarized, these investigations lead to the following conclusions:

1. Forgetfulness phase (GDS = 2), symptomatology in which there exist subjective complaints of cognitive decrement in the absence of clinically observable decrements in occupational or social functioning, appears to be benign. All 40 aged persons (mean age = 68.80 ± 5.29 yrs) with these symptoms remained alive and community functioning when followed up approximately 3½ years after the initial evaluation. Furthermore, only 5% demonstrated notable clinical deterioration (defined as a change of 2 points or greater on the 7-rating-point GDS, in order to make any judgment of change a conservative one) in cognitive functioning. The subjective deficits in this stage are characteristic. Elderly persons complain of no longer remembering names as well as formerly and of forgetting names that previously were well known to them. Frequently there are also complaints of inability to recall where one has placed familiar objects. The mild subjective symptomatology of the forgetfulness phase is accompanied by an increase in concern or anxiety in the patient. This anxiety is voiced by the patient (i.e., it is subjective); however, it is not manifest in a clinically overt manner.

2. The early confusional phase (GDS = 3), in which there occur the earliest clear-cut, clinically evident deficits in occupational and social functioning, appears to represent a borderline condition between normal aging and AD. Although the great majority of aged persons with these symptoms do not demonstrate further decline over an interval of approximately 3½ years, 6% of 32 individuals whom we followed at this stage (mean age at baseline = 71.09 ± 6.79 yrs) did worsen sufficiently to result in institutionalization or even death. Another 9% demonstrated notable clinical worsening (defined as stated above) over the follow-up interval.

Deficits become manifest in this stage in various ways. If the patient is engaged in a white-collar or similarly demanding occupation in terms of cognitive demands, then co-workers frequently become aware of the patient's relatively poor performance. In the early confusional phase, overt word-finding difficulties occur, and these deficits become evident to spouses and other intimates. Occasionally in this phase, the patient's verbalizations are interrupted intermittently as the patient gropes for the proper word. Mild stuttering may also occur on occasion. Persons at this stage may display decreased ability to handle complex tasks, and hence they may have become hopelessly lost when traveling to an unfamiliar location or may misplace objects of value, such as financial documents, or forget important appointments. Similarly, they may read a passage of a book and retain relatively little material and show demonstrably poor performance on concentration and calculation tasks. Decreased abilities in the performance of complex psychomotor tasks, such as sailing, or complex constructional tasks may also occur. Because these kinds of complex motor abilities are not necessarily a part of modern, everyday life, psychomotor deficits may not be noted by either patient or spouse at this phase.

In the early confusional phase, the stresses and demands of a life-style that the patient is no longer capable of successfully fulfilling frequently result in overt anxiety manifestations. The latter may be evident to the patient's spouse.

In general, the patients' reported awareness of their memory deficits tends to peak in this stage (Reisberg, Gordon, McCarthy, Ferris, & de Leon, 1985) (Figure 12-1). Spouses' awareness of memory problems in the patients tends not to differ markedly from the patients' assessments at this stage. Patients and their spouses experience some emotional problems as a result of the patients' memory difficulties. However, increased irritability and shame are transient phenomena that patients are able to suppress at this phase.

3. If we operationalize the clinical definition of AD and define it as beginning at the stage from which a majority of individuals demonstrate notable negative outcomes over a specified interval, and if, for convenience, we specify that interval as being approximately 3½ years, then the late confusional phase (GDS = 4) represents the earliest stage of AD. This stage can be defined succinctly for clinicians in terms of the functional deficit. Specifically, this is the stage in which individuals begin to manifest difficulties in marketing and in handling their finances. All of these subjects have declined notably from their premorbid level of functioning. None of these patients regain their former cognitive abilities. However, after an interval of approximately 3½ years, 27% of the 22 patients whom we followed at this stage (mean age at baseline = 72.32 ± 5.75 yrs) were not notably worse clinically, while 18% were notably worse but still resided in the community. Our results indicated that 27% were deceased.

Hence, more than two thirds of persons whom we followed at this stage demonstrated negative outcomes over the follow-up interval. Subjects at this stage were significantly more likely to be institutionalized ($p < .01$) and significantly more likely to be deceased ($p < .01$) than were subjects at either the forgetfulness phase (GDS = 2) or the early confusional phase (GDS = 3). For the subgroup of subjects who remained in the community, clinically notable deterioration (GDS change $\geq$ 2) was also significantly more likely at this stage than in subjects who were in the forgetfulness phase ($p < .01$) or the early confusional phase ($p < .05$).

Patients at this stage demonstrate decreased knowledge of current and recent events, although they are likely to recall such major aspects of their personal lives as their correct current address, such major aspects of their present activities as the current weather conditions, and such major aspects of public life as the name of the current president. However, they may not be able to recall their correct current telephone number or area code, their correct current postal code, the names of their grandchildren, the names of important business associates, or the names of important, and very well-known, public personages. Memory with respect to their personal past as well as with respect to major past events also suffers at this stage. This is frequently demonstrated by the finding that spouses recall more about the patients' past life than they recall about their own lives.

Concentration and calculation ability generally suffers to such an extent at this stage that a deficit is frequently elicited if the clinician asks the patient to subtract serial 4s from 40. Most patients at this stage, however, can perform the simple task of subtracting serial 2s from 20 without error.

As mentioned, patients in the late confusional phase manifest deficits in such complex tasks as shopping, handling a checking account, and planning a meal for

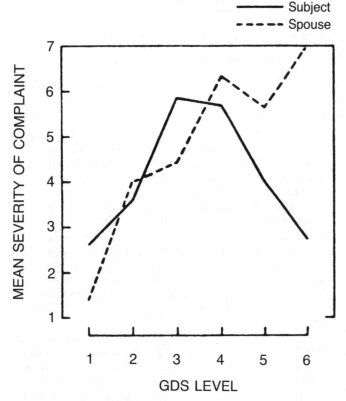

Figure 12-1. Patient and spouse assessment of the magnitude of memory deficit: Response to query "What kinds of problems do you (does your spouse) have with memory?" Adapted from Reisberg, Gordon, et al., (1985) by permission. Copyright 1985 by the American Psychiatric Association.

guests. However, patients at this stage are still capable of traveling, unassisted, to familiar locations and most often retain the ability to safely operate an automobile. Similarly, they are capable of making decisions with respect to such everyday matters as choosing the proper clothing to wear.

In the late confusional phase, the language deficit is most frequently manifested in a notable decrease in verbalizations. The patient becomes notably more "quiet" than formerly. The reasons for the late confusional phase patients' unaccustomed reticence are multiple and include decreased intellectual abilities generally, as well as decreased verbal abilities specifically. The reticence is also compatible with an affective flattening that occurs at this phase. Conversely, some patients react to this increased word finding deficit in the confusional phase with a tendency to ramble or "talk around the point." This form of adaptation to the deficit may lead to an overall increase in verbalization, although the precision of speech is compromised.

Motor abilities sometimes overtly decline in this stage. Those who know the patient well may note that the patient's gait has become slowed and that the patient is more cautious with respect to movements in general.

In the late confusional phase, denial becomes a dominant mechanism of defense (see Figure 12-1), and the patient frequently begins to adaptively withdraw from stresses. The net effects of these denial and withdrawal processes is a blunting of emotional responses, which psychiatrists term a "flattening of affect." The patient becomes less involved in activities, not only intellectually but also emotionally.

4. The early dementia phase (GDS = 5) is the second stage of AD. Functional deficits in this stage are manifest in decrements in the patient's ability to choose the proper clothing to wear, taking into consideration the weather and the social requirements of the day. Although, in accordance with our conceptualizations with respect to decline in so-called "degenerative dementia," the majority of these patients do show further decline, it is worthy of note that one third of six early dementia phase patients whom we followed (mean age at baseline = 72.33 ± 7.37 yrs) were not notably worse after an interval of approximately 4 years. Fifty percent were either institutionalized or deceased after this interval.

Patients at this stage are unable during a clinical interview to recall a major relevant aspect of their current lives, such as their correct address, or the names of close members of their family, such as their grandchildren. Similarly, they may be unable to recall such current major political events as the name of the current president and such important current personal matters as what the weather is like outside at the time of the interview. Memory with respect to personal history suffers at this stage such that patients are likely to be unable to recall the name of one or more of the schools (elementary, intermediate, secondary, or university level) that they had spent years attending. Conversely, persons at this stage generally can still correctly respond when queried with respect to their city and country of origin and their parents' first names.

Calculation and concentration deficit at this stage can generally be elicited by asking a well-educated patient to count backward from 20 by 2s. Most patients at this stage, however, will not manifest a deficit when asked to count backward from 10 by 1s.

Frequently persons in the early dementia phase are unable, when queried, to correctly state the current year. Similarly, they sometimes cannot give the correct name of the city or state in which the clinical interview is taking place.

The earlier reticence becomes an overt "paucity of speech" in this stage. Sentence production remains intact; however, the patient uncommonly offers much more than one-sentence responses to queries. Spontaneous speech is also notably decreased. Similarly, the slowing of gait and other movements sometimes observed by close relatives in the previous stage may become clearly observable even to a physician unfamiliar with the patient's previous level of functioning. Although arthritis, mild Parkinsonism, or other clinical causes of impaired movement may sometimes coexist in these aged patients, the Alzheimer's process alone is sufficient to account for the observed motor changes in the early dementia phase persons.

In the early dementia phase the flattening of affect and decreased involvement frequently noted by intimates earlier in the evolution of the disease become more overt and may be accompanied by a mourning process. The patient may suddenly begin to cry for no apparent reason over the course of the day—and then just as suddenly stop. Frequently, denial prevents a patient from expressing the reason for the crying episodes. In most cases, the patient is probably mourning, either consciously or unconsciously, the loss of his or her intellect.

Denial has been defined as a "defense mechanism, operating unconsciously, used to resolve emotional conflict and allay anxiety by disavowing thoughts, feelings, wishes, needs, or external reality factors that are consciously intolerable" (American Psychiatric Association, 1969, p. 28). Denial is generally betrayed by an obvious disparity between the condition of the patient and how he or she reports it. Such patients often smilingly insist that all is well or that a symptom does not exist (Martin, 1975).

The loss of one's intellectual and general thinking capacities is a terrible tragedy, too painful for conscious contemplation. As with any devastating illness or loss, the psychological mechanism of defense that is termed *denial* operates to prevent full conscious contemplation of the loss, which would be emotionally overwhelming. For many patients in the early dementia phase, denial protects entirely against overt emotional concomitants of the illness process.

Functional deficits in this stage are of sufficient magnitude that patients lose the ability to survive in the community without at least part-time assistance. In addition to inappropriate choice of clothing, deficits become manifest in such important everyday tasks as driving an automobile. For the first time patients at this stage begin to make errors in driving such as inappropriately accelerating the vehicle or failing to obey a stop sign or traffic light. Occasionally, patients will become involved in a vehicular accident for the first time in many years as a result of their compromised cognitive abilities. At this stage, patients can still put on their clothing, bathe, and toilet themselves without notable difficulty.

5. The middle dementia phase (GDS = 6) is the third stage of AD. At this stage patients manifest difficulties with such basic activities of daily living as dressing, bathing, and toileting. Approximately one third of six patients whom we followed at this stage (mean age = 72.50 ± 3.83 yrs) were deceased after a 4-year interval, and the remaining two thirds were in nursing homes. None of these six patients survived in a community setting over the 4-year interval.

Patients at this stage will be largely unaware of all recent events and experiences in their lives. They do not know their correct current address but may be capable of recalling rudiments of it. They generally do not recall the president's name; however, if told his first name, they can sometimes supply the last name. They do not know what the weather is like outside. They may occasionally forget the name of the spouse upon whom they are now entirely dependent for their survival.

Past memory suffers sufficiently at this stage that patients generally cannot recall the names of any of the schools they attended. They may or may not be able to recall their mother's name, their father's name, or their place of origin. Calculation and concentration ability declines to the extent that deficit is elicited in counting backward from 10 by 1s and, occasionally, even in counting forward from 1 to 10. Patients at this stage still know their own names. They have no idea of the year or season. Although, as mentioned, they may not recall their spouse's name, they can recognize their spouse as being a familiar person.

In the middle dementia phase, the patient may be no longer capable of speaking in sentences. Responses tend to be limited to one or at most a few words. Patients at this phase who have acquired new languages over the course of their lifetime frequently revert to using words from languages that have been acquired earlier in life. For instance, one man in the middle dementia phase had been born in Poland, as a child moved to Germany, where he met his wife, and subsequently moved with his wife to the United States, where they resided for the greater portion of their adult lives. This man began speaking to his wife not in their current English tongue, nor in their former mutual language, German, but rather in Polish, which was unintelligible to his wife and to others attending the patient.

In this stage the patient's steps often become very small and movements markedly slowed. Individuals at this stage also frequently have difficulty signing their names properly, even if some assistance is provided. Another psychomotor manifestation at this stage is increased difficulty in handling silverware. The ability to utilize a knife or fork properly is compromised.

The middle dementia phase is accompanied by overt agitation. The agitation may result from the constant threat of an environment that the patient can no longer successfully manipulate and that therefore becomes genuinely dangerous. The stresses of the illness, as well as the physiologic changes accompanying the illness, may result in severe psychiatric disturbances at this stage, as well as generalized agitation. Patients may begin "talking to themselves." They may also experience visual hallucinations, which may be related to their reveries. Frequently patients become paranoid or formally delusional. The paranoia may be the result of adaptive suspicion with respect to a world that is becoming frighteningly unfamiliar. The delusions may serve to provide one explanation for memory deficits that have befallen the patient. They may also serve to redirect anger that otherwise might be turned inward.

6. In the late dementia phase (GDS = 7), all verbal abilities are lost, although initially the patient is still capable of uttering occasional intelligible words and phrases. Frequently, there is no speech at all, only grunting. Neologisms, verbigeration, echolalia, and other major language disturbances may also occur at this stage. Some patients simply let out infrequent screams. One patient at this stage had a vocabulary consisting entirely of "okay," which she repeated innumerable times when she recognized a family member, in response to stress, or in response to other verbalization-provoking phenomena. Verbigeration is frequently manifested by repetition of the first syllable of a word. At some point in the late dementia phase, patients eventually lose all verbal abilities.

In the late dementia phase, patients eventually lose all ability to walk. They cannot even begin to sign their names and are frequently unable to grasp, in a usable fashion, a pen or pencil placed in their hand. They lose the ability to utilize utensils, and they either eat with their hands or must be fed.

Patients become relatively passive as they lose the ability to speak and to walk. Under these circumstances, agitation is utilized for communication. Excitement or crying out may indicate that the patient is about to have a bowel movement and requires assistance. It might also indicate that the patient has soiled himself or herself. Finally, increased respiration, increased verbalization, or a scream may indicate that the patient sees someone whom he or she formerly knew well.

Assessing Concordant Clinical Symptomatology in Normal Aging and Alzheimer's Disease: The Brief Cognitive Rating Scale

The global clinical symptoms of age-associated cognitive decline and PDD can be subdivided into five relatively concordant major axes of progressive cognitive decrement. The clinical characteristics of the five axes at each of the seven global stages of cognitive functioning can be seen in Table 12-3. The name Brief Cognitive Rating Scale (BCRS) was given to these assessments (Reisberg, Schneck, et al., 1983). The axes repre-

Table 12-3. Brief Cognitive Rating Scale (BCRS)[1] Part I

Axis	Rating	Item
	(Circle highest score)	
Axis I: Concentration and calculating ability	1	No objective or subjective evidence of deficit in concentration.
	2	Subjective decrement in concentration ability.
	3	Minor objective signs of poor concentration (e.g., on subtraction of serial 7s from 100).
	4	Definite concentration deficit for persons of their background (e.g., marked deficit on serial 7s; frequent deficit in subtraction of serial 4s from 40).
	5	Marked concentration deficit (e.g., giving months backwards or serial 2s from 20).
	6	Forgets the concentration task. Frequently begins to count forward when asked to count backwards from 10 by 1s.
	7	Marked difficulty counting forward to 10 by 1s.
Axis II: Recent memory	1	No objective or subjective evidence of deficit in recent memory.
	2	Subjective impairment only (e.g., forgetting names more than formerly).
	3	Deficit in recall of specific events evident upon detailed questioning. No deficit in the recall of major recent events.
	4	Cannot recall major events of previous weekend or week. Scanty knowledge (not detailed) of current events, favorite TV shows, etc.
	5	Unsure of weather; may not know current president or current address.
	6	Occasional knowledge of some recent events. Little or no idea of current address, weather, etc.
	7	No knowledge of any recent events.
Axis III: Remote memory	1	No subjective or objective impairment in past memory.
	2	Subjective impairment only. Can recall two or more primary school-teachers.
	3	Some gaps in past memory upon detailed questioning. Able to recall at least one childhood teacher and/or one childhood friend.
	4	Clear-cut deficit. The spouse recalls more of the patient's past than the patient. Cannot recall childhood friends and/or teachers but knows the names of most schools attended. Confuses chronology in reciting personal history.
	5	Major past events sometimes not recalled (e.g., names of schools attended).
	6	Some residual memory of past (e.g., may recall country of birth or former occupation).
	7	No memory of past.
Axis IV: Orientation	1	No deficit in memory for time, place, identity of self or others.
	2	Subjective impairment only. Knows time to nearest hour, location.
	3	Any mistake in time > 2 hrs; day of week > 1 day; date > 3 days.
	4	Mistakes in month > 10 days or year > one month.
	5	Unsure of month and/or year and/or season; unsure of locale.
	6	No idea of date. Identifies spouse but may not recall name. Knows own name.
	7	Cannot identify spouse. May be unsure of personal identity.
Axis V: Functioning and self-care	1	No difficulty, either subjectively or objectively.
	2	Complains of forgetting location of objects. Subjective work difficulties.
	3	Decreased job functioning evident to co-workers. Difficulty in traveling to new locations.
	4	Decreased ability to perform complex tasks (e.g., planning dinner for guests, handling finances, marketing, etc.).
	5	Requires assistance in choosing proper clothing.
	6	Requires assistance in feeding, and/or toileting, and/or bathing, and/or dressing.
	7	Requires constant assistance in all activities of daily life.

Note. Reprinted from Reisberg, Schneck, et al. (1983).
[1]Copyright 1984 by Barry Reisberg.

Table 12-4. BCRS: Pearson Correlations With Independent Psychometric and Mental Status Questionnaire Assessments

Independent assessment	BCRS					
	Axis I	Axis II	Axis III	Axis IV	Axis V	Total
Guild Test Battery						
Paragraph, initial recall	.69	.74	.64	.69	.67	.72
Paragraph, delayed recall	.68	.70	.61	.69	.68	.71
Paired-associate recall, initial	.60	.63	.51	.62	.62	.63
Paired-associate recall, delayed	.57	.60	.48	.56	.59	.59
Designs	.65	.71	.59	.66	.69	.70
Combined Guild score	.72	.76	.64	.72	.72	.75
WAIS Vocabulary subscale (raw scores)	.72	.78	.74	.68	.69	.76
Digit Symbol substitution test	.76	.78	.71	.71	.73	.78
Digit Span						
Forward	.64	.71	.71	.68	.66	.72
Backward	.69	.77	.71	.71	.65	.74
Total	.73	.84	.78	.77	.68	.79
Mental Status Questionnaire	.72	.75	.68	.78	.72	.77

Note. Adapted from Reisberg, Ferris, Anand, de Leon, Schneck, and Crook (1985) by permission. *N* = 50. All correlations are significant (*p* < .001).

sented are (a) concentration, (b) recent memory, (c) remote memory, (d) orientation, and (e) functioning and self-care. Items are scored from information obtained during a structured clinical interview conducted in the presence of a spouse or caregiver whenever possible. This interview procedure is particularly important in light of the denial that frequently accompanies moderate to severe memory loss (Reisberg, Gordon, et al., 1985) (see Figure 12-1).

Each axis utilizes seven rating points that correspond to seven definable and distinguishable stages of cognitive functioning within each axis. The axes were designed so that patients with normal aging or AD show a fairly uniform magnitude of cognitive and functional ability on each of the concordant axes. The clinical characteristics of the ratings on each axis are also designed to coincide with each corresponding Global Deterioration Scale (GDS) stage (Reisberg et. al., 1982) in patients with normal aging and AD (Reisberg & Ferris, 1982).

We have attempted to assess the validity of these assumptions with respect to the design of the clinical axes and also to obtain information on the validity of the axes in initial investigations with 18 subjects (Reisberg, Schneck, et al., 1983) and in further investigations with 50 subjects, 25 men and 25 women, mean age 71.2 ± 7.01 years (Reisberg, Ferris, Anand, et al., 1985). These subjects consisted of controls (GDS = 1) with average or superior cognitive function for their ages who demonstrated neither subjective nor objective evidence of cognitive deterioration (*n* = 9), subjects with very mild impairment (GDS = 2) consistent with the generally benign symptomatology of normal aging (*n* = 21), subjects with mild cognitive deterioration (GDS = 3) consistent with either age-associated decline or very early stage PDD (*n* = 4), and subjects

with moderate to severe cognitive deterioration (GDS = 4-6) consistent with PDD (*n* = 16). Patient evaluations were conducted by experienced geriatric clinicians who were not involved in the development of the clinical rating instruments. All subjects received extensive medical, psychiatric, neurologic, and neuroradiologic examinations prior to entry into the study. Subjects with factors other than normal aging or AD that might contribute to cognitive impairment were excluded from participation.

The relationships obtained between clinical assessments and the independently obtained psychometric and mental status evaluations can be seen in Table 12-4. All correlations were statistically significant (*p* < .001) and ranged from .51 to .84. The correlations with combined psychometric assessments (total Guild scores and digit span total scores) tended to be higher than the correlations with any individual psychometric assessment measures. Similarly, the correlations obtained for the WAIS vocabulary scores (Wechsler, 1955), the digit symbol substitution test scores, and Mental Status Questionnaire (Kahn, Goldfarb, Pollack, & Peck, 1960) scores were of comparable magnitude to the combined psychometric assessments. Hence, the clinical axes correlated most strongly with combined memory test scores, general assessment of language ability, coupled psychomotor interaction, and global mental status.

Interrelationships among the five clinical axes ranged between .83 and .94 (see Table 12-5). All individual axis correlations with total scores for the five axes combined and with GDS scores were .90 or greater.

These findings indicate that each of the clinical axes is consistently and significantly correlated with the magnitude of psychometrically determined cognitive

Table 12-5. Pearson Intercorrelations of BCRS Axes

	Axis I	Axis II	Axis III	Axis IV	Axis V
Axis I		.91	.89	.91	.88
Axis II			.88	.94	.90
Axis III				.88	.83
Axis IV					.94
BCRS Total	.96	.97	.94	.97	.95
GDS	.90	.94	.87	.94	.91

Note. Adapted from Reisberg, Ferris, Anand, et al., (1985) by permission. $N = 50$. All correlations are significant ($p < .001$).

impairment in subjects with age-associated cognitive decline and AD. These correlations appear to be particularly strong for combined and relatively "global" psychometric assessments. Furthermore, as intended in the design of the clinical assessments, the clinical axes do indeed show strong concordance over the range of normal aging and PDD. The magnitude of these interrelationships is sufficiently great as to raise the question of redundancy and whether multiple clinical modalities (or axes) are needed.

There are several reasons why multiple clinical assessments are desirable. These include (a) the utility of such measures in confirming the diagnosis and in differential diagnosis of normal age-associated cognitive changes and AD; (b) the utility of detailed assessments in sensitively and accurately gauging the value of putative treatment interventions; and (c) the utility of detailed assessments as research tools in increasing our understanding of the clinical characteristics and evolution of the disorder.

The clinical axes are specifically designed to parallel and to be concordant with the unique and characteristic clinical syndrome of age-associated cognitive decline and PDD. Cognitive impairment associated with other etiologies such as geriatric depression, multiinfarct dementia, and alcoholism would be expected to show different or less concordant patterns on the clinical axes. For example, patients with geriatric depression may show relatively greater impairment on the concentration assessments (Axis I) in comparison with recent memory (Axis II). If this hypothesis is confirmed, then increased scores on the concentration axis in comparison with the recent memory axis might alert clinicians to the possible presence of depression. Conversely, uniform scores on the various clinical axes can serve to help confirm a clinician's diagnosis of PDD. These brief procedures can be readily performed in an office setting and provide objective criteria that can be of value in the interchange of clinical information (Reisberg, 1982).

The ordinal clinical assessments may also be useful in the succinct staging of age-associated cognitive decline and PDD. With respect to succinct staging, Axis V, reflecting Functioning and Self-Care, may be particularly useful. Recent work has indicated that functionally, one can distinguish at least 16 distinct progressive stages in the continuum from normal aging to the end stages of Alzheimer's disease. These functional assessment stages (FAST) represent an expansion of Axis V of the BCRS and hence can be divided into seven major concordant stages with the GDS, as well as into further subdivisions, as seen in Table 12-6.

Observations reveal that in uncomplicated AD these FAST stages proceed in an ordinal fashion (Reisberg, Ferris, Anand, de Leon, et. al., 1984). Hence, AD patients who have difficulty marketing and handling their finances (FAST stage = 4) are always beyond the point at which they would demonstrate evident deficit in demanding employment settings (FAST = 3). Similarly, patients with uncomplicated AD always lose the ability to select their clothing properly (FAST stage = 5) after they have lost the ability to market and handle their finances (FAST stage = 4). Furthermore, AD patients always lose the ability to dress themselves properly (FAST stage = 6a) after they are no longer capable of choosing their clothing properly (FAST stage = 5).

In the sixth and seventh global stages, corresponding to the middle and late dementia phases, distinct functional substages are identifiable. Distinctions among these substages are relatively subtle. Nevertheless, in the majority of AD patients, functional progression appears to be ordinal for the substages as well as for the more distinct integer stages. The recognition of these stages represents a considerable advance in our understanding of AD, because they enable clinicians, scientists, and other professionals (Reisberg, 1984) to accurately quantify, in a readily comprehensible manner, the precise magnitude of impairment in AD much more readily and accurately than previously. They also represent an advance in enabling clinicians to accurately diagnose and differentially diagnose AD.

For example, if a patient with cognitive impairment of gradual onset loses the ability to walk (functional stage 7c), but the patient is still capable of articulating words, then an etiologic or confounding illness such as CNS neoplastic disease or stroke becomes much more likely to be the origin of the patient's impairment than AD. Similarly, a patient with so-called "depressive pseudodementia" may lose the ability to dress himself or herself but may still be capable of choosing the proper clothing to wear. An AD patient always loses the ability to choose clothing properly (functional stage 5) before losing the ability to put on clothing properly (functional stage 6a). Hence, the ordinal progression of functional loss in normal aging and AD provides a particularly useful tool for both the diagnosis and differential diagnosis of the age-associated cognitive disorders.

Other Clinical Features

In addition to the clinical features described in Table 12-3, other clinically observable changes also accompany the various stages of progressive cognitive decline. The most notable additional clinical features are those related to speech, to psychomotor abilities, and to

Table 12-6. Functional Assessment Stages (FAST)[1] in Normal Aging and Alzheimer's Disease

Global Deterioration Scale	Clinical phase	FAST characteristics
1 = No cognitive decline	Normal	No functional decrement, either subjectively or objectively manifest.
2 = Very mild cognitive decline	Forgetfulness	Complains of forgetting location of objects; subjective work difficulties.
3 = Mild cognitive decline	Early confusional	Decreased functioning in demanding employment settings evident to co-workers; difficulty in traveling to new locations.
4 = Moderate cognitive decline	Late confusional	Decreased ability to perform complex tasks such as planning dinner for guests, handling finances, and marketing.
5 = Moderately severe cognitive decline	Early dementia	Requires assistance in choosing proper clothing; may require coaxing to bathe properly.
6 = Severe cognitive decline	Middle dementia	(a) Difficulty putting on clothing properly. (b) Inability to bathe without assistance; requires assistance in adjusting the bath water. (c) Inability to handle mechanics of toileting. (d) Urinary incontinence. (e) Fecal incontinence.
7 = Very severe cognitive decline	Late dementia	(a) Ability to speak limited to approximately a half-dozen words. (b) Ability to speak limited to a single word. (c) All intelligible vocabulary lost. (d) Ability to ambulate is lost. (e) Ability to smile is lost. (f) Ability to hold up head is lost.

Note. Adapted from Reisberg, Ferris, Anand, de Leon, et al., (1984) by permission and from Reisberg, Ferris, and Franssen (1985) by permission.
[1]Copyright 1984 by Barry Reisberg.

mood and behavior (Tables 12-7 and 12-8).

It should be noted that motoric and mood changes are not as constant a concomitant of the progression of AD as the clinical features described previously. Stated differently, the changes in concentration, recent memory, remote memory, orientation, and functioning all correlate with the global progression of the illness process at .87 or greater. Hence, each of these clinical parameters individually accounts for at least three quarters of the total, global, clinical variance of the illness process. Loss of language abilities appears to also correlate with global clinical changes at approximately this magnitude (see Table 12-8). Motoric changes correlate with global changes in the illness at a lower level, approximately 0.62 (see Table 12-8). This implies that only 38% of the total variance in the illness process is accounted for by motoric changes. Hence, many patients with AD do not evince clinically observable motoric changes until very late in the illness process. Similarly, mood change correlates with global progression of the illness process at approximately the same magnitude as motor functioning. Many AD patients are entirely spared the emotional concomitants of the progression of AD that may be devastating for other AD patients and, in particular, for the family caregivers who must suffer the conse-

quences of the mood and behavioral changes. As emphasized previously, denial is a major factor in protecting the AD patient against the otherwise devastating emotional burden associated with the loss of one's memories and intellectual life.

Praxis

Historically, praxis disturbances have long been recognized as occurring in senile dementia at some stage in the illness process. In his 1837 textbook, James Prichard described an entity that he termed *senile incoherence,* which manifested itself in four successive stages: (a) impairment of recent memory, (b) loss of reason, (c) incomprehension, and (d) loss of instinctive action (Prichard, 1837). Prichard defined his third stage, incomprehension, as subsuming aphasia and apraxia. Subsequently, apraxia was noted as one feature in the illness constellation described by Alzheimer (1907), and in an epidemiologic study Sjogren, Sjogren, and Lindgren (1952) described apraxia in 80% of cases with "early onset dementia." Sjogren et al. believed that apraxia distinguished the early from the late-onset cases and hence did not believe apraxia to be a feature of most cases that would today be diagnosed

Table 12-7. Brief Cognitive Rating Scale (BCRS)[1]: Part II. Language, Motoric, and Mood Concomitants

Axis	Rating	Item
Axis VI: Language	1	No subjective or objective speech deficit.
	2	Subjective deficits in recalling names of persons and objects.
	3	Overt word-finding difficulties which may result in intermittent interruptions of speech or mild stuttering.
	4	Decrease of verbalization. Patient becomes more reticent. Alternatively, tendency to ramble.
	5	Overt paucity of spontaneous speech. Sentence production abilities remain intact.
	6	Inability to speak in sentences. Responses tend to be limited to one or a few words.
	7	Verbal abilities are lost. Vocabulary may be limited to one or two words, if any. Patient may repeat words or phrases (verbigeration), or make up new words or phrases (neologisms). Patient's vocabulary may be limited to grunts or screams.
Axis VII: Motoric functioning	1–2	No subjective or objective motor deficits.
	3	Decreased ability in the performance of complex psychomotor tasks, such as sailing, or complex constructional tasks.
	4	Gait becomes slowed. The deficit is noticeable to family members familiar with the patient, but not necessarily to clinicians who may not know the patient well. Patient becomes more cautious with respect to movements and activities in general, such as driving an automobile.
	5	Slowing of gait and movement is clearly evident, even to strangers. Auto driving ability is compromised or abandoned.
	6	Steps become small and movements are markedly slowed. Difficulty with signing name properly may occur.
	7	Ability to ambulate is lost. Inability to properly grasp a writing instrument.
Axis VIII: Mood and behavior	1	No subjective or objective changes in mood or behavior.
	2	Subjective increase in anxiety or concern with respect to cognitive functioning.
	3	Overt anxiety evident to clinician and/or patient's family.
	4	Blunting of emotional responses evident to family.
	5	Flattened affect evident to physician. Patient may have crying episodes.
	6	Overt agitation and/or formal thinking disorder (e.g., paranoia, hallucinations, delusions).
	7	Nonverbal agitation alternating with pathologic passivity.

Note. Reprinted from Reisberg, London, et al. (1983).
[1]Copyright 1984 by Barry Reisberg.

Table 12-8. Pearson Intercorrelations of BCRS Axes VI Through VIII With BCRS Major Axes I Through V and GDS Scores

	Axis I–V total scores	GDS
Axis VI: Language	.88	.86
Axis VII: Motoric functioning	.71	.62
Axis VIII: Mood and behavior	.72	.64

Note. $N = 30$. All correlations are significant ($p < .001$). Adapted from Reisberg, London, et al. (1983).

as AD. Subsequently, apraxia was identified in late-onset cases of senile dementia, as well as in the early-onset cases (Constantinidis, Garrone, Tissot, & de Ajuriaguerra, 1965; Lauter & Meyer, 1968; McDonald, 1969). Folstein and Breitner (1981) also found apraxia to be present in a substantial proportion of persons with dementia consistent with AD in American nursing homes. Folstein and Powell (1984) reviewed the history and evidence for apraxia and concluded that it is a late development, after "amnesia," in AD.

As discussed in this section, Reisberg and associates have described progressive, ordinal deficits in AD in such areas as concentration and calculation abilities, recent and remote memory, orientation, functioning, language, and motoric abilities. These progressive changes have been described on concordant, seven-point axes. An independent "Hierarchic Dementia Scale" based upon the hypothesis that dementia represents a reversal of Piaget's developmental stages, has recently been published (Cole, Dastoor, & Koszycki, 1983). This scale contains ordinal graphic praxis assessments. Hence, it was possible to determine the relationship between the ordinal graphic praxis scale and the GDS. The results can be seen in Table 12-9. It should be noted that these results are based on an analysis of only 22 patients with GDS scores of 2 to 7 and hence must be considered less than definitive.

Table 12-9. Praxis Concomitants of the Global Deterioration Scale (GDS) for Age-Associated Cognitive Decline and Alzheimer's Disease

GDS stage	Praxis ability
1–2	Can draw a cube.
3	Has difficulty drawing a cube with proper perspective.
4	Can draw a rectangle.
5	Can draw a circle inside a circle.
6 (a)[1]	Can draw a circle.
(b)	Can draw a line.
(c–e)	Can draw a scribble.
7	Will not write anything, but may grasp a writing implement in a usable fashion.

Note. Adapted from Reisberg, Ferris, & de Leon (1985) by permission.
[1]See Table 12-6 for substages.

Nevertheless, it appears that progressive decrement in praxic ability can be described as a concordant, ordinal phenomenon at all stages in the progression of AD.

II. Assessing the Stage of Cognitive Decline: The Mini-Mental Exam

A variety of instruments have been available for several years that are capable of assessing the magnitude of dementia symptomatology irrespective of the etiology of the dementia. These include the various mental status questionnaires (Folstein, Folstein, & McHugh, 1975; Jacobs, Bernhard, Delgado, & Strain, 1977; Kahn et al., 1960; Pfeiffer, 1975), functional assessment measures (Lawton, 1971), and at least one scale that combines mental status and functional assessments (Blessed, Tomlinson, & Roth, 1968).

One of the most useful and widely utilized of these instruments is the Mini-Mental State scale (MMS; Folstein et al., 1975). The MMS is a 30-item, brief assessment, which can be administered by clinicians, psychologists, or other professional or lay personnel with little training (Folstein, 1983). The 30 items include assessments of time (5 items), place (5 items), registration (i.e., ability to recall the names of three objects a few seconds after they are verbally presented), attention and calculation (i.e., ability to subtract 7s serially from 100 or to spell *world* backward), recall (of the three words presented before the distractor), and "language ability." The latter consists of diverse assessments of the ability to name simple items (a pencil and a watch), to repeat a complex but short phrase ("no ifs, ands, or buts"), to follow a three-stage command, to read and obey a simple command ("close your eyes"), to write a sentence, and to copy a complex polygon. Folstein has emphasized that the MMS differs from other similar mental status tests (including those of Kahn et al., 1960, and Pfeiffer, 1975) in that the

MMS includes measures of the use of language and constructional capacities.

Naturally, low scores on the MMS (or other mental status assessments) can be the result of dementia, delirium, pseudodementia, anxiety, amentia (i.e., perinatal mental subnormality), low educational status, or other conditions. With respect to dementia in later life, these instruments do not in any way distinguish between multi-infarct dementia, Huntington's chorea, medication-induced dementia, dementia secondary to metabolic disturbances, and so on. Within these acknowledged constraints relating to diagnostic accuracy, the advent of specific assessment instruments for grading the severity of symptomatology in normal aging and AD enables us to define the following MMS concomitants of normal aging and AD: (a) the MMS range at which true AD begins; (b) the MMS range of the borderline stage between that of normal aging and true AD; (c) the MMS range corresponding to the benign symptomatology of senescent forgetfulness; and (d) the stage in the progression of AD in which patients begin to score zero on the MMS, and hence the stage at which this parameter is no longer of real utility in the assessment of AD patients.

Preliminary answers to each of the above questions can be seen in Table 12-10. Table 12-10 demonstrates that the relationship between MMS scores and GDS scores in subjects with normal aging and AD is quite strong ($r = -0.92$, $p < .001$). In subjects for whom other possible etiologic factors that are capable of producing dementia have been eliminated, and with uncomplicated AD, the range of MMS scores corresponding to the late confusional phase (GDS = 4), and hence early AD, is 16 to 23. Consequently, subjects with MMS scores greater than 23 cannot be said to have true AD. Subjects with MMS scores from 25 to 30 may have symptomatology consistent with the benign prognosis of the forgetfulness phase (GDS = 2). The borderline between early AD and benign senescent forgetfulness occurs in the MMS range of 20 to 27, corresponding to the early confusional phase (GDS = 3). It may be possible for clinicians to further differentiate among these patients with respect to prognostic classification using the clinical criteria described in Table 12-1.

Table 12-10. Relationships Between Scores on the Global Deterioration (GDS) and Mini-Mental State (MMS) in Subjects With Normal Aging or PDD (Dementia of the Alzheimer's Type)

GDS	n	MMS (range)
2	4	25–30
3	7	20–27
4	8	16–23
5	11	10–19
6	10	0–12

Note. Subjects included 10 men and 30 women ranging in age from 51 to 83 years (mean = 70.73 ± 8.0 years). The Pearson correlation between GDS and MMS scores was −.924. Adapted from Reisberg, Ferris, de Leon, & Crook (1985) by permission.

Table 12-11. Utility of Psychometric Assessments in Differentiating Normal Aged Subjects (n = 71) From Subjects With Early Alzheimer's Disease (n = 37)

Test measures	F	p
Paragraphs, initial and delayed recall	139.43	$p < .0001$
Paired associates, initial and delayed recall	47.43	$p < .0001$
Digits, forward and backward	12.75	$p < .001$
Digit symbol substitution test	68.86	$p < .0001$
WAIS vocabulary (raw score)	39.38	$p < .0001$
Guild designs	42.61	$p < .0001$
MSQ	63.60	$p < .0001$
Names (first and last)	43.95	$p < .0001$
Finger tapping (right and left hands)	1.63	$ns\ (p > .05)$
Buschke $\dfrac{\dfrac{\text{trials }1\text{--}5}{5} + \text{delayed}}{2}$	75.70	$p < .0001$
Perceptual speed (number crossout)	4.24	$ns\ (p > .05)$
Category retrieval (sum of easy and hard categories)	6.34	$p < .05$
Hidden word: Number crossout	5.72	$p < .03$

Note. Adapted from Reisberg, Ferris, de Leon, & Crook (1985) by permission. Normal aged GDS scores = 2, early AD subjects' GDS scores = 4, after controlling for age.

It is interesting to note that these results with respect to the MMS borders between normal aging and AD, based upon prognostic studies of Reisberg, Ferris, Shulman, et al. (in press), are in very close agreement with earlier studies of Folstein et al. (1975) and others with respect to the borders between normal and pathologic aging. Folstein et al. found that all 63 surveyed residents of a retirement complex in Westchester County, New York (assumed, without examination, to be healthy) scored at least 24 points on the MMS. Subsequently, De Paulo and Folstein (1978) reported that diverse neurological patients with scores of 24 or greater did not have cerebral disturbance. Hence, Folstein's MMS cutoff of 23 or less as indicative of the presence of cerebral disturbance is identical to Reisberg et al.'s cutoff of 23 or less as indicative of the earliest stage of AD, for the subgroup of subjects meeting DSM-III and GDS criteria for early AD.

Subjects with middle-dementia-phase symptomatology, corresponding to GDS scores of 6, may score zero on MMS assessments. Independent studies indicate that even AD patients at FAST stage 6a (Table 12-6)

may score zero on the MMS. Hence, clinically one can distinguish 11 functional stages of AD (6a to 6e and 7a to 7f) in which the MMS has little or no utility in assessing the magnitude of AD symptomatology. For these reasons the MMS is not very useful as a sole criterion in the study of patients with severe AD or in longitudinal studies of AD.

III. Assessing the Stage of Cognitive Decline: Psychological Performance Tests

The advent of clinical definitions for the stages of AD enables us to reexamine the utility of various test measures in distinguishing early AD and in distinguishing the various stages of AD. The results of such a reexamination can be seen in Tables 12-11 and 12-12.

As evidenced in Table 12-11, 11 of 13 of the psychometric assessments examined demonstrated significantly ($p < .05$) lower scores in the subjects with clini-

Table 12-12. Utility of Psychometric Assessments in Differentiating Subjects With Early Alzheimer's Disease (n = 37) From Subjects With Moderately Severe and Severe Alzheimer's Disease (n = 15)

Test measure	F	p
Paragraphs, initial and delayed recall	7.71	$p < .01$
Paired associates, initial and delayed recall	6.06	$p < .05$
Digits, forward and backward	15.29	$p < .0001$
Digit symbol substitution test	5.16	$p < .05$
WAIS vocabulary (raw score)	7.56	$p < .01$
Guild designs	1.05	$ns\ (p > .05)$
MSQ	0.96	$ns\ (p > .05)$
Names (first and last)	1.22	$ns\ (p > .05)$
Finger tapping (right and left hands)	1.25	$ns\ (p > .05)$
Buschke $\dfrac{\dfrac{\text{trials }1\text{--}5}{5} + \text{delayed}}{2}$	6.83	$p < .05$
Perceptual speed (number crossout)	5.42	$p < .05$
Category retrieval (sum of easy and hard categories)	14.21	$p < .01$
Hidden word: Number crossout	7.23	$p < .05$

Note. Adapted from Reisberg, Ferris, de Leon, & Crook (1985) by permission. GDS = 4 for early AD, GDS = 5–6 for moderate and severe AD, after controlling for age.

cal symptomatology consistent with early AD (GDS = 4), as compared with scores in subjects with clinical symptomatology consistent with the generally benign forgetfulness phase. Furthermore, for the majority of test measures (8 of 13 tests), highly significant ($p <$ .0001) differences were obtained between scores of subjects with early AD and scores of normal aged subjects in the forgetfulness phase. However, with respect to the latter statement, it should be noted that many of the test measures examined included combined scores (e.g., digits forward and digits backward; paired associates initial recall and paired associates delayed recall), and independent evidence (e.g., see Table 12-4) indicates that these combined measures are superior in evincing relationships to the clinical symptomatology of AD.

The few test measures that did not demonstrate significantly lower scores in the subjects with early AD are also of interest in that at least one of these, namely finger tapping, is a relatively pure assessment of motoric ability as opposed to cognitive ability; and the other, perceptual speed, is more perceptual–motor in nature than strictly cognitive.

Although the results in Table 12-12 are not directly comparable with those obtained in Table 12-11 (for a variety of reasons, including fewer subjects), they do appear to demonstrate that test measures in general are less valuable in distinguishing the earliest stages of AD from later stages of the illness process. In this regard, it should be noted that all test measures bottom out (i.e., yield uniform scores of zero), at some point in the middle dementia phase or, depending upon degree of difficulty, at earlier stages in the illness process.

Perhaps because it is relatively impervious to this bottoming-out process, digit recall appears to be particularly useful in distinguishing early AD from later stages of the illness process. For the same reason (i.e., relative facility of the test procedure), digit recall was not as useful as some other test measures in distinguishing senescent forgetfulness patients from those with early AD.

It should also be noted that the test of relatively pure motoric ability, namely finger tapping, was not useful in distinguishing AD patients at any stage in the illness process. These findings are in concordance with the clinical observations previously discussed, of relatively low correlations between decrements in motoric ability and progressive AD.

IV. The Utility of Assessment Instruments in Differential Diagnosis

In the introduction to this chapter, the major mental disorders of the senium were enumerated. Subsequently, emphasis was given to the truism that knowledge of the clinical characteristics of the syndromes is a prerequisite for proper diagnosis and differential diagnosis. Because the characterization of normal aged cognition and progressive cognitive decline consistent with AD are the most germane with respect to diagno-sis and differential diagnosis in geriatric age-related mental disorder, and because these clinical characteristics had been the least known in the field, the assessment of global and concordant clinical symptomatology in these conditions was discussed in some detail in Part I. Parts II and III of this chapter reviewed the utility of general measures for the assessment of dementia irrespective of etiology, with particular reference to their utility in the assessment of normal aging and progressive AD. In this section we shall reexamine the more general differential diagnostic issues, taking into consideration the recent increments in clinical knowledge reviewed in the preceding sections of this chapter.

Normal Aging

This condition can now be viewed as a diagnosis of both inclusion and exclusion. With respect to clinical memory assessment in older adults, the following prerequisites should be met for a diagnosis of normal aged cognition:

Inclusion criteria:
1. Cognitive functioning consistent with GDS scores of 1 or 2, including subjective cognitive deficit and
2. An MMS score of at least 27.

Exclusion criteria:
1. Presence of dementia indicated by an MMS score equal to or less than 23 and a GDS score equal to or greater than 4 at the time of assessment.
2. Evidence of significantly fluctuating cognitive status from the clinical history.

The functional assessment staging criteria enable the clinical historian to anchor the definition of *significant* to readily obtainable historic material. Specifically, cognitive deterioration of sufficient severity as to impair ability to handle finances, market, or prepare meals, that is, a FAST score of 4 or greater, is incompatible with normal aging.

Borderline Cognitive Functioning

In most illness entities, a somewhat definable area exists between normality and pathology. A fairly distinct border exists between normal and pathologic aging with respect to clinical memory assessment of the older adult. This border can be defined by inclusion and exclusion criteria. As a border entity, it necessarily overlaps somewhat with both normal and pathologic age-associated cognitive impairment.

Inclusion criteria:
1. Symptomatology compatible with GDS 3 assignment. Assignment to this category for an otherwise normal aged individual necessitates a careful evaluation on the part of the clinician to determine the etiology of the patient's symptomatology. In addition to di-

agnostic tests, the following assessments may be useful:

• A Hamilton Scale. By definition, the "borderline patient" does not have a clearly definable affective disorder. Nevertheless, a substantial percentage of these patients will be found to have an underlying depressive disorder, and the Hamilton Scale (Hamilton, 1960) can be very useful in indicating symptomatology compatible with an underlying depression or a depressive component.

• A Hachinski Scale. By definition, the "borderline patient" does not have a clearly definable cerebrovascular accident. However, these patients may have a history of multi-infarct-like pathology which might account for their symptoms. A Hachinski score (Hachinski, 1983; Hachinski, Lassen, & Marshall, 1974) can be useful in elucidating these cerebrovascular etiologic factors.

• A Brief Psychiatric Rating Scale (BPRS). By definition, the borderline patient does not have a clearly definable psychotic disorder. However, an incipient involutional or toxic psychosis can produce these symptoms, and a BPRS (Overall & Gorham, 1962) can be useful in elucidating these symptoms.

Exclusion criteria:

1. A MMS score greater than 27, indicative of normal aging, or less than 20, indicative of clear-cut pathology.

2. A FAST score of 4 or greater, indicative of clear-cut pathology that must be explained on clinical grounds (e.g., the patient can no longer write checks because his or her vision is failing).

Alzheimer's Disease

This condition (defined as primary degenerative dementia by the American Psychiatric Association, 1980, p. 126), synonymous with dementia of the Alzheimer's type, can now be defined by specific inclusion and exclusion criteria.

Inclusion criteria:

1. Dementia, indicated by a history of adequate premorbid functioning, and subsequent deterioration, indicated by a MMS score of 23 or less.

2. Symptomatology compatible with primary degenerative dementia, indicated by gradual onset and overall symptoms consistent with GDS 4 to 7 assignment.

3. A score of 4 or greater on at least two of the five axes in Part I of the BCRS (see Table 12-3). This ensures a somewhat generalized dementing picture in contrast to, for example, a calculation/concentration disturbance from an increase in anxiety.

Exclusion criteria (for uncomplicated Alzheimer's disease):

1. Absence of dementia, indicated by a score of 24 or greater on the MMS or a GDS assignment of 3 or less.

2. A history of abrupt onset.

3. A clinical picture incompatible with GDS assignment. Examples include the following:

• A confabulatory dementia. This is virtually always indicative of pathology other than AD. A confabulatory dementia does occur in toxic psychoses secondary to alcohol or other neurotoxic substances. It may also occur as a result of encephalopathies of infectious etiology. In some instances, infectious or toxic encephalopathies may be present with a dementia of insidious onset, and the incompatible clinical picture may be the only means of exclusion.

• A dementia presenting with gait disturbance early in the course of the illness, apart from the slowing of gait described previously in this chapter. Early onset of marked gait disturbance may be indicative of Creutzfeldt-Jakob disease, which presents in this fashion in approximately one third of cases (Will & Matthews, 1984), a toxic dementia with cerebellar involvement, a stroke, or other non-Alzheimer's pathology.

• Any focal neurologic sign occurring prior to the seventh stage.

• Myoclonus prior to the seventh stage.

• Seizure disturbances prior to the seventh stage. At the very least, this is indicative of a confounded dementia associated with diverse neurologic impairment.

4. A clinical picture grossly incompatible with progression as described in the FAST (Tables 12-6 and 12-13). Examples of this were alluded to earlier in this chapter. Others can be cited at this time:

• If a patient loses the ability to ambulate but is still capable of speaking, this is indicative of non-Alzheimer's pathology or of pathology that is complicated by additional, non-Alzheimer's disease elements. A commonly observed example is that of psychotropic medications, initially prescribed to treat agitation in the AD patient, that produce an extrapyramidal syndrome, which prematurely limits ambulatory abilities in a patient who continues to articulate intelligible phrases. The continuation of some verbal ability in the patient is indicative of the possibility of restoration of ambulatory capabilities, if the psychotropic medication can be discontinued.

• If a patient develops urinary or fecal incontinence but remains capable of dressing and bathing without assistance, this is indicative of pathology complicating AD, and a urinary tract infection or gastrointestinal infection should be given strong consideration in the differential diagnosis. Infectious factors may, of course, complicate cognitive as well as functional components of the patient's presentation.

Multi-Infarct Dementia

A clinical entity is a constellation of symptoms that reflects a common underlying pathology and is therefore indicative of a characteristic prognosis, course, and etiology. In this sense of the word, the utility of the present nosology, which defines multi-infarct dementia (MID) as a distinct clinical entity, apart from overt stroke, is presently being questioned (Kenny, Stevens,

Table 12-13. Strengths and Limitations of Existing Measures for the Evaluation of Cognition and Functioning in the Aged Patient

Measurement characteristic	Clinical measures			Mental status assessments (e.g., MMS, MSQ, SPMSQ)	Psychometric assessments
	GDS	BCRS (Axes I–V)	FAST		
Specificity	Specific for AACD[1] and AD	Concordance and ordinal progression semi-specific for AACD and AD.	Ordinal progression specific for AACD and AD.	Nonspecific: for AACD, dementia, or pseudodementia of diverse etiology.	Nonspecific: for AACD, dementia, or pseudodementia of diverse etiology.
Diagnostic utility	Useful in the diagnosis and staging of AD	Useful in the diagnosis and differential diagnosis of AD and of dementia of diverse etiology.	Particularly useful in the staging and diagnosis of AD.	Useful in the assessment of the magnitude of dementia of diverse etiology.	Useful in the assessment of the magnitude of dementia of diverse etiology.
Range	Superior cognitive functioning to very severe dementia (for normal aging and GDS = 1–7).	Superior cognitive functioning to very severe dementia (for normal aging and GDS = 1–7).	Particularly useful in staging of AD; uniquely useful in staging of severe and very severe dementia (GDS = 6–7).	Mild cognitive impairment to severe dementia (GDS = 2–6).	Superior cognitive functioning to severe dementia (GDS = 1–6).

[1]AACD is age-associated cognitive decline.

& Hodkinson, 1984; Liston & La Rue, 1983a, 1983b). Hence, there is a possibility that the terminology *multi-infarct dementia* (Hachinski et al., 1974) may become obsolete. The pathological substrate for this disorder is presumably loose tissue and blood observed in postmortem brain tissue. Specifically, in the studies of Tomlinson, Blessed, and Roth, (1970), an increased volume of loose soft tissue and blood was believed to be indicative of a vascular contributant to the clinicopathologic entity of dementia. This vascular contributant has long been thought to be related to stroke-like pathology and risk factors, including extracranial vascular sources of embolism, hence the Hachinski criteria and scale (Hachinski, 1983; Hachinski et al., 1975). This scale is in many ways analogous to the GDS for age-associated cognitive decline and AD and to the Hamilton scale for depression, in that it both defines the presence of a clinical entity and, in many ways, defines the clinical features of that entity. It is computed from the following clinical features:

1. Abrupt onset,
2. Stepwise deterioration,
3. Fluctuating course,
4. Nocturnal confusion,
5. Relative preservation of personality,
6. Depression,
7. Somatic complaints,
8. Emotional incontinence,
9. History of hypertension,
10. History of strokes,
11. Evidence of arteriosclerosis,
12. Focal neurological symptoms, and
13. Focal neurological signs.

Hachinski has suggested that each of these factors be weighted with a score of one or two points and, more specifically, that items 1, 3, 10, 12, and 13 be weighted as two-point items, and that the remaining clinical features be weighted as one-point items. Using this system, two distinct populations are identified: (a) subjects scoring seven and above are defined as suffering from multi-infarct dementia, and (b) subjects scoring four points or less are labeled as having primary degenerative dementia (Alzheimer's disease). Presumptively, many patients with intermediate scores may have a mixed underlying pathology.

More recently, Rosen, Terry, Fuld, Katzman, and Peck (1980) have suggested a modification of the Hachinski scoring system based upon a clinical and neuropathologic study of 14 cases. Each case was classified neuropathologically as having senile dementia of the Alzheimer's type (SDAT), multi-infarct dementia, or a mixed pathology. An independent attempt was made to classify each subject on the Hachinski scale. Their results suggested that (a) the ischemic score of Hachinski et al. (1975) is quite successful in differentiation of SDAT from MID and (b) the ischemic score does not differentiate at autopsy between MID and pathology with mixed infarct, and Alzheimer's pathology. Furthermore, they noted that certain aspects of the Hachinski scoring system appeared to be useful in differential scoring, and other features were not useful in differentiation of SDAT from MID. They suggested a modification of the Hachinski scoring system in accordance with their findings. Specifically, they noted that features of primary importance were (a) abrupt onset, (b) stepwise deterioration, (c) history of stroke, (d) focal neurological signs, and (e) focal neurological symptoms. A history or presence of hypertension was noted to be of secondary importance. They concluded that somatic complaints and emotional incontinence were of secondary importance; however, they noted that these features occurred only in the 9 patients with vascular dementia (MID or mixed). The results of Rosen et al. have suggested a modification of the Hachinski scoring system that utilizes only the features that they noted to be of primary importance. In this modification, Hachinski's original weighting system is utilized, and a score of 4 or greater is believed to indicate the presence of vascular dementia either as a primary factor or as a contributant.

Taking into consideration the above discussion, the following inclusion and exclusion criteria for multi-infarct dementia in either its pure or mixed forms can be adumbrated:

Inclusion criteria:
1. Presence of dementia (although not necessarily unremitting).
2. A Hachinski et al. (1975) scale score of 7 or greater or a Rosen et al. (1980) score of 4 or greater.

Exclusion criteria:
1. Absence of dementia.
2. A Hachinski et al. (1975) scale score of 4 or less or a Rosen et al. (1980) score of 2 or less.

Geriatric Depression

The mood changes in AD have been discussed earlier in this chapter. Briefly, these changes are not sufficient for a formal diagnosis of major affective disorder (see also Table 12-14 and Section IV of this volume).

Hence, although AD patients commonly develop transient episodes of tearfulness, and although affective flattening is a concomitant, particularly of the early stages of AD, these symptoms do not accrue to the extent that AD patients achieve Hamilton scores of sufficient magnitude to meet the common research diagnostic criteria for depression. Consequently, a Hamilton score of 18 or greater is generally indicative of depression either as a primary factor or as a confound in subjects with or without AD.

It should be noted that the combination of denial and cognitive impairment in the dementing disorders of the elderly render self-rating scales for affective disorder useless in this population.

Involutional Psychoses

Agitation and delusions may occur as concomitants of AD and commonly occur in the 6th GDS stage (middle dementia phase). The nature of these symptoms in the AD patient is characteristic, and a rating scale designed to elicit this characteristic pathology in AD patients has recently been developed (Reisberg & Ferris, 1985).

Agitation and delusions may also occur as concomitants of geriatric depression. Similarly, these and other psychotic symptoms may also occur as part of a primary vascular dementia or of involutional psychosis, or as a result of other etiologies. Irrespective of the etiology of psychotic symptomatology, the BPRS of

Table 12-14. Differential Diagnoses of the Dementias

	Alzheimer's disease	Senescent forgetfulness (forgetfulness phase)	Geriatric depression	Chronic schizophrenia	Multi-infarct dementia
Onset of cognitive impairment	Gradual process extending generally over a period of years.	Gradual process extending over a period of several months to years.	Onset generally sudden and associated with present illness episode; however, a lifelong history of memory problems is sometimes obtained.	An accurate history of onset is generally not obtained, but the cognitive impairment is generally long-standing, extending for at least several years.	Sudden, stroke-like onset.
Course of cognitive impairment	Progression of the process is noted. Patient eventually becomes severely demented (with incontinence, loss of speech, loss of ambulatory ability, etc.).	No subjective or objective evidence of progression.	If associated with present episode, then the cognitive symptomatology will remit; if associated with chronic depression, then remains the same. Patients do not become severely demented.	If not associated with an acute episode of the illness, then the cognitive impairment generally continues to worsen over the course of decades. Patients do not become incontinent, do not lose ambulatory ability; speech is, however, sometimes severely compromised.	Stepwise course with remissions and exacerbations.

Continued

Table 12-14. Differential Diagnoses of the Dementias, continued

	Alzheimer's disease	Senescent forgetfulness (forgetfulness phase)	Geriatric depression	Chronic schizophrenia	Multi-infarct dementia
Clinical cognitive symptomatology	As described in Tables 12-1 and 12-3. Deficit proceeds relatively uniformly on concentration, recent memory, past memory, and functioning and orientation axes.	Subjective complaints of cognitive deficit only. No clinically objective evidence of cognitive deterioration is obtained.	Deficits are particularly notable, when present at all, in concentration and in functioning. Despite complaints of "memory problems," there may be no objective evidence of deficit whatever. Sometimes despite excellent recent recall, patients can remember little about their childhood, a deficit most frequently related to active denial.	Deficits in concentration and functioning are notable; memory for past may be denied. Recent memory is frequently intact. Deficits in concentration, attention, insight, judgment, orientation, and affect.	"Emotional incontinence" is frequently noted (e.g., patient may suddenly begin to cry for no apparent reason). Otherwise, clinical symptomatology is variable.
Associated clinical symptomatology	As discussed in text and in Tables 12-1, 12-3, 12-6, 12-7, and 12-9.	Very mild anxiety and/or depression are the only associated symptoms; alternatively, the patient may have no associated clinical symptomatology whatever.	Associated mood disturbances with dysphoria, depression, and sadness. Anxiety is frequently associated. "Vegetative symptoms" also frequently occur, including sleep and appetite disturbances (insomnia or hypersomnia; anorexia or hyperphagia). Anergia is another frequent complaint.	There is a history of florid psychotic symptomatology with delusions and/or hallucinations, and/or "suspiciousness," and/or paranoia.	Risk factors for cerebral vascular disease are generally present. There may be history of blackouts. Peripheral vascular and cardiovascular disease is frequently present, notably including hypertension.

Note. Adapted from Reisberg (1983) by permission. Copyright 1983 by Barry Reisberg.

Overall and Gorham (1962) can be very useful in formally quantifying the nature and magnitude of such symptoms.

Extrapyramidal Symptomatology

Various clinical and neuropathologic associations between AD and Parkinson's disease occur (Boller, 1983; Lieberman, 1983). Hence, AD patients and normal aged patients may both be sensitive to extrapyramidal symptomatology, either as a primary event or as a result of exogenous causes such as psychotropic medication. Irrespective of the etiology of such symptoms, a scale for the magnitude of extrapyramidal symptomatology, such as that of Simpson and Angus (1970), can be very useful in the assessment of the presence and magnitude of these symptoms.

Conclusion

Alzheimer's disease, an ancient problem, has been recognized since antiquity. The rudiments of accurate clinical descriptions of the disorder do not appear before the late 18th and early 19th centuries. Only in the past few years has this syndrome been described in detail. This newfound knowledge represents a considerable advance in our understanding not only of AD but also of the other mental disorders of the senium from which it must be distinguished. The implications of these recent findings for the evaluation of presenting symptoms in the aged patient have been reviewed.

References

Alzheimer, A. (1907). Über eine eigenartige erkrankung der hirnrinde. *Allegemine Zeitschrift für Psychiatrie und Psychisch-Gerichtliche Medicin. 64,* 146–148.

American Psychiatric Association. (1969). *A psychiatric glossary* (3rd ed.). Washington, DC: Author.

American Psychiatric Association. (1980). *Diagnostic and statistical manual of mental disorders* (3rd ed.). Washington, DC: Author.

Blessed, G., Tomlinson, B. E., & Roth, M. (1968). The association between quantitative measures of dementia and senile change in the cerebral grey matter of elderly subjects. *British Journal of Psychiatry, 114,* 797–811.

Boller, F. (1983). Alzheimer's disease and Parkinson's disease: Clinical and pathological associations. In B. Reisberg (Ed.), *Alzheimer's disease* (pp. 295–392). New York: Free Press/Macmillan.

Cole, M. G., Dastoor, D. P., & Koszycki, D. (1983). The Hierarchic Dementia Scale. *Journal of Clinical Experimental Gerontology, 5,* 219–234.

Constantinidis, J., Garrone, G., Tissot, R., & de Ajuriaguerra, J. (1965). L'incidence familiale des alterations neurofibrillaires corticales d'Alzheimer. *Psychiatria et Neurologia, 150,* 235–295.

de Leon, M. J., Ferris, S. H., George, A. E., Reisberg, B., Christman, D., Kricheff, I. I., & Wolf, A. P. (1983). Computed tomography and positron emission transaxial tomography evaluations of normal aging and Alzheimer's disease. *Journal of Cerebral Blood Flow and Metabolism, 3,* 391–394.

De Paulo, J. R., & Folstein, M. F. (1978). Psychiatric disturbances in neurological patients: Detection, recognition, and hospital course. *Annals of Neurology, 4,* 225–228.

Esquirol, J. E. D. (1838). *Des maladies mentales* [Mental illnesses]. Paris: Ballière.

Ferris, S. H., de Leon, M. J., Wolf, A. P., Farkas, T., Christman, D. R., Reisberg, B., Fowler, J. S., MacGregor, R., Goldman, A., George, A. E., & Rampal, S. (1980). Positron emission tomography in the study of aging and senile dementia. *Neurobiology of Aging, 1,* 127–131.

Folstein, M. (1983). The Mini-Mental State Exam. In T. Crook, S. Ferris, & R. Bartus (Eds.), *Assessment in Geriatric Psychopharmacology* (pp. 47–51). New Canaan, CT: Mark Powley.

Folstein, M. F., & Breitner, J. C. S. (1981). Language disorder predicts familial Alzheimer's disease. *The Johns Hopkins Medical Journal, 149,* 145–147.

Folstein, M. F., Folstein, S. E., & McHugh, P. R. (1975). Mini-Mental State: A practical method for grading the cognitive state of patients for the clinician. *Journal of Psychiatric Research, 12,* 189–198.

Folstein, M. F., & Powell, D. (1984). Is Alzheimer's disease inherited? A methodological review. *Integrative Psychiatry, 2,* 163–170.

Hachinski, V. C. (1983). Differential diagnosis of Alzheimer's dementia: Multi-infarct dementia. In B. Reisberg (Ed.), *Alzheimer's disease* (pp. 188–192). New York: Free Press/Macmillan.

Hachinski, V. C., Iliff, L. D., Zilhka, E., DuBoulay, G. H., McAllister, V. L., Marshall, J., Ross-Russell, R. W., & Symon, L. (1975). Cerebral blood flow in dementia. *Archives of Neurology, 32,* 632–637.

Hachinski, V. C., Lassen, N. A., & Marshall, J. (1974). Multi-infarct dementia: A cause of mental deterioration in the elderly. *Lancet, 2,* 207–210.

Hamilton, M. (1960). A rating scale for depression. *Journal of Neurology, Neurosurgery, and Psychiatry, 23,* 56–62.

Jacobs, J. W., Bernhard, M. R., Delgado, A., & Strain, J. F. (1977). Screening for organic mental syndromes in the mentally ill. *Annals of Internal Medicine, 80,* 40–46.

Kahn, R. L., Goldfarb, A. I., Pollack, M., & Peck, A. (1960). Brief objective measures for the determination of mental status in the aged. *American Journal of Psychiatry, 117,* 326–328.

Kenny, R. A., Stevens, S., & Hodkinson, H. M. (1984). Hachinski score in elderly patients. *Journal of Clinical Experimental Gerontology, 6,* 63–74.

Lauter, H., & Meyer, J. E. (1968). Clinical and nosological concepts of senile dementia. In C. Muller & L. Ciompi (Eds.), *Senile dementia* (pp. 13–26). Bern: Hans Haber.

Lawton, M. P. (1971). The functional assessment of elderly people. *Journal of the American Geriatric Society, 19,* 465–481.

Lieberman, A. N. (1983). Parkinsonian dementia and Alzheimer's dementia: Clinical and epidemiological associations. In B. Reisberg (Ed.), *Alzheimer's disease* (pp. 303–310). New York: Free Press/Macmillan.

Liston, E. H., & La Rue, A. (1983a). Clinical differentiation of primary degenerative and multi-infarct dementia: A critical review of the evidence: Part I. Clinical studies. *Biological Psychiatry, 18,* 1451–1465.

Liston, E. H., & La Rue, A. (1983b). Clinical differentiation of primary degenerative and multi-infarct dementia: A critical review of the evidence: Part II. Pathological studies. *Biological Psychiatry, 18,* 1467–1484.

Mace, N., & Rabins, P. (1981). *The 36-hour day.* Baltimore, MD: Johns Hopkins University Press.

Martin, M. J. (1975). Psychiatry and other specialties. In A. M. Freedman, H. I. Kaplan, & B. J. Sadock (Eds.), *Comprehensive textbook of psychiatry/II* (p. 1740). Baltimore, MD: Williams & Wilkins.

McDonald, C. (1969). Clinical heterogeneity in senile dementia. *British Journal of Psychiatry, 115,* 267–271.

Miller, N. E., & Cohen, G. D. (Eds.). (1981). *Clinical aspects of Alzheimer's disease and senile dementia.* New York: Raven Press.

Nandy, K., Reisberg, B., Ferris, S. H., & de Leon, M. J. (1981). Brain reactive antibodies and progressive cognitive decline in the aged. *Journal of the American Aging Association, 4,* 145.

Overall, J. E., & Gorham, D. R. (1962). The Brief Psychiatric Rating Scale. *Psychological Reports, 10,* 799–812.

Pfeiffer, E. A. (1975). A short portable mental status questionnaire for the assessment of organic brain deficit in elderly patients. *Journal of the American Geriatric Society, 23,* 433–441.

Prichard, J. C. (1837). *A treatise on insanity and other disorders affecting the mind.* Philadelphia: Haswell, Barnington, & Howell.

Reisberg, B. (1981). *Brain failure: An introduction to current concepts of senility.* New York: Free Press/Macmillan.

Reisberg, B. (1982). The office management of primary degenerative dementia. *Psychiatric Annals, 12,* 631–637.

Reisberg, B. (1983). Clinical presentation, diagnosis, and symptomatology of age-associated cognitive decline and Alzheimer's disease. In B. Reisberg (Ed.), *Alzheimer's disease* (pp. 173–187). New York: Free Press/Macmillan.

Reisberg, B. (1984). Stages of cognitive decline. *American Journal of Nursing, 84,* 225–228.

Reisberg, B., & Ferris, S. H. (1982). Diagnosis and assessment of the older patient. *Hospital and Community Psychiatry, 33,* 104–110.

Reisberg, B., & Ferris, S. H. (1985). A clinical rating scale for symptoms of psychosis in Alzheimer's disease. *Psychopharmacology Bulletin, 21,* 101–104.

Reisberg, B., Ferris, S. H., Anand, R., Buttinger, C., Borenstein, J., Sinaiko, E., & de Leon, M. J. (1984). Clinical assessments of cognition in the aged. In C. A. Shamoian (Ed.), *Biology and treatment of dementia in the elderly* (pp. 15–37). Washington, DC: American Psychiatric Press.

Reisberg, B., Ferris, S. H., Anand, R., de Leon, M. J., Schneck, M. K., Buttinger, C., & Borenstein, J. (1984). Functional staging of dementia of the Alzheimer's type. *Annals of the New York Academy of Sciences, 435,* 481–483.

Reisberg, B., Ferris, S. H., Anand, R., de Leon, M. J., Schneck, M. K., & Crook, T. (1985). Clinical assessment of cognitive decline in normal aging and primary degenerative dementia: Concordant ordinal measures. In P. Pinchot, P. Berner, R. Wolf, & K. Thau (Eds.), *Psychiatry* (Vol. 5, pp. 333–338). New York: Plenum Press.

Reisberg, B., Ferris, S. H., & de Leon, M. J. (1985). Senile dementia of the Alzheimer type: Diagnostic and differential diagnostic features with special reference to functional assessment staging. In J. Traber & W. H. Gispen (Eds.), *Senile dementia of the Alzheimer type* (pp. 18–37). Berlin: Springer-Verlag.

Reisberg, B., Ferris, S. H., de Leon, M. J., & Crook, T. (1982). The Global Deterioration Scale for the assessment of primary degenerative dementia. *American Journal of Psychiatry, 139*(9), 1136–1139.

Reisberg, B., Ferris, S. H., de Leon, M. J., & Crook, T. (1985). Age-associated cognitive decline and Alzheimer's disease: Implications for assessment and treatment. In M. Berginer, M. Ermini, & H. B. Stahelin (Eds.), *Thresholds in aging* (pp. 255–292). London: Academic Press.

Reisberg, B., Ferris, S. H., & Franssen, E. (1985). An ordinal functional assessment tool for Alzheimer's type dementia. *Hospital and Community Psychiatry, 36,* 593–595.

Reisberg, B., Ferris, S. H., Shulman, E., Steinberg, G., Buttinger, C., Sinaiko, E., Borenstein, J., de Leon, M. J., & Cohen, J. (in press). Longitudinal course of normal aging and progressive dementia of the Alzheimer's type: A prospective study of 106 subjects over a 3.6-year mean interval. *Progress in Neuro-Psychopharmacology and Biological Psychiatry, 10.*

Reisberg, B., Gordon, B., McCarthy, M., Ferris, S. H., & de Leon, M. J. (1985). Insight and denial accompanying progressive cognitive decline in normal aging and Alzheimer's disease. In B. Stanley (Ed.), *Geriatric psychiatry: Ethical and legal issues* (pp. 37–79). Washington, DC: American Psychiatric Press.

Reisberg, B., London, E., Ferris, S. H., Borenstein, J., Scheier, L., & de Leon, M. J. (1983). The Brief Cognitive Rating Scale: Language, motoric, and mood concomitants in primary degenerative dementia. *Psychopharmacology Bulletin, 19*(1), 702–708.

Reisberg, B., Schneck, M. K., Ferris, S. H., Schwartz, G. E., & de Leon, M. J. (1983). The Brief Cognitive Rating Scale (BCRS): Findings in primary degenerative dementia (PDD). *Psychopharmacology Bulletin, 19,* 47–50.

Reisberg, B., Shulman, E., Ferris, S. H., de Leon, M. J., & Geibel, V. (1983). Clinical assessments of age-associated cognitive decline and primary degenerative dementia: Prognostic concomitants. *Psychopharmacology Bulletin, 19,* 734–739.

Rosen, W. G., Terry, R. D., Fuld, P. A., Katzman, R., & Peck, A. (1980). Pathological verification of ischemic score in differentiation of dementias. *Annals of Neurology, 7,* 486–488.

Rush, B. (1793). An account of the state of mind and body in old age. In *Medical inquiries and observations* (Vol. 2, p. 311). Philadelphia: Dobson.

Simpson, G. M., & Angus, J. W. S. (1970). A rating scale for extrapyramidal side effects. *Acta Psychiatrica Scandinavica, 212,* 11–19.

Sjogren, T., Sjogren, H., & Lindgren, A. G. H. (1952). Morbus Alzheimer and Morbus Pick. *Acta Psychiatrica and Neurologica Scandinavica, 82*(Suppl.), 1–152.

Tomlinson, B. E., Blessed, G., & Roth, M. (1970). Observations on the brains of demented old people. *Journal of Neurological Sciences, 11,* 205–242.

Wechsler, D. (1955). *Manual for the Wechsler Adult Intelligence Scale.* New York: Psychological Corporation.

Will, R. G., & Matthews, W. B. (1984). A retrospective study of Creutzfeldt-Jakob disease in England and Wales, 1970–79: Part 1. Clinical features. *Journal of Neurology, Neurosurgery, and Psychiatry, 47,* 134–140.

Richard Scott McDonald

CHAPTER

13

Assessing Treatment Effects: Behavior Rating Scales

This chapter reviews behavior rating scales that have been designed to assess cognitive functioning and related impairments in aged patients. The scales examined differ in their purpose and focus. Some are more useful for descriptive purposes, others for assessment purposes. In addition, some focus on cognitive dysfunction, but others examine many facets of psychopathology. It is apparent that no one scale is suitable for all purposes; rather, it would be more advantageous, especially in geriatric drug trials, to use two or more scales together. This approach offers a more comprehensive profile of treatment-related changes.

Behavior rating scales have been widely used with aged patients to evaluate drug treatment for symptoms associated with cognitive dysfunctions, mood disturbances, and related impairments. For example, a review of 38 double-blind studies of treatment with ergoloid mesylates (Hydergine) revealed that 36 investigators employed some type of behavior rating scale as the primary means of evaluating the drug's efficacy (McDonald, 1982). Yet there is concern regarding the adequacy of such scales as measures of cognitive change, especially when they are not used in conjunction with psychometric tests or mental status examinations (Salzman, 1983). In addition, many of the scales used in geriatric drug trials were created for other purposes or populations (Salzman, Kochansky, & Shader, 1972). Scales that have been designed for use in geriatric drug trials are relatively new and, except for the Sandoz Clinical Assessment Geriatric scale (Shader, Harmatz, & Salzman, 1974), have not been widely used in such settings (Salzman, 1983).

The focus of the newer scales is assessment of a variety of cognitive impairments manifested in patients with Alzheimer's disease (AD). This direction is to be expected because the hallmark of Alzheimer's disease is pronounced decline in cognitive functioning. This chapter presents an overview of the newer scales and

some established ones following a review of general characteristics of behavior rating scales.

General Characteristics of Behavior Rating Scales

Behavior rating scales are instruments designed to assess a person's functional status as evaluated by an observer (usually by a professional mental health worker). Overall (1983) defined rating scales as instruments for quantifying the judgments and perceptions of trained clinicians. These tools are used in a variety of educational, industrial, and research settings (Anastasi, 1976) and vary in focus, approach, type, and format. For example, in research settings, scales may either focus on a single dimension of psychopathology (e.g., Hamilton Rating Scale for Depression, Hamilton, 1960) or assess a wide range of psychopathology (e.g., Brief Psychiatric Rating Scale, Overall & Gorham, 1962).

Likewise, scales vary in their approaches to gathering information. At one extreme, the information may be obtained haphazardly; at the other extreme, it may be gathered along prescribed and structured guidelines (Gurland, 1980). Two common and accepted approaches illustrating the latter extreme are the interview and ward observation. The complementary advantages and limitations of these two approaches help to account for their popularity in most evaluative contexts (Honigfeld, 1981). One factor that differentiates the two approaches, however, is the degree of interaction between the rater and the patient. In the interview approach, ratings are based on information obtained in a structured or semistructured interview, whereas in the ward observation approach, assessment is based on behavior as is, without direct intervention.

Thus, the interview approach is better suited for evaluating cognitive impairment because direct query is considered essential for such evaluation (Honigfeld, 1981). Most scales reviewed here were developed to be employed during an interview.

Three different types of behavior rating scales have been identified: descriptive, discriminatory, and predictive (Garside, 1976). A descriptive scale is used to assess and describe patients with reference to a certain defined psychiatric dimension. It is not primarily concerned with arriving at a diagnosis. In contrast, a discriminatory scale is useful in attempting to arrive at a differential diagnosis. A predictive scale is helpful for predicting the course and outcome of a particular psychiatric condition or the results of specific treatments. Many descriptive scales are likely to be used to measure treatment outcomes. However, it has been pointed out by some authors (Honigfeld, 1983; Smith, 1979) that scales that are useful for descriptive or diagnostic purposes are not necessarily sensitive to treatment-induced changes.

Formats of scales are usually distinguished in terms of specificity of the scales' anchors and obviousness of the scaling continua. Behaviorally specific scales provide explicit behavioral examples, whereas behaviorally general scales provide general descriptions (Campbell, Dunnette, Lawler, & Weick, 1970; Smith & Kendall, 1963). On a behaviorally specific scale, there are usually a title and definition of the dimension or symptom and a description of it along a vertical or ordinal scale anchored with specific behavioral examples. A typical behaviorally general measure has poorly defined scale values (e.g., *below average, average, and above average*) and poorly defined performance dimensions (Schwab, Heneman, & DeCotiis, 1975). If anchors are presented along a continuous scale, the scaling continuum is obvious. If anchors are mixed in random order, the continuum is disguised. Currently available behavior rating scales in geriatric psychopharmacology are behaviorally specific and present anchors along either 5- or 7-point ordinal scales. Blanz and Ghiselli (1972) argued that when dimensions and ordinal relationships are disguised, the rater is unable to detect an order of merit in the items or symptoms, and thus the reliability of the scale should increase.

Behavior rating scales are subject to a number of measurement errors: halo effect (when a single favorable or unfavorable trait colors a rater's judgment of the individual's other traits), error of central tendency (the tendency to place persons in the middle of the scale), and leniency error (due to a rater's reluctance to assign unfavorable ratings) (Anastasi, 1976; Wittenborn, 1967, 1972). Research findings do not support any one format as being less subject to measurement errors than others. Campbell, Dunnette, Arvey, and Hellervik (1973) found that ratings obtained with behaviorally specific scales showed less halo effect and leniency error and had greater discriminant validity. In contrast, Bernardin, Alvares, and Cranny (1976) found that ratings obtained with the summated format displayed less leniency error and greater interrater

agreement than ratings obtained with behaviorally specific scales. Several research studies (Blanz & Ghiselli, 1972; Dickinson & Zellinger, 1980; Saal & Landy, 1977) indicate that the mixed, or disguised, scale format does reduce measurement errors, but other studies (Arvey & Hoyle, 1974; Finley, Osburn, Dubin, & Jeanneret, 1977) do not support these findings.

The following review of currently available behavior rating scales emphasizes the assessment of drug-related effects; but this emphasis does not mean that these instruments should not be used in other types of treatment, for example, psychotherapy, milieu therapy, and reality orientation. The following scales are reviewed:

1. Global Deterioration Scale (GDS) (Reisberg, Ferris, de Leon, & Crook, 1982)
2. Sandoz Clinical Assessment Geriatric (SCAG) scale (Shader et al., 1974; Venn, 1983)
3. Inventory of Psychic and Somatic Complaints in the Elderly (IPSC-E) (Raskin & Crook, 1977)
4. Brief Cognitive Rating Scale (BCRS) (Reisberg, Schneck, Ferris, Schwartz, & de Leon, 1983)
5. Brief Psychiatric Rating Scale (BPRS) (Overall & Gorham, 1962)
6. Alzheimer's Disease Assessment Scale (ADAS) (Rosen, Mohs, & Davis, 1984)
7. Mental status examinations
8. Geriatric Evaluation by Relatives Rating Instrument (GERRI) (Schwartz, 1983).

Global Deterioration Scale

Reisberg et al. (1982) devised the Global Deterioration Scale (GDS) for assessing cognitive decline associated with primary degenerative dementia (Alzheimer's disease) and for delineating its stages. The scale was developed as a result of more than 1,000 hours of clinical observations of normal elderly subjects and elderly subjects with AD. It is based on the premise that three major clinical phases of this disease are identifiable: forgetfulness, confusion, and dementia. These phases can be further divided into seven identifiable and ratable clinical phases that range from Phase 1 (normal) to Phase 7 (late dementia). Each phase is associated with a GDS stage of cognitive decline and with clinical characteristics. A detailed description of the clinical symptomatology of progressive cognitive impairment is presented by Reisberg (1983b).

For example, at GDS Stage 4 (moderate cognitive decline), which corresponds to the late confusional phase, a careful clinical interview with the patient reveals a clear-cut deficit in knowledge of recent events, memory of personal history, concentration on serial subtractions, and ability to handle finances. There is frequently no deficit in orientation to time and person, recognition of family or familiar persons, or ability to travel to familiar locations. Denial is the dominant defense mechanism, and flattening of affect and with-

Table 13-1. Stages of Cognitive Decline on the Global Deterioration Scale (GDS)

GDS Stage	Clinical Phase
1. No cognitive decline	Normal
2. Very mild cognitive decline	Forgetfulness
3. Mild cognitive decline	Early confusional
4. Moderate cognitive decline	Late confusional
5. Moderately severe cognitive decline	Early dementia
6. Severe cognitive decline	Middle dementia
7. Very severe cognitive decline	Late dementia

Note. Adapted from Reisberg, Ferris, de Leon, and Crook (1982) by permission. Copyright 1982 by the American Psychiatric Association.

drawal from challenging situations is common. The patient also makes mistakes on three or more items on a 10-item mental status questionnaire. Table 13-1 presents the seven GDS stages and the respective clinical phases.

Reisberg (1983a) reported on a retrospective analysis of the relationship between GDS scores and independent psychometric assessments of 36 patients with very mild to moderately severe cognitive decline consistent with AD. The GDS scores correlated significantly with 14 of the 19 cognitive items in the Inventory of Psychic and Somatic Complaints in the Elderly (r = .31 to .66, p < .05) (Reisberg et al., 1981) and with 24 out of 25 psychometric measurements (r = .31 to .64, p < .05) (Reisberg et al., 1982).

Significant relations have also been demonstrated between GDS stages and both anatomic brain changes as visualized in computerized tomography (CT) scans and metabolic changes as determined by positron emission tomography in patients with AD. In a sample of 43 patients, GDS scores correlated at a statistically significant level (p < .01) with CT scan rankings of ventricular dilatation (r = .62) as well as with CT scan cortical assessments of sulcal enlargement (r = .53) (de Leon et al., 1980). Using the F-2-deoxy-2-fluro-D-glucose positron-emitting tracer for the rate of glucose utilization in the brain, in conjunction with positron emission tomography, Ferris et al. (1980) found significant relations (p < .05) between decreased metabolism and progressive cognitive decline. Decreased glucose utilization in the caudate, thalamic, and ganglia also correlated significantly (r = .69 to .83; N = 7) with GDS scores.

Although the GDS can be a useful tool for the staging of AD, it presupposes accurate clinical diagnosis of the syndrome (Reisberg, 1983a). Likewise, its diagnostic value is greatly enhanced by objective cognitive testing. Nevertheless, if employed during a structured or semistructured interview conducted in the presence of a family member, the GDS can be helpful in grading the degree of cognitive impairment and in selecting research patients for geriatric drug trials. Furthermore, it may be of value in assessing the severity of disease processes and treatment-related changes.

Sandoz Clinical Assessment Geriatric Scale

The Sandoz Clinical Assessment Geriatric scale (SCAG) (Shader et al., 1974) is a standard multiple psychopathological rating scale designed specifically for geriatric patients (Kochansky, 1979). It is the result of an extensive, ongoing clinical research program at Sandoz, Inc., and was developed in response to a need for an easily used general-purpose rating scale for evaluating the efficacy of drug treatment for AD and related conditions. Ratings should be made during or immediately following an interview with the patient and be based on the patient's verbal report or on observations of the patient's behavior (Venn, 1978).

The SCAG rates 18 symptoms and an overall impression on a 7-point scale (1 = *not present*, 2 = *very mild*, 3 = *mild*, 4 = *mild to moderate*, 5 = *moderate*, 6 = *moderately severe*, 7 = *severe*). A manual provides raters with definitions and a set of broad standards for assessing the severity of each of the symptoms and the global impression (Venn, 1983). In particular, the manual contains general guidelines for each symptom explaining what each of the three cardinal points (3, 5, and 7) on the rating key represents in terms of deviation from normal. In addition, there are short descriptors and brief instructions on the scale itself indicating the manner in which each item should be rated.

Shader et al. (1974) found the SCAG to be reliable and valid. They reported an average interrater reliability of SCAG items of about .75. They also documented discriminant validity of the SCAG in separating a group of patients with varying degrees of affective and cognitive impairment and found correlations between SCAG total scores and scores on a mental status examination.

Three factor-analytic studies of the SCAG have been undertaken (Gaitz, Varner, & Overall, 1977; Hamot, Patin, & Singer, 1984; Shader, Harmatz, & Tammerk, 1979). The study by Hamot et al., the most comprehensive of the three, was based on pretreatment scores of 1,165 geriatric patients with clinical diagnoses compatible with mild to moderate AD. The principal component analysis followed by varimax orthogonal rotation yielded five factors (Table 13-2) that accounted for 64 percent of the total variance: Cognitive Dysfunction, Interpersonal Relationships, Affect, Apathy, and Somatic Dysfunction. The factor structure suggests internal consistency among the items that load on each factor. The construct validity of the SCAG is also supported by the fact that ratings of items that are clinically expected to represent the same pathology correlate with each other, but ratings of items measuring different clinical phenomena do not (Hamot et al., 1984; Overall, 1983).

In the United States and Europe, the SCAG has been extensively used in the past 15 years to investigate the effects of treating AD patients with ergoloid mesylates (Fanchamps, 1983; McDonald, 1982; Venn, 1980). Its sensitivity to drug treatment has been documented in numerous studies, especially in the areas of cognitive

Table 13-2. Factor Analysis of the Sandoz Clinical Assessment Geriatric Scale

Factor	Symptoms
I. Cognitive Dysfunction	Impairment of mental alertness
	Confusion
	Impairment of recent memory
	Impairment of orientation
II. Interpersonal Relationships	Uncooperativeness
	Irritability
	Bothersomeness
	Hostility
III. Affect	Emotional lability
	Mood depression
	Anxiety
IV. Apathy	Impairment of motivation and initiative
	Indifference to surroundings
	Unsociability
	Impairment of self-care
V. Somatic Dysfunction	Appetite (anorexia)
	Dizziness
	Fatigue

Note. Adapted from Hamot, Patin, and Singer (1984).

dysfunction and mood depression.

The major strengths of the SCAG are that it is multidimensional (measures five symptom areas), is designed for use with older populations, is useful in defining clinical populations, discriminates between different levels of functioning, can be organized into different factors, is sensitive to drug-related changes, and has a manual to provide investigators with guidelines. Like all rating scales, it has limitations: Its 7-point scoring format is not necessarily linear (e.g., *moderately severe*, for which the rating is 6, may not be twice as severe as *mild*, for which the rating is 3). Also, it does not cover some important items (e.g., sleep), and some of its items are difficult to rate in an interview without the help of a significant other (e.g., spouse, child, or friend). Finally, substantiating cognitive function without the aid of psychometric tests is difficult.

Inventory of Psychic and Somatic Complaints in the Elderly

The Inventory of Psychic and Somatic Complaints in the Elderly (IPSC-E) (Raskin & Crook, 1977) was developed to assess a wide spectrum of complaints of the elderly. It consists of 80 items classified into 16 clusters and assesses mood depression, insomnia, anergia, anxiety, mania, paranoia, psychosis, somatic functioning, and sexual function, as well as cognition. Of the 80

items, 19 fall into the clusters of memory, attention–concentration, confusion–perplexity, and disorientation (Table 13-3). Most of these 19 items appear to reflect cognitive functioning. All items are rated for severity on a 6-point scale (0 = *unratable*, 1 = *not at all*, 2 = *a little*, 3 = *moderately*, 4 = *quite a bit*, 5 = *extremely*). Ratings are to be made during or immediately following an interview with the patient and should be based on observations of the patient's behavior or on the patient's verbal report.

Reisberg et al. (1981) examined the relationship between specific cognitive items on the IPSC-E and independent psychometric parameters in 35 mild to moderately impaired geriatric outpatients. More than 50% of the IPSC-E items correlated significantly with a majority of the psychometric measures of immediate

Table 13-3. Item Clusters of the Inventory of Psychic and Somatic Complaints in the Elderly

Cluster	Items
Memory	Forgetting where he or she has placed things
	Forgetting appointments, addresses, or phone numbers
	Forgetting recent events such as items in newspaper, on TV, in movies, etc.
	Forgetting people and events during childhood
	Having a good memory one day, bad the next
	Forgetting names of people immediately or soon after being introduced
	Having difficulty recalling appropriate words or names during conversation
Attention–Concentration	Acting as if lost in a dream world
	Failing to respond when called by name
	Having difficulty concentrating
	Having to check and doublecheck actions
Confusion–Perplexity	Appearing bewildered by events
	Forgetting the point of conversation
	Rambling or drifting off the topic being discussed
	Wandering at night
Disorientation	Failing to recognize surroundings
	Forgetting the day of the week
	Having difficulty recognizing close relatives and friends
	Being unaware of the time of the day

Note. Reprinted from Raskin and Crook (1977).

memory, recent memory, and remote memory. The range of significant correlations was .29 to .89, with a median of .44. The authors concluded that the cognitive items on the IPSC-E appear to be a sensitive tool for clinically assessing mild to moderately severe cognitive deterioration. Reisberg et al. (1982) also reported a significant correlation between 13 of the IPSC-E's cognitive items and GDS scores in patients with AD.

At present, however, there are few empirical data that demonstrate the scale's sensitivity to change due to time or treatment. Additional limitations of the scale are its length, the fact that the points on the rating scale are not well defined, and the lack of factor-analytic data supporting the cognitive clusters. Its major strengths are the broad range of symptomatology assessed and the relative value of the cognitive items.

Brief Cognitive Rating Scale

The Brief Cognitive Rating Scale (BCRS) (Reisberg et al., 1983) is a new instrument for the rapid, structured clinical assessment of cognitive decline, regardless of etiology. Using specified criteria, the rater assesses the magnitude of cognitive impairment and the progression of deficit on five axes: concentration, recent memory, past memory, orientation, and functioning and self-care. For each axis, the 7 points on the rating scale correspond to seven definable and distinguishable stages of cognitive decline. Items are scored using information obtained during a structured clinical interview conducted in the presence of a significant other whenever possible.

Reisberg et al. (in press) studied the validity of the BCRS using a sample of 50 community-dwelling elderly subjects whose degrees of cognitive impairment ranged from no impairment to severe dementia. All subjects received psychometric evaluations as well as clinical assessments. Half the subjects received CT scans.

The BCRS assessments and scores on psychometric tests and mental status examinations correlated significantly ($r = .51$ to .84, $p < .001$). The correlations tended to be higher when psychometric assessments were combined. The correlations between BCRS ratings and CT evaluations were all significant; they ranged from .57 to .65 for cortical atrophy and from .50 to .59 for ventricular dilatation. Interrelationships among BCRS axes ranged between .83 and .94. All correlations of individual axes with BCRS total scores and with GDS scores were .90 or greater.

Thus, in this sample of patients with AD, each of the BCRS axes correlated with the magnitude of psychometrically determined cognitive impairment, and correlations with global assessments were particularly strong. Decline on the BCRS axes corresponded to the successive stages of global cognitive deterioration measured by the GDS. Reisberg and his colleagues postulated that cognitive impairment associated with other etiologies, such as geriatric depression, would yield different or less concordant patterns on the BCRS axes.

Because the BCRS is so new, it is too early to predict its value as a research tool in assessing cognitive decline. Nevertheless, certain areas of potential usefulness are already apparent. It should aid in confirming a diagnosis of AD, be useful in demonstrating effects of drugs on one or more aspects of cognition, and provide information on the clinical characteristics and progress of AD. Limitations are the time needed to complete the BCRS and the lack of empirical data. Other research groups have not yet accepted the BCRS. Nevertheless, it appears that this instrument can provide investigators with an intensive and detailed evaluation of five components of cognitive functioning.

Brief Psychiatric Rating Scale

The Brief Psychiatric Rating Scale (BPRS) (Overall & Gorham, 1962) was developed to provide "a rapid and efficient evaluation of treatment response in both clinical drug trials and routine settings" (Guy, 1976, p. 159). Its focus is primarily inpatient psychopathology, but it has been used with outpatients (Overall, Hollister, Johnson, & Pennington, 1966). Even though the BPRS was designed for a general adult psychiatric population, it has clear relevance for measuring change in elderly psychiatric patients (Overall, 1983; Overall & Beller, 1984). Kochansky (1979) reported that the BPRS was used in six drug studies with the elderly and was sensitive to drug effects in five of them.

The BPRS comprises 18 items rated on an 8-point continuum (0 = *not assessed*, 1 = *not present*, 2 = *very mild*, 3 = *mild*, 4 = *moderate*, 5 = *moderately severe*, 6 = *severe*, 7 = *extremely severe*). For each item there is a descriptor printed on the scale itself. The Early Clinical Drug Evaluation Program (ECDEU) assessment manual (Guy, 1976) provides instructions and defines the items in greater detail. The manual reports five factors based on a large sample of adult schizophrenics: Anxiety–Depression, Anergia, Thought Disturbance, Activation, and Hostile-Suspiciousness.

Recently, Overall and Beller (1984) reported on a factor analysis for a sample of 87 geropsychiatric inpatients. The purpose of the undertaking was to evaluate the range of psychopathology the BPRS is capable of measuring in this patient population and the adequacy with which it does so. It was assumed that the correlational structure of ratings for elderly patients would differ from that observed in younger psychiatric patients.

The factor analysis resulted in five factors that accounted for 65 percent of the total variance. The five factors and respective item compositions are presented in Table 13-4. This factor structure differs in two important ways from structures previously observed in numerous analyses of BPRS ratings. The symptom of depressive mood combines with emotional withdrawal and motor retardation to define the Withdrawn Depression factor, whereas depressive mood has routinely related to anxiety and tension in a younger population.

Table 13-4. Factor Analysis of the Brief Psychiatric Rating Scale

Factor	Items
I. Withdrawn Depression	Emotional withdrawal Depressive mood Motor retardation Blunted affect
II. Agitation	Anxiety Tension Excitement
III. Cognitive Dysfunction	Conceptual disorganization Disorientation
IV. Hostile suspiciousness	Hostility Suspiciousness
V. Psychotic Distortion	Hallucinatory behavior Unusual thought content

Note. Adapted from Overall and Beller (1984) by permission.

Table 13-5. The Alzheimer's Disease Assessment Scale

Cognitive Items	Noncognitive Items
Spoken language ability	Tearful
Comprehension spoken language	Depressed mood
Recall test instructions	Concentration distractibility
Word-finding difficulty	Uncooperative: testing
Following commands	Delusions
Naming: objects, fingers	Pacing
Constructions: drawing	Motor activity: increase
Ideational praxis	Tremors
Orientation	Appetite change
Word recall	
Word recognition	

Note. Adapted from Rosen, Mohs, and Davis (1984) by permission. Copyright 1984 by the American Psychiatric Association.

In addition, the original Thought Disturbance factor is split into clearly distinguishable components: Conceptual disorganization and disorientation combine to form the Cognitive Dysfunction factor, and hallucinatory behavior and unusual thought content form the Psychotic Distortion factor.

Construct validity of the Cognitive Dysfunction factor was examined with reference to a mental status examination (Pfeiffer, 1975). All the mental status items related to this factor, confirming that the BPRS rating of disorientation is the single best measure of cognitive dysfunction.

Overall and Beller (1984) suggested that the difference in the symptom profile patterns in this geriatric population arises primarily from the prominence of organic dysfunction that results in ratings of conceptual disorganization and disorientation. Although the clinical utility of the factor structure in assessing drug effects must be demonstrated, it appears that the BPRS will have a role in geriatric psychopharmacology and, in particular, with inpatients.

Alzheimer's Disease Assessment Scale

The Alzheimer's Disease Assessment Scale (ADAS) (Rosen et al., 1984) is designed specifically to evaluate the severity of cognitive and noncognitive behavioral dysfunctions that are characteristic of persons with AD. The scale was developed according to the following guidelines: It should assess all major behavioral characteristics of AD, specific aspects of reliably identified behavior, and the range of dysfunction for mild to severe dementia; it should be short; and it should be appropriate for patients in different environments (Mohs, Rosen, & Davis, 1982).

The scale consists of 21 items. The cognitive section includes 9 items that have a maximum score of 48 points and 2 memory tasks that have a maximum score of 22 points. The 10 items in the noncognitive section have a maximum score of 50 points. Items are rated on a scale of severity of dysfunction ranging from 0 to 5 (0 = *no impairment*, 1 = *very mild*, 2 = *mild*, 3 = *moderate*, 4 = *moderately severe*, 5 = *severe*). The ADAS is administered in approximately 45 minutes. A manual outlines specific administration and scoring procedures. The scale is outlined in Table 13-5.

The original scale had 40 items; the final 21 items were chosen on the basis of interrater reliability and test–retest reliability. Normative data were obtained from a group of 27 Alzheimer's patients and a group of 28 normal elderly persons. Each person was evaluated by two trained raters to obtain interrater reliability. Test–retest reliability was obtained 2 months after the initial session with 18 of the patients and 26 of the normal elderly subjects. One year after the initial session, 10 persons from each group were again evaluated.

For the Alzheimer's patients, 37 items had significant interrater reliability ($r = .650$ to $.989$, $p < .01$), and for the normal elderly, 38 items had significant interrater reliability ($r = .658$ to 1.0, $p < .01$). Intraclass coefficients were determined for the cognitive subscale, noncognitive subscale, and total score. Correlation coefficients on these three measures ranged from $.826$ to $.989$. Test–retest reliability correlations were highly stable for 11 items in the cognitive subscale ($r = .58$ to $.92$) and for 10 items in the noncognitive subscale. These 21 items became the final form of the ADAS.

In a matched group of 15 subjects from each of the other two groups, significant differences were found between the patients and the normal elderly on every cognitive item, the total cognitive scale, and the total noncognitive scale. Test–retest data for 10 patients and 10 normal elderly subjects indicated that the scale reflects changes in symptoms of AD over time. No changes were noted in the normal elderly group.

Rosen et al. investigated external validity by correlating the subscales and total scores with the SCAG, the Memory-Information Test (Blessed, Tomlinson, & Roth, 1968) and Blessed's Dementia Rating Scale

(DRS) (Blessed et al., 1968). SCAG scores correlated significantly with cognitive and total scores on the ADAS ($r = .67$, $p < .01$ and $r = .52$, $p < .02$, respectively). Scores on the mental status examination correlated significantly with scores on the cognitive subscale, noncognitive subscale, and total ADAS ($r = .77$, $p < .001$; $r = -.42$, $p < .02$; and $r = -.67$, $p < .001$, respectively). The DRS scores correlated significantly with the cognitive, noncognitive, and total ADAS scores ($r = .48$, $p < .01$; $r = .45$, $p < .01$; and $r = .64$, $p < .001$, respectively).

Preliminary data support the claim that the ADAS is a potentially useful instrument for evaluating the severity of dysfunction in AD and a sensitive tool for psychopharmacological research. An ideal feature of the test is that the cognitive tasks are administered in the context of an interview; however, they are based on performance per se, not on the rater's clinical impression. (Thus, strictly speaking, the ADAS is not a behavior rating scale). Additional pluses are that the ADAS rates the major cognitive dysfunctions of AD, has standardized guidelines, and can be completed in a short time and administered in different environments. The major limitation is the lack of empirical data. Also, like all new instruments, it must withstand the passage of time.

Mental Status Examinations

The necessity of examining the mental state of the aged patient is unquestionable, but the reliability of behavior rating scales in assessing mental state is uncertain. Therefore, many investigators have added some form of quantitative assessment of cognitive performance to the standard clinical interview. The most widely used test of this nature is commonly known as the Mental Status Questionnaire (Kahn, Goldfarb, Pollack, & Peck, 1960).

Table 13-6 lists a few of the mental status questionnaires that have been developed during the past 25 years. All of the scales in the table were designed to provide a rapid means of assessing the presence or absence of cognitive impairment. In general, all are easily administered within 5 to 15 minutes and can be incorporated into standard psychiatric interviews. Also, all concentrate on the cognitive aspects of mental functions (e.g., attention, orientation, registration, memory) and exclude questions regarding mood and general behavior. All scales employ a similar standardized format for scoring, and responses are usually quantified in terms of an error score (a score of 1 point for each error). (See Gurland, 1980, for an excellent review of mental status questionnaires.)

The Mini-Mental State Examination (Folstein, Folstein, & McHugh, 1975) and the Dementia Rating Scale (Mattis, 1976) are particularly useful mental status questionnaires. Both are relatively extensive and comprehensive and, therefore, should aid in initial assessment, in diagnosis, and in the design of a treatment. In addition, when the two are used together, it is apparently possible to distinguish normal elderly from

Table 13-6. A Summary of Mental Status Examinations

Test	No. of Items	Scoring Range	Author(s)
Mental Status Questionnaire (MSQ)	10	0–10	Kahn et al. (1960)
Mini-Mental State Examination	11	0–30	Folstein, Folstein, & McHugh (1975)
Short portable MSQ	10	0–10	Pfeiffer (1975)
MSQ for organic brain syndrome	10	0–35	Fishback (1977)
Cerebral Function Test	19	0–45	Silver (1972)
Information-Memory-Concentration MSQ	26	0–26	Blessed, Tomlinson, & Roth (1968)
Short Version Information-Memory-Concentration	6	0–6	Katzman et al. (1983)
Mental status cognitive tasks	20	0–20	Taylor, Abrams, Faber, & Almy (1980)
Dementia Rating Scale	49	0–65	Mattis (1976)

mildly impaired Alzheimer's patients and mildly impaired from moderately impaired Alzheimer's patients (Vitaliano, Breen, Albert, Russo, & Prinz, 1984). However, these instruments cannot yield a diagnosis but can only support a diagnosis that has already been made.

Geriatric Evaluation by Relatives Rating Instrument

The assessment procedures reviewed so far were designed primarily for use in interviews. This approach offers a better opportunity to assess cognitive impairment than does ward observation. Ward rating scales, for example, do not lend themselves well to evaluating mental impairment because they usually rely on inference, not direct query (Honigfeld, 1981). In addition, many of the available ward rating scales do not evaluate mental impairments. One observational scale, the Geriatric Evaluation by Relatives Rating Instrument (GERRI) (Schwartz, 1983), however, does address memory and cognitive functioning as well as other factors.

The GERRI differs from other observational scales in that it was developed for use by significant others (e.g., spouses, children, or friends) to assess changes in outpatients. Significant others by definition usually have close contact (more than 20 hours a week) with the patient and are in an ideal position to observe the patient in the home environment. In addition, because significant others may not have the biases of professionals, their observations about the patient's behavior may be very reliable and valid (Zimmermann, Vestre, & Hunter, 1975).

The GERRI consists of 49 items in three clusters: cognitive functioning, social functioning, and mood. A 6-point rating key is used for evaluating each item (1 = *almost all the time*, 2 = *most of the time*, 3 = *often*, 4 = *sometimes*, 5 = *almost never*, 6 = *does not apply*). Most of the test items are descriptive and behavioral and were assigned by the author on the basis of face validity and content to one of the three clusters. Assessment is based on the patient's behavior during the preceding 2 weeks. The significant others making the assessment are instructed to answer each question to the best of their ability and are informed that there are no wrong or right answers.

Schwartz (1983) gathered preliminary data on 45 patients over the age of 55 (mean age of 78 years) who were presumed to have AD. Each patient was evaluated by two significant others using the GERRI. Interrater reliability correlations ranged from .06 to .89, with a median value of .72. Intraclass correlations were .94 for the total scale score, .92 for the cognitive functioning cluster, and .66 for the mood cluster. Cronback's alpha coefficients were also obtained to provide an overall measure of consistency. The alphas were remarkably similar for both sets of raters and ranged from .66 to .96. Cluster scores were all significantly correlated with each other. Validity of the scale was determined by dividing the patients into three groups based on their GDS scores (Reisberg et al., 1982): low deterioration, medium deterioration, and high deterioration. Mean GERRI scores were obtained for each of these three categories. Based on an analysis of variance, the GERRI total score and the three cluster scores significantly differentiated the three groups.

Schwartz (1983) reported that the GERRI meets acceptable standards of reliability and validity. It appears that the instrument will be a valuable means of measuring significant others' perceptions of geriatric patients who show symptoms of mental decline. The usefulness of this instrument in clinical drug trials, however, must be tested in outpatient studies.

Advantages of the scale are that items are short, easy sentences and that they assess a broad range of typical behavioral disturbances and complaints among the elderly. A possible limitation of the scale is that data may be biased because of the relationship between the informant and the patient. Likewise, value judgments and expectations on the part of an untrained observer may also produce a bias in behavioral reporting. Finally, as pointed out by Schwartz (1983), an untrained observer may be too insensitive to detect subtle changes in behavior, which would mean that certain behaviors would go unreported. Nevertheless, such an instrument offers the possibility of assessing changes in outpatients living in their own social environment, especially in relevant areas such as social functioning, activities of daily living, and cognitive functioning. In addition, significant others may be able to observe subtle treatment-related changes in behavior otherwise unnoticed in the context of a clinical interview.

Discussion

Because the assessment of cognitive functioning in the elderly via behavior rating scales leaves a lot to be desired, researchers in recent years have turned their attention to developing tests that provide more objective measurements (chapters 14 to 18 in this book; Corkin, Davis, Growdon, Usdin, & Wurtman, 1982; Crook, Ferris, & Bartus, 1983). Useful as these objective techniques are, Venn (1978) contended that it will be the degree of symptomatic change that determines whether the quality of life of the geriatric patient has been influenced by treatment, irrespective of changes found in objective measurements. In addition, many changes in cognitive behavior may be so subtle that a psychometric evaluation will not point them out. The clinical behavior rating scale will therefore remain an essential component in evaluating the effects of drug therapy on memory and cognitive functioning in aged patients. It must be emphasized, however, that behavior rating scales contribute only so much to the evaluation of treatment effects in geriatric patients and, whenever possible, should be supported by appropriate psychometric testing. As Overall (1983) indicated, rating scales are nothing more than vehicles for accurately quantifying the perceptions and judgments of trained clinical observers.

Most of the scales reviewed here appear to be adequate for their intended purposes. The usefulness of these instruments, however, would be enhanced if certain studies were performed. All of the scales would benefit if additional multicenter studies of reliability and validity were conducted. Furthermore, longitudinal studies should be conducted to determine the scales' sensitivity over time to the progression of disease and their correlation with other psychometric measurements. Finally, manuals like those for the SCAG and ADAS need to be developed for the other scales.

In summary, it is apparent that there is no scale that is suitable for all uses. The scales examined here have been designed for various purposes. Some may be useful for descriptive purposes and others may be more useful for assessing treatment-induced change. In addition, some were developed to provide an intensive examination of cognitive dysfunction whereas others were developed to provide a more comprehensive evaluation of cognitive functioning and associated symptoms, such as mood and general behavior. Since no existing instrument is broad enough to assess the complete range of cognitive dysfunctions and associated symptoms in the aged, it would appear to be worthwhile to use two or more of the scales together in clinical drug trials. Such an approach would generate valuable data from many perspectives and offer a more comprehensive profile of treatment-related change.

References

Anastasi, A. (1976). *Psychological testing* (4th ed.). New York: Macmillan.

Arvey, R. D., & Hoyle, J. C. (1974). A Guttman approach to the development of behaviorally based rating scales for systems analysts and programmer/analysts. *Journal of Applied Psychology, 59*, 61–68.

Bernardin, H. J., Alvares, K. M., & Cranny, C. J. (1976). A recomparison of behavioral expectation scales to summated scales. *Journal of Applied Psychology, 61*, 564–570.

Blanz, F., & Ghiselli, E. E. (1972). The mixed-standard scale: A new rating system. *Personnel Psychology, 25*, 185–199.

Blessed, G., Tomlinson, B. E., & Roth, M. (1968). The association between quantitative measures of dementia and senile change in the cerebral grey matter of elderly subjects. *British Journal of Psychiatry, 114*, 797–811.

Campbell, J. P., Dunnette, M. D., Arvey, R. D., & Hellervik, L. V. (1973). The development and evaluation of behaviorally based rating scales. *Journal of Applied Psychology, 57*, 15–22.

Campbell, J. P., Dunnette, M. D., Lawler, E. E., & Weick, K. E. (1970). *Managerial behavior, performance and effectiveness.* New York: McGraw-Hill.

Corkin, S., Davis, K. L., Growdon, J. H., Usdin, E., & Wurtman, R. J. (Eds.). (1982). *Alzheimer's disease: A report of progress in research.* New York: Raven Press.

Crook, T., Ferris, S., & Bartus, R. (Eds.). (1983). *Assessment in geriatric psychopharmacology.* New Canaan, CT: Mark Powley.

de Leon, M. J., Ferris, S. H., George, A. E., Reisberg, B., Kricheff, I. I., & Gershon, S. (1980). Computed tomography evaluations of brain-behavior relationships in senile dementia of the Alzheimer's type. *Neurobiology of Aging, 1*, 69–79.

Dickinson, T. L., & Zellinger, P. M. (1980). A comparison of the behaviorally anchored rating and mixed standard scale formats. *Journal of Applied Psychology, 65*(2), 147–154.

Fanchamps, A. (1983). Dihydroergotoxine in senile cerebral insufficiency. In A. Agnoli, C. Gaetano, P. F. Spano, & M. Trabucci (Eds.), *Aging brain and ergot alkaloids* (pp. 311–322). New York: Raven Press.

Ferris, S. H., de Leon, M. J., Wolf, A. P., Farkas, T., Christman, D. R., Reisberg, B., Fowler, J. S., MacGregor, R., Goldman, A., George, A. E., & Rampal, S. (1980). Positron-emission tomography in the study of aging and senile dementia. *Neurobiology of Aging, 1*, 127–131.

Finley, D. M., Osburn, H. G., Dubin, J. A., & Jeanneret, P. R. (1977). Behaviorally based rating scales: Effects of specific anchors and disguised scale continua. *Personnel Psychology, 30*, 659–669.

Fishback, D. B. (1977). Mental status questionnaire for organic brain syndrome, with a new visual counting test. *Journal of the American Geriatric Society, 25*, 167–172.

Folstein, M. F., Folstein, S. E., & McHugh, P. R. (1975). Mini-Mental State: A practical method for grading the cognitive state of patients for the clinician. *Journal of Psychiatric Research, 12*, 189–198.

Gaitz, C. M., Varner, R. V., & Overall, J. E. (1977). Organic brain syndrome in late life. *Archives of General Psychiatry, 34*, 839–847.

Garside, R. F. (1976). The comparative value of types of rating scale. *British Journal of Clinical Pharmacology,* (Suppl.), 61–67.

Gurland, B. J. (1980). The assessment of the mental health status of older adults. In J. E. Birren & R. B. Sloan (Eds.), *Handbook of mental health and aging* (pp. 671–700). New York: Prentice-Hall.

Guy, W. (1976). *ECDEU assessment manual for psychopharmacology* (DHEW Publication No. ADM 76-388). Washington, DC: U. S. Department of Health, Education, and Welfare.

Hamilton, M. (1960). A rating scale for depression. *Journal of Neurology, Neurosurgery, and Psychiatry, 23*, 56–62.

Hamot, H. B., Patin, J. R., & Singer, J. M. (1984). Factor structure of the Sandoz Clinical Assessment Geriatric (SCAG) scale. *Psychopharmacology Bulletin, 20*(Suppl. 1), 142–150.

Honigfeld, G. (1981). The evaluation of ward behavior rating scales for psychogeriatric use. *Psychopharmacology Bulletin, 17*(Suppl. 4), 82–95.

Honigfeld, G. (1983). Psychopathology rating scales for use by nursing personnel. In T. Crook, S. Ferris, & R. Bartus (Eds.), *Assessment in geriatric psychopharmacology* (pp. 81–96). New Canaan, CT: Mark Powley.

Kahn, R. L., Goldfarb, A. I., Pollack, M., & Peck, A. (1960). Brief objective measures for the determination of mental status in the aged. *American Journal of Psychiatry, 117*, 326–328.

Katzman, R., Brown, T., Fuld, P., Peck, A., Schechter, R., & Schimmel, H. (1983). Validation of a short orientation-memory-concentration test of cognitive impairment. *American Journal of Psychiatry, 140*(6), 734–739.

Kochansky, G. E. (1979). Psychiatric rating scales for assessing psychopathology in the elderly: A critical review. In A. Raskin & L. F. Jarvik (Eds.), *Psychiatric symptoms and cognitive loss in the elderly* (pp. 125–156). New York: Wiley.

Mattis, S. (1976). Mental status examination for organic mental syndrome in the elderly patient. In L. Bellak & T. B. Karasu (Eds.), *Geriatric psychiatry: A handbook for psychiatrists and primary care physicians* (pp. 79–121). New York: Grune & Stratton.

McDonald, R. J. (1982). Drug treatment in senile dementia. In D. Wheatley (Ed.), *Psychopharmacology of old age* (pp. 113–138). England: Oxford University Press.

Mohs, R. C., Rosen, W. G., & Davis, K. L. (1982). Defining treatment efficacy in patients with Alzheimer's disease. In S. Corkin, K. L. Davis, J. H. Growdon, E. Usdin, & R. J. Wurtman (Eds.), *Alzheimer's disease: A report of progress in research* (pp. 351–356). New York: Raven Press.

Overall, J. E. (1983). Psychiatric rating scales: State of the art and directions for future research. In T. Crook, S. Ferris, & R. Bartus (Eds.), *Assessment in geriatric psychopharmacology* (pp. 69–79). New Canaan, CT: Mark Powley.

Overall, J. E., & Beller, S. A. (1984). The Brief Psychiatric Rating Scale (BPRS) in geropsychiatric research: 1. Factor structure on an inpatient unit. *Journal of Gerontology, 39*(2), 187–193.

Overall, J. E., & Gorham, D. R. (1962). The Brief Psychiatric Rating Scale. *Psychological Reports, 10*, 799–812.

Overall, J. E., Hollister, L. E., Johnson M., & Pennington, V. (1966). Nosology of depression and differential response to drugs. *Journal of the American Medical Association, 195*, 946–948.

Pfeiffer, E. (1975). A short portable mental status questionnaire for the assessment of organic brain deficit in elderly patients. *Journal of the American Geriatrics Society, 23*, 433–441.

Raskin, A., & Crook, T. (1977). *The inventory of psychic and somatic complaints in the elderly.* Unpublished manuscript.

Reisberg, B. (1983a). The Brief Cognitive Rating Scale and Global Deterioration Scale. In T. Crook, S. Ferris, & R. Bartus (Eds.), *Assessment in geriatric psychopharmacology* (pp. 19–35). New Canaan, CT: Mark Powley.

Reisberg, B. (1983b). Clinical presentation, diagnosis, and symptomatology of age-associated cognitive decline and Alzheimer's disease. In B. Reisberg (Ed.), *Alzheimer's disease* (pp. 173–187). New York: Free Press/Macmillan.

Reisberg, B., Ferris, S., de Leon, M., Anand, R., Schneck, M., Geibel, V., & England, E. (in press). The Brief Cognitive Rating Scale: A clinical instrument for the assessment and diagnosis of primary degenerative dementia. *American Journal of Psychiatry*.

Reisberg, B., Ferris, S. H., de Leon, M. J., & Crook, T. (1982). The Global Deterioration Scale for assessment of primary degenerative dementia. *American Journal of Psychiatry*, *139*(9), 1136–1139.

Reisberg, B., Ferris, S. H., Schneck, M. K., de Leon, M. J., Crook, T., & Gershon, S. (1981). The relationship between psychiatric assessments and cognitive test measures in mild to moderately cognitively impaired elderly. *Psychopharmacology Bulletin*, *17*, 99–101.

Reisberg, B., Schneck, M. K., Ferris, S. H., Schwartz, G. E., & de Leon, M. J. (1983). The Brief Cognitive Rating Scale (BCRS): Findings in primary degenerative dementia (PDD). *Psychopharmacology Bulletin*, *19*(1), 47–50.

Rosen, W. G., Mohs, R. C., & Davis, K. L. (1984). A new rating scale for Alzheimer's disease. *American Journal of Psychiatry*, *14*(11), 1356–1364.

Saal, F. E., & Landy, F. J. (1977). The mixed standard rating scale: An evaluation. *Organizational, Behavioral, and Human Performance*, *18*, 19–35.

Salzman, C. (1983). The Sandoz Clinical Assessment–Geriatric Scale. In T. Crook, S. Ferris, & R. Bartus (Eds.), *Assessment in geriatric psychopharmacology* (pp. 53–58). New Canaan, CT: Mark Powley.

Salzman, C., Kochansky, G. E., & Shader, R. I. (1972). Rating scales for geriatric psychopharmacology: A review. *Psychopharmacology Bulletin*, *8*, 3–50.

Schwab, D. P., Heneman, H. G., & DeCotiis, T. A. (1975). Behaviorally anchored rating scales: A review of the literature. *Personnel Psychology*, *28*, 549–562.

Schwartz, G. E. (1983). Development and validation of the Geriatric Evaluation by Relatives Rating Instrument (GERRI). *Psychological Reports*, *53*, 479–488.

Shader, R. I., Harmatz, J. S., & Salzman, C. (1974). A new scale for clinical assessment in geriatric populations: Sandoz Clinical Assessment Geriatric (SCAG). *Journal of the American Geriatrics Society*, *22*, 107–113.

Shader, R. I., Harmatz, J. S., & Tammerk, H. A. (1979). Towards an observation structure for rating dysfunction and pathology in ambulatory geriatrics. In W. Meir-Ruge (Ed.), *Central nervous system aging and its neuropharmacology* (pp. 153–168). Basel: Karger.

Silver, C. P. (1972). Simple methods of testing ability in geriatric patients. *Clinical Gerontologist*, *14*, 110–114.

Smith, J. (1979). Nurse and psychiatric aide rating scales for assessing psychopathology in the elderly: A critical review. In A. Raskin & L. F. Jarvik (Eds.), *Psychiatric symptoms and cognitive loss in the elderly* (pp. 169–186). New York: Halsted Press.

Smith, P. C., & Kendall, L. M. (1963). Retranslation of expectations: An approach to the construction of unambiguous anchors for rating scales. *Journal of Applied Psychology*, *47*(2), 149–155.

Taylor, M. A., Abrams, R., Faber, R., & Almy, G. (1980). Cognitive tasks in the mental status examination. *The Journal of Nervous and Mental Disease*, *168*(Suppl. 3), 167–170.

Venn, R. D. (1978). Clinical pharmacology of ergot alkaloids in senile cerebral insufficiency. In B. Berde & H. O. Schild (Eds.), *Ergot alkaloids and related compounds* (pp. 533–566). Berlin: Springer.

Venn, R. D. (1980). Review of clinical studies with ergots in gerontology. In M. Goldstein, D. Calne, A. Lieberman, & M. Therwen (Eds.), *Ergot compounds and brain function* (pp. 363–380). New York: Raven Press.

Venn, R. D. (1983). The Sandoz Clinical Assessment Geriatric (SCAG) scale: A general purpose psychogeriatric rating scale. *Gerontology*, *29*, 185–198.

Vitaliano, P. P., Breen, A. R., Albert, M., Russo, J., & Prinz, P. N. (1984). Memory, attention, and functional status in community residing Alzheimer type dementia patients and optimally healthy aged individuals. *Journal of Gerontology*, *39*(1), 58–64.

Wittenborn, J. R. (1967). Do rating scales objectify clinical impression? *Comprehensive Psychiatry*, *8*, 386–392.

Wittenborn, J. R. (1972). Reliability, validity and objectivity of symptom-rating scales. *Journal of Nervous and Mental Disease*, *169*, 139–156.

Zimmerman, R. L., Vestre, N. D., & Hunter, S. H. (1975). Validity of family informants' rating of psychiatric patients: General validity. *Psychological Reports*, *37*, 619–630.

Steven H. Ferris, Thomas Crook, Charles Flicker, Barry Reisberg, and Raymond T. Bartus

CHAPTER

14

Assessing Cognitive Impairment and Evaluating Treatment Effects: Psychometric Performance Tests

Psychometric tests serve two important functions in treatment studies with elderly or demented subjects: They help both in selecting and assessing subjects initially and in evaluating treatment effects. The measures currently used for selecting subjects (standardized tests and mental status evaluations) are reviewed. Tests for evaluating treatment effects often differ from those used for selecting subjects because the former do not require normative data and may assess a wide variety of specific cognitive functions. The criteria for selecting or developing a treatment assessment battery are discussed, and a recommended battery that meets these criteria is described. A discussion of directions for future test development considers the need for human tasks that parallel the animal memory tests used in initial drug development, and a new human memory task that satisfies this need is described.

Psychometric performance tests are reliable, valid, and standardized measures (see Cunningham, chapter 4 in this volume). Such measures are particularly useful in research on aging in which the goal is to assess the effects of treatment on cognitively impaired subjects. Treatment studies with elderly subjects often involve evaluating drugs but also may assess memory training (e.g., use of mnemonics), psychotherapy, and other therapeutic approaches. The majority of these studies are conducted with outpatients, and the severity of cognitive impairment typically varies from very mild to only moderately severe. Objective cognitive testing plays two essential roles in treatment studies with this population: (a) diagnosing and selecting patients and (b) assessing treatment effects. Because the requirements for fulfilling these two functions may differ, different measures are often used.

Selecting Patients

Performance tests are quite valuable tools to verify objectively the presence of cognitive deficits in mildly to moderately impaired elderly subjects. Of course, documenting cognitive impairment is not equivalent to diagnosis, because the same cognitive symptoms can result from quite different underlying disorders. Rather, the task in selecting patients for treatment studies is to operationalize cognitive impairment and establish clear criteria for subject inclusion. When the intent is to select patients with mild symptoms of cognitive decline, as is often the case in treatment studies, the need for sensitive, objective measures becomes particularly important.

There are not many psychometric tests that are useful for selecting patients, because most of the tests that are otherwise suitable do not provide normative data for older age groups, which are needed to distinguish impaired from normal individuals. The measures that are available fall into two general categories: standardized memory tests and extended mental status evaluations.

Standardized memory tests include several versions of the Wechsler Memory Scale (WMS) (Wechsler, 1945), the Guild Memory Test (Crook, Gilbert, & Ferris, 1980; Gilbert & Levee, 1971; Gilbert, Levee, & Catalano, 1968), Fuld's (1980) Object Memory Test, and the New York University (NYU) Memory Test (Randt, Brown, & Osborne, 1980). Each of these tests has published norms for older age groups.

1. The original WMS includes several subtests (which assess information and orientation, concentration, paragraph recall, memory for designs, and paired-associate recall), but norms are available only for the overall Memory Quotient (Wechsler, 1945).

2. The Guild Memory Test has subtests that assess digit span, paragraph recall (immediate and delayed), paired-associate recall (immediate and delayed), and design recall. A unique feature of the normative data is that scores on each subtest are related not only to age but also to performance levels on the vocabulary subtest of the Wechsler Adult Intelligence Scale (WAIS) (Crook, Gilbert, & Ferris, 1980; Wechsler, 1981). Two alternate forms of the Guild test are available. Table 14-1 illustrates the use of standardized psychometric tests such as the WAIS and Guild for selecting research subjects. The table shows scores on the Guild test and WAIS for a sample of young, normal elderly, and impaired elderly subjects. All between-groups differences on the Guild subtests are statistically significant ($p < .01$). Thus, the Guild test assisted in selecting a group of elderly subjects with mild to moderate memory impairment.

3. Fuld's Object Memory Test is a verbal learning task in which the items are verbal labels of common objects that the subject must initially identify.

4. The NYU Memory Test has numerous subtests, which include general information, list learning, digit span, paired-associate learning, picture recognition, and incidental learning. Several of the subtests measure both delayed and 24-hour recall, and five alternate forms of the test are available for repetitive administrations. Detailed norms and an instruction manual are available.

For each of the four standardized tests described, the author or authors have reported reasonable evidence supporting the test's sensitivity, reliability, and valid-

ity. The Guild Memory Test has been used routinely for screening and selecting patients at the New York University (NYU) Geriatric Study and Treatment Program, and the other three tests have served a similar function for other research groups. The WMS, Guild Memory Test, and NYU Memory Test have been used in conjunction with clinical drug trials.

Mental status evaluations are not psychometric tests, but they bridge the gap between clinical rating-scale evaluations (see chapters 11–13, this volume) and psychometric tests. The mental status scales include the original Mental Status Questionnaire (MSQ) (Kahn, Goldfarb, Pollack, & Peck, 1960), Blessed's Dementia Rating Scale (Blessed, Tomlinson, & Roth, 1968), and the popular Mini-Mental State Examination (MMSE) (Folstein, Folstein, & McHugh, 1975). The 10-question MSQ formalizes the information and orientation questions traditionally used in a psychiatric interview (e.g., What is the day? the date? the name of the president?). Blessed's scale and the MMSE include, in addition, some specific items assessing memory, attention, and other cognitive functions, resulting in evaluations that are both broader and more specific. Because normal–abnormal cutoff scores are available for each of these mental status evaluations, these tests can objectively verify cognitive impairment consistent with some forms of dementia.

The comparative utility of one standardized memory test (the Guild) and one mental status measure (the MSQ) is illustrated in Figure 14-1. On this figure, level of impairment is indicated by level on the Global Deterioration Scale (GDS) (Reisberg, Ferris, de Leon, & Crook, 1982). For normal functioning to moderate levels of global clinical impairment (levels 1 to 4 on the GDS), the Guild Memory Test discriminates well be-

Table 14-1. Mean Scores of Three Subject Groups on WAIS and the Guild Memory Test

Measure	Impaired Elderly ($n = 60$)	Normal Elderly ($n = 44$)	Normal Young ($n = 63$)
WAIS			
Vocabulary[a]	13.7 (3.3)	15.4 (2.9)	14.7 (2.9)
Digit Symbol[a]	6.3 (2.7)	8.6 (2.0)	13.3 (2.5)
Digit Span			
Forward	6.8 (1.4)	7.2 (1.3)	7.3 (1.3)
Backward	4.5 (1.1)	5.5 (1.5)	5.7 (1.3)
Guild Memory Test			
Paragraph Recall			
Immediate	5.3 (2.9)	9.7 (2.3)	11.1 (3.1)
Delayed	5.0 (3.5)	12.3 (3.0)	14.6 (3.8)
Paired-Associate Recall			
Immediate	1.4 (1.3)	4.6 (1.8)	6.7 (1.9)
Delayed	1.4 (1.4)	5.4 (1.9)	8.1 (2.1)
Design Recall	2.4 (1.8)	6.3 (2.5)	8.1 (1.6)

Note. Standard deviations are in parentheses. Adapted from Ferris, Crook, Clark, McCarthy, and Rae (1980) by permission.
[a]Standard scaled scores.

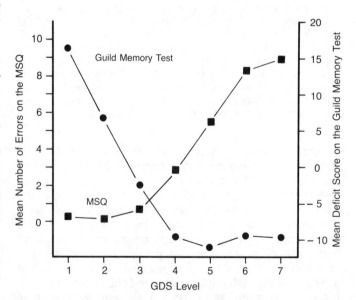

Figure 14-1. Mean transformed scores (difference from norm-based average) on the Guild Memory Test and MSQ (number of errors) for seven levels of global cognitive impairment as measured by the Global Deterioration Scale (GDS). The data are based on a total sample of 207 elderly subjects ranging in age from 60 to 85. Adapted from Ferris, Reisberg, de Leon, and Crook (1984) by permission.

tween impairment levels. But when the clinical symptoms become severe (levels 5 to 7 on the GDS), floor effects (i.e., absolute scores of zero) on the memory test limit its utility. The MSQ shows the opposite pattern: Ceiling effects limit the MSQ's utility for evaluating mild impairment, but the MSQ discriminates well between GDS levels for moderate to severe impairment. These results are specific to these tests, however. Easier psychometric tests certainly can be devised (e.g., by including recognition instead of recall tasks) that show floor effects at a higher level of severity. Also, Blessed's scale and the MMSE probably are more useful than the MSQ for differentiating between milder levels of impairment. However, the general conclusions regarding range of difficulty and severity of cognitive impairment are still applicable, namely, that psychometric tests are best for discriminating mild impairment, but mental status evaluations are best for discriminating levels of more severe impairment.

In summary, standardized psychometric tests and mental status evaluations are particularly valuable for selecting subjects for research. These assessment measures are also useful for assessing relative degree of impairment. Thus, the measures facilitate comparisons between samples in different studies.

Assessing Treatment

Measures used to assess effects of treatment for cognitive impairment often differ in one important respect from the standardized tests typically used for diagnosing patients and selecting subjects: Normative data are not essential for measures used to assess treatment, because change in performance, not the normality or abnormality of baseline function, is crucial. Thus, although the widely used, somewhat global standardized instruments certainly can be used for assessing treatment, in practice, investigators typically select more sophisticated experimental measures that evaluate more specific experimental constructs. Such measures tend to bridge the gap between the traditional psychometric measures and measures derived from cognitive psychology (see chapter 17, this volume).

The general requirements for batteries used to assess treatment are listed in Table 14-2. These require-

Table 14-2. Cognitive Battery for Treatment Assessment

1. Samples a variety of cognitive functions
2. Is sensitive to the deficits characteristic of aging or senile dementia
3. Is of appropriate difficulty for the sample being studied
4. Provides equivalent forms for repeated administration
5. Does not require more than one hour for administration
6. Is sensitive to effects of drugs
7. Has high reliability
8. Has high face validity
9. Has been validated against neuropathologic changes or performance in daily life

Note. Adapted from Ferris and Crook (1983) by permission.

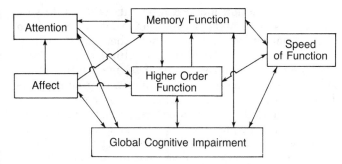

Figure 14-2. A simplified conceptual model of global cognitive impairment.

ments provide a rational framework for selecting or developing an optimal battery for cognitive assessment.

Figure 14-2 illustrates the major interacting factors that may combine to produce clinically observable global mental impairment. As the figure indicates, it is important that a battery for treatment assessment evaluate a wide variety of cognitive functions. A more detailed listing of the numerous subcomponents of this model is provided in Table 14-3. (Affect is discussed in section 4 of this book.)

Table 14-3. Cognitive Processes and Their Subcomponents

Cognitive Process	Subcomponents
Memory	
Primary memory (short-term; immediate)	
Secondary memory (long-term; recent)	Verbal and nonverbal/spatial memory
	Storage and retrieval
	Associative memory
	Depth of processing
	Effortful and automatic memory
	Declarative and procedural memory
Tertiary memory (remote)	Episodic and semantic memory
	Language ability
Other Cognitive Functions	
Attention	General arousal
	Selective attention
	Vigilance
Speed of function	Motor speed
	Perceptual speed
	Sensorimotor speed
	Central processing speed
Higher order cognition	Spatial orientation
	Constructional abilities
	Concept learning
	Problem solving
	Decision making

Memory function alone can be subdivided into several stages, processes, or constructs that are related to information-processing or other theoretical frameworks, and a test battery could evaluate each of these components and its contribution to age-related or dementia-related cognitive impairment. In practice, it is difficult to isolate fully each particular component or subcomponent for independent assessment, in part because of the mutual interactions among the various processes. However, by selecting appropriate tasks, it is possible to assess components that may be relevant in a particular study of treatment effects. This strategy is important, because a global change resulting from treatment may reflect underlying changes in attention, arousal, mood, memory, or other cognitive processes. Also, specific treatment effects that do not produce a global change may go undetected without a specialized battery. A well-constructed test battery makes it possible to determine the component or components responsible for changes in global or specific behavior.

A number of practical issues must also be considered in constructing a test battery for cognitive functions. The availability of equivalent forms is an important consideration. Although the number of test sessions depends on a study's design, tests must always be administered repetitively to evaluate change. Particularly with memory tasks, multiple equivalent forms are essential for retesting. Also, because elderly or demented patients become fatigued, lose motivation, or become uncooperative if a test battery is too long, a battery should last no longer than about 1 hour, if possible. If a study requires more extensive evaluation, rest periods or less demanding activities between sessions are useful. In studies designed to evaluate the effects of single doses of drugs with a short duration of action, very brief batteries are necessary.

The issue of task difficulty is important because ceiling or floor effects may mask changes due to treatment. Test reliability (consistency of individual results) is essential and relatively easy to demonstrate. But the important issues of sensitivity to drug effects and test validity present difficulties (see chapter 4, this volume). In cases of senile dementia, it is difficult to demonstrate a test's sensitivity to the effects of drugs because there are no clearly effective compounds. However, drugs that alter mental function can be administered to normal subjects to evaluate the sensitivity of cognitive measures to negative alterations. A classic example of this procedure is the study by Drachman and Leavitt (1974) in which scopolamine was used to depress cholinergic function in normal young subjects. On various measures, the subjects showed cognitive deficits similar to those seen in patients with senile dementia.

The issue of validity concerns whether a measure in the laboratory setting is related to the actual symptomatology of the patient who requires drug treatment. A test can be validated by showing it to be closely related either to the patient's actual performance of the principal tasks of daily life or to independent ratings by clinicians or family members of psychopathology shown by the patient in the community. In the case of disorders such as Alzheimer's disease, an alternate strategy is to validate a test against the characteristic brain changes. Unfortunately, at present few if any tests of psychological performance have been satisfactorily validated using any of these strategies. As discussed elsewhere in this book (see chapter 37 in this volume), validation is difficult because it is a somewhat circular, but convergent, process.

Some degree of validity can be inferred if a measure has "face validity," that is, if the nature of the task is realistic and bears an obvious relation to a difficulty in daily functioning. For example, memory tasks in which the subject must remember a grocery shopping list or recognize faces have greater face validity than tasks in which the stimuli are nonsense syllables or random shapes.

Tasks with high face validity have other important advantages. Tasks that are very abstract and artificial are adequate for studying memory in college students and other normal volunteers, but the tasks do not work so well with patients. Patients, and even normal elderly subjects, react quite negatively toward such tasks. They may, for example, feel threatened, develop anxiety, or refuse to cooperate. Face-valid tasks seem much more reasonable, relevant, and meaningful to elderly subjects and patients with dementia. Therefore, such tasks produce less anxiety, better cooperation, better motivation, and, consequently, more reliable data. Thus, a major challenge for the investigator is to develop sophisticated measures that address important memory constructs but also have high face validity.

Recommended Battery for Treatment Assessment

The battery recommended for use in treatment trials with normal elderly subjects or patients with mild to moderately severe dementia is summarized in Table 14-4. This particular battery assesses many, but not all, of the subcomponents listed in Table 14-3. The battery is weighted toward assessing memory, because memory impairment is generally the primary deficit in dementia.

Of the tests of primary memory (equivalent to immediate or short-term memory), the telephone task (Crook, Ferris, McCarthy, & Rae, 1980) has face validity, but the Brown-Peterson (Peterson & Peterson, 1959) and Sternberg (Sternberg, 1969) tasks do not. In the telephone task, 3-digit area codes, 7-digit phone numbers, and 10-digit combinations of the two are presented in random order. Immediately following each presentation, the subject must dial the number on a standard telephone dial. Accuracy of recall on the 7-digit and 10-digit numbers is sensitive to the effects of aging and dementia (Crook, Ferris, et al., 1980). Sensitivity to the effects of drugs has not as yet been demonstrated. The Brown-Peterson and Sternberg

Table 14-4. Recommended Cognitive Battery for Treatment Assessment

Cognitive Process	Test
Memory Tasks	
Primary memory	Telephone task
	Brown-Peterson task
	Sternberg task
Secondary memory	Verbal: shopping list task
	Nonverbal: facial recognition task
	Spatial: misplaced objects task
	Associative: first–last names task, name–face task
Tertiary memory	Category retrieval task
Other Cognitive Tasks	
Attention	Continuous performance test
Speed of function	Motor: finger-tapping task
	Perceptual: perceptual speed test
	Sensorimotor and central processing: Digit Symbol subtest, WAIS reaction time task

Note. Adapted from Ferris and Crook (1983) by permission.

tasks probe, respectively, retention of information in primary memory and speed of scanning in primary memory (see chapter 17 in this volume for descriptions of these tasks). Although both tasks are sensitive to aging and have shown sensitivity to the effects of drugs, the difficulty of these tasks is appropriate only for patients with very mild dementia. Easier, face-valid versions of these useful procedures are clearly needed.

The tests of secondary memory (equivalent to recent or long-term memory) all have excellent face validity. The shopping list task (McCarthy, Ferris, Clark, & Crook, 1981) currently utilizes Buschke and Fuld's (1974) selective reminding and scoring procedures. Each of the 18 available word lists for this task is composed of 10 common food items that can be purchased in a supermarket. The shopping list task is sensitive to the effects of aging and dementia (McCarthy et al., 1981), and it has been used in several drug studies (see, e.g., Ferris, Reisberg, Crook, et al., 1982; Ferris, Reisberg, Schneck, Mir, & Geibel, in press), in one case showing sensitivity to the effects of a drug (Ferris, Reisberg, Friedman, et al., 1982).

The first–last names task and name–face tasks (Clark, Ferris, Crook, & McCarthy, 1982) evaluate associative memory for verbal–verbal information (first and last names) and visual–verbal information (faces and first names). The tests evaluate associative span (accuracy of recall after a single presentation of 1, 3, 5, or 7 pairs) and paired-associate learning of 4 pairs (3 presentation and recall trials, followed by delayed recall). These tests of associative memory have been used in several drug trials (see, e.g., Ferris, Sathananthan,

Gershon, Clark, & Moshinsky, 1976; Ferris, Reisberg, Crook, et al., 1982), in one case showing sensitivity to the effects of a drug (Ferris et al., in press). Some representative data from performance on the name–face task (from Clark et al., 1982) are shown in Figure 14-3. The young, normal elderly, and impaired elderly groups differed significantly with respect to the list length that produced optimal recall.

In the facial recognition task (Ferris et al., 1980), the subject views a continuous sequence of unfamiliar faces and must indicate whether each face is "new" (first presentation) or was shown earlier in the sequence (second presentation). The time interval between first and second presentations may be varied systematically. This task may also be administered as a series of three learning trials, followed by a delayed recognition trial. The latter version of this test of visual recognition memory has been used in several drug trials (Crook, Ferris, Sathananthan, & Gershon, 1977; Ferris et al., in press; Ferris, Reisberg, Crook, et al., 1982; Ferris, Sathananthan, et al., 1976). The misplaced objects task (Crook, Ferris, & McCarthy, 1979) is a visuospatial memory task based on the common complaint of putting something away and not remembering where. The subject places representations of 10 common household objects (keys, glasses, book, etc.) into the various rooms of a representation of a 10-room

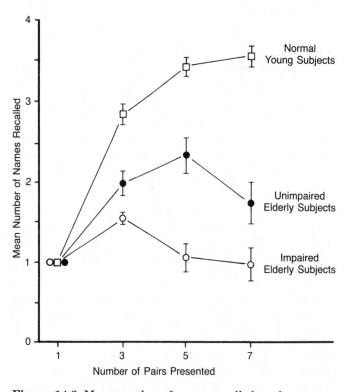

Figure 14-3. Mean number of names recalled on the name–face task for normal young subjects (ages 18–45, $N = 63$), normal elderly subjects (ages 60–85, $N = 44$), and elderly impaired subjects (ages 60–85, $N = 60$). Ranges shown by vertical lines are standard errors of measurement. Reprinted from Clark et al. (1982) by permission.

house. The subject later must recall where each object was placed. This task is sensitive to both normal aging and senile dementia (Crook et al., 1979).

The final memory task, category retrieval, assesses retrieval from semantic tertiary memory (equivalent to remote memory). The task involves producing words from either high- or low-frequency semantic categories selected on the basis of category norms (Battig & Montague, 1969). This task, which may also be considered a measure of language function, because it assesses verbal fluency, has been used in several drug studies (Ferris, Reisberg, Crook, et al., 1982; Reisberg et al., 1983).

The other cognitive measures listed in Table 14-4 generally lack face validity. However, the finger-tapping task (Lehmann & Ban, 1970), perceptual speed test (Moran & Mefferd, 1959), Digit-Symbol subtest from the WAIS, reaction time task (Ferris, Crook, Sathananthan, & Gershon, 1976), and continuous performance test (Kornetsky, 1972) are all well-established neuropsychological measures sensitive to aging and dementia that have frequently been used to assess the effects of drugs (see, e.g., Crook et al., 1977; Ferris et al., in press; Ferris, Sathananthan, et al., 1976; Ferris, Sathananthan, Reisberg, & Gershon, 1979; Reisberg et al., 1983).

The finger-tapping task involves rapid and repeated pressing of a lever with the right or left index finger for 15-second intervals. The perceptual speed test is a timed number-cancellation task in which rows of random numbers are presented. The Digit-Symbol subtest is a coding task (associating symbols with numbers). In the reaction time task, the subject is required to release a telegraph key only when one of three possible colored lights is presented. In the continuous performance test, a long sequence of capital letters is presented, one second each. The subject is required to press a key whenever an X is presented (X task) or whenever an X presented has been immediately preceded by presentation of an A (AX task).

The memory and other cognitive tests in the battery have been validated by showing relationships to both clinical-behavioral evaluations (Reisberg et al., 1981) and in vivo measures of changes in the brain (de Leon et al., 1979, 1980).

Overall, the recommended battery meets most of the requirements outlined in Table 14-2. It samples a variety of functions, the measures are sensitive to aging and dementia, the tasks provide an appropriate range of difficulty, and the measures are all available in multiple equivalent forms. In addition to having good face validity in most cases, the measures have shown good reliability, and validity with respect to activities of daily living or in vivo brain measures. Various shorter versions of this battery have been used successfully in drug trials at the New York University Geriatric Study and Treatment Program for more than 10 years. However, some of the measures have obvious weaknesses: Some are abstract and lack face validity, and others have not been shown to be sensitive to the effects of drugs. Furthermore, the battery as a whole is too long and somewhat redundant, although shorter versions can be selected to fit the needs of particular treatment studies. Finally, the battery does not adequately assess certain relevant cognitive functions, including language function, constructional abilities, spatial orientation, concept learning, problem solving, and decision making. Suitable measures in these areas remain to be developed and tested for the particular requirements of geriatric treatment trials.

Future Directions for Test Development

Compared with the cognitive measures used as recently as 10 years ago, the battery just outlined and others described in this book represent a major leap forward. Ten years ago, there were virtually no measures or batteries that met the criteria listed in Table 14-2. Measures typically used included the WMS, WAIS, and Halstead-Reitan Neuropsychological Test Battery (Reitan, 1979). Today there are a wide variety of good measures to choose from that meet all or many of the criteria in Table 14-2. Nevertheless, much work remains to be done in developing new or improved measures.

Abstract tasks that assess useful constructs (e.g., the Brown-Peterson and Sternberg tasks) should be replaced by the development of new versions with face validity. Also, cognitive processes such as language function and problem solving are not adequately covered by existing batteries, and tasks that assess these processes are needed. In addition, much work is needed to establish further the validity of many of the newer measures, as well as their sensitivity to the effects of drugs. Normative data would also be extremely valuable, so that the measures could be used for making diagnoses and selecting patients as well as for measuring treatment effects. The cognitive tests currently used for diagnosis lack many of the advantages of the newer tasks for assessing treatment (e.g., function specificity, face validity), and normative data are generally quite limited.

Another future direction concerns the computerization of the cognitive measures used in drug trials. Many of the tasks in the recommended battery are currently administered and scored using a microprocessor-based system. The advantages include improved consistency of administration, greater reliability, and greater ease of storing and analyzing data (see chapter 18 in this volume). Computerizing entire batteries may also lead to improved standardization across different research sites and may facilitate multicenter clinical trials. However, great care must be taken to avoid creating an artificial, mechanical testing environment, devoid of face validity. There is no substitute for human interaction as a means of minimizing stress, maximizing motivation and cooperation, and thereby ensuring reliable results.

A final issue concerns the development of tasks that are related to animal models of age-related memory or cognitive deficits. Drugs for improving memory may be highly effective in preclinical trials with animals but show no memory effects in humans. In such cases, it is unclear whether the drug does not work in humans or whether the clinical trial has failed to measure the same function as was measured in the animal trial. For this reason, it would be useful to develop and validate human tasks that closely parallel the animal models used for screening potential antidementia drugs. Similarity between animal and human tests would increase the probability of obtaining similar results across species, thereby facilitating the transition from preclinical to clinical testing. A new clinical task that parallels an animal task and conforms to the criteria in Table 14-2 is discussed next.

Visuospatial Delayed Recall Task

A new computerized delayed-recall task exemplifies our efforts to develop and evaluate new psychometric tests with increased face validity and similarity to both animal memory tests and human information-processing tasks. In this task, the subject is presented with a diagrammatic representation of a 25-room house. One of the rooms has a white square in it, and the subject is instructed to "try to remember which room has a light on in the window." The light remains on for 3 seconds and then the house disappears. After a delay interval of 0, 15, 30, 60, or 120 seconds, the house reappears, and the subject is asked to point to the previously illuminated room. During retention intervals greater than 0 seconds, the subject performs a choice reaction time task. In this task, the subject views a diagrammatic representation of two tall buildings. After a variable foreperiod, a lightning bolt appears, striking one of the towers. The subject is instructed to send in a fire alarm if a fire appears on the right or left building by pressing the corresponding button of a reaction time apparatus. On one third of the trials there is no fire, on one third of the trials there is a fire on the right, and on one third there is a fire on the left.

We selected a visuospatial stimulus for this test for several reasons, including the association between Alzheimer's disease and spatial disorientation (Blessed et al., 1968), the current availability of many verbal memory tests, and the potential for comparing a nonverbal task with animal memory tests. In fact, the design of this task was in large part based on a delayed-response task currently used to assess memory function in aged nonhuman primates.

A study was conducted to determine the discriminant validity of the new task (Flicker, Bartus, Crook, & Ferris, 1984). Subjects with senile dementia were recruited from a population of elderly outpatients at the NYU Geriatric Study and Treatment Program. Most of the normal aged subjects were spouses and siblings of the patients, and all elderly subjects were between 57 and 85 years of age. The group of normal young subjects consisted of laboratory personnel between the ages of 18 and 42. All elderly subjects had received a clinical interview with a psychiatrist and had been rated on the GDS. On the basis of this rating,

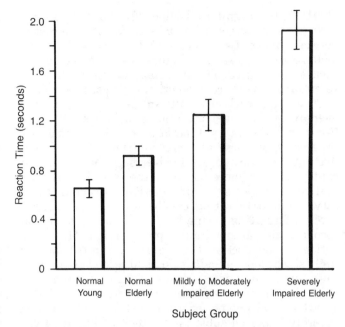

Figure 14-4. Mean response latency on the choice reaction time task for 20 normal young subjects (ages 18–42), 29 normal elderly subjects (ages 57–85, GDS 1–2), and 76 impaired elderly subjects (ages 57–85) divided into mildly to moderately impaired subjects (GDS 3–4) and severely impaired subjects (GDS 5–6). Ranges shown by vertical lines are standard errors of measurement. Adapted from Flicker et al. (1984) by permission.

subjects were classified as normal (GDS 1–2), mildly to moderately impaired (GDS 3–4), severely impaired (GDS 5–6), or very severely impaired (GDS 7).

Older and more impaired subjects showed significantly longer reaction times, $F(3, 34) = 24.16$, $p < .0001$ (see Figure 14-4). Pair-wise comparisons between groups were all significant ($p < .01$). Thus, normal aged subjects were slower than normal young subjects. These results are consistent with results from a previous study indicating that disjunctive reaction time can be used as a diagnostic measure for senile dementia, probably because disjunctive reaction time is more sensitive than simple reaction time to alterations in cognitive-processing ability (Ferris, Crook, et al., 1976). In the present study, severely impaired subjects made many incorrect responses and took a long time to respond (mean reaction time was 1.92 seconds; see Figure 14-4). These results imply that sensorimotor responsivity may not have been the primary determinant of the poor performance of severely impaired subjects on this task. About half of the severely impaired subjects were incapable of following the instructions for this task, and many of the moderately and severely impaired subjects appeared to have difficulty understanding and remembering the instructions.

Performance on the delayed-recall task, measured as the percentage of correct responses, exhibited significant effects of delay interval ($F[4, 144] = 38.99$, $p <$

.0001) and of cognitive decline ($F[3, 36] = 28.33$, $p < .0001$). There was also a significant interaction between these two factors, $F(12, 144) = 5.07$, $p < .0001$. As can be seen in Figure 14-5, the decrease in accuracy produced by increasing the duration of the retention interval occurred primarily over intervals up to 30 seconds, with no significant decrease in accuracy over intervals longer than 30 seconds. Except at the 0-second delay interval, performance on the task was progressively worse at increasing levels of cognitive dysfunction. Normal aged subjects performed significantly ($p < .01$) more poorly on the task than did normal young subjects. The interaction between delay interval and GDS rating can be ascribed to different rates of forgetting among the four groups over the 30-second period after stimulus presentation. This interaction can be discerned in Figure 14-5 in the increasingly steep slope for delays up to 30 seconds in increasingly more impaired groups. Excluded from data analysis were very severely impaired subjects (GDS = 7), who could not perform the task at all, and some severely impaired subjects who took a simplified version of the test.

It has been previously reported that primary memory is unaffected by normal aging (Craik, 1977) but is impaired in demented subjects (Miller, 1977). In support of these findings, on the delayed-recall task, per-

formance in the 0-second delay condition showed a significant ($p < .01$) effect for presence of dementia but not for age. The decline in accuracy of responses over delay intervals up to 30 seconds thus seems to reflect forgetting from primary memory, and the increasingly poor performance with increasing severity of dementia may reflect accelerated forgetting from primary memory. The less impaired subjects may also have been compensating better for decay from primary memory by utilizing alternative means of recall, such as rehearsal strategies or secondary memory processes. The demented subjects' capacity for longer term storage is apparent in the absence of any performance decrement for delay intervals between 30 and 120 seconds. Because rehearsal was presumably prevented by the interposed reaction time task, some secondary memory mechanism must have been acting to maintain recall percentages above the level expected by chance. It seems possible that between-groups differences in this secondary memory process may have been responsible for the between-groups differences in the rate of forgetting during the first 30 seconds after stimulus presentation. This suggestion is compatible with results from previous studies indicating that the most severe memory problem of the aged and demented is impaired encoding into secondary memory (Craik, 1977; Morley, Haxby, & Lundgren, 1980).

As mentioned, this delayed visuospatial recall task was designed for comparability with memory tests for animals. In fact, a similar delayed-response paradigm using a 3×3 stimulus–response matrix and food reinforcement has been applied to the study of nonhuman primates. Aged monkeys perform similarly to aged human subjects, exhibiting decreased accuracy of spatial localization at delay intervals greater than 0 seconds. This test for primates has been used to evaluate a wide variety of potential pharmacological treatments for age-related cognitive disorders (Bartus, Dean, & Beer, 1983). The similarity of this test and the delayed visuospatial recall task increases the likelihood of observing similar effects in animals and humans, thus reciprocally enhancing the predictive value and reliability of test results.

In conclusion, the delayed visuospatial recall task satisfies many of the criteria suggested for batteries that assess treatments for age-related cognitive dysfunction. It is a test of spatial information processing and memory, cognitive capacities that have been histopathologically confirmed to be impaired by Alzheimer's disease (Blessed et al., 1968). The test is sensitive to differences in cognitive ability between young and old subjects, between normal aged and demented subjects, and between subjects with senile dementia of different degrees of severity. It is comparable to animal tests currently in use, so pharmacological effects observed are likely to correspond to results obtained in preclinical evaluations. Test administration and data collection are almost fully automated, thus maximizing the test's efficiency and reliability. Finally, the test has a reasonable degree of face validity, which improves patients' compliance and enhances the test's relevance to day-to-day function.

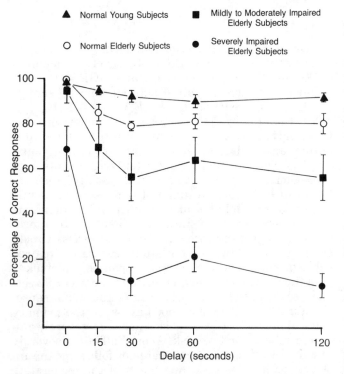

Figure 14-5. Percentage of correct responses on the delayed visuospatial recall task for 20 normal young subjects (ages 18–42), 29 normal elderly subjects (ages 57–85, GDS 1–2), and 76 elderly impaired subjects (ages 57–85) divided into mildly to moderately impaired subjects (GDS 3–4) and severely impaired subjects (GDS 5–6). Ranges shown by vertical lines are standard errors of measurement. Adapted from Flicker et al. (1984) by permission.

References

Bartus, R. T., Dean, R. L., & Beer, B. (1983). An evaluation of drugs for improving memory in aged monkeys: Implications for clinical trials in humans. *Psychopharmacology Bulletin, 19,* 168–184.

Battig, W. F., & Montague, W. E. (1969). Category norms for verbal items in 56 categories: A replication and extension of the Connecticut category norms. *Journal of Experimental Psychology Monographs, 80*(3, Pt. 2), 1–46.

Blessed, G., Tomlinson, B. E., & Roth, M. (1968). The association between quantitative measures of dementia and senile change in the cerebral grey matter of elderly subjects. *British Journal of Psychiatry, 114,* 797–811.

Buschke, H., & Fuld, P. A. (1974). Evaluating storage, retention, and retrieval in disordered memory and learning. *Neurology, 24*(11), 1019–1025.

Clark, E., Ferris, S. H., Crook, T., & McCarthy, M. (1982). *Paired-associate span and learning in aging and dementia.* Unpublished manuscript.

Craik, F. I. M. (1977). Age differences in human memory. In J. E. Birren & K. W. Schaie (Eds.), *Handbook of the psychology of aging* (pp. 384–420). New York: Van Nostrand Reinhold.

Crook, T., Ferris, S. H., & McCarthy, M. (1979). The misplaced-objects task: A brief test for memory dysfunction in the aged. *Journal of the American Geriatrics Society, 27,* 284–287.

Crook, T., Ferris, S. H., McCarthy, M., & Rae, D. (1980). The utility of digit recall tasks for assessing memory in the aged. *Journal of Consulting and Clinical Psychology, 48,* 228–233.

Crook, T., Ferris, S. H., Sathananthan, G., & Gershon, S. (1977). Methylphenidate and cognitive performance in geriatric patients. *Psychopharmacology, 52,* 251–255.

Crook, T., Gilbert, J. G., & Ferris, S. H. (1980). Operationalizing memory impairment in elderly persons: The Guild Memory Test. *Psychological Reports, 47,* 1315–1318.

de Leon, M. J., Ferris, S. H., Blau, I., George, A. E., Reisberg, B., Kricheff, I. I., & Gershon, S. (1979, October 20). Correlations between CT changes and behavioral deficits in senile dementia. *Lancet,* pp. 859–860.

de Leon, M. J., Ferris, S. H., George, A. E., Reisberg, B., Kricheff, I. I., & Gershon, S. (1980). Computed tomography evaluations of brain–behavior relationships in senile dementia of the Alzheimer's type. *Neurobiology of Aging, 1,* 69–79.

Drachman, D. A., & Leavitt, J. (1974). Human memory and the cholinergic system: A relationship to aging? *Archives of Neurology, 30,* 113–121.

Ferris, S. H., & Crook, T. (1983). Cognitive assessment in mild to moderately severe dementia. In T. Crook, S. Ferris, & R. Bartus (Eds.), *Assessment in geriatric psychopharmacology.* New Canaan, CT: Mark Powley.

Ferris, S. H., Crook, T., Clark, E., McCarthy, M., & Rae, D. (1980). Facial recognition memory deficits in normal aging and senile dementia. *Journal of Gerontology, 35,* 707–714.

Ferris, S. H., Crook, T., Sathananthan, G., & Gershon, S. (1976). Reaction time as a diagnostic measure of cognitive impairment in senility. *Journal of the American Geriatrics Society, 24,* 529–533.

Ferris, S. H., Reisberg, B., Crook, T., Friedman, E., Schneck, M. K., Mir, P., Sherman, K. A., Corwin, J., Gershon, S., & Bartus, R. T. (1982). Pharmacologic treatment of senile dementia: Choline, L-DOPA, piracetam, and choline/plus piracetam. In S. Corkin, K. L. Davis, J. H. Growdon, E. Usdin, & R. Wurtman (Eds.), *Alzheimer's disease: A report of progress in research* (pp. 475–481). New York: Raven Press.

Ferris, S. H., Reisberg, B., de Leon, M., & Crook, T. (1974). Recent developments in the assessment of dementia. In J. P. Abrahams & V. Crooks (Eds.), *Geriatric mental health* (pp. 55–73). Orlando, FL: Grune & Stratton.

Ferris, S. H., Reisberg, B., Friedman, E., Schneck, M. K., Sherman, K. A., Mir, P., & Bartus, R. T. (1982). Combination choline/piracetam treatment of senile dementia. *Psychopharmacology Bulletin, 18,* 94–98.

Ferris, S. H., Reisberg, B., Schneck, M. K., Mir, P., & Geibel, V. (in press). Effects of vasopressin on primary degenerative dementia. In J. M. Ordy, J. R. Sladek, & B. Reisberg (Eds.), *Neuropeptide and hormone modulation of brain function and homeostasis.* New York: Raven Press.

Ferris, S. H., Sathananthan, G., Gershon, S., Clark, C., & Moshinsky, J. (1976). Cognitive effects of ACTH 4–10 in the elderly. *Psychopharmacology, Biochemistry and Behavior, 5*(Suppl. 1), 73–78.

Ferris, S. H., Sathananthan, G., Reisberg, B., & Gershon, S. (1979). Long-term choline treatment of memory-impaired elderly patients. *Science, 205,* 1039–1040.

Flicker, C., Bartus, R. T., Crook, T., & Ferris, S. H. (1984). Effects of aging and dementia upon recent visuospatial memory. *Neurobiology of Aging, 5,* 275–283.

Folstein, M. F., Folstein, S. E., & McHugh, P. R. (1975). Mini-Mental State: A practical method for grading the cognitive state of patients for the clinician. *Journal of Psychiatric Research, 12,* 189–198.

Fuld, P. A. (1980). Guaranteed stimulus-processing in the evaluation of memory and learning. *Cortex, 16,* 255–271.

Gilbert, J. G., & Levee, R. F. (1971). Patterns of declining memory. *Journal of Gerontology, 26,* 70–75.

Gilbert, J. G., Levee, R. F., & Catalano, F. L. (1968). A preliminary report on a new memory scale. *Perceptual and Motor Skills, 27,* 277–278.

Kahn, R. L., Goldfarb, A. I., Pollack, M., & Peck, A. (1960). Brief objective measures for the determination of mental status in the aged. *American Journal of Psychiatry, 117,* 326–328.

Kornetsky, C. (1972). The use of a simple test of attention as a measure of drug effects in schizophrenic patients. *Psychopharmacologia, 24,* 99–106.

Lehmann, H. E., & Ban, T. A. (1970). Psychometric tests in evaluation of brain pathology responsive to drugs. *Geriatrics, 25,* 142–147.

McCarthy, M., Ferris, S. H., Clark, E., & Crook, T. (1981). Acquisition and retention of categorized material in normal aging and senile dementia. *Experimental Aging Research, 7,* 127–135.

Miller, E. (1977). *Abnormal ageing.* New York: Wiley.

Moran, L. J., & Mefferd, R. B. (1959). Repetitive psychometric measures. *Psychological Reports, 5,* 269–275.

Morley, G. K., Haxby, J. V., & Lundgren, S. L. (1980). Memory, aging, and dementia. In G. J. Maletta & F. J. Pirozzolo (Eds.), *The aging nervous system: Vol. I. Advances in neurogerontology* (pp. 211–240). New York: Praeger.

Peterson, L. R., & Peterson, M. J. (1959). Short-term retention of individual verbal items. *Journal of Experimental Psychology, 58,* 193–198.

Randt, C. T., Brown, E. R., & Osborne, D. P., Jr. (1980). A memory test for longitudinal measurement of mild to moderate deficits. *Clinical Neuropsychology, 2,* 184–194.

Reisberg, B., Ferris, S. H., Anand, R., Mir, P., Geibel, V., de Leon, M. J., & Roberts, E. (1983). Effects of naloxone in senile dementia: A double-blind trial. *New England Journal of Medicine, 308,* 721–722.

Reisberg, B., Ferris, S. H., de Leon, M. J., & Crook, T. (1982).

The Global Deterioration Scale for assessment of primary degenerative dementia. *American Journal of Psychiatry, 139*(9), 1136–1139.

Reisberg, B., Ferris, S. H., Schneck, M. K., de Leon, M. J., Crook, T., & Gershon, S. (1981). The relationship between psychiatric assessments and cognitive test measures in mild to moderately cognitively impaired elderly. *Psychopharmacology Bulletin, 17,* 99–101.

Reitan, R. M. (1979). *Halstead-Reitan Neuropsychological Test Battery*. Tucson, AZ: University of Arizona, Neuropsychology Laboratory.

Sternberg, S. (1969). Memory-scanning: Mental processes revealed by reaction-time experiments. *American Scientist, 57,* 421–457.

Wechsler, D. A. (1945). A standardized memory scale for clinical use. *Journal of Psychology, 19,* 87–95.

Wechsler, D. A. (1981). *Wechsler Adult Intelligence Scale-Revised (WAIS-R)*. New York: Psychological Corporation.

Richard C. Mohs, Youngjai Kim, Celeste A. Johns, Daniel D. Dunn, and Kenneth L. Davis

CHAPTER

15

Assessing Changes in Alzheimer's Disease: Memory and Language

The principal cognitive symptoms associated with Alzheimer's disease (AD) are memory loss, dysphasia, and dyspraxia. The longitudinal development of these symptoms has not been determined, and techniques for measuring change are not generally agreed on. Three memory tests (word recall, word recognition, paired-associate learning) and two language tests (naming and sentence reading) were given to patients with AD and 12 matched control subjects at the beginning of this study and after 12 months. Generally, patients were more impaired on the more difficult tests, such as the word recall test and naming test for low-frequency objects. However, the tests' sensitivity to change in the patients with AD depended on both test difficulty and the patients' baseline ability. It is recommended that tests with different degrees of difficulty be included in any longitudinal assessment of the severity of AD.

The principal symptoms associated with Alzheimer's disease (AD) have been described clinically by many investigators (e.g., Liston, 1979; Meyer-Gross, Slater, & Roth, 1969; Mohs, Rosen, & Davis, 1982; Sim & Sussman, 1962; Torack, 1978). Nearly all patients suffer a progressive loss of memory, language, and praxis functions. Associated with the cognitive loss in some patients are abnormalities in mood, agitation, disturbance of sleep, and, occasionally, violence and other grossly disturbed behavior. Although these impairments have been described clinically, several important questions regarding the evolution of AD symptoms remain unanswered. It is not yet known, for example, how to detect and measure the earliest symptoms of AD. Also, it is not yet known whether the apparently atypical symptom patterns observed in some patients (see, e.g., Crystal, Horoupian, Katzman, & Jotkowitz, 1981) are associated with either a clinically distinct prognosis or a distinct pattern of neurochemical deficits. One of the most important unanswered questions is how to evaluate change in symptomatol-

ogy. Currently, there is no generally accepted method of staging patients with AD throughout the course of the illness. Also, there is no generally accepted method for measuring the severity of symptoms that can serve as a standard in treatment studies.

The problems of staging, measuring the severity of symptoms, and evaluating treatments could be dealt with much more readily if information were available on the longitudinal course of the symptoms of AD. AD is clearly progressive and degenerative, yet only a few studies such as those of Blessed & Wilson (1982) and Kaszniak et al. (1978) have examined cognitive decline longitudinally. In no studies that we are aware of have patients been given a standard set of cognitive tests at regular intervals. A number of cross-sectional studies have been done (e.g., Miller, 1973), but it is not clear whether their results apply to all patients or only to those at a certain point in the disease process. Knowledge of the longitudinal course of this illness can be obtained only by examining patients along clinically relevant dimensions as the disease progresses. At the same time, our knowledge of what methods give meaningful data about these patients will increase as more patients are examined. Clinical knowledge and methodologic sophistication will both be increased by systematic administration of a variety of tests for specific impairments over the course of the disease.

Because AD is progressive, it is likely that different kinds of tests are sensitive indicators of increasing impairment at different stages of the disease. Subtle cognitive impairments early in the disease process might be detected most readily by very difficult memory tests, whereas changes later in the course of the disease might be detected more readily by simpler tests of memory, language, and praxis. Fortunately, research with normal individuals clearly indicates the

149

factors that increase or decrease the level of difficulty of tests of memory and language. For normal people, tests of recognition memory are usually much easier than are tests of recall (Atkinson & Juola, 1974), and there is evidence that tests of recall memory are more sensitive to age-related memory decrements than are tests of recognition (Schonfield, 1965). Given a constant mode of testing for verbal material, two stimulus characteristics that greatly affect memory performance are word familiarity or frequency (Christian, Bickley, Tarka, & Clayton, 1978) and word vividness or imagery (Paivio, Yuille, & Rogers, 1969). Word frequency is also an important determinant of the measured degree of dysphasia: Some patients show word-finding impairment relative to normal subjects only when asked to name relatively unfamiliar objects (Barker & Lawson, 1968).

The purpose of this chapter is to present data on five selected tests of memory and language given to patients with AD and to nondemented subjects at two times, one year apart. The data show cross-sectional differences between the two groups and, more important, which kinds of tests were most sensitive to increasing severity of the patients' symptoms.

The tests were selected so that factors known to affect level of difficulty were varied systematically. The effects of testing mode are assessed by comparing tests of recall and recognition memory. The effects of frequency are evaluated both for tests of memory and for tests of language (a paired-associate learning task, a sentence-reading task, and a naming task).

Study Design

Subjects

Characteristics of the subjects in the study are summarized in Table 15-1. Twelve patients and twelve normal subjects matched for sex, age, and years of education were included. Each patient had at least a one-year history of progressive cognitive impairment and had a score of less than 10 on the Memory and Information Test (MIT) or a score of greater than 4 on the Dementia Rating Scale (DRS) (Roth & Hopkins, 1953). (Kay, 1977, showed that people with these cutoff scores on the MIT and DRS differentiate people with progressive dementia from nondemented elderly people and from

other elderly psychiatric patients with a high degree of specificity.) Also, each patient was tested to rule out all other possible causes of dementia. The tests used included complete medical, neurologic, and psychiatric examinations; a computerized axial tomographic (CAT) scan; tests of thyroid function; and B-12, folate, and routine laboratory tests. Particular care was taken to rule out patients with cognitive loss secondary to vascular or other neurologic disease or secondary to psychiatric illness. Patients with multi-infarct dementia were ruled out by excluding patients with unmedicated resting blood pressure greater than 150/90 and patients with scores greater than 4 on the ischemia scale (Hachinski, Lassen, & Marshall, 1974). Also excluded were patients with a history of alcoholism as defined by the Research Diagnostic Criteria (RDC) (Spitzer, Endicott, & Robins, 1978) and patients with a history of major affective disorder as defined by the RDC. Subjects in the nondemented group were all without evidence of cognitive impairment and satisfied the same medical exclusion criteria as patients. All subjects were free of all psychoactive medications at both times of testing.

Testing Schedule

All subjects were participants in a longitudinal comparison of patients with AD and healthy elderly people. As part of this study, each patient was given a series of cognitive tests and behavioral evaluations every 6 months and a medical review every 12 months. The initial cognitive, behavioral, and medical evaluation was done in the Psychiatry Service at the Bronx Veterans Administration Medical Center. For some patients, follow-up visits to the hospital were difficult, usually because of the patients' cognitive impairment, and in those cases, follow-up cognitive testing was done at home. The entire cognitive and behavioral evaluation for each visit took about 3 hours, sometimes divided into two or three sessions, and included tests of perception, praxis, and behavior as well as the tests described in this report.

Data from each of the five tests were analyzed separately using analysis of variance (ANOVA). Diagnosis (AD vs. nondemented) was always treated as a between-subjects factor, whereas time (baseline vs. follow-up) and task parameters (e.g., learning trial and frequency) were treated as repeated measures. Two patients were completely unable to do one or more of the tests at follow-up, and their data were omitted from the analysis of those tasks so as not to distort the results.

Recommended Tests and Results

Word Recognition Test

For this test, the subject was given three trials to learn a set of 12 unrelated words. Each word was printed in large letters on a three-by-five-inch card. On each

Table 15-1. Characteristics of Subjects Tested Longitudinally

| Group | Sex | | Age[a] (years) | Education[a] (years) |
	Males	Females		
Nondemented elderly	9	3	64 ± 6.4	15.1 ± 2.6
Patients with AD	9	3	64 ± 7.2	14.7 ± 3.1

[a]Data presented as mean ± standard deviation.

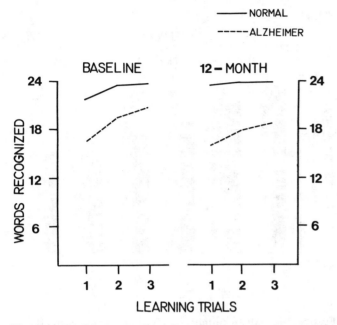

Figure 15-1. Mean number of words correctly classified as studied or new on the word recognition test by normal controls and Alzheimer's patients at baseline and follow-up.

learning trial, the cards were shown to the subject one at a time for 2 seconds each, and the subject was asked to read every word aloud to ensure that he or she paid attention to it. A test trial followed each learning trial. For the test trials, the 12 studied words were mixed with 12 new words (distractors) printed on identical cards. The 24 words were shown to the subject one at a time, and for each the subject was asked whether it was a word he or she had just seen. A new set of distractors was used for each test trial. To ensure that studied words and distractors were similar, sets were matched as closely as possible for frequency (Thorndike & Lorge, 1944) and for imagery (Paivio, Yuille, & Madigan, 1968). A similar list of study words was matched with three new sets of distractors for the retest after 12 months.

Figure 15-1 presents the results of the word recognition test. The main effects of diagnostic group ($F[1, 21] = 53.0$, $p < .001$) and learning trial ($F[2, 42] = 18.4$, $p < .001$) were significant, but the effect of time was not ($p > .10$). In addition, there were significant interactions of time with learning trial ($F[2, 42] = 7.5$, $p < .01$) and of diagnostic group with time ($F[1, 21] = 5.2$, $p < .03$). The interaction of group and trial was marginally significant ($F[2, 42] = 2.7$, $p = .08$). Both groups showed less improvement over trials at follow-up than at baseline. Although normal subjects improved slightly over the one-year period and obtained nearly perfect scores at baseline and retest, patients showed a decline in performance. Patients improved more over trials than did normal subjects—probably because the normal subjects obtained nearly perfect scores on all trials. Thus, the word recognition test clearly was sensitive to differences between patients and normal subjects and also was sensitive to increases in the severity of patients' symptoms over one year.

Word Recall Test

For this test, the subject tried to learn a list of 10 nouns belonging to the same semantic category. Categorized rather than unrelated words were used to make the test simple enough for patients and also to enable patients to clearly distinguish the words on this task from the ones used in the recognition task. The words selected for the lists were high-frequency instances from the following categories for which Battig and Montague (1969) provided norms: articles of furniture, parts of the body, parts of a building, articles of clothing, four-footed animals, weather phenomena, and birds. The lists were equated for mean frequency within category, and the subject saw different lists at baseline and follow-up. At the start of the first of four learning trials, the list was read to the subject at a rate of one word per second. Then the subject was asked to recall orally as many words on the list as possible. On the remaining three trials, selective reminding (Buschke, 1973) was used: The tester first reminded the subject of all of the words not recalled on the previous trial, and then the subject tried again to recall the entire list.

Figure 15-2 presents the results of this test. Patients performed much worse than did normal subjects ($F[1, 21] = 4.06$, $p < .001$), and performance of both groups improved across the four learning trials ($F[3, 36] = 19.7$, $p < .001$). There was no main effect due to time, and none of the interactions were significant ($p > .10$ in all cases). Thus, although the magnitude of the difference between groups on this test was very large at both baseline and follow-up, the test was not sensitive to any increase in symptom severity among the patients over the 12-month period.

Test of Paired-Associate Learning

For this test, the subject tried to learn a list of 15 pairs over three trials. Five of the pairs were high-frequency

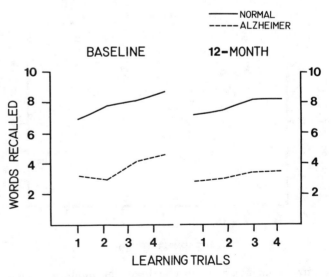

Figure 15-2. Mean number of words correctly recalled on the word recall test (Buschke, 1973).

associates (e.g., "table–chair"), five were medium-frequency associates (e.g., "head–think") and five were low-frequency associates (e.g., "king–green"). The kinds of pairs were mixed randomly on the list. Association frequencies were greater than 70, between 8 and 15, and less than 1 for the high-, medium- and low-frequency pairs, respectively (Palermo & Jenkins, 1964). Each pair was printed in large letters on a three-by-five-inch card. At the start of the first trial, the cards were presented one at a time for 2 seconds each, and the subject was asked to read each pair aloud. Then a set of cards showing only the first members of pairs was presented, and the subject was asked to supply the associated words. The same procedures were used on each trial, and a different, similarly constructed set of pairs was used at the follow-up session.

Figure 15-3 presents the data from this test. All four main effects (group, time, trial, and frequency) were significant ($p < .01$ in all cases) but are of little interest in light of the significant two- and three-way interactions. Most important was the significant interaction of group and frequency ($F[2, 38] = 30.1$, $p < .001$), which, as Figure 15-3 indicates, reflects the greater impairment of patients on low- and medium-frequency pairs than on high-frequency pairs. Also significant were interactions of group with trial ($p < .001$) and time with trial ($p < .01$) and the three-way interaction of group with trial and with frequency ($p < .01$). That is, improvement over trials was greatest for high-frequency items among patients but was greatest for low-frequency items among normal subjects; patients learned virtually no low-frequency items, but normal subjects learned most high-frequency items on the first trial. The interactions of group with time ($F[1, 19] = 3.9$, $p = .06$) and group with time with trial ($F[2, 38] = 2.6$, $p = .09$) were both marginally significant; as Figure 15-3 indicates, performance of the patients stayed nearly the same from baseline to follow-up, but performance of normal subjects tended to improve. Be-

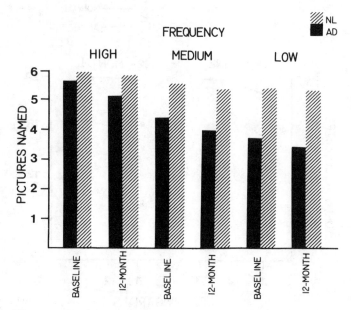

Figure 15-4. Mean number of pictures named correctly by normal subjects and AD patients in the test of confrontation naming.

cause there was no significant interaction of group, time, and frequency, however, it appears that none of the items used was more sensitive to change over time than others.

Test of Confrontation Naming

For the naming test, 18 black-and-white drawings of objects (e.g., bed, house) were selected from the Boston Naming Test (Kaplan, Goodglass, & Weintraub, 1978). Six of the objects had names with high frequencies (AA), six had names with medium frequencies (6 to 10), and six had names with low frequencies (less than 6) (Thorndike & Lorge, 1944). The subject viewed the drawings one at a time and was asked to name each.

Results are presented in Figure 15-4. The main effects of both group and frequency were significant ($p < .01$ in both cases), as was the interaction of group with frequency ($F[2, 42] = 6.4$, $p < .01$); all other effects were nonsignificant ($p > .10$ in all cases). As can be seen from the figure, patients correctly named fewer objects than normal subjects did, but the difference between groups was greater for objects with low-frequency names than for objects with medium- or high-frequency names. Because there was no interaction with time, apparently none of the conditions was sensitive to increasing language dysfunction among the patients over the one-year follow-up period.

Test of Sentence Reading

For this test, 10 sentences were selected from the Boston Diagnostic Aphasia Examination (Goodglass & Kaplan, 1972). The five high-frequency sentences contained only common words and were easy to pronounce (e.g., "I got home from work"). The five low-frequency

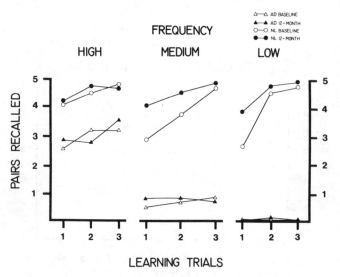

Figure 15-3. Mean number of high-, medium-, and low-frequency pairs correctly recalled on the test of paired-associate learning by AD patients and normal subjects.

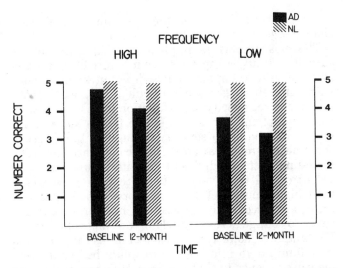

Figure 15-5. Mean number of sentences read correctly by AD patients and normal subjects in the test of sentence reading.

sentences contained low-frequency words and were more difficult to pronounce (e.g., "The barn swallow captured the plump worm"). Each sentence was typed in large letters on a separate card. Subjects were given as much time as they wanted to try to read each sentence aloud, and only those sentences read completely without error were scored as correct.

Figure 15-5 presents the results of this test. The effects of group and frequency and the interaction of group with frequency were significant ($p < .01$ in all cases). Also significant, however, was the effect of time ($F[1, 22] = 5.2$, $p < .03$). The interaction of time with group was marginally significant (F[1, 22] = 40, p = .06). As the figure indicates, normal subjects were able to read correctly nearly all sentences at both baseline and follow-up. Patients made more errors on low-frequency sentences than on high-frequency sentences and made more errors at follow-up than at baseline. Thus, the test was sensitive to differences between groups and to increasing language dysfunction among patients over the follow-up period.

Conclusions and Recommendations

Clinical descriptions (e.g., Roth, 1955) and cross-sectional studies employing formal psychological testing procedures have provided some insights into the longitudinal development of the symptoms of AD. In one follow-up study (Kaszniak et al., 1978), severe language impairment predicted decreased survival time in a mixed group of patients with AD or multi-infarct dementia. Kaszniak, Garron, and Fox (1979) examined the relationship of aging and cortical atrophy (measured by CAT scan) to performance on memory tests by comparing nondemented young adults, nondemented elderly people, and patients with AD. The investigators also found that aging impaired performance on tests that required storage of information into long-term memory but had no effect on tests that involved primary or immediate memory (e.g., digit span) as de-

fined by the model of Atkinson and Shiffrin (1971). The degree of cortical atrophy, however, was correlated with severity of impairment on both tests of immediate memory and tests involving storage into long-term memory. The one test that has been shown to correlate with both the neuropathologic (Blessed, Tomlinson, & Roth, 1968) and the neurochemical (Perry et al., 1978) changes associated with AD is a brief test emphasizing memory and orientation developed by Blessed et al. (1968). Thus, although the functional biological and possible diagnostic importance of memory and language changes in AD is apparent, important questions remain to be answered about the best ways to assess these symptoms, particularly as they develop longitudinally.

The results obtained in this study demonstrate that the sensitivity of memory and language tests to increasing severity of dysfunction in patients with AD depends both on the method of testing and on the kind of stimulus items used. Patients made more errors than normal subjects on tests of both verbal recall and recognition. Patients were more impaired on recall than on recognition, but recognition testing was sensitive to increasing dysfunction over 12 months whereas recall testing was not. On the test of paired-associate learning, patients were most impaired learning difficult, low-frequency items but showed only a marginally significant increase in memory impairment over 12 months. On both language tests, patients made more errors on the difficult, low-frequency items. The sentence-reading test showed only a marginally significant increase in language dysfunction in patients over the 12-month follow-up period, and the confrontation-naming test showed no increase.

To interpret these results, one must keep in mind the characteristics of the patients included in the study. Very mildly demented patients were excluded because of the one-year history and cognitive cutoff scores used for diagnosis, and very severely demented patients were excluded because they could not perform the tests. For patients of the kind included in this study, level of difficulty apparently determines, in different ways, the degree of measured cognitive impairment and the sensitivity of tests to increasing cognitive dysfunction.

On tests of both memory and language, the magnitude of the difference between patients and normal subjects was greatest for the most difficult versions of the tests: Patients showed greater impairment on recall than on recognition tests and were, on tests of paired-associate learning and language, more impaired on difficult, low-frequency items than on easier, high-frequency items. Thus, the difficulty of items is the most important determinant of measured impairment in this population.

Sensitivity to change in patients with AD, however, appears not to be a monotonic increasing function of task difficulty in this population. The most difficult memory tasks, verbal recall and learning low-frequency paired associates, were both insensitive to change over the one-year follow-up period. The easiest task (i.e., the one on which patients made fewest errors), naming common objects, was also insensitive. The tests that did show change over one year, the tests of word recognition, sentence reading, and paired-associate learning, were of intermediate difficulty; that is, patients made some errors but were still showing cognitive performance well above that expected by guessing alone. Thus, a test's sensitivity to longitudinal change in patients with AD apparently depends on the patients' cognitive abilities at the start of the study. Tests that are either too easy or too difficult will be insensitive to change, whereas those on which the patients show a modest degree of impairment will be most sensitive to immediately subsequent declines in ability.

These results have several implications for clinical evaluation and for future research. First, they suggest that relatively difficult tests of memory and language abilities are most useful for detecting and quantifying progressive cognitive change early in the course of AD. The use of such tests longitudinally in populations at high risk for AD might solve one of the most difficult problems encountered by clinicians and researchers trying to identify early cases of AD. Mental status examinations (e.g., the scale of Blessed et al., 1968, or the Mini-Mental State Examination of Folstein, Folstein, and McHugh, 1975) usually used for this purpose have two deficiencies: They are difficult to use longitudinally because alternate forms are not available, and they are usually very simple and can identify only patients with a marked degree of cognitive impairment. Thus, developing difficult tests with alternate forms sensitive to the abnormally rapid decline in cognition characteristic of early AD might be very useful for identifying incipient cases of true dementia in high-risk populations.

A second implication of these results is that it may be possible to measure and quantify changes in cognitive abilities of patients with fairly advanced AD. Recent studies (Blessed & Wilson, 1982; Christie, 1982) indicate that patients with dementia, particularly those with AD, are living much longer than formerly following the onset of symptoms (Roth, 1955), presumably because of better medical care. It is likely, then, that in the future more people with moderate to severe dementia will need evaluation for both clinical and research purposes. It is well known that in the terminal stages of AD patients are unable to complete any formal psychological tests (Larsson, Sjogren, & Jacobson, 1963; Roth & Hopkins, 1953). As a result of the difficulty in obtaining meaningful cognitive test results for these patients, some investigators have used more global behavioral rating scales to determine severity of symptoms (Reisberg, Schneck, Ferris, Schwartz, & de Leon, 1983; Shader, Harmatz, & Salzman, 1974) and to evaluate treatment efficacy (Summers, Viesselman, Marsh, & Candelora, 1981; Yesavage, Tinklenberg, Hollister, & Berger, 1979). Although this approach may be unavoidable for some patients, the present results indicate that patients who are severely demented can be meaningfully evaluated by tests of recognition memory and simple tests of reading and naming. As the present results indicate, even patients with moderate dementia followed for one year can score above a chance level on such tests.

The most important implication of the present results is that any comprehensive measure of severity of symptoms in AD must include different kinds of tests with different degrees of difficulty. Because a test's sensitivity to severity of dysfunction in AD varies with the stage of the illness, no single test is suitable for measuring change or severity throughout the course of the illness or in all patients. Some combination of tests, including tests of different cognitive functions and tests ranging from very difficult to very easy, would probably be most useful. For memory, a combination of recall and recognition procedures may provide sensitivity to change across a fairly broad range of patients. For language, some combination of items ranging from very familiar to relatively rare would be useful. One measure of severity that incorporates items of the type just described into a relatively brief scale is the Alzheimer's Disease Assessment Scale (ADAS) (Rosen, Mohs, & Davis, 1984). Currently, this scale is being used in several studies to evaluate proposed treatments for AD and to investigate the relationships between biological and behavioral changes in disease (Mohs et al., 1985). Additional studies are needed to determine whether this instrument or others can answer important questions about the etiology, course, diagnosis, and treatment of AD.

References

Atkinson, R. C., & Juola, J. F. (1974). Search and decision processes in recognition memory. In D. H. Krantz, R. C. Atkinson, R. D. Luce, & P. Suppes (Eds.), *Contemporary developments in mathematical psychology* (Vol. 1, pp. 243–293). San Francisco: Freeman.

Atkinson, R. C., & Shiffrin, R. M. (1971). The control of short-term memory. *Scientific American, 224,* 82–90.

Barker, M. G., & Lawson, J. S. (1968). Nominal aphasia in dementia. *British Journal of Psychiatry, 114,* 1351–1356.

Battig, W. F., & Montague, W. E. (1969). Category norms for verbal items in 56 categories: A replication and extension of the Connecticut category norms. *Journal of Experimental Psychology Monographs, 80*(3, Pt. 2), 1–46.

Blessed, G., Tomlinson, B. E., & Roth, M. (1968). The association between quantitative measures of dementia and of senile change in the cerebral grey matter of elderly subjects. *British Journal of Psychiatry, 114,* 797–811.

Blessed, G., & Wilson, I. D. (1982). The contemporary natural history of mental disorder in old age. *British Journal of Psychiatry, 141,* 59–67.

Buschke, H. (1973). Selective reminding for analysis of memory and learning. *Journal of Verbal Learning and Verbal Behavior, 12,* 543–550.

Christian, J., Bickley, W., Tarka, M., & Clayton, K. (1978). Measures of free recall of 900 English nouns: Correlations with imagery, concreteness, meaningfulness, and frequency. *Memory and Cognition, 6,* 379–390.

Christie, A. B. (1982). Changing patterns of mental illness in the elderly. *British Journal of Psychiatry, 140,* 154–159.

Crystal, H. A., Horoupian, D. S., Katzman, R., & Jotkowitz, S. (1981). Biopsy-proved Alzheimer disease presenting as a right parietal lobe syndrome. *Annals of Neurology, 12,* 186–188.

Folstein, M. F., Folstein, S., & McHugh, P. R. (1975). Mini-Mental State: A practical method for grading the cognitive state of patients for the clinician. *Journal of Psychiatric Research, 12,* 189–198.

Goodglass, H., & Kaplan, E. (1972). *The assessment of aphasia and related disorders.* Philadelphia: Lea and Febiger.

Hachinski, V. C., Lassen, N. A., & Marshall, J. (1974). Multi-infarct dementia: A cause of mental deterioration in the elderly. *Lancet, 2,* 207–210.

Kaplan, E., Goodglass, H., & Weintraub, S. (1978). *The Boston Naming Test.* Boston: Kaplan & Goodglass.

Kaszniak, A. W., Fox, J., Gandell, D. L., Garron, D. C., Huckman, M. S., & Ramsey, R. G. (1978). Predictors of mortality, in presenile and senile dementia. *Annals of Neurology, 3,* 246–252.

Kaszniak, A. W., Garron, D. C., & Fox, J. (1979). Differential effects of age and cerebral atrophy upon span of immediate recall and paired-associate learning in older patients suspected of dementia. *Cortex, 15,* 285–295.

Kay, D. W. K. (1977). The epidemiology and identification of brain deficit in the elderly. In C. Eisdorfer & R. O. Friedel (Eds.), *Cognitive and emotional disturbances in the elderly* (pp. 11–26). Chicago: Year Book Medical Publishers.

Larsson, T., Sjogren, T., & Jacobson, G. (1963). Senile dementia: A clinical sociomedical and genetic study. *Acta Psychiatrica Scandinavica, 63*(Suppl. 167), 1–259.

Liston, E. H. (1979). The clinical phenomenology of presenile dementia. *Journal of Nervous and Mental Disease, 167,* 329–336.

Meyer-Gross, W., Slater, E., & Roth, M. (1969). *Clinical psychiatry* (3rd ed.). London: Balliere.

Miller, E. (1973). Short- and long-term memory in patients with presenile dementia (Alzheimer's disease). *Psychological Medicine, 3,* 221–224.

Mohs, R. C., Davis, B. M., Johns, C. A., Mathe, A. A., Greenwald, B. S., Horvath, T. B., & Davis, K. L. (1985). Oral physostigmine treatment of patients with Alzheimer's disease. *American Journal of Psychiatry, 142*(1), 28–33.

Mohs, R. C., Rosen, W. G., & Davis, K. L. (1982). Defining treatment efficacy in patients with Alzheimer's disease. In S. Corkin, K. L. Davis, J. H. Growdon, E. Usdin, & R. J. Wurtman (Eds.), *Alzheimer's disease: A report of progress in research* (pp. 351–356). New York: Raven Press.

Paivio, A., Yuille, J. C., & Madigan, S. A. (1968). Concreteness, imagery, and meaningfulness values for 925 nouns. *Journal of Experimental Psychology Monographs, 76*(1, Pt. 2), 1–25.

Paivio, A., Yuille, J. C., & Rogers, T. B. (1969). Noun imagery and meaningfulness in free and serial recall. *Journal of Experimental Psychology, 79,* 509–514.

Palermo, D. S., & Jenkins, J. J. (1964). *Word association norms: Grade school through college.* Minneapolis: University of Minnesota Press.

Perry, E. K., Tomlinson, B. E., Blessed, G., Bergmann, K., Gibson, P. H., & Perry, R. H. (1978). Correlation of cholinergic abnormalities with senile plaques and mental test scores in senile dementia. *British Medical Journal, 2,* 1457–1459.

Reisberg, B., Schneck, M. K., Ferris, S. H., Schwartz, G. E., & de Leon, M. J. (1983). The Brief Cognitive Rating Scale (BCRS): Findings in primary degenerative dementia (PDD). *Psychopharmacology Bulletin, 19*(1), 47–50.

Rosen, W. G., Mohs, R. C., & Davis, K. L. (1984). A new rating scale for Alzheimer's disease. *American Journal of Psychiatry, 14*(11), 1356–1364.

Roth, M. (1955). The natural history of mental disorder in old age. *Journal of Mental Science, 101,* 281–301.

Roth, M., & Hopkins, B. (1953). Psychological test performance in patients over sixty: I. Senile psychosis and affective disorders of old age. *Journal of Mental Science, 99,* 439–450.

Schonfield, D. (1965). Memory changes with age. *Nature, 208,* 918.

Shader, R. I., Harmatz, J. S., & Salzman, C. (1974). A new scale for clinical assessment in geriatric populations: The Sandoz Clinical Assessment Geriatric (SCAG). *Journal of the American Geriatrics Society, 22,* 107–113.

Sim, M., & Sussman, I. (1962). Alzheimer's disease: Its natural history and differential diagnosis. *Journal of Nervous and Mental Disease, 135,* 489–499.

Spitzer, R. L., Endicott, J., & Robins, E. (1978). Research Diagnostic Criteria: Rationale and reliability. *Archives of General Psychiatry, 35,* 773–782.

Summers, W. K., Viesselman, J. O., Marsh, G. M., & Candelora, K. (1981). The use of THA in treatment of Alzheimer-like dementia: Pilot study in twelve patients. *Biological Psychiatry, 16,* 145–153.

Thorndike, E. L., & Lorge, I. (1944). *Teachers' word book of thirty thousand words.* New York: Teacher's College of Columbia University.

Torack, R. M. (1978). *The pathologic physiology of dementia.* Berlin: Springer-Verlag.

Yesavage, J. A., Tinklenberg, J. R., Hollister, L. E., & Berger, P. A. (1979). Vasodilators in senile dementias: A review of the literature. *Archives of General Psychiatry, 36,* 220–223.

Suzanne Corkin, John H. Growdon, Edith V. Sullivan, Mary Jo Nissen, and F. Jacob Huff

Assessing Treatment Effects: A Neuropsychological Battery

This chapter outlines the rationale for and use of a neuropsychological approach in assessing treatment effects. Rationale and procedures for evaluating attention, memory, language, visual perception, and praxis are discussed.

George Talland's (1965) approach to the study of Korsakoff's syndrome was to describe the spectrum of behavioral disorders associated with that multifocal disease. Our tack in investigating Alzheimer's disease (AD) is in the Talland tradition: We administer a series of tests that allow the assessment of the major areas of cognitive disability: attention, memory, language, visual perception, and praxis. Our laboratory has devoted considerable effort to developing tests that are appropriate for evaluating the cognitive status of patients with AD and measuring the outcome of treatment in such patients. The tests need to be simple enough for demented patients to perform and sensitive enough to detect any benefits of drug administration. It is important to vary the demands on behavior so that patients with AD of mild or moderate severity are able to answer at least a few items correctly on most or all of the tests. This kind of evaluation provides a quantitative baseline against which to measure the patients' subsequent performance during the administration of a drug.

Rationale for a Neuropsychological Approach

Neuropsychology is the discipline that quantifies behavior and accounts for it in terms of the underlying neuroanatomy, neurochemistry, and neurophysiology. We know that AD is relatively selective with respect to areas of degeneration and with respect to the neurotransmitter systems that are affected. The severity of degeneration in the cerebral cortex varies from one region to another (Brun & Englund, 1981). In normal aging, minimal involvement occurs in the frontal lobe; moderate involvement is found in the temporal and parietal neocortex; and the most severe involvement occurs in medial temporal-lobe structures, specifically the hippocampus and amygdala. This pattern of abnormality corresponds closely to the areas of involvement revealed by PET scans and by neurochemical studies (Chase, 1984; Rossor, Emson, Iversen, Mountjoy, & Roth, 1984).

A subcortical brain region known to be affected in AD is the nucleus basalis of Meinert in the basal forebrain (Whitehouse, Price, Clark, Coyle, & DeLong, 1981). This area is a major source of cholinergic projections to the cerebral cortex. Another subcortical nucleus, the locus coeruleus, is believed to be affected in some patients but not in others (Bondareff, Mountjoy, & Roth, 1982; Iversen et al., 1983; Mann, Yates, & Hawkes, 1982). The locus coeruleus has the greatest concentration of noradrenergic neurons in the central nervous system (Dahlstrom & Fuxe, 1964; Loizou, 1969). Axons from locus coeruleus neurons project throughout the cerebral cortex to several other subcortical structures and the spinal cord (Redmond, 1979).

A reasonable question to ask is "What classes of behavior would be expected to be compromised in patients with the alterations in brain morphology and brain chemistry just outlined?" Table 16-1 provides an answer to that question, but note that the material in the table is simplified for didactic purposes. The brain regions of interest are listed in the left column; the right-hand column shows some of the behaviors that are believed to be affected by focal lesions in those brain regions (see Hecaen & Albert, 1978). We therefore expect these behaviors to be compromised in AD. Table 16-2 lists the neurotransmitters that are affected in AD; on the right are our best guesses as to the behavioral correlates (see Wurtman, Corkin, & Growdon, 1984). The extent to which a particular patient shows

Table 16-1. Neuropathology of Alzheimer's Disease

Brain regions affected	Associated behaviors
Frontal lobe	Problem solving, fluency, temporal ordering
Temporal lobe	Visual and auditory perception, language
Parietal lobe	Language, praxis, spatial abilities
Hippocampus and amygdala	Memory, affect, spatial abilities
Basal forebrain	Memory and other cognitive functions
Locus coeruleus	Attention, arousal, spatial memory

Table 16-2. Neurochemistry of Alzheimer's Disease

Neurotransmitters affected	Associated behaviors
Acetylcholine	Memory, perhaps other cognitive functions
Somatostatin	Motor functions
Dopamine	Motor functions, mood, memory, cognition
Norepinephrine	Attention, arousal, mood, memory, spatial abilities
Serotonin	Arousal, circadian rhythms
Vasopressin	Cognition (via autonomic nervous system

impairment in each of these capacities depends on the distribution and severity of neuropathological changes in that person's brain.

Use of Neuropsychological Tests in Drug Protocols

All of the tests to be described are given during the baseline session and after the final washout period in order to characterize the symptoms of each patient and provide information regarding practice effects and de-

terioration. Of this group, selected tests are repeated following drug and placebo administration to measure the effects of treatment (Table 16-3). Different but comparable forms of each test are used on each occasion of repeat testing.

The series of tests that we administer in drug trials samples cognitive capacities in five domains: attention, memory, language, visual perception, and praxis. The methods for 27 tests will be described. For some of them, data are presented that compare the performance of patients with AD at baseline testing with the performance of healthy control subjects. The latter

Table 16-3. Tests Administered to Patients With AD During Drug Trials

Attention	Memory	Language	Visual perception	Praxis
Attentional focusing test[1]	Brown-Peterson distractor task[1]	Boston Naming Test[1]	Gollin incomplete-pictures test	Matchsticks test[1]
	Test of immediate memory span for digits[1]	Boston Naming Test, multiple choice	Test of contrast sensitivity function[1]	Drawing test
	Test of immediate memory span for blocks[1]	Category fluency test[1]		Test of use of common objects[1]
	Test of verbal paired-associate learning[1]	Object-nonobject discrimination test		
	Test of nonverbal paired-associate learning[1]	Nonmeaningful-form discrimination test[1]		
	Test of verbal recognition memory[1]	Naming latency test[1]		
	Story recall test[1]	Reading latency test[1]		
	Recency discrimination test[1]	Category recognition test		
	Test of rate of forgetting[1]	Name recognition test[1]		
		Wechsler Adult Intelligence Scale, Vocabulary subtest		
		Token Test		
		Reporter's Test		

[1]Tests administered during active drug and placebo conditions (all tests given during baseline and washout conditions).

group was matched to the patient group for age, sex, educational level, and socioeconomic status. It is impossible at this stage of our research to specify which tests are most sensitive to the effects of drugs, because we have not yet identified a drug that alters the course of AD dramatically.

Extra care should be taken to ensure that patients fully understand the testing procedures. Because it can be difficult for even mildly demented patients to make the transition from task instruction to task performance, instructions that are adequate for normal healthy subjects should be embellished with several examples and practice trials. Beyond that, some patients require extra coaching before they are ready to begin a test. Testing is always performed individually in a quiet room in order to ensure the patient's comfort and cooperation and to minimize distraction.

Patients with AD are expected to perform more poorly on the cognitive neuropsychological tests as the dementia progresses. Therefore, when analyzing their scores, researchers should take into account severity of dementia. Accordingly, for most of the analyses reported here, the patients were divided into three subgroups: mildly, moderately, and severely demented. The criteria for judging severity of dementia were qualitative and were based on how well the patient functioned independently in everyday life (Corkin, 1982).

Attention

The test of attention requires subjects to attend to a spatial location, and it evaluates the ability to focus attention, maintain attentional selectivity, and respond to unexpected stimuli.

Attentional focusing. This test evaluates several aspects of selective attention (Nissen, Corkin, & Growdon, 1982; Posner, Nissen, & Ogden, 1978). Each of 30 practice trials and 90 test trials begins with the presentation of the message "Get ready" on a video screen controlled by an Apple II microcomputer; 5 seconds later, the message is replaced by the presentation of a visual warning cue at the center of the screen. The warning cue is accompanied by an auditory beep. On one third of the trials, the cue is an arrow pointing right; on one third, it is an arrow pointing left; and on one third, it is a double arrow pointing both left and right (neutral trials). Either 2 or 3 seconds after the warning cue, an X appears 3.7 degrees to the right or 3.7 degrees to the left of the arrow. The subject's task is to press a single response key (the space bar on a keyboard) as fast as possible after the X appears in either position. The subject's reaction time is printed on the screen following each trial. If the subject responded before the X appeared, the word "Error" appears on the screen. Subjects are instructed that when a warning cue is a single arrow, the X will probably appear in the direction of the arrow, and when the warning is a double arrow, the two locations are equally likely. The single-arrow cues are valid 80% of the time (expected

trials); on the remaining 20% of single-arrow trials, the X appears on the side opposite the direction of the arrow (unexpected trials).

Median reaction time and standard deviation of reaction times are computed for neutral, expected, and unexpected trials. These measures are obtained separately for trials on which the warning interval was 2 seconds and trials on which it was 3 seconds. Trials on which subjects responded before the X appeared and trials with reaction times greater than 2 seconds are counted separately and are not included in the other analyses. The median and standard deviation of reaction time in the neutral condition are taken as measures of the speed and variability of subjects' response to visual stimuli. The difference in reaction time to expected and unexpected stimuli indicates whether subjects oriented their attention to the probable stimulus location. A comparison of the difference between expected and unexpected trials at the shorter and longer warning intervals shows whether, if oriented initially, attention is maintained at the possible location. Comparison of responses in the neutral condition following 2- and 3-second warning intervals indicates whether subjects benefit from the reduced temporal uncertainty at the longer interval. Comparisons of performance on neutral trials early versus late in the task indicate the effect of practice on performance.

Memory

Because memory failure is a universal symptom of AD, can be measured quantitatively, and may be palliated by drugs that increase cholinergic neurotransmission, we devote considerable time to the selective assessment of short-term memory and long-term memory. Because some patients with AD have word-finding difficulties that could interfere with their performance on tests of verbal memory, we include tests of memory for nonverbal materials as well. The test format is also varied: Some tests require recall, whereas others require recognition. A test is also included that allows comparison of memory for the content versus the temporal order of a list of words; other tests document each patient's short-term memory capacity and rate of forgetting information from short-term memory and longterm memory.

Brown-Peterson distractor task. This test assesses the duration of short-term memory (Brown, 1958; Peterson & Peterson, 1959). The general procedure requires a subject to hear a trigram of low association value and to report it after having engaged in a distractor task. At the outset of each trial, subjects hear the word "Ready," followed by a trigram, for example, "STV." Subjects then have 2 seconds in which to repeat the trigram aloud, after which they hear a 3-digit number, for example, "287." They repeat the number immediately and then count backward from that number as quickly as possible. The word "Recall" signals subjects to stop counting and to say the trigram aloud during a 10-second silent interval. The counting task is intended to prevent silent rehearsal of the trigram during retention intervals of 3, 6, 9, 15, and 30 seconds. When healthy young adults perform this test, the distractor task is to count backward by 3s or 7s from a particular 3-digit number. For many demented patients, however, we must simplify this task by having them count backward by ones, often with prompting by the examiner. In order to detect possible disorders of attention or sensory memory, we have included two control situations: First, after subjects hear the trigram, they have 2 seconds in which to repeat it aloud once before the onset of the distractor; and second, in a distractor-free immediate recall condition, subjects hear the trigram, repeat it aloud, hear the word "Recall," and attempt to repeat the trigram. Should a subject fail either of these simple tasks, it would indicate a defect of attention or sensory memory severe enough to invalidate memory testing with this task. If a subject fails all 4 trials at a retention interval, the test is discontinued.

The performance at each retention interval of the healthy control subjects and of the three subgroups of patients with AD was compared using 6 one-way analyses of variance (Figure 16-1). At the 0-second delay, the four groups did not differ significantly. At all of the other delays, the healthy control group recalled significantly more letters than did any of the subgroups of patients.

Test of immediate memory span for digits. This test provides a measure of auditory-verbal short-term memory capacity. It is established for each subject by the presentation of strings of digits at the rate of one digit per second and determining the longest string that can be recalled correctly (Wechsler, 1944). Backward digit span is also determined.

On forward digit span, the healthy control subjects

Table 16-4. Digit Span and Block Span: Comparison of Healthy Subjects and Patients With AD

Group	Forward digit span		Forward block span	
	Mean	Range	Mean	Range
Healthy (*n* = 14)	7.1	4–9	5.5	5–7
With Alzheimer's disease				
Mild (*n* = 11)	5.9	3–7	4.4	3–7
Moderate (*n* = 8)	5.8	5–6	4.4	3–6
Severe (*n* = 8)	4.7	4–6	2.5	1–4

Note. Reprinted from Corkin (1982) by permission.

performed significantly better than the moderately and the severely demented patients, who performed equally poorly (Table 16-4). The performance of the mildly demented patients was not significantly different from any of the other three groups (Corkin, 1982).

Test of immediate memory span for blocks. This procedure (Corsi, 1972; Milner, 1971) is modeled after the digit span test. The test material consists of nine black cubes impartially arranged on a black board. The examiner taps the top of the blocks with a white pen in a particular sequence, and immediately thereafter the subject is required to tap the cubes, with the forefinger of the preferred hand, in exactly the same pattern. Subjects' immediate span is the maximum number of blocks they are able to tap in correct order. Backward block span is also established.

The mean forward block span of the healthy control subjects was significantly longer than that of the mildly or the moderately demented patients (Table 16-4). The spans of these two subgroups of patients did not differ from each other, but they were significantly superior to those of the severely demented patients (Corkin, 1982).

Test of verbal paired-associate learning. This test evaluates the ability to remember pairs of unrelated words. Designed specifically for use with elderly subjects (Inglis, 1959), it consists of 3 stimulus–response pairs, which are read once by the examiner: for example, flower–sparks, table–river, bottle–comb. Then the stimulus words (flower, table, and bottle) are presented orally, one at a time, and the subject is asked to supply the response words (sparks, river, and comb, respectively) within 10 seconds. If the answer is correct, the examiner says "right"; if the subject's answer is wrong, the examiner says "no" and supplies the correct response. This correction procedure is continued until the subject reaches a criterion of 3 consecutive correct responses for each of the 3 stimulus words, or until each has been presented 30 times. The score is the total number of times the stimulus words are presented before criterion is reached.

The healthy control group reached criterion in significantly fewer trials than did the subgroups of pa-

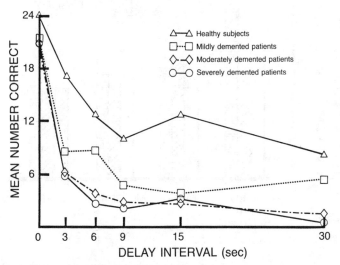

Figure 16-1. Brown-Peterson distractor task: performance of healthy control subjects (*n* = 15), mildly demented patients with AD (*n* = 10), moderately demented patients with AD (*n* = 8), and severely demented patients with AD (*n* = 4) at 6-month intervals. Adapted from Corkin (1982) by permission.

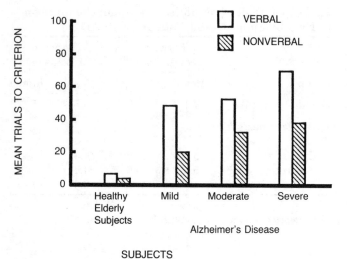

Figure 16-2. Tests of verbal and nonverbal paired-associate learning: performance of healthy control subjects (*n* = 15), mildly demented patients with AD (*n* = 11), moderately demented patients with AD (*n* = 7), and severely demented patients with AD (*n* = 7). Reprinted from Corkin (1982) by permission.

tients with AD, who did not differ from each other (Figure 16-2).

Test of nonverbal paired-associate learning. This test measures the ability to remember pairs of unrelated geometric shapes. It uses geometric drawings that are difficult to assign verbal tags and are therefore apt to be coded visually. Like the verbal test just described, the nonverbal test consists of 3 stimulus–response pairs that are shown once, one pair at a time, on stimulus cards. In the remainder of the test, the 3 stimulus figures are presented individually at the top of a card with all three response figures below. During each such presentation, the subject is asked to choose the response figure associated with that stimulus. If the choice is correct, the examiner says "right"; if the subject's choice is wrong, the examiner says "no" and indicates the correct response. As in the verbal analogue, this correction procedure is continued until the subject reaches a criterion of 3 consecutive correct responses for each of the 3 stimulus pairs, or until each has been presented 30 times.

In general, the nonverbal paired-associate learning test, which requires recognition, was significantly easier than the verbal one, which requires recall. The healthy elderly group achieved criterion in fewer trials than did the moderately or the severely demented subgroups (Figure 16-2). The scores of the mildly demented subgroup did not differ significantly from the other three groups.

Test of verbal recognition memory. This test evaluates the effect of level of processing on recognition memory for words. The levels of processing framework (Craik & Lockhart, 1972) embodies the idea that how a stimulus is processed when it is presented affects how well it is encoded and, therefore, remembered. Level of processing is manipulated in the first part of this test by the procedure of requiring subjects to answer a

question about each stimulus word when it is presented. There are 3 types of questions: (a) "Does a man/woman say the word?" (sensory level); (b) "Does the word rhyme with _____?" (phonological level); and (c) "Is the word a type of _____?" (semantic level). One type of question is asked for each of 10 stimulus words. Following the question, the word is presented and the subject answers "yes" or "no." Half of the questions of each type require a "yes" response and half require a "no" response. The questions and stimulus words are presented auditorily by tape recorder. The second part of the test begins after the 30 trials are completed, when an unexpected test of recognition memory for the stimulus words is administered. On each of 30 recognition trials, the examiner reads 3 words, and the subject is asked to choose which of the 3 words was presented before. The test yields a measure of recognition accuracy for the 3 levels of processing.

The overall performance of the healthy control group was superior to that of all subgroups of patients with AD (Figure 16-3). Further, only the healthy group showed the expected depth of processing effect, that is, best recognition of words encoded by category, moderately good recognition of words encoded by rhyme, and worst recognition of words encoded by physical characteristics (Corkin, 1982).

Story recall test. This test involves immediate and delayed retention of short prose passages (Randt, Brown, & Osborne, 1980). The subject is instructed to

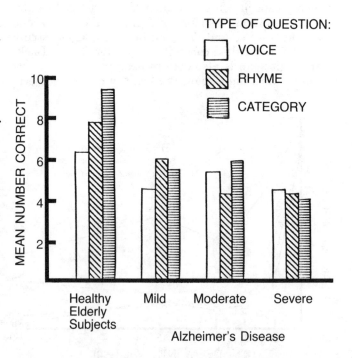

Figure 16-3. Test of verbal recognition memory: performance of healthy control subjects (*n* = 15), mildly demented patients with AD (*n* = 11), moderately demented patients with AD (*n* = 8), and severely demented patients with AD (*n* = 4) for three types of encoding strategies. Adapted from Corkin (1982) by permission.

listen carefully as the examiner reads a 4-to-5-line story and to repeat the story back immediately after it is read, keeping as close to the exact wording as possible. After a 10-minute delay, the subject is asked, without forewarning, to recall the story again. The scoring procedure awards 1 point for each word recalled correctly in the correct position and 1/2 point for a word recalled out of position or for the wrong tense of a word.

Recency discrimination test. This test allows a comparison of recognition memory for the content versus the temporal order of a list of words (Milner, 1971; Teuber, Corkin, & Twitchell, 1977). Subjects are read a list of 14 words that all belong to a particular semantic category, such as items on a farm. Immediately after presenting the list, the examiner asks four content questions and four order questions. In the content questions, subjects indicate which of two words was included in the list. In the order questions, subjects indicate which of two words, both from the list, was presented first. The two types of questions are presented in variable order. This procedure is followed for a total of four lists. The sums of the content errors and the order errors for all four lists are computed.

Test of rate of forgetting. In a test designed to evaluate the rate of forgetting from long-term memory (Freed, 1984; Huppert & Piercy, 1978, 1979), subjects are shown 90 colored slides of magazine pictures. Patients with AD are given sufficient time to inspect each slide to bring their initial recognition performance to the level achieved by healthy control subjects, who view each slide for one second. Initial recognition is tested 10 minutes later as follows: 30 target slides are paired with 30 foils (slides not shown before), and subjects are asked to identify the slide in each pair that has been shown previously. Recognition is again tested 24 and 72 hours after acquisition, with 30 different target slides and 30 new foils used in each session. Patients' rate of forgetting is compared with that of control subjects by noting the performance of the two groups 24 and 72 hours after acquisition.

Language

Anomia is a frequent early symptom of AD. It is evident in conversational speech and can be demonstrated if the patient is asked to name objects. We administer a group of tests designed to provide a quantitative measure of anomia and to understand its basis. Three disorders have been suggested to explain anomia in demented patients: impaired visual recognition, impaired semantic memory, and impaired word retrieval. We evaluate these three capacities with tests that do not depend upon a naming response. The results should permit determination of the relative importance of deficits in these three capacities as underlying causes of anomia in AD. Three additional language tests (a vocabulary test and tests of expressive and receptive language capacities) are also administered. They are described at the end of this section.

We have devised two empirically equivalent forms of the Boston Naming Test. Only one form of each of the other tests is available because of the difficulty of assembling multiple sets of stimulus material that are comparable. Although our experience to date is that practice effects in demented patients on these tasks are minimal, we look specifically for practice effects by comparing performance during the baseline and final washout sessions, and we take account of such effects in the analysis and interpretation of our results.

Boston Naming Test. This test provides a quantitative measurement of anomia (Kaplan, Goodglass, & Weintraub, 1978). It consists of 85 line drawings of objects, which the subject is requested to name. The subject is allowed 20 seconds in which to name each drawing. If the correct word is not produced in that time, a semantic cue (e.g., "a kind of building" for "house") is given, and an additional 20 seconds is allowed for response. If the name is not produced in that time, a phonemic cue (for example, "hou . . ." for "house") is offered, and another 20 seconds allowed for response. Correct responses during the uncued and semantically cued conditions are combined in calculating the test score.

Normative data are available for different age groups and levels of education. In order to develop two equivalent naming tests for use in pharmacologic trials in AD, the items in the Boston Naming Test were divided into two forms of 42 items each. The forms were matched for frequency of the target words (names) according to standard word-frequency norms (Carroll, Davies, & Richman, 1971) and for difficulty on the basis of an analysis of difficulty of individual items in a control sample of 221 normal subjects (Goodglass, 1975). In addition, the two forms were administered to 10 nondemented elderly people (ages 57 to 84) and 12 patients with dementing illnesses or focal brain lesions. Both subtests were administered in a single session, with the order of administration of the subtests alternated in successive subjects. The performance of these 22 control subjects was highly similar on the two forms. The correlation between scores on the two forms was .96 ($p < .001$). Both forms are administered to each patient during the baseline and final washout testing sessions. One form is given during drug treatment, and the other form is given during the placebo condition. The order of administration of the forms is counterbalanced from patient to patient. Practice effects can be assessed by a comparison of performance at baseline and after the final washout.

A multiple-choice version of the Boston Naming Test is administered after the standard version. In this version, 5 words are printed below each line drawing. One word is the correct response (e.g., "house"). Another is a semantically related distractor (e.g., "church"). A third is a phonemic distractor (e.g., "hound"), and the remaining two distractors are concrete nouns unrelated to the correct response but matched with it in word frequency (Carroll et al., 1971). The choices are randomly ordered for each item. The subject must read aloud the choices for each item; reading errors are corrected by the examiner as they occur. The subject then selects the name corresponding to the line drawing.

Category fluency test. This test evaluates word retrieval and also documents word-finding difficulty (Newcombe, 1969), a frequent symptom in the early stages of AD. The subjects list words aloud from a semantic category specified by the examiner, who writes the responses as they are produced. One minute is allowed per category; four categories (vehicles, vegetables, tools, and clothing) are tested. The instructions stress the importance of speed and accuracy of responses. Subjects are told in advance that repetitions are excluded from total counts. The category norms of Battig and Montague (1969) are the basis of judging the correctness of responses. The total number of correct and incorrect responses are scored for each category. This test also permits evaluation of intrusion errors, defined as incorrect repetitions of responses from categories tested previously. Fuld, Katzman, Davies, and Terry (1982) reported that intrusion errors are characteristic of AD and correlate with the number of senile plaques and CAT levels in the brain.

Object–nonobject discrimination test. In this test, line drawings of 20 nameable objects, 5 from each of the four categories used in the category fluency test, and 20 nonobject line drawings are presented to subjects in random order. The nonobject pictures are line drawings of closed figures with an object-like appearance, created when parts of real object drawings are traced and the resulting figures are regularized (Figure 16-4). Each item is presented by slide projection onto a blank white surface. Subjects are asked to decide whether or not each picture represents "something real" that they recognize having seen before and to indicate an answer "yes" or "no" by pressing one of two designated keys on a keyboard connected to an Apple II microcomputer. The onset of projection is detected by a photocell connected to the computer, and the interval between projection and the patient's response is measured in milliseconds. The instructions explain the nature of the nonmeaningful stimuli and stress speed and accuracy of response. The 20 nonmeaningful stimuli include 10 easy and 10 difficult items as determined by the latency of judgments by normal subjects (Kroll & Potter, 1984). Results are analyzed for false positive and false negative errors and for latency of correct responses.

Before the key-press response format is used for testing, a series of practice trials is given. The practice stimuli are slides displaying the words "yes" and "no." All slides used for key-press response display a visual reminder at the bottom that the right-side key means "yes" and the left means "no." At the start of each trial, the subject rests the index finger of the preferred hand on a platform between the two response keys, which are 2 centimeters apart. Subjects who are unable to perform reliably on these practice trials are instructed to respond verbally during the tests, and the examiner depresses the appropriate response keys.

Nonmeaningful-form discrimination test. This test evaluates discrimination of complex visual forms; unlike the object–nonobject discrimination test, it does not require recognition. The stimuli for this test, developed by LaBerge and Lawrence (1957), consist of 16

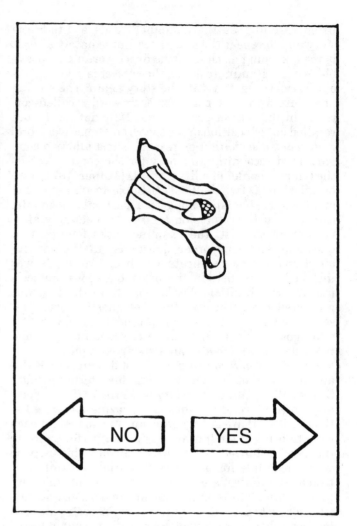

Figure 16-4. Sample stimulus from the object–nonobject discrimination test.

polygons that differ from each other in systematic and quantifiable ways. On each of 24 trials, two of these figures are presented by slide projection, one above the other. Subjects are asked to decide whether the two forms are "exactly the same or different." The presentation and response are the same as those used in the object–nonobject discrimination test. Half of the trials require a "same" response, and half require a "different" response. The 12 "different" trials include 4 trials at each of three levels of difficulty, based on the similarity between the paired forms. Results are analyzed for errors and latency of correct response.

Naming latency test. The same 20 line drawings of objects used in the object–nonobject discrimination test are presented by slide projection in the naming latency test. The subject is allowed 30 seconds to say the name of each object. The examiner presses a key if the subject responds correctly, and the latency of correct responses is recorded in seconds. The 20 items consist of 5 items in each of the four categories used in the category fluency test.

Reading latency test. In this test, the subject reads aloud printed words that are presented by slide projection. The examiner presses a key if the patient responds correctly, and the latency of correct responses is recorded in seconds. The 20 words used in this test are the names of the 20 objects used in the naming latency test and the object–nonobject discrimination test.

Category recognition test. This test requires judgments of category membership based on semantic memory. The 20 items used in the naming latency test are used in the 80 trials of this test. A drawing of each item is presented on 40 trials; the printed name of each item is presented on the other 40 trials. Subjects whose performance on the reading latency test is abnormal are not given this test. Before each stimulus is projected, the examiner asks, "Is this a kind of X?" where X is one of the four categories used in the test: vegetable, vehicle, tool, or clothing. The subject responds by pressing a button indicating "yes" or a button indicating "no." Half of the picture stimulus trials and half of the word stimulus trials require a "yes" response; the remaining half require a "no" response. The results are evaluated for accuracy and for latency of correct responses on picture and word trials.

Name recognition test. The same 20 pictures of objects are used in this test as were used in the previous tests. Before each picture is projected, the examiner asks "Is this called a(n) X?" where X is one of the 20 object names. Each picture is presented four times: once paired with its correct name, twice paired with names of other objects in the same category (inside-category false pairings), and once paired with the name of an object from a different category (outside-category false pairings). The subject responds by pressing a button indicating "yes" or a button indicating "no." The results are evaluated for accuracy and latency of correct responses, with particular attention to differences in these measures between the inside-category and outside-category false pairings.

Wechsler Adult Intelligence Scale (WAIS) Vocabulary subtest. Performance on the Vocabulary subtest of the WAIS provides an estimate of a subject's semantic knowledge (Wechsler, 1955). There is little drop in this measure with increasing age until about age 70 (Doppelt & Wallace, 1955). The test consists of 40 words

that the subject is asked to define orally. Items range in difficulty from such words as "bed" and "ship" at the beginning of the list to "impale" and "travesty" at the end. Each definition is scored 2, 1, or 0, depending upon the completeness of the definition.

The performance on the Vocabulary subtest by the three subgroups of patients with AD was significantly inferior to that of the healthy control group, despite the comparability of the four groups in years of formal education (Table 16-5). Performance by the patients was not related to severity of dementia (Corkin, 1982).

Token Test. This test provides a sensitive, quantitative measure of the subject's ability to understand and respond to increasingly complex verbal commands (De Renzi & Vignolo, 1962). An array of 20 wooden tokens, differing in size (large or small), shape (square or circle), and color (red, yellow, green, or white), is placed before the subject, who is given a series of 36 verbal commands of increasing complexity to manipulate the tokens. The subject receives 1 point for each correct response and 1/2 point for a correct response produced on a second attempt. Performance on this test of receptive language is evaluated together with performance on a companion test of expressive language, the Reporter's Test.

On the Token Test, the three subgroups of patients performed equally poorly and were impaired compared with healthy control subjects (Table 16-5) (Corkin, 1982).

Reporter's Test. This test provides a sensitive, quantitative measure of expressive language capacity (De Renzi & Ferrari, 1978). The same array of tokens used in the Token Test is placed before the subject, who must describe aloud a series of 26 increasingly complex manipulations of the tokens executed by the examiner. The subject receives 1 point for each correct answer and 1/2 point for a correct description produced on a second attempt.

On the Reporter's Test, the patients with AD as a group were significantly more handicapped than were the healthy control subjects (Table 16-5). Within the AD group, the scores of the severely demented patients

Table 16-5. Characteristics of Healthy Subjects and Patients With AD on Three Tests

Group	Age	Sex	Education (years)	Duration of amnesia (years)	WAIS Vocabulary subtest (scaled score)	Token Test (max. = 36)	Reporter's Test (max. = 26)
Healthy (n = 15)	66.9 (55–81)	4 female, 11 male	15.2 (10–19)	—	14.7 (10–19)	35.1 (34–36)	25.1 (24–26)
With Alzheimer's disease							
Mild (n = 11)	60.2 (51–75)	5 female, 6 male	14.6 (8–20)	3.05 (1–7)	10.8 (8–13)	29.3 (15–35)	17.8 (2.5–23)
Moderate (n = 8)	65.6 (56–78)	6 female, 2 male	12.6 (8–20)	2.04 (1–6)	10.2 (8–11)	30.6 (25–34)	12.6 (7–20)
Severe (n = 9)	67.4 (60–76)	2 female, 7 male	14.9 (9–20)	2.39 (1–4)	8.5 (1–14)	24.9 (20–34)	9.3 (6.5–15)

Note. Reprinted from Corkin (1982) by permission.

were significantly inferior to those of the mildly and the moderately demented patients (Corkin, 1982).

Visual Perception

Patients with AD sometimes report visual difficulties. In some cases, disorders of visual perception in AD are severe and overshadow any deficits in memory or language function (Cogan, 1979). We document perceptual disorders by administering the nonmeaningful-form discrimination test, described in the preceding section, and the Gollin incomplete-pictures test. We also measure spatial contrast sensitivity, because decreased sensitivity to low spatial frequencies may underlie deficits in picture recognition (Leibowitz, Post, & Ginsburg, 1980; Nissen et al., 1985; Owsley, Sekuler, & Boldt, 1981).

Gollin incomplete-pictures test. This test assesses the subject's ability to identify figures from incomplete information (Gollin, 1960). It can be used to evaluate both visual perception and perceptual learning. The test consists of five sets of line drawings of 20 animals and common objects, with the five sets differing in degree of fragmentation. The observer is first shown all 20 items in their most fragmented version and is asked to guess what each one is. Then the second, slightly more complete version of each of the 20 items is presented in a different order for identification, and so on through the successively more complete sets until all items are identified correctly or until the fifth, most complete version has been presented. Each stimulus is presented for about one second. Although the task requires a naming response, subjects are also given credit for a response that correctly describes the stimulus item or its use.

Perceptual learning is assessed by a repeat of the test procedure with the same stimulus materials after delays of 1 hour and 24 hours, followed by a calculation of the reduction in errors on retest. The statistical comparisons of the healthy control and the AD groups revealed significant effects at all three testing times and on all trials except trials 3 through 5 in the second-delay testing, when many subjects had already correctly recognized all 20 pictures (Figure 16-5). Trial-by-trial comparisons were made of the mean scores that the healthy control and the three AD groups achieved in the three test sessions. In trials 1 through 3, healthy elderly subjects made significantly fewer errors in the two retest sessions than they had made in the initial test, indicating marked savings. The mildly demented patients also showed significant improvements in retest scores, although only on trials 1 and 2. In contrast, analyses of the mean scores of the moderately and severely demented AD patients showed no statistically significant differences on any trial. Thus, their dementia prohibited perceptual learning, and impairment was related to severity of dementia (Corkin, 1982).

Test of contrast sensitivity function. This test summarizes a subject's ability to see objects of all possible spatial structures by assessing sensitivity to spatial

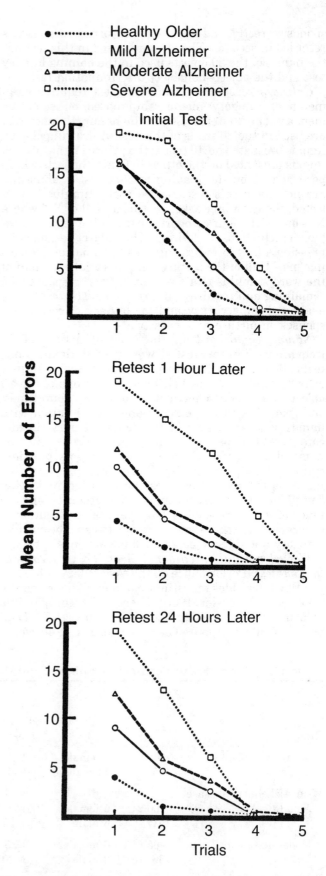

Figure 16-5. Gollin incomplete-pictures test: performance of healthy control subjects (*n* = 16) and patients with AD (*n* = 24) at three test sessions. Adapted from Corkin (1982) by permission.

structures ranging from the coarsest to the finest (Sekuler, 1974; Sekuler & Hutman, 1980). The stimuli for this test are vertical gratings whose contrasts vary sinusoidally along the horizontal axis. Each grating is presented for 700 milliseconds on an oscilloscope. On each trial, the examiner says "ready" and then either presents a grating stimulus or, on catch trials, does not present any stimulus. The subjects' task is to say "yes" if they saw the stimulus and "no" if they did not. A single staircase procedure is followed in which grating contrast (the difference between the grating's maximum and minimum luminance) is initially well above threshold and is reduced on each trial until the subjects can no longer see the grating. Contrast is then increased until the grating is visible again, at which point it is reduced, and so on. This procedure, which causes contrast to oscillate above and below threshold, continues for 30 trials. Contrast thresholds are measured in this way for gratings of 5 spatial frequencies: 0.5, 1, 2, 4, and 8 cycles per degree. (Spatial frequency is defined as the number of pairs of light and dark bars of the grating per degree of visual angle.) Viewing is monocular with the subject's preferred eye. Subjects are dark-adapted for 5 minutes before beginning the test.

Nissen et al. (1985) compared spatial contrast sensitivity functions for patients with AD and healthy control subjects (Figure 16-6). The two upper functions represent the mean values (with 95% confidence lim-

its) for control subjects and for 16 patients with AD. The patients showed reduced sensitivity to all frequencies; the difference between groups averaged 0.37 log unit and ranged from 0.31 log unit at 1 cpd to 0.43 log unit at 8 cpd. The two measurements of sensitivity to 0.5 cpd correlated 0.61 for control subjects and 0.87 for patients with AD. The false alarm rates of the two groups were similar: 14% for patients with AD and 11% for control subjects. These results indicate that AD leads to reduced sensitivity to spatial contrast, even in patients whose primary symptoms do not involve vision. The sensitivity loss is approximately the same across all frequencies from 0.5 to 8 cpd. Although the possibility that the results reflect a criterion difference between groups cannot be ruled out, the similarity of false alarm rates makes this interpretation unlikely. Rather, the neural degeneration of AD appears to produce a true sensitivity loss. Alternatively, Schlotterer, Moscovitch, and Crapper-McLachlan (1983) found no difference in contrast sensitivity between patients with AD and control subjects. These investigators matched the two groups on the basis of visual acuity, a procedure that would have equated them for sensitivity to high spatial frequencies.

Praxis

Apraxias, disorders in performing complex motor acts, are common in AD, even in mildly demented patients. Impairment may be observed in the performance of constructional tasks, such as drawing, or in the manipulation of objects used in daily activities, such as using a key to unlock a door. Dressing may also be a problem such that patients put their clothes on wrong side out or fail to line up the heel of the sock with the heel of the foot. We have assembled a series of tests in order to evaluate such capacities and to quantify the disability in each patient.

Matchsticks test. This test evaluates subjects' constructional abilities (Benson & Barton, 1970; Butters & Barton, 1970). The test includes a copy condition, in which subjects are required to reproduce stick patterns, and a rotation condition, in which subjects must construct an inverted version of each of the stick patterns arranged by the examiner. Subjects are given four wooden sticks, each about 5 inches long with one tip painted black. On each of 5 trials the subjects are asked to use these sticks to reproduce a stick design displayed in front of them. These copy trials, which use 5 different designs, are followed by 5 rotation trials in which the design the subjects must reproduce is rotated 180 degrees. During the rotation trials, the examiner sits facing the subject and gives the instruction to "make your pattern look to you like mine looks to me." Practice trials precede the copy and rotation conditions and continue until it is clear that the subject understands the task. The subjects are instructed to say "Finished" as soon as they believe that they have completed a design correctly. There is a generous time limit of 4 minutes for each design. The number of errors in each condition is recorded.

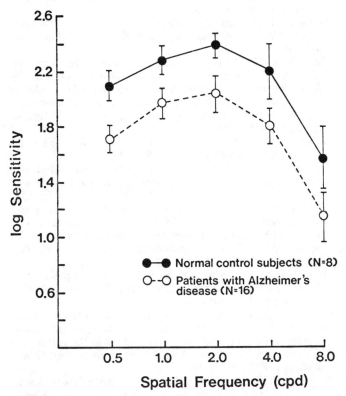

Figure 16-6. Spatial contrast sensitivity functions for healthy control subjects ($n = 8$) and patients with AD. Reprinted from Nissen et al. (1985) by permission. Copyright 1985 by the American Medical Association.

Drawing test. This test further assesses constructional abilities by requiring the subject to draw a bicycle, a daisy, and a clock showing the time as 11:10, and to copy a cube. Each drawing is scored quantitatively. The total achievement score for the four drawings may range from 0 to 30.

Test of use of common objects. This test evaluates complex motor abilities and documents difficulties that the subjects may have in tasks of daily life. The subject is asked to perform 24 tasks such as the following: unlock a door with a key, take a coat off a hanger, put on the coat, button the coat, hang the coat on a hanger, tie a shoelace, pour a glass of water, dial a telephone number, cut a piece of bread and lift it with a fork, open a jar, open an envelope, and sharpen a pencil. One point is given for each task completed in response to a verbal command; 1/2 point is awarded for each task the subject performed only by imitating the examiner.

Analysis of Treatment Effects

Treatment effects in AD are not all-or-none phenomena. A total cure from any treatment is unlikely because considerable cell death has already occurred by the time a clinical diagnosis of AD can be made. Current treatment efforts do not attempt to reverse the degenerative process but at best to retard it or palliate its symptoms. Although drugs cannot replace neurons that synthesize acetylcholine or other neurotransmitters, they may be able to optimize the efficiency of the surviving neurons. Investigators conducting drug studies must therefore establish criteria for deeming a treatment successful, when success falls short of a cure.

One approach in performing statistical analyses of the data obtained in drug trials is to calculate a group mean score for each test under drug and placebo conditions and then to determine whether the means for individual tests change significantly across conditions. This procedure may give disappointing results, however, because it is likely that in a given group of patients, some will be treatment responders and others nonresponders; positive effects in the former subgroup will be diluted by no effect in the latter. The reasons for differential response will not be well understood until more is known about the pathophysiology of AD; these reasons include misdiagnosis and differences in brain chemistry within an accurately diagnosed AD group.

We conclude with a note about the usefulness and limitations of test results as a criterion of treatment efficacy. Although we are encouraged when we see a significant gain in memory-test or language-test performance, a patient's remembering 2 or 3 more words in a list of 30 words may not translate into a meaningful change outside the laboratory. The main criterion of treatment success must be a marked improvement in the patient's daily behavior. Conversely, family impressions of improvement are not by themselves a satisfactory measure of drug efficacy. Objective measures of change must be used to help distinguish drug effects from placebo effects. Moreover, statistically significant improvement on neuropsychological or other laboratory tests, even if the change is small and not reflected in everyday life, can indicate that one is on the right track in pursuit of a treatment. If minimal benefit of a drug is observed, it may be possible to develop an analogue of that particular drug in order to achieve a more meaningful effect. We anticipate that when a clinically useful treatment becomes available, behavioral and biochemical tests can be used to confirm and document the benefit. The tests described here were designed with that purpose in view.

References

Battig, W. F., & Montague, W. E. (1969). Category norms for verbal items in 56 categories: A replication and extension of the Connecticut category norms. *Journal of Experimental Psychology Monographs, 80*(3, Pt. 2), 1–46.

Benson, D. F., & Barton, M. I. (1970). Disturbances in constructional ability. *Cortex, 6,* 19–46.

Bondareff, W., Mountjoy, C., & Roth, M. (1982). Loss of neurons of origin of the adrenergic projection to cerebral cortex (nucleus locus ceruleus) in senile dementia. *Neurology, 32,* 164–168.

Brown, J. (1958). Some tests of the decay theory of immediate memory. *Quarterly Journal of Experimental Psychology, 10,* 12–21.

Brun, A., & Englund, E. (1981). Regional patterns of degeneration in Alzheimer's disease: Neuronal loss and histopathological grading. *Histopathology, 5,* 549–564.

Butters, N., & Barton, M. (1970). Effect of parietal lobe damage on the performance of reversible operations in space. *Neuropsychologia, 8,* 205–214.

Carroll, J. B., Davies, P., & Richman, B. (1971). *The American heritage word frequency book.* New York: Houghton-Mifflin.

Chase, T. N. (1984). Focal abnormalities in Alzheimer's disease as determined by positron emission tomography. In R. J. Wurtman, S. Corkin, & J. H. Growdon (Eds.), *Alzheimer's disease: Advances in basic research and therapies.* Cambridge, MA: Center for Brain Sciences and Metabolism Charitable Trust.

Cogan, D. G. (1979). Visuospatial dysagnosia. *American Journal of Ophthalmology, 88,* 361–368.

Corkin, S. (1982). Some relationships between global amnesias and the memory impairments in Alzheimer's disease. In S. Corkin, K. L. Davis, J. H. Growdon, E. Usdin, & R. J. Wurtman (Eds.), *Alzheimer's disease: A report of progress in research* (pp. 149–164). New York: Raven Press.

Corsi, P. (1972). *Human memory and the medial temporal region of the brain.* Unpublished doctoral dissertation, McGill University, Montreal.

Craik, F. I. M., & Lockhart, R. S. (1972). Levels of processing: A framework for memory research. *Journal of Verbal Learning and Verbal Behavior, 11,* 671–684.

Dahlstrom, A., & Fuxe, K. (1964). Evidence for the existence of monoamine-containing neurons in the central nervous system: I. Demonstration of monoamines in the cell bodies of brain stem neurons. *Acta Physiologica Scandinavica, 62*(Suppl. 232), 1–55.

De Renzi, E., & Ferrari, C. (1978). The reporter's test: A sensitive test to detect expressive disturbances in aphasics. *Cortex, 14,* 279–293.

De Renzi, E., & Vignolo, L. A. (1962). The token test: A sensitive test to detect receptive disturbances in aphasics. *Brain, 85,* 665–678.

Doppelt, J. E., & Wallace, W. L. (1955). Standardization of the Wechsler Adult Intelligence Scale for older persons. *Journal of Abnormal and Social Psychology, 51,* 312–330.

Freed, D. M. (1984). *Rate of forgetting in Alzheimer's disease.* Paper presented at the annual meeting of the Eastern Psychological Association, Baltimore, MD.

Fuld, P. A., Katzman, R., Davies, P., & Terry, R. D. (1982). Intrusions as a sign of Alzheimer's dementia: Chemical and pathological verification. *Annals of Neurology, 11,* 155–159.

Gollin, E. S. (1960). Developmental studies of visual recognition of incomplete objects. *Perceptual and Motor Skills, 11,* 289–298.

Goodglass, H. (1975). [Norming of an experimental version of the Boston Naming Test]. Unpublished data.

Hecaen, H., & Albert, M. L. (Eds.). (1978). *Human neuropsychology.* New York: Wiley.

Huppert, F. A., & Piercy, M. (1978). Dissociation between learning and remembering in organic amnesia. *Nature, 275,* 317–318.

Huppert, F. A., & Piercy, M. (1979). Normal and abnormal forgetting in organic amnesia: Effect of locus of lesion. *Cortex, 15,* 385–390.

Inglis, J. (1959). A paired-associate learning test for use with elderly psychiatric patients. *Journal of Mental Science, 105,* 440–443.

Iversen, L. L., Rossor, M. N., Reynolds, G. P., Hills, R., Roth, M., Mountjoy, C. Q., Foote, S. L., Morrison, J. H., & Bloom, F. E. (1983). Loss of pigmented dopamine beta-hydroxylase positive cells from locus coeruleus in senile dementia of Alzheimer's type. *Neuroscience Letters, 39,* 95–100.

Kaplan, E., Goodglass, H., & Weintraub, S. (1978). *The Boston Naming Test.* Boston: Kaplan & Goodglass.

Kroll, J. F., & Potter, M. C. (1984). Recognizing words, pictures, and concepts: A comparison of lexical, object, and reality decisions. *Journal of Verbal Learning and Verbal Behavior, 23,* 39–66.

LaBerge, D. L., & Lawrence, D. H. (1957). Two methods for generating matrices of forms of graded similarity. *Journal of Psychology, 43,* 77–100.

Leibowitz, H. W., Post, R., & Ginsburg, A. P. (1980). Role of fine detail in visually controlled behavior. *Investigative Ophthalmology and Visual Science, 19,* 846–848.

Loizou, L. A. (1969). Projections of the nucleus locus coeruleus in the albino rat. *Brain Research, 15,* 563–566.

Mann, D., Yates, P., & Hawkes, J. (1982). The noradrenergic system in Alzheimer and multi-infarct dementias. *Journal of Neurology, Neurosurgery, and Psychiatry, 45,* 113–119.

Milner, B. (1971). Interhemispheric differences in the localization of psychological processes in man. *British Medical Bulletin, 27,* 272–277.

Newcombe, F. (1969). *Missile wounds of the brain: A study of psychological deficits.* London: University Park Press.

Nissen, M. J., Corkin, S., Buonanno, F. S., Growdon, J. H., Wray, S. H., & Bauer, J. (1985). Spatial vision in Alzheimer's disease: General findings and a case report. *Archives of Neurology, 42,* 667–671.

Nissen, M. J., Corkin, S., & Growdon, J. H. (1982). *Attentional focusing in amnesia and Alzheimer's disease.* Unpublished manuscript.

Owsley, C., Sekuler, R., & Boldt, C. (1981). Aging and low-contrast vision: Face perception. *Investigative Ophthalmology and Visual Science, 21,* 362–365.

Peterson, L. R., & Peterson, M. J. (1959). Short-term retention of individual verbal items. *Journal of Experimental Psychology, 58,* 193–198.

Posner, M. I., Nissen, M. J., & Ogden, W. C. (1978). Attended and unattended processing modes: The role of set for spatial location. In H. L. Pick, Jr., & E. Saltzman (Eds.), *Modes of perceiving and processing information.* Hillsdale, NJ: Erlbaum.

Randt, C. T., Brown, E. R., & Osborne, D. P., Jr. (1980). A memory test for longitudinal measurement of mild to moderate deficits. *Clinical Neuropsychology, 2,* 184–194.

Redmond, D. E., Jr. (1979). New and old evidence for the involvement of a brain norepinephrine system in anxiety. In W. E. Fann et al. (Eds.), *Phenomenology and treatment of anxiety* (pp. 153–203). New York: Spectrum Publications.

Rossor, M. N., Emson, P. C., Iversen, L. L., Mountjoy, C. Q., & Roth, M. (1984). Patterns of neuropeptide deficits in Alzheimer's disease. In R. J. Wurtman, S. Corkin, & J. H. Growdon (Eds.), *Alzheimer's disease: Advances in basic research and therapies.* Cambridge, MA: Center for Brain Sciences and Metabolism Charitable Trust.

Schlotterer, G., Moscovitch, M., & Crapper-McLachlan, D. (1983). Visual processing deficits as assessed by spatial frequency contrast sensitivity and backward masking in normal aging and Alzheimer's disease. *Brain, 107,* 309–325.

Sekuler, R. (1974). Spatial vision. *Annual Review of Psychology, 25,* 195–232.

Sekuler, R., & Hutman, L. P. (1980). Spatial vision and aging: I. Contrast sensitivity. *Journal of Gerontology, 35,* 692–699.

Talland, G. (1965). *Deranged memory.* New York: Academic Press.

Teuber, H.-L., Corkin, S., & Twitchell, T. E. (1977). A study of cingulotomy in man. In National Commission for the Protection of Human Subjects of Biomedical and Behavioral Research, *Psychosurgery: Report and recommendations* (DHEW Publication No. OS-77-0001). Washington, DC: U.S. Government Printing Office.

Wechsler, D. (1944). *The measurement of adult intelligence.* Baltimore, MD: Williams & Wilkins.

Wechsler, D. (1955). *Manual for the Wechsler Adult Intelligence Scale.* New York: Psychological Corporation.

Whitehouse, P. J., Price, D. L., Clark, A. W., Coyle, J. T., & DeLong, M. R. (1981). Alzheimer's disease: Evidence for selective loss of cholinergic neurons in the nucleus basalis. *Annals of Neurology, 10,* 122–126.

Wurtman, R. J., Corkin, S., & Growdon, J. H. (Eds.). (1984). *Alzheimer's disease: Advances in basic research and therapies.* Cambridge, MA: Center for Brain Sciences and Metabolism Charitable Trust.

Alfred W. Kaszniak, Leonard W. Poon, and Walter Riege

Assessing Memory Deficits: An Information-Processing Approach

This chapter provides an introductory review of approaches to memory assessment derived from the information-processing tradition in cognitive psychology. The focus is on application of these approaches in three areas of study: (a) normal aging, (b) Alzheimer's disease (AD), and (c) focal brain lesions. Review of literature in these three areas reveals that memory assessment procedures based on information-processing models have utility in differentiating impairment in the various aspects of complex memory processes. Normal aging appears to have its most marked effects on secondary memory, with other memory processes relatively spared. In AD, all memory processes appear to become eventually impaired, with increasing interdependence between performance on tasks designed to assess each of the theoretical storage capacities (i.e., sensory, primary, secondary, and tertiary memory). When the brain is focally damaged, various memory processes and storage capacities can be impaired, depending on the location and size of the lesion.

The purpose of this chapter is to provide an introductory review and evaluation of memory assessment procedures derived from the information-processing tradition in cognitive psychology. We focus on application in three major areas: (a) normal aging, (b) Alzheimer's disease (AD), and (c) focal brain lesions. The chapter begins with a descriptive introduction to the information-processing approach, continues with sections dealing with the three areas of application, and concludes with a brief summary.

The Information-Processing Approach to Memory Assessment

Both the psychometric and the information-processing traditions have contributed to the study of intellectual and cognitive functioning. In clinical, neuropsychologi-

cal, and intellectual testing, the psychometric approach is predominant. Psychometric instruments have the advantage of being portable, involving little or no equipment, being standardized, and having published norms. A common complaint regarding some psychometric tests, however, is that test scores alone do not isolate the underlying factor(s) associated with performance changes. For example, of the 11 subtests of the Wechsler Adult Intelligence Scale (WAIS), the Digit Symbol subtest shows the greatest difference between young and old adults (Botwinick, 1978). However, it is not clear what causes the poor performance of the aged—slow psychomotor skills, poor learning or retrieval of the digit symbol codes, poor visuomotor coordination, or a combination of these factors (Royer, 1978).

The information-processing approach is most often used in laboratory investigations of cognitive processes (Atkinson & Shiffrin, 1968; Estes, 1978; Murdock, 1974); it is relatively infrequently used for clinical diagnosis and treatment evaluation. The approach makes these basic assumptions: (a) that the subject is an active participant in the learning and decision-making processes and the effectiveness of the learner's cognitive processing can be measured and (b) that a response can be partitioned into theoretical components or stages so that they can be analyzed. The essence of the approach is that by controlling and manipulating the information input (e.g., instructions, stimulus complexity, and input modality), the clinician or researcher should be able to infer the integrity of the subject's processor on the basis of the patterns and quality of the response output (speed, accuracy, strategies, and biases).

For example, if a clinical syndrome is characterized by the slowing of decision processes, an information-processing procedure could determine if the slowing is due to either peripheral (motor) or central (decision-processing) functions, or to both. The clinician could select a choice reaction time task in which the complexity of the decision might vary from no decision (one choice) to complex decisions by increasing the number of choices. In a no-choice condition, the subject's sensorimotor efficiency for this particular task could be assessed. As the number of decision choices increases, the clinician could examine the patterns of speed and accuracy of decision making to ascertain the source of difficulty for the patient. The questions asked about the integrity of the "processor" guide the selection of the test paradigm, test stimuli, and dependent measures.

Four kinds of criticism have been leveled against the use of the information-processing approach in clinical testing. First, executing the various paradigms often requires complicated and expensive equipment, such as a cathode-ray tube display, reaction time keys, and a computer. Second, testing paradigms are often experimental and are frequently associated with specific theoretical models of behavior. Third, information-processing tasks are frequently so complicated that they could be beyond the capacity of some clinical populations. Fourth, these tests are often more time consuming than are psychometric tests.

The first criticism has become somewhat less important because new, inexpensive, personal-type microcomputers are sufficiently portable for bedside testing. The second and third criticisms are germane to existing problems in communication between clinicians and researchers dealing with cognitive and memory functions. In addressing this issue, Erickson, Poon, and Walsh-Sweeney (1980) wrote:

To the uninitiated the literature seems vast, intricate, endlessly laborious, and sometimes contradictory. It is with good reason that some clinicians feel overwhelmed and consequently reject the experimental models and literature as self-serving and irrelevant to their needs. Furthermore, lack of meaningful communication between laboratory and clinical personnel contributes to the practice, by some clinicians, of administering memory tests without knowing the theoretical rationale behind the tests. Likewise, this lack of communication contributes to an insensitivity to and/or an ignorance of clinical problems and procedures on the part of some laboratory researchers. (p. 394)

Laboratory procedures can increase the specificity of clinical techniques, and procedures can be designed to the capacity level of a specific patient population. However, a significant amount of work by both clinicians and researchers is needed to translate laboratory procedures into clinically relevant diagnostics.

Finally, information-processing procedures are indeed more time consuming than checklists or subjective behavioral rating scales, but the additional time is sometimes justifiable. Information processing is an approach and not a set of concrete tests or procedures. The test procedure can be innovative and flexible and must be guided by theoretical or clinical hypotheses.

Additional testing time is justified if greater assessment precision is required or if objective validation of rating scales and psychometric tests is needed.

A major source of difficulty in diagnosing and treating memory problems lies in the multidimensionality of memory. In the last several decades, psychologists, neurologists, and neuropsychologists have attempted to establish models of memory and of the relationship between memory and brain functions. Although no model is completely satisfactory, it is now possible to identify some major characteristics of memory (e.g., Cermak, 1982; Murdock, 1974) and the factors that influence its functioning. Imagine memory as a multidimensional entity with interacting dimensions. One dimension of memory consists of dynamic processes related to the encoding, storage, and retrieval of information. Another is a theoretical definition of different information storage capacities—iconic (sensory), primary (short-term), secondary (newly learned information), and tertiary (well-learned or very familiar) memory stores. A third dimension defines the modality-specific properties of the incoming information—verbal, spatial, visual, auditory, olfactory, and so on.

The different dimensions interact, and their functioning is affected by the characteristics of the person—patterns of responses to environmental stresses; changing affective states; personality and cognitive styles; health; intelligence; education; socioeconomic status; and transient and stable neurologic, hormonal, and physiologic states. Thus, the level of functional memory is fluid and subject to intra- and interpersonal variability. Obviously, no single instrument or battery could adequately assess the many facets of memory functioning. Furthermore, the combination of factors that could produce memory problems makes information processing an invaluable clinical tool for the testing of hypotheses regarding the locus of dysfunction.

Normal Aging

The information-processing approach has proved useful for studying age-related differences in memory functions. Table 17-1 presents a list of 20 recent reviews of the literature on memory and aging (Poon, 1985). The table demonstrates the prevalence of the information-processing approach in examining age-related differences in memory components, stages, and processes.

In reading our description of information-processing studies, it is important to keep in mind that some of the procedures were originally designed to test existing theoretical models of cognitive functioning. Results should be interpreted on the basis of those models and their assumptions. It should be noted that the representativeness of these models is constantly debated. When a model is thought not to be clearly representative, it does not mean that data supporting it are tenuous; rather, they may require modification of assumptions or fit a more appropriate model. For example, recognition of words in a list is claimed to contain two processing components, one based on intra-item "fa-

Table 17-1. Reviews of Recent Literature on the Effects of Aging on Memory Functions

Authors	Sensory memory	Primary memory	Secondary memory	Encoding	Storage	Retrieval	Remote memory	Speed	Contextual semantic processing	Spatial memory	Mnemonic organization	Meta-memory
Albert & Kaplan												
Burke & Light				X		X			X			
Cavanaugh & Perlmutter												X
Craik	X	X	X	X	X	X						
Craik & Simon				X		X						
Erber (1981)							X					
Erber (1982)	X	X	X	X	X	X	X					X
Erickson, Poon, & Walsh-Sweeney												
Fozard	X	X	X				X	X				
Hartley, Harker, & Walsh		X	X	X		X		X	X	X	X	
Hines & Fozard				X							X	
Kausler	X	X	X	X	X	X	X		X	X	X	X
Labouvie-Vief & Schell	X	X	X	X	X	X			X			
Poon	X	X	X	X	X	X	X	X	X		X	X
Poon, Walsh-Sweeney, & Fozard			X	X							X	
Salthouse	X	X	X	X	X	X	X	X	X	X		X
Schonfield & Stone		X	X			X		X	X		X	
Smith				X	X	X					X	
Smith & Fullerton	X	X	X	X	X	X	X		X		X	
Walsh & Prasse	X											

Note. Authors listed are cited in Poon (1985). Table adapted by permission.

miliarity processing" (Mandler, 1980), the other on inter-item associative processes. Age differences observed in word recognition have been assumed to involve the second but not the first component (Rabinowitz, 1984), and studies in word recognition generally support this assumption. However, age differences have also been observed in immediate and delayed recognition of nonverbal visual designs (Riege & Inman, 1981), which rely almost exclusively upon the first component; these findings indicate a need to reassess the model. It is important, then, to examine the replicability of data as well as their relevance to a proposed model.

A "linear" model of information processing has dominated research on memory and aging for the past 20 years (Labouvie-Vief & Schell, 1982). This model postulates that information flows from input to output through a series of stages. At the very early stage of information, registration is sensory (iconic and echoic) memory, a preattentive and highly unstable system. Primary (short-term) and secondary (long-term) memory (Waugh & Norman, 1965) are responsible for the acquisition and retention of new information. Primary memory is conceptualized as a limited-capacity store in which information is still "in mind" as it is being used. If the information is not rehearsed instantaneously so that it can be stored in secondary memory, the information will be lost. Secondary memory is a repository of newly acquired information. Finally, tertiary memory is a repository for well-learned and personal information. Difficulty in any stage of memory creates an information "bottleneck," and performance suffers (cf. Atkinson & Shiffrin, 1968; Neisser, 1967).

A global summary of normal age-related changes in

Table 17-1, continued

Authors	Noncognitive factors	Attentional resources	Diagnostic battery	Intervention
Albert & Kaplan		X	X	
Burke & Light				
Cavanaugh & Perlmutter				
Craik		X		
Craik & Simon		X		
Erber (1981)				
Erber (1982)	X			
Erickson, Poon, & Walsh-Sweeney			X	
Fozard				X
Hartley, Harker, & Walsh				
Hines & Fozard				X
Kausler	X	X		
Labouvie-Vief & Schell	X			
Poon			X	X
Poon, Walsh-Sweeney, & Fozard				X
Salthouse	X	X		
Schonfield & Stone				
Smith				
Smith & Fullerton				
Walsh & Prasse		X		

Note. Authors listed are cited in Poon (1985). Table adapted by permission.

memory is presented in Tables 17-2 and 17-3. Table 17-2 shows that there is a general age-related decline in speed of retrieval from the various theoretical memory stores, and Table 17-3 shows that the locus of the age-related decline in memory capacity is found primarily in secondary memory (Fozard, 1980). Thus, although sensorimotor slowing is inevitable with aging, this slowing apparently does not appreciably affect the capacities of sensory, primary, or tertiary memory. Aging, however, has been found to have profound influence in the acquisition and retrieval of new information in secondary memory. Although the reasons for the deficit in secondary memory are being actively debated and researched, it is encouraging to note that research in mnemonics (memory aids) and practice effects (see, e.g., Poon, Walsh-Sweeney, & Fozard, 1980; Treat, Poon, & Fozard, 1981) has shown that some sec-

Table 17-2. Cross-Sectional Evidence for Normal Age-Related Slowing in Memory

Component	Sensory memory	Primary memory	Secondary memory	Tertiary memory
Perceptual–motor	Yes	Yes	Yes	Yes
Decision-making	—	Yes	Yes	No

Note. Adapted from Fozard (1980) by permission.

ondary memory deficits can be dramatically reduced in the community-dwelling elderly.

From the standpoint of instrument review, it is important to emphasize again that information processing is an approach and not a set of prescribed procedures. The clinician has the flexibility to select or design information-processing procedure(s) that could evaluate observable symptoms as well as underlying processes. It should be noted that a set of procedures that may be appropriate for the testing of some hypotheses may not be appropriate for other hypotheses. Furthermore, procedures that are commonly employed in laboratory situations may need to be modified for clinical purposes. The following is a selection of information-processing procedures that have been used in the study of aging and memory. The procedures selected highlight how this approach can be used to elucidate underlying processes.

Sensory Memory

This brief storage of information is labeled *iconic memory* in the visual system and *echoic memory* in the auditory system (Crowder, 1980). Information on sensory memory and aging is derived primarily from work on iconic memory. A primary question in the study of iconic memory is whether there is a significant slowing in the initial registration of information that could compromise later stages of memory.

Iconic memory is often measured by using backward masking. A letter or number (the target) is presented for a very short duration (about 10 to 150 millisec-

Table 17-3. Evidence for Normal Age-Related Declines in Memory Capacity

Type of evidence	Sensory memory	Primary memory	Secondary memory	Tertiary memory
Cross-sectional				
Anecdotal	—	Yes	Yes	Yes
Psychometric	—	No	Yes	No
Experimental	Yes	No	Yes	No
Longitudinal				
Anecdotal	—	—	—	—
Psychometric	—	No	Yes	No
Experimental	—	—	Yes	—

Note. Adapted from Fozard (1980) by permission.

onds), followed by an interfering (masking) stimulus that effectively terminates the display. The target stimulus duration necessary for correct target identification is recorded (stimulus duration is systematically varied over trials). Walsh and his colleagues, in a series of studies using this technique, showed that the time needed to identify a single letter does not change or changes only a small amount (by a factor of 1.3) with age (Walsh, Till, & Williams, 1978).

Multiple targets may also be presented, in order to evaluate the identification rate, as well as speed and accuracy. When seven-letter strings were presented to subjects for 10 to 200 milliseconds, younger adults were able to identify three letters at a rate of 27 milliseconds per letter, a rate similar to those reported by Sperling (1963) and Coltheart (1972). Any additional letters were identified at a slower rate. In contrast, older subjects were able to identify two letters at a rate of 35 milliseconds per letter (Cerella, Poon, & Fozard, 1982). These rates indicate an age-related decline by a factor of 1.3, paralleling Walsh's results.

It is important to note that, in assessing aged people, investigators need to adjust stimulus size to equate for parafoveal discriminability in young and old subjects. Otherwise, differences in iconic readout can be due to differences in parafoveal discrimination. Although the elderly have significantly reduced parafoveal fields, in two experiments (Cerella & Poon, 1981), age differences in iconic readout became minimal after the sizes of parafoveal targets were adjusted to compensate for the loss in discrimination.

Other experimental methods that have been employed to examine age differences in iconic memory include the partial report method (Averbach & Coriell, 1961; Walsh & Prasse, 1980) and the stimulus persistence method (Haber & Standing, 1969; Walsh & Thompson, 1978). However, these methods have yielded conflicting results and may not be appropriate for use with the elderly (Grossberg, 1980; Kline & Schieber, 1981). They are therefore not clinically useful at present.

In summary, despite some decline in the visual system of older adults (see Fozard, Wolf, Bell, McFarland, & Podolsky, 1977, for a detailed review), research has revealed only small age differences in the ability to identify briefly presented visual stimuli.

Primary Memory

Minimal or no age difference is found in primary memory, an ephemeral, limited capacity memory store that is hypothesized to control and assimilate information prior to its entry into secondary memory (Craik, 1977; Waugh & Norman, 1965). The forward memory span is commonly used to evaluate primary memory capacity (e.g., Botwinick & Storandt, 1974), and minimal age difference has been found in either the capacity or speed of retrieval from primary memory, when the number of items is approximately seven or less. Age differences have been obtained in backward memory

span (Botwinick & Storandt, 1974); however, it is noted that the cognitive operations necessary to perform the task may exceed the primary memory capacity.

An example of one information-processing procedure that has been shown to elucidate underlying retrieval characteristics is a continuous recognition memory task employed by Poon and Fozard (1978). In this task the subject is presented a series of words one at a time and is told that some of the words will be repeated a second time. The task is to say whether a presented word is shown for the first or second time, and the speed of this decision is measured. The subject also provides an estimate of his or her confidence in the response. The intervening intervals between the first and second presentations of a word are manipulated so that they are within either the primary memory range (about seven items or less) or within the secondary memory range (from seven items and up). In this manner, both the speed and the accuracy of retrieval from primary and secondary memory can be assessed. Furthermore, d' (item detection sensitivity) and β (criterion bias), parameters from signal detection theory (Marcer, 1979; Swets, 1973), can also be evaluated.

Figure 17-1 presents retrieval times for young, middle-aged, and elderly samples. For each group, two types of retrieval rate are noted, a steeper retrieval function (or slope) that is evidenced for retrieval of items from primary memory range and a more moderate retrieval function for retrieval from the secondary memory range. Retrieval times for items in primary memory did not differ significantly between the groups, although a significant age-related difference was found in retrieval times for items in secondary memory. The analyses of accuracy, d', and β showed the same pattern.

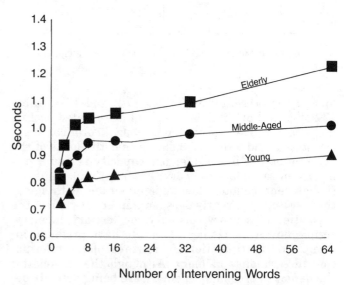

Figure 17-1. Median correct retrieval times for young, middle-aged, and elderly samples in a continuous recognition memory task. Adapted from Poon and Fozard (1978) by permission.

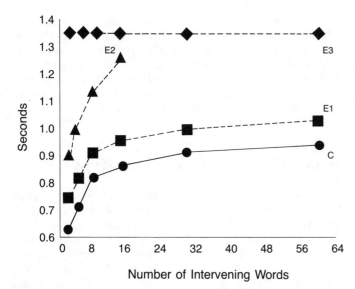

Figure 17-2. Hypothetical retrieval speed functions for a continuous recognition memory task. Function C represents performance of a hypothetical control subject. Function E1 shows normal retrieval but a slower than normal rate. E2 exemplifies secondary memory dysfunction, with successful retrieval of only those words in the primary memory range. E3 represents compromise of both accuracy and retrieval speed in a subject with both primary and secondary memory difficulty.

This paradigm could be used to differentiate different kinds of retrieval dysfunctions. Figure 17-2 shows four hypothetical retrieval speed functions. The performance of the control subject is represented by function C. Function E1 represents normal retrieval, but a slower rate. Function E2 shows the performance of a subject who has a secondary memory dysfunction and successfully retrieves only words in the primary memory range. Either accuracy or speed of retrieval may be compromised, and both set limits to performance. The performance of a subject who has difficulty in both primary and secondary memory is shown by function E3. A more comprehensive picture of a dysfunction could be obtained by examining also the other dependent measures associated with this paradigm. Because it can provide a wealth of data, this procedure is a potentially cost-effective instrument for both clinical diagnosis and treatment evaluation.

The Sternberg (1969) memory scan task has been employed to evaluate the speed of scanning primary memory. Each subject is presented with a memory set varying from one to seven items to hold in memory. The subject's task is to identify whether a probe item is a member of the memory set. Age differences have been reported using this task (Anders & Fozard, 1973); however it has been argued that scanning of the larger set sizes may also involve secondary memory functions (Labouvie-Vief & Schell, 1982), and a failure to find age differences has been reported (Bacon, Wilson, & Kaszniak, 1982) when the task is limited to smaller (two to four items) set sizes.

Secondary Memory

In contrast to the findings for iconic and primary memory, a comparatively larger age-related deficit is evident in secondary memory. Consequently, a great amount of effort has been expended to determine whether encoding, storage, or retrieval is responsible for this deficit. The flexibility of the information-processing approach is an asset in isolating learning and retrieval problems.

Reviews of the extant literature generally agree that normal age-related deficits are most evident in encoding and retrieval, whereas there is minimal age-related deficit in storage. If one can use a battery as an analogy to study memory processes, one method of evaluating the storage efficiency is the discharge rate over time. Analogously, in memory functioning, it is possible to evaluate the rate of forgetting (discharge) after information is properly encoded. Rates of forgetting, which are measured by the accuracy of recall at different retrieval intervals, are generally parallel in young and elderly adults for tasks involving paired-associate learning (Thomas & Ruben, 1973), word recognition (Poon & Fozard, 1978; Wickelgren, 1975), picture recognition (Fozard & Poon, 1976), and recall of colloquial events (Warrington & Silberstein, 1970). Proactive (Craik, 1968; Fozard & Waugh, 1969) and retroactive (Smith, 1975) inhibition procedures also have not shown an age-related deficit.

Encoding deficits in the aged have been studied using information-processing procedures that examined (a) verbal elaboration, the degree to which each item is distinctly encoded; (b) visual elaboration, the degree to which imagery is used in encoding; and (c) organization, the degree to which stimulus items are related to each other during acquisition (Smith, 1980).

To investigate the possibility of a deficit in verbal elaboration in older adults, Eysenck (1974) employed an incidental orienting task in which varying levels of elaboration of words were required. Subjects were required to count letters of words, to generate rhymes, or to generate appropriate adjectives. A control group received no elaboration instructions. In a later free-recall test, older subjects who generated adjectives performed worse than those who made up rhymes, who performed worse than those who counted letters. These results suggest that tasks requiring elaborate processing will show larger age differences in later recall.

There is also evidence for deficits in organization and visual elaboration. Studies have demonstrated a significant age-related deficit in learning when the material to be learned needs organization. Furthermore, this age difference is significantly reduced when visual mnemonics (see Poon, Walsh-Sweeney, & Fozard, 1980, for a review) or organizational cues (e.g., Hultsch, 1969) are provided.

Information-processing procedures can also be used to evaluate possible deficits in retrieval. It should be noted that efficiency of retrieval is dependent on efficiency of encoding; it is difficult, if not impossible, to untangle the two processes. Most often, deficit in retrieval is evaluated by comparing performances on recall and recognition tasks (Erber, 1974; Schonfield & Robertson, 1966). The well-replicated finding of small age-related deficits in recognition and large age-related deficits in recall suggests that retrieval rather than storage is impaired in the elderly. Other procedures for evaluating retrieval involve comparing performance on free- and cued-recall tasks (Hultsch, 1975) and in comparing performance when organization cues are provided at different times during a task (Smith, 1977).

Tertiary Memory

A common question about memory asked by elderly adults is why they experience difficulty in recalling recent events, whereas events that happened years ago can supposedly be recalled with accuracy. Perhaps this type of ancedotal evidence contributed to the formulation of Ribot's Law (1882), which states that information is forgotten in the reverse order from which it was acquired. A review of data on the retrieval of familiar information (i.e., tertiary or remote memory) suggests that age differences are minimal, and although remote memory stays fairly intact in older adults it is not superior to the recall of recent events (Erber, 1981).

Questionnaire testing for the recognition and/or recall of public events is a common means of evaluating remote memory (e.g., Botwinick & Storandt, 1974; Poon, Fozard, Paulshock, & Thomas, 1979; Warrington & Sanders, 1971). Information-processing procedures are available for the measurement of speed and accuracy of recalling information from remote and tertiary memory. Poon and Fozard (1978) employed a naming-latency procedure in measuring the time needed to name objects presented by a slide projector. Objects were selected on the basis of frequency of use (common versus unique) as well as the datedness of use (used in the 1920s versus 1970s). There were no age differences in the naming of frequently used objects. However, the younger subjects were significantly faster in correctly naming objects unique to the 1970s. The elderly subjects were faster in correctly naming the unique objects used in the 1920s, and the naming latencies of the middle-aged subjects were between those of the other two age groups. Thus, retrieval time from tertiary memory is a function of the familiarity of the information. Most test procedures employ stimuli that are more familiar to younger adults than to older adults; demonstrated deficits in performance could be a function of the test stimuli used—a cohort effect—rather than cognitive inefficiency.

In summary, information-processing studies of aging in community-dwelling adults indicate minimal age-related deficits in sensory, primary, and tertiary memory, although significant deficits are found in secondary memory. It should be noted that these findings reflected differences between groups; the data show a significant amount of individual variability (Fozard & Costa, in press; Poon, 1985).

Nevertheless, information processing procedures are available that could be used in clinically relevant ways to isolate the nature of sensory, primary, secondary, and tertiary memory deficits or to test hypotheses regarding such deficits. In the next section, the application of these procedures to the evaluation of memory deficit in dementia of the Alzheimer's type will be examined.

Dementia of the Alzheimer's Type

The essential feature of the syndrome of dementia is a loss of intellectual ability of sufficient severity to interfere with social or occupational functioning (American Psychiatric Association, 1980, p. 107). Additional diagnostic criteria include the presence of memory impairment and disturbance in at least one of the following: abstract thinking, judgment, higher cortical function (e.g., language, perception, reproduction of designs), and personality. Exclusionary criteria include evidence of clouded consciousness and conditions other than organic mental disorders. Although there are a large number of possible causes of dementia, Alzheimer's disease (AD) is now recognized as the cause of the majority of cases of dementia in older age (Roth, 1980; Terry & Davies, 1980; Terry & Katzman, 1983; Tomlinson, 1982).

Clinical observers (e.g., Schneck, Reisberg, & Ferris, 1982) have pointed out frequently that memory disturbance is one of the earliest symptoms of progressive dementia of AD and that memory is perhaps the most severely affected cognitive function as the disease progresses. Consequently, memory has received the most attention from neuropsychological and other investigators concerned with the nature and correlates of cognitive dysfunction in patients with AD. Most of this research has employed psychometric and neuropsychological methods, although an increasing number of these studies have applied an information-processing approach (for recent reviews of this research, see Fozard, 1980; Kaszniak, 1986; Miller, 1977a, 1981; Morley, Haxby, & Lundgren, 1980).

The present review focuses on studies illustrating the application of the information-processing approaches to clinical assessment of the memory deficit characteristic of AD. One potential criticism of the information-processing approach in research with patients with AD is that some tasks may be too difficult or the patient too demented to understand the procedures, the result being that poor performances occur in all such tasks. Although this criticism must be seriously considered, it should not necessarily discourage such application. First, task difficulty can be manipulated, via alteration of stimulus characteristics, timing, and response requirements to bring a task to a level of difficulty within the competency of many demented patients. However, dementia may progress to such an extreme, and involve so many cognitive functions, that patients cannot comprehend task instructions or make required responses. In such cases, the majority of information-processing tasks currently available would be useless. In general, the information-processing approach has been most revealing and productive with less severely demented patients (see Wilson & Kaszniak, chapter 29, this volume). However, this same limitation applies to most tasks derived from the psychometric and neuropsychological traditions. In the studies reviewed in this section, results are based on study of only those patients who could clearly comprehend and provide appropriate responses to the tasks employed.

Sensory Memory

Experimental paradigms for evaluating sensory memory, such as backward masking, are very difficult to execute with demented patients, in part because of the difficulty patients experience in understanding instructions and task demands (Kaszniak, 1986; Miller, 1981). Miller (1977b) reported on a preliminary study of iconic memory in patients with presenile dementia of the Alzheimer type (PSDAT). Patients and control subjects briefly viewed a six-letter array, followed after 50 to 250 milliseconds by a masking stimulus. Although the patients recalled fewer letters in the array than the control subjects, it is not clear whether this impairment was due to deficit in attention or iconic memory, to increased susceptibility to interference, or to some combination of these factors. One aspect of this ambiguity in interpretation reflects the difficulty in finding a task that is neither too easy for control subjects nor too difficult for patients with AD, so that basement and ceiling effects do not occur. Although there is insufficient information concerning the status of sensory memory in dementia, Miller's research does raise the possibility that PSDAT may result in impairment of even the earliest stages of information registration.

Primary Memory

Primary memory in patients with AD has most often been studied using the forward digit span test. Most studies comparing patients who have AD with normal subjects have found patients to be impaired on this test (e.g., Corkin, 1982; Crook, Ferris, McCarthy, & Rae, 1980; Kaszniak, Garron, & Fox, 1979; Larner, 1977), although mildly demented patients do not always exhibit impairment (Danziger & Storandt, 1982). Digit span performance deteriorates as dementia progresses (Danziger & Storandt, 1982), and impairment is correlated with the severity of electroencephalographic (EEG) slowing (Kaszniak, Garron, Fox, Bergen, & Huckman, 1979) and with the degree of impairment in activities of daily living (ADL) (Corkin, 1982). Forward digit span performance deteriorates over repeat (yearly) examination in patients with AD (Storandt, Botwinick, & Danziger, chapter 28, this volume; Wilson & Kaszniak, chapter 29, this volume). Tests of memory span for words or spatially arranged blocks show similar impairment in patients with AD (Corkin, 1982; Miller, 1973). However, these results cannot be

unambiguously interpreted as providing evidence of a deficit in primary memory. Although reflecting mostly primary memory, the digit span test and other span memory tasks probably also contain a small secondary memory component (Craik, 1977).

Another procedure that has been employed to examine primary memory in patients with AD is the Brown (1958) or Peterson and Peterson (1959) technique. In this procedure, either a consonant trigram (CCC) or three words are presented, with recall tested either immediately or following various delay intervals (typically ranging up to 18 seconds) filled with distracting cognitive activity (e.g., counting backward). The distracting activity presumably prevents rehearsal, and any decrease in recall with increasing distraction interval is taken to reflect loss of information from primary memory. Corkin (1982), employing the Brown-Peterson procedure, found no difference between patients and control subjects in immediate (zero delay interval) recall, but the groups differed at increasing distraction intervals. She also found impaired performance to be correlated with impairment in ADL. As is the case with span memory tasks just discussed, interpretation of the Brown-Peterson procedure is controversial. Baddeley (1976) has argued that the pattern of results, when different cognitive distracting tasks in the Brown-Peterson procedure are used with normal subjects, has been more consistent with results obtained from other secondary memory tasks rather than from primary memory tasks. Thus, span memory and Brown-Peterson tasks cannot be interpreted unambiguously as reflecting primary memory processes.

Primary memory can also be examined using the free-recall procedure. The subject is serially presented a supra-span list of words (a longer-than-average forward word span of seven items) and is instructed to recall as many words as possible, in any order, immediately following the last presented word. Traditionally, probability of recall is plotted against the serial position. For normal individuals, the plot is a U-shaped curve; the first few words and the last few words of the list are recalled more often than words in the middle of the list. Glanzer and Cunitz (1966) hypothesized that words from the end of the list are recalled from primary memory, whereas words from the beginning of the list are recalled from secondary memory.

Miller (1971) tested patients with PSDAT using the free-recall procedure. Compared with normal subjects, the dementia patients had poorer recall across all word positions. Words from the end of the list (primary memory component) were recalled more poorly by the PSDAT patients, although the group difference was even more marked for words from the beginning of the list (secondary memory component). A similar verbal free-recall procedure (Kaszniak, Wilson, & Fox, 1981) obtained similar evidence of reduced primary and secondary memory components in patients with AD, compared with age-matched control subjects.

Baddeley (1976) has questioned whether recall of words presented at the end of a list ("recency effect") results from a retrieval strategy that uses serial position as a cue, rather than reflecting primary memory.

Tulving and Colotla (1970) developed a scoring procedure that takes into account the order in which words are both presented and recalled. In this procedure, the number of word presentations and recall productions intervening between presentation and recall of a word is counted. If the number is 6 or less, the word is assigned to primary memory. All other recalled words are assigned to secondary memory. Empirical support for the interpretation of primary and secondary memory components derived from the scoring procedure has been found in experimental investigations of normal memory functions (Watkins, 1974), as well as in neuropsychological studies of amnesia (Moscovitch, 1982). Using this scoring procedure, Wilson, Bacon, Fox, and Kaszniak (1983) found primary memory to be impaired in AD patients, relative to the performance of control subjects. Annual reexamination of the subjects over a 3-year period demonstrated that the primary memory score deteriorated over time for the patients with AD but not for the control subjects (Wilson & Kaszniak, chapter 29, this volume).

In summary, although there has been theoretical debate concerning the validity of various experimental procedures for defining primary memory, the available research collectively suggests that primary memory is impaired in patients with AD. The impairment of primary memory appears to be mild early in the course of dementia and increases over time and with greater severity of dementia. Primary memory for both verbal and nonverbal material appears to be impaired, and the degree of deficit on at least one representative task (i.e., digit span) corresponds to the severity of EEG slowing. Table 17-4 summarizes the investigations reported on here.

Secondary Memory

Researchers have studied secondary memory in patients with AD, using a variety of tasks in which encoding processes (e.g., phonemic vs. semantic encoding), duration of storage (e.g., immediate vs. delayed recall), stimulus material (e.g., verbal vs. nonverbal stimuli), and aspects of retrieval (e.g., recall vs. recognition memory testing) have been manipulated systematically. Verbal learning tasks have been among those most frequently employed in such research. Recall of material presented in verbal learning tasks has been interpreted as reflecting at least some secondary memory component, because word lists used have been longer than presumed primary memory capacity.

McCarthy, Ferris, Clark, and Crook (1981) showed patients with AD to be impaired, relative to matched control subjects, in learning a list of 10 words representing common items found on shopping lists. (The number of trials to accurate recall was the dependent variable). They also found evidence of impairment in delayed recall and recognition, suggesting that both storage and retrieval are involved in the impairment. Similarly, patients have been shown to be impaired in learning and recalling lists of progressively longer length (Miller, 1973). Also, patients are impaired in both verbal and nonverbal paired-associate learning (Barbizet & Cany, 1969; Caird, Sanderson, & Inglis, 1962; Corkin, 1982; Danziger & Storandt, 1982; Inglis, 1959; Inglis & Caird, 1963; Kaszniak, Garron, & Fox, 1979; Rosen & Mohs, 1982; Wilson, Bacon, Kaszniak, & Fox, 1982). Degree of impairment in verbal paired-associate learning has been shown to be correlated with degree of cerebral atrophy seen on computed to-

Table 17-4. Investigations of Primary Memory in Patients With AD

Task	Measure	Results	Authors
Digit span	Accuracy	Patients impaired; impairment related to behavioral indices of dementia severity and physiological (EEG) index of cerebral dysfunction; increased impairment seen after one year for some patients	Larner (1977) Kaszniak, Garron, & Fox (1979) Kaszniak et al. (1979) Crook et al. (1980) Corkin (1982) Danziger & Storandt (1982)
Word span	Accuracy	Patients impaired	Miller (1973)
Block span	Accuracy	Patients impaired; degree of impairment related to severity of impairment in ADL	Corkin (1982)
Brown-Peterson distractor task (consonant trigrams)	Accuracy of recall after various retention intervals	Patients impaired for all but 0-S delay; impairment related to severity of impairment in ADL	Corkin (1982)
Immediate verbal free-recall task	Number of words recalled in each serial position of presentation	Patients impaired in recall of words at end of list; validated procedure for scoring primary memory confirms deficit; patients show deterioration in primary memory over 3 years	Miller (1971) Kaszniak, Wilson, & Fox (1981) Wilson, Bacon, Fox, & Kaszniak (1983) Wilson & Kaszniak (chapter 29, this volume)

Note. EEG = electroencephalogram, ADL = activities of daily living.

mography (CT) scans (de Leon et al., 1980; Kaszniak, Garron, Fox, Bergen, et al., 1979) and with severity of EEG slowing (Johannesson, Hagberg, Gustafson, & Ingvar, 1979; Kaszniak, Garron, Fox, Bergen, et al., 1979).

Recall of textual material such as short stories is another task considered to involve predominantly secondary memory. Patients with AD demonstrate impairment, relative to matched control subjects, in both immediate and delayed recall of spoken short stories (Brinkman, Largen, Gerganoff, & Pomara, 1983; Danziger & Storandt, 1982; Logue & Wyrick, 1979; Osborne, Brown, & Randt, 1982). As in the case of verbal paired-associate learning, level of performance is negatively correlated with degree of cerebral atrophy seen on CT scans and with degree of EEG slowing (de Leon et al., 1980; Kaszniak, Garron, Fox, Bergen, et al., 1979).

As already described, the portion of the serial position curve in free-recall tasks that is taken to reflect secondary memory (i.e., words presented early in the list) is lower in patients with AD than in matched control subjects (Miller, 1971; Kaszniak, Wilson & Fox, 1981). Employing Tulving and Colotla's (1970) scoring procedure for separating primary and secondary memory components on free-recall tasks also results in evidence of impaired secondary memory in patients with AD (Wilson, Bacon, Fox, & Kaszniak, 1983), with progressive impairment observed on longitudinal reexamination (Wilson & Kaszniak, chapter 29, this volume). Scores for primary and secondary memory are independent for normal elderly people but are significantly correlated for patients with AD (Wilson, Bacon, Fox, et al., 1983). This observation, together with the fact that the size of the patients' deficit in primary memory increases linearly as the number of items between presentation and attempted recall increases, suggests that the deficit in secondary memory is due at least partially to impaired primary memory (see also Diesfeldt, 1978; Miller, 1971).

Observations concerning proactive interference (previously learned information interfering with recall of more recent material) are also consistent with this view. Proactive interference can be examined by measuring decline in recall from secondary memory across consecutive list presentations (see Underwood, 1957) and by measuring the number of words from a previous list produced during attempts at recall of a subsequent list (intrusions). In an experiment following this approach (Wilson, Bacon, Fox, et al., 1983), control subjects showed the expected linear decline in recall from secondary memory over lists, but patients with AD did not. Furthermore, the patients showed fewer intrusions from a prior list than the control subjects (patients' intrusion errors were predominantly not from the list). Thus, the patients showed no substantial proactive interference. Both the lack of evidence of proactive interference and the marked impairment of recall from secondary memory in patients with AD seem to reflect failure in initial processing.

Additional insight into the mechanisms of secondary memory impairment associated with AD has been pro-

vided by recognition memory paradigms. These paradigms have typically involved a "study-test" procedure, in which stimuli to be remembered ("targets") are presented, followed by forced-choice recognition of mixed target and distractor stimuli. One advantage of recognition memory tasks is that they provide data on variables (e.g., response bias) not easily evaluated in free-recall tasks. Furthermore, recognition memory tasks are easier and therefore are not so prone to basement effects among more severely demented patients (see Wilson & Kaszniak, chapter 29, this volume). Performance on both verbal (Miller, 1975, 1978; Wilson, Kaszniak, Bacon, Fox, & Kelly, 1982) and nonverbal (i.e., facial) (Wilson, Kaszniak, Bacon, et al., 1982) recognition memory tasks is impaired in patients with AD. Signal detection analysis indicates that this deficit is due to a problem in the memory discrimination between target and distractor stimuli rather than to any response bias (Miller & Lewis, 1977; Wilson, Kaszniak, Bacon, et al., 1982).

Several recent observations have supported the interpretation that poor initial encoding of information into secondary memory may account for the deficit in recognition memory in patients with AD. Performance on verbal, but not facial, recognition memory tasks has been shown to be negatively correlated with the severity of language impairment (Wilson, Kaszniak, Bacon, et al., 1982), suggesting that linguistic deficits limit verbal encoding and make a specific contribution to impairment in verbal recognition memory. Furthermore, manipulating the depth of processing (Craik & Tulving, 1975) of verbal stimuli (by asking orienting questions prior to presenting each stimulus word, focusing the subject on either phonemic or semantic aspects of the word) has less effect on the verbal recognition memory performance of patients with AD than on that of matched control subjects (Corkin, 1982; Wilson, Kaszniak, Bacon, et al., 1982). Similarly, patients with AD have relatively more difficulty making use of verbal imagery (see Paivio, 1971) in free recall than do matched control subjects (Kaszniak et al., 1981). Patients with AD also fail to show the normal low-frequency word advantage in recognition memory hit rates (recognition memory for rare words is superior to that for common words in normal younger and older adults), despite a normal tendency to false alarm to common words (Wilson, Bacon, Kramer, Fox, & Kaszniak, 1983). The low-frequency word advantage in hit rates in recognition memory tasks is thought to be a function of incremental integration, dependent on active attention to and analysis of the stimulus words as they are presented.

Other experiments employing hypotheses derived from information-processing models of memory have provided evidence of additional encoding deficits in patients with AD. For example, patients appear deficient in ability to use visual context (relationships among pictured figures and objects) as an aid in pictorial secondary memory (Butters et al., 1983).

In summary, information-processing approaches to assessing both verbal and nonverbal secondary memory in patients with AD have provided evidence of deficit. Impairment of primary memory appears to contribute to the severity of this deficit, possibly by limiting the amount of information available to be processed into secondary memory. The possibility of impaired retrieval cannot be excluded, but recent research supports the hypothesis that the deficit in secondary memory is due to failure to encode contextual, featural, and intrastructural elements of information. Table 17-5 summarizes the studies reviewed here.

Tertiary Memory

Clinical observation of patients with dementia has suggested that tertiary or remote memory might be spared, as patients often seem able to recall childhood or other remote events despite severe deficits in recall of recent events. However, interpretation of such clinical observations is problematic because remote events recalled not only occurred in the more distant past but also are typically of greater emotional significance or have been more frequently rehearsed than recent events. Wilson, Kaszniak, and Fox (1981) evaluated remote memory in patients with AD with the procedure developed by Albert and her coworkers (Albert, Butters, & Levin, 1979) to examine the temporal gradient of deficit in remote memory in patients with Korsakoff's syndrome. This procedure involves two tests of memory for events and persons that became famous between 1930 and 1975 (equated for difficulty of recall). When these tests were administered to patients with AD and matched control subjects, patients were found to be significantly impaired (Wilson, Kaszniak, & Fox, 1981). They showed a relatively consistent deficit over the time period examined (i.e., 1930 to 1975), unlike the retrograde gradient found to characterize the remote memory deficit of patients with Korsakoff's syndrome.

In summary, in contrast to the available data on community-dwelling adults, in which age-related deficits are consistently observed only in secondary memory, AD-related deficit appears evident in sensory, primary, secondary, and tertiary memory. Information-processing procedures have contributed substantially to our understanding of the nature of memory deficit in patients with AD. Although such procedures are not now generally employed in the routine clinical examination of patients with known or suspected dementia, they may prove particularly useful as the similarities and differences among the memory disorders of various amnesic and demented patients become better understood (cf. Butters, 1984). Increased understanding of how the results of information-processing assessment of memory relate to patients' performance outside of the laboratory (e.g., Baddeley, Sunderland, & Harris, 1982) will also likely enhance the contributions of clinical memory assessment to patient management. Applying these assessment procedures to the evaluation of pharmacologic treatment, such as treatment involving manipulating cholinergic neurotransmission (see Bartus, Dean, Beer, & Lippa, 1982), may both facilitate the clinical specificity of treatment and assist in resolving some of the apparently contradictory results of research concerning pharmacological intervention.

Focal Cerebral Lesions

Many elderly patients who are suffering insult to the brain show some specific impairments in memory even though they are not globally amnesic in the clinical sense. These deficits are usually distinctly different from those memory changes associated with normal aging, although the effects of a focal lesion and aging appear to be additive. There are, however, to the best of our knowledge, no published reports that evaluate age differences in memory functions of patients with comparable lesions.

Table 17-6 offers a sample of information-processing tasks that have been used to differentiate patients with focal lesions affecting different memory stages. Age differences in mechanisms underlying capacity and transformation of information between stages seem to be reflected most reliably in secondary memory when tasks impose interference conditions. It is plausible that focal lesions might also differentially impair secondary memory, in contrast to primary or tertiary memory. The present review of focal lesion studies published during the past 8 years sought evidence for such differential impairments from reports that compare patients who have localized brain lesions with healthy subjects comparable in age and education. A "focal lesion" is here taken to mean a circumscribed injury or excision of cerebral tissue, often verified by CT scan. Our discussion is confined to a review of exemplary findings on impairments of one or another memory function within the information-processing model.

The interpretation of all research concerned with the effects of focal brain lesions must be approached with caution. A localized lesion can produce more than disruption of local neural mechanisms, and the impact on interrelated structures and functions needs to be considered (Sergent, 1984). The observation of a specific information-processing deficit associated with a lesion in a particular location does not allow the conclusion that that cognitive process is localized in that area in the normal brain.

Focal lesions may be followed by a number of impairments in perceptual, memory, and other cognitive functions (Smith, 1975). Numerous accounts have provided evidence for deficits in attention (Burditt, 1981), in speed of responding (Benton, 1977; Riege, Klane, Metter, & Hanson, 1982), in discrimination of faces (Damasio, Damasio, & Van Hoesen, 1982), in visuospatial contrasts (Sergent, 1984), and in WAIS Verbal and Performance IQ scores (Inglis, Ruckman, Lawson, MacLean, & Monga, 1982; McGlone, 1978) as sequelae to unilaterally confined brain lesions. Studies have implicated sensory coding and organization of information in the dysfunctions of primary and secondary memory, contending that if perceptual processing is

Table 17-5. Investigations of Secondary Memory in Patients With AD

Task	Measure	Results	Authors
Verbal shopping list task (10 words)	Trials to accurate recall; delayed recall; recognition	Patients impaired in learning, delayed recall, and recognition	McCarthy et al. (1981)
Learning progressively longer lists above word span	Accuracy of recall; trials to criterion	Patients impaired	Miller (1973)
Verbal paired-associate learning	Accuracy; trials to criterion	Patients appear consistently impaired, with some evidence of longitudinal deterioration; impairment correlated with severity of EEG slowing and cerebral atrophy seen on CT scan	Inglis (1959) Caird, Sanderson, & Inglis (1962) Inglis & Caird (1963) Barbizet & Cany (1969) Kaszniak, Garron, & Fox (1979) Kaszniak, Garron, Fox, Bergen, & Huckman (1979) de Leon et al. (1980) Corkin (1982) Danziger & Storandt (1982) Rosen & Mohs (1982) Wilson, Bacon, Kaszniak, & Fox (1982)
Nonverbal paired-associate learning (geometric forms)	Trials to criterion for recognition	Moderately and severely demented patients impaired	Corkin (1982)
Story recall test	Accuracy of immediate recall; percentage accuracy of retention after delay	Patients impaired in immediate and delayed recall and percentage retention	Logue & Wyrick (1979) Brinkman et al. (1983) Danziger & Storandt (1982) Osborne, Brown, & Randt (1982)
Verbal free-recall task (lists of 7 to 32 words)	Accuracy of recall	Patients impaired in recall, particularly in primacy component of serial position curve; severity of impairment increases over time; stimulus manipulations suggest patients are deficient in encoding semantic and organizational features; recent studies indicate scores for primary and secondary memory are correlated for patients with AD but not for the normal elderly	Miller (1971, 1975, 1978) Diesfeldt (1978) Kaszniak, Wilson, & Fox (1981) Wilson, Bacon, Fox, & Kaszniak (1983) Wilson & Kaszniak (chapter 29, this volume)
Verbal recognition memory task	Accuracy of forced-choice recognition	Patients impaired, with evidence for relative inability to make use of semantic cues; signal detection analysis reveals the deficit to be in memory efficiency and not in decision criteria; two studies show, at least for moderately demented patients, an absence of the normal low-frequency word advantage in hit rate	Miller (1975) Miller & Lewis (1977) Kaszniak, Wilson, & Fox (1981) Corkin (1982) Wilson, Kaszniak, Bacon, Fox, & Kelly (1982) Wilson, Bacon, Kramer, et al. (1983)
Facial recognition memory task	Accuracy of forced-choice recognition	Patients impaired; signal detection analysis indicates the impairment is due to memory inefficiency and not altered decision criterion	Wilson, Kaszniak, et al. (1982)

Note. CT = computerized tomography; EEG = electroencephalogram.

Table 17-6. Unilateral Brain Lesions That Impair Memory Stages for Specific Tasks

Site of lesion	Primary memory	Secondary memory	Tertiary memory
Left hemisphere	Visuospatial sequencing (Kim et al., 1980; Cremonini, De Renzi, & Faglioni, 1980) Recognition of designs (Gainotti et al., 1978)	Free recall of words (Lezak, 1979)	
Anterior cortex	Recognition of words (Cermak & Tarlow, 1978; Whitehouse, 1981)	Recognition of words (Whitehouse, 1981)	Word frequency and recall (Bentin & Gordon, 1979; Miceli, Caltagirone, Gainotti, Masullo, & Silveri, 1981)
Temporal lobe		Word paired-associate learning (Birri, Perret, & Weiser, 1982; De Renzi, Faglioni, & Reiser, 1977) Bisecting line (Capitani, DiCostanza, & Spinnler, 1978)	Declarative naming (Cavalli, De Renzi, Faglioni, & Vitale, 1981; Wilkins & Moscovitch, 1978)
Posterior-parietal area	Auditory span (Gardner et al., 1977; Gordon, 1983)		
Right hemisphere	Recognition of pictures (Whitehouse, 1981) Visuo-nonverbal sequencing (Bentin & Gordon, 1979)	Sentence completion (Cavalli et al., 1981; Hier & Kaplan, 1980) Visuotemporal sequencing (Cremonini et al., 1980; Capitani, Spinnler, Sterzi, & Vallar, 1980; De Renzi et al., 1977; Petrides & Milner, 1982) Recognition of unknown faces (Biber, Butters, Rosen, Gerstman, & Mattis, 1981; Dricker, Butters, Berman, Samuels, & Carey, 1978)	Recognition of well-known faces or voices (Van Lanker & Canter, 1982; Albert et al., 1979)
Anterior cortex	Digit span (Black & Strub, 1978; Cremonini et al., 1980)	Recognition of facial emotion (Prigatano & Pribram, 1982) Delayed recognition of pictures (Whitehouse, 1981)	
Temporal lobe		Recall of spatial location (Smith & Milner, 1981) Visual maze learning (Birri et al., 1982)	
Temporal-parietal area	Recognition of abstract designs (Miceli et al., 1981; Schwartz, Shipkin, & Cermak, 1979)	Recognizing abstract designs (Delaney, Rosen, Mattson, & Novelly, 1980; Riege, Klane, Metter, & Hanson, 1982)	Recognition of landmarks (Hecaen & Albert, 1978)

deprived of intact channeling, memory processes cannot be expected to remain unscathed.

Damage to a number of different cortical and subcortical brain structures is known to be accompanied by impairments in memory. Difficulties in learning new material or in recalling events across interference arise with damage to the temporal-hippocampal formation from herpes encephalitis, anoxia, surgical lesions for the treatment of epilepsy or tumor, or from a cerebrovascular accident (CVA) involving the posterior cerebral artery distribution (see Hirst, 1982; Squire, 1982). Other brain regions, such as the frontal or right parietal-occipital areas, are equally implicated in memory performance deficits, although visuoperceptual and memorizing difficulties have not always been sufficiently differentiated.

Severe deficits in secondary and tertiary memory are described for patients with lesions of the dorsomedial nucleus of the thalamus, possibly also involving the mammilary bodies and numerous punctate lesions bordering the third ventricle in patients with Korsakoff's syndrome, or the basal ganglia in patients with Huntington's disease. These "diencephalic amnesias" have been extensively described by Butters (1984) and Squire (1982). Squire has labeled as "bitemporal amnesia" the memory dysfunctions following bilateral electroconvulsive shock or temporal lobectomy, on the basis of differences in forgetting, in contrast to the diencephalic amnesia shown by patients with Korsakoff's syndrome and by patient N. A., who was accidentally stabbed in the left-dorsomedial thalamic and tectal regions (Squire & Moore, 1979).

The role of other subcortical structures is not clearly defined. Some investigators report memory deficits from bilateral lesions in the fornix (Heilman & Sypert, 1977), while others do not (Squire & Moore, 1979; Woolsey & Nelson, 1975). Debate over the involvement of the amygdala, uncus, or even hippocampus has still not abated (Birri et al., 1982; Squire, 1982).

Acquisition and Encoding Strategies

Strategies in acquiring and coding information in primary and secondary memory differ in their emphasis on labeling, categorizing, or chunking events to be remembered into associative strings. When information can be verbally coded, by far the most essential acquisition strategy is rehearsal. Spontaneous verbal rehearsal seems to be diminished following left-temporal or left-anterior lesions (Cremonini, De Renzi, & Faglioni, 1980; Smith & Milner, 1981). However, right-hemisphere lesions have been shown to affect rehearsal of visual sequence (Kim, Royer, Bonstelle, & Boller, 1980), and right-parietal damage impairs immediate recognition of abstract designs (Miceli, Caltagirone, Gainotti, Masullo, & Silveri, 1981).

Active rehearsal theoretically maintains information in primary memory so that coded items can be transferred to secondary memory. It permits more linkages between items, more elaborate processing (Craik & Simon, 1980), and, consequently, multiple

encoding. In contrast to initial perceptual encoding, which is mostly automatic, the encoding for secondary memory is more often deliberate than automatic. Because speed of processing is slowed by damage almost anywhere in the brain, deliberate encoding is also slowed. Encoding time seems to increase when the preferred mode of coding is no longer available. Under the hypothesis that coding is hemisphere specific (i.e., verbal encoding is the preferred mode of the left hemisphere, imaginal coding of the right), Whitehouse (1981) reported that patients with damage to the anterior left hemisphere benefited more than right-lesioned patients (Cermak & Moreines, 1976) from slowing the rate of presentation of picturable nouns (from one word every second to one word every 3 seconds). This was presumably because a slower rate allowed them to use imaginal (right-hemisphere) coding. Extra time did not aid, to the same degree, the right-lesioned patients in recognizing nameable pictures.

Memory for sequences of pictures appears to be mediated, in part, by encoding and rehearsing the pictures as names. Both aphasic and nonaphasic patients with damage to the left hemisphere were impaired, compared with control subjects and right-lesioned patients, on a task evaluating such encoding. When given the opportunity to learn sequences of eight nameable pictures to a criterion of three errorless trials, the right-lesioned but not the left-lesioned patients fell far short of normal learning (Cremonini et al., 1980). Cremonini et al. suggested that weak verbal coding was replaced by imaginal coding over trials in left-lesioned patients. In these patients, verbal coding was limited to rehearsal in primary memory. In contrast, acquisition of a pictorial sequence appears to be mediated mainly by visual images and is weakened by a right-hemisphere lesion.

The coding of the undamaged hemisphere after unilateral damage also does not seem to be optimal. In one study, left-lesioned patients with aphasia used an analytical strategy in reconstructing designs instead of the global planning employed by nonaphasic, right-lesioned, and control subjects (Semenza, Denes, D'Urso, Romano, & Montorsi, 1978). In another study, patients with right-hemisphere lesions of mainly vascular etiology had considerable difficulty constructing sentences from word parts (Cavalli, De Renzi, Faglioni, & Vitale, 1981). The difficulty was interpreted as participation of the right hemisphere in linguistic encoding but can also be seen as impaired interaction between hemispheres. It is questionable, then, whether a focal lesion can truly be called "localized."

Cuing with a letter cue did not markedly aid patients with left-temporal or right-temporal lesions in naming line drawings (Wilkins & Moscovitch, 1978). However, the instruction to invent sentences in order to link pairs of concrete words improved the paired-associate learning of patients with right-temporal lobectomy (Jones-Gotman & Milner, 1978). This improvement did not depend on the extent of hippocampal removal (including the pes). When no coding instructions were given for single-trial recall, patients with large right-hippocampal excisions scored significantly lower than those who had lost only up to one centimeter of the body of hippocampus; however, they still performed reliably better than patients with lesions in the left temporal region. Since there was no correlation of recall with the extent of lateral neocortex removed, the authors concluded that the right-hippocampal region is involved in the processing of image-mediated verbal learning. Similarly, patients who had right-hemisphere strokes were not so impaired as patients who had left-hemisphere strokes in recognizing word lists by phonemic similarity (e.g., sign–time, barn–farm) between target and distractor words (Riege, Metter, & Hanson, 1980) or when words were read aloud instead of printed on cards (Schwartz, Shipkin, & Cermak, 1979).

With cuing by word categories, neither patients with Korsakoff's syndrome (diencephalic amnesia) nor patients with Huntington's disease (primarily basal ganglia disease) improved their free-recall scores for concrete words (Butters, Tarlow, Cermak, & Sax, 1976). However, patients with Korsakoff's syndrome, but not patients with right-hemisphere damage, did improve their recognition of unfamiliar faces when instructed to judge the likability of faces (Bibner, Butters, Rosen, Gertsman, & Mattis, 1981). Left to their own strategies, both kinds of patients relied on superficial (visuoperceptual) coding (Dricker, Butters, Berman, Samuels, & Carey, 1978). Biber et al. (1981) interpreted these results as indicating that right-lesioned patients lack structures necessary to complete the configurational analyses of faces needed for effective processing strategies.

In most memory tasks, both the event and its context need to be encoded, and encoding may require more effort for brain-injured persons than for normal persons. Most persons encode several sources of information simultaneously and many of them automatically (Hasher & Zacks, 1979). This ability, however, is limited by the lack of attention and practice (Hirst, 1982). When the system is compromised, as by a focal lesion, encoding of both the event and its context is constrained. Information that is automatically encoded by normal adults may require considerable effort by brain-injured adults (Kinsbourne & Wood, 1975), so that either context cues may be sacrificed or the event may be imprecisely coded. In either case, information is inefficiently remembered.

Processing Capacity

Over the past several years many authors have suggested that the two cerebral hemispheres operate as separate information-processing systems, each with its own mode of processing and a limited capacity, different from those of the other hemisphere.

Data from visual laterality experiments (Hellige & Wong, 1983) suggest that the left hemisphere is more limited than the right in its information-processing capacity. Its advantage for processing verbal material is attenuated or reversed when concurrent processing demands are made. In a study of dichotic listening, rec-

ognition of a consonant–vowel series was reduced for the right ear (left hemisphere) but not the left ear (right hemisphere) when a concurrent interference task (remembering six printed words) was introduced. A nonverbal memory load (nonsense shapes) did not affect recognition for either the left or right ear (Hellige & Wong, 1983). These results indicate that initial processing capacity is hemisphere specific.

Experiments with lesioned subjects seem to confirm this interpretation. In a series of recognition experiments, Whitehouse (1981) asked patients with CVA in either the left anterior or right anterior quadrant to recognize a target from a distractor immediately after a target card had been shown for one second. The left-lesioned patients were impaired, in contrast to right-lesioned patients, when targets were picturable or abstract nouns; they improved more than right-lesioned patients when picturable nouns were presented more slowly, which presumably allowed them additional use of imaginal coding. In contrast, when targets were pictures of common objects or abstract designs, the right-lesioned patients performed more poorly than the left-lesioned patients. More important, patients with right-anterior lesions did not benefit from increased time when trying to recognize abstract designs, presumably because the abstract designs did not permit verbal coding. It can be argued, therefore, that the initial processing capacity for words and designs is limited to the residual or secondary coding that can be called up.

Whitehouse (1981) also demonstrated the separate and limited capacities for dual coding in secondary memory. In a second study, he introduced a 3-minute naming task for abstract designs (imaginal coding) or nouns (verbal coding) between the presentation of nameable pictures and the recognition test, thereby selectively overloading the coding process available to the patients. In left-lesioned patients, dependent on imaginal coding, recognition errors were increased only by interpolated imaginal interference; in right-lesioned patients, the results were reversed. Although the study did not address the question of whether capacity of secondary memory is simply reduced by limited hemispheric interaction in the presence of unilateral lesions (Hecaen & Albert, 1978), the results seem to show that a focal lesion selectively disrupts hemisphere-specific coding of information and leaves the primary coding process of the contralateral hemisphere relatively intact. Thus, right-lesioned patients were considerably aided in picture-context recognition by a story linking the salient figures in a picture (Butters, 1984).

Primary and Secondary Memory

Studies of primary and secondary memory relevant to focal lesions have shown that the capacity of both primary and secondary memory is diminished by the lesion. The side of the lesion determines, in general, which tasks are impaired and which are spared. When recognition or learning of words or a story was tested (Delaney, Rosen, Mattson, & Novelly, 1980; Jones-

Gotman & Milner, 1978; Whitehouse, 1981), secondary memory, in particular, but also primary memory, was found to be sensitive to lesions in the left anterior quadrant or left temporal regions. In comparison, performance on tasks requiring recognition memory for pictures of common objects, abstract designs, or unknown faces (forced-choice discrimination of target from distractors following interference) was found to be impaired by lesions in the right-temporal or right-posterior quadrant (Bentin & Gordon, 1979; Riege et al., 1982; Schwartz et al., 1979).

Primary memory was found to be affected by a number of testing variables, such as whether the task stimuli could be verbally labeled or not. The corresponding side of the focal lesion was found to influence performance as much as the presence of visual field defects or aphasia (Cremonini et al., 1980; Gainotti, Caltagirone, & Miceli, 1978). For example, in tasks requiring immediate recall or rehearsal, left-lesioned patients with or without aphasia used imagery coding of sequences of pictures (Cremonini et al., 1980) or abstract designs (Cermak & Tarlow, 1978).

As shown in Table 17-6, the continuous recognition of words in primary memory is impaired by a left-anterior lesion that produced aphasia, but the language difficulty is not responsible for the deficit in immediate recognition of printed words following a right posterior parietal lesion. A similar overlap of task and coding with side of lesion is seen in secondary memory. Recognition of picturable nouns or recall of nameable objects following an interpolated task (Lezak, 1979; Smith & Milner, 1981; Whitehouse, 1981) were decreased by the presence of left or right anterior or temporal lesions. The results do not seem to argue against laterality, but rather for hemispheric-specific coding in both secondary and primary memory.

In a study of forward digit span comparing four groups of patients, each with injury to one of the four cerebral quadrants, mean forward (as well as backward) scores did not differ among groups, but only patients with right-posterior lesions performed as well as control subjects (Black & Strub, 1978). When the influence of aphasia was partialed out (Cremonini et al., 1980), left-hemisphere patients did not score significantly more poorly on this task than control subjects. Testing auditory binary digit span, W. P. Gordon (1983) observed severe deficits in aphasic patients with a single left CVA involving Heschl's, angular, or middle-temporal gyri, or Wernicke's area. Damage to Broca's area or damage anterior to the precentral gyrus did not impair binary digit or tone span.

One way to separate performance of primary and secondary memory is to experimentally manipulate the coding deficit resulting from a focal lesion. Left-lesioned patients with and without aphasia could not retain a sequence of nine words as well as control subjects or right-lesioned patients (Kim et al., 1980). Neither did they retain as well six nameable pictures (Cremonini et al., 1980) that they were asked to point to in an array. Whatever correct scores they obtained were interpreted to result from relying on imaginal coding. The immediate sequencing of cube tapping

(De Renzi, Faglioni, & Previdi, 1977; Kim et al., 1980), light series (Bentin & Gordon, 1979), and melody (Gardner, Silverman, Denes, Semenza, & Rosenstiel, 1977), in contrast, was difficult for right-lesioned patients and was taken to indicate that sequencing in primary memory is not uniquely left lateralized.

By comparison, sequencing in secondary memory does not seem to be affected by a left-lateralized lesion, although performance is not optimal. When asked to learn a visual maze (Birri et al., 1982) or the sequence of eight nameable pictures (Cremonini et al., 1980), patients with right-temporal or right-posterior lesions were more impaired than patients with left lesions. Thus, depending upon task content, primary memory is distinguished from secondary memory in verbal sequencing by laterality of lesion; right-lesioned patients do not seem to have an efficient verbal rehearsal strategy for delayed sequence learning. In nonverbal sequencing, by comparison, a right lesion affects both primary and secondary memory.

A similar difference between primary and secondary memory is seen in visual recognition of abstract colored patterns. Although left-lesioned aphasic patients scored lower in immediate four-choice recognition of designs than did right-lesioned patients (Gainotti et al., 1978), recognition of designs across distractors in secondary memory was more difficult for patients with right-temporal epilepsy (Delaney et al., 1980) or with right CVA (Riege et al., 1982) than for patients with left lesions. These results seem to reinforce the interpretation that verbal coding aids right-lesioned patients in primary but not in secondary memory. Basic perceptual processes can be shown to be intact in these groups of patients, yet the discrimination of patterns and memory decisions lose their precision. Damage to postrolandic regions on the right correlate with impairments in immediate (primary memory) six-choice recognition of unfamiliar faces (Bentin & Gordon, 1979) and in delayed recognition of facial features (Cohn, Neumann, & Wood, 1977).

The reports cited show clearly that dual coding (verbal and imaginal) is dissociated by a unilateral lesion and can be manipulated in order to separate primary from secondary memory processes. As shown in Table 17-6, the two memory stores interact with side of lesion on similar tasks; however, this does not seem to have been experimentally verified in any single study.

Tertiary Memory

There is evidence that focal lesions have a conditional impact on tertiary or remote memory. With unilateral lesions, impairments in tertiary memory again depend upon laterality of the lesion. In the case of bitemporal amnesia, the events that constitute premorbid memory are relatively preserved (Squire, 1982), and the loss of information for the time periods before the trauma is temporally limited. Despite persistent impairment in recalling newly learned information, bitemporal amnesics, as well as diencephalic amnesics (Butters & Albert, 1982), recognize or recall facts pertaining to the distant past more accurately than facts concerning events just prior to the onset of their illness. In a test of recognition of famous faces and events prominent between 1930 and 1975, patients with Korsakoff's syndrome (diencephalic amnesia) showed loss in remote memory characterized by a steep temporal gradient in which the oldest memories remained relatively intact (Albert et al., 1979). Both a progressive failure to learn new material during the extended time of alcohol abuse and deficit in retrieving previously learned information may contribute to this impairment (Butters & Albert, 1982).

The amnesic's semantic memory also appears to be impaired. In memory search for conceptual naming of items for which category and adjective cues were given, patients with Korsakoff's syndrome made more errors than alcoholics or control subjects (Cermak, 1982), and their recall with or without semantic cues for public events or people did not approach the level of normal subjects (Albert et al., 1979). Their gradient of forgetting reflected a decline in memory from remote to recent events, whereas the gradient for patients with Huntington's disease was "flat," implying a uniform deficit in retrieval from tertiary memory.

Compared with normal elderly persons, patients with left-temporal lesions are considerably less accurate in naming items, given one-sentence descriptions (Hier & Kaplan, 1980). Their word fluency is also impaired, as is that of patients with left- or right-frontal lesions (Cavalli et al., 1981; Miceli et al., 1981; Weingartner, Grafman, Boutelle, Kaye, & Martin, 1983), and sentence completion is deficient in timed tasks. Because declarative naming was found to be spared by a right-sided lesion, Cavalli et al. concluded that a lesion in the right hemisphere leaves lexical memory intact. However, matching a name to a famous face or a name and face to a famous voice is markedly more difficult for right- than for left-lesioned patients (Van Lanker & Canter, 1982).

In summary, focal lesions may affect any level of information processing. At the stages of memorization and retrieval discussed in this chapter, effects are consistent with the lateralization of hemispheric functions. In general, lesions in the left hemisphere affect verbal processing of temporal order and recognition or learning of words, paragraphs, or nameable pictures. Although there is little direct evidence, lesions on the right appear to be somewhat more function specific; those in the right temporal region, with or without involvement of hippocampal structures, seem to impair nonverbal sequencing, maze learning, and recognition of abstract designs. By comparison, the recognition of faces and feature analysis are affected by right posterior parietal and by midline diencephalic lesions, and facial emotions by right-frontal lesions. However, the secondary effects of a lesion on interrelated structures and functions have rarely been taken into account.

On some tasks (e.g., verbal and nonverbal sequencing or recognition of abstract designs), primary and secondary memory are differentially affected by lesions, but other tasks (such as recognition of picturable nouns) do not show this effect. It seems plausible that a selective aid of verbal coding or rehearsal is provided to right-lesioned patients both in primary and in secondary memory, whereas left-lesioned patients benefit from use of imaginal coding only in secondary memory. The laterality of a focal lesion is also reflected in tertiary memory; left lesions weaken lexical recall, whereas right-posterior or diencephalic lesions impair recognition of famous faces or voices. We conclude, following a direct-access model, that initial processing of information to be remembered is hemisphere specific; a focal lesion weakens coding that is dependent on that hemisphere and subsequent output at any stage. Tasks that interfere with residual coding, such as in secondary memory, accentuate the weakness in processing.

Summary and Conclusions

Application of memory assessment procedures based on information processing appears to have utility in differentiating aspects of complex memory processes that can be differentially impaired by aging, progressive degenerative brain disease (AD), or focal cerebral lesions. Normal aging appears to have its most marked effects on secondary memory processes, with other stages of memory relatively spared. AD appears eventually to involve all memory processes, with increasing interdependence between the theoretical storage capacities (e.g., primary and secondary memory). This phenomenon both has potential diagnostic significance and limits the ability of clinicians and researchers alike to clearly measure theoretically distinct aspects of information processing, particularly with increasing severity of dementia (see Wilson & Kaszniak, chapter 29, this volume). When the brain is focally damaged, various memory processes and storage capacities can be impaired, depending on the location and size of the lesion.

The information-processing approach allows considerable flexibility in selecting procedures. Specific tasks selected for evaluating a given individual or group should be determined by the condition under study, theoretical considerations (e.g., the aspect of memory expected to be affected by a treatment), and the judged appropriateness of various criteria of reliability and construct and content validity. Although many theoretical issues remain to be resolved, and practical obstacles to be overcome, information-processing approaches to memory assessment of the elderly hold promise for increasing understanding of memory change, as well as for improving the clinical assessment and care of older memory-disordered patients.

References

Albert, M., Butters, N., & Levin, J. (1979). Temporal gradients in the retrograde amnesia of patients with alcoholic Korsakoff's disease. *Archives of Neurology, 36,* 211–216.

American Psychiatric Association. (1980). *Diagnostic and statistical manual of mental disorders* (3rd ed.). Washington, DC: Author.

Anders, T. R., & Fozard, J. L. (1973). Effects of age upon retrieval from primary and secondary memory. *Developmental Psychology, 9,* 411–415.

Atkinson, R. C., & Shiffrin, R. M. (1968). Human memory: A proposed system and its control process. In K. W. Spence & J. T. Spence (Eds.), *The psychology of learning and motivation: Advances in research and theory* (Vol. 2). New York: Academic Press.

Averback, E., & Coriell, H. D. (1961). Short-term memory in vision. *Bell System Technical Journal, 40,* 309–328.

Bacon, L. D., Wilson, R. S., & Kaszniak, A. W. (1982). Age differences in memory scanning? *Perceptual and Motor Skills, 55,* 499–504.

Baddeley, A. D. (1976). *The psychology of memory.* New York: Basic Books.

Baddeley, A., Sunderland, A., & Harris, J. (1982). How well do laboratory-based psychological tests predict patients' performance outside the laboratory? In S. Corkin, K. L. Davis, J. H. Growdon, E. Usdin, & R. L. Wurtman (Eds.), *Alzheimer's disease: A report of progress in research* (pp. 141–148). New York: Raven Press.

Barbizet, J., & Cany, E. (1969). A psychometric study of various memory deficits associated with cerebral lesions. In G. A. Talland & N. C. Waugh (Eds.), *The pathology of memory* (pp. 49–64). New York: Academic Press.

Bartus, R. T., Dean, R. L., Beer, B., & Lippa, A. S. (1982). The cholinergic hypothesis of geriatric memory dysfunction. *Science, 217,* 408–417.

Bentin, S., & Gordon, H. W. (1979). Assessment of cognitive asymmetries in brain-damaged and normal subjects: Validation of a test battery. *Journal of Neurology, Neurosurgery, and Psychiatry, 42,* 715–723.

Benton, A. L. (1977). Interactive effects of age and brain disease on reaction time. *Archives of Neurology, 34,* 369–370.

Biber, C., Butters, N., Rosen, J., Gerstman, L., & Mattis, S. (1981). Encoding strategies and recognition of faces by alcoholic Korsakoff and other brain-damaged patients. *Journal of Clinical Neuropsychology, 3*(4), 315–330.

Birri, R., Perret, E., & Wieser, H. G. (1982). Der Einfluss verschiedener Temporallappenoperationen auf das Gedaechtnis bei Epileptikern, *Nervenarzt, 53,* 144–149.

Black, F. W., & Strub, R. L. (1978). Digit repetition performance in patients with focal brain damage. *Cortex, 14,* 12–21.

Botwinick, J. (1978). *Aging and behavior* (2nd ed.). New York: Springer.

Botwinick, J., & Storandt, M. (1974). *Memory, related functions, and age.* Springfield, IL: Charles C Thomas.

Brinkman, S. D., Largen, J. W., Gerganoff, S., & Pomara, N. (1983). Russell's Revised Wechsler Memory Scale in the evaluation of dementia. *Journal of Clinical Psychology, 39,* 989–993.

Brown, J. (1958). Some tests of the decay theory of immediate memory. *Quarterly Journal of Experimental Psychology, 10,* 12–21.

Burditt, G. L., (1981, August). *Identifying processing disorders of the communicatively impaired adult stroke patient.* Paper presented at the 89th annual meeting of the American Psychological Association, Los Angeles, CA.

Butters, N. (1984). The clinical aspects of memory disorders: Contributions from experimental studies of amnesia and dementia. *Journal of Clinical Neuropsychology, 6,* 17–36.

Butters, N., & Albert, M. S. (1982). Processes underlying failures to recall remote events. In L. S. Cermak (Ed.), *Human memory and amnesia* (pp. 257–274). Hillsdale, NJ: Erlbaum.

Butters, N., Albert, M. S., Sax, D. S., Miliotis, P., Nagode, J., & Sterste, A. (1983). The effect of verbal mediators on the pictorial memory of brain-damaged patients. *Neuropsychologia, 21,* 307–323.

Butters, N., Tarlow, S., Cermak, L. S., & Sax, D. (1976). A comparison of the information processing deficits of pa-

tients with Huntington's chorea and Korsakoff's syndrome. *Cortex, 12,* 134–144.

Caird, W. K., Sanderson, R. E., & Inglis, J. (1962). Cross validation of a learning test for use with elderly psychiatric patients. *Journal of Mental Science, 108,* 368–370.

Capitani, E., DiCostanzo, M., & Spinnler, H. (1978). Do focal neocortical lesions hamper short-term recognition of visual spatial patterns? *Archives Suisses de Neurologie,*123I, 207–221.

Capitani, E., Spinnler, H., Sterzi, R., & Vallar, G. (1980). The hemispheric side of neocortical damage does not affect memory for unidimensional position. An experiment with Posner and Konick's test. *Cortex, 16,* 295–304.

Cavalli, M., De Renzi, E., Faglioni, P., & Vitale, A. (1981). Impairment of right-brain-damaged patients on a linguistic cognitive task. *Cortex, 17,* 545–556.

Cerella, J., & Poon, L. W. (1981). Age and parafoveal sensitivity. *The Gerontologist, 12,* 76.

Cerella, J., Poon, L. W., & Fozard, J. L. (1982). Age and iconic read-out. *Journal of Gerontology, 37,* 197–202.

Cermak, L. S. (Ed.). (1982). *Human memory and amnesia.* Hillsdale, NJ: Erlbaum.

Cermak, L. S., & Moreines, J. (1976). Verbal retention deficits in aphasic and amnesic patients. *Brain and Language, 3,* 16–27.

Cermak, L. S., & Tarlow, S. (1978). Aphasic and amnesic patients' verbal vs. nonverbal retentive abilities. *Cortex, 14,* 32–40.

Cohn, R., Neumann, M. A., & Wood, D. H. (1977). Prosopagnosia: A clinicopathological study. *Annals of Neurology, 1,* 177–182.

Coltheart, M. (1972). Visual information processing. In P. C. Dodwell (Ed.), *New horizons in psychology.* Harmondsworth, England: Penguin.

Corkin, S. (1982). Some relationships between global amnesias and the memory impairments in Alzheimer's disease. In S. Corkin, K. L. Davis, J. H. Growdon, E. Usdin, & R. J. Wurtman (Eds.), *Alzheimer's disease: A report of progress in research* (pp. 149–164). New York: Raven Press.

Craik, F. I. M. (1968). Two components in free recall. *Journal of Verbal Learning and Verbal Behavior, 7,* 996–1004.

Craik, F. I. M. (1977). Age differences in human memory. In J. E. Birren & K. W. Schaie (Eds.), *Handbook of the psychology of aging* (pp. 384–420). New York: Van Nostrand Reinhold.

Craik, F. I. M., & Simon, E. (1980). Attention and depth of processing. In L. W. Poon, J. L. Fozard, L. S. Cermak, D. Arenberg, & L. W. Thompson (Eds.), *New directions in memory and aging* (pp. 95–112). Hillsdale, NJ: Erlbaum.

Craik, F. I. M., & Tulving, E. (1975). Depth of processing and the retention of words in episodic memory. *Journal of Experimental Psychology: General, 104,* 268–294.

Cremonini, W., De Renzi, E., & Faglioni, P. (1980). Contrasting performance of right- and left-hemisphere patients on short-term and long-term sequential visual memory. *Neuropsychologia, 18,* 1–9.

Crook, T., Ferris, S., McCarthy, M., & Rae, D. (1980). Utility of digit recall tasks for assessing memory in the aged. *Journal of Consulting and Clinical Psychology, 48,* 228–233.

Crowder, R. G. (1980). Echoic memory and the study of aging memory systems. In L. W. Poon, J. L. Fozard, L. S. Cermak, D. Arenberg, & L. W. Thompson, (Eds.), *New directions in memory and aging* (pp. 181–204). Hillsdale, NJ: Erlbaum.

Damasio, A. R., Damasio, H., & Van Hoesen, G. W. (1982). Prosopagnosia: Anatomic basis and behavioral mechanisms. *Neurology, 32,* 331–341.

Danziger, W. L., & Storandt, M. (1982, November). *Psychometric performance of healthy and demented older adults:*

A one-year follow-up. Paper presented at the 35th Annual Meeting of the Gerontological Society of America, Boston, MA.

Delaney, R. C., Rosen, A. J., Mattson, R. H., & Novelly, R. A. (1980). Memory function in focal epilepsy: A comparison of non-surgical, unilateral temporal lobe and frontal lobe samples. *Cortex, 16,* 103–117.

de Leon, M. J., Ferris, S. H., George, A. E., Reisberg, B., Kricheff, I. I., & Gershon, S. (1980). Computed tomography evaluations of brain–behavior relationships in senile dementia of the Alzheimer's type. *Neurobiology of Aging, 1,* 69–79.

De Renzi, E., Faglioni, P., & Previdi, P. (1977). Spatial memory and hemispheric locus of lesion. *Cortex, 13,* 424–433.

Diesfeldt, H. F. A. (1978). The distinction between long-term and short-term memory in senile dementia: An analysis of free recall and delayed recognition. *Neuropsychologia, 16,* 115–119.

Dricker, J., Butters, N., Berman, G., Samuels, I., & Carey, S. (1978). The recognition and encoding of faces by alcoholic Korsakoff and right hemisphere patients. *Neuropsychologia, 16,* 683–695.

Erber, J. T. (1974). Age differences in recognition memory. *Journal of Gerontology, 29,* 177–181.

Erber, J. T. (1981). Remote memory and age: A review. *Experimental Aging Research, 1,* 189–199.

Erickson, R. C., Poon, L. W., & Walsh-Sweeney, L. (1980). Clinical memory testing of the elderly. In L. W. Poon, J. L. Fozard, L. S. Cermak, D. Arenberg, & L. W. Thompson (Eds.), *New directions in memory and aging* (pp. 379–402). Hillsdale, NJ: Erlbaum.

Estes, W. K. (1978). The information-processing approach to cognition: A confluence of metaphors and methods. In W. K. Estes (Ed.), *Handbook of learning and cognitive processes: Vol. 5. Human information processing* (pp. 1–18). New York: Wiley.

Eysenck, M. W. (1974). Age differences in incidental learning. *Developmental Psychology, 10,* 936–941.

Fozard, J. L. (1980). The time for remembering. In L. W. Poon (Ed.), *Aging in the 1980s: Psychological issues* (pp. 273–290). Washington, DC: American Psychological Association.

Fozard, J. (in press). Normal and pathological age differences in memory. In J. H. Brocklehurst (Ed.), *Textbook of geriatric medicine and gerontology* (3rd ed.). London: Churchill Livingstone.

Fozard, J. L., & Costa, P. T. (in press). Age differences in memory and decision making in relation to personality, abilities, and endocrine function: Implications for clinical practice and health planning policy. In M. Marios (Ed.), *Aging: A challenge for science and social policy*. London: Oxford University Press.

Fozard, J. L., & Poon, L. W. (1976, November). *Age-related differences in long-term memory for pictures*. Paper presented at the 29th annual meeting of the Gerontological Society of America, New York, NY.

Fozard, J. L., & Waugh, N. C. (1969). Proactive inhibition of prompted items. *Psychonomic Science, 17,* 67–68.

Fozard, J. L., Wolf, E., Bell, B., McFarland, R. A., & Podolsky, S. (1977). Visual perception and communication. In J. E. Birren & K. W. Schaie (Eds.), *Handbook of the psychology of aging* (pp. 497–534). New York: Van Nostrand Reinhold.

Gainotti, G., Caltagirone, C., & Miceli, G. (1978). Immediate visual–spatial memory in hemisphere-damaged patients: Impairment of verbal coding and of perceptual processing. *Neuropsychologia, 16,* 501–507.

Gardner, H., Silverman, J., Denes, G., Semenza, C., & Rosenstiel, A. K. (1977). Sensitivity to musical denotation and connotation in organic patients. *Cortex, 13,* 242–256.

Glanzer, M., & Cunitz, A. R. (1966). Two storage mechanisms in free recall. *Journal of Verbal Learning and Verbal Behavior, 5,* 351–360.

Gordon, W. P. (1983). Memory disorders in aphasia–I. Auditory immediate recall. *Neuropsychologia, 21,* 325–339.

Grossberg, M. (1980). Individual age-related differences in sensory memory. In L. W. Poon, J. L. Fozard, L. S. Cermak, D. Arenberg, & L. W. Thompson (Eds.), *New directions in memory and aging* (pp. 243–250). Hillsdale, NJ: Erlbaum.

Haber, R. N., & Standing, L. G. (1969). Direct measures of short-term visual storage. *Quarterly Journal of Experimental Psychology, 21,* 43–54.

Hasher, L., & Zacks, R. T. (1979). Automatic and effortful processes in memory. *Journal of Experimental Psychology: General, 108,* 356–388.

Hecaen, H., & Albert, M. L. (Eds.). (1978). *Human neuropsychology*. New York: Wiley.

Heilman, K., & Sypert, G. (1977). Korsakoff's syndrome resulting from bilateral fornix lesions. *Neurology, 27,* 490–493.

Hellige, J. B., & Wong, T. M. (1983). Hemisphere-specific interference in dichotic listening. *Journal of Experimental Psychology: General, 112,* 218–239.

Hier, D. B., & Kaplan, J. (1980). Verbal comprehension deficits after right hemisphere damage. *Applied Psycholinguistics, 1,* 279–294.

Hirst, W. (1982). The amnesic syndrome: Descriptions and explanations. *Psychological Bulletin, 91,* 435–460.

Hultsch, D. F. (1969). Adult age differences in the organization of free recall. *Developmental Psychology, 1,* 673–678.

Hultsch, D. (1975). Adult age differences in retrieval: Trace-dependent and cue-dependent forgetting. *Developmental Psychology, 11,* 197–201.

Inglis, J. (1959). A paired associate learning test for use with elderly psychiatric patients. *Journal of Mental Science, 105,* 440–448.

Inglis, J., & Caird, W. K. (1963). Modified-digit spans and memory disorder. *Diseases of the Nervous System, 24,* 46–50.

Inglis, J., Ruckman, M., Lawson, J. S., MacLean, A. W., & Monga, T. N. (1982). Sex differences in the cognitive effects of unilateral brain damage. *Cortex, 18,* 257–275.

Johannesson, G., Hagberg, B., Gustafson, L., & Ingvar, D. H. (1979). EEG and cognitive impairment in presenile dementia. *Acta Neurologica Scandinavica, 59,* 225–240.

Jones-Gotman, M., & Milner, B. (1978). Right temporal-lobe contribution to image-mediated verbal learning. *Neuropsychologia, 16,* 61–71.

Kaszniak, A. W. (1986). The neuropsychology of dementia. In I. Grant & K. Adams (Eds.), *Neuropsychological assessment of neuropsychiatric disorders* (pp. 172–220). New York: Oxford University Press.

Kaszniak, A. W., Garron, D. C., & Fox, J. H. (1979). Differential effects of age and cerebral atrophy upon span of immediate recall and paired-associate learning in older patients suspected of dementia. *Cortex, 15,* 285–295.

Kaszniak, A. W., Garron, D. C., Fox, J. H., Bergen, D., & Huckman, M. (1979). Cerebral atrophy, EEG slowing, age, education, and cognitive functioning in suspected dementia. *Neurology, 29,* 1273–1279.

Kaszniak, A. W., Wilson, R. S., & Fox, J. H. (1981). Effects of imagery and meaningfulness on free recall and recognition memory in presenile and senile dementia. *International Journal of Neuroscience, 12,* 264.

Kim, Y., Royer, F., Bonstelle, C., & Boller, F. (1980). Temporal sequencing of verbal and nonverbal materials: The effect of laterality of lesion. *Cortex, 16,* 135–143.

Kinsbourne, M., & Wood, F. (1975). Short term memory and

the amnesic syndrome. In D. Deutsch & J. A. Deutsch (Eds.), *Short term memory* (pp. 257–291). New York: Academic Press.

Kline, D. W., & Schieber, F. (1981). What are the age differences in visual sensory memory? *Journal of Gerontology, 36*, 86–89.

Labouvie-Vief, G., & Schell, D. A. (1982). Learning and memory in later life. In B. B. Wolman (Ed.), *Handbook of developmental psychology*. Englewood Cliffs, NJ: Prentice-Hall.

Larner, S. (1977). Encoding in senile dementia and elderly depressives: A preliminary study. *British Journal of Social and Clinical Psychology, 16*, 379–390.

Lezak, M. D. (1979). Recovery of memory and learning functions following traumatic brain injury. *Cortex, 15*, 63–72.

Logue, P., & Wyrick, L. (1979). Initial validation of Russell's revised Wechsler Memory Scale: A comparison of normal aging versus dementia. *Journal of Consulting and Clinical Psychology, 47*, 176–178.

Mandler, G. (1980). Recognizing: The judgment of previous occurrence. *Psychological Review, 87*, 252–271.

Marcer, D. (1979). Measuring memory change in Alzheimer's disease. In A. I. M. Glen & L. J. Whalley (Eds.), *Alzheimer's disease: Early recognition of potentially reversible deficits* (pp. 117–121). London: Churchill Livingstone.

McCarthy, M., Ferris, S. H., Clark, E., & Crook, T. (1981). Acquisition and retention of categorized material in normal aging and senile dementia. *Experimental Aging Research, 7*, 127–135.

McGlone, J. (1978). Sex differences in functional brain asymmetry. *Cortex, 14*, 122–128.

Miceli, G., Caltagirone, C., Gainotti, G., Masullo, C., & Silveri, M. C. (1981). Neuropsychological correlates of localized cerebral lesions in non-aphasic brain-damaged patients. *Journal of Clinical Neuropsychology, 3*, 53–63.

Miller, E. (1971). On the nature of the memory disorder in presenile dementia. *Neuropsychologia, 9*, 75–78.

Miller, E. (1973). Short- and long-term memory in presenile dementia (Alzheimer's disease). *Psychological Medicine, 3*, 221–224.

Miller, E. (1975). Impaired recall and the memory disturbance in presenile dementia. *British Journal of Social and Clinical Psychology, 14*(1), 73–79.

Miller, E. (1977a). *Abnormal ageing: The psychology of senile and presenile dementia*. New York: Wiley.

Miller, E. (1977b). Visual information processing in presenile dementia. *British Journal of Social and Clinical Psychology, 16*, 99–100.

Miller, E. (1978). Retrieval from long-term memory in presenile dementia: Two tests of an hypothesis. *British Journal of Social and Clinical Psychology, 17*, 143–148.

Miller, E. (1981). The nature of the cognitive deficit in senile dementia. In N. E. Miller & G. D. Cohen (Eds.), *Aging: Vol. 15. Clinical aspects of Alzheimer's disease and senile dementia* (pp. 103–120). New York: Raven Press.

Miller, E., & Lewis, P. (1977). Recognition memory in elderly patients with depression and dementia: A signal detection analysis. *Journal of Abnormal Psychology, 86*, 84–86.

Morley, G. K., Haxby, J. V., & Lundgren, S. L. (1980). Memory, aging, and dementia. In G. J. Maletta & F. J. Pirozzolo (Eds.), *Advances in neurogerontology: Vol. I. The aging nervous system* (pp. 211–240). New York: Praeger.

Moscovitch, M. (1982). Multiple dissociations of function in amnesia. In L. S. Cermak (Ed.), *Human memory and amnesia* (pp. 337–370). Hillsdale, NJ: Erlbaum.

Murdock, B. B., Jr. (1974). *Human memory: Theory and data*. Hillsdale, NJ: Erlbaum.

Neisser, U. (1967). *Cognitive psychology*. New York: Appleton-Century-Crofts.

Osborne, D. P., Brown, E. R., & Randt, C. T. (1982). Qualitative changes in memory function: Aging and dementia. In S. Corkin, K. L. Davis, J. H. Growdon, E. Usdin, & R. L. Wurtman (Eds.), *Alzheimer's disease: A report of progress in research* (pp. 165–169). New York: Raven Press.

Paivio, A. (1971). *Imagery and verbal processes*. New York: Holt, Rinehart & Winston.

Peterson, L. R., & Peterson, M. J. (1959). Short-term retention of individual verbal items. *Journal of Experimental Psychology, 58*, 193–198.

Petrides, M., & Milner, B. (1982). Deficits of subject-ordered tasks after frontal- and temporal-lobe lesions in man. *Neuropsychologia, 20*, 249–262.

Poon, L. W. (1985). Differences in human memory with aging: Nature, causes, and clinical implications. In J. E. Birren & K. W. Schaie (Eds.), *Handbook of the psychology of aging* (2nd ed., pp. 427–462). New York: Van Nostrand Reinhold.

Poon, L. W., & Fozard, J. L. (1978). Speed of retrieval from long-term memory in relation to age, familiarity, and datedness of information. *Journal of Gerontology, 33*, 711–717.

Poon, L. W., Fozard, J. L., Paulshock, D. R., & Thomas, J. C. (1979). A questionnaire assessment of age differences in retention of recent and remote events. *Experimental Aging Research, 5*, 401–411.

Poon, L. W., Walsh-Sweeney, L., & Fozard, J. L. (1980). Memory skill training for the elderly: Salient issues on the use of imagery mnemonics. In L. W. Poon, J. L. Fozard, L. S. Cermak, D. Arenberg, & L. W. Thompson (Eds.), *New directions in memory and aging* (pp. 461–484). Hillsdale, NJ: Erlbaum.

Prigatano, G. P., & Pribram, K. (1982). Perception and memory of facial affect following brain injury. *Perceptual and Motor Skills, 54*, 859–869.

Rabinowitz, J. C. (1984). Aging and recognition failure. *Journal of Gerontology, 39*, 65–71.

Ribot, T. (1882). *Diseases of memory*. New York: Appleton.

Riege, W. H., & Inman, V. (1981). Age differences in nonverbal memory tasks. *Journal of Gerontology, 36*, 51–58.

Riege, W. H., Klane, L. T., Metter, E. J., & Hanson, W. R. (1982). Decision speed and bias after unilateral stroke. *Cortex, 18*, 345–355.

Riege, W. H., Metter, E. J., & Hanson, W. R. (1980). Verbal and nonverbal recognition memory in aphasic and non-aphasic stroke patients. *Brain and Language, 10*, 60–70.

Rosen, W. G., & Mohs, R. C. (1982). Evolution of cognitive decline in dementia. In S. Corkin, K. L. Davis, J. H. Growdon, E. Usdin, & R. J. Wurtman (Eds.), *Alzheimer's disease: A report of progress in research* (pp. 183–188). New York: Raven Press.

Roth, M. (1980). Senile dementia and its borderlands. In J. O. Cole & J. E. Barrett (Eds.), *Psychopathology in the aged* (pp. 205–232). New York: Raven Press.

Royer, F. L. (1978). Intelligence and the processing of stimulus structure. *Intelligence, 2*, 11–40.

Schneck, M. K., Reisberg, B., & Ferris, S. H. (1982). An overview of current concepts of Alzheimer's disease. *American Journal of Psychiatry, 139*, 165–173.

Schonfield, D., & Robertson, B. A. (1966). Memory storage and aging. *Canadian Journal of Psychology, 20*, 228–236.

Schwartz, R., Shipkin, D., & Cermak, L. S. (1979). Verbal and nonverbal memory abilities of adult brain-damaged patients. *The American Journal of Occupational Therapy, 33*, 79–83.

Semenza, C., Denes, G., D'Urso, V., Romano, O., & Montorsi, T. (1978). Analytic and global strategies in copying designs by unilaterally brain-damaged patients. *Cortex, 14*, 404–410.

Sergent, J. (1984). Inferences from unilateral brain-damage about normal hemispheric functions in visual pattern recognition. *Psychological Bulletin, 96,* 99–115.

Smith, A. D. (1975). Aging and interference with memory. *Journal of Gerontology, 30,* 319–331.

Smith, A. D. (1977). Adult age difference in cued recall. *Developmental Psychology, 13,* 326–331.

Smith, A. D. (1980). Age differences in encoding, storage, and retrieval. In L. W. Poon, J. L. Fozard, L. S. Cermak, D. Arenberg, & L. W. Thompson (Eds.), *New directions in memory and aging* (pp. 23–46). Hillsdale, NJ: Erlbaum.

Smith, M. L., & Milner, B. (1981). The role of the right hippocampus in the recall of spatial location. *Neuropsychologia, 19,* 781–793.

Sperling, G. (1963). A model for visual memory tasks. *Human Factors, 5,* 19–31.

Squire, L. (1982). The neuropsychology of human memory. *Annual Review of Neurosciences, 5,* 241–273.

Squire, L. R., & Moore, R. Y. (1979). Dorsal thalamic lesion in a noted case of chronic memory dysfunction. *Annals of Neurology, 6,* 503–506.

Sternberg, S. (1969). Memory scanning: Mental processes revealed by reaction-time experiments. *American Scientist, 57,* 421–457.

Swets, J. A. (1973). The relative operating characteristic in psychology. *Science, 182,* 990–1000.

Terry, R. D., & Davies, P. (1980). Dementia of the Alzheimer type. *Annual Review of Neuroscience, 3,* 77–95.

Terry, R., & Katzman, R. (1983). Senile dementia of the Alzheimer type: Defining a disease. In R. Katzman & R. Terry (Eds.), *The neurology of aging* (pp. 51–84). Philadelphia: F. A. Davis.

Thomas, J. C., & Ruben, H. (1973, November). *Age and mnemonic techniques in paired associate learning.* Paper presented at the 26th annual meeting of the Gerontological Society, Miami, FL.

Tomlinson, B. E. (1982). Plaques, tangles and Alzheimer's disease. *Psychological Medicine, 12,* 449–459.

Treat, N. J., Poon, L. W., & Fozard, J. L. (1981). Age, imagery and practice in paired associate learning. *Experimental Aging Research, 7,* 337–342.

Tulving, E., & Colotla, V. A. (1970). Free recall of trilingual lists. *Cognitive Psychology, 1,* 86–98.

Underwood, B. J. (1957). Interference and forgetting. *Psychological Review, 64,* 49–60.

Van Lanker, D., & Canter, G. J. (1982). Impairment of voice and face recognition in patients with hemispheric damage. *Brain and Cognition, 1,* 185–195.

Walsh, D. A., & Prasse, M. J. (1980). Iconic memory and attentional processes in age. In L. W. Poon, J. L. Fozard, L. S. Cermak, D. Arenberg, & L. W. Thompson (Eds.), *New directions in memory and aging* (pp. 153–180). Hillsdale, NJ: Erlbaum.

Walsh, D. A., & Thompson, L. W. (1978). Age difference in visual sensory memory. *Journal of Gerontology, 33,* 383–387.

Walsh, D. A., Till, R. E., & Williams, M. V. (1978). Age differences in peripheral perceptual processing: A monoptic backward masking investigation. *Journal of Experimental Psychology: Human Perception and Performance, 4,* 232–243.

Warrington, E. K., & Sanders, H. I. (1971). The fate of old memories. *Quarterly Journal of Experimental Psychology, 23,* 432–442.

Warrington, E. K., & Silberstein, M. (1970). A questionnaire technique for investigating very long term memory. *Quarterly Journal of Experimental Psychology, 22,* 508–512.

Watkins, M. J. (1974). Concept and measurement of primary memory. *Psychological Bulletin, 81,* 695–711.

Waugh, N. C., & Norman, D. A. (1965). Primary memory. *Psychological Review, 72,* 89–104.

Wechsler, D. (1955). *Manual for the Wechsler Adult Intelligence Scale.* New York: Psychological Corporation.

Weingartner, H. Grafman, J., Boutelle, W., Kaye, W., & Martin, P. R. (1983). Forms of memory failure. *Science, 221*(4608), 380–382.

Whitehouse, P. J. (1981). Imagery and verbal encoding in left and right hemisphere damaged patients. *Brain and Language, 14,* 315–332.

Wickelgren, W. A. (1975). Age and storage dynamics in continuous recognition memory. *Developmental Psychology, 11,* 165–169.

Wilkins, A., & Moscovitch, M. (1978). Selective impairment of semantic memory after temporal lobectomy. *Neuropsychologia, 16,* 73–79.

Wilson, R. S., Bacon, L. D., Fox, J. H., & Kaszniak, A. W. (1983). Primary memory and secondary memory in dementia of the Alzheimer type. *Journal of Clinical Neuropsychology, 5,* 337–344.

Wilson, R. S., Bacon, L. D., Kaszniak, A. W., & Fox, J. H. (1982). The episodic–semantic memory distinction and paired associate learning. *Journal of Consulting and Clinical Psychology, 50,* 154–155.

Wilson, R. S., Bacon, L. D., Kramer, R. L., Fox, J. H., & Kaszniak, A. W. (1983). Word frequency effect and recognition memory in dementia of the Alzheimer type. *Journal of Clinical Neuropsychology, 5,* 97–104.

Wilson, R. S., Kaszniak, A. W., Bacon, L. D., Fox, J. H., & Kelly, M. P. (1982). Facial recognition memory in dementia. *Cortex, 18,* 329–336.

Wilson, R. S., Kaszniak, A. W., & Fox, J. H. (1981). Remote memory in senile dementia. *Cortex, 17,* 41–48.

Woolsey, R. M., & Nelson, J. S. (1975). Asymptomatic destruction of the fornix in man. *Archives of Neurology, 32,* 566–568.

Roland J. Branconnier

18

A Computerized Battery for Behavioral Assessment in Alzheimer's Disease

The Alzheimer's Disease Assessment Battery (ADAB) is a microcomputer-based behavioral assessment package that measures the intellectual deterioration, pathological memory loss, word-finding disturbance, and spatial disorientation that are the core cognitive symptoms of Alzheimer's disease (AD). A validation study comparing the cognitive performance of patients with AD and normal age-matched subjects found that all test instruments of the ADAB have substantial discriminative validity for, as well as sensitivity to, the severity of the dementia of Alzheimer's disease. The ADAB should prove to be a useful tool for evaluating the efficacy of new treatments designed to ameliorate the cognitive dysfunction of Alzheimer's disease.

Wells (1979) defined dementia as a clinical syndrome associated with chronic, diffuse cerebral hemispheric dysfunction, which, when pervasive, is characterized by intellectual deterioration, memory impairment, disordered abstract thinking, defective judgment, poor impulse control, personality changes, and lability of affect. Although dementia can result from a variety of underlying diseases, several carefully conducted differential diagnostic studies have shown that in the population over 65 years of age, 50 percent to 60 percent of all cases of dementia are due to Alzheimer's disease (AD) (Freeman, 1976; Seltzer & Sherwin, 1978) (see also Sections I and II of this volume).

To date, attempts to develop agents that improve the cognitive symptoms of AD have met with limited success (Crook, 1983). However, several classes of agents, such as the metabolic enhancers and cholinergics, appear to be promising (Branconnier, 1983; Johns, Greenwald, Mohs, & Davis, 1983).

Assessing the therapeutic efficacy of new drug treatments for the cognitive symptoms of AD poses major problems. First, there is no generally accepted standard therapeutic agent to validate test instruments. Second, without pharmacologically validated tests, it is debatable which cognitive symptoms should be assessed and with what instruments. The remainder of this chapter will describe the rationale, development, and validation of the Alzheimer's Disease Assessment Battery (ADAB), a computerized test battery for assessing efficacy of treatments for AD.

Determination of the Core Cognitive Deficits of AD

Sjogren, Sjogren, and Lindgren (1952) divided AD into three clinically distinct stages. At Stage I, the principal symptoms are incipient dementia, mnestic disturbance (including anomia), and spatial disorientation. At Stage II, the dementia becomes more pronounced, with marked mnestic disturbance and spatial disorientation. In addition, disorientation for time, place, and person as well as many focal neurological disturbances such as visual agnosia, aphasia, agraphia, alexia, and apraxia become superimposed on the earlier symptoms. Stage III is the terminal stage of the disease, in which cognitive activity is absent and the clinical picture is dominated by decerebrate vegetative status. These findings agree with more contemporary descriptions of the stages of the disease as detailed by Coblentz et al. (1973), Reisberg, Ferris, de Leon, and Crook (1982), and Sim and Sussman (1962). Thus, the core cognitive deficits that should be targeted for testing are incipient dementia, memory impairment, amnestic aphasia (word-finding disturbance), and spatial disorientation.

189

The Definition and Assessment of the Core Cognitive Symptoms of AD

Assessment of Intellectual Deterioration

Although Sjogren et al. (1952) do not define the term *incipient dementia,* clearly it connotes a decline in intellectual capacity. Intelligence is not a unitary process. Horn and Cattel (1967) described two broad categories of intelligence, fluid (Gf) and crystallized (Gc). Gf is nonverbal, independent of education, and measured by tests of figural and inductive reasoning. In contrast, Gc is the ability to use habits of judgment based on experience. It is dependent on education and is measured by tests of general information, verbal ability, and knowledge of specific topics.

The effects of normal aging on Gf and Gc are discordant. A preponderance of the evidence suggests that whereas Gf declines from maturity onward, the Gc dependent functions are relatively stable (Baer, 1972; Cunningham, Clayton, & Overton, 1975; Horn, 1976). Indeed, Goldstein and Shelly (1975) demonstrated that verbal abilities in normal elderly people may be superior to verbal abilities in normal young people.

The intellectual deterioration associated with AD is characterized by a global decline of both Gf and Gc dependent functions. Because verbal abilities are loaded on Gc and are stable in normal aging while declining in AD, tests of general verbal ability should be optimal measures of intellectual deterioration in patients with AD.

Nelson and McKenna (1975) reported that word-reading ability assessed with Nelson's National Adult Reading Test (NART) is highly predictive of intelligence as measured by the Wechsler Adult Intelligence Scale (WAIS) (Wechsler, 1955) and is preserved in dementia until the degree of dementia is moderately severe. Thus, reading ability scores on the NART can provide an estimate of premorbid intelligence in dementia when contrasted with current levels of performance on the WAIS.

The NART is composed of 50 irregular words that the subject reads aloud. The score is the number of pronunciation errors. In the initial standardization, normal subjects took both the NART and the WAIS. Nelson and McKenna then calculated regression equations to predict Verbal, Performance, and Full-Scale IQ based on NART performance. The obtained regression equations were then used to predict IQ scores in a group of patients with dementia. Although patients with dementia had significantly lower observed IQ scores on the WAIS than normal age-matched subjects, no significant differences in predicted IQs estimated from the NART were observed (Nelson & McKenna, 1975). Since this initial study was reported, the findings have been replicated and norms provided for predicted–obtained IQ discrepancies (Nelson, 1982; Nelson & O'Connell, 1978). Thus, the NART–WAIS combination appears to be a sensitive indicator of intellectual deterioration.

In the version adapted to the ADAB, intellectual deterioration is assessed by administering the NART and obtaining a predicted Verbal IQ based on the regression equations of Nelson (1982). Then scores on WAIS Information, Similarities, and Vocabulary subtests are prorated to yield an estimate of obtained Verbal IQ. These subtests were chosen for prorating because Duke (1967) showed that these three tests combined correlate with full Verbal IQ at $r = .96$. In addition, each subtest was shortened according to the method of Satz and Mogel (1962), a modification that also results in a high correlation with full Verbal IQ (Burns, Elias, Hitchcock, & St. Germain, 1980; Satz & Mogel, 1962). Only the Verbal IQ is evaluated, because this measure is loaded on Gc and therefore discriminates AD better than either Performance or Full-Scale IQ. A discrepancy of 8 points between predicted and obtained Verbal IQ is considered diagnostic of intellectual deterioration (Nelson, 1982).

The Assessment of Memory Impairment

The principal effect of normal aging on memory is characterized by a selective disruption of retrieval from, while sparing the storage into, Secondary Memory (SM) (Branconnier, Cole, Spera, & DeVitt, 1982). This interpretation is supported by the preponderance of experimental evidence showing that increasing age is associated with a marked deterioration of recall performance, while recognition is less affected (Schonfield & Stones, 1979). In contrast, the pathological memory loss seen in dementia is distinguished by a failure of both the storage and retrieval mechanisms of SM. Since recall and recognition are dependent on the availability of information, performance on both would be expected to be impaired in patients with AD. Indeed, Branconnier et al. (1982) demonstrated that failure of verbal recognition memory has high predictive value in differentiating memory impairment in normal aging from the pathological memory loss associated with AD. Since recognition is impaired in dementia but less affected in normal aging, assessment of recognition should provide an optimal measure for discriminating pathological memory dysfunction in AD.

To assess availability of information in SM, a two-step process is necessary. In the first step, new information must be learned. In the second, the recognition test for this material must be taken.

For the ADAB, learning is accomplished through the technique of selective reminding (Buschke, 1973). The patient views a list of 10 random words at a rate of one item every 2 seconds and is then asked to recall as many words as possible in any order (free recall). If some of the words are not recalled, the subject is selectively reminded of only those words missed on the previous trial and is then asked to recall the entire list again. This process is repeated until the subject recalls all 10 words on two consecutive trials or completes five trials.

After the criterion is reached, availability of the material learned during selective reminding is tested by a subject-paced recognition paradigm. Twenty words are presented to the patient, one at a time. Ten of the words are the target items learned previously; the other 10 are distractors that were not part of the list. The patient's task is to decide if each item was on the list he or she learned. Targets and distractors appear in a random order balanced for frequency in the English language (Thorndike & Lorge, 1944). Scoring this recognition task involves determining the rate at which targets are recognized (hits) and the rate at which distractors are incorrectly classified as targets (false alarms). These rates are used to determine the response criterion (β) and criterion-free estimate of sensitivity (d') by the application of signal detection theory (Freeman, 1973). A d' statistic of 2.6 or less is diagnostic of the pathological memory loss characteristic of AD (Branconnier et al., 1982).

The Assessment of Amnestic Aphasia

Aphasia, the disorder of language secondary to brain pathology, is not a consequence of the normal aging process. Indeed, as already noted, some language-related functions may improve with aging (Goldstein, 1980). For example, studies of the ability to generate examples of specific categories (category instance fluency, or CIF) have shown that normal aging does not affect the retrieval of lexical material under conditions of either free or cued recall (Drachman & Leavitt, 1972; Eysenck, 1975). Likewise, Waugh and Barr (1980) demonstrated that normal elderly subjects were slightly faster than normal young subjects in a naming-latency task that assessed the speed of retrieval of words from the internal lexicon. Thus, in normal aging the ability to retrieve lexical material does not deteriorate.

In contrast, the inability to retrieve lexical material is a frequently observed symptom of AD (Strub & Black, 1977). Moreover, in AD there is a characteristic progression and symptomatology of aphasia (Irigaray, 1973). In Stage I, the principal aphasic symptom of AD is a specific type of anomia or word-finding disturbance (Benson, 1979). Confrontation naming of objects is well preserved; however, there is a marked impairment in ability to generate category instances. As the disease progresses to Stage II, verbal output becomes "empty," with circumlocutory speech that reflects an increasingly impoverished lexical base. However, while both expressive and receptive lexical aspects of language are deteriorating rapidly, confrontation naming is only minimally impaired, and syntactic processes are not affected (Irigaray, 1973). At this stage, echolalia, the involuntary repetition of words spoken by others, is also common (Stengel, 1964). This total pattern has led Schwartz, Marin, and Saffran (1979) to conclude that the linguistic disturbance of advanced AD is a mixed sensorimotor transcortical aphasia in which the intact speech areas are isolated from the higher cortical func-

tions. At Stage III, all linguistic functions are lost, and a global aphasia results.

The observation that in AD, confrontation naming is preserved while category generation is impaired has psycholinguistic implications. Collins and Loftus (1975) proposed that semantic information is structured into two systems, a lexicon and a conceptual network. The lexicon is organized by the way words sound, while the conceptual network is structured by conceptual relatedness or semantic distance. Each word in the lexicon is linked to at least one concept in the conceptual network. Thus, a concept can be interfaced with a word that is used to designate the concept. This suggests that in AD the conceptual network (category generation) breaks down while the lexicon (confrontation naming) remains intact. Indeed, Warrington (1975) showed that the breakdown of the conceptual network in dementia is systematic and is characterized by a loss of specific concepts followed by a loss of general concepts. For example, the concept of *robin* would be lost before *bird*, and *bird* before *animal*. Because the conceptual network is disrupted in AD but is unaffected in normal aging, assessment of CIF should provide an optimal measure for discriminating the anomia (word-finding disturbance) specific to AD.

Clinicians assessing word-finding disturbance use CIF tests that require the patient to generate as many exemplars as possible from a category defined by a specific concept or letter (Benson, 1979). The performance criterion is either the number of instances generated within a specified time limit or the time taken to produce a specified number of instances (Schonfield & Stones, 1979).

The preferred paradigm to assess word-finding disturbance is the Word Fluency subtest of the Neurosensory Center Comprehensive Examination for Aphasia (Spreen & Benton, 1977). In the adaptation of this subtest that is included in the ADAB, the patient views a letter of the alphabet and tries to say aloud as many words as possible that begin with the specified letter. Three one-minute trials with the letters *F*, *A*, and *S* are given. The score is the sum of all admissible words produced after correction for age and education. A total production score of 26 or less is considered diagnostic for amnestic aphasia (Spreen & Benton, 1977).

The Assessment of Spatial Disorientation

Factor-analytic studies of primary mental abilities have demonstrated that there exists a factor of broad visualization (BV) that involves spatial concepts and orientation (Horn, 1976). Longitudinal investigations of BV have revealed that spatial ability is stable and does not decline with normal aging when generational differences are taken into account (Nesselroade, Schaie, & Baltes, 1972). However, Gaylord and Marsh (1975) showed that normal elderly people are significantly slower than normal young people at mental rotation in the spatial task of Shepard and Meltzer (1971). The observed mental rotation rates were

17.7 and 9.6 degrees, or an elderly:young performance ratio of 1.84:1. Cerella, Poon, and Fozard (1981) reported similar results, showing an age-related decline in ratio to 1.7:1. Thus, although subtle chronometric deficits in spatial performance are observed in normal aging, manifest spatial orientation is well preserved.

Geographic (or topographic) disorientation is a form of visual agnosia that results from a disturbance of the comprehension of spatial concepts (Luria, 1966). It is characterized by loss of the ability to orient places on maps, to estimate distances accurately, and to find routes in both familiar and new places (Lezak, 1976). Geographic disorientation has a devastating effect on functional capacity, and it is often the first recognizable symptom of AD (Strub & Black, 1977). Indeed, Sjogren et al. (1952) reported that 100 percent of their AD patients at Stage I had an obvious impairment in the ability to orient in space, while orientation for time was well preserved. The defect is so striking that Reisberg, Ferris, Horn, McCarthy, and de Leon (1981) have suggested that a positive finding of geographic disorientation is virtually pathognomonic of AD when observed in an elderly patient as part of a constellation of idiopathic cognitive dysfunctions. Thus, because manipulation of spatial information is markedly impaired in people with AD but only minimally affected by normal aging, assessment of spatial ability should provide an optimal measure for discriminating the spatial disorientation characteristic of AD.

In the ADAB, the instrument for assessing geographic disorientation is the Standardized Road-Map Test of Direction Sense (Money, Alexander, & Walker, 1965). The patient views a schematized city map on which is superimposed a dashed line representing a trail. The patient is told that this is a map of a city and that the task will involve following the trail. The dashed line is then sequentially replaced with a solid line starting at the origin and finishing at the end. The patient is shown each of 32 turns in the displayed trail and asked whether a right- or left-hand turn is required to follow the trail. Ten or more errors is considered diagnostic of geographic disorientation (Money et al., 1965).

The tests and performance criteria selected for the ADAB are listed in Table 18-1.

Table 18-1. Summary of the Alzheimer's Disease Assessment Battery

Symptom	Test	Performance criterion
Intellectual deterioration	IQ Reading ability	Predicted–observed discrepancy
Mnestic disturbance	Selective reminding recognition	d' statistic
Amnestic aphasia	Word fluency	Word production score
Spatial disorientation	Standardized road-map	Number of turn errors

Minimizing Error Variance With the Computer

The selection of performance criteria that provide optimal discrimination between the cognitive changes associated with normal aging and those associated with AD maximize the between-groups systematic variance. However, the efficacy of maximizing systematic variance can be attenuated unless procedures are implemented to minimize error variance.

Errors of measurement are principal sources of error variance (Kerlinger, 1973). Increasing the reliability of administering a test and decreasing human subjectivity in scoring it reduce measurement errors (Nunnally, 1978). Both of these objectives can be accomplished by using computerized testing procedures.

Computerized testing has several additional advantages over standard paper-and-pencil testing procedures. First, the indirect interaction between the patient and the experimenter via the computer reduces the anxiety associated with test taking. Second, computers can maximize staff efficiency, because paraprofessionals can administer complex testing procedures, thus minimizing professional staff involvement in testing. Last, computers can provide facile storage, retrieval, scoring, and statistical handling of patient data.

The Discriminative Validity and Sensitivity of ADAB

The study of the ADAB's discriminative validity involved 32 patients with AD and 20 normal aged control subjects. Patients with a presumptive diagnosis of AD were referred as possible candidates for AD treatment studies. The diagnosis of AD was established by findings on the Composite Mental Status Examination (Strub & Black, 1977) that were consistent with criteria in the *Diagnostic and Statistical Manual* (DSM-III) (American Psychiatric Association, 1980) for dementia. In each case, other organic or functional causes of dementia were excluded by history; physical, neurological, and psychiatric examinations; electroencephalogram (EEG); electrocardiogram (ECG); chest X-ray; computed tomography (CT) scan; blood chemistries, including thyroid function, B-12, and folate levels; tests for venereal disease; complete blood count; and urinalysis. Thus, all accepted patients met DSM-III criteria for Primary degenerative dementia, uncomplicated (DSM-III, 290.00).

Normal aged control subjects were recruited by newspaper advertisements. Each normal candidate took all of the medical tests that the AD patients did except for the EEG, chest X-ray, and CT scan. Potential candidates who met DSM-III criteria for any psychiatric disorder were excluded. Neither patients nor normal subjects were allowed to use drugs with intrinsic central nervous system activity during the study. The age and sex distribution of the sample is pre-

Table 18-2. Demographics of the Sample for the Validation Study

Variable	Normal aged subjects	Patients with Alzheimer's disease	p^1
Age[2]	69.16 (1.38)	69.15 (1.20)	ns
Sex[3]			
Male	10	8	ns
Female	10	24	

[1]Age was analyzed by one-way analysis of variance; sex was analyzed by chi-square analysis. [2]Data expressed as means with standard errors in parentheses. [3]Data expressed as number of subjects.

sented in Table 18-2. There was no statistically significant difference between the groups for sex or age even though there was a higher proportion of women in the AD group than in the control group.

The ADAB test battery was programmed in Microsoft BASIC and run under the CP/M disk operating system on the Psychometric Assessment System (PAS). The PAS consisted of an Apple II+ microcomputer system equipped with a 4MHz, Z80 CPU with 48K RAM. The operator (test administrator) used a Sanyo 12-inch green screen monitor with 24 × 80 character resolution, an Apple dual-drive floppy disk subsystem and CP/M disk operating system, and an Epson MX-80 dot matrix printer for hard-copy output. The patient used a separate station that consisted of a 15-inch Sanyo terminal, an RCA VP 3301 alphanumeric keyboard for accurate chronometric measurement of motor responses, and a NuTone Intercom for communication of verbal responses.

To determine the discriminative validity of the dependent variables as measures of diagnostic category, a one-way analysis of variance (ANOVA) was performed for each variable. The correlation ratio, η^2, was calculated (Winer, 1962) for each dependent variable to estimate the proportion of variance in that variable accounted for by the independent variable.

The sensitivity of the tests to increasing severity of dementia was evaluated using a criterion validation approach. Severity of cognitive impairment was assessed by administering the Mini-Mental State Examination (MMSE) (Folstein, Folstein, & McHugh, 1975) to all subjects. The MMSE yields a global score that is useful for grading severity of dementia (Anthony, LeResche, Unaiza, VonKoroff, & Folstein, 1982). Each

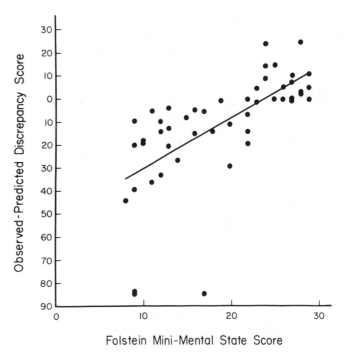

Figure 18-1. Scatterplot showing least squares linear regression of NART–WAIS verbal IQ discrepancy on Mini-Mental State score.

of the dependent variables (NART–WAIS discrepancy, d' statistic, word production score, and number of turn errors) was subjected to linear regression analysis using the MMSE score as the independent variable (criterion). A statistically significant linear relationship between the dependent variable and the criterion was considered evidence of sensitivity to increasing severity of dementia.

The discriminative validity analyses are summarized in Table 18-3. As expected, patients with AD had much greater IQ discrepancies than normal subjects and performed markedly worse on the other three tests. Moreover, the strength-of-association measure, η^2, reveals that diagnostic category accounts for a significant proportion of the variance observed for each variable. Thus, each parameter of cognitive dysfunction selected for the ADAB has substantial discriminative validity for the dementia characteristic of AD.

The data showing the sensitivity of Verbal IQ discrepancy to increasing severity of dementia are presented in Figure 18-1. Regression analysis revealed a highly significant linear relationship between the Ver-

Table 18-3. Discriminative Validity of the Alzheimer's Disease Assessment Battery

Variable	Normal aged subjects[1]	Patients with Alzheimer's disease[1]	F	p	η^2
IQ discrepancy	7.10 (1.67)	−21.75 (4.14)	28.3	<.001	.36
d' statistic	3.92 (0.14)	1.51 (0.16)	111.7	<.001	.69
Word production score	37.35 (2.39)	17.65 (1.62)	50.1	<.001	.50
Number of turn errors	7.95 (1.30)	12.84 (0.94)	9.6	<.004	.16

[1]Data expressed as means with standard errors in parentheses.

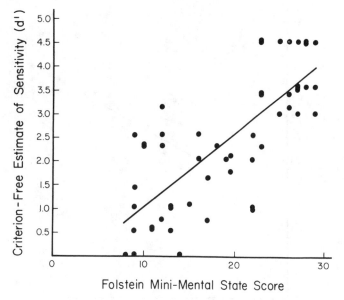

Figure 18-2. Scatterplot showing least squares linear regression of d' score (selective reminding and recognition task) on Mini-Mental State score.

bal IQ discrepancy and increasing severity of dementia as measured by the MMSE, $r = .647$, $F(1,50) = 36.07$, $p < .001$. The severity of dementia accounted for 42% of the variance in the deterioration of verbal intelligence.

Degree of MML, as assessed by the d' statistic, also shows sensitivity to increasing severity of dementia, $r = .767$, $F(1,50) = 71.57$, $p < .001$. Figure 18-2 illustrates the linear relationship between d' and MMSE

score. Severity of dementia accounts for 59% of the variance in d scores.

The relationship between word production score and severity of dementia is shown in Figure 18-3. Again, the linear regression is significant, $r = .763$, $F(1,50) = 69.64$, $p < .001$. Severity of dementia accounts for 58% of the variance in the word production score.

The association between performance on the Standardized Road-Map Test and the MMSE score is shown in Figure 18-4. Spatial disorientation (number of turn errors) exhibits a statistically significant negative correlation with MMSE score, $r = -.560$, $F(1,50) = 22.85$, $p < .001$. Degree of dementia accounts for 31% of the variance in the number of turn errors.

Conclusions

The results show that the ADAB's performance criteria (Verbal IQ discrepancy, d' statistic, word production score, and number of turn errors) have both substantial discriminative validity for, and sensitivity to, the severity of the dementia of AD. Moreover, these parameters assess the core symptoms of AD that are present even when the disease is incipient. Thus, the measurement of intellectual deterioration, pathological memory loss, word-finding disturbance, and spatial disorientation provides a homogeneous data base to assess change in severity of dementia after treatment.

At present, it is not possible to validate the sensitivity of the ADAB to decreased severity of dementia, because no standard pharmacologic agent has proven therapeutic efficacy in reducing the cognitive dysfunction of AD (Crook, 1983). However, the data presented

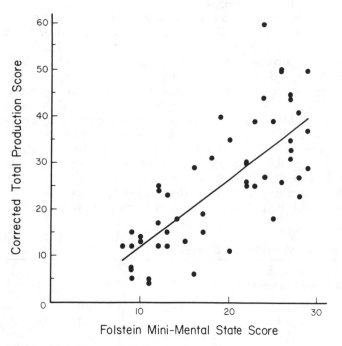

Figure 18-3. Scatterplot showing least squares linear regression of word production score (word fluency test) on Mini-Mental State score.

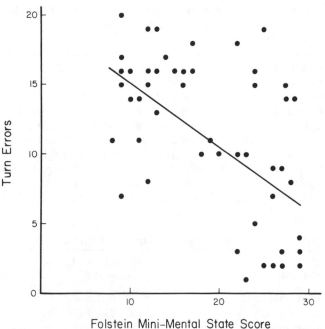

Figure 18-4. Scatterplot showing least squares linear regression of number of turn errors (Standardized Road-Map Test of Direction Sense) on Mini-Mental State score.

suggest that the instruments that compose the ADAB would be sensitive to amelioration of the cognitive symptoms of AD.

References

American Psychiatric Association. (1980). *Diagnostic and statistical manual of mental disorders* (3rd ed.). Washington, DC: Author.

Anthony, J. C., LeResche, L., Unaiza, N., VonKoroff, M. R., & Folstein, M. R. (1982). Limits of the "Mini-Mental State" as a screening test for dementia and delirium among hospital patients. *Psychological Medicine, 12*, 397–408.

Baer, P. E. (1972). Cognitive changes in aging: Competence and incompetence. In C. M. Gaitz (Ed.), *Aging and the brain* (pp. 5–13). New York: Plenum Press.

Benson, D. F. (1979). Neurologic correlates of anomia. In H. Whitaker & H. A. Whitaker (Eds.), *Studies in neurolinguistics* (Vol. 2, pp. 293–328). New York: Academic Press.

Branconnier, R. J. (1983). The efficacy of the cerebral metabolic enhancers in the treatment of senile dementia. *Psychopharmacology Bulletin, 19*, 212–219.

Branconnier, R. J., Cole, J. O., Spera, K. F., & DeVitt, D. R. (1982). Recall and recognition as diagnostic indices of malignant memory loss in senile dementia: A Bayesian analysis. *Experimental Aging Research, 8*(3–4), 189–193.

Burns, J. E., Elias, M. F., Hitchcock, A. G., & St. Germain, R. (1980). Corroboration of the utility of the Satz-Mogel abbreviated WAIS with hospitalized geriatric patients. *Experimental Aging Research, 6*(2), 181–184.

Buschke, H. (1973). Selective reminding for analysis of memory and learning. *Journal of Verbal Learning and Verbal Behavior, 12*, 543–550.

Cerella, J., Poon, L. W., & Fozard, J. L. (1981). Mental rotation and age reconsidered. *Journal of Gerontology, 36*, 620–624.

Coblentz, J. M., Mattis, S., Zingesser, L. H., Kasoff, S. S., Wisniewski, H. M., & Katzman, R. (1973). Presenile dementia: Clinical aspects and evaluation of cerebrospinal fluid dynamics. *Archives of Neurology, 29*(5), 299–308.

Collins, A. M., & Loftus, E. F. (1975). A spreading-activation theory of semantic processing. *Psychological Review, 82*, 407–428.

Crook, T. (1983). Geriatric psychopharmacology: Progress in the past decade and directions for the next. *Psychopharmacology Bulletin, 19*, 166–167.

Cunningham, W. R., Clayton, V., & Overton, W. (1975). Fluid and crystallized intelligence in young adulthood and old age. *Journal of Gerontology, 30*(1), 53–55.

Drachman, D. A., & Leavitt, J. (1972). Memory impairment in the aged: Storage versus retrieval deficit. *Journal of Experimental Psychology, 93*(2), 302–308.

Duke, R. B. (1967). Intellectual evaluation of brain-damaged patients with a WAIS short form. *Psychological Reports, 20*, 858.

Eysenck, M. W. (1975). Retrieval from semantic memory as a function of age. *Journal of Gerontology, 30*(2), 174–180.

Folstein, M. F., Folstein, S. E., & McHugh, P. R. (1975). Mini-Mental State: A practical method for grading the cognitive state of patients for the clinician. *Journal of Psychiatric Research, 12*, 189–198.

Freeman, P. R. (1973). *Tables of d' and β*. Cambridge, England: Cambridge University Press.

Freeman, P. R. (1976). Evaluation of patients with progressive intellectual deterioration. *Archives of Neurology, 33*, 658–659.

Gaylord, S. A., & Marsh, G. R. (1975). Age differences in the speed of spatial cognitive process. *Journal of Gerontology, 30*, 674–678.

Goldstein, G. (1980). Psychological dysfunction in the elderly: Discussion. In J. O. Cole & J. E. Barrett (Eds.), *Psychopathology in the aged* (pp. 205–232). New York: Raven Press.

Goldstein, G. C., & Shelly, C. H. (1975). Similarities and differences between psychological deficit in aging and brain damage. *Journal of Gerontology, 30*(4), 448–455.

Horn, J. L. (1976). Psychometric studies of aging and intelligence. In S. Gershon & A. Raskin (Eds.), *Aging* (Vol. 2, pp. 19–43). New York: Raven Press.

Horn, J. L., & Cattel, R. B. (1967). Age differences in fluid and crystallized intelligence. *Acta Psychologica, 26*, 107–219.

Irigaray, L. (1973). *Le langage des déments*. The Hague: Mouton.

Johns, C. A., Greenwald, B. S., Mohs, R. C., & Davis, K. L. (1983). The cholinergic treatment strategy in aging and senile dementia. *Psychopharmacology Bulletin, 19*, 185–197.

Kerlinger, F. N. (1973). *Foundations of behavioral research*. New York: Holt, Rinehart, & Winston.

Lezak, M. D. (1976). *Neuropsychological assessment*. New York: Oxford University Press.

Luria, A. R. (1966). *Higher cortical functions in man*. New York: Basic Books.

Money, J., Alexander, D., & Walker, H. T. (1965). *Manual for a Standardized Road-Map Test of direction sense*. Baltimore, MD: Johns Hopkins University Press.

Nelson, H. E. (1982). *National adult reading test*. Windsor, England: NFER-Nelson.

Nelson, H. E., & McKenna, P. (1975). The use of current reading ability in the assessment of dementia. *British Journal of Social and Clinical Psychology, 14*, 259–267.

Nelson, H. E., & O'Connell, A. (1978). Dementia: The estimation of premorbid intelligence levels using the new adult reading test. *Cortex, 14*, 234–244.

Nesselroade, J. R., Schaie, K. W., & Baltes, P. B. (1972). Ontogenetic and generational components of structural and quantitative change in adult behavior. *Journal of Gerontology, 27*, 222–228.

Nunnally, J. C. (1978). *Psychometric theory*. New York: McGraw-Hill.

Reisberg, B., Ferris, S. H., de Leon, M. J., & Crook, T. (1982). The Global Deterioration Scale for assessment of primary degenerative dementia. *American Journal of Psychiatry, 139*(9), 1136–1139.

Reisberg, B., Ferris, S. H., Horn, R., McCarthy, M., & de Leon, M. J. (1981, July). *Patterns of early age associated cognitive decline*. Paper presented at the meeting of the International Congress of Gerontology, Hamburg, Germany.

Satz, P., & Mogel, S. (1962). An abbreviation of the WAIS for clinical use. *Journal of Clinical Psychology, 18*, 77–79.

Schonfield, D., & Stones, M. J. (1979). Remembering and aging. In J. F. Kihlstrom & F. J. Evans (Eds.), *Functional disorders of memory* (pp. 103–139). Hillsdale, NJ: Erlbaum.

Schwartz, M. F., Marin, O. S. M., & Saffran, E. M. (1979). Dissociation of language function in dementia. *Brain and Language, 7*, 277–306.

Seltzer, B., & Sherwin, I. (1978). Organic brain syndromes: An empirical study and critical review. *American Journal of Psychiatry, 135*, 13–21.

Shepard, R. N., & Meltzer, J. (1971). Mental rotation of three-dimensional objects. *Science, 171*, 701–703.

Sim, M., & Sussman, I. (1962). Alzheimer's disease: Its natural history and differential diagnosis. *Journal of Nervous and Mental Disease, 135,* 489–499.

Sjogren, T., Sjogren, H., & Lindgren, A. G. H. (1952). Morbus Alzheimer and morbus pick. *Acta Psychiatrica et Neurologica Scandinavica, 82*(Suppl.), 1–152.

Spreen, O. F., & Benton, A. L. (1977). *Manual of instructions for the Neurosensory Center Comprehensive Examination for Aphasia.* Victoria, British Columbia, Canada: University of Victoria.

Stengel, E. (1964). Psychopathology of dementia. *Proceedings of the Royal Society of Medicine, 57,* 911–914.

Strub, R. L., & Black, F. W. (1977). *The mental status examination in neurology.* Philadelphia: F. A. Davis.

Thorndike, E. L., & Lorge, I. (1944). *Teachers' word book of thirty thousand words.* New York: Teacher's College of Columbia University.

Warrington, E. K. (1975). The selective impairment of semantic memory. *Quarterly Journal of Experimental Psychology, 27,* 635–657.

Waugh, N. C., & Barr, R. A. (1980). Memory and mental tempo. In L. W. Poon, J. L. Fozard, L. S. Cermak, D. Arenberg, & L. W. Thompson (Eds.), *New directions in memory and aging* (pp. 251–260). Hillsdale, NJ: Erlbaum.

Wechsler, D. (1955). *Manual for the Wechsler Adult Intelligence Scale.* New York: Psychological Corporation.

Wells, C. E. (1979). Diagnosis of dementia. *Psychosomatics, 20,* 517–522.

Winer, B. J. (1962). *Statistical principles in experimental design.* New York: McGraw-Hill.

SECTION
IV

Assessing the Effects of Depression

Larry W. Thompson, *Section Editor*

Larry W. Thompson

Measurement of Depression: Implications for Assessment of Cognitive Function in the Elderly

Over the past 20 years, considerable attention has been called to the adverse effects of depression on cognitive function in the elderly. Some authors have reported effects so severe that patients may evidence a level of impairment that is typically associated with organic dementia. The term *pseudodementia* is often used as a diagnostic classification for such individuals. Indeed, as Salzman and Gutfreund point out in the last chapter of this section, this relationship is so readily accepted into the clinical lore that clinicians are frequently called upon to make a differential diagnosis between depression and dementia in older patients with complaints of memory dysfunction. Yet other researchers have found no or very minimal negative effects of depression on a variety of cognitive processes. Attempts to reconcile such disparate findings have frequently led to intense scrutiny of methodologic differences among the various research reports. One problem contributing to the confusion in this area is that many clinicians and researchers alike have not made a clear distinction between memory complaints and memory performance. On the one hand, it is known that depression is related to an increase in complaints about memory loss, irrespective of actual performance on memory tests. Memory performance, on the other hand, may be related to depression only under certain conditions. Therefore, as the reader attempts to reconcile some of the discrepancies in the depression–performance controversy, it may be helpful to keep in mind that three constructs are involved: depression, memory complaints, and memory/cognitive performance.

A major purpose of this section is to highlight a number of the methodologic problems and controversial issues embedded in this literature. The authors in this section have taken this challenge seriously and to a greater or lesser degree have presented data from their own laboratories that clearly illustrate the discrepancies. For the most part they have also interspersed numerous references to the controversies throughout the manuscripts, along with a host of possible explanations.

The section begins with two chapters on the assessment of depression. Issues raised in these chapters could apply just as well to the measurement of other variables that reflect psychological distress, such as level and type of anxiety. The importance of proper assessment of such variables for classification purposes needs little justification here. Yet frequently researchers in the field of memory research pay only minimal attention to the potential impact of psychological distress on indices of memory function. Although this may not be a serious problem for the researcher who is studying memory function in normal young subjects, in the clinical setting careful documentation of the type and level of depression is essential.

A comprehensive evaluation of depression should include both a self-report measure and a behavioral rating. These two dimensions are highly correlated, but each provides unique information that greatly improves the precision of the assessment process. In chapter 20, Gallagher has reviewed several of the more traditional interview instruments used in clinical settings to classify the nature and severity of depressive disorders in the elderly. Similarly, in chapter 21, Yesavage provides a brief review of some of the more common self-report measures in use today. This compilation of interview and self-report assessment procedures is, by no means, intended to be exhaustive, nor is there any claim that those measures mentioned are necessarily more useful or psychometrically sound than many not included in these two chapters. Both authors emphasize the complexities involved in making a comprehensive assessment and encourage the researcher to pay careful attention to these complexities when evaluating the relationship of depression or other psychological distress measures to memory function in clinical populations.

In chapter 23, Niederehe questions the extent to which this relationship may hold in elderly populations. After a concise review outlining the positive and negative results in the area, he presents data showing no significant differences between depressed and nondepressed elderly on measures of semantic, episodic, and constructive memory. Furthermore, he found no age-by-depression interactions that would indicate that older depressives are more susceptible to memory impairment than are younger depressives. Attempting to reconcile these findings with others, Niederehe discusses his data in the context of four well-known validity considerations—an exercise that researchers all too often fail to complete. He emphasizes differences among studies, such as the setting, time, sampling, and specific experimental procedures. A comparison of these data with Raskin's data in chapter 25 highlights the importance of sampling differences. Raskin reports findings from several different samples that indicate that the impact of depression is more likely to be evident in hospitalized patients, in outpatients in an episode of very severe depressive disorder, in patients with low educational or socioeconomic status, and in patients with poor physical health. He also argues that the type of depression is important to consider: agitated and withdrawn depressed patients are likely to perform more poorly than others. Niederehe's subjects were female outpatients with fairly good education who were sufficiently interested in the project to make a trip to the laboratory. This factor may contribute to the absence of a depression effect.

This last subject feature—the patients' willingness to transport themselves to the laboratory—emphasizes the need to consider noncognitive factors, such as motivation, when one is attempting to assess cognitive changes associated with depression. Virtually all of the chapters mention the importance of this variable. Niederehe, for example, suggests that depression entails a reduction in the self-initiation of behaviors rather than an inability to complete them. Raskin (chapter 25) mentions, as does Weingartner (chapter 22), that the pattern of deficit seen in the wide array of cognitive procedures he employed could reflect a generalized deficit in a central motivational state of depressed individuals. From a slightly different perspective, Weingartner argues also that many of the cognitive impairments seen in depressed individuals could be subsumed under the construct of sustained cognitive effort.

Stylistic features of responding and attending to the environment are other factors that may affect performance of the elderly individual. Niederehe argues that depressed individuals are inclined to be more conservative, and the increased caution seen in older individuals may potentiate this effect. The likelihood is thus increased that elderly depressed patients would fail to provide answers in a memory assessment procedure or in other types of cognitive tasks unless they could be quite certain of the outcome. In line with this idea, Niederehe observed that a conservative response bias was more typical of the older depressed subjects on his memory tasks. They were more likely to have complete omissions of material to be remembered, whereas old normal subjects and younger subjects (both depressed and nondepressed) were more likely to have partial omissions. Kelley (in chapter 24) reminds us that in addition to the effects of a response bias, depressive mood affects what is attended to in the environment. Her data suggest that depressed individuals are likely to attend more closely to sad or negative stimulus material, whereas nondepressed individuals attend more to happy and neutral material. Depending on the nature of the material to be processed, such selective attention could markedly alter results on cognitive performance measures.

Taken together, these observations indicate that not only sampling problems but also procedural differences that affect motivation and attention must be given serious consideration in future research. Greater understanding of how these issues relate to various measures of performance would be helpful—first, in accounting for the discrepant findings already reported and second, in developing much-needed memory assessment devices to assist in differentiating between the detrimental effects of depression and of dementia. Researchers need to know which cognitive processes are most easily influenced by variations in these factors and which are relatively undisturbed. Weingartner's observation that cognitive impairments in depression appear to be determined by effort-demanding cognitive processes rather than by automatic processing provides useful leads in this direction and should encourage researchers to strive for greater precision in describing the differential impact of task and subject variables on a variety of cognitive processes. Specifically, within the arena of memory assessment, a distinction between tests of effort-demanding and automatic processes might prove very fruitful.

From the standpoint of the clinician, Salzman and Gutfreund (chapter 26) emphasize that the significance of this line of investigation cannot be overestimated. Given that clinicians are continually being asked to distinguish between depression and dementia in elderly individuals who complain of memory impairment, it is of paramount importance that clinicians be equipped with as much information as possible concerning noncognitive as well as cognitive correlates of memory dysfunction in the elderly. Errors of classification in either direction could have tragic consequences in terms of treatment outcomes. All too often another older person with a potentially reversible dementia is relegated to a "back ward" type of caretaker program because of a false positive diagnosis of progressive degenerative disease. Conversely, there are instances in which cognitive impairment in a patient with mild dementia has been further aggravated by the use of anticholinergics for the treatment of depression. Although many factors may play a role in misclassifications, greater clarification regarding the impact of psychological distress factors on cognitive function in different patient groups would be a welcome addition to the clinician's armamentarium.

Recent trends in the study of Alzheimer's disease (AD) have increased even further the need for continued concentration on the importance of noncognitive factors. In the past decade, data from the biological sciences have led to encouraging theoretical speculations about the underlying mechanisms responsible for the development of AD, and some of these findings have even resulted in several rudimentary treatment efforts. However, a major problem in evaluating any theories or their consequent treatment programs is that the dementia is usually detected only after massive amounts of brain tissue have been destroyed. Even if the model were correct and the treatment appropriate, the lack of viable tissue may make a fair test impossible. Thus, it would seem necessary to make an accurate diagnosis early in the course of the disease, when only minimal damage to the brain has occurred, in order to provide a useful evaluation of any theoretical formulation. Several researchers in this area have raised the question of whether AD may be the endpoint or final common pathway for a number of different disease processes. For example, psychologists have observed that there may well be distinctly different symptom profiles early in the disease but that these differences become obscured as the degenerative process progresses. If such observations are corroborated by future research, the hypothesis that different causes require different treatments would be supported.

The arguments of both biological and psychological researchers point toward the need for detection of the disease as early as possible. The development of more sensitive assessment procedures that are capable of detecting subtle changes in functioning in individuals who are otherwise reasonably intact will be extremely helpful in making positive diagnoses in the early stages. Efforts in this direction will likely involve the assessment of more complex abilities that are also readily disrupted by noncognitive processes that typically lead to distraction of attention. Therefore, it behooves researchers to determine the precise manner in which noncognitive features affect performance on tests that are potentially useful in detecting degenerative brain disease in the early stages. Clearly, more research is needed to ascertain whether changes in cognitive functioning that are uniquely characteristic of AD can be identified in the earlier stages of the disease. Being able to account for the influences of noncognitive features in the analysis and interpretation of test results is an important piece of the puzzle.

Dolores Gallagher

CHAPTER
20

CHAPTER
20

Assessment of Depression by Interview Methods and Psychiatric Rating Scales

This chapter describes what is meant by depression as a clinical syndrome. Diagnostic problems encountered with older adults are highlighted. Six specific interviewer-administered scales for the assessment of depression are then critically reviewed, and the advantages and disadvantages of each are noted. The importance of careful assessment of elders' affective status in future experimental and clinical memory research is emphasized.

Depressive disorders are the most common emotional problems found in older persons (Butler & Lewis, 1982). Severe depression is thought to impair cognitive functioning at any age (Miller, 1975). Depressions of moderate or lesser intensity in the elderly seem to be associated more with increased *complaints* about functioning than with actual performance deficits (Kahn, Zarit, Hilbert, & Niederehe, 1975; Popkin, Gallagher, Thompson, & Moore, 1982; Zarit, Gallagher, & Kramer, 1981). At present, it is not possible to state with certainty that elders with mild to moderate depression evidence significant cognitive deficits, although clinical experience with such patients certainly suggests that this is the case.

Irrespective of the controversy, it is critically important to evaluate affective status when one is conducting memory research with elders. It is necessary to find out if the person is clinically depressed, and if so, what the level of severity is. Mild as well as severe depressive symptoms should be noted. It may be that true cognitive deficits are associated with one or another type of depression or with certain severity levels. Unfortunately, at present not enough is known about these issues to permit the researcher to make confident predictions about memory and depression in the aged. Therefore, some "measurement overkill" will be necessary in the next few years, until a broader spectrum of lawful relationships have been demonstrated and replicated.

This chapter focuses on interview procedures that are useful in the assessment of depression, as well as on some of the problems encountered in the evaluation of older persons with symptoms of depression. Earlier community surveys (e.g., Gaitz, 1977) found that the majority of elderly respondents reported depressive symptoms such as sleep and appetite disturbances, blue mood, and pessimistic views of the future. However, an important distinction should be made between depressive complaints and depression as a clinical syndrome. As a syndrome, depression is a complex disorder that manifests itself in different individuals in a great variety of ways. A question asked frequently is whether the same diagnostic criteria should apply to older persons as to younger persons. For example, should the somatic complaints of a 70-year-old person with chronic rheumatoid arthritis and those of a 23-year-old person in good health be evaluated in the same way? What about memory complaints? Can clinicians be certain the complaints are not prodromal signs of a dementia? Some clinicians would argue that it is necessary for elders to undergo a medical examination before an accurate diagnosis of depression can be made. There are no simple "yes" or "no" answers to these concerns. There are, however, guidelines to assist the clinician in the differential diagnostic process.

Clinical Syndrome of Depression

Before discussing some recommended procedures for evaluating depression in the elderly, it might be helpful to review briefly the criteria used for making a diagnosis of clinical depression. In most instances, the

Preparation of this chapter was supported by grant RO1-MH37196 from the National Institute of Mental Health.

primary feature of depression is dysphoria—a feeling of being sad, down hearted, or blue. However *clinical* depression refers to a cluster of specific symptoms that have been present for a specified period of time; the term is not used simply to describe a feeling state. There are many different kinds of depressive disorders; diagnosis is usually based on whether the condition is chronic or episodic, as well as on the intensity of the disturbance. The following features, which are abstracted from the American Psychiatric Association's *Diagnostic and Statistical Manual of Mental Disorders* (DSM-III) (APA, 1980) and from the Research Diagnostic Criteria (RDC) (Spitzer, Endicott, & Robins, 1978) define an episode of clinical depression for older as well as for younger persons:

1. Duration of two or more weeks must be established for both mood and symptomatic disturbances. To qualify on this criterion, the patient has to report experiencing several of the symptoms to be detailed later, on a consistent basis, for at least that period of time. This stipulation rules out elders with transitory symptomatic distress that some have called "demoralization."

2. The primary feeling state during this interval must be determined. Typically, the patient reports feeling sad or depressed, with relatively little mood fluctuation. Some patients may report a cycling of moods from relatively low to relatively high during the period in question; this phenomenon should alert the interviewer to inquire about manic or hypomanic features. Other patients may report that they vary from experiencing a relatively normal mood state to having low periods that last several hours or several days but that they are not really continually depressed. It is important to clarify what the mood status has been, because different patterns imply different diagnostic decisions. Some older patients do not label their depression as such but, rather, use terms that are considered to be depressive equivalents, such as hopelessness, "don't care anymore", or intense irritability. Alternatively, they may report pervasive loss of interest and pleasure in everyday activities. Persons meet criterion 2 if either depression per se or an equivalent term is used to describe the mood state during the interval in question or if pervasive loss of interest and pleasure is reported while the dysphoric mood is not acknowledged (see Spitzer et al., 1978, for further discussion of this point).

3. According to the DSM-III, at least four of the following symptoms must have been present nearly every day of the episode in question if the patient is to be diagnosed as being in an episode of major depressive disorder; according to the RDC, at least five symptoms must have been present. Having two such symptoms will lead to a diagnosis of minor depression.

• Poor appetite or significant weight loss, or increased appetite or significant weight gain

• Insomnia (less sleep than usual) or hypersomnia (more sleep than usual)

• Psychomotor agitation or retardation, as evidenced by behavioral symptoms such as inability to sit still or slowed speech and strained conversation

• Anhedonia—loss of interest or pleasure in usual activities, including social contact

• Loss of energy, fatiguability, or tiredness

• Feelings of self-reproach or excessive or inappropriate guilt

• Complaints or evidence of diminished ability to think or concentrate (e.g., slowed thinking, indecisiveness)

• Recurrent thoughts of death or suicide, wishes to be dead, or evidence of suicidal behavior.

The RDC has the additional stipulation that the individual must evidence functional impairment *or* must be taking medication, *or* be seeking help for the disorder. It can be helpful to include this requirement when assessing elders, because a number of the symptoms listed may occur as normal concomitants of the aging process. For example, there are age-related changes in sleep patterns (Dement, Miles, & Carskadon, 1982); appetite changes in the elderly can occur for any number of reasons, such as decline in taste sensation or in funds to purchase nutritious, appetizing meals (Butler & Lewis, 1982); and physical fatigue may be due to specific health problems as often as to depression (Salzman & Shader, 1979). Moreover, bereavement is a common occurrence in later life, yet many of the symptoms that are part of a normal grief reaction can be confused with clinical depression. Recent work by Breckenridge, Gallagher, Thompson, and Peterson (1986) provides guidelines to distinguish between normal and abnormal grief in the elderly.

Besides the episodic depressive disorder just explained, there are other types of affective disorders that should be considered. For example, depressed individuals who also experience manic or hypomanic states constitute a distinct subgroup and should not be combined with "pure" depressives. There are classifications for chronic depressive conditions as well. Major depression is regarded as an episode with a fairly definite starting point that can be identified by the patient, whereas in chronic depression, usually a clear onset cannot be specified. In the DSM-III, chronic depressions are referred to as cyclothymic disorder or dysthymic disorder. For either of these diagnoses, a duration of two years is required along with certain characteristic symptoms (see APA, 1980, pp. 218–223 for more complete descriptions).

Sources of Confusion in the Diagnosis of Older Adults

Both episodic and chronic clinical depressions may at times be difficult to diagnose reliably in the elderly. Several factors may impinge on the accuracy of the diagnostic process.

Role of Physical Symptoms

Earlier it was noted that some of the symptoms that are used to qualify a person for a diagnosis of major depression can also be symptoms of physical illness—that is, they can truly reflect the patient's health status rather than his or her emotional status. Our research group (Dessonville, Gallagher, Thompson, Finnell, & Lewinsohn, 1982) studied this problem by comparing 59 elderly outpatients diagnosed as having a major depressive disorder with a sample of 69 normal elderly volunteers, using the Schedule for Affective Disorders and Schizophrenia (SADS) (Spitzer & Endicott, 1978). All subjects rated their perceived physical health on a 4-point scale, and the data of a subsample were checked against other indices of health status to verify that the 4-point scale was adequate for classifying subjects into two groups (healthy and unhealthy). We completed multivariate analyses of variance (MANOVAs) using two levels each of diagnosis (depressed and not depressed), health status (healthy and unhealthy), and age (young-old—55 to 69 years—and old-old—70 to 80 years).

Dependent variables were scores on five SADS summary scales designed to tap multiple aspects of depression. The scales were (a) depressed mood and associated features, (b) endogenous features, (c) depressive associated features, (d) suicidal ideation and behavior, and (e) anxiety. We found that depressive symptoms (as reflected in these summary scales) were substantially increased in the depressed group, irrespective of age, reported health status, or sex. Further analyses compared unhealthy old-old normal subjects with healthy young-old depressives (where the least differences might be expected if physical health and age were significant factors in these data). We found that differences were still highly significant on all summary scales.

Next, individual items were compared, to evaluate age and health effects on the somatic items in particular. Only 6 of 31 items tested had distributions that overlapped between one or more of the subgroups. As might be expected, most of those pertained to somatic processes. Normal elderly, particularly the old-old who reported that they were unhealthy, had insomnia, weight loss, weight gain, hypersomnia, somatic anxiety, and phobia scores that did not distinguish well among the groups. Therefore, our research group recommends that caution should be exercised in interpreting responses to such items by persons over 70 years of age who report that they are in poor health; and, whenever possible, data should be verified against a physician's report before a final diagnosis is made.

Role of Physical Illness and Medication

The role of physical illness and medication concerns many clinical researchers who work in medical centers with elders experiencing any of a broad range of diagnosed physical illnesses. It is likely that such patients may be taking quite a spectrum of medication for these disorders. Salzman and Shader (1979) offer information on diseases that may present with depression or be accompanied by it as well as information on drugs that may contribute to depression in the elderly. For example, brain tumors, anemia, and endocrine abnormalities may present with depression, or depression may be a physiological result of these disorders. Commonly prescribed medications (e.g., the antihypertensives) may contribute to depression in the elderly (Avorn, Everitt, & Weiss, 1986). The interviewer should study resource material on these issues prior to initiating assessment procedures in order to increase his or her sensitivity to the problem of differential diagnosis.

To understand how illnesses and medications may be affecting older persons, one must get accurate information on previous and current health status and on medications used. Our research group recommends that such information be elicited routinely to assist in interpreting interview responses. A variety of self-report measures are available for patients to complete prior to the diagnostic interview; interviewers can scan these reports to determine relevant areas to probe. In many instances, the researcher or clinician will need to consult with the patient's physician in order to understand the role of physical illness and medication usage in the overall clinical picture.

It should be noted that in the RDC classification system, episodic major depression may develop secondary to a physical illness. Again it is recommended that patients who are so subtyped should probably not be aggregated with elders whose depression does not seem to be biological in origin, because there are likely to be many uncontrolled differences between such groups that could confound results obtained from experimental and clinical studies of memory in the elderly.

Complaints About Impaired Cognitive Functioning

It was noted earlier that one of the symptoms used to diagnose clinical depression is the presence of either complaints about cognitive functioning (specifically, indecisiveness and inability to concentrate are noted in the DSM-III and the RDC) or actual impairment in functioning. In prior research our research group reported that complaints and performance were not necessarily isomorphic and that improvement in depression was associated with fewer complaints about memory capacity. However, many clinicians and researchers hold that complaints and impaired cognitive functioning may be more indicative of early organic disorder than of a functional problem such as depression. This is a controversial issue that has not been resolved in the literature to date. There has been little research on the cognitive functioning of elderly depressed people and little long-term follow-up to examine the relationship between affective improvement and cognitive status. Therefore, in a given case, it is difficult to know whether performance deficits are simply symptomatic of depression and are thus likely to improve with appropriate treatment of the affective disorder or whether they are prodromal indices of compromised cerebral functioning.

A clinically useful view on this issue is to regard cognitive complaints and performance deficits as part and parcel of the depressive disorder that are likely to improve as the disorder remits. To obtain some data that would either support or refute this view in a given case, the following steps are recommended: (a) administer cognitive performance tests of various kinds to determine the current level of performance and to evaluate whether complaints and performance are actually dysjunctive; (b) obtain a careful history to determine if the cognitive disturbance predated the development of depression, seems to accompany it, or even results from it. Typically, at least in cases of major depression, one finds that the individual functioned well before becoming depressed. It is also helpful to inquire about previous history of depressive episodes and whether cognitive problems have occurred before (in the earlier episodes) and (if they existed) whether they remitted with change in affective status. However, if there is no prior history of depressive episodes, and if fairly widespread cognitive problems have been present for some time, then it is desirable for the clinician to obtain a detailed neurological and neuropsychological workup prior to coming to a diagnostic decision.

Assessment of Depressive Disorders

Given that diagnosis of depression in elders may be a difficult process, depending on the situation, how does one go about conducting the assessment? What clinical interview procedures and psychiatric rating scales are available at present? What are their strengths and weaknesses? Many interview methods and rating scales have been designed to assess depressive symptoms, and several have been specifically designed to permit a diagnosis of depressive disorders (see reviews by Gallagher & Thompson, 1983; Kane & Kane, 1981; Kochansky, 1979; Mayer, 1978; McNair, 1979). The selection of what to include in this chapter was guided by the notion that a range of measures should be presented, including some developed to assess elders' general mental status, that would be useful to experimental cognitive psychologists who want a detailed description of a particular older person's affective state. I have selected six interviews to present in detail:

1. Schedule for Affective Disorders and Schizophrenia (SADS) (Spitzer & Endicott, 1978)

2. Diagnostic Interview Schedule (DIS) (National Institute of Mental Health, 1979)

3. Comprehensive Assessment and Referral Evaluation (CARE) (Gurland et al., 1977)

4. Older Americans Resources and Services (OARS) Multidimensional Functional Assessment Questionnaire (MFAQ) (Duke University Center for the Study of Aging, 1978)

5. Longitudinal Interval Follow-up Evaluation (LIFE) (Shapiro & Keller, 1979)

6. Hamilton Rating Scale for Depression (HRS-D) (Hamilton, 1960, 1967). This interview guide is in widespread current use to assess severity of depression, once a diagnosis has been established.

For each interview, the following information will be provided: description of the interview, including sample questions and scoring; the interview's use in prior research or in clinical contexts; and discussion of relative strengths and drawbacks of using that particular assessment device with elders.

Schedule for Affective Disorders and Schizophrenia

It should be noted that since the advent of the SADS, most depression researchers have used this instrument. It is currently regarded as representing the "gold standard" in this field. The SADS is a structured interview consisting of two parts (current status and historical information), each of which contains over 100 questions that explore in depth multiple aspects of the depressive syndrome, including affective distress, somatic complaints, and the full symptom picture used to make DSM-III and RDC diagnoses. At the start of the interview, patients are asked to talk about recent problems or difficulties, including what led to their coming in, when the problem began, what its course has been, whether they are feeling comparatively better or worse now, and when they last felt like their "usual" selves. This information enables the interviewer to determine if the person is, in fact, in an episode with a definite starting date that can be pinpointed, or if the condition is chronic.

The remainder of Part I concerns detailed representation of the current symptom picture. Ratings are made of symptoms when they were at their most severe; in addition, many items are scored again for their intensity in the week prior to the interview. Part I takes approximately 90 minutes. Part II is administered if the current illness is not a fairly clear-cut episode of depression of less than 5 years' duration or if the interviewer is interested in past psychiatric disturbance. At the end of the interview, ratings are made on the Global Assessment Scale (part of the SADS interview). These are summary judgments of functioning and psychopathology for the period when the condition was at its worst and for the past week. These global ratings have been found to be sensitive to change over time in patients' status.

The SADS is intended to be administered by a trained clinical interviewer who rates the presence or absence of each symptom and (if present) its degree of severity on a 7-point scale ranging from zero to 6 for most items. Ratings range from "absent" to "present in an extreme degree." Severity ratings at or above level 3 (indicating that the symptom is present to at least a "mild" degree) place it in the clinical range of significance. Examples of actual SADS items include "How have you been feeling? Describe your mood. Have you felt sad, moody, empty? How often? Does it come and go? How bad is the feeling?" A "mild" rating on this question (scale score of 3) indicates that the person often feels somewhat depressed or blue. A "moderate" rating (scale score of 4) means that the person felt this way during most of the time in question. An "extreme" rating (scale score of 6) means that the depressive feeling was extreme and present most of the time.

The SADS also contains sets of questions on psychotic processes, drug abuse and alcoholism, and previous history of depression. Information obtained from the SADS is weighed along with data about the patient from other sources and is used to classify the disorder in DSM-III or RDC terms. As previously noted, the SADS appears to be an instrument that is sensitive to detecting differences between depressed and nondepressed elders. In addition, there is a briefer version of the SADS, called the SADS-Change interview, that can be given at repeated intervals to evaluate both change in diagnosis and change in levels of distress on particular items.

The SADS interview is preferred for several reasons. First, it was developed specifically to control for *information variance* associated with typical diagnostic interviewing. All patients are asked the same questions, and, if the interviewer is properly trained, responses will be scored the same, regardless of who administers the interview (Endicott & Spitzer, 1978).

Second, it was designed to elicit information necessary for making RDC diagnoses. The organization of the interview and the item coverage enable the interviewer to go directly from the SADS to RDC criteria and to use the information to make standardized classifications. The RDC itself was designed specifically to reduce the *criterion variance* in the diagnosis of a selected group of functional disorders (Spitzer et al., 1978). It was the forerunner of the DSM-III for classification of affective disorders. These interrelated procedures were formulated by Endicott, Spitzer, and their colleagues at the New York State Psychiatric Institute, with assistance from other participants in the NIMH Clinical Research Branch Collaborative Program on the Psychobiology of Depression. Their aim was to develop procedures that would considerably improve the reliability, and thereby the validity, of diagnostic practice. Thus, using the SADS and the RDC in combination allows the clinical researcher to improve the precision of diagnostic classification.

Third, the SADS provides an excellent "cognitive map" of the territory of depression that goes beyond the scope of most other psychiatric rating scales (see Endicott & Spitzer, 1978). Fourth, the original reliability and validity data reported on this instrument were quite good (see Endicott & Spitzer, 1978), and our research group's work with it supports the notion that it is similarly reliable and valid with older adults. We have found, for example, that trained interviewers can achieve excellent agreement on the individual item level as well as on the classification level. Although future research may find that other interviewer-administered scales do equally well or better than the SADS, at present no such studies exist in the literature.

Some drawbacks to use of the SADS method involve the training time required to gain expertise in the interview and the amount of supervised clinical experience needed (even for skilled clinicians) before the technique can be used reliably. When used with elders, the SADS needs to be supplemented with data from other sources regarding health status, mental status,

medication usage, and so forth, to clarify the etiology of specific symptoms. Finally, the SADS is lengthy to administer and, at times, difficult to score because clinical judgment often must be exercised during the scoring process. Interviewers need periodic "reliability checks" so that drift from criterion standards is minimized.

Diagnostic Interview Schedule

The structured Diagnostic Interview Schedule (DIS) was developed by the National Institute of Mental Health (NIMH) and is currently being used in NIMH's multisite Epidemiological Catchment Area (ECA) survey of the prevalence of psychiatric disorders in adults in different regions of the country. Older adults are being oversampled in this survey so that eventually, extensive epidemiological data should be available on the prevalence of mental disorders in adults across the life span. The development and psychometric properties of the DIS are described in Robins, Helzer, Croughan, and Ratcliff (1981).

The DIS consists of 254 questions, of which only about 100 questions are asked of every subject interviewed (the remainder are contingency items). Scoring requires some judgment on the part of the interviewer in that decisions have to be made about whether or not the symptom meets all criteria as a *psychiatric* symptom. For example, for most items a code of "1" is scored if the answer is no, the symptom did not occur; a "2" is scored if the symptom occurred but did not meet criteria for severity when standard probes were applied; a "3" is scored if the symptom occurred and met severity criteria but this was explainable by the effects of medication, drugs, or alcohol; a "4" is scored if the symptom can be explained by physical illness or injury; and a "5" is scored only if the symptom is clearly psychiatric in origin. What is termed a "Probe Flow Chart" is used to assist the interviewer in making these decisions. An example of a question from the depression section of the interview is the following: "Have you ever had a period of a week or more when you had trouble falling asleep, staying asleep, or with waking up too early?" Other questions tap manic episodes, cognitive status, alcohol and drug abuse, and certain personality disorders.

A major advantage of the DIS is that it requires only between 45 and 75 minutes to complete and is routinely administered by paraprofessionals or trained technicians with minimal formal training in psychology or psychiatry. Thus it is less costly to use than interviews (e.g., the SADS) that need to be administered by specially trained mental health professionals. One to two weeks of training is generally sufficient to attain proficiency (see Robins et al., 1981, on this point).

A second advantage of the DIS is that it was designed specifically to generate the information needed to make most Axis I diagnoses in the DSM-III system, as well as most RDC diagnoses. Thus, it is broader in scope than the SADS, and its developers would argue that it is in some ways more accurate than the SADS for generating the information needed to make diagnoses. Their basis for this is that the DIS clearly specifies questions and probes (so that the interviewer is not called on to improvise questions) and that the scoring system follows automatically from answers to the questions posed (to minimize the clinical judgment required).

A third advantage is that final scoring and summary data are achieved by a computerized scoring system for which clear diagnostic algorithms have been written. According to Robins et al. (1981), "The computer, unlike the clinician, looks only at those items to which the program directs it in making a diagnostic decision" (p. 385). This feature may decrease bias and increase decision-making accuracy.

However, the DIS was developed primarily for use in epidemiological and survey research, not for use in clinical practice. This raises a question about its suitability for individualized clinical assessment. Also, depression constitutes only one section of the interview; although the requisite questions are included (regarding mood, cognitive/behavioral disturbances, and somatic symptoms), depressive syndromes are not as fully explored as on the SADS. The extent of information one needs to have about depression versus other psychiatric disorders would probably be a helpful criteria in deciding whether or not the DIS is adequate for one's research program. A final drawback concerns the lack of any published data at present on the reliability and validity of this interview with elderly samples. This lack may be remedied in the future, as ECA findings become available, but in the interim it is likely to be a concern for gerontological researchers.

Comprehensive Assessment and Referral Evaluation

The CARE is a semi-structured interview specifically designed to be used in community surveys of elders. It was developed by Gurland and associates as part of the United States/United Kingdom Cross National Project, which compared psychiatric practice and psychiatric disorders in these two countries. It has been extensively used in New York and London in household surveys and with patients in community service settings. Its psychometric properties and a full description of its historical development can be found in Gurland et al. (1977) and in several other articles (Golden, Teresi, & Gurland, 1984; Gurland & Wilder, 1984; Teresi, Golden, & Gurland, 1984; Teresi, Golden, Gurland, Wilder, & Bennett, 1984).

The CARE is a multidimensional interview used to describe the individual's psychiatric, medical, nutritional, economic, and social status and to determine if there are unmet needs requiring referrals for services. It can also be used to assess the effectiveness of services received. Its style, scope, and scoring method make it suitable for use with both elderly patients and elderly nonpatients. Typically, the CARE interview takes about 90 minutes to administer; it is usually given in the elder's home by a trained interviewer. Kane and Kane's (1981) review of this measure supports its use as an assessment device for detection of the nature and scope of common health and social problems of urban elders.

This instrument has gone through several modifications designed to reduce the number of questions (the original CARE contained about 1,500 items) and thus to develop an interview that is cost and time efficient. The CORE-CARE resulted; this contains 314 items that can be summarized in terms of 22 "indicator scales" that point out specific problems (e.g., cognitive impairment, demoralization, stroke effects, sleep disorder, ambulation problems, activity limitation, social isolation, etc.) and their severity and impact on the person's daily life. As with the full CARE, this information is used to determine if referrals are needed and to predict outcome (with or without treatment).

The interview was designed to be tactful; questions are asked in such a way that respondents can expand on their symptoms rather than be restricted to a monosyllabic answer. The rater, however, must judge the relevance of the information provided. Sample questions from the CARE that are designed to tap depression are the following: "Have you been sad or depressed during the past month? (If subject admits to depression): How long does the depression last? Just a few hours at a time or longer than that? Have you felt that life wasn't worth living?" Other depression items inquire about the presence, duration, and pervasiveness of vegetative symptoms (not accounted for by physical disease), the presence of self-depreciation, suicidal or psychotic thinking, and other features (like "excitement") that would assist in differential diagnosis. Scoring uses the following categories: "true" means that the symptom is present; "false" means that the symptom is not present; "?" means that the information obtained from the subject's response is insufficient for the rater to make a true or false rating (also, if the subject says "don't know," it is recorded here); "refusal" means that the subject refused to answer that particular question; and "not applicable" is used to indicate that a particular question was not asked because it was not appropriate. The time frame in this interview is the past month.

It is clear that the CARE was not designed to be a clinical diagnostic interview. However, much of the information obtained can be related to current diagnostic systems, because there is considerable overlap in content. Recently, Gurland's group has developed an interview schedule called the SHORT-CARE specifically to assess depression and dementia (see Gurland, Dean, Copeland, Gurland, & Golden, 1982; Gurland, Golden, & Challop, 1982; and Gurland, Golden, Teresi, & Challop, 1984, for actual questions and information on the psychometric properties of this interview).

Finally, this group has also developed a very brief 11-item Screen Schedule, used to assess quickly whether additional questioning for depression or dementia should occur, and a 31-item Short Behavioral Assessment Schedule that can be used in the same way. Items on cognitive and affective status compose these scales. The gerontological researcher interested in the CARE approach thus has several interview schedules to choose from, depending on the amount and kind of information to be gathered.

Advantages of the CARE-type interviews include careful conceptual and psychometric development; focus on the multiple problems that elders can experience, along with probes for etiology of psychiatric symptoms (which help to clarify the contribution of physical illness, medication usage, etc., to the presenting symptomatology); and extensive use in prior research with the elderly. However, these interviews must be administered by trained personnel; they can be costly and time-consuming if information is obtained that is not relevant to the researcher's questions; and because they were not designed with explicit reference to either the DSM-III or the RDC, they may not be the most appropriate diagnostic instruments to use when the focus is on detailed description of clinical depression. Finally, because these are multidimensional interviews, depression cannot be explored as fully as with the SADS interview.

Older Americans Resources and Services Instrument

The OARS is similar to the CARE in that it is a multidimensional, semistructured interview that has been used primarily in community and institutional survey-type research. The OARS is intended to describe elders' characteristics in the particular domains assessed and to determine needs for services. The revised version, called the Multidimensional Functional Assessment Questionnaire (MFAQ), contains 105 questions and is designed to be administered in approximately one hour. Training is required to administer the interview properly.

Information is collected about functional status in five domains: social resources, economic resources, mental health, physical health, and activities of daily living. From responses to questions in each domain, the rater makes a global judgment of functional status for that area on a 6-point scale. A rating of "1" means that excellent functioning is present; a rating of "6" means the person is totally impaired in that area. The five summary ratings can be combined to create a cumulative impairment score. Data indicate that validity and reliability are adequate for the OARS to be used for screening and for assessing change; the latter is possible because categories of potentially useful remedial services are included in the interview and can be recommended for the subject. Hence, on readministration, one can determine if these services were utilized and if change occurred in functional status in any of the domains. Psychometric properties of the interview are reviewed in Fillenbaum (1978) and in Kane and Kane (1981).

The mental health section (in the original version) contains items designed to tap the extent of psychiatric well-being and the presence of organicity. The OARS includes 18 questions that reflect DSM-III indicators of depressive symptomatology (although this interview was designed prior to the publication of DSM-III). These items were labeled the OARS Depressive Scale and were used by Blazer (1980) to determine the extent to which DSM-III criteria were useful for identifying elderly persons diagnosed as depressed. Blazer found that the scale performed well in identifying hospitalized elders with known diagnoses of depression but that it failed to reliably identify outpatient depressives. Blazer and Williams (1980) subsequently used this measure to determine the prevalence of depressive symptoms in a sample of nearly 1,000 elders in North Carolina. However, they noted that duration of symptoms is not adequately measured in the OARS Depressive Scale (duration is unspecified), and that there is no item on suicidal ideation or behavior. These two drawbacks detract seriously from the use of this instrument as a clinical diagnostic tool (despite its advantage of brevity).

Longitudinal Interval Follow-Up Evaluation

The LIFE interview was specifically designed to link with the diagnostic categories of the RDC system. It is a semistructured interview that yields a comprehensive picture of the course of a patient's depression over a specified time interval (usually 6 months). Questions are asked about the patterns of symptomatic distress over time, including variations in mood and symptom profile. Ratings are made for each week of the interval. Information is also obtained regarding any treatment that was received for the affective problem during the interval.

The LIFE may be administered at the point of entry into a clinical research study so that baseline diagnostic and severity ratings are obtained. It is of greater value, however, when used repeatedly over time, thus enabling the researcher to track the course of a patient's progress or worsening in terms of RDC diagnostic categories. The LIFE has been used in the NIMH Clinical Research Branch Collaborative Program on the Psychobiology of Depression to evaluate such issues as relapse, "lag" effects of treatment, and so on (see Shapiro & Keller, 1981; and Keller & Shapiro, 1981, for further explication). The LIFE may be of interest to cognitive psychologists, because it is the only interview currently available that takes a longitudinal perspective on depressive illness (and related RDC problems). The SADS-Change interview (noted earlier) gives cross-sectional data about the patient's affective status at a particular point in time—its ratings are based on symptomatic distress in the past week only. The SADS-Change and LIFE interviews may be used together in research projects in which both kinds of data are desired.

The interviewer begins by asking open-ended questions regarding what has happened to the subject in the past 6 months. The responses give a broad indication of whether the subject has recovered from a previous problem or has developed new problems. Ratings from previous LIFE interviews are available so that no problem that has already been diagnosed is overlooked in the current assessment. Screening questions are then asked for the following disorders: major (episodic) depression; intermittent depression; mania; schizophrenia; anxiety, panic, and phobic disorders; alcohol and drug abuse; and obsessive–compulsive disorder. If a positive response is given to any of the screening questions, or if preexisting conditions were noted, the interviewer follows up with specific questions designed to tap that disorder in more detail. Weekly ratings of symptomatic distress associated with that particular disorder are made. If more than one problem is noted, the procedure is repeated until all problems have week-to-week ratings. To reduce possible difficulties in remembering this amount of detailed information, probes are used to determine the occurrence of change points. Dates for the change points are pinpointed as accurately as possible and provide the structure for more detailed inquiry into the symptom picture preceding and following these nodal points.

For example, if the person had previously been diagnosed as being in an episode of major depression and indicated that he or she felt better for awhile and then worsened again, the interviewer would date the improvement period and the time when the depression seemed to return. The subject would then be asked about the presence and severity of each of the eight symptoms defining major depression (noted earlier in this chapter) to determine how extensive the improvement was (i.e., was it a full remission or a partial remission; was there a sustained period of at least 8 weeks when the subject felt like his "usual self" or had only mild residual symptoms? etc.). After the duration and degree of improvement were recorded, the interviewer would note when depressive symptoms returned as well as their duration and intensity. If a number of episodes have occurred in the interval or if the subject has difficulty being specific in recalling how he or she felt and what symptoms were present, this interview can take more than the one hour it usually requires.

Ratings are made on a 6-point severity scale for each disorder: "1" means the patient was his or her "usual self" with no symptoms of the disorder that is being evaluated; "2" is a residual rating, meaning one or more RDC criterion symptoms are present to a mild degree; "3" indicates partial remission, meaning that there is obvious evidence of the disorder, with moderate impairment but less psychopathology than is set forth in the full RDC criteria; "4" indicates marked disorder—the person does not meet RDC criteria for definite presence of the disorder, but there are major symptoms or impairment; "5" indicates that the person meets RDC criteria for definite presence of the disorder; and "6" indicates that the condition is severe, with extreme impairment or prominent psychotic features. Thus, one can evaluate both diagnosis and severity of all RDC classifications, using the LIFE interview method. Training is required, of course, to develop expertise in administering this interview. Those with prior SADS/RDC training appear to learn most

quickly, because most of the questions and decision rules are comparable.

One drawback to use of the LIFE interview is its cost, because trained clinical interviewers are needed. Time of administration will vary according to the number of new episodes (or other changes in clinical status) that have occurred during the interval. A more significant problem with the LIFE interview is that its almost total reliance on retrospective memories of the patient may make this interview method considerably less reliable with older adults than with younger patients. Although validity and reliability data in general appear to favor the use of this instrument in its intended manner, no information is available on the psychometric properties of this interview with elderly depressives. At the Palo Alto Veterans Administration Medical Center, we are currently undertaking a pilot study to address this issue. Preliminary data from our laboratory suggests that the use of a 6-month interval between LIFE interviews is too long for reliable data to be provided by many elderly depressives; it is likely that shortening the interval (e.g., to one month only) will improve this situation.

Hamilton Rating Scale for Depression

This scale was developed almost 25 years ago and continues to be widely used in contemporary research on depression to assess *severity* of depressive disorders. According to its author, it is not intended for use as a diagnostic instrument (Hamilton, 1967); however, the HRS-D is included in this chapter because of its ubiquity and longevity in the field.

The HRS-D is a clinical instrument "whose value depends on the skill of the interviewer in eliciting necessary information" to make the ratings (Hamilton, 1960, p. 56). It typically requires one half hour for a skilled clinician to obtain sufficient information to code all questions contained in the scale. The rating scale really provides a systematic method for quantifying the results of the interview, which should be conducted only with persons already diagnosed as suffering from a depressive disorder. The original HRS-D contained 21 areas of inquiry, 17 of which related to depression; items were chosen on the basis of the author's observations of symptoms.

Scoring criteria and scaling are not consistent across the 17 items. Eight items are scored on a 5-point severity scale, and nine are scored on a 3-point scale. For example, in order to score the "early insomnia" item, one needs to ask about the *frequency* of difficulty the patient has falling asleep. A zero rating means there is no difficulty; a "1" rating means occasional problems; and a "2" rating means nightly difficulty. In contrast, to score the "guilt" item, one has to determine the *severity* level. A zero rating means that feelings of guilt are absent; a "1" rating indicates some feelings of self-reproach; a "2" rating is given if there are clear ideas of guilt (not just self-reproach) or rumination over past errors or sinful deeds; a "3" is used if the person thinks that the present illness is a punishment and there are delusions of guilt; and a "4" is used to record presence of hallucinations. On most of the remaining questions, it is left to the rater's judgment to distinguish between intensity and frequency of symptoms and to decide how to weigh each attribute in the determination of the score for that item.

Scoring of the HRS-D was originally the sum of two independent ratings, one by the interviewer and the other by an observer who could ask additional questions for clarification. The maximum possible score was therefore 100. In current practice, this interview is typically given by one trained clinician, making 50 the maximum score at present (based on the 17-item version of the HRS-D). Recently the NIMH Collaborative Depression Research Project has developed a 23-item version that is more closely aligned with DSM-III and RDC criteria for major depressive disorder (Sotsky & Glass, 1982). Because of this feature, their revision may be an improvement over the original HRS-D.

Several issues should be considered before a decision is made on whether to use the HRS-D in clinical research with elders. First, considerable interviewer training is needed to develop skill in administering this measure. In his 1967 article, Hamilton provided some guidelines for rating; however, many of the ratings require a high level of inference and can be complex to make, particularly in the absence of additional information about the patient. Therefore, simply studying Hamilton's guidelines is generally not sufficient; rather, our research group has found that after training, supervised experience in about 20 more interviews is necessary before an interviewer can achieve adequate reliability in the use of this scale with elders. Sotsky and Glass (1982) have developed a manual with detailed, clear interview guidelines, which should prove helpful both for shortening training time and for increasing reliability among raters. In the manual, all scale points are clearly anchored, thus reducing the number of inferences required.

Second, on a more general level, the psychometric properties of this scale have not been adequately established. Although it is possible to obtain high reliability among similarly trained interviewers, data on the internal consistency and test–retest reliability of the scale are sparse, as are data on its content and construct validity (reviewed in Mayer, 1978). Similarly, no published data are available to support or reject the notion that the HRS-D is appropriate for use with depressed elders. However, it is used widely enough that comparisons can be made between samples in different studies and of different ages.

Third, it has been noted (Carroll, Fielding, & Blashki, 1973; Schwab, Bialow, Holzer, Brown, & Stevenson, 1967) that the HRS-D is heavily weighted toward somatic symptomatology: Nine of its 17 items have a somatic focus. This may present a problem when the scale is used with elders, particularly if the HRS-D is administered in the absence of accurate information about the person's health status. Scores can be inflated as a result of legitimate health problems (whether or not depressive disorder is present), thereby confounding interpretation. One study conducted with 49 older rheumatoid arthritic (RA) patients (mean age = 63; 84% male) highlights this issue (Gallagher, Slife, Rose, & Okarma, 1982).

The HRS-D was administered in two ways: first traditionally (i.e., the patient was asked if each symptom was present and if so, to what extent) and then again with an active interviewing style in which more questions were asked to determine the extent to which a particular symptom appeared to result from RA rather than from depression. This yielded "regular" and "adjusted" scores for each patient. The "regular" sample mean was 13.45, suggesting at least a mild level of depression; however, the "adjusted" sample mean was only 7.45, which is in the normal range. This difference was statistically significant ($t = 10.43, p < .001$). Items most likely to receive inflated scores concerned sleep problems, fatigue, poor appetite, and bodily concerns.

When probed, most patients were able to discuss what role they thought their disease played in each of these symptoms versus the role played by depression—when it was acknowledged to be present. Helpful questions concerned onset, whether the symptom was associated with changes in mood, and whether or not it was present on days when the RA was quiescent. In addition, we noted that the correlation between HRS-D scores and a self-report measure of depression, the Geriatric Depression Scale (GDS) (Yesavage et al., 1983), was stronger when the "adjusted" HRS-D score was used, compared to the "regular" HRS-D score ($r = .62$ vs. $r = .48$, respectively). Taken together, these data underscore the importance of carefully assessing the relative contribution of known physical illness to depressive symptoms.

In summary, the HRS-D has several strengths and weaknesses. The interview can be conducted by a skilled clinician in about 30 minutes. This is brief compared with the other interviews discussed in this chapter. The total score appears sensitive to treatment effects and changes over time in accord with change on other measures of affective status. However, the HRS-D was not designed with reference to DSM-III or RDC criteria (so not all relevant dimensions of depression are tapped), and it is psychometrically weak in comparison to other scales. Scoring of certain items can be significantly affected by the respondent's physical health status, so interviewers must be trained to sort out somatic versus psychic influences in the individual case. Finally, a recent revision has become available that has updated the HRS-D and provided more comprehensive interview guidelines; thus, its utility may be increased in the future. Our research group cannot heartily recommend the HRS-D because of the problems noted; however, it is clear that the HRS-D will continue to be widely used because of its long history and its use for comparisons across studies.

Conclusions and Recommendations

The main goals of this chapter were to describe clinical depression as it is currently understood, to alert the reader to several critical measurement issues involved in diagnosing depression in elders, and to argue for the importance of careful assessment of elders' affective status in future experimental and clinical memory research. In addition, our research group reviewed and critiqued selected interviewer-administered assessment procedures for diagnosis of depression and measurement of its severity. Six of the most prevalent interview methods were included. Others that deserve mention have had to be omitted because of space limitations (e.g., observational rating scales developed by Raskin & Crook to distinguish depression from dementia in elders; see Raskin & Rae, 1981, for discussion).

Our research group recommends the use of the SADS/RDC approach, supplemented by several additional measures (as noted earlier) to round out one's information base. Although this is an expensive investment in terms of training time and interviewer salary, we believe that the quality of the data obtained will offset the cost factor. In addition, we recommend consideration of the LIFE interview for information about the longitudinal course of depression, particularly if one's research design calls for repeated assessment over time. Although each of the other interviews reviewed has a number of strengths and may be more appropriate for use in a given study, we think that, in general, the SADS/RDC approach will be preferable.

For use in settings in which time and financial considerations preclude use of the SADS/RDC approach, we can suggest two alternative procedures that should yield reliable (though less fine-grained) information about depressive syndromes. First, we have observed excellent correspondence between the diagnosis of major depressive disorder and the use of specific cutoff scores on the Beck Depression Inventory (BDI) (Beck, Ward, Mendelson, Mock, & Erbaugh, 1961). The BDI is a widely used self-report measure for assessment of depressive symptoms (see Gallagher, Breckenridge, Steinmetz, & Thompson, 1983, for concordance between BDI scores and certain RDC diagnoses). This is important clinically; it suggests that the BDI can be administered as a screening measure and then patients selected for a more time-consuming interview when it is important to clarify the nature (and possibly the duration and subtype) of the depressive disorder. Second, one could construct a clinical interview, based on SADS questions, that would be comprehensive in terms of gathering all necessary information but could be shorter in that questions not likely to apply to an individual patient could be omitted. For example, questions pertaining to duration and those needed to establish specific DSM-III or RDC diagnoses could be the focus of the interview, and questions could be omitted that pertained to alcohol use, anxiety, and so forth. Although neither of these methods is perfect, each may prove to be an adequate substitute when practical concerns require it.

In conclusion, it is hoped that this chapter will help to significantly increase interaction between clinical and cognitive psychologists, who can really enrich each other's work only after such rapprochement exists.

References

American Psychiatric Association. (1980). *Diagnostic and statistical manual of mental disorders* (3rd ed.). Washington, DC: Author.

Avorn, J., Everitt, D., & Weiss, S. (1986). Increased antidepressant use in patients prescribed beta blockers. *Journal of the American Medical Association, 225*(3), 357–360.

Beck, A. T., Ward, C. H., Mendelson, M., Mock, J. E., & Erbaugh, J. (1961). An inventory for measuring depression. *Archives of General Psychiatry, 4,* 561–571.

Blazer, D. (1980). The diagnosis of depression in the elderly. *Journal of the American Geriatrics Society, 28,* 52–58.

Blazer, D., & Williams, C. D. (1980). Epidemiology of dysphoria and depression in an elderly population. *American Journal of Psychiatry, 137,* 439–444.

Breckenridge, J., Gallagher, D., Thompson, L. W., & Peterson, J. (1986). Characteristic depressive symptoms of bereaved elders. *Journal of Gerontology, 41,* 163–168.

Butler, R. N., & Lewis, M. I. (1982). *Aging and mental health* (3rd ed.). St. Louis, MO: Mosby.

Carroll, B. J., Fielding, J. M., & Blashki, T. G. (1973). Depression rating scales: A critical review. *Archives of General Psychiatry, 28,* 361–366.

Dement, W. C., Miles, L. E., & Carskadon, M. A. (1982). The white paper on sleep and aging. *Journal of the American Geriatrics Society, 30,* 26–50.

Dessonville, C., Gallagher, D., Thompson, L., Finnell, K., & Lewinsohn, P. M. (1982). Relation of age and health status to depressive symptoms in normal and depressed older adults. *Essence, 5,* 99–117.

Duke University Center for the Study of Aging. (1978). *Multidimensional Functional Assessment: The OARS methodology* (2nd ed.). Durham, NC: Duke University Press.

Endicott, J., & Spitzer, R. L. (1978). A diagnostic interview: The Schedule for Affective Disorders and Schizophrenia. *Archives of General Psychiatry, 35,* 837–844.

Fillenbaum, G. G. (1978). Validity and reliability of the Multidimensional Functional Assessment Questionnaire. In Duke University Center for the Study of Aging, *Multidimensional Functional Assessment: The OARS methodology* (2nd ed.). Durham, NC: Author.

Gaitz, C. M. (1977). Depression in the elderly. In W. Fann, I. Karacan, A. Pokorny, & R. Williams (Eds.), *Phenomenology and treatment of depression.* New York: Spectrum.

Gallagher, D., Breckenridge, J., Steinmetz, J., & Thompson, L. (1983). The Beck Depression Inventory and Research Diagnostic Criteria: Congruence in an older population. *Journal of Consulting and Clinical Psychology, 51,* 945–946.

Gallagher, D., Slife, B., Rose, T., & Okarma, T. (1982). Psychological correlates of immunologic disease in older adults. *Clinical Gerontologist, 1,* 51–58.

Gallagher, D., & Thompson, L. W. (1983). Depression. In P. Lewinsohn & L. Teri (Eds.), *Clinical geropsychology.* New York: Pergamon Press.

Golden, R., Teresi, J., & Gurland, B. J. (1984). Development of indicator scales for the Comprehensive Assessment and Referral Evaluation (CARE) interview schedule. *Journal of Gerontology, 39,* 138–146.

Gurland, B. J., Dean, L. L., Copeland, J., Gurland, R., & Golden, R. (1982). Criteria for diagnosis of dementia in the community elderly. *The Gerontologist, 22,* 180–186.

Gurland, B., Golden, R., & Challop, J. (1982). Unidimensional and multidimensional approaches to the differentiation of depression and dementia in the elderly. In S. Corkin, K. L. Davis, J. H. Growdon, E. Usdin, &

R. J. Wurtman (Eds.), *Alzheimer's disease: A report of progress in research (pp. 119–125)*. New York: Raven Press.

Gurland, B. J., Golden, R., Teresi, J., & Challop, J. (1984). The SHORT-CARE: An efficient instrument for the assessment of depression, dementia and disability. *Journal of Gerontology, 39,* 166–169.

Gurland, B., Kuriansky, J., Sharpe, L., Simon, R., Stiller, P., & Birkett, P. (1977). The Comprehensive Assessment and Referral Evaluation (CARE)—Rationale, development and reliability. *International Journal of Aging and Human Development, 8,* 9–42.

Gurland, B. J., & Wilder, D. E. (1984). The CARE interview revisited: Development of an efficient, systematic clinical assessment. *Journal of Gerontology, 39,* 129–137.

Hamilton, M. (1960). A rating scale for depression. *Journal of Neurology, Neurosurgery, and Psychiatry, 23,* 56–62.

Hamilton, M. (1967). Development of a rating scale for primary depressive illness. *British Journal of Social and Clinical Psychology, 6,* 278–296.

Kahn, R., Zarit, S., Hilbert, N., & Niederehe, G. (1975). Memory complaints and impairment in the aged. *Archives of General Psychiatry, 32,* 1569–1573.

Kane, R. A., & Kane, R. L. (1981). *Assessing the elderly: A practical guide to measurement.* Lexington, MA: Lexington Books.

Keller, M. B., & Shapiro, R. (1981). Major depressive disorder: Initial results from a one-year prospective naturalistic follow-up study. *Journal of Nervous and Mental Disease, 169,* 761–768.

Kochansky, G. E. (1979). Psychiatric rating scales for assessing psychopathology in the elderly: A critical review. In A. Raskin & L. F. Jarvik (Eds.), *Psychiatric symptoms and cognitive loss in the elderly (pp. 125–156).* Washington, DC: Hemisphere.

Mayer, J. M. (1978). Assessment of depression. In P. McReynolds (Ed.), *Advances in psychological assessment* (Vol. 4). San Francisco: Jossey-Bass.

McNair, D. M. (1979). Self-rating scales for assessing psychopathology in the elderly. In A. Raskin & L. F. Jarvik (Eds.), *Psychiatric symptoms and cognitive loss in the elderly.* Washington, DC: Hemisphere.

Miller, W. (1975). Psychological deficit in depression. *Psychological Bulletin, 82,* 238–260.

National Institute of Mental Health. (1979). *The Diagnostic Interview Schedule.* Washington, DC: National Institute of Mental Health, Center for Epidemiological Studies.

Popkin, S., Gallagher, D., Thompson, L. W., & Moore, M. (1982). Memory complaint and performance in normal and depressed older adults. *Experimental Aging Research, 8,* 141–145.

Raskin, A., & Rae, D. S. (1981). Psychiatric symptoms in the elderly. *Psychopharmacology Bulletin, 17,* 96–99.

Robins, L. N., Helzer, J. E., Croughan, J., & Ratcliff, K. S. (1981). National Institute of Mental Health Diagnostic Interview Schedule: Its history, characteristics, and validity. *Archives of General Psychiatry, 38,* 381–389.

Salzman, C., & Shader, R. I. (1979). Clinical evaluation of depression in the elderly. In A. Raskin & L. F. Jarvik (Eds.), *Psychiatric symptoms and cognitive loss in the elderly.* Washington, DC: Hemisphere.

Schwab, J. J., Bialow, M., Holzer, C. E., Brown, J. M., & Stevenson, B. E. (1967). Sociocultural aspects of depression in medical inpatients. *Archives of General Psychiatry, 17,* 533–536.

Shapiro, R. W., & Keller, M. B. (1979). *Longitudinal Interval Follow-up Evaluation (LIFE).* Boston: Massachusetts General Hospital.

Shapiro, R., & Keller, M. B. (1981). Initial 6-month follow-up of patients with major depressive disorder. *Journal of Affective Disorders, 3,* 205–220.

Spitzer, R. L., & Endicott, J. (1978). *NIMH Clinical Research Branch Collaborative Program on the Psychobiology of Depression: Schedule for Affective Disorders and Schizophrenia (SADS).* New York: New York State Psychiatric Institute, Biometrics Research Division.

Spitzer, R. L., Endicott, J., & Robins, E. (1978). Research Diagnostic Criteria: Rationale and reliability. *Archives of General Psychiatry, 35,* 773–782.

Sotsky, S., & Glass, D. (1982). *Guidelines to the Hamilton Depression Rating Scale.* Unpublished manuscript, George Washington University, Washington, DC.

Teresi, J., Golden, R., & Gurland, B. J. (1984). Concurrent and predictive validity of indicator scales developed for the Comprehensive Assessment and Referral Evaluation Interview Schedule. *Journal of Gerontology, 39,* 158–167.

Teresi, J., Golden, R., Gurland, B. J., Wilder, D., & Bennett, R. (1984). Construct validity of indicator scales developed from the Comprehensive Assessment and Referral Evaluation interview schedule *Journal of Gerontology, 39,* 147–157.

Yesavage, J., Brink, T., Rose, T., Lum, O., Huang, O., Adey, V., & Leirer, V. (1983). Development and validation of a geriatric depression screening scale: A preliminary report. *Journal of Psychiatric Research, 17,* 37–49.

Zarit, S., Gallagher, D., & Kramer, N. (1981). Memory training in the community aged: Effects on depression, memory complaint, and memory performance. *Educational Gerontology, 6,* 11–27.

Jerome A. Yesavage

CHAPTER

21

The Use of Self-Rating Depression Scales in the Elderly

Although a number of self-rating depression scales already exist, they have typically been developed and validated in younger populations, and hence, their applicability with older persons has yet to be demonstrated. This chapter will discuss several established self-rating scales that have been used in research with elderly patients, as well as a new scale that was designed specifically to assess the level of depression in elderly samples.

This chapter is intended as a complement to the one by Gallagher (chapter 20, this volume), which discusses interview approaches to the assessment of depression in the elderly. Many of the problems and issues in assessing elderly patients raised in that chapter are directly applicable to the self-assessment of depression. In particular, a major problem is the confusion of dementia with depression in the elderly. The syndrome of "pseudodementia"—depression with psychomotor retardation—is often mistaken for dementia (Jarvik, 1976; Wells, 1979). Furthermore, depression in the elderly often is accompanied by subjective experiences of memory loss and cognitive impairment (Kahn, Zarit, Hilbert, & Niederehe, 1975). Conversely, somatic symptoms, which are usually a key to diagnosis of depression in the young, are of less diagnostic help in the elderly. For instance, sleep disturbances are a common symptom of endogenous depression; but sleep disturbances are also common in the elderly in general (Coleman et al., 1981), occurring rarely in younger persons not suffering from depression.

Another problem in the assessment of any disorder experienced by the aged, including depression, is that the elderly are typically more resistant to psychiatric evaluation than are younger patients (Salzman & Shader, 1978; Wells, 1979). Consequently, one needs to design the items composing a scale to fit this population; questions appropriate for use with the young may

not be appropriate for the old. For example, questions about sexuality often make the elderly defensive, and yet they are included on many existing scales. Other questions may pose problems of patient acceptance as well as leading to problems of interpretation (Blumenthal, 1975). For example, questions about suicidal intent, whether life is worth living, or whether one is hopeful about the future may be viewed differently and reflect different motives or concerns among elderly persons who are reaching the end of their lifetimes and who may have serious medical illnesses than among younger individuals who are not yet dealing with these or similar issues. A final problem is that several of the self-rating scales currently available may be too difficult for the elderly to complete by themselves. Before turning to the development of a new scale designed to meet some of these problems, I shall briefly review several existing depression scales.

Established Rating Scales for Depression

Numerous depression rating scales are currently available. They have been subject to several reviews (Carroll, Fielding, & Blashki, 1973; Hedlund & Vieweg, 1979; Kochansky, 1979; McNair, 1979) and include such measures as the Zung Self-Rating Depression Scale (SDS) (Zung, 1965), Phenomena of Depression Scale (Grinker, Miller, Sabahin, Nunn, & Nunnally, 1961), Beck Depression Inventory (BDI) (Beck, Ward, Mendelson, Mock, & Erbaugh, 1961), Grading Scale for Depressive Reactions (Cutler & Kurland, 1961), Psychiatric Judgment of Depression Scale (Overall, Houister, Pokorny, Casey, & Katz, 1962), SAD-GLAD (Simpson, Hackett, & Kline, 1966), Verdun Depression

213

Rating Scale (Lehmann & Ban, 1975), NIMH Collaborative Depression Scale (GDS) (Raskin, 1965), Center for Epidemiologic Studies-Depression Scale (CES-D) (Radloff, 1977), Symptom Check List-90 (SCL-90) (Derogatis, 1977), Profile of Mood States (POMS) (McNair, Lorr, & Droppleman, 1971), and the MMPI-Depression Scale (Harmatz & Shader, 1973). This chapter focuses on selected self-rating instruments and attempts to cover material published since the last comprehensive review in 1979.

Zung Self-Rating Depression Scale

This scale is one of the most widely used self-rating measures. Although it has a reliable factor structure across studies, reliability has been questioned in its use with individuals above the age of 70 (McGarvey, Gallagher, Thompson, & Zelinski, 1982). In another attempt to validate the SDS in the aged, the ability of the SDS to discriminate nondepressed from depressed elderly was found to be limited (Zung & Green, 1973). Zung suggested using a classification criterion of 40 for depression; although this would correctly identify 88% of depressives, it would lead to the false identification of normal elderly as being depressed in 44% of the cases. Other comprehensive reviews suggest that there are still no better criteria that would reduce the number of false positives associated with the SDS (Carroll, 1978; Carroll et al., 1973). Thus, although this represents the best validation efforts in this population to date, the SDS still has limitations as a geriatric depression rating scale.

Carroll Rating Scale for Depression

This scale was designed to be a one-to-one transformation of the Hamilton Rating Scale for Depression (HRS-D, Hamilton, 1967) to a self-rating format (Carroll, Fieberg, Greden, Tarika, & Albala, 1981). In younger populations it has been shown to be highly correlated with the HRS-D ($r = .75$) and the BDI ($r = .86$). The disadvantages of the scale are that, like the HRS-D, it is highly loaded with somatic items that may lead to false positives in the elderly. No validity studies have yet been completed with elderly samples.

Beck Depression Inventory

The BDI (Beck et al., 1961) has recently been studied for validity and reliability in the elderly (Gallagher, Nies, & Thompson, 1982; Gallagher, Breckenridge, Steinmetz, & Thompson, 1983). Unlike the SDS, the BDI rates the intensity rather than the frequency of symptoms, which may be an advantage if intensity distinctions are easier for the elderly. However, it still requires a 4-point discrimination and includes items that may be misleading. For example, the most intense scoring for crying spells, which describes having cried so much that one has stopped, may be misinterpreted

to mean that one has no crying tendency at all. Furthermore, some elderly people may balk at the question on sexuality, thereby producing a scoring problem for the clinician or researcher. Nonetheless, the BDI has been carefully validated in the elderly and has been found to misclassify only 16% of subjects in relation to Research Diagnostic Criteria (RDC) (Gallagher et al., 1983).

Center for Epidemiologic Studies-Depression

This is a simple 20-item scale originally designed for epidemiological studies. Unfortunately, like the SDS, it requires a frequency estimation. Several of the items appear to relate to "morale" rather than to depression. Correlation between the CES-D and the HRS-D in younger patients on admission was found to be only .44 (Radloff, 1977). This may be because somatic complaints are not emphasized in the CES-D. Yet, just for this reason, validity and reliability might be better in the elderly. To date, such data have not been gathered.

Brief Symptom Inventory (BSI)

The BSI (Derogatis & Spencer, 1983) is an abbreviated version of the SCL-90 (Derogatis, 1977). According to Derogatis and Spencer, correlations between the two range from .92 to .99. The BSI, like the SCL-90, measures psychopathology along nine dimensions, including depression. The 53-item scale takes about 20 minutes to administer, and all items are suitable for the elderly. Norms are available for older persons grouped by sex (Hale, Cochran, & Hedgepeth, 1984). Internal consistency is adequate, ranging from alpha = .77 on the Interpersonal Sensitivity scale to alpha = .91 on the Depression scale (Pearson & Gatz, 1982). Because the BSI has a somatization scale, the depression scale is relatively free of somatic items. Although few research studies have reported using the BSI with the elderly, it appears sound psychometrically and will likely be included in clinical research studies with greater regularity in the future.

POMS and MMPI-D

Earlier reviews have examined the Profile of Mood States and the MMPI-Depression Scale (McNair, 1979). The POMS covers six mood items, including depression. It is reported to be sensitive to drug treatment in the elderly. McNair also noted that there are substantial differences according to age on the MMPI and that, therefore, further studies are needed on its reliability and validity with the elderly before it is used in research settings. It appears that no additional work has been completed on these scales since the 1979 reviews and that no prior reviews or validation work was done on the use of analog scales in the elderly, although data exist that suggest that such scales may have considerable utility in younger populations (Bond & Lader, 1974).

A New Scale: The Geriatric Depression Scale (GDS)

Two studies were conducted in the process of developing and validating the GDS and are described in detail elsewhere (Brink et al., 1982; Yesavage et al., 1983). Briefly, in the first study, a team of researchers and clinicians who were involved in geriatric psychiatry and gerontology selected 100 widely varied yes/no questions that were hoped to have potential for distinguishing elderly normal subjects from elderly depressed subjects. The 30 "best" questions were selected for final inclusion in the scale on the rationale that if the 100-item scale had prima facie validity for rating depression, those items that correlated best with the total score would be the best items to include in the final scale. Although 12 of the 100 original items assessed somatic complaints (e.g., sleep disturbance, weight loss, and gastrointestinal symptoms), none of these were among the 30 items that correlated best with the total score. Hence, these items were excluded from the final scale, because they did not meet the purely empirical criterion adopted as a basis for an item's inclusion.

In the second study, the 30 selected questions were readministered to a new sample of subjects and were validated against an independent criterion of depression. Because the latter study included the SDS and the HRS-D, it provided a basis for comparing properties of the GDS with these other existing measures of depression. Two groups of geriatric subjects were chosen for the validation phase. The first group ($n = 40$) consisted of normal community-residing elderly persons. These subjects had no histories of mental illness. The second group ($n = 60$) was composed of patients complaining of depression. It was decided to divide the group of clinically depressed subjects into "mild" and "severe" groups on the basis of whether or not they met Research Diagnostic Criteria (RDC) for major affective disorder (depressed) (Spitzer, Endicott, & Robins, 1978). On the basis of RDC criteria, it was possible to separate the depressed subjects into a "mild" group ($n = 26$), having an average of 3.4 RDC symptoms, and a "severe" group ($n = 34$), with an average of 5.9 RDC criteria symptoms. Statistical analyses in this study found evidence for the validity of each of these depression scales.

The correlation of each of the depression scales with the classification variable derived from these criteria was computed. Then, following Ferguson (1971, pp. 171–172), the magnitude of each correlation was compared with the other two. The obtained correlations between the classification variable and the GDS, SDS, and HRS-D were $r = .82$, $r = .69$, and $r = .83$, respectively. All of these represented statistically reliable correlations (all $p < .001$).

Information regarding the sensitivity (correctly classified depressed subjects) and specificity (correctly classified normal subjects) of the GDS indicates that among elderly persons drawn from the same centers as those used in the present study, a cutoff score of 11 on the GDS yielded an 84% sensitivity rate and a 95%

specificity rate. A more stringent cutoff score of 14 yielded a slightly lower 80% sensitivity rate but resulted in no nondepressed persons being incorrectly classified as depressed—that is, a 100% specificity rate. On the basis of these findings, the authors suggested that a score of 0 to 10 be viewed as within the normal range and 11 or greater as a possible indicator of depression. Criteria for the SDS and the HRS-D were also considered: scores of 46 and 11, respectively. A score of 46 on the SDS achieved 80% sensitivity and 85% specificity, whereas a score of 11 on the HRS-D achieved 86% sensitivity and 80% specificity. The three scales, however, are best compared by holding either sensitivity or specificity constant while comparing the scales in terms of the other index. Thus, holding specificity constant at 80%, the sensitivity of the GDS, the SDS, and the HRS-D were found to be 90%, 82%, and 86%, respectively.

A geriatric depression scale, however, should not only be applicable for screening depression in the physically healthy but should also be applicable for use with the physically ill, the cognitively impaired, and other select populations in which the aged are more heavily represented. A study by Gallagher et al. (1983) found that the GDS differentiated depressed from nondepressed elderly subjects, even though all of the subjects were suffering from physical illness. Furthermore, in an ongoing study by the same group, the GDS was found to differentiate depressed demented from nondepressed demented elderly subjects. These subjects ($n = 43$) were classified as demented by criteria of Folstein's Mini-Mental Status Exam (Folstein, Folstein, & McHugh, 1975). It was found that the subjects categorized as depressed by a therapist who was unaware of the GDS scores received a mean score of 14.72 (SD = 6.13) on the GDS versus a mean of only 7.49 (SD = 4.26) for nondepressed subjects (t [41] = 4.4; $p < .001$).

No evidence has been generated to indicate that the GDS is sensitive to drug treatment for depression. The GDS has, however, been used as a screening device in studies of alcoholics at the Veterans Administration Medical Center in Palo Alto, California, and has shown significant improvement of depression in alcoholics undergoing treatment. A 15-item version of the scale (see Table 21-1) has been validated (Sheikh & Yesavage, 1986). Current studies are testing its sensitivity to psychological and pharmacological treatments for depression in the elderly (Michiko, personal communication).

Conclusions

Ultimately, researchers can compare the scales best not only by focusing on their performance in current research but by considering practical aspects of their performance as well. In this regard, the GDS would appear to be a desirable scale for use as a screening device with elderly individuals. It was developed and specifically tailored for use with the elderly, and questions that might increase the defensiveness of subjects

Table 21-1. Geriatric Depression Scale (Short Form)

Choose the Best Answer for How You Felt
Over the Past Week

1. Are you basically satisfied with your life? . . . . . yes / no
2. Have you dropped many of your activities and interests? . . . . yes / no
3. Do you feel that your life is empty? . . . . yes / no
4. Do you often get bored? . . . . yes / no
5. Are you in good spirits most of the time? . . . . . . yes / no
6. Are you afraid that something bad is going to happen to you? . . . . yes / no
7. Do you feel happy most of the time? . . . . yes / no
8. Do you often feel helpless? . . . . yes / no
9. Do you prefer to stay at home, rather than going out and doing new things? . . . . yes / no
10. Do you feel you have more problems with memory than most? . . . . yes / no
11. Do you think it is wonderful to be alive now? . . . . yes / no
12. Do you feel pretty worthless the way you are now? . . . . yes / no
13. Do you feel full of energy? . . . . yes / no
14. Do you feel that your situation is hopeless? . . . yes / no
15. Do you think that most people are better off than you are? . . . . yes / no

The following answers count one point;
scores > 5 indicate probable depression:

1. NO	6. YES	11. NO
2. YES	7. NO	12. YES
3. YES	8. YES	13. NO
4. YES	9. YES	14. YES
5. NO	10. YES	15. YES

Note. Reprinted from Sheikh and Yesavage (1986) by permission.

or otherwise reduce cooperation and rapport were avoided. In addition, the yes/no format provides a simple task for elderly subjects (the GDS has never taken over 10 minutes in over 400 administrations).

It also appears that some of the self-rating depression scales that were originally developed for younger populations are also valid in the elderly. Unfortunately, no studies have directly compared all of these scales in the same population, a comparison that would illuminate the relative merits of each metric. Final choices about the most appropriate self-rating depression scales for use with the elderly should await the collection of such data.

References

Beck, A. T., Ward, C., Mendelson, M., Mock, J., & Erbaugh, J. (1961). An inventory for measuring depression. *Archives of General Psychiatry, 4,* 561–571.

Blumenthal, M. D. (1975). Measuring depressive symptomatology in a general population. *Archives of General Psychiatry, 32,* 971–978.

Bond, A., & Lader, M. (1974). The youth analog scales in rating subjective feelings. *British Journal of Medical Psychology, 47,* 211–218.

Brink, T. A., Yesavage, J. A., Lum, O., Heersema, P., Adey, V., & Rose, T. L. (1982). Screening tests for geriatric depression. *Clinical Gerontologist, 1,* 37–44.

Carroll, B. J. (1978). Validity of the Zung self-rating scale. Letter to the editor. *British Journal of Psychiatry, 133,* 379.

Carroll, B. J., Fieberg, M., Greden, F., Tarika, J., & Albala, A. A. (1981). A specific laboratory test for the diagnosis of melancholia. *Archives of General Psychology, 38,* 18–23.

Carroll, B. J., Fielding, J. M., & Blashki, T. G. (1973). Depression rating scales: A critical review. *Archives of General Psychiatry, 28,* 361–366.

Coleman, R. H., Miles, L. E., Guilleminault, C., Zarcone, V. P., van den Hoed, J., & Dement, W. C. (1981). Sleep–wake disorders in the elderly: A polysomnographic analysis. *Journal of the American Geriatric Society, 29,* 289–296.

Cutler, R. P., & Kurland, H. D. (1961). Clinical quantification of depressive reactions. *Archives of General Psychiatry, 5,* 280–285.

Derogatis, L. R. (1977). *The SCL-90 manual I: Scoring, administration and procedures for the SCL-90.* Baltimore, MD: Johns Hopkins University School of Medicine, Clinical Psychometrics Unit.

Derogatis, L. R., & Spencer, P. M. (1983). *BSI manual I: Administration and procedures.* Baltimore, MD: Johns Hopkins University School of Medicine, Clinical Psychometrics Unit.

Ferguson, G. A. (1971). *Statistical analysis in psychology and education,* (3rd ed.). New York: McGraw-Hill.

Folstein, M. F., Folstein, S. E., & McHugh, P. R. (1975). Mini-Mental State: A practical method for grading the cognitive state of patients for the clinician. *Journal of Psychiatry Research, 12,* 189–198.

Gallagher, D., Breckenridge, J., Steinmetz, J., & Thompson, L. W. (1983). The Beck Depression Inventory and Research Diagnostic Criteria: Congruence in an older population. *Journal of Consulting and Clinical Psychology, 51,* 945–946.

Gallagher, D., Nies, G., & Thompson, L. W. (1982). Reliability of the Beck Depression Inventory with older adults. *Journal of Consulting and Clinical Psychology, 50,* 152–153.

Grinker, R. R., Sr., Miller, J., Sabahin, M., Nunn, R., & Nunnally, J. C. (1961). *The phenomena of depressions.* New York: Hoeber.

Hale, W. D., Cochran, C. D., & Hedgepeth, B. E. (1984). Norms for the elderly on the Brief Symptom Inventory. *Journal of Consulting and Clinical Psychology, 52,* 321–322.

Hamilton, M. (1967). Development of a rating scale for primary depressive illness. *British Journal of Social and Clinical Psychology, 6,* 278–296.

Harmatz, J. S., & Shader, R. I. (1975). Psychopharmacologic investigations in healthy elderly volunteers: MMPI-Depression Scale. *Journal of the American Geriatrics Society, 23,* 350–354.

Hedlund, J. L., & Vieweg, B. W. (1979). The Zung Self-Rating Depression Scale: A comprehensive review. *Journal of Operational Psychiatry, 10,* 51–64.

Jarvik, L. F. (1976). Aging and depression: Some unanswered questions. *Journal of Gerontology, 31,* 324–326.

Kahn, R. L., Zarit, S. H., Hilbert, N. M., & Niederehe, G. (1975). Memory complaint and impairment in the aged: The effect of depression and altered brain function. *Archives of General Psychiatry, 32,* 1569–1573.

Kochansky, G. E. (1979). Psychiatric rating scales for assessing psychopathology in the elderly: A critical review. In A.

Raskin & L. F. Jarvik (Eds.), *Psychiatric symptoms and cognitive loss in the elderly* (pp. 125–156). New York: Wiley.

Lehmann, H. E., & Ban, T. A. (1975). Central nervous system stimulants and anabolic substances in geropsychiatric therapy. In S. Gershon & A. Raskin (Eds.), *Aging* (Vol. 2). New York: Raven Press.

McGarvey, B., Gallagher, D., Thompson, L. W., & Zelinski, E. (1982). Reliability and factor structure of the Zung Self-Rating Depression Scale in three age groups. *Essence, 5,* 141–151.

McNair, D. M. (1979). Self-rating scales for assessing psychopathology in the elderly. In A. Raskin & L. F. Jarvik (Eds.), *Psychiatric symptoms and cognitive loss in the elderly: Evaluation and assessment techniques.* (pp. 157–167). Washington, DC: Winston.

McNair, D. M., Lorr, M., & Droppleman, L. F. (1971). *Psychiatric Outpatient Mood Scale* (revised). Boston: Boston University Medical Center, Psychopharmacology Laboratory.

Overall, J. E., Houister, L. E., Pokorny, A. D., Casey, J. F., & Katz, G. (1962). Drug therapy in depressions: Controlled evaluation of imipramine, isocarboxazid, dextroamphetamine amobarbital, and placebo. *Clinical Pharmacological Therapeutics, 3,* 16–22.

Pearson, C., & Gatz, M. (1982). Health and mental health in older adults: First steps in the study of a pedestrian complaint. *Rehabilitation Psychology, 27,* 37–50.

Radloff, L. S. (1977). A self-report depression scale for research in the general population. *Applied Psychological Measurement, 3,* 385–401.

Raskin, A. (1965). *NIMH Collaborative Depression Mood Scale.* Rockville, MD: National Institute of Mental Health.

Salzman, C., & Shader, R. I. (1978). Depression in the elderly: Relationship between depression, psychologic defense mechanisms and physical illness. *Journal of the American Geriatric Society, 26,* 253–259.

Sheikh, J. I., & Yesavage, J. A. (1986). Geriatric Depression Scale (GDS): Recent evidence and development of a shorter version. In T. L. Brink (Ed.), Clinical gerontology: A guide to assessment and intervention (pp. 165–173). New York: Haworth Press.

Simpson, G. M., Hackett, E., & Kline, N. S. (1966). Difficulties in systematic rating of depression during outpatient drug treatment. *Canadian Psychiatric Association Journal, 1*(Suppl.), 116–122.

Spitzer, R., Endicott, J., & Robins, E. (1978). Research Diagnostic Criteria: Rationale and reliability. *Archives of General Psychiatry, 35,* 773–782.

Wells, C. E. (1979). Pseudodementia. *American Journal of Psychiatry, 136,* 895–900.

Yesavage, J., Brink, T., Rose, T., Lum, O., Huang, O., Adey, V., & Leirer, V. (1983). Development and validation of a geriatric depression screening scale: A preliminary report. *Journal of Psychiatric Research, 17,* 37–49.

Zung, W. W. K. (1965). A self-rating depression scale. *Archives of General Psychiatry, 12,* 63–70.

Zung, W. W. K., & Green, R. L., Jr. (1973). Detection of affective disorders in the aged. In C. Eisdorfer & W. E. Fann (Eds.), *Psychopharmacology and aging* (pp. 213–223). New York: Plenum Press.

Herbert Weingartner

Automatic and Effort-Demanding Cognitive Processes in Depression

This review provides a sketch of the determinants of cognitive impairments evident in depression. The ways in which depressed patients express difficulties in learning, memory, and related cognitive functions are compared with cognitive dysfunctions seen in other types of patients. A framework for the analysis of cognitive dysfunctions is presented and then used to characterize cognitive failures. The features of this approach are built on the following propositions: (a) Cognitive processes may fail because of dysfunctions in different types of processes; (b) each of these processes is linked to changes in distinct but overlapping psychobiological systems; and (c) these cognitive processes include episodic memory, knowledge memory, effort-demanding cognitive processes, automatic cognitive operations, and reward- or reinforcement-related cognitive behaviors. Cognitive impairments in depression appear to be determined by effort-demanding cognitive processes that are linked to alterations in the reward–reinforcement system of the brain.

A great deal has been learned about the cognitive, affective, and biological events that are associated with the experience of being depressed. Nevertheless, the psychobiology of depression remains poorly understood. To obtain a clear picture of cognitive processes in depression, researchers must be able to design studies that will allow them to map distinct cognitive and affective behaviors onto definable biological systems.

This chapter first examines issues pertinent to understanding cognitive changes in depression. Unresolved research problems that limit the value of currently available findings are discussed. Next follows a brief summary of some of the well-established empirical findings and theoretical explanations that have been used to describe cognitive changes in depression. A framework that may serve to integrate many of these findings is then proposed, and data from recent studies are used to test the adequacy of this framework. Other recent findings are presented to contrast

the cognitive dysfunction in depression with cognitive failures associated with other disorders. The analysis emphasizes that cognitive processes requiring effort and cognitive capacity are the ones most severely impaired in depression. Dysfunctions in effort-demanding cognitive operations are mediated by changes in those brain systems that determine motivation and appreciation of and sensitivity to reinforcing events.

Problems in Design and Conceptualization

The general problems that plague many types of clinical research have also been evident in studies of depressed patients. Adequately defining the nature of the sample studied (diagnostic specificity) is a chronically nagging clinical research problem. Whatever is learned about some aspect of cognitive functioning in depression may hold true for only some subgroups of patients. Measurement of mood in relation to some cognitive function, or manipulation of mood in unimpaired subjects and consequent effects on aspects of cognition, may reveal very different types of things about depressive cognition.

Basic problems in measuring depression remain unresolved. The issues transcend the rating scale used or, for example, the relative value of self-rated or observer-rated instruments. Uncertainties remain about how to view the continuity, or discontinuity, of the experience of depression. Are there different types of depression, a series of threshold phenomena, nonlinear mood functions?

Investigators bring to the study of cognitive processes in depression their own "favorite" cognitive theories, models, methods, and procedures, as well as their

218

choices of target cognitive behaviors. If, for example, a researcher is curious about attention, attention is what is studied, often in an isolated fashion, while systems requiring characterization and other types of cognitive and noncognitive behaviors that would also be clinically altered in depression are ignored. Frequently, research has focused on exploring a favored model of how memory might work or, for example, how reinforcing contingencies alter learned behaviors rather than on characterizing depressive cognition.

In contrast, more clinically defined efforts are less concerned with general theory about cognition or reinforcement theory and are directed at understanding depression as a clinical entity. The major problem that has plagued these more obviously clinically defined studies has been that "standard" psychometric tools are used to measure cognitive behaviors even though administered tests do not clearly measure what they purport to measure or, perhaps more to the point, are of questionable ethological value. Procedures that lack both sensitivity and specificity are often applied to measure aspects of cognition. For example, changes in performance as assessed by a memory scale may realistically reflect altered motivation rather than mood-related changes in memory. That is, standardized cognitive psychometric tests may incidentally measure cognition but may, in fact, reflect changes in behaviors outside the cognitive domain.

Although many of the studies outlined in this chapter have provided much useful information about both the qualitative and quantitative features of cognition in depressed patients, the cliché that "much more work needs to be done" is appropriate. Some of the broad questions that remain are as follows: Are there, in fact, different types of cognitive dysfunctions in distinct subgroups of depressed patients? If so, what are their psychobiological features and determinants? What are the links and relationships between dysfunctions in types of cognitive processes and noncognitive behaviors in the depressed patient? How unique or distinct is the expression of impaired cognition in depression compared with other syndromes that also show clear evidence of cognitive dysfunction? How is the cognitive dysfunction in depression altered by different treatments, and what are the implications of treatment-linked changes in cognition for understanding more about the mechanisms that mediate depressed mood?

Patterns of Findings That Describe Cognitive Changes in Depression

Depressed patients provide many clinically relevant clues and cues that their experience of themselves, significant others, and the physical environment is somehow altered. These subjectively experienced cognitive changes are both qualitative and quantitative. Depressed patients' interpretations of their histories and biographical experience are quite different from how they ordinarily view themselves. They also complain of disturbances in concentration, attention, learning, retention, retrieval, conceptualization, and other cognitive operations. Many of these qualitative and quantitative changes in cognition have been documented in laboratory studies. In general, however, these clinical symptoms and empirical findings remain fragmented. In addition, relatively little systematic research has been done to contrast cognitive changes in depressed patients with changes in other patient groups.

With respect to some of the qualitative changes in cognition, it is known that the accuracy and completeness of memory for previously stored information is mood state-dependent (Bower, 1981; Lishman, 1972; Nelson & Craighead, 1977; Teasdale & Fogarty, 1979; Weingartner, Miller, & Murphy, 1977; Weingartner, Murphy, & Stillman, 1978). That is, depressed mood can serve as a type of context that biases how information is encoded and how previously stored events are retrieved from memory. The biological representation of the cognitive context of the depressed mood state is likely to involve systems that modulate motivation and reinforcement. It is not surprising, therefore, that the depressed patient's experience of previous reinforcement history and self-expectations is biased and negative. This context-specific perception of reinforcing contingencies, a sense of the adaptive value of previously acquired skills and knowledge, determines how contemporary events are encoded and incorporated into ongoing biographical experience (Rizley, 1978). A learned-helplessness view of depression is one type of conceptualization of how mood-specific context effects bias the encoding and retrieval of (experience) information (Hiroto, 1974; Maier & Seligman, 1976; Seligman, 1971, 1975; Seligman, Abramson, Semmel, & von Baeyer, 1979). A parallel conceptualization has been defined in terms of perceived competence (Lewinsohn, Mischel, Chaplain, & Barton, 1980) and self-efficacy (Bandura, 1977).

Studies of quantitative cognitive changes in depression have emphasized learning-memory-related functions (primarily episodic memory) and have dealt less with the efficiency of how depressed patients use or manipulate information based on previously acquired knowledge (semantic memory). Every conceivable stage or type of information-processing system has been implicated in determining aspects of learning-memory (cognitive) dysfunction in depression (Miller, 1975). Hypothesized reasons that depressed patients find it difficult to learn and remember have included a generalized cognitive impairment, attentional dysfunctions, encoding problems, rehearsal problems, rapid memory decay, and retrieval difficulties (Breslow, Kocsis, & Belkin, 1981; Cohen, Weingartner, Smallberg, Pickar, & Murphy, 1982; Cronholm & Ottosson, 1961; Friedman, 1964; Henry, Weingartner, & Murphy, 1973; Huesman, 1978; Krantz & Hammen, 1979; Miller & Lewis, 1977; Sternberg & Jarvik, 1976; Weingartner, Cohen, Murphy, Martello, & Gerdt, 1981; Whitehead, 1973). Other mechanisms that have been used to explain cognitive dysfunctions in depression include reduced cognitive channel capacity, alterations in control or decision-making processes, disturbances in motivation, and a conservative response bias (Henry et al., 1973; Miller & Lewis, 1977; Sternberg &

Jarvik, 1976; Whitehead, 1973). Most of these postulated determinants have emerged from well-designed studies, using appropriate procedures that were then used to test moderately depressed patients.

Neuropsychological tests assessing the clarity and logic of the thinking processes also show quantitative changes in the cognition of depressed patients (Savard, Rey, & Post, 1980; Small, Small, Milstein, & Moore, 1972). Neuropsychological studies indicate that depressed patients can often successfully attend to information, remember, and perform logical operations under conditions of low information load, but they cannot effectively coordinate the cognitive functions necessary for solving problems under more demanding processing conditions (Silberman, Weingartner, & Post, 1983).

Findings in Search of a Hypothesis

Many components of cognitive processes appear to be altered in depression. That is, previous studies provide evidence that depressed patients perform more poorly than control subjects on a wide range of tasks that seemingly tap different stages or components of information processing. No single stage or component of information processing appears to account for the cognitive changes in depression. In some studies the impairments in cognitive performance appeared to be correlated with the intensity of depression. Most of the cognitive processes tested in the studies just summarized require subjects to perform on some highly directed task. An examination of the tasks typically used to test depressed patients reveals that they all require operations that demand considerable cognitive capacity; they invariably require concentration and sustained cognitive effort. Sustained cognitive effort is necessary for tasks that challenge attention, short-term memory, list learning, and concept formation. Impairments in cognitive processing may be linked to changes in other types of behavior that are typically seen in depression.

Alterations in motivation, drive, and sensitivity to reinforcing stimuli are central in the manifestation of depression. Learned-helplessness models of depression are built on findings of changes in motivation and reinforcement. Psychologically, the ability to sustain effort would be expected to be linked to conditions that affect motivation. Changes in motivation and, therefore, in effort would be reflected in altered cognitive efficiency, speed of processing, motor slowing, and related behaviors. Support for this view of the interrelationship between cognition and motivation in depression comes from neuroanatomical–neurochemical studies that demonstrate an intimate interrelationship between brain systems that mediate reward–reinforcement and motivation, and networks that mediate and modulate cognition (Esposito, in press; Esposito, Parker, & Weingartner, in press). This research has been built on explorations of brain systems that are involved in self-

stimulation behaviors. Although changes in both cognitive and motivational or hedonic behaviors are present in depression, little research has linked these systems.

The hypothesis proposed here, and the basis of the framework for the analysis of cognitive changes in depression, is as follows: In depression, cognitive changes are evident on effort-demanding, cognitive-capacity-demanding tasks but not under processing conditions that can be accomplished automatically. An effortful, cognitive-capacity-demanding process is one that is sensitive to motivation and reinforcement, set, attention, intention, and alertness and that would alter performance on effort-demanding tasks (Hasher & Zacks, 1979; Kahneman, 1973; Schneider & Shiffrin, 1977). When attention is shared with some other activity in executing an effort-demanding task, performance suffers. Automatic cognitive operations are hypothesized to be far less disrupted in comparison with effort-demanding operations. In contrast, some cognitive behaviors require relatively little sustained effort and can be accomplished almost automatically. Tasks, procedures, and processing conditions that can be accomplished automatically are those that are performed with almost equal effectiveness under incidental processing conditions in contrast to circumstances in which subjects are directed to focus on some task. One type of automatic task may involve executing over-learned habits in which performance is almost error-less. There is now increasing evidence that effort-demanding and automatic processes are determined by somewhat different psychobiological mechanisms.

This broad hypothesis can be readily tested, as demonstrated in the following studies. Depression-related impairments in performance under effort-demanding conditions can be predicted in a wide range of situations, including the acquisition of information, retrieval from memory, motor output, and concept learning. Furthermore, such a relatively specific impairment in effort-demanding processes may be attributable to those neurobiological processes that are known to mediate motivation, drive, self-stimulation, and reward. The following experiments were designed to test these points.

How Do Processing Conditions That Vary in Effort Demands Alter Memory Performance in Depression?

In this experiment, processing conditions were systematically varied and were followed later by tests of memory in 10 hospitalized depressed patients and an equal number of normal control subjects. All patients had been evaluated and diagnosed as depressed on the basis of a standardized research diagnostic evaluation (Endicott & Spitzer, 1978). Intensity of the mood disorder was assessed using a number of validated observer-rated scales as well as self-rating instruments (Bunney & Hamburg, 1963; Guy, 1976). The patients

Table 22-1. Effects of Effort-Demanding and Superficial Processing Conditions on the Acquisition and Recall of Information in Depressed Patients and Normal Controls

| | Number of items recalled | | | |
| | Effort-demanding processes | | Superficial processing conditions | |
	A	B	C	D
Depressed patients	4.0 ± 0.3	10.6 ± 2.3	2.6 ± .3	18.9 ± 2.9
Normal controls	7.1 ± 0.4	16.1 ± 1.9	3.1 ± .4	20.4 ± 2.1

Note. Values presented are means ± standard errors.
A = semantic processing conditions;
B = remembering unrelated words;
C = processing sound properties of words;
D = remembering highly related words.

were at least moderately depressed, with Hamilton ratings of above 20 (see Hamilton, 1960).

On separate occasions subjects were asked to listen to 20 different imageable (concrete) common English words. In response to each word, subjects were asked to respond with a word that was related in meaning to the stimulus (a semantic, effort-demanding, cognitive-processing condition). On another occasion, in response to a different but equivalent set of word stimuli, subjects were required to generate a word that sounded like each stimulus word (an acoustic, superficial, cognitive-processing condition). Twenty minutes after processing words, memory was tested by a free-recall method.

On still another testing occasion, subjects were asked to listen to a set of 20 unrelated common concrete words. Their instructions were to try to organize and relate them to one another (a cognitively demanding condition). One hour later, subjects were asked to recall these same words. In contrast, at another time, subjects were asked to listen to 20 highly related words requiring no organizing schema (e.g., types of vegetables). Again they were asked to relate these words (a superficial, far less effort-demanding cognitive operation). One hour later they were asked to recall these words.

The results of this experiment are presented in Table 22-1. Depressed patients reliably learn and remember less information than normal controls only under effort-demanding processing conditions. Memory for events that have been superficially processed does not distinguish patients from control subjects, nor does recall of highly related, easily encoded information distinguish depressed patients from normal control subjects. The contrast between control subjects and depressed patients, in terms of numbers of items recalled as a function of processing condition, provides support for the hypothesis that effort-demanding cognitive processes affect memory in depression.

How Do Retrieval Conditions That Vary in Effort Demands Alter Memory Performance in Depression?

This experiment was designed to test, in depressed patients, the effect on memory processes of cognitive effort demands made at the time of remembering. A group of 10 depressed patients who were demographically and clinically like those described in Experiment 1 served as subjects. An equal number of normal control subjects were also tested. The processing conditions were similar to those described in Experiment 1. Subjects listened to 30 words and were instructed to respond to each with a word that was semantically related (15 stimuli) or, alternatively, to generate a word that sounded like the stimulus (15 stimuli). Four hours later subjects were either asked to freely remember previously processed words or, alternatively, were provided with their own responses, which in normal volunteers served as strong retrieval cues that substantially aided recall. That is, providing subjects with their own responses would make the retrieved processes far less effort-demanding than a free-recall procedure.

The results from this experiment were similar to those obtained in Experiment 1. When tests of memory were relatively cognitively demanding, memory for events was impaired in depressed patients in comparison with normal control subjects. In contrast, depressed patients were indistinguishable from normal control subjects under less demanding, cued-retrieval conditions. These findings are summarized in Table 22-2.

This procedure was also used in another study, in which a small group ($N = 8$) of depressed patients were tested on two occasions, following administration of placebo and amphetamine (20 mg. administered intravenously). Information was processed 20 minutes prior to placebo and amphetamine administration. Four hours later, subjects' memory was tested using a free and then cued (subjects' associated responses) retrieval condition. Once again, findings showed that memory for words tested under cognitively demanding retrieval conditions (free recall) was reliably and selectively increased under amphetamine treatment conditions.

Table 22-2. Comparisons of Effort-Demanding and Superficial Retrieval Processes for Accessing Memory in Normal Controls and Depressed Patients

	Effort-demanding retrieval conditions: Free recall	Superficial retrieval conditions: Recognition memory
Depressed patients	3.2 ± 0.4	12.2 ± 0.9
Normal controls	9.9 ± 0.5	13.6 ± 1.1

Note. Values presented are means ± standard errors.

Cued recall of words was the same following amphetamine and placebo conditions. The findings are described in greater detail elsewhere (Reus, Silberman, Post, & Weingartner, 1979).

Direct Measures of Sustained Effort, Memory, and Mood in Depression.

This experiment was designed to investigate, somewhat more directly, the relationship between the intensity of depression, cognitive performance, and the ability to sustain effort. Eight hospitalized depressed patients and an equal number of normal volunteers matched for gender, education, and age were studied repeatedly over a period of weeks (a minimum of 4 weeks). Mood, motor effort, and memory were assessed at least twice weekly. Mood was measured prior to each motor and memory testing session using the Hamilton Depression Scale (Hamilton, 1960), the Bunney-Hamburg mood rating scale (Bunney & Hamburg, 1963), the Beck Depression Scale (Beck, 1974), and the Profile of Mood States or POMS (Guy, 1976). Motor effort was measured using a standard hand grip dynamometer for measured grip strength in the left and right hands. Subjects were asked to squeeze the dynamometer as hard as they could alternately with the left hand and the right hand. Then they were asked again to squeeze the hand-held dynamometer but to maintain their grip pressure as long as possible at a level predetermined by the examiner (60% of their peak response). Memory testing followed the evaluation of sustained motor effort using a procedure in which subjects heard different but equivalent 3-letter trigrams and were asked to repeat them after activity-filled delays of 3 to 18 seconds.

The results from this study were as follows: Depressed subjects had difficulty remembering the 3-letter trigrams, particularly after long delays between memory testing and presentation of stimuli. The longer information had to be maintained in memory, the more apparent the memory impairment in depressed patients. The intensity of patients' depressed mood was highly (negatively) correlated with memory performance ($r = -.82$, $p < .01$). The intensity of depressed mood was also highly negatively correlated with sustained motor effort ($r = -.68$, $p < .01$), which in turn was reliably negatively related to memory performance ($r = .72$, $p < .01$). Thus, sustained cognitive effort, sustained motor effort, and severity of depressed mood were highly linked in these patients. The results are presented in more detail elsewhere (Cohen et al., 1982).

In a separate experiment, memory performance and mood were assessed in similarly depressed patients. These patients had also given informed consent to allow collection of a small amount of cerebrospinal fluid (CSF). This permitted an examination of the relationship between levels of neurotransmitter metabolites and learning–memory performance. The level of 3 methoxy-4-hydroxyphenyl glycol (MHPG), the major metabolite of norepinephrine, was reliably related to both cognitive performance and depressed mood ($r = -.86$, $p < .01$). This neurotransmitter system is also the one most likely to fluctuate with changes in effort-demanding behaviors and also may play an important role in determining the expression of motivated, drive-associated behaviors. These findings demonstrate, in various ways, that there is a consistent relationship among the psychology and biology (psychobiology) of sustained effort, cognition, and the mood-state of depressed patients.

When Cognitive Processing Fails Despite Sustained Effort.

A series of studies were designed to examine the determinants and pattern of cognitive impairments in early-stage progressive dementia patients (SDAT). The findings from these studies show that the cognitive changes in SDAT are, in fact, qualitatively different from those seen in other severely memory-impaired, amnestic patients, including patients suffering from depression. This is particularly important, because the cognitive impairments seen in older individuals, and particularly in older depressed individuals, are clinically difficult to distinguish from the impairments associated with an early-stage progressive dementing disease such as SDAT.

The recent-memory failures in patients with progressive dementia of an Alzheimer's type (SDAT) appear to be directly correlated with the patients' inability to access previously acquired knowledge in long-term, or semantic, memory (Weingartner, Grafman, Boutelle, Kaye, & Martin, 1983; Weingartner, Kaye, et al., 1981). This is not the case in severely memory-impaired patients with Korsakoff's syndrome or in depressed patients. When several types of methods and procedures for assessing access to knowledge memory are used, and when sufficient time is provided, depressed patients are effective in retrieving knowledge, rules, and information from long-term memory. Only when a conceptual task requires extensive cognitive effort, either because of time constraints or information load, are cognitive dysfunctions evident in depression (Silberman et al., 1983). Are SDAT patients, like depressed patients, differentially sensitive to effort-demanding cognitive requirements of some task? Would they, like depressed patients, demonstrate relatively better performance on tasks that are less cognitively demanding? These questions regarding effort demands and the relative sensitivity of patients to those demands in memory and learning are discussed in the experiments that follow.

The experiment described here was designed to explore whether SDAT patients, like depressed patients, are more like normal controls under automatic processing conditions than when they are under effort-demanding cognitive conditions. The subjects studied were SDAT patients diagnosed and evaluated on the basis of a series of neurological and neuropsychological evaluations. Their average age was 62 years. Six were women and four were men. Their cognitive characteristics are described elsewhere (Weingartner et. al., 1983). All of these SDAT patients had graduated from college and had functioned in high-level work activities prior to becoming ill. Their Wechsler Memory Scale scores (MQs; Wechsler, 1945) were between 70 and 90, significantly lower than estimates of their expected MQs based on their pre-SDAT intellectual achievement.

This experiment employed a task that is one of the standardized methods for measuring and contrasting automatic and effort-demanding memory processes in unimpaired subjects (Hasher & Zacks, 1979). In this study, patients and age-matched normal control subjects were asked to listen to a list of 32 unrelated common words. These words were read to subjects slowly, every 3 seconds. Each word was presented (repeated) from one to seven times. On one occasion, subjects were asked to remember as many words as possible (an effort-demanding task). On another occasion, after listening to a different but equivalent word list, subjects were asked to judge the frequency with which each word had occurred in the list (automatic processing). That is, subjects were presented with each word at the time of recall and were asked to judge how often that word had appeared in the list that had just been presented to them.

The findings in unimpaired subjects were consistent with those from previously reported studies of younger subjects (Hasher & Zachs, 1979). That is, the probability of recall of any word in unimpaired subjects is a function of its frequency of presentation. In addition, unimpaired subjects are able to monitor the frequency of events so that their judged frequency of that event is sensitive to changes in the event's frequency of occurrence. Frequency monitoring appears to follow a psychophysical relationship, so that judged frequency varies in a linear manner with the log of actual frequency of occurrence. When depressed patients are tested with this same procedure, a similar relationship is observed. That is, despite their poor memory, under effort-demanding conditions depressed patients appear to be able to monitor how often some event occurred. Similarly, Hasher found accurate frequency monitoring in testing somewhat less depressed outpatients. In dramatic contrast, SDAT patients are equally memory-impaired in effort-demanding cognitive operations and in cognitive processing that normally can be accomplished relatively automatically. That is, memory in SDAT patients is not sensitive either to repetition of events—an effort-demanding process—or to frequency of occurrence, an automatic operation. These findings are summarized in Table 22-3.

Comments and Conclusions

The findings reviewed here would suggest that effort-demanding cognitive processes are differentially impaired in depression. In the experiments described, this has been seen both in the processing or acquisition of information and in the retrieval of information from memory. Treatments that lift depression appear to fa-

Table 22-3. Effects of Effort-Demanding and Automatic Processing Conditions on Memory–Learning Processes in SDAT Patients

Subjects	Presentation frequency		
	1–2	3–4	5–7
Effort-demanding processing[1]			
	Proportion of items recalled		
SDAT patients	.08	.10	.14
Normal controls	.43	.53	.68
Automatic processing[2]			
	Frequency judgment		
SDAT patients	1.9	2.1	2.1
Normal controls	1.6	2.9	3.4

[1]Values presented are mean proportions of words recalled.
[2]Values presented are mean frequency judgments.

cilitate memory-learning and related cognitive processes, particularly when processing conditions require effort. Biological systems that are associated with motivation, effort, and arousal also appear to be linked to the performance of effort-demanding cognitive operations in depressed patients. Although explicit or direct tests of selective impairment of effort-demanding processes have not been used in studies of attention, short-term memory, or other stages of the processing system, some of the findings from the studies cited would support the hypothesis of relatively selective impairment in effort-demanding cognitive operations.

It is also clear, however, that other types of cognitive dysfunctions can exhibit a similar selective pattern of dysfunction. It has been proposed recently that much of the cognitive impairment in schizophrenic patients can be accounted for by a selective disturbance in effort-demanding volitional control processes (Gjerde, 1983). Similarly, many types of cognitive processes have been studied in aged subjects, and their performance has been compared with performance in younger subjects. In general, where impairments have been apparent, they are also readily evident on the more demanding types of cognitive tasks (Cerella, Poon, & Williams, 1980). It is also clear, however, that impaired cognition is not necessarily reflected in a selective impairment in effort-demanding processes. In SDAT, memory-learning impairments are equally evident on effort-demanding and automatic processing tasks. Studies of other types of patients have also shown that it is possible to demonstrate unimpaired, effort-demanding, memory-learning processes with a selective disruption of automatic processes. Neuropharmacological studies in unimpaired subjects have also demonstrated selective effects on effort-demanding and automatic types of processes. These findings provide evidence for a double dissociation of automatic and effort-demanding processes, suggesting that these cognitive processes are psychobiologically distinct.

It would be appropriate to at least speculate about how the neurobiology of effort-demanding cognitive processes differs from that of automatic processes, or from accessing and using previously acquired knowledge. Most of the findings that would contribute to such speculation come from psychobiological studies of learning and memory in lower animals, a limited pool of neuropathological findings in humans, and relatively weak neuropharmacological findings. Those findings can be particularly useful when collated and integrated with what is known about cognitive processing in unimpaired and impaired humans. What I believe emerges is that effort-demanding cognitive processes are those that are substantially modulated by brain systems that are extrinsic to those directly involved in the storage and maintenance of memories. This extrinsic system is tied to those brain regions that regulate arousal and activation; these, in turn, are linked to subcortical regions and neurochemical events that regulate the appreciation of reinforcing properties of events (self-stimulation reward systems). The regions involved include limbic system structures, but other systems are also implicated. Neurochemically, the noradrenergic–dopaminergic system probably plays an important role in defining the biology of extrinsic, effort-related cognitive processing. In contrast, the types of cognitive processes that are involved in some automatic operations, particularly those that are engaged in the storage and retrieval of knowledge, are dependent upon neocortical structures. These structures are the ones compromised in SDAT with a consequent disruption in accessing knowledge memory. Neurochemically this system is linked to cholinergic processes. This intrinsic, memory–cognitive system interacts and overlaps with extrinsic, memory–cognitive, neurobiological networks.

Finally, it is clear that to move beyond speculation, models, and fantasy requires a great deal more research. It is also clear, however, that to solve basic problems, which process would help define a psychobiology of cognition, requires that investigators not only look at simple systems at a molecular level but integrate those findings with those that emerge from the study of intact and disordered cognition in humans.

References

Bandura, A. (1977). Self-efficacy: Toward a unifying theory of behavioral change. *Psychological Review, 84*(2), 191–215.

Beck, A. T. (1974). The development of depression: A cognitive model. In R. S. Friedman & M. M. Katz (Eds.), *The psychology of depression: Contemporary theory and research*. New York: Wiley.

Bower, G. H. (1981). Mood and memory. *American Psychologist, 36*, 129–148.

Breslow, R., Kocsis, J., & Belkin, B. (1981). Contribution of the depressive perspective to memory function in depression. *American Journal of Psychiatry, 138*, 227–230.

Bunney, W. E., Jr., & Hamburg, D. A. (1963). Methods for reliable longitudinal observation of behavior. *Archives of General Psychiatry, 9*, 280–294.

Cerella, J., Poon, L. W., & Williams, D. M. (1980). Age and the complexity hypothesis. In L. W. Poon (Ed.), *Aging in the 1980s: Psychological issues* (pp. 332–340). Washington, DC: American Psychological Association.

Cohen, R. M., Weingartner, H., Smallberg, S. A., Pickar, D.,

& Murphy, D. L. (1982). Effort and cognition in depression. *Archives of General Psychiatry, 39*, 593–597.

Cronholm, B., & Ottosson, J. O. (1961). Memory functions in endogenous depression: Before and after electroconvulsive therapy. *Archives of General Psychiatry, 5*, 193–199.

Endicott J., & Spitzer, R. L. (1978). A diagnostic interview: The Schedule for Affective Disorders and Schizophrenia. *Archives of General Psychiatry, 35*, 837–844.

Esposito, R. U. (in press). Cognitive–affective integration: Some recent trends from a neurobiological perspective. In H. Weingartner & E. S. Parker (Eds.), *Memory consolidation*. Hillsdale, NJ: LEA Press.

Esposito, R. U., Parker, E. S., & Weingartner, H. (in press). Enkephalinergic-dopaminergic "reward" pathways: A critical substrate for the stimulatory, euphoric and memory-enhancing actions of alcohol—A hypothesis. *Substance and Alcohol Actions and Misuse.*

Friedman, A. S. (1964). Minimal effects of severe depression on cognitive functioning. *Journal of Abnormal and Social Psychology, 69*, 237–243.

Gjerde, P. F. (1983). Attentional capacity dysfunction and arousal in schizophrenia. *Psychological Bulletin, 93*(1), 57–72.

Guy, W. (1976). *ECDEU assessment manual for psychopharmacology.* (DHEW Publication No. 76–338). Washington, DC: U. S. Department of Health, Education, and Welfare.

Hamilton, M. (1960). A rating scale for depression. *Journal of Neurology, Neurosurgery, and Psychiatry, 23*, 56–62.

Hasher, L., & Zacks, R. T. (1979). Automatic and effortful processes in memory. *Journal of Experimental Psychology: General, 108*, 356–388.

Henry, G. M., Weingartner, H., & Murphy, D. L. (1973). Influence of affective states and psychoactive drugs on verbal learning and memory. *American Journal of Psychiatry, 130*, 966–971.

Hiroto, D. S. (1974). Locus of control and learned helplessness. *Journal of Experimental Psychology, 102*, 187–193.

Huesman, L. R. (1978). Cognitive processes and models of depression. *Journal of Abnormal Psychology, 87*, 194–198.

Kahneman, D. (1973). *Attention and effort.* Englewood, Cliffs, NJ: Prentice-Hall.

Krantz, S., & Hammen, C. (1979). Assessment of cognitive bias in depression. *Journal of Abnormal Psychology, 88*, 611–619.

Lewinsohn, P. M., Mischel, W., Chaplain, W., & Barton, R. (1980). Social competence and depression: The role of illusory self-perceptions? *Journal of Abnormal Psychology, 89*, 203–212.

Lishman, W. A. (1972). Selective factors in memory. *Psychological Medicine, 2*, 248–253.

Maier, S. F., & Seligman, M. E. P. (1976). Learned helplessness: Theory and evidence. *Journal of Experimental Psychology: General, 105*, 3–46.

Miller, E., & Lewis, P. (1977). Recognition memory in elderly patients with depression and dementia: A signal detection analysis. *Journal of Abnormal Psychology, 87*, 84–86.

Miller, W. R. (1975). Psychological deficit in depression. *Psychological Bulletin, 82*, 238–260.

Nelson, R. E., & Craighead, W. E. (1977). Selective recall of positive and negative feedback, self-control behaviors, and depression. *Journal of Abnormal Psychology, 86*, 379–388.

Reus, V. I., Silberman, E., Post, R. M., & Weingartner, H. (1979). d-Amphetamine: Effects on memory in a depressed population. *Biological Psychiatry, 14*, 345–356.

Rizley, R. (1978). Depression and distortion in the attribution of causality. *Journal of Abnormal Psychology, 87*, 32–48.

Savard, R. J., Rey, A. C., & Post, R. M. (1980). Halstead-Reitan category test in bipolar and unipolar affective illness: Relationship to age and phase of illness. *Journal of Nervous and Mental Disease, 168,* 297–304.

Schneider, W., & Shiffrin, R. M. (1977). Controlled and automatic human information processing: I. Detection, search, and attention. *Psychological Review, 84*(1), 1–67.

Seligman, M. E. P. (1971). Depression and learned helplessness. In R. J. Freedman & M. M. Katz (Eds.), *The psychology of depression: Contemporary theory and research.* New York: Wiley.

Seligman, M. E. P. (1975). *Helplessness: On depression, development and death.* San Francisco: Freeman.

Seligman, M. E. P., Abramson, L. Y., Semmel, A., & von Baeyer, C. (1979). Depressive attributional style. *Journal of Abnormal Psychology, 88,* 242–248.

Silberman, E. K., Weingartner, H., & Post, R. M. (1983). Thinking disorder in depression. *Archives of General Psychiatry, 40,* 775–780.

Small, I. F., Small, J. C., Milstein, V., & Moore, J. E. (1972). Neuropsychological observations with psychosis and somatic treatment: Neuropsychological examinations of psychiatric patients. *Journal of Nervous and Mental Disease, 155,* 6–13.

Sternberg, D. E., & Jarvik, M. E. (1976). Memory functions in depression: Improvement with antidepressant medication. *Archives of General Psychiatry, 33,* 219–224.

Teasdale, J. D., & Fogarty, S. J. (1979). Differential effects of induced mood on retrieval of pleasant and unpleasant events from episodic memory. *Journal of Abnormal Psychology, 88,* 248–257.

Wechsler, D. (1945). A Standardized Memory Scale for clinical use. *Journal of Psychology, 19,* 87–95.

Weingartner, H., Cohen, R. M., Murphy, D. L., Martello, J. D. I., & Gerdt, C. (1981). Cognitive processes in depression. *Archives of General Psychiatry, 38,* 42–47.

Weingartner, H., Grafman, J., Boutelle, W., Kaye, W., & Martin, P. (1983). Forms of memory failure. *Science, 221* (4608), 380–382.

Weingartner, H., Kaye, W., Smallberg, S. A., Ebert, M. H., Gillin, J. C., & Sitaram, N. (1981). Memory failures in progressive idiopathic dementia. *Journal of Abnormal Psychology, 90,* 196–197.

Weingartner, H., Miller, H., & Murphy, D. L. (1977). Mood state-dependent retrieval of verbal associations. *Journal of Abnormal Psychology, 86,* 276–284.

Weingartner, H., Murphy, D. L., & Stillman, R. C. (1978). Mood state-dependent learning. In F. C. Colpaert & J. A. Rosecrans (Eds.), *Stimulus properties of drugs: Ten years of progress.* Amsterdam: Elsevier/North-Holland Biomedical Press.

Whitehead, A. (1973). Verbal learning and memory in elderly depressives. *British Journal of Psychiatry, 123,* 203–208.

George Niederehe

Depression and Memory Impairment in the Aged

It is commonly stated that memory function is impaired in depressed patients and that this pattern becomes more pronounced in older patients. This chapter reviews the equivocal research literature on this issue and describes a study of episodic, semantic, and constructive memory functions in both young and old depressed women. This study found differences between age groups but few significant differences between depressed and control subjects in level of memory performance. Also, the results showed a general lack of the age-by-depression interactions that would be expected if older depressives were more susceptible to memory impairment than younger depressives. The depressed subjects showed conservative response biases and differed from control subjects in some of their self-perceptions and self-monitoring of memory performance. Both substantive and methodological factors that may account for this pattern of findings are discussed.

Two sets of issues in clinical gerontology—differential diagnosis, and people's concerns about memory decline with age—make it important to determine whether depression produces changes in memory functioning. First, with more elderly patients, it is increasingly difficult to distinguish diagnostically between depression and organic brain disorders (Busse, 1973; Butler & Lewis, 1977). Late-life depressions often present in so-called "atypical" forms that make the depressive nature of the disorder more difficult to identify (Gabrynowicz, 1968; Gordon, 1973; Pfeiffer & Busse, 1973). Diagnosis is also complicated by the notion that cognitive impairments result from depression more commonly among older adults than among the young.

Despite scant research evidence on this matter, many clinicians believe that the older the patient, the more pronounced the impact of depression on cognitive functions. In general, clinicians have not viewed depression as affecting the basic cognitive ability of younger patients, despite their symptoms of impaired concentration, distractibility, or difficulties in making decisions. However, in the aged, depression is seen as sometimes producing a syndrome with sufficient cogni-

tive impairment to be misdiagnosed as an organic dementia—the so-called problem of "pseudodementia" (Kiloh, 1961). If the underlying depression is suspected and treated, or if it spontaneously remits, the patient may return to a state of normal cognitive functioning. Clearly, in evaluating memory deficits in older patients, clinicians would be aided by knowing definitively whether depression is likely to be an underlying cause of certain deficits and whether age is likely to potentiate the effects of depression.

Second, the great amount of concern that people have regarding memory changes with age also raises issues for the clinician who is evaluating the impact of depression on memory function. Lowenthal, Berkman, and associates (1967) found reports of memory decline to be so common and so associated with age among the community-dwelling elderly that they termed such reports one of the stereotypic complaints of aging (along with decreased energy). However, the actual performance of the community-dwelling elderly on the cognitive measures used by Lowenthal et al. did not demonstrate an age-related decline in memory. Gerontological research in general suggests that the cognitive declines seen in normal aging are relatively mild and are less substantial than is popularly thought. Certainly the number of persons showing marked decline is smaller than is suggested by the frequency with which the aged themselves complain about their cognitive losses. Questions about what these frequent complaints represent remain unanswered at this time.

In the research by Lowenthal et al., subjects with symptoms of functional psychopathology complained more about memory decline than those without such symptoms. Many clinical observers have noted that memory complaints are common in depression and

The research reported in this chapter was supported in part by National Institute of Mental Health Grant MH-30664.

may be connected with self-reports about other intellectual difficulties (e.g., problems of concentration). Until the advent of cognitive theories about depression, however, these symptoms were generally not labeled as "cognitive" effects of depression. Even today, many clinicians do not interpret this sort of complaint literally. Instead, they may view these complaints as reflecting a negative bias in the self-reports or self-concepts of depressives. This interpretation is in line with the traditional viewpoint that depression is a mood disorder rather than a thought disorder like schizophrenia or senile dementia. Thus, in evaluating older patients, the clinician needs to know whether depression is likely to affect actual cognitive and memory abilities, or merely the patient's appraisal of these abilities. Furthermore, when should a patient's complaints of memory difficulties be taken literally? And when memory complaints are associated with depression and are not literally accurate, how should they be understood?

Research Findings on Depression and Memory

Unfortunately, the research literature on whether depression has significantly detrimental effects on memory is equivocal and controversial. Numerous studies have reported that the performance of depressed patients on memory tests is comparatively poor or that it improves significantly after patients are treated with antidepressants or other therapies (Allison, 1955; Cronholm & Ottosson, 1961; Fraser & Glass, 1980; Gibson, 1981; Glass, Uhlenhuth, Hartel, Matuzas, & Fischman, 1981; Grinker, Miller, Sabahin, Nunn, & Nunnally, 1961; Henry, Weingartner, & Murphy, 1973; Hilbert, Niederehe, & Kahn, 1976; Raskin, Friedman, & DiMascio, 1982; Sternberg & Jarvik, 1976; Strömgren, 1977; Talland, 1968; Walton, 1958; Whitehead, 1973; 1974; Williams & Jaco, 1958; Zung, Rogers, & Krugman, 1968). However, the precise nature or prognostic significance of these memory deficits is unclear. In general, these studies suggest that depressed subjects demonstrate deficiencies in learning processes and short-term memory (i.e., arousal and attentional processes), whereas long-term memory and retentional processes seem to be intact. Some of the studies have also suggested that the results obtained might be attributable to response biases. Some neurobiological evidence indicates that depression involves changes in the same brain structures and substances that underlie memory functions (Akiskal & McKinney, 1975; Carroll, 1976; Kety, 1970; McGaugh, 1983), suggesting one theoretical basis for an association between memory and affective state.

At the same time, numerous other studies have reported no impairment in the overall level of memory performance in depressed subjects (Derry & Kuiper, 1981; Friedman, 1964; Golub, 1975; Granick, 1963; Kahn, Zarit, Hilbert, & Niederehe, 1975; Kendrick & Post, 1967; Miller & Lewis, 1977; Niederehe & Camp, 1985; Orme, 1957; Perlin & Butler, 1963; Popkin, Gallagher, Thompson, & Moore, 1982; Roth & Rehm, 1980). Furthermore, studies investigating whether depression might be associated with mild neurological impairment have generally failed to demonstrate such an interrelationship (Hemsi, Whitehead, & Post, 1968; Rochford, Detre, Tucker, & Harrow, 1970). In fact, Beck's (1972) review indicates that research has not consistently shown generalized inadequacy of cognitive functions even among severely depressed psychiatric patients.

A fair number of the studies of quantitative differences in the memory performance of depressives have focused on elderly patients, but research concerned with qualitative changes in memory as a result of depression has focused less on the aged. The findings in general indicate that depressed patients remember neutral and negatively toned information normally but may show reduced recall for positively toned information (Breslow, Kocsis, & Belkin, 1981; Derry & Kuiper, 1981) and a selective bias toward negative themes (Lishman, 1972). These patterns, however, may reflect a response bias rather than an intrinsic change in memory processes or in the strength of memory traces (Zuroff, Colussy, & Wielgus, 1983). Coyne and Gotlib (1983) argued that no measure of cognitive bias or distortion has yet been demonstrated to have a consistent and specific relationship to depression.

Thus, the research literature on memory functioning leaves a number of methodological and substantive issues to be sorted out regarding the impact of depression on memory functioning. The clinical literature on depression has yet to pay adequate attention to discrepancies between patients' complaints about memory difficulties and their basic abilities or performance levels on memory tests. Often a complaint or self-report about a difficulty is assumed to be isomorphic with the presence of a deficit. However, various studies suggest that self-report data about memory may often not be accurate, particularly for depressed persons. Kahn et al. (1975) found that depression was strongly related to the degree of memory complaint but that neither depression nor complaint was correlated with the actual level of performance on memory tests.

Similar results differentiating memory complaints from objective evidence of memory impairment in depression have been reported by other gerontological researchers (Gurland et al., 1976; Popkin et al., 1982; Zarit, Cole, & Guider, 1981). Such findings may relate to the general inaccuracy and unreliability of many depressed patients' self-reports about their clinical symptoms (Prusoff, Klerman, & Paykel, 1972). Acceptable research must maintain a clear distinction between the individual's subjective perceptions and complaints and his or her objective performance on memory tasks.

Another problem concerns the type of measurements used in clinical studies to operationalize memory and, more basically, the models of memory underlying these measurements. Many studies of depression have used clinical memory tests designed primarily to measure memory deficits characteristic of dementia, perhaps because memory dysfunction is often assumed to be a behavioral marker for organic pathology in the central nervous system (CNS), reflecting structural CNS damage, neuronal degeneration and cellular loss, or metabolic changes. Because memory is not a unitary phenomenon, however, not all types of memory impairment necessarily relate to abnormalities at the neurological level. It is questionable whether tests geared toward neurological deficits and the severe types of memory impairment seen in the dementias are appropriate for detecting the kind of changes that might more reasonably be expected in depressions. Research based on theoretical models of both depression and memory functions is needed to specify the kind of memory changes expected in depressives and to develop appropriate measuring instruments.

Recently, clinical memory research has been based on information-processing models of memory. This approach, and particularly some variants such as the levels-of-processing model (Craik & Lockhart, 1972), emphasize how important a person's mental activity as an information-processor is to eventual remembering of material. In this approach, the degree of recall depends on active processes of immediately encoding new information in a personally meaningful way and of reconstructing prior experiences from memory fragments at the point of retrieval. Memory is a by-product of these kinds of active processing. In gerontological research, such theoretical viewpoints have been fruitfully applied to the study of normal aging. Findings suggest that much of the memory decline seen in the aged may be due to less active information processing (in terms of encoding, using mnemonic strategies, etc.) (Perlmutter & Mitchell, 1982). The information-processing approach deserves to be applied in research on depression, and cognitive–behavioral models of depression seem to offer a natural framework within which to do so, with their emphasis on operationalizing various cognitive elements in the depressive process.

Analogously to information-processing models of memory, cognitive–behavioral models of depression emphasize the role of the individual as an active cognitive agent. A primary feature of depression is a reduced frequency of many customary and normally adaptive behaviors previously evident in the individual's activities (Ferster, 1966), and it is reasonable to suppose that this change may involve a reduction in instrumental cognitive processes as well as a restriction of overt physical activity. A critical implication of this viewpoint, however, is that depression entails reduced self-initiation of behaviors rather than loss of the ability to perform those behaviors. "Executive-level" changes in the self system are suggested.

Weingartner and his colleagues have taken a somewhat similar approach in a series of studies of memory processes that demand mental effort and activity (chapter 22, this volume; Cohen, Weingartner, Smallberg, Pickar, & Murphy, 1982). These researchers have reported that younger depressives show deficiencies in memory performance only when effortful as opposed to automatic information processing is required, and the researchers have proposed the notion of a "central motivational deficit" in depression.

A Study of Memory in Late-Life Depression

Research with elderly patients at the Gerontology Center at the Texas Research Institute of Mental Sciences (TRIMS) has been based on the viewpoint that depression frequently involves such features as inactivity, retardation, and sluggishness, at a mental as well as a physical level. Our research team hypothesized that memory impairment results not from structural limitations in the person's memory system but rather from the person's failure to maintain an active role in information processing. Therefore we sought evidence for executive-level failures in depressed patients and used tasks designed to highlight this aspect of memory. We were also concerned about the ecological validity of our memory assessment techniques and addressed this problem by including a task that involved semantic rather than episodic memory (Tulving, 1972) and that focused on memory for "real-world knowledge" (Lachman & Lachman, 1980).

The research investigated both whether significant memory impairments are associated with depression and whether the effects of depression are influenced by the patient's age (age potentiation). The study compared depressed outpatients with normal control subjects at both young (ages 20 to 45) and old (ages 55 to 80) age levels. There were 24 subjects in each of the four groups. A smaller group of 12 elderly patients with neuropsychological profiles suggestive of mild-to-moderate dementia was also tested. We examined their data to provide a standard for gauging the relative severity of depressive effects on memory but did not include these data in the statistical analyses when testing for effects of depression. The sample was limited to women to control for possible sex differences.

Subjects were recruited for the study after admission to one of the psychiatric outpatient clinics at TRIMS (either the geriatric or the general adult service) or after responding to publicity about the study in the local community (via newspaper stories and ads, posters, appeals to senior citizen organizations, and word of mouth). Each subject received a standardized clinical interview based on the Schedule for Affective Disorders and Schizophrenia (Endicott & Spitzer, 1978) and was classified as depressed if she met the research diagnostic criteria (RDC) (Spitzer, Endicott, & Robins, 1978) for major or minor depressive disorder. Subjects with indications or a history of bipolar or cyclothymic disorder were excluded, as were those with indications or a history of schizophrenia, mental retardation, brain damage, epilepsy, or other neurological illness and those who were currently abusing alcohol or drugs. Persons in a state of remission from a prior episode of a major depressive disorder were also excluded, even if they met criteria for being currently not mentally ill. "Normal control subjects" were all others who met the RDC for being "currently not mentally ill."

The National Institute of Mental Health's (NIMH) 24-item version of the Hamilton Rating Scale for Depression (Guy & Bonato, 1970; Hamilton, 1967) was used to assess symptomatic severity. The group means were 22.9 (*SD* = 9.89) for the young depressed subjects and an identical 22.9 (*SD* = 6.20) for the elderly depressed subjects. Mean ratings for the control groups were 1.04 (*SD* = 1.30) for the young and 1.38 (*SD* = 2.63) for the elderly. Nearly all of the subjects in both depressed groups met the RDC for major depressive disorder.

All subjects were screened in a physical examination for adequate sensory acuity and for acute health problems, and they were screened for evidence of diagnosable brain dysfunction on a brief battery of nonmemory neuropsychological tests. The tests administered included the Short Portable Mental Status Exam (Pfeiffer, 1975), the Face-Hand Test (Kahn, Goldfarb, Pollack, & Peck, 1960), the Aphasia Screening, Trail making and Tapping Tests from the Halstead-Reitan Neuropsychological Battery (Reitan & Davison, 1974), and the Bender-Gestalt Test with Background Interference Procedure (Canter, 1968). Twelve subjects who scored in the impaired range on multiple tests in this battery were classified in the "altered brain function" or "organic" group mentioned above.

At the mean ages of 30.9 and 30.8 years, the young control and young depressed groups did not differ significantly. Among the aged, the control subjects averaged about 5 years older than the depressed subjects (70.5 versus 64.9 years). Mean years of education ranged from 13.3 to 14.0 and did not differ significantly among the four groups. Scores on the Peabody Picture-Vocabulary Test differed by age but not by diagnosis. Both aged groups obtained higher vocabulary scores than both young groups. The groups did not differ in self-rated health nor in assessed visual acuity. There were significant age differences favoring the young on physician ratings of global health status and degree of activity limitation due to health. The control and depressed subjects did not differ within age levels on these health measures, except that the young depressed subjects were rated significantly lower than the young control subjects on global health status (by less than 1 point on a 7-point scale).

Measurement of Objective Memory Performance

Our research, which maintained the essential distinction between objective memory performance and more subjective phenomena (complaints, self-perceptions, metamemorial strategies), focused on three types of tasks measuring objective performance. These tasks were conceptualized as reflecting episodic, semantic, and constructive memory processes.

Episodic memory. In this task, subjects viewed lists of 40 high-frequency nouns that fell into 10 taxonomic categories (e.g., birds, weapons, footgear) comprising four nouns each. After each list was shown, free recall, cued recall, and recognition were tested in succession to see if retrieval processes affected performance differentially. For cued recall, the names of the various taxonomic categories were presented as the cues.

The encoding process was manipulated so as to evaluate whether depressed subjects showed "production deficiencies" in their encoding of information. Two equivalent word lists and the sequencing of the conditions were counterbalanced across the two encoding conditions (spontaneous vs. prompted). In the prompted encoding condition, when subjects viewed the list, they had to answer questions (out loud) regarding whether each item belonged to one or another of the taxonomic categories (e.g., "Is the next item a bird?" "Is the next item a weapon?"). A "yes" response was required for half of the stimuli and a "no" response for half. An executive-level failure to employ efficient encoding strategies would be inferred if subjects showed disproportionately better performance after being prompted to encode the stimulus material in a relatively "deep" fashion than after approaching the task spontaneously.

Retrieval mode had a highly significant effect; for all groups, performance was poorest under the free-recall condition and best under the recognition condition (Figure 23-1). Encoding had a small but statistically significant effect opposite to that expected. Subjects tended to perform more poorly following prompted encoding; this suggests that it interfered with rather than facilitated spontaneous encoding strategies.

In general, the young performed this task more effectively than the aged. As Figure 23-2 shows for the spontaneous encoding condition, the effects of age and retrieval mode interacted; the deficiencies of the aged, apparent in free recall, tended to disappear in recogni-

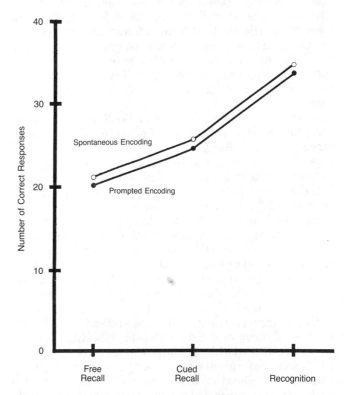

Figure 23-1. Episodic memory task performance for total sample as a function of encoding condition and retrieval mode.

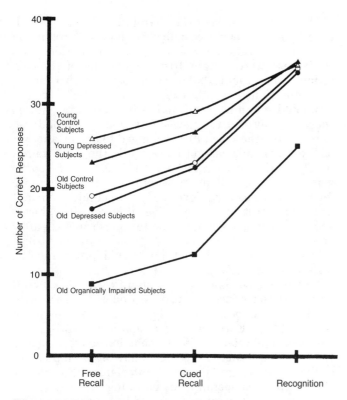

Figure 23-2. Episodic memory task performance under spontaneous encoding condition as a function of retrieval mode and five subject groups.

with the degree of conservative response bias shown in the test of recognition memory.

Several other indices of interest were investigated. The categorical clustering of free-recall responses (around the taxonomic categories inherent in the stimulus list) can be seen as an indicator of how actively subjects have processed the stimulus material. No significant group differences were found on a clustering index.

Similarly, for the prompted encoding condition, a check was made to see whether subjects were actually attending to the items and processing their meanings in the intended manner. This check involved simply counting incorrect responses to the categorical questions of the orienting task. In absolute terms, few errors were made by any of the groups, but the depressed groups made significantly more errors (about two errors out of 40 items, as opposed to less than one-half error for the control groups; the demented group made about six errors). The number of errors made correlated inversely with performance level. These data indicate that the impaired performance of at least some of the depressed subjects might have been due to deficits in attention rather than in memory.

The subjects were also assessed on several other brief standardized tests of visual memory functioning. The results obtained on the Facial Recognition Test (Milner, 1968) and the Visual Retention Test (Benton, 1974) fit the same basic pattern seen in the test of ver-

tion memory. Although in both age groups the depressed subjects scored below the control subjects on this task, the overall differences due to depression were not statistically significant, and interactions between age and depression were not found. If anything, the differences due to depression were smaller in absolute magnitude among the aged. Performance under the prompted encoding condition showed a similar pattern.

Signal detection analyses were done on the data for recognition memory. A nonparametric memory strength index (Grier, 1971) showed no significant differences in performance level due to subjects' age and diagnosis. The response bias index, however, showed a big difference between depressed and control groups (Figure 23-3). Both young and old depressed groups manifested conservative decision criteria (i.e., a tendency toward disproportionate numbers of false negative errors), whereas the control groups (and the organically impaired group) tended to use laxer criteria (i.e., to make more false positive errors). The tendency toward depressive "cautiousness" appeared greater among the aged.

Unfortunately, the data for free and cued recall cannot be similarly analyzed. However, if similar tendencies were in fact shown under these retrieval modes, the lower performance scores of the depressed groups might be attributable to a conservative response bias rather than to a reduced capability to retain and freely recall the information. Indeed, performance scores for free recall and cued recall were inversely correlated

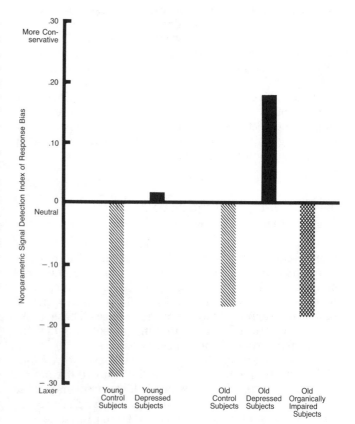

Figure 23-3. Mean subjective decision criteria in episodic recognition memory (averaged across encoding conditions) for five subject groups.

bal episodic memory: The aged performed less adequately than the young, but there were no significant differences between depressed and control groups.

Semantic memory. This study attempted to approximate more closely the memory demands encountered in everyday life, by using a questionnaire method to assess how well subjects could retrieve information from their "real-world knowledge" systems (Lachman & Lachman, 1980). In this method, the subject's exposure to the information is not experimentally controlled. Rather, acquisition is presumed to have occurred long ago (thus tapping what experimentalists have termed *tertiary memory* and clinicians *remote memory*). In order for scores on a task like this to reflect individual differences in retrieval from a knowledge system, differences between subjects in the amounts of baseline knowledge (i.e., in size of the system) must somehow be controlled. Our particular methodological concerns in this research were to assure that the items were relatively age fair, so that both young and old subjects could be assumed to have had roughly equal exposure to the information, and that the items were at an appropriate level of difficulty, so as to avoid floor and ceiling effects.

An initial pool of 100 items was drawn from eight content areas: politics; news events and celebrities; stage and screen; sports; the fine arts; science and technology; religion; and a miscellaneous category dealing mostly with U.S. history, geography, and folklore. Each item was prepared in three forms. In the free-recall form, an open-ended question was presented (e.g., "What cowboy had a horse named Silver?"). In cued recall, the same question was followed by a statement giving a second clue or hint (e.g., "The theme song of the cowboy's radio and TV show was the 'William Tell Overture'"). The recognition version included the question without the clue but with four multiple-choice responses (e.g., "Roy Rogers, Hopalong Cassidy, Gene Autry, and the Lone Ranger").

The initial 100 items were pretested with samples of young and old normal subjects to establish appropriate difficulty levels and to eliminate items that proved to be too hard or too easy. Then homogeneity of scaling procedures were used to pare the pool down to 40 items that correlated best with the scale total and that together yielded an internal consistency coefficient (Cronbach's alpha) greater than .90 in each retrieval mode. Scale totals on these 40 items were not correlated with age in the pilot sample. The questionnaire for the depression study included these 40 items, along with 10 easier "filler" items and 10 specifically age-correlated items. Each subject answered the entire set of items first in the free-recall mode, then in the cued-recall mode, and finally in the recognition mode.

As shown in Figure 23-4, performance on the core 40 items produced a very orderly pattern of results. All groups improved in performance across retrieval modes, going from free recall to recognition. The group differences stayed relatively constant across retrieval modes, which suggests that neither age nor affective status interacted significantly with retrieval mode on this task. Significant differences by age were apparent,

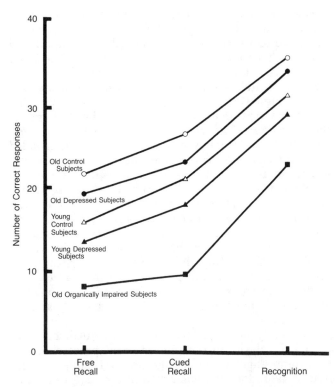

Figure 23-4. Performance on core subscale of semantic memory task (memory for world knowledge) as a function of retrieval mode and five subject groups.

but these results were opposite to those found in episodic memory: The aged recalled more of the information tested than did the younger subjects. Consistent with the results for episodic memory, in both age groups the depressed subjects scored somewhat lower than the control subjects, but, again, the differences were not statistically significant.

Although signal detection analyses of response bias cannot be derived from these data, response biases can be looked at, to some extent, by examining the types of errors made in free and cued recall (but not in recognition memory where the forced-choice format allowed no errors of omission). The number of errors of commission may reflect, in part, a subject's willingness to venture a response even when uncertain; however, the rate of such errors for both free and cued recall did not differ significantly between groups. Counts of "don't know" responses fail to differentiate true negative responses from false negative errors. Young subjects made more "don't know" responses than did aged subjects, but the diagnostic groups did not have different rates for this response.

Constructive memory. A third task studied was a story recall procedure designed to operationalize certain constructs from the "constructive memory" framework associated with the tradition of Bartlett (1932), Cofer (1977), and others. In this model, remembering is an active process in which the person's organized knowledge structures are used to reconstruct prior experiences from the features that have been stored; memory is not a matter of simply retrieving memory traces stored as wholes. Constructive memory research generally uses meaningful, connected stimulus material, such as narratives, to engage the individual and analyzes recall data qualitatively, with a focus on changes that the individual has introduced.

In this study, two prose narratives, each about 370 words long, were presented orally, as subjects read along on a written copy. Both passages left the ages of the characters indeterminate, because both young and old subjects were being tested. Also, both stories ended on an inconclusive note and left other connections unstated, so as to encourage subjects to draw their own conclusions or to read things into the stated sequence of events. Subjects gave their free recalls orally, and these recalls were recorded verbatim. A 24-item, true–false recognition test was also used after each narrative to assess whether subjects would falsely "recognize" statements that did not accurately paraphrase material in the original passage; the inaccuracies included text-based inferences, garbled relationships among story elements, and wild intrusions of extraneous material.

The analysis of the free-recall data utilized techniques developed in the field of prose processing and text comprehension to specify how well subjects were able to reproduce the basic meaning structure of each narrative. For one method, the hierarchy of propositions in the narrative (Kintsch, 1974) was determined, and subjects were scored for how many of the core elements (or macropropositions) fundamental to comprehending the gist of the story they recalled. For the second scoring method, meaning structure was specified in terms of idea units classifiable in one of the categories of a story grammar (e.g., settings, episodes, or outcomes) (Mandler & Johnson, 1977), and recall for these story grammar units was scored.

Analysis showed no significant differences between age groups or diagnostic groups for either the number of macropropositions or the number of story grammar units correctly recalled. Macropropositions and story grammar units that were not correctly recalled were also scored more qualitatively as being either completely omitted, partially omitted, or altered in some way (commission error). Again, similar results were obtained for the two scoring systems. The groups did not differ significantly in the overall number of commission errors, but there were three-way interactions among age, diagnosis, and type of omission. Figure 23-5 illustrates the results for story grammar units. As indicated, the young groups and the elderly control group made more partial than complete omissions. In contrast, the elderly depressed group (and the organically impaired group even more so) made more complete than partial omissions. These results suggest, but do not conclusively demonstrate, a conservative response bias in elderly depressives.

The groups did not differ in the frequency with which they introduced inferential or new material into their recalls. However, an index of the type of inferencing suggested that, compared with the young, the aged tended to make inferences that were further removed from the story schema.

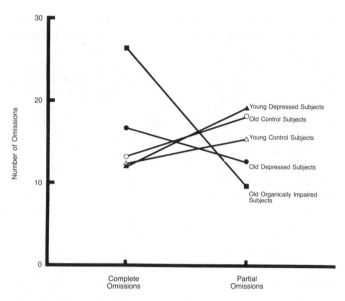

Figure 23-5. Omission of story grammar units in constructive memory task (Story J) as a function of omission type and five subject groups.

On the recognition tests, all groups correctly tended to recognize paraphrases as statements from the stories and, except for the organically impaired patients, correctly indicated lack of recognition for statements that distorted relationships between story elements or that contained intrusions of extraneous information. Responses to inferential statements that had not actually been stated in the narratives were more mixed in terms of accuracy. The aged tended to recognize fewer of the accurate paraphrases, but otherwise age differences were not shown on these tests. Effects of depression were not apparent in these data.

Measurements of Subjective Memory Phenomena: Metamemory

In addition to administering the objective memory performance tasks described, we also investigated various aspects of subjective perceptions, strategies, and complaints about memory, which can be loosely grouped under the heading "metamemory." Some of these dimensions were measured by self-assessments gathered during the memory tasks. Subjects also completed a 125-item Metamemory Questionnaire, which covered problems and concerns with memory, circumstances surrounding memory difficulty (e.g., the content or types of information involved, occasions of difficulty, and retention intervals involved), metamemory knowledge (e.g., how memory works or can be facilitated), the use of mnemonic strategies, beliefs about age-related changes in memory, and the personal significance attached to memory (see discussion by Gilewski and Zelinski in chapter 11, this volume).

Although the results cannot be discussed in detail here, in general, depression was associated with greater perceived difficulty with memory, with more concerns about memory, and with particular circumstances of difficulty. Depression was not significantly related to the degree of metamemory knowledge, to most beliefs about age-related changes, to the personal significance attached to memory, or to a generalized tendency toward a less active strategic approach to remembering things. In self-ratings gathered during the memory tasks, both older subjects and depressed subjects had somewhat lower expectations of their performance and, following testing, estimated having made fewer correct responses than did other subjects. However, these self-ratings very much followed the pattern of *actual* performance differences, so in general terms the subjects' self-monitoring was fairly accurate.

Methodological Considerations

In summary, this research failed to demonstrate deficits associated with depression along most of the memory dimensions investigated. However, a conservative response bias on the memory tasks was typical of the depressed subjects. The results also suggested that the depressed subjects had a mild attentional deficit and certain patterns of metamemory and self-perception. Another clear and consistent finding was that older age did not magnify the effects of depression on memory. How should these findings be interpreted? It may be useful to discuss the results relative to the four types of validity articulated by Cook and Campbell (1979).

Statistical Conclusion Validity

It is always problematic to discuss null findings. Because the depressed groups consistently scored in the predicted direction relative to the control groups but the group differences were not statistically significant, the question must be raised whether the null findings stem from inadequate statistical power to detect real trends due to depression. A concerted effort was made in this research to carefully diagnose homogeneous groups of patients with depressive disorders and to use sensible memory measures that would be sensitive to fairly subtle variations in memory performance and would be scorable in a fine-grained manner across an adequate scoring range. The sample sizes were substantial for this kind of research. Nonetheless, inadequate statistical power may have been a problem. It is difficult to specify how large a difference in scores on these tests would be expected if depression in fact does produce memory deficits on the dimensions assessed. The standard deviations for the episodic and semantic memory variables tended to run from 5 to 8 points, so the study had roughly 90% power to detect real differences between groups if these differences are as large as 4 to 6 items on these 40-item tests—but only 50% power or less if there are real differences of only 2 to 3 items.

The finding that age did not potentiate the effects of depression on memory, however, cannot be attributed to failure of age-by-depression interactions to reach statistical significance. Rather, a trend toward an interaction between age and diagnosis was entirely absent, and the group differences between control and depressed subjects were often smaller among the elderly than among the young.

Construct Validity

An issue regarding the construct validity of the memory measures used in this and most other studies is whether the measures are contaminated by response biases that cannot be partialed out from the measured rate of correct responding. In this study, the data associating depression with conservative response biases in recognition memory (for which the performance levels tended to be similar across groups) suggest that depressed groups might frequently score below the level of control groups on other non-forced-choice tests because of similar conservative biases and response withholding.

Unfortunately, conservative response biases (which result in errors of omission) cannot as readily be taken into account in free-recall tests, even though group differences tend to be greatest on such tests. In this study, response bias assessed on the recognition subsection of a memory task did correlate with performance levels on other parts of the task for which bias could not be assessed directly. Thus, other published reports that have attributed diminished or distorted memory performance to impaired information processing in depression may contain serious flaws if response biases have not been taken into account (Zuroff et al., 1983).

External Validity

If statistical power considerations do not account for the null findings in this study, what is to be made of the discrepancy between this study and other studies showing depressive impairments of memory? This is essentially an issue of the external validity, or generalizability, of the findings obtained in a study. Addressing this issue calls for consideration of the many differences between studies, such as setting, time, sampling, and procedures. For example, possibly the procedures used in this project did not require the kind of "effortful" processing that Weingartner has identified as affected by depression. However, even though we did not conceptualize our testing procedures along a continuum from effortful to automatic processes, it is unlikely that all of the tasks required only automatic processes.

It seems likely that conflicting studies have used significantly different samples. In addition to studying patients of different ages, studies may have used different diagnostic criteria to define depression, included different depressive subtypes, and included patients with disorders of different overall severity. Raskin (chapter 25, this volume) has identified and comprehensively discussed many of the attendant features of depressed samples that have been associated with positive (or negative) findings regarding memory impairment. Compared with researchers who have found no effects of depression on memory, researchers who have found impaired memory in depressed subjects have been dealing more often with hospitalized samples or patients with relatively severe depressive disorders and often also with patients from relatively uneducated and low socioeconomic status backgrounds. It has also been reported that men may be more susceptible to cognitive impairment in depression (Raskin et al., 1982) and that bipolar patients are more vulnerable than patients with other diagnostic subtypes of affective disorder (Weingartner & Silberman, 1984).

Thus, the sample in this study manifested many characteristics likely to mitigate the extent to which memory impairment would ensue from the patients' depression. The patients were all women, tended to be well educated, and were all psychiatric outpatients. Although the elderly subjects were comparable to the younger subjects in years of formal education (averaging a year or two beyond high school graduation), they were atypically well educated for their generation. The higher vocabulary scores of the elderly subjects compared with the young subjects probably reflects this fact. In addition, whereas some studies have included patients with bipolar disorders in their depressed samples (e.g., many of the studies by Weingartner and his colleagues), patients with any cyclothymic characteristics were excluded from our sample.

Although almost all of the depressed patients in this study met the RDC for major depressive disorder, their average rating on the Hamilton scale was in the moderately depressed range. Thus, this sample was probably less severely depressed than the samples in a number of other studies, particularly in studies of psychiatric inpatients hospitalized for affective disorders. Contrary to many treatment studies of depression, this study did not have a lower limit on Hamilton scale ratings as a criterion for entry. Instead, wanting to study the entire range of depressed patients, not just the most severe cases, we relied exclusively on whether subjects met the RDC for depression. Consequently, minor portions of the two depressed groups fell within the range on the Hamilton scale usually considered to indicate mild symptomatic severity. This is not to say, however, that these patients were not depressed. There is considerable question about which end of the range of depressions is statistically most representative of depressions occurring at large in the population, and which part of the range has the most complaints about memory dysfunction.

We conducted various secondary analyses of the data to examine whether the basic findings were contingent on peripheral characteristics or severity levels of the sample. We statistically controlled for the effects of education and vocabulary skills on performance, using analysis of covariance techniques. Also, we repeated our original analyses, eliminating those subjects who were rated as only mildly depressed. These variations did not alter the findings. We also ran separate correlational analyses within each of the four subgroups (and across each age group, as well) to determine whether performance levels corresponded with the severity of depressive symptoms, as measured by Hamilton scale ratings and by self-reports on the Self-Rating Depression Scale (Zung, 1965) and on the short-form Beck Depression Inventory (Beck & Beck, 1972). Within these subgroups, performance levels were consistently not correlated with symptom severity scores on the depression scales.

Internal Validity

Finally, there is an issue involving the internal validity of most of the studies that have examined effects of depression on memory, namely, whether the studies can validly claim diagnostic specificity for their findings. Most of the studies in the literature, including this one, have not used both a normal control group and another psychiatric control group. Thus, the positive findings of "depression effects" on memory in the patient groups have not been demonstrated as being specific to depression. If, in addition, it is true that the positive findings have been demonstrated largely in studies of psychiatric inpatients, it is questionable whether the memory impairments observed are attributable to depression per se or to psychoticism, severity of disturbance, or the like. Such a possibility is not unlikely. General reviews of research on various cognitive and motoric deficits in psychiatric patients have indicated that such impairments are linked primarily with severity of illness rather than with specific psychiatric diagnoses such as depression or schizophrenia (Hunt & Cofer, 1944; Lang & Buss, 1965; Miller, 1975).

Future Clinical and Research Directions

The research reviewed and reported in this chapter leaves unclear what impact depression has on memory functions. Therefore, what is the clinician to do when faced with practical decisions about evaluating and treating a patient who complains of memory dysfunction? Most obviously, besides evaluating the extent of depression, the clinican must carefully test the patient's memory functions. It will behoove the clinician to take special pains to assure that the patient is as motivated as possible to cooperate with testing procedures because performance on a test will not reflect the individual's ability level unless he or she is performing at peak motivation (Fiske & Butler, 1963).

Future research should address whether deficient performance on cognitive procedures may more frequently be observed in inpatient and severely disturbed depressives because such patients are poorly motivated and minimally compliant, rather than because they suffer from basic information-processing deficits. Outpatient samples must show at least enough motivation to travel to the study site specifically to participate. Future research may enhance evaluation of depression-memory linkages by developing assessment techniques that somehow take into account or quantify both the amount of motivation or "effort" the patient brings to the testing situation and the amount of "cognitive effort" or "processing resource" that each task demands.

Research on self-reporting and self-monitoring of memory activities by depressed patients (Roth & Rehm, 1980) may also produce significant payoffs for the practicing clinician. It may be possible to develop a taxonomy of memory complaints that will help clinicians to distinguish which complaints are typically depressive, which more likely reflect verifiable cognitive deficits, and so forth. Identification of patients' self-monitoring tendencies, mnemonic strategies, and other metamemorial processes may aid in understanding and treating complaints about memory.

Future research on memory performance deficits in depressives might fruitfully explore several promising leads. Foremost among these is the issue of response biases in depression and their effect on memory measures (Larner, 1977; Miller, 1975; Miller & Lewis, 1977; Zuroff et al., 1983). More attention should be paid to means of taking response biases into consideration and to the possibility that response biases could account for many reported findings. Closely related is the issue of qualitative bias in the types of information recalled by depressives (e.g., inadequacies specific to recall of positively toned items) (Breslow, Kocsis, & Belkin, 1981; Derry & Kuiper, 1981). Response biases constitute an intriguing focus for research, because the findings could cut across quantitative, qualitative, and metamemorial changes in the memory functioning of depressed persons.

Another prime target for future research should be the possibility of primary attentional deficits in elderly depressives (Thompson, 1980). Also intriguing are the reports that suggest that depression has an effect on memory only when mood at retrieval is incompatible with the mood context under which the material was encoded (i.e., that state-dependent learning or mood-dependent retrieval is involved) (Weingartner, Miller, & Murphy, 1977). These findings need to be replicated and elaborated.

Probably the biggest research challenge at the moment, however, has less to do with determining the nature of the deficit in depressed patients (assuming that some deficit does exist) than with refining the definition of depression to pinpoint which patients are likely to manifest a deficit. In this connection, researchers would do well to guard against falling into habits of thought or speech that suggest that depression can "cause" memory impairment, or cause anything else, for that matter. "Depression" is but a label applied when enough components of a broadly defined symptom complex are manifested—and a label for a very heterogeneous category of patients at that. If research establishes an association between a memory disorder and this generic diagnosis, this is only the first step in a search for the specific aspects of the syndrome that play a causal role in the disorder. Thus, the greatest priority currently should be placed on investigating how memory performance varies within the depressed population. For example, how does perform-ance vary between symptomatic subtypes? Do such characteristics as age, physical health, and underlying neurological status affect performance? Are chronic and episodic depressions associated with different levels of performance? Does performance vary in association with state versus trait components of depression, or in conjunction with mood versus somatic versus behavioral features? Answers to these questions will lead the way to a true understanding of the relationship between depression and memory impairment.

References

Akiskal, H. S., & McKinney, W. T., Jr. (1975). Overview of recent research in depression: Integration of ten conceptual models into a comprehensive clinical frame. *Archives of General Psychiatry, 32,* 285–305.

Allison, R. S. (1955). Changes in behavior and impairment of memory and intellect in later life: Differentiation of focal lesions from diffuse cerebral atrophy. *Geriatrics, 10,* 306–310.

Bartlett, F. C. (1932). *Remembering.* Cambridge, England: Cambridge University Press.

Beck, A. T. (1972). *Depression: Causes and treatment.* Philadelphia: University of Pennsylvania Press.

Beck, A. T., & Beck R. W. (1972). Screening depressed patients in family practice: A rapid technic. *Postgraduate Medicine, 52,* 81–85.

Benton, A. L. (1974). *The Revised Visual Retention Test* (4th ed.). New York: Psychological Corporation.

Breslow, R., Kocsis, J., & Belkin, B. (1981). Contribution of the depressive perspective to memory function in depression. *American Journal of Psychiatry, 138,* 227–230.

Busse, E. W. (1973). Mental disorders in later life—Organic brain syndromes. In E. W. Busse & E. Pfeiffer (Eds.), *Mental illness in later life* (pp. 89–106). Washington, DC: American Psychiatric Association.

Butler, R. N., & Lewis, M. I. (1977). *Aging and mental health: Positive psychosocial perspectives* (2nd ed.). St. Louis: C. V. Mosby.

Canter, A. (1968). The BIP-Bender Test for the detection of organic brain disorder: Modified scoring method and replication. *Journal of Consulting and Clinical Psychology, 32,* 522–526.

Carroll, B. J. (1976). Limbic system-adrenal cortex regulation in depression and schizophrenia. *Psychosomatic Medicine, 38,* 106–121.

Cofer, C. N. (1977). On the constructive theory of memory. In U. C. Uzgiris & F. Weizman (Eds.), *The structuring of experience.* New York: Plenum Press.

Cohen, R. M., Weingartner, H., Smallberg, S. A., Pickar, D., & Murphy, D. L. (1982). Effort and cognition in depression. *Archives of General Psychiatry, 39,* 593–597.

Cook, T. D., & Campbell, D. T. (1979). *Quasi-experimentation: Design and analysis issues for field settings.* Chicago: Rand McNally.

Coyne, J. C., & Gotlib, I. H. (1983). The role of cognition in depression: A critical appraisal. *Psychological Bulletin, 94,* 472–505.

Craik, F. I. M., & Lockhart, R. S. (1972). Levels of processing: A framework for memory research. *Journal of Verbal Learning and Verbal Behavior, 11,* 671–684.

Cronholm, B., & Ottosson, J. O. (1961). Memory functions in endogenous depression: Before and after electroconvulsive therapy. *Archives of General Psychiatry, 5,* 193–199.

Derry, P. A., & Kuiper, N. A. (1981). Schematic processing and self-reference in clinical depression. *Journal of Abnormal Psychology, 90,* 286–297.

Endicott, J. E., & Spitzer, R. L. (1978). A diagnostic interview: The Schedule for Affective Disorders and Schizophrenia. *Archives of General Psychiatry, 35,* 837–844.

Ferster, C. B. (1966). Animal behavior and mental illness. *Psychological Record, 16,* 345–356.

Fiske, D. W., & Butler, J. M. (1963). The experimental conditions for measuring individual differences. *Educational and Psychological Measurement, 23,* 249–266.

Fraser, R. M., & Glass, I. B. (1980). Unilateral and bilateral ECT in elderly patients. *Acta Psychiatrica Scandinavica, 62,* 13–21.

Friedman, A. S. (1964). Minimal effects of severe depression on cognitive functioning. *Journal of Abnormal and Social Psychology, 69,* 237–243.

Gabrynowicz, J. E. (1968). Depression in late life. *Medical Journal of Australia, 1,* 299–303.

Gibson, A. (1981). A further analysis of memory loss in dementia and depression in the elderly. *British Journal of Clinical Psychology, 20,* 179–185.

Glass, R. M., Uhlenhuth, E. H., Hartel, F. W., Matuzas, W., & Fischman, M. W. (1981). Cognitive dysfunction and imipramine in outpatient depressives. *Archives of General Psychiatry, 38,* 1048–1051.

Golub, S. (1975, September). *The effect of premenstrual anxiety and depression on cognitive function.* Paper presented at the 83rd Annual Convention of the American Psychological Association, Chicago.

Gordon, S. K. (1973). The phenomenon of depression in old age. *Gerontologist, 13,* 100–105.

Granick, S. (1963). Comparative analysis of psychotic depressives with matched normals on some untimed verbal intelligence tests. *Journal of Consulting Psychology, 27,* 439–443.

Grier, J. B. (1971). Nonparametric indexes for sensitivity and bias: Computing formulas. *Psychological Bulletin, 75,* 424–429.

Grinker, R. R., Miller, J., Sabahin, M., Nunn, R., & Nunnally, J. (1961). *The phenomena of depressions.* New York: Paul B. Hoeber.

Gurland, B. J., Fleiss, J. L., Goldberg, K., Sharpe, L., Copeland, J. R. M., Kelleher, M. J., & Kellet, J. M. (1976). The Geriatric Mental State Schedule: II. Factor analysis. *Psychological Medicine, 6,* 451–459.

Guy, W., & Bonato, R. R. (1970). *Manual for the ECDEU Assessment Battery.* Chevy Chase, MD: National Institute of Mental Health.

Hamilton, M. (1967). Development of a rating scale for primary depressive illness. *British Journal of Social and Clinical Psychology, 6,* 278–296.

Hemsi, L. K., Whitehead, A., & Post, F. (1968). Cognitive functioning and cerebral arousal in elderly depressives and dements. *Journal of Psychosomatic Research, 12,* 145–156.

Henry, G. M., Weingartner, H., & Murphy, D. L. (1973). Influence of affective states and psychoactive drugs on verbal learning and memory. *American Journal of Psychiatry, 130,* 966–971.

Hilbert, N. M., Niederehe, G., & Kahn, R. L. (1976). Accuracy and speed of memory in depressed and organic aged. *Educational Gerontology, 1,* 131–146.

Hunt, J. McV., & Cofer, C. N. (1944). Psychological deficit. In J. McV. Hunt (Ed.), *Personality and the behavior disorders* (Vol. 2). New York: Ronald Press.

Kahn, R. L., Goldfarb, A. I., Pollack, M., & Peck, A. (1960). Brief objective measures for the determination of mental status in the aged. *American Journal of Psychiatry, 117,* 326–328.

Kahn, R. L., Zarit, S. H., Hilbert, N. M., & Niederehe, G. (1975). Memory complaint and impairment in the aged: The effect of depression and altered brain function. *Archives of General Psychiatry, 32,* 1569–1573.

Kendrick, D. C., & Post, F. (1967). Differences in cognitive status between healthy, psychiatrically ill, and diffusely brain-damaged elderly subjects. *British Journal of Psychiatry, 113,* 75–81.

Kety, S. S. (1970). The biogenic amines in the central nervous system: Their possible roles in arousal, emotion and learning. In F. O. Schmitt (Ed.), *The neurosciences: The Second Study Program* (pp. 324–336). New York: Rockefeller University Press.

Kiloh, L. G. (1961). Pseudo-dementia. *Acta Psychiatrica Scandinavica, 37,* 336–351.

Kintsch, W. (1974). *The representation of meaning in memory.* Hillsdale, NJ: Erlbaum.

Lachman, J. L., & Lachman, R. (1980). Age and the actualization of world knowledge. In L. W. Poon, J. L. Fozard, L. S. Cermak, D. Arenberg, & L. W. Thompson (Eds.), *New directions in memory and aging: Proceedings of the George Talland Memorial Conference* (pp. 285–311). Hillsdale, NJ: Erlbaum.

Lang, P. J., & Buss, A. H. (1965). Psychological deficit in schizophrenia: II. Interference and activation. *Journal of Abnormal Psychology, 70,* 77–106.

Larner, S. (1977). Encoding in senile dementia and elderly depressives: A preliminary study. *British Journal of Social and Clinical Psychology, 16,* 379–390.

Lishman, W. A. (1972). Selective factors in memory: Part 2. Affective disorder. *Psychological Medicine, 2,* 248–253.

Lowenthal, M. F., Berkman, P. L., & associates. (1967). *Aging and mental disorder in San Francisco: A social psychiatric study.* San Francisco: Jossey-Bass.

Mandler, J. M., & Johnson, N. S. (1977). Remembrance of things parsed: Story structure and recall. *Cognitive Psychology, 9,* 111–151.

McGaugh, J. L. (1983). Preserving the presence of the past: Hormonal influences on memory storage. *American Psychologist, 38,* 161–174.

Miller, E., & Lewis, P. (1977). Recognition memory in elderly patients with depression and dementia: A signal detection analysis. *Journal of Abnormal Psychology, 86,* 84–86.

Miller, W. R. (1975). Psychological deficit in depression. *Psychological Bulletin, 82,* 238–260.

Milner, B. (1968). Visual recognition and recall after right temporal lobe excision in man. *Neuropsychologia, 6,* 191–209.

Niederehe, G., & Camp, C. J. (1985). Signal detection analysis of recognition memory in depressed elderly. *Experimental Aging Research, 11,* 207–213.

Orme, J. E. (1957). Non-verbal and verbal performance in normal old age, senile dementia, and elderly depression. *Journal of Gerontology, 12,* 404–413.

Perlin, S., & Butler, R. N. (1963). Psychiatric aspects of adaptation to the aging experience. In J. E. Birren, R. N. Butler, S. W. Greenhouse, L. Sokoloff, & M. R. Yarrow (Eds.), *Human aging: A biological and behavioral study* (PHS Publication No. 986, pp. 159–213). Washington, DC: U.S. Government Printing Office.

Perlmutter, M., & Mitchell, D. B. (1982). The appearance and disappearance of age differences in adult memory. In F. I. M. Craik & S. Trehub (Eds.), *Aging and cognitive processes* (pp. 127–144). New York: Plenum Press.

Pfeiffer, E. (1975). A short portable mental status questionnaire for the assessment of organic brain deficit in elderly patients. *Journal of the American Geriatrics Society, 23,* 433–441.

Pfeiffer, E., & Busse, E. W. (1973). Mental disorders in later life: Affective disorders; paranoid, neurotic, and situational reactions. In E. W. Busse & E. Pfeiffer (Eds.), *Mental illness in later life* (pp. 107–144). Washington, DC: American Psychiatric Association.

Popkin, S. J., Gallagher, D., Thompson, L. W., & Moore, M. (1982). Memory complaint and performance in normal and depressed older adults. *Experimental Aging Research, 8,* 141–145.

Prusoff, B. A., Klerman, G. L., & Paykel, E. S. (1972). Concordance between clinical assessments and patients' self-report in depression. *Archives of General Psychiatry, 26,* 546–552.

Raskin, A., Friedman, A. S., & DiMascio, A. (1982). Cognitive and performance deficits in depression. *Psychopharmacology Bulletin, 18,* 196–202.

Reitan, R. M., & Davison, L. A. (Eds.). (1974). *Clinical neuropsychology: Current status and applications.* New York: Wiley.

Rochford, J. M., Detre, T., Tucker, B. T., & Harrow, M. (1970). Neuropsychological impairments in functional psychiatric diseases. *Archives of General Psychiatry, 22,* 114–119.

Roth, D., & Rehm, L. P. (1980). Relationships among self-monitoring processes, memory, and depression. *Cognitive Therapy and Research, 4,* 149–157.

Spitzer, R. L., Endicott, J., & Robins, E. (1978). Research diagnostic criteria: Rationale and reliability. *Archives of General Psychiatry, 35,* 773–782.

Sternberg, D. E., & Jarvik, M. E. (1976). Memory functions in depression: Improvement with antidepressant medication. *Archives of General Psychiatry, 33,* 219–224.

Strömgren, L. S. (1977). The influence of depression on memory. *Acta Psychiatrica Scandinavica, 56,* 109–128.

Talland, G. A. (1968). *Disorders of memory and learning.* Harmondsworth, Middlesex, England: Penguin.

Thompson, L. W. (1980). Periodic "lapses" in attentional processes: A possible correlate of memory impairment in the elderly. In L. W. Poon, J. L. Fozard, L. S. Cermak, D. Arenberg, & L. W. Thompson (Eds.), *New directions in memory and aging: Proceedings of the George Talland Memorial Conference* (pp. 239–242). Hillsdale, NJ: Erlbaum.

Tulving, E. (1972). Episodic and semantic memory. In E. Tulving & W. Donaldson (Eds.), *Organization of memory* (pp. 381–403). New York: Academic Press.

Walton, D. (1958). The diagnostic and predictive accuracy of the Wechsler Memory Scale in psychiatric patients over sixty-five. *Journal of Mental Science, 104,* 1111–1116.

Weingartner, H., Miller, H., & Murphy, D. L. (1977). Mood-state-dependent retrieval of verbal associations. *Journal of Abnormal Psychology, 86,* 276–284.

Weingartner, H., & Silberman, E. (1984). Cognitive changes in depression. In R. M. Post & J. C. Ballenger (Eds.), *Frontiers of clinical neuroscience: Neurobiology of mood disorders.* (Vol. 1, pp. 121–135). Baltimore, MD: Williams & Wilkins.

Whitehead, A. (1973). Verbal learning and memory in elderly depressives. *British Journal of Psychiatry, 123,* 203–208.

Whitehead, A. (1974). Factors in the learning deficit of elderly depressives. *British Journal of Social and Clinical Psychology, 13,* 201–208.

Williams, W. S., & Jaco, E. G. (1958). An evaluation of functional psychoses in old age. *American Journal of Psychiatry, 114,* 910–916.

Zarit, S. H., Cole, K. D., & Guider, R. L. (1981). Memory training strategies and subjective complaints of memory in the aged. *Gerontologist, 21,* 158–164.

Zung, W. W. K. (1965). A self-rating depression scale. *Archives of General Psychiatry, 12,* 63–70.

Zung, W. W., Rogers, J., & Krugman, A. (1968). Effects of electroconvulsive therapy on memory in depressive disorders. *Recent Advances in Biological Psychiatry, 10,* 160–179.

Zuroff, D. C., Colussy, S. A., & Wielgus, M. S. (1983). Selective memory and depression: A cautionary note concerning response bias. *Cognitive Therapy and Research, 7,* 223–232.

Colleen M. Kelley

CHAPTER
24

Depressive Mood Effects on Memory and Attention

The effects of depressive mood on selective attention were investigated in a group of elderly outpatients and matched normal subjects. Subjects were allowed to view freely a collection of sad, happy, and neutral slides. Attention allocation was measured via a secondary reaction time task. The results indicated that elderly depressives attend more intensively to sad than to happy slides, whereas nondepressed control subjects attend to happy and sad photographs equally. On a later surprise recall test, the elderly depressives showed a decrement in memory compared with the nondepressed elderly. The findings are consistent with a spreading activation model of mood and cognition. Implications for clinical assessment of elderly depressives are discussed.

In this chapter, I focus on one aspect of depressive disorders, sad affect, and discuss its effects on memory and attention. I introduce some findings from experiments that induce moods by nonchemical means, namely, through verbal and imaginative techniques. The temporary moods induced by these techniques may have little impact on people's neurophysiology and thus allow investigators to isolate the effects of one aspect of depression—sad affect—on cognition. Sad affect appears to alter what people attend to, which leads to certain patterns of memory problems. Specifically, people experiencing sad moods attend to mood-congruent events more than to mood-incongruent events. This mood-congruent attention leads to better memory for mood-congruent events.

Mood and Cognition

Mood State-Dependent Learning

Mood acts as an important context for encoding events and as an important dimension for later retrieval of memories. A person's mood can be viewed as a context or cue to which different memories become associated. Just as walking back into a room may help a person

recapture a thought he or she had there, reinstating the mood in a particular situation may aid memory for the details of that situation. For example, a person's prevailing mood during learning seems to provide a distinctive context for the information learned, to such an extent that state-dependent learning occurs. To illustrate, Bower, Monteiro, and Gilligan (1978) induced happy and sad moods in subjects via hypnotic suggestion and had them learn a different list of words in each mood. Later recall in a happy or sad mood showed a state-dependent learning effect—a given list was better recalled when subjects were in the same mood at recall as when they had learned the list. The mood presumably served as an extra retrieval cue. Weingartner, Miller, and Murphy (1977) noted a similar state-dependent phenomenon in rapidly cycling manic depressives. In each testing session, the patients were asked to free associate 20 responses to each of two words. In the following testing session, the patients attempted to recall their associations to the cue words. Those associations were reproduced more completely when patients were in a similar mood state than when their mood changed between sessions. As Weingartner et al. noted, the task is a blend of retrieval from episodic memory ("which words did I say four days ago in response to the word *butterfly*"?) and a possible mood bias in free associations. Bower (1981) found that the particular associations given to words are skewed in the direction of the subject's mood. Thus, a subject in the same mood on two occasions will be more likely to generate the same associations to a cue word than will a subject in different moods on the two occasions.

A Model of Mood and Cognition

When mood is considered as a context or as a retrieval cue, it is essentially being treated as information. As such, it can be considered within the framework of current cognitive models. To explain the mood state-dependent learning effects, Bower (1981) and Clark and Isen (1982) proposed a modified semantic network model.

Network theories of memory (Anderson & Bower, 1973; Collins & Loftus, 1975; Schneider & Shiffrin, 1977) present human memory as a network of concepts and schemata, which are nodes in the network. The nodes are connected via associations. Activation is the basic process of thought. If a node (concept or proposition) is activated above some threshold, it comes into conscious awareness. Activation spreads from unit to unit according to the associative links between them. Thus, if one idea is currently in consciousness, the probability increases that an associated idea will soon come into consciousness. A novel event is represented by a set of nodes corresponding to concepts that describe the event. This configuration of nodes is activated by the event, and new connections are made among the elements. Learning is the establishment and strengthening of the connections between ideas.

Bower (1981) proposed adding a new kind of unit called the emotion node—a specific node in memory for each distinct emotion such as joy, sadness, or fear. The emotion node is linked to its pattern of autonomic arousal, expressive behaviors, verbal descriptors, and description of situations that can evoke that emotion. The experience of emotion corresponds to the activation of this emotion node and its surrounding contents, for example, its autonomic nervous system pattern, facial expressions, and the name of the emotion.

Like other nodes, emotion nodes may establish new connections by entering into association with concurrent events. Whenever an emotion is aroused, that emotion node will be linked to nodes describing the ongoing events. When that emotion is aroused again, the activated node sends out activation to the nodes describing previous instances when that emotion was experienced. Thus, those memories are "primed" (receiving subthreshold activation) and are more likely to be activated above threshold by some specific cue.

Such priming by the emotion node is the source of the mood state-dependent learning effect. Suppose, for example, that subjects in a sad mood read a list of words in preparation for a memory test. Because they are in a sad mood, associations are formed between their emotion nodes for sadness, nodes representing the words on the list, and nodes representing the physical context (the experimental room, the face of the experimenter). If these subjects are retested the following day, when half are in a sad mood and the other half are in a happy mood, the subjects who are retested in the sad mood should have better recall of words on the list. They are cued with the experimental context, which primes the word list, and with their mood, which also primes the word list. The interaction of these two sources of activation should lead to better access to the word list for the sad subjects than for their counterparts who are experiencing happy moods.

As noted, the model predicts that when people are in a particular mood, items in memory that occurred during earlier instances of that mood are being cued or primed. Thus, people in an anxious mood may recall times in the past when they felt the same anxiety; people feeling joy and excitement may find themselves thinking of an earlier event that was marked by those same feelings of joy. An experiment relevant to this priming of memories by a particular mood was conducted by Lloyd and Lishman (1975), who measured the speed at which subjects could retrieve pleasant versus unpleasant memories as a function of their level of depression. They found a state-dependent retrieval effect: Depressed patients were slower to recall pleasant experiences than unpleasant experiences, whereas subjects who were happy recalled pleasant experiences faster than unpleasant experiences. The same effect occurs when the elation or depression is induced experimentally (Teasdale & Fogarty, 1979) using the Velten technique (Velten, 1968).

Mood-Congruent Learning

In mood state-dependent studies, the emotional quality of events is an important retrieval cue, but does it affect learning, particularly learning of events that vary in emotional quality? Do moods change the type of information that subjects initially give attention to and encode into memory? During learning, a subject's mood may be congruent with the emotional quality of the events, neutral, or incongruent. For example, a subject in a sad mood may be asked to learn material that has a sad, happy, or neutral emotional quality to it. When the mood of the subject is varied, as well as the emotional quality of the material being learned, mood-congruent learning results. Positive material is learned more readily when the subject is in a happy mood, and negative material is learned more readily when the subject is in a sad mood. Bower, Gilligan, and Monteiro (1981) did one study that varied moods and studied the type of information learned. They studied selective learning, by subjects whose happy or sad mood had been induced by hypnosis, of happy versus sad material in a story. Happy subjects showed a bias toward learning the happy incidents, whereas sad subjects were biased toward learning the sad incidents.

Mood-congruent learning and depressives. Does mood-congruent learning occur in depressives? A study of mood-congruent learning was done by Breslow, Kocsis, and Belkin (1981) using hospitalized depressives and matched normal subjects. They compared the ability of the depressives and the normal subjects to recall a story containing material with positive, negative, and neutral affective tones. They found an overall deficit in the story recall of the depressed patients, most of which could be attributed to their decrement in recall of the positive themes. The depressed patients were, however, quite able to recall the negative and neutral themes in the story.

Mood-congruent learning is a qualitative change with mood, not a quantitative change. The sad affect that so predominates in depression may lead to better learning of material if it has a negative affective tone rather than a neutral or positive one. Given the focus on depression in the elderly, the question is whether such mood-congruent learning is a substantial factor in the memory of elderly depressives.

Slife, Miura, Thompson, and Gallagher (1983) studied mood-congruent learning in a group of elderly outpatients classified as major depressives in comparison with a group of age-matched control subjects. Subjects were informed that they were to be given a memory test; thus, this was a study of intentional memory. All subjects were asked first to state whether they liked or disliked a number of consonant-vowel-consonant trigrams. The experimenter then drew up a list of trigrams for each subject, half of which were liked and half disliked. Each subject was allowed to study briefly the personalized trigram list and then was asked for free recall. Again, a pattern of mood-congruent learning appeared. The depressed elderly learned more disliked than liked items, while the normal elderly learned more liked than disliked items. However, the depressed elderly still showed lower recall overall.

Mood-congruent attention. One question regarding mood-congruent learning in depressives is whether the depressives actually attend to and learn the negative information best or whether they simply have a response bias against reporting positive information (Zuroff, Colussy, & Wielgus, 1983). One way to answer this question is to track the degree to which depressives and nondepressive subjects attend to positive versus negative stimuli. Although the spreading activation model of mood has focused primarily on memory rather than on selective attention, it is possible to make predictions from the model regarding selective attention. First, it is important to note that when a person is in a certain mood, all memories and concepts associated with that mood are primed. Then when the person is exposed to two distinct stimuli—one that is mood congruent and one that is mood incongruent—he or she may attend to both stimuli for a short time; however, the node corresponding to the mood-congruent stimulus will receive additional activation because it is connected to the ongoing mood of the person. Thus, if more activated nodes dominate awareness, the mood-congruous stimulus should attract more attention.

Another reason to expect more attention to mood-congruent than to mood-incongruent stimuli is that emotions appear to inhibit one another. Emotions may exist as pairs of opposites (Plutchik, 1980) with inhibitory connections between them. Thus, fear and anger are said to be opposites, as are happiness and sadness. If one member of a pair exceeds threshold activation, it may send an inhibitory signal to the opposite member of its pair. Such inhibition may extend to associates of an emotion node. If those nodes are receiving inhibitory signals, they will require more activation than usual to exceed the threshold of conscious awareness. Thus, the impact of any mood-incongruent stimulus would be diminished.

To review some evidence relevant to the effect of mood on the direction of attention, I recently found a mood-congruent interaction between mood and the time people spent viewing happy versus sad slides. The subjects were college students experiencing experimentally induced happy and sad moods. Sad subjects spent more time viewing sad pictures than happy pictures, whereas happy subjects spent more time viewing happy pictures than sad pictures. Following such selective viewing of happy and sad pictures, the subjects exhibited mood-congruent recall: sad subjects remembered more sad pictures than did happy subjects, and happy subjects remembered more happy pictures than did sad subjects.

In a similar finding, Forgas, Bower, and Krantz (reported in Gilligan & Bower, 1982) found a mood-congruent effect that may be mediated by selective attention. In the first session of their experiment, subjects were videotaped during a short social interaction. In the second session, these same subjects were placed in happy or sad moods during a hypnotic induction. Then they watched the videotape of themselves and of another person and were asked to mark down every 10 seconds the occurrence of either a positive or a negative social behavior. People who were happy "saw" many more positive social actions than did the sad people, who were more likely to "see" themselves performing negative behaviors. This effect may be due to a bias in the interpretation of ambiguous body language or conversation as positive or negative, or it may be due to the subjects' selective attention to mood-congruent events.

Another study found that moods may selectively alter the type of information people seek out. Mischel, Ebbesen, and Zeiss (1973) manipulated subjects' moods by giving them a success or failure experience on an ego-involving task that, subjects were told, reflected their intelligence. Subjects were then left alone and allowed access to two folders, one of which contained negative information and one of which contained positive information about themselves (the material was allegedly the result of their prior personality test). Subjects spent more time reading the folder that contained negative information about themselves after a failure experience and more time reading the folder that contained positive information about themselves after a success experience. Such mood-congruent choices may reflect a general phenomenon of selective attention to mood-congruent material.

Mood-congruent attention in elderly depressives. I recently did a preliminary study of mood-congruent attention in elderly depressives using a dual task technique (Kahneman, 1973; Kerr, 1973). This technique rests on the assumption that attention capacity is a general, limited resource for cognitive processing (Kahneman, 1973). In the dual task technique, one task is designated the primary task, and the other is the secondary task. Subjects are instructed to focus on the primary task and not to allow their performance on the primary task to suffer when they must simultaneously perform the secondary task. Thus, the secondary task becomes a marker of the amount of attention or effort the primary task requires. As the primary task becomes more demanding, or as the subject attends more intensively to the primary task, performance on the secondary task will drop. The most commonly used secondary task is the probe reaction time task (Posner,

1978), in which subjects must react to an occasional signal as quickly as possible. Increased latencies to the signal reflect the increased attention demands of the primary task.

Subjects were 9 elderly depressives and 12 matched elderly controls; 7 of the depressives were outpatients, not currently taking medication, and 2 were newly hospitalized inpatients. The depressed and normal elderly subjects were asked to view a collection of happy, sad, and neutral slides. The slides were black-and-white reproductions of photographs in art and photojournalism books. The happy slides included scenes of smiling newlyweds, children playing, and people dancing. Sad slides included a picture of a funeral, starving people, and a war scene. The neutral scenes included a person reading a book, a city street scene, and a person working in a factory. As the subjects viewed the slides, a buzzer would occasionally sound. The subjects were instructed to press a button in reaction to that buzzer.

The hypothesis was that as subjects viewed the slides, they would attend more intensely to mood-congruent ones (happy pictures for the normal subjects versus sad pictures for the depressed subjects). Such variations in attention would be reflected in increased reaction times to buzzing that coincided with their viewing mood-congruent slides. That was indeed the pattern of reaction times that occurred. The difference between probe reaction time on happy trials and sad trials was positive for the normal elderly subjects ($M = +5$ msec), indicating more attention to happy slides. The opposite occurred for the depressed elderly subjects: The difference between reaction time on happy trials and sad trials was negative ($M = -78$ msec), indicating greater attention to negative slides. This difference was significant in the predicted direction, $t(19) = 1.88$, $p < .05$.

I also asked subjects to recall all of the slides at the end of the session. This was an incidental learning task, as no mention had been made that subjects were to memorize the slides. Depressives recalled significantly fewer photographs ($M = 7.9$) than did controls ($M = 12.5$), $t(19) = 2.29$, $p < .05$. However, no pattern of mood-congruent recall appeared in this study. Both depressed and normal elderly subjects recalled more sad than happy slides. This result is a puzzle, given the mood-congruent memory results of Breslow et al. (1981) and Slife et al. (1983). The simplest explanation is that there was a floor effect. The depressed elderly recalled only about 10% of the slides. One strategy for dealing with a possible floor effect in memory is to make the task simpler by using a recognition-memory test rather than a free-recall test. Doing so would probably produce a mood-congruent memory effect similar to the one found by Slife et al., with elderly depressives recalling more negative than positive material.

Alternatively, it is also possible that the emotional aspect of information is a fairly deep level of analysis, to use the levels-of-processing terminology (Craik & Lockhart, 1972). If interpreting the emotional quality of information, particularly the emotional tone of slides, requires a fairly deep level of processing (or is a fairly effortful, nonautomatic process), then elderly depressives may not always make such an assessment of the emotional impact of material. Before the subjects in the current study were debriefed, they rated the overall emotional impact of the slides on a scale of 1 to 7, with 1 meaning no emotional impact and 7 referring to a strong emotional impact. The depressed patients and the normal elderly subjects demonstrated a large difference in their average ratings of the emotional impact of the slides: 5.2 for the normal elderly subjects versus 1.9 for the depressed patients.

These ratings may reflect the relatively shallow processing of the slides by the elderly depressives, such that they did not access the emotional nature of the scenes represented. Researchers could evaluate this possibility by requiring elderly depressives to process the emotional quality of stimuli, perhaps by using an orienting task such as "decide if this photograph is pleasant or unpleasant" or "decide if you like or dislike this photograph." Ensuring that elderly depressives process the affective tone of the material may be a prerequisite for mood-congruent learning.

Memory, Attention, and Effort

Memory complaints in depressed elderly persons are not always accompanied by objective decrements in memory performance, as several studies have shown (Kahn, Zarit, Hilbert, & Niederehe, 1975; Popkin, Gallagher, Thompson, & Moore, 1982; Zarit, Gallagher, & Kramer, 1981). Those studies were of outpatient populations, and certainly, as pointed out in chapters 23 and 25 of this volume, memory deficits may depend on severity of depression. Investigators who test memory by using intentional memory tests, however, may not be tapping into the same processes that lead to memory complaints in everyday life. People are not normally attempting to memorize material for a memory test 2 or 10 minutes later. Depressed subjects may be able to concentrate and marshall their processing resources for a short intentional memory test but still experience many memory failures in their daily lives.

In the study reported here, I hypothesized that the memory complaints of elderly depressives stem partially from their lack of attention to events in their environments. If so, memory deficits in elderly depressives might be detected on an incidental memory test with no particular orienting instruction. Under those conditions, depressives, unlike normal control subjects, might attend primarily to their own thoughts rather than to external events, and so fail to encode the external events.

I tested this hypothesis by allowing subjects to view a collection of photographs at their own pace and with no instructions to memorize them. They were asked to imagine themselves browsing through photographs in a magazine or wandering through an art gallery. The task allowed them to attend freely and selectively to the photographs (or to their own thoughts and preoccupations). The elderly depressives showed a large decrement in incidental recall in comparison with normal subjects.

The performance of depressives on many tasks may be described as "disinterested." However, as Britton and Tesser (1982) noted, the construct of "interest" is not clear and remains loosely related to such concepts as concentration, attention, interaction between the stimulus and the subject's knowledge, and cognitive motivation. Niederehe (chapter 23 in this volume) notes that unless we maximize the motivation of depressed subjects, we are measuring not their cognitive abilities but their motivation. Indeed, Cohen, Weingartner, Smallberg, Pickar, and Murphy (1982) found a strong association between severity of depression and ability to sustain effort on motor tasks as well as on memory tasks. They entertained the hypothesis that memory deficits may not be separable from deficits of motivation, drive, and attention.

Automatic Versus Effortful Cognition

Perhaps one way to deal with this plethora of concepts is through the automatic versus effortful distinction of Hasher and Zacks (1979). Some cognitive operations require minimal attentional capacity, owing to either heredity or practice. Such processes are termed automatic. In contrast, "effortful" operations require considerable attentional capacity. An example of an automatic process may be the activation of a word's meaning. Because of a person's extensive exposure to a word by reading and by hearing it in the language, the presentation of a word may automatically activate the node corresponding to the word's meaning. But maintaining the activation of a word (which might correspond to rehearsing that word) would require attentional capacity. Attentional capacity may decline with age (Botwinick & Thompson, 1966; Hasher & Zacks, 1979; Rabinowitz, Craik, & Ackerman, 1982) and with depression (Hasher & Zacks, 1979). Thus, elderly depressives may show deficits on such effortful operations as rehearsal and elaboration, while less demanding operations, such as activating word meanings and monitoring the frequency of events, are not impaired.

Depressive Mood and Selective Attention

Age and depression may diminish attentional capacity, leading to a variety of cognitive deficits. However, attention varies in direction as well as in amount or intensity. The hypothesis that aging and depression cause a loss of attentional capacity refers only to the intensive aspect of attention. In the experiment reported here, the depressed elderly subjects attended more intensively to mood-congruent, sad photographs than to mood-incongruent, happy photographs. The mood-congruence hypothesis suggests that depression may also influence the direction of attention or the selection of stimuli for processing. Such selective attention corresponds roughly to "interest." Depressed people may be more likely to selectively attend to sad than to happy stimuli. However, a measure of selective attention to happy and sad external events is somewhat incomplete. People may also direct their attention to internal events, such as their thoughts or feelings. The spreading activation model predicts that depressed persons' thoughts will center on mood-congruent material: sad incidents from the past, problems in the present, and concerns for the future. These negative mood-congruent events may be magnified in intensity and seriousness (see Tversky & Johnson, 1981), and thus be quite compelling relative to any external event.

Conclusions

Depression may have general detrimental effects on cognitive functioning. In addition to these general quantitative effects, there may be qualitative differences in what depressives and normal people attend to and later remember, depending on the affective tone of the material; for example, depressives learn sad material more effectively than happy material. What does such mood-congruent learning imply for our concern with memory assessment in the elderly? In addition to expecting depression to have some general detrimental effects on memory, investigators should look for some qualitative changes due simply to sad affect.

The data discussed in this chapter applied to elderly outpatients suffering from depression. However, the spreading activation theory of mood and memory predicts mood-congruent learning whenever strong affect, including sadness, is present. Using neutral or positive material for a memory test may underestimate the elderly depressives' capabilities. It is important to find conditions under which they can learn, as well as to explore their memory deficits. Thus, testing patients' memory for material that has varying affective quality (such as the short story used by Breslow et al., 1981) may reveal detriments only on the neutral and positive themes while memory for negative themes may be preserved. This may be particularly true if the test is one of incidental recall, in which the patients are allowed to allocate their attention freely. Such testing with affective materials may help separate the effects of mood on memory from other sources of memory dysfunction.

References

Anderson, J., & Bower, G. H. (1973). *Human associative memory*. Washington, DC: Winston.

Botwinick, J., & Thompson, L. (1966). Components of reaction time in relation to age and sex. *Journal of Genetic Psychology, 108*, 175–183.

Bower, G. H. (1981). Mood and memory. *American Psychologist, 36*, 129–148.

Bower, G. H., Gilligan, S. G., & Monteiro, K. P. (1981). Selectivity of learning caused by affective states. *Journal of Experimental Psychology: General, 110*, 451–473.

Bower, G. H., Monteiro, K. P., & Gilligan, S. G. (1978). Emotional mood as a context for learning and recall. *Journal of Verbal Learning and Verbal Behavior, 17*, 573–587.

Breslow, R., Kocsis, J., & Belkin, B. (1981). Contribution of the depressive perspective to memory function in depression. *American Journal of Psychiatry, 138*, 227–230.

Britton, B. K., & Tesser, A. (1982). Effects of prior knowledge on use of cognitive capacity in three complex cognitive tasks. *Journal of Verbal Learning and Verbal Behavior, 21,* 421–436.

Clark, M. S., & Isen, A. M. (1982). The relationship between feeling states and social behavior. In A. H. Hastorf & A. M. Isen (Eds.), *Cognitive social psychology.* New York: Elsevier North-Holland, Inc.

Cohen, R. M., Weingartner, H., Smallberg, S. A., Pickar, D., & Murphy, D. L. (1982). Effort and cognition in depression. *Archives of General Psychiatry, 39,* 593–597.

Collins, A. M., & Loftus, E. F. (1975). A spreading-activation theory of semantic processing. *Psychological Review, 82,* 407–428.

Craik, F. I. M., & Lockhart, R. S. (1972). Levels of processing: A framework for memory research. *Journal of Verbal Learning and Verbal Behavior, 11,* 671–684.

Gilligan, S. G., & Bower, G. H. (1982). *Cognitive consequences of emotional arousal.* Unpublished manuscript, Stanford University, Palo Alto, CA.

Hasher, L., & Zacks, R. T. (1979). Automatic and effortful processes in memory. *Journal of Experimental Psychology: General, 108,* 356–388.

Kahn, R. L., Zarit, S. H., Hilbert, N. M., & Niederehe, G. (1975). Memory complaint and impairment in the aged: The effects of depression and altered brain function. *Archives of General Psychiatry, 32,* 1569–1573.

Kahneman, D. (1973). *Attention and effort.* Englewood Cliffs, NJ: Prentice-Hall.

Kerr, B. (1973). Processing demands during mental operations. *Memory and Cognition, 1,* 401–412.

Lloyd, G. G., & Lishman, W. A. (1975). Effect of depression on the speed of recall of pleasant and unpleasant experiences. *Psychological Medicine, 5,* 173–180.

Mischel, W., Ebbesen, E., & Zeiss, A. (1973). Selective attention to the self: Situational and dispositional determinants. *Journal of Personality and Social Psychology, 27,* 129–142.

Plutchik, R. (1980). *Emotion: A psychoevolutionary synthesis.* New York: Harper & Row.

Popkin, S. J., Gallagher, D., Thompson, L., & Moore, M. (1982). Memory complaint and performance in normal and depressed older adults. *Experimental Aging Research, 8,* 141–145.

Posner, M. I. (1978). *Chronometric explorations of mind.* Hillsdale, NJ: Erlbaum.

Rabinowitz, J. C., Craik, F. I. M., & Ackerman, B. P. (1982). A processing resource account of age differences in recall. *Canadian Journal of Psychology, 36,* 325–344.

Schneider, W., & Shiffrin, R. M. (1977). Controlled and automatic human information processing: I. Detection, search, and attention. *Psychological Review, 84(1),* 1–67.

Slife, B. D., Miura, S., Thompson, L., & Gallagher, D. (1983). *Learning style and depression: An empirical investigation of theoretical and therapeutic considerations.* Unpublished manuscript, University of Santa Clara, Santa Clara, CA.

Teasdale, J. D., & Fogarty, S. J. (1979). Differential effect of induced mood on retrieval of pleasant and unpleasant events from episodic memory. *Journal of Abnormal Psychology, 88,* 248–257.

Tversky, A., & Johnson, E. J. (1981). Affect and the perception of risk. In *Proceedings of the Third Annual Conference of the Cognitive Science Society* (p. 96). Berkeley, CA.

Velten, E. (1968) A laboratory task for induction of mood states. *Behavior Research and Therapy, 6,* 473–482.

Weingartner, H., Miller, H., & Murphy, D. L. (1977). Mood-state-dependent retrieval of verbal associations. *Journal of Abnormal Psychology, 86,* 276–284.

Zarit, S. H., Gallagher, D., & Kramer, N. (1981). Memory training in the community aged: Effects on depression, memory complaint, and memory performance. *Educational Gerontology, 6,* 11–27.

Zuroff, D. C., Colussy, S. A., & Wielgus, M. S. (1983). Selective memory and depression: A cautionary note concerning response bias. *Cognitive Therapy and Research, 7,* 223–232.

CHAPTER
25

Partialing Out the Effects of Depression and Age on Cognitive Functions: Experimental Data and Methodologic Issues

The literature contains conflicting reports regarding the negative effects of depression and age on cognitive functions. Data from a series of studies reviewed here indicate that severe depression can have far-ranging negative effects on both psychomotor and cognitive performance. Another series of studies reviewed demonstrates that depressed persons with early signs of senile dementia may have difficulty learning. Factors accentuating cognitive deficits in these groups included severity of depression, residence in a continuous care facility, poor premorbid social competence, low premorbid intelligence, and cognitive tasks requiring sustained effort or concentration.

Within the past decade there has been an exponential increase in publications devoted to the effects of both depression and aging on cognitive functioning. It is also noteworthy that both depression and aging have been reported to have no effects as well as adverse effects on cognitive functioning (Miller, 1975; Poon, 1985; Strömgren, 1977). A similar situation obtains with regard to studies on the effects of depression on cognitive functioning in the elderly, which have also burgeoned in the past decade (Friedman, 1964; Gibson, 1981; Kahn, Zarit, Hilbert, & Niederehe, 1975; Popkin, Gallagher, Thompson, & Moore, 1982). A variety of explanations have been offered to reconcile these disparate findings. For the most part, these have related to methodologic issues such as differences in the upper age ranges of subjects, their severity of illness, their socioeconomic and educational backgrounds, and the nature and difficulty of the cognitive tasks themselves (Browning & Spilich, 1981). In general, the trend is for older patients, those rated as more severely ill, and

those with low educational levels to perform most poorly on the cognitive tests. One is also more likely to see the effects of either age, depression, or both on cognitive tests that require sustained effort or attention.

One of the aims of this chapter is to focus on these and related variables as factors moderating or accentuating the effects of both depression and aging on cognitive functioning. An additional and more substantive aim is to identify some of the common as well as unique effects of depression and aging on cognitive functioning. Specifically, my colleagues and I have been collecting data over a period of years on cognitive tests and on symptom rating scales that will be used to describe (a) psychomotor and cognitive deficits in severely depressed patients; (b) the combined effects of depression and age on cognitive functioning; (c) the combined effects of depression and dementia on cognitive functioning; and (d) the differential effects of chronic versus acute depression on cognitive functioning in elderly persons. Some effort will also be made to tie these findings to current theories of the effects of depression and aging on cognition.

Cognitive Deficits in Depression

In the late 1960s, a National Institute of Mental Health (NIMH) multihospital collaborative study of drug treatment in depression was initiated and included a battery of psychomotor, learning, and perceptual tests (Raskin, Friedman, & DiMascio, 1982). The major reasons for including these tests were to examine differences on these measures between depressed patients and normal subjects and to assess their possible use as outcome measures for evaluating psychoactive drug effects. When this study was conceived, Friedman had just published a paper showing few cognitive, perceptual, and psychomotor deficits in 55 severely depressed patients compared with a matched sample of 65 normal subjects (Friedman, 1964). He concluded that the actual performance of the patients did not match their unrealistically low perceptions of themselves or of their performance on the tests. With the Friedman study in mind, NIMH researchers included in the test battery for the collaborative study a number of items asking subjects to evaluate their test performance and to estimate how well they did on the tests.

The collaborative study sample consisted of 277 inpatients (17 to 70 years of age) with moderate to severe depression as rated on the Three-Area Severity of Depression Scales (Table 25-1). The 112 normal subjects were matched to the patient sample by age, sex, and years of schooling. There were 13 separate psychomotor and cognitive tests yielding a total of 33 scores (see Raskin et al., 1982, for a description of the tests). Initial testing was done prior to patient assignment to drug treatment and after patients had been kept off all medication for a minimum of 4 days.

There were significant differences between patients and normal subjects on 11 of the 13 tests and on 25 of the 33 scores derived from these tests (Table 25-2). The number and breadth of the differences between patients and normal subjects were surprising, particularly in light of the prior findings by Friedman of few patient–normal differences on comparable measures in his sample of depressed patients. One possible explanation for this disparity was the fact that Friedman's subjects showed above-average verbal facility as reflected in their Wechsler Adult Intelligence Scale (WAIS) (Wechsler, 1955) vocabulary test scores and appeared to be brighter than those in the collaborative study. High IQ and high educational level tend to moderate or narrow the effects of aging and depression on cognitive tests.

Tests were selected for the collaborative study primarily on the basis of their prior ability to differentiate psychiatric populations from normal populations. No unifying theory of psychological deficit in depression guided the choice of measures. However, the differences between depressed patients and normal subjects that emerged support the hypothesis that a generalized deficit in central motivational state exists in depressed individuals. This information was recently proposed by Cohen, Weingartner, Smallberg, Pickar, and Murphy (1982), who found that the greatest depression-related impairment was on cognitive and motor tasks requiring sustained effort. Perhaps the best example of this finding in the collaborative study was on the tapping test where patients actually outperformed normal subjects under the free condition when instructed to tap at a comfortable rate. In contrast, under the speed condition, when they were instructed to tap "as fast and as steadily as possible," the normal subjects did substantially better than the patients (Table 25-2).

Additional corroboration can be found in the percentage accuracy scores on the unpaced and paced Digit Symbol Tests. In the unpaced Digit Symbol Test, subjects are given a Digit Symbol sheet to complete with the usual instructions to fill in as many squares

Table 25-1. Three-Area Severity of Depression Scales

Severity of depression: To what extent does the patient evidence depression or despondency in verbal report, behavior, and secondary symptoms of depression?

Cues		Not at all	Somewhat	Moderately	Considerably	Very much
Verbal report	Says he or she feels blue; talks of feeling helpless, hopeless, or worthless; complains of loss of interest; may wish he or she were dead; reports crying spells.	1	2	3	4	5
Behavior	Looks sad; cries easily; speaks in a sad voice; appears slowed down; lacks energy.	1	2	3	4	5
Secondary symptoms of depression	Insomnia; G.I. complaints; dry mouth; history of recent suicide attempt; lack of appetite; weight loss.	1	2	3	4	5
Total	Add the scale points checked for severity of depression in verbal report, behavior, and secondary symptoms of depression.				Total _____	

Note. Adapted from Raskin, Schulterbrandt, Reatig, and McKeon (1970). In the public domain.

Table 25-2. Mean Scores Showing Significant Differences Between Depressed Patients and Normal Subjects on Cognitive and Psychomotor Tests

Variable	Mean scores		*F*
	Depressed patients (*n* = 277)	Normal subjects (*n* = 112)	
Tapping Test			
Additional taps under speed condition	54.17	75.22	25.07**
Aiming Test			
Total no. of dots in circles	76.34	125.22	116.91**
Percentage accuracy on 4 trials	69.77	84.05	20.64**
Subject's estimate of no. of dots in circles	83.58	102.82	4.34*
Unpaced Digit Symbol Test			
No. of correct symbols on Trial 2	12.07	17.00	76.07**
Percentage accuracy on all trials	95.67	99.55	3.91**
Guess of time to complete test (sec)	177.79	137.35	4.67*
No. of additional symbols completed on Trial 4 vs. Trial 2	.36	1.73	5.26*
Paced Digit Symbol Test			
No. of correct symbols	22.40	34.55	63.20**
No. of errors	1.28	.47	4.20*
Percentage accuracy	69.56	86.10	20.32**
Clock Reversal Test			
No. correct on Trial 4	1.77	1.90	4.39*
Score for speed and accuracy	2.49	3.82	25.45**
Shift Test			
No. correct on Trial 3	15.88	21.72	62.39**
Stroop Color-Naming Test			
No. of errors in reading	3.20	1.82	5.32*
Ratio of time to complete Line 1, Card C, and to complete Card C	16.41	14.28	9.23**
Difference score in minutes in time to read Card C vs. Card B	42.34	34.07	6.62*
Area Tapping Test			
Estimate of time to complete (sec)	44.78	22.68	6.37*
Circle Tracing Test			
Time to trace (sec)	43.35	68.55	16.35**
Learning nonsense syllables			
No. attempted	3.38	6.75	102.48**
No. correct	1.26	2.17	27.60**
Gorham Proverbs Test			
Abstract sum	5.57	8.12	47.64**
Concrete sum	1.18	.59	18.06**
Abstract sum + concrete sum + 6	9.68	13.53	57.13**

*$p < .05$, two-tailed. **$p < .01$, two-tailed.

as they can without skipping any. In the paced Digit Symbol Test, the numbers are presented on a memory drum, and the subjects write the appropriate mark or symbol on a sheet in a box under the number. The paced Digit Symbol Test requires greater concentration and effort to keep up with the moving drum. The percentage accuracy score dropped for both patients and normal subjects from the unpaced to the paced task, but the drop for patients was more dramatic (normal subjects went from 99.6% to 86.1% accuracy, a 13.5% drop, and patients went from 95.7% to 69.6% accuracy, a 27.1% drop).

The motivational deficit hypothesis could also account for the differences between patients and normal subjects on the Clock Reversal, which requires sustained concentration, and in the difference between patients and normal subjects in the number of nonsense syllables each group attempted to learn. This latter difference was especially striking.

The earlier study by Friedman (1964) led us to expect patients to underestimate their actual performance on the tests. There was some evidence for this: Patients tended to overestimate the time it took them to complete the unpaced Digit Symbol Test and to overestimate the time spent on the Area Tapping Test. In one instance, however—in estimating the number of dots in circles on the Aiming Test—their estimates of poor performance accurately reflected their actual performance. In sum, although patients in the collaborative study tended to downplay their actual performance, there was ample evidence that they did, in fact, perform more poorly than the matched sample of normal controls.

The findings from this collaborative study also bear on recent reports of conceptual organization and abstract reasoning deficits in depressed patients (Savard, Rey, & Post, 1980; Silberman, Weingartner, & Post, 1983; Weingartner, Cohen, Murphy, Martello, & Gerdt, 1981). Two of the tests in the collaborative study measured abstracting ability. On the Stroop Color-Naming Test, the subject is required to read color names that are printed on the card in incongruous colors (e.g., the word *red* appears in blue ink). To succeed on this task, the subject has to break prior conceptual sets or organizations and demonstrate conceptual fluidity by accurately and quickly reading the color names despite the fact that they appear in incongruous colors on the card. The Gorham Proverbs Test provides the subject with four multiple-choice answers to explain each proverb. These answers differ in their level of abstraction. Patients performed more poorly than normal control subjects on both of these tests, showing less ability to reorganize their thinking and more concrete thinking.

Hypotheses other than the motivational deficit hypothesis have been offered to explain the depressed patients' deficits in abstracting ability and in reasoning. Included are the possibility of some form of right hemisphere dysfunction (Buchsbaum, Carpenter, & Fedio, 1979) or a disruption in brain state arousal and activation (Bloch, 1976; Weingartner, Murphy, & Weinstein, 1976). Silberman et al. (1983) noted that patients with both right and left temporal lobectomies in the Rausch (1977) study were found to be impaired to the same degree as the depressed patients in their study. However, whereas subjects with left lobectomies formulated fewer hypotheses than normal subjects, the right-lesioned subjects formulated as many hypotheses as normal subjects but tended to retain them even when they were disconfirmed. This parallel between right-lobectomized and depressed patients in the Silberman et al. (1983) study is consistent with other reports linking depression with right-hemisphere dysfunction (Buchsbaum et al., 1979; Yozawitz, Bruder, Sutton, Gurland, Fleiss, & Costa, 1979).

The tendency of persons with right-hemisphere lesions or depression to retain untenable hypotheses can be viewed as an example of conceptual rigidity. It is exemplified by the difficulty that depressed patients in the collaborative study had on the Stroop Color-Naming Test. The brain activation or arousal hypothesis is supported by research findings showing that drugs that activate depressed patients, such as L-dopa and *d*-amphetamine, enhance learning and cognition (Murphy & Weingartner, 1973; Reus, Silberman, Post, & Weingartner, 1979; Stein, Belluzzi, & Wise, 1975).

These biological or pharmacological hypotheses do not necessarily negate the psychological hypothesis of a motivational deficit in depression. Rather, these hypotheses should be viewed as representing different levels of explanation for the same phenomena. This is the position that Weingartner and associates appear to have adopted.

The Combined Effects of Depression and Age on Cognitive Functions

It has been shown that depression can have far-reaching effects on psychomotor tasks as well as on cognitive tasks. Are these effects magnified in older persons, or does depression have different effects in older persons as compared with younger persons? The collaborative study results suggest an answer to this question, but these results cannot be regarded as definitive, because the subjects in this study were limited to those age 70 or younger.

Study subjects were divided into four groups: depressed patients under 40 years of age, depressed patients 40 years old and older, normal subjects under age 40, and normal subjects 40 years old and older. When an overall *F*-ratio comparing these groups on the psychomotor and cognitive tests was significant, Tukey-b range tests were performed to locate the significant differences among the groups. The results of these analyses are seen in Table 25-3. The "Difference" column in Table 25-3 (and in Tables 25-4 and 25-7 to 25-11) is designed to illustrate the results obtained from the range tests. Each group of subjects is assigned a number (e.g., the number 1 is for patients under age 40, 2 is for normal subjects under age 40, and so on). The numbers are ordered from left to right in the Difference column according to the magnitude of the groups' mean scores; the group with the highest mean score is at the extreme left, followed by groups with successively lower mean scores. A hyphen between numbers in the "Difference" column indicates that there was a statistically significant difference between those groups; a comma between numbers indicates that the groups did not differ significantly on that variable.

There were 10 significant age-group differences out of 33 tests run. The depressed patients age 40 and older were least similar to the other groups. They performed more slowly, were less accurate, and showed more perceptual rigidity and concreteness in thinking than did normal subjects in the same age group. It is also noteworthy that on a number of measures, normal subjects over age 40 did at least as well as the subjects under age 40. Hence, it was the combination of age and depression rather than age per se that seemed to have the greatest negative impact on psychomotor and cognitive performance.

A similar finding was reported by Savard et al. (1980), who found that older bipolar depressive patients made significantly more errors on the Halstead-Reitan Category Test than younger bipolar and younger unipolar patients. This test has been used in the past to differentiate brain-damaged from nonbrain-damaged subjects and requires subjects to both differentiate and integrate percepts into categories, an ab-

Table 25-3. Mean Scores Showing Significant Age-Group Differences on Cognitive and Psychomotor Tests

Variable	Under age 40		Age 40 +			
	(1) Depressed patients ($n = 139$)	(2) Normal subjects ($n = 31$)	(3) Depressed patients ($n = 138$)	(4) Normal subjects ($n = 81$)	F	Difference[1]
Aiming Test						
Total no. of dots in circles	90.54	120.33	62.14	130.11	19.65**	4,2,1–3
Percentage accuracy on 4 trials	76.40	81.44	63.15	86.65	9.50**	4,2,1–3
Time Estimation Test						
Time off from 15 seconds	12.28	28.25	34.15	15.58	4.92*	3–2–4,1
Unpaced Digit Symbol Test						
No. of correct symbols on Trial 2	14.28	16.85	9.86	17.16	19.21**	4,2,1–3
Guess of time to complete test (sec)	124.83	140.35	230.76	134.35	9.86**	3–2,4,1
Shift Test						
No. correct on last trial	18.95	21.80	12.81	21.64	18.01**	2,4,1–3
Paced Digit Symbol Test						
Percentage accuracy	79.89	86.90	59.23	85.31	7.44**	2,4,1–3
Gorham Proverbs Test						
Abstract sum	6.37	8.23	4.76	8.00	3.85*	2,4,1–3
Concrete sum	.79	.57	1.57	.60	7.82**	3–1,4,2
Abstract sum + concrete sum + 6	11.08	13.66	8.28	13.40	6.84**	2,4,1–3

[1]Groups are listed in order of decreasing scores. A comma indicates no significant difference between scores; a hyphen indicates a significant difference
*$p < .05$, two-tailed. **$p < .01$, two-tailed.

stract organizing task. These results support the view that age tends to magnify psychological deficits associated with depression. However, depression also appears to have a greater negative impact in older persons on difficult tasks requiring a fairly high level of sustained effort and motivation.

The Effects of Depression on Cognitive Impairment in Early Dementia Patients

Depression is frequently seen in individuals with senile dementia, particularly in the early stages of this illness. Does depression also magnify psychomotor and cognitive deficits in these individuals? How do depressed demented patients compare with depressed nondemented patients? Partial answers to these questions are available from data collected at five settings on a geriatric test battery developed at the NIMH (Raskin & Rae, 1981). To be included in this study, subjects had to be 60 years of age or older; had to obtain an age-corrected scaled score of at least 8 on the vocabulary subtest of the WAIS; and had to have good comprehension, speaking, and reading skills in English. All subjects were assigned a diagnosis from the January 15, 1978, draft of the *Diagnostic and Statistical Manual* (DSM-III) (American Psychiatric Association, 1978). The diagnosis for the 32 patients in the two demented groups was progressive idiopathic dementia, senile onset. The 24 subjects characterized as

nonsenile depressed received a variety of depression diagnoses, including major depressive disorder and depressive personality. The study also included 150 normal subjects. Nonsenile depressed and depressed demented patients had to receive a total score of 7 or higher on the Three-Area Severity of Depression Scales (Table 25-1) in order to be included. (A score of 7 or higher on these scales has been used as an entry criterion in a number of outpatient depression studies.)

The results from only a few of the evaluation instruments in this study will be described. There were significant group differences on 19 of the 21 variables rated by psychiatrists and psychologists on the Global Assessments of Psychopathology Scale, a symptom-rating scale. Table 25-4 lists 8 of these 19 variables. The psychiatrists and psychologists believed that the depressed demented patients were the most severely ill, but these patients were not rated as showing more mental deterioration than the nondepressed demented patients. Furthermore, the psychiatrists and psychologists rated both demented groups as more mentally deteriorated than the depressed patients. In the cognitive sphere, the psychiatrists and psychologists consistently rated the two demented groups as appearing more confused, more disoriented, and more forgetful than the depressed or normal samples. The depression-alone group and the depressed demented group were also rated highest on depression and on anxiety, although the nondepressed demented patients showed more depression and anxiety than the matched sample of normal controls.

Table 25-4. Mean Scores Showing Significant Differences Among Groups on Selected Symptoms Rated by Psychiatrists and Psychologists (Geriatric Test Battery File)

| Variable | Demented | | Nondemented | | F | Difference[1] |
	(1) Depressed ($n = 13$)	(2) Nondepressed ($n = 19$)	(3) Depressed ($n = 24$)	(4) Normal subjects ($n = 150$)		
Appears confused, perplexed[2]	2.46	2.16	1.17	1.12	54.78*	1,2–3,4
Seems disoriented[2]	2.23	2.16	1.12	1.03	57.96**	1,2–3,4
Appears inattentive[2]	1.23	1.00	1.00	1.03	4.02**	1–4,2,3
Appears forgetful[2]	2.62	2.42	1.88	1.19	51.51**	1,2–3–4
Appears depressed, blue[2]	3.38	1.89	3.54	1.17	241.77**	3,1–2–4
Appears tense, anxious[2]	2.23	1.57	2.62	1.17	64.41**	3,1–2–4
Severity of illness[3]	3.00	2.47	2.33	1.11	108.60**	1–2,3–4
Severity of mental deterioration[4]	2.23	2.37	1.67	1.10	93.98**	2,1–3–4

[1]Groups are listed in order of decreasing scores. A comma indicates no significant difference between scores; a hyphen indicates a significant difference.
[2]Rated on a 5-point scale from *Not at all* to *Extremely*.
[3]Rated on a 7-point scale from *Normal, not ill at all* to *Among the most extremely ill patients*.
[4]Rated on a 5-point scale from *Normal, shows no signs of deterioration* to *Among the most deteriorated patients*.
*$p < .05$, two-tailed. **$p < .01$, two-tailed.

One test in this battery, the Mini-Mental State Examination by Folstein, Folstein, and McHugh (1975; Table 25-5), provides direct measures of cognitive functioning. There were significant group differences on 10 of the 33 scores derived from this test. Seven of these differences are listed in Table 25-5. In all instances, the demented patients performed more poorly than the depressed or normal subjects, but there were no significant differences between the depressed and nondepressed demented subjects. There were also significant differences between the nondemented depressed subjects and the normal comparison group on the three recall or short-term memory items, that is on the ability to recall "ball," "flag," and "tree."

These results suggest that depression adds little to the cognitive problems already extant in patients in the early stages of senile dementia. Results from an earlier study of the effects of hyper- and normobaric oxygen on cognitive functioning in the elderly, however, qualify these findings (Raskin, Gershon, Crook, Sathananthan, & Ferris, 1978). An operational definition of cognitive deficit was used as an entry criterion in that study. Subjects were between 60 and 85 years of age and had scored more than one standard deviation below the mean established for their age group and vocabulary level on at least three of the five subtests on the Guild Memory Test. Subjects were divided into two groups: those with and those without significant depression. Significant depression was defined as scoring 7 or higher on the Three-Area Severity of Depression Scales. Subjects were given a battery of cognitive tests that included tests developed by Crook, Ferris,

Table 25-5. Significant Differences Among Groups on Selected Items From the Mini-Mental Status Examination (Geriatric Test Battery File)

| Item | Demented | | Nondemented | | x^2 |
	(1) Depressed ($n = 13$)	(2) Nondepressed ($n = 19$)	(3) Depressed ($n = 24$)	(4) Normal subjects ($n = 150$)	
Knows date	46	53	79	90	29.70**
Knows country	38	21	83	87	53.24**
Can count backward from 100 by 7s to 72	45	53	87	71	8.60*
Can recall "ball"	23	21	50	83	50.75**
Can recall "flag"	8	5	17	52	29.42**
Can recall "tree"	15	16	21	52	19.58**
Can repeat, "No if, ands, or buts"	62	68	88	88	10.53*
Total score	19.08	20.32	25.54	26.43	45.16**[1]

Note. Scores indicate the percentage of subjects in each group attaining correct scores.
[1]This is the value of F, not x^2.
*$p = <.05$, two-tailed. **$p < .01$, two-tailed.

Table 25-6. Mean Scores Showing Significant Differences on Cognitive Measures Between Depressed and Nondepressed Elderly Subjects With Cognitive Impairment (Hyperbaric Oxygen Study)

Variable	Depressed ($n = 10$)	Non-depressed ($n = 46$)	t
Telephone numbers: verbal recall (10 digits)	23.30	30.35	2.19**
Telephone numbers: motor recall (10 digits)	14.70	20.02	2.02*
Facial recognition (2-minute delay)	5.30	7.27	2.40*
Name–face acquisition (delayed recall)	.50	1.27	2.03*
First-name acquisition (first presentation)	.50	1.02	2.34*
First-name acquisition (delayed recall)	1.00	1.78	2.70**

*$p < .05$, two-tailed. **$p < .01$, two-tailed.

and others. As Table 25-6 reveals, the depressed and nondepressed patients could be distinguished on these tests: The presence of depression resulted in both poorer immediate recall and poorer delayed recall.

The results of these two studies highlight the importance of test selection and sample characteristics. In the geriatric test battery study, the majority of the demented patients and almost half the depressed patients were in continuous care facilities. In contrast, all the cognitively impaired subjects in the hyperbaric oxygen study were still living in the community, most in their own homes. Also, these latter patients were recruited from ads in the *New York Times,* and their educational levels were higher than those of subjects in the geriatric test battery study. Thus, a fairly high degree of mental deterioration, coupled with a low-to-moderate educational background, is apparently associated with evidence of mental deterioration on relatively simple measures of cognitive functioning, but the presence of depression in such patients is not a significant factor in further lowering their ability to perform. Although the analogy is not exact, the result is similar to what is known in statistics as a floor effect. Institutionalization and hospitalization are also known to accelerate mental deterioration and confusion in some elderly persons. In contrast, when subjects are drawn from relatively high socioeconomic and educational backgrounds and are just beginning to show signs of senility and cognitive impairment, the presence of clinical depression can be detected in a further lowering of their levels of cognitive functioning. To demonstrate cognitive deficits secondary to depression in such subjects, however, it may be necessary to use highly technical or conceptually difficult cognitive tests.

Results of the geriatric test battery study also bear on the issue of the relationship between depressed patients' memory complaints and actual performance on memory tasks. This issue is examined in the next section.

The Differential Effects of Chronic Versus Acute Depression on Cognitive Functioning in the Elderly

To examine the differential effects on cognitive functioning of chronic versus acute depression in elderly subjects, the geriatric test battery study was expanded to include a larger sample of depressed outpatients. Psychiatrists and psychologists at the five collaborating centers made the diagnoses of chronic depressive disorder (now termed dysthymic disorder) and major depressive disorder (now termed major depression) on the basis of criteria contained in the 1978 draft of the DSM-III mentioned earlier (American Psychiatric Association, 1978).

There were important differences between these two depressed groups on a number of background variables. The chronic depression patients were older (mean age, 74.6) than the major depression patients (mean age, 67.1), more were widowed, and more were living in continuous care facilities. However, the chronic depression patients received lower ratings on global severity of illness than the major depression patients, a finding that is consistent with the prior characterization of the latter patients as acutely ill (Table 25-7).

On a symptom checklist completed by the subjects (the Inventory of Psychic and Somatic Complaints— Patient), the major depression patients rated themselves higher than the chronic depression patients on "feeling blue" and on "feeling no interest in things," two of the major signs of depression (see Table 25-8). However, the patients with major depression also rated themselves significantly higher than the chronic group and the senile group on all of the items listed under the heading "Attention–Concentration," such as, "feeling confused" and "having trouble concentrating." These patients also rated themselves highest on items subsumed under the headings "Recent Memory" and "Remote Memory." However, they did not differ signifi-

Table 25-7. Mean Scores on Global Assessment Scales (Psychiatric) (Expanded Data File—Geriatric Test Battery)

Item	(1) Senile patients (n = 34)	(2) Chronic depressives (n = 29)	(3) Major depressives (n = 102)	(4) Normal controls (n = 292)	F	Difference[1]
Severity of illness[2]	2.88	2.48	3.86	1.48	114.09*	3–1,2–4
Severity of mental deterioration[3]	2.29	1.78	1.89	1.25	42.02*	1–3,2–4

[1]Groups are listed in order of decreasing scores. A comma indicates no significant difference between scores; a hyphen indicates a significant difference.
[2]Rated on a 7-point scale ranging from *Normal, not ill at all* (1) to *Among the most extremely ill patients* (7).
[3]Rated on a 5-point scale ranging from *Normal, shows no sign of deterioration* (1) to *Among the most extremely deteriorated patients* (5).
*$p < .01$, two-tailed.

Table 25-8. Mean Scores on Selected Items From the Inventory of Psychic and Somatic Complaints (Patient) (Expanded Data File—Geriatric Test Battery)

Item	(1) Senile patients (n = 34)	(2) Chronic depressives (n = 29)	(3) Major depressives (n = 102)	(4) Normal subjects (n = 292)	F	Difference[1]
Depression						
1. Feeling blue	2.47	3.04	3.46	1.68	76.14**	3–2,1,4
2. Feeling no interest in things	1.76	2.07	2.87	1.61	29.48**	3–2,1,4
Attention–Concentration						
1. Feeling confused	1.53	1.56	2.44	1.36	31.49*	3–2,1,4
20. Having to do things very slowly to be sure you were doing them right	1.76	1.81	2.60	1.72	16.54**	3–2,1,4
22. Having difficulty making even simple decisions	1.41	1.37	2.46	1.36	31.77**	3–1,2,4
27. Having to check and double-check what you do	1.71	1.67	2.74	1.62	32.71**	3–1,2,4
41. Having difficulty organizing your thoughts	1.41	1.48	2.53	1.46	29.74**	3–2,4,1
52. Having trouble concentrating	1.65	1.56	2.96	1.53	46.36**	3–1,2,4
Recent Memory						
7. Having trouble remembering things	2.21	1.81	3.01	1.98	21.50**	3–1,4,2
62. Forgetting where you place things	2.15	1.67	3.01	1.91	21.91**	3–1,4,2
64. Forgetting people's names soon after being introduced	3.06	2.37	3.38	2.35	16.20**	3,1–2,4
Remote Memory						
21. Having trouble remembering people and events from childhood	2.00	1.48	2.01	1.53	7.31**	3,1–4,2
40. Forgetting appointments	1.47	1.19	1.68	1.42	3.14*	3–1,4,2

[1]Groups are listed in order of decreasing scores. A comma indicates no significant difference between scores; a hyphen indicates a significant difference.
*$p < .05$, two-tailed. **$p < .01$, two-tailed.

cantly from the senile patients on two items: "forgetting people's names soon after being introduced," and "having trouble remembering people and events from childhood." The senile patients resembled the chronic depression patients in being the oldest group (mean age, 79.0) and in being drawn almost exclusively from continuous care facilities.

A slightly different pattern emerged on a symptom checklist completed by psychiatrists and psychologists (Inventory of Psychic and Somatic Complaints—Psychiatrist; see Table 25-9). Although these mental health professionals rated the group with major depression highest on anergia ("feeling no interest in things"), they rated both depression groups high on depressed mood ("feeling blue"). They saw no significant differences between the subjects with major depression and the senile subjects on the attention–concentration items. On the recent and remote memory items they saw more pathology in the senile patients than in the other groups. As becomes evident later, these ratings are more consistent with the actual performance of the subjects on tests of memory function than are the subjects' self-report ratings.

Staff at the five sites also obtained ratings of psychopathology from close relatives or friends of the subjects in this study (Relative's Assessment of Global Symptomatology; see Table 25-10). These results paralleled those obtained from the subjects themselves. The major depression patients received the highest ratings on depressed mood, anergia, and appearing confused and forgetful. Hence, these ratings were apparently based primarily on complaints voiced by the subjects to their friends and relatives rather than on independent judgments.

Table 25-9. Mean Scores on Selected Items From the Inventory of Psychic and Somatic Complaints (Psychiatrist) (Expanded Data File—Geriatric Test Battery)

Item	(1) Senile patients ($n = 34$)	(2) Chronic depressives ($n = 29$)	(3) Major depressives ($n = 102$)	(4) Normal subjects ($n = 292$)	F	Difference[1]
Depression						
5. Feeling no interest in things	1.79	2.00	2.74	1.22	36.03*	3–2,1–4
8. Feeling blue	2.47	3.08	3.46	1.58	49.35*	3,2–1–4
Attention–Concentration						
40. Having difficulty concentrating	1.59	1.31	1.82	1.15	8.86*	3,1–2,4
41. Having to check and double-check what he or she does	1.62	1.23	1.62	1.17	4.69*	1,3–2,4
43. Forgetting the point she or he was trying to make	1.53	1.08	1.59	1.10	7.64*	3,1–4,2
44. Rambling or drifting off the topic discussed	1.59	1.15	1.54	1.35	1.38	1,3,4,2
Recent Memory						
31. Forgetting where she or he has placed things	2.38	1.77	2.00	1.62	7.16*	1,3–2,4
33. Having trouble remembering recent events such as items in newspaper, on TV, movies, etc.	2.85	1.54	1.69	1.30	36.54*	1–3,2–4
36. Forgetting names of people immediately or soon after being introduced	3.38	2.27	2.03	1.80	17.99*	1–2,3,4
37. During conversation, having difficulty recalling appropriate words or names	1.97	1.38	1.54	1.15	11.92*	1–3,2–4
Remote Memory						
32. Forgetting appointments, addresses, or phone numbers	2.38	1.46	1.67	1.35	16.43*	1–3,2,4
34. Having trouble remembering people and events during childhood	2.68	1.50	1.59	1.26	30.19*	1–3,2,4

[1]Groups are listed in order of decreasing scores. A comma indicates no significant difference between scores; a hyphen indicates a significant difference.
*$p < .01$, two-tailed.

Table 25-10. Mean Scores on Selected Items From Relative's Assessment of Global Symptomatology (Expanded Data File—Geriatric Test Battery)

Item	(1) Senile patients ($n = 10$)	(2) Chronic depressives ($n = 16$)	(3) Major depressives ($n = 51$)	(4) Normal subjects ($n = 190$)	F	Difference[1]
3. Appearing depressed, blue, or despondent	2.40	2.81	3.25	1.52	34.09*	3–2,1–4
12. Appearing slowed-down, fatigued, and lacking in energy	2.00	2.38	2.76	1.64	10.95*	3–2,1–4
16. Appearing inattentive	1.10	1.56	1.55	1.19	1.92	2,3,4,1
17. Appearing confused, perplexed	1.60	1.75	1.98	1.18	7.39*	3–2,1–4
19. Appearing forgetful	1.90	2.13	2.55	1.66	5.95*	3–2,1,4

[1]Groups are listed in order of decreasing scores. A comma indicates no significant difference between scores; a hyphen indicates a significant difference.
*$p < .01$, two-tailed.

As in the original geriatric test battery study, only one of the tests in the battery provided direct measures of cognitive functioning, the Mini-Mental State Examination by Folstein et al. (1975). This test is designed primarily as a screening device for detecting evidence of organic brain damage or senility. Table 25-11 illustrates the results obtained for two of the sections, "registration" and "recall." Registration taps immediate recall. The scores (2 = correct; 1 = incorrect) denote whether the subject is able to repeat the words "ball," "flag," and "tree," in that order, after one presentation. Later, the subject is again asked to recall these three words, which were previously repeated until learned. Recall—or, more accurately, delayed recall—of these words is elicited following a task requiring sustained attention and concentration. Results on this test indicated that the senile patients performed least well on

both immediate and delayed recall, and the major depression patients did not differ significantly from the normal control subjects on either immediate or delayed recall. The chronic depressed patients, however, did differ significantly from the normal control group on delayed recall but not on immediate recall.

These results clearly indicate that some depressed patients who complain of problems with their memory show no evidence of cognitive deficits on objective tests. This finding is consistent with the report by Kahn et al. (1975) and with a more recent publication by Popkin et al. (1982) that in elderly depressed persons who complained about memory problems, poor performance on a series of memory tests was related to altered brain function and not to depression. How does one reconcile these findings with the substantial literature that shows that depression does have negative

Table 25-11. Mean Scores on Selected Items From the Mini-Mental State Examination (Expanded Data File—Geriatric Test Battery)

Item	(1) Senile patients ($n = 34$)	(2) Chronic depressives ($n = 29$)	(3) Major depressives ($n = 102$)	(4) Normal subjects ($n = 292$)	F	Difference[1]
Registration (immediate recall)						
"Ball"	1.91[a]	1.96	1.98	1.99	14.44*	4,3,2–1
"Flag"	1.88	2.00	1.98	1.99	5.98*	2,4,3–1
"Tree"	1.88	1.96	1.98	1.99	5.27*	4,3,2–1
No. of trials until learned	1.32	1.15	1.63	1.27	2.33	3,1,4,2
Recall (delayed recall)						
"Ball"	1.21	1.56	1.82	1.80	25.43*	3,4–2–1
"Flag"	1.06	1.26	1.61	1.52	13.51*	3,4–2–1
"Tree"	1.15	1.33	1.67	1.53	7.17*	3,4–2–1
Total score	19.74	25.52	27.08	26.38	61.26*	3,4,2–1

[1]Groups are listed in order of decreasing scores. A comma indicates no significant difference between scores; a hyphen indicates a significant difference.
[a]A correct response or recall after the first presentation is scored 2, an incorrect response, 1. Hence, the closer the mean value is to 2, the better the score.
*$p < .01$, two-tailed.

effects on cognitive functioning? The results of the collaborative depression study described earlier is a case in point.

One methodologic factor that might be at least partially responsible for these disparate findings is the difference in overall severity of illness of subjects admitted to these studies. In the collaborative depression study, in which there were many significant differences between the patients and normal subjects on the psychomotor and cognitive tests, the patients were all hospitalized and had to receive total scores of 9 or higher on the Three-Area Severity of Depression Scales. In later studies with outpatient depressives, investigators required only a total score of 7 on these scales; hence, in the geriatric test battery studies this criterion was also used. Consequently, patients in the latter studies were less severely depressed than those in the earlier collaborative study. In the study by Kahn et al. (1975), the median total score for the depressed sample on the Hamilton Psychiatric Rating Scale for Depression (HAM-D) was only 10.5, which is considerably below the score of 18 or higher that is generally required for entrance into treatment assessment studies. Kahn et al. (1975) also characterized their depressed sample as being mildly to moderately depressed. Hence, to demonstrate cognitive deficits on objective tests, it may be necessary to sample patients who are more severely depressed.

It is also possible that depressed patients with certain symptom profiles may be more likely to perform poorly on cognitive tests than patients with other symptom profiles. Overall (1965), for example, has identified four subtypes of depression. One might expect his withdrawn–retarded and agitated types to do less well on psychomotor and cognitive tests than his hostile or anxious types. This premise is predicated on the belief that patients suffering from retardation in speech and behavior (withdrawn–retarded depressives) and patients with difficulty sustaining attention and concentration (agitated depressives) would perform less well on cognitive and psychomotor tasks than patients who were more intact in these areas, namely, hostile and anxious depressives. However, this premise has never been tested.

Although the psychiatrists and psychologists rated the chronic depression patients in the geriatric test battery study as less severely ill than the major depression patients, the former group were older and more physically infirm, necessitating residence in continuous care facilities. They also had greater problems with the recall items on the Mini-Mental State Examination than either the major depression patients or the normal subjects. Thus, in this case, three background variables—age, physical health, and institutionalization—affected performance on cognitive tests.

Another possible reason for inconsistent study results relates to the level of difficulty and nature of the cognitive tasks included in test batteries. As noted earlier, the Mini-Mental State Examination used in the geriatric test battery studies is designed to detect organic brain damage and performs this role quite well.

For example, the senile patients had a total mean score below 20 on this scale, as predicted by the authors of the scale, whereas the depressed patients and normal subjects had significantly higher mean scores. However, the test is relatively simple, particularly the items sampling immediate and remote memory. It was also previously demonstrated that the Mini-Mental State Examination was not able to distinguish depressed from nondepressed patients with early signs of senility, whereas a more difficult cognitive battery was able to show significant differences between these samples on both recent and remote memory.

Discussion

If nothing else, the data presented highlight methodologic issues to be considered when examining elderly depressed patients for evidence of cognitive decline. One of these issues that has not received the attention it deserves is the definition of depression. In many studies, the samples of depressed elderly subjects would not meet established DSM-III criteria for a diagnosis of depression and could best be characterized as suffering from mild to moderate dysphoria. Such people may complain of memory problems but generally do not show evidence of memory impairment on objective tests. Is there a certain level of severity of depression at which we begin to see evidence of impairment on objective cognitive tests? Also, it is possible, as previously noted, that severity of depression per se may not be the critical factor inducing cognitive dysfunction. Rather, certain key symptoms, or a specific profile of symptoms, or institutionalization may be associated with cognitive difficulties.

The cognitive measures in the studies described in this chapter are admittedly crude by today's standards, which may also account for the failure to demonstrate some of the unique effects of depression originally intended. Gibson (1981), for example, found that both depressed and demented patients, compared with normal subjects, showed memory loss in learning serially presented words and pictures, with the loss being more severe in the demented group. Furthermore, a qualitative analysis of serial position curves revealed that the curves for the depressed group had the same shapes as those for the normal group, albeit at a lower absolute level, but the curves for the demented group were quite different. Hence, a refined approach to data analysis was able to detect differences in memory deficits between depressed and demented subjects.

Tests for memory deficits in elderly subjects need to be designed so that they are clinically meaningful. This is particularly important because elderly persons may lose interest as well as patience when asked to perform tasks they view as meaningless. Some efforts have been made; for example, the Digit Span Test has been transformed into a series of telephone numbers and subjects are asked to dial the numbers and to repeat them verbally.

A major aim of this chapter was to identify idiosyncratic or unique patterns of cognitive loss in depressed elderly persons, in depressed persons with early signs of senility, and in acute and chronic depressions. The data at hand did not prove very helpful in this task, primarily because of limitations in the cognitive tests employed, but some differences among the groups did emerge.

Evidence from the collaborative depression study suggests that the effects of aging in a moderately to severely depressed sample were more likely to appear on tests tapping the ability to shift cognitive sets and to solve problems requiring skills in reasoning ability than on simple measures of recall and recognition.

It was also possible to detect the presence of depression in persons with early signs of senile dementia. On tests sampling both immediate and delayed recall, we could distinguish depressed senile patients from nondepressed senile patients only when the tests were made more difficult. For example, significant differences between these two groups emerged on the task requiring subjects to repeat 10 digits, but not on the task of repeating 5 or 7 digits. These findings have important clinical implications; they suggest that there may be a syndrome of depressive pseudodementia in persons who are in the early stages of senile dementia, and that treating the depression in these persons may result in at least a temporary improvement in their cognitive skills.

There seems little doubt that elderly persons who are mildly to moderately depressed do complain of problems with their memory, but they also complain of psychic and somatic distress on a wide range of symptoms. Furthermore, in the geriatric test battery study, this tendency to complain or to manifest what has been called the "sick set" was more prominent in persons with acute as opposed to chronic depression. It is not entirely clear whether these persons do, in fact, have problems with their memory and, if so, to what extent. More definitive studies are needed to compare the performance of persons with different degrees of depression, as well as different depression profiles, on cognitive tasks varying in complexity and difficulty. There is compelling evidence for cognitive deficits associated with depression in young and middle-aged persons, so it seems reasonable to believe that similar results would obtain in older depressed persons when attention is paid to the methodologic issues discussed here.

References

American Psychiatric Association. (1978). *Diagnostic and statistical manual of mental disorders* (3rd ed.). Washington, DC: Author. (January 15 draft)

Bloch, J. (1976). Brain activation and memory consolidation. In M. R. Rosenzweig & E. L. Bennett (Eds.), *Neural mechanisms of learning and memory* (pp. 583–590). Cambridge: MIT Press.

Browning, G. B., & Spilich, G. J. (1981). Some important methodological issues in the study of aging and cognition. *Experimental Aging Research, 7,* 175–187.

Buchsbaum, M. S., Carpenter, W. T., Jr., & Fedio, P. (1979). Hemispheric differences in evoked potential enhancement by selective attention to hemiretinally presented stimuli in schizophrenic, affective, and posttemporal lobectomy patients. In W. H. Gruzelier & P. Flor-Henry (Eds.), *Hemispheric asymmetrics of functions in psychopathology.* New York: Elsevier North-Holland.

Cohen, R. M., Weingartner, H., Smallberg, S. A., Pickar, D., & Murphy, D. L. (1982). Effort and cognition in depression. *Archives of General Psychiatry, 39,* 593–597.

Folstein, M. F., Folstein, S. E., & McHugh, P. R. (1975). Mini-Mental State: A practical method for grading the cognitive state of patients for the clinician. *Journal of Psychiatric Research, 12,* 189–198.

Friedman, A. S. (1964). Minimal effects of severe depression on cognitive functioning. *Journal of Abnormal and Social Psychology, 69,* 237–243.

Gibson, A. (1981). A further analysis of memory loss in dementia and depression in the elderly. *British Journal of Clinical Psychology, 20,* 179–185.

Kahn, R. L., Zarit, S. H., Hilbert, N. M., & Niederehe, G. (1975). Memory complaint and impairment in the aged. *Archives of General Psychiatry, 32,* 1569–1573.

Miller, W. R. (1975). Psychological deficit in depression. *Psychological Bulletin, 82,* 238–260.

Murphy, D. L., & Weingartner, H. (1973). Catecholamines and memory-enhanced verbal learning during L-DOPA administration. *Psychopharmacology Bulletin, 27,* 319–326.

Overall, J. E. (1965). Computer classifications of depressions and differential effect of antidepressants. *Journal of the American Medical Association, 192,* 561.

Poon, L. W. (1985). Differences in human memory with aging: Nature, causes, and clinical implications. In J. E. Birren & K. W. Schaie (Eds.), *Handbook of the psychology of aging* (pp. 427–462). New York: Van Nostrand Reinhold.

Popkin, S. J., Gallagher, D., Thompson, L. W., & Moore, M. (1982). Memory complaint and performance in normal and depressed older adults. *Experimental Aging Research, 8,* 141–145.

Raskin, A., Friedman, A. S., & DiMascio, A. (1982). Cognitive and performance deficits in depression. *Psychopharmacology Bulletin, 18(4),* 196–202.

Raskin, A., Gershon, S., Crook, T. H., Sathananthan, G., & Ferris, S. (1978). The effects of hyperbaric and normobaric oxygen on cognitive impairment in the elderly. *Archives of General Psychiatry, 35,* 50–56.

Raskin, A., & Rae, D. S. (1981). Psychiatric symptoms in the elderly. *Psychopharmacology Bulletin, 17,* 96–99.

Raskin, A., Schulterbrandt, J. G., Reatig, N., & McKeon, J. J. (1970). Differential response to chlorpromazine, imipramine, and placebo. *Archives of General Psychiatry, 23,* 164–171.

Rausch, R. (1977). Cognitive strategies in patients with unilateral temporal lobe excisions. *Neuropsychologia, 15,* 385–395.

Reus, V. I., Silberman, E., Post, R. M., & Weingartner, H. (1979). d-Amphetamine: Effects on memory in a depressed population. *Biological Psychiatry, 14,* 345–356.

Savard, R. J., Rey, A. C., & Post, R. M. (1980). Halstead-Reitan Category Test in bipolar and unipolar affective disorders: Relationship to age and phase of illness. *Journal of Nervous and Mental Disease, 168,* 207–304.

Silberman, E. K., Weingartner, H., & Post, R. M. (1983). Thinking disorder in depression: Logic and strategy in an abstract reasoning task. *Archives of General Psychiatry, 40,* 775–780.

Stein, K., Belluzzi, J. D., & Wise, C. D. (1975). Memory enhancement by central administration of norepinephrine. *Brain Research, 34,* 329–335.

Strömgren, L. S. (1977). The influence of depression on memory. *Acta Psychiatrica Scandinavica, 56,* 109–128.

Weingartner, H., Cohen, R. M., Murphy, D. L., Martello, J., & Gerdt, C. (1981). Cognitive processes in depression. *Archives of General Psychiatry, 38,* 42–47.

Weingartner, H., Murphy, D. L., & Weinstein, S. (1976). Imagery, affective arousal, and memory consolidation. *Nature, 263,* 311–312.

Yozawitz, A., Bruder, G., Sutton, S., Gurland, B., Fleiss, J., & Costa, L. (1979). Dichotic perception. Evidence for right hemisphere dysfunction in affective psychosis. *British Journal of Psychiatry, 135,* 224–237.

Wechsler, D. (1955). *Manual for the Wechsler Adult Intelligence Scale.* New York: Psychological Corporation.

Carl Salzman and M. Janice Gutfreund

CHAPTER

26

Clinical Techniques and Research Strategies for Studying Depression and Memory

In this chapter, a clinical perspective is presented on the relationship between decrements in cognitive functioning in depression and dementia, and some strategies for future research are suggested. First, personal experiences of older people who have memory loss are discussed, and the increased impact of personal losses in the lives of elderly patients is noted. Then the clinical evaluation of elderly patients is reviewed, and suggestions are made of ways to distinguish memory loss caused primarily by dementia from memory loss caused primarily by depression. The authors emphasize the importance in clinical practice of the combined picture of cognitive losses due to the interaction of depression (or dysphoric states) and dementia. The final section focuses on both biological and psychological approaches to future research. The two research goals are to differentiate between depression and dementia and to examine their combined effect on function in elderly persons.

Clinical Evaluation of Depression and Dementia in the Elderly

The Effects of Depression on Memory

A substantial body of research literature documents the fact that memory processes can be functionally impaired by depression. Some of these research topics are summarized as follows:

• Decreased acquisition and recall of new information (Breslow, Kocsis, & Belkin, 1981; Cohen, Weingartner, Smallberg, Pickar, & Murphy, 1982; Davis & Unruh, 1980; Friedman, 1964; Henry, Weingartner, & Murphy, 1973; Jarvik, Gritz, & Schneider, 1972);

• Increased errors of omission (Henry et al., 1973; Jarvik et al., 1972; McAllister, 1981; Whitehead, 1973);

• Transposition errors, mispairing, and reversal of stimulus–response words (Henry et al., 1973; Whitehead, 1973);

• Decreased ability to impose organization on unorganized information (Breslow et al., 1981; Weingartner, Cohen, & Bunney, 1982; Weingartner, Cohen, Murphy, Martello, & Gerdt, 1981);

• Less effective coding and memory strategies (level of processing) (Breslow et al., 1981; Weingartner et al., 1981, 1982);

• Fluctuating deficits in episodic memory; increased access to sad memories (Bower, 1981; Fogarty & Hemsley, 1983; Isen, Clark, Shalker, & Karp, 1978; Natale & Hantas, 1982; Teasdale & Fogarty, 1979) and, with increasing depression, decreased access to pleasant memories (Breslow et al., 1981);

• Altered guessing strategies; taking fewer risks in a task (Miller & Lewis, 1977), reluctance to give oneself the benefit of the doubt (Alloy & Abramson, 1979), or reluctance to use negative feedback as a basis for change in strategy (Silberman, Weingartner, & Post, 1983); and

• Decreased attention and reaction time (Breslow et al., 1981; Cohen et al., 1982; Glass, Uhlenhuth, Hartel, Matuzas, & Fischman, 1981).

Clinicians who work with elderly people frequently have personal confirmation of these research data. Many older patients with reasonably intact cognitive functions are brought to medical attention when, as a result of depression, they suddenly seem to lose their memory and ability to think clearly. This dramatic change in cognitive functioning may be seen following the death of a spouse or lifelong friend. In such circumstances, the older person is described as having "suddenly grown old" or as having "given up." Physicians at times may make a presumptive diagnosis of a "silent stroke" to account for the cognitive change, but rarely can such a diagnosis be verified.

It is not surprising that older persons who are experiencing a gradual decline in function and in the ability to care for themselves may be especially vulnerable to the psychological consequences of loss. The loss of a person with whom one has lived for three or four decades is an overwhelming experience. For the aging survivor, such a loss may raise the fundamental question about his or her ability to continue to live alone.

The effect of such acute loss, grief, and mourning on memory in the elderly is variable; as is discussed later, the effect depends partly on whether there is preexisting cognitive impairment. In some cases, cognitive impairment is limited to diminution of concentration and inability to retain new information. There may also be confusion and fluctuating disorientation. These problems may occur during obvious grief or even when the survivor seems to be coping well with the loss. In many cases, this period of acute cognitive dysfunction resolves if the grief resolves and the older person is able to continue to function without the lost loved one. Consider the following case:

Mrs. A. was a 71-year-old retired schoolteacher whose husband died after a 3-year bout with intestinal cancer. Although his death was expected and well prepared for, Mrs. A. was overcome with emotion. Formerly a highly functioning, intellectual woman who read widely, Mrs. A. suddenly found herself unable to think clearly. She noticed her marked forgetfulness, as did her children, who had come to stay with her during the period of mourning. She had trouble remembering where she had put things, occasionally misidentified the day of the week and the date, and felt unable to shop for groceries because making change seemed too difficult. She began to make lists as a means of reminding herself of the many tasks that needed to be done but quickly misplaced and forgot the lists. She could not read, found herself unable to concentrate on television; she could not remember what she watched or what she did try to read. She often called her children by the wrong name, particularly calling her son by her dead husband's first name. As the weeks passed, however, her forgetfulness, disorientation, and diminished concentration gradually disappeared. After 6 months, Mrs. A. returned to her former level of cognitive ability, and she has continued to do well.

Memory loss associated with depression in older people also occurs in circumstances other than acute grief. For example, older patients with recurrent depressive disorders may suffer dramatic changes in cognitive ability. Consider the following patient:

Mrs. B., an 80-year-old woman, was hospitalized for incapacitating depression characterized by an inability to take care of herself, severe early morning awakening, loss of appetite and weight, loss of energy, and loss of ability to enjoy life. She described herself as helpless, hopeless, and worthless and saw no future for herself. She sighed deeply when spoken to and answered questions slowly and with great effort. She looked and felt terribly sad. Mrs. B. had been hospitalized four times previously for depression, each time with similar symptoms.

Between hospitalizations, for periods lasting from 6 months to 3 years, she had been an active, well-functioning woman, who participated in senior citizens' volunteer organizations. She had had an active social life, been involved with her local church, and visited with family members frequently. Her husband had died 15 years earlier, and she had seemed quite capable of living alone and independently. She had managed her finances by herself, had shopped and prepared her own meals, and was not noted to have any significant memory loss or other cognitive impairment.

During her depressions, however, she was unable to answer any factual questions. She could repeat only three numbers forward and no numbers backward. She could not remember an address after 5 minutes and had difficulty recalling what her last meal had consisted of. She knew her own address and birth date but could not remember the birth dates of her children or the date of her husband's death. She was disoriented to time and place; when told the date and the name of the hospital, she acknowledged that she may have known it but seemed to be unable to concentrate on remembering it.

Mrs. B. responded rapidly to antidepressant treatment, and her prior cognitive functions returned completely. When interviewed again, she noted, with some humor, that during her depressions she had been "senile."

Mrs. A. and Mrs. B. both illustrate levels of reversible cognitive loss and memory impairment associated with depression that is often seen in older patients (Donnelly, Waldman, Murphy, Wyatt, & Goodwin 1980; LaRue, 1982; Rubinow, Post, Savard, & Gold, 1984). In the next section we consider the case of an older person who was actually losing his memory due to dementia and became depressed as he admitted his cognitive dysfunction.

Reactions to Loss of Memory

The loss of ability to remember produces different responses in people, depending on a number of factors. A major consideration is the importance of memory and cognitive functions in the person's life. For someone who has lived by his or her mind and memory, such a loss may be the equivalent of an athlete's losing a limb, or an artist's losing eyesight. Such people often feel that the whole purpose of life has been taken away, and they feel a profound sense of hopelessness and despair. Consider Professor C.:

Professor C., a well-known scientist, 79 years old, was brought to a physician because he was unable to continue with his work. Although retired, Professor C. had attempted to maintain an active correspondence and was engaged in writing articles for numerous scholarly journals. He was also frequently consulted by members of his profession who came to his home office seeking his guidance in their field of study. For at least 12 months, however, Professor C.'s ability to write, read, and speak with colleagues had seemed impaired. He would sit in his study for long periods and stare at the opposite wall. At times, he seemed not to know the day of the week, although, when asked, he often was able to fashion a satisfactory response. He also became less talkative and did not participate in dinner table discussions with his usual animation. His facial expression and reduced energy suggested sadness, and his sleep and appetite were diminished. At times, he would sigh deeply, but he always denied that he was sad, depressed, or feeling unwell. When the family brought Professor C. for medical help, they spoke of him as being depressed and described a prior depression 30 years earlier. They attributed his decreased functioning to his retirement and were convinced that if he had "something meaningful to live for," he would be his old self.

Examination revealed, however, that Professor C. was not only depressed but also quite demented. Mental status measurements of dementia revealed marked diminution of memory, orientation, and logical thinking. Neuroradiologic imaging techniques confirmed this diagnosis. Professor C., unfortunately, was suffering from severe progressive dementia. It was apparent that he had realized his cognitive impairments and become depressed about them, although he was too proud to admit his awareness. After a brief period of psychotherapy, he admitted his awareness of the loss of his mental faculties and the profound sadness that this engendered.

Whether or not they have lived by their wits, most older people experience some degree of sadness as they become aware of their loss of cognitive functions. If the losses are mild and the forgetfulness only an annoyance, memory loss may be joked about or defended against in some other manner, and depression may not be a prominent part of the picture. However, many older patients, like Professor C., develop some degree of depression.

The clinician, therefore, may see the early and middle stages of dementia accompanied by depression, just as one may see depression in late life accompanied by impairment of memory and cognitive function. Several studies have found an association between depressive symptoms and dementia. In a study of factors associated with presenile dementia, Gustafson (1975) found that mild to moderate cognitive impairment was associated with depressed mood, hypochondriasis, delu-

sions, and rigid thinking. As cognitive impairment became more severe, it was associated not with depressed mood but with affective lability. (A highly loaded component of the cognitive impairment factor was affective shallowness, that is, the more severe the impairment, the shallower the affect.) Miller (1980) and Reifler (1982) found this phenomenon in their samples of elderly demented/organically impaired subjects as well; Reifler also showed less reporting of depressed mood with increasing cognitive dysfunction. In conclusion, demented older people, most likely in reaction to their dementia, can also be depressed. This finding does not mean, however, that this depression is not to be considered a separate disorder. It has its own etiology and symptoms and may add, synergistically, to the severity of the presenting cognitive impairment.

To address this issue, Feinberg and Goodman (1984), in a recent review, presented four categories of the differential diagnosis of depression with dementia: depression presenting as dementia, depression with secondary dementia, dementia presenting as depression, and dementia with secondary depression. Their four-category model, however, does not take into account the differing interaction of both depression and dementia with the aging process. The next case illustrates dramatically the effect of a superimposed major depressive disorder on cognitive functioning in a very old demented person.

Dementia, Personal Loss, and Depression

Clinicians frequently see older patients with early or midstage dementia who are coping adequately until they experience a significant personal loss and become depressed. This depression impairs memory and cognitive function as does any depression. However, when superimposed on a preexisting dementia, a dramatic and sudden worsening in memory and cognitive functioning can occur. Consider the case of Miss D.:

Miss D. was a delightful, energetic woman of 82 in good physical health. She had run a stationery store in a small southern town where she had lived all of her life. Miss D. had never married and had lived with an older unmarried sister. She had many friends, had amassed sufficient capital to be financially secure, was active in church and community affairs, and was one of the town's better known storekeepers. When she was in her early 80s, her nieces and nephews noted that Miss D. was occasionally forgetful. She sometimes forgot their names and occasionally made mistakes in ordering stationery supplies for the store. However, she otherwise functioned well at the store and was able to care for herself and her sister. She seemed neither depressed nor overly forgetful for a woman of her age.

During the winter of her 83rd year, Miss D.'s sister suddenly and unexpectedly had a heart attack, was hospitalized, and despite a brief rally, died within 2 weeks. During this period of hospitalization, Miss D. was noted to be very upset and considerably more forgetful. In the months that followed her sister's death, Miss D. seemed grief stricken and remained considerably confused, occasionally disoriented, and forgetful. She wore the same dress to church each Sunday morning despite urging from her nieces and nephews to vary her attire. She regularly forgot the names of these relatives and, occasionally, of some of her cousins. The family became concerned that Miss D. was becoming senile; a local physician made the diagnosis of Alzheimer's disease on the basis of this behavior.

Miss D. lived for only a year after her sister's death. Although she continued to manage her store until her death, her functioning during this final year never returned to what it had been prior to her sister's death. She needed more assistance in handling her financial matters, and occasionally she made mistakes in ordering supplies for the store. Her grooming became rather shabby; she no longer cared for her long, beautiful hair, which had been a source of pride to her. Family members who visited her commented that she seemed to have lost her will to live.

Miss D. represents a common clinical situation facing physicians who treat older patients. True cognitive dysfunction combines with grief and depression to produce a worsening of both the cognitive function and the depression, making it almost impossible to determine the primary illness.

Older patients with both syndromes, dementia and depression, frequently present problems for clinicians. To date, little work has been done on the natural history of grief reactions in the elderly, and none that specifically focuses on grief reactions in the mildly to moderately demented person. This emphasis on the dementia and depression presenting in combination, synergistically affecting each other, is necessary because current research is more specifically devoted to distinguishing between depression and dementia than to understanding the clinical presentation of both.

Distinguishing Between Memory Loss Due to Dementia and Memory Loss Due to Depression

In the past three decades, the term *pseudodementia* (Kiloh, 1961) has been applied to memory loss associated with depression, and the diagnosis of pseudodementia has become an important focus for clinicians who work with older patients. Many discriminating criteria have been applied to pseudodementia versus true dementia, but pseudodementia is neither pseudo nor dementia. Rather, it is true impairment of memory processes secondary to depression but without impairment of other aspects of the mental status. This has led some authors to suggest abandoning the term pseudodementia (McAllister, 1981; Reifler, 1982; Shraberg, 1978).

Recent studies of the diagnosis of pseudodementia have yielded a number of concordant discriminating factors that help to verify this diagnosis (Caine, 1981; Gurland, Dean, Cross, & Golden, 1980; Wells, 1979).

These factors are summarized in Table 26-1. As seen in this table, the discrimination between "pseudo" and "true" dementia is made on the basis of prior history, onset of symptoms, and associated diagnostic variables.

Clinicians are often called on to make a differential diagnosis between true dementia and pseudodementia: Is the memory loss in an elderly patient due to depression or to dementia? Misdiagnosing depression-related memory loss as irreversible dementia would be a serious therapeutic mistake. In contrast to cognitive impairment due to central nervous system changes resulting from normal aging or to the pathology of dementia, cognitive impairment associated with depression may be reversed with appropriate treatment.

In many cases of patients with depression and memory loss, the clinician may attempt to distinguish empirically between depression-related dementia and senile dementia by using a trial of stimulant or antidepressant medication. In younger, healthy elderly patients, this trial may be diagnostically helpful. Patients who are indeed depressed may respond to stimulant medication through an improvement in memory dysfunction, whereas patients with dementia will often show an increase in confusion (Salzman & van der Kolk, 1984). Similarly, careful use of antidepressant medication will often reverse depression-related cognitive dysfunction. Not all depressed elderly patients for whom the etiology of memory loss is uncertain, however, should be given antidepressant medication as a diagnostic challenge for these reasons:

• Antidepressant drugs are extremely toxic, particularly in older patients (Davies, Tucker, & Harrow, 1971; Salzman & van der Kolk, 1984).

Table 26-1. Clinical Features of True Dementia and Pseudodementia

Features	True dementia	Pseudo-dementia
Onset and duration of symptoms	Extended	Brief
Depressed mood	Follows memory loss	Precedes memory loss
Sleep and appetite disturbance in early stages	Normal	Prominent
Emotional lability	Marked and frequent	Mild and infrequent
Confusion and disorientation	Marked and frequent	Mild and infrequent
Recent memory impairment	Marked and frequent	Mild and infrequent
Reduced mental alertness	Marked and frequent	Mild and infrequent
Unsociability and lack of cooperation	Marked and frequent	Mild and infrequent
Confabulation	Present	Absent

Note. Adapted from Salzman and van der Kolk (1984) by permission.

• Changes in memory function, although demonstrated in research with antidepressant drugs, tend to be measurable only by neuropsychologic testing (Glass et al., 1981; Henry et al., 1973; Sternberg & Jarvik, 1976; Thompson & Trimble, 1982).

• The anticholinergic properties of antidepressant drugs themselves may further impair memory function (Branconnier & Cole, 1981; Cole & Schatzberg, 1976; Liljequist, Mattila, & Linnoila, 1981; Mattila, Liljequist, & Seppala, 1978).

To discriminate between memory impairment that comes from mood disorder versus dementia, therefore, the clinician must rely on clues in the clinical interview itself. Before this differentiation between memory loss from dementia or from depression can be undertaken, it is helpful to categorize the patient in terms of level of cognitive and mood functioning as well as age, because depression and memory loss may have different characteristics at different ages. We suggest a breakdown into four categories:

1. Young old (under age 80) and mildly to moderately depressed
2. Young old (under age 80) and severely depressed
3. Old (over age 80) and mildly to moderately depressed
4. Old (over age 80) and severely depressed

On clinical grounds, diagnosing memory loss resulting from depression versus aging or dementia is relatively easy in Category 1, considerably more difficult in both Categories 2 and 3, and invariably difficult and sometimes impossible in Category 4.

Category 1. Clinical diagnosis of depression and memory loss in these patients usually does not require the assistance of biologic probes or sophisticated neuropsychological testing. The discriminating characteristics are (a) complaints of memory loss, (b) complaints of global dysfunction, (c) associated affective disturbance, (d) poor concentration, and (e) decreased ability to organize thinking.

These younger elderly, depressed patients tend to focus on the experience of their impaired memory, often describing it as more severe than it appears during the clinical interview. The degree of complaint has been associated with the severity of the depression (Kahn, Zarit, Hilbert, & Niederehe, 1975). The patient sometimes insists that the interviewer recognize the deficit in memory functioning as real and crippling.

Patients also complain of feeling hopeless, helpless, nonfunctional, and crippled by their experience of memory dysfunction. Simple tests that reveal relatively intact cognitive processes are of little use in reassuring the patients. In the absence of true physical pathology, complaints of memory loss resemble hypochondriacal, obsessional complaints of somatic dysfunction. In contrast, patients with amnestic syndromes often confabulate in an effort to cover up their symptoms, but older patients with depressive memory loss do not.

In addition, depressed patients usually have symptoms of affective disturbance, including depressed mood, diminished energy, decreased pleasure, and disturbed sleep and appetite. Patients sometimes express their depression through physical symptoms, such as aches and pains or gastrointestinal disturbance. These symptoms, called "depressive equivalents," may occur in the absence of a mood disturbance or may accompany it.

Poor concentration is a classic component of depression in all ages. Older patients who were depressed often described this poor concentration as an impairment of their usual thinking abilities as characterized by being unable to read or watch television. These patients are often distressed by their inability to concentrate, and they may have fantasies of having developed Alzheimer's disease (AD), brain cancer, or stroke. The appearance of worry, sadness, or even despair is prominent in such patients, in contrast with the situation in nondepressed demented patients, who often seem unaware of impairments or inappropriately unconcerned about them.

An inability to organize thinking is also characteristic of depression-associated cognitive impairment but it also occurs in all age groups. In older people, however, it may aggravate the existing cognitive impairment associated with the aging process. Thus, older people who may have some difficulties acquiring and retaining new information that enables them to plan future activities are further impaired by depression. This impairment, in turn, is perceived as evidence of loss of intelligence and often aggravates the sense of helplessness and hopelessness that is part of depression.

The inability to organize one's thinking also can be attributed to forgetfulness. Although the forgetfulness resembles that of the normal aging process (benign senile forgetfulness), depressed patients often do not use familiar cues or memory devices that nondepressed elderly persons would use (e.g., lists or associative techniques). It is as if these people do not want to remember or believe that they can remember. Depressed patients may respond to questions of memory function by saying "I don't know" instead of using techniques of memory assistance or making a reasonable guess.

Category 2. In younger elderly patients who are severely depressed, the cognitive dysfunction resembles that of depressed younger adults. In severe depression, however, older persons may be mute, bedridden, and unable to describe their feelings; they are often disoriented and think slowly. In general, these patients appear nearly moribund. They often cannot cooperate in mental or cognitive status testing and, when able to talk, complain generally about their dysphoria. At times, however, they have modest increases in energy, decreases in disorientation, and some amelioration of cognitive dysfunction, all of which suggests an affective basis for their symptoms.

Category 3. In very old patients with a mild to moderate depression, affective and cognitive disturbance may be obscured by physical illness, frailty, impaired hearing or vision, and reduced motor activity due to diminished physical energy. These older patients, when physically sick and very frail, are sometimes mistakenly considered to be demented because of their withdrawal and inability to care for themselves. They are also sometimes victims of "ageism"—that is, the observer assumes that they are sicker, more cognitively impaired, and less able to care for themselves than is, in fact, the case. Mildly to moderately depressed very old patients may respond dramatically to antidepressant treatment, but the drugs must be prescribed with care and allowances made for very advanced age (Salzman & van der Kolk, 1984).

Category 4. Severely depressed, very old patients with severe cognitive impairment are the most difficult patients to diagnose correctly. On the one hand, cognitive impairment due to depression may be so severe as to be indistinguishable from true, primary, progressive dementia. On the other hand, the depression may be so severe as to produce a state of near stupor, muteness, complete disorientation, and complete lack of self-care. Markedly decreased cognitive ability makes it increasingly difficult for these patients to experience or describe emotions accurately. The agitated behavior and affective lability of severely depressed elderly patients may be indistinguishable from the agitation of dementia. Psychological testing is often impossible in this group, and examination of available biological markers to distinguish between depression and dementia is often of little help (see the next section of this book).

In summary, in younger elderly patients whose depressive symptoms are not severe, the contribution of affective disturbance to the picture of cognitive dysfunction can be relatively easy to identify. For older patients or patients who are severely depressed and already demented, each syndrome often potentiates the other, making the differentiation of the two forms of memory impairment and the contribution of each form much more difficult. In these categories, the development of discriminating biological and psychological measures assumes increasing importance. Clinicians must understand elderly patients' emotional reactions to changes in memory function (whatever their cause) and how these reactions may affect cognitive functioning itself. This understanding leads to more research on the psychological and biological interactions between depression and aging.

Directions for Future Research

Psychological Research

As stated in the first section, we believe that there is an important psychological interplay among diminished memory, cognitive function, and depression in older people. Understanding this interplay and discriminating between the two syndromes are areas of increasing clinical importance and concern as the number of older people in our population continues to increase dramatically. We therefore encourage research on these topics.

It is particularly important to determine whether the older person has a true depression or a fluctuating state that includes periods of dysphoria but lacks the vegetative signs or symptoms of true affective illness. Qualitative differences between dysphoric states and depression may be reflected in differences in cognitive deficits. Studies testing the effect of mood changes on memory function have often tested normal subjects after a depressed or elated mood has been induced instead of testing depressed subjects. This practice suggests that fluctuating dysphoria affects cognitive functioning even in the absence of other signs of clinical depression. As is pointed out in chapter 24 of this volume, subjects with induced dysphoric mood show state-dependent changes in cognitive function, such as increased access to sad memories and increased self-doubt. People with major depression show these effects and also more deficits in organization, motivational state, and hypothesis testing, and decreased guessing (Breslow, Kocsis, & Belkin, 1980; Breslow et al., 1981; McAllister, 1981; Silberman et al., 1983; Weingartner et al., 1981, 1982).

The diagnostic picture may be further complicated if more than one form of depression is present. "Double depression," a major depressive disorder superimposed on an underlying chronic minor depression, has been described in several studies (Akiskal et al., 1980; Keller & Shapiro, 1982; Rounsaville, Sholomskas, & Prusoff, 1980). For these patients, the major depressive disorder is responsive to medication, but symptoms of the chronic depression remain. These depressions constitute a part of the patient's personality.

Comparison of the trends of cognitive changes in normal subjects with an induced dysphoric mood and in subjects with clinical depression implies that patients with both disorders may have more than one kind of memory dysfunction due to dysphoric states and minor as well as major depression. The longitudinal study of memory dysfunction in persons with and without double depression may shed light on the roles of major depression and minor depression and dysphoria in cognitive functioning.

The response to memory loss among older people may vary greatly. In his study of neurotic styles (1965), Shapiro maintained that both character structure and cognitive style influence the ways in which people select, organize, and remember information. For example, people who have a more detail-oriented cognitive style may view their failing memory (due to benign senescent forgetfulness or to dementia) with distress and depression, because the loss threatens to interfere with a primary method of coping with feelings. People who are generally less attentive to detail in their environments may be more philosophical or nonchalant about losing their memory. Whatever their primary cognitive style, people who have had rewarding and fulfilling experiences respond to memory loss somewhat differently than do those for whom life has been generally frustrating.

In one of his crucial discoveries in psychoanalysis, Freud demonstrated that vividly recalled "memories" were given shape by the presence of unconscious fantasies. The truth of these memories rested on emotional and personal interest as well as on fact. People seem to remember significant events in this manner (Neisser,

1981). Warrington (1981) recognized this form of memory as vital to the maintenance of the self-concept and termed it "event memory."

Longitudinal studies of normal ego function (Bellak, Hurvich, & Gediman, 1973; Vaillant, 1977) in the elderly also are necessary to demonstrate what forms natural responses to cognitive changes take. Comparison with depressed elderly people may then be made. Longitudinal studies of Erikson's (1950) final stage—Ego Integrity versus Despair—must be conducted as well: How do older people *adapt* to both cognitive and affective changes?

Biological Research

Both depression and memory loss are associated with biological dysfunction in older people (Rubinow et al., 1984; Schildkraut, 1978), and affective disturbance has been associated with dysfunction of the catecholamine neurotransmitter system in the central nervous system (Bartus, Dean, Beer, & Lippa, 1982; Drachman, Feinberg, & Goodman, 1978). The capacity to determine accurately the presence of a state of depression in older patients through the use of a biological marker would be of considerable help in the discrimination of cognitive dysfunction due to depression versus aging or dementia. Whereas psychological research should be directed toward describing the response of older people to depression, dementia, and the two together, biological research should be directed toward discriminating between depression and dementia.

One biological marker that has been extensively studied in this regard is the dexamethasone suppression test. This test, which is abnormal in approximately half of patients with true depression, is also, unfortunately, abnormal in some states of dementia (Carroll, Feinberg, & Greden, 1981; Spar & Gerner, 1982). In addition, a recent report demonstrated no differences in cognitive functioning between suppressors and nonsuppressors with major depression (Caine, Yerevanian, & Bamford, 1984). As the test is currently used, therefore, it cannot reliably discriminate between suppression and nonsuppression. Other biological markers with greater discriminating power apparently need to be developed.

One test now in the developmental stage is the thyroid-releasing hormone test, which has been used to establish the presence of depression (Loosen & Prange, 1982). Its use in older populations has been limited, however, and there are no data regarding its use in cognitive dysfunction in the elderly. A study that may help to discriminate between depression and dementia is a psychomotor stimulant challenge test with an amphetamine such as methylphenidate. A depressed or apathetic person may respond briefly by elevation of interest, motivation, and energy; in contrast, persons with dementia may seem more confused (Salzman & van der Kolk, 1984).

Other studies of neurotransmitter function may help to discriminate between depression and dementia. Most studies to date have focused primarily on acetyl-choline, the neurotransmitter thought to be responsible for aspects of memory function:

- Acetylcholine agonist challenge (phosphotidylcholine, arecholine) (Christie, 1982; Sitaram, Weingartner, & Gillin, 1978);
- Acetylcholine precursors (choline, lecithin) (Bajada, 1982; Ferris et al., 1982; Wurtman & Zeisel, 1982);
- Acetylcholine metabolism inhibitors (physostigmine) (Bajada, 1982; Peters & Levin, 1982); and
- Acetylcholine receptor binding (Ehlert, Roeske, & Yamamura, 1982).

An additional and active line of research inquiry has focused on neuropeptides such as ACTH and vasopressin and substances that affect neuropeptide functioning such as narcotic antagonists and endorphins (Reisberg, 1983).

Each of these investigations into biological markers of depression, dementia, or memory function may someday help clinicians to discriminate between memory loss due to depression and that which is due to dementia. In combination with longitudinal psychological studies of thinking and depression in old age, these investigations may further enhance our understanding of elderly patients and permit more accurate diagnostic assessment and treatment. However, an overall context in which to place both psychological and biological research data would, in addition, elucidate basic brain neurophysiological function as it relates to psychological processes of aging. The field of depression and dementia provides fertile ground for the development of this context.

Bringing Psychology and Biology Together: Depression and Memory Function in the Elderly

To unify biological and psychological research efforts in the area of depression and memory loss in the elderly, a model for memory loss would be useful. Such a model, if applicable to the clinical diagnostic dilemma, would provide the basis for exploring the etiology of memory loss with depression as well as with aging and would serve as a context for research into treatment.

The study of sleep and dreaming may be a key to the interaction of depression, dementia, and memory loss in the elderly, as well as to their differentiation. Studies of sleep physiology provide evidence of overlapping neurobiological control of sleep, depression, and memory systems. Sleep stages are associated with different types of dream content, a phenomenon that suggests that different sleep stages may play a role in the construction and maintenance of separate memory systems.

The reciprocal interaction model of the sleep–wake system proposed by Hobson, McCarley, and associates (Flicker, McCarley, & Hobson, 1981; Hobson & McCarley, 1977; McCarley, 1982) hypothesizes that arousal levels in organisms are controlled by regular, periodic changes in activity in neurons located in the nucleus locus ceruleus, the raphe nucleus, and the pontine reticular formation. Their pioneering work is briefly reviewed in the next paragraphs.

The duration and termination of REM sleep are controlled by a reciprocal balance between acetylcholine and monoamine neurotransmission in the brain. During waking, cholinergic neurons in the pons are under tonic inhibition by norepinephrine neurons in the locus ceruleus and by serotonin neurons in the raphe nucleus. REM onset is caused by a marked release of cholinergic neurons from the tonic inhibitory effect of aminergic neurons, producing a state of internal arousal without sensory input from the environment. During slow-wave sleep, the balance between monoamines and acetylcholine is at intermediate levels.

What might these arousal states have to do with memory and learning? One clue comes from what subjects, awakened during the night, reported about their dreams. Flicker et al. (1981) reported that subjects awakened during slow-wave sleep reported dreams that were preoccupied with the recent past and that had perserverative, nonprogressive, ruminative qualities. Attempts to relate the activities of this sleep stage to memory consolidation have produced equivocal results, so further exploration is needed. During REM sleep, however, dreams were "perceptually vivid, convincingly real, episodically narrative, emotionally charged, and formally bizarre. . . . Current concerns meld with remote past history in fantastic but plausible synthesis" (Flicker et al., 1981, p. 125).

Sleep could then represent an important component of the later stages of the learning process. Flicker et al. (1981) hypothesized that during waking, the organism is acquiring new information; during slow-wave sleep, it is consolidating this new information; and during REM sleep, it is comparing and fitting this new information into remote memory. This may be the way the entire memory system works.

Aging, dementia, and depression all cause changes in sleep structure. In major depression, slow-wave sleep is significantly decreased (Lowy, Kleghorn, & McClure, 1971; Mendels & Chernik, 1975). (This change also occurs in many other medical conditions, such as uremia, asthma, and hypothyroidism [Hauri, 1977].) Also in association with depression, REM latency (time from sleep onset until first REM period) is decreased and REM density is increased (Kupfer, 1976; McPartland, Kupfer, & Coble, 1979). McCarley (1982) hypothesized that this shortened REM latency is due to the premature release of acetylcholine neurons from inhibition by monoamine neurons; the strength of this release results in increased REM density. He argued that one or more changes in this system affecting the balance of neurotransmitter effects may cause depressive symptoms and account for various subtypes of depressions.

Absolute amounts of REM sleep may decrease with age—researchers disagree on this subject—but the relative amount of REM (REM time as percentage of total sleep time) remains steady until extreme old age (Kales, Wilson, & Kales, 1967; Prinz, Obrist, & Wang, 1975). These researchers also discovered that Stage 4 sleep is significantly decreased in elderly people. Prinz (1977) found that intellectual function is associated with REM time in aged subjects; decreases in REM time occur with decreases in measured intellectual function. In senile dementia and organic brain syndrome, the REM percentage decreases dramatically (Prinz & Raskind, 1978).

The third piece of this puzzle is to link alterations in neurotransmitters to the aging process as well as to depression. There is strong evidence that the synthesis and storage of neurotransmitters and the process of transmission are altered in aging and depression in several ways. First, acetylcholine and its synthesizing enzyme choline acetyltransferase are decreased in normal aging and markedly decreased in dementia (Goodnick, Gershon, & Salzman, 1984); and second, norepinephrine neurotransmission may be impaired in depression and to a lesser extent by the normal aging process.

These data show that alterations in neurotransmission associated with aging, dementia, and depression affect normal sleep stages. We may now ask, Is the forgetting of dreams (the dream "censor") a function of the balance of these neurotransmitter systems regardless of age or affective state? The cholinergic system in the brain has long been associated with memory function; in addition, there may be a time-dependent factor in the fluctuation of acetylcholine and consolidation of the memory trace (Deutsch & Rocklin, 1972). If so, decreases in acetylcholine would be expected to decrease dream recall if acetylcholine is, in fact, associated with memory function. Several lines of evidence support this hypothesis. For example, anticholinergic drugs impair memory function, but their effect on dream recall has not been sufficiently studied (Branconnier & Cole, 1981; Cole & Schatzberg, 1976; Drachman et al., 1978; Drachman & Leavitt, 1974; Sitaram et al., 1978). (Antidepressant drugs inhibit REM sleep by lengthening REM latency [Kupfer, 1976].) However, one might hypothesize that the natural reduction in acetylcholine with aging or the marked decrease in acetylcholine with dementia might contribute to impaired dream recall. The norepinephrine system also plays a role in memory formation. Delaney, Tussi, and Gold (1983) found that increased stimulation of noradrenergic neurons was associated with the establishment of long-term memory. Thus, a study of factors that affect dream recall might shed some light on memory disorders in aging.

Similar reasoning suggests that a study of norepinephrine functioning in depression may be useful in elucidating the role of depression in memory dysfunction in aging persons. Because norepinephrine neurotransmission dysfunction is hypothesized to play a central role in depression, and because norepinephrine is decreased in aging and dementia, one would expect that a reciprocal balance between norepinephrine and acetylcholine would be impaired in the depressed elderly person. The exact role of decreased reciprocal balance in the pons is not yet clear, but, in the elderly, decreases in both acetylcholine and norepinephrine function might play a central role in alterations in sleep–wake cycle. If so, dream production, and very likely dream recall, would be altered.

Having reviewed the biological data linking depression, memory, REM sleep, and neurotransmitter dysfunction in the aging brain, we turn to data from psychological studies of dreams and dream recall.

The scant data that exist on the study of dream content and dream recall in aged subjects suggest the following:

1. Dream recall in normal aged persons correlates positively with verbal intelligence (Kahn, Fisher, & Lieberman, 1969; Kramer, Roth, & Trinder, 1975).

2. Elderly people recall dreams less frequently than do young people (Kahn et al., 1969).

3. Elderly women recall dreams more frequently than do elderly men (Kahn et al., 1969).

4. Dreams of subjects with AD or organic brain syndrome are different from dreams of normal subjects. Torda (1969) found that the dreams of subjects with amnestic syndrome secondary to encephalitis were shorter, simpler, direct representations of physiological needs and were repetitions of past situations rather than present events. Kramer et al. (1975) found a significant decrease in dream recall: 8% for severely demented elderly subjects, as opposed to 57% for mildly demented younger patients, and 35% for severely demented younger patients. The dream reports differed in content from dreams of normal younger men by the degree of emotional blandness, lack of expression of aggression, and increase in number of characters in dreams. The authors attributed altered dream content mostly to subjects' external environment and their feelings of helplessness; they speculated that decreased dream recall might be associated with REM dysfunction in patients with dementia.

The question for future research is as follows: If dream amnesia is in some way related to acetylcholine and norepinephrine, and if these neurotransmitters are in fact related to memory and norepinephrine depression, what research variables can be studied to shed further light on the processes of memory, depression, dreaming, forgetting, and aging? Thus, we recommend the following research projects:

1. Natural study of sleep stages in aging, with particular reference to type and amount of dream recall, should be conducted. Normal elderly persons should be compared with young old, very old, mildly depressed, and very depressed elderly patients.

2. Sleep stages (especially REM) should continue to be studied in severely demented elderly people.

3. The effect of pharmacological agents (neurotransmitter precursors, antidepressants, stimulants, and peptides) should be studied in the categories of patients specified in 1.

4. Natural observations of dream production and dream recall with pharmacological probes shall be made, and physiological studies of brain function, such as brain electrical activity mapping (BEAM) and ago-nist binding studies of cholinergic receptor sites, should be undertaken.

5. In the clinical setting, clinicians should begin to ask elderly patients about dream recall and should begin to quantify the nature of dream recall in different populations of older people. Dream recall should be noted before and after treatment for depression, as well as before and after any treatment for memory loss, if such treatment is undertaken.

References

Akiskal, H. S., Rosenthal, T. L., Haykal, R. F., Lemmi, H., Rosenthal, R. H., & Scott-Strauss, A. (1980). Characterological depressions: Clinical and sleep EEG findings separating "subaffective dysthymias" from "character spectrum" disorders. *Archives of General Psychiatry, 37,* 777–783.

Alloy, L. B., & Abramson, L. Y. (1979). Judgment of contingency in depressed and nondepressed students: Sadder but wiser? *Journal of Experimental Psychology: General, 108,* 441–485.

Bajada, S. (1982). A trial of choline chloride and psysostigmine in Alzheimer's dementia. In S. Corkin, K. L. Davis, J. H. Growdon, E. Usdin, & R. J. Wurtman (Eds.), *Alzheimer's disease: A report of progress in research* (pp. 427–432). New York: Raven Press.

Bartus, R. T., Dean, R. L., Beer, B., & Lippa, A. S. (1982). The cholinergic hypothesis of geriatric memory dysfunction. *Science, 217,* 408–417.

Bellak, L., Hurvich, M., & Gediman, H. (1973). *Ego functions in schizophrenics, neurotics, and normals.* New York: Wiley.

Bower, G. H. (1981). Mood and memory. *American Psychologist, 36,* 129–148.

Branconnier, R. J., & Cole, J. O. (1981). Effects of acute administration of trazodone and amitriptyline on cognition, cardiovascular function, and salivation in the normal geriatric subject. *Journal of Clinical Psychopharmacology,* (Suppl.), 82S–88S.

Breslow, R., Kocsis, J., & Belkin, B. (1980). Memory deficits in depression: Evidence using the Weschler Memory Scale. *Perceptual and Motor Skills, 51,* 541–542.

Breslow, R., Kocsis, J., & Belkin, B. (1981). The contribution of the depressive perspective to memory function in depression. *American Journal of Psychiatry, 138,* 227–230.

Caine, E. D. (1981). Pseudodementia. *Archives of General Psychiatry, 38,* 1359–1364.

Caine, E. D., Yerevanian, B. I., & Bamford, K. A. (1984). Cognitive function and the dexamethasone suppression test in depression. *American Journal of Psychiatry, 141,* 116–117.

Carroll, B. J., Feinberg, M., & Greden, F. (1981). A specific laboratory test for the diagnosis of depression. *Archives of General Psychiatry, 38,* 15–22.

Christie, J. E. (1982). Physostigmine and arecholine infusions in Alzheimer's disease. In S. Corkin, K. L. Davis, J. H. Growdon, E. Usdin, & R. J. Wurtman (Eds.), *Alzheimer's disease: A report of progress in research* (pp. 413–420). New York: Raven Press.

Cohen, R. M., Weingartner, H., Smallberg, S. A., Pickar, D., & Murphy, D. L. (1982). Effort and cognition in depression. *Archives of General Psychiatry, 39,* 593–597.

Cole, J. O., & Schatzberg, A. F. (1976). Memory difficulty and tricyclic antidepressants. *McLean Hospital Journal, 102,* 102–107.

Davies, R. K., Tucker, G. J., & Harrow, M. (1971). Confusional episodes and antidepressant medication. *American Journal of Psychiatry, 128,* 127–131.

Davis, H., & Unruh, W. R. (1980). Word memory in non-psychotic depression. *Perceptual and Motor Skills, 51,* 699–705.

Delaney, R., Tussi, D., & Gold, P. E. (1983). Long-term potentiation as a neurophysiological analog of memory. *Pharmacology, Biochemistry, and Behavior, 18,* 137–139.

Deutsch, J. A., & Rocklin, K. (1972). Anticholinesterase amnesia as a function of massed or spaced retest. *Journal of Comparative Physiology and Psychology, 81,* 64–68.

Donnelly, E. F., Waldman, I. N., Murphy, D. L., Wyatt, R. J., & Goodwin, F. K. (1980). Primary affective disorder: Thought disorder in depression. *Journal of Abnormal Psychology, 89*(3), 315–319.

Drachman, D. A., Feinberg, T., & Goodman, B. (1978). Central cholinergic systems and memory. In M. A. Lipton, A. DiMascio, & K. F. Killam (Eds.), *Psychopharmacology: A generation of progress.* New York: Raven Press.

Drachman, D. A., & Leavitt, J. (1974). Human memory and the cholinergic system: A relation to aging? *Archives of Neurology, 30,* 113–121.

Ehlert, F. J., Roeske, W. R., & Yamamura, H. I. (1982). A radioreceptor assay for estimation of acetylcholine. *Proceedings of the Western Pharmacological Society, 25,* 237–239.

Erikson, E. H. (1950). *Childhood and society.* New York: Norton.

Feinberg, T., & Goodman, B. (1984). Affective illness, dementia, and pseudodementia. *Journal of Clinical Psychiatry, 45,* 99–103.

Ferris, S. H., Reisberg, B., Crook, T., Friedman, E., Schneck, M. K., Mir, P., Sherman, K. A., Corwin, J., Gershon, S., & Bartus, R. T. (1982). Pharmacologic treatment of senile dementia: Choline, L-DOPA, piracetam, and choline plus piracetam. In S. Corkin, K. L. Davis, J. H. Growdon, E. Usdin, & R. J. Wurtman (Eds.), *Alzheimer's disease: A report of progress in research* (pp. 475–481). New York: Raven Press.

Flicker, C., McCarley, R. W., & Hobson, J. A. (1981). Aminergic neurons: State control and plasticity in three model systems. *Cellular and Molecular Neurobiology, 1,* 123–166.

Fogarty, S. J., & Hemsley, D. R. (1983). Depression and the accessibility of memories: A longitudinal study. *British Journal of Psychiatry, 142,* 232–237.

Friedman, A. S. (1964). Minimal effects of severe depression on cognitive functioning. *Journal of Abnormal and Social Psychology, 69,* 237–243.

Glass, R. M., Uhlenhuth, E. H., Hartel, F. W., Matuzas, W., & Fischman, M. W. (1981). Cognitive function and imipramine in outpatient depressives. *Archives of General Psychiatry, 38,* 1048–1051.

Goodnick, P., Gershon, S., & Salzman, C. (1984). Treatment of dementia and memory loss. In C. Salzman (Ed.), *Clinical geriatric psychopharmacology* (pp. 171–198). New York: McGraw-Hill.

Gurland, B., Dean, L., Cross, P., & Golden, R. (1980). The epidemiology of depression and dementia in the elderly. In J. O. Cole & J. E. Barrett (Eds.), *Psychopathology in the aged* (pp. 37–62). New York: Raven Press.

Gustafson, L., (1975). Psychiatric symptoms in dementia with onset in the senile period. *Acta Psychiatrica Scandinavica, 257*(Suppl.), 9–35.

Hauri, P. (1977). *The sleep disorders.* Kalamazoo, MI: Upjohn.

Henry, G. M., Weingartner, H., & Murphy, D. L. (1973). Influence of affective states and psychoactive drugs on verbal learning and memory. *American Journal of Psychiatry, 130,* 966–971.

Hobson, J. A., & McCarley, R. W. (1977). The brain as a dream state generator: An activation–synthesis hypothesis of the dream process. *American Journal of Psychiatry, 134,* 1335–1347.

Isen, A. M., Clark, M., Shalker, T. E., & Karp, S. (1978). Affect, accessibility of material in memory, and behavior: A cognitive loop? *Personality and Social Psychology, 36,* 1–12.

Jarvik, M. E., Gritz, E. R., & Schneider, N. G. (1972). Drugs and memory disorders in human aging. *Behavioral Biology, 7,* 643–688.

Kahn, E., Fisher, C., & Lieberman, A. (1969). Dream recall in the normal aged. *Journal of the American Geriatric Society, 17,* 1121–1126.

Kahn, R. L., Zarit, S. H., Hilbert, N. M., & Niederehe, G. (1975). Memory complaint and impairment in the aged. *Archives of General Psychiatry, 32,* 1569–1573.

Kales, A., Wilson, T., & Kales, J. (1967). Measurements of all-night sleep in normal elderly persons: Effects of aging. *Journal of the American Geriatric Society, 15,* 405–414.

Keller, M. B., & Shapiro, R. W. (1982). "Double depression": Superimposition of acute depressive episodes on chronic depressive disorders. *American Journal of Psychiatry, 139,* 438–442.

Kiloh, L. G. (1961). Pseudodementia. *Acta Psychiatrica Scandinavica, 37,* 336–351.

Kramer, M., Roth, T. N., & Trinder, J. (1975). Dreams and dementia: A laboratory exploration of dream recall and dream content in chronic brain syndrome patients. *International Journal of Aging and Human Development, 6,* 169–178.

Kupfer, D. (1976). REM latency: A psychobiologic marker for primary depressive disease. *Biological Psychiatry, 11,* 159–174.

LaRue, A. (1982). Memory loss and aging: Distinguishing dementia from benign senescent forgetfulness and depressive pseudodementia. *Psychiatric Clinics of North America, 5,* 89–104.

Liljequist, R., Mattila, M. J., & Linnoila, M. (1981). Alterations in human memory following acute maprotiline, diazepam, and codeine administration. *Acta Pharmacology and Toxicology, 48,* 190–192.

Loosen, P. T., & Prange, A. J., Jr. (1982). Serum thyrotropin response to thyrotropin-releasing hormone in psychiatric patients: A review. *American Journal of Psychiatry, 139,* 405–416.

Lowy, F. H., Kleghorn, J. M., & McClure, D. J. (1971). Sleep patterns in depression. *Journal of Nervous and Mental Disease, 153,* 10–26.

Mattila, M. J., Liljequist, R., & Seppala, T. (1978). Effects of amitriptyline and mianserin on psychomotor skills and memory in man. *British Journal of Clinical Pharmacology, 5,* 53S–55S.

McAllister, T. W. (1981). Cognitive functioning in the affective disorders. *Comprehensive Psychiatry, 22,* 572–586.

McCarley, R. W. (1982). REM sleep and depression: Common neurobiological control mechanisms. *American Journal of Psychiatry, 140,* 565–570.

McPartland, R. J., Kupfer, D. J., & Coble, P. A. (1979). An automated analysis of REM sleep in primary depression. *Biological Psychiatry, 14,* 767–776.

Mendels, J., & Chernik, D. A. (1975). Sleep changes and affective illness. In F. F. Flach & S. C. Draghi (Eds.), *The nature and treatment of depression* (pp. 77–92). New York: Wiley.

Miller, E., & Lewis, P. (1977). Recognition memory in elderly patients with depression and dementia: A signal detection analysis. *Journal of Abnormal Psychology, 86,* 84–86.

Miller, N. E. (1980). The measurement of mood in senile brain disease: Examiner ratings and self-reports. In J. O. Cole & J. E. Barrett (Eds.), *Psychopathology in the aged* (pp. 97–122). New York: Raven Press.

Natale, M., & Hantas, M. (1982). Effect of temporary mood states on selective memory about the self. *Journal of Personality and Social Psychology, 42,* 927–934.

Neisser, U. (1981). John Dean's memory: A case study. *Cognition, 9,* 1–22.

Peters, B. H., & Levin, H. S. (1982). Chronic oral physostigmine and lecithin administration in memory disorders of aging. In S. Corkin, K. L. Davis, J. H. Growdon, E. Usdin, & R. J. Wurtman (Eds.), *Alzheimer's disease: A report on progress in research* (pp. 421–426). New York: Raven Press.

Prinz, P. (1977). Sleep patterns in the healthy aged: Relationship with intellectual function. *Journal of Gerontology, 32,* 179–186.

Prinz, P. Obrist, W., & Wang, H. (1975). Sleep patterns in healthy elderly subjects: Individual differences as related to other neurophysiological variables. *Sleep Research, 4,* 132.

Prinz, P., & Raskind, M. (1978). Aging and sleep disorders. In R. Williams & I. Karacan (Eds.), *Sleep Disorders.* New York: Wiley.

Reifler, B. V. (1982). Arguments for abandoning the term pseudodementia. *Journal of the American Geriatric Society, 30,* 665–668.

Reisberg, B. (Ed.). (1983). *Alzheimer's disease.* New York: Free Press/Macmillan.

Rounsaville, B. J., Sholomskas, D., & Prusoff, B. A. (1980). Chronic mood disorders in depressed outpatients. *Journal of Affective Disorders, 2,* 73–88.

Rubinow, D. R., Post, R. M., Savard, R., & Gold, P. W. (1984). Cortisol hypersecretion and cognitive impairment in depression. *Archives of General Psychiatry, 41,* 279–283.

Salzman, C., & van der Kolk, B. A. (1984). Treatment of depression. In C. Salzman (Ed.), *Clinical geriatric psychopharmacology* (pp. 77–115). New York: McGraw-Hill.

Schildkraut, J. J. (1978). Current status of the catecholamine hypothesis of affective disorders. In M. A. Lipton, A. DiMascio, & K. F. Killam (Eds.), *Psychopharmacology: A generation of progress* (pp. 1223–1234). New York: Raven Press.

Shapiro, D. (1965). *Neurotic styles.* New York: Norton.

Shraberg, D. (1978). The myth of pseudodementia: Depression and the aging brain. *American Journal of Psychiatry, 135,* 601–603.

Silberman, E. K., Weingartner, H., & Post, R. M. (1983). Thinking disorder in depression. *Archives of General Psychiatry, 40,* 775–780.

Sitaram, N., Weingartner, H., & Gillin, J. C. (1978). Human serial learning: Enhancement with arecholine and choline and impairment with scopolamine. *Science, 201,* 274–276.

Spar, J. E., & Gerner, R. (1982). Does the dexamethasone suppression test distinguish between dementia and depression? *American Journal of Psychiatry, 139,* 238–239.

Sternberg, D. E., & Jarvik, M. E. (1976). Memory functions in depression. *Archives of General Psychiatry, 33,* 219–225.

Teasdale, J. D., & Fogarty, S. J. (1979). Differential effects of induced mood on retrieval of pleasant and unpleasant events from episodic memory. *Journal of Abnormal Psychology, 88,* 248–257.

Thompson, P. J., & Trimble, M. R. (1982). Non-MAOI antidepressant drugs and cognitive functions: A review. *Psychological Medicine, 12,* 539–548.

Torda, C. (1969). Dreams of subjects with loss of recent memory for recent events. *Psychophysiology, 6,* 358–365.

Vaillant, G. (1977). *Adaptation to life.* Boston: Little, Brown & Co.

Warrington, E. K. (1981). Neuropsychological evidence for multiple memory systems. *Acta Neurologica Scandinavica, 64*(Suppl. 89), 13–19.

Weingartner, H., Cohen, R. M., & Bunney, W. E. (1982). Memory-learning impairments in progressive dementia and depression. *American Journal of Psychiatry, 139,* 135–136.

Weingartner, H., Cohen, R. M., Murphy, D. L., Martello, J., & Gerdt, C. (1981). Cognitive processes in depression. *Archives of General Psychiatry, 38,* 42–47.

Wells, C. E. (1979). Pseudodementia. *American Journal of Psychiatry, 136,* 895–900.

Whitehead, A. (1973). Verbal learning and memory in elderly depressives. *British Journal of Psychiatry, 123,* 203–208.

Wurtman, R. J., & Zeisel, S. H. (1982). Brain choline: Its sources on the synthesis and release of acetylcholine. In S. Corkin, K. L. Davis, J. H. Growdon, E. Usdin, & R. J. Wurtman (Eds.), *Alzheimer's disease: A report of progress in research* (pp. 303–314). New York: Raven Press.

Instrument and Data Review: The Quest for External Validators

Alfred W. Kaszniak and Kenneth L. Davis, *Section Editors*

Alfred W. Kaszniak and Kenneth L. Davis

CHAPTER

27

Instrument and Data Review: The Quest for External Validators

This chapter provides an introduction and overview of issues in the external validation of instruments for the clinical memory assessment of older adults. The authors of chapters in this section were selected as representing various approaches to external validation, with particular focus on longitudinal change, clinical diagnosis, and neurobiologic measures as validational criteria. In introducing the reader to this section of the handbook, we address five general questions: (a) What are the justifications for selecting the specific external validators employed by each team of investigators? (b) What evidence is available concerning the reliability and validity of the external validator itself (e.g., sources of technical artifact or accuracy of clinical diagnosis)? (c) What problems are encountered with respect to relating the memory assessment measures to the external validators? (d) Does the research support the validity of the clinical memory assessment instruments? (e) What are the implications for clinical application of the assessment instruments? Overall, the chapters in this section provide considerable support for the validity of various assessment instruments. However, the authors of these contributions also indicate limitations of such validity and argue that the selection of any particular memory assessment approach must be guided by the purpose of the assessment (e.g., diagnosis vs. longitudinal follow-up), by considerations regarding the relationship of task difficulty to severity of memory impairment, and by the present state of knowledge regarding the nature of memory impairment in different disease processes.

In the clinical assessment of older individuals, the informed selection of particular memory measures is dependent upon knowledge of the validity of such measures. In judging the validity of an assessment instrument, questions regarding both what the test measures and how well it does so must be asked (Anas-

tasi, 1982). The question of what an assessment instrument measures has generally been addressed with procedures classified under the titles "content" validity and "construct" validity (Anastasi, 1982; Cunningham, chapter 4, this volume). The question of how well an instrument measures what it is presumed to measure is generally addressed via criterion-related validation procedures. It is this latter approach, in which performance on a measure is assessed against some independent measure, with which this section of this handbook is concerned.

In selecting the authors for the chapters of this section, the editors have attempted to provide a representative sample of approaches to the criterion validation of clinical memory assessment instruments that are appropriate for older persons. It must be emphasized that this selection was designed to be representative rather than exhaustive. Although the choice of selections could certainly be faulted for exclusion of specific assessment instruments, of particular approaches to external validation, or of specific outstanding investigators, the chapters included do represent fairly a cross-section of work within this area. The chapters in this section represent research that involves validational criteria in three broad categories: clinical diagnosis, longitudinal change within particular diagnostic groups, and various neurobiologic measures of presumed relevance to memory functioning in older persons. In examining the validity of a particular memory assessment instrument against such criteria, we must address several specific issues.

Critical Issues in External Validation

The first issue faced by the investigator concerns the choice of the criterion measure to be employed. The external criterion must be justified on the basis of a theoretical rationale that relates the memory assessment measure to the criterion. Preferably, this theoretical rationale will rest upon prior empirical information that links the criterion measure to the particular construct the memory assessment instrument is attempting to operationalize. The second issue facing the investigator concerns the availability of empirical information on the reliability and validity of the external criterion itself. If the criterion cannot be measured reliably (either in terms of internal consistency, test–retest reliability, or scorer reliability), error variance will be high, and the relationship between the criterion measure and the memory assessment instrument will necessarily be attenuated (Anastasi, 1982, pp. 102–130). Even if the external criterion can be reliably measured, it may not be validly related to the phenomenon it attempts to operationalize. This lack of validity may be due to systematic contributions of technical artifact as well as to the influence of other intervening variables. Such problems are particularly prevalent when neurobiologic measures are employed as external criteria, because techniques available for noninvasive study of humans may be several steps removed from the neurobiologic phenomenon of interest (e.g., radiographic imaging of anatomic structure rather than tissue examination of the anatomy itself; statistical averages of bioelectric phenomena; or plasma or cerebrospinal fluid measures of centrally active neurotransmitter activity).

Once an external criterion has been rationally selected and its own reliability and validity have been determined, the investigator can begin to examine its relationship to the particular memory assessment measure. A variety of problems may be encountered in this endeavor. One of the more serious difficulties relates to issues in sampling. If the subjects selected for study (e.g., patients with Alzheimer's disease [AD]) are not reasonably representative of the full range of severity of the illness (e.g., either all are very severely impaired or all are very mildly impaired), then this truncation of range will affect the magnitude of any relationship that can be observed between the external criterion (e.g., anatomic, physiologic, or neurochemical measures) and the memory assessment instrument. Similarly, if the memory assessment instrument samples only a limited range of variability in the construct it is designed to operationalize (e.g., task difficulty is either very high or very low), the potential magnitude of relationship between the assessment instrument and the external criterion will be limited. Finally, logistical problems may be encountered that limit the generality of any conclusions. For example, although a sample of patients may representatively reflect the full range of illness severity, the most severely impaired patients may be unable or unwilling to sufficiently cooperate with procedures required for measurement of either the memory construct or the external criterion. Validational studies that use longitudinal change within a particular patient group as the external criterion are notoriously plagued by selective attrition due to death, disappearance, and failure to cooperate with repeat assessments (Schaie, 1977).

It is only after these issues are given due consideration that the investigator can address the question of whether the magnitude of relationship between the memory assessment instrument and the external criterion supports the instrument's validity. Confidence in the answer to this question is dependent directly upon the issues just addressed. Obviously, all of these issues have a significant impact on the ultimate question of implications for clinical application of the memory assessment instrument. Thus, validity studies may reveal that a particular memory assessment instrument is validly related to clinical diagnosis for a particular disorder (e.g., AD) but does not validly reflect expected differences in longitudinal change between AD patients and age-matched healthy control subjects. The lack of longitudinal validity may be secondary to issues in sampling (e.g., either the initial severity of illness or the difficulty of the memory assessment task results in a truncation of measurement range and consequent "floor" or "basement" effects at repeat assessment). Such observations would imply that the memory assessment instrument in question is likely to be more appropriate for purposes of initial clinical diagnosis than for clinical applications in which change over time must be assessed.

In the remainder of this chapter, the contributions to this section of the handbook will be discussed in relation to the foregoing issues.

What Are the Justifications for the Selection of Specific External Validators?

As noted, the chapters in this section are concerned with validation studies involving three major classes of external validators: clinical diagnosis, longitudinal change within particular diagnostic groups, and neurobiologic measures. Although the rationale for selection of external criteria that fall within these categories may appear obvious, they are worthy of brief discussion. Memory disorder is a pervasive symptom of a wide variety of central nervous system diseases (Butters, 1979; Russell, 1981; Squire & Butters, 1984; Squire & Cohen, 1984). Although many such diseases can and do occur within the older adult population, chapters in this section focus primarily on the most prevalent diseases: AD, multi-infarct dementia (MID), and disorders associated with relatively focal cerebral damage, such as that seen in cerebrovascular infarct, space-occupying lesions, and some toxic/nutritional diseases (e.g., Korsakoff's syndrome).

Of particular clinical concern is the differential diagnosis of disorders presenting as dementia, in which memory impairment is one part of a syndrome that involves progressive impairment of a range of cognitive functions (American Psychiatric Association, 1980, p. 107). Based on studies carried out primarily in northern Europe, estimates of the prevalence of dementia in persons over 65 years of age have ranged from 1.3% to 6.2% for severe dementia and from 2.6% to 15.4% for those with milder dementia (Mortimer, Schuman, & French, 1981; Pfeffer, in press). The prevalence of dementia appears to be age associated; for example, it is four to seven times more prevalent in persons over 80 years of age than in the 70-to-79 age group (Mortimer et al, 1981). Neuropathologic studies have found AD (with its characteristic neuropathology of neurofibrillary tangles, neuritic plaques, and granulovacuolar degeneration) to account for between 50% and 70% of older patients with dementia who are seen in psychiatric practice. An additional 15% to 25% are found to have multiple infarctions of the brain, either alone or in combination with AD (Roth, 1980; Terry & Davies, 1980; Terry & Katzman, 1983; Tomlinson, 1982). Several of the remaining causes of dementia are potentially reversible (Cummings, Benson, & LoVerme, 1980). Studies indicate that a range of from 10% to over 20% (with an average of approximately 15%) of apparent dementing illness in elderly patients has treatable causes (see review by Hutton, 1980).

Such figures underscore the importance of accurate differential diagnosis. The potential of clinical memory assessment instruments to contribute to differential diagnosis provides several of this section's chapter authors with a major rationale for the employment of clinical diagnosis as an external validator. Chapters 32 and 34 (by Brinkman, Largen, Cushman, Braun, & Block and by Butters, Martone, White, Granholm, and White) are specifically concerned with the validity of different memory assessment instruments in differentiating particular clinical diagnostic groups presenting with memory impairment. Both studies emphasize the importance of examining patterns of performance across theoretically distinct aspects of memory and other cognitive functions.

Current diagnostic criteria for AD emphasize the progressive nature of impairment in memory and in other cognitive functions (McKhann et al., 1984). Valid measures of memory impairment, when used in longitudinal studies of patients with AD, would hence be expected to reflect such deterioration. Three of this section's chapters (by Rosen, Mohs, & Davis; by Storandt, Botwinick, & Danziger; and by Wilson & Kaszniak) are explicitly concerned with longitudinal change in AD. Each of the three studies reported in these chapters provides some support for the validity of a particular memory assessment instrument against the criterion of longitudinal change. However, each study also indicates specific limits to such validity, dependent upon memory task difficulty, type of memory process assessed, and severity of dementia at the time patients enter the study.

Most of the remaining chapters of this section employ various neurobiologic measures as external criteria, primarily in studies of patients with AD. Since the earliest neuropathologic descriptions of AD (Alzheimer, 1907), brain atrophy has been thought to be characteristic of the disease. Gross postmortem examination of the brains of AD patients reveals such atrophy in the characteristic appearance of widened cortical sulci and enlarged lateral and third ventricles (Terry & Katzman, 1983). Because computerized tomographic (CT) scanning has the ability to noninvasively visual-

ize enlarged sulcal and ventricular spaces (as well as tissue density), the procedure has frequently been employed, since its introduction (Ambrose, 1973; Hounsfield, 1973), in the study of AD patients. Several of the following chapters are therefore concerned with CT scanning as a potential external criterion. These chapters underscore the technical difficulties and other limitations that must be considered when such measures are used. Although brain atrophy has been thought to be characteristic of AD, marked individual variability among the postmortem brain weights of AD patients (as well as substantial overlap between the brain weight distributions of AD patients and nondemented control groups) has been documented (Terry, Peck, DeTeresa, Schecter, & Horoupian, 1981). A more clearly identifying neuropathologic feature of AD is the quantity and distribution of microscopic lesions (primarily neuritic plaques and neurofibrillary tangles). In chapter 31 Fuld illustrates how such histopathologic features of autopsy material from AD patients can be used to examine the validity of particular patterns of performance on measures of memory and other cognitive functions.

Not only anatomic changes but also physiologic changes are observed to be characteristic of AD. One physiologic change that can be noninvasively studied is diffuse electroencephalographic (EEG) slowing (e.g., Muller & Schwartz, 1978). However, the EEGs of AD patients early in the course of their dementia may show normal or only mildly slowed activity (Sim, 1979), resulting in considerable overlap between groups of AD patients and healthy control subjects. Albert and her colleagues (chapter 38) illustrate the potential of EEG computer spectral analysis (with its attendant improvement in sensitivity and accuracy over clinical evaluation of EEG slowing) as a neurobiologic criterion against which memory assessment instruments can be judged. More recently, interest has developed in the application of measures of brain electrical activity that are temporally related to specifiable sensory stimuli and hence are termed *evoked potentials* (EP) or *event-related potentials* (ERP). Such measures require sophisticated computer averaging techniques for their measurement. The chapter by Horvath clarifies issues concerning the rationale of employing ERPs as external criteria, and the chapter by Albert and her colleagues illustrates the application of ERPs in relation to measures of memory and other cognitive functions. The recent development of positron emission tomography (PET), which allows imaging of intracranial regional metabolism, has generated considerable interest among investigators concerned with AD. The potential applications of PET as an external validator in studies of AD is illustrated by de Leon and his colleagues in chapter 37. In chapter 33 Riege, Harker, and Metter illustrates the application of PET methodology in memory disorders that are secondary to focal cerebral disease.

Finally, no discussion of potential neurobiologic criteria for assessing the validity of memory assessment instruments would be complete without attention to neurochemical and neuroendocrine measures. Intensive research over the past several years has resulted in general agreement (Bartus, Dean, Beer, & Lippa, 1982; Coyle, Price, & DeLong, 1983) that deficiency of acetylcholine (ACh) is the most frequently documented and important neurotransmitter abnormality in AD. Postmortem study of the brains of AD patients shows marked decrease in cerebral choline acetyltransferase (ChAT) activity compared with the brains of age-matched nondemented patients (Bowen, Smith, White, & Davison, 1976; Davies & Maloney, 1976; Perry, Perry, Blessed, & Tomlinson, 1977). The chapter by Mohs and his colleagues illustrates the potential of measures of cholinergic serum and cerebrospinal fluid, as well as anticholinergic pharmacologic manipulation, as external validators for clinical memory assessment instruments.

What Evidence is Available Concerning the Reliability and Validity of the External Validator?

Several of the chapters in this section use clinical diagnosis as the external validating criterion. Others use longitudinal change or neurobiologic measures within clinically diagnosed patient groups. Reliable and valid clinical diagnosis is therefore of primary importance in most attempts to externally validate clinical memory assessment instruments. The differential diagnosis of disorders presenting as dementia poses particular difficulties. These difficulties appear to be most marked when (a) the dementia is relatively early in its course (and therefore mild), (b) signs and symptoms of dementia are confused with those of other disorders, or (c) patients without organic mental disorders present with significant cognitive deficit (i.e., pseudodementia) (Kaszniak, 1986). Empirical data on the accuracy of clinical diagnosis of dementia indicate that such diagnostic difficulty is of significant proportion. Ron, Toone, Garralda, and Lishman (1979) obtained 5-to-15-year follow-up on 51 patients who were discharged from hospital with a firm diagnosis of presenile dementia. At follow-up, the diagnosis of dementia was confirmed in only 69% of cases. Among those 31% that were apparently misdiagnosed, one half received follow-up diagnoses of affective disorder. Garcia, Reding, and Blass (1981) reported comparable data on misdiagnosis from their study of 100 older patients referred to a specialized outpatient dementia clinic. Twenty-six of the patients referred were found not to be demented; 15 of these received a diagnosis of depression.

One contributor to this high rate of misdiagnosis in the past appears to have been the relative lack of specificity in diagnostic criteria. With the publication of the DSM-III and its more explicit criteria (as compared with the DSM-II) for the diagnosis of dementias, acceptably high interclinician reliabilities have been achieved (American Psychiatric Association, 1980, p. 470). The most recent criteria for the clinical diagnosis of AD, as put forward by the Department of Health and Human Services Task Force on AD (McKhann

et al., 1984), include even greater specificity than the DSM-III criteria and would thus be expected to produce at least as high a rate of interdiagnostician agreement. Hence, it appears that clinical diagnosis, at least of AD, can be made reliably, using current criteria. There is currently insufficient information, however, concerning the validity of these criteria. Such information would require follow-up studies, such as those employing previous, less specific criteria, as just described. Even with recent improvements in the specificity of diagnostic criteria, it is likely that there will continue to be difficulties in the accurate differential diagnosis of AD versus pseudodementia (e.g., dementia syndrome of depression) or of AD versus MID (see Kaszniak, 1986; Kaszniak, Sadeh, & Stern, 1985; Roth, 1980; Shore, Overman, & Wyatt, 1983).

Although the reliability and validity of longitudinal change used as an external validator are typically presumed, they may be limited by particular problems in the longitudinal study of both normally aging persons and AD patients. One of the more serious problems concerns selective subject attrition at follow-up. The three chapters in this section that use longitudinal change as a validating criterion illustrate the magnitude of such attrition, particularly among AD patients. Wilson and Kaszniak (chapter 29, this volume) explicitly discuss the impact of such attrition upon generalizability of results.

A major issue in judging the reliability and validity of various neurobiologic measures relates to technical artifact inherent in the measurement procedures. The chapters by Jernigan, by Albert and her colleagues, and by de Leon and his colleagues describe the sources of potential artifact in CT scanning. Other chapters contain similar discussions of methodologic issues in PET scanning (de Leon, George, and Ferris, chapter 37, this volume), ERPs (Horvath, chapter 39, this volume), and pharmacologic intervention (Mohs and his colleagues, chapter 40, this volume).

What Problems Are Encountered in Relating Memory Assessment Measures to External Validators?

Even when a rationally selected external validator has been shown to be reliable and valid, one can encounter a variety of problems when attempting to relate the validator to the memory assessment measure. One particularly problematic issue concerns the interaction between task difficulty and severity of memory impairment. The chapters by Wilson and Kaszniak and by Storandt and her colleagues discuss this issue in detail. This issue is of particular relevance in studies that employ longitudinal change as the validating criterion. Because memory and other cognitive impairment becomes more severe over time, "floor" or "basement" effects may occur in AD patients at follow-up examinations on measures of clinical or theoretical interest. The severity of illness may also interact with the construct validity of a clinical memory assessment instrument. Particularly in AD, as an increasing range of cognitive functions become more severely impaired over time, the construct validity of a measure may change by being "contaminated" by other cognitive processes that do not significantly contribute to the memory task performance of healthy control subjects. The chapter by Wilson and Kaszniak illustrates this problem in its application of primary and secondary memory measures derived from a free verbal recall task. The problems posed by the interaction between task difficulty and severity of illness also affect the relationship between clinical memory measures and neurobiologic criteria.

Does the Research Support the Validity of the Clinical Memory Assessment Instruments?

Despite the foregoing range of problems, the chapters in this section provide considerable support for the validity of their respective assessment instruments. However, consideration of the issues discussed also reveals particular limitations of validity. What emerges most clearly is that the validity of an assessment instrument is very dependent upon what validational criterion is employed. An assessment instrument with demonstrated validity against clinical diagnostic criteria may lack validity when judged against the criterion of longitudinal change. Similarly, performance on an assessment instrument may be validly related to one neurobiologic measure but not to another. Such differences in the association of an assessment instrument with different neurobiologic criteria may relate to the nature and localization of brain dysfunction that the criterion indexes (see Riege et al., chapter 33, this volume). It is also clear that the validity of a memory assessment instrument against clinical diagnostic criteria is very dependent upon the particular diagnostic group examined. This is most clearly illustrated in chapter 34 by Butters et al. Different disease processes affect different aspects of memory functioning, which are reflected in differential performance across various memory assessment instruments. As will be described, the limitations to and qualifications of the validity of various assessment instruments have significant implications for the clinical application of these tools.

What Are the Implications for Clinical Application of the Assessment Instruments?

Several important clinical implications can be derived from the research reported in this section. First, the assessment of memory cannot be approached as if memory were a unitary psychological function. Memory is multidimensional, and processes contributing to overall memory efficiency are highly differentiated. The more closely this differentiation is reflected within the memory assessment instruments, the more likely it is that researchers and clinicians will come to better understand diseases producing memory impairment;

and better understanding, one hopes, will lead to improved treatment and management of such patients. Although traditional instruments, such as the Wechsler Memory Scale (Wechsler, 1945), may continue to play a role as screening instruments, currently available research dictates the need for more sophisticated approaches.

Second, the selection of a particular memory assessment instrument must be informed by the purpose for which it is to be used. Some instruments seem best suited for diagnostic application, particularly when the signs and symptoms of the disorder in question are subtle and the memory impairment is mild. Other instruments appear most appropriate for longitudinal study, for evaluation of treatment effects, or for examination of more severely impaired patients. The chapters in this section provide considerable information to help guide the clinician or clinical investigator in selecting instruments.

Finally, the validation studies reported here also contribute to an understanding of the nature of memory disorder in older age and ultimately will have an impact on approaches to clinical patient management. As illustrated in chapter 33 by Riege et al., the evaluation of memory assessment instruments against current sophisticated neurobiologic criteria may lead to a questioning of many previous assumptions about the relationship of brain structure and function to memory disorder. Such questioning holds the promise for generating new hypotheses concerning the treatment of memory disorders in older age.

References

Alzheimer, A. (1907). Über eigenartige Krankereits falle des späteran alters. *Allegemeine Zeitschrift für Psychiatrie, 64,* 146–148.

Ambrose, J. (1973). Computerized transverse axial scanning (tomography): Part 2. Clinical application. *British Journal of Radiology, 46,* 1023–1047.

American Psychiatric Association. (1980). *Diagnostic and statistical manual of mental disorders* (3rd ed.). Washington, DC: Author.

Anastasi, A. (1982). *Psychological testing* (5th ed.). New York: Macmillan.

Bartus, R. T., Dean, R. L., Beer, B., & Lippa, A. S. (1982). The cholinergic hypothesis of geriatric memory dysfunction. *Science, 217,* 408–417.

Bowen, D. M., Smith, C. B., White, P., & Davison, A. N. (1976). Neurotransmitter-related enzymes and indices of hypoxia in senile dementia and other abiotrophies. *Brain, 99,* 459–496.

Butters, N. (1979). Amnesic disorders. In K. M. Heilman & E. Valenstein (Eds.), *Clinical neuropsychology* (pp. 439–474). New York: Oxford University Press.

Coyle, J. T., Price, D. L., & DeLong, M. R. (1983). Alzheimer's disease: A disorder of cortical cholinergic innervation. *Science, 219,* 1184–1190.

Cummings, J., Benson, D. F., & LoVerme, S. (1980). Reversible dementia: Illustrative cases, definition and review. *Journal of the American Medical Association, 243,* 2434–2439.

Davies, P., & Maloney, A. J. F. (1976). Selective loss of central cholinergic neurons in Alzheimer's disease. *Lancet, 2,* 1403.

Garcia, D., Reding, M. J., & Blass, J. P. (1981). Overdiagnosis of dementia. *Journal of the American Geriatrics Society, 29,* 407–410.

Hounsfield, G. N. (1973). Computerized transverse axial scanning (tomography): Part I. Description of a system. *British Journal of Radiology, 46,* 1016–1022.

Hutton, J. T. (1980). Clinical nosology of the dementing illnesses. In F. J. Pirozzolo & G. J. Maletta (Eds.), *Advances in neurogerontology: Vol. 1. The aging nervous system* (pp. 149–174). New York: Praeger.

Kaszniak, A. W. (1986). Neuropsychology of dementia. In I. Grant & K. Adams (Eds.), *Neuropsychological assessment of neuropsychiatric disorders* (pp. 172–220). New York: Oxford University Press.

Kaszniak, A. W., Sadeh, M., & Stern, L. Z. (1985). Differentiating depression from organic brain syndromes in older age. In G. M. Chaisson-Stewart (Ed.), *Depression in the elderly: An interdisciplinary approach* (pp. 161–189). New York: Wiley.

McKhann, G., Drachman, D., Folstein, M., Katzman, R., Price, D., & Stadlan, E. M. (1984). Clinical diagnosis of Alzheimer's disease: Report of the NINCDS-ADRDA work group under the auspices of the Department of Health and Human Services Task Force on Alzheimer's disease. *Neurology, 34,* 939–944.

Mortimer, J. A., Schuman, L. M., & French, L. R. (1981). Epidemiology of dementing illness. In J. A. Mortimer & L. M. Schuman (Eds.), *The epidemiology of dementia* (pp. 3–23). New York: Oxford University Press.

Muller, H. F., & Schwartz, G. (1978). Electroencephalograms and autopsy findings in geropsychiatry. *Journal of Gerontology, 33,* 504–513.

Perry, E. K., Perry, R. H., Blessed, G., & Tomlinson, B. E. (1977). Necropsy evidence of central cholinergic deficits in dementia. *Lancet, 1,* 189.

Pfeffer, R. I. (in press). Degenerative neurologic disease: Alzheimer's disease, senile dementia of the Alzheimer's type, and related disorders. In D. Holland (Ed.), *Textbook of public health.* New York: Oxford University Press.

Ron, M. A., Toone, B. K., Garralda, M. E., & Lishman, W. A. (1979). Diagnostic accuracy in presenile dementia. *British Journal of Psychiatry, 134,* 161–168.

Roth, M. (1980). Senile dementia and its borderlands. In J. O. Cole & J. E. Barrett (Eds.), *Psychopathology in the aged* (pp. 205–232). New York: Raven Press.

Russell, E. W. (1981). The pathology and clinical examination of memory. In S. B. Filskov & T. J. Boll (Eds.), *Handbook of clinical neuropsychology* (pp. 287–317). New York: Wiley.

Schaie, K. W. (1977). Quasi-experimental research designs in the psychology of aging. In J. E. Birren & K. W. Schaie (Eds.), *Handbook of the psychology of aging* (pp. 39–58). New York: Van Nostrand Reinhold.

Shore, D., Overman, C. A., & Wyatt, R. J. (1983). Improving accuracy in the diagnosis of Alzheimer's disease. *Journal of Clinical Psychiatry, 44,* 207–212.

Sim, M. (1979). Early diagnosis of Alzheimer's disease. In A. I. M. Glen & L. J. Whalley (Eds.), *Alzheimer's disease: Early recognition of potentially reversible deficits* (pp. 78–85). New York: Churchill Livingstone.

Squire, L. R., & Butters, N. (Eds.). (1984). *Neuropsychology of memory.* New York: Guilford.

Squire, L. R., & Cohen, N. J. (1984). Human memory and amnesia. In G. Lynch, J. L. McGaugh, & N. M. Weinberger (Eds.), *Neurobiology of learning and memory* (pp. 3–64). New York: Guilford.

Terry, R. D., & Davies, P. (1980). Dementia of the Alzheimer type. *Annual Review of Neuroscience, 3,* 77–95.

Terry, R., & Katzman, R. (1983). Senile dementia of the Alzheimer type: Defining a disease. In R. Katzman & R. Terry (Eds.), *The neurology of aging* (pp. 51–84). Philadelphia: F. A. Davis.

Terry, R. D., Peck, A., DeTeresa, R., Schecter, R., & Horoupian, D. S. (1981). Some morphometric aspects of the brain in senile dementia of the Alzheimer type. *Annals of Neurology, 10,* 184–192.

Tomlinson, B. E. (1982). Plaques, tangles and Alzheimer's disease. *Psychological Medicine, 12,* 449–459.

Wechsler, D. (1945). A standardized memory scale for clinical use. *Journal of Psychology, 19,* 87–95.

Martha Storandt, Jack Botwinick, and Warren L. Danziger

CHAPTER

28

Longitudinal Changes: Patients With Mild SDAT and Matched Healthy Controls

The test responses of patients with mild senile dementia of the Alzheimer's type (SDAT) were compared with those of normal control subjects in the course of a longitudinal study. The 1.5- to 2.0-hour test battery was administered three times over 2.5 years. Patients and control subjects differed in all but one test at the start of the study, with patients declining in all tests over time and control subjects maintaining performance levels. A subsample of patients was identified that maintained function over the 2.5-year period.

Senile dementia is a devastating health problem of later life. It impairs the patient's quality of life and imposes great emotional and economic burdens on the patient's family. The occupancy of chronic institutional beds mounts, increasing the drain on the national health care budget. Between 5% and 10% of elderly persons in this country suffer from senile dementia (Slater & Roth, 1969). Alzheimer's disease (AD) is by far the most common senile dementia (Terry & Wisniewski, 1975).

AD has an insidious onset. Initially the patient has minor memory problems, not unlike the memory deficits experienced by many healthy older adults. The course of AD, however, is inevitably progressive. Memory continues to deteriorate, and the person experiences difficulty with orientation and concentration. Eventually the person is unable to carry out even the most basic aspects of personal care and everyday living (e.g., dressing and eating). Although the cause of the disease is unknown, unique associated changes in the brain, principally neuritic plaques and neurofibrillary tangles, indicate the physiological nature of this primary neuronal degeneration. Because of the gradual degenerative course of the disease, longitudinal studies are necessary to describe the cognitive changes that accompany it. Thus, the Washington University Memory and Aging Project has been concerned with the nat-

ural history of senile dementia of the Alzheimer's type (SDAT). We on the project are also trying to identify the disorder as early as possible so that effective interventions, when developed, will have maximum impact. Therefore, we have identified patients in the mild stage of the disease, and we are following these people in a longitudinal study.

It is important to compare SDAT with the normal aging process. It is often difficult to make a differential diagnosis between persons in the very early stages of the disease and normal aged persons who may be functioning at less than top level. Differential diagnosis with respect to other disease processes is less difficult. Although most investigators consider SDAT to be a disease process, some researchers have suggested that the underlying bases (i.e., changes in brain cells) are not qualitatively different from the changes seen in healthy older adults—there are just more plaques and tangles in the brains of persons with AD (Tomlinson, Blessed, & Roth, 1970). Thus, as the *quantity* of these changes in the brain cells increases, perhaps clinicians and researchers make a *qualitative* distinction between normal aging and SDAT. For this complex set of reasons, we included in our study patients in the mild stages of SDAT and a matched group of healthy older adults.

The project involves a broadly based interdisciplinary research team that is studying longitudinally the clinical features of the disease from the perspectives of

This research was supported in part by grant number MH 31054 from the National Institute of Mental Health. Our appreciation is extended to Drs. Leonard Berg (principal investigator), Charles P. Hughes, Lawrence A. Coben, Ronald L. Martin, and John Knesevich, who conducted the structured interviews; to Mrs. Emily LaBarge, who did the psychological testing; and to Dr. Patricia Lacks, who scored the Bender Gestalt Tests.

neurology, psychological test performance, spontaneous electroencephalography, visual-evoked potentials in the occipital region, and quantitative computed tomography. This chapter reports the results from the psychological tests across three times of testing (spaced over 2.5 years), comparing the SDAT patients and the control subjects. In view of the careful and detailed screening of subjects before their placement into the categories of mild SDAT patients and healthy control subjects, the results reported here bear on the validity of the test battery with respect to diagnosis. The results also indicate the level of psychological dysfunction that accompanies SDAT in its early stages and the course the dysfunction takes as the disease progresses.

The Study Sample

The original SDAT study sample included 43 persons (20 men and 23 women) with mild AD who were living in the community. The diagnostic procedure is described in the next section; here, we note only that the patients were diagnosed as having mild SDAT. Most of the impaired participants were recruited when their families responded to widespread community announcements in newspapers and on the radio and television. A few patients were referred by physicians in response to letters of solicitation sent to the medical community. The recruitment procedure has been described in detail elsewhere (Berg et al., 1982).

Each patient was matched on the basis of age, sex, and social position (Hollingshead, 1957) with a healthy older adult also recruited from the community. The healthy participants responded to the same public announcements or had volunteered for other studies at the university. Although the recruitment procedure was not designed to exclude any racial or ethnic group, all participants were white. Thus, the sample initially comprised 43 patients with mild SDAT and 43 healthy control subjects. Table 28-1 shows the range, mean, and standard deviation of the ages, years of education, and socioeconomic categories for the two groups. These values are shown in the first two columns of the table labeled "original sample."

Not every person could be tested on each of the three occasions. Thus, the analyses reported in this chapter were based on the 22 SDAT patients and 39 healthy control subjects who were tested at all three times, beginning in late 1979. The first and second times of testing were separated by 1 year, the second and third times of testing by 1.5 years, on the average. The range, mean, and standard deviation of each of the demographic variables for the analyzed sample are shown in the last two columns of Table 28-1.

Researchers conducting any longitudinal study must realize that sample attrition may be selective, that is, particular types of participants may drop out during the course of the study. Riegel, Riegel, and Meyer (1967) reported an example of such selective attrition in a study of intelligence in adults. Persons with lower scores at the initial testing were overrepresented in

Table 28-1. Demographic Characteristics at Initial Testing of the Original and Analyzed Samples

Variables	Original sample		Analyzed sample	
	SDAT ($n = 43$)	Control ($n = 43$)	SDAT ($n = 22$)	Control ($n = 39$)
Age				
Range	63–81	64–82	63–80	64–82
Mean	71.4	71.6	71.1	71.3
Standard deviation	5.0	5.2	4.7	5.0
Education (years)				
Range	8–21	8–20	8–21	8–20
Mean	12.5	12.5	12.6	12.6
Standard deviation	4.1	3.2	4.0	3.3
Socioeconomic status[1]				
Range	1–5	1–4	1–4	1–4
Mean	3.0	3.0	3.3	3.0
Standard deviation	1.2	1.2	1.1	1.3

[1]Socioeconomic status categories as determined by the Hollingshead (1957) Two-Factor Index of Social Position.

the group that was lost to follow-up. Thus, the representativeness of the longitudinal analysis was threatened because the analysis was conducted largely on the subjects who were scored initially as more able.

Accordingly, we conducted Hotelling's T^2 analyses, comparing the initial scores of persons who were not available for all three testings with the initial scores of those who were. These analyses were conducted separately for the SDAT and control groups. Neither T^2 analysis was significant ($p > .05$). Thus, we concluded that the attrition we experienced in this longitudinal study was not selective.

The reasons for attrition were varied. In the control group, one woman developed cancer and refused to be tested at the last time of testing. One man moved out of state. One man died from what was called "infirmities of old age." One woman who was diagnosed initially as healthy was diagnosed at the second and third times of testing as having some degree of dementia. The reasons for attrition among persons in the SDAT group included death, placement in out-of-state nursing homes, and refusal to continue participating. (Families, rather than the patients, often made the refusal decisions.) Scheduling difficulties prevented assessment of one man with SDAT on the psychometric battery at the initial time of testing, although he was tested on subsequent occasions.

An additional Hotelling's T^2 analysis was conducted, comparing the initial scores of the healthy older people matched with SDAT patients who remained in the sample and the healthy older people matched with SDAT patients who dropped out. The purpose of this analysis was to determine if the entire remaining sample of healthy aged persons could be included in the longitudinal analyses without compromising the purposes of the original matching strategy. This T^2 analysis was not significant ($p > .05$). Therefore, all 39 remaining control subjects were included.

Diagnosis

Diagnosis was based on a 90-minute structured interview and neurological examination conducted in the outpatient offices of the Department of Neurology of the Washington University Medical School. Part of the interview was with the subject and part with a collateral source (usually the spouse or an adult child). This procedure was followed with all participants—those diagnosed as having SDAT and the healthy control subjects. The structured interview included questions concerning medical and psychiatric history; family history; and social, educational, and cultural background. Several published procedures used to rate individuals with dementia were also included in the diagnostic examination. These included the Dementia Scale (Blessed, Tomlinson, & Roth, 1968), the Short Portable Mental Status Questionnaire (Pfeiffer, 1975), and the Face–Hand Test (Fink, Green, & Bender, 1952). Each person was given tasks in memory, orientation, abstraction, calculation, judgment, and problem solving. Collateral sources were asked about the subject's ability to dress and care for himself or herself.

The information obtained from the structured interview and examination formed the basis of the clinician's global rating of each participant in the study (see Hughes, Berg, Danziger, Coben, & Martin, 1982, for a more detailed description of the Clinical Dementia Rating Scale). This rating scale ranges from 0 (healthy) to 3 (severe dementia). All persons in our sample diagnosed as healthy and without the disease were given a rating of 0. All of those in our study diagnosed as mildly demented were given a rating of 1; everyone in this mildly demented group had suffered from gradual intellectual deterioration for 6 months or longer.

Interviews and examinations were conducted by one of three neurologists or two psychiatrists. Each interview was videotaped for an independent rating by one of the other physicians. In six cases, the two raters disagreed on the subjects' stage of *mild* SDAT; these cases were not included in the sample. Six possibly healthy control subjects were also eliminated because of contradictory ratings.

Other reasons for exclusion from the study included presence of reversible dementias and medical disorders (or treatment with medication) that cause mental impairment. Persons with psychiatric disorders such as alcohol abuse, major depression, or pseudodementia were also excluded, as were persons with other neurological diseases, such as Parkinsonism, Huntington's chorea, communicating hydrocephalus, multi-infarct dementia, stroke, and seizure disorders. In addition, persons with severe loss of vision or hearing, insulin-dependent diabetes mellitus, malignancy, or other serious medical illnesses were excluded. All told, we eliminated, either by telephone screening or the structured interview, 489 potential subjects in the search for our sample. The goal was to study persons with mild SDAT who had no interfering conditions that might obfuscate or mimic the behavioral and other effects of the AD process.

Confirmation of the diagnosis of AD can be obtained only at autopsy. Prior to autopsy, the suspected Alzheimer's condition is labeled senile dementia of the Alzheimer type (SDAT). Of the 9 persons in the original sample of 43 mildly demented persons who had died at the time this chapter was written, autopsies were obtained for 6; all were confirmed as having had AD.

Measures

A 1.5- to 2-hour psychological test battery (shown in Table 28-2) was used to assess different types of memory, reasoning, mental control, speed of mental processing, and general brain damage. Most of the tests were standard verbal and nonverbal procedures selected on the basis of a review of the literature reporting previous research on dementia and normal aging.

We decided to employ measures that were portable and relatively easy to administer so that the battery could be taken to an institution or to a patient's home when necessary. We also thought that a portable battery might be easier to use later as a screening device to help in the early identification of SDAT on a widespread scale. Four tests from the battery have, in fact, been found useful in identifying 98% of the cases as either healthy or mildly demented (Storandt, Botwinick, Danziger, Berg, & Hughes, 1984).

Two tests (the Personal Information and Orientation subtests of the Wechsler Memory Scale, WMS) that were similar to parts of the physician's interview were excluded from the battery in order to avoid part–whole correlations with the criterion (i.e., the diagnosis).

Procedure

All participants were tested individually by the same research assistant, who was uninformed with respect to group classification, although in most cases it was not hard to tell which person belonged to which classification, especially as the study progressed. All standard tests were administered according to the test manuals, but patients were given encouragement to assure their continued cooperation. For example, successful performance was often praised, and exceedingly poor performance might be followed by a statement such as, "Some of these are really hard." All standard tests except the Bender Gestalt Test (Bender, 1938) were scored according to the test manuals. This test was scored by a clinical psychologist who had long experience with the Hutt and Briskin (1960) scoring method; she was uninformed with respect to diagnostic classification of the subjects.

Results

The means and standard deviations for the mild SDAT and control groups on each of the procedures in the test

Table 28-2. Means and Standard Deviations of SDAT and Control Groups on Psychological Tests at Three Times of Testing and Results of Analyses of Variance

Test	SDAT			Control			F ratios[1]		
	Initial	1 year	2.5 years	Initial	1 year	2.5 years	Group	Time	Interaction
Wechsler Memory Scale									
Mental Control									
Mean	4.9	3.3	2.6	7.3	6.9	7.6	53.93****	7.78***	14.74****
Standard deviation	2.2	2.7	2.9	1.7	1.9	1.9			
Logical Memory									
Mean	2.3	1.8	1.1	9.1	10.2	10.1	213.78****	2.43	10.47****
Standard deviation	2.1	2.3	1.4	2.1	2.6	2.8			
Digit Span forward									
Mean	6.3	5.5	4.3	6.7	6.5	6.7	15.04**	8.51***	16.11****
Standard deviation	1.1	1.7	2.3	1.1	1.4	1.2			
Digit Span backward									
Mean	3.3	3.0	1.7	5.1	4.6	5.1	42.54****	7.71***	23.11****
Standard deviation	1.5	1.6	1.6	1.4	1.3	1.6			
Associate Learning									
Mean	5.9	5.3	3.7	13.2	13.4	13.6	129.19****	1.42	7.87***
Standard deviation	2.7	2.5	2.9	3.3	3.4	3.4			
Wechsler Adult Intelligence Scale									
Information[2]									
Mean	10.8	8.7	5.3	19.8	20.4	20.1	68.02****	18.08****	40.93****
Standard deviation	6.3	6.6	6.5	4.9	4.9	5.0			
Comprehension[2]									
Mean	13.2	10.1	7.2	22.5	23.0	23.5	108.36****	9.79****	48.42****
Standard deviation	6.5	7.5	7.6	2.8	2.9	2.9			
Block Design[2]									
Mean	13.5	12.1	7.0	29.6	30.8	28.8	72.86****	11.57****	7.28**
Standard deviation	11.4	12.0	9.7	7.5	7.2	7.7			
Digit Symbol[2]									
Mean	21.0	14.7	9.2	45.2	44.9	45.4	102.11****	11.85****	22.82****
Standard deviation	13.2	12.8	12.3	11.0	11.6	11.4			
Benton Test of Visual Retention									
Memory (10-second delay)[3]									
Mean	16.2	18.8	20.9	7.1	7.0	7.5	118.12****	10.91****	13.33****
Standard deviation	4.9	5.1	5.4	3.8	4.3	3.6			
Copying[3]									
Mean	3.3	7.3	13.5	0.6	0.9	0.8	37.51****	16.31****	26.29****
Standard deviation	5.1	8.4	11.7	0.8	1.8	1.5			
Boston Naming Test									
Mean	43.7	31.7	20.3	70.8	69.6	69.5	100.16****	29.29****	37.61****
Standard deviation	22.5	20.4	22.8	8.7	9.9	11.2			
Word Fluency[4]									
Mean	15.3	13.6	7.7	27.5	31.4	31.9	56.12****	3.40*	24.05****
Standard deviation	9.9	10.6	10.5	8.2	9.4	10.6			
Trailmaking, Form A[5]									
Mean	13.2	10.7	6.4	26.5	24.6	24.7	65.18****	10.94****	5.79**
Standard deviation	7.3	9.2	8.9	7.5	5.8	8.8			
Bender Gestalt									
Mean	4.3	6.4	8.1	2.1	2.5	2.3	86.29****	18.23****	24.33****
Standard deviation	4.0	8.5	11.1	1.3	1.4	2.4			
Crossing-off									
Mean	134.3	121.5	76.3	180.1	179.8	168.9	51.21****	21.12****	12.70****
Standard deviation	38.6	40.4	63.4	39.4	34.3	29.1			

[1]The degrees of freedom for the group effect were 1 and 59, and for the time and interaction effects, 2 and 118.
[2]Raw scores.
[3]Number of errors.
[4]Number of S words in 1 minute plus number of P words in 1 minute.
[5]The reciprocal of time to completion in seconds times 1,000.
*$p < .05$ **$p < .01$.   ***$p < .001$.   ****$p < .0001$.

battery are shown in Table 28-2. The scores from each procedure were subjected to a two-way analysis of variance. That is, the patients with mild SDAT were compared with the healthy control subjects, and the scores at the three times of testing were compared (time of testing was a within-subjects variable). As shown in Table 28-2, all but one F ratio (both main effects and interactions) were significant, usually at the .0001 probability level.

In general, the performance of the mild SDAT group deteriorated over the 2.5-year period, whereas the performance of the control group remained steady. In addition, the mildly demented participants demonstrated poorer performance on many of the tests at the initial time of testing. A notable exception was the measure of primary (short-term) memory, the WMS Digit Span forward subtest (Wechsler, 1945). As shown in Figure 28-1, the two groups performed at comparable levels initially, although the mild SDAT group deteriorated progressively. It appears that primary memory is affected mainly later in the course of the disease. Figure 28-1 suggests that, if one is to follow the demented patients over time, it is important to include in the battery some tests that seem inadequate in discriminating between mild SDAT and healthy aged persons. Moreover, the Digit Span forward subtest may be helpful in determining the stage, or severity, of the disease.

Measures of secondary (longer-term) memory in the battery included the Associate Learning and Logical Memory subtests of the WMS. The level of significance for the main effect of time was only about .03 for the Associate Learning subtest, although the interaction between group and time was significant. The time effect was not significant for the Logical Memory subtest, although, again, the group × time interaction was. The problem with the Logical Memory subtest, and with the Associate Learning subtest to a lesser degree, is that a number of the mild SDAT patients

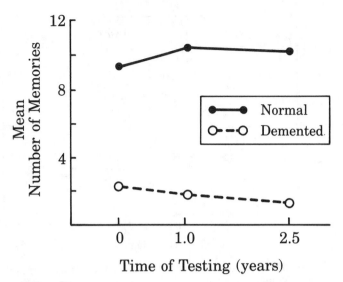

Figure 28-2. Performance by the SDAT and control groups on the Logical Memory subtest of the Wechsler Memory Scale at three times of testing.

reached floor relatively rapidly. Nonetheless, the Logical Memory subtest is very important in the battery. In fact, in terms of explained variance, it was the most powerful in discriminating between the SDAT and control groups initially (Storandt et al., 1984). Thus, it would seem that logical memory is affected very early in the disease process. A good test battery should have tests such as Digit Span that do not discriminate well at first but do later, as well as tests such as the Logical Memory that discriminate very well at first but may be unusable later. As seen in Figure 28-2, the group effect on Logical Memory subtest performance is so powerful that it accounts for a large percentage of the variance, leaving relatively little for the time effect.

The nonverbal test of secondary memory (Benton Test of Visual Retention, Benton, 1974) is scored in terms of number of errors and provides an advantage in that two forms of the test can be used, one involving memory and one simply copying. The performances of the SDAT and control groups on these two forms of the test can be compared in Figure 28-3. Again, the demented group performed less well initially and made more errors in subsequent testing on both forms. The controls produced nearly perfect performance on the copying form, although they averaged about seven errors on the memory form.

Three tests of relatively long-term memory were included in the battery: the Information subtest of the Wechsler Adult Intelligence Scale (WAIS; Wechsler, 1955), word fluency for the letters S and P, and the Boston Naming Test (Kaplan, Goodglass, & Weintraub, 1978). On all three of these tests of well-learned information, the SDAT group started lower and declined progressively, whereas the control group was stable over time. The WAIS Information subtest (Figure 28-4) may be especially useful in differentiating between normal aging and SDAT, because performance on this test is known to "hold" with age, but these data show clearly that performance on this subtest de-

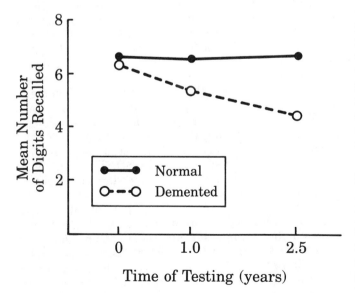

Figure 28-1. Performance by the SDAT and control groups on the Digit Span forward subtest of the Wechsler Memory Scale at three times of testing.

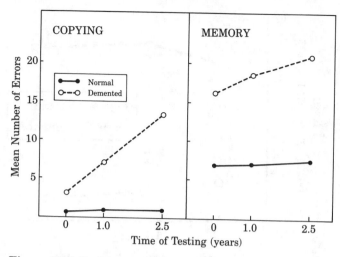

Figure 28-3. Performance of the SDAT and control groups on the 10-second delay (memory) and copying forms of the Benton Test of Visual Retention.

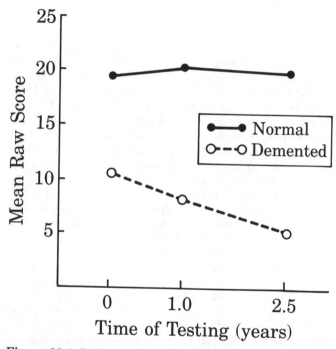

Figure 28-4. Performance by the SDAT and control groups on the Information subtest of the Wechsler Adult Intelligence Scale at three times of testing.

teriorates with SDAT. (The same is true of the WAIS Comprehension subtest; performance on the subtest holds with age but deteriorates with SDAT.) Although the basic pattern of results was similar to those of the word fluency measure, there did appear to be a slight practice effect on this measure in the control group. This was not so with most of the tests in the battery. The Boston Naming Test is interesting because decrement with SDAT was observed at the first time of testing, even though moderate to severe aphasia had been ruled out in the screening for AD in the diagnostic interview.

The pattern of deterioration among participants with SDAT and of stability in the control group was pervasive on all of the psychological tests we administered, including those that hold with age and those that do not. We obtained exactly the same pattern on the WAIS Digit Symbol subtest, even though this test shows the greatest decline among all the WAIS subtests with normal aging. Tests that are used often to measure general brain damage (e.g., Trailmaking and Bender Gestalt), and tests on which older adults perform less well than do younger adults, showed the same pattern as well.

We also administered the simple crossing-off test, which has a minimum cognitive load and was designed to be a purer measure of speed of response (Botwinick & Storandt, 1974). The test was very effective in predicting mortality in a large sample of community-dwelling older adults (Botwinick, West, & Storandt, 1978). It consists of a sheet of 8.5-×-11-inch paper with 12 rows of 8 typed dashes. The person is instructed to cross the dashes (that is, make the dashes into pluses) as quickly as possible, moving from left to right on each line. The score is the number of lines crossed per second (multiplied by 100). The person is given a maximum of 3 minutes to complete the page. Most elderly people, even if demented, can do this task. It is a good test to include in studies of AD because it can be used to measure psychomotor speed at almost all degrees of impairment. The pattern of initially poorer scores and steady decline was observed even with this simple measure of psychomotor speed.

A Subsample

The pattern of deterioration in cognitive function over the 2.5-year course of the study revealed in the analyses reported in the previous section agrees with the clinical observation of progressive deterioration as reflected in increased ratings of severity of SDAT given by the physicians to almost all members of the AD group. There was, however, a small group (n = 5) of SDAT patients who received a rating of *mild* SDAT at each of the three times of assessment.

These five SDAT patients may have had the disease for a shorter time and therefore may not have deteriorated as much as those who had had the disease longer (Berg et al., 1984). Support for this interpretation can be found by comparing the estimated durations of the disease at the time of entry into the study for these five patients (2.9 years) with those for SDAT patients who progressed from ratings of mild to moderate (3.6 years) or mild to severe (3.9 years).

Alternatively, these five SDAT patients may have been more able in their premorbid state than their controls matched for age, sex, and socioeconomic status. If such were the case, the impact of the disease would have diminished their performance levels prior to entry into the study but, because of their greater reserve or capacity, not to the point of interfering with function so as to appear more than mildly demented. Because of their initially greater capacity, these people

Table 28-3. Groupings of Tests on the Basis of Comparison of Initial Scores of Five SDAT Patients With Controls and Course Over Time

Course over time	Comparison of initial scores	
	Equal to scores of controls	Lower than scores of controls
	Group 1	Group 2
Downward	WMS Mental Control WAIS Information WAIS Comprehension WAIS Block Design Boston Naming Test Bender Gestalt Test Crossing-off	WMS Logical Memory Benton (memory)
	Group 3	Group 4
Stable	WMS Digit Span forward Benton (copying)	WMS Digit Span backward WMS Associate Learning WAIS Digit Symbol Trailmaking, Form A

Note. These groupings of tests are based on inspection of the performance of five demented persons who remained in the mild stage of the disease over the course of the study in comparison with the performance of their five matched controls and of the entire control group.

might take longer to progress through the mild stage of the disease.

If the reason for the stability in the severity ratings of these five SDAT patients is shorter duration of the disease or greater premorbid ability, these five patients should show the same *pattern* of deterioration as did the remainder of the SDAT sample. That is, some tests should be affected sooner than others and all should show a downward course, unless they reach floor.

The sample size was too small to allow meaningful statistical analyses; however, the scores of these five SDAT patients were compared by inspection with those of their own matched controls and with those of the total SDAT group. The results are shown in Table 28-3, which lists the various procedures in the battery in terms of initial differences and course over time. Scores on nine of the tests followed a downward course, seven (Group 1) beginning at levels comparable to the scores of the controls and two (Group 2) at levels lower than those of the controls. Thus, the patterns observed for the tests listed in Groups 1 and 2 as well as in Group 3 are consistent with either of the explanations already offered (i.e., shorter duration or greater premorbid ability). The WMS Logical Memory subtest and the memory form of the Benton test represent verbal and nonverbal secondary memory, which is thought to be affected very early in the course of the disease. The two tests in Group 3 (WMS Digit Span forward and the copying form of the Benton) are very easy, involve primary memory, and are probably affected later in the course of the disease.

The four tests that fall into Group 4 of Table 28-3, however, support neither of the explanations already suggested. Some functions, as represented by these tests, did not follow a course of steady deterioration. Perhaps these five patients have a distinct and different form of SDAT that affects some cognitive functions in the same way as was observed in the remainder of the SDAT sample but allows for a plateau in the downward course in other functions.

Summary

Our tests differentiated patients with mild SDAT and normal age-matched control subjects. Except for their primary memory, the mildly demented patients performed less well than the control subjects at the initial testing on all measures and then declined over the 2.5-year period. Thus, it would appear that primary memory is affected later in the course of the disease; but once affected it, too, follows a downward course.

It is important to include in a battery of cognitive tests designed to assess this type of dementia some measures that are sensitive to early symptoms of the disease (e.g., deficits in secondary memory and psychomotor speed). At the same time, however, it is important to include measures (e.g., forward digit span) that can be performed by persons in the more advanced stages of the disease. Overall, however, most persons with SDAT, whatever the stage of the disease, will perform poorly on almost all psychological tests.

References

Bender, L. (1938). *A Visual Motor Gestalt Test and its clinical use.* New York: Orthopsychiatric Association.

Benton, A. L. (1974). *The Revised Visual Retention Test* (4th ed.). New York: Psychological Corporation.

Berg, L., Danziger, W. L., Storandt, M., Coben, L. A., Gado, M., Hughes, C. P., Knesevich, J., & Botwinick, J. (1984). Predictive features in mild senile dementia of the Alzheimer type. *Neurology, 34,* 563–569.

Berg, L., Hughes, C. P., Coben, L. A., Danziger, W. L., Martin, R. L., & Knesevich, J. (1982). Mild senile dementia of the Alzheimer type (SDAT): Research diagnostic criteria, recruitment, and description of a study population. *Journal of Neurology, Neurosurgery, and Psychiatry, 45,* 962–968.

Blessed, G., Tomlinson, B. E., & Roth, M. (1968). The association between quantitative measures of dementia and of senile change in the cerebral grey matter of elderly subjects. *British Journal of Psychiatry, 114,* 797–811.

Botwinick, J. & Storandt, M. (1974). *Memory, related functions, and age.* Springfield, IL: Charles C Thomas.

Botwinick, J., West, R., & Storandt, M. (1978). Predicting death from behavioral test performance. *Journal of Gerontology, 33,* 755–762.

Fink, M., Green, M. A., & Bender, M. B. (1952). The Face–Hand Test as a diagnostic sign of organic mental syndrome. *Neurology, 2,* 46–58.

Hollingshead, A. B. (1957). *Two-factor index of social position.* (Available from 1965 Yale Station, New Haven, CT.)

Hughes, C. P., Berg, L., Danziger, W. L., Coben, L. A., & Martin, R. L. (1982). A new clinical scale for the staging of dementia. *British Journal of Psychiatry, 140,* 566–572.

Hutt, M., & Briskin, G. (1960). *The clinical use of the revised Bender Gestalt test.* New York: Grune & Stratton.

Kaplan, E., Goodglass, H., & Weintraub, S. (1978). *The Boston Naming Test.* Boston: Kaplan & Goodglass.

Pfeiffer, E. (1975). A Short Portable Mental Status Questionnaire for the assessment of organic brain deficit in elderly patients. *Journal of the American Geriatric Society, 23,* 433–441.

Riegel, K. F., Riegel, R. M., & Meyer, G. (1967). A study of the dropout rates in longitudinal research on aging and the prediction of death. *Journal of Personality and Social Psychology, 5,* 342–348.

Slater, E., & Roth, M. (1969). *Clinical psychiatry* (3rd ed.). Baltimore, MD: Williams & Wilkins.

Storandt, M., Botwinick, J., Danziger, W. L., Berg, L., & Hughes, C. P. (1984). Psychometric differentiation of mild senile dementia of the Alzheimer type. *Archives of Neurology, 41,* 497–499.

Terry, R. B., & Wisniewski, H. M. (1975). Structural and chemical changes of the aged human brain. In S. Gershon & A. Raskin (Eds.), *Genesis and treatment of psychologic disorders in the elderly* (pp. 127–141). New York: Raven Press.

Tomlinson, B. E., Blessed, G., & Roth, M. (1970). Observations on the brains of demented old people. *Journal of Neurological Sciences, 11,* 205–242.

Wechsler, D. (1945). A standardized memory scale for clinical use. *Journal of Psychology, 19,* 87–95.

Wechsler, D. (1955). *Manual for the Wechsler Adult Intelligence Scale.* New York: Psychological Corporation.

Robert S. Wilson and Alfred W. Kaszniak

CHAPTER

29

Longitudinal Changes: Progressive Idiopathic Dementia

One approach to the validation of memory assessment instruments involves the longitudinal study of patients with degenerative disorders of the brain, in which memory is progressively impaired. Alzheimer's disease (AD) is one such disorder that has recently received increased attention. In the study described here, a sample of 31 patients with clinically diagnosed AD and 39 normal control subjects of equivalent age and education were given three annual examinations. The performance of the control group did not change, but the AD patients showed progressive decline on a mental status examination, the Wechsler Memory Scale, and the Northwestern Word Latency Naming Test. Subjects were also given a verbal free-recall task from which measures of primary (short-term) and secondary (long-term) memory were derived. The AD patients showed decline of both primary and secondary memory, but control subjects declined only on the latter. The study demonstrates that the instruments employed reflected the expected longitudinal deterioration in AD. The results also argue that researchers and clinicians must consider both the overall severity of dementia and the level of difficulty of the task to be performed by the patient in selecting a particular approach to memory assessment.

In the past 10 years research interest has increased in the progressive dementias, particularly in Alzheimer's disease (AD). The prominence of AD, the availability of various models to study it, and the development of theoretically relevant (i.e., cholinergic) pharmacologic intervention have undoubtedly contributed to this interest. At this point, AD has been reasonably well described, if not completely understood (see Kaszniak, 1986; Kaszniak, Poon, & Riege, chapter 17 in this volume). Patients present with pronounced secondary memory deficits (Miller, 1977; Sjogren, Sjogren, & Lindgren, 1952; Wilson, Bacon, Fox, & Kaszniak, 1983). Primary memory is less impaired (Kaszniak, Garron, & Fox, 1979), although there is some evidence that deficits in primary memory contribute to impair-

ment on secondary memory tasks (Wilson et al., 1983). The secondary memory deficit is seen for both verbal and nonverbal material (Wilson, Kaszniak, Bacon, Fox, & Kelly, 1982). This deficit is not independent of dementia severity (Corkin, 1982) or of subtle linguistic deficits (Butters et al., 1983; Weingartner et al., 1981; Wilson, Kaszniak, et al., 1982). Remote (or tertiary) memory is impaired as well, but the deficit may be mild and shows no temporal gradient, contrary to Ribot's (1882) original postulation (Wilson, Kaszniak, & Fox, 1981).

A major problem in trying to describe AD, treat it, or simply help with management of the patient is the relative lack of empirical data concerning the natural history of this disorder. Classical clinical descriptions (e.g., Sjogren et al., 1952) and current diagnostic criteria (McKhann et al., 1984) both emphasize the progressive nature of memory impairment and other cognitive impairment in AD. Remaining life expectancy has been estimated to be reduced by as much as 50% to 67% in persons with AD, depending on the age of onset (Go, Todorov, Elston, & Constantinidis, 1978; Katzman, 1976). The time from diagnosis to death is difficult to specify, given the variable lag from symptom onset to diagnosis. Estimates suggest survival of from 1 to 10 years following diagnosis, with a mean of 3 to 4 years (Coblentz et al., 1973). Proximity to death is positively correlated with dementia severity (Kaszniak et al., 1978). Beyond such general information, few empirical data have been available on the course of deterioration in AD.

There are many reasons for this dearth of research. In particular, it is difficult to follow a group of patients who are suffering from a disorder for which there is no effective treatment and in whom the phenomena of interest become increasingly difficult to measure as the disorder progresses. Yet, such knowledge is of more than academic interest and is vital to attempts to treat, manage, or even adequately describe such patients.

The work reported on here is based on a longitudinal study of AD patients and normal control subjects. Three broad questions are addressed: First, do the memory assessment instruments employed validly reflect the expected longitudinal deterioration in AD? Second, do these patients whose memory is severely impaired at the study entry point continue to deteriorate at a rate greater than the rate associated with normal aging? Third, does memory decline uniformly or is there differential decline in theoretically different areas of memory?

Subjects

The initial sample consisted of 122 subjects—62 patients and 60 controls—who satisfied the selection criteria for entry into the study. The control subjects were healthy volunteers from the community who were paid to participate in the project. All subjects received a physical and neurological examination, a computerized tomographic (CT) scan, an electroencephalogram (EEG), a psychiatric interview, and an extensive neuropsychological examination. The AD patients met DSM-III criteria (American Psychiatric Association, 1980) for primary degenerative dementia and underwent a series of laboratory procedures to rule out various infectious, toxic, or metabolic disturbances (see Kaszniak, Garron, Fox, Bergen, & Huckman, 1979). The diagnosis of AD required a history of cognitive decline and an absence of evidence of focal lesion, major systemic illness, delirium, or major psychotic symptoms. The Hachinski Ischemic Scale (Hachinski, Lassen, & Marshall, 1974) was used to help exclude patients suspected of having multi-infarct dementia. The current sample of AD patients meets the NINCDS-ADRDA (McKhann et al., 1984) criteria for clinical

diagnosis of probable AD. No patients were institutionalized at the time of entry into the sample. The initial examinations required 2 full days, followed by 1-day examinations at annual intervals.

The total duration of the study was 5 years, with new subjects entering during Years 1 through 4. Eight patients and 14 control subjects entered in Year 4 and therefore received only two annual examinations. This reduced the potential sample that could be followed for 3 years to 54 patients and 46 controls. Of these, 31 patients and 39 controls were actually followed for at least three annual examinations. Five controls (11%) were lost to follow-up because of two deaths, one medical complication, and two refusals. Two more controls, although followed, were not included in analyses because neurological examination raised the possibility of minor focal neurologic abnormality at reexamination. Twenty-three patients (43%) were lost to follow-up because of five deaths, four medical complications, five moves out of state, and nine refusals. Demographic data for the subjects followed for 3 years, and for those lost to follow-up are shown in Table 29-1. These 70 subjects did not differ significantly from the original sample of 122 in age, sex, education, physical and neurologic examination, or initial examination memory test and mental status scores.

Mental Status Examination

At each annual evaluation, the subjects were given a 24-item mental status examination consisting of eight orientation questions and four questions about public figures drawn primarily from the Wechsler Memory Scale (WMS) (Wechsler, 1945) and 12 language items (naming common objects, repeating phrases, following spoken commands) drawn primarily from the Boston Diagnostic Aphasia Examination (Goodglass & Kaplan, 1972). This examination provides only a relatively crude index of mental status, but it has proved useful

Table 29-1. Demographic Description of Subjects Followed for Three Annual Examinations Versus Subjects Lost to Follow-up[1]

Characteristics	Sample followed		Sample lost to follow-up	
	Controls (n = 39)	AD patients (n = 31)	Controls (n = 7)	AD patients (n = 23)
Age	69.28	68.81	68.86	66.70
Education (years)	10.82	11.81	13.10	10.80
Sex[2]				
Female	17.6%	18.5%	9.2%	11.8%
Male	15.1%	7.6%	9.2%	10.9%
Race[2]				
White	32.0%	23.5%	18.5%	22.7%
Black	0.8%	2.5%	0.0%	0.0%
Length of illness (months)	—	33.14	—	44.18

[1]N = 100
[2]Expressed as a percentage of total sample.

because it is highly correlated ($r = .85$, $p < .001$) with the WMS total raw score (for all 122 subjects at initial examination). Furthermore, it can be administered to even severely demented patients who are not always able to complete other measures (e.g., WMS) at follow-up examinations.

Wechsler Memory Scale

The WMS was administered also at each annual examination. The primary rationale for inclusion of this instrument is its frequent use in clinical memory assessment (Prigatano, 1978). Although the WMS has been criticized (Erickson, 1978; Erickson & Scott, 1977; Prigatano, 1978) for its psychometric deficiencies, some of its subtests have been shown to validly differentiate AD patients from controls matched by age, sex, and education (Brinkman, Largen, Gerganoff, & Pomara, 1983; Logue & Wyrick, 1979). A secondary rationale for inclusion of the WMS is that it contains various subtests that differentially tap theoretically distinct memory processes. One example is the familiar Digit Span subtest, involving repetition of increasingly long strings of digits spoken by the examiner, in both forward and reverse order. The Digit Span forward portion of this subtest has generally been considered to reflect mostly operations of the primary, or short-term, memory system, although a small secondary, or long-term, memory component may also be involved (Craik, 1977). Primary memory is conceptualized as a limited-capacity storage system in which information is still "in mind" as it is being used. Rehearsal of items allows for the action of various coding processes enabling the information to be stored in secondary memory, a theoretically relatively permanent store with unlimited capacity (Waugh & Norman, 1965; Kaszniak et al., chapter 17 in this volume). The WMS Logical Memory subtest has been considered to involve predominantly secondary memory (see Kaszniak, 1986), as it requires immediate recall of spoken stories that are of sufficient length to exceed primary memory capacity.

Previous research has shown WMS digit span forward performance in AD patients to be impaired relative to the performance of age-matched controls (Danziger & Storandt, 1982; Kaszniak, Garron, & Fox, 1979), although this impairment may not be seen in mildly demented patients (Danziger & Storandt, 1982). Performance on the WMS Digit Span forward test has been found to be negatively correlated with severity of electroencephalographic (EEG) slowing in AD patients (Kaszniak, Garron, Fox, et al., 1979), and preliminary longitudinal data (Danziger & Storandt, 1982) have documented deterioration in the performance of such patients relative to the performance of matched controls. Similarly, the WMS Logical Memory subtest shows impairment in AD patients (Brinkman et al., 1983; Danziger & Storandt, 1982; Kaszniak, Garron, & Fox, 1979). Performance is negatively correlated with severity of EEG slowing and degree of cerebral atrophy (by CT scanning) (Kaszniak, Garron, Fox, et al., 1979)

and shows deterioration over a one-year retesting interval (Danziger & Storandt, 1982).

Northwestern Word Latency Naming Test

Tulving (1972) proposed that long-term memory may be divided into two theoretically distinct storage systems, episodic and semantic memory. Episodic memory refers to "memory for personal experiences and their temporal relations," and semantic memory is "a system for receiving, retaining and transmitting information about meaning of words, concepts and classification of concepts" (Tulving, 1972, pp. 401–402). Within this conceptual framework, tasks such as the WMS Logical Memory subtest involve episodic memory. The Northwestern Word Latency Naming Test (Rutherford, 1973) was selected for the current study as a measure of semantic memory. This task involves the sequential presentation of 63 pictures of common objects, with three temporally separated, reordered repetitions. The subject is required to name each object. Response latency and type of error (e.g., appropriate substitution, verbal paraphasia, and literal paraphasia) are recorded, but this study is concerned only with the total number of correct namings, averaged across the three lists. Previous research has shown the total number of correct namings on this task to have the largest rotated factor loading on a factor identifying semantic memory in AD patients (Wilson, Bacon, et al., 1982), whereas WMS logical memory was unrelated to this factor but had the highest loading on an episodic memory factor.

Free-Recall Task

On each examination, the subjects were also presented with four 12-word lists for free recall. This task was included in order to provide additional measures of primary memory and episodic secondary memory, with somewhat firmer grounding in the experimental psychologic literature than the measures provided by the WMS. The words were read and shown on index cards at a rate of 2 seconds per word with recall immediately after presentation. Seven forms of these list sets were assembled; the lists were balanced within and across forms for free recallability (Christian, Bickley, Tarka, & Clayton, 1978). All subjects were given Form 1 in Year 1, Form 2 in Year 2, and Form 3 in Year 3. Word order within lists and list order within forms were randomly arranged.

Following Tulving and Colotla (1970), free recall was divided into primary memory and secondary memory components on the basis of the number of words between presentation and recall, with six items representing the cutoff point between primary and secondary memory (Watkins, 1974). Thus, a word presented in the ninth position and recalled fifth has seven items intervening between presentation and recall and would be assigned to secondary memory. This procedure for measuring primary and secondary memory has been supported by both experimental (Watkins, 1974) and neuropsychological (Moscovitch, 1982) research.

Previous research employing this free-recall task (Wilson et al., 1983) found primary memory to be impaired in AD patients (relative to matched healthy controls) and indicated that the size of the patients' primary memory deficit increased linearly with the increasing number of items between presentation and recall. Secondary memory was more severely impaired than primary memory in the patient group. These findings provide support for the validity of the primary and secondary memory free-recall measures in differentiating AD patients from healthy older persons. Support for the validity of the distinction between primary and secondary memory was obtained in correlation analyses performed on the control group data ($N = 31$). For controls, the primary and secondary memory measures were not significantly correlated. Furthermore, as predicted by the literature concerning memory in normal aging (see Kaszniak et al., chapter 17 in this volume; Poon, 1985), age was related to secondary memory ($r = .33$) but not to primary memory ($r = .09$). Interestingly, for the AD patient group ($N = 47$), the primary and secondary memory measures were not independent ($r = .45$). This observation suggests that the AD patients' secondary memory deficit is at least partially due to impaired primary memory. Other investigators (Diesfeldt, 1978; Miller, 1971) employing free-recall tasks to investigate primary and secondary memory in AD patients have come to the same conclusion.

Longitudinal Validation

Figure 29-1 shows the performance of the longitudinal sample on the 24-item mental status examination. Multivariate analysis of variance (MANOVA) revealed

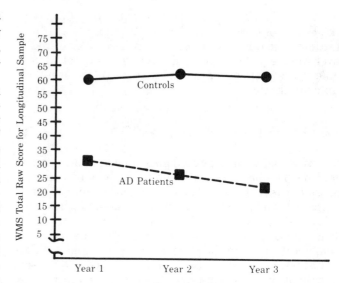

Figure 29-2. Wechsler Memory Scale total raw scores for longitudinal sample.

a significant group effect [$F (1,68) = 107.63$], a significant year effect [$F (2,67) = 15.43$], and a significant group-by-year interaction [$F (2,67) = 19.40$]. On this measure the progressive deterioration that is the hallmark of AD is apparent. Thus, in answer to the first two questions raised in the beginning of this chapter, the mental status measure here employed, which assesses a mixture of episodic and semantic secondary memory (as well as simple language expression and comprehension), validly reflects the expected longitudinal deterioration in AD patients, with no change over time in the performance of normal controls.

Figure 29-2 illustrates the WMS total raw score means for the longitudinal sample. Ten of the AD patients were too demented at either the second or third examination for meaningful collection of all subtest data on the WMS (i.e., they were unable to demonstrate comprehension of or compliance with instructions). MANOVA performed on this smaller sample (21 AD patients and 39 controls) demonstrated a significant group effect [$F (1,58) = 231.71$], a significant year effect [$F (2,57) = 11.62$], and a significant group-by-year [$F (2,57) = 22.93, p < .01$] interaction. As with the mental status measure, the WMS total raw score, reflecting a mixture of primary memory and both episodic and semantic secondary memory (see Wilson, Bacon, et al., 1982), appears to have validity in documenting the expected deterioration over time in AD patients, while showing stability in performance, over the same interval, in normal controls.

Longitudinal data for the Digit Span forward and Logical Memory WMS subtests are shown in Figures 29-3 and 29-4 (23 AD patients and 39 controls). MANOVA of the Digit Span forward data demonstrated a significant group effect [$F (1,60) = 18.15$], and group-by-year interaction [$F (2,59) = 3.11, p = .052$]. MANOVA of the Logical Memory subtest showed a significant group effect [$F (1,60) = 140.73$], a significant year effect [$F (2,59) = 3.47$], and a significant group-by-year interaction [$F (2,59) = 4.31$]. Thus,

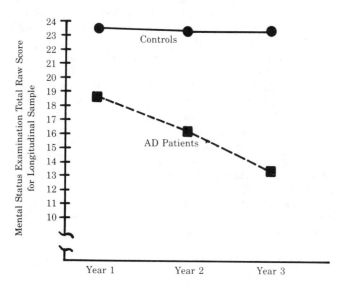

Figure 29-1. Mental status examination total raw scores for longitudinal sample.

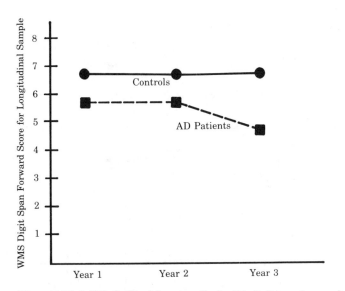

Figure 29-3. Wechsler Memory Scale Digit Span forward scores for longitudinal sample.

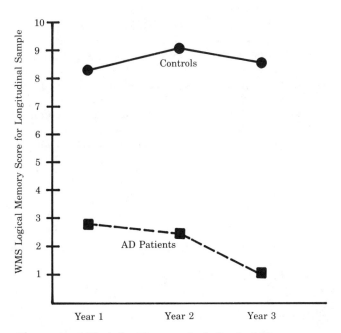

Figure 29-4. Wechsler Memory Scale Logical Memory scores for longitudinal sample.

although WMS measures of both verbal primary memory (Digit Span) and secondary memory (Logical Memory) appear to validly reflect the expected longitudinal deterioration in AD patients and stability in normal control subjects, inspection of Figures 29-3 and 29-4, as well as their respective multivariate F values, suggests that memory impairment in AD patients at the initial examination (and, hence, earlier in the course of their disease) is more severe for verbal secondary memory than for primary memory. Results of the Storandt, Botwinick, and Danziger (chapter 28 in this volume) longitudinal study of WMS performance in AD patients and matched healthy control subjects are

nearly identical to those reported here. Although both memory processes show deterioration over time in AD patients, this deterioration seems somewhat more gradual for primary memory. (Digit Span forward mean scores are identical for Years 1 and 2 [5.78 for both], dropping only by Year 3 [4.74].) Given the magnitude of the AD patients' secondary memory (logical memory) deficits revealed at their initial examinations, basement effects may have been reached by subsequent examinations. As a result, the researchers' ability to measure any further change was limited. Indeed, several patients showed zero recall of material presented in the Logical Memory paragraphs at the second and third examinations. Furthermore, the current analyses are based on a subsample of the AD patients who were available for follow-up examinations; the more severely demented patients were eliminated because they could not comprehend and/or follow task instructions.

Figure 29-5 presents the Northwestern Word Latency Naming Test (total correct namings) score means for the follow-through sample. For this task, six of the AD patient sample were too demented at either the second or third examination to cooperate with the task. MANOVA revealed significant group effect [F (1,62) = 71.95], a significant year effect [F (2,61) = 4.76], and a significant group-by-year interaction [F (2,61) = 11.82]. Thus, much as the currently employed WMS measures of episodic secondary memory do, the Northwestern Naming Test measure of semantic memory validly reflected the expected deterioration, over the 3 years, for AD patients, compared with the stable performance of the normal control subjects. Other confrontation naming tasks, such as the Boston Naming Test (Kaplan, Goodglass, & Weintraub, 1978) and the object and body-part naming subtests of the Boston Diagnostic Aphasia Examination (Goodglass & Kaplan, 1972), also have validity in demonstrating significantly more naming errors in AD patients, as com-

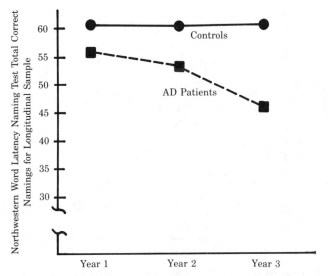

Figure 29-5. Northwestern Word Latency Naming Test mean total correct namings for longitudinal sample.

pared with normal subjects matched by age and education (Bayles & Tomoeda, 1983; Kirshner, Webb, & Kelly, 1984; Martin & Fedio, 1983; Wilson, Kaszniak, Fox, Garron, & Ratusnik, 1981). Longitudinal studies employing these tasks have not yet been published. It has been suggested that AD leads to a disruption in semantic knowledge (Martin & Fedio, 1983), often characterized by difficulty in differentiating between items within the same semantic category. This difficulty probably contributes to the encoding deficit in episodic secondary memory functioning of AD patients (Weingartner et al., 1981).

Of the 31 AD patients in the follow-through sample, 15 were too demented at either the second or third examination for meaningful collection of the verbal free-recall data. A MANOVA comparing performance on the mental status examination for the 16 patients able to complete the verbal learning examinations, as opposed to the 15 who could not, revealed a significant main effect for group [F (1,29) = 6.01], a significant year effect [F (2,28) = 25.52], and a significant group-by-year interaction [F (2,28) = 5.23]. These two subgroups were only slightly different at Year 1, but, not surprisingly, persons lost to follow-up with regard to the verbal learning measure showed a greater rate of deterioration on the mental status examination (see Figure 29-6). Thus, the analyses of the verbal learning data are based on a select group of patients and would be expected to minimize the extent of deterioration in the entire patient group.

Figure 29-7 shows the number of words recalled from primary memory as a function of group membership and year of examination. For primary memory, there was a significant group effect [F (1,53) = 82.4], no significant main effect for year (F = 1.21), and a nearly significant group-by-year interaction [F (2,52) = 3.12, $.05 > p > .10$]. The control subjects showed no decline on this measure, a finding that is consistent with the

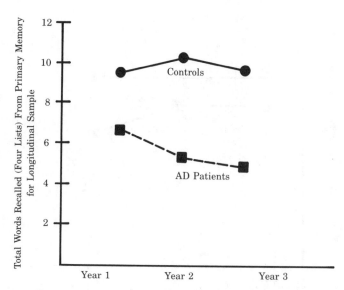

Figure 29-7. Free-recall task primary memory scores for longitudinal sample.

general finding that primary memory functions show little to no adult age change (Craik, 1977; Poon, 1985). The patients, however, did show some decline in primary memory. Figure 29-8 shows results for the secondary memory measure. There were significant effects for group [F (1,53) = 131.4] and for year [F (2,52) = 17.5] but no group-by-year interaction ($F < 1$). The patients who presented with a severe secondary memory deficit at entry into the study declined, but apparently at a rate not appreciably different from the

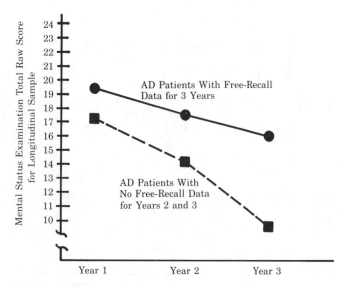

Figure 29-6. Mental status examination total raw scores for AD patients who could be tested on free-recall task for all 3 years versus those who could not (longitudinal sample).

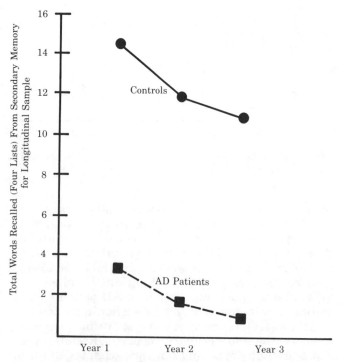

Figure 29-8. Free-recall task secondary memory scores for longitudinal sample.

rate for the control group. This finding must be interpreted with great caution, however, given both the select nature of the AD patients who could actually be tested with the free-recall task at the second and third reexaminations and the obvious basement effects obtained on the secondary memory measure. (By the third examination, AD patients averaged less than one word recalled from all four 12-word lists).

Thus, although the free-recall measures of primary and secondary memory validly reflect the initial deficit in the AD patients as compared with normal controls, the validity of these measures is limited for purposes of longitudinal follow-up (or, by extrapolation, for assessment of more severely demented patients). This limitation appears to be due to the difficulty level of the task. Further limiting the validity of the primary–secondary memory distinction purportedly provided by the measure is the fact that these primary and secondary memory measures are correlated in AD patients (although not in normal controls), as was previously observed by Wilson et al. (1983). The free-recall measures may thus be better suited for the assessment of memory changes in normally aging individuals than in AD patients. Indeed, the free-recall decline in secondary memory observed for the healthy control sample suggests that the measure is quite sensitive to normal aging changes in secondary memory over a relatively brief interval (3 years).

Conclusions

At the beginning of this chapter three questions were asked. First, can the mental deterioration that is the main feature of AD be validly documented psychometrically? The answer is yes. All of the currently employed instruments showed deterioration of the AD patient group over the three annual reexaminations.

The second question concerned whether these patients, whose memory was severely impaired at study entry point, continued to deteriorate at a rate greater than the rate associated with normal aging. The answer here appears to be a qualified yes. The mental status examination, the WMS total raw score, the WMS Digit Span and Logical Memory subtests, and the Northwestern Word Latency Naming Test all showed the expected longitudinal deterioration of the AD patient group and the stability of the healthy control group. The free-recall measure of secondary memory lacked validity in demonstrating the expected differential group change over time. Perhaps this should not be surprising. A confident diagnosis of AD requires a clinically apparent memory impairment that probably reflects a profound deficit in secondary memory. To rely on such a profound deficit as a baseline may be misguided, because there is little memory left to measure. The mental status examination instrument used in this study was useful not only because it is appropriate for even severely demented patients but also because it measures, albeit crudely, behaviors that are

typically normal or nearly so when patients initially come to professional attention and that become impaired only as the disorder progresses. The WMS measures and the naming task also appear to involve cognitive processes (largely primary memory and semantic memory) less severely impaired at the first examination and hence not showing basement effects as quickly at follow-up. In the assessment of these patients it is important to distinguish between measures useful for diagnosis and those useful for following the course of dementia. Diagnosis depends, in large part, on a profile of cognitive strengths and weaknesses, and it usually takes place when the general level of impairment is mild. Once the diagnosis is made, however, the focus of longitudinal measurement should be on relatively preserved abilities (e.g., certain aspects of language).

The third question was whether memory declined in a uniform or a differentiated manner. The answer to this question is qualified, because it can be addressed only in a select group of patients: those who did not die, refuse to continue, develop medical complications, or simply deteriorate too rapidly. In this select group of patients some evidence was found of differential mnemonic decline: Primary memory, as assessed by both the WMS Digit Span forward task and the free-recall measure of primary memory, apparently declined in patients, with no such trend evident in the controls; the WMS measure of secondary memory (Logical Memory), which very likely involves contributions of both primary and secondary memory, showed longitudinal deterioration in AD patients and stability in healthy controls. However, the free-recall measure of secondary memory (probably a "purer" measure of secondary memory, at least in normally aging individuals) showed roughly parallel decline in the two groups.

In many of these patients, secondary memory was so impaired initially that there was no room for further deterioration to be measured ("floor" or "basement" effect). Because AD patients, even apparently early in their disease, typically present with secondary memory deficits out of proportion to other cognitive and mnemonic deficits, it can be inferred that secondary memory rapidly declines but usually before the patient comes to medical attention. This inference, along with the current findings, suggests a rapid, early decline in secondary memory that continues in the middle stages of AD but possibly at a decreasing rate.

Primary memory may show a different but complementary course: relatively normal functioning early, followed by deterioration in the middle to late stages. Storandt, Botwinick, and Danziger (chapter 28 in this volume) arrive at a similar conclusion, on the basis of their longitudinal study of AD and matched control performance on WMS Digit Span forward and Logical Memory subtests. However, the highly select nature of the current AD patients who could be followed and tested on the primary and secondary measures, the fact that primary and semantic memory deficits probably contribute to the severity of patients' secondary memory deficit (Weingartner et al., 1981; Wilson et al., 1983), and the possibility that the basement effects obtained in this study by free-recall secondary memory measures may reflect inappropriate difficulty level (e.g., measures of recognition memory might be easier for AD patients), all limit what conclusions may be drawn regarding differential decline in memory process.

Thus, although deterioration in AD can be documented psychometrically, a number of problems are encountered by researchers in moving from a mental status screening examination to measures of specific areas of cognition. The term *dementia* implies a global decline in mental abilities and in this sense appears to be an appropriate term. Performance, even on disparate mental ability tests, is often highly intercorrelated in dementia. Within the current AD patient sample, all the cognitive measures were significantly intercorrelated at the time of initial examination (which was not true for the normal control sample). Furthermore, the magnitude of the average intercorrelation among these measures increased at each subsequent annual examination. It becomes increasingly difficult to maintain that measures of specific cognitive functions are not largely measuring some general cognitive factor in these patients. This point is relevant to the choice of measures used to follow such patients, the expectations with regard to differential cognitive decline, and the search for neuroanatomical correlates of specific cognitive deficits.

References

American Psychiatric Association. (1980). *Diagnostic and statistical manual of mental disorders* (3rd ed). Washington, DC: Author.

Bayles, K. A., & Tomoeda, C. K. (1983). Confrontation naming impairment in dementia. *Brain and Language, 19,* 98–114.

Brinkman, S. D., Largen, J. W., Gerganoff, S., & Pomara, N. (1983). Russell's Revised Wechsler Memory Scale in the evaluation of dementia. *Journal of Clinical Psychology, 39,* 989–993.

Butters, N., Albert, M. S., Sax, D. S., Miliotis, P., Nagode, J., & Sterste, A. (1983). The effect of verbal mediators on the pictorial memory of brain-damaged patients. *Neuropsychologia, 21,* 307–323.

Christian, J., Bickley, W., Tarka, M., & Clayton, K. (1978). Measures of free recall of 900 English nouns: Correlations with imagery, concreteness, meaningfulness, and frequency. *Memory and Cognition, 6,* 379–390.

Coblentz, J. M., Mattis, S., Zingesser, L. H., Kasoff, S. S., Wisniewski, H. M., & Katzman, R. (1973). Presenile dementia. *Archives of Neurology, 29*(5), 299–308.

Corkin, S. (1982). Some relationships between global amnesias and the memory impairments in Alzheimer's disease. In S. Corkin, K. L. Davis, J. H. Growdon, E. Usdin, & R. J. Wurtman (Eds.), *Alzheimer's disease: A report of progress in research* (pp. 149–164). New York: Raven Press.

Craik, F. I. M. (1977). Age differences in human memory. In J. E. Birren & K. W. Schaie (Eds.), *Handbook of the psychology of aging* (pp. 384–420). New York: Van Nostrand Reinhold.

Danziger, W. L., & Storandt, M. (1982, November). *Psychometric performance of healthy and demented older adults:*

A one-year follow-up. Paper presented at the annual meeting of the Gerontological Society of America, Boston, MA.

Diesfeldt, H. F. A. (1978). The distinction between long-term and short-term memory in senile dementia: An analysis of free recall and delayed recognition. *Neuropsychologia, 16,* 115–119.

Erickson, R. C. (1978). Problems in the clinical assessment of memory. *Experimental Aging Research, 4,* 255–272.

Erickson, R. C., & Scott, M. L. (1977). Clinical memory testing: A review. *Psychological Bulletin, 84,* 1130–1149.

Go, R. C. P., Todorov, A. B., Elston, R. C., & Constantinidis, J. (1978). The malignancy of the dementias. *Annals of Neurology, 3,* 559–561.

Goodglass, H., & Kaplan, E. (1972). *The assessment of aphasia and related disorders.* Philadelphia: Lea and Febiger.

Hachinski, V. C., Lassen, N. A., & Marshall, J. (1974). Multi-infarct dementia: A cause of mental deterioration in the elderly. *Lancet, 2,* 207–210.

Kaplan, E., Goodglass, H., & Weintraub, S. (1978). *The Boston Naming Test.* Boston: Kaplan & Goodglass.

Kaszniak, A. W. (1986). Neuropsychology of dementia. In I. Grant & K. Adams (Eds.), *Neuropsychological assessment of neuropsychiatric disorders (pp. 172–220).* New York: Oxford University Press.

Kaszniak, A. W., Fox, J. H., Gandell, D. L., Garron, D. C., Huckman, M. S., & Ramsey, R. G. (1978). Predictors of mortality in presenile and senile dementia. *Annals of Neurology, 3,* 246–252.

Kaszniak, A. W., Garron, D. C., & Fox, J. H. (1979). Differential effects of age and cerebral atrophy upon span of immediate recall and paired-associate learning in older patients suspected of dementia. *Cortex, 15,* 285–295.

Kaszniak, A. W., Garron, D. C., Fox, J. H., Bergen, D., & Huckman, M. (1979). Cerebral atrophy, EEG slowing, age, education, and cognitive functioning in suspected dementia. *Neurology, 29,* 1273–1279.

Katzman, R. (1976). The prevalence and malignancy of Alzheimer's disease. *Archives of Neurology, 33,* 217–218.

Kirshner, H. S., Webb, W. G., & Kelly, M. P. (1984). The naming disorder of dementia. *Neuropsychologia, 22,* 23–30.

Logue, P., & Wyrick, L. (1979). Initial validation of Russell's revised Wechsler Memory Scale: A comparison of normal aging versus dementia. *Journal of Consulting and Clinical Psychology, 47,* 176–178.

Martin, A., & Fedio, P. (1983). Word production and comprehension in Alzheimer's disease: The breakdown of semantic knowledge. *Brain and Language, 19,* 124–141.

McKhann, G., Drachman, D., Folstein, M., Katzman, R., Price, D., & Stadlan, E. M. (1984). Clinical diagnosis of Alzheimer's disease: Report of the NINCDS-ADRDA work group under the auspices of the Department of Health and Human Services Task Force on Alzheimer's disease. *Neurology, 34,* 939–944.

Miller, E. (1971). On the nature of the memory disorder in presenile dementia. *Neuropsychologia, 9,* 75–78.

Miller, E. (1977). *Abnormal ageing.* New York: Wiley.

Moscovitch, M. (1982). Multiple dissociations of function in amnesia. In L. S. Cermak (Ed.), *Human memory and amnesia* (pp. 337–370). Hillsdale, NJ: Erlbaum.

Poon, L. W. (1985). Differences in human memory with aging: Nature, causes, and clinical implications. In J. E. Birren & K. W. Schaie (Eds.), *Handbook of the psychology of aging* (2nd ed., pp. 427–462). New York: Van Nostrand Reinhold.

Prigatano, G. P. (1978). Wechsler Memory Scale: A selective review of the literature. *Journal of Clinical Psychology, 34,* 816–832.

Ribot, T. (1882). *Diseases of memory*. New York: Appleton.

Rutherford, D. (1973). *The Northwestern University Word Latency Test*. Evanston, IL: Northwestern University Press.

Sjogren, T., Sjogren, H., & Lindgren, A. G. H. (1952). Morbus Alzheimer and morbus pick: Genetic, clinical and patho-anatomical study. *Acta Psychiatrica et Neurologica Scandinavica, 82*(Suppl.), 1–152.

Tulving, E. (1972). Episodic and semantic memory. In E. Tulving & W. Donaldson (Eds.), *Organization of memory* (pp. 381–403). New York: Academic Press.

Tulving, E., & Colotla, V. A. (1970). Free recall of trilingual lists. *Cognitive Psychology, 1,* 86–98.

Watkins, M. J. (1974). Concept and measurement of primary memory. *Psychological Bulletin, 81,* 695–711.

Waugh, N. C., & Norman, D. A. (1965). Primary memory. *Psychological Review, 72,* 89–104.

Wechsler, D. A. (1945). A standardized memory scale for clinical use. *Journal of Psychology, 19,* 87–95.

Weingartner, H., Kaye, W., Smallberg, S. A., Ebert, M. H., Gillin, J. C., & Sitaram, N. (1981). Memory failures in progressive idiopathic dementia. *Journal of Abnormal Psychology, 90,* 187–196.

Wilson, R. S., Bacon, L. D., Fox, J. H., & Kaszniak, A. W. (1983). Primary memory and secondary memory in dementia of the Alzheimer type. *Journal of Clinical Neuropsychology, 5,* 337–344.

Wilson, R. S., Bacon, L. D., Kaszniak, A. W., & Fox, J. H. (1982). The episodic–semantic memory distinction and paired associate learning. *Journal of Consulting and Clinical Psychology, 50,* 154–155.

Wilson, R. S., Kaszniak, A. W., Bacon, L. D., Fox, J. H., & Kelly, M. P. (1982). Facial recognition memory in dementia. *Cortex, 18,* 329–336.

Wilson, R. S., Kaszniak, A. W., & Fox, J. H. (1981). Remote memory in senile dementia. *Cortex, 17,* 41–48.

Wilson, R. S., Kaszniak, A. W., Fox, J. H., Garron, D. C., & Ratusnik, D. L. (1981, February). *Language deterioration in dementia*. Paper presented at the annual meeting of the International Neuropsychological Society, Atlanta, GA.

Wilma G. Rosen, Richard C. Mohs, and Kenneth L. Davis

CHAPTER

30

Longitudinal Changes: Cognitive, Behavioral, and Affective Patterns in Alzheimer's Disease

This chapter discusses the issues of validity and reliability that pertain to developing a scale to assess cognitive, behavioral, and affective functioning in Alzheimer's disease (AD). Scales designed specifically to assess AD patients are reviewed. Particular attention is focused on the Alzheimer's Disease Assessment Scale (ADAS) and its ability to detect increasing deficits in the cognitive and behavioral functioning of AD patients as the disorder progresses.

Numerous scales and tests are available for the assessment of cognitive, behavioral, and affective functioning in the elderly (Salzman, Kochansky, & Shader, 1972), but very few instruments are specific to Alzheimer's disease (AD). This lack of specificity has its historical roots in the simple dichotomy of functional versus organic disorders and, within the category of organic disorders, in the dichotomy between the acute, reversible states and the chronic, irreversible conditions often labeled organic brain syndrome, organic mental syndrome, or chronic brain syndrome. Consequently, scales were constructed in order to make these broad distinctions more useful. However, the finding of a specific biochemical deficit in the cholinergic system of the brains of persons with AD (Davies & Maloney, 1976), coupled with the recognition that AD is one of the major medical disorders of the elderly (Katzman, 1976), has led to a recognition of the importance of distinguishing among dementias that have different etiologies (Brust, 1983; Cummings, 1983), different clinical features (Rosen, Terry, Fuld, Katzman, & Peck, 1980), and presumed different methods of treatment.

The efforts expended by numerous investigators to develop a rational treatment strategy for AD based on the cholinergic deficit hypothesis (Greenwald & Davis, 1983) have created the need for a specific means of evaluating treatment efficacy in AD patients. Adequate assessments can also assist in the management of these patients, because they provide information about the patients' remaining abilities and weaknesses. In this chapter we discuss the requirements for a rating scale specific to AD as they relate to issues of validity and reliability, examine some of the scales specific to dementia, and present a longitudinal assessment of AD using the Alzheimer's Disease Assessment Scale (ADAS) (Rosen, Mohs, & Davis, 1984).

Requirements for a Rating Scale Specific to AD

Report of a scale specific to AD should provide evidence of validity and reliability consistent with the changes in cognition, behavior, affect, neuropathology, and biochemistry characteristic of AD. Validity of a test or scale is actually an inference or judgment based on the outcomes of particular statistical procedures applied to the test scores (American Psychological Association, 1974). Three kinds of validity—content, criterion-related, and construct—are interrelated. Demonstration of content validity requires that the behaviors appearing during testing are representative of the behaviors in the performance domain, which must be carefully defined. For example, the performance domain for a rating scale applicable to cognitive dysfunc-

This report was supported by grant AG02219 from the National Institute on Aging, the Medical Research Service of the Veterans Administration, and the Department of Neurosurgery, Mount Sinai School of Medicine.

tion in AD could be defined in terms of the language, memory, and praxis dysfunctions characteristic of AD. Specifically, language disturbances include word-finding difficulty in spontaneous speech, anomia, poverty of speech, and comprehension of oral speech (Appel, Kertesz, & Fishman, 1982; Barker & Lawson, 1968; Coblentz et al., 1973; de Ajuriaguerra & Tissot, 1975; Rochford, 1971; Rosen, 1983; Sim & Sussman, 1962). Memory dysfunctions include disorientation, impairment in recent memory, and deficits in learning both visual and verbal material (Fuld, 1978; Hagberg, 1978; Kaszniak, Garron, Fox, Bergen, & Huckman, 1979; Rosen, 1983). Praxis dysfunctions include constructional, ideomotor, and ideational apraxia (de Ajuriaguerra & Tissot, 1968; Hagberg & Ingvar, 1976; Rosen, 1983, 1984; Rosen & Mohs, 1982).

Criterion-related validity is an inference from one test score to the most likely performance or standing on another variable, called the criterion. This type of validity is composed of concurrent and predictive validity. Concurrent validity refers to the extent to which performance on one test can be used to estimate the current performance or standing on another variable. In AD, concurrent validity for a scale could be established in relation to other test scores, biochemical measures, or anatomical measurements. It could also reflect the diagnostic utility of the scale in discriminating dementing from nondementing conditions or in differentiating among types of dementias (Anastasi, 1982). Predictive validity refers to the degree to which the current performance is predictive of a standing on the criterion measure at some future point. For example, the current measure might predict mortality status in a certain number of years.

Construct validity is the extent to which a test reflects a specified psychological construct or trait. Construct validity of a rating scale specific to AD can refer to the internal consistency or homogeneity of test items, correlations among subscales, and the expected increasing dysfunction as the disorder progresses (longitudinal changes). Construct validity is also necessary for a scale that purports to determine stages of AD.

Reliability refers to the extent to which systematic sources of variance account for test results (APA, 1974). Some sources of variance and related types of reliability include time of measurement and test–retest reliability, content sampling and alternate-form or split-half reliability, and the examiners' and interscorers' or interraters' reliability. Because of the heterogeneity among AD patients, examiners must be familiar with the wide range of dysfunction; patient fluctuations (random or otherwise) may lead to spurious conclusions in experimental studies that use scores on the scale to evaluate treatment effects.

Scales for Assessing AD

The few recently developed scales designed specifically to assess AD include the Dementia Rating Scale (Cole & Dastoor, 1980), another Dementia Rating Scale

(Mattis, 1976), the Global Deterioration Scale (Reisberg, Ferris, de Leon, & Crook, 1982), the Brief Cognitive Rating Scale (Reisberg, Schneck, Ferris, Schwartz, & de Leon, 1983), and the Alzheimer's Disease Assessment Scale (Rosen et al., 1984). In this section, we describe each scale briefly and then examine it with regard to the different types of validity and reliability.

Dementia Rating Scale of Cole and Dastoor

The Dementia Rating Scale (Cole & Dastoor, 1980) is unique in that it is based on Piagetian developmental psychology. Previous longitudinal and cross-sectional studies showed that in AD patients, regression in instrumental behaviors and through levels of operations was essentially the opposite of the development of these functions (Constantinidis, Richard, & de Ajuriaguerra, 1978; de Ajuriaguerra & Tissot, 1968). In this scale, test items illustrative of various types of functions such as gnosis, ideomotor praxis, and graphic praxis are organized in order of increasing difficulty. This is the only published report on this scale, and the authors acknowledge that the reliability and validity of the scale have not been examined. Nevertheless, the scale appears to have acceptable content validity. On the basis of the performances of 30 patients, ranging from nondemented to severely demented, the scale was shortened from 40 to 50 functions to 27, and from 10 to 15 items within each function to 5 to 10. The final hierarchy of items in each function was determined from the performance of these patients.

Dementia Rating Scale of Mattis

A different Dementia Rating Scale (DRS) was developed by Mattis (1976) because standard psychological tests, such as the Wechsler Adult Intelligence Scale (WAIS; Wechsler, 1955) and the Wechsler Memory Scale (Wechsler, 1945), cannot provide quantifiable measures of mental ability in severely demented patients. This DRS has five subscales: attention, perseveration and initiation, construction, conceptualization, and memory. Items in each subscale are arranged in an assumed, but untested, hierarchic organization of difficulty. Content validity appears reasonable in that the items examine the major characteristic cognitive dysfunctions of AD. To determine whether subscales are representative of particular psychological constructs, however, a factor analysis of the items would be more appropriate than the a priori classification of the items.

Concurrent validity was demonstrated on 20 patients who had organic mental syndromes (AD was not the specified diagnosis), resulting in a correlation of $r = .75$ between the WAIS Full-Scale IQ and total DRS score. Concurrent validity was also demonstrated on a subset of 15 patients with severely impaired verbal memory, with $r = .86$ (Coblentz et al., 1973). There was a significant positive correlation between DRS scores and cerebral blood flow in the frontal lobes of patients with presenile dementia. No information is available on the internal consistency of the scale, such as correlations among subscales. Test–retest reliability, which was determined from the administration of the scale twice (with a one-week interval between test sessions) to 30 clinically diagnosed AD patients, ranged from $r = .61$ to $r = .94$ for the subscales and $r = .97$ for the total score.

Another study using split-half forms of Mattis's scale, which required the elimination of some items, yielded a split-half reliability correlation coefficient of .90 (Gardner, Oliver-Munoz, Fisher, & Empting, 1981). However, AD was not carefully diagnosed in the 25 elderly nursing-home residents who were tested.

Global Deterioration Scale

The Global Deterioration Scale (GDS) was developed to assess primary degenerative dementia (PDD), which the authors believe to be equivalent to AD, and to delineate seven stages of PDD. Each stage is characterized by both clinical manifestations and several psychometric measures. In the first publication of the GDS (Reisberg et al., 1982) it is unclear whether the ratings were determined from the clinical characteristics or from test scores, although a later publication (Reisberg, Shulman, Ferris, de Leon, & Geibel, 1983) seemed to indicate that ratings were based on intensive clinical interviews.

Each stage corresponds to a particular clinical phase, both of which are hypothetical constructs. The first stage (GDS 1) is normal; the second stage (GDS 2) is thought to reflect "benign senescent forgetfulness." GDS ratings of 3 and 4 correspond to early and late confusional phases, respectively. GDS ratings of 5, 6, and 7 correspond to early, middle, and late dementia phases, respectively. No evidence is provided for the distinction between the constructs of confusional and dementing phases. Perhaps GDS Stages 3 and 4 should be considered as early dementia, since the descriptions of these stages or phases indicate that clear-cut deficits are apparent, and patients classified in these phases showed increased cognitive decline when reexamined 18 to 37 months postbaseline (Reisberg, Shulman, et al., 1983). There are no reports of interrater and test–retest reliability of the GDS.

Examination of concurrent validity reveals that GDS ratings correlated significantly with performance on a number of psychometric tests (Reisberg et al., 1982), computed tomography (CT) scan rankings of ventricular dilatation and CT scan measures of sulcal enlargement (de Leon, Ferris, Blau, et al., 1979; de Leon, Ferris, George, et al., 1980), and metabolic rates using positron emission tomography (Ferris et al., 1983). A longitudinal study of 41 community-dwelling PDD patients with GDS ratings of 2 to 5, who were assessed on additional measures of orientation, cognition, and daily functioning at baseline and then reassessed 16 to 37 months later, revealed no decline in patients with a GDS 2 rating but significant decline in patients with GDS ratings of 3 to 5 on one or more of these measures (Reisberg, Shulman, et al., 1983). This finding suggests that the GDS has some predictive validity. There is no mention of change in GDS levels from baseline to retest, so that construct validity of the GDS with respect to longitudinal changes is unverified.

Brief Cognitive Rating Scale

The Brief Cognitive Rating Scale (BCRS) was originally presented as a "rapid, structured clinical assessment of cognitive decline, regardless of etiology" (Reisberg, Schneck, et al., 1983, p. 47). However, a later publication claimed that the BCRS was specific to PDD (Reisberg, London, et al., 1983). The original BCRS had five axes (concentration, recent memory, past memory, orientation, and functioning and self-care), with a single rating given on each axis. These five axes cover only a small aspect of cognition; three of the axes pertain to memory. Consequently, definition of the performance domain is severely limited. The BCRS was expanded to include the three additional axes of speech and language, motor functioning, and mood and behavior (Reisberg, London, et al., 1983). The language axis is limited in scope, poorly defined, and based on an unproved hierarchy. Minimal dysfunction (rating = 2) is defined in terms of recall (memory) for names. Ratings 3 to 7 simply pertain to amount of speech. Comprehension of spoken speech is not evaluated. The motor-functioning axis is narrowly defined, being limited primarily to gait disturbance. Other functions, such as complex constructional tasks, automobile driving, and signing one's name, also are considered in determining the rating, but an impairment in these abilities does not necessarily reflect motor dysfunction. The mood and behavior axis rates anxiety, blunting and flattened affect, agitation, and psychotic disturbances. These four different concepts have been hierarchically arranged on the rating scale to represent one construct without evidence for validation.

Concurrent validity for the BCRS was documented in the finding that the first five axes of the BCRS correlated significantly with the Guild Memory Test total scores (Reisberg, Schneck, et al., 1983). Very high correlations among axes, ranging from .88 to .93, were found in 18 patients, but two thirds of these patients had a GDS rating of 1 or 2, both of which are nondementing conditions. For the BCRS to be appropriate to AD, it must be validated on such patients. In a later study in which 26 of 30 PDD patients had GDS ratings of 4 to 6, there were significant correlations among the three new axes and the original five axes, ranging from .56 to .84 (Reisberg, London, et al., 1983).

In the same study, the authors stated that the levels of impairment tended to be relatively uniform across the BCRS axes and that this uniformity may distinguish PDD patients from patients with other disorders, such as depression. In order to substantiate this claim, however, they must analyze the correlations among axes at each GDS level, because evidence from neuropsychological studies of AD patients suggests that cognitive functions do not decline at the same rate (Hagberg & Ingvar, 1976; Rosen & Mohs, 1982). As with the GDS, there is no report of interrater and test–retest reliability of the BCRS.

The Alzheimer's Disease Assessment Scale

The Alzheimer's Disease Assessment Scale (ADAS) was developed to assess the major cognitive, behavioral, and affective dysfunctions characteristic of AD (Rosen et al., 1984). None of the scales already mentioned, except the BCRS, rates these three primary areas. Selection of the original 40 items was based on clinical observations of memory dysfunction, disorientation, behavioral disturbances, and affective dysfunction and on experimental investigations of various components of language, memory, and praxis. The original 40-item ADAS was administered to 27 persons with a clinical diagnosis of AD and to 28 normal elderly persons. The final form of the scale comprised 21 items with significant interrater reliability (ranging from .659 to 1) and significant test–retest reliability (one-month interval between test sessions), ranging from .514 to 1 for AD patients. The 21 items constituting the final form of the scale are shown in Table 30-1. The cognitive subscale, composed of items evaluating memory, language, and praxis functions, had an interrater reliability of .989 and a test–retest reliability of .915 (excluding the two memory tests). The noncognitive behaviors subscale, whose items evaluate components of depression, concentration, cooperation, psychotic disturbances, and motoric activity, had an

interrater reliability of .947 and a test–retest reliability of .588. For the total score, interrater reliability was .986 and test–retest reliability was .838.

Concurrent validity of the ADAS was demonstrated by the significant correlations among the subscales and total scores with scores on the Memory Information Test, MIT (Blessed, Tomlinson, & Roth, 1968), for which r's ranged from $-.419$ to $-.775$, and the Dementia Rating Scale (Blessed et al., 1968), with r's ranging from .455 to .642. Scores on both of these instruments correlated significantly with measures of the histopathological changes characteristic of AD (Blessed et al., 1968). Similarly, the concentration of acetylcholine in the cerebrospinal fluid of AD patients, a possible antemortem marker of AD, was correlated with the total ADAS score ($r = -.63$), suggesting increasing cholinergic cell loss with increasing symptom severity (Mohs, Rosen, Greenwald, & Davis, 1983). Another indication of the criterion-related validity of the ADAS was that all cognitive subscale items, memory tasks, and the noncognitive subscale score demonstrated significant differences between 15 AD patients and 15 normal elderly persons who had been matched for age, sex, and education. Construct validity was evidenced by the significant correlations between the two subscales ($r = .588$) and between the total score and cognitive subscale ($r = .824$) and noncognitive subscale ($r = .666$).

A Longitudinal Analysis Using the ADAS

The construct validity of the ADAS would also be indicated by its sensitivity to increased dysfunction over time in the same patients as the disorder progresses (i.e., longitudinal evaluation). A longitudinal study also permits examination of decline in different cognitive functions by analyzing individual items on the scale that test the components of these functions. For example, comparisons between decline in expressive language (the ability to convey ideas and to find the appropriate words) and in receptive language (auditory comprehension in conversation and the ability to follow commands) can be evaluated. We present the changes that occur at intervals of 12 and 18 months following a baseline examination in cognitive and noncognitive behaviors in patients with a clinical diagnosis of AD. Particular attention is directed toward the pattern of change detected in different memory tasks and components of language.

Table 30-1. Alzheimer's Disease Assessment Scale

Cognitive subscale

1. Spoken language ability
2. Comprehension of spoken language
3. Recall of test instructions
4. Word-finding difficulty
5. Commands
6. Naming objects and fingers
7. Constructions—copying forms
8. Ideational praxis
9. Orientation to time, place, and person
10. Word recall memory test
11. Word recognition memory test

Noncognitive subscale

12. Tearful appearance
13. Appearance/report of depressed mood
14. Concentration/distractibility
15. Lack of cooperation in testing
16. Delusions
17. Hallucinations
18. Pacing
19. Increased motor activity
20. Tremors
21. Appetite change

Procedure

Participants in this longitudinal study were 12 persons (9 men, 3 women) with a clinical diagnosis of AD and 10 (7 men, 3 women) community-dwelling, normal elderly volunteers. AD patients ranged between 54 and 74 years old ($\overline{X}=63.5$, $SD = 7.0$) and had 12 to 20 years of education ($\overline{X}=14.8$, $SD = 3.2$). Eight patients had presenile onset (under age 65) of the disorder. Diagnosis of AD was made after complete neurological and psychological examinations and appropriate laboratory tests to rule out other causes of dementia, confounding neurologic disorder, and history or presence of significant psychiatric disorder. All had a history of cognitive impairment with insidious onset and progressive decline of, at minimum, one year's duration at the time of initial assessment. Patients' dementia ranged from mild to moderately severe, as the number of correct responses on the 20-point MIT mental status examination ranged from 0 to 17 ($\overline{X}$=7.4, SD = 5.7).

The normal elderly participants ranged between 55 and 73 years old ($\overline{X}$=63.9, SD = 6.6) and had 12 to 18 years of education ($\overline{X}$=15.4, SD = 2.4). None had a history of neurological or psychiatric disorder. All were nondemented and free of significant medical disease. Their scores on the MIT ranged from 16 to 20 ($\overline{X}$=18.7, SD = .4). The AD patients and the normal elderly volunteers did not differ in age [$t(20) < 1$] and years of education [$t(20) < 1$]. MIT scores were significantly lower for the AD group [$t(20) = 5.88, p < .01$].

The ADAS was administered and scored by two raters according to the guidelines of the manual for the ADAS (Rosen et al., 1984). Items 1 through 8 and 12 through 20 were scored on a 5-point rating scale (0 = not present to 5 = severe). The score for each of these items was equal to the mean of the two raters' scores. Maximum error score for orientation questions (Item 9) was 8, for word recall test (Item 10) was 10, and for word recognition test (Item 11) was 12. All 22 subjects were evaluated at a baseline examination and then approximately 12 months later (11- to 13-month range). Eight AD subjects were also evaluated 18 months postbaseline.

Results

The three basic scores derived from ADAS ratings are the cognitive subscale score, which is the sum of ratings obtained on Items 1 through 9; the noncognitive subscale score, which is the sum of ratings on Items 12 through 21; and the total score, which equals the sum of all 21 items. The mean subscales and total scores for the AD patients and the normal elderly volunteers at baseline are shown in Table 30-2. AD patients were significantly more dysfunctional on all three measures at baseline.

Comparison of baseline and 12-month retest revealed that subscale and total scores increased significantly for the AD patients only. On each of these measures, 10 of 12 AD patients showed a decline in functioning. The two patients who showed a slight improvement in the cognitive subscale score exhibited a decline in the noncognitive subscale score, and two patients with minimal improvement in noncognitive behaviors showed increased cognitive dysfunction.

Performances at baseline and 12 months by AD patients on the four items evaluating memory function were compared with the Wilcoxon Matched Pairs Signed-Ranks Test (Table 30-3). On Item 3, which

Table 30-2. Mean ADAS Scores at Baseline and 12-Month Retest for AD Patients and Normal Elderly Volunteers

Group	Baseline	12-month retest
AD patients (n = 12)		
Cognitive subscale	15.7****	20.4***
Noncognitive subscale	2.5****	4.0*
Total score	30.0****	38.3**
Normal elderly volunteers (n = 10)		
Cognitive subscale	1.0	0.8
Noncognitive subscale	1.3	1.2
Total score	5.7	4.3

*$p < .025$, **$p < .01$, ***$p < .005$, one-tailed Wilcoxon Matched Pairs Signed-Ranks Test, compared with their baseline scores. ****$p < .001$, two-tailed Mann-Whitney U-Test, compared with normal elderly volunteers at baseline.

Table 30-3. Mean Scores for Memory and Language Functions for AD Patients (n = 12) at Baseline and 12-Month Retest

Item	Baseline	12-month	p^1
Memory Functions			
3. Recall test instructions	1.2	2.3	.007
9. Orientation	3.7	5.0	.005
10. Word recall	6.8	7.4	ns
11. Word recognition	5.2	6.6	ns
Language functions			
1. Spoken language	1.4	1.8	.07
2. Comprehension	1.0	1.2	ns
4. Word-finding difficulty	1.8	2.2	.033
5. Commands	1.5	1.9	ns
6. Naming	1.9	1.9	ns
Total language	7.6	9.0	.036

[1]One-tailed Wilcoxon Matched Pairs Signed-Ranks Test.

rated recall of the word recognition test instructions during performance of the test, seven patients declined significantly in their ability to retain the task requirements, and five subjects showed no change. Nine patients showed significantly increased disorientation. Only six subjects showed increased memory dysfunction on the word-recall task. Although eight patients were more impaired on the word-recognition task at retest, these changes were not significant for the group as a whole, because scores for four patients improved. One third of the group showed increased impairment on all four memory measures; another one-quarter showed a decrease on three measures. Only one patient showed no decline on any memory measure.

Analysis of specific components of language (Table 30-3) revealed that the primary decline at 12 months in language abilities rated on the ADAS occurred in word-finding ability (Item 4) for seven patients, with a concomitant, but nonsignificant, decrease for eight patients in expressive language ability (Item 1). The total score for all five language items combined showed significantly increased impairment for nine patients.

As shown in Figure 30-1, the eight AD patients examined at 18 months showed increasing severity of dysfunction from baseline testing. All showed a significant increase (i.e., greater dysfunction) in cognitive subscale score on the one-tailed Wilcoxon Matched Pairs Signed-Ranks Test from baseline ($\overline{X}$=21.4) to 18-month retest ($\overline{X}$=28.6, p = .005), and in total score (baseline, $\overline{X}$=37.3; 18 months, $\overline{X}$=52.6, p = .0005). Seven patients showed significantly increased noncognitive behavioral dysfunction (baseline, $\overline{X}$=2.4; 18 months, $\overline{X}$=6.4, p = .01).

Analysis of individual memory tasks (Table 30-4) revealed a significant increase in dysfunction in three of four measures. Seven patients were more disoriented and recalled fewer words at the 18-month retest, and six patients declined on word recognition. Spoken language and word-finding and naming abilities declined significantly for seven, six, and five patients, respectively, while auditory comprehension and following commands remained stable for the majority of patients.

Discussion

The current longitudinal study of the ADAS revealed that the entire scale, as well as the individual cognitive and noncognitive subscales, detected increasing deficits in AD patients during the course of the disorder at 12- and 18-month postbaseline evaluations. Analysis of specific memory tasks and language functions indicated that not all patients declined on every measure after 12 or even 18 months. This finding raises a number of issues about evaluation of the construct validity of a scale measuring longitudinal changes in AD.

Table 30-4. Mean Scores for Memory and Language Functions for AD Patients (n = 8) at Baseline and 18-Month Retest

Item	Baseline	18-month	p^1
Memory functions			
3. Recall test instructions	1.8	2.5	*ns*
9. Orientation	4.9	6.4	.005
10. Word recall	7.4	8.7	.025
11. Word recognition	6.1	8.8	.05
Language functions			
1. Spoken language	2.0	3.1	.01
2. Comprehension	1.4	2.1	*ns*
4. Word-finding difficulty	2.4	3.2	.025
5. Commands	2.1	3.3	*ns*
6. Naming	2.7	3.2	.025
Total language	10.6	14.9	.005

[1]One-tailed Wilcoxon Matched Pairs Signed-Ranks Test.

The tasks or specific items may be insensitive to change. If we assume that decline must occur in the function presumably measured by the task or evaluated by an item, then, in fact, the task or item is insensitive. However, other longitudinal studies (Wilson & Kaszniak, chapter 29, this volume; Storandt, Botwinick, & Danziger, chapter 28, this volume) have shown that decline may not be apparent on certain tasks because AD patients perform at such a low level at initial evaluation that further decline cannot be measured; moreover, some functions remain intact in mild dementia, and there may be a distinct subgroup of AD patients with a different pattern of decline. Furthermore, in a cross-sectional study, the level of difficulty of the stimulus materials in oral sentence reading and in repetition tasks was a significant factor in the detection of increased impairments (Rosen, 1983). Comparison of persons who had mild AD with persons who had moderate to severe AD revealed that both groups read and repeated more sentences composed of high-frequency words equally well, but the more impaired group performed worse on both tasks with sentences containing primarily low-frequency words.

Ideally, attempts to determine the course of decline in AD should (a) compare different cognitive functions, because they have differential rates of decline, and then (b) clearly identify and examine the components of a function, because decline in these components does not appear to be uniform. In this study, orientation to time and place declined at 12 months, whereas increased impairment in the ability to learn a new list of words was not found until 18 months. Expressive (spoken) language declined over an 18-month period, while receptive language remained relatively constant.

Patients may decline at different rates. This variability may be related to the degree of premorbid competence in particular abilities, the rate of change in pathological conditions in the brain, the presence of other

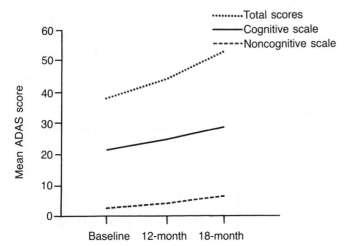

Figure 30-1. Mean ADAS scores at baseline, 12- and 18-month retest for AD patients (n = 8).

illnesses and social and environmental stressors, and the stage or stages of the dementing process in which the patient is examined. Thus, the slope of the decline in dementia may not be constant throughout the disorder, and one must consider the length of the time interval selected for evaluation of deterioration.

These ideas about differential rates of decline underscore the difficulty of evaluating the construct validity of a scale used for determining longitudinal changes in AD. The total ADAS score indicates impairment in many areas combined. The scale appears significantly sensitive to overall decline. Comparison of the two subscales reveals differential decline or stability in cognitive and behavioral disturbances. Finally, within each of the subscales, the deterioration of components of cognitive and noncognitive behaviors can be followed longitudinally. This study gives a preliminary picture of differential decline in these components. The adequacy of the items for evaluating these components—that is, the construct validity—requires further study.

References

American Psychological Association. (1974). *Standards for educational and psychological tests*. Washington, DC: Author.

Anastasi, A. (1982). *Psychological testing* (5th ed.). New York: Macmillan.

Appel, J., Kertesz, A., & Fishman, M. A. (1982). A study of language functioning in Alzheimer's patients. *Brain and Language, 17,* 73–91.

Barker, M. G., & Lawson, J. S. (1968). Nominal aphasia in dementia. *British Journal of Psychiatry, 114,* 1351–1356.

Blessed, G., Tomlinson, B. E., & Roth, M. (1968). The association between quantitative measures and senile change in the cerebral grey matter of elderly patients. *British Journal of Psychiatry, 114,* 797–811.

Brust, J. C. M. (1983). Dementia and cerebrovascular disease. In R. Mayeux & W. G. Rosen (Eds.), *Advances in neurology: Vol. 38. The dementias* (pp. 131–147). New York: Raven Press.

Coblentz, J. M., Mattis, S., Zingesser, L. H., Kasoff, S. S., Wisniewski, H. M., & Katzman, R. (1973). Presenile dementia: Clinical aspects and evaluation of cerebrospinal fluid dynamics. *Archives of Neurology, 29*(5), 299–308.

Cole, M. G., & Dastoor, D. (1980). Development of a dementia rating scale: Preliminary communication. *Journal of Clinical Experimental Gerontology, 2,* 46–63.

Constantinidis, J., Richard, J., & de Ajuriaguerra, J. (1978). Dementias with senile plaques and neurofibrillary changes. In A. D. Isaacs & F. Post (Eds.), *Studies in geriatric psychiatry* (pp. 119–152). New York: Wiley.

Cummings, J. L. (1983). Treatable dementias. In R. Mayeux & W. G. Rosen (Eds.), *Advances in neurology: Vol. 38. The dementias* (pp. 165–183). New York: Raven Press.

Davies, P., & Maloney, A. J. F. (1976). Selective loss of central cholinergic neurons in Alzheimer's disease. *Lancet, 2,* 1403.

de Ajuriaguerra, J., & Tissot, R. (1968). Some aspects of psychoneurologic disintegration in senile dementia. In C. H. Mueller & L. Ciompi (Eds.), *Senile dementia* (pp. 69–79). Switzerland: Huber.

de Ajuriaguerra, J., & Tissot, R. (1975). Some aspects of language in various forms of senile dementia (comparisons with language in childhood). In E. H. Lenneberg & E. Lenneberg (Eds.), *Foundations of language development (Vol. 1)*. New York: Academic Press.

de Leon, M. J., Ferris, S. H., Blau, I., George, A. E., Reisberg, B., Kricheff, I. I., & Gershon, S. (1979). Correlations between CT changes and behavioral deficits in senile dementia. *Lancet, 2,* 859–860.

de Leon, M. J., Ferris, S. H., George, A. E., Reisberg, B., Kricheff, I. I., & Gershon, S. (1980). Computed tomography evaluations of brain–behavior relationships in senile dementia of the Alzheimer's type. *Neurobiology of Aging, 1,* 69–79.

Ferris, S. H., de Leon, M. J., Wolf, A. P., George, A. E., Reisberg, B., Christman, D. R., Yonekura, Y., & Fowler, J. S. (1983). Positron emission tomography in dementia. In R. Mayeux & W. G. Rosen (Eds.), *Advances in neurology: Vol. 38. The dementias* (pp. 123–129). New York: Raven Press.

Fuld, P. A. (1978). Psychological testing in the differential diagnosis of the dementias. In R. Katzman, R. D. Terry, & K. L. Bick (Eds.), *Alzheimer's disease: Senile dementia and related disorders* (pp. 185–193). New York: Raven Press.

Gardner, R., Jr., Oliver-Munoz, S., Fisher, L., & Empting, L. (1981). Mattis Dementia Rating Scale: Internal reliability study using a diffusely impaired population. *Journal of Clinical Neuropsychology, 3,* 271–275.

Greenwald, B. S., & Davis, K. L. (1983). Experimental pharmacology of Alzheimer's disease. In R. Mayeux & W. G. Rosen (Eds.), *Advances in neurology: Vol. 38. The dementias* (pp. 87–102). New York: Raven Press.

Hagberg, B. (1978). Defects of immediate memory related to the cerebral blood flow distribution. *Brain and Language, 5,* 366–377.

Hagberg, B., & Ingvar, D. H. (1976). Cognitive reduction in presenile dementia related to regional abnormalities of the cerebral blood flow. *British Journal of Psychiatry, 128,* 209–222.

Kaszniak, A. W., Garron, D. C., Fox, J. H., Bergen, D., & Huckman, M. (1979). Cerebral atrophy, EEG slowing, age, education, and cognitive functioning in suspected dementia. *Neurology, 29,* 1273–1279.

Katzman, R. (1976). The prevalence and malignancy of Alzheimer's disease. *Archives of Neurology, 33,* 217–218.

Mattis, S. (1976). Mental status examination for organic mental syndrome in the elderly patient. In L. Bellak & T. Karasu (Eds.), *Geriatric psychiatry: A handbook for psychiatrists and primary care physicians*. New York: Grune & Stratton.

Mohs, R. C., Rosen, W. G., Greenwald, B. S., & Davis, K. L. (1983). Neuropathologically validated scales for Alzheimer's disease. In T. Crook, S. Ferris, & R. Bartus (Eds.), *Assessment in geriatric psychopharmacology* (pp. 37–45). New Canaan, CT: Mark Powley Associates.

Reisberg, B., Ferris, S. H., de Leon, M. J., & Crook, T. (1982). The Global Deterioration Scale for assessment of primary degenerative dementia. *American Journal of Psychiatry, 139*(9), 1136–1139.

Reisberg, B., London, E., Ferris, S. H., Borenstein, J., Scheier, L., & de Leon, M. J., (1983). The Brief Cognitive Rating Scale: Language, motoric, and mood concomitants in primary degenerative dementia. *Psychopharmacology Bulletin, 19,* 702–708.

Reisberg, B., Schneck, M. K., Ferris, S. H., Schwartz, G. E., & de Leon, M. J. (1983). The Brief Cognitive Rating Scale (BCRS): Findings in primary degenerative dementia (PDD). *Psychopharmacology Bulletin, 19,* 47–50.

Reisberg, B., Shulman, E., Ferris, S. H., de Leon, M. J., & Geibel, V. (1983). Clinical assessment of age-associated cognitive decline and primary degenerative dementia:

Prognostic concomitants. *Psychopharmacology Bulletin, 19,* 734–739.

Rochford, G. (1971). A study of naming errors in dysphasic and in demented patients. *Neuropsychologia, 91,* 437–443.

Rosen, W. G. (1983). Neuropsychological investigation of memory, visuoconstructional, visuoperceptual, and language abilities in senile dementia of the Alzheimer type. In R. Mayeux & W. G. Rosen (Eds.), *Advances in Neurology: Vol. 38. The dementias* (pp. 65–73). New York: Raven Press.

Rosen, W. G. (1984, February). Neuropsychological patterns with focus on constructional apraxia. In S. Brinkman & J. Largen (Chair), *Longitudinal studies of dementia of the Alzheimer's type: Neuropsychological and neurophysiological patterns.* Symposium conducted at the meeting of the International Neuropsychological Society, Houston, TX.

Rosen, W. G., & Mohs, R. C. (1982). Evolution of cognitive decline in dementia. In S. Corkin, K. L. Davis, J. H. Growdon, E. Usdin, & R. J. Wurtman (Eds.), *Alzheimer's disease: A report of progress in research* (pp. 183–188). New York: Raven Press.

Rosen, W. G., Mohs, R. C., & Davis, K. L. (1984). A new rating scale for Alzheimer's disease. *American Journal of Psychiatry, 14*(11), 1356–1364.

Rosen, W. G., Terry, R. D., Fuld, P. A., Katzman, R., & Peck, A. (1980). Pathologic verification of ischemic score in differentiation of dementias. *Annals of Neurology, 7,* 486–488.

Salzman, C., Kochansky, G. E., & Shader, R. I. (1972). Rating scales for geriatric psychopharmacology: A review. *Psychopharmacology Bulletin, 8,* 3–50.

Sim, M., & Sussman, I. (1962). Alzheimer's disease: Its natural history and differential diagnosis. *Journal of Nervous and Mental Disease, 135,* 489–499.

Wechsler, D. A. (1945). A standardized memory scale for clinical use. *Journal of Psychology, 19,* 87–95.

Wechsler, D. A. (1955). *Manual for the Wechsler Adult Intelligence Scale.* New York: Psychological Corporation.

Paula Altman Fuld

CHAPTER
31
Pathological and Chemical Validation of Behavioral Features of Alzheimer's Disease

This chapter describes studies identifying and validating behavioral features of AD. A specific WAIS profile identifies a proportion of testable patients highly accurately, and the absence of word intrusions in a mildly to moderately demented patient suggests the presence of a syndrome other than AD. These behavioral features are both correlated with the cholinergic deficiency in AD and have been found in patients with histopathological evidence of AD from biopsy or autopsy. Additional work is needed to identify other features that would be useful in characterizing patients who are not sufficiently testable on the WAIS.

Distinguishing among the dementias of late life is often difficult. Part of this difficulty results from the past unavailability of studies delineating useful clinical features (Eisdorfer & Cohen, 1978), but part is inherent in the nature of the dementias themselves.

Clinicopathological studies by Jellinger (1976) and Tomlinson (1977) have shown that 50% to 60% of dementia cases are accounted for by changes in the brain associated with Alzheimer's disease (AD), senile or presenile, and 12% to 22% are accounted for entirely by cerebrovascular disease. An additional 12% to 22% are accounted for by both kinds of pathology together. The histopathological diagnosis of AD or of multi-infarct dementia (MID) depends on the quantity of such changes found in the brain at autopsy. The diagnosis of AD is made in the widespread presence of large numbers of senile plaques and neurofibrillary tangles in the cells of the cerebral cortex as well as of the hippocampus (Blessed, Tomlinson, & Roth, 1968). The diagnosis of MID is made when more than 50 to 100 ml of brain tissue have been destroyed by stroke (Tomlinson, 1977).

The extent to which smaller quantities of the patho-logical changes of AD or MID may produce dementia in or alter the clinical presentation of patients with both types of changes is unknown. Roth (1978) suggested that the occurrence of a single infarct may bring out AD earlier than dementia would otherwise have occurred.

Despite these quantitative limits for making the diagnosis of AD or MID, these brain pathologies have a continuous and often overlapping distribution. Over 70% of dementia patients are found to have plaques and tangles sufficient to cause dementia, and over two thirds of nondemented, unselected patients over the age of 60 in Tomlinson, Blessed, and Roth's (1968) autopsy study had some infarcts. Thus, the coincident occurrence of some changes associated with AD and some degree of cerebrovascular disease must be common. Undoubtedly, the continuous and overlapping distribution of these pathologies results in a wide range of clinical symptoms and courses in living patients. Consequently, it is not surprising that the clinical differentiation of the dementias has, in the past, been reported to show error rates as high as 50% when followed up by autopsy (Jellinger, 1976; Nott & Fleminger, 1975; Ron, Toone, Garralda, & Lishman, 1979; Shapiro, Post, Lofving, & Inglis, 1956). It seems likely that diagnostic accuracy has improved somewhat in centers that now have computed tomography

The author thanks David Masur for editorial assistance. Writing of this chapter was supported in part by NINCDS grants NS19234 and NS18248 and NIA grants AG03949 and AG02478.

(CT) scanners, but there is evidence that even the fourth generation of CT scanners may not identify the majority of infarcts that occur in dementia patients (Kuhl, 1983). It therefore remains important to identify clinical features that may help differentiate the dementias.

Studies of Performance on the Wechsler Adult Intelligence Scale

Because dementia always involves a loss of intellectual ability, studies involving the Wechsler Adult Intelligence Scale and its predecessor have been in the literature since 1945 (Botwinick & Birren, 1951; Crookes, 1974; Hopkins & Roth, 1953; Miller, 1977; Perez, Stump, Gay, & Hart, 1976; Rabin, 1945; Ron et al., 1979; Roth & Hopkins, 1953; Sim, Turner, & Smith, 1966; Storrie & Doerr, 1980). None of these resulted in the delineation of any features specific enough to be of significant help in the diagnosis of individual patients, but Rabin (1945) and Hopkins and Roth (1953) showed that MID patients are likely, on the average, to be less impaired than AD patients and more impaired than nonpsychotic patients. Also, the Verbal–Performance score discrepancy tends to increase from nonpsychotic to MID and AD patients. Hopkins and Roth pointed out that the scores of most AD patients overlapped with scores from the other two groups, although some AD patients had scores on the Vocabulary subtest that were lower than those of any other patients.

Sim et al. (1966) compared two patients with AD (diagnosed by biopsy) with two patients with Korsakoff's syndrome (associated with cerebral aneurysm excision). Their results differed from those of Hopkins and Roth; the patient with AD scored near zero on the Performance subtest but had relatively normal Vocabulary, Comprehension, and Similarities scores. The patients with Korsakoff's syndrome showed dull-average to average performance on all subtests except for the Digit Symbol (rapid coding) test, on which they scored much lower. Loranger et al. (1972) similarly reported, for a group of patients with Parkinson's disease, no subtest means below the average range for their age. There was an extraordinarily wide range of scores on each subtest, however, which could be associated with the later development of AD in 33% of such patients (Boller, Mizutani, Toessmann, & Purluigi, 1980).

These studies seem to indicate that while patients with AD may score very low on some tests, patients with other common dementias seem, on the average, relatively unimpaired. Clinical experience suggests that patients with AD may initially retain their ability to perform tasks involving no learning, novelty, or complexity, but that after the disease advances they lose this ability. This change over time probably accounts for the difference in Vocabulary subtest scores reported by Hopkins and Roth (1953) and Sim et al. (1966). It also indicates that group averages may be unhelpful to the clinician or researcher dealing with an individual patient.

In 1977, Miller reported WAIS scores from a group of patients with presenile dementia and argued that be-

cause of the unusual spread in this group's scores on any given test, a specific AD profile could not exist. Because presenile dementia progresses faster and more severely than AD in the elderly, it is not surprising that greater than normal variability occurred. But these results do not necessarily mean the typical patient with AD does not maintain an identifiable pattern for at least part of the course of the disease.

Because of the frequency of extremely low test scores of patients with AD and the very wide range of performance on each test, group averages are likely to be misleading. The strengths and weaknesses indicated by the mean scores of a group may not be reflected in many individual patients' data or may not be reproducible from study to study because of the great influence of extreme scores on group averages. But if data from carefully selected patients are examined individually, recognizable patterns can be found for each patient and may even be common.

The WAIS Profile Study

The WAIS profile study (Fuld, 1984) grew out of experience evaluating dementia patients with a neuropsychological test battery that included seven WAIS subtests: Information, Vocabulary, Similarities, Digit Span, Digit Symbol, Block Design, and Object Assembly (Wechsler, 1955). (The subtests eliminated were believed to be overly sensitive to cultural differences or to involve visual stimuli too small to be seen easily by many patients.) For many patients, the Information and Vocabulary scores were preserved relative to the Similarities and Digit Span scores; two of the three Performance test scores were much lower, but the Object Assembly score was relatively preserved, although usually not very high (see chapter 28 in this volume).

Because of the high frequency of AD (50% of patients), as well as its nonfocal, nonacute nature, it seemed likely that this pattern, which occurred in large numbers of demented patients, was associated with AD. The second most frequent dementia, MID, is multifocal and therefore unlikely to produce any frequently repeated pattern. The pattern also seemed to make sense in view of the fact that patients with AD have the greatest difficulty with the new and unfamiliar (Fuld, 1983a) and the finding that impaired cholinergic functioning produces difficulty with stimulus discrimination and response differentiation (Gonzalez & Altschuler, 1979).

The first step in this study was to look for the pattern in WAIS subtest scores obtained by Drachman and Leavitt (1972) for 22 untreated young adults and 19 young adults treated with scopolamine, an anticholinergic drug. The following pattern in age-corrected scores was discovered:

If A = (Information + Vocabulary) ÷ 2,
  B = (Similarities + Digit Span) ÷ 2,
  C = (Digit Symbol + Block Design) ÷ 2, and
  D = Object Assembly, then $A > B > C \leq D$ and
  $A > D$.

(The size of the differences between the part-scores was not deemed important.) Of the 19 anticholinergically treated subjects, 10 showed this pattern, while only 4 of the 22 untreated subjects did. The difference was significant ($p = .0014$), which indicates that the profile is likely to be associated with deficient functioning of the cholinergic system.

The next step was to determine if this profile is also characteristic of patients with AD. The scores of 31 Caucasian dementia patients aged 49 to 81 were examined. Of 17 patients with a clinical neurological diagnosis of probable AD, 10 had the profile, while only one of the 14 patients with other dementias had it ($p = .0027$). Of the 12 patients who met research criteria for AD, 8 had the profile, in contrast to only one of the 14 with other dementias ($p = .0028$). These results have been replicated (Brinkman & Braun, 1984).

In a group of seven dementia patients whose diagnoses were histopathologically confirmed (by biopsy or autopsy), both of two patients with AD displayed the profile, but only one other patient did. This patient had widespread cortical micro-infarcts without any gross focal lesions. He displayed the profile the first time tested, but became aphasic and too emotionally labile to be given all the tests 2 years later. Three patients who met research diagnostic criteria for AD (Eisdorfer & Cohen, 1980) did not display the profile the first time tested but did so 1 or 2 years later.

The profile may be characteristic of a particular part of the course of AD, a hypothesis that can be studied when data from a sufficient number of patients are obtained. As a clinical test for AD with only fully testable patients, the profile was 90% specific and 67% sensitive. Unfortunately, 50% of the patients with AD are not fully testable on the WAIS, in our experience, and even testable patients with AD may not display the profile because of coincidental handicaps due to strokes, educational limitations, or foreign language background. Patterns of strengths and weaknesses on other tests are likely to be found for patients with AD who are not fully testable on the WAIS, and these patterns should make possible the behavioral identification of a larger proportion of patients. Only a small proportion (33%) of all patients with AD can be identified in this way using the WAIS, so that additional behavioral signs of AD must be found.

The Intrusion Studies

Studies by Bowen et al. (1976), Davies and Maloney (1976), and Perry et al. (1978) demonstrated that the cholinergic neurotransmitter system was impaired in AD, and Drachman (1978) suggested that behavioral abnormalities associated with anticholinergic medication might also be characteristic of dementia. Fuld examined the psychological test data from Drachman and Leavitt's (1972) study of the effects of scopolamine on healthy college-aged subjects. Many of the subjects had been unable to say words rapidly in specific categories when asked to do so. Their responses included words not related to the specific category named by the examiner, and those responses were categorized as intrusions. The intrusion errors of the subjects in Drachman and Leavitt's (1972) study resembled the intrusion errors of the dementia patients tested by Fuld in her clinical practice (a detailed report may be found in Fuld, Katzman, Davies, & Terry, 1982).

The purpose of this study was to evaluate the relationship between premorbid clinical test results and postmortem autopsy findings for 29 nursing home patients. The clinical testing of the patients had included the Blessed Mental Status Test (Fuld, 1983b) and the Fuld Object-Memory Evaluation (Fuld, 1981), which includes a task requiring the subject to say words from familiar categories rapidly. The responses of the patients were examined to identify intrusion errors of the kind made by Drachman and Leavitt's (1972) anticholinergically medicated college students.

For this study, an intrusion was operationally defined as the inappropriate recurrence of a response (or type of response) from a preceding test item, test, or procedure. Immediate repetitions (perseverations) were not counted, nor were guesses on the memory test; both of these phenomena were very rare in testable patients. Three raters identified the intrusions consensually, and a fourth rater working independently agreed with 97% of these determinations. The consensual procedure was necessary because each patient made no more than one or two intrusions during the half-hour screening, and only an exceptionally vigilant examiner, or one working under a challenge (as was the fourth rater), could sustain attention when searching through the test records.

Autopsy material from these patients was examined both neurochemically and histopathologically (see Fuld et al., 1982). Neurochemical data was available for 26 of the patients. Eight of the 26 subjects with neurochemical data made intrusions and 18 did not, showing a significant association between low cholinergic activity and intrusions (Mann-Whitney U-test, $p < .05$). Of the demented subjects, 8 of 10 who had choline acetyltransferase (ChAT) levels of 225 or less made intrusions; the 3 demented subjects who had higher ChAT levels did not make intrusions ($p = .03$). Among the 26 subjects with histopathological data, there was a highly significant association between intrusions and the finding of 10 or more senile plaques per low-power microscopic field ($p = .001$). Of the 11 subjects with 10 or more plaques, 8 made intrusions; of the 15 subjects with fewer plaques, only 1 made intrusions. The association was significant also when only demented subjects were considered.

When intrusions were sought in the neuropsychological test data of patients with clinical research neurological diagnoses of AD, 19 of the 21 with AD made intrusions (90% sensitivity), but only 6 of the 17 with other diagnoses did so (65% specificity; $p = .0005$). Patients with AD did not make intrusions merely because of severe aphasia, serious frontal lobe dysfunction, or Korsakoff-like memory impairment. Older patients did not make intrusions more frequently than younger patients. Patients with serious dementia tended to respond too inadequately to make intrusions (such patients tended to give no response, to be unintelligible, or to perseverate).

In this retrospective analysis, there were so few instances of intrusions per patient that the data could not be used as ordinal data. Subsequent work has therefore involved a procedure that produces intrusions in sufficient numbers to correlate the number of different intrusions with the degree of dementia or with chemical or pathological data. This procedure, the Buschke-Fuld Test (Buschke & Fuld, 1974), is based on selective reminding and evaluates storage and retrieval in learning and memory. In a study of eight patients given oral physostigmine and lecithin, the number of different intrusions into recall of a list of 12 unrelated words was sensitive to the drug manipulation, suggesting that this test may be a way to measure the cholinergic functioning of the brain (Thal, Fuld, Masur, Sharpless, & Davies, 1983).

Studies of Mental Status and Memory

The mental status test scores of patients who were tested in life and autopsied at death have been found to be highly correlated with both senile plaques in the cerebral cortex and measures of cholinergic functioning upon autopsy. In 1968, Blessed, Tomlinson, and Roth found a significant correlation between the scores on the Blessed Mental Status Test and the number of plaques in the cerebral cortex. In 1983, Katzman et al. successfully replicated Blessed et al.'s (1968) study, using a version of the Blessed Mental Status Test adapted for use in the United States (Fuld, 1983b). Perry et al. (1978) found that scores on the Blessed Mental Status Test showed a stronger correlation with CAT levels than with the number of senile plaques. In an ongoing study, my colleagues and I analyzed the scores of a large number of autopsied patients who had been tested during their lives with both the Fuld Object-Memory Evaluation (which is a test of new learning) and the Blessed Mental Status Test. Data from the first recall on the memory test of the Object-Memory Evaluation as well as scores on the Blessed Mental Status test showed consistently high correlations with the number of senile plaques and neurofibrillary tangles, as well as with ChAT levels in several areas of the cerebral cortex.

Scores on rapid word-listing in categories and difficulty in naming common objects accounted for part of the association between the Blessed test and the number of cortical plaques, but scores on recall of newly learned information (Fuld memory test) accounted for most of the variance from patient to patient. This study supports the hypothesis that memory impairment is a central feature of AD, while language impairment may not play as important a part in producing the dramatic changes in mental status that are typically seen.

Implications for Clinical Assessment

This chapter has described studies attempting to identify and validate behavioral features of AD. Pioneered by Blessed et al. (1968), this work has led to the identification of a profile of WAIS subtest scores that appears highly specific for AD and a behavioral feature (word intrusions) that occurs in about 90% of AD patients.

Although each of these behavioral features is helpful in identifying patients with AD, each has limitations: The WAIS profile appears to identify only about 33% of all AD patients because only about 50% of all such patients are testable on the seven necessary subtests; and of these, only 44% appear to show the profile. The intrusion phenomenon is most useful in its absence; if a mildly or moderately demented patient fails to make intrusions, given ample opportunity, a dementia other than AD is likely. Despite these limitations, using the requisite tests and attempting to make these observations does significantly increase the accuracy of the differentiation of the dementias.

References

Blessed, G., Tomlinson, B. E., & Roth, M. (1968). The association between quantitative measures of dementia and of senile change in the cerebral grey matter of elderly subjects. *British Journal of Psychiatry, 114,* 797–811.

Boller, F., Mizutani, T., Toessmann, V., & Purluigi, G. (1980). Parkinson's disease, dementia and Alzheimer disease: Clinicopathological correlations. *Annals of Neurology, 7*(4), 329–335.

Botwinick, J., & Birren, J. (1951). Differential decline in the Wechsler-Bellevue subtests in the senile psychoses. *Journal of Gerontology, 6*(4), 365–368.

Bowen, D. M., Smith, C. B., White, P., & Davison, A. N. (1976). Senile dementia and related abiotrophies: Biochemical studies on histologically evaluated human postmortem specimens. In R. D. Terry & S. Gershon (Eds.), *Neurobiology of Aging* (pp. 361–378). New York: Raven Press.

Brinkman, S. D., & Braun, P. (1984). Classification of dementia patients by a WAIS profile related to central cholinergic deficiencies. *Journal of Clinical Neuropsychology, 6*(4), 393–400.

Buschke, H., & Fuld, P. A. (1974). Evaluating storage, retention, and retrieval in disordered memory and learning. *Neurology, 24*(11), 1019–1025.

Crookes, T. G. (1974). Indices of early dementia on WAIS. *Psychological Reports, 34,* 734.

Davies, P., & Maloney, A. J. F. (1976). Selective loss of central cholinergic neurons in Alzheimer's disease. *Lancet, 2,* 1403.

Drachman, D. A. (1978). Memory, dementia, and the cholinergic system. In R. Katzman, R. D. Terry, and K. L. Bick (Eds.), *Alzheimer's disease: Senile dementia and related disorders* (pp. 141–148). New York: Raven Press.

Drachman, D. A., & Leavitt, J. (1972). Memory impairment in the aged: Storage versus retrieval deficit. *Journal of Experimental Psychology, 93*(2), 302–308.

Eisdorfer, C., & Cohen, D. (1978). In M. Storandt, I. C. Siegler, & M. F. Elias (Eds.), *Clinical psychology of aging* (p. 7). New York: Plenum Press.

Eisdorfer, C., & Cohen, D. (1980). Diagnostic criteria for primary neuronal degeneration of the Alzheimer's type. *The Journal of Family Practice, 11*(4), 553–557.

Fuld, P. A. (1981). *The Fuld Object-Memory Evaluation.* Chicago, IL: Stoelting Instrument Co. (1350 S. Kostner Ave.)

Fuld, P. A. (1983a). Psychometric differentiations of the dementias: An overview. In B. Reisberg (Ed.), *Alzheimer's disease: The standard reference.* New York: Free Press.

Fuld, P. A. (1983b). Word intrusion as a diagnostic sign in Alzheimer's disease. *Geriatric Medicine Today, 2,* 33–41.

Fuld, P. A. (1984). Test profile of cholinergic dysfunction and of Alzheimer-type dementia. *Journal of Clinical Neuropsychology, 6*(4), 380–392.

Fuld, P. A., Katzman, R., Davies, P., & Terry, R. D. (1982). Intrusions as a sign of Alzheimer's dementia: Chemical and pathological verification. *Annals of Neurology, 11*(2), 155–159.

Gonzalez, L. P., & Altschuler, H. L. (1979). Scopolamine effects on suppression of operant responding. *Physiological Psychology, 7,* 156–162.

Hopkins, B. A., & Roth, M. (1953). Psychological test performance in patients over sixty: II. Paraphrenia, arteriosclerotic psychosis and acute confusion. *Journal of Mental Science, 99,* 451–463.

Jellinger, K. (1976). Neuropathological aspects of dementias resulting from abnormal blood and cerebrospinal fluid dynamics. *Acta Neurologica Belgium, 76,* 83–102.

Katzman, R., Brown, T., Fuld, P., Peck, A., Schechter, R., & Schimmel, H. (1983). Validation of a short orientation-memory-concentration test of cognitive impairment. *American Journal of Psychiatry, 140*(6), 734–739.

Kuhl, D. (1983, December). Paper presented at the meeting of the Association for Research in Nervous and Mental Disease, New York.

Loranger, A. W., Goodell, H., McDowell, F. H., Lee, J. E., & Sweet, R. (1972). Intellectual impairment in Parkinson's syndrome. *Brain, 95* (2), 405–412.

Miller, E. (1977). *Abnormal ageing: The psychology of senile and presenile dementia.* New York: Wiley.

Nott, P. N., & Fleminger, J. J. (1975). Presenile dementia: the difficulties of early diagnosis. *Acta Psychiatrica Scandinavica, 51,* 210–217.

Perez, F. I., Stump, D. A., Gay, J. R. A., & Hart, V. (1976). Intellectual performance in multi-infarct dementia and Alzheimer's disease: A replication study. *Le Journal Canadian des Sciences Neurologiques, 3*(3), 181–187.

Perry, E. K., Tomlinson, B. E., Blessed, G., Bergmann, K., Gibson, P. H., & Perry, R. H. (1978). Correlation of cholinergic abnormalities with senile plaques and mental test scores in senile dementia. *British Medical Journal, 2,* 1457–1459.

Rabin, A. (1945). Psychometric trends in senility and psychosis of the senium. *Journal of General Psychology, 32,* 149–162.

Ron, M. A., Toone, B. K., Garralda, M. E., & Lishman, W. A. (1979). Diagnostic accuracy in presenile dementia. *British Journal of Psychiatry, 134,* 161–168.

Roth, M. (1978). Diagnosis of senile and related forms of dementia. In R. Katzman, R. D. Terry, & K. L. Bick (Eds.), *Alzheimer's disease: Senile dementia and related disorders* (pp. 71–85). New York: Raven Press.

Roth, M., & Hopkins, B. A. (1953). Psychological test performance in patients over sixty: I. Senile psychoses and the affective disorders of old age. *Journal of Mental Science, 99,* 439–451.

Shapiro, M. B., Post, F., Lofving, B., & Inglis, J. (1956). Memory function in psychiatric patients over sixty; some methodological and diagnostic implications. *Journal of Mental Science, 102,* 233–246.

Sim, M., Turner, E., & Smith, W. T. (1966). Cerebral biopsy in the investigation of presenile dementia. *British Journal of Psychiatry, 112,* 119–125.

Storrie, M. C., & Doerr, H. O. (1980). Characterization of Alzheimer type dementia utilizing an abbreviated Halstead-Reitan Battery. *Clinical Neuropsychology, 11*(2), 78–82.

Thal, L., Fuld, P. A., Masur, D. M., Sharpless, N. S., & Davies, P. (1983). Oral physostigmine and lecithin improve memory in Alzheimer's disease. *Annals of Neurology, 13*(5), 491–496.

Tomlinson, B. E. (1977). Morphological changes and dementia in old age. In W. L. Smith & M. Kinsbourne (Eds.), *Aging and dementia* (pp. 25–56). New York: Spectrum Publications.

Tomlinson, B. E., Blessed, G., & Roth, M (1968). Observations on the brains of non-demented old people. *Journal of Neurological Sciences, 7,* 331–356.

Wechsler, D. (1955). *Manual for the Wechsler Adult Intelligence Scale.* New York: Psychological Corporation.

Samuel D. Brinkman, John W. Largen, Jr., Laura Cushman, Paul R. Braun, and Robert Block

32

Clinical Validators: Alzheimer's Disease and Multi-Infarct Dementia

This chapter is concerned with the validity of some neuropsychological indicators in the differential diagnosis of Alzheimer's disease (AD) and multi-infarct dementia (MID). Early studies of the Wechsler Adult Intelligence Scale (WAIS) and Wechsler Memory Scale (WMS) failed to take into account global differences between groups. When MID and AD patients were matched for global indices of severity, two trends were noted: First, a WAIS subtest pattern derived from scopolamine-treated normal adults appeared characteristic of many AD cases. Second, the tendency toward intrusion errors (reported by Fuld and colleagues to be correlated with neuropathological and neurochemical parameters) was greater in AD patients than in MID patients. Results suggest the utility of pharmacological (especially cholinergic) models for studying the neuropsychological aspects of dementia.

The term *dementia* refers to a wide range of conditions that have in common a generalized reduction in neuropsychological abilities. The two most common forms of irreversible dementia in the elderly are Alzheimer's disease, AD, and multi-infarct dementia, MID (Tomlinson, Blessed, & Roth, 1970). Although both of these disorders are characterized by widespread neuropsychological deficits, the nature of the neuropsychological disturbance may not be the same in the two conditions. If the neuropsychological characteristics of each disorder can be compared and contrasted, investigators will be in a better position to study and conceptualize neurobiological–behavioral correlates in dementia. The purpose of this chapter is to review recent research concerned with neuropsychological differences between AD and MID.

Alzheimer's Disease

AD is a degenerative disorder of the central nervous system characterized by insidious onset and relatively smooth, that is, continuous, worsening of symptoms. Memory failure is usually the earliest symptom of AD; patients usually develop deficits in language, praxis, gnosis, and attention as well (Liston, 1979). Personality and emotional changes may evolve during the course of the disorder.

Microscopic examination of brain tissue reveals neuritic plaques and neurofibrillary tangles in many areas, especially the hippocampi, temporal lobes, and parietal lobes (Brun & Englund, 1981; Tomlinson et al., 1970). There is evidence of predominant disruption in central cholinergic systems, although other neurotransmitter systems are probably affected but to a lesser extent (Davies & Maloney, 1976; Perry, 1980; Perry, Perry, Blessed, & Tomlinson, 1977).

The patient who is suspected of having AD normally undergoes a wide range of physical, chemical, neurological, and psychiatric diagnostic studies to rule out treatable etiologies and focal lesions. A clinical diagnosis of AD may be accepted by exclusion, but a conclusive diagnosis requires biopsy or autopsy. With a characteristic clinical history, the neuropathological diagnosis is based on a preponderance of neuritic plaques and neurofibrillary tangles in the appropriate anatomical distribution.

Multi-Infarct Dementia

Unlike AD, MID is a manifestation of cerebrovascular disease. Until fairly recently (Neumann & Cohn, 1953; Tomlinson, Blessed, & Roth, 1968, 1970), MID was thought to be the primary cause of dementia in late life. In the "textbook" case, the symptoms of MID are abrupt in onset and follow a stepwise progression. Sudden changes in the symptoms are thought to reflect new infarctions. The clinical diagnosis of MID is similar to that of AD. Extensive diagnostic studies are completed to rule out reversible etiologies. If there is a history of one or more strokes or transient ischemic attacks, a diagnosis of MID is more likely but not definite (Brust, 1983). Hachinski's Ischemic Score may help to differentiate between AD and MID (Hachinski et al., 1975; Rosen, Terry, Fuld, Katzman, & Peck, 1980). Of course, AD and MID may coexist in the same patient.

Perez and colleagues (Perez, Gay, & Taylor, 1975; Perez, Gay, Taylor, & Rivera, 1975; Perez, Rivera, et al., 1975; Perez, Stump, Gay, & Hart, 1976) completed a number of studies to determine whether the performance of patients with MID was different from the performance of patients with AD on the Wechsler Adult Intelligence Scale (WAIS) (Wechsler, 1955) and the Wechsler Memory Scale (WMS) (Wechsler, 1945). Each study involved analyses of variance and discriminant function to determine group differences, followed by classification analyses employing stepwise regression.

Perez and colleagues reported that patients with AD tended to be more impaired than patients with either MID or vertebrobasilar insufficiency (VBI). Overall accuracy of classification of MID and AD patients in the various studies ranged from 74% to 100%. Unfortunately, this series of studies had two flaws: Patient groups were not matched for education, and differences were found in global indices of severity, suggesting that the dementia in AD groups had simply progressed more than in the MID groups or in the VBI groups.

This latter point requires some clarification. Both MID and AD are progressive disorders, and therefore differences between groups may be attributed to differences in time points on the progression when the evaluations were performed. Because AD has a continuously changing clinical appearance, apparent differences between groups at one point may not be found at another time point. Two approaches may be taken to circumvent this problem: (a) Multiple assessments in each group over time may elucidate the potential differences between groups, as suggested by Storandt and colleagues (see chapter 28, this volume), and (b) groups may be equated on the basis of a global index of severity so that potential patterns of neuropsychological impairments may be identified.

The latter approach was employed with 16 AD patients and 20 MID patients. To rule out treatable etiologies, all patients received extensive clinical evaluations, including physical examination, psychiatric history and evaluation, neurological examination, clinical laboratory investigations (urinalysis, complete blood count, SMA-17, thyroid function tests, and B12 and folate tests), electrocardiogram (ECG), electroencephalogram (EEG), and computerized tomography (CT) scan. Exclusion criteria were history of alcoholism, schizophrenia, or major affective disorder; history of other neurological disorder; significant medical illness; or evidence of focal lesion (other than infarction) on CT scan. No patients were taking psychotropic medications or other medications that might have induced or contributed significantly to the dementia. All patients scored below 12 on the Hamilton Depression Scale (Hamilton, 1960) and all patients were categorized as 3 or 4 on the Global Deterioration Scale (Reisberg, 1983).

Additional criteria for the diagnosis of probable AD were history of memory and cognitive impairment of at least 6 months' duration; insidious onset of disorder with smooth progression; no evidence of focal lesion by neurological examination, EEG, or CT scan; and Hachinski Ischemic Score of 4 or below.

Additional criteria for the diagnosis of probable MID were presence of one or more risk factors for cerebrovascular disease (e.g., hypertension, hyperlipidemia, obesity, or diabetes mellitus); symptoms of sudden onset and stepwise progression; Hachinski Ischemic Score of 7 or higher; and radiographic evidence of cerebrovascular disease, either as infarctions in the CT scan or as obstructions of cerebral arteries by routine cerebral arteriography. These MID cases often had histories of stroke, but none had a hemiparesis, hemisensory deficit, hemianopia, or other visual field defect. None of the MID patients had experienced an ischemic event within one week of the neuropsychological assessment.

The groups were equated for WAIS Full-Scale IQ and the WMS MQ (Memory Quotient). The groups did not differ in age or education. As noted in Table 32-1, no significant differences were noted on any WAIS or WMS subtests, and when groups of AD and MID patients were equated for global indices of severity, the mean data for the groups were nearly identical. The diagnostic criteria for these patients were essentially the same as the diagnostic criteria employed by Perez and colleagues. The AD group, however, was less impaired than the AD groups studied by Perez and colleagues. The disparity in results between the current analysis and earlier studies accentuates the importance of considering the progressive characteristics of AD.

The Scopolamine-Related WAIS Profile

Because of the marked reduction in levels of brain choline acetyltransferase (ChAT) in AD, Drachman and colleagues (Drachman, 1977; Drachman & Leavitt, 1974) suggested that researchers might gain an understanding of the neuropsychological aspects of AD through the administration of scopolamine to normal young adults. Scopolamine blocks cholinergic neurotransmission by competitively binding muscarinic receptors (Goodman & Gilman, 1975). Scopolamine produces marked learning impairments in normal young adults (Ghoneim & Mewaldt, 1977; Petersen, 1977). These learning deficits may be reversed by administration of physostigmine (Drachman & Leavitt, 1974), which inhibits the enzymatic degradation of acetylcholine and maintains the acetylcholine in the synaptic area for a greater period of time.

Fuld (1984; see also chapter 31, this volume) reviewed the WAIS protocols of the scopolamine-treated young adults of Drachman and Leavitt (1974) and

Table 32-1. Scores of MID and AD Groups on WAIS and WMS (X ± Se)

Subtests	Group[1] MID (n = 20)	AD (n = 16)	t[*]
WAIS			
Age	60.50 ± 1.2	63.44 ± 1.7	1.43
Education	10.20 ± 0.5	11.81 ± 0.7	1.86
VIQ	89.58 ± 2.2	91.69 ± 2.4	0.64
PIQ	88.53 ± 4.0	84.63 ± 4.5	0.65
FSIQ	88.63 ± 3.0	88.00 ± 3.3	0.14
Information	9.53 ± 0.6	8.50 ± 0.7	1.13
Comprehension	9.05 ± 0.5	8.56 ± 0.8	0.49
Arithmetic	8.11 ± 0.5	8.56 ± 0.6	0.60
Similarities	7.68 ± 0.5	7.94 ± 1.0	0.24
Digit Span	7.89 ± 0.5	8.56 ± 0.8	0.74
Vocabulary	8.21 ± 0.5	9.19 ± 0.6	1.33
Digit Symbol	7.11 ± 0.7	6.94 ± 1.2	0.12
Picture Completion	9.16 ± 1.0	7.88 ± 0.8	1.03
Block Designs	7.21 ± 0.8	6.63 ± 1.0	0.44
Picture Arrangement	8.63 ± 0.8	6.94 ± 1.2	1.18
Object Assembly	7.84 ± 0.9	7.19 ± 0.9	0.51
WMS			
MQ	87.30 ± 2.6	84.94 ± 3.4	0.55
Information	5.15 ± 0.2	4.25 ± 0.4	1.78
Orientation	4.25 ± 0.3	3.75 ± 0.3	1.15
Mental Control	4.50 ± 0.5	4.69 ± 0.6	0.25
Logical Memory	4.88 ± 0.5	3.84 ± 0.6	1.39
Digit Span	8.55 ± 0.4	8.63 ± 0.4	0.13
Visual Reproduction	4.55 ± 0.9	2.75 ± 0.7	1.57
Associate Learning	9.53 ± 0.5	11.03 ± 0.9	1.43
Easy	15.15 ± 0.6	15.86 ± 0.5	0.91
Hard	1.95 ± 0.4	3.50 ± 0.9	1.56

[1]All test scores are presented as mean ± standard error.
[*]All ps were not significant at the .05 level.

noted that more than half of these subjects had a common profile of WAIS subtest scores while under the drug condition. Fuld described the profile by the following formula:

$$A > B > C \leq D, \text{ and } A > D, \text{ where}$$
$$A = 1/2 \text{ (Information + Vocabulary)},$$
$$B = 1/2 \text{ (Similarities + Digit Span)},$$
$$C = 1/2 \text{ (Digit Symbol + Block Designs)}, \text{ and}$$
$$D = \text{Object Assembly}.$$

When Fuld (1984) applied this formula to a small group of demented patients, she reported that 8 of 12 patients with clinical diagnoses of AD, but only 1 of 14 other demented patients, demonstrated this WAIS profile.

Brinkman and Braun (1984) compared the scopolamine-related WAIS profile with Wechsler's deterioration quotient (Lezak, 1983) in 23 patients diagnosed clinically as having AD and 39 patients diagnosed clinically as having MID. The groups were equated for WAIS Full-Scale IQ. The scopolamine-related WAIS profile correctly identified 13 of the 23 AD patients, whereas only 2 of the 39 MID patients demonstrated this WAIS profile. The profile was unrelated to age, sex, or severity of impairments. Considerable overlap was noted with Wechsler's deterioration quotient, but the scopolamine-related WAIS profile was more specific to AD.

The striking feature of this WAIS profile is its specificity. Although the formula does not appear to be especially sensitive to the AD group, correctly identifying just over half the AD cases in these analyses, these studies support Drachman's (1977; Drachman & Leavitt, 1974) earlier contention that a more complete understanding of AD may be reached by the study of pharmacologically induced cholingeric deficits in normal young adults.

Intrusion Errors in AD

Fuld and co-workers (Fuld, Katzman, Davies, & Terry, 1982; see also chapter 31, this volume) also reported that patients with neuropathologically diagnosed AD tended to make intrusion errors on a mental status examination. Intrusion errors, "the inappropriate recurrence of a response (or type of response) from a preceding test item, test, or procedure" (Fuld et al., 1982), have been reported in patients with massive frontal lobe lesions (Luria, 1966) and in patients with Korsakoff's syndrome (Baddeley & Warrington, 1970; Moudell, Butters, & Montgomery, 1978). Drachman and Leavitt (1974) reported that normal young adults tended to make intrusion errors when treated with scopolamine. Brinkman and Gershon (1983) reported that intrusion errors on word-list-learning tasks were among the most likely parameters to be modified by cholinomimetics during drug trials with patients thought to have AD. These studies suggested that intrusion errors may often be seen in AD. In addition, the reports of Drachman and Leavitt (1974) and of Brinkman and Gershon (1983) provide some basis for the hypothesis that the tendency to make intrusion errors may be related to the central cholinergic deficiency of AD.

Systematic evaluations by Fuld et al. (1982) were correlated with biochemical studies at autopsy and supported this hypothesis. Patients who had lower levels of ChAT in cortex tended to make more intrusion errors. Moreover, the tendency toward intrusion errors was associated with larger numbers of neuritic plaques in cerebral cortex. Classification analysis by Fuld et al. (1982) provided significant accuracy of discrimination among patients with AD (n = 19) and patients with various other causes of dementia (n = 17), correctly identifying 90% of patients thought to have AD.

In the analysis of Fuld et al. (1982), intrusions were scored from the Fuld Memory Test (Fuld, 1980), the mental status examination of Blessed and colleagues (Blessed, Tomlinson, & Roth, 1968), and the Information, Similarities, and Vocabulary subtests of the WAIS. Patients were rated as either demonstrating the tendency toward intrusion errors or failing to demonstrate this tendency. To follow up the report of Fuld et al. (1982), we studied 36 patients with apparently irreversible dementia. According to diagnostic criteria listed earlier, 20 patients had probable MID and 16 had probable AD. Groups were equated for age, education, WAIS Full-Scale IQ, and WMS MQ. Buschke's Selective Reminding Procedure (Buschke & Fuld, 1974; Levin & Grossman, 1976) was selected for analysis because it readily provides an index of intrusions. Intrusion errors were scored in two ways: First, total intrusion errors were calculated by counting the number of times that words were reported incorrectly as being from the list. Second, intrusive elements were calculated by determining the number of *different* words that were incorrectly reported as being from the word list that had been presented. Both indices were summed over the 12 trials on the 12-word list.

As reflected in Table 32-2, the MID and AD groups did not differ significantly in terms of total number of items correctly recalled over the 12 trials. Although there was a tendency for the MID group to score higher on the total long-term recall and total consistent long-term recall indices (Buschke & Fuld, 1974), these differences were not statistically significant. Patients with probable AD, however, had significantly more intrusion errors and intrusive elements. Although both patient groups performed in the impaired range on the Buschke procedure, the data in Table 32-2 suggest that the groups may have performed poorly for different reasons. The reasons for the differences in the nature of the poor performance in these two groups cannot be derived from a single procedure such as the Buschke test. This avenue of research, however, is likely to be fruitful.

Summary and Conclusions

There have been relatively few studies of neuropsychological differences between AD and MID. When AD and MID groups were equated for global indices of severity of cognitive dysfunction (WAIS IQ and WMS MQ), the groups appeared remarkably similar in performance on WAIS and WMS subtests. When two indices derived from the study of pharmacologically induced cholinergic deficiencies in normal young adults have been employed, however, some neuropsychological differences between MID and AD have been reported. Both indices have been replicated in separate laboratories.

Just over half of the patients with AD tended to produce a WAIS profile as originally defined by Fuld (1984). This profile was strikingly rare in non-AD cases of dementia. To determine the robustness of this finding, several studies are indicated: First, Fuld's WAIS profile should be evaluated in normal elderly individuals to determine the degree to which the profile may reflect qualitative distinctions between AD and normal age-related cognitive changes. Second, the stability of the profile over time should be evaluated by multiple assessments in patients with AD and MID. Third, the formula may be applied to clinical diagnoses

Table 32-2. Buschke Scores of MID and AD Groups Summed Across 12 Trials

| Test indices | Group[1] | | |
	MID (n = 20)	AD (n = 16)	t^*
Total recall	56.05 ± 5.2	51.31 ± 4.4	0.69
Total long-term recall	30.20 ± 5.8	23.25 ± 5.6	0.87
Total long-term storage	38.70 ± 6.1	34.38 ± 7.2	0.46
Total consistent long-term recall	14.40 ± 4.1	5.44 ± 2.6	1.83
Total intrusion errors	4.10 ± 1.4	10.88 ± 3.0	2.07
Total intrusive elements	1.16 ± 0.3	4.9 ± 1.3	2.77

[1]All test scores are presented as mean ± standard error.
*All ps were not significant (NS) at the .05 level.

of greater concern to determine whether the profile is useful in helping to detect reversible etiologies in patients who present with symptoms similar to those of AD. Fourth, the degree to which cholinomimetics (such as oral physostigmine) may modify this profile in patients with mild AD may clarify the relationship between central cholinergic deficiencies and neuropsychological functioning in AD.

As Fuld observed, the study of intrusion errors is potentially useful and is worthy of further investigation. Intrusion errors may be related to central cholinergic activity (Brinkman & Gershon, 1983; Drachman & Leavitt, 1974) and may be relatively more prominent in AD than in other dementing disorders (Fuld et al., 1982). It would be helpful to determine why this tendency has been observed in AD. A tendency toward intrusion errors may reflect inadequate encoding, poor discriminability of an item during retrieval, disruption in metamemorical processes, loss of trace excitability, or any of a wide range of other deficits. There is now a greater need for research anchored in experimental cognitive psychology such as that of Miller (1971, 1972, 1973, 1975, 1978) or Wilson and colleagues (Wilson, Bacon, Fox, & Kaszniak, 1983; Wilson, Bacon, Kramer, Fox, & Kaszniak, 1983), so that these observations may be translated into more generalized principles of neuropsychological functioning in AD, MID, and other dementing disorders. A series of investigations into the differential diagnosis of AD and MID might lead to the identification of the best tests for making this clinical distinction, but few neuropsychological tests have been evaluated in this context.

Some types of dementia may be associated with particular neuropsychological patterns. Neuropsychological patterns, however, may be seen in areas other than memory assessments. The WAIS, which may require adequate memory functioning for successful performance on some subtests, assesses a wide range of intellectual abilities. Perhaps the broad range of abilities assessed by the WAIS underlies its apparent sensitivity to differences between AD and MID.

The WMS has not provided acceptable discrimination between AD and MID. Although the WMS is a widely used instrument (Lezak, 1983), its theoretical basis and psychometric foundations are inadequate (Prigatano, 1978). The WMS taps some aspects of attention and memory and provides a global index (the MQ) that may be of questionable validity (Prigatano, 1978). Although the WMS may discriminate between early probable AD patients and normal elderly people (Brinkman, Largen, Gerganoff, & Pomara, 1983), as do many other assessment procedures, the optimal use of the WMS may be in equating groups for general severity of impairments. The Global Deterioration Scale (Reisberg, 1983), which is based on a wider range of abilities and a broader elderly normative sample, is probably a better instrument for matching purposes, provided that the observations on which the rating is based are standardized.

The study of intrusion errors in dementia is especially interesting because the results of these investigations have transcended the specific assessment instrument used. Fuld et al. (1982) derived an index of intrusions from a mental status examination, some subtests of the WAIS, and the Fuld Memory Test. Our investigations were based on Buschke's Selective Reminding Procedure (Buschke, 1973). The assessment of tendencies toward intrusion errors, therefore, may be derived from a number of assessment instruments. Because clinical situations often dictate the specific tests to be employed during assessments (based on considerations of sensory or motor loss, the patient's idiosyncratic strengths and weaknesses prior to onset of symptoms, etc.), the validity of Fuld's initial findings provides greater flexibility in assessment.

Our currently inadequate understanding of AD, MID, and other dementias can be attributed not to a paucity of research subjects but to certain characteristics of the dementias that have presented formidable challenges to neuropsychological research.

1. Progressive characteristics. AD and many other dementias are progressive disorders. The time-dependent changes in symptoms of AD are so pronounced that it has been difficult to monitor specific areas of dysfunction over the course of the disease. In addition, the lack of a generally acceptable method for documenting the stage or degree of progression of the disease has made comparisons across studies difficult. Words such as *early* and *mild* are not equivalent; *early* refers to the time since symptoms became noticeable, and *mild* refers to the severity of symptoms. Both expressions lack operational definitions. The progressive nature of many of the dementias, therefore, has limited our neuropsychological understanding of these disorders.

2. Age-related cognitive changes. Maturity and the accumulation of idiosyncratic experiences doubtlessly lead to unique neuropsychological organizations of cognitive abilities in individuals. Superimposed on the increasingly unique cognitive organization with age are marked changes in brain morphology, fine structure, neurotransmission, and neurochemistry. The complex behavior that arises from unique experiences and age-related neurobiological changes occurs in markedly variable psychosocial contexts. Because AD occurs with increased frequency in older age groups, an adequate understanding of the disease requires an understanding of the context in which the disease occurs. The range of variables that must be taken into account in the neuropsychological study of an age-related disorder such as AD is substantial.

3. Nature of the symptoms. The most prominent symptoms of AD during the first several years of the progression are in higher order cognitive processes. Basic sensory, motor, and arousal processes are generally intact. Higher level cognitive processes may be subject to the disruptive influence of a wider range of variables than are more basic processes. A modality-specific deficit in information-processing abilities suggests the involvement of a fairly limited set of neural circuitry, regardless of education, occupational status, premorbid personality, and affective state. In the dementias, information-processing deficits are seldom modality specific and may be influenced by a wide range of biological, psychological, and social factors. At our present level of comprehension of AD, the early symptoms may be caused by a wide range of factors.

4. Heterogeneity of patients. In view of points 2 and 3, it is not surprising to find much intersubject variability in AD patients. Patients may vary in age at onset, family histories of dementia, rate of progression, nature of early symptoms, and coping abilities. The degree to which neurobiological factors determine the unique characteristics of the disease in any individual will not be determined until clinicopathological correlations are completed with a larger number of subjects.

Patients with cognitive deficits due to cerebrovascular disease are markedly heterogeneous with respect to neuropsychological abilities. Some aspects of the arteriographic characteristics may be useful in reducing the heterogeneity, as seen in the preoperative data of Jacobs, Ganji, Shirley, Morrell, and Brinkman (1983). The degree of neuropsychological impairment may fluctuate when there are episodes of temporary ischemia (Brinkman, Braun, Ganji, Morrell, & Jacobs, 1984; Delaney, Wallace, & Egelko, 1980). In studies that compare AD patients with MID patients, therefore, consideration of the intrasubject variability over time in the MID group may be essential.

The cognitive deficits of AD may reflect the simultaneous decline in a number of distinct cognitive areas or a unitary disruption in some aspect of information-processing abilities that manifests itself differently in memory, attention, language, and the like. Unfortunately, the most widely used clinical assessment instruments are not likely to clarify this issue. There is a growing need for the application of research techniques developed in experimental cognitive psychology so that cognitive functioning in AD and other dementias can be clarified. This approach has been very beneficial to the study of memory functioning in the amnesic syndrome. The integration of experimental techniques into the repertoire of clinical researchers should be of similar benefit in the study of dementia.

Relatively little has been published regarding neuropsychological distinctions between AD and MID.

Published studies have involved the use of standardized, widely employed clinical procedures rather than experimental cognitive analyses. Early studies were hampered by poor matching of groups and failure to account for the progressive nature of the disorders. More recent research, however, has developed from the study of the manner in which cholinergic systems may subserve some aspects of cognition, and this area of study appears promising. Continued research is hampered by a number of methodological issues related to characteristics of the disease, factors involved in normal aging, and conceptual approaches to the study of cognitive processes. Although the dementias have in common a generalized reduction in neuropsychological abilities, one form of dementia may be found to be neuropsychologically distinct from another form. As these distinctions become more evident, our ability to identify the most salient neurobiological and psychosocial aspects of AD may be significantly enhanced.

References

Baddeley, A. D., & Warrington, E. K. (1970). Amnesia and the distinction between long- and short-term memory. *Journal of Verbal Learning and Verbal Behavior, 9,* 176–189.

Blessed, G., Tomlinson, B. E., & Roth, M. (1968). The association between quantitative measures of dementia and of senile change in the cerebral grey matter of elderly subjects. *British Journal of Psychiatry, 114,* 797–811.

Brinkman, S. D., & Braun, P. (1984). Classification of dementia patients by a WAIS profile related to central cholinergic deficiencies. *Journal of Clinical Neuropsychology, 6(4),* 393–400.

Brinkman, S. D., Braun, P., Ganji, S., Morrell, R. M., & Jacobs, L. A. (1984). Neuropsychological abilities one week after carotid endarterectomy reflective of intra-operative ischemia. *Stroke, 15,* 497–503.

Brinkman, S. D., & Gershon, S. (1983). Measurement of cholinergic drug effects on memory in Alzheimer's disease. *Neurobiology of Aging, 4,* 139–145.

Brinkman, S. D., Largen, J. W., Jr., Gerganoff, S., & Pomara, N. (1983). Russell's Revised Wechsler Memory Scale in the evaluation of dementia. *Journal of Clinical Psychology, 39,* 989–993.

Brun, A., & Englund, E. (1981). Regional patterns of degeneration in Alzheimer's disease: Neuronal loss and histopathological grading. *Histopathology, 5,* 549–564.

Brust, J. C. M. (1983). Vascular dementia—still overdiagnosed. *Stroke, 14,* 298–300.

Buschke, H. (1973). Selective reminding for analysis of memory and learning. *Journal of Verbal Learning and Verbal Behavior, 12,* 543–550.

Buschke, H., & Fuld, P. A. (1974). Evaluating storage, retention, and retrieval in disordered memory and learning. *Neurology, 24(11),* 1019–1025.

Davies, P., & Maloney, A. J. F. (1976). Selective loss of central cholinergic neurons in Alzheimer's disease. *Lancet, 2,* 1403.

Delaney, R. C., Wallace, J. D., & Egelko, S. (1980). Transient cerebral ischemic attacks and neuropsychological deficits. *Journal of Clinical Neuropsychology, 2,* 107–114.

Drachman, D. A. (1977). Memory and cognitive function in man: Does the cholinergic system have a specific role? *Neurology, 27,* 783–790.

Drachman, D. A., & Leavitt, J. (1974). Human memory and the cholinergic system: A relationship to aging? *Archives of Neurology, 30,* 113–121.

Fuld, P. A. (1980). Guaranteed stimulus-processing in the evaluation of memory and learning. *Cortex, 16,* 255–271.

Fuld, P. A. (1984). Test profile of cholinergic dysfunction and of Alzheimer-type dementia. *Journal of Clinical Neuropsychology, 6(4),* 380–392.

Fuld, P. A., Katzman, R., Davies, P., & Terry, R. D. (1982). Intrusions as a sign of Alzheimer's dementia: Chemical and pathological verification. *Annals of Neurology, 11,* 155–159.

Ghoneim, M. M., & Mewaldt, S. P. (1977). Studies on human memory: The interactions of diazepam, scopolamine, and physostigmine. *Psychopharmacology, 52,* 1–6.

Goodman, L. S., & Gilman, A. (1975). *The pharmacological basis of therapeutics* (5th ed.). New York: Macmillan.

Hachinski, V. C., Iliff, L., Zilhka, E., DuBoulay, G. H., McAllister, V. L., Marshall, J., Ross-Russell, R. W., & Symon, L. (1975). Cerebral blood flow in dementia. *Archives of Neurology, 32,* 632–637.

Hamilton, M. (1960). A rating scale for depression. *Journal of Neurology, Neurosurgery, and Psychiatry, 23,* 56–62.

Jacobs, L. A., Ganji, S., Shirley, J. G., Morrell, R. M., & Brinkman, S. D. (1983). Cognitive improvement after extra-cranial reconstruction for the low flow endangered brain. *Surgery, 93,* 683–687.

Levin, H. S., & Grossman, R. G. (1976). Storage and retrieval. *Journal of Pediatric Psychology, 1,* 38–42.

Lezak, M. D. (1983). *Neuropsychological assessment* (2nd ed.). New York: Oxford University Press.

Liston, E. H. (1979). The clinical phenomenology of presenile dementia: A critical review of the literature. *Journal of Nervous and Mental Diseases, 167,* 329–336.

Luria, A. R. (1966). *Higher cortical functions in man.* New York: Basic Books.

Miller, E. (1971). On the nature of the memory disorder in presenile dementia. *Neuropsychologia, 9,* 75–78.

Miller, E. (1972). Efficiency of coding and the short-term memory defect in presenile dementia. *Neuropsychologia, 10,* 133–136.

Miller, E. (1973). Short- and long-term memory in patients with presenile dementia (Alzheimer's disease). *Psychological Medicine, 3,* 221–224.

Miller, E. (1975). Impaired recall and the memory disturbance in presenile dementia. *British Journal of Social and Clinical Psychology, 14,* 73–79.

Miller, E. (1978). Retrieval from long-term memory in presenile dementia: Two tests of an hypothesis. *British Journal of Social and Clinical Psychology, 17,* 143–148.

Moudell, P., Butters, N., & Montgomery, K. (1978). Role of rehearsal in the short-term memory performance of patients with Korsakoff's and Huntington's disease. *Neuropsychologia, 16,* 507–510.

Neumann, M. A., & Cohn, R. (1953). Incidence of Alzheimer's disease in a large mental hospital. *Archives of Neurology, 69,* 615–636.

Perez, F. I., Gay, J. R. A., & Taylor, R. L. (1975). WAIS performance of neurologically impaired aged. *Psychological Reports, 37,* 1043–1047.

Perez, F. I., Gay, J. R. A., Taylor, R. L., & Rivera, V. M. (1975). Patterns of memory performance in the neurologically impaired aged. *Canadian Journal of Neurological Sciences, 1,* 347–355.

Perez, F. I., Rivera, V. M., Meyer, J. S., Gay, J. R. A., Taylor, R. L., & Matthew, N. T. (1975). Analysis of intellectual and cognitive performance in patients with multi-infarct dementia, vertebrobasilar insufficiency with dementia, and

Alzheimer's disease. *Journal of Neurology, Neurosurgery, and Psychiatry, 38,* 533–540.

Perez, F. I., Stump, D. A., Gay, J. R. A., & Hart, V. R. (1976). Intellectual performance in multi-infarct dementia and Alzheimer's disease: A replication study. *Canadian Journal of Neurological Sciences, 3,* 181–187.

Perry, E. K. (1980). The cholinergic system in old age and dementia. *Age and Aging, 9,* 1–9.

Perry, E. K., Perry, R. H., Blessed, G., & Tomlinson, B. E. (1977). Necropsy evidence of central cholinergic deficits in senile dementia. *Lancet, 1,* 189.

Petersen, R. C. (1977). Scopolamine induced learning failures in man. *Psychopharmacology, 52,* 283–289.

Prigatano, G. P. (1978). Wechsler Memory Scale: A selective review of the literature. *Journal of Clinical Psychology, 34,* 816–832.

Reisberg, B. (1983). The Brief Cognitive Rating Scale and Global Deterioration Scale. In T. Crook, S. Ferris, & R. Bartus (Eds.). *Assessment in geriatric psychopharmacology* (pp. 19–35). New Canaan, CT: Mark Powley Associates.

Rosen, W. G., Terry, R. D., Fuld, P. A., Katzman, R., & Peck, A. (1980). Pathological verification of ischemic score in differentiation of dementias. *Annals of Neurology, 7,* 486–488.

Tomlinson, B. E., Blessed, G., & Roth, M. (1968). Observations on the brains of non-demented old people. *Journal of the Neurological Sciences, 7,* 331–356.

Tomlinson, B. E., Blessed, G., & Roth, M. (1970). Observations on the brains of demented old people. *Journal of the Neurological Sciences, 11,* 205–242.

Wechsler, D. (1945). A standardized memory scale for clinical use. *Journal of Psychology, 19,* 87–95.

Wechsler, D. (1955). *Manual for the Wechsler Adult Intelligence Scale.* New York: Psychological Corporation.

Wilson, R. S., Bacon, L. D., Fox, J. H., & Kaszniak, A. W. (1983). Primary memory and secondary memory in dementia of the Alzheimer type. *Journal of Clinical Neuropsychology, 5,* 337–344.

Wilson, R. S., Bacon, L. D., Kramer, R. L., Fox, J. H., & Kaszniak, A. W. (1983). Word frequency effect and recognition memory in dementia of the Alzheimer type. *Journal of Clinical Neuropsychology, 5,* 97–104.

Walter H. Riege, Judith O. Harker, and E. Jeffrey Metter

CHAPTER

33

Clinical Validators: Brain Lesions and Brain Imaging

Evidence from review of brain lesion studies raises questions about a direct correlation between task-specific deficits in memory and a focal lesion. A deficit detected by a test may correlate with a lesion at many different sites, and a focal lesion may be accompanied by deficits on many different tasks. To obtain a patient profile that can be correlated with clinical phenomenology, the investigator must evaluate performance on many tests measuring several dimensions in memory processing. Through such multivariate memory assessment, the authors have been able to separate disease parameters from the effects of age—the findings have been validated in chronic alcoholics and in people who have suffered unilateral stroke—and to support a neuropathological interpretation of a dysfunction. Along with new techniques of noninvasive brain imaging and new lesion evidence, multivariate assessment of memory dysfunctions can help to distinguish clinically the early signs of memory impairment in older adults. Metabolic scans using positron emission tomography, which seem to reflect a complex interplay among neural subprocessors involved in memory test performances, show particular promise for more exact brain localization.

Many instruments that are used to measure memory are validated by testing people who have impaired memory. Memory assessment tools related to brain functioning are used in two distinct, yet interrelated ways—in treatment and in research. Clinical memory testing has a number of applications: It contributes to medical diagnosis of syndromes in which normal mentation is in question, such as Korsakoff's syndrome or Alzheimer's disease (AD), and to preliminary evaluation of brain pathology when memory impairments may suggest the side or site of a lesion. The outcome of such testing is then validated by more refined brain-imaging techniques.

Use of well-constructed memory tests also helps produce more precise descriptions of patient behavior to flesh out general clinical impressions. Test results may provide the physician or family with information essential for the patient's care and recovery; for example,

memory deficits may explain noncompliance with medication instructions. Reliable assessment tools permit monitoring of treatment programs or a rehabilitation regimen for a patient or patient groups.

Clinical memory testing requires reliable evaluation of several components of memory processing. Use of a single memory test gives a view of only one particular aspect of memory. This may be useful in distinguishing between two or more groups of patients, as required in research studies, but it will not provide enough information for diagnosing memory deficits in an individual case. Unless a person fails on that task, we cannot infer which component processes of that task may be faulty. Nor do we have information about other aspects of memory. A battery of tests organized around theories of memory or modeled on the structural organization of the brain, however, should tap a variety of components in memory processing and permit a more clinically valid interpretation of the pattern of deficits.

The use of memory tests in research is prompted by the need to understand brain functions in normal as well as in brain-damaged persons. Goals in research can be primarily descriptive, such as discovering the pattern of abilities and deficits characteristic of a disease, or they can be explanatory, such as testing hypotheses about conditions that affect memory. In either case, the choice of tests is dictated by the research question at hand. In research on aging, memory testing more often attempts to define the conditions in which age-related impairments are observed. In neuropsychological studies, memory tests often are selected to bring out the deficits correlated with a specific brain dysfunction. The underlying brain pathology is verified by a neurological or computed tomography (CT) exam, which may confirm test accuracies and outcome.

Thus, memory tests may be considered the behavioral tools used in the clinical assessment of brain dysfunctions. Although studies find considerable complexity in brain–memory correlations, a number of tests measuring basic memory processes seem to be able to sketch the differences among lateralized brain lesions or diseases. Such results add to the knowledge base on which clinical interpretation relies.

There are, then, three major components in assessment of memory: the knowledge base about the correlations among memory and brain dysfunctions, the memory assessment instruments based on that knowledge, and the neurological validators such as CT or other brain-imaging techniques that relate regional brain dysfunctions to memory test outcomes. The knowledge base serves as a starting point for developing the memory assessment tools. The results of memory testing, especially those from research studies, add to the knowledge base and may lead to revisions of current models of memory. Similarly, the results of clinical memory testing coupled with a clinical validator (such as a CT scan) are a basis for diagnosis or therapy evaluation. Each of the three components (knowledge base, assessment tools, validators) contributes to and draws from the others.

In the first section of the chapter, we focus on the knowledge base derived from research and clinical studies. We summarize divergent findings from brain lesion investigations, present conclusions important for clinical memory assessment, and evaluate current knowledge about localization of memory functions in the brain.

In the second section, we discuss the advantages and shortcomings of some existing memory assessment tools and the difficulty of constructing tests that adequately reflect the complex dimensions in memory performance. We also give an example of multivariate memory testing and demonstrate its validation in clinical research.

In the third section, we discuss brain-imaging techniques as diagnostic and localizing tools, also described in subsequent chapters of this volume (i.e., chapters 35, 36, 37, and 38). Our studies using positron emission tomography (PET) with glucose scans shows specific correlations of cerebral regional metabolism with memory functions in brain-injured patients and normal older adults.

Localization of Memory Functions: Current Knowledge

Hemispheric Lateralization

The enormous body of evidence for memory impairments following brain damage is mainly consistent with the notion of hemispheric lateralization. A review of studies through October of 1983 easily demonstrated that deficits in performance on material-specific tests may be systematically related to left- or right-hemispheric impairment, as illustrated in Table 33-1. The

Table 33-1. Tasks Impaired by a Lateralized Brain Lesion

Task	Impaired hemisphere Left	Impaired hemisphere Right	Reference[1]
Digit span, forward	X		Cremonini, De Renzi, & Faglioni, 1980
Sequence of nameable pictures			
• Pointing to pictures	X		Cremonini et al., 1980
• Arranging pictures on a table		X	Cremonini et al., 1980
Sequence of words, digits	X		Kim, Royer, Bonstelle, & Boller, 1980
Sequence of lights	X		Bentin & Gordon, 1979
4 × 4 block sequence		X	Kim et al., 1980
Nameable pictures or objects			
• Recognizing after design interference		X	Whitehouse, 1981
• Recognizing after verbal interference	X		Whitehouse, 1981
Abstract designs		X	Whitehouse, 1981
Abstract designs		X	Riege, Metter, et al., 1982
Abstract designs (Raven's)	X <	X	Gainotti, Caltagirone, & Miceli, 1978
Unknown faces		X	Bentin & Gordon, 1979
Famous faces	X <	X	Van Lancker & Canter, 1982
Famous voices		X	Van Lancker & Canter, 1982
Sentence anagrams (scrambled sentences)		X	Cavalli, De Renzi, Faglioni, & Vitale, 1981

[1]Only studies that compared patients having a left-hemisphere or a right-hemisphere lesion with normal control subjects were included; impairment on a task is denoted by an "X."

verbal tasks (word learning, digit span, recognition after verbal interference) and sequencing tasks (using nameable pictures, words, digits, lights) are characteristically sensitive to left-hemispheric impairments. Deficits in nonverbal reconstruction or recognition tasks (famous and unknown faces, voices, abstract designs) and imaginal coding (shown by impaired recognition of nameable pictures and common objects after interference) are generally seen following right-hemispheric damage.

Such lesion evidence has reinforced a view that material-specific memory processing is necessarily lateralized. Thus, some researchers have examined only functions of a single hemisphere in performances on function-specific tests. For example, Cermak and Tarlow (1978) included only left-anterior aphasic patients in comparison with Korsakoff patients and control subjects on recognition of words or nameable pictures; and in studying visuospatial functions of the human cortex, Fried, Mateer, Ojemann, Wohns, and Fedio (1982) electrically stimulated only the right hemisphere of patients undergoing surgery, assuming that the left hemisphere is not involved in such functions.

Despite the widely held view that the right hemisphere is critical for visuospatial processing and the left for verbal, there is evidence that neither hemisphere by itself is sufficient for optimal processing of information and that each hemisphere contributes to contralateral functions (Sergent, 1984). Table 33-1 lists several studies that report decreased performance on tasks thought to be dependent on processing by the "intact" hemisphere contralateral to that of the lesion. Control subjects had higher scores than left-hemisphere damaged patients in recognizing abstract designs (Gainotti, Caltagirone, & Miceli, 1978) and learning a sequence of lights (Bentin & Gordon, 1979).

Several studies demonstrated further that the dichotomy between the verbal left and nonverbal right hemispheres is overly simplistic. A number of verbal functions seemed to involve the right hemisphere and were impaired with damage to that area. For example, right-hemisphere-damaged patients were impaired in ability to reorder words in a scrambled sentence (Cavalli, De Renzi, Faglioni, & Vitale, 1981) and to reorder sentences in a scrambled story (Wapner, Hamby, & Gardner, 1981). They also were less able than control subjects to infer the point of a story (Wapner et al., 1981) or to correctly infer coherent punch lines to jokes (Brownell, Michel, Powelson, & Gardner, 1983). In addition, the left hemisphere is implicated in nonverbal face recognition (Damasio, Damasio, & Van Hoesen, 1982). These investigators found that face recognition after left-posterior damage was impaired relative to control subjects and concluded from autopsy evidence that bilateral posterior damage was needed for complete prosopagnosia.

Patients with left-hemispheric lesions were also impaired relative to control subjects in immediate memory for sequencing nameable pictures, when the recall task was pointing to pictures (Cremonini, De Renzi, & Faglioni, 1980). However, the left-hemisphere-impaired group was not impaired in learning a sequence of eight nameable pictures when the recall task was arranging the pictures in order on a table. The reverse effects were found with right-hemispheric damage. Sequencing of dually codable materials such as nameable pictures may be selectively impaired by damage to either hemisphere, depending on subtle task demands. Again, a simple dichotomous view of laterality of function is insufficient.

Lateralization is also in question when sex differences in tests of intellect are considered. Men with left unilateral stroke were impaired on the Wechsler Adult Intelligence Scale (WAIS; Wechsler, 1955) Verbal IQ, but not on Performance IQ; men with right-unilateral stroke showed the reverse pattern, as expected. However, women with unilateral stroke (either left or right) showed similar impairments in both WAIS Verbal and Performance IQ; their test scores did not fit clearly the expected hemispheric lateralization (Inglis, Ruckman, Lawson, MacLean, & Monga, 1982; McGlone, 1978).

Several other investigators have challenged the assumptions of a verbal-nonverbal hemispheric lateralization. Some contend that the hemispheres rely on different processing modes, such as analytic or temporal-sequential operation by the left hemisphere and holistic or simultaneous processing by the right hemisphere (see Moscovitch, 1979). Others cite evidence that structures, although different on the left and on the right, retain some capacity to process information usually handled by the other side (Gazzaniga, 1983; Zaidel, 1982). Memory deficits after commissurotomy, for example, have been interpreted to result from loss of intercallosal excitation, and evidence for right-hemisphere language is growing (Zaidel, 1983).

In contrast to the view that structures in one hemisphere are functionally different from corresponding structures in the other hemisphere, Moscovitch (1979) proposed that homologous structures in the two hemispheres are interchangeable and that no basic differences distinguish them. He argued that a memory impairment from a unilateral lesion should not be accentuated by a lesion to the mirror structure, if the two structures are functionally different. If the two are basically similar, however, bilateral damage should result in more severe memory deficits than a unilateral lesion "even for those functions that appear to be lateralized" (p. 410). That is, damage to both should be additive. Evidence from patients with bitemporal-hippocampal lesions seems to support this hypothesis for added lesion effects (Milner, 1971).

In general, hemispheric lateralization has become a useful concept for understanding a large body of data on deficits. Diagnostically, however, any impaired performances on complex tasks involving memory only suggest brain dysfunction localized to a hemisphere, and such a suggestion is often restricted to adult, right-handed males. In the damaged brain, the contributions of adjacent or even contralateral structures may become more relevant. Specific diagnoses based on correlations between particular memory deficits and circumscribed lesion sites require more detailed assessment techniques.

Correlation of Memory Deficit With Lesion

In order for memory tests to be accepted as clinically valid, they must effectively demonstrate impairments (against a norm) that correlate with a recognized brain dysfunction or clinical syndrome. The probability of correlating a specific memory deficit with damage to a regional brain structure is relatively high in some disease states, such as stroke, but it is tenuous in others, such as major depression or chronic schizophrenia. The inference from memory impairment to an underlying lesion is not straightforward, even when a lesion is verified neurologically.

Some investigations of memory impairments in a variety of tasks associated with focal lesions are summarized in Table 33-2. Readers with a diagnostic orientation may ask whether an observed impaired performance on a task is indicative of damage to a particular brain region. Readers with a descriptive or rehabilitative orientation may ask which cognitive performances are impaired and which are spared by this focal lesion. The table makes it clear that testing of a single function is inadequate.

The link between a lesion and a task-specific deficit is more complex than a direct correlation. The table indicates that impairments on one task may be produced by a lesion at a number of different sites. For example, reading across from left to right, performance on forward digit span was impaired in patients with either left or right frontal-lobe lesions, or left-parietal damage (Black & Strub, 1978). Impaired performance on binary digit span was related to left-hemispheric lesions in Heschl's gyrus, Wernicke's and deep to Wernicke's area, temporal pole, medial temporal gyrus, or angular gyrus (Gordon, 1983). Impairments in nonverbal memory span, as measured with spatial and temporal sequencing tasks have been found after either left or right parietal-occipital damage (De Renzi, Faglioni, & Previdi, 1977).

Several lesion sites are also implicated in word-learning deficits. Impaired learning of pairs of words was associated with both left and right temporal-lobe damage (Jones-Gotman & Milner, 1978), right parietal-occipital damage (Hecaen, Tzortzis, & Rondot, 1980), damage to dorsomedial thalamus (patient N.A., Squire & Slater, 1978), and lesions due to Korsakoff's syndrome (Ryan, Butters, Montgomery, Adinolfi, & DiDaro, 1980) as illustrated in Table 33-2. The delayed recall of paired associates was affected by a left temporal-lobe lesion but not by a selective left hippocampal lesion (Birri, Perret, & Wieser, 1982).

Nonverbal paired-associate learning was also sensitive to lesions in one of several areas. Petrides and Milner (1982) found that patients with either left or right frontal-lobe lesions had difficulty learning to associate spatial positions with lights or hand posture with lights. Right-temporal patients were impaired on the spatial position task, while left-temporal patients were deficient in the hand posture task. It is apparent that impairments on one particular task are not exclusively related to damage at one site but may be produced by lesions at a number of different sites.

When reviewing the table from the point of lesion impact, we also find diversity and complexity. The major point here is that a focal lesion can impair performance on a number of different memory tasks, and these tasks are not limited to one memory process or another. This may be illustrated by reading down the columns of the table.

For example, a lesion in the left frontal quadrant may affect digit span (primary memory, Black & Strub, 1978), paired-associate learning (Milner, 1982) or delayed recognition of pictures (secondary memory), and the tertiary memory reflected in word fluency (Bentin & Gordon, 1979; Petrides & Milner, 1982). Several studies show that a right temporal-hippocampal lesion may impair self-ordered recognition of representational pictures (Petrides & Milner, 1982), learning of concrete words (Jones-Gotman & Milner, 1978), visual maze learning (Birri et al., 1982), and use of spatial location (Smith & Milner, 1981). In addition, lesions in the left parietal-occipital region produce impairments in digit span (Black & Strub, 1978), spatial sequencing (De Renzi et al., 1977), facial recognition (Cohn, Neumann, & Wood, 1977), and recall of a list of words (Miceli, Caltagirone, Gainotti, Masullo, & Silveri, 1981).

The comparisons within and across lesion sites in the table suggest that left- and right-hemispheric interaction, rather than specialization, may be the more valid model for interpretation of deficits in learning and memory tasks. A focal lesion may disrupt performance on several, apparently different memory tasks. In addition, even relatively simple tasks such as digit span may be more complex than would be expected and seem to depend on intact functioning of a number of brain areas.

Role of Temporal and Diencephalic Structures in Memory

Bilateral impairment. Attempts at specifying the neuroanatomical substrate underlying severe memory dysfunctions early focused on temporal and hippocampal regions (Barbizet, 1970; Bekhterev, 1900). Since the well-known work of Milner and her colleagues on patient H.M. (Milner, 1971; Scoville & Milner, 1957), the hippocampus has been considered important in memory processing. Most textual citations referring to severe difficulties in secondary memory have been to reports of just this one patient, who underwent bitemporal excision with bilateral involvement of the anterior two thirds of the hippocampus, the uncus, and the amygdaloid nuclei in 1953. Subsequent reports described several cases of mesio-temporal-lobe resections that disturbed organization and recall of items from delayed (secondary) but not from immediate memory when hippocampal regions were damaged on both sides (Lhermitte & Signoret, 1976).

The often severe learning and recall deficits of these patients have been called "bitemporal amnesia," in contrast to the diencephalic amnesias seen in patients with lesions to the dorsomedial nucleus of the thala-

Table 33-2. Summary of Memory Impairments by Lesion Site and Task

Frontal		Temporal-hippocampal		Parietal-occipital		Diencephalic (Korsakoff)	Reference
Left (1)	Right (2)	Left (3)	Right (4)	Left (5)	Right (6)	(7)	(8)
Memory Span							
		Binary digit span, tones					Gordon, 1983
Digit span, forward	Digit span, forward			Digit span, forward			Black & Strub, 1978
				Cube sequence	Cube sequence		De Renzi, Faglioni, & Previdi, 1977
		Consonant trigrams					Corsi, 1972
						Consonant trigrams	Butters et al., 1976
						Consonant trigrams	Squire & Slater, 1978 (patient N.A.)
Paired-Associate Learning							
		Concrete words	Concrete words				Jones-Gotman & Milner, 1978
		Words					Birri et al., 1982[1]
			Words				Hecaen et al., 1980
						Words	Squire & Slater, 1978 (patient N.A.)
						Words	Ryan et al., 1980
Spatial location & hand posture	Spatial location & hand posture	Hand posture	Spatial location				Milner, 1982
Learning							
Tactile maze							Kolb & Whishaw, 1980
		Visual maze					Birri et al., 1982[1]
			Visual maze				Hecaen et al., 1980
						Release from PI	Moscovitch, 1982
Recognition							
Low-, high-image words		Low-image words					Petrides & Milner, 1982
			Words				Schwartz, Shipkin, & Cermak, 1979
					Words		Haxby, Lundgren, & Marley, 1983
						Words	Cohen & Squire, 1980
Abstract designs	Abstract designs		Abstract designs				Petrides & Milner, 1982
						Designs	Haxby et al., 1983
		Designs					Delaney, Rosen, Mattson, & Novelly, 1980 (epileptic)
					Designs		Miceli et al., 1981
Pictures	Pictures		Pictures				Petrides & Milner, 1982

[1]Two-thirds temporal excision alone.

Continued

Table 33-2, continued

| Frontal | | Temporal-hippocampal | | Parietal-occipital | | Diencephalic | |
Left (1)	Right (2)	Left (3)	Right (4)	Left (5)	Right (6)	(Korsakoff) (7)	Reference (8)
		Pictures (details)					Zaidel & Rausch, 1981
					Pictures (delay)		Schwartz et al., 1979
					Faces	Faces	Dricker, Butters, Berman, Samuels, & Carey, 1978
				Faces			Cohn et al., 1977

Recall

| Frontal | | Temporal-hippocampal | | Parietal-occipital | | Diencephalic | |
Left (1)	Right (2)	Left (3)	Right (4)	Left (5)	Right (6)	(Korsakoff) (7)	Reference (8)
		Words	Prose				Delaney et al., 1980 (epileptic)
				Words			Miceli et al., 1981
						Cued words	Butters et al., 1976
						Words	Weingartner, Grafman, Boutelle, Kaye, & Martin, 1983
			Prose				Wieser & Yasargil, 1982
						Prose	Cohen & Squire, 1980
					Landmarks		Hecaen et al., 1980
Facial affect	Facial affect						Prigatano & Pribram, 1982
		Objects	Objects & locations				Smith & Milner, 1981
			Spatial location				Corsi, 1972

Recall From Semantic Memory

| Frontal | | Temporal-hippocampal | | Parietal-occipital | | Diencephalic | |
Left (1)	Right (2)	Left (3)	Right (4)	Left (5)	Right (6)	(Korsakoff) (7)	Reference (8)
Word fluency	Word fluency						Miceli et al., 1981
		Object naming					Wilkins & Moscovitch, 1978
		Word fluency	Word fluency				Zaidel & Rausch, 1981

mus (Squire, 1982). The latter categorization includes the disproportionate impairments in secondary memory of Korsakoff patients (Victor, Adams, & Collins, 1971) and of the well-studied patient N.A., who suffered a stab wound to the dorsomedial thalamus (Squire & Moore, 1979; Teuber, Milner, & Vaughan, 1968). Punctate periventricular lesions, damage to mammillary bodies, or craniopharyngiomas involving these structures (Kahn & Crosby, 1972) have also been correlated with Korsakoff's syndrome (Brierley, 1977), but the separate role of these structures in memory disorders is debated (Hirst, 1982; Mishkin, 1978).

Korsakoff patients often have normal intellectual capacity and a normal rate of forgetting for material they have learned (Huppert & Piercy, 1979); they are competent to recall distant premorbid events and experiences (Butters & Albert, 1982), but remote memory loss is severe and characterized by a temporal gradient. Although they are unable to generate previously processed events on demand, which is taken as failure in episodic memory (Weingartner, Grafman, Boutelle, Kaye, & Martin, 1983), they have normal access to lexical (semantic) memory, as seen with word fluency tests, sentence completion, or narration.

Amnesic patients can learn reading of mirror-inverted text (Cohen & Squire, 1980) and they may retain this procedural skill at a normal level for 3 months (Butters, 1983; Squire, 1982). Information about the testing situation, however, or the words that had been read was lost almost instantaneously (Cohen & Squire, 1980). Korsakoff patients can recognize across successive trials and distractors the complex nonverbal designs they failed to recognize earlier (Riege, 1977), and they have shown learning of fragmented pictures or words upon repetition or partially cued recall (Warrington & Weiskrantz, 1982). In contrast to these relatively automatic memorization tasks are those on which the amnesic performs dismally, such as multiple choice or recurrent recognition of words or faces, free recall, story recall, or reconstruction of newly acquired information. They fail to show better recognition of words encoded semantically than words identified by letter size (Wetzel & Squire, 1980). However, bitemporal amnesics normally recognized words differentiated by graphic, phonemic, or semantic encoding.

As reviewed by Butters and Albert (1982) and Squire (1982), the evidence so far has tended to support the limited encoding hypothesis for Korsakoff amnesics. In contrast, in bitemporal amnesia, the storing of a new memory seems to be disrupted. Bitemporal amnesics, of which patient H.M. is an example, showed rapid forgetting of pictures over a 32-hour interval, despite comparable recognition at 10 minutes after learning (Squire, 1981). These findings have been taken to suggest that at least two memory systems are differently organized and rely upon separate brain structures (Squire, 1982).

Debate over the involvement of related and distant structures in diencephalic amnesias is still intense. A number of memory disorders have been common to Korsakoff patients and to patients who had sustained surgical removal of portions of the frontal lobe: increased susceptibility to interference, poor memory for temporal order, difficulty in using imagery mediation, and impaired release from proactive interference (Moscovitch, 1982). These findings suggest that frontal-lobe dysfunctions determine some of the information-processing deficits of Korsakoff patients. Their diencephalic amnesia involves the putative lesions of mammillary bodies and medial thalamus, which, via mammilothalamic and thalamocingulate fibers, exercise control over frontal regions (Lhermitte & Signoret, 1976).

Warrington and Weiskrantz (1982) suggested that lesions in the diencephalon disconnect medial thalamic structures from frontal cortical areas that are essential for the processing of "cognitive mediation" in memory in which information is interrelated, organized, elaborated, and "stored in a continually changing record of events" (p. 242). Memory dysfunctions have been repeatedly demonstrated in patients with frontal-lobe lesions (Black & Strub, 1978; Petrides & Milner, 1982; Prigatano & Pribram, 1982); these lesions render the memory without content, meaning, or affect.

Unilateral focal impairments. Laterality-specific memory impairments following lesions made in unilateral temporal regions to treat tumors or focal epilepsy have been documented. The results have suggested to some that hippocampal structures are critical for coding and processing of information across interference (Butters, 1979; Squire, 1982), because lesions that spared the hippocampus but not the temporal gyrus were said to have no noticeable effect upon verbal or nonverbal memorizing.

Investigators have considered interrelated structures within the limbic-diencephalic circuit as being necessary if not also sufficient for memory processes. In particular, they have viewed projections from hippocampus and subiculum through fornix to mammillary bodies and hence to anterior and medial thalamus and to frontal cortex (Nauta, 1972), as well as hippocampal connections to amygdala and to cingulate gyrus, as sensitive to memory dysfunctions from injury.

Investigators do not agree, however, on the role that one or the other structure plays in memory dysfunc-

tions. Several hold that fornix lesions do not induce memory dysfunctions (Squire & Moore, 1979; Woolsey & Nelson, 1975), whereas others report that they do (Heilman & Sypert, 1977). Some contend that amnesia occurs only after combined amygdala-hippocampus lesions (Mishkin, 1978; Zola-Morgan, Squire, & Mishkin, 1982); others find the involvement of these two structures in question (Horel, 1978; Wieser & Yasargil, 1982). A third group holds the size of damage to temporal and hippocampal structures critical for deficit in one or more memory tests (Jones-Gotman & Milner, 1978). It has been suggested that all these regions collaborate in a "memorization system" with redundant interaction (Luria, 1976).

Unilateral damage to the amygdala itself does not seem to seriously affect memorizing. Anderson (1978) observed no reduction in general intelligence of patients with temporal-lobe epilepsy 1 year after right- or left-amygdala coagulation. Although their memory for delayed recall of story improved against preoperative level, picture recognition declined; however, cueing with picture fragments increased performance in both groups.

Many memory tasks are sensitive to temporal-hippocampal lesion, and in several the impairment is directly correlated with the extent of hippocampal damage. Reports describe learning of concrete but not abstract word pairs more impaired by a large lesion (with additional lesioning of the body of the hippocampus and parahippocampal gyrus) than by a small temporal-hippocampal lesion in the right hemisphere (Jones-Gotman & Milner, 1978). Some researchers concluded that hippocampal structures were necessary for inhibiting interference and for "image-mediated verbal learning," because both a large and a small lesion in the left hemisphere affected learning of paired associates, as well as delayed recall for names, but not for location, of 16 toys on a board (Smith & Milner, 1981). Recall of location was deficient only after a large hippocampal excision on the right. Patients with such an excision on the right were also impaired on a task asking them to point to a different item on successive pages printed with an array of different abstract words or designs (Petrides & Milner, 1982). Patients with a small mesio-temporal lesion on left or right not extending posteriorly beyond the foot of the hippocampus were unimpaired, indicating that small hippocampal damage does not seem to disrupt this sequencing.

Debate over the involvement of hippocampal structures was rekindled by Horel (1978). From review of studies on temporal lesions in humans and animals, Horel suggested that the memory dysfunctions seen after temporal-lobe excision are due not to damaged hippocampal structures but rather to damage to the temporal stem. This is described as a band of white matter that lies adjacent to the hippocampus across the lateral ventricle and connects the amygdala and temporal neocortex to several diencephalic structures, including the dorsolateral thalamus. Although surgical excisions of large temporal-hippocampal areas rarely spare the temporal stem, small lesions do. Recent evidence from experimental lesions in monkeys suggested that bilateral damage to the temporal stem did not affect performance on a delayed recognition task (Zola-Morgan et al., 1982) but did impair skill learning. The reverse results were found in monkeys with amygdala-hippocampus lesions. Both types of lesions, on the other hand, removed a considerable amount of tissue bilaterally so that correlation of a relevant structure to a memory deficit seems tenuous.

Another line of recent evidence has left this correlation even more equivocal. With a skillful microsurgical technique that selectively excised the amygdala and hippocampus but not the mesio-temporal lobe in 22 patients with tumor or epileptogenic focus in these structures, Wieser and Yasargil (1982) found improved intellectual skills and no memory deficits in all but three patients. Compared with selective amygdala-hippocampectomy, which left memory performance intact, a lesion of two thirds of the temporal lobe alone (Figure 33-1) impaired paired-associate learning and story recall when lesioned in the left-temporal area and visual maze learning when lesioned in the right-temporal area (Birri et al., 1982). Although the find-

ings were limited by the small number of patients and by the epileptic history of patients, the inference from hippocampal damage directly to memory impairment seems somewhat in question.

Problems With Assumptions Underlying Brain–Memory Correlations

Most of what is known about the correlation between brain structure and information processes relies heavily on results of studies of patients with verified focal lesions. Neurological populations and case studies have outlined specific impairments. Studies of lateralization of functions in normal, healthy persons have sought confirmation in results from the damaged brain. Lesion studies have pointed out the implicit ambiguity in the interpretation of correlation between the two basic variables: brain structure and function. Several recent reviews and textbooks have debated the validity of inferring function from the disruptive effects of a lesion (Hirst, 1982; Kertesz, 1983; Kolb & Whishaw, 1980; Sergent, 1984), while others have skirted the issue (Hecaen & Albert, 1978; Heilman & Valenstein, 1979).

For the purpose of diagnostically associating a symptom with a cerebral structure or inferring the normal function of a cerebral area from a lesion, however, investigators must not see the impact of the injury in isolation, and they must carefully constrain their conclusions. Even when brain damage is limited to a single structure, which rarely occurs, interaction with other brain structures or neuronal systems is likely to be affected. Investigators often seem to forget that knowing how a damaged brain processes information may not always reveal how a normal brain works, although as early as 1874 Jackson cautioned against confusing the location of a function with the location of a lesion that impairs a function.

A lesion symptom need not reflect disturbed function, which can be localized at the lesion site, but may implicate a number of processes involved in the disrupted function (Luria, 1976). In fact, in the past decade, it has become apparent that localized lesions can disrupt more than the localized neural mechanisms that are responsible for specific neurobehavioral functions assumed to reside in discrete nuclei or fiber tracts.

For example, data showing that patients with a right parietal-occipital lesion cannot use or learn to use landmarks (Hecaen et al., 1980) do not necessarily mean that topographical memory is localized in the right-posterior hemisphere. The data may simply mean that this brain region is, at one stage or another, involved in the processing of the information. Therefore, instead of seeking to ascertain where the impaired function is localized, we should seek to discover how a lesion modifies the brain systems so that a specific memory deficit is observed. This throws a different light on the diagnostic question. We not only look for a circumscribed structure associated with a mem-

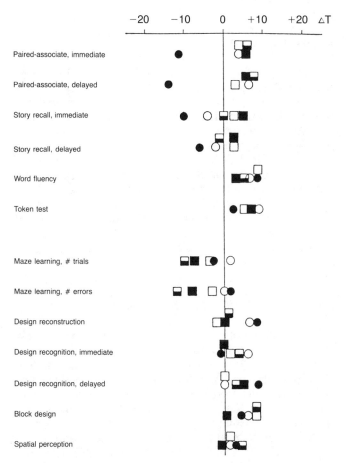

Figure 33-1. Deviations from median performances (in *t*-scores) on verbal and nonverbal learning tasks in patients (*n* = 3/group) after selective excision of either left (○) or right (□) amygdala-hippocampus, two-thirds temporal lobe (●=left, ■=right), or foot of temporal lobe plus right amygdala-hippocampus (◨). Reproduced in translation from Birri, Perret, and Wieser (1982) with permission from Springer Verlag.

ory deficit, but also seek the correlation among those brain structures that subserve "one of several different memory systems" (Weiskrantz, 1978).

Several other difficulties hinder valid comparisons between lesion results. Many studies fail to consider the heterogeneity within their patient samples. Measures of the age of the patient at onset of the trauma, as well as of the extent and the chronicity of the lesion, have not been systematically considered as covariates or as variables separating groups. In particular, the dynamics of the lesion have been mostly left out of consideration. Neurological dysfunctions may be observed without accompanying neuropsychological impairments; conversely, neuropsychological functions such as abstracting or memorization may be impaired when neurological signs are intact (Smith, 1975). The spectra of sensory-perceptual, motor, language, or cognitive disturbances vary with the patient and with the frequency, origin, and size of the trauma.

There is growing evidence that the extent of the lesion dysfunction is not clearly determined from structural evidence. What looks like focal structural damage on CT scan may involve more widespread and interrelated brain structures. CT scans have failed to detect lesions later observed in postmortem evaluation or in more fine-grained PET scans. In our studies of stroke patients, the area of metabolic abnormality determined by a PET scan of cerebral glucose use far exceeded the area of infarction or hemorrhage seen on CT and consistently involved the caudate and thalamic regions (Metter, Wasterlain, Kuhl, Hanson, & Phelps, 1981). More than a month after a mesial frontal infarct, an aphasic patient still showed significant depression of cerebral glucose metabolism throughout the left hemisphere (Kuhl et al., 1980).

Lesion studies report that distal changes in the brain induced by a lesion, which can account for an impaired function, can be a more significant neurological deficit (Schoenfeld & Hamilton, 1977; Sergent, 1984). Secondary neuropathological changes, such as necrosis, transneuronal degeneration, supersensitivity, changes in vascularity, and diaschisis may be involved in the altered cerebral functions to which the behavioral change can be attributed. Consequently, the secondary changes, as well as recovery and adaptation, following a focal lesion argue against any direct or specific link with a memory deficit.

A broader view: Neural subprocessors. In recent reviews, the view of hemispheric lateralization has made room for more flexible accounts of functional brain systems that serve information-processing needs (Allen, 1983; Luria, 1973, Moscovitch, 1979; Sergent, 1984). Researchers propose viewing the lateralized tasks and functions as complexes of subprocesses that rely on one or more interrelated cerebral structures. They believe that a number of processes are involved in both verbal and nonverbal memory, and they seek a careful analysis of the components of the task. Statements such as "verbal recall is a left-hemisphere function" or "face recognition is a right-hemisphere task," for example, can mislead one into assuming the task is a somewhat indivisible and localizable entity (Allen, 1983). How-

ever, most (lateralized) memory tasks can be divided into a number of components, the execution of which may involve several subprocessors (Allen, 1983); these subprocessors can be viewed as neural processing units that handle, transform, and pass on neural input. It follows, then, that damage to any of the subprocessors would disrupt performance on a given task. Similarly, a number of apparently different tasks that have one or more common components may be affected by a lesion, as was suggested earlier in Table 33-2. Interplay among such putative subprocessors need not be serial and can be time- or task-dependent as processing demands require.

Because it is believed that the processes involved in memory are managed at a number of different cerebral sites, it seems obvious that a memory impairment does not imply that brain dysfunction occurs at a single locus. This is seen in attempts to order aphasic dysfunctions (Hanson, Riege, Metter, & Inman, 1982; Kertesz, 1979) or amnesic dysfunctions (Squire, 1982; Weingartner et al., 1983) into clusters of underlying processes for which no localized cerebral dysfunction is made responsible.

Clinical Memory Assessment

The ability to forge diagnostic links between brain and memory dysfunctions depends on the accuracy of three methodologies: memory assessment and neuroanatomical description from lesion evidence and from noninvasive brain scans. All three have been considerably advanced, but memory assessment has lagged behind nuclear medical technology in developing valid, sensitive instruments for deficit assessment. Researchers have been attempting to overcome this problem; in this section, we discuss an approach based on multivariate memory tests. Measures of different dimensions of memory processing have been entered into clinical memory testing so that more than one aspect of impairment can be considered.

Need for a Multivariate Approach

The assessment of memory in older adults, particularly in those with brain impairments, has often been complicated by little knowledge of their pretraumatic levels of performance. The best recourse has been the use of age-differentiated norms on a number of separate memory tasks that span different dimensions of processing. Deviations from a norm profile can then be evaluated with multivariate analysis techniques and may implicate a component dysfunction underlying performances on several different, but related tasks.

Support for a multivariate assessment approach is illustrated by Table 33-2, presented earlier, when we made the point that impairment on a particular task (e.g., memory for paired-associate words) could not localize damage to the temporal lobe. However, performance on that task in a battery of tests could help to differentiate the constellation of impaired performances consistent with a particular lesion site. For example, if we read down the third column of Table 33-2 we see an impairment pattern associated with left temporal-lobe damage, which is different from that seen with left-frontal lesions (reading down the first column).

In addition, available statistical techniques to evaluate and interpret multivariate test results permit a more detailed interpretation. Although they are less straightforward than a single test, multivariate analysis techniques may tease apart subtle group differences, define relationships among variables, predict impairment on the basis of multiple test scores, and sort performances by principal components. These may be powerful tools for finding the patterns of differences not apparent on the surface or in a single test. The value gained in reliability and in the level of detail outweighs the costs in effort. In addition, a more descriptive clinical picture of memory impairments is obtained for diagnostic consult around which to construct a therapeutic regimen.

Multivariate memory tests also have disadvantages. Obviously such tests take much longer to administer, the order of tests is critical, and task interference and patient's fatigue must be considered, as well as cost in staff time. Some batteries may have come about using a "stew" approach—throwing a number of tests together regardless of a theoretical basis for choosing tests. There may be a tendency to attempt to use the same instrument in all situations, instead of revising and adapting it to the specific research or clinical question at hand. For example, tests developed to separate Huntington's from multi-infarct dementia patients might not be applicable to identifying subtle age-related differences in normal adults.

Examples of Multivariate Instruments

Several memory test batteries have been developed for use with the aged and the brain impaired. Among these, the Wechsler Memory Scale (WMS) (Wechsler, 1945) has been the most frequently used memory battery. However, the WMS quotient (MQ) is not a sufficient index of memory functioning (Brooks, 1976). Despite its frequent clinical use, the WMS has been criticized because it does not have a measure of long-term retention, does not differentiate modality-specific memory functions, is not validated for the elderly, and has limited diagnostic value (Erickson & Scott, 1977). The WMS is widely used as a screening and reference test, despite its restriction to tests of immediate verbal memory (Prigatano, 1978). Although the MQ is of little use for differential diagnosis, scores are sensitive to aging and especially to left-hemispheric and diffuse damage. However, subtests are highly verbal and do not reliably detect right-hemispheric damage. Follow-up testing is limited to one alternate form.

The five subtests of the Guild Memory Test (Gilbert, Levee, & Catalano, 1968) include immediate and delayed recall of paragraphs, paired associates, and designs. Although this test does relate memory scores to different levels of verbal intelligence as measured by the WAIS, it is too complex for use with persons with more than mild deficits and it neglects tertiary memory.

The Randt Memory Test (Randt, Brown, & Osborne, 1980) is less complex than the Guild test, requiring only 30 minutes to administer, plus a 24-hour telephone follow-up. The Randt test consists of seven subtests that assess acquisition and retrieval from both primary and secondary memory. The Randt test adopted and improved a number of tests from the WMS; for example, the Logical Memory subtest was rewritten and modernized. Digits (forward and backward) and paired associates are also similar to WMS. One subtest similar to Buschke's Selective Reminding Task (1973) was designed to separate storage from retrieval, an important goal in diagnostic memory testing. One problem is the reliance on verbal measures while nonverbal memory is neglected. It provides five alternate forms, so that repeat testing is possible, but at present it lacks reliability measures.

Multivariate Memory Tests

The need for tests to measure different memory functions is obvious. Using the information-processing model (Waugh & Norman, 1965), we have put together a set of multivariate memory tests sensitive to age differences (Riege & Inman, 1981) and able to measure the effects of chronic alcohol abuse (Riege, Holloway, & Kaplan, 1981; Riege, Tomaszewski, Lanto, & Metter, 1984) as well as unilateral stroke (Riege, Klane, Metter, & Hanson, 1982; Riege, Metter, & Williams, 1980) and chronic schizophrenia (Riege, Metter, Kuhl, Phelps, & Kling, 1984).

Several variables determined the composition of our set of 16 different tasks designed to assess recognition, recall, reasoning, and decision bias in memory, as illustrated in Table 33-3. One distinction was between tasks that asked for and those that clearly discouraged verbal coding: seven tests are nonverbal, four are verbal, two involve both verbal and nonverbal components, and three tests require visuo-constructive reasoning and primary memory.

The verbal and nonverbal tests are subdivided along several other dimensions of memory. One is task demand; comparing recognition and recall allows the test user to assess possible retrieval deficits, and acquisition difficulties can be assessed by observing subjects' performance in recognizing nameable and abstract designs. Another task demand is separation by sensory modalities: visual, auditory, and tactual. Effects of interference are examined in the modality-specific recognition tests presented after a 1-minute delay without, and a 15-minute delay with, interpolated testing.

The recurrent recognition tests follow the same paradigm. A supra-span number of target items, presented once, are to be recognized in a series intermingled with an equal number of distractors. For nonverbal memory, tested in visual, auditory, and tactual recognition, items are purposely selected for re-

Table 33-3. Dimensions of Memory Assessed by the Multivariate Memory Tests (Riege)

	Verbal	Nonverbal
Recognition tests	Verbal: Supraspan list of common nouns Oral or visual (tachistoscopic) presentation, 1-minute delay and 15-minute delay	Visual: Geometric art designs, 1-minute delay and 15-minute delay
		Auditory: Bird calls, 1-minute delay and 15-minute delay
		Tactual: Random flat wire forms
		Seashore Rhythm Test
	Faces: Match names to photographs of faces in the news (1950–1980)	
Recall tests	Sentence Memory: Repeat & recall after interference	Memory-for-designs: Draw designs after 5-second delay
	Story recall: Immediate recall of fable	Pattern reconstruction: Recall pattern of dots on grid, 5-second delay
	WAIS Vocabulary (also a measure of verbal intelligence)	Visual sequences: Recall order of 3 to 6 symbols, 5-second delay
	Delayed picture recall: Verbalized pictures, 15-minute delay	
Reasoning tests	Shipley Hartford	WAIS Block Design
		Raven's Colored Progressive Matrices

sistance to verbal labeling. Target items in the visual tests are 20 geometric art patterns that recur twice in fixed-random order in the two-test series (Riege, 1977). In the auditory tests, 3-second sections of bird calls are selected as target and distractor items. The tactual test uses flat, hand-size random wire figures presented out of sight to separate hands (Riege et al., 1980).

In the Faces test, a person is given names of targets and foils and is asked to recognize, by pointing out from an array of photographs, the faces of prominent persons in the news during one of three decades (1950–1980). Sixteen concrete nouns are targets in the word recognition tests. The recognition performances are transformed into measures derived from signal detection theory, which provide estimates of discriminability (d') and within-test decision bias (log beta) (Riege & Inman, 1981). In addition, decision time is tallied (in milliseconds) for correct and for false recognitions. All remaining tasks listed in Table 33-3 are scored as percentage correct.

Several verbal recall tasks assess secondary memory and interference. Recall of pairs of sentences is made difficult by retroactive interference from repetition of the first, then the second, sentence before a 20-second delayed recall of the first and then the second. All sentences are syntactically correct but of increasing semantic anomaly. Verbal memory is tested also in immediate recall of an orally presented 141-word fable. Paraphrases of selected key ideas are accepted. Delayed picture recall asks for verbal descriptions of nine pictures, each containing two or three elements, after a 15-minute filled interval. Primary memory for visual designs is evaluated with tests that require reconstruc-

tion of designs, patterns, or sequences across an unfilled 5-second interval (Riege & Inman, 1981).

All tests are brief and moderately demanding; ample response time is allowed to avoid confounding with motor speed slowing. Persons are tested individually, and Yes/No hand signs are adopted for patients with language impairments.

Any person's performance on the 18 tests, plotted test by test on this profile, can be interpreted in terms of deviations from the mean scores of his or her age group. An example of such a patient profile is shown in Figure 33-2. This presents, as deviations from the relevant norm averages of his age group ($n = 77$), the memory test measures of a 63-year-old patient with diagnosis of early AD (2-year duration). The standard deviations for each task are based on the total standardization sample of more than 270 adults, ranging in age from 18 to 84 years, and indicate the range of normal limits. The patient's profile reflects severe deficits in recognition of words from a list and in verbal recall after interference, although his vocabulary (78%) and nonverbal memory scores were relatively preserved. These deficits implicate impairments in verbal coding and organizing of information also seen in the low scores on memory-for-designs and abstraction tasks.

Memory Deficits Caused By Chronic Alcoholism

Memory dysfunctions characteristic of alcoholism have included impairments in learning new associations of symbols or designs, deficits in tactual memory, nonver-

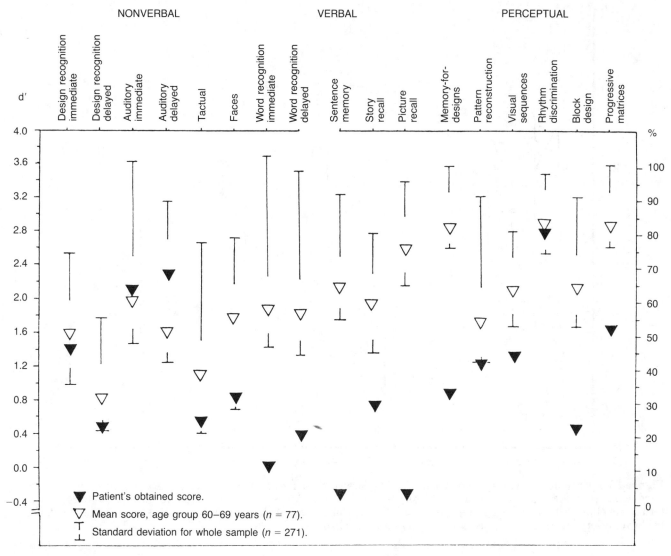

Figure 33-2. Memory performance profile of a 63-year-old male adult (▼) with diagnosis of early Alzheimer's disease in comparison with average scores (▽) of healthy adults in the 60 to 69-year age group. Standard deviations are based on a validation sample ($N > 270$) ranging in age from 18 to 84 years.

bal abstracting, and perceptuo-spatial processing (Eckardt, Parker, Noble, Feldman, & Gottschalk, 1978; Parsons & Leber, 1981). Comparatively few studies have used measures of brain pathology as validators of memory measures in chronic alcoholics. Those that did have reported moderate negative correlation of the WMS quotient with CT intercaudate span and cerebral atrophy, not significant enough to outweigh the age influence (Carlen et al., 1981; Ron, Acker, & Lishman, 1982). Several studies, including ours, have used measures of rate or length of alcohol abuse obtained from self-reported drinking history as correlates of memory test performances. To demonstrate the clinical validity of multivariate tests, we summarize two studies (Riege et al., 1981; Riege, Tomaszewski et al., 1984) that showed that impairment on specific memory tests separated the effects of chronic alcohol abuse from the effects of aging.

Specific deficits caused by alcoholism. In the first study we categorized chronic alcoholics with a mean age of 48.4 into three groups of alcohol abusers: short-term (less than 12 years), long-term (13 to 22 years), and extended-term (more than 22 years), and compared them with 18 healthy men (with a mean age of 46.9) on tests of recognition memory. Measures of memory accuracy (d') and decision certainty (log beta) were tabulated for each of five recognition tests (visual, auditory, tactual, words, and faces). Estimates of years of alcohol abuse and total consumption were derived from extensive interviews and medical records.

Hierarchical regression analyses indicated that age accounted for a significant portion (adjusted $p < .05$) of the total explained variance in auditory, tactual, and faces tests. Length of alcohol abuse contributed considerably ($p < .01$) to the explained variance in visual, auditory, and faces scores over and above the variance

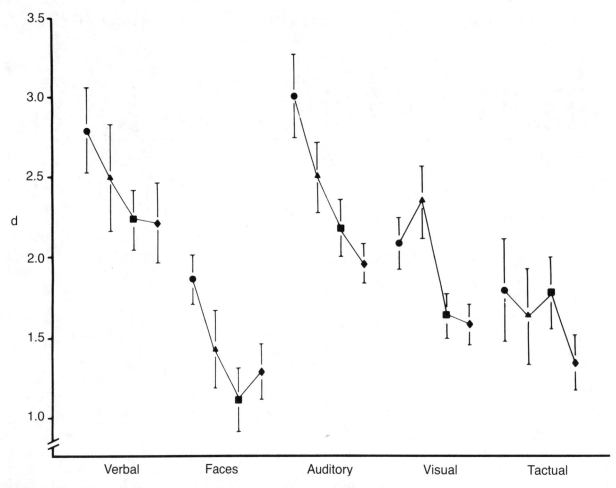

Figure 33-3. Chronic alcoholics with extended (> 22 years = ◆) or long-term (> 12 years = ■) lengths of heavy drinking were impaired in recognition of visual or auditory patterns, or well-known faces in contrast to controls (●) but not to short-term alcoholics (< 12 years = ▲). Reprinted from Riege, Holloway, and Kaplan (1981) with permission of the American Medical Society on Alcoholism, Research Society on Alcoholism.

already explained by age. Patients with a longer history of heavy drinking generally scored low on these tests. The interaction of higher age and longer drinking adversely affected auditory recognition. A measure of lifetime consumption contributed mainly to visual scores, whereas education predicted performance in verbal and faces recognition.

The alcoholic groups were most reliably differentiated by their performances on visual and auditory recognition tests ($p < .002$), even after correcting for the covariate effect of age. This is shown in Figure 33-3. The long-term alcoholics did not differ from the extended-term alcoholics on any of the five tests, but were more impaired than short-term alcoholics in visual recognition. However, most alcoholics differed from controls in nonverbal visual, auditory, and faces recognition. Verbal recognition was less affected by alcoholism than by age or education. The recognition tests used in this study were sensitive to detect specific deficits resulting from alcohol abuse, independent from the effects of age and education.

Independent memory decrements from alcoholism and aging. In the second study, we also used multivariate memory testing to differentiate deficits of alcohol-

ism from those of aging, but we used the entire set of tests. At the same time, we sought to confirm one of three hypotheses: (1) The "premature aging" hypothesis suggests that alcoholism accelerates the normal aging processes so that a pattern of cognitive deficits observed in older adults should also occur in chronic alcoholics, but several years earlier. (2) The "age sensitivity" hypothesis proposes that the aged brain may be more susceptible to alcohol toxicity; greater deficits from alcoholism will occur with increasing age. (3) The "independent decrement" hypothesis postulates that various insults to the brain (including alcoholism) produce cognitive impairments that are independent from and additional to decrements associated with normal aging (Ryan, 1982).

We closely matched 26 young (mean age = 37.8 years) and 30 older alcoholics (mean age = 58.1 years) on average length (16.4 years and 18.8 years) and annual rate of heavy drinking and equated them with young and older control subjects in age, education, and vocabulary levels. To determine whether groups could be differentiated on a few independent factors underlying the memory test battery, we applied factor analyses to all 25 measures, including memory accuracy (d´)

and decision certainty (log beta) obtained from the 112 persons under study.

A five-factor principal components solution produced factor scores for each person, which revealed that age and alcoholism had different effects on the factors, as demonstrated in Figure 33-4. Groups were separated by age on Factor I (largely perceptuo-constructive tests), on Factor III (immediate and delayed recognition of visual patterns), and on Factor V (decision criteria in auditory and tactual tests). These factors did not separate alcoholics from controls.

By comparison, alcoholics differed significantly from nonalcoholic control subjects on Factor II, but no age difference was observed. This factor consisted of tests requiring memory for auditorily presented information: story recall and immediate and delayed recognition of words or auditory patterns (bird calls). Both young and older alcoholics seemed less skilled in memory processing of auditory information than did the nonalcoholic control subjects. Neither age nor alcoholism had an effect on Factor IV, which included decision criteria adopted on verbal and visual recognition tests.

A discriminant analysis based on the factor scores correctly classified more than two thirds of the persons according to age and alcoholism. The accurate classification of both young (79%) and older (77%) persons was evidence for the age sensitivity of the measures.

Impairments from alcoholism stood out only when a battery of modality-specific memory tests was used and when alcohol decrements were compared against age-related decrements. Memory and decision measures were found sensitive to differentiate young from older persons and the alcoholic from the nonalcoholic, but it required factor analytic adjustment to sort these measures into nonoverlapping factors. The "independent decrement" hypothesis seemed to provide the most plausible interpretation of the results. According to this, alcoholism is responsible for some brain dysfunctions, "as well as decrements in neuropsychological performance, which adds to, but is independent of, those changes produced during the course of normal aging" (Ryan, 1982, p. 27).

When taken together, the results of these two studies emphasize that specific memory deficits accompany chronic alcoholism, which can be separated from age-related deficits. Only multivariate testing revealed this. However, the memory decrements alone are only suggestive of the brain dysfunctions responsible for them.

Brain Imaging and Memory

Recently developed localization techniques have been of considerable use in helping to solve the problem of correlating memory dysfunctions with cerebral anatomical sites or systems. Measures of regional cerebral blood flow with xenon, x-ray CT, or nuclear magnetic resonance provide noninvasive imaging of brain structures. In particular, the PET brain scan using F-18-Fluorodeoxyglucose (FDG) as measure of regional cerebral glucose metabolism is potentially capable of the

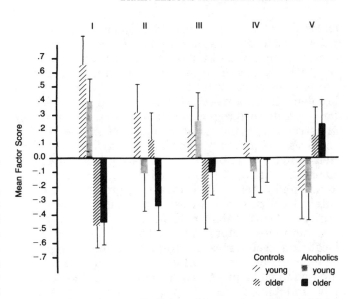

Figure 33-4. Chronic alcoholics ($N = 56$) are distinguished from controls by factor (II) of auditory memory processing; young persons are separated from older persons by factors (I, III, and V) of verbal and visuo-perceptual memory and decision bias. Reprinted from Riege, Tomaszewski, Lanto, and Metter (1984) with permission of the American Medical Society on Alcoholism, Research Society on Alcoholism.

fine resolution required for determining circumscribed regions of subnormal activity (Phelps et al., 1979). Moreover, with this technique it is now possible to visualize metabolic changes in the brain related to age (Kuhl, Metter, Riege, & Phelps, 1982; Riege, Metter, et al., 1982; Riege, Metter, Kuhl, & Phelps, 1983), to stroke (Kuhl et al., 1980), or to degenerative disease (Ferris et al., 1980; Friedland et al., 1983; Kuhl et al., 1983).

Advanced Brain Imaging

The most commonly used localizing tool at present is x-ray CT which, with current equipment, demonstrates all but the smallest abnormal structures. Linear measures of enlarged ventricles or cortical sulci or of increased caudate span have been taken as indices of brain atrophy related with age or dementing illness (see de Leon, George, & Ferris, chapter 37 in this volume). Volumetric CT measures of CSF spaces hold considerably more promise (Gado, Hughes, Danziger, & Chi, 1983). Evaluation of structural damage, however, relies on a static cerebral anatomy.

But many neuropsychological functions, in particular, memory, occur in dynamic and interacting brain systems, which change activity on demand and probably across time. Tools that measure and trace dynamic changes in the damaged and the normal brain should be valuable for determining brain–behavior correlations. Most developed of these tools are event-related potentials, ERPs (complex waveforms highly sensitive to local as well as distal changes in neuronal activity; Hillyard & Woods, 1979), stimulation mapping of the exposed cortex (Ojemann, 1982; Ojemann & Mateer, 1979), and measures of regional cerebral blood flow (Lassen, Ingvar, & Skimhoj, 1978). These reports have considerably advanced our understanding of regional cerebral responses to task activation, but each presents problems to the investigator. ERPs tend to be specific for large, defined regions and not necessarily for a single structure. Stimulation mapping of exposed cortex requires a craniotomy and thus is restricted to a limited number of patients with existing brain dysfunctions (Ojemann, 1982). Blood flow measures with xenon and external detectors have problems in accurately localizing structures, in particular, subcortical regions (Benson, Metter, Kuhl, & Phelps, 1983).

Other investigators have used parallel application of localizing techniques in brain mapping of regional changes in dementing illness. With computer-generated volumetric measures of the fluid spaces, particularly in lateral ventricles, progressive brain pathology of AD could be discriminated from age changes in normal age-matched control subjects (Albert, Naeser, Duffy, & McAnulty, chapter 38 in this volume; Gado et al., 1983). Similarly, topographic mapping by EEG and evoked potential data in dementia patients identified posterior parietal-temporal and bilateral frontal regions as sources of abnormal function in AD patients.

Linear CT measures have not yet entered criteria for diagnosis of dementia, because a number of influences, including age, may affect their high variability. Nevertheless, the dementia-related widening seen in ranking of linear measures of cortical sulci and ventricles was reported to be negatively correlated with measures of cognitive impairment (de Leon et al., 1979). The CT-derived mapping, however, is confined to relatively clear demarcation of tissue: fluid boundaries in large regions, and even the reported loss in discriminability between gray and white matter on CT in AD patients, which correlated with cognitive impairments, remains to be verified (see de Leon et al., chapter 37 in this volume).

Positron Emission Tomography Scan of Brain Metabolism

The PET scanning methods, by comparison, hold promise for more exact brain localization. Transverse images of the brain demonstrate radioactivity from labeled compounds that emit positrons as they decay (Phelps, Hoffman, Mullani, & Ter-Pogossian, 1975). Each positron collides with an electron, generating two gamma rays that travel 180 degrees apart and can be monitored by electronic coincidence counting. Spatial resolutions of cerebral structures of less than 1 centimeter, full-width-half maximum, have been achieved (Phelps, Kuhl, & Mazziotta, 1981) using the Neuro-ECAT tomograph and FDG for mapping local cerebral metabolic rate of glucose utilization (LCMRGlc).

Studies using PET with FDG have examined the relation of brain and memory dysfunctions more closely. Metabolic scans have been done in normal states (Kuhl, Metter, et al., 1982; Metter, Riege, Kuhl, &

Phelps, 1982, 1983; Raichle, 1982; Riege et al., 1983) and in clinical states including degenerative disease (Benson et al., 1983; Chase et al., 1983; Ferris et al., 1980; Friedland et al., 1983; Kuhl et al., 1983; Kuhl, Phelps, et al., 1982, Metter, Riege, Kameyama, Kuhl, & Phelps, 1984). If LCMRGlc is assumed to be a measure of the function of a specific brain region (i.e., the index of neuronal and dendritic activity), then the cross-sectional image of the brain FDG metabolism presents a functional map of brain activity in regions of interest.

Determination of LCMRGlc by the FDG scan requires an intravenous injection of 5 to 10 mCi of the tracer, continuous sampling of arteriolized venous blood to determine FDG concentration, and multiple brain scans beginning 40 minutes after injection when the uptake of FDG has reached steady state. Local CMRGlc's are determined in milligrams per minute per 100 grams of tissue, using constants from normal young adults (Phelps et al., 1979) that have been shown to remain unchanged in normal older persons (Hawkins et al., 1983). The metabolic scans are then displayed on a videomonitor in transverse sections, from which regions of interest are outlined. In our earlier studies, we selected 13 regions in each hemisphere from three transverse slices as shown at the right of Figure 33-5: (1) one supraventricular slice at the level of the centrum semiovale in which a more or less continuous cortical midline is seen but not yet central gray masses; (2) a midventricular slice with high uptake regions around the Sylvian fissure and insula and, mesial to this, thalamic regions and the head of caudate; and (3) an infra-ventricular slice with frontal lower cortex and inferior temporal and occipital regions. Regions selected included measures of superior and inferior frontal, Broca's (and corresponding contralateral right posterior frontal), parietal, Wernicke's, posterior temporal, occipital, caudate, and thalamic regions.

We then expressed each local metabolic rate in reference to a person's mean CMRGlc by dividing a LCMRGlc value of the region by the mean of all regions for a person. These local metabolic reference ratios correct in part the large variations among individuals and permit comparisons between patients and regions.

Regional metabolic correlates of memory impairments in aphasia. In two studies we have tested multivariate memory functions contiguous with PET metabolic scans in patients with cortical and with subcortical aphasia, including patient N.A. (Metter, Riege, Hanson, et al., 1983; Metter, Riege, Hanson, Phelps, & Kuhl, 1981). The metabolic measures were expressed as the ratio of each LCMRGlc to average right-hemisphere CMRGlc because we had found that metabolic indices of the right hemisphere in aphasia were not different from normal.

Abnormalities that were common to both subcortical and cortical aphasics were seen in the severely depressed metabolic ratio of the left-thalamic region and in marked deficits in verbal recall of sentences, stories, pictures, or word lists. However, these impairments in

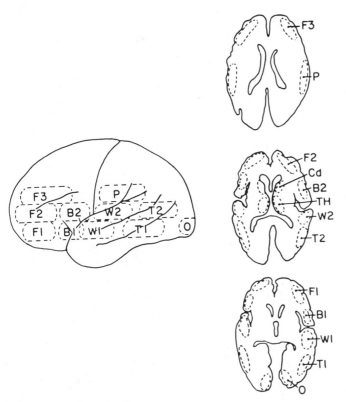

Figure 33-5. Transverse sections of FDG brain scan (right side graphs) parallel to the canthomeatal line (middle graph) provided demarcation of 13 regions of interest in each hemisphere. These include superior (F3), middle (F2), and inferior frontal (F1), high Broca's (B2) and low Broca's (B1), high Wernicke's (W2) and low Wernicke's (W1), parietal (P), posterior (T2), and posterior middle inferior temporal (T1), occipital regions (O), and subcortical caudate (Cd) and thalamic areas (Th). Broca's and Wernicke's region fold into the Sylvian fissure and do not cross it.

verbal memory were unlike the mild language difficulties in the subcortical patients; moreover, their metabolic ratios of cortical regions were not significantly different from normal, whereas those of cortical aphasics were depressed. The metabolic indices, therefore, clearly pointed out left-thalamic dysfunctions, and these were correlated with memory dysfunctions relatively independent of aphasic impairments.

When the right-hemisphere metabolic ratios of aphasic patients (the putatively normal local metabolic indices) were correlated with multivariate memory tests, the diagnostic link seemed to become at the same time more pronounced and complex (Figure 33-6). Performances on several tasks—by no means only nonverbal—were reliably and positively correlated with right posterior middle and inferior temporal (MIT) metabolic ratio. In other words, patients who had high MIT metabolic ratios also had high scores in delayed recognition of nonverbalizable geometric art pictures, auditory (bird call) segments, or well-known faces, as expected. Yet, their recall of sentences was also positively correlated with right MIT ratio, but negatively with metabolic ratio of right thalamus. In view of the fact that these are local metabolic measures

of the right hemisphere of patients with unilateral left damage, the evidence for diverse and multiple processing of memory seems enhanced. The right hemisphere may be adapting to task demands by assuming functions of the left or by using strategies other than the apparently verbal and intensive coding required by the tests. Quite often more than one region appeared to be involved in the metabolic correlations with memory tasks.

The extent of metabolic depression in thalamus was similar in cortical and subcortical aphasic patients and has been noted in all stroke patients who were studied (Kuhl et al., 1980); only a few of them had structural damage of the thalamus as estimated by x-ray CT. Similarly, patient N.A., who sustained medial thalamic damage, had low thalamic metabolic ratio coupled with verbal recall difficulties that left visuospatial memorization intact (Metter, Riege, Hanson, et al., 1983). The thalamic and temporal neocortical correlations with memory suggest strong thalamocortical interactions.

Studies of word naming and recall in thalamotomy patients during deep electrode stimulation have shown that more lateral regions of the thalamus including parts of the ventrolateral nucleus and the pulvinar are involved with verbal short-term memory (Fedio & Van Buren, 1975; Ojemann, 1982). These studies suggested a more general role for these lateral thalamic areas, providing an arousing or organizational step to language and memory functions. The thalamic organizational process may allow for focusing or alerting of neuronal complexes in the posterior temporal and parietal lobes, as the pulvinar projects extensively to these regions. Left-pulvinotomy or left-ventrolateral thalamotomy produced difficulties in word fluency or face-matching tasks (Vilkki & Laitinen, 1976).

Regional brain activity and memory in schizophrenia and depression. Patients with chronic schizophrenia and patients with depression have consistently shown impairments in tasks of delayed recall and verbal abstraction, although they may not have undergone acute episodes of illness while being tested. Recent studies using PET metabolic brain scans have attempted to determine the regional dysfunctions characteristic of schizophrenia, but have been less concerned with the correlation of regional metabolic and memory functions in these patients (Buchsbaum et al., 1982; Farkas et al., 1984). These studies showed that chronic schizophrenic patients in the resting state had lower metabolic ratios in frontal cortices, indicating relatively lower glucose use than control subjects. This finding was consistent with results from cerebral blood flow studies (Ingvar & Franzen, 1974), which had used the nitrous oxide or Xe133 methods showing relatively normal mean cerebral blood flow but "hypofrontal" flow distribution in chronic schizophrenic patients in contrast with the "hyperfrontal" pattern seen in normal adults. Such "hypofrontality" was not seen in depressed patients—not even in those who had shown wider sulci.

If frontal glucose metabolism and blood flow are decreased in chronic schizophrenia, abnormal cognition

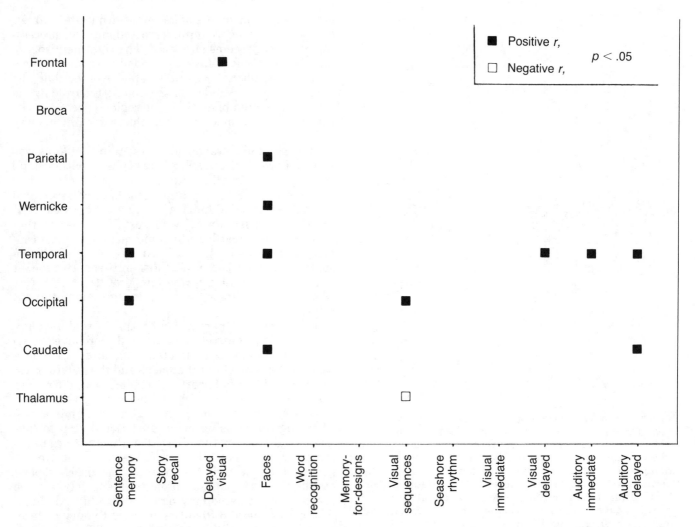

Figure 33-6. Reliable correlations of memory measures with regional cerebral metabolic ratios in right hemisphere of aphasics. ■ = positive r, □ = negative r. $p < .05$.

or memory should reflect these decreases. We compared 8 patients with depression (mean age = 62.2 years) and 6 chronic schizophrenic patients (mean age = 37.8 years, 3 with paranoid and 3 with residual-undifferentiated schizophrenia) with two groups of healthy adults age matched to each patient group. All 14 patients were being treated with neuroleptics and none had florid psychotic symptoms. Seven patients showed normal CT scan by clinical criteria, but 7 patients (3 schizophrenic and 4 depressed patients) were categorized as having enlarged lateral ventricles.

When the regional metabolic rates were corrected by dividing each local measure by the overall cerebral metabolic rate for each person, the metabolic ratios did not differ. Such a correction is needed because regional metabolic indices are highly intercorrelated and group variances are quite heterogeneous. Multivariate and step-down analyses failed to reveal any specific regional metabolic measure that could reliably separate the chronic schizophrenic or depressed patients from the corresponding controls or from one another.

When the uncorrected measures of regional metabolic rates were used as the basis for group compari-

sons, the 6 chronic schizophrenic patients had lower values which exceeded the standard deviations in two regions on the left, Broca's and Wernicke's regions. The group differences could not be attributed to wider sulci or enlarged ventricles, because Broca's and Wernicke's metabolic indices had been obtained from regions that did not cross the fissure, and categorization by large ventricles had shown no reliable group differences.

Neither did the two groups differ in any of the regional left–right hemispheric ratios nor in a ratio of frontal to parietal metabolic rates, so that we did not find evidence for "hypofrontality" seen by others with glucose metabolic or blood flow methods. With the high resolution of the Neuro-ECAT scanner, we were able to see differences only in uncorrected metabolic indices, and these pointed out only Broca's and Wernicke's regions.

When metabolic and memory measures were combined in a cross-correlation matrix, several reliable correlations (adjusted critical $r = .84$, $p < .05$) were apparent: Impairments in immediate verbal memory and sequencing were positively correlated with inferior and posterior frontal metabolic indices, whereas delayed recognition of pictures, patterns, or faces was associated with inferior frontal and parieto-temporal metabolic measures in the schizophrenic patients. In depressed patients, however, there was a consistently negative correlation between memory for designs or word lists and left superior and inferior frontal metabolic ratios. These correlations implicate lower metabolic activity of anterior and lateral regions in the memory dysfunctions of chronic schizophrenic patients and validate the sensitivity of the memory tests in separating the disease profiles.

PET Measures, Memory, and Age

The link between regional metabolic and memory dysfunctions has been seen in the injured brain. What correlations are seen between brain function and memory in the aging brain? We know that, with age, loss occurs in neurons and in volume of cortical tissue, up to 17 percent in bilateral frontal lobes and more than 20 percent in basal ganglia (Haug et al., 1983). Devaney and Johnson (1980) reported a decrease in the density of neurons but not in the volume of the occipital cortex, and others have reported widening of sulci and ventricles (Brizzee, Ordy, Knox, & Jirge, 1980). Cerebral oxygen consumption is not significantly lowered (Lammertsma et al., 1981), but overall utilization of glucose by the brain, as well as that of Broca's region (Riege et al., 1983), decreases gradually with increasing age (Kuhl, Metter, et al., 1982). Impairment of glucose and pyruvate metabolism may selectively compromise cerebral cholinergic functions (Blass & Gibson, 1979), which have been linked with memory and aging (Drachman & Glosser, 1981). Regions of lower glucose utilization are probably involved in the decline of memory ability with aging.

In one of our studies, 23 healthy adults between the ages of 27 to 78 years underwent FDG tomography. All were right-handed and no one had evidence of cardio- or cerebrovascular disease. Within a week of their brain scan, they were also tested with our set of multivariate memory tests.

When correlations were calculated between the 18 regional metabolic ratios and the 18 memory and decision scores, the glucose metabolic index of superior frontal regions correlated positively with accuracy in immediate memory tasks (after Bonferoni adjustment; critical $r = .48$, $p < .05$). Recall of sentences and reconstruction of designs or sequences from memory were positively correlated with superior frontal metabolic ratio but negatively with the ratios of caudate and thalamic areas (Table 33-4). The ability to analyze the relational cues in complex sentences or in geometric designs may involve inherently the high frontal or the low subcortical metabolic ratio or both. However, neither frontal nor subcortical metabolic indices were by themselves correlated with age, so that their interaction may be more important than their direct influence on age-dependent memory decline.

A similar interplay between anterior and subcortical metabolic measures was seen in the positive correla-

tion of immediate recognition memory and superior frontal indices and the negative correlation of delayed recognition memory with caudate-thalamic measures. Tasks that required recall of words or complex sentences from secondary memory showed correlation with age as well as with Broca's regional metabolic ratio, which alone was highly age-sensitive. The decrease of test scores in parallel with metabolic ratio validates the use of such tests in aging studies.

The local metabolic measures also seemed to delineate correspondence among regions. In particular, reliable metabolic relations were found among superior frontal, parietal, and occipital areas. It has been suggested that these regions form a functionally interrelated brain system that may be involved in the processing of visual sequential information and in the control of eye movements (Metter et al., 1982). These areas are known to be connected by the superior longitudinal fasciculus and to correspond to those regions that have been postulated as involved with attention and the ability to focus or follow sequentially presented items (Mesulam, 1981).

The ability to code and organize complex information in memory is known to be more difficult for older adults or for people with brain disease, yet there seem to be no reports correlating this processing deficit with local brain functions. Thus, it is of interest that recognition of complex lists of words, symbols, or nonverbal patterns is low in persons with basic impaired inferior frontal or high thalamic metabolic ratio. The interrelation of frontal-subcortical metabolic indices with memory processing was more prominent in younger persons under study and indicates decreasing thalamo-frontal interaction with age.

Conclusion

Most tests of learning and memory are sensitive to brain pathology, some more so than others, and the tests have a greater correlation to damage in certain brain regions than in other regions. Nonetheless, it has been difficult to show that damage to any single cerebral structure alone induces memory dysfunctions. In fact, some reports assume a functional link among distant neuroanatomical structures implicated in a specific memory deficit. A review of the neuropathological and memory evidence suggests that material-specific memory dysfunctions are consistent mainly with the left–right hemispheric specialization.

Most of the tests that measure memory dysfunctions are research tools rather than diagnostic tools. The instruments that measure specific memory deficits have comparatively low resolution and it is difficult to isolate the basic memory-impaired mental processes and relate them to structural brain damage. This difficulty may be reflected in the interplay among regional brain activities of which metabolic scans seem to offer us a glimpse.

In choosing tests, the investigator is not restricted by models or criteria other than the need to be inclusive, within constraints of test time and patient cooperation.

Table 33-4. Correlations Among Test Scores and Local Cerebral Metabolic Ratios in 23 Adults, Ages 27–78 Years

| | Frontal | | | | Broca's | | Parietal | | Wernicke | | Temporal | | Occipital | | Caudate | | Thala-mus | |
| | Superior | | Inferior | | | | | | | | | | | | | | | |
	L	R	L	R	L	R	L	R	L	R	L	R	L	R	L	R	L	R
Word recognition															●		●	
Sentence recall	■				■												●	
Story recall	■																	
Picture recall																		
Immed. recognition:																		
Visual patterns	■												●	●				
Auditory patterns																		
Tactual patterns			■															
Rhythm matching	■		■															
Progressive matrices	■														●			
Delayed recognition:																		
Visual patterns																	●	●
Auditory patterns															●	●		
Faces																		
Reconstruction:																		
Patterns																	●	●
Designs	■														●	●		
Sequences	■		■															
Decision criteria:																		
Immediate											●	●						
Delayed			■										●	●				●
Education					■													
Vocabulary					■													
Age					●	●												

Note: ■ indicates positive correlations, ● indicates negative correlations exceeding an adjusted critical *r* of ± .47, *p* < .05.

For clinical memory testing, it is obvious that only a profile of impaired and correct performances can characterize disease entities. Researchers need to select tests that sample not only the disease-specific performances, but also performances that are preserved, such as some forms of auditory recognition in early AD. Some tests are clearly sensitive to memory difficulties in older adults; examples include the delayed picture recall and the pattern reconstruction test, presented in Table 33-3.

It is important to consider a number of requirements before including a test. The test must measure one of the functions of diagnostic or rehabilitative interest (e.g., reconstruction of abstract designs after delay or interference). The test also should have a sensitive range of scoring and rely on a norm relevant for the group in question; it should be brief, contain items of increasing complexity, and provide alternate forms.

The investigator should find tests representative of different components in memory, and, in particular, should avoid testing predominantly verbal memory functions (e.g., word list learning) or relying on tasks that older adults may find unfamiliar or irrelevant. The composition of the test set is dictated by the clinical question to be answered or hypothesis to be tested. In either case, the patient's ability to process information is the focus of measurement.

Information processing depends upon the complexity of the task and is not a question of simple encoding and storing, limited by age or disease. The information has to be manipulated according to some strategy, the result of which is to make possible a reduction in its quantity, as well as a chunking, and a link to already existing coded information. This processing according to a strategy is one of the recognized functions of the frontal lobes (Luria, 1976), whereas encoding deficits have been related to temporal-hippocampal damage. The attention process required in both acquisition and retrieval has been associated with intact lateral thalamic activity. It is important, therefore, to view interrelated brain structures as subserving memory processing and to consider a one-to-one correlation of memory deficit and lesion as tenuous. Even when brain damage is limited to a single structure, which rarely occurs, its effect is widespread and cannot be clearly determined from structural damage. In evidence, we pointed out two conclusions: (1) a focal lesion can be related to impaired performance on a number of apparently different memory tasks and (2) impairment on one task may follow a lesion at a number of different cerebral sites.

To obtain a patient profile that can be correlated with clinical phenomenology, the investigator must evaluate performance on many tests measuring several dimensions in memory processing. Through such multivariate memory assessment, we have been able to separate disease parameters from the effects of age— our findings have been validated in chronic alcoholics and in people who have suffered unilateral stroke— and to support a neuropathological interpretation of a dysfunction. Along with the recently developed techniques of noninvasive brain imaging and lesion evidence, multivariate assessment of memory dysfunctions can help to distinguish clinically the early signs of memory impairment in older adults.

References

Allen, M. (1983). Models of hemispheric specialization. *Psychological Bulletin, 93,* 73–104.

Anderson, R. (1978). Cognitive changes after amygdalotomy. *Neuropsychologia, 16,* 439–451.

Barbizet, J. (1970). *Human memory and its pathology.* San Francisco: Freeman.

Bekhterev, V. M. (1900). Demonstration eines Gehirns mit Zerstoerung der vorderen und inneren Theile der Hirnrinde beider Schlaefenlappen. *Zentralblatt fuer Neurologie, 19,* 990–991.

Benson, D. F., Metter, E. J., Kuhl, D. E., & Phelps, M. E. (1983). Positron-computed tomography in neurobehavioral problems. In A. Kertesz (Ed.), *Localization in neuropsychology* (pp. 121–139). New York: Academic Press.

Bentin, S., & Gordon, H. W. (1979). Assessment of cognitive asymmetries in brain-damaged and normal subjects: Validation of a test battery. *Journal of Neurology, Neurosurgery, and Psychiatry, 42,* 715–723.

Birri, R., Perret, E., & Wieser, H. G. (1982). Der Einfluss verschiedener Temporallappenoperationen auf das Gedaechtnis bei Epileptikern. *Nervenarzt, 53,* 144–149.

Black, F. W., & Strub, R. L. (1978). Digit repetition performance in patients with focal brain damage. *Cortex, 14,* 12–21.

Blass, J. P., & Gibson, G. E. (1979). Carbohydrates and acetylcholine synthesis: Implications for cognitive disorders. In K. L. Davis & P. A. Berger (Eds.), *Brain acetylcholine and neuropsychiatric disease* (pp. 215–236). New York: Plenum Press.

Brierley, J. B. (1977). Neuropathology of amnesic states. In C. W. M. Whitty & O. L. Zangwill (Eds.), *Amnesia.* London: Butterworths.

Brizzee, K. R., Ordy, J. M., Knox, C., & Jirge, S. K. (1980). Morphology in the aging brain. In G. Maletta & F. Pirozzolo (Eds.), *The aging nervous system* (pp. 10–39). New York: Praeger.

Brooks, D. N. (1976). Wechsler Memory Scale performance and its relationship to brain damage after severe closed head injury. *Journal of Neurology, Neurosurgery, and Psychiatry, 39,* 593–601.

Brownell, H. H., Michel, D., Powelson, J., & Gardner, H. (1983). Surprise but not coherence: Sensitivity to verbal humor in right-hemisphere patients. *Brain and Language, 18,* 20–27.

Buchsbaum, M. S., Ingvar, D. H., Kessler, R., Waters, R. N., Cappelletti, J., van Kammen, D. P., King, A. C., Johnson, J. L., Manning, R. G., Flynn, R. W., Mann, L. S., Bunney, W. E., & Sokoloff, L. (1982). Cerebral glucography with positron tomography. *Archives of General Psychiatry, 39,* 251–259.

Buschke, H. (1973). Selective reminding for analysis of memory and learning. *Journal of Verbal Learning and Verbal Behavior, 12,* 543–550.

Butters, N. (1979). Amnesic disorders. In K. M. Heilman & E. Valenstein (Eds.), *Clinical neuropsychology* (pp. 439–474). New York: Oxford University Press.

Butters, N. (1983, August). Clinical aspects of memory disorders: Contributions from experimental studies of amnesia and dementia. Paper presented at the 91st Annual Convention of the American Psychological Association, Anaheim, CA.

Butters, N., & Albert, M. S. (1982). Processes underlying failures to recall remote events. In L. S. Cermak (Ed.), *Human memory and amnesia* (pp. 257–274). Hillsdale, NJ: Erlbaum.

Butters, N., Tarlow, S., Cermak, L. S., & Sax, D. (1976). A comparison of the information processing deficits of patients with Huntington's chorea and Korsakoff's syndrome. *Cortex, 12,* 134–144.

Carlen, P. L., Wilkinson, D. A., Wortzman, G., Holgate, R., Cordingley, J., Lee, M. A., Huzar, L., Moddel, G., Singh R., Kiraly, L., & Rankin, J. G. (1981). Cerebral atrophy and functional deficits in alcoholics without clinically apparent liver disease. *Neurology, 31,* 377–385.

Cavalli, M., De Renzi, E., Faglioni, P., & Vitale, A. (1981). Impairment of right-brain-damaged patients on a linguistic cognitive task. *Cortex, 17,* 545–556.

Cermak, L. S., & Tarlow, S. (1978). Aphasic and amnesic patients' verbal vs. nonverbal retentive abilities. *Cortex, 14,* 32–40.

Chase, T. N., Foster, N. L., Fedio, P., DiChiro, G., Brooks, R., & Patronas, N. J. (1983). Alzheimer's disease: Local cerebral metabolism studies using the F18-Fluoro-deoxyglucose-positron emission tomography technique. *Aging of the Brain,* pp. 143–154.

Cohen, N. J., & Squire, L. R. (1980). Preserved learning and retention of pattern analyzing skill in amnesia: Dissociation of knowing how and knowing that. *Science, 210,* 207–209.

Cohn, R., Neumann, M. A., & Wood, D. H. (1977). Prosopagnosia: A clinicopathological study. *Annals of Neurology, 1,* 177–182.

Corsi, P. M. (1972). *Human memory and the medial temporal region of the brain.* Unpublished PhD thesis, McGill University, cited in Milner, B. (1974). Hemispheric specialization: Scope and limits. In F. O. Schmitt & F. G. Worden (Eds.), *The neurosciences: Third study program.* Cambridge, MA: MIT Press.

Cremonini, W., De Renzi, E., & Faglioni, P. (1980). Contrasting performance of right- and left-hemisphere patients on short-term and long-term sequential visual memory. *Neuropsychologia, 18,* 1–9.

Damasio, A. R., Damasio, H., & Van Hoesen, G. W. (1982). Prosopagnosia: Anatomic basis and behavioral mechanisms. *Neurology, 32,* 331–341.

Delaney, R. C., Rosen, A. J., Mattson, R. H., & Novelly, R. A. (1980). Memory function in focal epilepsy: A comparison of non-surgical, unilateral temporal lobe and frontal lobe samples. *Cortex, 16,* 103–117.

de Leon, M. J., Ferris, S. H., Blau, I., George, A. E., Reisberg, B., Kricheff, I. I., & Gershon, S. (1979, October 20). Correlations between CT changes and behavioral deficits in senile dementia. *Lancet,* 859–860.

De Renzi, E., Faglioni, P., & Previdi, P. (1977). Spatial memory and hemispheric locus of lesion. *Cortex, 13,* 424–433.

Devaney, K. O., & Johnson, H. A. (1980). Neuron loss in the aging visual cortex of man. *Journal of Gerontology, 35,* 836–841.

Drachman, D. A., & Glosser, G. (1981). Pharmacologic strategies in aging and dementia: The cholinergic hypothesis. In T. Crook & S. Gershon (Eds.), *Strategies for the development of an effective treatment for senile dementia* (pp. 35–51). New Canaan, CT: Mark Powley Associates.

Dricker, J., Butters, N., Berman, G., Samuels, I., & Carey, S. (1978). The recognition and encoding of faces by alcoholic Korsakoff and right hemisphere patients. *Neuropsychologia, 16,* 683–695.

Eckardt, M. J., Parker, E. S., Noble, E. P., Feldman, D. J., & Gottschalk, L. A. (1978). Relationship between neuropsychological performance and alcoholic consumption in alcoholics. *Biological Psychiatry, 13,* 551–565.

Erickson, R. C., & Scott, M. L. (1977). Clinical memory testing: A review. *Psychological Bulletin, 84,* 1130–1149.

Farkas, T., Wolf, A. P., Jaeger, J., Brodie, J. D., Christman, D. R., & Fowler, J. S. (1984). Regional brain glucose metabolism in chronic schizophrenia. *Archives of General Psychiatry, 41,* 293–300.

Fedio, P., & Van Buren, J. M. (1975). Memory and perceptual deficits during electrical stimulation in the left and right thalamus and parietal subcortex. *Brain and Language, 2,* 78–100.

Ferris, S. H., de Leon, M. J., Wolf, A. P., Farkas, T., Christman, D. R., Reisberg, B., Fowler, J. S., MacGregor, R., Goldman, A., George, A. E., & Rampal, S. (1980). Positron emission tomography in the study of aging and senile dementia. *Neurobiology of Aging, 1,* 127–131.

Fried, I., Mateer, C., Ojemann, G., Wohns, R., & Fedio, P. (1982). Organization of visuospatial functions in human cortex: Evidence from electrical stimulation. *Brain, 105,* 349–371.

Friedland, R. P., Budinger, T. F., Ganz, E., Yano, Y., Mathis, C. A., Koss, B., Ober, B. A., Huesman, B. H., & Derenzo, S. E. (1983). Regional cerebral metabolic alterations in dementia of the Alzheimer type: Positron emission tomography with F18-Fluorodeoxyglucose. *Journal of Computer Assisted Tomography, 7,* 590–598.

Gado, M., Hughes, C. P., Danziger, W., & Chi, D. (1983). Aging, dementia, and brain atrophy: A longitudinal computed tomographic study. *American Journal of Neuroscience Research, 4,* 699–702.

Gainotti, G., Caltagirone, C., & Miceli, G. (1978). Immediate visual-spatial memory in hemisphere-damaged patients: Impairment of verbal coding and of perceptual processing: *Neuropsychologia, 16,* 501–507.

Gazzaniga, M. S. (1983). Right hemisphere language following brain bisection: A 20-year perspective. *American Psychologist, 38*(5), 525–537.

Gilbert, J. G., Levee, R. F., & Catalano, F. L. (1968). A preliminary report on a new memory scale. *Perceptual and Motor Skills, 27,* 277–278.

Gordon, W. P. (1983). Memory disorders in aphasia. I. Auditory immediate recall. *Neuropsychologia, 21,* 325–339.

Hanson, W. R., Riege, W. H., Metter, E. J., & Inman, V. W. (1982). Factor-derived categories of chronic aphasia. *Brain and Language, 15,* 369–380.

Haug, H., Barmwater, U., Eggers, R., Fischer, D., Kuehl, S., & Sass, N. L. (1983). Anatomical changes in aging brain: Morphometric analysis of the human prosencephalon. In J. Cervos-Navarro & H. I. Sarkander (Eds.), *Brain aging: Neuropathology and neuropharmacology* (pp. 1–12). New York: Raven Press.

Hawkins, R. A., Mazziotta, J. C., Phelps, M. E., Huang, S. C., Kuhl, D. E., Carson, R. E., Metter, E. J., & Riege, W. H. (1983). Cerebral glucose metabolism as a function of age in man: Influence of the rate constants in the Fluorodeoxyglucose method. *Journal of Cerebral Blood Flow and Metabolism, 3,* 250–253.

Haxby, J., Lundgren, S., & Marley, G. (1983). Short-term retention of verbal, visual shape and visuospatial location information in normal and amnesic subjects. *Neuropsychologia, 21,* 25–33.

Hecaen, H., & Albert, M. L. (Eds.). (1978). *Human neuropsychology.* New York: Wiley.

Hecaen, H., Tzortzis, C., & Rondot, P. (1980). Loss of memory with learning deficits. *Cortex, 16,* 525–542.

Heilman, K. M., & Sypert, G. (1977). Korsakoff's syndrome resulting from bilateral fornix lesions. *Neurology, 27,* 490–493.

Heilman, K. M., & Valenstein, E. (Eds.). (1979). *Clinical neuropsychology.* New York: Oxford University Press.

Hillyard, S. A., & Woods, D. L. (1979). Electrophysiological analysis of human brain function. In M. S. Gazzaniga (Ed.), *Handbook of behavioral neurobiology: Vol. 2,* (pp. 345–378). New York: Plenum Press.

Hirst, W. (1982). The amnesic syndrome: Descriptions and explanations. *Psychological Bulletin, 91,* 435–460.

Horel, J. A. (1978). The neuroanatomy of amnesia: A critique of the hippocampal memory hypothesis. *Brain, 101,* 403–445.

Huppert, F. A., & Piercy, M. (1979). Normal and abnormal forgetting in organic amnesia: Effect of locus of lesion. *Cortex, 15,* 385–390.

Inglis, J., Ruckman, M., Lawson, J. S., MacLean, A. W., & Monga, T. N. (1982). Sex differences in the cognitive effects of unilateral brain damage. *Cortex, 18,* 257–275.

Ingvar, D. H., & Franzen, G. (1974). Abnormalities in cerebral blood flow distribution in patients with chronic schizophrenia. *Acta Neurologica Scandinavica, 50,* 425–462.

Jackson, H. J. (1874). On the nature and duality of the brain. *Medical Press and Circular, 1,* 19–41.

Jones-Gotman, M., & Milner, B. (1978). Right temporal-lobe contribution to image-mediated verbal learning. *Neuropsychologia, 16,* 61–71.

Kahn, E. A., & Crosby, E. C. (1972). Korsakoff's syndrome associated with surgical lesions involving the mammillary bodies. *Neurology, 22,* 117–125.

Kertesz, A. (1979). Recovery and treatment. In K. M. Heilman & E. Valenstein. (Eds.), *Clinical neuropsychology* (pp. 503–534). New York: Oxford University Press.

Kertesz, A. (Ed.). (1983). *Localization in neuropsychology.* New York: Academic Press.

Kim, Y., Royer, F., Bonstelle, C., & Boller, F. (1980). Temporal sequencing of verbal and nonverbal materials: The effect of laterality of lesion. *Cortex, 16,* 135–143.

Kolb, B., & Whishaw, I. (1980). *Fundamentals of human neuropsychology.* San Francisco: Freeman.

Kuhl, D. E., Metter, E. J., Riege, W. H., Hawkins, R. A., Mazziotta, J. C., Phelps, M. E., & Kling, A. S. (1983). Local cerebral glucose utilization in elderly patients with depression, multiple infarct dementia, and Alzheimer's disease. *Journal of Cerebral Blood Flow and Metabolism, 3*(Suppl. 1), S494–S495.

Kuhl, D. E., Metter, E. J., Riege, W. H., & Phelps, M. E. (1982). Effects of human aging on patterns of local cerebral glucose utilization determined by the F18-Fluorodeoxyglucose method. *Journal of Cerebral Blood Flow and Metabolism, 2,* 163–171.

Kuhl, D. E., Phelps, M. E., Kowell, A. P., Metter, E. J., Selin, C., & Winter, J. (1980). Effects of stroke on local cerebral metabolism and perfusion: Mapping by emission computed tomography of 18FDG and 13NH3. *Annals of Neurology, 8,* 47–60.

Kuhl, D. E., Phelps, M. E., Markham, C. M., Metter, E. J., Riege, W. H., & Winter, J. (1982). Cerebral metabolism and atrophy in Huntington's disease determined by 18FDG and computed tomographic scan. *Annals of Neurology, 12,* 425–434.

Lammertsma, A. A., Frackowiak, R. S. J., Lenzi, G. L., Heather, J. D., Pozzilli, C., & Jones, T. (1981). Accuracy of the oxygen-15 steady state technique for measuring CBF and CMR02. *Journal of Cerebral Blood Flow and Metabolism, 1,* S3-S4.

Lassen, N. A., Ingvar, D. H., & Skimhoj, E. (1978). Brain functions and blood flow. *Scientific American, 239,* 62–71.

Lhermitte, F., & Signoret, J.-L. (1976). The amnesic syndromes and the hippocampal-mammillary system. In M. R. Rosenzweig & E. L. Bennett (Eds.), *Neuronal mechanisms of learning and memory* (pp. 49–56). Cambridge, MA: MIT Press.

Luria, A. R. (1973). *The working brain. An introduction to neuropsychology.* New York: Basic Books.

Luria, A. R. (1976). *The neuropsychology of memory.* Washington, DC: V. H. Winston.

McGlone, J. (1978). Sex differences in functional brain asymmetry. *Cortex, 14,* 122–128.

Mesulam, M. M. (1981). A cortical network for directed attention and unilateral neglect. *Annals of Neurology, 10,* 309–325.

Metter, E. J., Riege, W. H., Hanson, W. R., Kuhl, D. E., Phelps, M. E., Squire, L. R., Wasterlain, C. G., & Benson, D. F. (1983). Comparison of metabolic rates, language, and memory in subcortical aphasias. *Brain and Language, 19,* 33–47.

Metter, E. J., Riege, W. H., Hanson, W., Phelps, M. E., & Kuhl, D. E. (1981). Correlation of metabolic and language abnormalities in aphasia. *Annals of Neurology, 10,* 102.

Metter, E. J., Riege, W. H., Kameyama, M., Kuhl, D. E., & Phelps, M. E. (1984). Cerebral metabolic relationships for selected brain regions in Alzheimer's, Huntington's, and Parkinson's diseases. *Journal of Cerebral Blood Flow and Metabolism, 4,* 500–506.

Metter, E. J., Riege, W. H., Kuhl, D. E., & Phelps, M. E. (1982). Relation among measures of local cerebral glucose utilization in healthy adults. *Neuroscience Abstracts, 8,* 917.

Metter, E. J., Riege, W. H., Kuhl, D. E., & Phelps, M. E. (1983). Differences in regional glucose metabolic intercorrelations with aging. *Journal of Cerebral Blood Flow and Metabolism, 3*(Suppl. 1), S482–S483.

Metter, E. J., Wasterlain, C. G., Kuhl, D. E., Hanson, W. R., & Phelps, M. E. (1981). 18FDG positron computed tomography: A study of aphasia. *Annals of Neurology, 10,* 173–183.

Miceli, G., Caltagirone, C., Gainotti, G., Masullo, C., & Silveri, M. C. (1981). Neuropsychological correlates of localized cerebral lesions in non-aphasic brain-damaged patients. *Journal of Clinical Neuropsychology, 3,* 53–63.

Milner, B. (1971). Interhemispheric differences in the localization of psychological processes in man. *British Medical Bulletin, 27,* 272–277.

Milner, B. (1982). Some cognitive effects of frontal-lobe lesions in man. *Philosophical Transactions of the Royal Society of London,* Series B, *298,* 211–226.

Mishkin, M. (1978). Memory in monkeys severely impaired by combined but not by separate removal of amygdala and hippocampus. *Nature, 273,* 297–298.

Moscovitch, M. (1979). Information processing and the cerebral hemispheres. In M. S. Gazzaniga (Ed.), *Handbook of behavioral neurobiology: Vol. 2, Neuropsychology* (pp. 379–446). New York: Plenum Press.

Moscovitch, M. (1982). Multiple dissociations of function in amnesia. In L. S. Cermak (Ed.), *Human memory and amnesia* (pp. 337–370). Hillsdale, NJ: Erlbaum.

Nauta, W. J. H. (1972). Neural associations of the frontal cortex. *Acta Neurobiologica Experimentia, 32,* 125–140.

Ojemann, G. (1982). Interrelationships in the localization of language, memory, and motor mechanisms in human cortex and thalamus. In R. A. Thompson & J. R. Green (Eds.), *New perspectives in cerebral localization.* New York: Raven Press.

Ojemann, G., & Mateer, C. (1979). Human language cortex: Localization of memory, syntax, and sequential motor-phoneme identification systems. *Science, 205,* 1401–1402.

Parsons, O. A., & Leber, W. R. (1981). The relationship between cognitive dysfunction and brain damage in alcoholics: Causal, interactive, or epiphenomenal. *Alcoholism: Clinical and Experimental Research, 5,* 326–343.

Petrides, M., & Milner, B. (1982). Deficits of subject-ordered tasks after frontal- and temporal-lobe lesions in man. *Neuropsychologia, 20,* 249–262.

Phelps, M. E., Hoffman, E. J., Mullani, N. A., & Ter-Pogossian, M. M. (1975). Application of annihilation coincidence detection to transaxial reconstruction tomography. *Journal of Nuclear Medicine, 16,* 210–224.

Phelps, M. E., Huang, S. C., Hoffman, E. J., Selin, S. C., Sokoloff, L., & Kuhl, D. E. (1979). Tomographic measurement of local cerebral metabolic rate in humans with (F-18) 2-fluoro-2-deoxyglucose: Validation of method. *Annals of Neurology, 6,* 371–388.

Phelps, M. E., Kuhl, D. E., & Mazziotta, J. C. (1981). Metabolic mapping of the brain's response to visual stimulation: Studies in humans. *Science, 211,* 1445–1448.

Prigatano, G. P. (1978). Wechsler Memory Scale: A selective review of the literature. *Archives of the Behavioral Sciences, 54,* 3–19.

Prigatano, G. P., & Pribram, K. (1982). Perception and memory of facial affect following brain injury. *Perceptual and Motor Skills, 54,* 859–869.

Raichle, M. E. (1982). Positron emission tomography. In R. A. Thompson & J. R. Green (Eds.), *New perspectives in cerebral localization.* New York: Raven Press.

Randt, C. T., Brown, E. R., & Osborne, D. P., Jr. (1980). A memory test for longitudinal measurement of mild to moderate deficits. *Clinical Neuropsychology, 2,* 184–194.

Riege, W. H. (1977). Inconstant nonverbal recognition memory in Korsakoff patients and controls. *Neuropsychologia, 15,* 269–276.

Riege, W. H., Holloway, J. A., & Kaplan, D. W. (1981). Specific memory deficits associated with prolonged alcohol abuse. *Alcoholism: Clinical and Experimental Research, 5,* 378–385.

Riege, W. H., & Inman, V. (1981). Age differences in nonverbal memory tasks. *Journal of Gerontology, 36,* 51–58.

Riege, W. H., Klane, L. T., Metter, E. J., & Hanson, W. R. (1982). Decision speed and bias after unilateral stroke. *Cortex, 18,* 345–355.

Riege, W. H., Metter, E. J., Kuhl, D. E., Hawkins, R. A., & Phelps, M. E. (1982). Multivariate memory and local cerebral glucose metabolism in human aging. *The Gerontologist, 22*(5), 131.

Riege, W. H., Metter, E. J., Kuhl, D. E., & Phelps, M. E. (1983). Brain glucose metabolism and memory functions: Age differences in factor scores. *The Gerontologist, 23,* 264.

Riege, W. H., Metter, E. J., Kuhl, D. E., Phelps, M. E., & Kling, A. S. (1984). PET with F-18 Fluorodeoxyglucose measures of local brain activity and memory in schizophrenia and in depression. *Journal of Nuclear Medicine, 25,* 57.

Riege, W. H., Metter, E. J., & Williams, M. V. (1980). Age and hemispheric asymmetry in nonverbal tactual memory. *Neuropsychologia, 18,* 707–710.

Riege, W. H., Tomaszewski, R., Lanto, A., & Metter, E. J. (1984). Age and alcoholism: Independent memory decrements. *Alcoholism: Clinical and Experimental Research, 8*(1), 42–47.

Ron, M. A., Acker, W., & Lishman, W. A. (1982). Morphological abnormalities in the brains of chronic alcoholics: A clinical, psychological and computerized axial tomographic study. *Brain, 105,* 497–514.

Ryan, C. (1982). Alcoholism and premature aging: A neuropsychological perspective. *Alcoholism: Clinical and Experimental Research, 6,* 22–30.

Ryan, C., Butters, N., Montgomery, K., Adinolfi, A., & DiDario, B. (1980). Memory deficits in chronic alcoholics: Continuities between the "intact" alcoholic and the alcoholic Korsakoff patient. In H. Begleiter & B. Kissin (Eds.), *Biological Effects of Alcohol.* New York: Plenum Press.

Schoenfeld, T. A., & Hamilton, L. W. (1977). Secondary brain changes following lesions: A new paradigm for lesion experimentation. *Physiology and Behavior, 18,* 951–967.

Schwartz, R., Shipkin, D., & Cermak, L. S. (1979). Verbal and nonverbal memory abilities of adult brain-damaged patients. *The American Journal of Occupational Therapy, 33,* 79–83.

Scoville, W. B., & Milner, B. (1957). Loss of recent memory after bilateral hippocampal lesions. *Journal of Neurology, Neurosurgery, and Psychiatry, 20,* 11–21.

Sergent, J. (1984). Inferences from unilateral brain-damage about normal hemispheric functions in visual pattern recognition. *Psychological Bulletin, 96,* 99–115.

Smith, A. D. (1975). Aging and interference with memory. *Journal of Gerontology, 30,* 319–325.

Smith, M. L., & Milner, B. (1981). The role of the right hippocampus in the recall of spatial location. *Neuropsychologia, 19,* 781–793.

Squire, L. R. (1981). Two forms of human amnesia: An analysis of forgetting. *Journal of Neuroscience, 1,* 635–640.

Squire, L. R. (1982). The neuropsychology of human memory. *Annual Review of Neurosciences, 5,* 241–273.

Squire, L. R., & Moore, R. Y. (1979). Dorsal thalamic lesion in a noted case of chronic memory dysfunction. *Annals of Neurology, 6,* 503–506.

Squire, L. R., & Slater, P. C. (1978). Anterograde and retrograde memory impairment in chronic amnesia. *Neuropsychologia, 16,* 313–322.

Teuber, H.-L., Milner, B., & Vaughan, H. G. (1968). Persistent anterograde amnesia after stab wound of the basal brain. *Neuropsychologia. 6,* 267–282.

Van Lancker, D., & Canter, G. J. (1982). Impairment of voice and face recognition in patients with hemispheric damage. *Brain and Cognition, 1,* 185–195.

Victor, M., Adams, R. D., & Collins, G. H. (1971). *The Wernicke-Korsakoff Syndrome.* Philadelphia: F. A. Davis.

Vilkki, J., & Laitinen, L. V. (1976). Effects of pulvinotomy and ventrolateral thalamotomy on some cognitive functions. *Neuropsychologia, 14,* 67–78.

Wapner, W., Hamby, S., & Gardner, H. (1981). The role of the right hemisphere in the apprehension of complex linguistic materials. *Brain and Language, 14,* 15–33.

Warrington, E. K., & Weiskrantz, L. (1982). Amnesia: A disconnection syndrome? *Neuropsychologia, 20,* 233–248.

Waugh, N. C., & Norman, D. A. (1965). Primary memory. *Psychological Review, 72,* 89–104.

Wechsler, D. (1945). A standardized memory scale for clinical use. *Journal of Psychology, 19,* 87–95.

Wechsler, D. (1955). *Manual for the Wechsler Adult Intelligence Scale.* New York: Psychological Corporation.

Weingartner, H., Grafman, J., Boutelle, W., Kaye, W., & Martin, P. R. (1983). Forms of memory failure. *Science, 221*(4608), 380–382.

Weiskrantz, L. (1978). A comparison of hippocampal pathology in man and other animals. In *Functions of the septo-hippocampal system,* CIBA Foundation Symposium 58. Oxford: Elsevier.

Wetzel, C. D., & Squire, L. R. (1980). Encoding in anterograde amnesia. *Neuropsychologia, 18,* 177–184.

Whitehouse, P. J. (1981). Imagery and verbal encoding in left and right hemisphere damaged patients. *Brain and Language, 14,* 315–332.

Wieser, H. G., & Yasargil, M. G. (1982). Selective amygdalohippocampectomy as a surgical treatment of mesiobasal limbic epilepsy. *Surgical Neurology, 17,* 445–457.

Wilkins, A., & Moscovitch, M. (1978). Selective impairment of semantic memory after temporal lobectomy. *Neuropsychologia, 16,* 73–79.

Woolsey, R. M., & Nelson, J. S. (1975). Asymptomatic destruction of the fornix in man. *Archives of Neurology, 32,* 566–568.

Zaidel, D. W., & Rausch, R. (1981). Effects of semantic organization on the recognition of pictures following temporal lobectomy. *Neuropsychologia, 19,* 813–817.

Zaidel, E. (1982). Disconnection syndrome as a model for laterality effects in the normal brain. In J. Hellige (Ed.), *Cerebral hemisphere asymmetry: Method, theory, and application.* New York: Praeger.

Zaidel, E. (1983). A response to Gazzaniga: Language in the right hemisphere, convergent perspectives. *American Psychologist, 38*(5), 542–546.

Zola-Morgan, S., Squire, L. R., & Mishkin, M. (1982). The neuroanatomy of amnesia: Amygdala-hippocampus versus temporal stem. *Science, 218,* 1337–1339.

Nelson Butters, Maryann Martone, Betsy White, Eric Granholm, and Jessica Wolfe

CHAPTER

34

Clinical Validators: Comparisons of Demented and Amnesic Patients

Recent investigations have demonstrated that the memory disorders of patients with alcoholic Korsakoff's syndrome (AKS) and of demented patients with Huntington's Disease (HD) involve different underlying cognitive processes. Although the AKS and HD patients' performances on recall tests are often quantitatively similar, the two patient groups differ in their sensitivity to proactive interference (PI), in their acquisition of procedural or skill learning, and in recognition memory. The AKS patients' deficits involve a preserved capacity to acquire skills, poor recognition memory, and an increased sensitivity to PI. In contrast, HD patients demonstrate deficits in skill learning, relatively intact recognition memory, and no increments in sensitivity to PI. It is concluded that the memory deficiencies of HD involve a failure to initiate efficient search strategies to recall stored information.

Introduction

Even fledgling clinical neuropsychologists know that memory disorders are ubiquitous after brain damage and that standardized tests exist for documenting the presence and severity of these memory deficits. Severe impairments in the learning of new information and in the recall of public and personal events from the remote past occur after head trauma, long-term alcohol abuse, strokes, encephalitis, and bilateral ECT and are also an early sign of progressive dementing illnesses. Tests such as the Wechsler Memory Scale (Wechsler, 1945) and the Benton Visual Retention Test (Benton, 1974) have proven to be valuable but not perfect tools for the assessment of these problems.

Despite this awareness of memory impairments, most neuropsychologists have been insensitive to the multidimensional nature of the symptoms. Usually implicitly, but sometimes explicitly, neuropsychologists have assumed that all debilitating memory deficits, regardless of etiology, may be treated as a single symptom or cognitive problem. Amnesic patients with bilateral hippocampal lesions and patients with medial diencephalic damage have often been treated as two exemplars of a single underlying clinical entity. In recent years this situation has changed as evidence has accumulated that the amnesias are as heterogeneous as the aphasias and the apraxias (for review, see Butters & Miliotis, 1985; Butters, Miliotis, Albert, & Sax, 1984; Squire, 1981, 1982). On the basis of studies from several laboratories, it now appears that there are important qualitative differences among the anterograde and retrograde memory deficits of various neurological populations. Although failures in retention and recall following diencephalic and hippocampal lesions may have some superficial similarities, close scrutiny has shown these amnesic populations to have distinctive patterns of deficits when a broad range of memory capacities is assessed. Similarly, direct comparisons of the memory deficits of amnesic and demented patients have uncovered differences that may be of some importance in making prognostic and rehabilitative judgments and in future attempts to evaluate the decline in memory associated with normal aging.

The main purpose of this chapter is to emphasize the differences between the memory disorders of amnesic patients with alcoholic Korsakoff's syndrome (AKS) and demented patients with Huntington's Disease (HD). We wish not only to convince the readers of the clinical importance of a thorough memory assessment

The studies reported in this chapter were supported by funds from the Medical Research Service of the Veterans Administration, by NIAAA Grant AA00187 to Boston University, by NINCDS Grant NS16367 to Massachusetts General Hospital, and by NIA Grant AG02269 to Beth Israel Hospital.

but also to illuminate the ongoing symbiotic relationship between experimental and clinical neuropsychology. The discovery that memory tests are among the most sensitive psychometric instruments for distinguishing among various patient populations and for the early diagnosis of dementing illnesses has evolved from basic research into brain–behavior relationships.

The AKS patients to be discussed in this chapter were male veterans with a mean age of approximately 55 years. They all had 20-to-30-year histories of alcohol addiction accompanied by malnutrition prior to the onset of their AKS. At the time of testing, all of the AKS patients were residing in a Veterans Administration facility or nursing home. They had severe anterograde and retrograde amnesias, as measured by the Wechsler Memory Scale (WMS) and on the basis of clinical assessment, but their general intellectual functioning, as measured by the Wechsler Adult Intelligence Scale (WAIS), was within normal limits (mean = 101). Their MQs (mean = 78) were a minimum of 18 points lower than their full-scale IQs. According to the neuropathological reports of Victor, Adams, and Collins (1971), the AKS patient's severe amnesia is related to hemorrhagic lesions in the medial diencephalon (i.e., the dorsomedial nucleus of the thalamus and the mammillary bodies).

The patients with Huntington's Disease (HD) have a genetically transmitted disorder that results in a progressive atrophy of the basal ganglia, especially the caudate nucleus. The most common behavioral symptoms include involuntary choreiform movements and a progressive dementia in which severe memory problems form an integral part of a broader intellectual decline (Caine, Ebert, & Weingartner, 1977; Weingartner, Caine, & Ebert, 1979). Approximately 70% of the HD patients described in the present chapter were men. In most cases, personality changes (e.g., increased irritability, depression) and complaints of forgetfulness were apparent at the time of diagnosis. These HD patients had a mean age of 45 years and had been diagnosed 3 months to 19 years (mean = 9 years) prior to testing. The median full-scale IQ (WAIS) and MQ (WMS) of these patients were in the middle 80s and high 70s, respectively. Although many of the HD patients had moderate-to-severe choreiform movements, very few were institutionalized and none were considered to be in the terminal stages of the illness.

Comparisons of the Memory Disorders of Patients With Huntington's Disease and Patients With Alcoholic Korsakoff's Syndrome

Severe memory disorders are not unique to amnesic patients. In fact, complaints about memory (anterograde and retrograde) are among the first symptoms of progressive dementing disorders (Miller, 1977). The major difference between pure amnesia and progressive dementia is that the memory loss of the demented patient is part of a general loss of cognitive capacities.

Although the amnesic patient's IQ usually remains within the normal range despite a severely impaired memory quotient, both the IQ and the MQ of the demented patient decline progressively as the illness advances (Butters, Sax, Montgomery, & Tarlow, 1978).

Several studies comparing the memory disorders of amnesic patients with AKS patients and of demented patients with HD patients have indicated that the anterograde and retrograde memory deficits of these two patient populations are distinguishable (Albert, Butters, & Brandt, 1981a, 1981b; Biber, Butters, Rosen, Gerstman, & Mattis, 1981; Butters & Grady, 1977; Butters, Tarlow, Cermak, & Sax, 1976; Meudell, Butters, & Montgomery, 1978; Oscar-Berman & Zola-Morgan, 1980a, 1980b). Because most of these investigations have been reviewed in detail elsewhere (Butters, Albert, & Sax, 1979; Butters & Cermak, 1980), we discuss them briefly and then concentrate more fully on some recent findings concerned with pictorial memory, with differences between the learning of declarative and the learning of procedural information, with recall versus recognition memory, and with semantic memory. It should be evident from this presentation that the memory impairments of HD and AKS patients involve different underlying processes and that our conception of the demented HD patients' deficits has undergone a natural evolution over the years. Although our initial studies led us to suggest that storage problems were the primary processes involved in the HD patients' memory failures, the results of several investigations completed during the past several years have demonstrated that retrieval deficits are perhaps the most important factors in the HD patients' learning and retentive difficulties.

Sensitivity to Interference

In our initial studies, the abilities of HD and AKS patients to retain information in short-term storage were compared using the Peterson distractor technique (Peterson & Peterson, 1959). On each trial the subjects were read or shown verbal stimuli (i.e., consonant trigrams, like *JZD*, or word triads, such as *neck-chair-belt*) and then asked to count backwards by 3s until the examiner said "stop." After 0, 3, 9, or 18 seconds of such counting (i.e., distraction), the examiner stopped the subjects and asked them to recall the stimulus material that had just been presented. It was found that although the HD patients performed as poorly as did the AKS patients after 3-, 9-, and 18-second delays, only the AKS patients' impaired recall was affected by proactive interference, rehearsal time, and encoding (Butters et al., 1976; Butters & Grady, 1977; Meudell et al., 1978). Manipulations of proactive interference (PI) and rehearsal time (i.e., time between the end of stimulus presentation and the beginning of the counting task) improved the AKS patients' performance on distractor tasks, whereas such changes in experimental conditions had virtually no effect upon the HD patients' ability to recall materials presented 9 or 18 seconds previously. Although the results of these investigations did not reveal the specific nature of the HD patients' anterograde memory deficits, they did suggest that these patients have difficulty storing new information (i.e., a deficit in consolidation). The HD patients' failure to improve with low proactive interference (PI) conditions and with increased time for rehearsal suggested that HD patients may lack some of the neuroanatomical structures necessary for consolidating and storing new information.

Oscar-Berman and Zola-Morgan have compared AKS and HD patients on a series of visual and spatial discrimination tasks. In an initial experiment (Oscar-Berman & Zola-Morgan, 1980a), visual and spatial reversal learning tests were administered. The AKS patients were impaired on both types of reversal problems, whereas the HD patients had difficulty only with the visual reversals. An inspection of the types of errors made on the visual reversal tasks suggested that the HD and AKS patients' deficiencies involved different learning, cognitive, and motivational mechanisms. In a second experiment (Oscar-Berman & Zola-Morgan, 1980b), the AKS and HD patients learned a series of two-choice simultaneous and concurrent pattern discriminations. Again, both patient groups were impaired, but they differed in the nature of their deficits. The HD patients were equally impaired on simultaneous and the concurrent discriminations, whereas the AKS patients encountered more difficulty with the concurrent than with the simultaneous tests. In summarizing their findings, Oscar-Berman and Zola-Morgan (1980b) suggested that, although both groups of patients were deficient in their ability to form stimulus–reinforcement associations, the AKS but not the HD patients' deficiencies also involved an increased sensitivity to proactive interference and a lack of sensitivity to reinforcement contingencies.

Retrograde Amnesia

To determine whether the HD patients also differ from the AKS patients in their ability to recall people and public events from the remote past, Albert, Butters, and Levin's (1979) remote memory battery was administered to AKS and HD patients (Albert et al., 1981a; Butters & Albert, 1982). As shown in Figure 34-1, the AKS patients had a severe impairment in their ability to recall remote memories. Although this deficiency included all periods of their lives, it was characterized by a temporal gradient in which the AKS patients' most remote memories (e.g., from the 1930s and 1940s) were relatively preserved. Like the AKS patients, the HD patients were severely impaired in their ability to identify famous people and to recall public events, but their retrograde amnesia was not characterized by a temporal gradient in which famous faces and public events from the 1930s and 1940s were relatively spared. That is, the HD patients had as much difficulty identifying faces and events from the 1930s and 1940s as faces and events from the 1960s and 1970s. Wilson, Kaszniak, and Fox's (1981) report of very similar results for patients with senile dementia of the Alzhei-

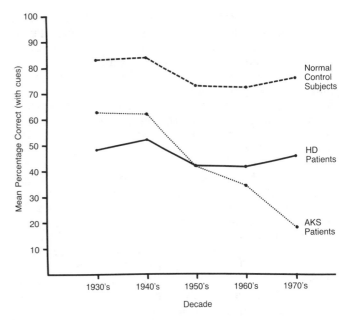

Figure 34-1. Performance of patients with AKS, patients with HD, and normal control subjects on the Famous Faces Test. Adapted from Butters (1984) by permission.

mer type suggests that flat retrograde amnesias may be associated with a number of dementing illnesses.

In a second study, Albert et al. (1981b) compared the performances of patients with advanced HD (diagnosed 3 to 7 years prior to testing) and patients with recently diagnosed HD (less than 12 months prior to testing) on a remote memory battery. The recently diagnosed HD patients, who showed only a mild cognitive loss at this early stage of the disease, had a retrograde amnesia that was quantitatively less severe than, but qualitatively similar to, that of the advanced patients. Like the advanced HD patients, the recently diagnosed HD patients' impairments in the identification of remote events and famous faces extended equally over all decades of their lives. On the basis of these results for the recently diagnosed HD patients, Albert et al. (1981b) concluded that the flat retrograde amnesia that seems to characterize all stages of the disease cannot be attributed to the dementing process per se. They also noted that the equal loss of remote memories over all time periods sampled was consistent with the thesis that these patients have a storage deficit affecting both the consolidation of new memory traces and the maintenance of memories formed prior to the onset of the disease.

Memory for Faces and Pictures

Biber et al. (1981) used an orientation procedure in an attempt to improve the HD and AKS patients' memory for faces. Bower and Karlin (1974) reported that requiring normal subjects to make global-evaluative judgments (e.g., likability) about a face prompted a thorough analysis of facial features, which, in turn, resulted in improved recognition. In contrast, requiring normal subjects to judge some isolated facial features (e.g., straightness of hair) supposedly leads to a limited, inadequate analysis of facial features and ultimately to poor recognition performance. When Biber et al. (1981) administered these "high-level" and "low-level" orientation tasks to HD and AKS patients, they found that only the AKS patients showed a significant improvement in face recognition after being required to judge the likability of the faces. The HD patients' recognition deficit was unaffected by the nature of the orientation task.

The results of the Biber et al. investigation are consistent with the conclusions drawn from the previously cited comparisons of the memory disorders of AKS and HD patients. Once again, the AKS patients' impaired memory was aided by a procedure that promotes encoding, whereas the impairments of the demented HD patients remained impervious to the same experimental manipulation. This failure of the HD patients to improve significantly with the high-level orientation task, although not precluding other possible explanations, supported the notion that deficits in storage and consolidation play a vital role in the HD patients' memory problems and perhaps are characteristic of all dementing illnesses.

Four recently completed studies that forced us to alter our conception of the HD patients' memory impairment have uncovered significant cognitive distinctions among patients with HD, Alzheimer's disease (AD), and AKS. In the first of these four investigations, Butters et al. (1983) evaluated the beneficial effects that verbal mediation and labeling might have on the amnesic and demented patients' ability to remember pictorial materials. In the other studies reviewed in this chapter, it was found that manipulations of experimental variables, such as rehearsal time, intertrial rest intervals, and orientation instructions, resulted in improved performance only for AKS patients. However, because HD is a progressive dementia, in which many aspects of language abilities remain relatively intact until the terminal stages of the disease (Butters et al., 1978), the possibility remained that providing HD patients with verbal labels and mediators might reduce their severe difficulties in remembering pictorial stimuli. In view of numerous reports that AKS patients do not encode all of the semantic attributes of verbal material (for review, see Butters & Cermak, 1980), there was reason to believe that verbal mediators would have little impact on their memory problems. Similarly, the very prevalent and severe language impairments that usually accompany AD (Miller, 1977) could eliminate any beneficial consequences that verbal mediators might have on an AD patient's ability to remember pictorial materials.

In this study, Schneidman's (1952) Make a Picture Story (MAPS) test was modified to assess the pictorial memory of HD patients, patients with AD, AKS patients, patients with lesions restricted to the right hemisphere, young-normal control subjects, and old-normal control subjects. Two conditions were employed: a no-story condition followed by a story condition. In the no-story condition, the subjects were shown pictures of six backgrounds (e.g., a raft floating on a large body of water, or a living room) on which three cut-out human or animal figures had been placed. For example, a superman figure, a figure of an angry man, and a figure of a happy little boy were placed on the living room scene. The subjects were instructed to remember the identity and location of the specific figures on each scene and were allowed 30 seconds to study each of the six scenes. Five minutes following the presentation of the sixth scene, the subjects were administered a forced-choice recognition test consisting of 15 pairs of figures. For all 15 pairs, one of the figures had been exposed previously, and the other was a distractor item not previously seen by the subjects. The subjects were required to indicate for each pair which of the two cut-out figures they had seen in one of the previously exposed scenes.

Ten minutes after the recognition test, a picture-context recognition test was administered. The six backgrounds were placed, one at a time, in front of the subjects, and 33 cut-out figures (18 targets and 15 distractors) were distributed symmetrically around the background. The subjects were asked to select from the 33 figures the ones that had been associated with each scene during the original exposure (i.e., learning) trial and to place them on the scene. The examiner recorded the identity of the figures selected, the location of the figures on the backgrounds, and the figures' spatial orientations.

After a 15-minute rest interval, the story condition was administered. Six different background scenes, each with three new cut-out figures, were shown to the subjects. The major difference in procedure was that, during the 30-second study period provided for each picture, the subjects were read a story about the events transpiring in the stimulus scene. Each story related not only what was occurring in the scene but also what had led to the depicted situation and how the situation would be resolved in the immediate future. As in the no-story condition, forced-choice and picture-context recognition tests followed the presentation of the sixth background.

The groups' performances on the forced-choice recognition tests are shown in Figure 34-2. Although for both story and no-story conditions, the patients correctly recognized slightly fewer figures than did the normal control subjects, their performance was considerably better than chance (7.5 correct). Thus, it appeared that amnesic and demented patients could accurately discriminate familiar from unfamiliar figures.

Despite the patients' relatively intact performance on the forced-choice task, their performance on the picture-context test, as seen in Figure 34-3, was severely impaired. A two-way analysis of variance yielded highly significant group, condition (story vs. no-story), and interaction (Group × Condition) effects. In the no-story condition, all four patient groups recognized significantly fewer figures than did the normal control group. Of the four patient groups, the AKS and the AD patients were the most impaired, although there was considerable variability within each patient group in terms of degree of impairment.

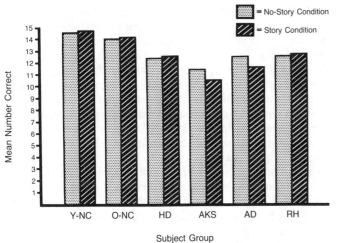

Figure 34-2. Performance results of young-normal control (Y-NC) and old-normal control (O-NC) subjects and four patient subject groups on the forced-choice recognition subtest of the Make a Picture Story (MAPS) test under the story and no-story conditions. Adapted from Butters (1984) by permission.

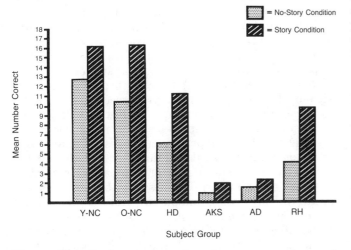

Figure 34-3. Performance results of young-normal control (Y-NC) and old-normal control (O-NC) subjects and four patient subject groups on the picture-context recognition subtest of the Make a Picture Story (MAPS) test under the story and no-story conditions. Adapted from Butters (1984) by permission.

The results for the story condition (Figure 34-3) clearly show that the four patient groups were aided differentially by the presentation of verbal mediators. The recognition scores of the HD and right-hemisphere patients were significantly improved by the recitation of the story, but the recognition scores of the AKS and AD patients appeared to be insensitive to this mnemonic aid. It is important to note that the improvement of the HD and right-hemisphere patients was not due to their superior performance in the no-story condition. When the amount of improvement between the story and no-story conditions was analyzed with a covariance design that statistically corrected for performance in the no-story condition, the HD and right-

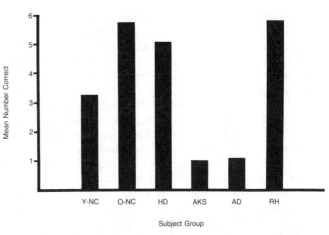

Figure 34-4. Improvement scores of young-normal control (Y-NC) and old-normal control (O-NC) subject groups and four patient subject groups on the Make a Picture Story (MAPS) test. Scores are based on covariance design with performance in the no-story condition as the covariate. Adapted from Butters (1984) by permission.

hemisphere patients continued to demonstrate significantly more improvement than did the other two patient groups (Figure 34-4). Furthermore, no significant correlation was found between performance in the no-story condition and the amount of improvement induced by the story.

The findings of this investigation, especially those relating to the HD and AKS patients, are of special importance because they provide additional legitimacy for other dissociations noted in this chapter. Although the studies of the patients' short-term memory, retrograde amnesia, and memory for faces suggested significant differences between HD and AKS patients, none of them provided the elusive double dissociation needed to firmly establish our claim of qualitative differences in the memory disorders of the two groups. The fact that the AKS, but not the HD, patients were affected by rehearsal time, intertrial rest intervals, and orientation procedures might have been a reflection of the totally debilitating effects of dementia rather than an indicator of qualitative differences in information processing.

In the present study, however, the double dissociation between groups and tasks has been completed. For the first time in our comparative studies of AKS and HD patients, an experimental manipulation (i.e., the introduction of verbal mediators) enhanced the learning performance of the HD patients more than that of the AKS patients. As anticipated on the basis of their lack of aphasic symptoms, the HD patients were able to utilize language cues to facilitate associations between the cut-out figures and specific scenes and thereby improve their contextual memory. Conversely, the AKS patients, who are reputed to have deficits in verbal encoding (see Butters & Cermak, 1980), were unable to utilize the stories in such a beneficial manner. (It has been reported by Winocur and Kinsbourne (1978) that the contextual memory of AKS patients can be improved by increasing the saliency of cues present in the learning environment, but none of the procedures employed by these investigators involved the introduction of verbal mediators.)

Although these findings may support the thesis that demented HD and AKS patients have qualitatively distinct memory deficits, they offer little help in specifying the exact nature of the cognitive disorders. Clearly, our suggestion that HD patients lack the neuroanatomical structures necessary for storing information is untenable in light of this last study. If the HD patients had a storage problem, the introduction of verbal mediators should have been as unsuccessful in improving performance as Biber et al.'s (1981) orientation task and Butters et al.'s (1979) use of increased rehearsal times and intertrial rest intervals. One point worth noting is that, unlike most of our previous studies, which employed recall measures of retention, this investigation of pictorial memory required only recognition of the correct figure–background relationships.

Like the HD patients, the patients with right-hemisphere lesions also benefited significantly from the introduction of the verbal mediators. The recitation of the stories apparently prompted a more complete analysis of the elements of the pictures and may also have provided valuable cues for linking the figures with specific contexts. Although there has been abundant documentation of the severe visuoperceptual deficits that accompany right-hemisphere damage (e.g., Benton, 1979; Milner, 1971), the feasibility of employing the linguistic capacities of the intact left hemisphere in rehabilitative efforts has not received adequate attention. Boller and De Renzi (1967) have reported that right-hemisphere patients, as well as patients with left-hemisphere lesions and intact normal control subjects, find it easier to form associations between meaningful (i.e., verbalizable) figures than between meaningless (i.e., nonverbalizable) figures, but they did not evaluate whether their two patient groups would be differentially affected by the imposition of explicit verbal labels on the figures. The findings reported here suggest that it may be worthwhile to explore both the rehabilitative limits of verbal mediators and the mechanisms by which language can alter the perceptual and memory disorders of patients with right-hemisphere lesions.

It is evident from the picture-recognition study that the dementias (like the amnesias) should not be treated as a single disorder. Although the HD patients can utilize language as a mnemonic for circumventing their pictorial memory problems, patients with AD apparently have lost this ability to employ linguistic mnemonics because of the aphasic symptoms usually associated with AD. This difference has important implications for the ability of demented patients to remain in a noninstitutional setting.

Memory for Procedural and Declarative Knowledge

A second recent investigation (Martone, Butters, Payne, Becker, & Sax, 1984) emanated from a desire to examine what learning capacities were preserved in

HD. For the past 15 years, research concerned with severe memory disorders has focused primarily on the patients' extensive anterograde and retrograde memory deficits (for review, see Butters & Cermak, 1980; Butters & Miliotis, 1985; Hirst, 1982; Squire, 1982). There has been a growing interest, however, in those memory capacities that appear to be well preserved even in severely amnesic patients (Brooks & Baddeley, 1976; Cohen & Squire, 1980). There have been numerous demonstrations of the amnesics' ability to acquire and retain a variety of perceptual–motor skills on mirror-tracing, bimanual tracking, and pursuit–rotor tasks (Cermak, Lewis, Butters, & Goodglass, 1973; Corkin, 1968) despite the absence of any recollection by the patients of having performed the test previously. Good performances by amnesic patients have also been observed on tasks that are not primarily perceptual–motor in nature, such as rule-based paired-associate learning, in which word pairs are linked by a semantic or phonological rule (Winocur & Weiskrantz, 1976). Less formal demonstrations of preserved memory capacity have been reported by researchers who have noted that amnesic patients are often able to retain testing procedures across experimental sessions even when unable to recall the specific stimulus material (Corkin, 1968; Milner, Corkin, & Teuber, 1968). Such observations suggest that the acquisition and retention of at least some types of information are intact in patients with severe memory impairments.

Mirror-reading task. A recently proposed model to account for the pattern of preserved and impaired memory functions (Cohen & Squire, 1980; Squire, 1982) suggests that memory for information consisting of skills or rule-based procedures is spared in amnesia, whereas memory for information that is data based or declarative (e.g., specific facts) is impaired. According to this view, amnesic patients are able to learn and retain mirror-tracing and pursuit–rotor tasks because successful performance on these tests depends on the ability to learn and retain the procedures involved but not on the ability to recall the specific content of the tasks.

This proposed dissociation between two types of memory in amnesia was demonstrated experimentally by Cohen and Squire (1980) with a pattern-analyzing task that involved both skill learning (procedural knowledge) and verbal recognition (declarative knowledge). Subjects were required to read blocks of word triads that appeared as mirror images of themselves. Half of the words were unique to each block, and half were repeated on every block during the three test sessions. Both the amnesic and normal control subjects showed significant and equivalent improvement in reading the unique, mirror-reflected triads over the three test days. Although the control subjects were much faster at reading the repeated words than the unique words, the amnesic patients demonstrated only a slight improvement in reading speed for the repeated word triads. It seemed, then, that although the amnesic patients were able to learn and retain the general skills underlying mirror reading, they, unlike the normal subjects, did not recognize that specific word triads had been presented on numerous trials. A verbal recognition test administered following the skill-learning task confirmed that the AKS patients could not identify the words employed in the mirror-reading task. In a recent report, Moscovitch (1984) replicated Cohen and Squire's (1980) findings with a task that required patients with amnesic symptoms to read sentences written in transformed script rotated along the vertical axis.

This distinction between procedural and declarative information appears to characterize the memory defects of amnesic patients of numerous etiologies, but whether it can be generalized to other populations of brain-damaged patients with memory disorders, such as progressive dementias, has yet to be fully evaluated. In the Martone et al. (1984) study, Cohen and Squire's mirror-reading task (1980) was used to evaluate the skill learning and verbal recognition of HD patients, AKS patients, and normal control subjects. Testing on the mirror-reading task was conducted on three successive days, with 60 trials (three blocks of 20 word triads each) administered each day. Because the mirror reading of unique words is a relatively pure indicator of skill learning, it was expected that normal acquisition would be reflected by a steady decrease in the time needed to read the unique mirror-reflected word triads. The ability of the subjects to recognize verbal materials (i.e., declarative knowledge) was assessed by two criteria: (a) by any differences between the mirror reading of unique and repeated word triads and (b) by scores on a verbal recognition test administered after the last trial of the mirror-reading task. Normal subjects were expected to read the repeated word triads much faster than the unique triads and to be able to

identify on the recognition test the words used on the mirror-reading task. Of these two measures, the word recognition test seemed to be the more uncontaminated indicator of declarative knowledge, because the mirror reading of repeated words is affected by skill learning and priming effects (i.e., the recognition of one word elicits the recall of another), as well as by simple word recognition.

The major finding of this study (Martone et al., 1984) was a double dissociation between the HD and AKS patients on rule learning and recognition memory. Figure 34-5 shows the mean latencies (log transformed) of the three groups of subjects for the unique word triads used on the mirror-reading task. Although both patient groups read the unique mirror-reflected words more slowly than did the normal subjects, only the AKS patients demonstrated a normal rate of rule-learning over the three test days. The AKS patients and the normal control subjects showed significant improvement from Day 1 to Day 2 and from Day 2 to Day 3, whereas the HD patients improved only from Day 1 to Day 2. The HD patients' mean latencies on Days 2 and 3 were essentially identical.

Figure 34-6 presents the performance of the three groups of subjects on both the unique and the repeated triads for each of the three blocks of 20 trials on each test day. The important result to note is the difference in latencies between the unique and the repeated triads. This difference score (unique–repeated) is significantly greater for the normal control subjects and the HD patients than for the AKS patients. That is, the HD patients and the normal control subjects seemed to recognize that certain triads were being repeated on

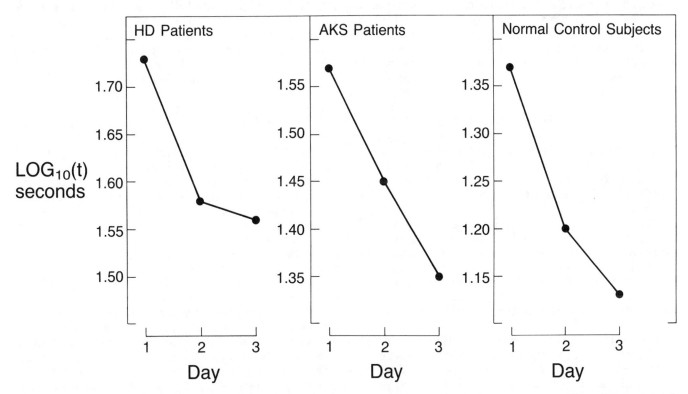

Figure 34-5. Performance of HD patients, AKS patients, and normal control subjects on the mirror reading of unique word triads. Mean time (log 10 seconds) to read a word triad for 3 test days (collapsing blocks) is shown. Adapted from Butters (1984) by permission.

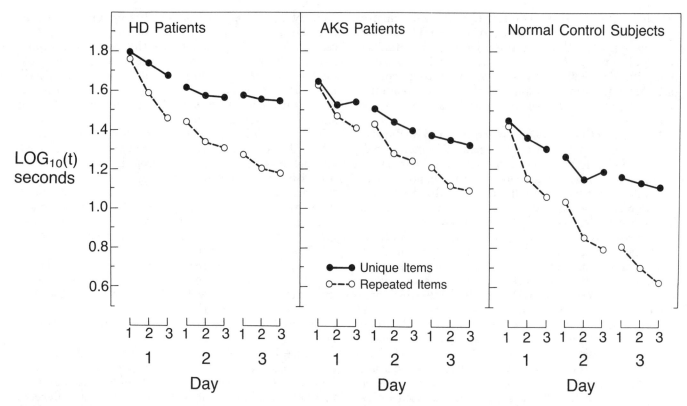

Figure 34-6. Performance of HD patients, AKS patients, and normal control subjects on the mirror reading of unique and repeated word triads. Mean time (log 10 seconds) to read a word triad is shown for each block on each test day. Adapted from Butters (1984) by permission.

each block of trials and subsequently identified these repeated mirror-reflected words in a short period of time. In contrast, the AKS patients, who acquired the general rule in normal fashion, did not seem to recognize that specific word triads were being repeated on every block of 20 trials. This finding suggests that the AKS patients were much more impaired in recognition memory than were the HD patients.

This conclusion was supported by the patients' performance on the recognition test that immediately followed administration of the mirror-reading task on Day 3. This test required the subjects to identify from a 60-word list the words that had been used on the mirror-reading task. Of the 60 words, 30 (15 unique words and 15 repeated words) had been presented in the rule-learning task; the other 30 words were distractor (new) items. As shown in Figure 34-7, the HD patients could recognize both unique and repeated words at a level comparable to the performance of the normal control subjects. However, the recognition scores of the AKS patients for both unique and repeated words were significantly impaired in comparison to the performance of the HD and normal control groups.

The results of this investigation (Martone et al., 1984) suggest that the anterograde memory disorder of demented HD patients cannot be characterized by normal skill learning (i.e., procedural knowledge) paired with severely deficient recognition of specific verbal materials (i.e., declarative knowledge). In fact, the re-

sults demonstrate a double dissociation between amnesic AKS and demented HD patients on skill learning and verbal recognition. The AKS patients, as had been reported previously by Cohen and Squire (1980), can acquire motor and visuoperceptual skills at a normal rate despite being severely impaired in their recognition memory. On the other hand, HD patients are impaired in their ability to acquire skills but retain their capacity to recognize previously presented verbal stimuli. The unsolicited casual remarks of the HD patients while performing the mirror-reading tasks were consistent with these quantitative results. Most of the HD patients and normal control subjects often uttered remarks like "I have seen these (i.e., words) before" while being shown the repeated words. Such acknowledgments were not offered by any of the AKS patients.

It is important to note that the HD patients' lack of skill learning cannot be attributed to the dysarthria that often accompanies their disorder. If dysarthria had limited the HD patients' mirror reading of unique word triads, it should have had the same debilitating effect for the repeated words. Given the large difference between HD patients' reading speed of the unique and the repeated words, dysarthria does not appear to be a crucial factor in limiting the patients' acquisition of the mirror-reading skills. Furthermore, the HD patients who participated in this study were primarily in the middle stages of the disease process, and their dysarthria was not considered a serious impediment to verbal communication.

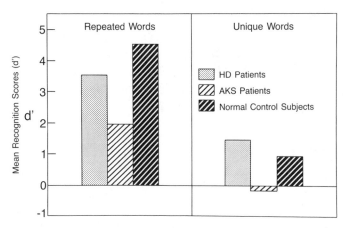

Figure 34-7. Mean recognition scores (d') of HD patients, AKS patients, and normal control subjects for unique and repeated word triads used in the mirror-reading task. Adapted from Martone et al. (1984) by permission.

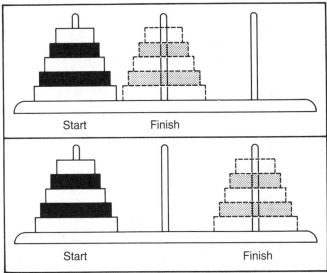

Figure 34-8. Illustration of the Tower of Hanoi puzzle showing starting position of five blocks on peg 1 (solid lines) and two possible solutions (dotted lines), with either peg 2 (top) or peg 3 (bottom) as the end peg (i.e., goal). Adapted from Butters et al. (1985) by permission.

Tower of Hanoi puzzle. Our most recent attempt to evaluate the HD patients' skill-learning capacities has involved the use of the Tower of Hanoi puzzle (Butters, Wolfe, Martone, Granholm, & Cermak, 1985). According to Cohen (1984), the Tower puzzle can be learned and retained in normal fashion by severely amnesic patients (including patient H.M.). Cohen cited this successful performance by amnesic patients as evidence that their intact procedural learning encompasses cognitive as well as motor and perceptual skills. Intrigued by Cohen's (1984) brief report, we administered the Tower puzzle to six patients in the early stages of HD (EHD), to nine patients in the middle-to-advanced stages of HD (AHD), to six amnesics whose memory disorders were associated with damage to the medial diencephalic region (five of these patients had AKS syndrome), to 12 normal control subjects, and to Cermak's well-studied amnesic patient S.S. (Cermak, 1976; Cermak & O'Connor, 1983). Because patient S.S. had a very severe anterograde amnesia associated with bilateral damage to the temporal lobes, it seemed pertinent to determine whether he also could acquire this cognitive skill. On the basis of our previous findings with the mirror-reading task (Martone et al., 1984), we anticipated that the amnesic patients would perform normally on the Tower puzzle but that the HD patients (especially the AHD patients) would show little learning on this skill-based cognitive task.

The Tower of Hanoi puzzle is shown in Figure 34-8. It consists of three pegs and five wooden blocks. At the beginning, all five blocks are arranged according to size (with the largest on the bottom and the smallest on top) on the leftmost peg (peg 1). Subjects are asked to move the blocks from this "start" peg to either the center peg (peg 2) or the rightmost peg (peg 3), maintaining the established order by size. Subjects are permitted to move only one block at a time and can never place a larger block on top of a smaller one. To solve the puzzle, subjects have to shuffle the blocks back and forth among all three pegs. The optimal solution can be accomplished with a minimum of 31 moves. For each "end" peg (pegs 2 and 3), there is only one sequence of movements that will lead to an optimal 31-move solution. Subjects are allowed to select either peg 2 or 3 as the "end peg."

The subjects in the experiment reported here were asked to solve the Tower puzzle eight times on two consecutive days. The eight trials (one trial = one solution) were administered in two blocks of four trials separated by a 15-minute rest interval. Thus, by the end of Day 2, the subjects had solved the puzzle a total of 16 times. Before testing began on the second day, each subject was administered a written recognition test to assess memory (i.e., declarative) for facts about the Tower of Hanoi puzzle and to determine whether dissociations (single or double) between skill learning and recognition memory noted with the mirror reading test could be confirmed with the Tower of Hanoi puzzle. The test consisted of 10 multiple-choice questions on details of the previous day's testing (e.g., "What was the name of the game?"). Four choices were provided for each question: three distractors plus the correct answer. Subjects were asked to circle the correct answer for each question.

Figure 34-9 shows the results for the acquisition of the Tower of Hanoi puzzle. As can be seen on the right half of the figure, patients in the early stages of HD were indistinguishable from normal subjects in the learning of the puzzle; the improvement (i.e., reduction in the number of moves to solve the puzzle) from the first block of four trials (Day 1) to the fourth block of four trials (Day 2) was 75% for the normal control subjects and 74% for the early HD patients. In contrast to these performances by the normal control subjects and the early HD patients, the advanced HD patients (30%), the diencephalic amnesics (35%) and patient

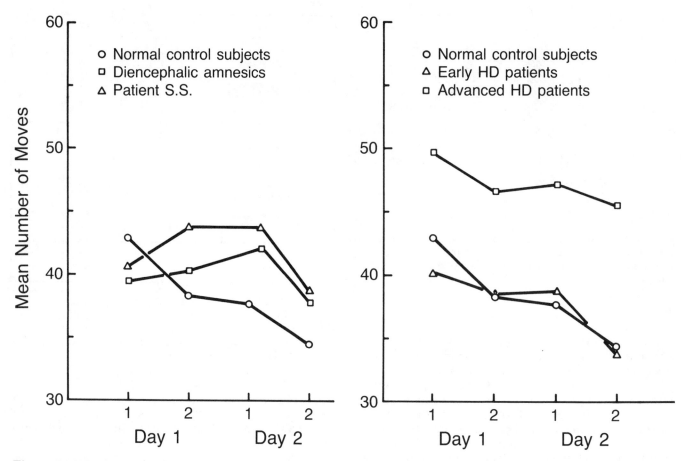

Figure 34-9. Performance of subjects on the Tower of Hanoi puzzle. Mean number of moves needed to solve the puzzle for both blocks of four trials on Days 1 and 2 of testing are shown. Adapted from Butters et al. (1985) by permission.

S.S. (21%) evidenced significantly less improvement over the two days of testing.

The findings for the written recognition test about the Tower puzzle yielded results consistent with Martone et al.'s (1984) report. The normal subjects (96%), early HD (93%), and advanced HD (81%) subjects recognized significantly more facts about the puzzle than did the diencephalic amnesics (58%) and patient S.S. (21%).

Although the impairment of the advanced HD patients supports the notion that the basal ganglia are vital for skill learning, the importance of this result is diminished by the failure of our amnesic patients to acquire the solution of the Tower puzzle over the 16 trials. In fact, all of the diencephalic amnesics and patient S.S. required almost as many moves on the final block of four trials (13 through 16) on Day 2 as they had on the first block of trials (1 through 4) on Day 1. This failure of our amnesic subjects to acquire the solution to the puzzle is especially disappointing in view of Cohen's (1984) report that his amnesic patients could consistently solve the Tower puzzle in 31 moves after 16 test trials. Unfortunately, without a dissociation between the performance of the HD and amnesic patients similar to that reported with the mirror-reading task (Martone et al., 1984), it is impossible to conclude

from this experiment that the caudate nucleus plays a special role in skill or procedural learning.

At least two factors could account for the differences between the findings reported here and those of Cohen (1984). First, the mastery of the Tower of Hanoi puzzle may represent too complex a cognitive skill for all but the mildest of amnesic patients. Cohen did not provide any independent psychometric indices of the severity of his amnesic populations' anterograde memory deficits, but his demonstration that patient H.M., whose severe amnesia has been well-documented (Corkin, 1984; Milner, 1966), also shows significant improvement in solving the Tower puzzle over 16 test trials reduces somewhat the possibility of this factor. However, it should be noted that patient H.M., unlike the other amnesics reported by Cohen, required 32 trials before he could consistently solve the puzzle in 31 moves. Given the questionable performances of patients H.M. and S.S., both of whose amnesias have been attributed to damage to mesial temporal lobe structures (especially the hippocampus), Cohen's claim that severely amnesic patients are normal in the acquisition and retention of cognitive procedural tasks may be overly optimistic.

A second possible contribution to our results is that the Tower of Hanoi relies heavily on other cognitive abilities in addition to the capacity to acquire skill-based procedural knowledge. Like many other problem-solving tasks, the Tower puzzle requires the identification, sequencing, and retention of moves (i.e., strategies) to ensure an efficient solution. On such tasks, subjects can rarely confine themselves to the specific move or choice immediately confronting them; rather, the current move must be considered in the context of the immediately succeeding situation. Because AKS patients are impaired in the initiation and ordering of problem-solving strategies (Oscar-Berman, 1973; Talland, 1965), the failure of the five AKS patients in the experiment reported here may not be indicative of a deficit in acquiring skill-based information.

The most compelling evidence that the diencephalic amnesics in the study reported here failed the Tower puzzle because of the problem-solving demands of the task emanates from the performance of the AKS patients on other skill-learning tests. Four of the five patients had participated in Martone et al.'s mirror-reading study and had been able to acquire this reading skill at the same rate as did intact control subjects. This suggests that the AKS patients' deficits on the Tower puzzle cannot be attributed to a general impairment in acquiring skills and procedural knowledge. Furthermore, because the mildly demented, early HD patients were able to perform normally on the Tower problem, the amnesics' difficulties with this task are probably due to a specific problem-solving deficit rather than to a general intellectual decline.

Given the findings reported here, the clinician (and experimenter) should exercise considerable caution when interpreting findings with the Tower of Hanoi and other "procedural" tasks. It may be true that normal rates of improvement by amnesic, or demented, patient populations may be an indicator of intact skill learning, but failure to learn the puzzle's solution does not necessarily indicate a general impairment in procedural learning. Cohen's (1984) tendency to define procedural learning by enumerating the memory tests performed normally by amnesic patients rather than by the conventional use of common features and operations further complicates (and limits) the concept's clinical utility.

Despite the ambiguities surrounding the Tower puzzle, it must be stressed that the results of the recognition test administered at the beginning of the second day of testing are consistent with the recognition data reported by Martone et al. (1984). The advanced HD patients were impaired in comparison with the normal control subjects, but both the early and advanced HD patients' recognition of details concerning the Tower of Hanoi puzzle were still superior to that of the seven amnesic patients. Interestingly, when the Tower puzzle was first shown to the patients at the beginning of Day 2, none of the amnesics, but all of the demented patients, remembered attempting to solve the puzzle on the immediately preceding day.

In addition to emphasizing that important differences exist between the memory disorders of HD and AKS patients, the Martone et al. (1984) and Butters, Wolfe, Granholm, & Martone (1986) studies provide some clues about the nature of the demented HD patients' anterograde memory deficits. A review of our previous investigations reveals that the memory performance of HD patients seems most impaired when recall paradigms are employed. For example, when HD patients were asked to recall verbal materials after 3 to 18 seconds of distraction (i.e., the Brown-Peterson technique), their impaired performance was quantitatively similar to that of amnesic AKS patients. However, in both of the procedural-learning studies, which used verbal recognition tests rather than a recall paradigm, and on the previously discussed picture-context recognition task (Butters et al., 1983), the HD patients' performance was significantly superior to that of the AKS patients. The AKS patients, like all amnesics, are impaired equally on recall and recognition tests of memory (for review, see Butters & Cermak, 1980; Hirst, 1982; Piercy, 1977), whereas the HD patients' impairments appear more prevalent and severe when recall rather than recognition is demanded. In retrospect, it appears likely that HD patients may have very low MQs because the Associative-Learning, Logical Memories, and Visual Reproduction tests of the unmodified WMS all require recall rather than recognition of previously presented materials.

If this proposed dissociation between the HD patients' recall and recognition abilities is substantiated by future studies, it will suggest that the HD patients' memory problems involve primarily an inability to search their recent and remote memories. Because recognition tests eliminate most of the patients' need to search their short- and long-term memories, they result in relatively intact performance by HD patients. The HD patients may adequately process and store verbal information but be unable to generate the search strategies needed to recover this material when a recall paradigm is employed. This interpretation is consistent with the HD patients' flat retrograde amnesia and with the previously discussed failures to improve recall from short-term memory by reducing proactive interference and by providing additional rehearsal time. Any patient with a general retrieval problem will have as much difficulty retrieving information from the remote past as well as the recent past.

Recall Versus Recognition of Verbal Material

Further evidence to support the conclusion that verbal retrieval processes are impaired in HD patients has been reported in the Butters et al. (1985) study. The Rey Auditory Verbal Learning Test (Lezak, 1983) was administered with a recall and a recognition procedure to nine amnesic (six AKS, two post-encephalitics, and one patient with a neoplasm located in the medial diencephalic region), 10 subjects with HD, and 14 normal control subjects. In the recall condition, five presentation-recall trials were followed by a single delayed-recall trial 30 minutes after the fifth presentation-recall trial. On each presentation-recall trial, a list of 15 words (having high frequency in the English language) were read to the subject at the rate of one word per second. Immediately after the presentation of the 15th word, the subjects were asked to recall in any order as many of the words as possible. Ten seconds after the first recall was completed, the entire list was read again to the subjects and was followed immediately by a second test of recall. This procedure was followed for all five presentation-recall trials. The ordering of the words on each presentation trial was randomized.

For the recognition procedure, five presentation-recognition learning trials were followed 30 minutes later by a single delayed-recognition test. On each presentation-recognition learning trial, a 15-word list (different from the one used for recall testing) was read to the subjects at the rate of one word per second. Immediately following the reading of the 15th word, a 30-item yes-no recognition test was administered orally. Thirty words (15 from the presented list and 15 distractors that had not been presented previously) were read to the subject sequentially, and the subject was asked to indicate whether each word was or was not on the previously presented list. There was a 10-second delay between the end of the recognition test and the beginning of the next presentation-recognition trial. As with the recall paradigm, the 15 words on each trial were presented in random order. Different distractors were used on each recognition trial, and the ordering of the 30 words in each recognition test was random.

The results of this study are shown in Figures 34-10 and 34-11. On the verbal recall test (Figure 34-10), both the demented HD and the amnesic patients were severely impaired in their acquisition and delayed recall of the 15-word lists. Statistical analyses failed to uncover any significant differences between the HD and amnesic patients on the five presentation-recall trials, although on the delayed-recall trials the amnesic patients were significantly worse than the HD patients. This failure to differentiate the HD and amnesic patients on the acquisition trials of the recall test stands in marked contrast to their performance on the verbal recognition test (Figure 34-11). Both the HD and amnesic patients were again impaired in comparison with the normal control subjects, but the recognition scores of the HD patients on the five acquisition trials and on the delayed-recognition test were significantly better than those of the amnesic patients. As with the picture-context recognition (Butters et al., 1983) and procedural learning studies (Martone et al., 1984), the patients with HD evidenced far better performance when recognition rather than recall measures were employed.

It is obvious from an inspection of Figure 34-11 that the HD patients' recognition performance, although superior to that of the amnesic patients, was not normal. The major reason for this deficit was discovered when the number of false positive and false negative errors the subjects made on the recognition test (Figure 34-12) was examined. Unlike the amnesic patients,

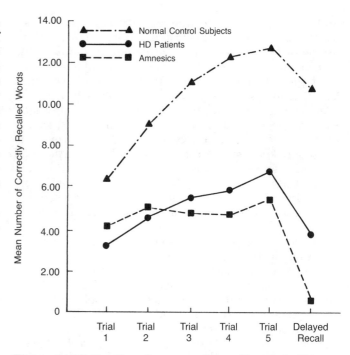

Figure 34-10. Recall performance of normal control subjects, HD patients, and amnesics on a 15-word list. Thirty minutes intervened between the fifth acquisition trial and delayed recall. Adapted from Butters et al. (1985) by permission.

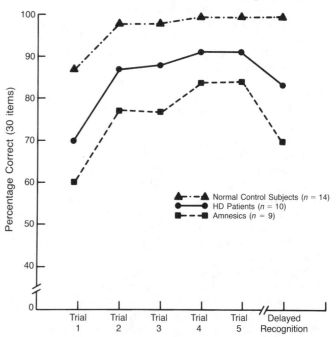

Figure 34-11. Recognition performance of normal control subjects, HD patients, and amnesics on a 30-word list (15 target words and 15 distractors). Thirty minutes intervened between the fifth acquisition trial and delayed recognition. Adapted from Butters et al. (1985) by permission.

who made many errors of both types, the HD patients differed from the normal control subjects primarily in the number of false positive errors they made during testing. That is, although HD patients usually detected a word that had been presented on the list, they tended to say "yes" when some of the distractor words were presented. Thus, the HD patients usually recognized words that had been presented, but when they were uncertain about some of the distractor words, they tended to adopt rather liberal judgment criteria. The fact that the amnesic patients made numerous false negative errors (i.e., failed to detect a word that had been presented) again emphasized that they were unable to recognize (as well as recall) the words used on our two verbal tests.

It should be noted that Biber et al.'s (1981) earlier mentioned findings on a facial recognition task are not consistent with this most recent evidence concerning recall and recognition in demented HD patients. Biber's investigation used a forced-choice recognition test to determine whether HD patients (as well as other patient populations) could identify photographs of faces they had viewed previously. The results showed that for all experimental conditions (baseline, "high-," and "low-" level orientation procedures) the HD patients were severely impaired in their recognition of faces. One possible explanation for the HD patients' poor recognition performance on this task involves the nature of the stimuli and the length of the exposure time. To ensure that subjects could not rely on superficial cues (e.g., clothing and hair styles) to identify faces, Biber et al. selected photographs of cadets from the yearbook of a military academy. All of these cadets wore the same uniform and had short haircuts at the time their photographs were taken. Thus, to discriminate among the photographs, subjects had to focus their attention upon the configurational features of the faces (e.g., the relationships among the eyes, nose, and mouth). Biber et al. further increased the difficulty of their test by limiting the exposure (i.e., study) time for each photograph to 7 seconds. Given the designed complexity of this task and the HD patients'

inability to control their involuntary choreiform movements, the HD patients may not have had sufficient time to analyze the critical configurational features of the faces. For example, because of their involuntary movements, the HD patients may have required 3 or 4 seconds to focus their attention on a given stimulus and subsequently had only 3 or 4 seconds to analyze the photograph of each cadet. If such were the case, it is not surprising that the HD patients performed so poorly in comparison to normal control subjects and AKS patients, both of whom had a full 7 seconds to analyze the critical features of each photograph.

Verbal Fluency

Further evidence that the memory disorders of AKS and HD patients involve different underlying processes is found in a fourth study, which focuses on their performance on a letter fluency task (Butters et al., 1986). Because such verbal tests place great demands on the subjects' ability to systematically search their semantic memories (Martin & Fedio, 1983), HD patients should retrieve fewer words than do AKS patients. However, in view of the AKS patients' increased sensitivity to proactive interference, they should emit more incorrect perseverative errors (i.e., repetitions of words previously emitted) than should patients with HD. To assess this predicted dissociation, the letter fluency (FAS) task, developed by Benton and his colleagues (Benton, 1968; Borkowski, Benton, & Spreen, 1967) was administered to 9 early HD patients, 11 advanced HD patients, 9 AKS patients, and 26 normal control subjects. The subjects were read the letters *F, A,* and *S* successively and were asked to produce as many words as they could think of that began with the given letter. They were instructed that giving proper nouns or the same word with a different suffix was not permitted. For each of the three letters, the subjects were allowed 60 seconds to generate words orally. All of the subjects' responses (correct and incorrect) were recorded by the examiner.

The results are shown in Figure 34-13. In terms of total correct responses, both the early and the advanced HD groups generated fewer words to the three letters than did the AKS patients and the normal control subjects. The AKS patients' performance, although superior to that of the two HD patient populations, was impaired in comparison with the scores of the normal control subjects. The results for perseverative errors and for perseverations as a proportion (percentage) of total responses indicate that the AKS patients were more likely to commit such repetitions than were the other three subject groups. Thus, although the HD patients were able to retrieve fewer correct words than were the Korsakoff patients, the latter were the most likely to make perseverative errors.

The results of this letter fluency task are directly relevant to the HD patients' performance on recognition tests. Although HD patients have demonstrated normal verbal recognition memory in a number of experimental paradigms, their performance could be ex-

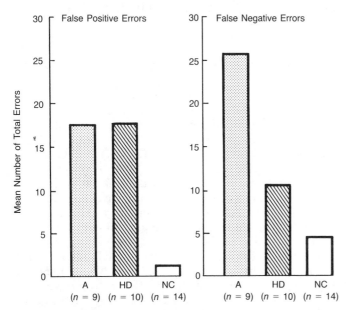

Figure 34-12. Mean total false positive and false negative errors made by amnesic patients (A), HD patients, and normal control subjects on Trials 1–6 of the verbal recognition test. Adapted from Butters et al. (1985) by permission.

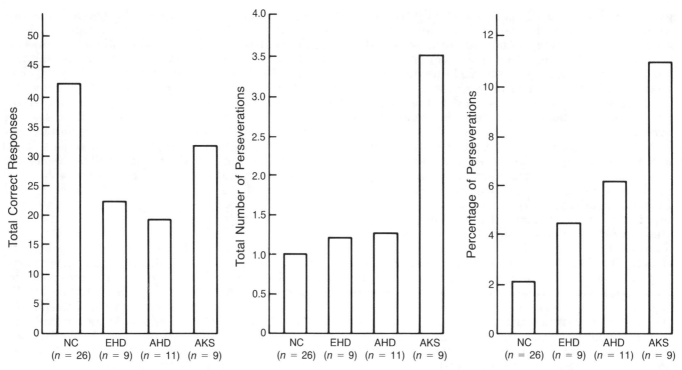

Figure 34-13. Performance of normal control subjects (NC), patients with early HD (EHD), patients with advanced HD (AHD), and AKS patients on a letter fluency (FAS) task. Adapted from Butters et al. (1986) by permission.

plained by assuming that recognition tests are simply easier (i.e., less complex) and consequently less sensitive than recall tasks. That is, one could argue persuasively that AKS and HD patients share a qualitatively similar memory disorder that differs only in severity. It is vital to note, then, that the patients' performance on the letter fluency task greatly reduces the value of such an appeal to task complexity. That HD patients produced fewer correct responses and a lower proportion of perseverative errors than did the AKS patients suggests that retrieval impairments and increased sensitivity to proactive interference are differentially influencing the verbal memory capacities of these two patient groups. Furthermore, when the results for the various recognition tests (e.g., the skill-learning tests and the Rey list-learning task) and the letter fluency test are considered together, a double dissociation between tasks and patient groups emerges. The HD patients demonstrate a greater difference between recognition and recall memory than do the AKS patients, whereas the amnesic AKS patients retrieve significantly more correct words than do the HD patients on the semantic memory (i.e., fluency) test. This double dissociation indicates that the memory deficiencies of HD patients represent a unique pattern of retrieval and perhaps other processes, rather than a mild form of an amnesic syndrome.

The results for the early and advanced HD patients are consistent with previous reports (Butters, et al., 1978; Josiassen, Curry, & Mancall, 1983) that the memory disorder associated with HD is apparent very early in the disease process and shows only a moderate progression as the patients' functional disabilities and

general dementia worsen. On the letter fluency task, the performances of early and advanced HD patients were virtually identical, with both groups retrieving fewer words than did the amnesic AKS patients. It appears then that the severe deficits in the initiation of retrieval processes are evident when the HD patient's functional disability is only mild to moderate and that these deficits change relatively little as the abnormal movements and general intellectual deterioration progress.

Summary and Conclusions

The findings of the studies reported here and of past studies suggest that the memory disorders of amnesic and of some demented populations have qualitatively distinct characteristics. Although amnesic patients with bilateral hippocampal or medial diencephalic lesions (e.g., AKS patients) are severely impaired in their recall and recognition of data-based verbal and nonverbal information, they retain the ability to learn and remember rule-based visuoperceptual and motor skills. The claim that amnesic patients can learn and retain cognitive skills remains controversial and complicated by the lack of an operational definition for procedural learning. In contrast, patients whose dementia results from atrophy or dysfunction of the basal ganglia (e.g., HD patients) may be retarded in their acquisition of general skills while they continue to demonstrate a considerable ability to learn new facts when recognition tests of memory are employed. The memory failures that HD patients evidence on verbal-recall tasks appear to be related to severe deficits in the initiation of systematic retrieval strategies. The possibility that limbic and basal ganglia structures may play qualitatively different roles in memory functions is intriguing and deserves further study with patients who have other subcortical neurological disorders (e.g., patients with Parkinson's disease).

The results of these comparative studies of HD and AKS patients reinforce conclusions based on a scrutiny of various forms of amnesia (for review, see Butters & Miliotis, 1985; Squire, 1982). These recent investigations of pictorial memory, of declarative and procedural knowledge, of verbal recall and recognition, and of verbal fluency, as well as the studies concerned with short-term memory, remote memory, and discrimination learning, suggest that HD, amnesic, and even AD patients fail to acquire and retrieve information for quite different reasons. That all of the amnesic and demented groups discussed in this chapter had low MQs revealed little about the nature of their impairments. Thus, relying on a single quantitative measure of memory (e.g., the MQ) for assessing amnesic symptoms may have as many limitations as does using an isolated score on a naming or a fluency test for the full description of aphasia. Because Huntington's disease, Alzheimer's disease, and Korsakoff's syndrome all involve different combinations of brain damage and dysfunctions, it should not be surprising that the pattern of memory impairments associated with each disorder is likely to prove unique.

References

Albert, M. S., Butters, N., & Brandt, J. (1981a). Development of remote memory loss in patients with Huntington's disease. *Journal of Clinical Neuropsychology, 3,* 1–12.

Albert, M. S., Butters, N., & Brandt, J. (1981b). Patterns of remote memory in amnesic and demented patients. *Archives of Neurology, 38,* 495–500.

Albert, M. S., Butters, N., & Levin, J. (1979). Temporal gradients in the retrograde amnesia of patients with alcoholic Korsakoff's disease. *Archives of Neurology, 36,* 211–216.

Benton, A. L. (1968). Differential behavioral effects in frontal lobe disease. *Neuropsychologia, 6,* 53–60.

Benton, A. L. (1974). *The Revised Visual Retention Test* (4th ed). New York: Psychological Corporation.

Benton, A. L. (1979). Visuoperceptive, visuospatial, and visuoconstructive disorders. In K. M. Heilman & E. Valenstein (Eds.), *Clinical neuropsychology,* New York: Oxford University Press.

Biber, C., Butters, N., Rosen, J., Gerstman, L., & Mattis, S. (1981). Encoding strategies and recognition of faces by alcoholic Korsakoff and other brain-damaged patients. *Journal of Clinical Neuropsychology, 3,* 315–330.

Boller, F., & De Renzi, E. (1967). Relationship between visual memory defects and hemispheric locus of lesion. *Neurology, 17,* 1052–1058.

Borkowski, J. G., Benton, A. L., & Spreen, O. (1967). Word fluency and brain damage. *Neuropsychologia, 5,* 135–150.

Bower, G. H., & Karlin, M. B. (1974). Depth of processing pictures of faces and recognition memory. *Journal of Experimental Psychology, 103,* 751–757.

Brooks, D. N., & Baddeley, A. D. (1976). What can amnesic patients learn? *Neuropsychologia, 14,* 111–122.

Butters, N. (1984). The clinical aspects of memory disorders: Contributions from experimental studies of amnesia and dementia. *Journal of Clinical Neuropsychology, 6,* 17–36.

Butters, N., & Albert, M. S. (1982). Processes underlying failures to recall remote events. In L. S. Cermak (Ed.), *Human memory and amnesia* (pp. 257–274). Hillsdale, NJ: Erlbaum.

Butters, N., Albert, M. S., & Sax, D. (1979). Investigations of the memory disorders of patients with Huntington's disease. In T. Chase, N. Wexler, & A. Barbeau (Eds.), *Advances in neurology: Vol. 23. Huntington's disease.* New York: Raven Press.

Butters, N., Albert, M. S., Sax, D. S., Miliotis, P., Nagode, J., & Sterste, A. (1983). The effect of verbal mediators on the pictorial memory of brain-damaged patients. *Neuropsychologia, 21,* 307–323.

Butters, N., & Cermak, L. S. (1980). *Alcoholic Korsakoff's syndrome: An information-processing approach to amnesia.* New York: Academic Press.

Butters, N., & Grady, M. (1977). Effect of predistractor delays on the short-term memory performance of patients with Korsakoff's and Huntington's disease. *Neuropsychologia, 13,* 701–705.

Butters, N., & Miliotis, P. (1985). Amnesic disorders. In K. M. Heilman & E. Valenstein (Eds.), *Clinical neuropsychology* (2nd ed.). New York: Oxford University Press.

Butters, N., Miliotis, P., Albert, M. S., & Sax, D. (1984). Memory assessment: Evidence of the heterogeneity of amnesic symptoms. In G. Goldstein (Ed.), *Advances in clinical neuropsychology* (Vol. 1). New York: Plenum Press.

Butters, N., Sax, D., Montgomery, K., & Tarlow, S. (1978). Comparison of the neuropsychological deficits associated with early and advanced Huntington's disease. *Archives of Neurology, 35,* 585–589.

Butters, N., Tarlow, S., Cermak, L. S., & Sax, D. (1976). A comparison of the information processing deficits of patients with Huntington's chorea and Korsakoff's syndrome. *Cortex, 12,* 134–144.

Butters, N., Wolfe, J., Granholm, E., & Martone, M. (1986). An assessment of verbal recall, recognition and fluency abilities in patients with Huntington's disease. *Cortex, 22,* 11–32.

Butters, N., Wolfe, J., Martone, M., Granholm, E., & Cermak, L. (1985). Memory disorders associated with Huntington's disease: Verbal recall, verbal recognition and procedural memory. *Neuropsychologia, 23,* 729–743.

Caine, E. D., Ebert, M. H., & Weingartner, H. (1977). An outline for the analysis of dementia: The memory disorder of Huntington's disease. *Neurology, 27,* 1087–1092.

Cermak, L. S. (1976). The encoding capacity of a patient with amnesia due to encephalitis. *Neuropsychologia, 14*(3), 311–326.

Cermak, L. S., Lewis, R., Butters, N., & Goodglass, H. (1973). Role of verbal mediation in performance of motor tasks by Korsakoff patients. *Perceptual and Motor Skills, 37,* 259–262.

Cermak, L. S., & O'Connor, M. (1983). The anterograde and retrograde retrieval ability of a patient with amnesia due to encephalitis. *Neuropsychologia, 21*(3), 213–234.

Cohen, N. (1984). Preserved learning capacity in amnesia: Evidence for multiple memory systems. In L. Squire & N. Butters (Eds.), *The neuropsychology of memory.* New York: Guilford Press.

Cohen, N. J., & Squire, L. R. (1980). Preserved learning and retention of pattern-analyzing skill in amnesia: Dissociation of knowing how and knowing that. *Science, 210,* 207–210.

Corkin, S. (1968). Acquisition of motor skill after bilateral medial temporal-lobe excision. *Neuropsychologia, 6,* 255–265.

Corkin, S. (1984). Lasting consequences of bilateral medial temporal lobectomy: Clinical course and experimental findings of H.M. *Seminars in Neurology, 4,* 249–259.

Hirst, W. (1982). The amnesic syndrome: Descriptions and explanations. *Psychological Bulletin, 91,* 435–460.

Josiassen, R., Curry, L., & Mancall, E. (1983). Development of neuropsychological deficits in Huntington's disease. *Archives of Neurology, 40,* 791–796.

Lezak, M. (1983). *Neuropsychological assessment* (2nd ed.). New York: Oxford University Press.

Martin, A., & Fedio, P. (1983). Word production and comprehension in Alzheimer's disease: The breakdown of semantic knowledge. *Brain and Language, 19,* 124–141.

Martone, M., Butters, N., Payne, M., Becker, J., & Sax, D. S. (1984). Dissociations between skill learning and verbal recognition in amnesia and dementia. *Archives of Neurology, 41,* 965–970.

Meudell, P., Butters, N., & Montgomery, K. (1978). Role of rehearsal in the short-term memory performance of patients with Korsakoff's and Huntington's disease. *Neuropsychologia, 16,* 507–510.

Miller, E. (1977). *Abnormal ageing: The psychology of senile and presenile dementia.* New York: Wiley.

Milner, B. (1966). Amnesia following operation on the temporal lobes. In C. W. M. Whitty & O. L. Zangwill (Eds.), *Amnesia.* London: Butterworths.

Milner, B. (1971). Interhemispheric differences in the localization of psychological processes in man. *British Medical Bulletin, 27,* 272–277.

Milner, B., Corkin, S., & Teuber, H.-L. (1968). Further analysis of the hippocampal amnesic syndrome: 14-year follow-up study of H.M. *Neuropsychologia, 6,* 215–234.

Moscovitch, M. (1984). The sufficient conditions for demonstrating preserved memory in amnesia. In L. Squire & N. Butters (Eds.), *The neuropsychology of memory.* New York: Guilford Press.

Oscar-Berman, M. (1973). Hypothesis testing and focusing behavior during concept formation by amnesic Korsakoff patients. *Neuropsychologia, 11,* 191–198.

Oscar-Berman, M., & Zola-Morgan, S. M. (1980a). Comparative neuropsychology and Korsakoff's syndrome: I. Spatial and visual reversal learning. *Neuropsychologia, 18,* 499–512.

Oscar-Berman, M., & Zola-Morgan, S. M. (1980b). Comparative neuropsychology and Korsakoff's syndrome II. Two-choice visual discrimination learning. *Neuropsychologia, 18,* 513–526.

Peterson, L. R., & Peterson, M. J. (1959). Short-term retention of individual verbal items. *Journal of Experimental Psychology, 58,* 193–198.

Piercy, M. (1977). Experimental studies of the organic amnesic syndrome. In C. W. M. Whitty & O. L. Zangwill (Eds.), *Amnesia,* (2nd ed). London: Butterworths.

Schneidman, E. S. (1952). *Make a Picture Story test.* New York: The Psychological Corporation.

Squire, L. R. (1981). Two forms of human amnesia: An analysis of forgetting. *The Journal of Neuroscience, 1,* 635–640.

Squire, L. R. (1982). The neuropsychology of memory. *Annual Review of Neurosciences, 5,* 241–273.

Talland, G. (1965). *Deranged memory.* New York: Academic Press.

Victor, M., Adams, R., & Collins, G. (1971). *The Wernicke-Korsakoff syndrome,* Philadelphia: F. A. Davis Co.

Wechsler, D. A. (1945). A standardized memory scale for clinical use. *Journal of Psychology, 19,* 87–95.

Weingartner, H., Caine, E., & Ebert, M. H. (1979). Imagery, encoding, and retrieval of information from memory: Some specific encoding-retrieval changes in Huntington's disease. *Journal of Abnormal Psychology, 88,* 52–58.

Wilson, R. S., Kaszniak, A. W., & Fox, J. H. (1981). Remote memory in senile dementia. *Cortex, 17,* 41–48.

Winocur, G., & Kinsbourne, M. (1978). Contextual cueing as an aid to Korsakoff amnesics. *Neuropsychologia, 16,* 671–682.

Winocur, G., & Weiskrantz, L. (1976). An investigation of paired-associate learning in amnesic patients. *Neuropsychologia, 14,* 97–110.

Terry L. Jernigan

CHAPTER

35

Anatomical Validators: Issues in the Use of Computed Tomography

In this chapter, specific relationships between brain changes and cognitive deficits in dementia are described. The brain changes are measured with semiautomated analyses of computed tomography (CT) scans. The logical problems that attend inferences of specificity are reviewed, as are other methodological issues that arise in CT research. A multivariate technique, canonical correlation, is used to detect the presence of two separate neurobehavioral relationships within a group of demented patients. The use of canonical correlation for defining the cognitive effects of specific neuropathological processes is discussed.

Introduction

The association of decreasing memory function with advancing age presents a number of challenges to investigators who clinically assess the mental status of older patients. First, the significance of these changes must be ascertained from both a functional and a biological point of view. Also, they must be distinguished from memory changes that are symptomatic of brain diseases common in the elderly. The treatment offered a patient should vary according to whether the changes observed in the patient's memory are associated with changing interests, depressed mood, or compromised brain systems. Research to identify which symptoms, under which circumstances, are due to which cerebral alterations requires that information about the brain be available for comparison with clinical assessments.

Computed tomography (CT) provides a wealth of information about the structure of the brain in vivo. In CT studies of the memory-impaired elderly, investigators are attempting to exploit this information to validate the assessment instruments with which they hope to draw inferences about cerebral dysfunction. Unfor-

tunately, many practical and conceptual difficulties accompany CT research. In this chapter, I discuss some of these difficulties, particularly those that attend the interpretation of positive correlations of CT changes with memory assessments. Readers should keep in mind, however, that the absence of association between CT results and memory assessments has few implications for the neurobehavioral basis of the memory dysfunction, because many brain abnormalities are not detectable with CT.

In this chapter, I also describe the process by which investigators approach the validation of memory assessments. This description focuses on CT, but it is relevant to research with other multidimensional biological variables now used to probe the brain. My colleagues and I are using a process similar to the one described here in studies with positron emission tomography (PET) and we will soon begin such a process in studies of magnetic resonance images. These questions logically precede the design and execution of neurobehavioral studies: What will we attempt to measure in the brain scans? How will we measure it? How successful will we be? What else will we be measuring?

In our research, we are seeking to learn which brain changes are associated with memory disorders. The complexity arises because CT shows no obvious lesion in most patients with disordered memory, although they may have diffuse morphological changes. This may be said of memory-disordered older people, demented persons, alcoholics, many posttraumatic amnesics, and some patients with amnesia of suspected vascular origin. Because CT yields information that has never before been available in vivo, it is not known whether the images hold unrecognized clues about the anatomical correlates of the amnesia. To pursue this possibility, it is important to adopt an exploratory approach that exploits the multidimensional nature of the image data but does not give rise to spurious post-hoc results.

The selection of CT variables in clinical studies has traditionally been guided by earlier work with other methods, such as pneumoencephalography. Because the ventricular system is well visualized with both techniques, a variety of measurements of the dimensions of its different parts have been developed. Other fluid areas, such as cisterns and sulci, are seen more easily on CT, and various methods for measuring them have been used. These fluid measurements are generally made to estimate the degree of "cerebral atrophy" present. Although clinical studies have linked global increases in fluid to various degenerative brain disorders, it is impossible to localize the neural changes presumed to accompany the fluid increases. Focal enlargement of the frontal horns (into the basal ganglia) has often been observed to accompany Huntington's disease (Terrence, Delaney, & Alberts, 1977), and it is well known that the ventricles sometimes enlarge toward an area of infarction, but the evidence that increases in fluid generally reflect changes in proximal tissue is very weak. Recent observations of altered CT values in the parenchyma itself have led to optimism about detecting localized changes with measurements of CT values taken from specific structures. In the next section, I outline attempts to develop a set of measurements from CT scans.

Measurements of the Brain From Computerized Tomography

Most investigators have made measurements from CT by obtaining lengths, widths, or areas of fluid structures as they are seen in films or prints of the images (Banna, 1977; Barron, Jacobs, & Kinkel, 1976; Gyldensted, 1977; Hahn & Rim, 1976; Huckman, Fox, & Topel, 1975; Synek & Reuben, 1976). Sometimes measurements are made from graphics consoles with the images displayed electronically (Penn, Belanger, & Yasnoff, 1978). My colleagues and I have performed semiautomated analyses, by computer, on the matrices of CT values themselves (Jernigan, Zatz, Feinberg, & Fein, 1980; Jernigan, Zatz, & Naeser, 1979; Zatz, Jernigan, & Ahumada, 1982a, 1982b).

Figure 35-1 shows the screen of our console with a CT image displayed. Inspection readily reveals one feature of CT scans. There is an irregularly shaped, lighter colored area just inside the skull near the skull-brain border. This lighter colored area is due to the artifactual elevation of CT values near a boundary separating high- from low-density material. The artifact is referred to as spectral shift artifact (DiChiro, Brooks, Dubal, & Chew, 1978). In our previous studies we have shown that this effect influences CT values even if they are taken from the medial part of the scan, away from the skull. To increase the sensitivity of our measures and to remove some of the variance due to

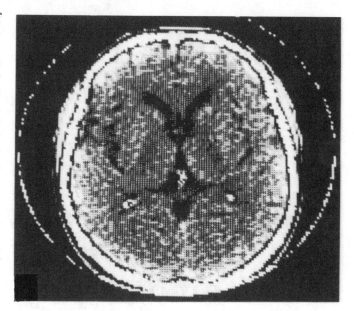

Figure 35-1. A CT image as seen on a console screen.

the spectral shift artifact, we derived corrections for CT values (Zatz et al., 1982b).

In measures of fluid volume such as ventricular volume, another source of irrelevant variation is natural biological variability in head size. People with larger heads tend to have larger ventricles. This difference in volume is obviously not due to ventricular dilatation. To control for this effect we have also derived corrections for the volume measures. To apply these corrections and those for the spectral shift artifacts mentioned earlier, we collect measures of the intracranial area and of the thickness and density of the skull. We also select points manually on the structural midline of the brain and within visually identified structures. These latter points are used to guide an automatic sampling of CT values within the structures. The samples are taken in frontal and temporal white matter, caudate, putamen, and thalamus. We take care to select these samples from outside the streak artifacts and wholly within the structures. To prevent partial voluming of the structures and to minimize inclusion of adjacent tissue or fluid, we inspect sections above and below the sampled section. Figure 35-2 shows the locations of the manually selected points for a typical scan.

Another consideration for selection of samples is sample size. Enough pixels should be included in the sample so that the inherent noise in the scan is overcome. Of course, the larger the sample, the more difficult it is to avoid partial voluming. We compromise with 25-pixel samples, obtained bilaterally.

At the next stage, the image is analyzed by a computer program that uses the input points to compute the sample means and the location of the midline. It also separates each hemisphere into a peripheral and a medial zone. Figure 35-3 shows the result of this algorithm. Each zone is then further subdivided into ante-

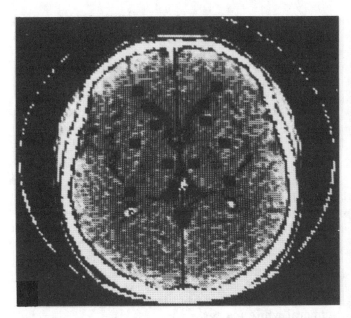

Figure 35-2. Dark squares within the CT image are points selected for automatic sampling of CT values within identified structures.

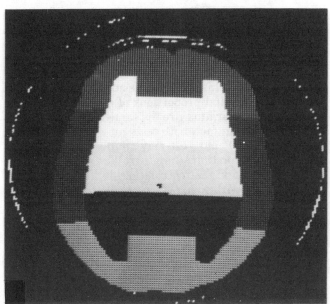

Figure 35-4. The hemispheres are further subdivided into anterior, central, and posterior subsegments.

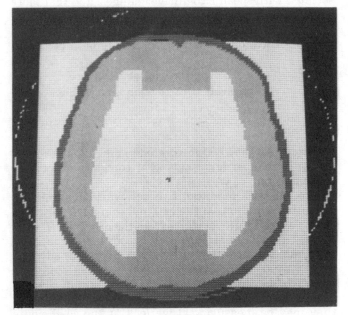

Figure 35-3. CT image showing each hemisphere separated into a peripheral and a medial zone.

rior, central, and posterior subsegments (see Figure 35-4). We compute CT values separately for each subsegment. Then we can estimate fluid volumes, such as ventricular volume, by combining specific sets of the subsegments.

Using the techniques outlined, we compute estimates of ventricular volume, sylvian fissure volume, frontal sulcal volume, and tissue density in the listed structures. Using these measures, we have found changes with normal aging in fluid volumes and tissue density (Zatz et al., 1982a, 1982b). A recent study with

normal elderly subjects replicated these earlier findings and revealed modest correlations between changes in the brain and measures of concentration, memory, and perceptual organization. Other investigators also have found morphological changes on CT in elderly or demented subjects and correlations with memory and other cognitive changes (de Leon et al., 1980; Ford & Winter, 1981; Gutzmann & Avdaloff, 1980; Jacoby & Levy, 1980; Kaszniak, Garron, & Fox, 1979). Unfortunately, the specific mechanisms by which this association occurs are unknown. In the following section we describe an attempt to begin to elucidate these mechanisms in dementia.

The Problem of Specificity

Although numerous studies have indicated an association of diffuse brain changes with cognitive deterioration in dementia, few have implicated specific brain systems or structures in specific cognitive impairments. Indeed, establishing a specific relationship between a cognitive change and a cerebral change is exceedingly difficult in clinical neuropsychological work. It can be demonstrated fairly easily that scores on a test are significantly correlated with a brain measure. Obviously, this correlation does not establish a specific relationship, because the same correlation might have occurred regardless of which test, or CT measure, was used.

At the least, one expects to observe unequal correlations between the brain measure and two cognitive measures. If an inference of specificity is to be made, the difference must be statistically significant. But even when this condition is met the inference may be incorrect. Suppose that scores on a test of memory are shown to have a higher correlation with temporal-lobe density than scores on a test of psychomotor speed. It may be tempting to infer that the temporal-lobe change has a greater impact on memory than on psychomotor speed. This inference assumes, however, that the reliabilities and proportions of specific factor and common factor variance are the same for the two cognitive measures. In fact, both tests may be measuring a single factor, but one test may simply be more sensitive to the factor than the other. The more sensitive test will yield a higher correlation, but this may have nothing to do with memory or psychomotor speed.

A much stronger inference may be drawn if a double dissociation can be demonstrated. Such would be the case if, in addition to the foregoing result, scores on the test of psychomotor speed were shown to have a significantly higher correlation than scores on the memory test with a second brain measure, for example, frontal-lobe density. In this case, the discrepancy between the two correlation patterns obtained with the two brain measures ensures that at least two separate cognitive factors and two separate brain factors are involved. The two tests measure the two cognitive factors to different degrees, and one may examine the cognitive differences between the two tasks in an attempt to define the factors.

Although double dissociation of this type ensures specificity, the failure to observe it in a set of variables does not mean that the hypothesized specificity does not exist. Separate specific factors might be present and might be measured by tests and brain measures, but the double dissociation might not be observed because the variables are intercorrelated. Factor-analytic studies consistently demonstrate that most clinical tests are multifactorial. Less attention has been given to the factor structure of brain scan measures, but in our work they have usually been highly intercorrelated. In this real-world circumstance, a strong finding of double dissociation like the one outlined above is rare. Fortunately, a multivariate technique, canonical correlation, can help to untangle the different factors operating in the cognitive disorder.

Two Factors in the Decline of Dementia

My colleagues and I analyzed the neuropsychological test scores of a group of 16 elderly subjects. Within this group all levels of intellectual function were represented, from normal superior intelligence to severe dementia. The group is not representative of any population but was deliberately constructed to provide the greatest range of variability in the cognitive measures. The intent was to increase the power in the analyses. No subjects with abrupt onset of symptoms or focal abnormalities were included. All subjects had had CT scans, but the findings did not influence subject selection, except to exclude patients with focal findings. No prevalence estimates or clinical predictions are permissible from these analyses; they were conducted for the sole purpose of examining the processes occurring

in cognitive deterioration, with the hope that some further information would emerge about the mechanisms by which dementia progresses.

Included in the cognitive assessments were the Wechsler Adult Intelligence Scale (WAIS) (Wechsler, 1955), the Wechsler Memory Scale (Wechsler, 1945), and the Boston Naming Test (Kaplan, Goodglass, & Weintraub, 1978). For the purposes of our analysis we selected three measures on the basis of their sensitivity to measures of atrophy in a previous study of normal elderly subjects: the scores on the Boston Naming Test, the Digit Symbol subtest from the WAIS, and the Visual Reproduction subtest from the WMS. The number of measures was restricted to preserve the power in the analysis.

Because we hoped that the results might implicate specific structures, we decided to examine only tissue sample measures of the brain. Again, the number of measures was restricted to preserve power. Those selected were CT values from frontal white matter and temporal white matter.

We entered the two sets of measures, CT and cognitive, into a canonical correlation analysis to test the hypothesis that specific changes in the brain were associated with specific cognitive changes, and that more than one such neuro-cognitive process was present in this group. The results support this conclusion. Two significant canonical correlations were obtained.

	Eigenvalue	Canonical correlation	Chi-square	Significance
Correlation 1	.65	.81	18.4	.005
Correlation 2	.46	.68	6.8	.034

These results may be interpreted to mean that two statistically independent sources of correlation between these two sets of variables exist.

This analysis produced two new variables that are linear combinations of the original cognitive variables and two new brain variables from the original CT variables. These four new variables are, by definition, a set of variables that satisfy the requirements already outlined for a double dissociation. They are not our original variables, however, and interpretation of them is problematic. Nevertheless, we can get some idea what they may be measuring if we look at the coefficients weighting the original variables in the new combinations of them. The coefficients for the first pair are as follows:

Cognitive set		CT set	
Boston naming	−.80	Temporal white matter	1.52
Visual reproduction	1.29	Frontal white matter	−.86
Digit symbol	.26		

The coefficients for the second pair are as follows:

Cognitive set		CT set	
Boston naming	.96	Temporal white matter	−.53
Visual reproduction	−1.08	Frontal white matter	1.36
Digit symbol	.89		

The coefficients reflect the relative contributions of the different original variables in the construction of the new canonical variables. For the first correlation, .81, the cognitive variable constructed is strongly and positively related to the visual reproduction scores. The brain variable constructed is strongly and positively related to the temporal white matter measure. This suggests that the correlation is due to an effect involving relatively lower temporal-lobe values and relatively lower visual reproduction scores, although to describe the correlation this way is to oversimplify the variables somewhat.

The second canonical correlation, .68, produces very different variables. In fact, these variables are, by definition, uncorrelated with the first two. The cognitive variable is positively related to the Boston Naming and Digit Symbol tests to about the same degree. The brain measure is positively related to the frontal white matter values. Relatively low frontal values are apparently associated with relatively lower Boston Naming and Digit Symbol scores.

It is tempting to interpret these results as evidence that the cognitive processes involved in registration and short-term retention of information are specifically disrupted by a process differentially affecting the temporal lobes (relative to the frontal lobes). Furthermore, it would appear that a separate process, affecting the two lobes in the opposite way, specifically impairs naming and psychomotor coordination. These interpretations are based on the variable weightings, however, and these are the products of the analysis with least reliability. That two independent processes are occurring within this group of patients may be inferred. This inference rests only on the significance of the second canonical correlation. Understanding the nature of these processes, either their neuropathological nature or their cognitive nature, requires more information than we now have.

What we have gained in this regard is chiefly some guidelines for beginning to formulate the cognitive and neuropathological characteristics. It is appropriate that we constrain our hypotheses about the cognitive processes to those that are consistent with the relative contributions of the tests, and our hypotheses about the brain mechanisms to those that are consistent with the pattern observed for the two white matter measures, since such hypotheses represent educated guesses. Many plausible explanations remain. To gain more information, we will study more patients, so that we will have adequate power to include more brain variables and more cognitive variables. The results of these planned analyses may further clarify the results.

Although the analyses described here do not validate memory assessments in a straightforward way, they may provide a basis for validating cognitive measures specifically for use in dementia. If two separate cerebral processes, and possibly more, are occurring within the demented population, it would probably be very useful to have cognitive measures that are highly sensitive to one process and relatively insensitive to others. The new composite variables are our best substitutes for such measures at this point, and they provide

a score on each factor for each subject. Ideally, though, we would like to discover the cognitive distinctions between the two factors. If we design a cognitive task that we think is strongly affected by one of the processes and only weakly affected by others, the measure should be highly weighted in our canonical analysis. In this sense the analysis can be used to test our hypotheses about the specific cognitive impairments associated with these particular patterns of cerebral change.

Conclusions

I have outlined the approach that my colleagues and I have used to exploit CT in the investigation of human brain–behavior relationships. It is clearly an exploratory approach, in that our hypothesis is only that specific relationships exist; the nature of these relationships is emerging post hoc. We have tried to avoid the pitfalls of much exploratory research by not drawing inferences from significant results obtained after many tests. We have also refrained from making assumptions about the unknown relative reliabilities and factor structure of our variables.

We conclude that our neuropsychological tests and CT measurements enable us to measure the structural and cognitive aspects of two cerebral processes with sufficient sensitivity to confirm their presence. Using these tests, we can now compute for any subject an estimate of the extent to which each process is occurring. Although we do not yet fully understand the processes involved, such estimates should have some utility in research with other biological measurements. For example, these estimates might help to predict drug response within the demented population. We hope that this question and others will be investigated with CT and with other neuroimaging techniques in the near future.

References

Banna, M. (1977). The ventriculo-cephalic ratio on computed tomography. *Journal of the Canadian Association of Radiology, 28,* 205–210.

Barron, S. A., Jacobs, L., & Kinkel, W. R. (1976). Changes in size of normal lateral ventricles during aging determined by computerized tomography. *Neurology, 26,* 1011–1013.

de Leon, M. J., Ferris, S. H., George, A. E., Reisberg, B., Kricheff, I. I., & Gershon, S. (1980). Computed tomography evaluations of brain–behavior relationships in senile dementia of the Alzheimer's type. *Neurobiology of Aging, 1,* 69–79.

DiChiro, G., Brooks, R. A., Dubal, L., & Chew, E. (1978). The apical artifact: Elevated attenuation values toward the apex of the skull. *Journal of Computer Assisted Tomography, 2,* 65–70.

Ford, C. V., & Winter, J. (1981). Computerized axial tomograms and dementia in elderly patients. *Journal of Gerontology, 36,* 164–169.

Gutzmann, H., & Avdaloff, W. (1980). Mental impairment (dementia) and cerebral atrophy in geriatric patients. *Mechanisms of Aging and Development, 14,* 459–468.

Gyldensted, C. (1977). Measurements of the normal ventricular system and hemispheric sulci of 100 adults with computed tomography. *Neuroradiology, 14,* 183–192.

Hahn, F. J. Y., & Rim, K. (1976). Frontal ventricular dimensions on normal computed tomography. *American Journal of Radiology, 126,* 593–596.

Huckman, M. S., Fox, J., & Topel, J. (1975). The validity of criteria for the evaluation of cerebral atrophy by computed tomography. *Radiology, 116,* 85–92.

Jacoby, R. J., & Levy, R. (1980). Computed tomography in the elderly: 2. Senile dementia: Diagnosis and functional impairment. *British Journal of Psychiatry, 136,* 256–269.

Jernigan, T. L., Zatz, L. M., Feinberg, I., & Fein, G. (1980). Measurement of cerebral atrophy in the aged by computed tomography. In L. W. Poon (Ed.), *Aging in the 1980's: Psychological issues* (pp. 86–94). Washington, DC: American Psychological Association.

Jernigan, T. L., Zatz, L. M., & Naeser, M. A. (1979). Semiautomated methods for quantitating CSF volume on cranial computed tomography. *Radiology, 132,* 463–466.

Kaplan, E. F., Goodglass, H., & Weintraub, S. (1978). *The Boston Naming Test.* Boston: E. Kaplan & H. Goodglass.

Kaszniak, A. W., Garron, D. C., & Fox, J. (1979). Differential effects of age and cerebral atrophy upon span of immediate recall and paired associate learning in older patients suspected of dementia. *Cortex, 15,* 285–295.

Penn, R. D., Belanger, M. G., & Yasnoff, W. A. (1978). Ventricular volume in man computed from CAT scans. *Annals of Neurology, 3,* 216–223.

Synek, V., & Reuben, J. R. (1976). The ventricular brain ratio using planimetric measurement of EMI scans. *British Journal of Radiology, 49,* 233–237.

Terrence, C. F., Delaney, J. F., & Alberts, M. C. (1977). Computed tomography for Huntington's disease. *Neuroradiology, 13,* 173–175.

Wechsler, D. (1945). A standardized memory scale for clinical use. *Journal of Psychology, 19,* 87–95.

Wechsler, D. (1955). *Manual for the Wechsler Adult Intelligence Scale.* New York: Psychological Corporation.

Zatz, L. M., Jernigan, T. L., & Ahumada, A. J., Jr. (1982a). Changes on computed cranial tomography with aging: Intracranial fluid volume. *American Journal of Neuroradiology, 3,* 1–11.

Zatz, L. M., Jernigan, T. L., & Ahumada, A. J., Jr. (1982b). White matter changes in cerebral computed tomography related to aging. *Journal of Computer Assisted Tomography, 6,* 19–23.

Samuel D. Brinkman, John W. Largen, Jr., Laura Cushman, and Mohammad Sarwar

CHAPTER

36

Anatomical Validators: Progressive Changes in Dementia

Limited progress has been made in relating characteristics of computed tomography (CT) to neuropsychological functioning in memory-impaired elderly persons. Many patients with probable Alzheimer's disease (AD) have abnormally large ventricular systems, and the size of the lateral or third ventricles is related to the degree of functional impairment. Ventricular size may change more rapidly in patients with probable AD than in normal elderly persons or in patients with stable cerebrovascular disease. The utility of CT scanning as an external validator, however, appears to be limited by at least three factors: the variability among subjects in clinical symptoms and in the course of their disease, a lack of understanding of how CT parameters may be related to biochemistry or other aspects of the disease, and the multidetermined nature of neuropsychological functioning.

This chapter is concerned with the usefulness of computed tomography (CT) for validating neuropsychological tests of the elderly. As an index of age-related or disease-related changes in brain morphology, CT scanning seems to be a useful tool for determining the relative sensitivity of various tests to the aging process or to age-related disorders such as Alzheimer's disease (AD). Unfortunately, limited progress has been made in understanding the relationship between morphological changes and neuropsychological changes in impaired elderly persons.

Since its introduction to clinical practice (Ambrose, 1973), CT scanning has contributed significantly to the diagnostic evaluation of patients with dementia. Because of the relative safety of CT scanning in comparison with other neurodiagnostic procedures such as pneumocencephalography (PEG) or angiography, it has been possible to study in greater detail brain changes in normal elderly individuals and in larger numbers of patients with probable AD. With more detailed analyses of CT images, there has been a continu-

ing hope that CT scanning would provide the capability for more specific diagnosis of AD. This hope, however, has never been realized. The clinical application of CT scanning in the dementia workup is limited to ruling out mass lesions or other disorders that may produce dementia.

When CT scanning was introduced in clinical practice, AD was conceptualized as a progressive central nervous system (CNS) disorder characterized by degenerative changes in posterior cortical and limbic regions. Just 2 years later, reports of reduced CNS ability to synthesize acetylcholine (ACh) shifted the emphasis from morphological changes reflected in CT scans to specific cholinergic pathways (Davies & Maloney, 1976; Perry, 1980). Further investigation of these pathways has suggested that specific degeneration in the nucleus basalis of Meynert, with consequent loss of much of the cholinergic input to cortex, may produce a pattern of functional cortical disturbance, even though the primary site of anatomical change is in the basal forebrain (Struble, Cork, Whitehouse, & Price, 1982; Whitehouse, Price, Clark, Coyle, & Delong, 1981). The nucleus basalis of Meynert has rather poorly defined anatomical limits. It may be difficult for the untrained eye to visualize this structure in tissue sections, and it has not been possible to study the structure morphometrically by CT scanning. As a result, the major "discovery" in AD research in the past decade has had little to do with gross morphological changes as seen in the CT scan.

Although the findings of reduced ability to synthesize brain ACh do not invalidate the results of CT investigations of AD, no clear link between cholinergic deficits and cortico-cerebral atrophy has been established. The study of CT scanning in dementia, therefore, has led to some disappointment. But CT scanning is well suited to the study of brain morphology in vivo with minimal risk to the subject, so research emphasis has now shifted from the study of morphology toward the study of neurochemistry and neurotransmission.

Current Status of CT Scanning in Diagnosing Dementia

In clinical practice, the CT scan is employed to rule out mass lesions or other similar CNS disturbances that may produce dementia. Although the analysis of pixel values or Hounsfield units holds promise (Jernigan, chapter 35, this volume; Albert and colleagues, chapter 38, this volume), there is no experimental CT analysis or measurement that significantly increases the accuracy of a specific diagnosis of AD. Cortico-cerebral atrophy, which may be seen in the CT scan as enlarged ventricles and prominent cortical sulci, has often been reported in cases of AD. When the CT-demonstrated components of cortico-cerebral atrophy have been measured from x-ray images in cross-sectional studies, several trends have emerged.

Age-Related CT Changes

The degree to which brain morphology changes with age has been recognized for some time through autopsy studies (Haug et al., 1983). Measurement of the lateral ventricles from CT scans provided corroborative evidence that there is a gradual increase in the size of cerebrospinal fluid (CSF)-containing compartments as aging occurs. Barron and colleagues (Barron, Jacobs, & Kinkel, 1976) identified a marked increase in the rate of ventricular enlargement beginning around the sixth decade of life. These results are consistent with studies of brain weight at different ages (Brody, 1978; Pakkenberg & Voigt, 1964) and with ventricular measurements from CT scans of older persons reported by other investigators (Brinkman, Sarwar, Levin, & Morris, 1981; Gonzales, Lantieri, & Natha, 1978; Jacoby, Levy, & Dawson, 1980; Ito, Hatazawa, Yamamura, & Matsuzawa, 1981). Investigations of the third ventricle, sylvian fissure, cortical sulci, and other structures have suggested a strong relationship with age as well, but these structures have been studied less extensively in the normal elderly population.

Cortical Sulci and Neuropsychological Abilities

Although the cortical sulci may appear more prominent with age, there has been little evidence that the degree of enlargement of cortical sulci is related to neuropsychological functioning in patients with AD. Prior to the advent of CT scanning, the excessive filling of subarachnoid space with air during PEG (sulcus width greater than 3 mm) was taken as an index of cortical atrophy. PEG studies failed to demonstrate that the degree of filling of the subarachnoid space with air was related to the severity of cognitive deficits in patients with dementia (Mann, 1973; Niessen, Petersen, Thygesen, & Willanger, 1966). Subsequent studies with CT scanning have generally confirmed these findings, as no statistically significant correlations between measurements of cortical sulci and performance on neuropsychological tests have been found in patients with dementia (Brinkman et al., 1981; Ford & Winter, 1981; Roberts & Caird, 1976; Roberts, McGeorge, & Caird, 1978; Soininen, Puranen, & Riekkinen, 1982). To some extent, this lack of a relationship between size of cortical sulci and neuropsychological abilities may reflect the technical difficulties in measurement, because apparent widening of a sulcus in a CT image may be due to the reduction of a three-dimensional structure to a two-dimensional x-ray image. Even with the marked improvements in resolution of modern CT scanners, no significant relationship between prominence of cortical sulci and degree of cognitive impairment has been established.

Classification Analyses

Early studies were concerned with establishing an optimal cutoff to differentiate between cortico-cerebral atrophy associated with normal aging and that associated with dementia due to AD (e.g., Fox, Topel, & Huckman, 1975; Huckman, Fox, & Topel, 1975). Subsequent descriptions of age-related changes in the normal CT scan (Barron et al., 1976; Gyldenstedt, 1977) indicated that the optimal cutoff may be different at different ages. When classification as normal or demented was based on deviation from the expected normal ventricular size for age, the accuracy of classification improved, but a large percentage of subjects continued to be misclassified or to be classified in the equivocal range (Brinkman et al., 1981).

Correlational Analyses

Although CT classification of patients with AD and normal persons has been disappointing, it has become clear that specific measurements from the CT scan are significantly related to the degree of neuropsychological impairment. Recent studies have been concerned with the strength of the relationship, the best method of characterizing the CT scan, and the best method of quantifying the neuropsychological impairments.

The most extensive correlational analyses were completed by de Leon and colleagues (de Leon et al., 1980), who reported that a wide range of psychometric scores were significantly correlated with a number of CT parameters in a sample of patients with AD. The strongest correlations with psychometric variables involved measurements in the area of the third ventricle. Various indices of the size of the lateral ventricles, such as the bifrontal or bicaudate ratios, width of the lateral ventricles, or ventricular–brain ratio (VBR) (Synek & Reuben, 1976), also correlated significantly with neuropsychological measures. As noted earlier, measurements of cortical sulci were not related to cognitive deficits.

The strength of the relationships between CT parameters and indices of cognitive impairment has varied from study to study primarily because of sampling differences. In one of the early correlational studies, Roberts and Caird (1976) reported modest correlations from a heterogeneous group of patients with dementia ($r = .49$, employing a 4-point multidimensional scale). De Leon and colleagues (de Leon et al., 1980) evaluated a larger number of subjects who had milder deficits as well as patients who had more severe impairments (scores of 3 to 5 on the Global Deterioration Scale [GDS] [Reisberg, 1983]). With the more homogeneous sample and a broader range of severity, stronger correlations were reported (most rs were in the .40s and .50s). Brinkman et al. (1981) studied a homogeneous sample with greater impairments and reported that the correlations between the age-corrected VBR and Wechsler Adult Intelligence Scale (WAIS) (Wechsler, 1955) Verbal and Performance IQ scores were $-.53$ and $-.65$, respectively.

In general, therefore, CT parameters may at best account for up to 30% of the variance in neuropsychological performance in patients with dementia of the Alzheimer's type. In most analyses and with most samples, the variance in cognitive abilities that may be related to variance in the CT scan has been less than this. The study of neuropsychological correlates of CT parameters provides the opportunity to evaluate the relative sensitivity of various assessment devices to morphological change in AD. AD impairs a wide range of neuropsychological abilities. These areas of neuropsychological impairment may not be affected equally at all points in the progression of the disease. Early in the progression, more precise measurements of relatively specific neuropsychological abilities may be possible. Late in the progression, most standard neuropsychological tests may be inapplicable because of the patient's poor ability to comprehend or respond. In advanced AD, therefore, it may be necessary to employ more global rating scales to provide meaningful neuropsychological data.

Most of the correlational analyses have been concerned with the mild to moderate stages of AD, when patients are able to perform meaningfully on standardized tests. The extensive correlational matrix of de Leon et al. (1980) suggested two possible conclusions: First, certain aspects of the neuropsychological test performance may be most highly correlated with certain aspects of morphological change. Memory impairments, for example, may be related to changes in the area around the third ventricle and sylvian fissures more than to changes in other brain areas (de Leon et al., 1980). Second, some behavioral parameters may be more sensitive than other behavioral parameters to CT changes. In the study of de Leon et al. (1980), for example, the GDS correlated more strongly and with a wider range of CT variables than did a mental status questionnaire score.

There appears to be little preference for either memory tests or nonmemory cognitive tests for correlating CT variables with mental impairment in mild to moderate AD. Both types of psychometric data have been studied with approximately equal success (Brinkman et al., 1981; de Leon et al., 1980). Perhaps the psychometric properties of the assessment instrument are of greater importance than the specific area of cognition that the instrument purports to measure. Although there are insufficient data to identify the best assessment procedure, it appears that any test that measures higher order integrative abilities (whether within the context of memory or not) may reflect the anatomical changes in AD, if the scale is reliable, has acceptable validity, is within the range of performance potential for the patient (floor and ceiling effects), and is scaled so that discrimination among patients can be achieved in the mild to moderate range. Tests such as the Buschke Selective Reminding Procedure (Buschke & Fuld, 1974), the Guild Memory Test (Crook, Gilbert, & Ferris, 1980), the Peterson and Peterson procedure (Peterson & Peterson, 1959), and the WAIS have been correlated significantly with CT parameters. The conclusion drawn from the review of correlational studies is that there is no "best test" for correlating CT measurements with neuropsychological impairments. There are several possible explanations for this conclusion.

First, it may not be possible to express the progressive neuropsychological impairments associated with AD in terms of a single dimension. Although memory impairments are certainly prominent, they are usually associated with deficiencies in praxic, gnostic, attentional, and other processes as well. Attempts to quantify the impairments employing relatively unidimensional tests, therefore, may have inherent limitations.

Second, the progression of AD symptoms varies with the patient. In some patients, verbal-linguistic deficits may be especially prominent in early stages of the disease. In other patients, early symptoms may be characterized primarily by apraxia or memory impairments. Data analyses that collapse across this intersubject variability may underestimate the strength of anatomical–behavioral correlations.

Third, progression along multiple neuropsychological dimensions may have one underlying factor that cannot be assessed adequately by any individual test. A deficiency in some aspects of attention, for example, may require a number of behavior operations for adequate characterization and quantification. If this is the case, the recommendation of Riege, Harker, and Metter (see chapter 33, this volume) regarding the use of factor scores derived from multidimensional assessment may be valid.

Relationship of CT Scans to Other Clinical Measures

The results of CT scanning may not always agree with the results of other clinical studies. Employing a multiple regression analysis, Kaszniak and co-workers (Kaszniak, Garron, Fox, Bergen, & Huckman, 1979) found that the electroencephalograph (EEG) may be significantly more sensitive than the CT scan to mild degrees of cognitive change associated with AD. In addition, much of the variability in test performances of AD patients may be due to premorbid factors such as education level. Because most of the studies of CT scanning in dementia have not included other factors, the multiple regression approach of Kaszniak et al. (1979) enables the investigator to appreciate the relative contributions of different factors in determining cognitive functioning in these patients.

The EEG and the CT scan often disagree or are poorly correlated in patients with dementia (Kaszniak et al., 1979; Merskey et al., 1980; Roberts et al., 1978). Similarly, CT parameters may be poorly correlated with results of cerebral blood flow studies (Melamed, Lavy, Siew, Bentin, & Cooper, 1978).

De Leon, George, et al. (1983) reported on the relationship between CT parameters and results of positron emission tomography (PET) in a mixed group of normal elderly people and patients with probable AD. The CT analysis in this study involved assessment of the pixel values, rather than the linear measurement of compartments containing cerebrospinal fluid, which have been emphasized in this chapter. The study is included in the review because the CT data suggested that the anatomical area of primary importance for understanding more diffuse cerebral dysfunction may be adjacent to the third ventricle. CT attenuation values (pixel values or Hounsfield units) from the frontal white matter, caudate nucleus, and anterior limb of the internal capsule were not related to PET changes. CT attenuation values from the thalamus, posterior limb of the internal capsule, and temporal lobes were significantly correlated with widespread reductions in glucose utilization as measured by PET. These results suggest that the relationship between alterations in brain morphology and deterioration in brain function may be more complex than has been expected.

＊　　＊　　＊

This brief review of studies of CT scanning in dementia indicates that alterations in brain morphology are statistically significantly related to changes in neuropsychological functioning in patients with probable AD. The studies of de Leon et al. (1980) suggested that some CT parameters are more closely related to changes in brain function than other CT parameters; morphological change in the area adjacent to the third ventricle and in the temporal lobes may be especially relevant to cerebral functioning in AD. As pointed out by Kaszniak et al. (1979), neuropsychological functioning is determined by multiple factors in AD, and a single index of morphological change may not be the most powerful of these determinants (also see Riege et al., chapter 33 this volume). Classification analyses have been poor because of the wide variability in morphological change associated with normal aging.

In clinical practice, the role of CT scanning is limited to ruling out mass lesions or other etiologies. Cortical atrophy has not been related significantly to cognitive deficits. There is as yet no experimental CT index that improves the specific diagnostic accuracy beyond current clinical application.

Longitudinal CT Analyses

Nearly all published studies of CT scanning in dementia have been cross-sectional. AD, however, is a progressive disorder with a continuously changing clinical appearance. Because of the progressive characteristics of AD, the rate of morphological change might be a more powerful behavior correlate than the morphological characteristics at any single point in time. Several analyses were undertaken in a pilot effort to determine whether analysis of repeated CT scans would provide new data to facilitate an understanding of brain–behavior relationships in AD.

The diagnosis of AD was made using generally accepted standards. Reductions in intellectual and memory abilities were demonstrated through detailed history and neuropsychological evaluations. All patients received physical, neurological, and psychiatric evaluations. Laboratory studies were extensive and included thyroid screening. All patients underwent CT scanning (to rule out mass or focal lesions or other identifiable conditions), EEG, and ECG, and all scored below 5 on Hachinski's Ischemic Score (Hachinski et al., 1975). Medications were reviewed in order to rule out medication-induced dementia. No patients reported significant symptoms of depression, and "depressive pseudododementia" was thought to be unlikely on the basis of the psychiatric and neuropsychological evaluations.

Analysis 1

The purpose of the first analysis was to determine whether the rate of change in the ventricular–brain ratio (VBR) in patients with probable AD was greater than the ratio expected in normal elderly individuals. Unfortunately, there are no published data regarding repeated measurements of VBR in normal elderly individuals. As a result, it was necessary to infer rate of change of VBR from cross-sectional normative data.

Five patients with probable AD (three women, two men) met the diagnostic criteria (Brinkman & Largen, 1984) and had undergone two CT scans; the interval between CT scans ranged from 15 to 35 months. VBRs were measured blindly by planimetry. The average annual change in VBR was calculated and compared with the expected annual rate of change from data published by Barron et al. (1976).

According to the data of Barron et al. (1976), the VBR may be expected to change from .052 at age 54 to .064 at age 64, an average of .0012 (or 2%) each year. In contrast to these expectations, the five patients with probable AD had an average change of .0223 (or 20%) per year, a considerably greater rate of ventricular enlargement. At the time of the first CT scan, mean VBR (+ standard error) was .112 (+.017). At the time of the second CT scan, the mean VBR was .160 (+.021). The Randomization Test (Siegel, 1956) indicated that the

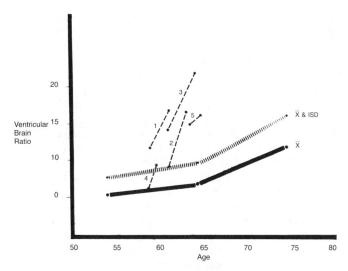

Figure 36-1. Change in ventricular–brain ratio (VBR) in five cases of probable Alzheimer's disease relative to expected VBR for age. Adapted from Brinkman and Largen (1984) by permission. Copyright © 1984, American Psychiatric Association.

change in VBR was unlikely to be due to chance ($p <$ .05), but no statistical test could be applied to determine whether the rate of change in the AD patients was greater than the normative rate of change, because the normative data were cross-sectional.

Individual cases are plotted in relation to the cross-sectional data in Figure 36-1. In four of the five AD cases, the slopes (which reflect rate of change of the VBR) are markedly steeper than the slope of the normative graph. Subject 4 is especially interesting because the second VBR was significantly larger than the first, even though the VBR on both occasions was within one standard deviation of the mean for age. This patient, a 61-year-old woman, had severe deficits at the time of the second CT scan. The patient's full-scale IQ on the WAIS was 55, and the memory quotient (MQ) from the Wechsler Memory Scale (WMS) was 58.

Figure 36-1 also shows that Subject 5 had relatively little change in VBR during the 15-month interval between CT scans. At the time of each CT scan, however, the VBR was markedly larger than expected for the patient's age. This patient's deficits were relatively less severe than those of other patients. The patient's high education level (16 years and a BA degree) suggested that the WAIS full scale IQ of 97 actually may have been in the abnormal range relative to her premorbid abilities. Objective evidence of functional impairments (including inability to perform her job) and the lack of evidence of depression or other reversible etiology during several years of participation in a longitudinal study supported the diagnosis of AD. Following the second CT scan, this patient's intellectual capacity degenerated rapidly.

These data suggest that morphological change and cognitive change may follow more or less parallel paths. The rate of loss in memory and intellectual abilities varies from patient to patient. Some patients (such as Subject 5) may experience an initial decline in

adaptive abilities followed by a period of relative stabilization. Other patients (such as Subject 4) experience a steady worsening of intellectual deficits from the time of initial symptoms. Although a large number of factors doubtless influence the temporal course of symptoms, the analysis of this small set of cases suggests that there may be morphological parallels to the clinical symptoms in some cases of AD.

Analysis 2

The first analysis suggested that the rate of morphological change, as reflected in the VBR, may be more strongly related to cognitive abilities than a cross-sectional correlation between CT parameters and intellectual performance measures. The second analysis was undertaken to explore this possibility using the limited pilot data that were available.

At the time of the second CT scan, thorough neuropsychological evaluations of nine patients between the ages of 59 and 70 had been completed. Spearman rank-order correlation coefficients were then calculated in two ways. First, correlation coefficients were calculated between the parameters derived from the second CT scan and the scores on these neuropsychological tests: WAIS Full Scale IQ, Buschke Selective Reminding Procedure, WMS Visual Reproduction, Seashore Rhythm (Halstead, 1947), Digit Cancellation and Hidden Words tasks (Moran & Mefferd, 1959), Embedded Figures (Thurstone, 1944), and the Blessed Dementia Rating Scale. Second, the change in CT parameters (expressed as percentages) was correlated with the neuropsychological test scores.

Eight neuropsychological scores were correlated with 11 CT parameters for a total of 88 correlation coefficients. With a cross-sectional analysis, only one of 88 correlation coefficients was statistically significant. Because of the small sample size, these results were not surprising. When the neuropsychological scores were correlated with the *change* in CT parameters, however, 16 of 88 correlation coefficients were statistically significant. The strongest correlations were noted with the 3V–SF ratio (Brinkman et al., 1981) and septum–caudate ratio.

Analysis 3

A comparison of correlations derived from a cross-sectional analysis with correlations derived from repeated CT scans provided additional support for the suggestion that the rate of morphological change may be an important determinant of the severity of clinical symptoms in AD. Changes in both morphology and cognitive abilities, however, may accompany normal aging. The first two analyses failed to provide evidence that morphological–behavioral relationships were specific to AD. In view of the lack of longitudinal CT data in the normal elderly population, the decision was made to compare the rate of VBR change in AD patients with the rate in patients with multi-infarct dementia (MID).

MID patients were classified according to Hachinski's Ischemic Scale (Hachinski et al., 1975). In addition, there was radiographic evidence of cerebrovascular disease (either by CT scanning or by four-vessel angiography) in all MID cases. Five patients with presumed MID had had multiple CT scans as part of a longitudinal study of cerebrovascular disease. Five patients with probable AD were matched as closely as possible to the MID cases for age and interval between CT scans. Patients with clinical diagnoses of AD tended to have greater rates of change in the VBR than did patients with probable MID:

Average VBR change* per month

	MID patients (n = 5)	AD patients (n = 5)
$\overline{X}$	−.09	.19
Standard deviation	.14	.07
Median	−.06	.21

*$p < .01$ by Randomization Test

There was no overlap between groups in the rate of VBR change, because all five AD cases had greater rates of change than any of the MID cases.

Changes in CT Scans of AD Patients

Although our sample size was small, we found unusually high rates of morphological change so consistently in the AD patients studied that we believe it is accurate to conclude that high rates of morphological change are characteristic of AD patients. In comparison with published cross-sectional norms for the VBR, AD patients tended to have a more rapid enlargement of the VBR over a period of 15 to 35 months. When compared with clinically stable MID patients, AD patients had significantly higher rates of enlargement of the VBR. Significant correlations between CT parameters and neuropsychological data were more likely to be found if the CT data were derived from multiple CT scans on the same patients.

AD patients are markedly heterogeneous in their initial presentation and clinical course. Some patients reach a point of relative stability in the progression of symptoms; the only patient like this in the present series of analyses tended to have little morphological change during the period of relative stabilization. Other patients may have a continuous progression of symptoms, and these patients may be more likely to undergo considerable change in brain morphology, even though specific CT parameters may continue to be in the normal range.

Summary and Conclusion

The concept of repeated estimates of ventricular size from CT scans during the progression of a degenerative CNS disorder is not new. Rao, Brennan, and Garcia (1977) reported dramatic increases in the appearance of atrophy in the CT scans of two cases of Creutzfeldt-

Jacob disease during a 1- to 2-month progression. Naguib and Levy (1982) reported that a few patients with clinical diagnoses of AD may have little change in mental abilities over a 2-year period. Serial CT scans in these patients tended to demonstrate little change in ventricular size over the same period. The majority of AD patients, however, experienced a normal clinical progression, with parallel changes in ventricular size. The appearance of the lateral ventricles in the initial CT scan did not predict the subsequent clinical course of CT changes. There was some suggestion, however, that attenuation density values at the time of the original CT scan may be of predictive value.

In general, the results presented in this chapter are consistent with the observations of Naguib and Levy (1982). Four of the five patients in the initial sample demonstrated an unremarkable progression of symptoms. The clinical course was associated with abnormally high rates of ventricular enlargement over a period of 15 to 35 months. The one patient whose cognitive abilities appeared to change least during the interval between CT scans also had the least amount of change in the VBR (although the VBR was abnormally large on both occasions).

Analysis 2 suggested that knowledge of the rate of change in the VBR may permit greater predictability of cognitive functioning than knowledge of the VBR at a single time-point. Although the observations of Kaszniak et al. (1979) regarding the multidetermined nature of cognitive functioning in AD are especially poignant in such a follow-up analysis, data from this pilot analysis of nine patients supported the results of our first analysis. The pilot data suggest that patients with the greatest change in VBR over a short interval may tend to undergo the most rapid progression of symptoms.

The difficulty investigators have in exploiting these observations more completely may be attributed to the lack of knowledge about the expected rate of ventricular enlargement in unimpaired elderly individuals. Published cross-sectional data suggest that there are marked changes in ventricular size from the sixth to the ninth decade of life (Barron et al., 1976; Earnest, Heaton, Wilkinson, & Manke, 1979; Gonzales et al., 1978; Jacoby et al., 1980). Unless one hypothesizes an intermittent or sporadic pattern of change in brain morphology, however, published cross-sectional data probably provide a reasonable estimate of rate of VBR change associated with normal aging. In view of the minimal ventricular change noted in a small group of MID patients (Analysis 3), who experienced relatively little concurrent clinical change, it appears reasonable to conclude that most patients with clinical diagnoses of AD may demonstrate significantly greater changes in VBR over a short period of time (15 to 35 months) than would be expected on the basis of aging alone.

Technical, Methodological, and Conceptual Issues

A thorough discussion of technical and methodological issues is beyond the purpose and scope of the present chapter, as such discussions have been published elsewhere (Bird, 1982; Brinkman & Largen, 1984; Naguib & Levy, 1982). The difficulties in making accurate clinical diagnosis of AD are especially noteworthy in pilot investigations with small samples (Sulkava, Haltia, Paetau, Wikstrom, & Palo, 1983). The consistency of findings in these analyses, however, provides an empirical rationale for a more detailed study of serial CT scans in normal elderly persons and in AD patients.

Perhaps the greatest obstacle to more effective use of CT scanning in dementia is our lack of understanding of the relationship between alterations in gross morphology, as seen in the CT scan, and other neuropsychological changes. The CT scan is thought to be a general reflection of pathology, but it is not a very direct measure. The relationship of changes in the CT scans to disruption of cellular functions and reductions in the ability to synthesize ACh is not known. Hubbard and Anderson (1981) reported that ventricular enlargement is not an accurate index of cerebral atrophy. Of 23 patients with the histopathological changes of AD (64 to 92 years old), only 13 were found to have had a ventricular volume clearly above the normal upper limit when measurements were taken from postmortem tissue. Although postmortem changes may alter the relationship between CT characteristics and necropsy measurements (Sarwar & McCormick, 1978), the results of Hubbard and Anderson (1981) appear to be valid, because a normal elderly sample had essentially the same degree of ventricular enlargement in necropsy measurements.

Results of the analyses presented in this chapter indicate the need for more detailed longitudinal study of individual cases of AD. Much of our current understanding of AD has been derived from the unidimensional study of AD at a single time-point. Because of the variable clinical progression of AD, comparisons of AD samples with other samples of patients or normal people may be misleading when data derived from different patients at different points in the progression are collapsed into a single measure of central tendency. There is a need for greater attention to the progressive features of AD. Two separate groups of investigators (Brinkman & Largen, 1984; Naguib & Levy, 1982) have provided data to suggest that more rapid clinical progression in AD may be associated with more rapid changes in the CT scans. More detailed understanding of the determinants of rate of progression may lead to more effective patient management. A small reduction in the rate of progression would lead to significant reductions in human suffering as well as in federal expenditures.

The study of CT scanning in dementia has raised interesting challenges for researchers. Future advances in biomedical technology will undoubtedly permit increasingly better characterization of the neurobiology of AD. Better neurobiological measurements will probably result in higher correlation between neuropsychological measures and neurobiological parameters. The search for a better neuropsychological test, however, should not depend excessively on developments in biomedical technology. Fundamental questions regarding the neuropsychological impairments of AD are becoming more urgent. These questions involve a conceptual

shift to the determinants of the *progression* of impairments of AD, rather than the cross-sectional neuropsychological correlates, and more theoretically based investigation of the seemingly multidimensional nature of the progression. Because AD is at present an irreversible disorder, a reduction in rate of progression through an understanding of and manipulation of various determinants of the progression may be a reasonable therapeutic goal while more effective treatments are under development.

References

Ambrose, J. (1973). Computerized transverse axial scanning (tomography): Part 2. Clinical application. *British Journal of Radiology, 46,* 1023–1047.

Barron, S. A., Jacobs, L., & Kinkel, W. R. (1976). Changes in size of normal lateral ventricles during aging determined by computerized tomography. *Neurology, 26,* 1011–1013.

Bird, J. M. (1982). Computerized tomography, atrophy, and dementia: A review. *Progress in Neurobiology, 19,* 91–115.

Brinkman, S. D., & Largen, J. W., Jr. (1984). Changes in brain ventricular size with repeated CAT scans in suspected Alzheimer's disease. *American Journal of Psychiatry, 141,* 81–83.

Brinkman, S. D., Sarwar, M., Levin, H. S., & Morris, H. H. (1981). Quantitative indexes of computed tomography in dementia and normal aging. *Neuroradiology, 138,* 89–92.

Brody, H. (1978). Cell counts in cerebral cortex and brainstem. In R. Katzman, R. D. Terry, and K. L. Bick (Eds.), *Aging: Vol. 7. Alzheimer's disease: Senile dementia and related disorders* (pp. 345–351). New York: Raven Press.

Buschke, H., & Fuld, P. A. (1974). Evaluating storage, retention, and retrieval in disordered memory and learning. *Neurology, 24*(11), 1019–1025.

Crook, T., Gilbert, J. G., & Ferris, S. (1980). Operationalizing memory impairment in elderly persons: The Guild Memory Test. *Psychological Reports, 47,* 1315–1318.

Davies, P., & Maloney, A. J. F. (1976). Selective loss of central cholinergic neurons in Alzheimer's disease. *Lancet, 2,* 1403.

de Leon, M. J., Ferris, S. H., George, A. E., Reisberg, B., Kricheff, I. I., & Gershon, S. (1980). Computed tomography evaluations of brain–behavior relationships in senile dementia of the Alzheimer's type. *Neurobiology of Aging, 1,* 69–79.

de Leon, M. J., George, A. E., Ferris, S. H., Rosenbloom, S., Christman, D. R., Gentes, C. I., Reisberg, B., Kricheff, I. I., & Wolf, A. P. (1983). Regional correlation of PET and CT in senile dementia of the Alzheimer type. *American Journal of Neuroradiology, 4,* 553–556.

Earnest, M. P., Heaton, R. K., Wilkinson, W. E., & Manke, W. F. (1979). Cortical atrophy, ventricular enlargement, and intellectual impairment in the aged. *Neurology, 29,* 1138–1143.

Ford, C. V., & Winter, J. (1981). Computerized axial tomograms and dementia in elderly patients. *Journal of Gerontology, 36,* 164–169.

Fox, J. H., Topel, J. L., & Huckman, M. S. (1975). Use of computerized tomography in senile dementia. *Journal of Neurology, Neurosurgery, and Psychiatry, 38,* 948–953.

Gonzales, C. F., Lantieri, R. L., & Natha, R. J. (1978). The CT scan appearance of the brain in a normal elderly population: A correlative study. *Neuroradiology, 16,* 120–122.

Gyldensted, C. (1977). Measurements of the normal ventricular system and hemispheric sulci of 100 adults with computed tomography. *Neuroradiology, 14,* 183–192.

Hachinski, V. C., Iliff, L., Zilhka, E., DuBoulay, G. H., McAllister, V. L., Marshall, J., Ross-Russell, R. W., & Symon, L. (1975). Cerebral blood flow in dementia. *Archives of Neurology, 32,* 632–637.

Halstead, W. C. (1947). *Brain and intelligence.* Chicago: University of Chicago Press.

Haug, H., Barmwater, U., Eggers, R., Fischer, D., Kuhl, S., & Sass, N. L. (1983). Anatomical changes in the aging brain: Morphometric analysis of the human prosencephalon. In J. Cervos-Navarro & H. I. Sarkander (Eds.), *Brain aging: Neuropathology and neuropharmacology* (pp. 1–12). New York: Raven Press.

Hubbard, B. M., & Anderson, J. M. (1981). Age, senile dementia and ventricular enlargement. *Journal of Neurology, Neurosurgery, and Psychiatry, 44,* 631–635.

Huckman, M. S., Fox, J., & Topel, J. (1975). The validity of criteria for the evaluation of cerebral atrophy by computed tomography. *Radiology, 116,* 85–92.

Ito, M., Hatazawa, J., Yamamura, H., & Matsuzawa, T. (1981). Age-related brain atrophy and mental deterioration: A study with computed tomography. *British Journal of Radiology, 54,* 384–390.

Jacoby, R. J., Levy, R., & Dawson, J. M. (1980). Computed tomography in the elderly: 1. The normal population. *British Journal of Psychiatry, 136,* 249–255.

Kaszniak, A. W., Garron, D. C., Fox, J. H., Bergen, D., & Huckman, M. (1979). Cerebral atrophy, EEG slowing, age, education, and cognitive functioning in suspected dementia. *Neurology, 29,* 1273–1279.

Mann, A. H. (1973). Cortical atrophy and air encephalography: A clinical and radiological study. *Psychological Medicine, 3,* 374–378.

Melamed, E., Lavy, S., Siew, F., Bentin, S., & Cooper, G. (1978). Correlation between regional cerebral blood flow and brain atrophy in dementia. Combined study with 133-Xenon inhalation and computerized tomography. *Journal of Neurology, Neurosurgery, and Psychiatry, 41,* 894–899.

Merskey, H., Ball, J. J., Blume, W. T., Fox, A. J., Fox H., Hersch, E. L., Kral, V. A., & Palmer, R. B. (1980). Relationships between psychological measurements and cerebral organic changes in Alzheimer's disease. *Canadian Journal of Neurological Sciences, 7,* 45–49.

Moran, L. J., & Mefford, R. B., Jr. (1959). Repetitive psychometric measures. *Psychological Reports, 5,* 269–275.

Naguib, M., & Levy, R. (1982). CT scanning in dementia. A follow-up of survivors. *British Journal of Psychiatry, 141,* 618–620.

Niessen, R., Petersen, O., Thygesen, P., & Willanger, R. (1966). Encephalographic ventricular atrophy. Relationships between size of ventricular system and intellectual impairment. *Acta Radiologica Diagnosis, 4,* 240–256.

Pakkenberg, H., & Voigt, J. (1964). Brain weight of the Danes. *Acta Anatomica, 56,* 297–307.

Perry, E. K., (1980). The cholinergic system in old age and dementia. *Age and Aging, 9,* 1–9.

Peterson, L. R., & Peterson, M. J. (1959). Short-term retention of individual verbal items. *Journal of Experimental Psychology, 58,* 193–198.

Rao, C. V. G. K., Brennan, T. G., & Garcia, J. H. (1977). Computed tomography in the diagnosis of Creutzfeldt-Jacob disease. *Journal of Computer Assisted Tomography, 1,* 211–215.

Reisberg, B., (1983). The brief Cognitive Rating Scale and Global Deterioration Scale. In T. Crook, S. Ferris, & R. Bartus (Eds.), *Assessment in geriatric psychopharmacology* (pp. 19–35). New Canaan, CT: Mark Powley Associates.

Roberts, M. A., & Caird, F. I. (1976). Computerized tomography and intellectual impairment in the elderly. *Journal of Neurology, Neurosurgery, and Psychiatry, 39,* 986–989.

Roberts, M. A., McGeorge, A. P., & Caird, F. I. (1978). Electroencephalography and computerized tomography in vascular and non-vascular dementia in old age. *Journal of Neurology, Neurosurgery, and Psychiatry, 41,* 903–906.

Sarwar, M., & McCormick, W. F. (1978). Decrease in ventricular and sulcal size after death. *Radiology, 127,* 409–411.

Siegel, S. (1956). *Nonparametric statistics for the behavioral sciences.* New York: McGraw-Hill.

Soininen, H., Puranen, M., & Riekkinen, P. J. (1982). Computed tomography findings in senile dementia and normal aging. *Journal of Neurology, Neurosurgery, and Psychiatry, 45,* 50–54.

Struble, R. G., Cork, L. L., Whitehouse, P. J., & Price, D. L. (1982). Cholingergic innervation in neuritic plaques. *Science, 216,* 413–415.

Sulkava, R., Haltia, M., Paetau, J., Wikstrom, J., & Palo, J. (1983). Accuracy of clinical diagnosis in primary degenerative dementia: Correlation with neuropathological findings. *Journal of Neurology, Neurosurgery, and Psychiatry, 46,* 9–13.

Synek, V., & Reuben, J. R. (1976). The ventricular–brain ratio using planimetric measurement of EMI scans. *British Journal of Radiology, 49,* 233–237.

Thurstone, L. L. (1944). *A factorial study of perception.* Chicago: University of Chicago Press.

Wechsler, D. (1945). A standardized memory scale for clinical use. *Journal of Psychology, 19,* 87–95.

Wechsler, D. (1955). *Manual for the Wechsler Adult Intelligence Scale.* New York: Psychological Corporation.

Whitehouse, P. J., Price, D. L., Clark, A. W., Coyle, J. T., & Delong, M. R. (1981). Alzheimer's disease: Evidence for selective loss of cholinergic neurons in the nucleus basalis. *Annals of Neurology, 10,* 122–126.

Mony J. de Leon, Ajax E. George, and Steven H. Ferris

CHAPTER

37

Computed Tomography and Positron Emission Tomography Correlates of Cognitive Decline in Aging and Senile Dementia

This chapter documents the search for clinically useful diagnostic criteria for senile dementia from the perspective of brain-imaging techniques, namely, computed tomography (CT) and positron emission tomography (PET). This search has improved our understanding of the brain and of the behavioral changes associated with normal aging and with suspected Alzheimer's disease (AD). Our research using CT has indicated that normal aging causes pronounced changes in brain structure, changes that are modestly exacerbated in AD patients. Our measurements of brain metabolism using PET, however, have revealed that although the brain's utilization of glucose changes little with normal aging, marked metabolic diminutions are associated with AD. These results suggest the importance of biochemical changes in AD and the potential utility of specific neuroimaging strategies.

New imaging techniques permit probing the nervous system with behavioral and pharmacologic perturbations and quantitating regional brain responses. Furthermore, new developments in radiochemistry permit examination of more specific metabolic pathways.

In this chapter we describe the value and limitations of in vivo brain imaging in the study and diagnosis of the major cause of AD. Our findings suggest that PET may be more useful than CT in the in vivo diagnosis of AD.

Clinical and Pathological Evaluations of Dementia

It is commonly understood that symptoms of dementia may arise from structural brain changes (e.g., disease-related brain atrophy) or from factors that interfere with normal brain functioning (e.g., toxins or nutritional deficiencies). Among the varied causes of dementia that affect the elderly, the most prevalent are the brain changes caused by Alzheimer's disease (AD)

and cerebrovascular or multi-infarct dementia (MID). As reported by Tomlinson and Kitchner (1972) and Jellinger (1976), clinicopathological studies have indicated that approximately 50% of the dementias are due to AD and about 20% are due to MID. Another 12% of the dementias were found to be due to a combination of the two. In the remaining cases, other pathologies, such as Pick's disease or tumors, were found to account for the dementia.

Clinically, the early diagnosis of AD and its differentiation from other causes of dementia, such as vascular disease, are important for prognosis and choice of treatment strategies. Rosen, Terry, Fuld, Katzman, and Peck (1980) reported in a clinicopathological study that several clinical features distinguished patients with vascular disease from patients with AD. The clinical features that best identified patients with vascular disease at postmortem were abrupt onset, stepwise deterioration, somatic complaints, emotional incontinence, history of hypertension, history of strokes, and focal neurologic symptoms. According to Roth and Meyers (1975), AD has the following features: (a) gradual and progressive deterioration over the years, (b) selective recent memory impairment that produces disorientation and that eventually encompasses all memories, (c) decline in intellectual functioning (the capacity for abstract thinking is particularly vulnerable), and (d) changes in personality that often present as caricatures of its worst features.

When this chapter was submitted (March 1984), magnetic resonance imaging was not available at our center. Currently we are actively using this modality in the study of normal aging and Alzheimer's disease. The present chapter does not reflect our recent findings.

Evaluations of Cognitive Deficits in AD

Global evaluations of mental functioning such as the Mental Status Questionnaire (MSQ) (Kahn, Goldfarb, Pollack, & Peck, 1960) have demonstrated their validity and reliability in differentiating brain-injured from functional and normal patients. Among the dementias, this type of test has little differential diagnostic utility. However, Gurland (1978) reported that the MSQ is predictive of mortality, discharge from hospital, institutionalization, nursing needs, and scores on other psychological tests that are indicative of dementia.

In the evaluation of dementia, the MSQ and other global evaluations need to be supplemented by other psychological measures that can help specify the nature and extent of cerebral dysfunctions (see Section 3 of this volume). There is general agreement that memory measures, particularly measures of recent memory, are useful in the evaluation of AD. There is also some evidence that perceptual–motor tasks, such as tests of reaction times, are useful in evaluating the nonmemory aspects of AD (Ferris, Crook, Sathananthan, & Gershon, 1976).

Pathological Diagnosis of AD

According to Corsellis (1976), gross examination of the brains of demented patients reveals two major disease processes. In MID patients, examiners have found arteriosclerotic changes in blood vessels that can compromise the supply of blood to the brain. The more severe the vascular breakdown, the more likely there will be cerebral softenings resulting from ischemic events.

In AD patients, histopathological studies have revealed specific diagnostic features. Senile plaques, neurofibrillary tangles, and granulovacuolar degeneration have been identified as the major lesions. Pathological study has not distinguished between senile dementia of the Alzheimer's type and presenile AD. If these two conditions are different entities, they are currently distinguished by the age of onset. Clinical pathological studies of AD patients have reported correlations between the number of these lesions and measures of cognitive impairment (Blessed, Tomlinson, & Roth, 1968). Nevertheless, these microscopic lesions are found to a limited extent in the brains of nondemented old people thus making the pathological diagnosis quantitative rather than qualititative.

Gross postmortem observation of the AD brain and the normal aged brain have demonstrated shrinkage of the cerebral convolutions and widening of the cortical sulci. In an age-controlled study of normal and demented persons, Tomlinson, Blessed, and Roth (1970) found that moderate or severe cortical atrophy was evident only in the brains of the demented old people. Evidence for selective degeneration of the temporal lobes also was found only in the demented group. Earlier, the same group of researchers (1968) had found that senile plaques in the cerebral gray matter correlated with cortical atrophy in general and in several cases were particularly associated with marked temporal lobe atrophy. Recently the same researchers (Tomlinson, 1980) reported that the most prominent macroscopic change in AD is the gyral atrophy of the frontal and temporal lobes. This appears to be especially true of the middle- and superior-temporal gyri, the hippocampus, and adjacent gyri. The volume of white matter also appears to be reduced. Quantitative investigations of neuronal populations have been contradictory, but recent studies have reported cellular losses in AD primarily in the frontal and temporal regions (Mountjoy, Roth, Evans, & Evans, 1983; Terry, Peck, deTeresa, Schecter, & Horoupian, 1981).

Further evidence for regionally selective neuronal changes in AD comes from neurochemical analyses of tissue from postmortem and biopsy studies (Bowen, Smith, White, & Davison, 1976; Davies & Maloney, 1976; Perry, Perry, Blessed, & Tomlinson, 1977). These studies have clearly demonstrated significant deficits of choline acetyltransferase (CAT) in the brain regions of AD patients, demonstrating the histopathological changes. CAT catalyzes the synthesis of the neurotransmitter acetylcholine and is specific to cholinergic neurons (Kuhar, 1976). Therefore, it appears that these neurons are selectively impaired in AD. Evidence from experiments with rats has shown that lesions of the nucleus basalis of Meynert produce marked cortical reductions in CAT (Johnston, Young, & Coyle, 1981). Significant neuronal losses in this nuclear group have been reported in AD patients (Whitehouse et al., 1982). Because cholinergic changes have long been associated with memory functioning, this selective basal forebrain lesion may account for some of the memory and intellectual dysfunctions characteristic of AD.

At autopsy, ventricular enlargement also has been observed as a pathological feature of AD (Corsellis, 1976). Tomlinson et al. (1970) found that moderate and severe ventricular dilatation was significantly more frequent in demented old patients than in age-matched control subjects. In these authors' pathological series, 70% of the brains were described as having moderately or severely dilated ventricles.

The ventricular dilatation, however, is not pathognomonic for AD. Many conditions, including normal aging, may affect ventricular size (Last & Tompsett, 1953). In general, the hypothesized mechanisms for ventricular dilatation are atrophic changes in brain parenchyma (hydrocephalus ex vacuo) and disturbances of cerebrospinal fluid physiology, that is, obstructions, defective absorption, and overproduction of cerebrospinal fluid (Fishman, 1980). Corsellis (1976) has suggested that ventricular dilatation in AD may reflect changes in the white matter of the brain.

Pathological Anatomy and Its Relation to Computed Tomography

Computed tomography (CT) has been especially useful in the identification of focal intracranial disease. For this reason, CT is an essential component in the clinical workup of the AD patient who requires a diagnosis by exclusion of other causes of dementia.

The CT Study of the Atrophic Brain

Changes associated with aging and AD have been limited in part by both the spatial resolution and the contrast resolution of the scanner. The spatial resolution of many current CT scanners is approximately 1 mm × 1 mm × 10 mm, but some machines are capable of an increased resolution mode of approximately 1 mm × 1 mm × 1.5 mm. This increased resolution may be helpful in further describing atrophy, but this possibility remains to be tested. The major problem is that many of the structural changes characteristic of the AD patient's brain at neuropathology are microscopic and well beyond the spatial-resolving power of CT.

Early CT studies were restricted to examining the intracranial contents as two compartments, either brain or cerebrospinal fluid. Recent developments in CT technology have extended these investigations into the study of brain parenchyma. As a consequence, white matter, specific subcortical gray matter structures, and, to a more limited extent, cortical gray matter can be studied. Furthermore, from the computer displays, these tissue areas can be sampled for their CT attenuation values.

According to Brooks, DiChiro, and Keller (1980), the different CT attenuation (x-ray absorption) values for white matter and gray matter can be explained by the chemical composition of these tissues. Specifically, white matter contains 8% more carbon and 8% less oxygen because of its higher lipid and lower water content. Because of the lower atomic number of carbon, the photoelectric x-ray absorption for white matter is lower.

CT Studies

Our understanding of the CT changes in the aging brain has been limited by methodological questions related to the selection of subjects, the methods of CT scan analysis, and the comparability of data across CT scanners. Several CT investigators have used normal patients, people who were undergoing evaluation for complaints such as headache and dizziness and whose studies proved negative. Such patients can provide only gross estimates of the true characteristics of the normal population, because they actually may have subtle pathological changes. This may be a concern in studies that attempt to distinguish the brain changes that occur in the earlier stages of degenerative brain disease from the brain changes that are found with normal aging.

Methods of CT scan analysis need to be appraised before the study results are interpreted. Researchers who have relied on traditional clinical CT ratings that range from normal to severely abnormal have had to make these subjective judgments in the absence of a normative CT data base. The rating-scale approach truncates the naturally occurring variation to three or four groupings, potentially obscuring some qualitative changes. In other studies, researchers have attempted to estimate ventricular size objectively with linear measures that have been selected without regard to pathological anatomy. Until recently, no CT studies have attempted to validate the predictive value of the often-used linear ventricular volume (George, de Leon, Rosenbloom, et al., 1981; Zatz, Jernigan, & Ahumada, 1982). No attempts have been made to validate linear sulcal measures as indicators of overall cortical atrophy.

The potential application of uniform research methodology across research centers has raised questions regarding image comparability. The current generation of CT machines generally permits enhanced visualization of smaller and less contrasting anatomical features. Therefore, as detail in the image (including the pathological features under investigation) increases, the comparison of groups studied with different scanners could introduce bias. The assessment of an individual's longitudinal CT changes across CT scanners is subject to the same cautions.

For example, Figure 37-1 shows the results of two CT studies of a single demented patient. These studies were conducted within a few months of each other, and during this time the patient was stable. The scans on the top were done with a current-generation scanner; the scans on the bottom were done with an earlier model. From left to right, the scans depict the centrum semiovale and the high convexities. As is evident, only the largest sulci are visible from the older scanner.

The Normal Aging Brain

There appears to be a consistent observation, across several different methods of CT scan analysis, that both ventricular size and cortical sulcal prominence increase with age (Barron, Jacobs, & Kinkel, 1976; de Leon et al., 1984; Gyldensted & Kosteljanetz, 1976; Haug, 1977; Yamamura, Ito, Kubota, & Matsuzawa, 1980; Zatz et al., 1982). These age-related changes apparently are found for both normal volunteer subjects and for neurologic patients diagnosed as normal. This finding is less interesting for the latter group, because subclinical intracranial disease would be expected to increase with age.

These reports suggest that studies examining limited portions of the life span rather than the entire continuum are less likely to reveal age-related brain changes (Cala, Thickbroom, Black, Collins, & Mastaglia, 1981; Jacoby & Levy, 1980). It remains unclear from these data whether the age-related changes that were reported occur gradually throughout the life span or are more likely to occur in the later years. Overall, it appears that there is increasing variability in ventricular size and in sulcal prominence with age.

The AD Patient's Brain

The use of CT in the study of the AD patient has been disappointing, because no reliable diagnostic criteria have emerged. In fact, several CT studies have reported the absence of a statistically significant disease effect. It may be that these studies used patient groups

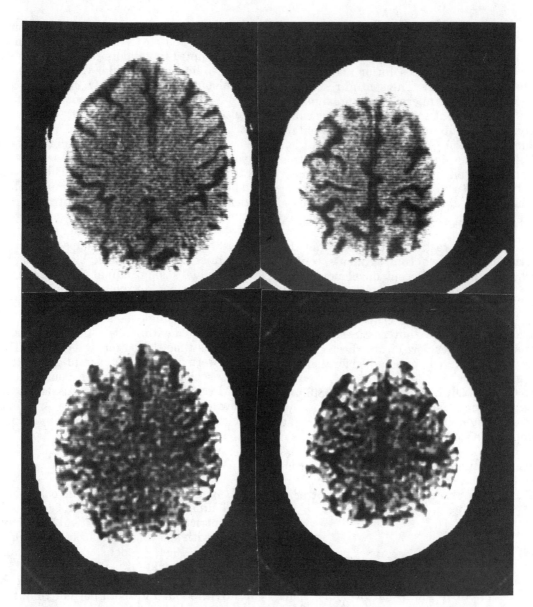

Figure 37-1. Shows two CT studies of a single dementia patient. Top-row scans were done with a current-generation scanner, and bottom-row scans were done with an earlier model. From left to right, the studies depict the centrum semiovale and the high convexities.

that were more heterogeneous with respect to age (Brinkman, Sarwar, Levin, & Morris, 1981; Kaszniak et al., 1978) or to clinical diagnosis (Claveria, Moseley, & Stevenson, 1977; Hughes & Gado, 1981) than were those studies that reported positive findings. Furthermore, some of these disappointing results may reflect methodological approaches based on the hypothesis that AD affects the brain diffusely. In the diffuse-change hypothesis, all brain regions are presumed to be affected by the disease; as a result, an examination of general structural changes is appropriate. It also appears that little attention has been paid to measurement strategies; as will be seen, measurement strategies vary in sensitivity.

In contrast to the diffuse-change hypothesis, the pathological data suggest that there are different degrees of regional change in AD patients. Thus,

hypothetically, certain measurements may be superior for identifying certain types of regional change. Although this question remains to be adequately addressed, preliminary evidence suggests that this line of thinking may be productive.

The use of CT in the study of brain changes in AD patients has been restricted to examining pathological brain changes as indirectly seen by cerebrospinal fluid distributions. Investigators have focused on two brain variables: ventricular dilatation and the size of the cortical sulci.

Huckman, Fox, and Topel (1975) compared 35 AD patients with a group of 20 control subjects (neurological patients complaining of headache). Patients in both groups were described as being over 60 years of age. The CT studies were evaluated using linear estimates of ventricular size (bifrontal and bicaudate) and subarachnoid cerebrospinal fluid (width of the four largest sulci). With all measurements combined into a single atrophy measure, the authors reported that 71% of the dementia cases had mild to severe atrophy but only 15% of the control subjects were similarly classified.

Roberts, Caird, Grossart, and Steven (1976) studied a group of 66 AD patients between the ages of 62 and 90. They estimated ventricular size using the ventricular area from a single CT slice; they estimated sulcal prominence using a linear and an area measure of the largest sulcus. The results indicated that the ventricular area, but not the sulcal measures, was significantly associated with increasing cognitive deficit.

In our laboratory, we studied 43 outpatients with a presumptive diagnosis of AD based on psychiatric, neuropsychological, neurologic, and biochemical study (de Leon et al., 1979). All patients were between 60 and 84 years of age (mean age = 70 ± 6.0). Each patient received a CT study and a cognitive test battery that was selected to focus on those cognitive areas known to be affected in AD (orientation, memory, and perceptual motor performance).

In the cognitive evaluations, we measured orientation with the MSQ (Kahn et al., 1960) and the Global Deterioration Scale (Reisberg, Ferris, de Leon, & Crook, 1982). We evaluated memory performance with the following tests of immediate and delayed recall (which resulted in 28 measures): paragraphs, paired associates, designs, (Gilbert & Levee, 1971), digits forward and backward, memory for faces (Moran, Kimble, & Mefferd, 1960), memory for names (French, Erkstrom, & Leighton, 1974), recall of meaningless trigrams with variable delays (Peterson & Peterson, 1959), Buschke Selective Reminding Task (Buschke & Fuld, 1974), Category Retrieval Test (Battig & Montague, 1969), and the Wechsler Adult Intelligence Scale (WAIS) Vocabulary subtest (Wechsler, 1955). We evaluated perceptual–motor functioning with measures of finger-tapping speed, simple and disjunctive reaction time, the perceptual speed test (Moran et al., 1960), and the Digit Symbol substitution test (WAIS).

We studied the CT images depicting the ventricles and the cortical sulci separately, using a rank-ordering procedure. In this procedure, we placed each study within a continuum of increasing pathology, ranging from most normal at one extreme to most abnormal at the other extreme. Using the ranking method, the observer compared each study with all of the other studies, thereby avoiding the diagnostic issue of separating the normal from the pathological and gaining some flexibility in establishing criteria for estimating size of the complexly shaped ventricles and sulci.

The results from this study indicated that both the ventricular and the cortical measures were significantly associated with measures of cognitive impairment. This was the first CT study of AD patients to report a relationship between cortical atrophy and cognitive impairment. We also reported that ventricular dilatation was more consistently associated with the cognitive deficits than was sulcal prominence.

Encouraged by these preliminary findings, we decided to investigate the relative efficacy of different methods of CT scan evaluation in determining brain–behavior relationships in AD patients. In this methodological study (de Leon et al., 1980), we reexamined the CT scans from our earlier study, using CT evaluation methods for ventricles and sulci that had been previously reported in the literature. These methods included a 4-point rating scale and linear and area measurements. The rating-scale approach required that the observer categorize the CT atrophy as normal, mild, moderate, or severe. The measurement approach required that the following linear measures be taken: (a) the bifrontal span of the lateral ventricles, (b) the bicaudate diameter, (c) the width of the third ventricle, (d) the widths of the anterior horns of the lateral ventricles, (e) the widths of the sylvian fissures, (f) the minimal width of the bodies of the lateral ventricles, and (g) the widths of the three most prominent cortical sulci (see Figure 37-2). We corrected the ventricular measures for head size using a linear estimate of brain

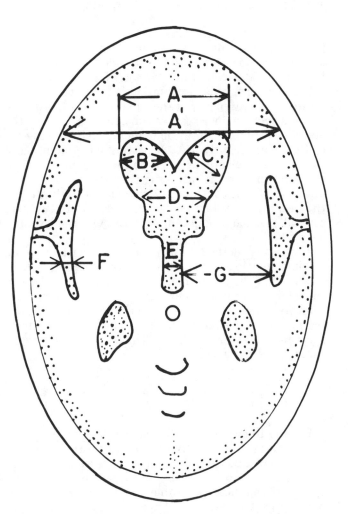

Figure 37-2. Illustration of commonly used measurements of ventricular and cortical features: A = bifrontal span of the lateral ventricles; A[1] = brain width correction for measurement A; B = transverse diameter of the left frontal horn; C = oblique diameter of the right frontal horn; D = bicaudate diameter; E = width of the third ventricle; F = width of the left sylvian fissure; G = distance between the third ventricle and the sylvian fissure; H = minimal width of the ventricular bodies; and I = the width of an enlarged sulcus.

Table 37-1. Percentages of Cognitive Measures Significantly Correlated ($p \leq .01$) With CT for the Three Methods of CT Evaluation

CT Measure	Memory	Performance	Global	Average
Ranking				
Ventricle	61	71	100	65
Cortical	25	14	100	27
4-point rating				
Ventricle	21	14	100	24
Cortical	32	43	100	37
Measurement				
Ventricle	18	26	36	20
Cortical	0	0	0	0

Note. Adapted from de Leon et al. (1980) by permission.

size (inner table to inner table of the skull) taken at the specific measurement site by determining a ventricle–brain ratio. All of the foregoing measurements were taken by each of two independent observers, and we used the mean of these observations in computing brain–behavior correlations. In addition, we calculated interrater reliability for each CT method.

For the ventricular evaluations, the results demonstrated the superiority of the subjective rank-ordering method over the more coarse subjective rating and the objective anatomical measurement method. Specifically, a significantly greater percentage of significant correlations was produced by the ranking method than by either the 4-point ratings or the measurements (see Table 37-1). The continuous comparisons facilitated by the ranking procedure permit the observer to evaluate several pathological features of the enlarged ventricles.

The rating method requires the observer to have an a priori knowledge of what is normal for a given age. It follows that the rating method would be more likely to reflect differences in experience among observers. This interpretation is consistent with the fact that the ranking method was superior to the rating method with respect to interrater reliability. The coefficients of interrater reliability were as follows:

	Ranking	Rating
Ventricular	.82	.63
Sulcal	.89	.79

For the linear ventricular measurements, only 20% of the correlations with the psychometric measures were significant ($p < .01$). Some measurements, however, were much more closely related to pathological change than others (see Table 37-2). The measurement of the third ventricle correlated with 54% of the cognitive measure in the test battery, the area of the lateral ventricles with 35%, and the bicaudate diameter with 27%. All of the other ventricular measures were associated with fewer than 15% of the cognitive measure.

The unequal value of these ventricular measurements may be of diagnostic importance. Although there are no neuropathological data indicating the anatomic significance of enlargement of the third ven-

tricle in AD patients, alterations of certain subcortical structures may be indirectly related to changes in the adjacent third ventricle. For example, Whitehouse et al. (1982) found selective destruction of the nucleus basalis of Meynert in AD. In our CT and PET work, described later, we have demonstrated both structural and metabolic changes in the thalamus.

For cortical evaluations, the subjective ranking and rating methods were both superior to the objective measurement methods, but the percentages of significant correlations they produced were not statistically different. This result suggests that multiple comparisons of the ranking method are not useful in the evaluation of diffuse sulcal prominence. Although ranking is a more reliable procedure, there is perhaps a limit on the disease-related information that an observer can extract using subjective cortical evaluations of a CT image.

Merskey et al. (1980) reported a CT and a psychometric study of 22 patients with progressive dementia. These authors used linear measures of ventricular (bifrontal and bicaudate) and sulcal sizes and produced results consistent with ours: Linear ventricular measures were correlated significantly with measures of cognitive impairment, whereas linear sulcal measures did not produce a pattern of correlation.

Jacoby and Levy (1980) studied 40 dementia patients with a mean age of 78.6 years and 50 control subjects with a mean age of 73.3 years. The CT evaluation procedures for the ventricular system included subjective ratings, linear measurements, and an area

Table 37-2. Percentages of Cognitive Measures Significantly Correlated ($p \leq .01$) With Brain Measurements

Measure	Memory	Performance	Global	Average
Ventricular				
Bifrontal	4	0	0	3
Bicaudate diameter	25	29	50	27
Third ventricle width	50	57	100	54
Body-lateral ventricle	4	29	50	11
Anterior horn, left	7	43	0	14
Anterior horn, right	0	0	0	0
Area lateral ventricle	36	29	50	35
Cortical				
Sum 3 largest sulci	0	0	0	0
Sylvian fissure, left	0	0	0	0
Sylvian fissure, right	0	0	0	0

Note. Reprinted from de Leon et al. (1980) by permission.

measurement. Cortical changes were evaluated by the subjective rating of five cortical areas. All measures showed significantly more dilatation in the dementia groups than in the control subjects. Enlargements on both the ventricular and the cortical measures were significantly correlated with decreasing performance on psychometric measures. This study thus replicates our observations of ventricular and cortical changes in AD patients.

Another replication of this work was conducted by Gado, Patel, Hughes, Danziger, and Berg (1983). These authors ranked the ventricular and the sulcal images of 33 AD patients and 25 control subjects. Gado reported that both ventricular and sulcal changes occurred in the presence of dementia but that the ventricular changes were the most prominent.

Measurement of ventricular volume avoids the bias of selective locations for linear or area measurements and provides the best estimate of overall ventricular size. Gado et al. (1982) determined that ventricular volume was significantly increased in 20 AD patients relative to the volume in 27 control subjects.

We conducted a ventricular volume and a psychometric study of 35 AD patients and 29 normal control subjects ranging in age from 61 to 80 years (George et al., 1983). Volume was defined as the sum of the ventricular area for each contiguous CT slice, multiplied by the CT slice thickness. The ventricular area was determined by using the computer interactively to outline the ventricular structures, empirically identifying a CT attenuation range for cerebrospinal fluid and quantitating the number of pixels (total area) that fell within the cerebrospinal fluid density range. The results indicated significantly greater ventricular volume (44% more) in the patients than in the control subjects. The severity of the cognitive deficits was significantly related to increasing ventricular volume.

We have also examined the effects of age on ventricular volume for both normal and AD patients (see Figure 37-3). These results suggest both an aging effect and a disease effect with marked ventricular size increases as a function of cognitive decline. However, the curves converge, and the severely impaired groups do not show an aging difference. These results suggest the importance of controlling for age in diagnostic studies of less advanced AD patients. In a related study of 16 AD patients, we (George, de Leon, Rosenbloom, et al., 1981) evaluated the extent to which the commonly used linear ventricular measures were related to total ventricular volume. We found that the best linear predictor of ventricular volume was the width of the third ventricle ($r = .72$, $p < .001$).

CT Parenchymal Evaluations

The improved capacity for scanners to resolve structures spatially, to distinguish between low-contrast tissues such as gray matter and white matter, and to facilitate retrieval of quantitative image data have permitted the definition of new CT variables. The studies discussed in this section represent the first at-

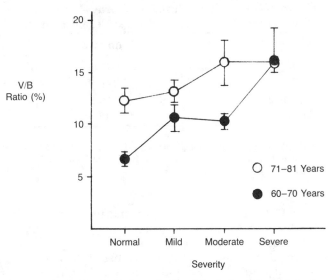

Figure 37-3. Depicts the relationship between ventricular volume and intellectual functioning for AD patients and normal persons in two age groups.

tempts, using CT, to quantitate regional changes in AD.

In a study of 14 presenile dementia patients and 6 control patients, Naeser, Gebhardt, and Levine (1980) reported that the average CT number derived from a white matter sample taken at the centrum semiovale level of the brain was significantly lower in dementia patients than in control subjects. In a related study, Albert, Naeser, Duffy, and McAnulty (chapter 38, this volume) found that 12 presenile AD patients could be differentiated from 8 control subjects by the use of an estimate of cerebrospinal fluid volume from the CT slice that depicts the bodies of the lateral ventricles. Contrary to the findings of Naeser et al., Albert et al. found that attenuation values of brain tissue did not differentiate between these groups. For a group of 12 late-onset AD patients and 18 control subjects, however, Albert et al. found the attenuation of the brain tissue but not the cerebrospinal fluid measure to differentiate the two groups.

Bondareff, Baldy, and Levy (1981) reported that the attenuation values in several brain regions are different in AD patients and control patients. These authors reported decreased attenuation in approximately one third of the regions sampled including head of caudate, frontal periventricular white matter, and uncus.

In our laboratory, George, de Leon, Ferris, and Kricheff (1981) studied 26 AD outpatients who were between the ages of 60 and 85. We examined subjectively the extent to which the gray and white matter could be differentiated. Subjective gray–white discrimination ratings of the CT scans, using a 5-point scale were obtained at three different brain levels (basal ganglia and two levels of ventricles: centrum semiovale, low, and centrum semiovale, high). The results indicated that the loss of discriminability of the gray and white matter was significantly associated with increasing cognitive impairment. In other words, the

Table 37-3. Significant Pearson Correlations ($p \leq .05$) Between Subjective Measures of Gray–White Matter Discriminability and of Structural Cerebral Atrophy

	Brain levels		
	Basal ganglia	Centrum semiovale	High convexity
Ventricular	−.58	−.53	−.58
Cortical	−.35	−.49	ns

Note. Reprinted from George, de Leon, Ferris, et al. (1981) by permission. Copyright by the American Society of Neuroradiology, 1981.

visual appearance of the gray matter and the white matter was found to be more homogeneous with increasing cognitive impairment.

We also examined the relationship between these parenchymal changes and both ventricular and cortical changes. The results (see Table 37-3) indicated a fairly strong relationship between ventricular size (as estimated by the ranking method) and gray–white matter discriminability.

We also studied linear measures of ventricular size. Several measurements correlated significantly with gray–white matter discriminability at the three brain levels studied. These findings suggest that parenchymal changes (possibly in white matter) may be closely related to the ventricular changes in this group, but this relationship does not necessarily imply cause and effect. From the available evidence, it is tempting to suggest that the tissue changes may be primary. It is of interest that the gray–white discriminability loss is not consistently correlated with the prominence of the cortical sulci. From CT scans we infer that multiple and possibly weakly interrelated changes are taking place in the cortex.

We concluded from this study that gray matter–white matter discriminability evaluations may be a useful new parameter in the evaluation of the AD patient. As an extension of these results, we also attempted to quantitate gray and white matter attenuation values for the three brain levels. The results indicated that only a few of the regional changes were associated with measures of cognitive deficit.

Gado, Danziger, Chi, Hughes, and Coben (1983) found no attenuation differences between 25 AD patients and 33 control subjects, but they found limited evidence for an association between increasing attenuation values and increasing cognitive deficit. Gado also calculated gray–white difference scores in an effort to quantitate discriminability. The results indicated that although decreasing difference scores were not related to cognitive performance, they were related to ventricular size. Therefore, Gado's study does in part support our own data, namely that gray–white changes are related to ventricular enlargement.

Recently, with a GE8800 scanner, we studied CT attenuation changes in 69 AD outpatients and 39 control subjects 64 to 84 years of age (unpublished data). CT attenuation values were derived from gray-matter and white-matter regions for four levels of brain. The results indicated that there were no attenuation differences between these groups. There were, however, some significant correlations between brain attenuation values and cognitive impairment, especially at the basal ganglia level. The consistency of this relationship decreased at higher (more dorsal) levels. For all levels studied, brain density was found to decrease with increasing cognitive impairment. However, given the absence of any consistent anatomic pattern for these correlations and their relative weakness, these data are difficult to interpret. At the highest brain level (the high convexities), the density measures were most consistently correlated with age rather than with dementia. This age correlation was found to decrease at lower (more ventral) brain levels.

The issue regarding attenuation changes in AD patients remains complex and unresolved. This situation exists in part because of several possible sources of contamination. Several studies reporting decreased attenuating values in AD patients may have included an unknown number of cases with white-matter lucencies, which lowered attenuation values. Our studies indicate that these changes are commonly found in the elderly and in patients with the clinical diagnosis of AD. We have reported (George et al., 1986) on the CT study of 275 elderly AD patients and control subjects. We found that 30% of the 151 AD patients, 16% of the 89 elderly normal subjects, and none of the 35 young normal subjects demonstrated white matter latencies. Postmortem examinations have consistently revealed subcortical small-vessel disease with demyelination.

Functional Measures in Aging and AD

Cerebral Blood Flow

The study of cerebral blood flow and cerebral oxygen utilization (a measure of cerebral metabolism) had its origins in the work of Kety and Schmidt (1948), who developed a technique to measure the total cerebral blood flow of the brain.

The subsequent development of this technique, using xenon-133, has expanded these measures to include the noninvasive local analysis of cerebral hemodynamics. These studies have reported topographical differences in cerebral blood flow, between passive and dynamic conditions, and between normal patients and patients with different neurologic and psychiatric disorders. The xenon-133 studies using surface detectors provide a lateral view of the brain with relatively poor measurement of depth. Consequently, these cerebral blood flow studies are limited with respect to anatomic identification of functional brain areas. The technique also tends to neglect regions of very low blood flow, as when regions of very low flow are concealed by highly perfused foreground or background tissue.

In part, the use of cerebral blood flow to estimate local cerebral metabolism has been based on the assumption that blood flow and metabolism are coupled.

As summarized by Fishman (1980), one of the end products of metabolism, carbon dioxide, plays an important role in the autoregulation of the vasculature and thereby in the control of cerebral blood flow. Therefore, changes in neuronal metabolism may be reflected directly in cerebral blood flow.

The literature on cerebral blood flow has been inconsistent with respect to normal aging changes over the life span. According to a review by Davis et al. (1983), several studies have reported age-related decreases in cerebral blood flow, but most studies have not found significant changes. In an attempt to explain this inconsistency, reviewers have raised the issue of subject selection. Some have suggested that studies of uniformly healthy aged people may be less likely to show these age-related reductions. The effect of dementia on the cerebral blood flow measure is more robust with age-matched control subjects. Most studies of patients with presumed degenerative dementia (e.g., AD) have reported disease-related diminutions in cerebral blood flow (Freyhan, Woodford, & Kety, 1951; Hagberg & Ingvar, 1976; Lassen, Feinberg, & Lane, 1960; Obrist, Chivian, Cronquist, & Ingvar, 1970; Yamaguchi, Meyer, Yamamoto, Sakai, & Shaw, 1980).

Although the specific explanation for the cerebral blood flow reduction in AD remains unknown, two general hypotheses are most salient. In the first hypothesis, cerebral blood flow is reduced because of vascular changes. Neuropathological evidence, however, has not supported this explanation (Brun, Gustafson, & Ingvar, 1974; Corsellis, 1976). In vivo data as reported by Ingvar and Gustafson (1970) indicate that these patients have cerebrovascular systems that are normally responsive to manipulations of blood carbon dioxide levels. Also, the cerebral arteriovenous oxygen difference in these patients was found to be normal, suggesting that these patients are not chronically ischemic.

The second hypothesis relates to a primary metabolic defect or to neuronal degeneration. With this explanation, brain tissue has reduced metabolic demands; therefore, less glucose is required to fuel neuronal activity, and, consequently, the byproducts of cerebral metabolism and the cerebral blood flow are reduced. Although this second hypothesis appears to be consistent with the neuropathological findings, there is little direct evidence to link the functional in vivo studies with the pathological examination. In an attempt to validate the cerebral blood flow measures, Brun et al. (1974) conducted an autopsy study of 14 presenile dementia patients of various etiologies who had been evaluated during life using measures of cerebral blood flow. These investigators reported qualitative relationships among regional neuronal loss, regional reductions in cerebral blood flow, and clinical symptoms. For example, in the four AD cases studied, a correspondence was reported between accentuated neuropathological changes in the temporo-parietal regions and marked reduction of cerebral blood flow in these regions. According to the authors, these patients were characterized by amnesia, apraxia dysgraphia, sensory aphasia, spatial disorientation, and restlessness. These changes were contrasted with those found in patients with Pick's disease, for whom the pathological and cerebral blood flow studies indicated frontal involvement and the clinical picture was of personality change and expressive dysphasia.

Positron Emission Tomography

Positron emission tomography (PET) has incorporated the image reconstruction technique of computed tomography in order to produce in vivo spatial studies of physiological processes. The PET technology represents a considerable advance over the cerebral blood flow techniques just discussed. With specific radio tracers and a PET imaging station, it is now possible to measure, noninvasively, regional brain glucose consumption, oxygen consumption, tissue pH, and dopaminergic and opiate receptor sites.

Methodologically, it is important to be aware of the assumptions that are an integral part of the PET technique. Of primary importance is the assumption regarding the behavior of the positron-emitting labeled compounds. Those compounds used to trace physiological function must be transported to the brain in the same way as the naturally occurring compound. For tracer compounds, validated models of the physiological process are necessary to translate the measured brain radioactivity into biological terms (Reivich et al., 1979; Sokoloff et al., 1977). If analogue compounds such as 18-F-2-deoxy-2-fluoro-D-glucose (FDG) are used to study glucose consumption, any differences between the analogue and the natural compound must be appropriately corrected for. Clearly, changes in transport or tracer metabolism need to be investigated in both normal and pathological aging.

Using FDG, investigators begin measurement of the tracer after a brain uptake period of approximately 30 minutes. During this period the tracer becomes bound in the brain and other organs in concentrations that mirror the regional metabolic demand. In some applications—for example, in studies of more than an hour's duration—it is necessary to make corrections for egress of the compound from brain tissue.

Of great importance in the interpretation of PET images is the issue of stimulus control during the uptake period. This is especially true when one is examining metabolic activity in various psychiatric and neurological disorders. From our experience with neuropsychiatric patients, we have found that experimental control over the subject's behavior varies with the severity of the disorder. This finding is particularly relevant to studies that report on resting or nonchallenged subjects, which typically do not yield measures of attention and cooperation.

Because the PET technique is designed to measure isotope concentration in specific brain volumes, another important consideration is the size of the anatomic structure or region of interest relative to the spatial-resolving power of the scanner. In our early studies with PET III, we used a resolving power of 1.7 cm $\times$ 1.7 cm $\times$ 1.7 cm. Currently, with PET VI, we are using a resolution of 1.2 cm × 1.2 cm × 1.4 cm. If we accept the recommendation of Mazziotta, Phelps, Plummer, and Kuhl (1981) that the object size be twice the resolving power, many brain structures are too small to be accurately measured with this machine. Therefore, in most PET studies, including our own, reports of metabolic changes across relatively small structures must be interpreted cautiously.

PET in Aging and AD

PET studies of glucose metabolism (FDG) in normal aging have resulted in contradictory findings. An early PET study of normal aging reported diminishing metabolic rates of oxygen only until the fifth decade of life (Lammertsma et al., 1981). Kuhl, Metter, Riege, and Phelps (1982) reported "definite" but highly variable diminutions with aging. This aging change was most apparent in the ratio of frontal to parietal regional metabolic rates (hypofrontality). Our data (de Leon, Ferris, George, Christman, et al., 1983; Ferris et al., 1983), those of Rapoport et al. (1983), and those of the Kuhl group in a later study (Hawkins et al., 1983) suggest the absence of specific glucose metabolism changes in normal aging. We also found no evidence of a relationship between hypofrontality and increasing age (de Leon et al., 1984).

In our first AD study, we reported results for seven patients, aged 72.7 ± 4.9 years, and three elderly normal subjects, aged 63.0 ± 6.6 years (Ferris et al., 1980). In these studies, as in our CT studies, the patients received an extensive medical, neurological, and psychiatric workup. Regions of interest were determined on PET using the patient's corresponding CT image as the anatomic reference. Our results indicated significant regional diminutions in metabolic rates for the AD patients, relative to the control subjects, that ranged between 33% and 37% (see Figure 37-4, color photo inserted in this volume). We also demonstrated significant positive correlation ($p < .05$) between the magnitude of the regional metabolic rates and the measures of the cognitive performance. For example, the correlation between the rate of glucose utilization in the temporal lobes was significantly associated with the level of performance on the GDS ($r = .70$, $p < .01$).

Frackowiak et al. (1981) used labeled oxygen ($^{15}O_2$) and the PET technique to study 22 dementia patients. Labeled oxygen is a positron emitter with a half-life of approximately 2 minutes, as compared with the 110 minutes for FDG. Frackowiak et al.'s technique permits the study of cerebral blood flow and cerebral oxygen utilization (an index of metabolism). Thirteen of the patients were classified as having degenerative dementias and nine as having vascular dementias. The mean age of the degenerative group was 65 ± 7 years. The results of this study indicated that, compared with 14 age-matched control subjects, the degenerative group had a diminished cerebral blood flow and a diminished metabolic rate for oxygen. The regions at the basal ganglia level showed diminutions of the metabolic rate ranging from 23% to 29%. No right–left

hemisphere differences were observed. There was a greater reduction in metabolic rates for the more severe dementia cases.

In this study, Frackowiak et al. also demonstrated a regional coupling of cerebral blood flow to cerebral metabolism in both degenerative and vascular dementia. This result substantiates the use of cerebral blood flow as an estimate of brain metabolism. Furthermore, in both degenerative and vascular dementia groups, there was no change in the oxygen extraction ratio across different severity levels of dementia. This result supports the view that the cognitive changes are not a consequence of chronic ischemia. Alternatively, the brain's metabolic demands and cognitive performance may be reduced as a consequence of damaged tissue.

In more recent PET–FDG studies, we examined both normal aging and dementia (de Leon, Ferris, George, Christman, et al., 1983; de Leon et al., 1984; Ferris et al., 1983). No significant differences were found between young normal volunteers (mean age = 26.2 ± 5.1 years, $n = 15$) and older normal control subjects (mean age = 66.6 ± 7.6 years, $n = 22$) for 11 brain regions at the basal ganglia level or for 9 regions at the centrum semiovale.

The dementia results indicated a significant diminution of the glucose utilization in AD patients (mean age = 73.4 ± 6.9 years, $n = 24$) relative to the elderly control subjects. At the basal ganglia level, the diminution ranged from 17% to 23%. At the centrum semiovale level, the diminution ranged from 18% to 24% (see Table 37-4). These results indicated a widespread pattern of metabolic changes, with the largest changes found in parietal, temporal, and frontal lobes. Other recent studies have identified similar patterns (Chase, Foster, & Mansi, 1983; Friedland, Brun, & Budinger, 1985). We have also found highly significant correlations between measures of cognitive impairment and the metabolic rates obtained from resting patients (see Table 37-5).

With the current availability of ^{11}C-deoxyglucose (^{11}CDG), we have begun to do multiple studies on the same patient on the same day for the first time. Because this tracer for glucose metabolism has a half-life of 20 minutes compared with the 110 minutes of 18FDG, the patient can now receive up to three PET studies in a single day. Although previous PET studies of aging and dementia examined the brain in a passive resting state, it is possible that both age and disease-related changes may be enhanced and better defined during perturbation.

Recently, we had the opportunity to study seven AD patients and seven age-matched control subjects using a procedure that included a memory test during the PET study (Miller et al., in press). Using a randomly ordered resting PET baseline and a verbal recognition memory task during isotope uptake, we found a shift of metabolic activity across right and left brain samples that distinguished patients from control subjects. Specifically, the temporal lobes of all seven AD patients demonstrated a relative shift in glucose metabolic rates to the right during the memory conditions relative to the baseline condition, and five out of seven con-

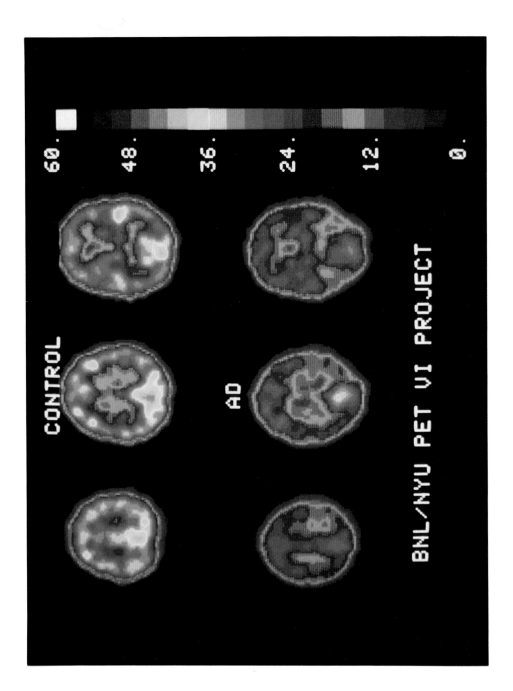

Figure 37-4. Representative PET scans for a normal elderly control subject (top) and an AD patient (bottom) at three brain levels. The color scale at right represents the rate of glucose utilization (mg/100g/min).

Table 37-4. Rates of Regional Glucose Utilization in Aging Control Subjects and Demented Subjects

| Region | Mean rates (SEM) | | t test | % change |
	Elderly controls	Demented patients		
Level of basal ganglia (CM + 40 mm)				
No. of subjects	21	23		
Frontal white matter				
Right	3.50(0.13)	2.75(0.14)	3.91**	−21
Left	3.38(0.12)	2.60(0.15)	3.91**	−23
Caudate				
Right	4.37(0.15)	3.62(0.15)	3.57**	−17
Left	4.33(0.17)	3.46(0.17)	3.63**	−20
Thalamus				
Right	4.31(0.16)	3.51(0.14)	3.72**	−19
Left	4.22(0.17)	3.33(0.15)	4.01**	−21
Temporal				
Right	3.77(0.17)	3.03(0.16)	3.12*	−20
Left	3.38(0.14)	2.68(0.16)	3.28*	−21
Centrum semiovale level (CM + 70 mm)				
No. of subjects	15	13		
Frontal				
Right	3.72(0.12)	2.91(0.18)	3.78**	−22
Left	3.60(0.13)	2.87(0.18)	3.35**	−20
Parietal				
Right	3.49(0.12)	2.65(0.17)	4.12**	−24
Left	3.19(0.15)	2.43(0.17)	3.36**	−24
White matter				
Right	3.09(0.15)	2.54(0.18)	2.35*	−18
Left	3.00(0.17)	2.41(0.17)	2.43*	−20

Note. Reprinted from de Leon, Ferris, George, Christman, et al. (1983) by permission. Copyright by the American Society of Neuroradiology, 1983.
*$p \leq .01$
**$p \leq .001$

trol subjects showed a shift to the left. For diagnostic applications, these results suggested that the activation procedure was more useful than the resting procedure in differentiating patients from control subjects. Furthermore, the lack of a shift or other response from other brain regions during the task condition suggests a temporal lobe abnormality in AD that is related to memory performance.

CT and PET Structure–Function Correlations

In the absence of age-associated changes of regional glucose utilization, we find evidence for structural brain changes on CT. Using a rank-ordering procedure (de Leon et al., 1979) we studied ventricular dilatation and cortical sulcal prominence in a group of CT scans from both young and elderly normal volunteers. For ventricular dilatation, 69% of the elderly had scores greater than the median, and 71% of the young had

scores below the median. For the measure of cortical change, 91% of the elderly were above the median, and 92% of the young were below the median. For both CT measures, these percentage distributions are significantly different ($p < .05$). In addition to rank ordering, we estimated ventricular size using linear and volumetric measurements (George et al., 1983). The measurements indicated consistently significant increases in ventricular size with age. Furthermore, there were no significant correlations between sulcal or ventricular size and glucose metabolism (CT–PET) in normal aging. These data therefore suggest structural but not metabolic brain changes in normal aging (de Leon et al., 1984).

In contrast with the results for normal aging, we have identified structure–function correlations in AD. We have learned that the ventricular enlargements and enlarged cortical sulci in AD patients are associated with marked metabolic diminutions. In particular, using linear measures, we found an 11% increase in ventricular size in AD patients (a 14% increase was found between young and old normal volunteers) that is accompanied by a 23% decrease in metabolic rate. Overall, in our studies of normal aging and dementia, we infer that in AD patients, the metabolic deficit proportionately exceeds the structural changes; but in normal aging patients, the structural changes appear to occur without any metabolic changes. These results suggest that PET may be more useful than CT in the in vivo diagnosis of AD (de Leon, Ferris, George, Reisberg et al., 1983).

We also reported that the correlation of CT and PET regions of interest may reveal structure–function relationships in AD (de Leon, George, Ferris, Rosenbloom, et al., 1983). We studied 22 patients who received both PET and CT scans (GE8800 scanner). The correlations between the PET measures of glucose utilization and CT-derived attenuation values for the same anatomic regions are found in Table 37-6. These data show consistent relations between widespread PET regions and structural (CT) measures from the temporal lobes, the thalamus, and the posterior limbs of the internal capsule. However, other CT regions, including the head of the caudate nucleus, the frontal white matter, and the anterior limbs of the internal capsule, did not show a pattern of significant correlation with the PET measures. These data support previous findings of temporal lobe involvement in AD and suggest that the structural changes in relay centers and pathways (i.e., thalamus and internal capsule) in the region of the third ventricle are related to more widespread metabolic changes.

Conclusions

Neuropathological studies have revealed the diagnostic criteria of AD and have described many brain changes associated with it. There is a consensus on the clinical description of the AD patient: The major behavioral defect is in recent memory, the symptoms are progressive, and there is little evidence to suggest focal

Table 37-5. Significant Pearson Product Correlations ($p \leq .05$) Between Rate of Glucose Utilization and Cognitive Impairment in Aging Control Subjects and Demented Subjects

| | CM + 40mm (−44) | | | | | | | | CM + | | | | | |
| | Frontal white matter | | Caudate | | Thalamus | | Temporal | | Frontal | | Parietal | | White matter | |
Measure	R	L	R	L	R	L	R	L	R	L	R	L	R	L
Guild Memory Test														
Paragraph recall														
Immediate	.61	.64	.60	.57	.58	.62	.60	.58	.67	.62	.73	.67	.54	.52
Delayed	.60	.62	.56	.52	.58	.60	.55	.53	.65	.59	.69	.64	.49	.48
Paired associate														
Immediate	.61	.61	.54	.57	.55	.60	.57	.57	.63	.54	.66	.53	.55	.46
Delayed	.57	.57	.52	.50	.49	.54	.49	.56	.50	.48	.56	.52	.45	.43
Memory for designs	.58	.55	.56	.57	.49	.50	.41	.42	.39	.33	.41	.25[a]	.17[a]	.17[a]
Wechsler Adult Intelligence Scale														
Vocabulary	.58	.62	.50	.47	.51	.53	.55	.54	.66	.62	.63	.57	.39	.43
DSST	.61	.61	.56	.51	.52	.55	.55	.54	.59	.52	.64	.52	.40	.41
Digits forward	.48	.52	.47	.39	.45	.45	.61	.49	.60	.57	.66	.59	.42	.49
Digits backward	.43	.44	.42	.37	.45	.44	.56	.47	.52	.48	.61	.47	.38	.41
Global Impairment														
Mental Status Questionnaire	−.61	−.61	−.56	−.55	−.53	−.57	−.52	−.55	−.60	−.61	−.66	−.57	−.50	−.52
Global Deterioration Scale	−.65	−.67	−.60	−.61	−.59	−.64	−.60	−.61	−.63	−.60	−.73	−.62	−.49	−.47

Note. Reprinted from de Leon, Ferris, George, Christman, et al. (1983) by permission. Copyright by the American Society of Neuroradiology, 1983.
R = right; L = left.
[a]Not significant.

Table 37-6. Pearson Correlations Between Regional PET and CT Brain Measures

| | Region of brain studied by CT for structural change | | | | | | | | | | | | Significance (%) |
| Region of brain studied by PET for metabolic change | Frontal lobe | | Caudate nucleus | | Thalamus | | Temporal lobe | | Anterior internal capsule | | Posterior internal capsule | | |
	R	L	R	L	R	L	R	L	R	L	R	L	
Frontal lobe:													
R	.21	.31	.24	.29	.45*	.55*	.73*	.67*	.17	.20	.49*	.55*	50
L	.16	.25	.17	.23	.41*	.49*	.69*	.65*	.12	.13	.49*	.51*	50
Caudate nucleus:													
R	.19	.27	.31	.29	.39*	.54*	.64*	.58*	.21	.27	.53*	.57*	50
L	.11	.17	.18	.24	.32	.45*	.64*	.56*	.14	.22	.51*	.51*	42
Thalamus:													
R	.18	.20	.22	.21	.43*	.52*	.53*	.50*	.12	.17	.46*	.48*	50
L	.07	.11	.12	.13	.31	.44*	.51*	.45*	.05	.15	.39	.46*	33
Temporal lobe:													
R	.15	.21	.18	.20	.44*	.48*	.58*	.51*	.11	.14	.41	.57*	42
L	.04	.13	.08	.06	.35	.39	.46*	.45*	.04	.05	.37	.49*	25
Whole slice	.19	.23	.20	.23	.46*	.52*	.58*	.48*	.08	.15	.46*	.51*	50
Significance (%)	0	0	0	0	67	89	100	100	0	0	67	100	

Note. Reprinted from de Leon, George, et al. (1983) by permission. Copyright by the American Society of Neuroradiology.
The 19-member study group comprised eight patients with Alzheimer's disease and 11 normal controls. R = right; L = left.
*$p \leq .05$.

disease. The evidence suggests multiple areas of brain involvement. Nevertheless, despite these well-documented brain changes, CT studies of these patients have not yet been able to establish diagnostic criteria or to describe consistently the lesions responsible for the symptoms. In part, this situation may be explained by several methodological shortcomings.

Some studies have examined groups of presumed AD patients that were heterogeneous in age or in possible diagnosis. Age heterogeneity may have the effect of obscuring the disease-related changes, especially when the investigator is using a relatively low-resolution technique, such as CT, to study this pathology. Our studies of ventricular volume clearly point up this concern.

Diagnostic heterogeneity is a more complex question in the absence of pathological confirmation (biopsy or postmortem) of cases studied with CT. Without CT criteria for identifying the AD patient, it is premature to reason that selecting subjects on the basis of excessive atrophic change will enhance the probability of a correct presumptive diagnosis. Therefore, studies that have included subjects primarily because of atrophy may not have had a representative sample of AD patients. Furthermore, CT attenuation studies that, for technical or other reasons, have not identified lucent white-matter cases in the AD population for separate analysis may be inadvertently including some unknown percentage of AD patients with concurrent vascular changes.

The selection of very demented patients for study following extensive medical, neurological, and psychiatric workup may improve the chances of identifying AD patients. For this select group of demented patients, however, many clinical measures will no longer be of much descriptive value, as these patients will have extreme scores. As a result, the correlation between the pathological feature under investigation and the behavioral or other clinical measure will be restricted. Furthermore, such studies tell us less about the course of the disease than would cross-sectional or longitudinal designs. But this type of study can be of value. The pathological anatomy of severe dementia has not been adequately evaluated with CT. Study of groups of severely demented patients using CT could provide clues to the involvement or relative preservation of specific brain regions. In addition, such groups are (presumably) close to death and hence will offer evidence for validation of in vivo measures.

Investigators have encountered further difficulty in generating adequate age-matched control subjects. In some studies, investigators have used as examples of normal neurological patients, patients who were being worked up for complaints such as headache and dizziness and who were diagnosed as normal. Logic leads us to expect increased variability for both brain and behavioral measures from such a group, but we do not know to what extent this presumed variability can affect the search for early indicators of AD.

Methodological constraints related to the CT evaluations may further explain the inconsistent CT findings.

In particular, we have found that not all CT parameters are of equal sensitivity for describing structural brain change. Our findings suggest that, in the absence of diagnostic criteria, trained readers will evaluate the complex ventricular system more reliably and with greater clinical meaning when using rank ordering than when using a rating scale.

We found linear measures, anatomically arbitrary with respect to the pathological changes they purport to measure, also to be of unequal sensitivity. In a multi-measurement study we found that the width of the third ventricle proved to be the best linear indicator of cognitive decline. In our recent ventricular volume studies, we have in part validated the anatomic significance of the width of the third ventricle, determining that this measure was the best linear correlate of the total ventricular volume. For cortical evaluations, we found subjectively determined CT measures to be better than objective measures. This finding is not surprising, given the great variations in the appearance of the cortical sulci. It appears that the eye of the skilled observer is best able to integrate this information. Linear measurements of sulcal size in our study, as in all AD investigations reporting this measure, were of no value in describing the clinical changes. We have not compared computer-derived quantification of the cortical sulci with subjective methods.

Overall, the evidence suggests that both ventricular and sulcal changes are superimposed on the more robust age-related changes and that the magnitude of these disease-related changes are associated with the magnitude of the cognitive deficit. Clearly, ventricular changes are more important than are sulcal changes in AD patients.

Regional parenchymal evaluations of gray and white matter are providing new measures (albeit not entirely understood) of evaluating directly the pathologically changing parenchyma in AD. We have found subjective discriminability evaluations to be more clinically useful for AD than are objective (CT attenuation) studies. Our results suggest that evaluations of gray–white discriminability may be a new parameter for the AD workup. We find this parameter to be significantly associated with both the cognitive changes and other anatomical changes characteristic of AD. Future studies may reveal the apparently complex relationship between discriminability and attenuation changes. In this regard, magnetic resonance imaging may become the modality of choice for parenchymal evaluations.

In a new and exciting development, PET has already made a contribution to the study of aging and AD. The studies reported in this area have demonstrated significant diminution in the metabolic rates for the AD patients, as compared with the rates for control subjects. Measures of recent memory and mental status demonstrate highly consistent patterns of correlation with the metabolic rates. Furthermore, we have used PET in conjunction with ^{11}CDG to directly measure the changes in the brain's response to specific experimental perturbations (e.g., memory tests).

Preliminary diagnostic attempts using PET data have yielded highly accurate classification of patients and control subjects. Moreover, when both CT and PET measures are derived from young normal subjects, old normal subjects, and AD patients, increases in ventricular size are found with both normal aging and disease. But the regional glucose metabolic rate is not affected by age, whereas it is markedly reduced in AD patients. These data suggest that PET may be more useful than CT in the in vivo diagnosis of AD. This also suggests that biochemical changes may be more important than structural changes in the evaluation and diagnosis of AD. We also examined the correlation of regional CT and regional PET measures for the AD patients. Structural (CT) changes in the left thalamus and in both posterior limbs of the internal capsule were consistently associated with metabolic changes (PET) in other brain regions. The metabolic mapping of such anatomic changes may also help with the description of AD. For the present, it is intriguing that structural changes in known relay and pathway areas are associated with more widespread metabolic changes. These structure–function relationships will be of interest in our planned stimulation studies (drug and behavioral).

In conclusion, these findings suggest that more extensive investigation of normal and pathological brain aging both in vivo and at pathology is warranted. In future work, it is important for researchers to begin to emphasize the replication and validation of old and new measures. Clearly, the issue of validation is complex and has no obvious starting point. Validation requires multiple comparisons and is a continuous process across different domains of data derived during life as well as postmortem. Only through such a process will we begin to understand the stages that mark the natural history of AD and the subgroups of patients that may constitute this entity.

References

Barron, S. A., Jacobs, L., & Kinkel, W. R. (1976). Changes in size of normal lateral ventricles during aging determined by computerized tomography. *Neurology, 26,* 1011–1013.

Battig, W. F., & Montague, W. E. (1969). Category norms for verbal items in 56 categories: A replication and extension of the Connecticut category norms. *Journal of Experimental Psychology Monographs, 80*(3, Pt. 2), 1–46.

Blessed, G., Tomlinson, B. E., & Roth, M. (1968). The association between quantitative measures of dementia and of senile change in the cerebral grey matter of elderly subjects. *British Journal of Psychiatry, 114,* 797–811.

Bondareff, W., Baldy, R., & Levy, R. (1981). Quantitative computed tomography in senile dementia. *Archives of General Psychiatry, 38,* 1365–1368.

Bowen, D. M., Smith, C. B., White, P., & Davison, A. N. (1976). Neurotransmitter-related enzymes and indices of hypoxia in senile dementia and other abiotrophics. *Brain, 99,* 459–496.

Brinkman, S. D., Sarwar, M., Levin, H. S., & Morris, H. H. (1981). Quantitative indexes of computed tomography in dementia and normal aging. *Neuroradiology, 138,* 89–92.

Brooks, R. A., DiChiro, G., & Keller, M. R. (1980). Explanation of cerebral white–gray contrast in computed tomography. *Journal of Computer Assisted Tomography, 4*(4), 489–491.

Brun, A., Gustafson, L., & Ingvar, D. H. (1974, October). *Neuropathological findings related to neuropsychiatric symptoms and regional cerebral blood flow in presenile dementia.* Paper presented at the 7th International Congress of Neuropathology, Budapest.

Buschke, H., & Fuld, P. A. (1974). Evaluating storage, retention, and retrieval in disordered memory and learning. *Neurology, 24*(11), 1019–1025.

Cala, L. A., Thickbroom, G. W., Black, J. L., Collins, D. W. K., & Mastaglia, F. L. (1981). Brain density and cerebrospinal fluid space size: CT of normal volunteers. *American Journal of Neuroradiology, 2,* 41–47.

Chase, T. N., Foster, N. L., & Mansi, L. (1983). Alzheimer's disease and the parietal lobe. *Lancet, 2,* 225.

Claveria, L. W., Moseley, I. F., & Stevenson, J. F. (1977). The clinical significance of "cerebral atrophy" as shown by C.A.T. In G. H. DuBoulay & I. F. Moseley (Eds.), *The first European seminar on computerized axial tomography in clinical practice* (pp. 213–217). Berlin: Springer-Verlag.

Corsellis, J. A. N. (1976). Aging and the dementias. In W. Blackwell & J. A. N. Corsellis (Eds.), *Greenfield's neuropathology* (3rd ed., pp. 796–848). Chicago: Yearbook Medical Publishers.

Davies, P., & Maloney, A. J. F. (1976). Selective loss of central cholinergic neurons in Alzheimer's disease. *Lancet, 2,* 1403.

Davis, S. M., Ackerman, R. H., Correla, J. A., Alpert, N. M., Chand, J., Buonanno, F., Kelley, R. E., Rosner, B., & Taveras, J. M. (1983). Cerebral blood flow and cerebrovascular CO_2 reactivity in stroke-age normal controls. *Neuroradiology, 33,* 391–399.

de Leon, M. J., Ferris, S. H., Blau, I., George, A. E., Reisberg, B., Kricheff, I. I., & Gershon, S. (1979). Correlations between CT changes and behavioral deficits in senile dementia. *Lancet, 2,* 859–860.

de Leon, M. J., Ferris, S. H., George, A. E., Christman, D. R., Fowler J. S., Gentes, C., Reisberg, B., Gee, B., Emmerich, M., Yonekura, Y., Brodie, J., Kricheff, I. I., & Wolf, A. P. (1983). Positron emission tomographic studies of aging and Alzheimer's disease. *American Journal of Neuroradiology, 4*(3), 568–571.

de Leon, M. J., Ferris, S. H., George, A. E., Reisberg, B., Christman, D., Kricheff, I. I., & Wolf, A. P. (1983). Computed tomography and positron emission transaxial tomography evaluations of normal aging and Alzheimer's disease. *Journal of Cerebral Blood Flow and Metabolism, 3,* 391–394.

de Leon, M. J., Ferris, S. H., George, A. E., Reisberg, B., Kricheff, I. I., & Gershon, S. (1980). Computed tomography evaluations of brain–behavior relationships in senile dementia of the Alzheimer's type. *Neurobiology of Aging, 1,* 69–79.

de Leon, M. J., George, A. E., Ferris, S. H., Christman, D. R., Fowler, J. S., Gentes, C., Brodie, J., Reisberg, B., & Wolf, A. P. (1984). Positron emission tomography and computed tomography assessments of the aging human brain. *Journal of Computer Assisted Tomography, 8*(1), 88–94.

de Leon, M. J., George, A. E., Ferris, S. H., Rosenbloom, S., Christman, D. R., Gentes, C. I., Reisberg, B., Kricheff, I. I., & Wolf, A. P. (1983). Regional correlation of PET and CT in senile dementia of the Alzheimer's type. *American Journal of Neuroradiology, 4*(3), 553–556.

Ferris, S. H., Crook, T., Sathananthan, G., & Gershon, S. (1976). Reaction time as a diagnostic measure of cognitive impairment in senility. *Journal of the American Geriatric Society, 24,* 529–533.

Ferris, S. H., de Leon, M. J., Wolf, A. P., Farkas, T., Christman, D. R., Reisberg, B., Fowler, J. S., MacGregor, R., Goldman, A., George, A. E., & Rampal, S. (1980). Positron emission tomography in the study of aging and senile dementia. *Neurobiology of Aging, 1,* 127–131.

Ferris, S. H., de Leon, M. J., Wolf, A. P., George, A. E., Reisberg, B., Christman, D. R., Yonekura, Y., & Fowler, J. S. (1983). Positron emission tomography in dementia. In R. Mayeux & W. G. Rosen (Eds.), *Advances in neurology: Vol. 38. The dementias* (pp. 123–129). New York: Raven Press.

Fishman, R. A. (1980). *Cerebrospinal fluid in diseases of the nervous system.* Philadelphia: Sanders.

Frackowiak, R. S. J., Pozzilli, C., Legg, N. J., DuBoulay, G. H., Marshall, J., Lenzi, G. L., & Jones, T. (1981). Regional cerebral oxygen supply and utilization in dementia: A clinical and physiological study with oxygen-15 and positron tomography. *Brain, 104,* 753–778.

French, J. W., Erkstrom, R. B., & Leighton, A. (1974). *Kit of reference tests for cognitive factors* (rev. ed.). Princeton, NJ: Educational Testing Service.

Freyhan, F. A., Woodford, R. B., & Kety, S. S. (1951). Cerebral blood flow and metabolism in psychoses of senility. *Journal of Mental Diseases, 113,* 449–456.

Friedland, R. P., Brun, A., & Budinger, T. F. (1985). Pathological and positron emission tomographic correlations in Alzheimer's disease. *Lancet, 1,* 228.

Gado, M., Danziger, W. L., Chi, D., Hughes, C. P., & Coben, L. A. (1983). Brain parenchymal density measurements by CT in demented subjects and normal controls. *Radiology, 147,* 703–710.

Gado, M., Hughes, C. P., Danziger, W., Chi, D., Jost, G., & Berg, L. (1982). Volumetric measurements of the cerebrospinal fluid spaces in demented subjects and controls. *Radiology, 144,* 535–538.

Gado, M., Patel, J., Hughes, C. P., Danziger, W., & Berg, L. (1983). Brain atrophy in dementia judged by CT scan ranking. *American Journal of Neuroradiology, 4,* 499–500.

George, A. E., de Leon, M. J., Ferris, S. H., & Kricheff, I. I. (1981). Parenchymal CT correlates of senile dementia (Alzheimer's disease): Loss of grey–white matter discriminability. *American Journal of Neuroradiology, 2,* 205–211.

George, A. E., de Leon, M. J., Gentes, C. I., Miller, J., London, E., Budzilovich, G., Ferris, S., & Chase, N. (1986). Leukoencephalopathy in normal and pathologic aging: 1. CT of brain lucencies. *American Journal of Neuroradiology, 7,* 561–566.

George, A. E., de Leon, M. J., Rosenbloom, S., Ferris, S. H., Gentes, C., Emmerich, M., & Kricheff, I. I. (1981). *CT ventricular volume and its relationship to cognitive impairment in dementia.* Paper presented at the 11th annual meeting of the American Aging Association, New York.

George, A. E., de Leon, M. J., Rosenbloom, S., Ferris, S. H., Gentes, C., Emmerich, M., & Kricheff, I. I. (1983). Ventricular volume and cognitive deficit: A computed tomographic study. *Radiology, 149,* 493–498.

Gilbert, J. G., & Levee, R. F. (1971). Patterns of declining memory. *Journal of Gerontology, 26,* 70–75.

Gurland, B. (1978). *The influence of socio-cultural characteristics on rates of dementia occurring in the senium.* Paper presented at the Conference on the Clinical Aspects of Alzheimer's Disease and Senile Dementia, Washington, DC.

Gyldensted, C., & Kosteljanetz, M. (1976). Measurements of the normal ventricular system with computer tomography. *Neuroradiology, 10,* 205–215.

Hagberg, B., & Ingvar, D. H. (1976). Cognitive reduction in presenile dementia related to regional abnormalities of the cerebral blood flow. *British Journal of Psychiatry, 128,* 209–222.

Haug, G. (1977). Age and sex dependence of the size of normal ventricles on computed tomography. *Neuroradiology, 14,* 201–204.

Hawkins, R. A., Mazziotta, J. C., Phelps, M. E., Huang, S. C., Kuhl, D. E., Carson, R. E., Metter, E. J., & Riege, W. H. (1983). Cerebral glucose metabolism function of age in man: Influence of the rate constants in the fluorodeoxyglucose method. *Journal of Cerebral Blood Flow and Metabolism, 3,* 250–253.

Huckman, M. S., Fox, J., & Topel, J. (1975). The validity of criteria for the evaluation of cerebral atrophy by computed tomography. *Radiology, 116,* 85–92.

Hughes, C. P., & Gado, M. (1981). Computed tomography and aging of the brain. *Radiology, 139,* 391–396.

Ingvar, D. H., & Gustafson, L. (1970). Regional cerebral blood flow in organ dementia with early onset. *Acta Neurologica Scandinavica, 46*(Suppl. 43), 42–73.

Jacoby, R. J., & Levy, R. (1980). Computed tomography in the elderly. 2. Senile dementia: Diagnosis and functional impairment. *British Journal of Psychiatry, 136,* 256–269.

Jellinger, K. (1976). Neuropathological aspects of dementia resulting from abnormal blood and cerebrospinal fluid dynamics. *Acta Neurologica Belgica, 76,* 83–102.

Johnston, M. V., Young, A. C., & Coyle, J. T. (1981). Laminar distribution of cholinergic markers in neocortex: Effects of lesions. *Journal of Neuroscience Research, 6,* 597–607.

Kahn, R. L., Goldfarb, A. I., Pollack, M., & Peck, A. (1960). Brief objective measures for the determination of mental status in the aged. *American Journal of Psychiatry, 117,* 326–328.

Kaszniak, A. W., Fox, J., Gandell, D. L., Garron, D. C., Huckman, M., & Ramsey, R. G. (1978). Predictors of mortality in presenile and senile dementia. *Annals of Neurology, 3,* 246–252.

Kety, S. S., & Schmidt, C. F. (1948). The nitrous oxide method. The quantitative determination of cerebral blood flow in man: Theory, procedure, and normal values. *Journal of Clinical Investigation, 27,* 476–483.

Kuhar, M. H. (1976). The anatomy of cholinergic neurons. In A. M. Goldberg & I. Hanin (Eds.), *Biology of cholinergic function* (pp. 3–27). New York: Raven Press.

Kuhl, D. E., Metter, E. J., Riege, W. H., & Phelps, M. E. (1982). Effects of human aging on patterns of local cerebral glucose utilization determined by the (^{18}F) Fluorodeoxyglucose method. *Journal of Cerebral Blood Flow and Metabolism, 2,* 163–171.

Lammertsma, A. A., Frackowiak, R. S. J., Lenzi, G. L., Heather, J. D., Pozzilli, C., & Jones, T. (1981). Accuracy of the oxygen-15 steady state technique for measuring CBF and $CMRO_2$: Tracer modeling, statistics and spatial sampling. *Journal of Cerebral Blood Flow and Metabolism, 1*(Suppl. I), S3–S4.

Lassen, N. A., Feinberg, I., & Lane, M. H. (1960). Bilateral studies of cerebral oxygen uptake in young and aged normal subjects and in patients with organ dementia. *Journal of Clinical Investigation, 39,* 491–500.

Last, R. J., & Tompsett, D. H. (1953). Casts of cerebral ventricles. *British Journal of Surgery, 40,* 525–543.

Mazziotta, J. C., Phelps, M. E., Plummer, D., & Kuhl, D. (1981). Quantitation in positron emission computed tomography: 5. Physical anatomical effects. *Journal of Computer Assisted Tomography, 5*(5), 734–743.

Merskey, H., Ball, M. J., Blume, W. T., Fox, A. J., Hersch, E. L., Kral, V. A., & Palmer, R. B. (1980). Relationships between psychological measurements and cerebral organic changes in Alzheimer's disease. *Le Journal Canadien des Sciences Neurologiques, 7,* 45–49.

Miller, J. V., de Leon, M. J., Ferris, S. H., Kluger, A., George, A. E., Reisberg, B., Sachs, H., & Wolf, A. P. (in press). Abnormal temporal lobe response in Alzheimer's disease during cognitive processing as measured by ^{11}C-2-deoxyglucose ([11]CDG) and PET. *Journal of Cerebral Blood Flow and Metabolism.*

Moran, L. J., Kimble, J. P., & Mefferd, R. B. (1960). Repetitive psychometric measures: Memory-For-Faces. *Psychological Reports, 7,* 407–413.

Mountjoy, C. Q., Roth, M., Evans, N. J. R., & Evans, H. M. (1983). Cortical neuronal counts in normal elderly controls and demented patients. *Neurobiology of Aging, 6,* 119–132.

Naeser, M. A., Gebhardt, C., & Levine, H. L. (1980). Decreased computerized tomography numbers in patients with presenile dementia. *Archives of Neurology, 37,* 401–409.

Obrist, W. D., Chivian, E., Cronquist, S., & Ingvar, D. H. (1970). Regional cerebral blood flow in senile and presenile dementia. *Neurology, 20,* 315–322.

Perry, E. K., Perry, R. H., Blessed, G., & Tomlinson, B. E. (1977). Necropsy evidence of central cholinergic deficits in senile dementia. *Lancet, 1,* 189.

Peterson, L. R., & Peterson, M. J. (1959). Short-term retention of individual verbal items. *Journal of Experimental Psychology, 58,* 193–198.

Rapoport, S. I., Duara, R., London, E. D., Margolin, R. A., Schwartz, M., Cutler, N. E., Partanen, M., & Shinohara, N. L. (1983). Glucose metabolism of the aging nervous system. In D. Samuel, S. Algeri, S. Gershon, V. E. Grimm, & G. Toffano (Eds), *Aging of the brain* (pp. 111–121). New York: Raven Press.

Reisberg, B., Ferris, S. H., de Leon, M. J., & Crook, T. (1982). The Global Deterioration Scale for assessment of primary degenerative dementia. *American Journal of Psychiatry, 139*(9), 1136–1139.

Reivich, M., Kuhl, D., Wolf, A., Greenberg, J., Phelps, M., Ido, T., Casella, V., Fowler, J., Hoffman, E., Alavi, A., Som, P., & Sokoloff, L. (1979). The (^{18}F) Fluorodeoxyglucose method for the measurement of local cerebral glucose utilization in man. *Circulation Research, 44,* 127–137.

Roberts, M. A., Caird, F. I., Grossart, K. W., & Steven, J. L. (1976). Computerized tomography in the diagnosis of cerebral atrophy. *Journal of Neurology, Neurosurgery, and Psychiatry, 39,* 905–915.

Rosen, W. G., Terry, R. D., Fuld, P. A., Katzman, R., & Peck, A. (1980). Pathological verification of ischemic score in differentiation of dementias. *Annals of Neurology, 7,* 486–488.

Roth, M., & Meyers, D. H. (1975). The diagnosis of dementia [Special publication no. 9]. *British Journal of Psychiatry,* 87–99.

Sokoloff, L., Reivich, M., Kennedy, C., DesRosiera, M. H., Patlak, C. S., Pettigrew, K. D., Sakurada, D., & Shinohara, M. (1977). The (^{14}C) deoxyglucose method for the measurement of local cerebral glucose utilization: Theory, procedure, and normal values in the conscious and anesthetized albino rat. *Journal of Neurochemistry, 28,* 897–916.

Terry, R. D., Peck, A., DeTeresa, R., Schechter, R., & Horoupian, D. S. (1981). Some morphometric aspects of the brain in senile dementia of the Alzheimer's type. *Annals of Neurology, 10,* 184–192.

Tomlinson, B. E. (1980). The structural and quantitative aspects of the dementias. In P. J. Roberts (Ed.), *Biochemistry of dementia.* New York: Wiley.

Tomlinson, B. E., Blessed, G., & Roth, M. (1968). Observation on the brains of non-demented old people. *Journal of Neurological Sciences, 7,* 331–356.

Tomlinson, B. E., Blessed, G., & Roth, M. (1970). Observation on the brains of demented old people. *Journal of Neurological Sciences, 11,* 205–242.

Tomlinson, B. E., & Kitchner, D. (1972). Granulovacuolar degeneration of hippocampal pyramidal cells. *Journal of Pathology, 106,* 165–185.

Wechsler, D. (1955). *Manual for the Wechsler Adult Intelligence Scale.* New York: Psychological Corporation.

Whitehouse, P. J., Price, D. L., Struble, R. G., Clark, A. W., Coyle, J. T., & DeLong, M. R. (1982). Alzheimer's disease and senile dementia: Loss of neurons in the basal forebrain. *Science, 215,* 1237–1239.

Yamaguchi, F., Meyer, J. S., Yamamoto, M., Sakai, F., & Shaw, T. (1980). Noninvasive regional cerebral blood flow measurements in dementia. *Archives of Neurology, 37,* 410–418.

Yamamura, H., Ito, M., Kubota, K., & Matsuzawa, T. (1980). Brain atrophy during aging: A quantitative study with computed tomography. *Journal of Gerontology, 4,* 492–498.

Zatz, L. M., Jernigan, T. L., & Ahumada, A. J. (1982). Changes on computed cranial tomography with aging: Intracranial fluid volume. *American Journal of Neuroradiology, 3,* 1–11.

Marilyn S. Albert, Margaret A. Naeser, Frank H. Duffy, and Gloria McAnulty

CHAPTER

38

CT and EEG Validators for Alzheimer's Disease

This chapter reports on research comparing the computed tomographic scans (CTs) and electroencephalograms (EEGs) of patients who have mild to moderate manifestations of Alzheimer's disease (AD), presenile and senile, with the CTs and EEGs of healthy age-matched normal control subjects. Two semi-automated computer programs were used to examine the CT scans. Topographic analysis of the EEG data was carried out by means of a technique known as brain electrical activity mapping (BEAM)[1]. These procedures delineated a small number of neuroanatomical and neurophysiological features that retrospectively discriminated between the patients and the normal control subjects with 89% to 93% accuracy. The discriminating CT and EEG features tended to be highly correlated with cognitive function. The results suggest that computerized measurements of CT scans and EEGs may provide external validation for the diagnosis of AD.

In recent years, numerous researchers have examined the computed tomography (CT) scans and electroencephalograms (EEGs) of patients with presenile and senile dementia of the Alzheimer's type. Researchers agree, on the basis of the CT studies, that ventricular size is significantly different in patients and age-matched normal control subjects (Brinkman, Sarwar, Levin, & Morris, 1981; Gado et al., 1982; Jacoby, Levy, & Dawson, 1980) and that the severity of cognitive deficits in patients with Alzheimer's disease (AD) correlates significantly with ventricular size (de Leon et al., 1980, Roberts & Caird, 1982; Soininen, Puranen, & Riekkinen, 1982). The EEG studies commonly report an increase in EEG slow activity (i.e., delta and theta), accompanied by diminished or absent alpha activity (Constantinidis, Krassoievitch, & Tissot, 1969; Gordon & Sim, 1967). The late components of the evoked potential (EP) show a prolonged latency and a reduced amplitude, especially in the P-300 event-related component (Goodin, Squires, & Starr, 1978; Squires, Goodin, & Starr, 1979). However, even when statistically significant differences between AD patients and normal control subjects are found, the groups tend to overlap; therefore the diagnostic utility of the data is limited.

It nevertheless seems possible that CT scans and EEGs contain as yet untapped information for identifying patients with AD. To test this theory, we applied computerized techniques previously used in the examination of other patient populations with cognitive disorders (Duffy, Denckla, Bartels, & Sandini, 1980; Naeser, Hayward, Laughlin, & Zatz, 1981) to patients with AD. It was hoped that these computerized analyses would identify regions of difference between patients and normal control subjects that might be used to assist in the diagnosis of AD.

Subject Selection

For purposes of the analyses, patients with presenile and senile dementia of the Alzheimer's type were examined separately. Thus, the subjects were divided into two age groups, ages 40 to 64 and ages 65 to 80. Within each group, AD patients who were otherwise healthy were compared with healthy age-matched normal control subjects. The number of patients and normal control subjects in each study are detailed in the figure captions.

In the study of EEGs and EPs, the younger group consisted of 9 patients with presenile AD (4 women and 5 men) and 15 age-matched normal control subjects (7

---

[1]BEAM is a registered trademark of Braintech, Inc.

The research for this chapter was supported by Grant PO1-AG-04953 from the National Institute on Aging. We would like to thank Susan LoCastro, Hope Heller, Stephen Woodward, Janis Fang, Alice Domar, Carol Cordier, Mary Hyde, PhD, and Kenneth Jones, PhD, for their assistance in the conduct of the work. Michael Jenike, MD, John Growdon, MD, Harvey Sagar, MD, Marsel Mesulam, MD, John Tellers, MD, and Sandra Weintraub, PhD, assisted in the selection of the patients.

women and 8 men). The mean ages of the younger patients and control subjects were 58.3 and 57.8, respectively. There was no significant difference in the ages of the control subjects and dementia patients. The older group consisted of 10 AD patients (8 women and 2 men) and 10 age-matched control subjects (6 women and 4 men). The mean ages of the older AD patients and control subjects were 70.3 and 70.2, respectively, and they did not differ significantly from one another.

In the CT investigation, the younger group consisted of 8 patients (6 women and 2 men) with presenile dementia of the Alzheimer's type and 10 male age-matched control subjects. The mean ages for patients and control subjects were 58.1 and 57.4, respectively. There was no significant difference in the ages of the two groups. Thirteen patients (11 women and 2 men) with senile dementia of the Alzheimer's type and 18 male age-matched control subjects were included in the CT study of older individuals. The mean age for the patients was 71.6; for the normal control subjects the mean age was 72.6. There was no significant difference between the groups.

The diagnosis of AD was based on the judgment of a staff neurologist, with independent agreement from the staff psychiatrist and neuropsychologist. Medical conditions known to produce dementia were excluded. A large number of laboratory tests (e.g., a standard metabolic screen, thyroid function tests, folate levels) were given to rule out various metabolic, neoplastic, infectious, or traumatic causes for dementia. Patients with a record of severe head trauma, alcoholism, serious psychiatric illness, learning disabilities, epilepsy, hypertension, lung disease, kidney disease, coronary artery disease, or cancer were excluded. All AD patients received an Ischemic Score of 4 or less on Hachinski's scale for ruling out multi-infarct dementia (Hachinski, 1978). Retrospective studies suggest that approximately 90% of patients classified by these procedures are correctly diagnosed as having AD (Davies, Katz, & Crystal, 1982; Wells, 1977). Only subjects with a score of 100 to 140 on a Dementia Rating Scale (Mattis, 1976) were admitted to the study in order to prevent the inclusion of patients in moderately advanced stages of the disease (Vitaliano, Breen, Albert, Russo, & Prinz, 1984).

The male control subjects were members of the Normative Aging Study at the Boston Veterans Administration (VA) Outpatient Clinic. Complete medical records were available on these persons for the previous 18 years. The female control subjects were community volunteers. Control subjects were screened and excluded from further examination on the basis of the exclusionary criteria already described and were therefore as free of systemic disease as the AD patients.

CT Scan Methodology

CT scans were done without contrast on an Ohio Nuclear Delta 2010 CT scanner at the Boston VA Medical Center. The scans were taken approximately 20° to the

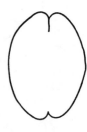  

Figure 38-1. Schematic representation of the three CT scan slices chosen for evaluation. A slice at the widest portion of the third ventricle (left), a slice at the maximum width of the bodies of the lateral ventricles (center), a supraventricular slice at the level of the centrum semiovale. Adapted from Albert et al. (1984b).

canthomeatal line. The picture element (pixel) size was 1 mm x 1 mm, and the image was reconstructed on a 256 x 256 matrix. The CT density number scale was air, −1,000 (±2 HU) and water, 0. Approximately 12 slices were obtained per subject (7 mm thick).

Figure 38-1 depicts three CT slices from each scan that were selected for evaluation: (a) a slice at the widest portion of the third ventricle, (b) a slice at the maximum width of the bodies of the lateral ventricles, and (c) a supraventricular slice at the level of the centrum semiovale selected on the basis of the slice size (i.e., 8,000 to 10,000 pixels). These slices were chosen because they represented the brain at three different levels: midventricular, high ventricular, and supraventricular.

Each slice was analyzed by two computer programs, known as ASI-I and ASI-II (Jernigan, Zatz, & Naeser, 1979; Naeser, Albert, & Kleefield, 1982; Naeser et al., 1981; Zatz, Jernigan, & Ahumada, 1982). The ASI-I program was used primarily for its information concerning the mean CT density number of the brain tissue on each slice. The ASI-I program uses a t-test to compare the mean CT density number and the standard deviation of a standard tissue sample (169 pixels) with each 4-pixel sample throughout the brain. It then calculates the total number of intracranial pixels on the slice (a measure of head size), the number of pixels in significantly low CT density number areas (i.e., an estimate of fluid area on the slice), and the mean CT density number of the "remaining" brain tissue (i.e., the density of all regions that were shown to be neither bone nor fluid by the method just described).

Because the smaller the head is, the higher the CT density numbers are (DiChiro, Brooks, Dubal, & Chew, 1978; Jernigan et al., 1979), all mean CT number data were corrected for head size using a regression procedure described in previous publications (Albert, Naeser, Levine, & Garvey, 1984b; Jernigan et al., 1979).

The ASI-II program was used primarily for its information concerning the amount of fluid on a CT slice. This program does not identify the origin of the fluid areas; it essentially provides a summation of sulcal and ventricular regions of fluid. It also attempts to take into account the fact that some pixels are entirely brain, some are entirely cerebrospinal fluid (CSF), and some are partially volumed (i.e., partially brain and partially CSF). To do this, the ASI-II program uses a previously established ideal CT density number difference between brain tissue and CSF for the Ohio Nuclear Delta Scanner (23.8 HU) to determine which 4-pixel samples are totally brain, which are CSF, and which are partially volumed samples. The ratio of actual-to-ideal difference constitutes the CSF fraction for a 4-pixel sample.

The presenile patients were administered a large battery of neuropsychological tests for assessing the relationship between cognitive function and the CT measures. The tests included tests of auditory and visual attention, the Boston Naming Test (Kaplan, Goodglass, & Weintraub, 1978), the Wechsler Memory Scale (Wechsler, 1945), a word list learning test, the Block Design subtest of the Wechsler Adult Intelligence Scale (Wechsler, 1955), clock drawing, proverb interpretation, competing motor programs, the Visual-Verbal Test (Feldman & Drasgow, 1951), and a test of verbal fluency. The senile dementia patients were administered an abbreviated test battery consisting of the Mattis Dementia Rating Scale and the National Adult Reading Test (Nelson, 1982).

CT Data Analysis

The results of the analysis with presenile AD patients showed that they could be differentiated from age-matched normal control subjects with a high degree of accuracy (89% or greater). In the presenile age range, the most powerful measure was the fluid volume of the bodies of the lateral ventricles (Figure 38-2). The computerized measure of fluid volume on the slice at the maximum width of the bodies of the lateral ventricles (Figure 38-1, center) was not only significantly different in presenile patients and controls ($p < .005$) but, in a discriminant function, this measure correctly predicted the group membership of 89% of the subjects. Fluid volume estimates on the other slices did not discriminate the groups. Measures of tissue density on the

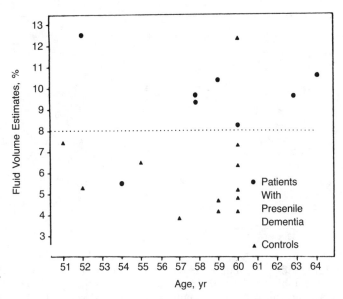

Figure 38-2. Computerized determinations of fluid volume (using the ASI-II program) on the slice at the bodies of the lateral ventricles for patients with presenile AD and for healthy age-matched control subjects. The comparison includes 8 patients and 10 control subjects. Seven out of eight presenile AD patients had more than 8% fluid volume on the bodies of the lateral ventricles slice (note dotted line). Only one healthy age-matched control subject had greater than 8% fluid volume on this slice. Adapted from Albert et al. (1984a).

same CT slices similarly failed to differentiate between presenile AD patients and normal control subjects (see Table 38-1).

In the senile age range, the computer measure that discriminated patients and normal control subjects with the highest degree of accuracy was the measure of the mean CT density number of the remaining brain tissue on the slice at the bodies of the lateral ventricles (Figure 38-3). This mean CT density number was significantly different in AD patients and control subjects ($p < .0001$, Table 38-2) and was selected in Step 1 of a

Table 38-1. Comparison of Computerized Analyses of Three CT Scan Slices in Presenile AD (PAD) Patients and Normal Control Subjects (NC)

Slice	Group	Mean CT density of brain tissue (in Hounsfield units)			Mean CT density of standard tissue sample (in Hounsfield units)			Fluid volume (%)		
		X̄	S.D.	p	X̄	S.D.	p	X̄	S.D.	p
Third ventricle	PAD	37.9	3.9	ns	24.8	3.9	ns	10.2	1.7	ns
	NC	36.7	5.2		24.7	3.3		8.7	2.0	
Body of lateral ventricle	PAD	40.1	3.8	ns	27.4	3.3	ns	9.9	1.4	.005
	NC	36.4	5.0		24.3	3.6		6.0	2.3	
Centrum semiovale	PAD	52.1	3.2	ns	37.3	3.2	ns	2.6	1.1	ns
	NC	50.1	5.7		35.6	4.1		1.9	1.1	

Note. Reprinted from Albert et al. (1984a).

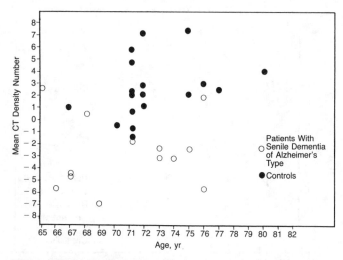

Figure 38-3. Computerized determination of mean CT density number of the remaining tissue (using the ASI-I program) on the slice at the bodies of the lateral ventricles for patients with senile AD and for healthy age-matched control subjects. The comparison includes 13 patients with senile AD and 18 control subjects. Adapted from Albert et al. (1984b).

discriminant function analysis comparing patients and controls (correctly classifying 77% of the subjects). When this mean CT density measure was combined with a computerized determination of CSF volume on the slice at the level of the maximum width of the third ventricle, 93% of the subjects were correctly classified. The addition of a third computerized measure, fluid volume on the slice at the bodies of the lateral ventricles, increased accuracy of classification from 93% to 97% (i.e., in all but one patient). The addition of this third variable did not, however, represent a significant increase in classification rate.

A stepwise discriminant function analysis was then performed in which the data from the presenile and senile AD patients were combined in one analysis. The variables selected at Steps 1, 2, and 3 were (a) the fluid volume measure from the third ventricle slice, (b) the mean CT density number of the remaining tissue at the lateral ventricle slice level, and (c) the mean CT density number of the standard tissue sample on the lateral ventricle slice. The percentages of the subjects correctly classified following the stepwise addition of each of these variables were 68.63%, 72.55%, and 80.39%, respectively.

These data suggest that computerized measures of CT scans can be used to discriminate patients with presenile and senile AD from healthy age-matched normal control subjects. However, there appear to be important age–disease interactions that greatly affect the outcome of the analysis. If the data from the presenile and senile patients are combined in one discriminant function, no more than 80% of the patients can be differentiated from the control subjects (6 patients and 4 control subjects were misclassified). By contrast, if the presenile and senile patients are examined separately, 89% to 93% of the subjects can be correctly discriminated from one another.

In both age groups it is clear that volumetric measurements of cerebrospinal fluid spaces are important. However, the regions that are most helpful differ; the degree of importance of the measurements themselves also varies. In the presenile age range, the slice at the bodies of the lateral ventricles contributes the important CT information for discriminating AD patients. In the senile age range, fluid volume measures at the slice at the maximum width of the third ventricle are useful but of secondary importance to a mean CT density measure of the remaining tissue.

These findings concerning estimates of fluid volume complement the findings of previous investigators who have shown that demented patients and normal control subjects differ significantly in CSF fluid volume (Gado et al., 1982), that CSF fluid volume increases in relation to the severity of illness (George et al., 1983), and that patients scanned longitudinally over time

Table 38-2. Comparison of Computerized Analyses of Three CT Scan Slices of Senile AD (SAD) Patients and Normal Control Subjects (NC)

Slice	Group	Mean CT density of brain tissue (in Hounsfield units)			Mean CT density of standard tissue sample (in Hounsfield units)			Fluid volume (%)		
		X̄	S.D.	p	X̄	S.D.	p	X̄	S.D.	p
Third ventricle	SAD	32.92	2.96	.003	24.16	2.37	ns	16.49	8.64	.003
	NC	36.62	3.27		24.52	3.29		10.39	2.34	
Body of lateral ventricle	SAD	34.29	2.91	.0001	23.95	2.99	ns	10.93	5.71	ns
	NC	39.38	2.44		25.75	2.72		8.42	2.65	
Centrum semiovale	SAD	46.31	4.85	.02	31.11	3.06	.007	8.58	5.39	ns
	NC	50.40	4.48		33.99	2.48		6.25	2.68	

Note. Reprinted from Albert et al. (1984b).

have significantly larger ventricles (Gado et al., 1982). The mean CT density number data is more controversial; some reports support the finding that CT density numbers are powerful discriminators between AD patients and controls (Bondareff, Baldy, & Levy, 1981; Naeser et al., 1982), whereas others do not (George et al., 1983; Hughes & Gado, 1981). The age–disease interaction suggested by the present findings may be one cause of the discrepancy between published studies, but technical aspects of CT density number analysis have varied widely across past studies as well.

Some factors that have not always been taken into account in previous investigations and that may have contributed to the appearance of conflict in the data are (a) the fluctuations of CT numbers from day to day, (b) the effect of head size on CT numbers, (c) the variation in CT numbers from one scanner to another, (d) the size of the tissue sample on which CT numbers are taken, and (e) the effect of bone density on CT numbers. These factors are discussed in greater detail elsewhere (Albert, Naeser, Levine, & Garvey, 1984b), but it is interesting to note that studies that have found no decrease in mean CT density number in dementia patients have not controlled for head size (Gado, Danziger, Chi, Hughes, & Coben, 1983; George, de Leon, Ferris, & Kricheff, 1981; Wilson, Fox, Huckman, Bacon, & Lobick, 1982), and that only those studies with sample sizes of 169 pixels or greater (Albert et al., 1984a; Bondareff et al., 1981; Naeser et al., 1982) have reported significant differences in mean CT density number between AD patients and normal control subjects.

Correlations were performed between major neuropsychological test scores for the presenile patients and the most discriminating CT variable for that population (i.e., fluid volume at the bodies of the lateral ventricles). Four neuropsychological test scores were correlated at the .01 significance level or greater (Table 38-3).

The CT measures that were most useful in discriminating senile AD patients and control subjects were correlated with subtest scores on the abbreviated neuropsychological test battery. Because fewer correlations were performed between the behavioral and CT variables, correlations that were significant at the .05 significance level or greater are reported (Table 38-4).

Table 38-3. Correlations Between Neuropsychological Test Scores and CT Measures in Presenile AD Patients

Neuropsychological test	Fluid volume bodies of lateral ventricle	
	r	p
Wechsler Memory Scale	−.68	.004
Verbal fluency	−.59	.01
Proverb interpretation	−.74	.001
Clock drawing	−.60	.009

Note. Reprinted from Albert et al. (1984a).

Table 38-4. Correlations Between Neuropsychological Test Scores and CT Measures in Senile AD Patients

Neuropsychological test	Mean CT density, bodies of lateral ventricle		Fluid volume, bodies of lateral ventricle	
	r	p	r	p
Dementia Rating Scale (Total)	—	—	−.56	.04
Initiation Subtest of DRS	—	—	−.71	.006
Confrontation Naming	+.65	.02	−.65	.02

Note. Third ventricle correlations are not reported because they are not significant at the .05 level.

Correlations between the CT and cognitive variables for both the presenile and senile patients were consistently negative; therefore, lower test scores were associated with increased fluid volume. Among the senile AD patients, lower CT density numbers were associated with lower test scores, whereas increases in fluid volume were associated with lower test scores.

EEG Methodology

Both EEG and EP data was gathered for all subjects. The EEGs were gathered during 10 behavioral states: resting with eyes open (EOP), resting with eyes closed (ECL), listening to speech (SPE) and music (MUS), memorizing (KFI) and being tested (KFT) on the recall of geometric shapes, reading paragraphs (RTI) and being tested on the recall of specific sentences (RTT), and forming (PAI) and being tested on (PAT) sound-symbol associations. The EPs were derived during three states: flash visual evoked potential (VEP); tone pip auditory evoked potential (AEP); and the P-300, or event-related, potential using high- and low-frequency auditory stimuli (P-300). Off-line data processing employed spectral analysis for the EEG states and signal averaging for the EP states. Because data were obtained from 20 scalp electrodes, the end product consisted of 20 spectra and 20 EPs (one from each electrode).

The 20 spectra and 20 EPs were transformed into a corresponding series of topographic maps of brain electrical activity that were visually displayed by means of a color-coded image. For EEG data, each image represents the topographic distribution of eight 4-Hz wide-frequency bands: delta (0.5 to 32 Hz), theta (4 to 7.75 Hz), alpha (8 to 11.75 Hz), and beta 1 (12 to 15.75 Hz), beta 2 (16 to 19.75 Hz), beta 3 (20 to 23.75 Hz), beta 4 (24 to 27.75 Hz), and beta 5 (28 to 31.75 Hz). Spectral values for any given band were also expressed as a percentage of total energy—a normalization process. For EP data, each image represented the topographic distribution of actual EP voltage during a single 4-msec epoch following stimulation.

The presenile and senile AD patients in our study were administered a battery of neuropsychological tests identical to the one employed in the study of CT variables in presenile patients. To simplify interpretation of the correlational analysis, we grouped the test results into four major cognitive skill areas (verbal memory, nonverbal memory, visuospatial ability, and attention/abstraction skills) on the basis of a priori theoretical judgment.

EEG Data Analysis

To delineate regional EEG and EP differences between groups, we used the significance probability mapping (SPM) technique (Duffy, Bartels, & Burchfiel, 1981). By this method, a new image was formed in which the maps of raw EEG and EP data were replaced by images representing the statistical difference between the groups (i.e., the presenile and senile AD patients and their controls). In our investigation, differences were determined with Student's t-statistic.

We identified numerous cortical areas that showed large and relatively contiguous regions of between-group difference. These regions acted as templates or masks for the development of features (Figure 38-1). Cortical activity was summated in the areas underlying the templates to produce a single numerical value in each subject.

The numerical values or features that were generated in this fashion were evaluated by the Mann-Whitney U-test (Siegel, 1956). Features significant at the .02 level or better were included in a merit value analysis (Bartels, 1979; Genchi & Mori, 1965; Selin, 1965; Sherwood, Bartels, & Wied, 1976). This procedure identified the features that were most useful in classifying subjects. Then we performed a discriminant function analysis using the features identified by the merit value analysis.

In the presenile age range, we identified four features that, in combination, correctly identified 95.8% of the subjects (all but one dementia patient). The best feature was AFEA 26c, which was derived primarily from the right posterior quadrant for 4-to-8-Hz normalized theta. The second-best feature was BFEA 4, derived from the bilateral posterior parietotemporal region in the 16-to-20-Hz normalized beta 2 range. The third-best feature, BFEA 22, was derived from the left anterior temporal region of the AER in the 84-to-104-msec latency epoch. The fourth-best feature, AFEA 14, was derived from the left midtemporal region during geometric figure recall testing in the 4-to-8-Hz normalized theta range. The templates from which these features were derived are shown in Figure 38-4.

In the senile age range, we identified four features that together correctly classified 90% of the subjects (all but one control subject and one patient). Three of the features (CFEA 7, CFEA 1, and CFEA 8) represented increased EEG slowing (0-4-Hz delta or 4-8-Hz theta) in the frontal lobes bilaterally. The fourth feature (CFEA 24) involved increased 4-8-Hz theta activity in the bilateral occipital region. The templates used to form these features are shown in Figure 38-5.

These data suggest that a computerized analysis of EEG and EP data based on topographic mapping techniques may also be used to differentiate patients in the

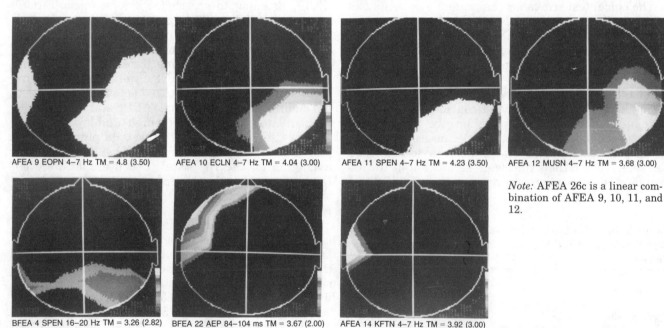

AFEA 9 EOPN 4–7 Hz TM = 4.8 (3.50)   AFEA 10 ECLN 4–7 Hz TM = 4.04 (3.00)   AFEA 11 SPEN 4–7 Hz TM = 4.23 (3.50)   AFEA 12 MUSN 4–7 Hz TM = 3.68 (3.00)

BFEA 4 SPEN 16–20 Hz TM = 3.26 (2.82)   BFEA 22 AEP 84–104 ms TM = 3.67 (2.00)   AFEA 14 KFTN 4–7 Hz TM = 3.92 (3.00)

Note: AFEA 26c is a linear combination of AFEA 9, 10, 11, and 12.

Figure 38-4. Seven BEAM images (t-SPMs—significance probability map) obtained by comparing presenile AD patients with normal control subjects. The state from which each t-SPM was derived is indicated below each image. The maximum t value in each image is shown as Tm. The t cutoff value used to form templates for feature development is shown in parentheses. The name of the feature derived from each t-SPM is also shown. The four best features by final merit value are, in order: AFEA 26c, BFEA 4, BFEA 22, and AFEA 14. Note that the differences between patients and control subjects involved the temporal lobes prominently, especially on the right. Adapted from Duffy, Albert, and McAnulty (1984) by permission.

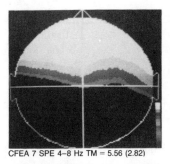 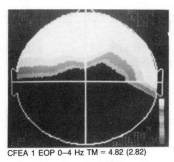 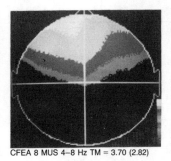 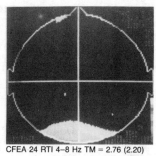

CFEA 7 SPE 4–8 Hz TM = 5.56 (2.82)   CFEA 1 EOP 0–4 Hz TM = 4.82 (2.82)   CFEA 8 MUS 4–8 Hz TM = 3.70 (2.82)   CFEA 24 RTI 4–8 Hz TM = 2.76 (2.20)

Figure 38-5. Four BEAM images obtained by comparing senile AD patients with normal control subjects. The display conventions are the same as in Figure 4. The four best features by final merit value are, in order: CFEA 7, CFEA 1, CFEA 8, and CFEA 24. Note that the differences between patients and control subjects involve the frontal lobes prominently and the occipital pole. Adapted from Duffy et al. (1984) by permission.

early stages of presenile and senile AD from age- and sex-matched control subjects. The topographic dissimilarities between the features derived for the younger and older age groups indicate that there are important differences between the groups. Although both patient groups demonstrate synchronization (i.e., increased slowing), the topographic distribution of these changes differs. In the older age range, the regions that best discriminate the AD patients from control subjects are in the frontal lobes; in the younger age range, temporal lobe features are powerful discriminators. Thus an age–disease interaction appears to be evident in the EEG data as well as in the CT data.

The highest correlations between cognitive test scores and EEG features are shown in Tables 38-5 and 38-6. Negative correlations were consistently associated with the theta and delta features, whereas beta features were positively related to test scores. Thus, better test performance was associated with less theta and delta activity and more beta.

Conclusions

There appears to be some concordance between the EEG and CT data with respect to the topographic regions that show the greatest change in AD patients, particularly among older individuals. Senile AD patients have lower CT density numbers on the slice level at the bodies of the lateral ventricles, at least half of which consist of frontal lobes. Similarly, the electrophysiological studies indicate that older AD patients differ most from normal control subjects in frontal regions. One might speculate that as people age, their frontal lobes become more vulnerable to the effects of disease; therefore, older patients show the greatest difference from the age-matched normal control subjects in frontal regions. The EEG data indicate that patients in the presenile age range differ most in the temporal lobes, but the temporal lobes are more difficult to evaluate using CT than the frontal lobes because of the interference of bone artifact from the base of the brain. Because magnetic resonance imaging is not affected by bone artifact, this technique may provide some data relevant to this issue.

It is also interesting to speculate on the neuropathological and neurochemical origins of the CT and EEG changes that have been revealed by these computerized analyses. One explanation for the lower mean CT density numbers for the remaining tissue is that they are a reflection of the reduced number of axons in white matter. Other investigators also have hypothesized a loss of white matter volume in AD patients (Gado et al., 1982; George et al., 1981). This hypothesis is based on findings of a reduced difference in grey–white matter discriminability for some demented patients and control subjects (George et al., 1981) and an inverse relationship between the differences in grey–

Table 38-5. Correlations Between Neuropsychological Test Scores and BEAM Features in Presenile AD Patients

BEAM feature	EEG frequency	Verbal memory		Nonverbal memory		Visuospatial ability		Attention/ abstraction skills	
		r	p	r	p	r	p	r	p
AFEA 26C	Theta	−.78	.0005	−.70	.002	−.70	.003	−.67	.006
BFEA 4	Beta 2	+.80	.0004	+.78	.003	+.79	.0004	+.71	.002
BFEA 22	AER	ns	ns	−.68	.01	ns	ns	ns	ns
AFEA 14	Theta	ns	ns	−.67	.01	ns	ns	−.65	.01

Note. Adapted from Duffy et al. (1984) by permission.

Table 38-6. Correlations Between Neuropsychological Test Scores and BEAM Features in Senile AD Patients

BEAM feature	EEG frequency	Verbal memory		Nonverbal memory		Visuospatial ability		Attention/ abstraction skills	
		r	p	r	p	r	p	r	p
CFEA 7	Theta	−.85	.0005	−.82	.003	−.78	.003	ns	ns
CFEA 1	Delta	−.77	.003	−.92	.003	−.78	.002	−.80	.009
CFEA 8	Theta	−.85	.001	ns	ns	−.91	.001	ns	ns
CFEA 24	Theta	−.77	.009	−.88	.002	ns	ns	ns	ns

Note. Adapted from Duffy et al. (1984) by permission.

white matter density and the size of the CSF space (Gado et al., 1983). There is pathologic evidence of reduced white matter in AD patients as well (Katzman & Terry, 1983). It is also possible that reduced CT density numbers are related to the presence of the neurofibrillary tangles and neuritic plaques in subcortical and cortical structures. Magnetic resonance imaging may be helpful in addressing these hypotheses.

The EEG slowing that was found in our investigations may be related to changes in cholinergic activity. It is well known that anticholinergic drugs such as atropine produce prominent EEG slowing (Niedermeyer & Lopes da Silva, 1982). Moreover, Gloor has postulated that delta activity may reflect the relative cholinergic deafferentation of the cortex (Testa & Gloor, 1974). The EEG changes seen in presenile and senile AD patients may therefore be the result of decreased regional brain cholinergic activity. This finding would be consistent with the findings of decreased amounts of choline acetyltransferase (CAT) found in the cortex on postmortem examination (Davies et al., 1982; Davies & Maloney, 1976) and decreased synthesis of acetylcholine in cortical biopsy tissue (Sims, Bowen, & Davison, 1981) reported for presenile and senile patients. The nucleus basalis of Meynert, a region of the basal forebrain that contains cholinergic positive neurons that project to widespread areas of the cerebral cortex, also is reported to show considerable neuronal loss in AD patients (Price et al., 1982). Moreover, there is a parallel between the location of the EEG features that best discriminate presenile and senile patients from control subjects, and the location of CAT decreases in the cortex of these patients on postmortem. Among 49-to-68-year-old patients, decreases in CAT are reported to be greatest in temporo-parietal regions, whereas patients aged 76 to 93 show the greatest decrease in fronto-parietal areas (Davies et al., 1982).

The significant correlations between cognitive test scores and the CT and EEG features reported here ranged from .59 to .92. However, it appears that the strength of the correlation between neurobiological and neurobehavioral variables depends greatly upon the types of measures employed.

The EEG features tended to show the strongest correlations with behavior. These features are based on group differences rather than simple summations of electrical activity and, therefore, maximize group differences. This analytic process appears to increase the likelihood of finding significant brain–behavior correlations.

The fewest and least striking correlations were found in the CT study with senile AD patients. Because the CT measures in this investigation were powerful discriminators of patients and normal control subjects, it seems likely that the correlational results were affected by the type of neuropsychological tests that were used. Both the Dementia Rating Scale and the National Adult Reading Test were designed for use with dementia patients and therefore contain tasks whose range of difficulty is greatly reduced in comparison to those in the more extensive test battery administered to the other patient populations. Thus, variations in both the selection of neuropsychological test items and the analytic techniques applied to the CTs and EEGs affect the ability to assess the relationship between cognitive function and neurobiological external validators.

Taken together, these studies demonstrate that a computerized analysis of CT scans and EEGs delineate neuroanatomical and neurophysiological features that retrospectively discriminate with a high degree of accuracy between healthy control subjects and age-equivalent presenile and senile AD patients. Although the number of subjects in each of our studies was small, the ratio of sample size to number of variables was carefully controlled to reduce the likelihood of a Type I error. Nevertheless, in order to prospectively evaluate the sensitivity of the finding, a cross-validation of these results on an independent sample is essential. To examine specificity it will be necessary to determine whether other neurological, medical, or psychiatric conditions (e.g., multi-infarct dementia, cardiovascular disease, or depression) produce CT or EEG changes similar in nature and location to those seen in AD patients. However, if these findings are replicated and extended, they will have important clinical utility. They offer the possibility that a small number of computerized measurements on CT scans or EEGs or both may provide external validation for the diagnosis of AD.

References

Albert, M. S., Naeser, M. A., Levine, H. L., & Garvey, A. J. (1984a). Mean CT density numbers in patients with senile dementia of the Alzheimer's type. *Archives of Neurology, 41*, 1264–1269.

Albert, M. S., Naeser, M. A., Levine, H. L., & Garvey, A. J. (1984b). Ventricular size in patients with presenile dementia of the Alzheimer's type. *Archives of Neurology, 41*, 1258–1263.

Bartels, P. H. (1979). Numerical evaluation of cytologic data III: Selection of features for discrimination. *Analytical and Quantitative Cytology, 1*, 153–159.

Bondareff, W., Baldy, R., & Levy, R. (1981). Quantitative computed tomography in dementia. *Archives of General Psychiatry, 38*, 1365–1368.

Brinkman, S. D., Sarwar, M., Levin, H. S., & Morris, H. H. (1981). Quantitative indexes of computed tomography in dementia and normal aging. *Neuroradiology, 138*, 89–92.

Constantinidis, J., Krassoievitch, M., & Tissot, R. (1969). Correlations entre les perturbations electroencephalographiques et les lesions anatomo-histologiques dans les demence. *Encephale, 58*, 19–52.

Davies, P., Katz, D. A., & Crystal, H. A. (1982). Choline acetyltransferase, somatostatin, and substance p in selected cases of Alzheimer's disease. In S. Corkin, K. L. Davis, J. H. Growdon, E. Usdin, & R. J. Wurtman (Eds.), *Alzheimer's disease: A review of progress in research* (pp. 9–14). New York: Raven Press.

Davies, P., & Maloney, A. J. F. (1976). Selective loss of central cholinergic neurons in Alzheimer's disease. *Lancet, 2*, 1403.

de Leon, M. J., Ferris, S. H., George, A. E., Reisberg, B., Kricheff, I. I., & Gershon, S. (1980). Computed tomography evaluations of brain–behavior relationships in senile dementia of the Alzheimer's type. *Neurobiology of Aging, 1*, 69–79.

DiChiro, G., Brooks, R. A., Dubal, L., & Chew, E. (1978). The apical artifact: Elevated attenuation values toward the apex of the skull. *Journal of Computer Assisted Tomography, 2*, 65–70.

Duffy, F. H., Albert, M. S., & McAnulty, G. (1984). Brain electrical activity in patients with presenile and senile dementia of the Alzheimer's type. *Annals of Neurology, 16*, 439–448.

Duffy, F. H., Bartels, P. H., & Burchfiel, J. L. (1981). Significance probability mapping: An aid in the topographic analysis of brain electrical activity. *Electroencephalography and Clinical Neurophysiology, 51*, 455–462.

Duffy, F. H., Denckla, M. B., Bartels, P. H., & Sandini, G. (1980). Dyslexia: Regional differences in brain electrical activity by topographic mapping. *Annals of Neurology, 7*, 412–420.

Feldman, M. J., & Drasgow, J. A. (1951). A visual–verbal test for schizophrenia. *Psychiatric Quarterly Supplement, 25*, 55–64.

Gado, M., Danziger, W., Chi, D., Hughes, C. P., & Coben, L. A. (1983). Brain parenchymal density measurements by CT in demented subjects and normal controls. *Radiology, 147*, 703–710.

Gado, M., Hughes, C. P., Danziger, W., Chi, D., Jost, G., & Berg, L. (1982). Volumetric measurements of the cerebrospinal fluid spaces in demented subjects and controls. *Radiology, 144*, 535–538.

Genchi, H., & Mori, K. (1965). Evaluation and feature extraction on automated pattern recognition system. *Denki-Tsuchin Gakkai, Part I.*

George A., de Leon, M., Ferris, S., & Kricheff, I. I. (1981). Parenchymal CT correlates of senile dementia (Alzheimer's disease) loss of grey–white matter discriminability. *American Journal of Neuroradiology, 2*, 205–213.

George, A., de Leon, M., Rosenbloom, S., Ferris, S., Gentes, C., Emmerich, M., & Kricheff, I. I. (1983). Ventricular volume and cognitive deficit: A computed tomographic study. *Radiology, 149*, 493–498.

Goodin, D. S., Squires, K. C., & Starr, A. (1978). Long latency event-related components of the auditory evoked potential in dementia. *Brain, 101*, 635–648.

Gordon, E. G., & Sim, M. (1967). The EEG in presenile dementia. *Journal of Neurology, Neurosurgery, and Psychiatry, 30*, 285.

Hachinski, J. (1978). Cerebral blood flow differentiation of Alzheimer's disease from multi-infarct dementia. In R. Katzman, R. D. Terry, & K. T. Bick (Eds.), *Alzheimer's disease: Senile dementia and related disorders* (pp. 97–104). New York: Raven Press.

Hughes, C. P., & Gado, M. (1981). Computed tomography and aging of the brain. *Radiology, 139*, 391–396.

Jacoby, R. J., Levy, R., & Dawson, J. M. (1980). Computed tomography in the elderly: 1. The normal population. *British Journal of Psychiatry, 136*, 249–255.

Jernigan, T. L., Zatz, L. M., & Naeser, M. A. (1979). Semiautomated methods for quantitating CSF volume on cranial computed tomography. *Radiology, 132*, 463–466.

Kaplan, E. F., Goodglass, H., & Weintraub, S. (1978). *The Boston Naming Test.* Boston: E. Kaplan & H. Goodglass.

Katzman, R., & Terry, R. (1983). *The neurology of aging.* Philadelphia: Davis.

Mattis, S. (1976). Dementia rating scale. In L. Bellak & T. B. Karasu (Eds.), *Geriatric psychiatry.* New York: Grune & Stratton.

Naeser, M. A., Albert, M. S., & Kleefield, J. (1982). New methods of CT scan diagnosis of Alzheimer's disease: Examination of white and gray matter CT density numbers. In S. Corkin, K. L. Davis, J. H. Growdon, E. Usdin, & R. J. Wurtman (Eds.), *Alzheimer's disease: A review of progress in research* (pp. 63–78). New York: Raven Press.

Naeser, M. A., Hayward, R. W., Laughlin, S., & Zatz, L. M. (1981). Quantitative CT scan studies in aphasia: Part II. Comparison of the right and left hemisphere. *Brain and Language, 12*, 165–189.

Nelson, H. E. (1982). National Adult Reading Test. *Test manual.* Windsor, England: NFER-Nelson Publishing Co.

Niedermeyer, E., & Lopes da Silva, F. (1982). *Electroencephalography: Basic principles, clinical applications and related fields.* Baltimore: Urban & Schwarzenberg.

Price, D. L., Whitehouse, P. J., Struble, R. G., Clark, A. W., Coyle, J. T., DeLong, M. R., & Hedreen, J. C. (1982). Basal forebrain cholinergic system in Alzheimer's disease and related dementias. *Neuroscience, 1*, 84–92.

Roberts, M. A., & Caird, F. I. (1982). Computerized tomography and intellectual decline in the elderly. *Journal of Neurology, Neurosurgery, and Psychiatry, 45*, 50–54.

Selin, I. (1965). *Detection theory.* Princeton, NJ: Princeton University Press.

Sherwood, E. M., Bartels, P. H., & Wied, G. L. (1976). Feature selection in cell image analysis. Use of the ROC curve. *Acta Cytology, 20*, 254–260.

Siegel, S. (1956). *Nonparametric statistics for the behavioral sciences.* New York: McGraw-Hill.

Sims, N. R., Bowen, D. M., & Davison, A. N. (1981). Acetylcholine synthesis and carbon dioxide production from glucose by tissue prisms from human neocortex. *Biochemical Journal, 196*, 867–976.

Soininen, H., Puranen, M., & Riekkinen, P. J. (1982). Computed tomography findings in senile dementia and normal aging. *Journal of Neurology, Neurosurgery, and Psychiatry, 45,* 50–54.

Squires, K., Goodin, D., & Starr, A. (1979). Event related potentials in development, aging, and dementia. In D. Lehman & E. Callaway (Eds.), *Human evoked potentials: Applications and problems* (pp. 383–396). New York: Plenum Press.

Testa, G., & Gloor, P. (1974). Generalized penicillin epilepsy in the cat: Effects of midbrain cooling. *Electroencephalography and Clinical Neurophysiology, 36,* 517–524.

Vitaliano, P., Breen, A., Albert, M., Russo, J., & Prinz, P. (1984). Memory, attention, and functional status in community residing Alzheimer type dementia patients and optimally healthy aged individuals. *Journal of Gerontology, 39*(1), 58–64.

Wechsler, D. (1945). A standardized memory scale for clinical use. *Journal of Psychology, 19,* 87–95.

Wechsler, D. (1955). *Manual for the Wechsler Adult Intelligence Scale.* New York: Psychological Corporation.

Wells, C. E. (1977). Diagnostic evaluation and treatment in dementia. In C. E. Wells (Ed.), *Dementia* (pp. 247–276). Philadelphia: Davis.

Wilson, R. S., Fox, J. H., Huckman, M. S., Bacon, L. D., & Lobick, J. J. (1982). Computed tomography in dementia. *Neurology, 32,* 1054–1057.

Zatz, L. M., Jernigan, T. L., & Ahumada, A. J. (1982). Changes on computed cranial tomography with aging: Intra-cranial fluid volume. *American Journal of Neuroradiology, 3,* 1–11.

Thomas B. Horvath

Event-Related Potential Validators in Alzheimer's Disease

Computer-averaged event-related potentials (ERPs) are thought to be electrical signals of information processing in the brain (Donchin, 1979). The components of the waveform are defined by their poststimulus onset and their scalp distribution. The components have been related to various physiological and psychological processes, and attempts have been made to locate their generators (Goff, Allison, & Vaughan, 1978). In cerebral disorders in which information processing is disturbed by pathological lesions, one might expect corresponding alterations in some of the components of the waveform of the ERPs. The purposes of this chapter are to examine briefly the evidence for the construct validity of ERPs as indices of information processing and then, in some detail, to review the changes of the late components with aging and dementia and their predictive validity in diagnosis. This hypothesis is offered to connect the ERP changes in aging and dementia to the cholinergic deficit in the hippocampus.

Event-Related Potentials

Measurement and Reliability

The methodology of recording event-related potentials (ERPs) and some of its pitfalls have been reviewed by, among others, Desmedt (1977, 1979) and Cooper, Osselton, and Shaw (1980). In brief, surface scalp electrodes are used to record the electroencephalogram (EEG), with due attention to electrical skin resistance and the elimination of artifacts. The number of electrodes used depends on the available amplifier and computer channel capacity; the selection of locations among the conventional 10 to 20 sites (Jasper, 1958) depends on the known scalp distribution of the ERP component to be studied. The amplifiers should have their high- and low-frequency filters set to record with-

out distortion the frequency range of the component of interest, and to eliminate, as much as possible, low-frequency artifacts, (skin potential, baseline drift, eye movement), and high-frequency contaminants (muscle and movement potentials, electrode "pop"). The poststimulus epoch to be studied should include the expected upper time limits of the component of interest. This may range from 10 msec in the case of brainstem auditory evoked potentials (BAEPs) to 750 msec in studies of the late positive components (P3).

The stimuli used in neurological studies may be simple and repetitive and require no response from the subject. Such stimuli include light flashes, checkerboard reversals, brief tones or clicks, and mild electrical impulses. The stimuli used in cognitive psychophysiological studies, however, may be more complex and require a variety of responses from the subject. The stimuli include geometric figures, words from different semantic classes, or tones of differing frequencies presented with different probabilities. The responses usually required include sensory discrimination, classification and silent counting, or the performance of a choice reaction-time (RT) task.

The analog EEG signal is then digitized by the computer, with the appropriate sampling rate and the poststimulus sweep time for the latency and frequencies of the component to be studied. The waveforms of the ERP are generally smaller than the background EEG and would be lost without further processing. By adding and averaging a sufficient number of stimulus-locked epochs, the computer cancels out the random background activity, allowing the time-locked ERP to emerge from the noise. Unfortunately, certain extraneous potentials are also time-locked to the stimulus: the startle electromyogram to loud tones, eye blinks to bright light flashes, skin potential orienting responses

393

to any novel stimuli. The judicious use of head rests, eye fixation and relaxation techniques, and appropriate filters on the amplifiers can reduce but not entirely eliminate these artifacts. Computer programs are now available that identify and exclude from averaging those epochs that contain unusually large or irregular voltages (this process is called automatic artifact rejection). If the raw data are preserved on magnetic tape or in high-density digital memory, the record can be manually edited before off-line averaging is done. Even with the use of all these techniques, the study of the low-frequency, late components of the ERP requires the parallel averaging of the electroculogram to display the adequacy of artifact control techniques.

In the early years of ERP work, each investigator set up a unique set of stimulators, component amplifiers, analog-to-digital converters, central processors, and averaging computer programs. Now a number of reliable, user-friendly, turnkey programmable amplifiers that are integrated with averaging computers are available.

Definitions

The availability of laboratory minicomputers led to the recording and measurement of ERPs, first in psychophysiology (Begleiter, 1977; Callaway & Lehman, 1979; Callaway, Tueting, & Koslow, 1978), then in neurology as well (Courjon, Mauguière, & Revol, 1982; Starr, 1978). Hillyard and Picton (1979) have recently reviewed these scalp-derived, computer-averaged manifestations of information processing in the brain. The early (10 msec) *brainstem auditory evoking potentials* (BAEPs) represent successive activations of relay stations in the auditory pathway; they are not affected by attention or other cognitive processes. The early components of the somatosensory evoked potential and visual evoked potential show similar resistance to cognitive manipulations.

The midlatency auditory evoked potentials (AEP) are best seen over the central scalp and vertex region, and consist of P1 (40 to 60 msec), N1 (80 to 130 msec), and P2 (150 to 200 msec). Somatosensory and visual stimuli produce similar vertex potentials with some latency variations. The functional neuroanatomy of the generators of these potentials is being established (Goff et al., 1978) and seems to involve areas of the frontal and secondary association cortex driven by the primary sensory cortex, possibly via thalamic pathways. Hillyard, Hink, Schwent, and Picton (1973) showed that selective attention in a dichotic listening task produced a reciprocal increase in N1 amplitude in the attended ear and attentuation in the ignored ear. This attentional effect on the vertex potential is seen only under conditions of high sensory load. Hillyard and Picton (1979) reviewed the evidence that N1 is a sign of a selective attentional filter in the various sensory modalities.

Sutton (1979), Donchin (1979), and Pritchard (1981) reviewed the advances in the study of a late (300 to 600 msec) positive potential initially described by Sutton, Braren, Zubin, and John in 1965. This wave, the P3 or P300, occurs when an unpredictable stimulus becomes relevant to an ongoing task (e.g., when a subject is asked to count the number of infrequent, low-pitched tones interspersed with a sequence of frequent, predictable, high-pitched tones). Frequent stimuli are usually not associated with P3s, but even low-probability stimuli fail to evoke P3s if the stimuli are task irrelevant or if the subject ignores them. Some researchers prefer to make distinctions between a centroparietal, task relevant component, (P3b) and a more frontally distributed component related to intrusive, novel stimuli (P3a) (Roth, Ford, Lewis, & Kopell, 1976; Roth & Kopell, 1973).

The N2 or N200 (200 to 300 msec) and the slow wave (SW) (400 to 800 msec) are other components of this late complex (Donchin, Ritter, & McCallum, 1978). The N2 is modality sensitive; it is elicited when an unexpected event occurs and is related to the P3a. It is often best elicited when a stimulus is missing from its regular sequence; otherwise the P2 component tends to interfere with its detection. It may have a novelty detection and classification function, and it is generated without active subject involvement (Ritter, Simpson, & Vaughan, 1972). The *slow wave* (SW), which is positive parietally and negative in frontal regions, may last beyond 600 msec. Ford and Pfefferbaum (1980) speculated that the negative SW may be generated by the dendritic trees of frontal lobe neurons during a decision-making process.

Halgren et al. (1980) were able to correlate endogenous limbic potentials detected by depth electrodes from the hippocampus and amygdala with vertex recorded P3s. Limbic potentials and P3 evolved in response to infrequent, attended stimuli and to the omission of expected stimuli. Okada, Kaufman, and Williamson (1983) evoked a visual P3 and N2 and measured the corresponding magnetic fluxes with a superconducting quantum interference device. The fluxes corresponding with the positive and negative potentials had different polarities and somewhat different projections, but their origin pointed to the hippocampus. Claims for evoked potential component generators are often controversial (Goff et al., 1978), and multiple generators may exist. In this instance it may be sufficient to state that the hippocampus is known to be involved in several functions during which P300s are generated, and the correlations found between scalp-recorded late potentials and depth-electrode recorded limbic potentials, as well as evoked magnetic fluxes, fit into recent models of information processing of rare and important events and their cerebral sites (Grossberg, 1982).

In summary, the early 0-to-200-msec components of the evoked potential are influenced by the stimulus modality and quality and are often referred to as "extrinsic" or sensory evoked potentials. Their use in neurological diagnosis has been reviewed by Greenberg and Ducker (1982). The late, 200-msec and beyond, components are not modality specific and are influenced not by sensory factors, but by a variety of cognitive mediators, such as attention, memory, and response selection. These "endogenous," cognitive ERPs may be useful in detecting abnormalities in cognitive disorders such as dementia, schizophrenia, and dyslexia. This literature has been reviewed by Syndulko, Cohen, Tourtellotte, and Potvin (1982).

Cognitive Determinants of the P3 Component

Hillyard and Picton (1979), using a distinction between "stimulus set" and "response set," contrasted the attentional processes indexed by N1 and P3. The ordinary conditions of stimulus processing call for adoption of a stimulus set for selecting between channels (e.g., between visual and auditory inputs) and a further memory-dependent target selection within a channel, the response set. N1 amplitude represents the former, and P3 amplitude represents the latter. The P3 is relatively independent of stimulus parameters and depends on cues that may be complex variations of task relevance and probability.

Donchin et al. (1978) discussed the determinants of P3 amplitude. A consistent feature of the nine studies reviewed was that P3 amplitude was the inverse function of the a priori probability of the eliciting event (i.e., the less frequent the event, the larger the elicited P3). This is the basis for the so-called oddball paradigm. In this commonly used stimulus sequence, the subject is asked to respond to infrequent, random target stimuli embedded in a sequence of frequent, nontarget stimuli (i.e., to pick the oddball). A subject must perceive and compute the objective probabilities of a sequence; as a result, there may be differences between different runs with the same objective probabilities. This phenomenon may help to explain the finding of Squires, Wickens, Squires, and Donchin (1976) that the P3 was affected by the sequence of immediately preceding stimuli and not simply the objective overall probability. Duncan-Johnson and Donchin (1977) found that a priori probability and sequential structure, involving processing through short-term memory, combined to determine P3 amplitude and accounted for 78% of its variance.

Task relevance is another determinant of P3 amplitude (Ford, Roth, & Kopell, 1976). Performing a reaction time response to a target stimulus increases the P3 (Roth, Ford, & Kopell, 1978), but it is not the motor response itself that affects P300 amplitude (McCarthy & Donchin, 1976). Task relevance depends more on the subject's estimate of what is important than on the experimenter's determination. Begleiter, Porjesz, Chou, and Aunon (1983) demonstrated that equiprobable and task-relevant stimuli elicited differential P300 amplitudes depending on the incentive or motivational value of the stimuli.

Thus the subjective importance and probability of stimuli determine P3 amplitude. Memory may also play a part. Donchin (1981) hypothesized, and obtained some preliminary data showing, that P3 amplitude was related to recall: Items that evoked a bigger P3 were subsequently recalled better.

The latency of the P3 correlates positively with reaction time (RT) (Ritter et al., 1972), but the extent of the positive correlation between single-trial RTs and P3s can be reduced if instructions are given to sacrifice speed for accuracy (Kutas, McCarthy, & Donchin, 1977). There are other important instances of dissociation as well (Squires et al., 1976). The discordance can be resolved if P3 latency is seen as an index of stimulus evaluation time (Kutas et al., 1977) and is independent of response selection, neural conduction, and movement time. Increased task difficulty delays the P3 in discrimination tasks (Ford, Pfefferbaum, Tinklenberg, & Kopell, 1982; Squires, Donchin, Squires, & Grossberg, 1977). Increasing the number of items to be scanned in a memory paradigm also increases P3 latency (Donchin et al., 1978; Ford, Roth, Mohs, Hopkins, & Kopell, 1979). Duncan-Johnson and Donchin (1982) presented evidence that the latency of the P3 was the time required to identify the stimulus, evaluate its task relevance, and assess its expectancy. Increased task difficulty delays the P3 in discrimination tasks (Ford, et al., 1982; Squires et al., 1977), and increasing the number of items to be scanned in a memory paradigm also increases P3 latency (Donchin et al., 1978; Ford, Roth, et al., 1979). McCarthy and Donchin (1981) showed that P3 latency was affected by the presence of noise. Duncan-Johnson (1981) showed increased P3 latency in the presence of a Stroop color–word conflict. Donchin (1981) thus concluded that the task difficulty affecting P3 latency is a perceptual one. Callaway (1984) summarized the cognitive and psychopharmacological evidence for a model of serial information processing. He concluded that the latency of the P3 represents stimulus evaluation and not response selection, whereas reaction time is the sum of both of these processes.

Donchin (1979) argued that the P3 is not simply the correlate of some overt behavioral process but rather is the manifestation of neural activity that relates the processing of expected events to unexpected ones. It is perhaps the manifestation of a neural program "subroutine" that gets called upon in a variety of contexts, such as in orienting, vigilance, incentive evaluation, and memorization. The P3 does not appear to be a tactical response to a specific stimulus, like the peripheral components of the orienting response (OR); instead, the P3 appears to be an aspect of strategic information processing, reevaluating the context in which stimuli occur for future reference, on the basis of experience. This may bring the P3 within a theoretical framework dealing with tonic readiness to respond (basal ganglia), phasic responses to input (amygdala), and the coordination between them (hippocampus) (Pribram & McGuiness, 1975). Grossberg (1982) also presented a model in which cholinergic and catecholaminergic interactions regulate a motivational baseline, with the hippocampus as a final common path. In his model, attentional and short-term memory functions may be related to the N2 and P3 components of evoked potentials.

ERP Changes in Cognitive Decline

Early Components in Aging and Dementia

Changes in ERP latency and amplitude may occur in those experiments of nature associated with varieties of cognitive decline, memory failure, and poor stimulus processing, particularly if the hippocampal-amygdaloid complexes are pathologically affected. Aging, senile AD, and possibly some delirious states may fill this requirement, as may some types of brain damage caused by chronic alcoholism.

Harkins and Lenhardt (1980) reported that in healthy elderly subjects there is little change in BAEPs that cannot be accounted for by high-frequency hearing loss. However, the latency of a BAEP component (Wave V) is prolonged in AD patients, as compared with normal subjects, a result that suggests a significant delay in central transmission time from the eighth nerve (Wave I) to the inferior colliculus (Wave V). Klorman, Thompson, and Ellingson (1978) reviewed the development of ERPs across the life span, and Smith, Thompson, and Michalewski (1980) looked at the aging end of the spectrum. A modest increase in the latency of midlatency visual and somatosensory EP components is seen with old age, but little extra delay with age is seen in the auditory midlatency components. The earlier (40-to-100-msec) components show increased amplitude with old age, whereas the later (100-to-300-msec) components seem to decrease in all three sensory modalities (Beck, Swanson, & Dustman, 1980; Celesia & Daly, 1977; Coben, Danziger, & Hughes, 1983; Dustman, Snyder, & Schlehuber, 1981).

The midlatency ERP changes in chronic brain syndromes were reviewed by Shagass, Ornitz, Sutton, and Tueting (1978). Straumanis, Shagass, and Schwartz, (1965) showed early visual EP amplitude increases, with latency prolongations. Visser, Stam, and Van Tilburg (1976) confirmed this. Levy, Isaacs, and Behrman (1971) found latency prolongations and N1 amplitude reduction in senile dementia. Hendrickson, Levy, and Post (1979) also found some midlatency ERP prolongation in senility. Drechsler (1978) attempted to explain age-related ERP changes from the perspective of a loss of inhibitory control. This accounts for increased amplitude of some early components and for the wider distribution of some components. But Ford, Hink, et al. (1979) found little difference in the responsiveness of aged and young subjects. In particular, N1 amplitudes were as well modulated by attention in the old as in the young subjects.

Compared with the often dramatic brainstem and midlatency EP changes in neurological diseases, where sensory pathology often exists (multiple sclerosis, intracranial tumors, etc.) (Greenberg & Ducker, 1982), the changes in ERPs within 200 msec of stimuli in aging and in dementia are modest indeed. There appears to be little correlation between the level of cognitive failure and the extent of changes in these exogenous evoked potentials (Shagass et al., 1978).

Late ERP Components and Aging

Klorman et al. (1978) reviewed the changes in the late or endogenous ERPs induced by aging. In a comparison between young and old subjects in an auditory sensory discrimination task, P3 amplitudes were equal, but P3 latencies were prolonged in the old subjects (Marsh & Thompson, 1972). Goodin, Squires, Henderson, and Starr (1978) studied 40 normal subjects between the ages of 15 and 76, using an auditory oddball sensory discrimination paradigm. For young subjects, the mean P3 latency was about 300 msec, which increased with a slope of 1.64 msec/year with standard deviation bands of ±20 msec around the regression line. P2 latency increased more slowly (.74 msec/year), and N1 did not show a significant change in latency. The amplitudes of P3 and N1 to P2 decreased slightly with age. Pfefferbaum, Ford, Wenegrat, Tinklenberg, and Kopell (1982) reported similar increases in P3 latency with age (1.45 msec/year) with visual ERPs, but their standard deviation bands around the regression line were wider (±40 msec).

Brown, Marsh, and LaRue (1983) also found the expected correlations of ERP latencies with age: The N2 latency slope was 0.7 msec/year, and the P3 latency slope was 1.12 msec/year. (There was also a negative correlation between age and P3 amplitude.) But when these researchers split their sample into two groups around the age of 45, the younger group did not show any correlations between age and evoked potential latency. For the older group, there was a correlation, and the slopes were steeper than those described by others: 1.35 msec/year for N2 and 3.14 msec/year for P3. Further analysis of their data and a reanalysis of two other papers suggest that the addition of a curvilinear, quadratic factor to the linear regression accounts for more variance. Thus P3 latency may be a positively accelerated function of age.

Pfefferbaum, Ford, Roth, and Kopell (1980a, 1980b) explored in detail the differences in P3 between young and old subjects and the different cognitive strategies that may have led to them. The paradigm included 1000 Hz tones 80% of the time, and 500 Hz and 2000 Hz tones 10% of the time, each serving as a target in a counterbalanced way. The latency of P3 was increased in the old subjects for both target and nontarget stimuli. P3-RT correlations were similar in the old and the young. However, mean P3 preceded the mean RT in most of the young subjects but in only 5 of the 12 old ones. Single trial analysis of P3-RT relationships revealed high P3-RT correlation and the use of an accuracy strategy by the young, but not by the older, subjects (Kutas et al., 1977). Ford, Roth, et al. (1979) demonstrated that on a memory scan task, the old subjects had longer RTs that increased with increasing memory set size. The P3 latency function, which represents encoding time, was slightly longer in the old subjects, but the shape of the function, representing scanning speed, was not different from that of the young. The major delay in RT could be accounted for by the increased difference between RT and P3 latency in the aged. This period may represent processes following the decision, such as motor preparation and execution time. In summary, aging increases P3 latency, perhaps in an accelerated manner, and reduces the likelihood of the use of an accuracy strategy. However, in the prolongation of reaction times, stimulus evaluation, indexed by P3 latency, is not the major source of delay; motor selection and execution time are also prolonged.

Late ERP Components and Dementia

An important clinical application of P3 appeared when Goodin, Squires, and Starr (1978) reported on 27 "demented" patients and 26 neurologically ill, but cognitively intact, subjects. Dementia was defined by a Mini-Mental State Exam (Folstein, Folstein, & McHugh, 1975) score of 25 out of 30, and included cases that would now be classified as suffering from delirium as well as from dementia. The patients were compared with the normal control subjects previously reported (Goodin, Squires, Henderson, & Starr, 1978). The nondemented patients did not differ from the normal subjects in any amplitude or latency measures. The "demented" patients did not differ in the age-normalized N1 and P2 components. However, the latencies of their P3s were longer and the amplitude of their P3 was smaller than that of age-matched controls. Squires, Chippendale, Wrege, Goodin, and Starr (1980) reporting on an enlarged sample, used a P3 latency, 2 standard deviation units (SD) longer than an age-matched mean to diagnose dementia. They claimed an 80% correct categorization of demented patients and a 4% false positive rate. In several patients, fluctuations in mental state were correlated with changes in P3 latency.

Syndulko, Hausch, et al. (1982) confirmed these results in 12 demented patients, all with presumptive AD. All exceeded 1 SD above the age mean, and 10 exceeded 2 SD. Canter, Hallett, and Growden (1982) reported on 10 AD patients whose P3 latency was significantly related to their performance on an auditory discrimination task. However, neither P3 latency nor the performance index correlated with the severity of their dementia. (But, slow-wave activity in the frequency-analyzed EEG did correlate with the severity of their dementia.)

Pfefferbaum et al. (1982) cautioned against a hasty acceptance of P3 latency deviation as a practical diagnostic test for dementia. Their standard deviations (39 msec) were about twice as large as Goodin's (21 msec) and Syndulko's (20 msec). The wide individual variability implies that P3 latency changes may be more useful for within-subject studies of cognitive decline or improvement rather than for between-subject comparisons for the early detection of mild degrees of cognitive impairment. In any case, one should not expect a tight coupling of P3 to age alone, as individual variations of cognitive function should make some difference. In fact, Brown, Marsh, and LaRue (1982) reported that in older normal adults, P3 latency correlated with performance on some cognitive tests: Digit Symbol substitution, Trail Making A, and Digit Span. Pfefferbaum et al. (1982) report that increases in the ventricular–brain ratio on computerized tomography (CT) may be correlated with later P3s and inversely related to frontal negative slow waves. More studies are needed to correlate the clinical and CT features of dementia to changes in the latency and amplitude of late ERP components.

P3 and N2 in AD

The definitive diagnosis of AD is still a postmortem or, rarely, a cerebral biopsy diagnosis. Clinical assessment based on strict criteria (Blessed, Tomlinson, & Roth, 1968; Kay, 1977) and detailed neuropsychological testing can go a long way toward an in vivo diagnosis, but new biological validators would be of significant help to the clinician. In evaluating a proposed external validator, the first step is to determine whether a physiological procedure can distinguish between putative AD patients and age-matched normal control subjects. A second step is to use nondemented, aged psychiatric patients as control subjects. Finally, samples of demented patients of differing etiologies should be compared with one other to determine the specificity of the finding to AD. A study such as the one described as follows takes the first step toward the predictive validation of the diagnosis of AD.

Patients with dementia of varying severity and normal, nonhospitalized subjects who have passed a thorough medical exam are enrolled in a longitudinal study of aging and putative AD. The following inclusion and exclusion criteria are employed for subjects in the studies for AD:

1. Memory and Information Test (MIT) score less than 10 (Blessed et al., 1968);
2. Dementia Rating Scale (DRS) score above 4 (Kay, 1977);
3. an insidious, not acute onset of memory loss, with a continuous and not steplike course of deterioration;
4. no focal localizing neurological signs;
5. no history of stroke;
6. an unmedicated resting blood pressure lower than 150/95;
7. no evidence of meeting DSM-III criteria for alcoholism;
8. no evidence of meeting research diagnostic criteria for primary affective disorder;
9. no evidence of Huntington's disease, Parkinson's disease, or Wilson's disease;
10. no history of head trauma with loss of consciousness;
11. normal electrolytes, renal, liver, and endocrine functions by laboratory tests;

12. no laboratory signs of neurosyphillis;

13. normal serum folate and B_{12} levels;

14. normal skull x-ray and chest x-ray;

15. CT scan, which rules out a focal lesion, and often displays cortical atrophy;

16. normal cerebrospinal fluid protein, cell count, and glucose; and

17. an EEG showing a slowing of frequencies without focal features.

These criteria were designed to exclude patients with multi-infarct dementia, alcoholic dementia, pseudodementia secondary to depression, and delirium due to metabolic encephalopathy.

A Nicolet Pathfinder II is used to record ERPs. Cup electrodes with Beckman adhesive paste are applied to carefully abraded locations (impedance less than 2k) according to the 10–20 system (Jasper, 1958). Electroculogram is recorded with electrodes above and below the right eye. The active EEG electrode on the vertex, Cz, is referred to linked mastoids. The physiological amplifiers have digitally controlled two-pole Butterworth filters with 12 dB per octave roll-off. The EEG is amplified at 10k, with a band pass from 0.5 to 100 Hz. Eye movements larger than 50 μV or other artifacts that saturate the amplifiers are automatically rejected. The sweeptime is 750 msec. The stimuli consist of pure tones, of 9.9-msec rise and fall time, and a plateau of 20 msec, set at 65 dB sensation level (after determination of hearing level at appropriate frequencies). Stimuli are delivered at a rate of 7 stimuli per 10 sec. A standard oddball paradigm is used, in which a series of "frequent" tones at 500 Hz are heard 85% of the time and "rare" tones at 2,000 Hz are interspersed at 15%. Subjects are required to press a button to the "rares" and to count them. Each run of 400 stimuli is replicated.

The waveforms are stored on floppy disc, on which patient information is also edited for archival purposes. The waves are currently visually recognized and labeled with a processor-controlled cursor program. After digital smoothing, the highest +ve or −ve point in the epochs of interest are labeled. Measurements are taken by the program both from prestimulus baseline and from peak to peak. Stimulus–wave and peak-to-peak latencies are also measured. The group mean latencies and amplitudes of the ERPs of the AD patients and their age-matched controls are compared. Multiple correlations between ERP measures and disease severity are also tested.

Fifteen patients with AD and 16 normal elderly subjects were tested. Data from only 12 of the patients could be used, as 1 protocol had too much artifact for a meaningful study and 2 patients were too restless to complete the recording. The patients were quite demented: The mean Blessed score was high (18 ± 10), reflecting poor memory; the DRS also was high (5.1 ± 3.4), reflecting social deterioration; the Memory and Information Test scores of the patients were quite low (7.6 ± 6.9). The scores for the control subjects were within normal limits: Blessed = 1.7 ± 1.0, DRS =

Table 39-1. Responses to "Frequent" Tones

	Latency in msec, mean ± SD		
	P1	N1	P2
AD Patients	40 ± 13	85 ± 13	168 ± 18
Control Subjects	42 ± 12	91 ± 11	179 ± 15

	Amplitudes in μV, mean ± SD		
	P1	N1	P2
AD Patients	2.5 ± 1.1	−3.1 ± 1.6	5.4 ± 1.4
Control Subjects	3.5 ± 1.2	−3.6 ± 1.1	6.2 ± 2.2

0.6 ± 0.5, MIT = 18 ± 1.5. There were no differences in latency or in amplitude of early and mid components between AD patients and normal control subjects (Table 39-1). There were no latency differences between AD and normal control subjects in the early and mid components to the rare tone, but there was a distinct prolongation of the N2 and P3 components in the AD groups (Table 39-2). These late components also showed a difference in amplitude: N2 amplitude in AD seems increased, but P3 amplitude was definitely diminished (Table 39-2). Finally, 13 of the 16 normal control subjects showed an SW but none of the AD patients did.

The strongest finding was the latency delay of the N2 and P3. The mean N2 for control subjects was 222 ± 23; of the AD patients, 3 fell within 2 SD of this mean. The mean P3 for control subjects was 333 ± 38; of the AD patients, 3 fell within 2 SD of the mean for normal control subjects. Thus, the overlap was too large for any of the single measures to be diagnostic. The ERP variables were then examined for predictive power through the construction of a stepwise discriminant function. Four coefficients were found that were not correlated with each other, and, when taken together in a discriminant function, could be used to classify 12 out of 12 cases as AD and to correctly identify 15 out of 16 patients as normal (see Table 39-3). This will clearly need to be replicated on a separate group of patients. Five more AD patients and nine normal elderly control subjects have subsequently been tested. Four of the five AD patients and eight of the nine normal subjects were correctly classified by the original discriminant function. Finally, an attempt was made to correlate the EP measures with simple severity measures (DRS, MIT, Blessed), but no significant correlations were found (Table 39-4).

The finding that a discriminant function using several late ERP components was a better diagnostic validator than any single measure suggests that future studies of ERPs should not only look at P3 latency but also combine it with amplitude measures and include other late components (N2 and perhaps SW) as well. Control groups for future studies should include elderly patients with psychiatric illnesses and with other dementing disorders. Only after these steps are taken can one argue for the use of the changes of the late components of the ERP as a diagnostic validator for AD or for a broader category of cognitive disorders.

Table 39-2. Responses to "Rare" Tones

	Latency in msec, mean ± SD				
	P1	N1	P2	N2	P3
AD Patients	41 ± 15	88 ± 22	168 ± 22	284 ± 27	441 ± 56
Control Subjects	41 ± 12	84 ± 12	162 ± 14	222 ± 23	333 ± 38
	ns	ns	ns	$p < .0005$	$p < .005$

	Amplitude in μV, mean ± SD				
	P1	N1	P2	N2	P3
AD Patients	3.3 ± 3.0	−3.4 ± 3.3	5.9 ± 2.9	−4.0 ± 2.9	4.1 ± 3.7
Control Subjects	3.8 ± 1.6	−1.4 ± 1.9	−5.2 ± 1.4	−1.7 ± 2.5	6.8 ± 2.6
	ns	ns	ns	$p = .046$	$p = .039$

The Cholinergic Hypothesis of AD and the Alterations in ERPs

The concentrations of various neurotransmitters have been measured in a variety of brain regions of patients with a diagnosis of AD. Although changes in the concentrations of norepinephrine, serotonin, and dopamine have been reported (Gottfries, 1980), the important change in patients with AD is a very large reduction in choline acetyltransferase (CAT) activity (Davies, 1979; Davies & Maloney, 1976; Perry et al., 1978). CAT is localized in cholinergic neurons and as such is marker for the cholinergic neuron. Hence a loss of CAT activity suggests a loss of cholinergic neurons or their distal synapses.

There appears to be a band of cholinergic cells, extending from the basal forebrain region of the substantia innominata, ventral globus pallidus through the diagonal band and medial septum. The most caudal cell bodies project to the neocortex, and the more dorsal cells (septal) to the hippocampus (Swanson, 1980). Probably 90% of acetylcholine in the hippocampus is medial septal in origin, and the cholinergic terminals impinge on pyramidal and dentate granular cells. These are intimately involved in the regulation of the theta rhythm (Gaztelu & Bruno, 1982), an important manifestation of hippocampal activity.

A number of factors link diminished cholinergic activity with the memory deficit of AD. CAT activity is particularly low in the hippocampus and frontal cortex, which are brain areas involved in the memory and mental organization, and areas in which the highest concentration of neurofibrillary tangles and senile plaques is found in AD patients (Torack, 1978). The likelihood that a cholinergic abnormality is involved in the symptoms of AD is further supported by the significant negative correlation between CAT activity and mental test scores (Perry et al., 1978), and CSF acetylcholine levels and disease severity (Davis, Hsieh, et al., 1982). Whitehouse, Price, Clark, Coyle, and DeLong (1981) have reported on several AD patients who had selective loss of cholinergic neurons in the nucleus basalis.

The effect of cholinergic agents on human memory is specific: The drugs consistently affect the ability to store new information into long-term memory (LTM). However, cholinomimetics have no effect on the retrieval of information from LTM nor on any short-term memory (STM) processes (Davis, Mohs, et al., 1982). The distinction between STM and LTM is an essential feature of current psychological theories of memory (Squire, 1982). STM is presumed to be of limited capacity and can be measured in seconds. (The digit span is a measure of STM.) LTM is the mechanism underlying permanent storage of information; its capacity appears unlimited. (Learning a long list of words involves encoding information into LTM.) Transfer of memories from STM to LTM involves hippocampus and diencephalic areas. It is this aspect of memory that is sensitive to cholinergic manipulation (Bartus, Dean, Beer, & Lippa, 1982; Davis, Mohs, et al., 1982).

Table 39-3. Discriminant Function Coefficients

P2 Latency to "Frequents"	−.41
N2 Latency to "Rares"	.62
P3 Latency to "Rares"	.49
P3 Amplitude to "Rares"	−.43

Actual Group	N	Predicted Membership	
		Correct:	Incorrect:
AD Patients	12	12	0
Control Subjects	16	15	1

Percentage of "grouped" cases correctly identified: 96.4%.

Table 39-4. Correlations Between Discriminant Function Variable and Severity of Illness in AD Patients

	FP2L	RN2L	RP3L	RP3A	Discriminant
Blessed	−.43	.33	.10	.16	.37
(p)	(.16)	(.30)	(.75)	(.62)	(.24)
MIT	.48	−.26	−.01	−.31	−.22
(p)	(.12)	(.41)	(.98)	(.33)	(.49)
DRS	−.31	.50	.28	.05	.57
(p)	(.33)	(.10)	(.38)	(.87)	(.06)

$N = 12$; p values are two-tailed.

The P3 wave of an ERP may also be sensitive to cholinergic manipulation. Callaway (1983) noted that although methylphenidate speeds up the reaction time and scopolamine delays it, the latency of the associated P3 is not affected by the adrenergic stimulant but is prolonged by the anticholinergic agent. Thus stimulus evaluation and context updating are at least partly cholinergic functions, whereas response speed is partly adrenergic (Callaway, 1984).

In AD and aging, the outstanding ERP change is the delay of N2 and P3, and the generator of these waves is thought to be the hippocampus, and possibly the amygdala. In AD and aging, the constant and early clinical finding is a memory problem of the type described in disorders of the hippocampus and amygdala. The important pathological feature of AD is the loss of CAT and other cholinergic markers, probably related to a "dying back" neuropathy of nucleus basalis and septal cholinergic neurons (Terry & Davies, 1980). Nucleus basalis cells project to the neocortex, especially to the frontal lobes, and to the hippocampus where plaques and CAT decline are prominent in AD. Synaptosomal debris from cholinergic cells contributes to the plaques, whose density correlates with the severity of dementia. P3 and N2 are seen in AD and aging and may be markers of cholinergic activity. Further empirical studies are needed to study the relationship of P3, N2, and SW to cholinergic markers, cognitive function, and disease severity and structural changes in AD and normal aging. Even if the changes in the late components are not unique to AD they may still have a common hypocholinergic basis. Hence the use of cholinergic pharmacological probes to dissect components of cognitive processing, as recommended by Callaway (1983) may throw further light on the biology of some aspects of memory.

References

Bartus, R. T., Dean, R. L., Beer, B., & Lippa, A. S. (1982). The cholinergic hypothesis of geriatric memory dysfunction. *Science, 217,* 408–417.

Beck, E. C., Swanson, C., & Dustman, R. E. (1980). Long latency components of the visually evoked potential in man: Effects of aging. *Experimental Aging Research, 6,* 523–545.

Begleiter, H. (Ed.). (1977). *Evoked brain potentials and behavior.* New York: Plenum Press.

Begleiter, H., Porjesz, B., Chou, C. L., & Aunon, J. L. (1983). P3 and stimulus incentive value. *Psychophysiology, 20,* 95–101.

Blessed, G., Tomlinson, B. E., & Roth, M. (1968). The association between quantitative measures of dementia and senile change in the cerebral grey matter of elderly subjects. *British Journal of Psychiatry, 114,* 797–811.

Brown, W. S., Marsh, J. T., & LaRue, A. (1982). Cognitive performance and P300 latency correlation in older normal adults. *Psychophysiology, 19,* 307ff.

Brown, W. S., Marsh, J. T., & LaRue, A. (1983). Exponential electrophysiological aging: P3 latency. *Electroencephalography and Clinical Neurophysiology, 55,* 277–285.

Callaway, E. (1983). The pharmacology of human information processing. *Psychophysiology, 20,* 359–370.

Callaway, E. (1984). Human information-processing: Some effects of methylphenidate, age, and scopolamine. *Biological Psychiatry, 19*(5), 649–662.

Callaway, E., & Lehman, D. (Eds.). (1979). *Human evoked potentials: Application and problems.* New York: Plenum Press.

Callaway, E., Tueting, P., & Koslow, S. H. (1978). *Event-related brain potentials in man.* New York: Academic Press.

Canter, N., Hallett, M., & Growden, J. H. (1982). Lecithin does not affect EEG spectral analysis or P300 in Alzheimer's disease. *Neurology (NY), 32,* 1260–1266.

Celesia, G. G., & Daly, R. F. (1977). Effects of aging on visual evoked response. *Archives of Neurology, 34,* 403–407.

Coben, L. A., Danziger, W. L., & Hughes, C. P. (1983). Visual evoked potentials in mild senile dementia of Alzheimer type. *Electroencephalography and Clinical Neurophysiology, 55,* 121–130.

Cooper, R., Osselton, J. W., & Shaw, J. C. (1980). *EEG Technology.* London: Butterworth.

Courjon, J., Mauguière, F., & Revol, M., (Eds.). (1982). *Clinical applications of evoked potentials in neurology.* New York: Raven Press.

Davies, P. (1979). Neurotransmitter-related enzymes in senile dementia of the Alzheimer type. *Brain Research, 171,* 319–326.

Davies, P., & Maloney, A. J. F. (1976). Selective loss of central cholinergic neurons in Alzheimer's disease. *Lancet, 2,* 1403.

Davis, K. L., Mohs, R. C., Davis, B. M., Levy, M. I., Horvath, T. B., Rosenberg, G. S., Ross, A., Rothpearl, A. B., & Rosen, W. G. (1982). Cholinergic treatment in Alzheimer's disease: Implications for future research. In S. Corkin, K. L. Davis, J. H. Growdon, H. Usdin, & R. J. Wurtman (Eds.), *Alzheimer's disease: A report of progress in research.* New York: Raven Press.

Davis, K. L., Hsieh, J. Y-K., Levy, M. I., Horvath, T. B., Davis, B. M., & Mohs, R. C. (1982). Cerebrospinal fluid acetylcholine, choline and senile dementia of the Alzheimer's type. *Psychopharmacological Bulletin, 18,* 193–195.

Desmedt, J. E. (1977). Some observations in the methodology of cerebral evoked potentials in man. In J. E. Desmedt (Ed.), *Attention, voluntary contraction and event-related cerebral potentials.* Basel, Switzerland: S. Karger.

Desmedt, J. E. (Ed.). (1979). *Cognitive components in cerebral event-related potentials and selective attention.* Basel, Switzerland: S. Karger.

Donchin, E. (1979). Event-related potentials: A tool in the study of human information processing. In H. Begleiter (Ed.), *Evoked brain potentials and behavior.* New York: Plenum Press.

Donchin, E. (1981). Surprise! . . . Surprise? *Psychophysiology, 18,* 493–513.

Donchin, E., Ritter, W., & McCallum, W. C. (1978). Cognitive psychophysiology: The endogenous components of the ERP. In E. Callaway, P. Tueting, & S. Koslow (Eds.), *Event-related brain potentials in man* (pp. 349–411). New York: Academic Press.

Drechsler, F. (1978). Quantitative analysis of neurophysiological processes of the aging CNS. *Journal of Neurology, 218,* 197–213.

Duncan-Johnson, C. C. (1981). P3 latency a new metric of information processing. *Psychophysiology, 18,* 207–215.

Duncan-Johnson, C. C., & Donchin, E. (1977). On quantifying surprise: The variation of event-related potentials with subjective probability. *Psychophysiology, 14,* 456–467.

Duncan-Johnson, C. C., & Donchin, E. (1982). The P300 latency component of the event-related brain-potentials as an index of information processing. *Biological Psychology, 14,* 1–52.

Dustman, R. E., Snyder, E. W., & Schlehuber, C. J. (1981). Life span alterations in visual evoked potentials and inhibitory function. *Neurobiology of Aging, 2,* 187–192.

Folstein, M. F., Folstein, S. E., & McHugh, P. R. (1975). Mini-Mental State: A practical method for grading the cognitive state of patients for the clinician. *Journal of Psychiatry Research, 12,* 189–198.

Ford, J. M., Hink, R. F., Hopkins, W. F., Roth, W. T., Pfefferbaum, A., & Kopell, B. S. (1979). Age effects on event-related potentials in a selective attention task. *Journal of Gerontology, 34,* 388–395.

Ford, J. M., & Pfefferbaum, A. (1980). The utility of brain potentials in determining age-related changes in central nervous system and cognitive functioning. In L. W. Poon (Ed.), *Aging in the 1980s* (pp. 115–124). Washington, DC: American Psychological Association.

Ford, J. M., Pfefferbaum, A., Tinklenberg, J. R., & Kopell, B. S. (1982). Effects of perceptual and cognitive difficulty on P3 and RT in young and old adults. *Electroencephalography and Clinical Neurophysiology, 54,* 311–321.

Ford, J. M., Roth, W. T., & Kopell, B. S. (1976). Attention effects on auditory evoked potentials to infrequent events. *Biological Psychiatry, 4,* 65–77.

Ford, J. M., Roth, W. T., Mohs, R. C., Hopkins, W. F., III, & Kopell, B. S. (1979). Event-related potentials recorded from young and old adults during memory retrieval task. *Electroencephalography and Clinical Neurophysiology, 47,* 450–459.

Gaztelu, J. M., & Bruno, W. (1982). Septo hippocampal relationships during EEG theta rhythm. *Electroencephalography and Clinical Neurophysiology, 48,* 375–387.

Goff, W. R., Allison, T., & Vaughan, H. G. (1978). The functional neuroanatomy of event-related potentials. In E. Callaway, P. Tueting, & S. H. Koslow (Eds.), *Event-related brain potentials in man* (pp. 1–81). New York: Academic Press.

Goodin, D., Squires, K. C., Henderson, B., & Starr, B. (1978). Age-related variations in evoked potentials to auditory stimuli in normal human subjects. *Electroencephalography and Clinical Neurophysiology, 44,* 447–458.

Goodin, D. S., Squires, K. C., & Starr, A. (1978). Long latency event-related components of the auditory evoked potential in dementia. *Brain, 101,* 635–648.

Gottfries, C. G. (1980). Biochemical aspects of dementia. In H. Praag, M. H. Lader, O. J. Rafaelson, & E. J. Sachar (Eds.), *Handbook of biologic psychiatry: 4. Brain mechanisms and abnormal behavior.* New York: Marcel Decker.

Greenberg, R. P., & Ducker, T. B. (1982). Evoked potentials in the clinical neurosciences. *Journal of Neurosurgery, 56,* 1–18.

Grossberg, S. (1982). Processing of expected and unexpected events during conditioning and attention: A psychophysiological theory. *Psychological Review, 89,* 529–572.

Halgren, E., Squires, N. K., Wilson, C. L., Rohrbaugh, J. W., Babb, T. L., & Crandall, P. H. (1980). Endogenous potentials generated in the human hippocampal formation and amygdala by infrequent events. *Science, 210,* 803–805.

Harkins, S. W., & Lenhardt, M. (1980). Brainstem auditory evoked potentials in the elderly. In L. W. Poon (Ed.), *Aging in the 1980s* (pp. 101–114). Washington, DC: American Psychological Association.

Hendrickson, C., Levy, R., & Post, F. (1979). Averaged evoked responses in relation to cognitive affective state of elderly psychiatric patients. *British Journal of Psychiatry, 134,* 494–501.

Hillyard, S. A., Hink, R. F., Schwent, V. L., & Picton, T. W. (1973). Electrical signs of selective attention in the human brain. *Science, 182,* 177–180.

Hillyard, S. A., & Picton, T. W. (1979). Event-related brain potentials and selective information processing in man. In J. E. Desmedt (Ed.), *Progress in clinical neurophysiology: Cognitive components in cerebral event-related potentials and selective attention* (Vol. 6, pp. 1–53). Basel, Switzerland: S. Karger.

Jasper, H. H. (1958). The ten twenty electrode system of the International Federation. *Electroencephalography and Clinical Neurophysiology, 24,* 371–375.

Kay, D. W. K. (1977). The epidemiology and identification of brain deficit in the elderly. In C. Eisdorfer & R. O. Friedel (Eds.), *Cognitive and emotional disturbances in the elderly* (pp. 11–26). Chicago: Year Book Medical Publishers.

Klorman, R., Thompson, L. W., & Ellingson, R. J. (1978). Event-related brain potentials across the life span. In E. Callaway, P. Tueting, & S. H. Koslow (Eds.), *Event-related potentials in man* (pp. 511–520). New York: Academic Press.

Kutas, M., McCarthy, G., & Donchin, E. (1977). Augmenting mental chronometry: The P300 as a measure of stimulus evaluation time. *Science, 197,* 792–795.

Levy, R., Isaacs, A., & Behrman, J. (1971). Neurophysiological correlates of senile dementia: 2. The somato-sensory evoked response. *Psychological Medicine, 1,* 159–165.

Marsh, G. R., & Thompson, L. W. (1972). Age differences in evoked potentials during an auditory discrimination task. *Gerontologist, 12,* 44–54.

McCarthy, D., & Donchin, E. (1976). The effects of temporal and event uncertainty in determining waveforms of the auditory event-related potentials. *Psychophysiology, 13,* 581–591.

McCarthy, D., & Donchin, E. (1981). A metric for thought: A comparison of P300 latency and reaction time. *Science, 211,* 77–80.

Okada, Y. C., Kaufman, L., & Williamson, S. J. (1983). The hippocampal formation as a source of the slow endogenous potential. *Electroencephalography and Clinical Neurophysiology, 55,* 417–426.

Perry, E. K., Tomlinson, B. E., Blessed, G., Bergmann, K., Gibson, P. H., & Perry, R. H. (1978). Correlation of cholinergic abnormalities with senile plaques and mental test scores in senile dementia. *British Medical Journal, 2,* 1457–1459.

Pfefferbaum, A., Ford, J. M., Roth, W. T., & Kopell, B. S. (1980a). Age differences in P3–reaction time associations. *Electroencephalography and Clinical Neurophysiology, 49,* 257–265.

Pfefferbaum, A., Ford, J. M., Roth, W. T., & Kopell, B. S. (1980b). Age-related changes in auditory event-related potentials. *Electroencephalography and Clinical Neurophysiology, 49,* 266–276.

Pfefferbaum, A., Ford, J. M., Wenegrat, B., Tinklenberg, J. R., & Kopell, B. S. (1982). Electrophysiological approaches to the study of aging and dementia. In S. Corkin, K. L. Davis, J. H. Growdon, H. Usdin, & R. J. Wurtman (Eds.), *Alzheimer's disease: A report of progress in research* (pp. 83–91). New York: Raven Press.

Pribram, K. J., & McGuiness, L. (1975). Arousal, activation and effect in the control of attention. *Psychological Review, 82,* 116–149.

Pritchard, W. S. (1981). Psychophysiology of P300. *Psychological Bulletin, 89,* 506–540.

Ritter, W., Simpson, R., & Vaughan, H. G. (1972). Association cortex potentials and reaction time in auditory discrimination. *Electroencephalography and Clinical Neurophysiology, 33,* 547–555.

Roth, W. T., Ford, J. M., & Kopell, B. S. (1978). Long latency-evoked potentials and reaction time. *Psychophysiology, 15,* 17–23.

Roth, W. T., Ford, J. M., Lewis, S. J., & Kopell, B. S. (1976). Effects of stimulus probability and task relevance on event-related potentials. *Psychophysiology, 13,* 311–317.

Roth, W. T., & Kopell, B. S. (1973). P300: An orienting reaction in the human auditory evoked response. *Perceptual and Motor Skills, 36,* 219–225.

Shagass, C., Ornitz, E. M., Sutton, S., & Tueting, P. (1978). Event related potentials and psychopathology. In E. Callaway, P. Tueting, & S. H. Koslow (Eds.), *Event-related potentials in man* (pp. 443–447) New York: Academic Press.

Smith, D. B. D., Thompson, L. W., & Michalewski, H. J. (1980). Averaged evoked potential research in adult aging—Status and prospects. In L. W. Poon, (Ed.), *Aging in the 1980s* (pp. 135–151). Washington, DC: American Psychological Association.

Squire, L. R. (1982). The neuropsychology of human memory. *Annual Review of Neuroscience, 5,* 241–273.

Squires, K. C., Chippendale, T. J., Wrege, K. S., Goodin, D. S., & Starr, A. (1980). Electrophysiological assessment of mental function in aging and dementia. In L. W. Poon (Ed.), *Aging in the 1980s* (pp. 125–134). Washington, DC: American Psychological Association.

Squires, K. C., Wickens, C., Squires, N. K., & Donchin, E. (1976). The effect of stimulus sequence on the waveform of the cortical event-related potential. *Science, 193,* 1142–1146.

Squires, N. K., Donchin, E., Squires, K. C., & Grossberg, S. (1977). Bisensory stimulation: Inferring decision-related processes from the P300 component. *Journal of Experimental Psychology, 3,* 299–315.

Starr, A. (1978). Sensory evoked potentials in clinical disorders of the nervous system. *Annual Review of Neuroscience, 1,* 103–127.

Straumanis, J. J., Shagass, C., & Schwartz, M. (1965). Visually evoked cerebral response changes associated with chronic brain syndrome and aging. *Journal of Gerontology, 20,* 498–506.

Sutton, S. (1979). P300: Thirteen years later. In H. Begleiter (Ed.), *Evoked potentials and behavior* (pp. 107–126). New York: Plenum Press.

Sutton, S., Braren, M., Zubin, J., & John, E. R. (1965). Evoked potentials correlates of stimulus uncertainty. *Science, 150,* 1187–1188.

Swanson, L. W. (1980). The anatomy of the septo-hippocampal pathway. In S. Corkin, K. L. Davis, J. H. Growdon, H. Usdin, & R. J. Wurtman, (Eds.), *Alzheimer's disease: A report of progress in research.* New York: Raven Press.

Syndulko, K., Cohen, S. N., Tourtellotte, W. W., & Potvin, A. R. (1982). Endogenous event-related potentials. *Bulletin of the Los Angeles Neurological Society, 47,* 124–140.

Syndulko, K., Hausch, E. C., Cohen, S. N., Pearce, J. W., Goldberg, Z., Montan, B., Tourtellotte, W. W., & Potwin, F. R. (1982). Long latency event-related potentials in normal aging and dementia. In J. Courjon, F. Mauguière, & M. Revol (Eds.), *Clinical applications of evoked potentials in neurology.* New York: Raven Press.

Torack, R. M. (1978). *The pathological physiology of dementia.* Berlin: Springer-Verlag.

Terry, R. D., & Davies, P. (1980). Dementia of the Alzheimer type. *Annual Review of Neuroscience, 3,* 77–95.

Visser, S. L., Stam, F. C., & Van Tilburg, W. (1976). Visual evoked response in senile and presenile dementia. *Electroencephalography and Clinical Neurophysiology, 40,* 385–392.

Whitehouse, P. J., Price, D., Clark, A., Coyle, J. T., & De-Long, M. (1981). Alzheimer's disease: Evidence for a selective loss of cholinergic neurons in the nucleus basalis. *Annals of Neurology, 10,* 122–126.

Richard C. Mohs, Celeste A. Johns, Daniel D. Dunn, Nancy A. Sherman, Wilma G. Rosen, and Kenneth L. Davis

CHAPTER

40

Anticholinergic Dementia as a Model of Alzheimer's Disease

Many studies have demonstrated that anticholinergic drugs produce, in normal people, memory impairments similar to those seen in patients in the early stages of Alzheimer's disease (AD). However, the extent to which other cognitive impairments of AD can be produced by anticholinergics is not clear. To help clarify the utility of anticholinergic dementia as a model of AD, 16 healthy young adults were given a test of free-recall memory, two tests of verbal fluency and a test of constructional praxis shortly after administration of 0.43 mg s.c. scopolamine and, 2 days later, following administration of a placebo. As has been shown in previous studies, scopolamine markedly impaired performance on the free-recall test; but had no effect on performance of the verbal fluency tests or on constructional praxis ability. These results suggest that the loss of cholinergic cells observed in patients with AD may not be sufficient to produce all of the cognitive deficits observed in these patients.

In this chapter we review data concerning the cognitive effects of anticholinergic drugs and discuss the implications of these findings for theories about the role of specific neurochemical deficits in producing the various cognitive impairments associated with aging and dementia. When administered to normal people, drugs can produce neurochemical imbalances or deficiencies that are more specific than those associated with aging and disease. Comparison of the effects of drugs with the effects due to dementing illness can provide clues about the extent to which specific chemical imbalances are responsible for dementia symptoms. Comparative studies can also indicate the extent to which certain kinds of cognitive tests are a valid reflection of the psychological consequences of a specific neurochemical imbalance. We first review the evidence implicating a cholinergic deficit in Alzheimer's disease (AD). We then discuss the symptoms of AD and the existing evidence regarding the similarity of these symptoms to cognitive impairments produced by anticholinergic drugs. Finally, we briefly present results of a recent study investigating how various cognitive functions affected in AD patients are affected in normal subjects by a moderate dose of scopolamine.

The Cholinergic Hypothesis of AD

Current interest in the role of the cholinergic system in dementia stems from two kinds of research. Neurochemical studies have demonstrated that patients dying with AD have dramatically reduced levels of markers for cholinergic neurons in the brain (Coyle, Price, & DeLong, 1983; Terry, Davies, DeTeresa, & Katzman, 1982). Furthermore, the extent of cholinergic cell loss is correlated both with the degree of histopathologic change of the type associated with AD (Perry et al., 1978; Price et al., 1982) and with the degree of cognitive impairment measured prior to death (Fuld, Katzman, Davies, & Terry, 1982; Perry et al., 1978). Supporting these neurochemical data are psychopharmacological studies investigating the cognitive effects of anticholinergic drugs. When administered to normal young adults, anticholinergics cause cognitive impairments that are phenomenologically similar to those seen in elderly people showing age-related memory loss (Drachman & Leavitt, 1974). The fact that the amnestic effects of anticholinergics are reversible by physostigmine, a cholinesterase inhibitor, but not by amphetamine, a central nervous system stimulant, indicates that these effects are directly related to the action of anticholinergics at the cholinergic synapse and are not simply a result of the sedative properties of these drugs (Drachman, 1977).

Together the neurochemical and psychopharmacological data have prompted many investigators (Bartus, Dean, Beer, & Lippa, 1982; Coyle et al., 1983; Terry et al., 1982) to adopt, at least as a working hypothesis, the view that the loss of cholinergic cells is the primary neurochemical defect in AD and that this cell loss is responsible for the principal cognitive impairments observed in AD patients. Whether or not this hypothesis is correct, it has certainly stimulated much productive and innovative research into the biological basis of dementia and into the neurochemistry of cognition. Attempts to replicate and expand on the original neurochemical studies demonstrating a cholinergic deficit have been particularly productive. Analyses have been made of a large number of neurotransmitter systems in brains of AD patients, and it now appears that two peptidergic systems, somatostatin and substance P (Terry & Katzman, 1983), and, at least in some patients, the noradrenergic (Cross et al., 1981) and serotonergic systems (Bowen et al., 1983) are affected in AD. A great number of other systems apparently remain intact in patients with AD (Terry & Katzman, 1983).

Anticholinergic Dementia

On the pharmacological side, most efforts have been devoted to developing and testing drugs that might increase cholinergic activity and thereby alleviate some of the symptoms of AD (Johns et al., 1983). Relatively few studies have attempted to define further the cognitive effects of anticholinergics, even though it is not yet clear to what extent the symptoms of AD can actually be mimicked in normal subjects by blocking cholinergic transmission. Numerous studies have now confirmed the pattern of memory impairments first reported by Drachman and Leavitt (1974) following the administration of scopolamine; specifically this drug and other anticholinergics have relatively little effect on tests of immediate memory such as the digit span, but they substantially impair performance on tasks such as free recall (Mohs, Kim, Johns, Dunn, & Davis, chapter 15, this volume; Petersen, 1977), serial recall (Sitaram, Weingartner, & Gillin, 1978; Tune, Strausse, Lew, Breitlinger, & Coyle, 1982), and supraspan digit learning (Drachman, 1977), in which subjects must learn information that exceeds the span of immediate memory. An impairment of the ability to learn new information is usually the earliest and most prominent symptom of AD (Roth & Hopkins, 1953; Sim & Sussman, 1962); although immediate memory eventually is impaired in AD, this impairment is not thought to be present in the earliest stages of the disease (Drachman & Leavitt, 1974; Miller, 1973, 1975).

In addition to their effects on memory storage, anticholinergics have a variety of other behavioral and cognitive effects some of which are evident on clinical examination and others of which can be assessed only by formal testing. An obvious effect of anticholinergics is their tendency to make people drowsy, but the drowsiness is often associated with restlessness at low doses; at higher doses there may even be a suppression of sleep with hyperactivity (Ketchum, Sidell, Crowell, Aghajanian, & Hayes, 1973). Mood is also affected; some patients report a feeling of euphoria (Ketchum et al., 1973), but most people report lower mood, in-

creased tension, confusion, and inertia (Mohs, Davis, & Levy, 1973). Formal testing indicates that overall response speed is decreased by anticholinergics (Callaway, 1984). Recently, complex reaction-time tasks have been used in an effort to determine the stage of cognitive processing most affected by anticholinergics. It was found that encoding variables such as stimulus complexity interacted with drug effects, whereas response variables such as response compatibility did not (Callaway, 1984). These results are consistent with those of the memory studies in that they suggest that the cholinergic system plays a major role in stimulus encoding and storage.

Symptoms of AD

The phenomenological similarity of memory deficits in normal subjects following the administration of anticholinergic drugs and in patients with early manifestations of AD supports the cholinergic hypothesis of AD and indicates the kinds of tests likely to be sensitive to changes in cholinergic activity. However, other symptoms produced by anticholinergics in normal subjects, particularly drowsiness and mood changes, have not yet been clearly shown to have parallels in AD patients. Mood disturbance is frequently mentioned in clinical descriptions of AD patients but drowsiness or somnolence is rarely noted (Liston, 1979; Sim & Sussman, 1962). These findings raise the possibility that cholinergic pathways involved in mood and arousal may be less susceptible to disruption by AD than are the pathways involved in memory storage. More important, it is not yet clear to what extent the other core cognitive impairments characteristic of AD can be produced by anticholinergics.

Clinical descriptions (Liston, 1979; Sim & Sussman, 1962) as well as formal psychological tests (Miller, 1975; Mohs, Rosen, & Davis, 1982; Rosen, Mohs, & Davis, 1984) indicate that the two other most prominent cognitive symptoms observed in patients with AD are dysphasia and dyspraxia (Mohs et al., 1982; Sim & Sussman, 1962). The longitudinal development of these symptoms has not been measured precisely, but clinical descriptions provide some information about their characteristics in the early stages of the disease (de Ajuriaguerra, 1975; Miller, 1973; Mohs et al., 1982; Sim & Sussman, 1962). Difficulty in finding appropriate words appears to be the earliest symptom of dysphasia in AD, although nearly all aspects of language are eventually impaired. Constructional praxis is also impaired relatively early in the course of the disease, whereas ideational and ideomotor praxis are probably impaired only later (de Ajuriaguerra & Tissot, 1968).

In one study of the effects of anticholinergics, it was found that a relatively high dose of scopolamine (1 mg s.c.) caused a slight but statistically significant reduction in the number of words that normal young adults could retrieve from familiar categories (Drachman & Leavitt, 1974). A later study (Caine, Weingartner, Ludlow, Cudahy, & Wehry, 1981) using a somewhat smaller dose (0.8 mg i.m.) also found a slight effect on retrieval of category instances. Whether similar effects might occur at other doses or on other kinds of language tasks has not been investigated, and no systematic studies of anticholinergic effects on constructional praxis have appeared.

Effects of Anticholinergic Drugs on Praxis and Language

A study designed to compare anticholinergic drug effects on memory with effects on praxis and language is under way in our laboratory. We administered a relatively low dose (0.43 mg s.c.) of scopolamine to 16 normal subjects; previous data had indicated that this dosage reliably impairs memory in young adults (Mohs et al., 1973). We then gave the subjects two tests of verbal fluency, a test of constructional praxis, and a test of memory known to be sensitive to anticholinergic drug effects.

Methods

Subjects were 16 men ranging in age from 20 to 38 years, with a mean age of 28.9 years. Most were students recruited from colleges in the New York area. Prior to entering the study, each prospective subject was given physical and psychiatric examinations. People with active medical conditions, including cardiac abnormalities, were excluded, as were people with a history of psychiatric illness. Smokers were excluded to eliminate the possible confounding effects of nicotine. Subjects were requested to abstain from all psychoactive drugs and alcohol beginning one week prior to the first test session until after the last session. All subjects gave written informed consent.

The design of the study is presented in Table 40-1. All subjects were tested on one day following administration of 0.43 mg subcutaneous scopolamine and on another day when no drug was given. The conditions were given in randomized order. Nine subjects were tested on Monday and Wednesday of the same week, and seven subjects were tested on Tuesday and Thursday of the same week. Testing began 45 minutes after drug administration. Because of scopolamine's marked subjective effects and its effects on behavior, a double-blind study was not possible. Both the tester and the subject knew on which day the subject received scopolamine, but both were blind to the specific hypotheses being tested by the tasks used in the study. At the time of their physical and psychiatric exams, all subjects were given a practice session to familiarize them with the cognitive testing procedures.

In each session, subjects were given one memory test, two tests of verbal fluency, and a test of constructional praxis. The memory test was four trials of a free-recall task for 24 words (Mohs et al., 1973) using the

Table 40-1. Design of Scopolamine Study

Schedule 1 $(n = 9)$			
Time	Monday	Time	Wednesday
12:15 pm	scopolamine or placebo[1]	12:15 pm	scopolamine or placebo
1:00 pm	cognitive testing	1:00 pm	cognitive testing

Schedule 2 $(n = 7)$			
Time	Tuesday	Time	Thursday
12:15 pm	scopolamine or placebo	12:15 pm	scopolamine or placebo
1:00 pm	cognitive testing	1:00 pm	cognitive testing

Note: Subjects are randomly assigned to either schedule 1 or schedule 2.
[1]Subjects randomly received 0.43 mg s.c. scopolamine on one day and placebo on the other day.

selective reminding procedure (Buschke, 1973). Eight different forms of the test were constructed using different words with lists equated for mean frequency of occurrence in English (Carroll, Davies, & Richman, 1971) and for imagery (Paivio, Yuille, & Madigan, 1968). The forms were assigned randomly to conditions with the constraint that no subject was given the same form twice.

The verbal fluency tests were category naming and word naming. For the category naming task, subjects were given 60 seconds to produce verbally as many examples as they could from one of four semantic categories—vehicles, fruits, sports, or four-footed animals. The Battig and Montague (1969) norms indicate that people can produce approximately the same number of instances from each of these categories. For the current study, two categories determined randomly were given in the first session and the remaining two were given in the second session. For the word naming task, subjects were given 60 seconds to produce as many words as possible beginning with a specified letter. On one test day, the letters *C, F,* and *L* were given; on the other test day, the letters *P, R,* and *W* were given. Studies with AD patients demonstrate that their performance on both these tests of verbal fluency is impaired relative to the performance of normal control subjects (Rosen, 1980).

To measure constructional praxis ability, subjects were given forms A and B of the Revised Visual Retention Test (Benton, 1974), each on one of the two test days. Each form consists of 10 cards on which one or more geometric figures is drawn. The cards progress from simple figures such as a circle to complex ones involving overlapping complex shapes. The subjects' task was to reproduce each drawing on a separate sheet of paper. Each figure was scored as correct or incorrect according to the criteria described by Benton (1974).

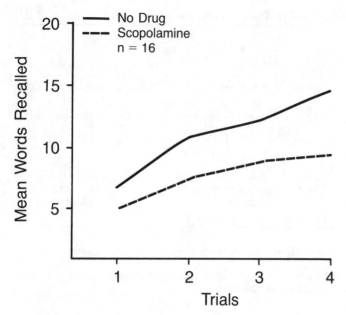

Figure 40-1. Mean number of words recalled on four trials of the free-recall (verbal learning) task.

Results

Figure 40-1 presents the results of the verbal learning task. A repeated measures analysis of variance demonstrated a significant main effect due to drug condition (F (1, 15) = 57.3, $p < .0001$), indicating that, as in previous studies, this dose of scopolamine markedly impaired memory performance. There was also a significant effect of learning trials (F (3, 45) = 49.0, $p < .0001$) and a significant trials-by-groups interaction (F (3, 45) = 7.7, $p < .0003$) indicating that recall improved over the four learning trials but that learning was slower in the scopolamine condition.

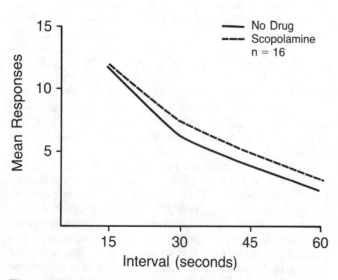

Figure 40-2. Mean number of category members named in each 15-second interval of a 1-minute period of the category naming task.

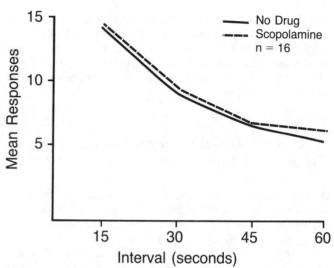

Figure 40-3. Mean number of words produced in each 15-second interval of the 1-minute period of the word fluency task.

Figures 40-2 and 40-3 present the results from the tests of category naming and word fluency, respectively. Repeated measures analysis of variance indicate that in both tasks the number of words produced declined from the first to the fourth 15-second segment of the 1-minute period ($p < .001$ in both cases). There was, however, no significant difference between the action of time with drug condition for either task ($p > .05$ in all cases). As the figures indicate, numbers of scopolamine and the no-drug conditions and no inter-examples produced were nearly identical in the two conditions.

Figure 40-4 presents the mean number of correctly drawn figures from the test of constructional praxis.

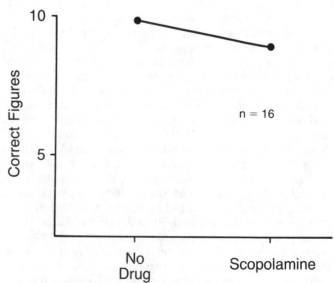

Figure 40-4. Mean number of figures drawn correctly on the constructional praxis task of Benton's Revised Visual Retention Test.

There was a slight but nonsignificant trend for subjects to make more errors in the scopolamine condition ($p >$ .05), although subjects clearly made few errors in either condition.

Conclusions

Anticholinergic Dementia

The results reported here reconfirm that relatively low doses of anticholinergic drugs cause substantial impairment of performance on tasks that involve storage of information into long-term memory. On two measures of verbal fluency and on one measure of constructional praxis, however, the same dose of scopolamine has no effect.

These results suggest that anticholinergic drugs administered to normal subjects do not produce all of the symptoms characteristic of AD and that there are limitations to the use of anticholinergic dementia as a model of AD. Determining the nature of those limitations, however, requires examination of possible explanations for these results. One possible explanation is that no effect of cholinergic blockade was found on the language and praxis tests because the tests were simply too easy to reveal anticholinergic drug effects on these aspects of cognition. This explanation is at least plausible for the praxis test, on which the subjects made almost no errors; thus the possibility of a ceiling effect cannot be ruled out. However, this explanation is considerably less plausible in the case of the verbal fluency tests, where no ceiling or floor effects were evident.

A second possibility is that no effect on language or praxis was found because the dose of scopolamine was too low. One study using a very high dose of scopolamine (1 mg s.c.) did find a small but significant impairment of verbal fluency (Drachman & Leavitt, 1974), but the effect was much smaller than the effect on memory measures. Similarly, a very high dose of scopolamine might cause some impairment in constructional praxis. Nevertheless, such results with higher doses of anticholinergics do not diminish the importance of the fact that language and praxis functions are clearly less susceptible to disruption by anticholinergics than are aspects of memory. In addition, given the fact that no impairment at all was seen at the doses used in the study reported on here, it appears that massive doses of anticholinergics might be required to produce anything like the language and praxis impairment observed even in mild cases of AD (Rosen et al., 1984).

A third possibility is that substantial language and praxis impairments cannot be produced by disruption of the cholinergic system alone and that disruption of other neurotransmitter or neuromodulator systems is necessary for these symptoms to appear. The results reported here suggest that this explanation is quite likely. One implication of this final explanation is that neurochemical abnormalities in addition to the cholinergic abnormality must be present in patients with AD before substantial language and praxis problems appear.

Test Validity

Just as the studies of anticholinergic drug effects have implications for the anticholinergic dementia model of AD, so too do they have implications for the validity of certain classes of tests and for research programs designed to develop valid tests. In this context a valid test is one that measures what it is supposed to measure. The number of different things a researcher or clinician might want to measure is almost limitless and could include a psychological construct such as memory, symptoms of a disease such as AD, or the effects of a neurochemical manipulation, for example, in the cholinergic system. It should be clear that a given test might be valid for one purpose, such as measuring symptoms of AD, but might be invalid for another, such as measuring the cognitive effects of anticholinergic agents. The results reviewed in this report indicate that certain kinds of memory tests may be both good measures of the severity of AD symptoms and good indicators of the cognitive effects of anticholinergic drugs. But tests of language and praxis appear to be much more useful in evaluating AD symptoms than in measuring the effects of cholinergic drugs.

Test validation must continue, however, and more work must be done to develop tests that are sensitive to pharmacological manipulations of specific neurochemical systems. Among the implications of these results for future research are the following:

1. Attempts should be made to develop tests of language and praxis that are more sensitive to neurochemical disturbances. This might be done by making more difficult tests. Language tests involving uncommon words could be developed (Barker & Lawson, 1968; Mohs et al., 1973), and praxis tests involving complex drawings might be used (Taylor, 1969).

2. The relative sensitivity of different aspects of cognition to disruption by anticholinergics should be investigated with a range of drug doses. At high doses, anticholinergics cause gross behavioral disturbances that make even normal subjects unable to undergo formal cognitive testing (Ketchum et al., 1973). This fact, together with the fact that our main interest should be in the relative sensitivity of different cognitive functions, suggests that studies with low to moderate doses will be most informative.

3. Studies of the cognitive effects of drugs that interfere with other neurotransmitter systems thought to be involved in AD might also be of some value. Studies of noradrenergic and serotonergic blockers might be particularly interesting, because some neurochemical studies have implicated these systems in AD (Bowen et al., 1983; Cross et al., 1981). Studies of these three types should provide valuable information both on the

role of various neurochemical systems in normal cognition and on the significance of various neurochemical deficits in producing specific symptoms in AD patients. Such studies also provide data on the extent to which various cognitive tests can be used as measures of specific neurochemical disturbances.

References

Barker, M. G., & Lawson, J. S. (1968). Nominal aphasia in dementia. *British Journal of Psychiatry, 114,* 1351–1356.

Bartus, R. T., Dean, R. L., Beer, B., & Lippa, A. S. (1982). The cholinergic hypothesis of geriatric memory dysfunction. *Science, 217,* 408–417.

Battig, W. F., & Montague, W. E. (1969). Category norms for verbal items in 56 categories: A replication and extension of the Connecticut category norms. *Journal of Experimental Psychology Monographs, 80*(3, Pt. 2), 1–46.

Benton, A. L. (1974). *The Revised Visual Retention Test (4th ed.).* New York: Psychological Corporation.

Bowen, D. M., Allen, S. J., Benton, M. J., Goodhardt, M. J., Haan, E. A., Palmer, A. M., Sims, N. R., Smith, C. C. T., Spillane, J. A., Esiri, M. M., Neary, D., Snowdon, J. S., Wilcock, G. K., & Davison, A. N. (1983). Biochemical assessment of serotonergic and cholinergic dysfunction and cerebral atrophy in Alzheimer's disease. *Journal of Neurochemistry, 41,* 266–273.

Buschke, H. (1973). Selective reminding for analysis of memory and learning. *Journal of Verbal Learning and Verbal Behavior, 12,* 543–550.

Caine, E. D., Weingartner, H., Ludlow, C. L., Cudahy, E. A., & Wehry, S. (1981). Qualitative analysis of scopolamine-induced amnesia. *Psychopharmacology, 74,* 74–80.

Callaway, E. (1984). Human information-processing: Some effects of methylphenidate, age, and scopolamine. *Biological Psychiatry, 19*(5), 649–662.

Carroll, J. B., Davies, P., & Richman, B. (1971). *The American Heritage word frequency book.* New York: Houghton Mifflin.

Coyle, J. T., Price, D. L., & DeLong, M. R. (1983). Alzheimer's disease: A disorder of cortical cholinergic innervation. *Science, 219,* 1184–1190.

Cross, A. J., Crow, T. J., Perry, E. K., Perry, R. H., Blessed, G., & Tomlinson, B. E. (1981). Reduced dopamine-beta-hydroxylase activity in Alzheimer's disease. *British Medical Bulletin, 282,* 93–94.

de Ajuriaguerra, J. (1975). Some aspects of language in various forms of senile dementia. In E. H. Lenneberg & E. Lenneberg (Eds.), *Foundation of language development.* New York: Academic Press.

de Ajuriaguerra, J., & Tissot, R. (1968). Some aspects of psychoneurologic disintegration in senile dementia. In C. Muller & L. Ciompi (Eds.), *Senile dementia* (pp. 69–79). Basel, Switzerland: Huber.

Drachman, D. A. (1977). Memory and cognitive function in man: Does the cholinergic system have a specific role? *Neurology, 27,* 783–790.

Drachman, D. A., & Leavitt, J. (1974). Human memory and the cholinergic system. *Archives of Neurology, 30,* 113–121.

Fuld, P. A., Katzman, R., Davies, P., & Terry, R. D. (1982). Intrusions as a sign of Alzheimer's dementia: Chemical and pathological verification. *Annals of Neurology, 11,* 155–159.

Johns, C. A., Levy, M. I., Greenwald, B. S., Rosen, W. G., Horvath, T. B., Davis, B. M., Mohs, R. C., & Davis, K. L. (1983). Studies of cholinergic mechanisms in Alzheimer's disease. In R. Katzman (Ed.), *Banbury report 15: Biological aspects of Alzheimer's disease* (pp. 435–449). New York: Cold Spring Harbor Laboratory.

Ketchum, J. S., Sidell, F. R., Crowell, E. B., Aghajanian, G. K., & Hayes, A. H. (1973). Atropine, scopolamine and ditran: Comparative pharmacology and antagonists in man. *Psychopharmacology, 28,* 121–145.

Liston, E. H. (1979). The clinical phenomenology of presenile dementia. *Journal of Nervous and Mental Disease, 167,* 329–336.

Miller, E. (1973). Short- and long-term memory in patients with presenile dementia (Alzheimer's disease). *Psychological Medicine, 3,* 221–224.

Miller, E. (1975). Impaired recall and the memory disturbance in presenile dementia. *British Journal of Social and Clinical Psychology, 14*(1), 73–79.

Mohs, R. C., Davis, K. L., & Levy, M. I. (1973). Partial reversal of anticholinergic amnesia by choline chloride. *Life Sciences, 29,* 1317–1323.

Mohs, R. C., Rosen, W. G., Davis, K. L. (1982). Defining treatment efficacy in patients with Alzheimer's disease. In S. Corkin, K. L. Davis, J. H. Growdon, E. Usdin & R. J. Wurtman (Eds.), *Alzheimer's disease: A report of progress in research* (pp. 351–356). New York: Raven Press.

Paivio, A., Yuille, J. C., & Madigan, S. A. (1968). Concreteness, imagery, and meaningfulness values for 925 nouns. *Journal of Experimental Psychology Monographs, 76*(1, Pt. 2), 1–25.

Perry, E. K., Tomlinson, B. E., Blessed, G., Bergmann, K., Gibson, P. H., & Perry, R. H. (1978). Correlation of cholinergic abnormalities with senile plaques and mental test scores in senile dementia. *British Medical Journal, 2,* 1457–1459.

Petersen, R. C. (1977). Scopolamine induced learning failures in man. *Psychopharmacology, 52,* 283–289.

Price, D. L., Whitehouse, P. J., Struble, R. G., Clark, A. W., Coyle, J. T., DeLong, M. R., & Hedreen, J. C. (1982). Basal forebrain cholinergic systems in Alzheimer's disease and related dementias. *Neuroscience Commentaries, 1,* 84–92.

Rosen, W. G. (1980). Verbal fluency in aging and dementia. *Journal of Clinical Neuropsychology, 2,* 135–146.

Rosen, W. G., Mohs, R. C., & Davis, K. L. (1984). A new rating scale for Alzheimer's disease. *American Journal of Psychiatry, 41*(11), 1356–1364.

Roth, M., & Hopkins, B. (1953). Psychological test performance in patients over sixty. *Journal of Mental Science, 99,* 439–450.

Sim, M., & Sussman, I. (1962). Alzheimer's disease: Its natural history and differential diagnosis. *Journal of Nervous and Mental Disease, 135,* 489–499.

Sitaram, N., Weingartner, H., & Gillin, J. C. (1978). Human serial learning: Enhancement with arecholine and choline and impairment with scopolamine. *Science, 201,* 274–276.

Taylor, E. M. (1969). Localization of cerebral lesions by psychological testing. *Clinical Neurosurgery, 16,* 269–287.

Terry, R. D., Davies, P., DeTeresa, R., & Katzman, R. (1982). Are both plaques and tangles required to make it Alzheimer's disease? *Journal of Neuropathology and Experimental Neurology, 41,* 364.

Terry, R. D., & Katzman, R. (1983). Senile dementia of the Alzheimer type. *Annals of Neurology, 14,* 497–506.

Tune, L. E., Strausse, M. E., Lew, M. F., Breitlinger, E., & Coyle, J. T. (1982). Serum levels of anticholinergic drugs and impaired recent memory in chronic schizophrenic patients. *American Journal of Psychiatry, 139,* 1460–1462.

Author Index

Page numbers in *italics* indicate the chapters in this volume that were written or co-written by the respective authors.

Subject Index

Index of Tests